MW01566648

EDITORIAL BOARD

ROBERT C. CLARK
DIRECTING EDITOR
Distinguished Service Professor and Austin Wakeman Scott
Professor of Law and Former Dean of the Law School
Harvard University

DANIEL A. FARBER
Sho Sato Professor of Law and Director, Environmental Law Program
University of California at Berkeley

HEATHER K. GERKEN
J. Skelly Wright Professor of Law
Yale University

SAMUEL ISSACHAROFF
Bonnie and Richard Reiss Professor of Constitutional Law
New York University

HERMA HILL KAY
Barbara Nachtrieb Armstrong Professor of Law and
Former Dean of the School of Law
University of California at Berkeley

HAROLD HONGJU KOH
Sterling Professor of International Law and
Former Dean of the Law School
Yale University

SAUL LEVMORE
William B. Graham Distinguished Service Professor of Law and
Former Dean of the Law School
University of Chicago

THOMAS W. MERRILL
Charles Evans Hughes Professor of Law
Columbia University

ROBERT L. RABIN
A. Calder Mackay Professor of Law
Stanford University

CAROL M. ROSE
Gordon Bradford Tweedy Professor Emeritus of Law and Organization and
Professional Lecturer in Law
Yale University
Lohse Chair in Water and Natural Resources
University of Arizona

UNIVERSITY CASEBOOK SERIES®

CRIMINAL LAW

CASES AND COMMENTS

TENTH EDITION

GERALD G. ASHDOWN
James H. and June M. Harless Professor of Law
West Virginia University

RONALD J. BACIGAL
Professor of Law
University of Richmond, Virginia

ADAM M. GERSHOWITZ
Associate Dean for Research and Faculty Development &
Professor of Law
William & Mary Law School

FOUNDATION
PRESS

To my wife, Marcia, and daughter, Brett
G.G.A.

To my parents
R.J.B.

To Ben and Emily
A.M.G.

PREFACE

The 2017 tenth edition of Cases and Comments on Criminal Law retains the structure and substance of previous editions, but with a substantial modernization. In addition to the standard updating of notes and principal cases, users will find two entirely new chapters: "Drug Possession and Distribution" and "Driving While Intoxicated and Texting While Driving."

Drug possession and drunk driving are an enormous part of the American criminal justice system. Nearly one-quarter of prison and jail inmates are incarcerated for drug offenses, and each year there are more than one million drivers arrested for driving while intoxicated. Texting while driving is also emerging as a serious problem, with almost all states recently adopting criminal statutes forbidding the practice. Yet, the crimes of possession of a controlled substance, possession with intent to distribute, driving while intoxicated, and texting while driving are almost completely absent from the standard first-year Criminal Law course. The tenth edition aims to change that by confronting issues such as constructive possession of drugs, the computation of drug quantities, and the challenge of separating mere possession from intent to distribute. In the drunk driving context, students will explore difficult questions such as what constitutes "operating" a vehicle, whether certain modes of transportation count as vehicles, what the prosecution must prove to demonstrate intoxication, and whether parked vehicles in public or quasi-public places come within driving while intoxicated statutes. The tenth edition also explores issues of statutory interpretation and whether it is possible for legislatures to impose a ban on texting while driving that is actually enforceable and that can keep pace with modern technology.

The tenth edition has maintained the substantial changes we made to the chapters on sexual assault, theft, uncompleted conduct, and the insanity defense in the ninth edition. The ninth edition added well-known cases such as Commonwealth v. Berkowitz and In the Interest of MTS, to explore the development of the law of acquaintance rape, while also including lesser-known cases analyzing fraud in the inducement, withdrawn consent, the spousal exception, and rape shield laws. The ninth edition expanded the theft chapter to include demarcations for the crimes of larceny by trick, false pretenses, and embezzlement. We included classic cases—such as The King v. Pear and The King v. Bazeley—as well as new modern day decisions and statutes showing the consolidation of theft offenses. The uncompleted conduct chapter considerably reduced the materials on RICO liability to make room for expanded analysis of the law of attempt, accessoryship, and conspiracy. We included cutting edge questions about aborted drug purchases, attempts to manufacture methamphetamine, and distinguishing between people who were merely present in drug neighborhoods and those who act as accomplices by serving as lookouts. We also added materials from the digital world, such as recent cases about internet predators attempting to solicit undercover officers, and high school students disseminating child pornography. Finally, the ninth edition revised the insanity defense chapter to include classic cases (such as Parsons and Durham) as well as a discussion of attempts to abolish or limit the insanity defense and the importance of expert testimony. The tenth edition retains all of these significant improvements that we introduced in the ninth edition and continues to reference the most current issues and cases.

While we have made substantial changes to the ninth and tenth editions, we have retained the basic structure of the book, by beginning with a focus on general concepts of criminality. The coverage and organization of these materials have been geared carefully to the goals of the first-year class in criminal law. Thus, we begin with a study of act, intent, lack of intent, proximate cause, and burdens of proof. In the selection of cases, we have sought to focus on those dealing with criminal law developments in modern code states, which frequently liberally discuss the Model Penal Code's suggested revisions of the law. At the same time, we have sought to demonstrate traditional common law concepts, which are important both for their historical perspective and because they are still very much the law in a number of jurisdictions.

As in the past, our book starts with a brief outline of criminal procedure. We believe it is essential that students have an insight into the criminal justice process as a prerequisite to a proper understanding of the cases on substantive criminal law. As in prior editions, the book ends with an Appendix containing pertinent provisions of the United States Constitution and its Amendments.

We hope that the tenth edition is a thoughtful modernization of a casebook that began in 1973 with the venerable Fred E. Inbau of Northwestern University, and which was steered for many years by Andre A. Moenssens of the University of Missouri and University of Richmond.

G.G.A.
R.J.B.
A.M.G.

April, 2017

SUMMARY OF CONTENTS

TABLE OF CONTENTS

TABLE OF CASES

The principal cases are in bold type.

UNIVERSITY CASEBOOK SERIES®

CRIMINAL LAW

CASES AND COMMENTS

TENTH EDITION

PART 1

THE CRIMINAL JUSTICE SYSTEM LEGAL CONCEPTS OF CRIMINALITY

CHAPTER 1

OVERVIEW OF CRIMINAL PROCEDURE

INTRODUCTION

Criminal law is an intricate and fascinating subject. The American Bar Association maintains that criminal law is the proper concern of all lawyers, and it also is of primary concern to the general public. Any skeptics may view a typical night of television programs and compare the number of "cop" shows with the number of shows that focus on contract law or property law.

People have an understandable curiosity and fascination with a branch of law that deals with thieves, rapists, robbers, and murderers—the seamy side of life. At the other end of the spectrum, however, criminal law, primarily constitutional procedure, addresses our highest aspirations: the right to privacy, liberty, freedom, and the need to limit government power over "we the people." Prosecutors often see themselves as protecting the community from dangerous lawbreakers, while defense counsel frequently characterize themselves as "Liberty's Last Champion," the motto of the National Association of Criminal Defense Lawyers.

These diametrically opposed views of criminal law have produced a criminal justice system like no other in the world. The United States leads the Western world in the number of persons incarcerated and condemned to death. At the same time, this country outstrips all nations in the constitutional and procedural protections given to those accused of crime. Similar paradoxes are manifested in the substantive law which defines criminal conduct. For example, the U.S. Supreme Court has elevated freedom of speech to unprecedented heights and guards against legislative attempts to criminalize the exercise of free speech (e.g., burning the American flag). At times, however, that same court has deferred to state legislatures that promulgate what some perceive to be puritanical laws against private sexual conduct (e.g., pre-marital or "deviate" sexual acts). You may judge for yourself whether these contradictions are part of the strength or weakness of the American criminal justice system.

A. PROCEDURE BETWEEN ARREST AND TRIAL

The procedural stages in a criminal case are not the same for all States. This overview focuses on a "typical case" in a "typical" jurisdiction.

3

1. TIMING FACTORS

In *Betterman v. Montana*, 136 S. Ct. 1609 (2016) the U.S. Supreme Court observed that criminal proceedings generally unfold in three discrete phases. First, the State investigates to determine whether to arrest and charge a suspect. Once charged, the suspect stands accused but is presumed innocent until conviction upon trial or guilty plea. After conviction, the court imposes sentence. There are checks against delay though out this progression, each geared to its particular phase.

In the first stage—before arrest or indictment, when the suspect remains at liberty—statutes of limitations provide the primary protection against delay, with the Due Process clause as a safeguard against fundamentally unfair prosecutorial conduct.

The Sixth Amendment's Speedy Trial Clause hones in on the second period: from arrest or indictment through conviction. The constitutional right does not attach until this phase begins, that is, when a defendant is arrested or formally accused. The right detaches upon conviction, when this second stage ends.

At the third phase of the criminal-justice process, i.e., between conviction and sentencing, a defendant retains an interest in a sentencing proceeding that is fundamentally fair under due process considerations.

2. PRE-ARREST INVESTIGATIONS

When there is a report or discovery of an alleged crime, the police must investigate to determine whether a crime was committed, and if so, by whom. This is the "cops and robbers" stage, because the principal participants are the police and those whom they suspect of criminal activity. The courts, prosecutors and defense counsel normally address the investigatory process in retrospect when determining whether the police acted in accordance with constitutional or statutory provisions governing police investigative practices.

3. ARREST

An arrest generally occurs when the police investigation uncovers facts sufficient to constitute probable cause to arrest (i.e., a reasonable belief that the suspect committed a crime). Although a judicial officer, normally a magistrate, may determine the adequacy of the facts constituting probable cause and issue an arrest warrant, the vast majority of arrests are made without a judicially issued warrant.

An arrest, of course, does not mean the end of police investigation of the crime. Incident to arrest, the police officer usually will search the suspect's person and remove any weapons, contraband, or evidence relating to the crime. Following arrest, police investigation may continue in the form of interrogation of the suspect, further searches for additional evidence, or placing the suspect in a lineup or using other identification procedures such as fingerprint or DNA analysis.

4. BOOKING PROCESS

In a typical arrest, the arrestee is transported to the police station and subjected to what is known as a booking process. The process is primarily clerical in nature and consists of: (1) completing the arrest report and preparing the arrestee's permanent police record; (2) fingerprinting and photographing the arrestee; and (3) entering on the police "blotter" the name of the arrestee, the personal effects found in his possession, and the date, time, and place of arrest.

5. FIRST APPEARANCE BEFORE A JUDICIAL OFFICER—BAIL

A person held in police custody has a right to a hearing before a judicial officer (perhaps a lower court judge, often a magistrate). With certain exceptions, the hearing must take place within forty-eight hours of the accused's arrest. The hearing determines whether there were proper grounds for arresting the suspect. If probable cause for the arrest is lacking, the suspect must be released from custody. If the arrest was lawful, the judicial officer must determine whether to hold the arrestee in pretrial custody, or set bail, in which case the accused will be released pending trial. Bail may consist of posting cash or a secured bond with the court, or the accused may be released on "personal recognizance," which is an unsecured promise to appear for trial.

6. PRELIMINARY HEARING

Many jurisdictions have eliminated the preliminary hearing stage and allow the prosecutor to go forward with the case by filing an "information" stating the charges or by taking the case directly to a grand jury, which may indict the accused for specific crimes. When a preliminary hearing is held, it is a judicial proceeding to determine whether there are reasonable grounds to require the accused to stand trial. The prime distinction between a preliminary hearing and a first appearance is that the preliminary hearing is an adversary proceeding in which the accused is allowed to introduce evidence, whereas a first appearance is normally an *ex parte* proceeding in which the judge or magistrate hears only the evidence which constituted probable cause to arrest the accused.

If the preliminary hearing judge determines that reasonable grounds to try the accused are lacking, he must be released from custody. This release, however, is not an acquittal, thus a grand jury may subsequently indict the accused for the crime and force him to go to trial on the indictment.

7. GRAND JURY INDICTMENT

Many jurisdictions require that all felony charges be submitted to a grand jury composed of citizens selected to review the evidence and determine whether there is sufficient evidence to justify a trial on the charge sought by the prosecution. A grand jury has significant power to investigate crime, primarily by subpoenaing witnesses and documentary evidence relevant to the charge. Generally, only the prosecution's evidence is presented to the grand jury, and the accused is not heard nor is defense counsel permitted to be present or offer any evidence.

8. ARRAIGNMENT AND PLEA

Arraignment consists of bringing the accused before the court, informing him of the charges against him, and asking him to enter a plea to the charges. In some jurisdictions, arraignment may take place weeks in advance of the actual trial, while other jurisdictions postpone arraignment until the trial is scheduled to begin.

In most jurisdictions, the accused may enter a plea of guilty, not guilty, or *nolo contendere*. A plea of *nolo contendere* has the same effect as a plea of guilty, except that the admission of guilt cannot be used as evidence in any other action. For example, former Vice President Spiro Agnew pled *nolo contendere* to bribery charges, but the plea was not admissible in subsequent civil litigation concerning whether taxes were due on the unreported bribes.

In the majority of cases, the defendant's guilt and the applicable range of sentences are determined by a plea agreement struck between the prosecutor and defense counsel. In most plea agreements, the defendant agrees to plead guilty to a charge in exchange for the prosecutor's promise to drop other charges or to recommend a reduced sentence.

In Missouri v. Fyre, 132 S.Ct. 1399, 182 L.Ed.2d 379 (2012), and Lafler v. Cooper, 132 S.Ct. 1376, 182 L.Ed.2d 398 (2012), the Court extended the Sixth Amendment right to counsel to the pleas bargaining stage because ours "is for the most part a system of pleas, not a system of trials." The Court noted that ninety-seven percent of federal convictions and ninety-four percent of state convictions are the result of guilty pleas.

9. PRE-TRIAL MOTIONS

Pretrial motions are requests that the trial court take some action such as dismissing a defective indictment, ruling on the admissibility of illegally obtained evidence, or ordering the parties to disclose certain information. In essence, these are matters which can or must be disposed of prior to the trial on the merits of the case. All jurisdictions have rules governing the time period within which pretrial motions must be filed with the trial court. A motion is merely a request for a court ruling or order that will afford the defendant what is being sought. The court will ordinarily hold a hearing to determine whether the motion was properly filed and whether the moving party is entitled to relief. Some of the more commonly used motions are the following:

Motion to Quash the Indictment. With this motion the defendant may question the legal sufficiency of the indictment. If the court decides that the indictment adequately charges a criminal offense, and that it was obtained in accordance with the prescribed legal procedures, the motion will be denied; otherwise the indictment will be considered invalid and "quashed." Even after an indictment has been thus rejected and set aside, the prosecutor may proceed to obtain another and proper indictment. At this stage of the proceedings the defendant has not been placed in jeopardy, and consequently a subsequent indictment and trial would not constitute a violation of the constitutional privilege against double jeopardy.

Motion for a Bill of Particulars. Although the indictment, if valid, will ordinarily contain all the allegations of fact necessary for the defendant to prepare a defense, a motion for a "bill of particulars" may seek to obtain further details respecting the accusation.

Motion for Discovery. This motion may be far more encompassing than a motion for a bill of particulars. The prosecution and the defense may seek to learn not only the details of the crime, but also additional relevant facts such as the names of the other side's witnesses and what they are expected to say.

Motion for a Change of Venue. A defendant may attempt to avoid trial in the city, county, or district where the crime occurred by seeking a "change of venue." In instances where this appears to be necessary in order that the defendant may receive a fair trial, the motion for a change of venue will be granted.

Motion to Suppress Evidence. A defendant may file with the court a "motion to suppress" evidence that is contended to have been obtained by the police in an unconstitutional manner. The evidence in question may be, on the one hand, a tangible item such as a gun, narcotics, or stolen property or, on the other hand, an intangible item such as a confession of the defendant. If the court is satisfied that the evidence has been illegally obtained, it will order the evidence suppressed, which means that it cannot be used at the trial. If the court decides that the evidence was lawfully obtained, it is usable against the defendant at the trial.

B. THE TRIAL

The American criminal justice system is an adversarial process which assigns each participant in the trial a defined role. The judge is not an advocate for either side, but is concerned with enforcing procedural rules. The prosecutor's primary task is to marshall the evidence against the defendant. The defendant has no obligation to present any evidence or play any part in the trial because of the presumption of innocence. Thus, the defendant may remain passive during the trial. The defense attorney is an advocate for the accused, whose prime responsibility is to win the case without violating the law, or, to insure that the prosecution meets its constitutional burden of proving guilt beyond a reasonable doubt. The jury (or the judge alone in a bench trial) hears the evidence from both sides and must decide whether the defendant committed the charged offense.

1. THE RIGHT TO A SPEEDY TRIAL

In all states, and in the federal system, the accused is entitled to a "speedy trial." This right is guaranteed by constitutional provisions, generally supplemented by legislative enactments that particularize and specifically limit the permitted time period. In some states, once a person is jailed upon a criminal charge, he must be tried within six months, unless the defendant requested or consented to a delay. The time period may also be extended if the prosecution offers acceptable explanations for the delay.

Time limits vary from state to state, but the consistent rule is that unless the accused person is tried within the specified period of time he must be released and is thereafter immune from prosecution for that offense.

2. DEFENDANT'S RIGHT TO THE ASSISTANCE OF AN ATTORNEY

The Sixth Amendment to the Constitution of the United States provides that "in all criminal prosecutions, the accused shall enjoy the right . . . to have the assistance of Counsel for his defense." The Supreme Court of the United States has held that where any incarceration may be a consequence of the prosecution, the defendant is entitled to court-appointed counsel in the event he cannot afford one. In 2006, the Court held that the erroneous denial of the right to counsel necessitates reversal of any conviction obtained without counsel.

The Sixth Amendment Right to Counsel applies not only at trial, but also at all critical stages of the proceedings. For example, at certain pretrial lineups and at post-conviction appeals of the conviction.

3. THE RIGHT TO A JURY TRIAL

A person accused of a "serious crime," which is considered to be one for which there may be incarceration beyond six months, has a constitutional right to trial by jury. However, the accused may waive this right and elect to be tried by a judge alone. In some jurisdictions the defendant has an absolute right to this waiver; in other states and in the federal system, it is conditioned upon the concurrence of the judge and the prosecution.

If the case is tried without a jury—called a "bench trial"—the judge hears the evidence and decides whether the defendant is guilty or not guilty. Where the trial is by a jury, the jury determines the facts and the judge serves primarily as an umpire or referee; it is the judge's function to determine what testimony or evidence is legally "admissible," that is, to decide what should be heard or considered by the jury. But the ultimate decision as to whether the defendant is guilty is one to be made by the jury alone.

4. JURY SELECTION

If the defendant has elected to be tried by a jury, the trial commences with the selection of the jurors who will try the case. In the selection of the jurors, usually twelve in number, most states permit the defendant's attorney as well as the prosecuting attorney to question a larger number of citizens who have been chosen for jury service from the list of registered voters. In the federal system and a growing number of states, however, the trial judges will do practically all of the questioning, with very little opportunity for questioning accorded the prosecutor and defense counsel. Nevertheless, each lawyer has a certain number of "peremptory challenges" which means that the attorney can arbitrarily refuse to accept as jurors a certain number of those who appear as prospective jurors, so long as the peremptory challenge is not based on race or gender. In all cases, if any prospective juror's answers to the questions of either attorney or the judge reveal a prejudice or bias that prevents the juror from fairly and impartially deciding the disputed facts, the judge, either on his own initiative or at the suggestion of either counsel, will dismiss that person from jury service. Although the desired result is not always achieved, the avowed purpose of this practice of permitting lawyers to question prospective jurors is to obtain twelve jurors who will be fair to both sides of the case.

As a safeguard against a juror becoming ill or disabled for some other reason, many states and the federal system provide for alternate jurors (usually two) who will hear all the evidence but not participate in the deliberation of the jury unless there is a replacement of one of the original jurors.

5. OPENING STATEMENTS

After the jury is selected, both the prosecuting attorney and the defense lawyer are entitled to make "opening statements" in which each outlines what he intends to prove. Such statements are not evidence, but serve to acquaint the jurors with each side of the case, so that it will be easier for them to follow the evidence as it is presented.

6. THE PROSECUTION'S EVIDENCE

The prosecutor has the burden of proving the state's case "beyond a reasonable doubt." [The prosecution has the obligation to notify the defense of any evidence that would be of significance in exculpating the accused or in mitigating his sentence, if the prosecution is aware of this evidence.] After the opening statements the prosecuting attorney has an opportunity to present testimony and evidence. If at the close of the prosecution's case the judge is of the opinion that reasonable jurors could not conclude that the charge against the defendant has been proved, the court will "direct a verdict" of acquittal. That ends the matter and the defendant goes free—forever immune from further prosecution for the crime, just the same as if a jury had heard all the evidence and found him not guilty.

7. THE DEFENDANT'S EVIDENCE

If at the close of the prosecution's case the court does not direct the jury to find the defendant not guilty, the defendant may, but is not required to, present evidence in refutation. The defendant has a constitutional right not to testify, but can waive that right by taking the stand. If a defendant chooses not to appear as a witness, the prosecuting attorney is not permitted to comment upon that fact to the jury.

After the defense has presented evidence, the prosecution is given an opportunity to rebut that evidence by presenting rebuttal witnesses or other evidence. The presentation of testimony usually ends at that point. Then, once more, defense counsel will try to persuade the court to "direct a verdict" in favor of the defendant. If the court decides to let the case go to the jury, the prosecuting attorney and defense counsel make their closing arguments.

8. CLOSING ARGUMENTS

In their closing arguments the prosecutor and defense counsel review and analyze the evidence and attempt to persuade the jury to render a favorable verdict.

9. INSTRUCTIONS OF THE COURT TO THE JURY

After the closing arguments are completed, or in some jurisdictions before the closing arguments, the judge will read and give to the jury certain written instructions as to the legal principles that should be applied to the facts of the case as determined by the jury. The judge also gives the jury written forms of possible verdicts. The jury then retires to the jury room where they are given an adequate opportunity to deliberate upon the matter, away from everyone, including the judge.

10. THE VERDICT OF THE JURY

When the jurors have reached a decision, they advise the bailiff of that fact and then return to the courtroom. The foreman, usually selected by the jurors themselves to serve as their leader and spokesman, announces the verdict of the jury. Jury participation in the case may end at that point, or the jury may play a role in sentencing the defendant.

If the defendant is acquitted, he is free forever from any further prosecution by that particular state or jurisdiction for the crime for which he was tried. If he is found guilty, then, in most types of cases and in most jurisdictions, it becomes the function of the trial judge to fix the sentence within the legislatively prescribed limitations.

In the event the jurors are unable to agree upon a verdict—and it must be unanimous in most states and in federal prosecutions—the jury, commonly referred to as a "hung jury," is discharged, and a new trial date may be set for a retrial of the case before another jury. The retrial does not constitute a violation of the constitutional protection against double jeopardy—trying a person twice for the same offense—because failure of the jury to agree upon a verdict constitutes "manifest necessity" for ending that trial.

11. THE MOTION FOR A NEW TRIAL

After a verdict of guilty the defendant has several opportunities to set aside his conviction. A "motion for a new trial" may be filed, in which the defendant alleges that certain "errors" were committed in the course of his trial; if the trial judge agrees, the conviction is set aside and the defendant may be tried again by a new jury and usually before a different judge.

The defendant may also seek a new trial on the grounds of newly discovered evidence favorable to the defense. Such motions are rarely granted, because the defendant must establish that she was not aware of the evidence, that she could not have discovered the evidence by exercising due diligence, and that the evidence would probably have changed the result of the trial had it been presented to the jury.

12. SENTENCING

In cases tried without a jury, the judge determines the sentence to be imposed. Where a jury trial was held, a small number of states also permit the jury to set the punishment, but most jurisdictions entrust sentencing to the trial judge. By statute, certain convictions require a mandatory sentence, in which case the judge has no discretion. In most cases, the judge exercises some discretion and may impose any sentence within statutory limitations, or the judge may determine the appropriate sentence according to sentencing guidelines enacted by the legislature. As part of the sentencing determination, the judge also may be empowered to suspend a portion of the sentence and place the defendant on probation. Parole and time off for "good behavior" are awarded by correctional authorities and are not part of the initial sentencing process.

The Federal Government and many states have adopted "sentencing guidelines." Prior to 2005, the federal guidelines were mandatory and limited the sentencing discretion of judges. Each criminal offense was assigned a "point value," while additional points were added for previous criminal record, use of a firearm, having a leading role in the criminal activity (such as racketeering), or other circumstances which increased the culpability of the offender. The point value could be reduced for mitigating reasons such as acceptance of responsibility and cooperation with authorities. Once a final point value had been calculated, the judge consulted a chart that provided the minimum and maximum sentence for that point value. With some exceptions, judges could not depart from the established sentencing range. But the U.S. Supreme Court held that such mandatory sentencing guidelines violated the defendant's Sixth Amendment right to trial by jury. At present, sentencing guidelines generally operate in an advisory capacity, giving the sentencing judge much greater freedom to choose the appropriate sentence. The concept of sentencing guidelines, advisory or otherwise, works to ensure some commonality in sentencing for offenders convicted of the same crime. Additionally, the guidelines can facilitate the criminal procedure process. Because the sentence can be easily calculated, prosecutors and defense attorneys are better able to work together to negotiate plea agreements.

C. POST-TRIAL PROCEEDINGS

1. PROBATION

In certain types of cases, a judge is empowered, by statute, to grant "probation" to a convicted person. This means that instead of sending the defendant to the penitentiary the court may allow him to remain at liberty upon certain conditions prescribed by law and by the judge. A probation officer typically begins the process by investigating the defendant's background for the purpose of determining the chances that the defendant is a person who may have "learned his lesson" by the mere fact of being caught and convicted, or whether he could be rehabilitated outside of prison better than behind prison walls.

Among the conditions of a defendant's probation, the court may require restitution of money stolen or reparations to a person physically injured by the criminal. Some state statutes provide that, for a period of up to six months in misdemeanor cases and up to five years in felony cases, a defendant on probation will be subjected to the supervision of a probation officer and, in general, must remain on "good behavior" during the period fixed by the court. A failure to abide by the conditions prescribed by the court will subject the defendant to a sentence in the same manner and form as though he had been denied probation and sentenced immediately after his conviction for the offense.

2. PAROLE

A penitentiary sentence of a specified term or number of years does not necessarily mean that a convicted person will remain in the penitentiary for that particular period of time. Under certain conditions and circumstances the offender may be released earlier "on parole," which means a release under supervision until the expiration of his sentence or until the expiration of a period otherwise specified by law. A violation of the conditions of the parole will subject the parolee to possible return to prison for the remainder of the unexpired sentence. Some states have abolished parole by providing mandatory release dates, less time off for good behavior, which means that there can be no parole release prior to that date.

In states maintaining the conventional parole system, revocation of probation or parole cannot be arbitrary. In either case there must be a hearing. The hearing need not be like a full scale trial (i.e., there is no jury), but it must be a fair determination of whether the conditions of probation and parole were violated.

3. THE APPEAL

A convicted defendant may appeal the conviction to an appellate court which will review the trial proceedings and will either reverse or affirm the trial court decision. If the conviction is "reversed and remanded," it means that the defendant's conviction is set aside, but a new trial may be conducted on the same charge of which the defendant was convicted. A second trial may be precluded, however, if the appellate court reverses the conviction because there is insufficient evidence to justify the conviction.

The excerpts of cases in this book are the written opinions of appellate courts, announcing and often explaining their decision. Most opinions are signed by one judge, and when joined by a majority of the judges, this opinion constitutes the judgement of the court. Judges who agree with the decision but wish to address other considerations may write separate concurring opinions. Judges who disagree with the court's decision may write dissenting opinions.

4. COLLATERAL ATTACK AND HABEAS CORPUS

If the defendant fails to obtain a reversal of his conviction on appeal, he may file a collateral attack on the conviction, the most common form of collateral attack being a habeas corpus petition. A habeas corpus petition is a collateral attack because it is not a continuation of the criminal process, but a civil suit brought to challenge the legality of the restraint under which a person is held. Because the action is a civil suit, the petitioner (the confined person) has the burden to prove that the confinement is illegal. The petitioner in this civil suit, having lost the presumption of innocence upon conviction, has the burden to prove by a preponderance of evidence that continued confinement is illegal. The respondent in a habeas action is the prisoner's custodian—the warden or other prison official.

Although the writ of habeas corpus has been called "the most celebrated writ in the English Law" and the "Great Writ of Liberty," there is a common misconception that federal courts sit as courts of last resort to correct any and all injustice. Justice Scalia, a frequent critic of expansive federal habeas review, discounted this view.

> It would be marvelously inspiring to be able to boast that we have a criminal-justice system in which a claim of "actual innocence" will always be heard, no matter how late it is brought forward, and no matter how much the failure to bring it forward at the proper time is the defendant's own fault. But of course we do not have such a system, and no society unwilling to devote unlimited resources to repetitive criminal litigation ever could. *Bousley v. U.S.*, 523 U.S. 614 (1998).

In the Antiterrorism and Effective Death Penalty Act of 1996, Congress created a one year time limitation on the filing of habeas corpus petitions and required federal courts to give great deference to prior determinations made by the State courts.

D. CRIMINAL JUSTICE PROFESSIONALS

Like any organization, the operation of our criminal justice system is dependent on the people who administer the system. Because of the popularity of movies and television shows focusing on criminal justice, most people are familiar with the roles played by police officers, prosecutors, defense attorneys, and judges. Less publicized, but no less important, is the vital role played by coroners, magistrates, court clerks, probation officers, and paralegals.

1. LAW ENFORCEMENT AGENCIES

Law enforcement agencies are charged with enforcing criminal laws which range from traffic offenses to serious felonies. At the national level, the Federal Bureau of Investigation is the largest agency empowered to deal with violations of federal criminal laws. In addition to the FBI, other federal agencies investigate specific types of violations of federal law. For example, the Drug Enforcement Administration; the Bureau of Alcohol, Tobacco, and Firearms; the Customs Service; the Secret Service; and the Immigration and Naturalization Service. Following the terrorist attacks in New York City, on the Pentagon, and in Pennsylvania on September

11, 2001, the Department of Homeland Security was created and now exercises significant law enforcement powers.

At the state level, the state police are charged with prevention and investigation of all crimes covered by state law. At the local level, police departments or sheriff's offices exercise broad powers as the chief law enforcement officers of their communities. Their responsibilities include enforcing state law as well as local ordinances.

2. PROSECUTORIAL AGENCIES

Prosecutorial agencies are responsible for reviewing the information gathered by law enforcement agencies, and deciding whether to proceed with formal charges. At the national level, the U.S. Department of Justice and U.S. Attorney's Offices, distributed geographically throughout the country, initiate a prosecution for a federal offense. At the state level, the State Attorney General's Office may initiate certain prosecutions, but such offices normally limit their function to handling appeals of convictions. Most state prosecutions are initiated by district attorneys (sometimes called "state's attorneys" or "commonwealth attorneys") geographically distributed throughout the state.

3. THE DEFENSE FUNCTION

Criminal defendants may hire attorneys to represent them in all criminal prosecutions, no matter how minor the offense. Indigents, who cannot afford to hire counsel, may have defense counsel appointed at public expense whenever the indigent faces possible imprisonment. Many states have established a Public Defender's Office to represent indigents. As a supplement to, or in place of, a public defender's office, many states utilize a court appointed list of attorneys who have volunteered or been recruited to represent indigents.

4. THE COURTS

In the federal system, the principle trial court is the U.S. District Court which presides over the prosecution of serious federal crimes. Trials of federal misdemeanors are often handled by federal magistrate judges, who are appointed by federal district judges. The U.S. Circuit Courts of Appeal hear appeals from convictions in the District Court. There are thirteen judicial circuits which cover the United States and its possessions. The U.S. Supreme Court reviews the decisions of the lower federal courts and many decisions of the state courts.

There is considerable variation in the structure of state court systems, but every state has one or more levels of trial courts and at least one appellate court. A common arrangement of a state court system includes: a lower court, often called police court, magistrate court, or, in some states, a court-not-of-record, which tries minor or petty offenses; a general jurisdiction trial court, always a court of record, which tries more serious offenses; and an appellate court which reviews the decisions of the lower courts.

5. THE CORONER AND THE MEDICAL EXAMINER

A coroner is either an elected or appointed individual charged with determining the cause of death in homicide cases. Coroners, by and large, need have no special training or degrees. The office is frequently held by funeral directors. In order to fulfill the function of the office, the coroner may conduct a coroner's inquest when a homicide has occurred. Just as the office of coroner is ancient, indeed archaic, the coroner's inquest is a very old proceeding and its function was and still is to determine the cause of death. The verdict of the coroner's jury, which is made up, in some states, of six lay persons selected by the coroner or a deputy, is not binding on the prosecuting attorney, the grand jury or the court. It is merely an advisory finding which can be either accepted or completely ignored. For instance, even though a coroner's jury returns a verdict of accidental death, a grand jury, either upon its own initiative or upon evidence presented by the prosecutor, may find that death resulted because of someone's criminal act and charge that person with the offense.

In some jurisdictions the office of coroner has been replaced by what is known as a medical examiner system. In other jurisdictions, the coroner and medical examiner systems operate side by side depending on the size of population centers served. Whereas the coroner is usually an elected official (who may or may not be a physician), a medical examiner ("M.E.") must be a physician appointed by a state or county officer or agency. Moreover, in many jurisdictions, the M.E. must be a forensic pathologist, specially trained for the position. The M.E. has, in turn, the power of appointing assistants who are physicians already trained for the purpose or at least in the process of receiving such training.

6. MAGISTRATES

In some jurisdictions, magistrates are judges who preside over lower courts (often called magistrate or police court) where traffic violations and minor misdemeanors are tried. In other jurisdictions, magistrates have no trial jurisdiction; their primary function is to determine whether there is probable cause to issue search or arrest warrants, and to determine the conditions of any pretrial release of an arrested suspect.

7. COURT CLERKS

Court clerks, who may be elected or appointed in different jurisdictions, handle the vast amount of paper work involved in bringing a case to trial. For example, the clerk's office may be responsible for issuing subpoenas for witnesses or documents; filing the formal charge upon which the accused will stand trial; summoning the jurors and administering requests to be excused from jury duty; scheduling the court's docket and use of multiple courtrooms; and receiving pretrial motions requesting the court to take some form of action.

8. PROBATION OFFICERS

Convicted defendants are sometimes granted a suspended sentence and may avoid incarceration so long as they are of good behavior and comply with the terms of the court's granting of probation. Probation officers supervise the conduct of the individual on probation by monitoring whether the individual is gainfully employed, has made restitution to any victim of the crime, and is avoiding any further breaches of the law. Prior to conviction, probation officers may be ordered to investigate the background of the defendant and prepare a presentence report recommending an appropriate sentence.

9. PARALEGALS

Like court clerks, paralegals may be responsible for organizing the vast amount of paper work sometimes generated by a criminal case. For example, obtaining and filing police reports; coroner's and medical examiner's findings; transcripts of preliminary hearings; grand jury indictments; and requests for and responses to pretrial discovery motions. Paralegals are also involved in the factual investigation and legal research surrounding the case.

As part of their tasks related to *factual* investigation, paralegals may be asked to: interview victims, witnesses, and police officers; draft preliminary charges when assisting a prosecutor; draft motions to dismiss the complaint when assisting defense counsel; draft subpoenas and locate witnesses; and prepare trial notebooks organizing the presentation of evidence, particularly any documents or exhibits to be used at trial. In that sense, paralegals employed by an attorney may fulfill roles that approach that of an investigator.

Criminal justice paralegals are also responsible for many *legal* tasks requiring them to: research the substantive law governing the charged offense; draft pretrial motions or responses to such motions; draft legal memoranda and briefs on contested points of law; prepare presentence reports or responses to such reports; and draft post-trial motions.

NOTE

In the past decade, there has been a tremendous increase in comparative law tomes discussing the legal systems of countries around the world. *See, e.g.*, Craig M. Bradley, Criminal Procedure: A Worldwide Study (2d ed. 2007); H. Patrick Glenn, Legal Traditions of the World: Sustainable Diversity of Law (4th ed. 2010).

CHAPTER 2

ESSENTIAL CONCEPTS OF CRIMINALITY

A. THE PROHIBITED CONDUCT—"*ACTUS REUS*"

1. VOLUNTARY ACT

State v. Hinkle
Supreme Court of Appeals of West Virginia, 1996.
200 W.Va. 280, 489 S.E.2d 257.

■ CLECKLEY, JUSTICE:

* * *

At approximately 7:30 p.m., the defendant was traveling north on Route 2 in St. Marys, West Virginia. Robert Barrett was driving south on Route 2 with his wife, Charlotte Ann Barrett. It appears the defendant's car gradually crossed the centerline and traveled in a straight line for approximately two hundred yards in the southbound lane before it collided head-on with the Barrett automobile.[5] As a result of the accident, the defendant and Mr. Barrett suffered severe injuries. Mrs. Barrett also sustained serious injuries, and died as a result of those injuries. Eyewitnesses reported the defendant crossed the centerline in a consistent, even fashion without attempting to swerve, brake, change directions, or stop.[6] Witnesses also indicated that both the defendant and Mr. Barrett were traveling at the posted speed limit. A bystander stated the defendant was semi-conscious immediately after the accident, and his breath smelled of alcohol.

An investigation of the defendant's vehicle immediately after the accident revealed one open can of beer, which was one-half full, in the driver's door compartment; several empty beer cans on the passenger's floor; four full beer cans on the rear floor; three empty beer cans on the driver's floor; and an empty glass, which smelled of beer, on the ground near the car. The defendant was transported to Camden Clark Memorial Hospital where testing revealed he had a blood alcohol level of less than one hundredth of one percent. Officer Charles Templeton of the Pleasants County Sheriff's Department, who investigated the accident, also requested that a blood sample from the defendant be tested by the crime lab. The crime lab found the defendant's blood alcohol level to be less

---

[5] Witness accounts indicate Mr. Barrett attempted to avoid the collision by swerving off the road and braking.

[6] There was no evidence of skid marks at the accident scene.

than one thousandth of one percent, well below the statutory definition of intoxication. While treating the defendant's injuries, he was given a Magnetic Resonance Imaging [MRI] scan to determine whether he had sustained any head injuries. The MRI results indicated the defendant had an undiagnosed brain disorder in the portion of his brain that regulates consciousness.

On September 13, 1993, a Pleasants County grand jury returned an indictment charging the defendant with the misdemeanor offense of involuntary manslaughter while driving a motor vehicle in an unlawful manner in violation of W. Va. Code, 61–2–5 (1923). The defendant stood trial, by jury, for this charge in Pleasants County on March 1, 1995. During the trial, the defendant's son testified that the defendant had been having memory loss for several months prior to the accident, and that he believed the defendant had seen a doctor in New Martinsville, West Virginia. Similarly, [another witness] stated the defendant had complained of feeling ill during the months preceding the collision, and he had complained of dizziness, memory loss, and double vision on the night of the accident. She, too, believed the defendant recently had been treated by a physician.

Defense witness, Ronald Washburn, M.D., reported the defendant's MRI scan showed an undiagnosed brain disorder affecting the reticular activating system of his brain. Dr. Washburn reasoned that because this portion of the brain affects one's consciousness, this disorder could have caused the defendant to suddenly lose consciousness immediately before the collision.[10] He also indicated the defendant had developed this brain abnormality approximately four to eight months prior to the accident[11] and the disease was not caused by chronic alcohol abuse. Testifying further, Dr. Washburn surmised the defendant's prior memory loss was a symptom of his brain disorder, but his other complaints of not feeling well, dizziness, and blurred or double vision were not related to this disease.[12] Concluding his opinion, Dr. Washburn determined the defendant's brain disorder would not have been diagnosed if he had not had an MRI scan after the accident. Finally, both the defendant and Mr. Barrett testified they could not recall any details of the automobile accident.

The trial court denied the defendant's motion to dismiss the indictment, his motion to suppress all evidence obtained immediately after the accident showing the presence of alcoholic beverage containers in or around the defendant's car, and statements indicating the defendant and his car smelled of alcohol; and his motions for a directed

---

[10] It does not appear the defendant ever had lost consciousness prior to the accident of June 12, 1993.

[11] Dr. Washburn based his opinion, in part, on the defendant's medical records from March, 1993.

[12] Dr. Washburn attributed the remaining symptoms not associated with the defendant's brain disorder to his chronic sinusitis.

verdict of acquittal. The trial court further denied the defendant's proposed jury instruction regarding the insanity defense,[16] to which defense counsel objected. Determining that the defendant's blood alcohol level did not establish that he was under the influence of alcohol, the trial court instructed the jury to find the defendant was not intoxicated at the time of the accident. Likewise, the trial court directed the jury to find that the defendant suffered from a brain disorder affecting the consciousness-regulating portion of his brain. . . .

Following deliberations, the jury, on March 2, 1995, returned a verdict of guilty of involuntary manslaughter. By order dated May 17, 1995, the circuit court denied the defendant's motions for a judgment of acquittal and a new trial, and sentenced him to one year in the Pleasants County Jail.

. . . [T]he appeal in this case has been limited to one issue: Whether the jury was instructed properly as to the defense of unconsciousness. The defendant claims the trial court committed reversible error when it refused to give his insanity instruction. On the other hand, the State contends the instruction offered by the defendant was imperfect, and the evidence did not support an insanity instruction. . . . This case requires us to harmonize a conflict between the defense of unconsciousness and that of insanity.

* * *

The defendant argues he was entitled to an insanity instruction. Of course, the State contends otherwise. We agree partially with the State that technically the defense was one of unconsciousness as opposed to insanity. The law on the notion of unconsciousness in West Virginia is terribly undeveloped. This is, no doubt, the reason why the defendant requested an insanity instruction in this case, since that is where our older cases seem to place this claim. *See State v. Painter*, 135 W.Va. 106,

---

16   The defendant's proposed jury instruction Number Ten provides:

> The Court instructs the jury the driver of a motor vehicle is not liable criminally for conduct which they [sic] otherwise would [sic] if he or she was "insane" at the time. "Insanity" is a legal term of art which means when at the time of the offense the defendant has a mental disease or defect from which the criminal acts resulted and which caused the defendant to lack the capacity to appreciate the wrongfulness [sic] of his conduct or to conform his actions to the requirements of the law, what the law refers to [sic] condition [sic] as "insanity". The State of West Virginia has the burden to prove the sanity of the defendant along with the other elements of the crime alleged by proof beyond a reasonable doubt once the defendant presents some evidence of insanity. Therefore, before you may find the defendant, Charles Rhea Hinkle [sic] guilty of involuntary manslaughter as otherwise instructed, the State of West Virginia must prove to the satisfaction of the jury that on or about June 12, 1993 Charles Rhea Hinkle did not suffer from a mental disease or defect from which the criminal action resulted which either prevented him from appreciating the wrongfulness [sic] of his actions or prevented him from conforming his actions to the requirements of the law. If the jury has a reasonable doubt as to any one of these elements, you shall find the defendant, Charles Rhea Hinkle, not guilty by reason of insanity.

The trial court noted on the refused instruction that it was "not supported by [the] evidence" and that it was "misleading given [the] other instructions."

63 S.E.2d 86 (1950); *State v. Alie*, 82 W.Va. 601, 96 S.E. 1011 (1918). Indeed, there is only a paucity of American appellate courts that have discussed this defense. With regard to those jurisdictions, Section 44 of Wayne R. LaFave & Austin W. Scott, Jr., *Criminal Law* (1972), one of the few treatises that gives this defense any extensive coverage, states: "A defense related to but different from the defense of insanity is that of unconsciousness, often referred to as automatism: one who engages in what would otherwise be criminal conduct is not guilty of a crime if he does so in a state of unconsciousness or semi-consciousness." *Id.* at 337.

Interpreting this defense, the weight of authority in this country suggests that unconsciousness, or automatism as it is sometimes called, is not part of the insanity defense for several reasons. First, unconsciousness does not necessarily arise from a mental disease or defect. Although always containing a mental component in the form of loss of cognitive functioning, the causes and conditions are diverse; examples include epilepsy, concussion, gunshot wounds, somnambulism, coronary episodes, and certain brain disorders, as here. Additionally, these unconscious disorders tend to be acute, unlike most cases of insanity which are typically chronic. Because cases of unconsciousness are temporary, they do not normally call for institutionalization, which is the customary disposition following a successful insanity defense.

A further, and probably the most significant, distinction between insanity and unconsciousness rests on the burden of proof issue. Because insanity leading to criminal behavior usually does not eliminate the mental state necessary for a finding of criminal culpability, the burden can be placed on the defendant to prove insanity.[21] *See Rivera v. Delaware*, 429 U.S. 877, 879–80, 97 S.Ct. 226, 227, 50 L.Ed.2d 160, 161 (1976) (*appeal dismissed*; BRENNAN, J., *dissenting*); *Leland v. Oregon*, 343 U.S. 790, 796–801, 72 S.Ct. 1002, 1006–09, 96 L.Ed. 1302, 1307–10 (1952). On the contrary, unconsciousness eliminates one of the basic elements of the crime—either the mental state or the voluntary nature of the act.[22] As such, once the issue of unconsciousness or automatism is raised by the defense, the State must disprove it beyond a reasonable doubt in order to meet its burden of proof with respect to the elements of the crime. *Patterson v. New York*, 432 U.S. 197, 215, 97 S.Ct. 2319, 2329,

---

[21] West Virginia law nevertheless places the burden on the State to disprove insanity beyond a reasonable doubt once the issue is raised by a defendant. *See* Edwards v. Leverette, 163 W.Va. 571, 576–78, 258 S.E.2d 436, 439–40 (1979). This approach is contrary to the current trend in the country which is to place the burden on the defendant to prove his insanity. We leave open for another day whether the burden of proof in insanity cases should be changed in West Virginia.

[22] The defense of unconsciousness is analogous to the defense of accident or alibi, in that these defenses negate an essential element of the crime charged. In these two situations, the reason the burden of proof cannot be placed on the defendant is that a prosecutor cannot secure a conviction unless the prosecution proves the killing was culpable or the defendant was present and participating at the time of the crime. The same legal analysis applies to unconsciousness. Proof that the act was done voluntarily necessarily negates unconsciousness. On the other hand, voluntary action and unconsciousness cannot co-exist.

53 L.Ed.2d 281, 295 (1977); *Mullaney v. Wilbur*, 421 U.S. 684, 701–04, 95 S.Ct. 1881, 1891–92, 44 L.Ed.2d 508, 521–22 (1975); *In re Winship*, 397 U.S. 358, 361–63, 90 S.Ct. 1068, 1071–72, 25 L.Ed.2d 368, 373–74 (1970).

Unconsciousness is thus a separate and distinct defense from insanity. In order to keep this distinction conceptually clear, it is better to view unconsciousness as eliminating the voluntary act requirement rather than negating the mental component of crimes. Thinking of unconsciousness in this conceptual fashion helps to avoid the temptation to collapse it into insanity which, of course, also deals with mental conditions. The defense of unconsciousness should be recognized in a criminal trial and equated with epilepsy rather than insanity. We believe this is the way the claim of unconsciousness should be viewed jurisprudentially in West Virginia.

Accordingly, we hold that unconsciousness (or automatism) is not part of the insanity defense, but is a separate claim which may eliminate the voluntariness of the criminal act. Moreover, the burden of proof on this issue, once raised by the defense, remains on the State to prove that the act was voluntary beyond a reasonable doubt. An instruction on the defense of unconsciousness is required when there is reasonable evidence that the defendant was unconscious at the time of the commission of the crime.[24] In the instant case, it is contended the defendant was, in fact, rendered unconscious at the time of the commission of the crime by reason of an undiagnosed brain disorder affecting the reticular activating system of his brain.[25]

Even if the trier of fact believes the defendant was unconscious at the time of the act, there is another consideration which occasionally arises. If the defendant was sufficiently apprised and aware of the condition and experienced recurring episodes of loss of consciousness, e.g., epilepsy, then operating a vehicle or other potentially destructive implement, with knowledge of the potential danger, might well amount to reckless disregard for the safety of others. Therefore, the jury should be charged that even if it believes there is a reasonable doubt about the defendant's consciousness at the time of the event, the voluntary operation of a motor vehicle with knowledge of the potential for loss of consciousness can constitute reckless behavior.

---

[24] The defense of unconsciousness must be distinguished from "blackouts" caused by the voluntary ingestion of alcohol or nonprescription drugs. If the evidence indicates that the unconsciousness is due to alcohol or drugs, as we discussed above, the case must be handled as an intoxication defense. *See* State v. Less, 170 W.Va. 259, 294 S.E.2d 62 (1981); State v. Vance, 168 W.Va. 666, 285 S.E.2d 437 (1981); State v. Keeton, 166 W.Va. 77, 272 S.E.2d 817 (1980); State v. Bailey, 159 W.Va. 167, 220 S.E.2d 432 (1975), *overruled on other grounds by* State *ex rel.* D.D.H. v. Dostert, 165 W.Va. 448, 269 S.E.2d 401 (1980).

[25] Although we hold unconsciousness to be a defense separate and apart from insanity, in that unconsciousness does not result from a disease or mental defect, it does not follow that the procedural requirements of the two should be different. Thus, where a defendant elects to assert the defense of unconsciousness, it is fair to require the defendant to comply with all the procedural requirements of Rule 12.2 of the West Virginia Rules of Criminal Procedural, including the pretrial notice requirement.

... Jurisdictions appear divided as to whether the defense can be put in issue by only the defendant's testimony. In *Starr v. State*, 134 Ga.App. 149, 150, 213 S.E.2d 531, 532 (1975), the court found that additional corroboration was required and, without corroboration, such an instruction was not required. On the other hand, in *People v. Wilson*, 66 Cal.2d 749, 762, 59 Cal. Rptr. 156, 165, 427 P.2d 820, 829 (1967), the court said because a defendant is entitled to an instruction as to his defense, no matter how incredible his theory is, there need be no corroboration for the instruction to be given. In this case, we need not decide this issue since the defendant's testimony was sufficiently corroborated by expert testimony and other eyewitness testimony.[26] We find the evidence was sufficient to require an unconsciousness instruction. . . .

. . . [A]lthough the trial court instructed the jury that the defendant was suffering from a brain disorder, no further instruction was given (on insanity or otherwise) which required the jury carefully to focus on how the nature of the defendant's brain disorder related to the elements of the crime. The jury should have been told that, in light of the evidence of the defendant's brain disorder and apparent blackout, he could not be convicted unless the State proved beyond a reasonable doubt that his act was *voluntary and that he acted in reckless disregard of the safety* of others.

* * *

Reversed and Remanded.

NOTES AND QUESTIONS

1. What if Hinkle had suffered previous blackouts?

What result in People v. Decina, 2 N.Y.2d 133, 157 N.Y.S.2d 558, 138 N.E.2d 799 (1956), where, after apparently suffering an epileptic seizure, defendant's car ran off the road striking six "schoolgirls," killing four of them? The defendant's medical history established

> that at the age of 7 he was struck by an auto and suffered a marked loss of hearing. In 1946 he was treated in this same hospital for an illness during which he had some convulsions. Several burr holes were made in his skull and a brain abscess was drained. Following this operation defendant had no convulsions from 1946 through 1950. In 1950 he had four convulsions, caused by scar tissue on the brain. From 1950 to 1954 he experienced about 10 to 20 seizures a year, in which his right hand would jump although he remained

---

[26] Even though we decline to address the issue of corroboration head-on, in order to avoid a flood of false and manufactured unconsciousness defenses, an impressive number of jurisdictions seems to favor the corroboration requirement. In these jurisdictions, some substantial corroboration is necessary to trigger the unconsciousness defense. For example, evidence that a defendant does not remember, without other eyewitnesses or expert testimony, is insufficient to carry the issue to the jury. To require otherwise, it is suggested, would place an almost impossible burden on the prosecution to prove the absence of unconsciousness.

fully conscious. In 1954, he had 4 or 5 generalized seizures with loss of consciousness, the last in September, 1954, a few months before the accident. Thereafter he had more hospitalization, a spinal tap, consultation with a neurologist, and took medication daily to help prevent seizures.

138 N.E.2d at 802–03.

2. Can you carefully explain the differences identified by the West Virginia Court between the concept of unconsciousness and the *defense* of insanity?

3. Is a defendant who suffers from a post-traumatic stress disorder entitled to an unconsciousness instruction? In State v. Fields, 324 N.C. 204, 376 S.E.2d 740 (1989), a defendant convicted of first-degree murder claimed that he was suffering from a post-traumatic stress disorder caused by killing his father while defending his mother from his father's physical attacks when the defendant was fourteen years old. At the time of the killing for which he was on trial, he claimed that he was in a disassociative state caused by the victim's violence toward his sister.

The North Carolina Supreme Court responded first by quoting from one of its previous cases:

> ... [T]he defense of unconsciousness does not apply to a case in which the mental state of the person in question is due to insanity [or] mental defect ..., but applies only to the case of the unconsciousness of persons of sound mind as, for example, somnambulists or persons suffering from the delirium of fever, epilepsy, [or] a blow on the head ..., and other cases in which there is no functioning of the conscious mind and the person's acts are controlled solely by the subconscious mind.

376 S.E.2d at 743 (quoting State v. Mercer, 275 N.C. 108, 118, 165 S.E.2d 328, 336 (1969)).

The court nevertheless went on to conclude:

> [D]efendant's evidence here ... merited the requested instruction on unconsciousness or automatism ... [F]amily members testified to a substantial history going back to the defendant's childhood of defendant's acting as if he were "in his own world." In the context of this testimony, and the basis of a personal and family history obtained from defendant and family members, Dr. Harrell clearly testified that in his opinion defendant was unable to exercise conscious control of his physical actions at the moment of the fatal shooting. He stated further: "I think he was acting sort of like a robot. He was acting like an automaton ... [W]hen he goes into the altered state of consciousness, ... then he engages in a motor action." This testimony, combined with the family members' testimony, if accepted by the jury, "exclude[d] the possibility of a voluntary act without which there can be no criminal liability." ... Therefore, an instruction on the legal principles applicable to the unconsciousness or automatism defense was required.

Id. at 744–45 (citations omitted).

Are these statements by the court consistent? Are you persuaded that the defendant was entitled to an unconsciousness instruction?

4. Is a defendant who alleges that he "blacked out" from the consumption of alcohol or drugs, and who claims that he has no recollection of the criminal incident for which he has been charged, entitled to an unconsciousness instruction? Is the response "it depends"? Is this the situation to which the West Virginia Court referred in footnote 24 of the *Hinkle* opinion? *See also* State v. Utter, 4 Wash.App. 137, 479 P.2d 946 (1971).

2.   THE ACT OF POSSESSION

State v. Fox
Supreme Court of Utah, 1985.
709 P.2d 316.

■ STEWART, JUSTICE:

Defendants Gary and Clive Fox were convicted of possession with intent to distribute and production of a controlled substance in violation of U.C.A., 1953, § 58–37–8(1)(a)(i) and § 58–37–8(1)(a)(ii). On appeal, both defendants argue that the evidence is insufficient to sustain the charges. We affirm the conviction of Gary Fox and reverse the conviction of Clive Fox.

In June 1983, the Weber County Sheriff's Office received an anonymous letter stating that 7-foot marijuana plants growing at 249 Harris Street in Ogden were soon to be harvested. The residence belonged to Gary Fox. Acting on the tip, an officer went to the residence to investigate. He saw that the yard contained two opaque greenhouses, one of which was attached to the house. The officer was able to determine that one greenhouse contained marijuana because a marijuana leaf was pressed against the greenhouse. That same day, the officer obtained a search warrant for the house and the greenhouses and conducted a search while the premises were unoccupied.

The home had two bedrooms. One bedroom contained men's clothing, carpentry tools, and a plastic identification card for Clive which had expired April 15, 1982. The second bedroom contained men's clothing, women's underclothing, a checkbook and bank deposit slips with Gary's name on them, a book entitled Marijuana Grower's Guide, marijuana and drug paraphernalia. The kitchen contained marijuana and other paraphernalia. Both greenhouses contained marijuana plants. One of the greenhouses was accessible from the kitchen and had no outside entrance. The kitchen and greenhouse were not separated or blocked off from the remainder of the house, and the entire house was very humid. In searching the house the officers found mail addressed to both Gary and Clive.

Gary owned the property. He arranged for the delivery of gas to the house, and the gas bills were sent to him. The telephone listing, however, was in Clive's name, and had been since 1979.

Neither Gary nor Clive had been seen near the house by the police. Mr. Seamon, a neighbor, testified that he thought Gary and Clive lived at the house: "I would see them on weekends would be all," doing yard work. Mrs. Seamon testified in response to a question whether she knew who lived at 249 Harris: "Well, I had seen Clive and Gary Fox over there." Neither witness remembered seeing either Gary or Clive at the house on any specific occasion during the month preceding the arrest, but remembered they were absent for a period following the arrest. An officer testified that the house appeared to be occupied because the refrigerator and cupboards contained food, and the kitchen had both clean and dirty dishes in it.

At the close of the State's case, both Gary and Clive moved to dismiss the charges because of insufficient evidence. The motion was denied. The trial court stated that the defendants lived in or occupied the home, and that there was "enough marijuana growth for sale."

Both were convicted of production of a controlled substance and possession of a controlled substance with intent to distribute for value in violation of U.C.A., 1953, § 58–37–8(1)(a)(i) and § 58–37–8(1)(a)(ii). On appeal, the defendants renew their claim that there was insufficient evidence to prove that they grew marijuana and that the marijuana found in the residence belonged to them or was for distribution.

* * *

A conviction for possession of a controlled substance with intent to distribute requires proof of two elements: (1) that defendant knowingly and intentionally possessed a controlled substance, and (2) that defendant intended to distribute the controlled substance to another. U.C.A., 1953, § 58–37–8(1)(a)(ii). Actual physical possession presupposes knowing and intentional possession. However, actual physical possession is not necessary to convict a defendant of possession of a controlled substance. A conviction may also be based on constructive possession. In *State v. Carlson*, 635 P.2d 72, 74, we held that constructive possession exists "where the contraband is subject to [defendant's] dominion and control." However, persons who might know of the whereabouts of illicit drugs and who might even have access to them, but who have no intent to obtain and use the drugs can not be convicted of possession of a controlled substance. Knowledge and ability to possess do not equal possession where there is no evidence of intent to make use of that knowledge and ability.

To find that a defendant had constructive possession of a drug or other contraband, it is necessary to prove that there was a sufficient nexus between the accused and the drug to permit an inference that the accused had both the power and the intent to exercise dominion and control over the drug.

Whether a sufficient nexus between the accused and the drug exists depends upon the facts and circumstances of each case. Ownership and/or occupancy of the premises upon which the drugs are found, although important factors, are not alone sufficient to establish constructive possession, especially when occupancy is not exclusive. Some other factors which might combine to show a sufficient nexus between the accused and the drug are: incriminating statements made by the accused, *Allen v. State*, 158 Ga. App. 691, 282 S.E.2d 126, 127 (1981) (defendant told unnamed individual that defendant had $500 worth of marijuana); incriminating behavior of the accused, *United States v. Garcia*, 655 F.2d 59 (5th Cir.1981) (defendant nodded affirmatively when introduced as owner of cocaine, and remained with drug during negotiations); *Francis v. State*, Ala. App., 410 So.2d 469 (1982) (defendant slammed door in face of police and ran back into the house yelling, "throw it in the fire"); presence of drugs in a specific area over which the accused had control, such as a closet or drawer containing the accused's clothing or other personal effects, *Walker v. United States*, 489 F.2d 714, 715 (8th Cir.) (drugs found in closet containing defendant's clothing), *cert. denied*, 416 U.S. 990, 94 S.Ct. 2399, 40 L. Ed.2d 768 (1974); presence of drug paraphernalia among the accused's personal effects or in a place over which the accused has special control, *United States v. James*, 494 F.2d 1007, 1030–31 (D.C.Cir.) (drug paraphernalia found in a locked box in defendant's dresser), *cert. denied sub nom.*, *Jackson v. United States*, 419 U.S. 1020, 95 S.Ct. 495, 42 L. Ed.2d 294 (1974); *Petley v. United States*, 427 F.2d 1101, 1106 (9th Cir.) (pipe containing marijuana residue found in defendant's duffel bag), *cert. denied*, 400 U.S. 827, 91 S.Ct. 55, 27 L. Ed.2d 57 (1970). In every case, the determination that someone has constructive possession of drugs is a factual determination which turns on the particular circumstances of the case. Among these circumstances must be facts which permit the inference that the accused intended to use the drugs as his or her own. . . .

The evidence as to Gary sufficiently supports his convictions for production of a controlled substance and possession of marijuana with an intent to distribute. Gary owned the property where the marijuana was found. Although he may not have had exclusive control or possession (in a practical non-legal sense) of the premises, his non-exclusive possession and control combined with other incriminating evidence to provide an adequate foundation for the convictions. Gary owned the house. His occupancy and control was evidenced by the presence of his personal effects in the same room as marijuana, drug-related paraphernalia, and a book entitled Marijuana Grower's Guide. Another room also contained marijuana and drug paraphernalia. Because he was the owner and occupier of the property and because of the manner in which the greenhouses were constructed in proximity to the house, one being accessible only through the house, there is a reasonable inference that he not only knew of the greenhouses and their contents but also had the power and intent to exercise dominion and control over the marijuana located in them, and was responsible for growing the marijuana. Furthermore, there was sufficient evidence that he intended to distribute the marijuana. Where one possesses a controlled substance in a quantity too large for personal consumption, the trier of fact can infer that the possessor had an intent to distribute. The police found approximately 2,850 mature marijuana plants growing on Gary's property, an amount of marijuana unquestionably too large for personal use.

On these facts the evidence was sufficient to sustain the conviction of Gary Fox of possession of a controlled substance with intent to distribute, and production of a controlled substance.

Because one of the greenhouses was attached to the house and was openly accessible from the kitchen, the trier of fact could reasonably find that Clive Fox knew that marijuana was being grown in the house. However, to prove that he had constructive possession of the marijuana, the evidence must also show that he had the power and intent to exercise dominion or control over the marijuana. There is no evidence that Clive Fox had any intent to grow or to possess the marijuana in the greenhouses. While he may have had knowledge of the existence of marijuana on the premises, that is not the equivalent of constructive possession. Indeed, evidence supporting the theory of "constructive possession" must raise a reasonable inference that the defendant was engaged in a criminal enterprise and not simply a bystander. That is, the evidence in its totality must show that defendant's dominion or control over the area must have been such that he in fact intended to exercise dominion and control over the marijuana.

The evidence showed that the telephone at 246 Harris Street was in Clive's name, that he was seen there on an undated occasion doing yard work, that mail addressed to him was found at unspecified locations within the house, and that his expired identification card was found in the room that apparently was his sleeping quarters, which contained no marijuana or related paraphernalia. On the totality of the evidence, a reasonable person could not find beyond a reasonable doubt that Clive had even non-exclusive dominion or control over the area where the marijuana was found. There was not any evidence at all beyond the possibility that Clive sometimes occupied the premises to link Clive Fox to the marijuana. In addition, there is no evidence that Clive grew the marijuana plants or participated in producing or distributing the marijuana.

The conviction of Gary Fox is affirmed. The conviction of Clive Fox is reversed, and that case is remanded for the purpose of discharging him.

■ DURHAM and ZIMMERMAN, JJ., concur.

■ HALL, CHIEF JUSTICE (concurring and dissenting):

I do not join the Court in overturning the convictions of defendant Clive Fox because I am not persuaded that the evidence is insufficient to prove guilt beyond a reasonable doubt.

This Court's standard of review when faced with a claim of insufficiency of the evidence is to view the evidence, and the facts reasonably to be inferred therefrom, in the light most favorable to the determination made by the trier of fact. We will only interfere when the evidence is so lacking and insubstantial that a reasonable person could not possibly have determined guilt beyond a reasonable doubt.

The evidence was that defendant's identification card and mail addressed to him were found in the residence. Phone service was in his name. The neighbors testified that defendant had lived there with defendant Gary Fox over a period of three years and that they had constructed the greenhouse which was only accessible through a door off the kitchen. No one else but defendant was identified as living in the house. Items of men's clothing were in the bedrooms, dirty dishes were in the sink, beds were unmade, and food was stocked in cupboards and in the refrigerator, all of which indicated the house was used as a dwelling.

The entire house was a virtual marijuana production center. The attached greenhouse was filled with growing marijuana plants which made the premises uncomfortably humid. The doorway from the kitchen afforded an unobstructed view of the greenhouse and its contents. A large bag of harvested marijuana was found in the kitchen, a common area of the house likely to be used daily by the occupants.

It was certainly reasonable to infer that not just one but *both* defendants knew of the greenhouse and its contents, had the power and intent to exercise dominion and control over the marijuana, and were jointly engaged in growing the marijuana and holding it for sale.

I would affirm the convictions of both defendants.

■ HOWE, J., concurs in the concurring and dissenting opinion of CHIEF JUSTICE HALL.

NOTES AND QUESTIONS

1. In *Fox*, is the court discussing the *act* of possession or the *mental element* of the crime for which the defendants have been convicted or both?

In *Fox* the defendants were charged not just with possession of marijuana (which is itself criminal), but with possession with intent to distribute. How can the state prove this latter intent? Why was Clive Fox's conviction not also affirmed by the Supreme Court of Utah? Was he just lucky? Would it have made a difference if he had been present either at the time the officer originally investigated the anonymous tip or at the time of the execution of the search warrant subsequently obtained? Incidentally, should the police be able to obtain a warrant to search private property on the basis of an anonymous tip?

What if a number of people are found at the scene of the execution of a search warrant where narcotics are found? Are they all guilty of possession? *See* Feltes v. People, 178 Colo. 409, 498 P.2d 1128 (1972); Speight v. United States, 599 A.2d 794 (D.C.Ct.App. 1991). Incidentally, do police have to obtain a warrant in order to search a private dwelling?

In addition to the defendant's presence at the scene where contraband is found, are his or her fingerprints on the receptacle containing the narcotics enough to establish possession? *See* State v. Spruell, 57 Wash.App. 383, 788 P.2d 21 (1990).

Is the discovery of a large quantity of drugs in plain view enough to establish possession on the part of all joint occupants of the premises? Are the only alternatives conviction of all or conviction of none? *See* United States v. Davis, 562 F.2d 681, 183 U.S. App. D.C. 162 (1977). Note especially Judge Bazelon's often cited dissenting opinion on the issue of constructive possession. *Id.* at 694–701.

2. Note the following statutory presumptions:

    a.   A person who is present in a dwelling where narcotics are found is presumed to be in possession thereof.

    b.   A person who is present in a vehicle where narcotics are found is presumed to be in possession thereof.

    c.   A person who is present in a dwelling [vehicle] where over ten ounces of marijuana [one hundred grams of cocaine] is found is presumed to be in possession thereof.

    d.   A person in possession of over ten ounces of marijuana [one hundred grams of cocaine] is presumed to be in possession with the intent to deliver the same.

See infra Chapter 2, Section D.2.

3. Does the *act of possession* require knowledge of the physical character or qualities of the property possessed in addition to awareness of the presence of the object, i.e., does *possession* require knowledge that a green leafy substance is, in fact, marijuana or that white powder one controls is cocaine? *See* State v. Carson, 941 S.W.2d 518 (Mo. 1997); Dawkins v. State, 313 Md. 638, 547 A.2d 1041 (1988); Model Penal Code, § 2.01(4) (below). If so, is such knowledge required by the definition of possession or because the relevant possessory crime also has a mental state component?

4. The Model Penal Code, § 2.01(4) defines possession in the following manner:

> Possession is an act within the meaning of this Section, if the possessor knowingly procured or received the thing possessed or was aware of his control thereof for a sufficient period to have been able to terminate his possession.

3. INACTION

State v. Miranda

Supreme Court of Connecticut, 1998.
245 Conn. 209, 715 A.2d 680.

■ KATZ, ASSOCIATE JUSTICE.

The issue in this appeal is whether a person who is not the biological or legal parent of a child but who establishes a familial relationship with a woman and her infant child, voluntarily assumes responsibility for the care and welfare of the child, and considers himself the child's stepfather, has a legal duty to protect the child from abuse, such that the breach of that duty exposes the person to criminal liability pursuant to General Statutes § 53a–59(a)(3). After a court trial, the defendant, Santos Miranda, was convicted of six counts of assault in the first degree in violation of § 53a–59 (a)(3), and one count of risk of injury to a child in violation of General Statutes § 53–21. The court concluded that the defendant had established a familial relationship with the victim and her mother, that his failure to help and protect the child from abuse constituted a gross deviation from the standard of conduct that a reasonable person would observe in the situation, and that such reckless conduct resulted in serious physical injuries to the child. . . .⁴ The court imposed a total effective sentence of forty years imprisonment.

* * *

As set forth in its memorandum of decision, the trial court found the following facts. The defendant commenced living with his girlfriend and her two children in an apartment in September, 1992. On January 27, 1993, the defendant was twenty-one years old, his girlfriend was sixteen, her son was two, and her daughter, the victim in this case, born on September 21, 1992, was four months old. Although he was not the biological father of either child, the defendant took care of them and considered himself to be their stepfather. He represented himself as such to the people at Meriden Veteran's Memorial Hospital where, on January 27, 1993, the victim was taken for treatment of her injuries following a 911 call by the defendant that the child was choking on milk. Upon examination at the hospital, it was determined that the victim had multiple rib fractures that were approximately two to three weeks old, two skull fractures that were approximately seven to ten days old, a brachial plexus injury to her left arm, a rectal tear that was actively "oozing blood" and bilateral subconjunctival nasal hemorrhages. On the basis of extensive medical evidence, the trial court . . . found that the

---

⁴ Although the trial court never stated who actually had caused the injuries, we take judicial notice that the child's mother entered a plea of nolo contendere to the crimes of intentional assault in the first degree and risk of injury to a minor. She received a sentence of twelve years incarceration suspended after seven years.

injuries, many of which created a risk of death, had been caused by great and deliberate force.

The trial court further found in accordance with the medical evidence that, as a result of the nature of these injuries, at the time they were sustained the victim would have screamed inconsolably, and that her injuries would have caused noticeable physical deformities, such as swelling, bruising and poor mobility, and finally, that her intake of food would have been reduced. The court also determined that anyone who saw the child would have had to notice these injuries, the consequent deformities and her reactions. Indeed, the trial court found that the defendant had been aware of the various bruises on her right cheek and the subconjunctival nasal hemorrhages, as well as the swelling of the child's head, that he knew she had suffered a rectal tear, as well as rib fractures posteriorly on the left and right sides, and that he was aware that there existed a substantial and unjustifiable risk that the child was exposed to conduct that created a risk of death. The trial court concluded that despite this knowledge, the defendant "failed to act to help or aid [the child] by promptly notifying authorities of her injuries, taking her for medical care, removing her from her circumstances and guarding her from future abuses. As a result of his failure to help her, the child was exposed to conduct which created a risk of death to her and the child suffered subsequent serious physical injuries. . . ."

The trial court concluded that the defendant had a legal duty to protect the health and well-being of the child based on the undisputed facts that he had established a familial relationship with the child's mother and her two children, that he had voluntarily assumed responsibility for the care and welfare of both children, and that he considered himself the victim's stepfather. On the basis of these circumstances, the trial court found the defendant guilty of one count of § 53–21 and six counts of § 53a–59 (a)(3).

I

* * *

The trend of Anglo-American law has been toward enlarging the scope of criminal liability for failure to act in those situations in which the common law or statutes have imposed an affirmative responsibility for the safety and well-being of others. See generally 1 W. LaFave & A. Scott, Substantive Criminal Law (1986) § 3.3; annot., 61 A.L.R.3d 1207 (1975); annot., 100 A.L.R.2d 483 (1965). Criminal liability of parents based on a failure to act in accordance with common-law affirmative duties to protect and care for their children is well recognized in many jurisdictions. See, e.g., *People v. Stanciel*, 153 Ill.2d 218, 180 Ill.Dec. 124, 606 N.E.2d 1201 (1992) (mother guilty of homicide by allowing known abuser to assume role of disciplinarian over child); *Smith v. State*, 408 N.E.2d 614 (Ind.App.1980) (mother held criminally responsible for failing to prevent fatal beating of child by her lover); *State v. Walden*, 306 N.C.

466, 293 S.E.2d 780 (1982) (mother guilty of assault for failure to prevent beating); *State v. Williquette*, 129 Wis.2d 239, 385 N.W.2d 145 (1986) (mother guilty of child abuse for allowing child to be with person known previously to have been abusive and who subsequently abused child again). In light of this duty to protect and care for children, courts in these jurisdictions have concluded that, where this duty exists and injury results, the failure to protect the child from harm will be "deemed to be the cause of those injuries" and the person bearing the duty may face criminal sanctions. *State v. Peters*, 116 Idaho 851, 855, 780 P.2d 602 (1989).

. . . We agree that criminal conduct can arise not only through overt acts, but also by an omission to act when there is a legal duty to do so. "Omissions are as capable of producing consequences as overt acts. Thus, the common law rule that there is no general duty to protect limits criminal liability where it would otherwise exist. The special relationship exception to the 'no duty to act' rule represents a choice to retain liability for some omissions, which are considered morally unacceptable." *State v. Williquette*, supra, 129 Wis.2d at 253, 385 N.W.2d 145. Therefore, had the defendant been the victim's parent—someone with an undisputed affirmative legal obligation to protect and provide for his minor child—we would conclude that his failure to protect the child from abuse could constitute a violation of § 53a–59(a)(3).

II

We next turn to the issue of whether the duty to protect can be imposed on the defendant, an adult member of the household unrelated to the child. Both the state and the defendant recognize that the determination of the existence of a legal duty is a question of law subject to de novo review by this court. . . .

The defendant argues that there is no statutory or common-law precept "authorizing the expansion of assault under § 53a–59(a)(3)." The state argues that there is both. We conclude that, based on the trial court's findings that the defendant had established a family-like relationship with the mother and her two children, that he had voluntarily assumed responsibility for the care and welfare of both children, and that he had considered himself the victim's stepfather, there existed a common-law duty to protect the victim from her mother's abuse, the breach of which can be the basis of a conviction under § 53a–59(a)(3). . . .

There are many statutes that expressly impose a legal duty to act and attach liability for the failure to comply with that duty. . . . With other statutes, however, the duty to act can be found outside the statutory definition of the crime itself, either in another statute; . . . or in the common law. 1 W. LaFave & A. Scott, supra, § 3.3(a), p. 283.

* * *

. . . The issue, therefore, is whether the principle should be recognized as a matter of policy under the circumstances of this case. We conclude that, under the facts of this case, it is appropriate to recognize an affirmative duty to act and to impose criminal liability for the failure to act pursuant to that duty.

" 'Duty is a legal conclusion about relationships between individuals, made after the fact. . . . The nature of the duty, and the specific persons to whom it is owed, are determined by the circumstances surrounding the conduct of the individual.' " *Clohessy v. Bachelor*, 237 Conn. 31, 45, 675 A.2d 852 (1996). Although one generally has no legal duty to aid another in peril, even when the aid can be provided without danger or inconvenience to the provider, there are four widely recognized situations in which the failure to act may constitute breach of a legal duty: (1) where one stands in a certain relationship to another; (2) where a statute imposes a duty to help another; (3) where one has assumed a contractual duty; and (4) where one voluntarily has assumed the care of another. 1 W. LaFave & A. Scott, supra, § 3.3(a)(1)–(4), pp. 284–87. The state argues that this case falls within both the first and fourth situations, or some combination thereof.

We begin with the duty based upon the relationship between the parties. One standing in a certain personal relationship to another person has some affirmative duties of care with regard to that person. . . .

* * *

In addition to biological and adoptive parents and legal guardians, there may be other adults who establish familial relationships with and assume responsibility for the care of a child, thereby creating a legal duty to protect that child from harm. See, e.g., *Cornell v. State*, 159 Fla. 687, 32 So.2d 610 (1947) (grandmother guilty of manslaughter in death of grandchild where she had assumed care of child but became so intoxicated that she allowed child to smother to death). "Recognizing the primary responsibility of a natural parent does not mean that an unrelated person may not also have some responsibilities incident to the care and custody of a child. Such duties may be regarded as derived from the primary custodian, i.e., the natural parent, or arise from the nature of the circumstances." . . .

Most courts deciding whether, under a particular set of facts, liability for an omission to act may be imposed under a statute that does not itself impose a duty to act, have looked to whether a duty to act exists in another statute, in the common law or in a contract. 1 W. LaFave & A. Scott, supra, § 3.3(a), p. 283. Of those courts acting outside the context of a statutory or contractual duty that have held a defendant criminally liable for failing to protect a child from injury, most have relied on a combination of both the first and fourth situations described by Professors LaFave and Scott to establish a duty as the predicate for the defendant's conviction. More specifically, these courts have examined the nature of the relationship of the defendant to the victim and whether the defendant, as part of that relationship, had assumed a responsibility for the victim. We find the reliance by these courts on this combination of factors persuasive.

* * *

. . . The traditional approach in this country is to restrict the duty to save others from harm to certain very narrow categories of cases. We are not prepared now to adopt a broad general rule covering other circumstances. We conclude only that, in accordance with the trial court findings, when the defendant, who considered himself the victim's parent, established a familial relationship with the victim's mother and her children and assumed the role of a father, he assumed, under the common law, the same legal duty to protect the victim from the abuse as if he were, in fact, the victim's guardian. Under these circumstances, to require the defendant as a matter of law to take affirmative action to prevent harm to the victim or be criminally responsible imposes a reasonable duty. That duty does not depend on an ability to regulate the mother's discipline of the victim or on the defendant having exclusive control of the victim when the injuries occurred. Nor is the duty contingent upon an ability by the state or the mother to look to the defendant for child support. . . .

* * *

The judgment of the Appellate Court is reversed and the case is remanded to that court for consideration of the defendant's remaining claims.[25]

* * *

■ BERDON, ASSOCIATE JUSTICE, dissenting.

Cases, such as the one before us, that present revolting facts concerning the physical abuse of a four month old child, test the foundation of our democracy. The rule of law must be upheld even when confronted with alarming allegations of improper acts, indeed allegations of loathsome conduct on the part of the defendant. The question for this court, in cases such as this, is whether the legislature intended to make the conduct with which the defendant was charged criminal under General Statutes § 53a–59 (a)(3), assault in the first degree. It is not whether this court, were it sitting as a legislature, would have proscribed the conduct at issue. "Such action by a legislature may well be commendable, but by a court condemnable." *State v. Williquette*, 129 Wis.2d 239, 263, 385 N.W.2d 145 (1986) (HEFFERNAN, C.J., dissenting).

---

25   The defendant has argued that he did not actually know that the child had been abused by her mother and that knowledge of her injuries should not be equated with knowledge of their cause. He also argues that there was no evidence that he had the ability to prevent any harm from occurring to the child. Those claims of insufficiency of evidence are to be considered on the merits by the Appellate Court on remand. . . .

Simply put, we cannot craft a substantive offense ex post facto in order to include conduct that we find abhorrent to our sensitivities and that of the general public. It is this judicial restraint that sharply puts into focus one of the essential differences between democratic and totalitarian forms of government.

The facts of this case, as they pertain to the issues before us, are as follows: The trial court concluded that the defendant, Santos Miranda, was guilty of six counts of assault in the first degree in violation of § 53a–59 (a)(3), not because he physically abused the child, nor because he aided in the abuse of the child, but, rather, as a result of the following: (1) that he lived with the physically abused child and the child's mother in the same household as a "live-in boyfriend"; (2) that he established a "family-like" relationship with the child—he considered himself her stepfather and he took care of her like a father; and (3) that he was aware of the child's injuries but failed to notify the authorities, failed to obtain medical treatment for her, failed to remove her from the circumstances and failed to guard her from future abuse. The Appellate Court reversed the defendant's assault convictions, holding that the "failure to act when one is under no legal duty to do so, thereby permitting a dangerous condition to exist, is not sufficient to support a conviction for assault in the first degree pursuant to § 53a–59 (a)(3)." . . . I agree with the Appellate Court.

* * *

II

The majority addresses . . . whether the "conduct" referred to in § 53a–59(a)(3) includes the failure to act. I disagree with the majority's very tenuous argument that it does. Section 53a–59(a) provides in part that "[a] person is guilty of assault in the first degree when . . . (3) under circumstances evincing an extreme indifference to human life he recklessly engages in conduct which creates a risk of death to another person, and thereby causes serious physical injury to another person. . . ." Although "conduct" can include the failure to act under circumstances when there is a duty to act; 1 W. LaFave & A. Scott, Substantive Criminal Law (1986) § 3.3., p. 282; the majority points to nothing in the text of § 53a–59(a)(3), or its legislative history, to support its conclusion that conduct under § 53a–59 (a)(3) includes the failure to act. In fact, both the common definition of assault—"a violent attack with physical means"; Webster's Third New International Dictionary; and the legal definition of assault—"[a]ny wilful attempt or threat to inflict injury upon the person of another"; Black's Law Dictionary (6th Ed.1990); belie the majority's claim.

* * *

III

Nevertheless, even if the majority were correct that one person can assault another person under § 53a–59(a)(3) by failing to act, the defendant's conviction in this case cannot stand. By superimposing on § 53a–59(a)(3) a common-law duty on the part of a person to act in order to protect a child from harm when that third person voluntarily assumes responsibility for the care and the welfare of the child and considers himself to have a stepfather-stepchild relationship with the child, the majority has created *a new crime*. . . . In crafting this new crime, the majority ignores the fact that it is the legislature that defines substantive crimes. . . .

* * *

IV

The legislature will be very much surprised to discover that we have in place, under § 53a–59(a)(3), a law that provides that the failure to act is punishable criminal conduct. Although the legislature recently has grappled with the issue of imposing an affirmative obligation on the part of a parent and an unrelated adult to protect children from abuse; see Substitute House Bill No. 5283 (1988) (H.B. No. 5283), entitled "An Act Concerning Facilitation of Abuse of a Child";[10] it did not enact the proposed legislation. Nevertheless, the majority of this court, without any understanding of the implications of its decision today and without the aid of expert advice that is available to the legislature through the public hearing process, impetuously and presumptuously crafts a crime of assault that was never intended by the legislature. Clearly, if the legislature agreed with the majority that, pursuant to § 53a–59(a)(3), parents as well as unrelated adults had an affirmative legal obligation to protect children from abuse, it never would have had a need to consider H.B. No. 5283, a bill that explicitly criminalizes the conduct with which the defendant was charged in the present case.

The representatives of several state agencies and several non-profit groups created to support victims of abuse spoke out against H.B. No. 5283 at the public hearing before the legislature's select committee on children. The remarks of these speakers set forth several significant reasons why this court should not undertake the legislative function and declare by judicial fiat that, "as a matter of policy under the circumstances of this case," the defendant in this case had an affirmative legal obligation under § 53a–59(a)(3) to protect the child from abuse.[12]

---

[10] The select committee on children issued a favorable report on H.B. No. 5283 to the judiciary committee. The judiciary committee took no action on H.B. No. 5283 and, as of this date, the bill remains dormant.

Substitute House Bill No. 5283, § 1(a) provides: "A person is guilty of facilitation of abuse of a child when, as a parent, guardian or caretaker of a child, such person fails to act to protect the child from death or serious physical injury by another person under circumstances where there is a continuing course of abusive conduct and the parent, guardian or caretaker reasonably should have known of such conduct."

[12] Paul Robinson, in his article *Criminal Liability for Omissions: A Brief Summary and Critique of the Law in the United States*, 29 N.Y.L. SCH. L. REV. 101, 104 (1984), also points out several reasons why the issue of imposing affirmative legal obligations on persons to protect children from abuse is best left for the legislature. "There is a general, albeit declining,

I would affirm the judgment of the Appellate Court.

Accordingly, I dissent.

NOTES AND QUESTIONS

1. In 2002, the Connecticut Supreme Court again heard the *Miranda* case, ruling that their earlier decision did not violate the notice requirements of the Due Process Clause or amount to *ex post facto* law-making. The court also ruled that there was sufficient evidence to support finding that the defendant was actually aware of and consciously disregarded the abuse of the victim, and that the evidence of the defendant's ability and opportunity to report the abuse also was sufficient. State v. Miranda, 260 Conn. 93, 794 A.2d 506 (2002).

Then, in 2004, the Connecticut Supreme Court again granted review on a sentencing issue in the case, but also requested a supplemental brief on whether the defendant could be convicted of assault in the first degree for failing to protect the victim from physical abuse by the mother. In a 2005 per curiam opinion, the court, in a split decision, reversed the conviction for first-degree assault. Three judges concluded that a person in the defendant's position—neither a parent or legal guardian—could not be found to owe a legal duty to the child such as to be held liable for an omission. Three separate judges concluded that a failure to act cannot constitute an assault within the meaning of the Connecticut first-degree assault statute. Only Justice Katz, who wrote the original opinion, dissented. Miranda's conviction for risk of injury to a child, based on his own negligence, was affirmed. State v. Miranda, 274 Conn. 727, 878 A.2d 1118 (2005).

2. A number of courts have imposed criminal liability in cases similar to *Miranda. See, e.g.*, Leet v. State, 595 So.2d 959 (Fla.App. 1991) (defendant in family-like relationship criminally responsible for abuse of a child by his mother although he was not the child's father); State v. Orosco, 113 N.M. 789, 833 P.2d 1155 (1991) (defendant who lived with victim's mother guilty of abuse for failing to intervene when one of his friends sexually abused the victim); People v. Wong, 182 App.Div.2d 98, 588 N.Y.S.2d 119 (1992), *rev'd on other grounds*, 81 N.Y.2d 600, 601 N.Y.S.2d 440, 619 N.E.2d 377 (1993) (babysitters for the child victim's parents); People v. Salley, 153 App.Div.2d 704, 544 N.Y.S.2d 680 (1989) (female live-in companion of three-year-old's assailant properly convicted of manslaughter).

---

reluctance in the United States to impose affirmative duties and to punish nonperformance of those duties. Various explanations for the reluctance to criminalize inactivity have been offered. First, there is difficulty in defining with sufficient clarity the effort that must be expended in order to satisfy the duty. Second, the inherent ambiguity in defining the scope of a duty leads to speculation about guilt and thereby poses a threat to society more serious than the harm prevented by requiring affirmative conduct. Third, because 'prevailing attitudes draw sharp distinctions between overt action and passivity[, the] legislature cannot ignore the mores, nor should it implement them beyond necessary limits.' Finally, a governmental demand to perform is significantly more intrusive than a command to refrain from harmful action and therefore must be justified by a significant overriding public interest and must be imposed in a way that minimizes the extent of intrusion." *Id.*

Problem 2–1. Reverend David Konz, while serving as a teacher, counselor, and chaplin at United Wesleyan College, became acquainted with Erikson, a student at the college. A close friendship, based on their common interest in religion, formed between Erikson and Reverend Konz as the former became a regular visitor at the latter's residence. Reverend Konz was a thirty-four-year-old diabetic and had, for seventeen years, administered to himself daily doses of insulin. However, following an encounter on campus with a visiting evangelist speaker, Reverend Konz publicly proclaimed his desire to discontinue insulin treatment in reliance on the belief that God would heal the diabetic condition. He assured the president of the College and members of the student body that he would carefully monitor his condition and would, if necessary, take insulin. On only one or two occasions did the Reverend thereafter administer insulin. Shortly thereafter, however, Erikson and Reverend Konz formed a pact to pray together to enable the latter to resist the temptation to administer insulin.

Dorothy Konz, the Reverend's wife, being informed of the prayer pact, later concealed insulin from her husband, and, along with Erikson, prevented Reverend Konz from telephoning police to obtain assistance. Nevertheless, all was settled amicably and no further request for insulin was ever made by Reverend Konz. He told relatives that "It's all settled now" and "Everything is fine" and that he did not intend to take insulin.

In the next twenty-four hours, Reverend Konz developed symptoms of insulin deficiency, including fatigue, nausea, and vomiting, and remained in bed the following day. As his condition worsened, his wife and Erikson administered cracked ice but did not summon medical aid. Reverend Konz died of diabetic ketoacidosis the following morning.

Should the state file charges in the death of Reverend Konz? Against whom? Under what theory or theories of criminal responsibility? Did Dorothy Konz (or Erikson) owe a legal duty of care to Reverend Konz? *See* Commonwealth v. Konz, 498 Pa. 639, 450 A.2d 638 (1982).

3. What is the nature of the difference between a legal duty and a moral obligation? Should state legislatures consider adopting a criminal statute generally requiring a person to go the aid of another in distress? If so, how should such a statute be worded?

Consider the cases of Katherine ("Kitty") Genovese who was murdered outside her apartment building on Queens, N.Y., while thirty-eight persons ignored her screams for help and failed to summon police. *See* ABRAHAM M. ROSENTHAL, THIRTY-EIGHT WITNESSES (1964). Also consider the more recent case of David Cash, a high school senior at the time, who was aware that his friend, Jeremy Strohmeyer, was attacking a seven-year-old girl (she was raped and murdered) in the bathroom of a Las Vegas casino, but did nothing to aid the victim or otherwise prevent the crime. *See Campus Peers Shun Student Who Did Not Report Child's Killing*, N.Y. TIMES, Oct. 4, 1998, at A29.

Some states have statutes requiring persons to summon assistance for victims of assaults or imposing a statutory duty on bystanders to give reasonable assistance in an emergency. *See* Hawai'i Rev. Stat. § 663–1.6; Vt.

Stat. Ann. tit. 12, § 519; Wis. Stat. Ann. 940.34. The Vermont statute reads as follows:

> A person who knows that another is exposed to grave physical harm shall, to the extent that the same can be rendered without danger or peril to himself or without interference with important duties owed to others, give reasonable assistance to the exposed person unless that assistance or care is being provided by others.

4. The duty to act may be imposed by statute. Under 26 U.S.C.A. § 7203 a person who is required by the Internal Revenue Act to file tax returns "who willfully fails to . . . make such a return" shall be guilty of a misdemeanor.

Also, most states have statutes requiring a driver involved in an accident to stop at the scene. *See, e.g.*, W.V. Code § 17C–4–1. Under such a provision, should the jury be instructed that the defendant must have known of the accident? *See* State v. Tennant, 173 W.Va. 627, 319 S.E.2d 395 (1984).

5. Although the "act" requirement has a well-established meaning from the common law, modern criminal codes that have done away with the common law crimes must define these concepts statutorily. *See, e.g.*, Mo. Rev. Stat. § 562.011:

> Voluntary Act.
>
> 1. A person is not guilty of an offense unless his liability is based on conduct which includes a voluntary act.
>
> 2. A "voluntary act" is
>
> > (1) A bodily movement performed while conscious as a result of effort or determination; or
> >
> > (2) An omission to perform an act of which the actor is physically capable.
>
> 3. Possession is a voluntary act if the possessor knowingly procures or receives the thing possessed, or having acquired control of it was aware of his control for a sufficient time to enable him to dispose of it or terminate his control.
>
> 4. A person is not guilty of an offense based solely on an omission to perform an act unless the law defining the offense expressly so provides, or a duty to perform the omitted act is otherwise imposed by law.

B. MENTAL STATE—"*MENS REA*"

1. SPECIFIC AND GENERAL INTENT

State v. Trinkle

Supreme Court of Illinois, 1977.
68 Ill.2d 198, 12 Ill.Dec. 181, 369 N.E.2d 888.

■ MR. JUSTICE DOOLEY delivered the opinion of the court.

Here the issue is whether a specific intent is requisite for the crime of attempted murder under the Criminal Code of 1961.

On February 28, 1974, the defendant drank 20 to 30 glasses of beer in Suppan's Tavern. The bartender, believing defendant to be intoxicated, refused him further service. After consuming more drinks in another bar, defendant purchased a .357 handgun. He returned to the area of Suppan's Tavern, fired a shot at the building, and wounded a patron within. He was indicted and convicted of the crime of attempted murder (Ill. Rev. Stat. 1973, ch. 38, pars. 8–4, 9–1). The appellate court held that a specific intent is an indispensable element to this crime, and hence the indictment and instructions relating to this crime were fatally erroneous.

* * *

The indictment charged:

"David Francis Trinkle committed the offense of ATTEMPT (MURDER) in that said defendant did perform a substantial step toward the commission of that offense in that he did without lawful justification shoot Gayle Lane with a gun knowing that such act created a strong probability of death or great bodily harm to Gayle Lane or another . . ."

The jury was instructed:

"A person commits the crime of attempt who, with intent to commit the crime of murder, does any act which constitutes a substantial step toward the commission of the crime of murder. The crime attempted need not have been committed."

"A person commits the crime of murder who kills an individual if, in performing the acts which cause the death he knows that such acts create a strong possibility of death or great bodily harm to that individual or another."

* * *

The State would urge that actual intention to kill is not a requisite mental state for attempted murder, and it suffices so long as the accused acted with such disregard of human life knowing his conduct created a strong probability of bodily harm.

Here, under the terms of the indictment as well as the instructions, the jury could have found the defendant guilty of attempted murder sans specific intent to kill. So long as he shot a gun "knowing such act created a strong probability of death or great bodily harm to Gayle Lane or another," the defendant could be guilty of attempted murder. But the General Assembly has exacted that the defendant must be guilty of an action "with intent to commit a specific offense" (Ill. Rev. Stat. 1973, ch. 38, par. 8–4(a)), namely, to kill. Hence the indictment and the instructions did not meet the criterion of the law. It is not sufficient that the defendant shot a gun "knowing such act created a strong probability of death or great bodily harm to Gayle Lane or another." If this were the test, then a defendant who committed a battery with knowledge that such conduct could cause great bodily harm would be guilty of attempted murder. . . .

* * *

Our position here is consistent with *People v. Viser* (1975), 62 Ill. 2d 568. There a conviction of attempted murder was reversed for failure of the indictment to charge "an attempt to commit a specific offense." . . .

* * *

It was there held reversible error to instruct the jury that the defendants could be found guilty of attempted murder without the specific intent, noting that under the terms of the instructions the defendants could have been found guilty of attempting to murder the deceased if the jury believed the defendants had committed an aggravated battery upon him.

The requirement that a conviction for attempted murder must be based on a charge and upon evidence that defendant had the intent to take a life is followed in many jurisdictions. See, *e.g., People v. Miller* (1935), 2 Cal. 2d 527, 42 P.2d 308; *Thacker v. Commonwealth* (1922), 134 Va. 767, 114 S.E. 504; Annot., 54 A.L.R.3d 612 (1973); Smith, *Two Problems in Criminal Attempts*, 70 Harv. L. Rev. 422, 429 (1957); W. LaFave and A. Scott, Criminal Law sec. 59, at 428–29 (1972); Perkins, Criminal Law sec. 3, at 573–74 (2d ed. 1969).

In *Thacker v. Commonwealth* (1922), 134 Va. 767, 114 S.E. 504, defendant and two companions were standing outside a tent which was, as defendant knew, occupied by a woman. Stating that he wanted to shoot out a lamp which was burning inside, defendant fired a gun into the tent, narrowly missing the occupant. Defendant's conviction for attempted murder was reversed for lack of proof of specific intent to kill. The court said: "And where it takes a particular intent to constitute a crime, that particular intent must be proved either by direct or circumstantial evidence . . ." (134 Va. 767, 770, 114 S.E. 504, 505.) The court also went on to quote from 1 Bishop, Criminal Law sec. 730 (8th ed.), as follows: " '. . . Thus . . . to commit murder, one need not intend to take life, but to be guilty of an attempt to murder, he must so intend. . . .' " There the facts are, of course, stronger against the defendant than here, where there is no evidence that this defendant knew someone was standing behind the door to the bar. 134 Va. 767, 771, 114 S.E. 504, 506.

LaFave and Scott (Criminal Law sec. 59, at 428–29 (1972)) point out how in the crime of attempted murder there must be a specific intent to commit the specific offense, unlike the crime of murder, which does not exact that specific intent:

"Some crimes, such as murder, are defined in terms of acts causing a particular result plus some mental state which need not be an intent to bring about that result. Thus, if *A, B,* and *C* have each taken the life of another, *A* acting with intent to kill, *B* with an intent to do serious bodily injury, and *C* with a reckless disregard of human life, all three are guilty of murder because the crime of murder is defined in such a way that any one of these mental states will suffice. However, if the victims do not die from their injuries, then only *A* is guilty of attempted murder; on a charge of attempted murder it is not sufficient to show that the defendant intended to do serious bodily harm or that he acted in reckless disregard for human life. Again, this is because intent is needed for the crime of attempt, so that attempted murder requires an intent to bring about that result described by the crime of murder (i.e., the death of another)."

To obtain a conviction on the charge of attempted murder, the indictment must charge a specific intent to commit the specific offense, and the jury must be accordingly instructed.

For the reasons expressed here, the judgment of the appellate court is affirmed.

Judgment affirmed.

State v. Rocker

Supreme Court of Hawai'i, 1970.
52 Hawai'i 336, 475 P.2d 684.

■ RICHARDSON, CHIEF JUSTICE. Defendants-appellants, having waived a jury trial, were tried in the circuit court of the second circuit and found guilty as charged for violation of HRS § 727–1 for creating a common nuisance. The complaint read: "That Richard Barry Rocker and Joseph Cava [defendants] at Pu'u Olai, Makena, District of Makawao, County of Maui, State of Hawaii, on the 26th day of February, 1969, did openly sun bathe in the nude, which was offensive and against common decency or common morality, thereby committing the offense of common nuisance, contrary to the provisions of Section 727–1 of the Hawaii Revised Statutes."

It is undisputed that on February 26, 1969, police officers of the Maui Police Department received a phone call from an anonymous person and, thereafter, on the day of the call, proceeded to the Pu'u Olai beach at

Makena to look for nude sunbathers. On reaching their destination, the police surveyed the beach from a ridge using both their naked eyes and binoculars and saw the defendants lying on the beach completely nude, one on his stomach and the other on his back. The officers then approached the defendants and arrested them for indecent exposure. It was admitted by the police officers that defendants were not at any time engaged in any activity other than sunbathing. At the time of the arrest there were several other people on the beach where the defendants were nude. Defendant Rocker was nude at the Pu'u Olai beach on other days before and after he was arrested on February 26, 1969. Defendant Cava likewise frequently sunbathed in the nude at the same beach prior to his arrest on February 26, 1969.

I.   *Indecent Exposure: Elements*

The first issue we are asked to decide on this appeal is whether defendants created a common nuisance by sunbathing in the nude on a public beach.

The statute (HRS § 727–1) reads as follows:

> The offense of common nuisance is the endangering of the public personal safety or health, or doing, causing or promoting, maintaining or continuing what is offensive, or annoying and vexatious, or plainly hurtful to the public; or is a public outrage against common decency or common morality; or tends plainly and directly to the corruption of the morals, honesty, and good habits of the people; the same being without authority or justification by law:
>
> As for example: * * *

* * *

> Open lewdness or lascivious behavior, or indecent exposure;

* * *

HRS § 727–1, unlike statutes of most states, incorporates indecent exposure as an example of what the legislature has defined to constitute common nuisances. The statute does not specifically delineate the elements of the crime of indecent exposure, and although reference to the common law or to cases decided in other jurisdictions based upon statutes different from ours may be helpful, neither is controlling. The question of whether sunbathing in the nude on a public beach is punishable as a common nuisance is one of construction of our statute.

* * *

. . . To create a common nuisance there must be an indecent exposure of the person in a public place where it may be seen by others if they pass by, and it need actually be seen by one person only.

However, to answer the specific questions presented to us on this appeal and to clarify and examine our construction of the statute in light of recent decisions in this and other jurisdictions, a further discussion of the elements of the crime of indecent exposure is needed.

A. Intent

Sunbathing in the nude is not per se illegal. It must be coupled with the intent to indecently expose oneself. Intent is an element of the crime of common nuisance defined by HRS § 727–1. The King v. Grieve, 6 Haw. 740 (1883). The intent necessary is a general intent, not a specific intent; i.e., it is not necessary that the exposure be made with the intent that some particular person see it, but only that the exposure was made where it was likely to be observed by others. Thus, the intent may be inferred from the conduct of the accused and the circumstances and environment of the occurrence. The criminal intent necessary for a conviction of indecent exposure is usually established by some action by which the defendant either (1) draws attention to his exposed condition or (2) by a display in a place so public that it must be presumed it was intended to be seen by others.

The defendants argue that there is no circumstantial evidence in the record from which a trier of fact could conclude that the element of intent had been proved beyond a reasonable doubt. The issue, therefore, is whether defendants' nude sunbathing at Pu'u Olai beach at Makena, Maui, was at a place *so public* that a trier of fact could infer it was intended to be seen by others. The prosecution offered testimony of one of the arresting police officers that the beach was a popular location for fishermen and was in fact one of his favorite fishing spots. Defendants testified that the public in general used the beach, that it was used by fishermen and local residents, and that they observed between 20 and 25 people on the beach over a two-month period. Although the Pu'u Olai beach is isolated by a hill and a ledge, away from the view of the public road and adjoining beaches, it is accessible by a well-worn path and known to be a favorite location of fishermen to cast and throw fish nets. In view of this and other evidence in the record, we cannot agree with defendants' argument that the trier of fact could not find the beach so public as to justify an inference of intent on the part of defendants to be seen by others.

* * *

III. *Motion for Acquittal: Test on Appeal*

The third issue raised on this appeal is whether the trial court erred in denying the defendants' motion for judgment of acquittal at the end of the prosecution's case. Rule 29(a), Motion for Judgment of Acquittal, of the Hawaii Rules of Criminal Procedure states in relevant part:

> The court on motion of a defendant or of its own motion shall order the entry of judgment of acquittal of one or more offenses charged in the indictment or information after the evidence on

either side is closed if the evidence is insufficient to sustain a conviction of such offense or offenses.

* * *

This court will not disturb the ruling of a lower court if the evidence of the prosecution is such that "a reasonable mind might fairly conclude guilt beyond a reasonable doubt." As discussed under section I of this opinion, the elements of the crime of indecent exposure that the prosecution must prove in order to establish a prima facie case against the defendants are that (1) the defendants expose themselves, (2) in a public place where it may be seen by others and (3) under circumstances that a trier of fact could infer a general intent of the defendants to offend the community's common sense of decency, propriety, and morality.

At the close of the prosecution's case it had been established that the defendants were seen by two police officers sunbathing in the nude at Pu'u Olai beach, a beach isolated by a hill and a ledge but accessible by a well worn path. One of the officers testified that the beach was a popular location for fishermen and was in fact one of his favorite fishing spots. From these facts the trial judge ruled that a prima facie case had been established and denied the defendants' motion for acquittal. We affirm this ruling. There was sufficient evidence at the close of the prosecution's case to justify an inference beyond a reasonable doubt that the Pu'u Olai beach was so public that the defendants could be attributed with the necessary knowledge to know that their acts under the circumstances were likely to offend members of the general public.

* * *

Affirmed.

■ LEVINSON, JUSTICE (dissenting).

* * *

III. *The Evidence Adduced by the Government at the Close of the Prosecution's Case Was Insufficient to Sustain a Conviction of the Offense Charged*

Before proceeding to my analysis of the insufficiency of the evidence offered by the prosecution I feel compelled to state the facts in the record at the close of the prosecution's case. I do this because I believe that the majority has failed to segregate clearly the prosecution's evidence from that offered by the defense and has omitted stating a key fact which I believe raises a reasonable doubt as to the defendants' guilt.

A. *The Evidence in the Record at the Close of the Prosecution's Case-in-Chief*

The State's case consisted solely of the testimony of the two arresting police officers. They both testified that the Pu'u Olai beach is isolated by a hill and a ledge, away from the view of the public road and adjoining beach. The beach is accessible by two trails. One is a well-worn path leading over the hill. The other is a trail on the Wailuku side of the beach, which is not well-used and connects the beach to a small road. The officers testified to being able to see, with the naked eye, the nudity of the defendants, from the crest of the hill.

One of the officers, George Matsunaga, testified that this beach was one of his favorite fishing spots and that it was a popular location for other fishermen. He also stated that the fishermen went to the beach in the "day or night." On examination by the court, Officer Matsunaga admitted that he had never seen the beach used for picnics or family recreation, and the only non-fishermen that he recalled having observed on this beach were what he called "hippie type characters." It was on this evidence alone that the State rested its case.

B.   *Intent to Be Seen by Others*

My reading of the majority opinion leads me to conclude that in order to prove a prima facie case against the defendants it was necessary for the prosecution to demonstrate that the defendants possessed a general intent to expose themselves in a place where it would be likely that they would be observed by others. To prove this, it would be enough for the prosecution to establish the defendants' awareness of sufficient facts and circumstances from which a trier of fact could infer such intent beyond a reasonable doubt. From the evidence in the record at the close of the prosecution's case I do not think that a trier of fact could be justified in inferring beyond a reasonable doubt that the defendants possessed the necessary general intent to be seen by others.

Although there was testimony that the beach was visited by fishermen there was no link established between the visits by the fishermen and visits to the beach by the defendants. Officer Matsunaga, one of the fishermen who used the beach, did not testify to ever having observed the defendants on this beach prior to arresting them. Thus, this evidence could not be used to support an inference that the defendants were aware that this beach was used by fishermen and therefore public.

Nor could a trier of fact infer beyond a reasonable doubt that the defendants were aware of the "well-worn" path leading over the hill to the beach and therefore knew that they were sunbathing in an area readily accessible to the public. One of the police officers testified that the beach was accessible by another trail which was *not* "well-used." There was no other evidence that would eliminate as a reasonable doubt the possibility that the defendants had used this other path and therefore inferred from its unused nature that the public would not be likely to see them. . . .

* * *

Since the prosecution failed to prove a prima facie case against the defendants the motion for acquittal was erroneously denied. I would reverse the convictions.

NOTES

1. Model Penal Code § 213.5 classifies indecent exposure as a sexual offense and defines it in the following manner:

> A person commits a misdemeanor if, for the purpose of arousing or gratifying sexual desire of himself or any person other than his spouse, he exposes his genitals under circumstances in which he knows his conduct is likely to cause affront or alarm.

Would Rocker and Cava have been guilty of violating this statute?

The Hawaii indecent exposure statute, Haw. Rev. Stat. § 707–734(1), currently reads:

> A person commits the offense of indecent exposure if, the person intentionally exposes the person's genitals to a person to whom the person is not married under circumstances in which the actor's conduct is likely to cause affront.

What would be the result under this provision? *See* State v. Kalama, 94 Hawai'i 60, 8 P.3d 1224 (2000).

2. The California Supreme Court, in In re Smith, 7 Cal.3d 362, 102 Cal.Rptr. 335, 497 P.2d 807 (1972), ruled that nude sunbathing on an isolated beach without any other sexual act being performed does not satisfy the requirements of the crime prohibiting the willful or lewd exposure of the private parts of the body.

In People v. Hardy, 77 Misc.2d 1092, 357 N.Y.S.2d 970 (1974), the court held that nude sunbathing on a public beach by the defendant, along with several other persons, did not in itself violate the New York public exposure statute: "Since no evidence was introduced establishing that defendant had intentionally exposed her private parts in a public place in a 'lewd' manner or otherwise committed a 'lewd act,' her guilt was not established beyond a reasonable doubt." N.Y. Pen. Laws § 245.00.

In Duvallon v. State, 404 So.2d 196 (Fla.App. 1981), defendant was protesting what she considered judicial and police corruption and picketed in front of the state's capitol and across from its Supreme Court building "dressed" in a 44.5 by 28 piece of cardboard suspended by a cord around her neck. She was arrested and charged with exposure of sexual organs. In reversing her conviction, the court said:

> We find no evidence in the present record that the petitioner exposed or exhibited her sexual organs in [a lewd and lascivious] manner. The arresting officer testified that the placard allowed exposure of her bare backside and the sides of her breasts, but he saw nothing lewd or lascivious about her conduct. The petitioner's behavior was, at a minimum, bizarre, but it falls short of being a vulgar and indecent exposure of her sexual organs.

3. In United States v. Jewell, 532 F.2d 697 (9th Cir. 1976), defendant was caught attempting to transport marijuana across the border from Mexico into the United States. The marijuana was concealed in a secret compartment between the rear seat and the trunk of the vehicle defendant was driving. Although he admitted knowing of the secret compartment he disclaimed knowledge of the marijuana. He claimed that a stranger named "Ray" had payed him $100 to drive the car north across the border and told a DEA agent that "he thought there was probably something wrong and something illegal in the vehicle, but that he checked it over. He looked in the glove box and under the front seat and in the trunk, prior to driving it. He didn't find anything, and, therefore, he assumed that the people at the border wouldn't find anything either."

The defendant was charged with *knowingly* bringing marijuana into the United States and *knowingly* possessing marijuana. He contended that the government was required to prove that he had positive knowledge of the presence of marijuana. However, the trial judge instructed the jury that

> [t]he Government can complete their burden of proof by proving, beyond as reasonable doubt, that if the defendant was not actually aware that there was marijuana in the vehicle he was driving when he entered the United States his ignorance in that regard was solely and entirely a result of his having made a conscious purpose to disregard the nature of that which was in the vehicle, with a conscious purpose to avoid learning the truth.

Who do you think is correct, the defendant or the trial judge? *See also* Alan C. Michaels, *Acceptance: The Missing Mental State*, 71 S. CAL. L. REV. 953 (1998).

2. MODEL PENAL CODE APPROACH

Section 2.02. General Requirements of Culpability.

(1) *Minimum Requirements of Culpability.* Except as provided in Section 2.05, a person is not guilty of an offense unless he acted purposely, knowingly, recklessly or negligently, as the law may require, with respect to each material element of the offense.

(2) *Kinds of Culpability Defined.*

(a) *Purposely.*

A person acts purposely with respect to a material element of an offense when:

> (i) if the element involves the nature of his conduct or a result thereof, it is his conscious object to engage in conduct of that nature or to cause such a result; and

> (ii) if the element involves the attendant circumstances, he is aware of the existence of such circumstances or he believes or hopes that they exist.

(b) Knowingly.

A person acts knowingly with respect to a material element of an offense when:

> (i) if the element involves the nature of his conduct or the attendant circumstances, he is aware that his conduct is of that nature or that such circumstances exist; and

> (ii) if the element involves a result of his conduct, he is aware that it is practically certain that his conduct will cause such a result.

(c) *Recklessly.*

A person acts recklessly with respect to a material element of an offense when he consciously disregards a substantial and unjustifiable risk that the material element exists or will result from his conduct. The risk must be of such a nature and degree that, considering the nature and purpose of the actor's conduct and the circumstances known to him, its disregard involves a gross deviation from the standard of conduct that a law-abiding person would observe in the actor's situation.

(d) *Negligently.*

A person acts negligently with respect to a material element of an offense when he should be aware of a substantial and unjustifiable risk that the material element exists or will result from his conduct. The risk must be of such a nature and degree that the actor's failure to perceive it, considering the nature and purpose of his conduct and the circumstances known to him, involves a gross deviation from the standard of care that a reasonable person would observe in the actor's situation.

(3) *Culpability Required Unless Otherwise Provided.* When the culpability sufficient to establish a material element of an offense is not prescribed by law, such element is established if a person acts purposely, knowingly or recklessly with respect thereto.

(4) *Prescribed Culpability Requirement Applies to All Material Elements.* When the law defining an offense prescribes the kind of culpability that is sufficient for the commission of an offense, without distinguishing among the material elements thereof, such provision shall apply to all the material elements of the offense, unless a contrary purpose plainly appears.

(5) *Substitutes for Negligence, Recklessness and Knowledge.* When the law provides that negligence suffices to establish an element of an offense, such element also is established if a person acts purposely, knowingly or recklessly. When recklessness suffices to establish an element, such element also is established if a person acts purposely or

knowingly. When acting knowingly suffices to establish an element, such element also is established if a person acts purposely.

(6) *Requirement of Purpose Satisfied if Purpose Is Conditional.* When a particular purpose is an element of an offense, the element is established although such purpose is conditional, unless the condition negatives the harm or evil sought to be prevented by the law defining the offense.

(7) *Requirement of Knowledge Satisfied by Knowledge of High Probability.* When knowledge of the existence of a particular fact is an element of an offense, such knowledge is established if a person is aware of a high probability of its existence, unless he actually believes that it does not exist.

(8) *Requirement of Wilfulness Satisfied by Acting Knowingly.* A requirement that an offense be committed wilfully is satisfied if a person acts knowingly with respect to the material elements of the offense, unless a purpose to impose further requirements appears.

(9) *Culpability as to Illegality of Conduct.* Neither knowledge nor recklessness or negligence as to whether conduct constitutes an offense or as to the existence, meaning or application of the law determining the elements of an offense is an element of such offense, unless the definition of the offense or the Code so provides.

(10) *Culpability as Determinant of Grade of Offense.* When the grade or degree of an offense depends on whether the offense is committed purposely, knowingly, recklessly or negligently, its grade or degree shall be the lowest for which the determinative kind of culpability is established with respect to any material element of the offense.

3. TRANSFERRED INTENT

Sagner v. State

Court of Appeal of Florida, Fourth District, 2001.
791 So.2d 1156.

■ TAYLOR, J.

Maurice William Sagner appeals his conviction and sentence for aggravated battery. We affirm on all issues raised by appellant, and write only to address his contention that the trial court improperly applied the doctrine of transferred intent to his aggravated battery offense.

* * *

Although the information charged appellant with intentionally touching or striking Michelle Green, the state's evidence showed that appellant intended to strike someone else, but hit Green instead. On the night of this incident, just before the attack, appellant was in a heated argument with William "Chino" Marquez. The two were still arguing when appellant got in his car to leave. As he was leaving, appellant threw a bottle out his car window. According to Chino, appellant looked directly at him when he threw the bottle. The bottle, however, hit bystander Chris Taupe in his head and shattered. A piece of glass from the shattered bottle flew into Michelle Green's eye, causing permanent damage. Green was a bystander, completely uninvolved in the strife between appellant and Chino.

At the close of the state's evidence, appellant moved for a judgment of acquittal, arguing that there was no evidence that appellant intended to hit Green with the bottle and that the state was improperly relying upon the concept of transferred intent to convict him of aggravated battery. The trial court denied the motion. During the jury charge conference, the state requested the court to instruct the jury on the doctrine of transferred intent. The court gave the following requested instruction, over appellant's objection:

> Now if a person has an intent to strike one person and in attempting to strike that person actually—accidentally strikes another person the striking is intentional.

In Florida, the doctrine of transferred intent has traditionally been applied in homicide cases as a means of holding a defendant criminally responsible for premeditation or intent to commit murder that results in the death of another person. *See Provenzano v. State*, 497 So. 2d 1177, 1180 (Fla.1986); *Wilson v. State*, 493 So. 2d 1019 (Fla.1986); *Lee v. State*, 141 So. 2d 257 (Fla.1962); *Coston v. State*, 139 Fla. 250, 190 So. 520 (Fla. 1939); *Hall v. State*, 70 Fla. 48, 69 So. 692 (1915). As the Florida Supreme Court observed in *Provenzano*, "the usual case involving the doctrine of transferred intent is when a defendant aims and shoots at A intending to kill him but instead misses and kills B." . . . Explaining that the original malice is transferred to the person who suffered the consequence of the unlawful act, the court said:

> The law, as well as reason, prevents (a defendant) from taking advantage of his own wrongdoing, or excusing himself when the unlawful act, if committed by (the defendant), strikes down an unintended victim.

* * *

Florida courts, however, have also applied the doctrine of transferred intent in aggravated battery prosecutions when a blow intended for one victim struck another. *See Edler v. State*, 616 So. 2d 546 (Fla. 1st DCA), *quashed in part on other grounds*, 630 So. 2d 528 (Fla.1993); *Battles v. State*, 498 So. 2d 1028 (Fla. 1st DCA 1986); *Brown v. State*, 599 So. 2d 132 (Fla. 2d DCA 1992) (ALTENBERND, J., concurring). . . .

In several cases, our courts have recognized the doctrine of transferred intent in aggravated battery prosecutions but held that it was inapplicable to enhance the severity of the crime against an unintended victim. *See B.L.L. v. State*, 764 So. 2d 837 (Fla. 2000) (where defendant intended to hit a fellow student and not a school employee, the defendant could only be adjudicated of simple battery); *V.M. v. State*, 729 So. 2d 428 (Fla. 1st DCA 1999) (doctrine of transferred intent did not operate to elevate defendant's general intent to commit a simple battery on her brother to the specific intent required to commit aggravated battery on a pregnant woman); *D.J. v. State*, 651 So. 2d 1255 (Fla. 1st DCA 1995) (where juvenile's intent was only to strike student, doctrine could not support finding of guilt of attempted battery upon school employee); *Mordica v. State*, 618 So. 2d 301 (Fla. 1st DCA 1993) (where the defendant swung at an inmate and hit a guard instead, the doctrine of transferred intent could not be used to enhance defendant's crime from simple battery to battery of a law enforcement officer). *See also In the Interest of J.G.*, 655 So. 2d 1284 (Fla. 4th DCA 1995) (where juvenile intended to hit another student, but instead missed the student and hit the student's car and shattered the rear window, juvenile should have been acquitted of criminal mischief, because juvenile's intent to strike another person could not be transferred to an intent to damage another's property).

Here, where the evidence showed that appellant struck a victim occupying the same status as the intended victim, i.e. just "another person," we conclude that the trial court properly instructed the jury on the doctrine of transferred intent.[1]

Further, we reject appellant's argument that, even under a transferred intent theory, the court erred in denying his motion for judgment of acquittal because the evidence failed to establish that he intended to hit Chino with the bottle. Evidence of the heated discussion and name calling between appellant and Chino, immediately followed by appellant's looking Chino "straight in the eyes" and throwing the bottle "pretty hard" in his direction, was sufficient to show appellant's specific intent to commit the offense. *See S.D.W. v. State*, 746 So. 2d 1232 (Fla. 1st DCA 1999) (in a battery prosecution the doctrine of transferred intent requires evidence of an intent to strike someone).

AFFIRMED.

■ FARMER, J., and MAY, MELANIE G., ASSOCIATE JUDGE, concur.

NOTES AND QUESTIONS

1. What do you think is the justification for the doctrine of transferred intent?

---

[1] § 784.045, Florida Statutes (1999) provides that a person commits aggravated battery who, in committing battery: (1) Intentionally or knowingly causes great bodily harm, permanent disability, or permanent disfigurement; or (2) Uses a deadly weapon.

§ 784.03 defines a "battery" as an offense occurring when a person actually and intentionally touches or strikes "another person" against the will of the other or intentionally causes bodily harm to "another person."

2. In *Sagner*, the court refers to several Florida cases, which seem to hold that the doctrine of transferred intent cannot be applied when the identity or character of the actual, unintended victim (e.g., a law enforcement officer) would aggravate the crime. Why not? *See also* State v. Phillips et al., 842 So.2d 27 (Ala.Crim.App. 2002); Michigan v. Hurse, 152 Mich.App. 811, 394 N.W.2d 119 (1986). If a defendant actually intended to assault or kill someone in a protected class but injured or killed a bystander instead, could the doctrine of transferred intent be applied to aggravate the crime?

3. Where the doctrine of transferred intent applies to an innocent, unintended victim, is the defendant entitled to rely on the defense of self-defense that arguably would have been available with respect to the intended victim? *See* V.M. v. State, 766 So.2d 280 (Fla.App. 2000).

4. If A and B are assailants engaged in a gun battle with C, who is shooting back in self-defense, and in the gun battle an innocent bystander located roughly behind C is killed, can A be convicted of the homicide under the doctrine of transferred intent even if it is impossible to establish who fired the bullet that killed the bystander? *See* Riddick v. Commonwealth, 226 Va. 244, 308 S.E.2d 117 (1983).

5. Does the doctrine of transferred intent apply when the unintended victim is not killed (either hit but only wounded or not hit but only endangered)? In such a case can the defendant be convicted of attempted murder or assault with intent to kill the actual victim (the one actually injured or endangered)? *See* Harvey v. State, 111 Md.App. 401, 681 A.2d 628 (1996).

6. Similarly, can a defendant who shot at one person but hit another be convicted of the attempted murder of the intended victim and, by way of the doctrine of transferred intent, the murder of the actual, unintended victim? *See* People v. Scott, 14 Cal.4th 544, 59 Cal.Rptr.2d 178, 927 P.2d 288 (1996).

7. Model Penal Code § 2.03 provides:

> (2) When purposely or knowingly causing a particular result is an element of an offense, the element is not established if the actual result is not within the purpose or the contemplation of the actor unless:
>
>> (a) the actual result differs from that designed or contemplated, as the case may be, only in the respect that a different person or different property is injured or affected or that the injury or harm designed or contemplated would have been more serious or more extensive than that caused; . . .

8. After an altercation between A and B, A fled with the promise that he will be back to kill B. Sometime later, A and two of his friends drive by B's house, at a time when B and several other friends are sitting on the front porch. As A drives by the house, he yells, "I'm going to kill you." When the car returns, all of the people who are on the porch run inside; A fires two shots into the home through a closed window shade, killing a woman inside. The woman was never in any altercation with A. A is charged with intentional murder under a statute that states: "A person commits the crime of murder if: (1) With intent to cause the death of another person, he causes the death of that person or of another person. . . . To be guilty of murder one must have the intention to kill a human being but it does not have to be toward the person who was killed." Can A be found guilty of intentional murder under a transferred intent theory? *See* Dubose v. State, 563 So.2d 18 (Ala.Crim.App. 1990).

9. A throws a rock into B's window, intending to frighten B and to damage B's property. By accident, the rock knocks over a burning oil lamp, which starts a blaze that destroys B's home. Can A be convicted of the arson of B's home under the transferred intent doctrine? *See* In the Interest of J.G., 655 So.2d 1284 (Fla.App. 1995) (referred to by the court in *Sagner*).

4. RECKLESSNESS AND CRIMINAL NEGLIGENCE

Santillanes v. State
Supreme Court of New Mexico, 1993.
115 N.M. 215, 849 P.2d 358.

■ FROST, JUSTICE.

We granted the defendant Vincent Santillanes' writ of certiorari to review the Court of Appeals decision affirming his conviction of child abuse under NMSA 1978, Section 30–6–1(C) (Repl. Pamp.1984). Santillanes' primary argument is that the provision in the statute under which he was convicted is unconstitutional because it improperly criminalizes ordinary civil negligence. He raises due process and fundamental fairness issues as well as equal protection and cruel and unusual punishment arguments. Santillanes also contests his conviction on the grounds of insufficiency of evidence, improper venue, prosecution under the wrong statute, and prosecutorial misconduct. Finding that all of his assigned errors are without merit except for his argument regarding the proper interpretation of the statute under which he was convicted, we address only that issue.

Santillanes cut his 7-year-old nephew's neck with a knife during an altercation. The jury convicted him of child abuse involving no death or great bodily injury under Section 30–6–1(C) on February 1, 1991. Section 30–6–1(C) reads as follows:

Abuse of a child consists of a person knowingly, intentionally or negligently, and without justifiable cause, causing or permitting a child to be:

(1) placed in a situation that may endanger the child's life or health;

(2) tortured, cruelly confined or cruelly punished; or

(3) exposed to the inclemency of the weather.

After the close of all evidence, defense counsel submitted a requested jury instruction to the court setting forth a criminal negligence standard rather than a civil negligence standard to define the negligence element under the statute. Defendant's Requested Instruction No. 3 stated:

> An act, to be "negligence" or to be done "negligently," must be one which a reasonably prudent person would foresee as creating a substantial and unjustifiable risk of injury to Paul Santillanes. The risk created must be of such a nature and degree that the reasonably prudent person's failure to perceive it involves a gross deviation from the standard of care that a reasonably prudent person would observe in the same situation.

The requested instruction was patterned after the definition of criminal negligence in Model Penal Code Section 2.02(2)(d) (1985). The trial court refused Santillanes' instruction and instead instructed the jury on a civil negligence standard. That instruction, Instruction No. 7, read:

> The term "negligence" may relate either to an act or a failure to act.

> An act, to be "negligence," must be one which a reasonably prudent person would foresee as involving an unreasonable risk of injury to himself or to another and which such a person, in the exercise of ordinary care, would not do. . . .

* * *

In this Court, Santillanes maintains that felony punishment should attach only to criminal behavior, in this case criminal negligence, not to ordinary civil negligence. Santillanes asserts that according felony status to acts of civil negligence violates substantive due process because the civil negligence standard is not tailored to meet the statutory goal of protecting children from abuse. Finally, Santillanes claims that as the Court of Appeals interpreted the statute, the civil negligence standard overreaches its mark and incorporates conduct that is not criminal, but rather simply negligent. Thus, he claims that the term "negligently," as interpreted, is overbroad in violation of due process of law.

The State counters that the statute, as applied, only pertains to child abuse that goes beyond merely normal action or inaction. *See State v. Coe*, 92 N.M. 320, 321, 587 P.2d 973, 974 (Ct.App.), *cert. denied*, 92 N.M. 353, 588 P.2d 554 (1978). According to the State, the Court in *Coe* limited the scope of the ordinary negligence standard because it interpreted the term "abuse" to require a showing of something more than just simple negligence or inadvertence even if it fell short of requiring a showing of criminal negligence. Thus, the State argues that the term "negligently," as interpreted in *Coe* and as applied in numerous other cases, is not constitutionally overbroad or vague. In addition, the State emphasizes that our courts have long interpreted the statute as requiring only a civil negligence standard and that there is no reason to change it now.

* * *

It is . . . well-settled that the legislature has the authority to make negligent conduct a crime. The issue in this case, then, is not whether we must read the *mens rea* element into a criminal statute because the child abuse statute contains a *mens rea* element. Rather, the question is when the legislature has included but not defined the *mens rea* element in a criminal statute, here the term "negligently," what degree of negligence is required.[2]

* * *

In addressing the issue of whether a civil or criminal negligence standard must be applied under the child abuse statute, the courts of this state consistently have applied a civil negligence standard. . . .

* * *

The opinion in *State v. Grubbs*, 85 N.M. 365, 512 P.2d 693 (Ct.App.1973), seems to be the foundation for the application of the civil negligence standard in the child abuse statute. In *Grubbs*, the Court of Appeals upheld the defendant's conviction of involuntary manslaughter by unlawful act. The unlawful act of which the defendant was found guilty was negligent use of a weapon under what is now Section 30–7–4(A)(3). The defendant claimed that "negligence" should be interpreted as criminal negligence, but the *Grubbs* court disagreed and held that ordinary negligence was all that was required. Noting that the statute failed to define "negligent," the Court applied its ordinary meaning because the legislature failed to indicate that it intended a different construction of the terms.

* * *

We have stated, however, in the context of a reckless driving conviction, that mere civil negligence "not amounting to wilful or wanton disregard of consequences cannot be made the basis of a criminal action." *See Raton v. Rice*, 52 N.M. 363, 365, 199 P.2d 986, 987 (1948). In *Raton v. Rice*, we went on to say broadly:

> [m]ere negligence is not sufficient. It may be sufficient to compel the driver to respond in damages. However, when it comes to responding to an accusation of involuntary manslaughter, with the possibility of a penitentiary sentence, a different rule is called into play.

We can find no clearly articulated basis for the rationale in *Raton v. Rice* except for the intuitive notion that a higher standard than tort negligence should be applied when the crime is punishable as a felony.

Indeed, most commentators urge the application of criminal negligence for felonies instead of the civil negligence standard. Typically,

---

2 It appears from our research that New Mexico's child abuse statute is unique in defining the proscribed conduct in terms of negligence rather than in terms of criminal or culpable negligence.

the commentators explain their preference for criminal negligence over civil negligence as a standard in criminal law by relying on common-sense justifications based upon the traditional application of heightened standards of culpability to crimes punishable with jail sentences.[4]

* * *

It is well-settled in our state that a statute defining criminal conduct must be strictly construed. Any doubts about the construction of penal statutes must be resolved in favor of lenity. A criminal statute may not be applied beyond its intended scope, and it is a fundamental rule of constitutional law that crimes must be defined with appropriate definiteness.

* * *

We believe that there is a reasonable doubt as to the intended scope of proscribed conduct under the child abuse statute. Strictly construing the statutory language in favor of lenity, and in the absence of a clear legislative intention that ordinary civil negligence is a sufficient predicate for a felony, we conclude that the civil negligence standard, as applied to the child abuse statute, improperly goes beyond its intended scope and criminalizes conduct that is not morally contemptable. *See State v. Grover*, 437 N.W.2d 60, 63 (Minn.1989) (interpreting element of negligence in criminal statute as requiring criminal negligence, absent clear legislative declaration that civil negligence is sufficient standard for crime). Although not constitutionally protected, such conduct nevertheless lies beyond the intended scope of the statute. We construe the intended scope of the statute as aiming to punish conduct that is morally culpable, not merely inadvertent.

We interpret the *mens rea* element of negligence in the child abuse statute, therefore, to require a showing of criminal negligence instead of ordinary civil negligence. That is, to satisfy the element of negligence in Section 30–6–1(C), we require proof that the defendant knew or should have known of the danger involved and acted with a reckless disregard for the safety or health of the child.

We do not find the absence of a definition of negligence in the statute indicative of legislative intent, and we are not persuaded by the State's

---

4 Noted scholars LaFave and Scott stated for example:

It came to be the general feeling of the judges when defining common law crimes (not always so strongly shared later by the legislatures when defining statutory crimes) that something more was required for criminal liability than the ordinary negligence which is sufficient for tort liability. The thought was this: When it comes to compensating an injured person for damages suffered, the one who has negligently injured an innocent victim ought to pay for it; but when the problem is one of whether to impose criminal punishment on the one who caused the injury, then something extra—beyond ordinary negligence—should be required.

1 Wayne R. LaFave & Austin W. Scott, Jr., Substantive Criminal Law § 3.7, at 326 (1986); *see also* Rollin M. Perkins & Ronald N. Boyce, Criminal Law 842 (3d ed. 1982) ("Common sense compels the conclusion that there may be a grade or degree of fault sufficient to call for the payment of damages in a civil suit, but quite insufficient to authorize criminal punishment, and this is exactly the result reached by the common law.").

contention that when the legislature has meant to apply a criminal negligence standard, it has specifically done so as in the case of negligent arson. *See* NMSA 1978, § 30–17–5(B) (Repl. Pamp.1984) (requiring recklessness as element of negligent arson). . . . Instead, we find this concept firmly rooted in our jurisprudence: When a crime is punishable as a felony, civil negligence ordinarily is an inappropriate predicate by which to define such criminal conduct.

Because the child abuse statute contains no indication that the legislature intended felony punishment to attach to ordinary negligent conduct under Section 30–6–1(C), we do not address the constitutionality of that provision. We simply construe the statute as requiring at least a showing of criminal negligence in the absence of some contrary indication from the legislature that "the public interest in the matter is so compelling or that the potential for harm is so great that the interests of the public must override the interests of the individual" so as to justify civil negligence as a predicate for a felony.

Having determined that the trial court committed error in failing to instruct the jury on a criminal negligence standard, we must now consider whether the error was harmless or whether it so undermined the reliability of the conviction or prejudiced the defendant's rights as to warrant reversal of his conviction. Failure to instruct the jury on an essential element of the charged offense has been held to be reversible error. When there can be no dispute that the essential element was established, however, failure to instruct on that element does not require reversal of the conviction.

Santillanes' defense was that his nephew injured himself when he jumped into a fishing line strung between two trees. He did not argue that he inadvertently caused the boy's throat to be cut. In addition, evidence in the record shows that his nephew's throat was cut from just below his right ear across to the left side of his neck below his jaw.

The jury found that Santillanes cut his nephew's throat with a knife during a scuffle. We believe that no rational jury could have concluded that Santillanes cut his nephew's throat, resulting in the injury described above, without satisfying the standard of criminal negligence that we have adopted today. Concluding that there could be no dispute that the element of criminal negligence was established by the evidence in the case, we hold that the error in instructing the jury on a civil negligence standard instead of a criminal negligence standard was not reversible error.

* * *

NOTES AND QUESTIONS

1. Does the legislature have the power to make harms due to civil negligence a crime? If so, why does the New Mexico Supreme Court in *Santillanes* interpret the word "negligence" in the New Mexico child abuse statute to require criminal negligence?

2. What is the difference between civil or ordinary negligence and criminal negligence? Model Penal Code § 2.02(2)(d) describes the kind of negligence sufficient for criminal liability in the following manner:

> A person acts negligently with respect to a material element of an offense when he should be aware of a substantial and unjustifiable risk that the material element exists or will result from his conduct. The risk must be of such a nature and degree that the actor's failure to perceive it, considering the nature and purpose of his conduct and the circumstances known to him, involves a gross deviation from the standard of care that a reasonable person would observe in the actor's situation.

Is this definition helpful to an understanding of gross or criminal negligence? Would such a definition aid a jury? Can you think of examples to distinguish civil from criminal negligence?

3. Model Penal Code § 2.02(2)(c) defines "recklessness" in the following fashion:

> A person acts recklessly with respect to a material element of an offense when he consciously disregards a substantial and unjustifiable risk that the material element exists or will result from his conduct. The risk must be of such a nature and degree that, considering the nature and purpose of the actor's conduct and the circumstances known to him, its disregard involves a gross deviation from the standard of conduct that a law-abiding person would observe in the actor's situation.

Does this definition adequately distinguish "reckless" behavior from criminal negligence? What is the basic difference? What would be an example of recklessness under the Model Penal Code formulation?

4. Where should the criminal law draw the line with respect to the type of mental state or behavior that will give rise to criminal responsibility?

5. Wherever one attempts to draw the definitional line, will it necessarily vary depending on the occasion or instrumentality involved? *See* People v. Lowe, 214 A.D.2d 1, 631 N.Y.S.2d 298 (1995) (gun); King v. Commonwealth, 217 Va. 601, 231 S.E.2d 312 (1977) (automobile).

5. STRICT LIABILITY AND LACK OF CRIMINAL INTENT AS A DEFENSE

State v. Loge
Supreme Court of Minnesota, 2000.
608 N.W.2d 152.

■ GILBERT, JUSTICE.

This case presents the question of whether knowledge is an element of the crime under the open bottle law when the driver is the sole occupant of a motor vehicle. Appellant Steven Mark Loge was cited on September 2, 1997, for a violation of Minn.Stat. § 169.122, subd. 3 (1998), which makes it unlawful for the driver of a motor vehicle, when the owner is not present, "to keep or allow to be kept in a motor vehicle when such vehicle is upon the public highway any bottle or receptacle containing intoxicating liquors or 3.2 percent malt liquors which has been opened." Violation of the statute is a misdemeanor. After a bench trial, the district court held that subdivision 3 imposed "absolute liability" on the driver/owner. Loge appealed. The court of appeals affirmed the conviction, holding that proof of knowledge that the open container was in the motor vehicle was not required. We affirm.

On September 2, 1997, Loge borrowed his father's pick-up truck to go to his evening job. Driving alone on his way home from work, he was stopped by two Albert Lea city police officers on County Road 18 at approximately 8:15 p.m. because he appeared to be speeding. Loge got out of his truck and stood by the driver's side door. While one officer was talking with Loge, the second officer, who was standing by the passenger side of the truck, observed a bottle, which he believed to be a beer bottle, sticking partially out of a brown paper bag underneath the passenger's side of the seat. He retrieved that bottle, which was open and had foam on the inside. He searched the rest of the truck and found one full, unopened can of beer and one empty beer can. After the second officer found the beer bottle, the first officer asked Loge if he had been drinking. Loge stated that he had two beers while working and was on his way home. Loge passed all standard field sobriety tests. The officers gave Loge citations for having no proof of insurance and for a violation of the open bottle statute but not for speeding. . . .

Loge testified that the bottle was not his, he did not know it was in the truck and had said that to one of the officers. . . . Based on an analysis of section 169.122 as a whole, the trial court held that subdivision 3 creates "absolute liability" on a driver/owner to "inspect and determine . . . whether there are any containers" in the motor vehicle in violation of the open bottle law and found Loge guilty. Loge was sentenced to five days in jail, execution stayed, placed on probation for one year, and fined $150 plus costs of $32.50.

Loge appealed the verdict. . . . In a published opinion, the court of appeals affirmed the decision of the trial court finding that the evidence, which establishes that one of the officers saw an open bottle containing intoxicating liquor underneath the passenger seat of the truck Loge was driving on a public highway, was sufficient to support Loge's conviction. The court of appeals held that proof of knowledge that the bottle was in the truck is not required to sustain a conviction.

* * *

Loge is seeking reversal of his conviction because, he argues, the trial court and court of appeals erroneously interpreted subdivision 3 of the open bottle statute[1] not to require proof of knowledge. Loge argues that the words "to keep or allow to be kept" implicitly and unambiguously require a defendant to have knowledge of the open container in the motor vehicle in order for criminal liability to attach. He argues that "keep" means "to maintain, or cause to stay or continue, in a specified condition, position, etc." Loge argues that that definition suggests that a person must purposely choose to continue possession. Further, Loge argues that the word "allow" from the phrase "allow to be kept" means "to permit; to grant license to," suggesting awareness at the minimum.

The state argues that the language of subdivision 3 creates a strict liability offense. The statute was enacted in 1959 and subdivision 3 has not had any substantive change since its enactment. The state relies heavily on the presumption that the legislature intends the statute as a whole to be effective and certain, with no surplusage. The state argues that subdivision 3's "keep or allow to be kept" language must mean more than mere possession of alcohol because owners/drivers are already subject to liability under subdivision 2 for mere possession, which applies to all persons in the motor vehicle. The state further argues that to read

---

[1]   Minnesota Statutes § 169.122 reads in part:

Subdivision 1. No person shall drink or consume intoxicating liquors or 3.2 percent malt liquors in any motor vehicle when such vehicle is upon a public highway.

Subdivision 2. No person shall have in possession while in a private motor vehicle upon a public highway, any bottle or receptacle containing intoxicating liquor or 3.2 percent malt liquor which has been opened, or the seal broken, or the contents of which have been partially removed. For purposes of this section, "possession" means either that the person had actual possession of the bottle or receptacle or that the person consciously exercised dominion and control over the bottle or receptacle. This subdivision does not apply to a bottle or receptacle that is in the trunk of the vehicle if it is equipped with a trunk, or that is in another area of the vehicle not normally occupied by the driver and passengers if the vehicle is not equipped with a trunk.

Subdivision 3. It shall be unlawful for the owner of any private motor vehicle or the driver, if the owner be not then present in the motor vehicle, to keep or allow to be kept in a motor vehicle when such vehicle is upon the public highway any bottle or receptacle containing intoxicating liquors or 3.2 percent malt liquors which has been opened, or the seal broken, or the contents of which have been partially removed except when such bottle or receptacle shall be kept in the trunk of the motor vehicle when such vehicle is equipped with a trunk, or kept in some other area of the vehicle not normally occupied by the driver of passengers, if the motor vehicle is not equipped with a trunk. A utility compartment or glove compartment shall be deemed to be within the area occupied by the driver and passengers.

subdivision 3 as requiring conscious or continuing possession would make it mere surplusage.

* * *

We are guided in our interpretation of section 169.122, subdivision 3 by the statutory presumption that the legislature intends an entire statute to be effective and certain. We must therefore look to all subdivisions of section 169.122 together to help us determine whether the legislature intended to impose liability under subdivision 3 on a driver/owner without proof of knowledge. Subdivision 1 prohibits the consumption of alcohol by any person in a motor vehicle on a public highway. Subdivision 2 prohibits the actual possession of, or conscious exercise of dominion and control over, an open bottle of alcohol by any person in the vehicle. In contrast, subdivision 3 provides that the owner, or if the owner is not present, the driver is responsible for ensuring that no open bottles of alcohol are present in a vehicle on a public highway, regardless of consumption, actual possession or conscious exercise of dominion and control. Consumption, possession and presence of an open container of alcohol in a motor vehicle are each separate risks. The legislature separately addressed each risk in section 169.122, subdivisions 1 through 3 in an effort to promote highway safety by decreasing the opportunity for alcohol consumption and drunken driving that an open container of alcohol anywhere in the vehicle creates. It is clear from reading the statute as a whole that the legislature intended to categorically prohibit open bottles of alcohol in a motor vehicle on a public road except under the limited circumstances that the legislature expressly addressed and carved out.[4] Thus, we find no ambiguity in the legislature's use of the word "keep."

We are mindful of Loge's argument that, as a criminal statute, section 169.122 must be strictly construed. Where we have found a statute ambiguous, we have said, "if criminal liability, particularly gross misdemeanor or felony liability, is to be imposed for conduct unaccompanied by fault, the legislative intent to do so should be clear." However, we have held that the rule of strict construction does not require this court to assign the narrowest possible interpretation to the statute or to adopt a construction that would render the statute or one of its subdivisions meaningless. Furthermore, where, as here, we have interpreted the statute and find no ambiguity, "the so-called 'rule of lenity,' which holds that *ambiguity* concerning the ambit of criminal statutes should be resolved in favor of lenity towards the defendant," has no application. . . .

* * *

_____

4   Minnesota Statutes § 169.122, subd. 5 (1998) exempts charter buses and limousines from the scope of the statute.

Here, if knowledge was a necessary element of the open container offense, there would be a substantial, if not insurmountable, difficulty of proof. The legislature may have weighed the possible injustice of subjecting a driver to a penalty against the opportunity of the driver to discover any open bottle and the difficulty of proof of knowledge. It is therefore reasonable to conclude that the legislature, weighing the significant danger to the public, decided that proof of knowledge under subdivision 3 was not required.

The legislature has made knowledge distinctions within its traffic statutes that also guide our interpretation. For example, with respect to marijuana in a motor vehicle, the Minnesota legislature has used language similar to the language found in section 169.122, subdivision 3 ("keep or allow to be kept") but added a knowledge requirement. An owner, or if the owner is not present, the driver, is guilty of a misdemeanor if he "*knowingly* keeps or allows to be kept" marijuana in a motor vehicle. Minn.Stat. § 152.027, subd. 3 (1998) (emphasis added). The use of the word "knowingly" in section 152.027, subdivision 3 to modify the same language as contained in section 169.122, subdivision 3 indicates that the legislature does not perceive the word "keep" alone to imply or contain a knowledge element. . . .

* * *

In the absence of such a modifier, we believe that the parallels between subdivision 3 and other non-alcohol related traffic statutes also support our holding. The phrases "it shall be unlawful" or "no person shall" appear throughout the traffic code and have never been understood to require a showing of intent to prove a violation of the statute. In fact, Loge concedes that other provisions of the traffic code that use such language are strict liability offenses.

* * *

In order to avoid violating this statute, Loge had an affirmative duty to ensure that there were no open containers in the area of a motor vehicle normally occupied by the driver or passenger on a public highway. He had the opportunity and was in the best position to find out the fact of the open bottle's presence "with no more care than society might reasonably expect and no more exertion than it might reasonably exact from one who assumed his responsibilities." (citing Morissette v. United States, 342 U.S. 246, 256, 72 S.Ct. 240, 96 L.Ed. 288 (1952)). Here, all Loge had to do was observe an open beer bottle protruding from a bag under the passenger's seat, which the trial court found was visible even to the officer who was standing outside the truck looking in.

The "to keep" an open bottle language of subdivision 3 means more than knowingly continuing possession because such conduct is already made illegal by subdivision 2. Any other interpretation would render subdivision 3 mere surplusage and would violate the statutory presumption that the legislature intends an entire statute to be effective and certain. Therefore, we hold that in a prosecution under section 169.122, subdivision 3, the state need not prove that the driver and sole occupant of a motor vehicle on a public highway knew of the existence of the open bottle containing intoxicating liquors in the motor vehicle.

Affirmed.

■ PAUL H. ANDERSON, J. (dissenting).

* * *

The majority's analysis of the language of Minn.Stat. § 169.122 does not demonstrate the level of certainty necessary to allow me to conclude that the statute manifests a clear intent by the legislature to impose criminal liability regardless of intent or knowledge. The plain language of the statute, the unreasonable results that arise from the majority's interpretation, the differing application of the statute by district courts, and even the cases cited by the majority lead me to this conclusion. Minnesota Statutes § 169.122, subd. 3, simply lacks the requisite clarity to support the imposition of criminal liability without any showing of intent or knowledge.

* * *

The majority cannot avoid the implications of the term "allow" because it is convenient to do so. In other contexts, we have held that the inclusion of words like "permit" (a synonym of "allow") clearly indicates a legislative intent to require some level of knowledge or intent. *See, e.g.,* Peterson v. Pawelk, 263 N.W.2d 634, 637 (Minn.1978) (stating that the use of the term "permit" in a statute clearly indicates that the legislature did not intend to impose strict liability). While it is possible to find definitions of "keep" that do not appear to implicate knowledge or intent, there are, as Loge points out, many definitions of "keep" that imply some level of conscious knowledge or intent. The multiple definitions of the word "keep" cited by the parties underscore the lack of clarity in the statute's language. None of these definitions clearly indicate that proof of knowledge or intent is either required or clearly excluded.

The majority asserts that because the legislature used the similar language "keeps or allows to be kept" in Minn.Stat. § 152.027, but added the word "knowingly," the lack of the word "knowingly" in Minn.Stat. § 169.122 means that no knowledge requirement was intended. While we do presume that the legislature uses words in a consistent manner, here such analysis yields no clear answers. It is clear that the use of the word "knowingly" in section 152.027 indicates that the legislature intended to require knowledge for the possession of marijuana in a vehicle. However, the fact that it is not included in section 169.122, a law passed some 20 years earlier and on a different subject, does not indicate that the legislature intended to disregard any requirement of knowledge or intent.

* * *

Under subdivision 2 of the statute, criminal liability is imposed for possession of an open container of alcohol by any person in a motor vehicle. Possession here means actual possession of or the conscious exercise of dominion or control over the container. The majority claims that because this subdivision already imposes liability for the knowing possession of an open container of alcohol in a vehicle, to do so again in subdivision 3 is unnecessary. This line of reasoning only works in the majority's interpretation and only in the case where one person is in the vehicle. When more than one person is in the vehicle, the purpose of the different subdivisions becomes clear. A passenger may have an open container of alcohol and not have disclosed that fact to the driver. Clearly subdivision 2 applies to that passenger. But it is also clear that because the passenger concealed this fact from the driver, the driver should not be held liable. To do otherwise would be to hold the driver criminally liable for an act he did not intend to commit and over which he had no control. In the case when a container is open and visible in the passenger compartment of a vehicle and none of the passengers are shown possessing it, then the owner, or driver, remains ultimately responsible. Simply because the subdivision may not have application in a unique fact pattern does not make it surplusage for the purposes of our analysis.

The above example highlights one of the unreasonable results of the majority's interpretation. A driver could be held responsible for the acts of passengers that they conceal from him. An absent owner could be held liable for acts of passengers he has never met. In interpreting a statute, we assume that the legislature does not intend an unreasonable or absurd result. *See* Minn.Stat. § 645.17.

* * *

Finally, under the majority's holding, we now will impose criminal liability on a person, not simply for an act that the person does not know is criminal, but also for an act the person does not even know he is committing. While the district court and the majority seem to assume that everyone who drives a motor vehicle knows that he or she is obligated to search the entire passenger compartment of the vehicle before driving on the state's roads, the law imposes no such requirement. Most drivers would be surprised to discover that after anyone else used their vehicle—children, friends, spouse—they are criminally liable for any open containers of alcohol that are present, regardless of whether they know the containers are there. This also means that any prudent operator of a motor vehicle must also carefully check any case of packaged alcohol before transport and ensure that each container's seal is not broken. *See* Minn.Stat. § 169.122 (defining an open bottle as a container that is open, has the contents partially removed, or has the seal broken). Under the majority's interpretation, all of these situations would render the driver criminally liable under Minn.Stat. § 169.122. Without a more clear statement by the legislature that this is the law, I cannot agree with such an outcome.

■ JUSTICES PAGE and STRINGER join in the dissent of JUSTICE PAUL H. ANDERSON.

NOTES AND QUESTIONS

1. Does the majority opinion in *Loge* provide an adequate explanation of why the legislature would want to impose strict liability *for a criminal offense—* liability without a mental state which establishes fault?

2. Would Section 3 of the Minnesota open container law be meaningless and redundant if not read to impose strict liability, or has the dissent provided a convincing explanation and example of how the section operates in the absence of strict liability?

3. Should a person ever be held vicariously responsible for a criminal act committed by a third person for whom he may be responsible in a supervisory capacity but who acts without his knowledge? *See* United States v. Park, 421 U.S. 658, 95 S.Ct. 1903, 44 L.Ed.2d 489 (1975); Ex parte Marley, 29 Cal.2d 525, 175 P.2d 832 (1946). See also the case that follows: *State v. Guminga.*

State v. Guminga
Supreme Court of Minnesota, 1986.
395 N.W.2d 344.

■ YETKA, JUSTICE:

* * *

On March 29, 1985, in the course of an undercover operation, two investigators for the City of Hopkins entered Lindee's Restaurant, Hopkins, Minnesota, with a 17-year-old woman. All three ordered alcoholic beverages. The minor had never been in Lindee's before, and the waitress did not ask the minor her age or request identification. When the waitress returned with their orders, the minor paid for all the drinks. After confirming that the drink contained alcohol, the officers arrested the waitress for serving intoxicating liquor to a minor in violation of Minn. Stat. § 340.73 (1984). The owner of Lindee's, defendant George Joseph Guminga, was subsequently charged with violation of section 340.73 pursuant to Minn. Stat. § 340.941 (1984), which imposes vicarious criminal liability on an employer whose employee serves intoxicating liquor to a minor. The state does not contend that Guminga was aware of or ratified the waitress's actions.

Guminga moved to dismiss the charges on the ground that section 340.941 violates the due process clauses of the federal and state constitutions. . . . After holding a hearing on August 28, 1985, the court denied the motion to dismiss.

* * *

The certified question of law before this court is as follows:

Whether Minn. Stat. § 340.941, on its face, violates the defendant's right to due process of law under the Fourteenth Amendment to the United States Constitution and analogous provisions of the Constitution of the State of Minnesota.

We find that the statute in question does violate the due process clauses of the Minnesota and the United States Constitutions and thus answer the question in the affirmative.

Guminga argues that section 340.941 violates due process as an unjustified and unnecessary invasion of his personal liberties. He maintains that the public interest in prohibiting the sale of liquor to minors does not justify vicarious criminal liability for an employer since there are less burdensome ways to protect the public interest. The constitutionality of the statute has not been squarely addressed by the court, he argues, since earlier cases did not directly raise the issue of whether the statute is unconstitutional.

The state contends that this court originally upheld the constitutionality of section 340.941 in *State v. Lundgren*, 124 Minn. 162, 144 N.W. 752 (1913), which it recently reaffirmed in [State v.] *Young*, 294 N.W.2d 128 (Minn. 1980)]. According to the state, vicarious criminal liability for employers whose employees sell alcohol to minors is a necessary part of liquor control.

Minn. Stat. § 340.73 (1984) provides criminal penalties for any person selling intoxicating liquor to a minor ... Minn. Stat. § 340.941 (1984) imposes vicarious criminal liability on the employer for an employee's violation of section 340.73:

> Any sale of liquor in or from any public drinking place by any clerk, barkeep, or other employee authorized to sell liquor in such place is the act of the employer as well as that of the person actually making the sale; and every such employer is liable to all the penalties provided by law for such sale, equally with the person actually making the same.

Under Minn. Stat. § 609.03 (1984), a defendant who commits a gross misdemeanor may be sentenced to "imprisonment for not more than one year or to payment of a fine of not more than $3,000 or both." In addition, a defendant convicted under section 340.941 may, at the discretion of the licensing authority, have its license suspended, revoked or be unable to obtain a new license. As a gross misdemeanor, a conviction under section 340.941 would also affect a defendant's criminal history score were he or she to be convicted of a felony in the future.

* * *

We find that criminal penalties based on vicarious liability under Minn. Stat. § 340.941 are a violation of substantive due process and that only civil penalties would be constitutional. A due process analysis of a statute involves a balancing of the public interests protected against the intrusion on personal liberty while taking into account any alternative means by which to achieve the same end. Section 340.941 serves the public interest by providing additional deterrence to violation of the liquor laws. The private interests affected, however, include liberty, damage to reputation and other future disabilities arising from criminal prosecution for an act which Guminga did not commit or ratify. Not only could Guminga be given a prison sentence or a suspended sentence, but, in the more likely event that he receives only a fine, his liberty could be affected by a longer presumptive sentence in a possible future felony conviction. Such an intrusion on personal liberty is not justified by the public interest protected, especially when there are alternative means by which to achieve the same end, such as civil fines or license suspension, which do not entail the legal and social ramifications of a criminal conviction.

* * *

. . . [F]ar from endorsing criminal sanctions for violation of vicarious liability statutes, commentators LaFave and Scott believe that such sanctions are a mistake.

> To the extent that vicarious liability can be justified in the criminal law, it should not be utilized to bring about the type of moral condemnation which is implicit when a sentence of imprisonment is imposed. On the other hand, imposition of a fine is consistent with the rationale behind vicarious criminal liability. Vicarious liability is imposed because of the nature and inherent danger of certain business activities and the difficulties of establishing actual fault in the operation of such businesses. A fine, unlike imprisonment, is less personal and is more properly viewed as a penalty on the business enterprise.

* * *

> Yet, it must be recognized that the imposition of criminal liability for faultless conduct is contrary to the basic Anglo-American premise of criminal justice that crime requires personal fault on the part of the accused. Perhaps the answer should be the same as the answer proposed in the case of strict-liability crimes: it is proper for the legislature to single out some special areas of human activity and impose vicarious liability on employers who are without personal fault, but the matter should not be called a "crime" and the punishment should not include more than a fine or forfeiture or other civil penalty; that is, it should not include imprisonment. As the law now stands, however, in almost all jurisdictions imprisonment and the word

"criminal" may be visited upon perfectly innocent employers for the sins of their employees.

LaFave & Scott, HANDBOOK ON CRIMINAL LAW § 32 at 227–28 (1972).

Moreover, this court, in *State v. Young*, 294 N.W.2d 728 (Minn.1980), was dealing only with the imposition of a fine, not imprisonment. We suggested in that case that imprisonment might dictate a different result.

The dissent argues that vicarious liability is necessary as a deterrent so that an owner will impress upon employees that they should not sell to minors. However, it does not distinguish between an employer who vigorously lectures his employees and one who does not. According to the dissent, each would be equally guilty. We believe it is a deterrent enough that the employee who sells to the minor can be charged under the statute and that the business is subject to fines or suspension or revocation of license.

* * *

We specifically and exclusively decide the question under the provisions of the Minnesota Constitution herein cited. We find that, in Minnesota, no one can be convicted of a crime punishable by imprisonment for an act he did not commit, did not have knowledge of, or give expressed or implied consent to the commission thereof.

* * *

■ KELLEY, JUSTICE (dissenting):

I respectfully dissent. The strong public interest in prohibiting the sale of liquor to minors justifies the imposition of vicarious liability on the bar owner—employer for illegal sales to minors made by an employee. I respectfully suggest that in ruling Minn. Stat. § 340.941 (1984) unconstitutional, the majority has failed to give adequate weight to the clearly expressed, long-standing public policy of this state as reflected in Section 340.941. Imposition of vicarious liability and criminal punishment for sale of intoxicating liquor to minors has been the law in this state since 1905.

In explaining the meaning and the purpose of a nearly identical predecessor of this statute, the court in 1913 stated:

This language plainly means that the act of the barkeeper is the act of the proprietor, that the proprietor must pay the penalty for sales made by his barkeeper in violation of the law, and that the delinquency of the barkeeper is the only evidence required to prove the guilt of the proprietor. The fact that the sale was made without the knowledge or assent of the proprietor and contrary to his general instructions furnishes no defense. The language of this statute is susceptible of no other construction.

The offense is one of the class where proof of criminal intent is not essential. The statute makes the act an offense, and imposes a penalty for violation of the law, irrespective of knowledge or intent.

The statute is drastic in its terms, but the Legislature was doubtless of the opinion that drastic measures are required to accomplish the purpose of enforcement of laws regulating the sale of intoxicating liquors. The law was in existence when the offense was committed. It was a notice to every man choosing to follow this line of business that he must control his own business and the men he employs in it, and that he is bound under penalty of the law to employ only men who will not commit crime in his name. *State v. Lundgren*, 124 Minn. 162, 167–68, 144 N.W. 752, 754 (1913) (citations omitted).

* * *

The Lundgren reasoning seems even more compelling today now that the state has raised the drinking age to 21 from 19. In so doing, the legislature recognized the societal dangers of the consumption of alcoholic beverages by younger people, even though they are adults for other legal purposes. In the same chapter, the legislature enacted a law requiring every application for a driver's license to include information on the effect of alcohol on driving ability and the levels of alcohol-related fatalities and accidents. The state legislature has had a long-standing and continuing concern about problems associated with minors who consume alcoholic beverages. The defendant cannot claim a due process violation for lack of notice of a law on the books for more than eight decades.

Furthermore, imposition of vicarious liability and the threat of a short jail, not prison, sentence is reasonably related to the legislative purpose: enforcement of laws prohibiting liquor sales to minors. Without the deterrent of possible personal criminal responsibility and a sentence, the legislature could have rationally concluded that liquor establishment owners will be less likely to impress upon employees the need to require identification of age before serving liquor. Limiting punishment to a fine allows bar owners to view their liability for violations as nothing more than an expense of doing business. The gravity of the problems associated with minors who consume alcoholic beverages justifies the importance by the legislature of harsher punishment on those who help contribute to those problems. The state has the right to impose limited criminal vicarious liability on bar proprietors as a reasonable exchange for the state-granted privilege of a liquor license.

* * *

The majority's holding today not only fails to give deference to decades of legislative policy, but it is likewise at odds with rulings of the majority of the courts of our sister jurisdictions. It can be stated as a general rule, that statutes imposing vicarious criminal liability upon the "innocent" employer for the illegal conduct of the employee have been generally upheld as constitutional. *See* Annot., 139 A.L.R. 306 (1942); Annot., 89 A.L.R.3d 1256 (1979). . . .

As lucidly stated in *Hershorn v. People*, 108 Colo. 43, 113 P.2d 680 (1941), the Colorado Supreme Court in upholding the conviction of the president and general manager of a corporation which operated a nightclub for selling liquor to an intoxicated minor and affirming the imposition of a sentence of 60 days in the county jail said, "To make unlawful the sale of intoxicants to minors and inebriates, regardless of intent, is a reasonable legislative regulation of the liquor traffic, so long as the proscribed act amounts only to a misdemeanor."

* * *

Every legislative enactment comes to the courts with a presumption in favor of its constitutionality. The burden of proof is on the challenging parties to show beyond a reasonable doubt that the act violates some particular constitutional provision. I do not believe the defendant has met his burden in challenging the constitutionality of Minn. Stat. § 340.941 of demonstrating that the act is "arbitrary and unreasonable." . . . I suggest the court errs in the holding that as a matter of substantive due process under Minnesota's Constitution that Minn. Stat. § 340.941 violates the due process clause. I would follow our own precedents and remain consistent with the great majority of states in recognizing the legislatively stated public policy of strict enforcement of liquor laws prohibiting sales to minors by imposing vicarious criminal liability on the owner-employer for such illegal sales.

■ SCOTT, JUSTICE, dissenting.

■ I join in the dissent of JUSTICE KELLEY.

NOTES AND QUESTIONS

1. How exactly is due process violated in *Guminga*? Doesn't due process refer to the procedures by which someone is arrested, charged and convicted of crime? Does it mean more than this, i.e., does it also have a substantive component? If so, when is it implicated?

2. Why does the Minnesota Supreme Court rely exclusively on the due process clause of its own state constitution instead of the due process provision in the Fourteenth Amendment to the United States Constitution? *See* Michigan v. Long, 463 U.S. 1032, 103 S.Ct. 3469, 77 L.Ed.2d 1201 (1983). In *Long* the Court, per Justice O'Connor, stated:

> [W]hen, as in this case, a state court decision fairly appears to rest primarily on federal law, or to be interwoven with the federal law, and when the adequacy and independence of any possible state law ground is not clear from the face of the opinion, we will accept as

the most reasonable explanation that the state court decided the case the way it did because it believed that federal law required it to do so. If a state court chooses merely to rely on federal precedents as it would on the precedents of all other jurisdictions, then it need only make clear by a plain statement in its judgment or opinion that the federal cases are being used only for the purpose of guidance, and do not themselves compel the result that the court has reached. In this way, both justice and judicial administration will be greatly improved. If the state court decision indicates clearly and expressly that it is alternatively based on bona fide separate, adequate, and independent grounds, we, of course, will not undertake to review the decision.

3. Why would Justice Kelley, dissenting in *Guminga*, uphold the Minnesota statute? Is reliance on *Lundgren*, a decision from 1913, helpful?

Morissette v. United States

Supreme Court of the United States, 1952.
342 U.S. 246, 72 S.Ct. 240, 96 L.Ed. 288.

■ MR. JUSTICE JACKSON delivered the opinion of the Court. . . .

On a large tract of uninhabited and untilled land in a wooded and sparsely populated area of Michigan, the Government established a practice bombing range over which the Air Force dropped simulated bombs at ground targets. These bombs consisted of a metal cylinder about forty inches long and eight inches across, filled with sand and enough black powder to cause a smoke puff by which the strike could be located. At various places about the range signs read "Danger—Keep Out—Bombing Range." Nevertheless, the range was known as good deer country and was extensively hunted.

Spent bomb casings were cleared from the targets and thrown into piles "so that they will be out of the way." They were not stacked or piled in any order but were dumped in heaps, some of which had been accumulating for four years or upwards, were exposed to the weather and rusting away.

Morissette, in December of 1948, went hunting in this area but did not get a deer. He thought to meet expenses of the trip by salvaging some of these casings. He loaded three tons of them on his truck and took them to a nearby farm, where they were flattened by driving a tractor over them. After expending this labor and trucking them to market in Flint, he realized $84.

Morissette, by occupation, is a fruit stand operator in summer and a trucker and scrap iron collector in winter. An honorably discharged veteran of World War II, he enjoys a good name among his neighbors and has had no blemish on his record more disreputable than a conviction for reckless driving.

The loading, crushing and transporting of these casings were all in broad daylight, in full view of passers-by, without the slightest effort at concealment. When an investigation was started, Morissette voluntarily, promptly and candidly told the whole story to the authorities, saying that he had no intention of stealing but thought the property was abandoned, unwanted and considered of no value to the Government. He was indicted, however, on the charge that he "did unlawfully, wilfully and knowingly steal and convert" property of the United States of the value of $84, in violation of 18 U.S.C. § 641, 18 U.S.C.A. § 641, which provides that "whoever embezzles, steals, purloins, or knowingly converts" government property is punishable by fine and imprisonment. Morissette was convicted and sentenced to imprisonment for two months or to pay a fine of $200. The Court of Appeals affirmed, one judge dissenting.

On his trial, Morissette, as he had at all times told investigating officers, testified that from appearances he believed the casings were cast-off and abandoned, that he did not intend to steal the property, and took it with no wrongful or criminal intent. The trial court, however, was unimpressed, and ruled: "[H]e took it because he thought it was abandoned and he knew he was on government property. . . . That is no defense. . . . I don't think anybody can have the defense they thought the property was abandoned on another man's piece of property." The court stated: "I will not permit you to show this man thought it was abandoned. . . . I hold in this case that there is no question of abandoned property." The court refused to submit or to allow counsel to argue to the jury whether Morissette acted with innocent intention. It charged: "And I instruct you that if you believe the testimony of the government in this case, he intended to take it. . . . He had no right to take this property. . . . [A]nd it is no defense to claim that it was abandoned, because it was on private property. . . . And I instruct you to this effect: That if this young man took this property (and he says he did), without any permission (he says he did), that was on the property of the United States Government (he says it was), that it was of the value of one cent or more (and evidently it was), that he is guilty of the offense charged here. If you believe the government, he is guilty. . . . The question on intent is whether or not he intended to take the property. He says he did. Therefore, if you believe either side, he is guilty." Petitioner's counsel contended, "But the taking must have been with a felonious intent." The court ruled, however: "That is presumed by his own act."

The Court of Appeals suggested that "greater restraint in expression should have been exercised", but affirmed the conviction because "As we have interpreted the statute, appellant was guilty of its violation beyond a shadow of doubt, as evidenced even by his own admissions." Its construction of the statute is that it creates several separate and distinct offenses, one being knowing conversion of government property. The court ruled that this particular offense requires no element of criminal intent. This conclusion was thought to be required by the failure of

Congress to express such a requisite and this Court's decisions in United States v. Behrman, and United States v. Balint.

In those cases this Court did construe mere omission from a criminal enactment of any mention of criminal intent as dispensing with it. If they be deemed precedents for principles of construction generally applicable to federal penal statutes, they authorize this conviction. . . .

The contention that an injury can amount to a crime only when inflicted by intention is no provincial or transient notion. It is as universal and persistent in mature systems of law as belief in freedom of the human will and a consequent ability and duty of the normal individual to choose between good and evil. A relation between some mental element and punishment for a harmful act is almost as instinctive as the child's familiar exculpatory "But I didn't mean to," and has afforded the rational basis for a tardy and unfinished substitution of deterrence and reformation in place of retaliation and vengeance as the motivation for public prosecution. Unqualified acceptance of this doctrine by English common law in the Eighteenth Century was indicated by Blackstone's sweeping statement that to constitute any crime there must first be a "vicious will." Common-law commentators of the Nineteenth Century early pronounced the same principle. . . .

Crime as a compound concept, generally constituted only from concurrence of an evil-meaning mind with an evil-doing hand, was congenial to an intense individualism and took deep and early root in American soil. As the states codified the common law of crimes, even if their enactments were silent on the subject, their courts assumed that the omission did not signify disapproval of the principle but merely recognized that intent was so inherent in the idea of the offense that it required no statutory affirmation. Courts, with little hesitation or division, found an implication of the requirement as to offenses that were taken over from the common law. The unanimity with which they have adhered to the central thought that wrongdoing must be conscious to be criminal is emphasized by the variety, disparity and confusion of their definitions of the requisite but elusive mental element. However, courts of various jurisdictions, and for the purposes of different offenses, have devised working formulae, if not scientific ones, for the instruction of juries around such terms as "felonious intent," "criminal intent," "malice aforethought," "guilty knowledge," "fraudulent intent," "wilfulness," "*scienter*," to denote guilty knowledge or "*mens rea*," to signify an evil purpose or mental culpability. By use or combination of these various tokens, they have sought to protect those who were not blameworthy in mind from conviction of infamous common-law crimes.

However, the Balint and Behrman offenses belong to a category of another character, with very different antecedents and origins. The crimes there involved depend on no mental element but consist only of forbidden acts or omissions. This, while not expressed by the Court, is made clear from examination of a century-old but accelerating tendency, discernible both here and in England, to call into existence new duties and crimes which disregard any ingredient of intent. The industrial revolution multiplied the number of workmen exposed to injury from increasingly powerful and complex mechanisms, driven by freshly discovered sources of energy, requiring higher precautions by employers. Traffic of velocities, volumes and varieties unheard of came to subject the wayfarer to intolerable casualty risks if owners and drivers were not to observe new cares and uniformities of conduct. Congestion of cities and crowding of quarters called for health and welfare regulations undreamed of in simpler times. Wide distribution of goods became an instrument of wide distribution of harm when those who dispersed food, drink, drugs, and even securities, did not comply with reasonable standards of quality, integrity, disclosure and care. Such dangers have engendered increasingly numerous and detailed regulations which heighten the duties of those in control of particular industries, trades, properties or activities that affect public health, safety or welfare.

While many of these duties are sanctioned by a more strict civil liability, lawmakers, whether wisely or not,[14] have sought to make such regulations more effective by invoking criminal sanctions to be applied by the familiar technique of criminal prosecutions and convictions. This has confronted the courts with a multitude of prosecutions, based on statutes or administrative regulations, for what have been aptly called "public welfare offenses." These cases do not fit neatly into any of such accepted classifications of common-law offenses, such as those against the state, the person, property, or public morals. Many of these offenses

---

[14] Consequences of a general abolition of intent as an ingredient of serious crimes have aroused the concern of responsible and disinterested students of penology. Of course, they would not justify judicial disregard of a clear command to that effect from Congress, but they do admonish us to caution in assuming that Congress, without clear expression, intends in any instance to do so.

Radin, Intent, Criminal, 8 Encyc.Soc.Sci. 126, 130, says, ". . . as long as in popular belief intention and the freedom of the will are taken as axiomatic, no penal system that negates the mental element can find general acceptance. It is vital to retain public support of methods of dealing with crime." Again, "The question of criminal intent will probably always have something of an academic taint. Nevertheless, the fact remains that the determination of the boundary between intent and negligence spells freedom or condemnation for thousands of individuals. The watchfulness of the jurist justifies itself at present in its insistence upon the examination of the mind of each individual offender."

Sayre, Public Welfare Offenses, 33 Col.L.Rev. 55, 56, says: "To inflict substantial punishment upon one who is morally entirely innocent, who caused injury through reasonable mistake or pure accident, would so outrage the feelings of the community as to nullify its own enforcement."

Hall, Prolegomena to a Science of Criminal Law, 89 U. of Pa.L.Rev. 549, 569, appears somewhat less disturbed by the trend, if properly limited, but, as to so-called public welfare crimes, suggests that "There is no reason to continue to believe that the present mode of dealing with these offenses is the best solution obtainable, or that we must be content with this sacrifice of established principles. *The raising of a presumption of knowledge might be an improvement.*" (Italics added.)

In Felton v. United States, 96 U.S. 699, 703, 24 L.Ed. 875, the Court said, "But the law at the same time is not so unreasonable as to attach culpability, and consequently to impose punishment, where there is no intention to evade its provisions. . . ."

are not in the nature of positive aggressions or invasions, with which the common law so often dealt, but are in the nature of neglect where the law requires care, or inaction where it imposes a duty. Many violations of such regulations result in no direct or immediate injury to person or property but merely create the danger or probability of it which the law seeks to minimize. While such offenses do not threaten the security of the state in the manner of treason, they may be regarded as offenses against its authority, for their occurrence impairs the efficiency of controls deemed essential to the social order as presently constituted. In this respect, whatever the intent of the violator, the injury is the same, and the consequences are injurious or not according to fortuity. Hence, legislation applicable to such offenses, as a matter of policy, does not specify intent as a necessary element. The accused, if he does not will the violation, usually is in a position to prevent it with no more care than society might reasonably expect and no more exertion than it might reasonably exact from one who assumed his responsibilities. Also, penalties commonly are relatively small, and conviction does no grave damage to an offender's reputation. Under such considerations, courts have turned to construing statutes and regulations which make no mention of intent as dispensing with it and holding that the guilty act alone makes out the crime. This has not, however, been without expressions of misgiving.

The pilot of the movement in this country appears to be a holding that a tavernkeeper could be convicted for selling liquor to an habitual drunkard even if he did not know the buyer to be such. . . . Later came Massachusetts holdings that convictions for selling adulterated milk in violation of statutes forbidding such sales require no allegation or proof that defendant knew of the adulteration. . . . Departures from the common-law tradition, mainly of these general classes, were reviewed and their rationale appraised by Chief Justice Cooley, as follows: "I agree that as a rule there can be no crime without a criminal intent, but this is not by any means a universal rule. . . . Many statutes which are in the nature of police regulations, as this is, impose criminal penalties irrespective of any intent to violate them, the purpose being to require a degree of diligence for the protection of the public which shall render violation impossible." . . .

Neither this Court nor, so far as we are aware, any other has undertaken to delineate a precise line or set forth comprehensive criteria for distinguishing between crimes that require a mental element and crimes that do not. We attempt no closed definition, for the law on the subject is neither settled nor static. The conclusion reached in the Balint and Behrman cases has our approval and adherence for the circumstances to which it was there applied. A quite different question here is whether we will expand the doctrine of crimes without intent to include those charged here.

Stealing, larceny, and its variants and equivalents, were among the earliest offenses known to the law that existed before legislation; they are invasions of rights of property which stir a sense of insecurity in the whole community and arouse public demand for retribution, the penalty is high and, when a sufficient amount is involved, the infamy is that of a felony, which, says Maitland, is ". . . as bad a word as you can give to man or thing." State courts of last resort, on whom fall the heaviest burden of interpreting criminal law in this country, have consistently retained the requirement of intent in larceny-type offenses. If any state has deviated, the exception has neither been called to our attention nor disclosed by our research.

Congress, therefore, omitted any express prescription of criminal intent from the enactment before us in the light of an unbroken course of judicial decision in all constituent states of the Union holding intent inherent in this class of offense even when not expressed in a statute. Congressional silence as to mental elements in an Act merely adopting into federal statutory law a concept of crime already so well defined in common law and statutory interpretation by the states may warrant quite contrary inferences than the same silence in creating an offense new to general law, for whose definition the courts have no guidance except the Act. Because the offenses before this Court in the Balint and Behrman cases were of this latter class, we cannot accept them as authority for eliminating intent from offenses incorporated from the common law. Nor do exhaustive studies of state court cases disclose any well-considered decisions applying the doctrine of crime without intent to such enacted common-law offenses. . . .[20]

The Government asks us by a feat of construction radically to change the weights and balances in the scales of justice. The purpose and obvious effect of doing away with the requirement of a guilty intent is to ease the prosecution's path to conviction, to strip the defendant of such benefit as he derived at common law from innocence of evil purpose, and to circumscribe the freedom heretofore allowed juries. Such a manifest impairment of the immunities of the individual should not be extended to common-law crimes on judicial initiative. . . .

We hold that mere omission from § 641 of any mention of intent will not be construed as eliminating that element from the crimes denounced.

It is suggested, however, that the history and purposes of § 641 imply something more affirmative as to elimination of intent from at least one of the offenses charged under it in this case. The argument does not contest that criminal intent is retained in the offenses of

---

[20] Sayre, Public Welfare Offenses, 33 Col.L.Rev. 55, 73, 84, cites and classifies a large number of cases and concludes that they fall roughly into subdivisions of (1) illegal sales of intoxicating liquor, (2) sales of impure or adulterated food or drugs, (3) sales of misbranded articles, (4) violations of antinarcotic Acts, (5) criminal nuisances, (6) violations of traffic regulations, (7) violations of motor-vehicle laws, and (8) violations of general police regulations, passed for the safety, health or well-being of the community.

embezzlement, stealing and purloining, as incorporated into this section. But it is urged that Congress joined with those, as a new, separate and distinct offense, knowingly to convert government property, under circumstances which imply that it is an offense in which the mental element of intent is not necessary.

Congress has been alert to what often is a decisive function of some mental element in crime. It has seen fit to prescribe that an evil state of mind, described variously in one or more such terms as "intentional," "wilful," "knowing," "fraudulent" or "malicious," will make criminal an otherwise indifferent act, or increase the degree of the offense or its punishment. Also, it has at times required a specific intent or purpose which will require some specialized knowledge or design for some evil beyond the common-law intent to do injury. The law under some circumstances recognizes good faith or blameless intent as a defense, partial defense, or as an element to be considered in mitigation of punishment. . . . In view of the care that has been bestowed upon the subject, it is significant that we have not found, nor has our attention been directed to, any instance in which Congress has expressly eliminated the mental element from a crime taken over from the common law.

Congress, by the language of this section, has been at pains to incriminate only "knowing" conversions. But, at common law there are unwitting acts which constitute conversions. In the civil tort, except for recovery of exemplary damages, the defendant's knowledge, intent, motive, mistake, and good faith are generally irrelevant. If one takes property which turns out to belong to another, his innocent intent will not shield him from making restitution or indemnity, for his well-meaning may not be allowed to deprive another of his own.

Had the statute applied to conversions without qualification, it would have made crimes of all unwitting, inadvertent and unintended conversions. Knowledge, of course, is not identical with intent and may not have been the most apt words of limitation. But knowing conversion requires more than knowledge that defendant was taking the property into his possession. He must have had knowledge of the facts, though not necessarily the law, that made the taking a conversion. In the case before us, whether the mental element that Congress required be spoken of as knowledge or as intent, would not seem to alter its bearing on guilt. For it is not apparent how Morissette could have knowingly or intentionally converted property that he did not know could be converted, as would be the case if it was in fact abandoned or if he truly believed it to be abandoned and unwanted property.

It is said, and at first blush the claim has plausibility, that, if we construe the statute to require a mental element as part of criminal conversion, it becomes a meaningless duplication of the offense of stealing, and that conversion can be given meaning only by interpreting it to disregard intention. But here again a broader view of the evolution of these crimes throws a different light on the legislation.

It is not surprising if there is considerable overlapping in the embezzlement, stealing, purloining and knowing conversion grouped in this statute. What has concerned codifiers of the larceny-type offense is that gaps or crevices have separated particular crimes of this general class and guilty men have escaped through the breaches. The books contain a surfeit of cases drawing fine distinctions between slightly different circumstances under which one may obtain wrongful advantages from another's property. The codifiers wanted to reach all such instances. . . . Knowing conversion adds significantly to the range of protection of government property without interpreting it to punish unwitting conversions. . . .

We find no grounds for inferring any affirmative instruction from Congress to eliminate intent from any offense with which this defendant was charged.

As we read the record, this case was tried on the theory that even if criminal intent were essential its presence (a) should be decided by the court (b) as a presumption of law, apparently conclusive, (c) predicated upon the isolated act of taking rather than upon all of the circumstances. In each of these respects we believe the trial court was in error. . . .

We think presumptive intent has no place in this case. A conclusive presumption which testimony could not overthrow would effectively eliminate intent as an ingredient of the offense. A presumption which would permit but not require the jury to assume intent from an isolated fact would prejudge a conclusion which the jury should reach of its own volition. A presumption which would permit the jury to make an assumption which all the evidence considered together does not logically establish would give to a proven fact an artificial and fictional effect. In either case, this presumption would conflict with the overriding presumption of innocence with which the law endows the accused and which extends to every element of the crime. Such incriminating presumptions are not to be improvised by the judiciary. Even congressional power to facilitate convictions by substituting presumptions for proof is not without limit. Tot v. United States, 319 U.S. 463, 63 S.Ct. 1241, 87 L.Ed. 1519.

Moreover, the conclusion supplied by presumption in this instance was one of intent to steal the casings, and it was based on the mere fact that defendant took them. The court thought the only question was, "Did he intend to take the property?" That the removal of them was a conscious and intentional act was admitted. But that isolated fact is not an adequate basis on which the jury should find the criminal intent to steal or knowingly convert, that is, *wrongfully* to deprive another of possession of property. Whether that intent existed, the jury must determine, not only from the act of taking, but from that together with defendant's testimony and all of the surrounding circumstances.

Of course, the jury, considering Morissette's awareness that these casings were on government property, his failure to seek any permission for their removal and his self-interest as a witness, might have disbelieved his profession of innocent intent and concluded that his assertion of a belief that the casings were abandoned was an afterthought. Had the jury convicted on proper instructions it would be the end of the matter. But juries are not bound by what seems inescapable logic to judges. They might have concluded that the heaps of spent casings left in the hinterland to rust away presented an appearance of unwanted and abandoned junk, and that lack of any conscious deprivation of property or intentional injury was indicated by Morissette's good character, the openness of the taking, crushing and transporting of the casings, and the candor with which it was all admitted. They might have refused to brand Morissette as a thief. Had they done so, that too would have been the end of the matter.

Reversed.

NOTES AND QUESTIONS

Problem 2–2. The National Firearms Act criminalizes possession of an unregistered "machine gun," which is defined as a weapon that automatically fires more than one shot with a single pull of the trigger. Defendant's home is searched by federal agents who seize a semiautomatic rifle—a weapon that normally fires only one shot with each trigger pull—that apparently had been modified for fully automatic fire. Defendant claims that the rifle never had fired automatically while he possessed it and that he had been ignorant of any automatic firing capability.

The Government argues that the Act fits within the Court's line of precedent concerning "public welfare" or "regulatory" offenses, and thus the presumption favoring *mens rea* does not apply. Citing precedents involving drugs and hand grenades, the claim is that, as long as the defendant knows that he is dealing with a dangerous device, he should be alerted to the probability of strict regulation, and no further mental state is necessary. What result? *See* Staples v. United States, 511 U.S. 600, 114 S.Ct. 1793, 128 L.Ed.2d 608 (1994).

Problem 2–3. The 1977 Protection of Children Against Sexual Exploitation Act prohibits "knowingly" transporting, shipping, receiving, distributing, or reproducing a visual depiction of a minor engaged in sexually explicit conduct. The defendant argues that the term "knowingly" in the statute modifies only the verbs, that there is no requirement that the actor know that person involved is a minor, and as such, the statute is an unconstitutional infringement of freedom of speech. Does the Act impose strict liability with respect to the involvement of a minor? If so, would such a construction of the statute leave it in violation of the First Amendment?

See United States v. X-Citement Video, Inc., 513 U.S. 64, 115 S.Ct. 464, 130 L.Ed.2d 372 (1994).

1. What function is the Court performing in cases like *Morissette* and *X-Citement Video*? Is the Court simply engaging in statutory construction—trying to determine the intent of the legislature (i.e., Congress)? Or is the Court doing something else as well?

2. Professor Jerome Hall in his book, GENERAL PRINCIPLES OF CRIMINAL LAW (2d ed. 1960), devotes a chapter to the problems of strict liability. In connection with proposed substitutes for strict liability, he suggests the following:

> Any current estimate of strict liability must take account of the vastly improved procedural and administrative facilities that now abound. Summary judicial hearings have been greatly improved; various techniques for arriving at judgments by conference, requiring mere recordation in court, are available; administration and administrative law have been greatly improved and expanded in the past quarter of a century. In short, the sole *raison d'être* of strict liability no longer exists—the problem posed by statistics can now be met by available legal institutions. . . . The continued recital of the rationalizations of a century ago loses any modicum of persuasiveness when the insistent claims of principle can be satisfied.

> The elimination of punitive strict liability would not restrict the inducements made by prosecutors to obtain pleas of guilty to the relevant criminal charges. The general features of contemporary criminal procedure, characterized by the disposal of the greatest part of the business by prosecutors and judges sitting without juries, would obtain here too. The bulk of the problem of protecting public welfare would be transferred to licensing and administrative agencies, . . . leaving the willful violations to be disposed of by specialized criminal courts or by special procedure. Against these unscrupulous individuals, the criminal law, sharpened to allow adequate dealing with crimes that are very serious in modern conditions, would be used much more frequently than in the past. On the other hand, the trial of reputable persons in a criminal court would be discontinued. Instead, sound legislation, . . . inspection, licensing, information, . . . investigation by boards, informal conferences, and publicity would provide much more likely means of influencing legitimate business.

> For the incompetents who simply cannot conform to decent standards, even after warning, information and counsel by regulatory boards, there is no alternative save to bar them from the pursuit of activities which are harmful to the public—whether that is driving an automobile, supplying milk or operating a public bar. It is undoubtedly true that the penal law functions much less onerously than would revocation of a license to do business. But this does not support the continuance of an anomalous strict

"penal" liability. The community is entitled to protection from inefficient persons who engage in potentially dangerous vocations or activities. They are certainly not restrained or improved by the perfunctory imposition of petty fines, nor for that matter by much severer penalties. The only proper recourse in some cases (very few, presumably, by comparison with those who improve their course of business after notice and assistance are received) must be the termination of the business or other activity. To make that depend on criminal behavior is to confuse immorality with inefficiency. To confine revocation of a license to the former is to ignore a major cause of injury to important social interests.

Id. at 351–53.

6. MISTAKE AND IGNORANCE

People v. Hernandez
Supreme Court of California, 1964.
61 Cal.2d 529, 39 Cal.Rptr. 361, 393 P.2d 673.

■ PEEK, JUSTICE. By information defendant was charged with statutory rape. (Pen.Code, § 261, subd. 1.) Following his plea of not guilty he was convicted as charged by the court sitting without a jury and the offense determined to be a misdemeanor.

Section 261 of the Penal Code provides in part as follows: "Rape is an act of sexual intercourse, accomplished with a female not the wife of the perpetrator, under either of the following circumstances: 1. Where the female is under the age of 18 years; * * *."

The sole contention raised on appeal is that the trial court erred in refusing to permit defendant to present evidence going to his guilt for the purpose of showing that he had in good faith a reasonable belief that the prosecutrix was 18 years or more of age.

The undisputed facts show that the defendant and the prosecuting witness were not married and had been companions for several months prior to January 3, 1961—the date of the commission of the alleged offense. Upon that date the prosecutrix was 17 years and 9 months of age and voluntarily engaged in an act of sexual intercourse with defendant.

In support of his contention defendant relies upon Penal Code § 20, which provides that "there must exist a union, or joint operation of act and intent, or criminal negligence" to constitute the commission of a crime. He further relies upon section 26 of that code which provides that one is not capable of committing a crime who commits an act under an ignorance or mistake of fact which disapproves any criminal intent.

Thus the sole issue relates to the question of intent and knowledge entertained by the defendant at the time of the commission of the crime charged.

Consent of the female is often an unrealistic and unfortunate standard for branding sexual intercourse a crime as serious as forcible rape. Yet the consent standard has been deemed to be required by important policy goals. We are dealing here, of course, with statutory rape where, in one sense, the lack of consent of the female is not an element of the offense. In a broader sense, however, the lack of consent is deemed to remain an element but the law makes a conclusive presumption of the lack thereof because she is presumed too innocent and naive to understand the implications and nature of her act. (People v. Griffen . . .) The law's concern with her capacity or lack thereof to so understand is explained in part by a popular conception of the social, moral and personal values which are preserved by the abstinence from sexual indulgence on the part of a young woman. An unwise disposition of her sexual favor is deemed to do harm both to herself and the social mores by which the community's conduct patterns are established. Hence the law of statutory rape intervenes in an effort to avoid such a disposition. This goal, moreover, is not accomplished by penalizing the naive female but by imposing criminal sanctions against the male, who is conclusively presumed to be responsible for the occurrence. . . .

The assumption that age alone will bring an understanding of the sexual act to a young woman is of doubtful validity. Both learning from the cultural group to which she is a member and her actual sexual experiences will determine her level of comprehension. The sexually experienced 15-year-old may be far more acutely aware of the implications of sexual intercourse than her sheltered cousin who is beyond the age of consent. A girl who belongs to a group whose members indulge in sexual intercourse at an early age is likely to rapidly acquire an insight into the rewards and penalties of sexual indulgence. Nevertheless, even in circumstances where a girl's actual comprehension contradicts the law's presumption, the male is deemed criminally responsible for the act, although himself young and naive and responding to advances which may have been made to him.

The law as presently constituted does not concern itself with the relative culpability of the male and female participants in the prohibited sexual act. Even where the young woman is knowledgeable it does not impose sanctions upon her. The knowledgeable young man, on the other hand, is penalized and there are none who would claim that under any construction of the law this should be otherwise. However, the issue raised by the rejected offer of proof in the instant case goes to the culpability of the young man who acts *without* knowledge that an essential factual element exists and has, on the other hand, a positive, reasonable belief that it does not exist.

The primordial concept of *mens rea*, the guilty mind, expresses the principle that it is not conduct alone but conduct accompanied by certain specific mental states which concerns, or should concern the law. In a broad sense the concept may be said to relate to such important doctrines as justification, excuse, mistake, necessity and mental capacity, but in the final analysis it means simply that there must be a "joint operation of act and intent," as expressed in section 20 of the Penal Code, to constitute the commission of a criminal offense. The statutory law, however, furnishes no assistance to the courts beyond that, and the casebooks are filled to overflowing with the courts' struggles to determine just what state of mind should be considered relevant in particular contexts. In numerous instances culpability has been completely eliminated as a necessary element of criminal conduct in spite of the admonition of section 20 to the contrary. . . (membership in organizations advocating criminal syndicalism); . . . (violation of Corporate Securities Act); . . . (sale of liquor). More recently, however, this court has moved away from the imposition of criminal sanctions in the absence of culpability where the governing statute, by implication or otherwise, expresses no legislative intent or policy to be served by imposing strict liability. . . .

Statutory rape has long furnished a fertile battleground upon which to argue that the lack of knowledgeable conduct is a proper defense. The law in this state now rests, as it did in 1896, with this court's decision in People v. Ratz, . . . where it is stated: "The claim here made is not a new one. It has frequently been pressed upon the attention of courts, but in no case, so far as our examination goes, has it met with favor. The object and purpose of the law are too plain to need comment, the crime too infamous to bear discussion. The protection of society, of the family, and of the infant, demand that one who has carnal intercourse under such circumstances shall do so in peril of the fact, and he will not be heard against the evidence to urge his belief that the victim of his outrage had passed the period which would make his act a crime." The age of consent at the time of the Ratz decision was 14 years, and it is noteworthy that the purpose of the rule, as there announced, was to afford protection to young females therein described as "infants." The decision on which the court in Ratz relied was The Queen v. Prince, L.R. 2 Crown Cas. 154. However England has now, by statute, departed from the strict rule, and excludes as a crime an act of sexual intercourse with a female between the ages of 13 and 16 years if the perpetrator is under the age of 24 years, has not previously been charged with a like offense, and believes the female "to be of the age of sixteen or over and has reasonable cause for the belief." . . .[2]

---

[2]   The American Law Institute in its model Penal Code (1962) provides in part as follows at pages 149 and 150:

"Section 213.6. Provisions Generally Applicable (Article 213 [Sexual Offenses].)

"(1) *Mistake as to Age.* Whenever in this Article the criminality of conduct depends upon a child's being below the age of 10, it is no defense that the actor did not know the child's age, or reasonably believed the child to be older than 10. When criminality depends upon the child's being below a critical age other than 10, it is a defense for the actor to prove that he reasonably believed the child to be above the critical age."

The rationale of the Ratz decision, rather than purporting to eliminate intent as an element of the crime, holds that the wrongdoer must assume the risk; that, subjectively, when the act is committed, he consciously intends to proceed regardless of the age of the female and the consequences of his act, and that the circumstances involving the female, whether she be a day or a decade less than the statutory age, are irrelevant. There can be no dispute that a criminal intent exists when the perpetrator proceeds with utter disregard of, or in the lack of grounds for, a belief that the female has reached the age of consent. But if he participates in a mutual act of sexual intercourse, believing his partner to be beyond the age of consent, with reasonable grounds for such belief, where is his criminal intent? In such circumstances he has not consciously taken any risk. Instead he has subjectively eliminated the risk by satisfying himself on reasonable evidence that the crime cannot be committed. If it occurs that he has been misled, we cannot realistically conclude that for such reason alone the intent with which he undertook the act suddenly becomes more heinous.

While the specific contentions herein made have been dealt with and rejected both within and without this state, the courts have uniformly failed to satisfactorily explain the nature of the criminal intent present in the mind of one who in good faith believes he has obtained a lawful consent before engaging in the prohibited act. As in the Ratz case the courts often justify convictions on policy reasons which, in effect, eliminate the element of intent. The Legislature, of course, by making intent an element of the crime, has established the prevailing policy from which it alone can properly advise us to depart.

We have recently given recognition to the legislative declarations in sections 20 and 26 of the Penal Code, and departed from prior decisional law which had failed to accord full effect to those sections as applied to charges of bigamy. (People v. Vogel, . . .) We held there that a good faith belief that a former wife had obtained a divorce was a valid defense to a charge of bigamy arising out of a second marriage when the first marriage had not in fact been terminated. Pertinent to the instant contention that defendant's intent did not suddenly become more criminal because it later developed that he had been misled by the prosecutrix, are the following comments appearing in Vogel at page 804 of 46 Cal.2d, at page 854 of 299 P.2d: "Nor would it be reasonable to hold that a person is guilty of bigamy who remarries in good faith in reliance on a judgment of divorce or annulment that is subsequently found not to be the 'judgment of a competent Court' * * *. Since it is often difficult for laymen to know when a judgment is not that of a competent court, we cannot reasonably expect them always to have such knowledge and make them criminals if their bona fide belief proves to be erroneous." Certainly it cannot be a greater wrong to entertain a bona fide but erroneous belief that a valid consent to an act of sexual intercourse has been obtained.

Equally applicable to the instant case are the following remarks, also appearing at page 804 of 46 Cal.2d, at page 855 of 299 P.2d of the Vogel decision: "The severe penalty imposed for bigamy, the serious loss of reputation conviction entails, * * * and the fact that it has been regarded for centuries as a crime involving moral turpitude, make it extremely unlikely that the Legislature meant to include the morally innocent to make sure the guilty did not escape."

We are persuaded that the reluctance to accord to a charge of statutory rape the defense of a lack of criminal intent has no greater justification than in the case of other statutory crimes, where the Legislature has made identical provision with respect to intent. " 'At common law an honest and reasonable belief in the existence of circumstances, which, if true, would make the act for which the person is indicted an innocent act, has always been held to be a good defense. * * * So far as I am aware it has never been suggested that these exceptions do not equally apply to the case of statutory offenses unless they are excluded expressly or by necessary implication.' " . . . Our departure from the views expressed in Ratz is in no manner indicative of a withdrawal from the sound policy that it is in the public interest to protect the sexually naive female from exploitation. No responsible person would hesitate to condemn as untenable a claimed good faith belief in the age of consent of an "infant" female whose obviously tender years preclude the existence of reasonable grounds for that belief. However, the prosecutrix in the instant case was but three months short of 18 years of age and there is nothing in the record to indicate that the purposes of the law as stated in Ratz can be better served by foreclosing the defense of a lack of intent. This is not to say that the granting of consent by even a sexually sophisticated girl known to be less than the statutory age is a defense. We hold only that in the absence of a legislative direction otherwise, a charge of statutory rape is defensible wherein a criminal intent is lacking.

For the foregoing reasons People v. Ratz, supra, and People v. Griffin, supra, are overruled, and People v. Sheffield, 9 Cal.App. 130, 98 P. 67, is disapproved to the extent that such decisions are inconsistent with the views expressed herein. . . .

The judgment is reversed.

NOTES

1. J.B. Haddad, in *The Mental Attitude Requirement in Criminal Law—And Some Exceptions*, 59 J. CRIM. L.C. & P.S. 4, 15 (1968), suggests, in relation to prosecutions for bigamy:

Strict liability in these cases is indefensible, whatever be the nature of the underlying mistake of fact. Defendants would not have been engaged in any legal or moral wrong had the facts been as they reasonably believed them to be; hence the principle of substituted intent is unavailable. Penalties from blameless defendants may be heavy, but they are unlikely to deter people who reasonably believe that they are free to marry, so that it makes little sense to say that the stability of the family depends upon a strict-liability standard. Even if such a standard would prevent more bigamous marriages than would a negligence standard, any *in terrorem* effect would also deter people whose marriages would not be bigamous from marrying because they lacked absolute certainty that the first spouse was dead or that a decree existed. This would be a significant deprivation of an important human right. Nor is there proof that juries would be deceived frequently by false claims of reasonable mistake of fact.

2. According to Wayne R. LaFave, in CRIMINAL LAW (3d ed. 2000):

Largely based on the influence of the Model Penal Code, The prevailing (but not universal) position taken in contemporary ["statutory rape"] statutes is that reasonable mistake *is* a defense when the age at issue is a higher age setting the very upper limits of the crime, but is *not* a defense when the age at issue is a lower age which determines whether a more serious version of the crime has occurred. Although undeniably a solid argument can be made for mistake as a defense no matter what the situation, this prevailing pattern makes some sense. When the age level is, say, ten, then strict liability is at least tolerable, "for no credible error regarding the age of a child in fact less than 10 years old would render the actor's conduct anything less than a dramatic departure from societal norms." But when the age at issue is in the high teens, the defendant who mistakenly but reasonably believes his partner is above the critical age should have a defense, for he "evidences no abnormality, no willingness to take advantage of immaturity, no propensity to corruption of minors."

Id. at § 7.20, at 779 (citations omitted).

For example, Model Penal Code § 213.6(1) provides:

Mistake as to Age. Whenever in this Article the criminality of conduct depends on a child's being below the age of 10, it is no defense that the actor did not know the child's age, or reasonably believed the child to be older than 10. When criminality depends on the child's being below a critical age other than 10, it is a defense for the actor to prove that he reasonably believed the child to be above the critical age.

Also see footnote 2 in *Hernandez.*

Not all jurisdictions agree. *See, e.g.*, People v. Cash, 419 Mich. 230, 351 N.W.2d 822 (1984) (construing legislative intent to dispense with reasonable mistake of fact as to complainant's age as a defense to statutory rape charge); Garnett v. State, *infra* Chapter 6 (second-degree rape statute prohibiting sexual intercourse with underage persons defines strict liability offense that does not require the state to prove *mens rea*, and makes no allowance for mistake-of-age defense).

United States of America v. United States District Court for the Central District of California (Kantor)

United States Court of Appeals for the Ninth Circuit, 1988.
858 F.2d 534.

■ KOZINSKI, CIRCUIT JUDGE:

Defendants are charged with violating 18 U.S.C. § 2251(a) (Supp. IV 1986), which prohibits the production of materials depicting a minor engaged in sexually explicit conduct. We consider whether they may present evidence that they reasonably believed the minor in question was an adult.

Facts

The basic facts are uncontested. In 1984, defendant James Marvin Souter, Jr., a so-called talent agent, hired 16-year-old Traci Lords to appear in a film to be produced by defendants Ronald Renee Kantor and Rupert Sebastian McNee. The film, *Those Young Girls*, was produced on August 2, 1984, and showed Lords engaging in sexually explicit conduct. While the depicted conduct, as described in the briefs, falls far outside the bounds of good taste, the government does not claim that the film is obscene under the standard of *Miller v. California*, 413 U.S. 15, 37 L.Ed.2d 419, 93 S.Ct. 2607 (1973). Rather, the theory of the prosecution, founded on solid Supreme Court authority, is that defendants may be punished for producing nonobscene films that depict minors engaging in sexually explicit conduct. *See New York v. Ferber*, 458 U.S. 747, 73 L.Ed.2d 1113, 102 S.Ct. 3348 (1982).

Defendants do not dispute the government's theory, nor do they suggest that Lords was in fact an adult. They protest only that they were seriously misled. According to their counsel, Lords and her agent perpetrated a massive fraud on what is euphemistically called the adult entertainment industry; purveyors of smut from coast to coast were taken in by an artful, studied and well-documented charade whereby Lords successfully passed herself off as an adult. Defendants proposed to introduce evidence of the charade at trial.

The government moved in limine to bar defendants from presenting this evidence. Because knowledge of the minor's age is not an element of the offense as defined by section 2251(a), the government argued, good-faith mistake could not be a defense. Defendants in turn moved to dismiss the indictment for failure to specify knowledge of the minor's age as an element, arguing that the statute would violate the first amendment and due process if the government were not required to prove scienter as part of its prima facie case.

The district court denied both motions. It concluded that neither the statute, nor due process, nor the first amendment requires the government to prove that defendants knew their subject was a minor. *United States v. Kantor*, 677 F. Supp. 1421, 1426–29 (C.D.Cal.1987). Nevertheless, the court noted that strict liability for criminal offenses appears to be justified only "(1) where the legislature grants the privilege to engage in the activity; (2) where the deterrent effect of a severe penalty is necessary to prevent harm to the public interest; and (3) where basic notions of fairness are not upset by criminal conviction." *Id.* at 1433. Finding that the first condition did not apply and the other two cut in favor of permitting a reasonable mistake of age defense, the district court ruled that defendants would be allowed to present their evidence.

* * *

Discussion

* * *

II

Our initial inquiry is whether scienter as to age is an element of the offense that the government must establish as part of its prima facie case. As always, we begin with the language of the statute:

> Any person who employs, uses, persuades, induces, entices, or coerces any minor to engage in, or who has a minor assist any other person to engage in, . . . any sexually explicit conduct for the purpose of producing any visual depiction of such conduct, shall be punished as provided under subsection (d), if such person knows or has reason to know that such visual depiction will be transported in interstate or foreign commerce or mailed, or if such visual depiction has actually been transported in interstate or foreign commerce or mailed.

18 U.S.C. § 2251(a) (Supp. IV 1986). The statute sets the age of majority at 18. 18 U.S.C. § 2256(1) (Supp. IV 1986). On its face, section 2251(a) requires only that a defendant arrange for a minor to engage in sexually explicit conduct for the purpose of creating a visual depiction, and that there be a nexus to interstate commerce.

The defendant's awareness of the subject's minority is not an element of the offense. This omission was quite clearly deliberate. Both Houses of Congress originally considered bills making it unlawful for any person "knowingly" to employ, entice or coerce a minor to engage in sexually explicit conduct for the purpose of producing or promoting a film or other print or visual medium. Department of Justice representatives urged deletion of "knowingly" so as to avoid the inference that producers could be prosecuted only if they knew the minor's age. Assistant Attorney General Patricia M. Wald stated as follows in a letter to the Senate Judiciary Committee:

Unless "knowingly" is deleted here, the bill might be subject to an interpretation requiring the Government to prove the defendant's knowledge of everything that follows "knowingly", including the age of the child. We assume that it is not the intention of the drafters to require the Government to prove that the defendant knew the child was under [the age of majority] but merely to prove that the child was, in fact, less than [the age of majority]. . . .

Expressly adopting this view, the House of Representatives struck "knowingly" from its bill. *See* H.R. Rep. 696, at 12 (citing *United States v. Hamilton*, 456 F.2d 171, 172 (3d Cir.) (federal statute punishing transportation of a minor in interstate commerce for the purpose of engaging in immoral practices does not require knowledge of minor's age), *cert. denied*, 406 U.S. 947, 32 L.Ed.2d 335, 92 S.Ct. 2051 (1972)). The conference committee accepted the House version "with the intent that it is not a necessary element of a prosecution that the defendant knew the actual age of the child." H.R. Rep. No. 811, 95th Cong., 1st Sess. 5 (1977), *reprinted in* 1978 U.S. Code Cong. & Admin. News 69, 69; S. Rep. No. 601, 95th Cong., 1st Sess. 5 (1977). There is thus little doubt that knowledge of the minor's age is not necessary for conviction under section 2251(a). . . .

III

Defendants concede that section 2251(a) also does not, on its face, make reasonable mistake of age an affirmative defense. Nevertheless, they contend that we must construe the statute as implicitly providing for such a defense in order to save it from constitutional infirmity. Specifically, they argue that the defense is required by the free speech and press clause of the first amendment, and by the due process clause of the fifth amendment. We need consider only the first of these.

A. We begin by acknowledging that the statute at issue regulates speech, albeit speech that is not protected by the first amendment. *See Ferber*, 458 U.S. at 763–64. Because protected and unprotected speech are "often separated . . . only by a dim and uncertain line," *Bantam Books, Inc. v. Sullivan*, 372 U.S. 58, 66, 9 L.Ed.2d 584, 83 S.Ct. 631 (1963), however, we must be careful to ensure that, in regulating unprotected speech, Congress does not also chill speech that is protected. *See Bose Corp. v. Consumers Union of the United States, Inc.*, 466 U.S. 485, 505, 508, 80 L.Ed.2d 502, 104 S.Ct. 1949 (1984) (the Court must "confine the perimeters of any unprotected category within acceptably narrow limits in an effort to ensure that protected expression will not be inhibited"). As the Supreme Court stated in *Smith v. California*, 361 U.S. 147, 152–53, 4 L.Ed.2d 205, 80 S.Ct. 215 (1959), "there is no specific constitutional inhibition against making the distributors of food the strictest censors of their merchandise, but the constitutional guaranties of the freedom of speech and of the press stand in the way of imposing a similar requirement on the bookseller."

As noted, no one claims that *Those Young Girls* is obscene; the film would therefore enjoy the protection of the first amendment were it not for its depiction of a minor. The age of the subject thus defines the boundary between speech that is constitutionally protected and speech that is not. The question we must resolve is whether Congress may subject a defendant to strict liability for misjudging the precise location of that boundary.

* * **

We read . . . Supreme Court cases as holding that a speaker may not be put at complete peril in distinguishing between protected and unprotected speech. Otherwise, he could only be certain of avoiding liability by holding his tongue, causing him "to make only statements which 'steer far wide of the unlawful zone.'" *New York Times Co. v. Sullivan*, 376 U.S. 254, 279, 11 L.Ed.2d 686, 84 S.Ct. 710 (1964) (quoting *Speiser v. Randall*, 357 U.S. 513, 526, 2 L.Ed.2d 1460, 78 S.Ct. 1332 (1958)). As the Court noted only this Term, "a rule that would impose strict liability on a publisher for [unprotected speech] would have an undoubted 'chilling' effect on speech . . . that does have constitutional value." *Hustler Magazine v. Falwell*, 485 U.S. 46, 108 S.Ct. 876, 880, 99 L.Ed.2d 41 (1988).

Section 2251(a) will have precisely this effect, defendants tell us, unless they are permitted to present a reasonable mistake of age defense. They point out that an actor's chronological age cannot be precisely ascertained from his appearance. Some 16- or 17-year-olds may look older and more sophisticated than their peers; 19- or 20-year-olds may look youthful and immature. . . . Age may also be ascertained on the basis of other evidence: birth certificates, driver's licenses or other identification; statements of those acquainted with the actor; reputation in the community. But, defendants argue, none of these sources is infallible: Documents can be, and frequently are, forged; people can be mistaken or lie; reputations may be based on unfounded rumor rather than fact.

Defendants contend that they were the victims of such deceit and misapprehension, proffering a catalogue of materials with which they expect to prove their contention if allowed to address the issue at trial. . . .

This scenario points to a serious dilemma faced by those who produce and distribute adult films: There is no way of being absolutely sure that an actor or actress who is youthful in appearance is not a minor. Even after taking the most elaborate steps to determine how old the subject is, as defendants claim they did here, a producer may still face up to ten years in prison and a $100,000 fine for each count. 18 U.S.C. § 2251(d) (Supp. IV 1986) (first offense). This must be a sobering thought for individuals wishing to cast young adults in sexually explicit films and other materials. Producers will almost certainly be deterred from producing such materials depicting youthful-looking adult actors; such actors may have considerable difficulty in finding producers willing to cast them; audiences wishing to view films featuring such actors would be denied the opportunity. . . .

Our reading of the relevant Supreme Court opinions, particularly *Smith v. California*, suggests that the first amendment does not permit the imposition of criminal sanctions on the basis of strict liability where doing so would seriously chill protected speech. While Congress may take steps to punish severely those who knowingly subject minors to sexual exploitation, and even those who commit such abuse recklessly or negligently, it may not impose very serious criminal sanctions on those who have diligently investigated the matter and formed a reasonable good-faith belief that they are engaged in activities protected by the first amendment. "Freedoms of expression require 'breathing space,'" *Hustler Magazine*, 108 S.Ct. at 880 (quoting *Philadelphia Newspapers, Inc. v. Hepps*, 475 U.S. 767, 772, 89 L.Ed.2d 783, 106 S.Ct. 1558 (1986)); imposition of major criminal sanctions on these defendants without allowing them to interpose a reasonable mistake of age defense would choke off protected speech.

* * *

B. Having concluded that the first amendment requires a reasonable mistake of age defense, we must next consider whether we have the authority to engraft such a defense onto a statute that does not expressly provide it. . . .

As noted, the statute is silent on whether reasonable mistake of age may serve as an affirmative defense. Moreover, unlike the question whether scienter should be an element of the government's prima facie case, there is no evidence that Congress considered and rejected the possibility of providing for such a defense. Engrafting such a defense would therefore not require us "to ignore the legislative will in order to avoid constitutional adjudication." *Schor*, 478 U.S. at 841.

* * *

We have little doubt that Congress would prefer section 2251(a) with a reasonable mistake of age defense to no statute at all. Allowing defendants to prove their reasonable, good-faith belief as to the age of an actor would not seriously disrupt the effective operation of section 2251(a), or materially hamper the vital effort to protect minors from sexual abuse. Such a defense would be entirely implausible under most circumstances, particularly in cases involving children or prepubescent teenagers. Even when dealing with older teenagers, a defendant would have a tough row to hoe in convincing a jury that he had acted with appropriate prudence in ensuring that the actor or actress was an adult.

Cases like this one, where the actress allegedly engaged in a deliberate and successful effort to deceive the entire industry, are likely to be exceedingly rare; even in those rare instances, juries may well be skeptical and choose to convict. As to those rare cases where otherwise culpable defendants may be exonerated on the basis of a reasonable mistake of age defense, we can only note that even as compelling a societal interest as the protection of minors must occasionally yield to specific constitutional guarantees. . . . We are convinced that if put to a choice between a statute that punishes severely the use of minors in sexually explicit materials, subject to a reasonable mistake of age defense, and no such statute at all, Congress would choose the former. Under the circumstances, we conclude that section 2251(a) is susceptible to the type of narrowing construction that would save it from fatal collision with the first amendment.

While the district court allowed defendants to present evidence of their reasonable mistake of age, it neither grounded the right to such a defense in the first amendment nor indicated the precise scope of such a defense. *See Kantor*, 677 F. Supp. at 1433. A defense grounded in common law notions of public policy might well be broader than one reflecting a mere constitutional minimum. As we read the constitutional requirement, the defense need be only a very narrow one: A defendant may avoid conviction only by showing, by clear and convincing evidence,[5] that he did not know, and could not reasonably have learned, that the actor or actress was under 18 years of age.[6] We instruct the district court to adopt this formulation in advising the jury on this issue.

* * *

---

[5] A section 2251(a) defendant who presents a reasonable mistake defense essentially alleges fraud on the part of the underage actor or actress. Clear and convincing evidence is the standard normally used to establish fraud in civil cases. *See Addington v. Texas*, 441 U.S. 418, 424, 60 L.Ed.2d 323, 99 S.Ct. 1804 (1979); *Woodby v. Immigration Serv.*, 385 U.S. 276, 285 n. 18, 17 L.Ed.2d 362, 87 S.Ct. 483 (1966).

While it is unusual to require a criminal defendant to prove an affirmative defense by clear and convincing evidence, *see* C.E. Torcia, 1 Wharton's Criminal Law § 39, at 205 (1978), it is not unheard of. The federal insanity defense, for instance, must be proved by clear and convincing evidence. 18 U.S.C. § 17(b) (Supp. IV 1986). The compelling government interest in enforcing section 2251(a) requires that we craft a reasonable mistake of age defense that is as narrow as possible without sacrificing the first amendment values it is designed to protect.

[6] Defendants would have us go farther and hold that the first amendment requires the government to prove scienter as part of its case. They rely on the Supreme Court cases holding that the government must carry such a burden in cases involving booksellers and other downstream distributors. *See, e.g., Hamling*, 418 U.S. at 123. We do not view these cases as controlling here. Those who arrange for minors to appear in sexually explicit materials are in a far different position from those who merely handle the visual images after they are fixed on paper, celluloid or magnetic tape. While it would undoubtedly chill the distribution of books and films if sellers were burdened with learning not only the content of all of the materials they carry but also the ages of actors with whom they have had no direct contact, *see Smith*, 361 U.S. at 153–54, producers are in a position to know or learn the ages of their employees. We note that several states have taken this approach. *See, e.g.*, Ky. Rev. Stat. Ann. § 531.330(2) (Michie 1985); N.Y. Penal Law § 263.20(1) (McKinney 1980); N.D. Cent. Code § 12.1–27.205(1) (1985); Or. Rev. Stat. § 163.690 (1987); Tenn. Code Ann. § 39–6–1138(d) (Supp. 1987); Tex. Penal Code Ann. § 43.25(f)(1) (Vernon Supp. 1988).

■ BEEZER, CIRCUIT JUDGE, dissenting:

The question we consider is whether Congress constitutionally may subject a person to criminal penalties for employing a minor to engage in sexually explicit conduct in a film intended for distribution in commerce, *see* 18 U.S.C. § 2251(a), regardless of whether that person made a "reasonable mistake" about the minor's age. The touchstone for our inquiry is *New York v. Ferber*, 458 U.S. 747, 73 L.Ed.2d 1113, 102 S.Ct. 3348 (1982). Pursuant to the Supreme Court's teaching in *Ferber*, I would weigh the government's interest in protecting children from sexual exploitation against the possibility of inhibiting expression protected by the first amendment. In my opinion, the balance tips sharply in favor of upholding section 2251(a) as written. Protecting children from sexual exploitation is a compelling government interest, and the statute does not pose a substantial threat of inhibiting protected expression. As a result, the first amendment does not require us to judicially interpose a reasonable mistake defense to section 2251(a).

* * *

NOTES

1. Why do you think the case is styled *United States v. United States District Court for the Central District of California*?

2. What kind of a mistake is made by the defendants in *Hernandez* and *U.S. District Court*? Is it the same kind of mistake? If so, do the courts treat it in the same fashion for legal purposes? If not, why not?

People v. Urziceanu

Court of Appeal of the Third District of California, 2005.
132 Cal.App.4th 747, 33 Cal.Rptr.3d 859.

■ ROBIE, J.

Defendant Michael C. Urziceanu claims he created a legal cooperative, FloraCare, to grow and supply medical marijuana for himself as a patient qualified to use it under the Compassionate Use Act and for other patients and primary caregivers who also qualify under the Compassionate Use Act. The People assert defendant and his codefendant, Susan B. Rodger,[2] were illegally cultivating and selling marijuana.

After trial, the jury acquitted defendant of cultivating marijuana, sale of marijuana, and being a felon in possession of ammunition. The jury, however, found him guilty of conspiracy to sell marijuana and being a felon in possession of a firearm and ammunition.

Defendant argues the recently enacted Medical Marijuana Program Act supplies him with a defense. As to his conviction for conspiracy,

---

[2] Rodger is not a party to this appeal.

defendant argues the court should have instructed the jury on the defenses of mistake of law and the vagueness of the Compassionate Use Act. He further contends the trial court erred in its ruling on his motion to suppress evidence obtained in violation of the knock-notice law.

As we shall demonstrate, the Compassionate Use Act, alone, does not authorize collective growing and distribution of marijuana by a group of qualified patients and caregivers. However, defendant's mistake of law as to whether that law provided him with a defense constitutes a defense to the charge of conspiracy to sell marijuana. . . . Thus, we shall reverse defendant's conspiracy conviction and remand for a new trial on that count.

In August 2000, the police learned that marijuana was being distributed from defendant's home in Citrus Heights. From newspaper articles and the Internet, Detective Steven Weinstock discovered defendant claimed to be engaged in medical marijuana activity. Police set up surveillance on the home and questioned people who came from that home. All but one of the subjects questioned had a medical marijuana recommendation—but that one person had a cooperative card from the Oakland Cannabis Buyers' Cooperative.

In January 2001, Detective Weinstock sent Detective Sue McCurry into defendant's residence without a medical certificate in an attempt to buy marijuana. She was unsuccessful.

After defendant was shot in 2001 during an apparent drug ripoff, Detective Weinstock visited him in the hospital. During their conversation, defendant told Detective Weinstock that he planned to establish a medical marijuana cooperative like the ones operating in the San Francisco Bay Area.

On August 9, 2001, Sacramento County Sheriff's Sergeant Karlene Doupe drove to defendant's Citrus Heights home. She had a laminated medical certificate for marijuana and a Department of Motor Vehicles driver's license in her undercover name.

Sergeant Doupe knocked on the door and Rodger opened it. Sergeant Doupe asked to speak with defendant and explained that she wanted to purchase some marijuana for her headaches. While she was in the house, Sergeant Doupe saw defendant in the kitchen and noticed about 15 to 20 marijuana plants in the backyard.

Rodger explained they normally only saw new members on Tuesdays or Wednesdays, but because it was slow, she could fill out the application paperwork. When Sergeant Doupe said she did not have her medical certificate, Rodger told her she could fill out the paperwork and bring her certificate in the next day. Rodger, however, would not provide Doupe with marijuana without a certificate. Sergeant Doupe went out to her car and brought in her certificate.

* * *

The medical cannabis farm consent form signed by Sergeant Doupe designated FloraCare as her "primary caregiver of health care services for the provision of medical cannabis as per the compassionate Use Act of 1996." Further, by signing the form, Sergeant Doupe confirmed under penalty of perjury that she had a qualifying medical condition and a doctor's prescription and agreed to reimburse FloraCare for the costs of gardening to cultivate her medical cannabis. . . .

* * *

After Sergeant Doupe filled out the paperwork, she returned it to Rodger. She also presented Rodger with her driver's license and the medical certificate. Rodger made a copy of the certificate and explained that the documents would be entered into a computer and then removed from the site so that law enforcement would be unable to obtain them.

* * *

Rodger then went into the kitchen and brought back a coffee can filled with small bags of marijuana. Rodger told Sergeant Doupe to take what she needed and that the bags were $50 each. Rodger also told Sergeant Doupe that the marijuana in the can had been donated by members of FloraCare, but there were 100 plants growing in the backyard.

Doupe took three bags and gave Rodger $160. Each bag contained 3.5 grams of marijuana and had a sticker with the word "FloraCare" on it. The sticker also bore the words: "The cannabis contained herein is intended for approved medical uses only pursuant to Health and Safety Code sections 11362.5 and 11357–11358 in accordance with the laws of the state of California." . . .

* * *

On September 18, 2001, Detective Dan Donelli served a search warrant on defendant's home. During that search, officers found a greenhouse structure in the backyard that contained at least 51 plastic drinking cups, each with a marijuana plant two to four feet tall. Around the pool and backyard, police found several different marijuana gardens that contained 159 plants which weighed a total of 410.65 pounds.

Inside the house, in the garage and in a separate drying room, officers found more marijuana, drying marijuana buds, plastic cups with potting soil in them, fertilizer, growing medium, and "grow lights." They also found glass marijuana pipes, a triple beam scale, a receipt book, marijuana leaves, various items of food made from marijuana, three guns, and assorted ammunition. Officers also discovered over $2,800 in cash and what they concluded were pay/owe sheets in the home. Defendant began to smoke marijuana during the search.

* * *

Defendant claimed that each of the members of FloraCare were caregivers for each of the other members of the cooperative. Defendant claimed FloraCare and its members were caring for the health and safety of the members of FloraCare. When he founded FloraCare, defendant spoke with law enforcement officials, members of district attorneys' offices, and attorneys.

Defendant downloaded the membership application documents used by FloraCare from the Internet. He also consulted with other cooperatives to obtain further information about those forms. Each member was required to fill out those forms as a condition of membership. Defendant testified that he used these forms so that he could follow the law. Further, each member was required to produce a valid California driver's license or type of identification and his or her original physician's recommendation. FloraCare also followed up each application with a telephone call to the physician to verify the information unless the member had a card from another club.

* * *

There were a few hundred members of FloraCare. At least a dozen of the members assisted with pruning and growing the marijuana. Often defendant or one of the members would deliver marijuana to patients. Upwards of 15 members assisted FloraCare in processing new members. Members who assisted with the intake of new members were often reimbursed for intake work, in the form of gas money or marijuana, for example.

* * *

We conclude the trial court did not err in concluding defendant could not raise the Compassionate Use Act defense to the conspiracy charge by arguing that he lawfully and cooperatively used, cultivated, and assisted others in obtaining medicinal marijuana. . . .

* * *

A cooperative where two people grow, stockpile, and distribute marijuana to hundreds of qualified patients or their primary caregivers, while receiving reimbursement for these expenses, does not fall within the scope of the language of the Compassionate Use Act or the cases that construe it.

* * *

Defendant argues he "was denied his constitutional right to present a mistake of law defense to the conspiracy charge . . ." [D]efendant asserts his good faith mistaken belief that his formation of FloraCare was legal, constituted a defense to the conspiracy charge because it negated his specific intent to violate the law. . . .

* * *

During trial, the trial court repeatedly rebuffed defendant's attempts to argue and present evidence that he believed the formation and operation of FloraCare was legal. . . .

* * *

Here, defendant's mistake that his formation and operation of FloraCare complied with the Compassionate Use Act was a mistake of law. Had he been convicted of selling marijuana, this mistake of law would provide no defense. Here, however, defendant was convicted of conspiracy to sell marijuana. To commit the crime of conspiracy, defendant must have had the specific intent to violate the marijuana laws (i.e., he must have known what he was doing was illegal and he must have intended to violate the law) before he can properly be convicted of conspiracy to violate those law. Because conspiracy requires a specific intent, a good faith mistake of law would provide defendant with a defense.

The elements of the crime of conspiracy are generally described as follows: "A criminal conspiracy exists where it is established that there was an unlawful agreement to commit a crime between two or more people, and an overt act in furtherance of the agreement. (See [Pen.Code,] § 182, subd. (a)(1).)" (*People v. Prevost* (1998) 60 Cal.App.4th 1382,1399, 71 Cal.Rptr.2d 487.) Other cases frame the elements as follows: "Pursuant to [Penal Code] section 182, subdivision (a)(1), a conspiracy consists of two or more persons conspiring to commit any crime. A conviction of conspiracy requires proof that the defendant and another person had the specific intent to agree or conspire to commit an offense, as well as the specific intent to commit the elements of that offense, together with proof of the commission of an overt act 'by one or more of the parties to such agreement' in furtherance of the conspiracy." (*People v. Morante* (1999) 20 Cal.4th 403, 416, 84 Cal.Rptr.2d 665, 975 P.2d 1071, fn. omitted.)

* * *

The defendant may not prove a good faith mistake of law by arguing he was unaware of the precise statute he was violating. In *People v. Smith* (1966) 63 Cal.2d 779, 48 Cal.Rptr. 382, 409 P.2d 222, the Supreme Court held it was irrelevant whether a defendant knew the crime he was about to commit was burglary as defined under California law when he entered a store in an attempt to cash a forged check. In that case, the defendant's specific *criminal* intent was demonstrated by his judicial admission that he entered the store with the intent to cash checks he knew were forged and he knew that was unlawful. (*Id.* at pp. 792–793, 48 Cal.Rptr. 382, 409 P.2d 222.) Thus, whether he knew he had violated a particular statute did not demonstrate the type of mistake that would disprove his criminal intent and therefore was not relevant. (*Ibid.*) The court explained, "the law recognizes honest purpose, not dishonest ignorance of the law, as a defense to a charge of committing a crime requiring 'specific intent.' " (*Id.* at p. 793, 48 Cal.Rptr. 382, 409 P.2d 222.)

As these cases demonstrate, defendant's good faith belief he was not violating the law is relevant in the context of the charge of conspiracy to sell marijuana. If the jury believed that defendant had a good faith belief, based on the Compassionate Use Act, that his actions were legal, this would negate the specific intent to violate the law required for a conspiracy conviction. That, ultimately, is a question of fact for a properly instructed jury.

Defendant presented evidence that he contacted law enforcement officers and public officials to ensure that his operation met the requirements of the Compassionate Use Act and attempted to cooperate with the police and authorities in an effort to bring his organization in line with the Compassionate Use Act. As noted above, however, the trial court repeatedly sustained objections to the admission of evidence on this subject, refused defendant the ability to argue this point to the jury, and specifically and erroneously concluded that defendant's mistake of law was not a defense.

* * *

The trial court's consistent rejection of this argument, its exclusion of evidence supporting this defense, and its prohibitions on defendant's arguments were error.

NOTES AND QUESTIONS

Problem 2–4. Is the court correct that Urziceanu's claim is one based on a mistake of law, which eliminates the necessary mental state for the crime of conspiracy, or rather is the claim one based on ignorance of the law, which is generally not regarded as a defense? *See* People v. Vogel, 46 Cal.2d 798, 299 P.2d 850 (1956) (also discussed in People v. Hernandez, *supra*; United States v. Ratzlaff, *supra*).

1. Model Penal Code § 2.04—Ignorance or Mistake provides:

(1) Ignorance or mistake as to a matter of fact or law is a defense if:

(a) the ignorance or mistake negatives the purpose, knowledge, belief. recklessness or negligence required to establish a material element of the offense; or

(b) the law provides that the state of mind established by such ignorance or mistake constitutes a defense.

(2) Although ignorance or mistake would otherwise afford a defense to the offense charged, the defense is not available if the defendant would be guilty of another offense had the situation been as he supposed. In such case, however, the ignorance or mistake of the defendant shall reduce the grade and degree of the offense of

which he may be convicted to those of the offense of which he would be guilty had the situation been as he supposed.

(3)   A belief that conduct does not legally constitute an offense is a defense to a prosecution for that based upon such conduct when:

(a)   the statute or other enactment defining the offense is not known to the actor and has not been published or otherwise reasonably made available prior to the conduct alleged; or

(b)   he acts in reasonable reliance upon an official statement of the law, afterward determined to be invalid or erroneous, contained in (i) a statute or other enactment; (ii) a judicial decision, opinion or judgement; (iii) an administrative order or grant of permission; or (iv) an official interpretation of the public officer or body charged by law with responsibility for the interpretation, administration or enforcement of the law defining the offense.

(4)   The defendant must prove a defense arising under Subsection (3) of this Section by a preponderance of evidence.

For examples of the application of § 2.04(1)(a), see Morissette v. United States, *supra* p. 74 (mistake as to ownership of property taken); Director of Public Prosecutions v. Morgan, [1976] A.C. 182, [1975] 2 W.L.R. 913, [1975] 2 All E.R. 347 (English House of Lords 1975) (mistaken belief that rape victim was consenting).

For examples of the application of § 2.04(3)(b), see United States v. Qualls, 172 F.3d 1136 (9th Cir. 1999) (reliance on judicial decision whose reversal was not reasonably forseeable); People v. Marrero, 69 N.Y.2d 382, 515 N.Y.S.2d 212, 507 N.E.2d 1068 (1987) (belief by federal corrections officer that he was "peace officer" within statutory language and therefore exempted from weapons statute).

Problem 2–5. Defendant, a guard at a federal prison in Connecticut, was arrested in a New York social club for possession of an unlicensed, loaded automatic pistol in alleged violation of a New York law that exempted "peace officers" defined to include "corrections officers of any state correctional facility or of any penal correctional facility." A New York appellate court ruled that this exemption did not cover a federal corrections officer; defendant then claimed that he should be excused from criminal liability because of his mistake about the exemption for "peace officers" in New York law. What result? *See* People v. Marrero, 69 N.Y.2d 382, 515 N.Y.S.2d 212, 507 N.E.2d 1068 (1987).

2. Professor Kenneth W. Simons describes the difference between mistake of fact and mistake of law in the following fashion: "Mistake and ignorance of fact involve perceptions of the world and empirical judgments derived from those perceptions. Mistake and ignorance of law involve assessment of whether, given a certain set of facts, the actor would or would not be violating the law." Kenneth W. Simons, *Mistake and Impossibility, Law and Fact, and Culpability: A Speculative Essay*, 81 J. CRIM. L. & CRIMINOLOGY 447, 469 (1990). Professor Simons says that a mistake of law can be identified by imagining an actor who knew all the facts. If this actor nevertheless failed to realize that certain conduct violated the law, then this would constitute a mistake of law. A mistake of fact could be identified by imagining an actor who had a perfect understanding of the law in its application to any set of facts, but failed to comprehend that certain conduct violated the law. This would constitute a mistake of fact. *Id.* at 469–70.

As an illustration of the difference between mistake of fact and mistake of law, Professor Gerald Leonard cites the case of Idaho v. Fox, 124 Idaho 924, 866 P.2d 181 (1993). He states:

> . . . Fox was charged with possession of a "controlled substance" without a prescription. He knew perfectly well that he possessed quite a lot of ephedrine and nothing in the way of prescriptions. What he did not know, insisted his lawyer, was the "fact" that ephedrine was on the list of controlled substances for which Idaho required a prescription. This mistake was, in a colloquial sense, clearly "factual," but, just as clearly, it counted as [a mistake of law] for the purposes of criminal law. Fox misunderstood that ephedrine was a "controlled substance" in Idaho. He thus mistook the scope of the term "controlled substance." And the court thus held, as any disinterested criminal lawyer would expect, that Fox's misunderstanding of statutory meaning was [a mistake of law].
>
> Had Fox claimed instead that, when he mail-ordered his 100,000 tablets, he had said "Excedrin" to the salesperson rather than "ephedrine" and had subsequently assumed that the pills that arrived were all pain-relievers, he would have had a good claim of [mistake of fact]. Since Idaho did not, in fact, require a prescription to buy Excedrin (even in such quantities, let us suppose) such a mistake would not have suggested any misunderstanding of the law but only a misperception of the actual nature of the substance in Fox's possession. . . . Such a mistake would be [a mistake of fact] and likely would provide a good defense. In fact, Idaho apparently requires any [mistake of fact] under this statute to be reasonable; so the hypothetical Fox who claims to have ordered Excedrin would have to convince the factfinder, for example, that he had good reason to think that the salesperson understood him properly and also had no obvious reason to believe that the pills he received were something different from what he had ordered. (citations omitted).

Gerald Leonard, *Rape, Murder, and Formalism: What Happens If We Define Mistake of Law?*, 72 U. COLO. L. REV. 507, 516–17 (2001).

Ratzlaf v. United States

Supreme Court of the United States, 1994.
510 U.S. 135, 114 S.Ct. 655, 126 L.Ed.2d 615.

■ JUSTICE GINSBURG delivered the opinion of the Court.

Federal law requires banks and other financial institutions to file reports with the Secretary of the Treasury whenever they are involved in a cash transaction that exceeds $10,000. 31 U.S.C. § 5313; 31 CFR § 103.22(a) (1993). It is illegal to "structure" transactions—*i.e.*, to break up a single transaction above the reporting threshold into two or more separate transactions—for the purpose of evading a financial institution's reporting requirement. 31 U.S.C. § 5324. "A person willfully violating" this antistructuring provision is subject to criminal penalties. § 5322. This case presents a question on which Courts of Appeals have divided: Does a defendant's purpose to circumvent a bank's reporting obligation suffice to sustain a conviction for "willfully violating" the antistructuring provision?[1] We hold that the "willfulness" requirement mandates something more. To establish that a defendant "willfully violat[ed]" the antistructuring law, the Government must prove that the defendant acted with knowledge that his conduct was unlawful.

I

On the evening of October 20, 1988, defendant-petitioner Waldemar Ratzlaf ran up a debt of $160,000 playing blackjack at the High Sierra Casino in Reno, Nevada. The casino gave him one week to pay. On the due date, Ratzlaf returned to the casino with cash of $100,000 in hand. A casino official informed Ratzlaf that all transactions involving more than $10,000 in cash had to be reported to state and federal authorities. The official added that the casino could accept a cashier's check for the full amount due without triggering any reporting requirement. The casino helpfully placed a limousine at Ratzlaf's disposal, and assigned an employee to accompany him to banks in the vicinity. Informed that banks, too, are required to report cash transactions in excess of $10,000, Ratzlaf purchased cashier's checks, each for less than $10,000 and each from a different bank. He delivered these checks to the High Sierra Casino.

Based on this endeavor, Ratzlaf was charged with "structuring transactions" to evade the banks' obligation to report cash transactions exceeding $10,000; this conduct, the indictment alleged, violated 31 U.S.C. §§ 5322(a) and 5324(3). The trial judge instructed the jury that the Government had to prove defendant's knowledge of the banks' reporting obligation and his attempt to evade that obligation, but did not have to prove defendant knew the structuring was unlawful. Ratzlaf was convicted, fined, and sentenced to prison.

Ratzlaf maintained on appeal that he could not be convicted of "willfully violating" the antistructuring law solely on the basis of his knowledge that a financial institution must report currency transactions in excess of $10,000 and his intention to avoid such reporting. To gain a conviction for "willful" conduct, he asserted, the Government must prove

---

[1] Compare, *e.g.*, *United States v. Scanio*, 900 F.2d 485, 491 (C.A.2 1990) ("proof that the defendant knew that structuring is unlawful" is not required to satisfy § 5322's willfulness requirement), with *United States v. Aversa*, 984 F.2d 493, 502 (C.A.1 1993) (en banc) (a "willful action" within the meaning of § 5322(a) "is one committed in violation of a known legal duty or in consequence of a defendant's reckless disregard of such a duty").

he was aware of the illegality of the "structuring" in which he engaged. The Ninth Circuit upheld the trial court's construction of the legislation and affirmed Ratzlaf's conviction. 976 F.2d 1280 (1992). We granted certiorari, ... and now conclude that, to give effect to the statutory "willfulness" specification, the Government had to prove Ratzlaf knew the structuring he undertook was unlawful. We therefore reverse the judgment of the Court of Appeals.

II

* * *

B

Section 5324 forbids structuring transactions with a "purpose of evading the reporting requirements of section 5313(a)." Ratzlaf admits that he structured cash transactions, and that he did so with knowledge of, and a purpose to avoid, the banks' duty to report currency transactions in excess of $10,000. The statutory formulation (§ 5322) under which Ratzlaf was prosecuted, however, calls for proof of "willful[ness]" on the actor's part. . . .

* * *

The United States urges, however, that § 5324 violators, by their very conduct, exhibit a purpose to do wrong, which suffices to show "willfulness". . . .

" '[S]tructuring is not the kind of activity that an ordinary person would engage in innocently,' " the United States asserts. . . . It is therefore "reasonable," the Government concludes, "to hold a structurer responsible for evading the reporting requirements without the need to prove specific knowledge that such evasion is unlawful." Brief for United States 29.

Undoubtedly there are bad men who attempt to elude official reporting requirements in order to hide from Government inspectors such criminal activity as laundering drug money or tax evasion. But currency structuring is not inevitably nefarious. Consider, for example, the small business operator who knows that reports filed under 31 U.S.C. § 5313(a) are available to the Internal Revenue Service. To reduce the risk of an IRS audit, she brings $9,500 in cash to the bank twice each week, in lieu of transporting over $10,000 once each week. That person, if the United States is right, has committed a criminal offense, because she structured cash transactions "for the specific purpose of depriving the Government of the information that Section 5313(a) is designed to obtain." . . . Nor is a person who structures a currency transaction invariably motivated by a desire to keep the Government in the dark. But under the Government's construction an individual would commit a felony against the United States by making cash deposits in small doses, fearful that the bank's reports would increase the likelihood of burglary, or in an endeavor to keep a former spouse unaware of his wealth.

Courts have noted "many occasions" on which persons, without violating any law, may structure transactions "in order to avoid the impact of some regulation or tax." . . . This Court, over a century ago, supplied an illustration:

> The Stamp Act of 1862 imposed a duty of two cents upon a bank-check, when drawn for an amount not less than twenty dollars. A careful individual, having the amount of twenty dollars to pay, pays the same by handing to his creditor two checks of ten dollars each. He thus draws checks in payment of his debt to the amount of twenty dollars, and yet pays no stamp duty. . . . While his operations deprive the government of the duties it might reasonably expect to receive, it is not perceived that the practice is open to the charge of fraud. He resorts to devices to avoid the payment of duties, but they are not illegal. He has the legal right to split up his evidences of payment, and thus to avoid the tax.

United States v. Isham, 84 U.S. (17 Wall.) 496, 506, 21 L.Ed. 728 (1873).

In current days, as an *amicus* noted, countless taxpayers each year give a gift of $10,000 on December 31 and an identical gift the next day, thereby legitimately avoiding the taxable gifts reporting required by 26 U.S.C. § 2503(b). . . .

In light of these examples, we are unpersuaded by the argument that structuring is so obviously "evil" or inherently "bad" that the "willfulness" requirement is satisfied irrespective of the defendant's knowledge of the illegality of structuring. . . .

C

In § 5322, Congress subjected to criminal penalties only those "willfully violating" § 5324, signaling its intent to require for conviction proof that the defendant knew not only of the bank's duty to report cash transactions in excess of $10,000, but also of his duty not to avoid triggering such a report. . . .

* * *

We do not dishonor the venerable principle that ignorance of the law generally is no defense to a criminal charge. See *Cheek v. United States*, 498 U.S. 192, 199, 111 S.Ct. 604, 609, 112 L.Ed.2d 617 (1991); *Barlow v. United States*, 32 U.S. (7 Pet.) 404, 410–412, 8 L.Ed. 728 (1833) (Story, J.). In particular contexts, however, Congress may decree otherwise. That, we hold, is what Congress has done with respect to 31 U.S.C. § 5322(a) and the provisions it controls. To convict Ratzlaf of the crime with which he was charged, violation of 31 U.S.C. §§ 5322(a) and 5324(3), the jury had to find he knew the structuring in which he engaged was unlawful.[19] Because the jury was not properly instructed in this regard,

---

[19] The dissent asserts that our holding "largely nullifies the effect" of § 5324 by "mak[ing] prosecution for structuring difficult or impossible in most cases." . . . Even under the dissent's reading of the statute, proof that the defendant knew of the bank's duty to report is required for

we reverse the judgment of the Ninth Circuit and remand this case for further proceedings consistent with this opinion.

It is so ordered.

■ JUSTICE BLACKMUN, with whom THE CHIEF JUSTICE, JUSTICE O'CONNOR, and JUSTICE THOMAS join, dissenting.

* * *

I

"The general rule that ignorance of the law or a mistake of law is no defense to criminal prosecution is deeply rooted in the American legal system." *Cheek v. United States*, 498 U.S. 192, 199, 111 S.Ct. 604, 609, 112 L.Ed.2d 617 (1991). The Court has applied this common-law rule "in numerous cases construing criminal statutes." *Ibid.*, citing *United States v. International Minerals & Chemical Corp.*, 402 U.S. 558, 91 S.Ct. 1697, 29 L.Ed.2d 178 (1971); *Hamling v. United States*, 418 U.S. 87, 119–124, 94 S.Ct. 2887, 2908–2911, 41 L.Ed.2d 590 (1974); and *Boyce Motor Lines, Inc. v. United States*, 342 U.S. 337, 72 S.Ct. 329, 96 L.Ed. 367 (1952).

Thus, the term "willfully" in criminal law generally "refers to consciousness of the act but not to consciousness that the act is unlawful." *Cheek*, 498 U.S., at 209, 111 S.Ct., at 614 (SCALIA, J., concurring in judgment); see also *Browder v. United States*, 312 U.S. 335, 341, 61 S.Ct. 599, 603, 85 L.Ed. 862 (1941); *Potter v. United States*, 155 U.S. 438, 446, 15 S.Ct. 144, 147, 39 L.Ed. 214 (1894); *American Surety Co. of New York v. Sullivan*, 7 F.2d 605, 606 (C.A.2 1925) (L. Hand, J.) ("[T]he word 'willful' . . . means no more than that the person charged with the duty knows what he is doing," not that "he must suppose that he is breaking the law"); American Law Institute, Model Penal Code § 2.02(8) (1985) ("A requirement that an offense be committed wilfully is satisfied if a person acts knowingly with respect to the material elements of the offense, unless a purpose to impose further requirements appears").

* * *

Unlike other provisions of the subchapter, the antistructuring provision identifies the purpose that is required for a § 5324 violation: "evading the reporting requirements." The offense of structuring, therefore, requires (1) *knowledge* of a financial institution's reporting requirements, and (2) the structuring of a transaction for the *purpose* of evading those requirements. These elements define a violation that is "willful" as that term is commonly interpreted. The majority's additional requirement that an actor have actual knowledge *that structuring is*

---

conviction; we fail to see why proof that the defendant knew of his duty to refrain from structuring is so qualitatively different that it renders prosecution "impossible." A jury may, of course, find the requisite knowledge on defendant's part by drawing reasonable inferences from the evidence of defendant's conduct, . . . See, *e.g., United States v. Dichne*, 612 F.2d 632, 636–638 (C.A.2 1979) (evidence that Government took "affirmative steps" to bring the reporting requirement to the defendant's attention by means of visual notices supports inference that defendant "willfully violated" § 5316).

prohibited strays from the statutory text, as well as from our precedents interpreting criminal statutes generally and "willfulness" in particular.

* * *

The Court next concludes that its interpretation of "willfully" is warranted because structuring is not inherently "nefarious." . . . It is true that the Court, on occasion, has imposed a knowledge-of-illegality requirement upon criminal statutes to ensure that the defendant acted with a wrongful purpose. See, *e.g., Liparota v. United States*, 471 U.S. 419, 426, 105 S.Ct. 2084, 2088, 85 L.Ed.2d 434 (1985). I cannot agree, however, that the imposition of such a requirement is necessary here. First, the conduct at issue—splitting up transactions involving tens of thousands of dollars in cash for the specific purpose of circumventing a bank's reporting duty—is hardly the sort of innocuous activity involved in cases such as *Liparota*, in which the defendant had been convicted of fraud for purchasing food stamps for less than their face value. Further, an individual convicted of structuring is, by definition, aware that cash transactions are regulated, and he cannot seriously argue that he lacked notice of the law's intrusion into the particular sphere of activity. Cf. *Lambert v. California*, 355 U.S. 225, 229, 78 S.Ct. 240, 243, 2 L.Ed.2d 228 (1957). By requiring knowledge of a bank's reporting requirements as well as a "purpose of evading" those requirements, the antistructuring provision targets those who knowingly act to deprive the Government of information to which it is entitled. In my view, that is not so plainly innocent a purpose as to justify reading into the statute the additional element of knowledge of illegality. . . .

In interpreting federal criminal tax statutes, this Court has defined the term "willfully" as requiring the " 'voluntary, intentional violation of a known legal duty.' " *Cheek v. United States*, 498 U.S., at 200, 111 S.Ct., at 610, quoting *United States v. Bishop*, 412 U.S. 346, 360, 93 S.Ct. 2008, 2017, 36 L.Ed.2d 941 (1973); see also *United States v. Murdock*, 290 U.S. 389, 394–396, 54 S.Ct. 223, 225–226, 78 L.Ed. 381 (1933). Our rule in the tax area, however, is an "exception to the traditional rule," applied "largely due to the complexity of the tax laws." *Cheek*, 498 U.S., at 200, 111 S.Ct., at 609; see also *Browder v. United States*, 312 U.S., at 341–342, 61 S.Ct., at 603. The rule is inapplicable here, where, far from being complex, the provisions involved are perhaps among the simplest in the United States Code.

* * *

III

The petitioner in this case was informed by casino officials that a transaction involving more than $10,000 in cash must be reported, was informed by the various banks he visited that banks are required to report cash transactions in excess of $10,000, and then purchased $76,000 in cashier's checks, each for less than $10,000 and each from a different bank. Petitioner Ratzlaf, obviously not a person of limited intelligence, was anything but uncomprehending as he traveled from bank to bank converting his bag of cash to cashier's checks in $9,500 bundles. I am convinced that his actions constituted a "willful" violation of the antistructuring provision embodied in 31 U.S.C. § 5324. As a result of today's decision, Waldemar Ratzlaf—to use an old phrase—will be "laughing all the way to the bank."

NOTES AND QUESTIONS

1. In *Ratzlaf*, the Supreme Court refers to both Cheek v. United States, 498 U.S. 192, 111 S.Ct. 604, 112 L.Ed.2d 617 (1991) (holding that term "willfully" in federal tax statutes requires the "voluntary, intentional violation of a known legal duty"), and Liparota v. United States, 471 U.S. 419, 105 S.Ct. 2084, 85 L.Ed.2d 434 (1985) (holding that the federal statute governing food stamps requires proof that the defendant knew that his acquisition or possession of food stamps was in a manner unauthorized by statute or regulations). These cases, along with *Ratzlaf*, seem to indicate that knowledge of and intent to violate the law are necessary for conviction. But, as both Justice Ginsburg and dissenting Justice Blackmun note, the general principle is that ignorance of the law is no excuse. Why then do these cases require knowledge of the law in order to satisfy the statutory mental state necessary for its violation?

2. Shortly after the decision in *Ratzlaf*, Congress amended § 5324 to eliminate any separate requirement that a defendant act "willfully." *See* 31 U.S.C. § 5324(c). Congress clearly indicated that it intended to remedy the error that it felt the majority had made in *Ratzlaf* interpreting the statutory term "willfully" to require proof that defendant knew that structuring was illegal. The 1994 amendment was made "to correct" the holding in *Ratzlaf* and to "restore the clear Congressional intent that a defendant need only have the intent to evade the reporting requirement" to violate the statute. *See* H.R. Rep. No. 103–438, at 22 (1994); H.R. Conf. Rep. No. 103–652, at 194 (1994), *reprinted in* 1994 U.S.C.C.A.N. 1881, 2024.

The term "willfully" nevertheless remains in other statutory schemes. And, as suggested by Professor Sharon L. Davies, in *The Jurisprudence of Willfulness: An Evolving Theory of Excusable Ignorance*, 48 Duke L.J. 341, 403–05 (1998):

> Despite the clear congressional disapproval of the judicial interpretation of "willfulness" in this post-Ratzlaf amendment, Congress's decision to override the Court's construction has had no effect on later constructions of "willfulness" in other criminal statutory schemes. Rather, the courts have continued to treat the Ratzlaf construction of "willfully" as an accurate reading of congressional intent and have used the same bases that led to the mistake, and the mistake itself, to determine what Congress meant in other statutes. Worse than mere obstinacy, this refusal to recognize the mistake undermines the legislative function and may violate separation of powers principles.

Critics of this view might argue that Ratzlaf was no mistake at all. By removing only the structuring offense set out in section 5324 from the willfulness requirement but allowing other related offenses to remain subject to that requirement, one might argue that Congress was signaling its agreement with the Court's construction of "willfully" and reaffirming its desire to make knowledge of the law an element of other structuring offenses to which the willfulness requirement of section 5322(a) continued to apply. After all, Congress could easily have taken the word "willfully" out of the statute altogether. Its decision to retain it while making the word inapplicable to the particular subsection under which Ratzlaf was prosecuted could indicate that it concurred with, or at least acquiesced in, the Court's interpretation of the term. Under this view, Ratzlaf-like structuring behavior would no longer be subject to an ignorance or mistake of law claim, but other structuring conduct falling under the reserved willfulness requirement would.

The difficulty with this view is that it completely ignores the best available source of information about Congress's view of the Ratzlaf construction of the term "willfully." The committee reports explain the impetus for the statutory change in no uncertain terms. As noted above, the reports roundly criticize the Court's construction and explain that the statutory change was intended to "correct" the error made by the Ratzlaf Court when it interpreted the term to impose a knowledge of the law requirement. The reports also clarify the legislative intent behind the initial use of the term in the structuring provision: prosecutors were expected to prove an accused's intent to evade a financial institution's reporting obligations, but not the accused's knowledge that structuring was illegal.

Moreover, even assuming that the structuring provisions which remain subject to the willfulness requirement after the amendment could be fairly construed to require proof of knowledge of the law, the legislative history overruling the Ratzlaf construction of section 5324 at least demonstrates the incorrectness of any claim that Congress equates "willfully" with knowledge of the law whenever it places the term in a criminal statute. The term was employed in section 5324, and Congress has denounced the suggestion that it used the word to make knowledge of the law an element of the offense. It is sensible to conclude from this congressional commentary that the use of the term "willfully" in other statutory contexts was not necessarily intended to provide a mistake of law defense. Finally, Congress's powerful repudiation of the Court's interpretation of "willfully" in Ratzlaf was also a repudiation of the Court's argument that conduct like Ratzlaf's evasions was not nefarious or that the crime of structuring was so technical that Congress must have wanted ignorance of the law to excuse. That repudiation should have led the Court to appreciate the gross subjectivity in such determinations and to hesitate before making them in the future. If *Bryan* [holding that "willfully" in statute prohibiting sale of firearm without a federal license requires knowledge that the conduct is unlawful] is any indication, however, the Court is unbowed.

3. Why do you suppose that ignorance of the law generally is not an excuse? *See* Mark D. Yochum, *Cheek is Chic. Ignorance of the Law Is an Excuse for Tax Crimes—A Fashion That Does Not Wear Well*, 31 DUQ. L. REV. 249 (1993).

Problem 2–6. Defendant is charged with the federal crime of carjacking "with the intent to cause death or serious bodily harm." His accomplice testified that the plan was to steal cars without harming the victim but that he would have used his gun if any of the drivers had given him a "hard time." The district judge instructed the jury that the Government was required to prove beyond a reasonable doubt that the taking of a vehicle was committed with the intent "to cause death or serious bodily harm to the person from whom the car was taken." He added:

> In some cases, intent is conditional. That is, a defendant may intend to engage in certain conduct only if a certain event occurs.

> In this case, the Government contends that the defendant intended to cause death or serious bodily harm if the alleged victims had refused to turn over their cars. If you find beyond a reasonable doubt that the defendant had such an intent, the Government has satisfied this element of the offense.

The defendant objected to this instruction, arguing that the statutory mental state covered only those carjackings in which the defendant's sole and unconditional purpose at the time of the carjacking was to kill or maim the victim. In other words, the federal statute covered "only those carjackings in which the offender actually attempted to harm or kill the driver (or at least intended to do so whether or not the driver resisted)." Which interpretation is correct, the instruction given by the trial judge or the one for which the defendant contended? *See* Holloway v. United States, 526 U.S. 1, 119 S.Ct. 966, 143 L.Ed.2d 1 (1999).

C. THE CAUSAL CONNECTION

People v. Dlugash
Court of Appeals of New York, 1977.
41 N.Y.2d 725, 395 N.Y.S.2d 419, 363 N.E.2d 1155.

■ JASEN, JUDGE. The criminal law is of ancient origin, but criminal liability for attempt to commit a crime is comparatively recent. At the root of the concept of attempt liability are the very aims and purposes of penal law. The ultimate issue is whether an individual's intentions and actions, though failing to achieve a manifest and malevolent criminal purpose, constitute a danger to organized society of sufficient magnitude to warrant the imposition of criminal sanctions. Difficulties in theoretical analysis and concomitant debate over very pragmatic questions of blameworthiness appear dramatically in reference to situations where the criminal attempt failed to achieve its purpose solely because the factual or legal context in which the individual acted was not as the actor supposed them to be. Phrased somewhat differently, the concern centers on whether an individual should be liable for an attempt to commit a crime when, unknown to him, it was impossible to successfully complete the crime attempted. For years, serious studies have been made on the subject in an effort to resolve the continuing controversy when, if at all, the impossibility of successfully completing the criminal act should preclude liability for even making the futile attempt. The 1967 revision of the Penal Law approached the impossibility defense to the inchoate crime of attempt in a novel fashion. The statute provides that, if a person engages in conduct which would otherwise constitute an attempt to commit a crime, "it is no defense to a prosecution for such attempt that the crime charged to have been attempted was, under the attendant circumstances, factually or legally impossible of commission, if such crime could have been committed had the attendant circumstances been as such person believed them to be." (Penal Law, § 110.10.) This appeal presents to us, for the first time, a case involving the application of the modern statute. We hold that, under the proof presented by the People at trial, defendant Melvin Dlugash may be held for attempted murder, though the target of the attempt may have already been slain, by the hand of another, when Dlugash made his felonious attempt.

On December 22, 1973, Michael Geller, 25 years old, was found shot to death in the bedroom of his Brooklyn apartment. The body, which had literally been riddled by bullets, was found lying face up on the floor. An autopsy revealed that the victim had been shot in the face and head no less than seven times. Powder burns on the face indicated that the shots had been fired from within one foot of the victim. Four small caliber bullets were recovered from the victim's skull. The victim had also been critically wounded in the chest. One heavy caliber bullet passed through the left lung, penetrated the heart chamber, pierced the left ventricle of the heart upon entrance and again upon exit, and lodged in the victim's torso. A second bullet entered the left lung and passed, through to the chest, but without reaching the heart area. Although the second bullet was damaged beyond identification, the bullet tracks indicated that these wounds were also inflicted by a bullet of heavy caliber. A tenth bullet, of unknown caliber, passed through the thumb of the victim's left hand. The autopsy report listed the cause of death as "[m]ultiple bullet wounds of head and chest with brain injury and massive bilateral hemothorax with penetration of [the] heart." Subsequent ballistics examination established that the four bullets recovered from the victim's head were .25 caliber bullets and that the heart-piercing bullet was of .38 caliber.

Detective Joseph Carrasquillo of the New York City Police Department was assigned to investigate the homicide. On December 27, 1973, five days after the discovery of the body, Detective Carrasquillo and a fellow officer went to the defendant's residence in an effort to locate him. The officers arrived at approximately 6:00 p.m. The defendant answered the door and, when informed that the officers were investigating the death of Michael Geller, a friend of his, defendant invited the officers into the house. Detective Carrasquillo informed defendant that the officers desired any information defendant might have regarding the death of Geller and, since defendant was regarded as a suspect, administered the standard preinterrogation warnings. The defendant told the officers that he and another friend, Joe Bush, had just returned from a four- or five-day trip "upstate someplace" and learned of Geller's death only upon his return. Since Bush was also a suspect in the case and defendant admitted knowing Bush, defendant agreed to accompany the officers to the station house for the purposes of identifying photographs of Bush and of lending assistance to the investigation. Upon arrival at the police station, Detective Carrasquillo and the defendant went directly into an interview room. Carrasquillo advised the defendant that he had witnesses and information to the effect that as late as 7:00 p.m. on the day before the body was found, defendant had been observed carrying a .25 caliber pistol. Once again, Carrasquillo administered the standard preinterrogation statement of rights. The defendant then proceeded to relate his version of the events which culminated in the death of Geller. Defendant stated that, on the night of December 21, 1973, he, Bush and Geller had been out drinking. Bush had been staying at Geller's apartment and, during the course of the evening, Geller several times demanded that Bush pay $100 towards the rent on the apartment. According to defendant, Bush rejected these demands, telling Geller that "you better shut up or you're going to get a bullet". All three returned to Geller's apartment at approximately midnight, took seats in the bedroom, and continued to drink until sometime between 3:00 and 3:30 in the morning. When Geller again pressed his demand for rent money, Bush drew his .38 caliber pistol, aimed it at Geller and fired three times. Geller fell to the floor. After the passage of a few minutes, perhaps two, perhaps as much as five, defendant walked over to the fallen Geller, drew his .25 caliber pistol, and fired approximately five shots in the victim's head and face. Defendant contended that, by the time he fired the shots, "it looked like Mike Geller was already dead". After the shots were fired, defendant and Bush walked to the apartment of a female acquaintance. Bush removed his shirt, wrapped the two guns and a knife in it, and left the apartment, telling Dlugash that he intended to dispose of the weapons. Bush returned 10 or 15 minutes later and stated that he had thrown the weapons down a sewer two or three blocks away.

After Carrasquillo had taken the bulk of the statement, he asked the defendant why he would do such a thing. According to Carrasquillo, the defendant said, "gee, I really don't know". Carrasquillo repeated the question 10 minutes later, but received the same response. After a while, Carrasquillo asked the question for a third time and defendant replied, "well gee, I guess it must have been because I was afraid of Joe Bush."

* * *

Defendant was indicted by the Grand Jury of Kings County on a single count of murder in that, acting in concert with another person actually present, he intentionally caused the death of Michael Geller. . . .

* * *

The trial court declined to charge the jury, as requested by the prosecution, that defendant could be guilty of murder on the theory that he had aided and abetted the killing of Geller by Bush. Instead, the court submitted only two theories to the jury: that defendant had either intentionally murdered Geller or had attempted to murder Geller.

The jury found the defendant guilty of murder. The defendant then moved to set the verdict aside. He submitted an affidavit in which he contended that he "was absolutely, unequivocally and positively certain that Michael Geller was dead before [he] shot him." Further, the defendant averred that he was in fear for his life when he shot Geller, "This fear stemmed from the fact that Joseph Bush, the admitted killer of Geller, was holding a gun on me and telling me, in no uncertain terms, that if I didn't shoot the dead body I, too would be killed." This motion was denied.

On appeal, the Appellate Division reversed the judgment of conviction on the law and dismissed the indictment. The court ruled that "the People failed to prove beyond a reasonable doubt that Geller had been alive at the time he was shot by defendant; defendant's conviction of murder thus cannot stand." Further, the court held that the judgment could not be modified to reflect a conviction for attempted murder because "the uncontradicted evidence is that the defendant, at the time that he fired the five shots into the body of the decedent, believed him to be dead, and * * * there is not a scintilla of evidence to contradict his assertion in that regard".

Preliminarily, we state our agreement with the Appellate Division that the evidence did not establish, beyond a reasonable doubt, that Geller was alive at the time defendant fired into his body. To sustain a homicide conviction, it must be established, beyond a reasonable doubt, that the defendant caused the death of another person. The People were required to establish that the shots fired by defendant Dlugash were a sufficiently direct cause of Geller's death. While the defendant admitted firing five shots at the victim approximately two to five minutes after Bush had fired three times, all three medical expert witnesses testified that they could not, with any degree of medical certainty, state whether the victim had been alive at the time the latter shots were fired by the defendant. Thus, the People failed to prove beyond a reasonable doubt that the victim had been alive at the time he was shot by the defendant. Whatever else it may be, it is not murder to shoot a dead body. Man dies but once.

* * *

The procedural context of this matter, a nonappealable but erroneous dismissal of the issue of accessorial conduct, contributes to the unique nature of the attempt issue presented here. Where two or more persons have combined to murder, proof of the relationship between perpetrators is sufficient to hold all for the same degree of homicide, notwithstanding the absence of proof as to which specific act of which individual was the immediate cause of the victim's death. On the other hand, it is quite unlikely and improbable that two persons, unknown and unconnected to each other, would attempt to kill the same third person at the same time and place. Thus, it is rare for criminal liability for homicide to turn on which of several attempts actually succeeded. In the case of coconspirators, it is not necessary to do so and the case of truly independent actors is unlikely. However, procedural developments make this case the unlikely one and we must now decide whether, under the evidence presented, the defendant may be held for attempted murder, though someone else perhaps succeeded in killing the victim.

The concept that there could be criminal liability for an attempt, even if ultimately unsuccessful, to commit a crime is comparatively recent. The modern concept of attempt has been said to date from Rex v. Scofield (Cald 397), decided in 1784. (Sayre, Criminal Attempts, 41 Harv.L.Rev. 821, 834.) In that case, Lord Mansfield stated that "[t]he intent may make an act, innocent in itself, criminal; nor is the completion of an act, criminal in itself, necessary to constitute criminality. Is it no offence to set fire to a train of gunpowder with intent to burn a house, because by accident, or the interposition of another, the mischief is prevented?" The Revised Penal Law now provides that a person is guilty of an attempt to commit a crime when, with intent to commit a crime, he engages in conduct which tends to effect the commission of such crime. The revised statute clarified confusion in the former provision which, on its face, seemed to state that an attempt was not punishable as an attempt unless it was unsuccessful.

The most intriguing attempt cases are those where the attempt to commit a crime was unsuccessful due to mistakes of fact or law on the part of the would-be criminal. A general rule developed in most American jurisdictions that legal impossibility is a good defense but factual impossibility is not. Thus, for example, it was held that defendants who shot at a stuffed deer did not attempt to take a deer out of season, even though they believed the dummy to be a live animal. The court stated that there was no criminal attempt because it was no crime to "take" a stuffed deer, and it is no crime to attempt to do that which is legal. (State

v. Taylor, 345 Mo. 325, 133 S.W.2d 336 [no liability for attempt to bribe a juror where person bribed was not, in fact, a juror].) These cases are illustrative of legal impossibility. A further example is Francis Wharton's classic hypothetical involving Lady Eldon and her French lace. Lady Eldon, traveling in Europe, purchased a quantity of French lace at a high price, intending to smuggle it into England without payment of the duty. When discovered in a customs search, the lace turned out to be of English origin, of little value and not subject to duty. The traditional view is that Lady Eldon is not liable for an attempt to smuggle. (1 Wharton, Criminal Law [12th ed.], § 225, p. 304, n. 9; for variations on the hypothetical see Hughes, One Further Footnote on Attempting the Impossible, 42 N.Y.U.L.Rev. 1005.)

On the other hand, factual impossibility was no defense. For example, a man was held liable for attempted murder when he shot into the room in which his target usually slept and, fortuitously, the target was sleeping elsewhere in the house that night. (State v. Mitchell, 170 Mo. 633, 71 S.W. 175.) Although one bullet struck the target's customary pillow, attainment of the criminal objective was factually impossible. State v. Moretti, 52 N.J. 182, 244 A.2d 499, cert. den. 393 U.S. 952, 89 S.Ct. 376, 21 L.Ed.2d 363, presents a similar instance of factual impossibility. The defendant agreed to perform an abortion, then a criminal act, upon a female undercover police investigator who was not, in fact, pregnant. The court sustained the conviction, ruling that "when the consequences sought by a defendant are forbidden by the law as criminal, it is no defense that the defendant could not succeed in reaching his goal because of circumstances unknown to him." On the same view, it was held that men who had sexual intercourse with a woman, with the belief that she was alive and did not consent to the intercourse, could be charged for attempted rape when the woman had, in fact, died from an unrelated ailment prior to the acts of intercourse.

The New York cases can be parsed out along similar lines. One of the leading cases on legal impossibility is People v. Jaffe, 185 N.Y. 497, 78 N.E. 169, in which we held that there was no liability for the attempted receipt of stolen property when the property received by the defendant in the belief that it was stolen was, in fact under the control of the true owner. Similarly, in People v. Teal, 196 N.Y. 372, 89 N.E. 1086, a conviction for attempted subornation of perjury was overturned on the theory that the testimony attempted to be suborned was irrelevant to the merits of the case. Since it was not subornation of perjury to solicit false, but irrelevant, testimony, "the person through whose procuration the testimony is given cannot be guilty of subornation of perjury and, by the same rule, an unsuccessful attempt to that which is not a crime when effectuated, cannot be held to be an attempt to commit the crime specified." Factual impossibility, however, was no defense. Thus, a man could be held for attempted grand larceny when he picked an empty pocket.

As can be seen from even this abbreviated discussion, the distinction between "factual" and "legal" impossibility was a nice one indeed and the courts tended to place a greater value on legal form than on any substantive danger the defendant's actions posed for society. The approach of the draftsmen of the Model Penal Code was to eliminate the defense of impossibility in virtually all situations. Under the code provision, to constitute an attempt, it is still necessary that the result intended or desired by the actor constitute a crime. However, the code suggested a fundamental change to shift the locus of analysis to the actor's mental frame of reference and away from undue dependence upon external considerations. The basic premise of the code provision is that what was in the actor's own mind should be the standard for determining his dangerousness to society and, hence, his liability for attempted criminal conduct.

In the belief that neither of the two branches of the traditional impossibility arguments detracts from the offender's moral culpability, the Legislature substantially carried the code's treatment of impossibility into the 1967 revision of the Penal Law. Thus, a person is guilty of an attempt when, with intent to commit a crime, he engages in conduct which tends to effect the commission of such crime. It is no defense that, under the attendant circumstances, the crime was factually or legally impossible of commission, "if such crime could have been committed had the attendant circumstances been as such person believed them to be." Thus, if defendant believed the victim to be alive at the time of the shooting, it is no defense to the charge of attempted murder that the victim may have been dead.

Turning to the facts of the case before us, we believe that there is sufficient evidence in the record from which the jury could conclude that the defendant believed Geller to be alive at the time defendant fired shots into Geller's head. Defendant admitted firing five shots at a most vital part of the victim's anatomy from virtually point blank range. Although defendant contended that the victim had already been grievously wounded by another, from the defendant's admitted actions, the jury could conclude that the defendant's purpose and intention was to administer the coup de grace. The jury never learned of defendant's subsequent allegation that Bush had a gun on him and directed defendant to fire at Geller on the pain of his own life. Defendant did not testify and this statement of duress was made only in a postverdict affidavit, which obviously was never placed before the jury. In his admissions that were related to the jury, defendant never made such a claim. Nor did he offer any explanation for his conduct, except for an offhand aside made casually to Detective Carrasquillo. Any remaining doubt as to the question of duress is dispelled by defendant's earlier statement that he and Joe Bush had peacefully spent a few days together on vacation in the country. Moreover, defendant admitted to freely assisting Bush in disposing of the weapons after the murder and, once the weapons were out of the picture, defendant made no effort at all to flee from Bush. Indeed, not only did defendant not come forward with his story immediately, but when the police arrived at his house, he related a false version designed to conceal his and Bush's complicity in the murder. All of these facts indicate a consciousness of guilt which defendant would not have had if he had truly believed that Geller was dead when he shot him.

Defendant argues that the jury was bound to accept, at face value, the indications in his admissions that he believed Geller dead. Certainly, it is true that the defendant was entitled to have the entirety of the admissions, both the inculpatory and the exculpatory portions, placed in evidence before the trier of facts. However, the jury was not required to automatically credit the exculpatory portions of the admissions. The general rule is, of course, that the credibility of witnesses is a question of fact and the jury may choose to believe some, but not all, of a witness' testimony. The general rule applies with equal force to proof of admissions. Thus, it has been stated that "where that part of the declaration which discharges the party making it is in itself highly improbable or is discredited by other evidence the [jury] may believe one part of the admission and reject the other." (People ex rel. Perkins v. Moss, 187 N.Y. 410, 428, 80 N.E. 383, 389.) In People v. Miller, 247 App.Div. 489, 493, 286 N.Y.S. 702, 706, relied upon by defendant, Justice Lewis (later Chief Judge) concluded that the damaging aspects of an admission should not be accepted and the exculpatory portion rejected *"unless the latter is disputed by other evidence in the case, or is so improbable as to be unworthy of belief"* (emphasis added). In this case, there is ample other evidence to contradict the defendant's assertion that he believed Geller dead. There were five bullet wounds inflicted with stunning accuracy in a vital part of the victim's anatomy. The medical testimony indicated that Geller may have been alive at the time defendant fired at him. The defendant voluntarily left the jurisdiction immediately after the crime with his coperpetrator. Defendant did not report the crime to the police when left on his own by Bush. Instead, he attempted to conceal his and Bush's involvement with the homicide. In addition, the other portions of defendant's admissions make his contended belief that Geller was dead extremely improbable. Defendant, without a word of instruction from Bush, voluntarily got up from his seat after the passage of just a few minutes and fired five times point blank into the victim's face, snuffing out any remaining chance of life that Geller possessed. Certainly, this alone indicates a callous indifference to the taking of a human life. His admissions are barren of any claim of duress[2] and reflect, instead, an unstinting co-operation in efforts to

---

[2] Notwithstanding the Appellate Division's implication to the contrary, the record indicates that defendant told the Assistant District Attorney that Bush, after shooting Geller, kept his gun aimed at Geller, and not at Dlugash. As defendant stated, "this was after Joe had his .38 on him, I started shooting on him."

dispose of vital incriminating evidence. Indeed, defendant maintained a false version of the occurrence until such time as the police informed him that they had evidence that he lately possessed a gun of the same caliber as one of the weapons involved in the shooting. From all of this, the jury was certainly warranted in concluding that the defendant acted in the belief that Geller was yet alive when shot by defendant.

The jury convicted the defendant of murder. Necessarily, they found that defendant intended to kill a live human being. Subsumed within this finding is the conclusion that defendant acted in the belief that Geller was alive. Thus, there is no need for additional fact findings by a jury. Although it was not established beyond a reasonable doubt that Geller was, in fact, alive, such is no defense to attempted murder since a murder would have been committed "had the attendant circumstances been as [defendant] believe them to be." The jury necessarily found that defendant believed Geller to be alive when defendant shot at him.

The Appellate Division erred in not modifying the judgment to reflect a conviction for the lesser included offense of attempted murder. An attempt to commit a murder is a lesser included offense of murder and the Appellate Division has the authority, where the trial evidence is not legally sufficient to establish the offense of which the defendant was convicted, to modify the judgment to one of conviction for a lesser included offense which is legally established by the evidence. Thus, the Appellate Division, by dismissing the indictment, failed to take the appropriate corrective action. Further, questions of law were erroneously determined in favor of the appellant at the Appellate Division. While we affirm the order of the Appellate Division to the extent that the order reflects that the judgment of conviction for murder cannot stand, a modification of the order and a remittal for further proceedings is necessary.

Accordingly, the order of the Appellate Division should be modified and the case remitted to the Appellate Division for its review of the facts pursuant to CPL § 470.15 and for further proceedings with respect to the sentence (see CPL § 470.20, subd. 4) in the event that the facts are found favorably to the People. As so modified, the order of the Appellate Division should be affirmed.

■ BREITEL, C.J., and GABRIELLI, JONES, WACHTLER, FUCHSBERG and COOKE, JJ., concur.

Order modified and the case remitted to the Appellate Division, Second Department, for further proceedings in accordance with the opinion herein and, as so modified, affirmed.

United States v. Hatfield

United States Court of Appeals for the Seventh Circuit, 2010.
591 F.3d 945.

■ POSNER, CIRCUIT JUDGE.

A jury convicted the defendants of conspiracy to burglarize pharmacies, 18 U.S.C. §§ 2118(b), (d), and to distribute controlled substances (including morphine, methadone, oxycodone, fentanyl, alprazolam, cocaine, and hydrocodone), the use of which resulted in death or serious bodily injury, 21 U.S.C. §§ 841(a)(1), (b)(1)(C), 846—specifically, four deaths, plus a serious bodily injury to a fifth user of the defendants' drugs. The defendants were sentenced to life in prison, as authorized by section 841(b)(1)(C). The principal issue presented by the appeals concerns the wording of the jury instruction explaining the meaning of the statutory term "results from." The exact statutory language is "if death or serious bodily injury results from the use of such substance [the defendant] shall be sentenced to a term of imprisonment of not less than twenty years or more than life."

The instruction began by stating that the jury had "to determine whether the United States has established, beyond a reasonable doubt, that the [victims] died, or suffered serious bodily injury, as a result of ingesting a controlled substance or controlled substances distributed by the defendants or by a defendant." But then it added that the controlled substances distributed by the defendants had to have been "a factor that resulted in death or serious bodily injury," and that although they "need not be the primary cause of death or serious bodily injury" they "must at least have played a part in the death or in the serious bodily injury." The defendants' lawyer asked that the addition, suggested by the prosecutor, be stricken as a confusing gloss on "results from." The district judge refused.

Causation is an important issue in many cases in a variety of fields of law and has been so for centuries. Yet it continues to confuse lawyers, in part because of a proliferation of unhelpful terminology (for which we judges must accept a good deal of the blame). . . . The prosecutor was unable at oral argument satisfactorily to differentiate or explain the causal terms listed in his brief, or the three causal terms added to the instruction—"a factor that resulted in," "primary cause," and "played a part."

The parties agree that the statutory term "results from" required the government to prove that ingestion of the defendants' drugs was a "but for" cause of the deaths and the bodily injury. The death or injury need not have been foreseeable, e.g., *United States v. Houston,* 406 F.3d 1121, 1124–25 (9th Cir.2005); *United States v. Soler,* 275 F.3d 146, 152–53 (1st Cir.2002), but the government at least must prove that the death or injury would not have occurred had the drugs not been ingested: "but for" (had it not been for) the ingestion, no injury. That is the minimum concept of cause . . .

* * *

. . . Suppose a defendant sells an illegal drug to a person who, not wanting to be seen ingesting it, takes it into his bathroom, and while he is there the bathroom ceiling collapses and kills him. Had he not ingested the drug, he would not have been killed. But it would be strange to think that the seller of the drug was punishable under 21 U.S.C. § 841(b)(1)(C).

"Cause" in law, as in life generally, is an opportunistic concept: ordinarily it is the name we attach to a but-for cause . . . that we're particularly interested in, often because we want to eliminate it. We want to eliminate arson, but we don't want to eliminate oxygen, so we call arson the cause of a fire set for an improper purpose rather than calling the presence of oxygen in the atmosphere the cause, though it is a but-for cause just as the arsonist's setting the fire is. We say that the cause of the death of the drug taker in the bathroom was the improper design or construction of the ceiling rather than the sale of the drug. The reason is that the sale of the drug did not increase the risk posed by the unsafe ceiling—did not increase the risk that *this* sort of mishap would occur. *Brackett v. Peters,* 11 F.3d 78, 82 (7th Cir.1993); *Zuchowicz v. United States,* 140 F.3d 381, 387–89 and n. 7 (2d Cir.1998); *Restatement (Third) of Torts* § 30 and comment a and illustration 1 (2005). Punishing a drug seller does not reduce building accidents. Punishing him more severely because of the buyer's death in the bathroom would not cause drug dealers to take care to prevent their sales of drugs from leading by so indirect a route to the death of a buyer; there is no way, in our example, that the seller could have prevented the ceiling from collapsing.

The concept of "marginal deterrence" is pertinent here. More-serious crimes are punished more severely than less-serious ones in part to ensure that criminals are not made indifferent between committing the lesser and the greater crime; if they're going to commit crimes, at least they should commit the less serious ones. As we explained in *United States v. Beier,* 490 F.3d 572, 575 (7th Cir.2007), "were robbery punished as severely as murder, a robber would have an increased incentive to murder his victim in order to eliminate a key witness." . . . We want drug dealers not to kill their customers inadvertently. But in our hypothetical case of the falling ceiling, nothing the drug dealer did made death more likely. So we would not call the sale of the drugs the "cause" of the death in that case even though it was a necessary condition of it because, had the sale not occurred, the buyer probably would not have been in the bathroom when the ceiling collapsed.

We cannot see what the government's list of causal terms contributes to an understanding of causation as we have just explained it—especially a jury's understanding of it since the terms in the list are for the most part unfamiliar to people who haven't studied law. We particularly don't understand what a jury would make of "primary cause" and "played a part," even though those do not sound like technical legal terms, albeit "primary cause" is listed in Black's law dictionary as a synonym for "proximate cause"—which confuses things further because "proximate cause" usually implies foreseeability, . . . which we know is not required in our case.

* * *

The defendants' objection to the instruction was well taken. All that would have been needed to satisfy it was to eliminate the addition to the statutory language, which was a good deal clearer than the addition and probably clear enough. Elaborating on a term often makes it less rather than more clear (try defining the word "time" in a noncircular way); it is on this ground that some courts, including our own, tell district judges not to try to explain to a jury the meaning of "beyond a reasonable doubt." *United States v. Bruce,* 109 F.3d 323, 329 (7th Cir.1997); *United States v. Desimone,* 119 F.3d 217, 226–27 (2d Cir.1997); *United States v. Oriakhi,* 57 F.3d 1290, 1300 (4th Cir.1995). Probably the same is true of "results from."

* * *

We have some misgivings about interpreting "results from" in the statute to impose strict liability. That could lead to some strange results. Suppose that, unbeknownst to the seller of an illegal drug, his buyer was intending to commit suicide by taking an overdose of drugs, bought from that seller, that were not abnormally strong, and in addition the seller had informed the buyer of the strength of the drugs, so that there was no reasonable likelihood of an accidental overdose. Yet the cases are unanimous and emphatic that section 841(b)(1)(C) imposes strict liability. . . . The cases emphasize the "plain meaning" of the statute, by which they mean simply the omission of any reference to foreseeability or state of mind, and point out that criminal statutes commonly do specify the required state of mind or other ground of culpability (such as negligence) rather than leaving it to be filled in by the judges (as under the Model Penal Code, which provides that proof of guilt of a statute that does not specify a state of mind or other standard of culpability requires proof of at least recklessness, American Law Institute, *Model Penal Code* § 2.02(3) (1962)). And from this they infer that the omission of any such requirement from section 841(b)(1)(C) was deliberate, and so liability must be strict.

A realistic consideration, however, supports the conclusion: strict liability creates an incentive for a drug dealer to warn his customer about the strength of the particular batch of drugs being sold and to refuse to supply drugs to particularly vulnerable people. And strict liability does not offend against the principle of marginal deterrence in this instance because it does not give the seller an incentive to commit a more serious crime, as in the case where robbery is punished as severely as murder.

In any event, the defendants in this case do not challenge the interpretation of the statute as imposing strict liability on them for death or injury to recipients of their drugs.

Still, there was error in the instruction, as we have found. But errors in instructions are not reversible if they are harmless. . . . But we do not think it *was* harmless. The evidence regarding the cause of the serious injury of the one victim and the deaths of the others, though strong enough to justify a verdict of guilt beyond a reasonable doubt, was not conclusive. In each case the victim was found to have taken multiple drugs, some probably or possibly not distributed by the defendants. In the case of the nonfatal injury (respiratory arrest), the testifying physician thought it more likely that the drug probably supplied by the defendants had caused the injury rather than the cocaine that the victim had also ingested, but he did not rule out the possibility that the cocaine was responsible. With regard to another victim, the medical evidence was that the methadone he apparently received from one of the defendants "would have been sufficient to kill him." But he had another drug in his system and it is unclear how a juror would have fitted that evidence to the "played a part" and "primary cause" templates that he was asked to use to interpret "results from."

* * *

REVERSED AND REMANDED.

NOTES AND QUESTIONS

1. In *Hatfield*, what does Judge Posner mean when he says that foreseeability is not required and that the statute imposes strict liability with respect to death from drugs? From your previous reading on strict liability (pp. 62–84), is that result sound? Does the court adequately defend that conclusion? Why doesn't it matter in *Hatfield*?

2. What, exactly, is wrong with the jury instruction in *Hatfield*?

People v. Rideout
Court of Appeals of Michigan, 2006.
727 N.W.2d 630.

■ SAWYER, P.J.

Defendant was convicted, following a jury trial, of operating a motor vehicle while intoxicated (OWI) or while visibly impaired (OWVI) and thereby causing death. He was sentenced to serve 3 to 15 years in prison. He now appeals and we reverse and remand.

At 2:00 a.m. on November 23, 2003, defendant was driving his sport utility vehicle (SUV) east on 17 Mile Road in northern Kent County. He attempted to turn north onto Edgerton Avenue and drove into the path of an oncoming car driven by Jason Reichelt. Reichelt's car hit defendant's SUV and spun 180 degrees, coming to rest on the centerline of 17 Mile Road. The SUV came to rest on the side of the road. It was later determined that defendant had a blood alcohol concentration of 0.16, which is twice the legal limit. Reichelt and his passenger, Jonathan Keiser, were not seriously injured, but Reichelt's car was severely damaged and the headlights stopped working. Both men left the car and walked to the SUV to determine if anyone was injured. After speaking briefly with defendant, the two men walked back to Reichelt's car. Reichelt indicated that he was aware that oncoming cars could hit his darkened car and that he wanted to determine if he could turn on the flashers. As Reichelt and Keiser stood by the car, an oncoming car driven by Tonya Welch hit Keiser, killing him.

At the center of this appeal is the issue of causation. Defendant argues that not only did the trial court improperly instruct the jury on causation, there was also insufficient evidence of causation to establish defendant's guilt. Because the two issues are intertwined with the question of what must be proven to establish causation in such a case, we shall analyze both issues together beginning with a determination of what the prosecutor must show to establish causation.

As the Supreme Court discussed in *People v. Schaefer,* causation consists of two components:

In criminal jurisprudence, the causation element of an offense is generally comprised of two components: factual cause and proximate cause. The concept of factual causation is relatively straight forward. In determining whether a defendant's conduct is a factual cause of the result, one must ask, "but for" the defendant's conduct, would the result have occurred? If the result would not have occurred absent the defendant's conduct, then factual causation exists.

The existence of factual causation alone, however, will not support the imposition of criminal liability. Proximate causation must also be established. . . . [P]roximate causation is a "legal colloquialism." It is a legal construct designed to prevent criminal liability from attaching when the result of the defendant's conduct is viewed as too remote or unnatural. Thus, a proximate cause is simply a factual cause "of which the law will take cognizance." We initially note that there is no dispute at this point that defendant was intoxicated and that his driving was the cause of the initial accident.[5] Furthermore, there is no argument that defendant's driving was the factual or "but-for" cause of the second accident. This analysis is relatively straightforward: but for defendant causing the initial accident, the subsequent accident would not have occurred.

---

[5] *Schaefer, supra* at 434–435, 703 N.W.2d 774, clarified that, under MCL 257.625(4), it must be shown that defendant was driving while intoxicated and that his driving caused the death, but the prosecutor does not have to show that it was defendant's intoxicated driving that caused the death.

. . . But the question whether defendant is the proximate cause of the subsequent accident, and thus of the victim's death, is not so easily resolved. *Schaefer* discussed this requirement in further detail:

For a defendant's conduct to be regarded as a proximate cause, the victim's injury must be a "direct and natural result" of the defendant's actions. In making this determination, it is necessary to examine whether there was an intervening cause that superseded the defendant's conduct such that the causal link between the defendant's conduct and the victim's injury was broken. If an intervening cause did indeed *supersede* the defendant's act as a legally significant causal factor, then the defendant's conduct will not be deemed a proximate cause of the victim's injury.

The standard by which to gauge whether an intervening cause supersedes, and thus severs the causal link, is generally one of reasonable foreseeability. For example, suppose that a defendant stabs a victim and the victim is then taken to a nearby hospital for treatment. If the physician is negligent in providing medical care to the victim and the victim later dies, the defendant is still considered to have proximately caused the victim's death because it is reasonably foreseeable that negligent medical care might be provided. At the same time, *gross* negligence or intentional misconduct by a treating physician is not reasonably foreseeable, and would thus break the causal chain between the defendant and the victim.

The linchpin in the superseding cause analysis, therefore, is whether the intervening cause was foreseeable based on an objective standard of reasonableness. If it was reasonably foreseeable, then the defendant's conduct will be considered a proximate cause. If, however, the intervening act by the victim or a third party was not reasonably foreseeable—e.g., *gross* negligence or intentional misconduct—then generally the causal link is severed and the defendant's conduct is not regarded as a proximate cause of the victim's injury or death.

With these basic principles in mind, we conclude that the trial court improperly instructed the jury on the issue of proximate cause. We review claims of instructional error de novo. The trial court is required to instruct jurors on "all elements of the crime charged and must not exclude consideration of material issues, defenses, and theories for which there is supporting evidence." Instructions are to be read as a whole and not piecemeal to determine if error requiring reversal occurred. "It is error for the trial court to give an erroneous or misleading jury instruction on an essential element of the offense."

The trial court gave detailed and extensive instructions on factual causation, including reinforcement of the concept that defendant had to be "a" cause of the accident, but not necessarily "the" cause of the accident. But the trial court's instructions on proximate cause and superseding intervening causes were virtually nonexistent. The trial court did implicitly touch on the issue of proximate cause when it instructed the jury that one of several causes "is a substantial factor in causing a death if, but for that cause's contribution, the death would not have occurred, unless the death was an utterly unnatural result of whatever happened." But the instructions also told the jury that another cause could be a superseding cause only if it was the sole cause:

> Now it also necessarily follows that somebody else's conduct, for example, by Mr. Keiser, or by some third party, even if that other conduct was wrong or itself negligent, does not cut off criminal liability unless the other cause was the only cause. Obviously, if somebody else's conduct was the only reason Mr. Keiser died, then it can't possibly be something to which Mr. Rideout contributed.

This is not a correct statement of the law. A superseding intervening cause does not need to be the only cause. Indeed, as the Court noted in *Schaefer*, while the defendant's conduct in that [case] was a factual cause of the accident, the victim's conduct may also have been a cause and, more to the point, potentially a superseding cause. The effect of the trial court's instructions was that the jury could convict defendant if they found him to be a factual cause of the accident and that the jury could find the existence of a superseding intervening cause only if that superseding intervening cause was the only cause of the second accident. The jury was not adequately instructed on the issues of proximate and intervening causes.[15]

This conclusion is enough to set aside defendant's conviction, with directions to the trial court to properly instruct the jury on the causation issue. But we agree with defendant that the problem in this case goes even deeper, because there was insufficient evidence to establish proximate cause at all. We review a claim of insufficient evidence in a criminal trial de novo. We view the evidence in a light most favorable to the prosecution to determine if a rational trier of fact could find beyond a reasonable doubt that the essential elements of the crime were established.

The troubling aspect of this case is that the second accident only occurred after Keiser had reached a position of safety (the side of the road) and then chose to reenter the roadway with Reichelt to check on the car. While foreseeability is the "linchpin" of the superseding causation analysis, and it is at least arguably foreseeable that a person involved in an accident would check on his or her vehicle even if it remains on the road, the analysis does not end there . . .

* * *

---

[15] The fact that the jurors struggled with the issue of causation is reflected by the fact that they sent questions on the issue to the trial court during deliberations.

. . . Keiser had reached a position of apparent safety: he had gotten out of the vehicle and was alongside the road, off the pavement. Had the second accident occurred before Keiser could extricate himself from the Reichelt vehicle and get to the side of the road, then the causal chain would have been intact. But he was able to get out of harm's way and to a relatively safe position at the side of the road. He then made the choice to return to the roadway and place himself in a more dangerous position . . . Keiser made a decision regarding his actions after the immediate danger was over. And that decision, . . . ended the initial causal chain and started a new one, one for which defendant was not responsible.

* * *

. . . Keiser made the voluntary decision to return to the vehicle on the roadway, despite the danger that it posed. He could have chosen to remain on the side of the road. He chose instead to reenter the roadway, with the danger of standing in the roadway next to an unlit vehicle in the middle of the night being readily apparent.

In sum, we conclude that the prosecution failed to present sufficient evidence to establish that defendant's actions were a proximate cause of Keiser's death. Therefore, we vacate defendant's conviction for OWI/OWVI causing death.

* * *

NOTES AND QUESTIONS

1. In People v. Rideout, 477 Mich. 1062, 728 N.W.2d 459 (2007), the Michigan Supreme Court affirmed the intermediate appellate court's reversal of defendant's conviction based on the erroneous jury instruction, but reversed its conclusion that the evidence was not sufficient for a jury to conclude that the defendant was the proximate cause of the victim's death. What is the effect of this ruling?

2. Can you explain the test for proximate cause articulated by the court, especially given the Michigan Supreme Court's ruling based on the sufficiency of the evidence?

3. What is the meaning of footnote 3 in the court's opinion?

4. For a similar case, see People v. Cook, 957 NE 2d 563 (Ill.Ct.App. 2011). After reviewing the facts of *Cook*, how is it different from *Rideout*?

State v. Grose

Court of Criminal Appeals of Tennessee, 1997.
982 S.W.2d 349.

FACTS

The appellant and the victim in this case, Jamie Forbes, were romantically acquainted. However, prior to the homicide their relationship had deteriorated. Forbes instituted stalking and harassment charges against the appellant. The day before the scheduled hearing on these charges, the appellant stated to a friend, William Carter, that he was going to kill Forbes. He showed Carter the rifle he planned to use. The appellant explained that he was going to have to do "a year anyway" on the stalking charges, so he figured that he would kill Forbes and "they would just think he was crazy and he could get off on insanity." The appellant took the rifle and left. Carter, convinced the appellant was seriously planning to kill Forbes, drove to a phone and called the Millington police. Unfortunately, the appellant found Forbes driving down the road before the police could prevent the homicide. The appellant pulled up behind her car and shot her with a high-powered rifle. The appellant sped away in his vehicle. Forbes suffered tremendous trauma and was in the hospital for several weeks. At the time of her release, she was a quadriplegic.

Approximately two weeks after Forbes' release from the hospital, her fever became extremely high, and she was readmitted to the hospital. She quickly fell into a coma. After suffering this condition for almost eight days, her family decided that she should not be resuscitated in the event of cardiac or pulmonary arrest. She died soon thereafter.

The pathologist testified that the cause of death was gunshot wounds. The pathologist further testified that there were two entry wounds, two exit wounds and two re-entry wounds.

I

In his first issue the appellant contends that the trial court erred in overruling his motion for judgment of acquittal. He claims the state failed to prove he caused Forbes' death. Specifically, he argues that the victim's immediate cause of death was the decision of her family to instruct medical personnel not to resuscitate the victim in the event of cardiac or pulmonary arrest. In support of this contention, the appellant relies primarily on *State v. Ruane*, 912 S.W.2d 766 (Tenn.Crim.App.1995). In *Ruane*, this Court held that the decision of a competent victim to refuse medical care is not a supervening cause that removes a criminal defendant's responsibility. *Id.* at 776. The rationale behind this decision was the fact that a victim's conscious decision to remove artificial life-support, while an act of intervention, only carries out the natural result of the defendant's wrongful act. *Id.* The appellant argues that because Forbes did not participate in the decision to refuse further medical treatment, her family's action was a wholly unexpected and unforeseeable supervening event which was the cause of her death.

In order for this Court to sustain a criminal conviction for homicide, the evidence must establish that the appellant's actions caused the harm. This is generally established by showing that the victim's death was the natural and probable result of the defendant's unlawful act.[2] *State v.*

---

[2] As common sense would suggest, the perimeters of legal causation are more closely drawn when the intervening cause is a matter of coincidence. For example, coincidence is where

Barnes, 703 S.W.2d 611 (Tenn.1985). Our Supreme Court has established a general rule on the issue of causation:

> One who unlawfully inflicts a dangerous wound upon another is held for the consequences flowing from such injury, whether the sequence be direct or through the operation of intermediate agencies dependent upon and arising out of the original cause. *Odeneal v. State*, 128 Tenn. 60, 157 S.W. 419, 421 (Tenn.1913).

Basically, the appellant asks this Court for largess because his actions only put Forbes in a vegetative coma from which she could not exercise her right to participate in her own medical decisions. We find that such a holding would be illogical. Offenders failing to kill their victims immediately, merely leaving them in a vegetative state, could escape punishment for homicide if the family chooses to end the victim's suffering. In the instant case, we find that Forbes' family acted as her agent in making the decision not to resuscitate her in the event of cardiac or pulmonary arrest. In so finding, we are merely extending *Ruane*. We hold that when a person, acting in the best interest of the victim, issues a nonresuscitation order, and such order is accepted by the attending medical personnel, that person is acting only as an agent for the victim and is not a supervening cause that releases the offender from criminal responsibility. The attending physicians and the family of the victim owe no duty to the accused to treat the victim so as to mitigate his or her potential criminal liability.

The appellant shot his victim with a high-powered rifle. The state offered proof at trial that the victim would have died within hours after the initial gunshot wounds had she not been administered emergency medical treatment. The decision to end Forbes' suffering and allow her to die with dignity was the natural and probable result of the appellant's gunshot wounds. He began a chain of events which in their natural and probable sequence caused the victim's death. The decision to abstain from providing extraordinary or heroic medical intervention merely allowed the natural and probable result of the appellant's actions to come to fruition. The jury resolved the factual question of causation in favor of the state. The record supports the jury's finding on the issue of causation beyond a reasonable doubt. . . .

A shoots at B, B changes his route in an attempt to escape harm and is struck by a car driven by C. This would be a coincidence and not subject A to liability for homicide. There is less reason to hold the defendant liable for the bad result when he has merely caused the victim to be at a particular place at a particular time, than when he has brought other agencies into play in response to a danger or injury he directly inflicted. Therefore, in order to warrant a conviction for homicide, the death must be the natural and probable consequence of the unlawful act. If an independent intervening agency also contributes to the victim's death, the defendant will still be held liable so long as the intervening agency was a foreseeable response to his or her initial injury.

NOTES AND QUESTIONS

1. Would it make a difference if the victim would not have died under normal circumstances, such as when a minor wound is inflicted but the victim has hemophilia and dies from loss of blood, see State v. Frazier, 98 S.W.2d 707 (Mo. 1936), or refuses treatment for religious reasons? See cases holding that the refusal of the victim to undergo a blood transfusion because of religious beliefs, even though it probably would have saved the victim's life, does not relieve the defendant from criminal responsibility for the victim's death. Klinger v. State, 816 So.2d 697 (Fla.App. 2002); State v. Welch, 135 N.C.App. 499, 521 S.E.2d 266 (1999); Regina v. Blaue, 1 W.L.R. 1411, 3 All.E.R. 446 (Eng.Crim.App. 1975). And see cases holding that intervening negligent medical treatment of victim does not relieve defendant of responsibility for homicide. People v. Saavedra-Rodriguez, 971 P.2d 223 (Colo. 1998); People v. Griffin, 173 A.D.2d 120, 578 N.Y.S.2d 782 (1991); Baylor v. United States, 407 A.2d 664 (D.C.App. 1979); Wright v. State, 374 A.2d 824 (Del. 1977).

2. Compare the foregoing with the result reached in People v. Flenon, 42 Mich.App. 457, 202 N.W.2d 471 (1972), where the defendant shot his victim in the leg (a non-mortal wound), necessitating amputation above the knee. The victim was discharged from the hospital several weeks later, but within a short time thereafter was readmitted to the hospital. He died from serum hepatitis contracted as a result of exposure to the disease while receiving blood transfusions during the course of the amputation operation. Defendant was convicted of homicide and the Court of Appeals of Michigan affirmed, holding that the defendant could prevail only if it be determined that the contraction of serum hepatitis was due to gross medical negligence. Short of that, it must be considered, the court said, that the consequences of a defendant's attack upon a victim are foreseeable. Because doctors are not infallible, ordinary medical negligence must be considered as foreseeable.

3. While the rule that ordinary medical negligence is deemed not to be an independent intervening act sufficient to cut off the chain of causation leading from the initial wrongful act of the defendant to the ultimate death is well established, should the rule be applied where, as in *Flenon*, the original wound inflicted was non-mortal?

Problem 2–7. After striking a pedestrian attempting to cross the street at an intersection, defendant drove some 600 feet and left his car parked on a side street, where it was shortly discovered by the police with the victim's body wedged beneath the vehicle. "[T]he court charged the jury that there was no evidence in the case of culpable negligence on the part of the defendant up to and including the time at which [the victim] was struck by the station wagon." The medical testimony established that the victim died of a massive skull fracture. Is there a causation problem in the case? *See* State v. Rose, 112 R.I. 402, 311 A.2d 281 (1973).

Velazquez v. State

Court of Appeal of Florida, Third District, 1990.
561 So.2d 347.

■ Opinion by: HUBBART

. . . The sole issue presented for review is whether a defendant driver of a motor vehicle who participates in a reckless and illegal "drag race" on a public road may be properly convicted of vehicular homicide . . . for the death of one of the co-participant drivers suffered in the course of the "drag race"—when the sole basis for imposing liability is the defendant's participation in said race. We hold that the defendant may not be held criminally liable under the above statute in such case because the co-participant driver, in effect, killed himself by his voluntary and reckless driving in the subject "drag race" and thus the defendant's actions in engaging in the said race was not a proximate cause of the co-participant's death.

I

* * *

On April 23, 1988, at approximately 2:30 A.M., the defendant Velazquez met the deceased Adalberto Alvarez at a Hardee's restaurant in Hialeah, Florida. The two had never previously met, but in the course of their conversation agreed to race each other in a "drag race" with their respective automobiles. They, accordingly, left the restaurant and proceeded to set up a quarter-mile "drag race" course on a nearby public road which ran perpendicular to a canal alongside the Palmetto Expressway in Hialeah; a guardrail and a visible stop sign stood between the end of this road and the canal. The two men began their "drag race" at the end of this road and proceeded away from the canal in a westerly direction for one-quarter mile. Upon completing the course without incident, the deceased Alvarez suddenly turned his automobile 180 degrees around and proceeded east toward the starting line and the canal; the defendant Velazquez did the same and followed behind Alvarez. Alvarez proceeded in the lead and attained an estimated speed of 123 m.p.h.; he was not wearing a seat belt and subsequent investigation revealed that he had a blood alcohol level between .11 and .12. The defendant Velazquez, who had not been drinking, trailed Alvarez the entire distance back to the starting line and attained an estimated speed of 98 m.p.h. As both drivers approached the end of the road, they applied their brakes, but neither could stop. Alvarez, who was about a car length ahead of the defendant Velazquez, crashed through the guardrail first and was propelled over the entire canal, landing on its far bank; he was thrown from his car upon impact, was pinned under his vehicle when it landed on him, and died instantly from the resulting injuries. The defendant also crashed through the guardrail, but landed in the canal where he was able to escape from his vehicle and swim to safety uninjured.

* * *

II

The vehicular homicide statute, under which the defendant was charged and convicted, provides as follows:

"Vehicular homicide" is the killing of a human being by the operation of a motor vehicle by another in a reckless manner likely to cause the death of, or great bodily harm to, another. Vehicular homicide is a felony of the third degree. . . .

§ 782.071(1), Fla. Stat. (1987). There are two statutory elements to vehicular homicide: (1) the defendant must operate a motor vehicle in a reckless manner likely to cause the death of, or great bodily harm to, another, and (2) this reckless operation of a motor vehicle must be the proximate cause of the death of a human being. . . .

Contrary to the defendant's argument, we have no trouble in concluding that the first element of this offense is clearly established on this record. Plainly, the defendant operated a motor vehicle in a reckless manner, likely to cause death or great bodily harm to another, in that (a) he participated in a highly dangerous "drag race" with the deceased on a public road in which both lanes were used as a speedway, and (b) he drove his vehicle at the excessive speed of 98 m.p.h. during the "drag race." Without question, the defendant's motor vehicle operation endangered the lives of all persons in the vicinity of the "drag race," namely, people in other motor vehicles and nearby pedestrians. *See McCreary v. State*, 371 So.2d 1024 (Fla.1979).

The second element of this offense, however, has given us considerable pause, as no doubt it did the trial court, because no endangered third party in the vicinity of the "drag race" was killed in this case; . . .

A

At the outset, it seems clear that the proximate cause element of vehicular homicide in Florida embraces, at the very least, a causation-in-fact test; that is, the defendant's reckless operation of a motor vehicle must be a cause-in-fact of the death of a human being. In this respect, vehicular homicide is no different than any other criminal offense in which the occurrence of a specified result, caused by a defendant's conduct, is an essential element of the offense—such as murder, . . . Clearly there can be no criminal liability for such result-type offenses unless it can be shown that the defendant's conduct was a cause-in-fact of the prohibited result, whether the result be the death of a human being, personal injury to another, or injury to another's property. To be sure, this cause-in-fact showing is insufficient in itself to establish the aforesaid "proximate cause" element in a vehicular homicide case, but it is clearly a sine qua non ingredient thereof. 1 W. LaFave & A. Scott, *Substantive Criminal Law* § 3.12(a), (b), at 390–96 (1986); *Model Penal Code and Commentaries* § 2.03 explanatory note, at 254 (1985).

Courts throughout the country have uniformly followed the traditional "but for" test in determining whether the defendant's conduct was a cause-in-fact of a prohibited consequence in result-type offenses such as vehicular homicide. Under this test, a defendant's conduct is a cause-in-fact of the prohibited result if the said result would *not* have occurred "but for" the defendant's conduct; stated differently, the defendant's conduct is a cause-in-fact of a particular result if the result would *not* have happened in the absence of the defendant's conduct. Thus, a defendant's reckless operation of a motor vehicle is a cause-in-fact of the death of a human being under Florida's vehicular homicide statute . . . if the subject death would *not* have occurred "but for" the defendant's reckless driving or would *not* have happened in the absence of such driving. . . .

In relatively rare cases, however, the "but for" test for causation-in-fact fails and has been abandoned in favor of the "substantial factor" test. This anomaly occurs when two defendants, acting independently and not in concert with one another, commit two separate acts, each of which alone is sufficient to bring about the prohibited result—as when two defendants concurrently inflict mortal wounds upon a human being, each of which is sufficient to cause death. In such case, each defendant's action was not a "but for" cause of death because the deceased would have died even in the absence of each defendant's conduct—although obviously not in the absence of both defendants' conduct considered together. In these rare cases, the courts have followed a "substantial factor" test, namely, the defendant's conduct is a cause-in-fact of a prohibited result if the subject conduct was a "substantial factor" in bringing about the said result. Thus, each defendant's conduct in independently and concurrently inflicting mortal wounds on a deceased clearly constitutes a "substantial factor" in bringing about the deceased's death, and, consequently, is a cause-in-fact of the deceased's death. . . .

B

The "proximate cause" element of vehicular homicide in Florida embraces more, however, than the aforesaid "but for" causation-in-fact test as modified by the "substantial factor" exception. Even where a defendant's conduct is a cause-in-fact of a prohibited result, as where a defendant's reckless operation of a motor vehicle is a cause-in-fact of the death of a human being, Florida and other courts throughout the country have for good reason declined to impose criminal liability (1) where the prohibited result of the defendant's conduct is beyond the scope of any fair assessment of the danger created by the defendant's conduct, or (2) where it would otherwise be unjust, based on fairness and policy considerations, to hold the defendant criminally responsible for the prohibited result. . . .

In deaths resulting from illegal "drag racing" on a public road, as here, it has been held in Florida that the driver of one of the racing vehicles was properly convicted of manslaughter when the driver of another vehicle in the race collided head on with a non-participant motor vehicle which was lawfully using the subject highway, killing the driver of same. *Jacobs v. State*, 184 So.2d 711 (Fla. 1st DCA 1966). The court reasoned that the defendant, by participating in the "drag race," was aiding and abetting each of the other participant drivers in the race in committing reckless driving—so that when one of the participants committed a manslaughter in the course of the race against a third party, the defendant was also guilty of manslaughter. . . .

* * *

Where, however, a participant passenger in such an illegal "drag race," accidently grabs the steering wheel of a vehicle involved in the race, instead of the gear shift he was assigned to operate, causing the vehicle to go out of control, crash, and kill the passenger—this court has held that the defendant driver of the subject motor vehicle was improperly convicted of vehicular homicide. *J.A.C. v. State*, 374 So.2d 606 (Fla. 3d DCA 1979), *rev. denied*, 383 So. 2d 1203 (Fla.1980). The court reasoned that the passenger's reckless act of grabbing the steering wheel was an independent intervening act which superseded the respondent's wrongful conduct in participating in the "drag race." *Id.* at 607. Although, obviously, the respondent's participation in the subject race was *a* "but for" cause-in-fact of the passenger's death and such death was plainly within the scope of the danger created by the defendant's conduct in participating in the race—this court nonetheless implicitly concluded that it would be unjust to hold the defendant criminally responsible for the passenger's death because the passenger, in effect, killed himself by his own reckless conduct.

The result reached in *J.A.C.* is in accord with the weight of better-reasoned decisions on this subject throughout the country. These courts have uniformly concluded that a driver-participant in an illegal "drag race" on a public road cannot be held criminally responsible for the death of another driver participant when (a) the deceased, in effect, kills himself by his own reckless driving during the race, and (b) the sole basis for attaching criminal liability for his death is the defendant's participation in the "drag race."[3] The policy reasons for reaching this result are best expressed in *State v. Petersen*, 17 Ore. App. 478, 495, 522

---

[3] *Thacker v. State*, 103 Ga.App. 36, 117 S.E.2d 913 (1961); *State v. Uhler*, 61 Ohio Misc. 37, 402 N.E.2d 556, 14 Ohio Op. 3d 158 (1979); *State v. Petersen*, 17 Ore. App. 478, 522 P.2d 912, 920 (1974) (Schwab, C.J., dissenting) (dissent adopted by Oregon Supreme Court in *State v. Petersen*, 270 Or. 166, 526 P.2d 1008 (1974)); *Commonwealth v. Root*, 403 Pa. 571, 170 A.2d 310 (1961).

P.2d 912, 920 (1974) (SCHWAB, C.J., dissenting) (dissent adopted by the Oregon Supreme Court in *State v. Petersen*, 270 Or. 166, 526 P.2d 1008 (1974)):

> [T]he question is whether defendant's reckless conduct "caused" the death of the victim. The problem here is not "causation in fact," it is "legal causation." In unusual cases like this one, whether certain conduct is deemed to be the legal cause of a certain result is ultimately a policy question. The question of legal causation thus blends into the question of whether we are willing to hold a defendant responsible for a prohibited result. Or, stated differently, the issue is not causation, it is responsibility. In my opinion, policy considerations are against imposing responsibility for the death of a *participant* in a race on the surviving racer when his sole contribution to the death is the participation in the activity mutually agreed upon.

> * * *

> My point is that people frequently join together in reckless conduct. As long as all participants do so knowingly and voluntarily, I see no point in holding the survivor(s) guilty of manslaughter if the reckless conduct results in death. . . .

522 P.2d at 920–21 (citations and footnote omitted). LaFave and Scott also summarize the legal basis for these decisions:

> It is submitted that the true reason for the holding [in these cases] is the court's feeling . . . that A should not, in all justice, be held for the death of B who was an equally willing and foolhardy participant in the bad conduct which caused his death.

1 W. LaFave and A. Scott, *Substantive Criminal Law* § 3.12, at 418 (1986).

III

Turning now to the instant case, it is clear that the defendant's reckless operation of a motor vehicle in participating in the "drag race" with the deceased was, technically speaking, a cause-in-fact of the deceased's death under the "but for" test. But for the defendant's participation in the subject race, the deceased would not have recklessly raced his vehicle at all and thus would not have been killed. However, under the authority of *J.A.C.* and the better reasoned decisions throughout the country, the defendant's participation in the subject "drag race" was not a proximate cause of the deceased's death because, simply put, the deceased, in effect, killed himself by his own volitional reckless driving—and, consequently, it would be unjust to hold the defendant criminally responsible for this death.

We agree that if the deceased had collided with an oncoming motorist who happened to be in the vicinity lawfully using the subject road resulting in the said motorist's death, the defendant would be criminally liable for this death on an aiding-and-abetting theory; clearly, the deceased would be guilty of vehicular homicide in killing the oncoming motorist, and the defendant, in participating in the illegal "drag race," would be aiding and abetting the deceased in the latter's reckless driving and ultimate negligent homicide. *Jacobs v. State*, 184 So.2d 711 (Fla. 1st DCA 1966). In such a case, however, the oncoming motorist could in no way be said to be responsible for his own death and, consequently, no policy or fairness reason would exist for finding no proximate cause. Clearly, this cannot be said in the instant case.

The state nonetheless relies on cases from other jurisdictions which have reached a contrary result to the one we reach herein.[4] We have reviewed these cases, but are not persuaded by their reasoning because we think they lead to an unjust result. In our judgment, it is simply unfair, unjust, and just plain wrong to say that the defendant in the instant case is criminally responsible for the death of the deceased when it is undisputed that the deceased, in effect, killed himself. No one forced this young man to participate in the subject "drag race"; no one forced him to whirl around and proceed back toward the canal after the race was apparently over; no one forced him to travel 123 m.p.h., vault a canal, and kill himself upon impact. He did all these things himself, and was, accordingly, the major cause of his own death. We are constrained by law to construe criminal statutes strictly in favor of the accused, § 775.021(1), Fla. Stat. (1989), and, given this salutary principle of statutory construction, we are unwilling to construe our vehicular homicide statute to impose criminal liability on the defendant under the circumstances of this case.

The final judgment of conviction and sentence under review is reversed, and the cause is remanded to the trial court with directions to grant the defendant's motion to dismiss.

Reversed and remanded.

NOTES AND QUESTIONS

1. The appropriate standard of causation to be applied in negligent vehicular homicide cases in Massachusetts is that employed in tort law, the Massachusetts Supreme Judicial Court held in Commonwealth v. Berggren, 398 Mass. 338, 496 N.E.2d 660 (1986). The court held that the homicide statute could be applied, under this standard, to a defendant who led a policeman on a high speed chase that ended when the policeman lost control of his vehicle and was killed. The court said:

The defendant essentially contends that since he was one hundred yards ahead of the patrolman's cruiser and was unaware of the accident, his conduct cannot be viewed as directly traceable to the

---

[4]   *State v. Melcher*, 15 Ariz.App. 157, 487 P.2d 3 (1971); *State v. McFadden*, 320 N.W.2d 608 (Iowa 1982); *State v. Escobar*, 30 Wash.App. 131, 633 P.2d 100 (1981).

resulting death of the patrolman. The defendant, however, was speeding on a motorcycle at night on roads which his attorney at oral argument before this court characterized as "winding" and "narrow." He knew the patrolman was following him, but intentionally did not stop and continued on at high speeds for six miles. From the fact that the defendant was "in fear of his license," it may be reasonably inferred that he was aware that he had committed at least one motor vehicle violation. Under these circumstances, the defendant's acts were hardly a remote link in the chain of events leading to the patrolman's death. . . . The officer's pursuit was certainly foreseeable, as was, tragically, the likelihood of serious injury or death to the defendant himself, to the patrolman, or to some third party.

The vehicular homicide statute of Maryland, among others, employs tort concepts of causation requiring a causal connection between driving while intoxicated and the fatal accident. Under Maryland law, the State must prove that the accident causing the fatal death of another was a result of the driver's negligent driving while intoxicated, but the mere fact of intoxication is not enough, the court said in Webber v. State, 320 Md. 238, 577 A.2d 58 (1990). To avoid a "strict liability" result, there must be "a causal relationship between the intoxicated motorist's negligence and the death of another." Contrast this with People v. Garner, 781 P.2d 87 (Colo. 1989), where the court said that proof of a causal connection between drinking and a fatal collision is not required; all that is needed is a showing that the defendant's voluntary act of driving while intoxicated resulted in the death of another. Likewise, in State v. Rivas, 126 Wash.2d 443, 896 P.2d 57 (1995), the Washington Supreme Court recognized that the legislature had amended the vehicular homicide statute in 1991 to overturn an earlier decision and eliminate the requirement of any causal connection between a driver's intoxicated condition and the death. The only causal connection required in the case of an intoxicated driver was between operation of the vehicle and the victim's death. *See also* State v. Benoit, 650 A.2d 1230 (R.I. 1994).

2. Consider a case situation involving the death of a participant in the "game" of "Russian Roulette." May the surviving participants be held guilty of manslaughter? Such a conviction was upheld in Commonwealth v. Atencio, 345 Mass. 627, 189 N.E.2d 223 (1963), in which the court distinguished the root case on the ground that "skill" is involved in a "drag race," whereas "Russian Roulette" involves only a matter of chance and someone is very likely to be killed. In Commonwealth v. Malone, 354 Pa. 180, 47 A.2d 445 (1946), the defendant's conviction for murder was affirmed when it was shown he had placed a gun against the decedent and pulled the trigger three times. He erroneously believed that he had placed the bullet in such a manner that the gun would not fire.

3. Does the discontinuance of respirator support for a person who has been severely injured in an accident while a passenger in a defendant's car relieve the defendant of liability for first-degree manslaughter while driving under the influence of drugs? *See* Eby v. State, 702 P.2d 1047 (Okl.Crim.App. 1985);

see also State v. Inger, 292 N.W.2d 119 (Iowa 1980) (holding that premature removal of a life support system does not relieve a defendant of criminal liability if the defendant was responsible for causing the trauma that placed the doctors in the position to exercise judgment as to whether the victim was dead).

chain of causation

4. In Commonwealth v. Cheeks, 423 Pa. 67, 223 A.2d 291 (1966), the victim of a robbery and stabbing was taken to the hospital where he required surgery. Following the operation and after coming out of the anesthesia, the victim was disoriented, resisted treatment, and demonstrated delirium tremens and hallucinations. He also extracted the Levin tube, which was inserted through the nostril to the stomach on four occasions, as a result of which he ultimately died. In affirming the conviction of murder, the majority of the court said: "The fact that the victim, while in weakened physical condition and disoriented mental state, pulled out the tubes and created the immediate situation, which resulted in his death, is not such an intervening and independent act sufficient to break the chain of causation of events between the stabbing and the death."

5. In State v. Preslar, 48 N.C. 421 (1856), the defendant and his wife had quarreled, and the defendant inflicted a severe beating upon her. The wife left the house and sat down in the yard. A short time later, she walked to the home of her father. Instead of entering the house, however, she laid down on a bedquilt in the woods, telling her son, who had accompanied her, that she would wait until morning to go inside. The next morning she was unable to walk due to the effects of exposure. She died the next day. The defendant was convicted of murder, but the conviction was set aside on appeal. The court stated that "if, to avoid the rage of a brutal husband, a wife is compelled to expose herself, by wading through a swamp, or jumping into a river, the husband is responsible for the consequences." The court further stated, however, that "if she exposes herself thus, without necessity, and of her own accord, we know of no principle of law, by which he is held responsible."

Consider the language of the Supreme Court of Missouri in State v. Glover, 330 Mo. 709, 50 S.W.2d 1049 (1932), where the defendant was convicted of first-degree murder as a result of the death of a fireman who died fighting a fire allegedly set by the defendant for the purpose of collecting insurance proceeds on the premises and contents:

> If the appellant had reason to think members of the fire department of Kansas City and citizens generally would congregate at the drug store to fight the fire, and thus would place themselves within perilous range of the flames and potentially destructive forces that had been set at work, the ensuing homicide was a natural and probable consequence of the arson; and the fact that the deceased fireman came after the fire began to burn did not break the causal relation between the arson and the homicide or constitute an independent intervening cause.

See also State v. Leopold, 110 Conn. 55, 147 A. 118 (1929), where defendant was convicted of the murder of two boys who died in a fire maliciously set by the defendant. The boys, in the building when the fire was set, had ample opportunity to escape; however, after starting to leave (or in fact leaving the building), they returned to save some property and, as a result, died in the fire. The Supreme Court of Connecticut noted that the boys' effort to save property from destruction was "such a natural and ordinary course of conduct that it cannot be said to break the sequence of cause and effect."

In People v. Kibbe, 35 N.Y.2d 407, 362 N.Y.S.2d 848, 321 N.E.2d 773 (1974), the defendants stole money from a helplessly drunken victim and left him in near zero temperatures on a rural two-lane highway, having stripped him of his outer clothing with his trousers down around his ankles and shoeless. Sometime later, the victim was killed when he was struck by a vehicle driven by one Blake. Is Blake's act an independent intervening act, cutting the chain of causation? The court said:

> Under the conditions surrounding Blake's operation of his truck (i.e., the fact that he had his low beams on as the two cars approached; that there was no artificial lighting on the highway; and that there was insufficient time in which to react to Stafford's [the victim] presence in his lane), we do not think it may be said that any supervening wrongful act occurred to relieve the defendants from the directly foreseeable consequences of their actions.

6. During a bar holdup, the robbers line up the victims along a wall and proceed to take money from the cash register. While this is going on, a lady among the victims topples over and falls to the floor. The defendants, on seeing this, run out the front of the bar and disappear. It is later determined that the lady suffered cardiac arrest, having had a history of heart disease in the past, due to fright during the holdup. Are the robbers guilty of murder? *See* Phillips v. State, 289 So.2d 447 (Fla.App. 1974); State v. Chavers, 294 So.2d 489 (La. 1974); State v. McKeiver, 89 N.J.Super. 52, 213 A.2d 320 (1965).

D. BURDEN OF PROOF

1. FROM THE COMMON LAW TO THE CONSTITUTION

In re Winship

Supreme Court of the United States, 1970.
397 U.S. 358, 90 S.Ct. 1068, 25 L.Ed.2d 368.

■ BRENNAN, J.

* * *

The requirement that guilt of a criminal charge be established by proof beyond a reasonable doubt dates at least from our early years as a Nation. The "demand for a higher degree of persuasion in criminal cases was recurrently expressed from ancient times, though its crystallization into the formula 'beyond a reasonable doubt' seems to have occurred as late at 1798. It is now accepted in common law jurisdictions as the measure of persuasion by which the prosecution must convince the trier of all the essential elements of guilt." McCormick, Evidence, § 321, at 681–682 (1954). Although virtually unanimous adherence to the reasonable-doubt standard in common-law jurisdictions may not conclusively establish it as a requirement of due process, such adherence does "reflect a profound judgment about the way in which law should be enforced and justice administered." . . .

Expressions in many opinions of this Court indicate that it has long been assumed that proof of a criminal charge beyond a reasonable doubt is constitutionally required [citing authorities].

* * *

The reasonable-doubt standard plays a vital role in the American scheme of criminal procedure. It is a prime instrument for reducing the risk of convictions resting on factual error. The standard provides concrete substance for the presumption of innocence—that bedrock "axiomatic and elementary" principle whose "enforcement lies at the foundation of the administration of our criminal law." . . .

The requirement of proof beyond a reasonable doubt has this vital role in our criminal procedure for cogent reasons. The accused during a criminal prosecution has at stake interests of immense importance, both because of the possibility that he may lose his liberty upon conviction and because of the certainty that he would be stigmatized by that conviction. Accordingly, a society that values the good name and freedom of every individual should not condemn a man for commission of a crime when there is reasonable doubt about his guilt. As we said in Speiser v. Randall, 357 U.S. 513, 525 . . . . "There is always in litigation a margin of error, representing error in factfinding, which both parties must take into account. Where one party has at stake an interest of transcending value—as a criminal defendant his liberty—this margin of error is reduced as to him by the process of placing on the other party the burden of . . . persuading the factfinder at the conclusion of the trial of his guilt beyond a reasonable doubt. Due process commands that no man shall lose his liberty unless the Government has borne the burden of . . . convincing the factfinder of his guilt. To this end, the reasonable-doubt standard is indispensable. . . ."

Moreover, use of the reasonable-doubt standard is indispensable to command the respect and confidence of the community in applications of the criminal law. It is critical that the moral force of the criminal law not be diluted by a standard of proof which leaves people in doubt whether innocent men are being condemned. It is also important in our free society that every individual going about his ordinary affairs have confidence that his government cannot adjudge him guilty of a criminal offense without convincing a proper factfinder of his guilt with utmost certainty.

———

■ [In his concurring opinion, JUSTICE HARLAN observed, in part:]

. . . In a civil suit between two private parties for money damages . . . we view it as no more serious in general for there to be an erroneous verdict in the defendant's favor than for there to be an erroneous verdict in the plaintiff's favor. A preponderance of the evidence standard therefore seems peculiarly appropriate for, as explained most sensibly, it simply requires that trier of fact "to believe that the existence of a fact is more probable than its nonexistence before [he] may find in favor of the party who has the burden to persuade the [judge] of the fact's existence."

In a criminal case, on the other hand, we do not view the social disutility of convicting an innocent man as equivalent to the disutility of acquitting someone who is guilty. . . .

In this context, I view the requirement of proof beyond a reasonable doubt in a criminal case as <u>bottomed on a fundamental value</u> determination of our society <u>that it is far worse to convict an innocent man than to let a guilty man go free.</u> It is only because of the nearly complete and longstanding acceptance of the reasonable-doubt standard by the States in criminal trials that the Court has not before today had to hold explicitly that due process, as an expression of fundamental procedural fairness, requires a more stringent standard for criminal trials than for ordinary civil litigation. . . .

———

■ [MR. JUSTICE BLACK'S dissenting opinion is omitted.]

NOTES AND QUESTIONS

1. Although the concept of requiring proof of guilt beyond a "reasonable doubt" is firmly embedded in our criminal justice system, the meaning of the term has been and continues to be a troublesome one, particularly with respect to the trial judge's instructions to the jury. The California legislature, in Section 1096 of its Penal Code, has sought to define it by stating, essentially, that a jury verdict of guilty requires "an abiding conviction, to a moral certainty, of the truth of the charge." On the other hand, the Supreme Court of Pennsylvania has held that the use of the words "moral certainty" merely "serves to confuse and befog the jury instead of enlightening them." Commonwealth v. Kloiber, 378 Pa. 412, 106 A.2d 820 (1954). The United States Court of Military Appeals has defined reasonable doubt as "a doubt based on reason." United States v. Kloh, 10 U.S.C.M.A. 329, 27 C.M.R. 403 (1959). In England the Court of Criminal Appeals experimented with the expression that reasonable doubt means the jury must "feel sure" about a verdict of guilty. R. v. Summers, 36 Cr.App.R. 14, [1952] 1 All E.R. 1059. But this too was found to be in need of clarification in a subsequent case. *See* R. v. Hepworth, [1955] 2 All Eng.Rep. 918. The Illinois Supreme Court, after exploring the possibility of assisting jurors in applying the "beyond a reasonable doubt" requirement, finally concluded that the term "needs no definition" and that trial judges should not give instructions "resulting in an elaboration of it." People v. Schuele, 326 Ill. 366, 372, 157 N.E. 215, 217 (1927). Wigmore, in his treatise WIGMORE ON EVIDENCE § 2497 (3d ed. 1940), expressed a similar viewpoint.

With respect to the application of the "reasonable doubt" requirement by trial courts, see R.J. Allen & L.A. DeGrazzia, *The Constitutional Requirement of Proof Beyond a Reasonable Doubt in Criminal Cases: A Comment Upon Incipient Chaos in the Lower Courts*, 20 AMER. CRIM. L. REV. 1 (1982).

2. Should a trial judge attempt to define or elaborate on the meaning of "reasonable doubt"? Which side is likely to make this request of the judge? Which side is likely to be benefitted or disadvantaged? See, in this regard, Victor v. Nebraska, 511 U.S. 1, 114 S.Ct. 1239, 127 L.Ed.2d 583 (1994) ("[A]biding conviction, to a moral certainty."); Cage v. Louisiana, 498 U.S. 39, 111 S.Ct. 328, 112 L.Ed.2d 339 (1990) (reviewing jury instruction that defined reasonable doubt as "a grave uncertainty" and "an actual substantial doubt"); Commonwealth v. Rembiszewski, 391 Mass. 123, 461 N.E.2d 201 (1984) (instruction that "proof beyond a reasonable doubt is the same kind of proof and degree of satisfaction or conviction which you wanted for yourself when you were considering one of those very important decisions" such as getting married, buying a house, changing jobs or undergoing surgery).

3. The two most often mentioned and utilized definitions of reasonable doubt are based on variations of the following:

(a) Proof beyond a reasonable doubt is such as you would be willing to rely and act upon without hesitation in the most important of your own affairs.

(b) Proof beyond a reasonable doubt is <u>proof that leaves you firmly convinced of the defendant's guilt</u>.

See Lawrence M. Solan, *Refocusing the Burden of Proof in Criminal Cases: Some Doubt About Reasonable Doubt*, 78 TEX. L. REV. 105 (1999). Which, if either, of the above elaborations of reasonable doubt do you prefer? The federal circuit courts of appeal are currently about evenly divided on the question of whether, and under what circumstances, the concept of reasonable doubt should be further explained to the jury. For a recent case where the United States Court of Appeals for the Fourth Circuit, sitting *en banc*, split 6–6 on the issue, hence affirming a three-judge panel decision not to define the term. *See* United States v. Walton, 207 F.3d 694 (4th Cir. 2000). As indicated in Note 1, the practice in the states varies widely.

Problem 2–8. Ann and Betty are hired to babysit a three-month old infant in a small apartment for about two hours. When the parents come home early, they find the baby dead in its crib. The babysitters say they do not know what happened—the baby was quiet and slept the whole time. The medical examiner performs an autopsy and concludes that the baby died, within thirty minutes of the time the parents arrived home, of the "shaken baby syndrome"—a shaking that is violent enough to cause fatal brain damage. The medical examiner testifies that the overt symptoms of the child's injuries would include a sharp scream by the infant followed within thirty minutes by the onset of a coma that could be mistaken for sleep. The prosecution files homicide charges against both babysitters. The State's theory is that one of the babysitters shook the baby very violently because it was crying, while the other stood by and did nothing to prevent this and failed to call medical help. The legal theory of the State is that both are independently liable for murder because one inflicted the violent shaking which caused death and the other, aware of the harm being done, failed to perform a duty imposed by law—to protect the child and summon medical help. Has the prosecution proved the defendants' guilt beyond a reasonable doubt? *See* People v. Wong, 81 N.Y.2d 600, 601 N.Y.S.2d 440, 619 N.E.2d 377 (1993).

4. Consider the words of Chief Justice Carrico of the Virginia Supreme Court who, while addressing lawyers, made this statement about the presumption of innocence:

> The second thing . . . was the shocking revelation that a large segment of the public misconceived certain basic rights which we, as lawyers, assumed everyone understood. For example, a national survey revealed that 50% of our citizenry believed a person accused of crime must prove himself or herself innocent. Worse yet, 49.9% of those who had served on juries harbored this mistaken belief.
>
> It takes but little imagination to understand why there is lack of respect for courts and lawyers when the public is so grossly misinformed concerning such a fundamental principle of law as the presumption of innocence. With half the people believing the defense must prove innocence, they cannot help but wonder why so many acquittals occur, and they cannot be faulted when they blame lawyers and judges for what they perceive as an obvious breakdown in the system. (Virginia Bar News, p. 26 [Aug. 1987].)

What special burdens does this place upon criminal defense lawyers? How does a lawyer overcome the common understanding on the part of the public, reflected in the opinions polls, that "where there's smoke there's fire," and "the police wouldn't have brought him to court if he weren't guilty"?

2. PRESUMPTIONS AND SHIFTING THE BURDEN OF PROOF

Patterson v. New York

Supreme Court of the United States, 1977.
432 U.S. 197, 97 S.Ct. 2319, 53 L.Ed.2d 281.

■ MR. JUSTICE WHITE delivered the opinion of the Court.

The question here is the constitutionality under the Fourteenth Amendment's Due Process Clause of burdening the defendant in a New York State murder trial with proving the affirmative defense of extreme emotional disturbance as defined by New York law.

[handwritten margin note: issue]

After a brief and unstable marriage, the appellant, Gordon Patterson, became estranged from his wife, Roberta. Roberta resumed an association with John Northrup, a neighbor to whom she had been engaged prior to her marriage to appellant. On December 27, 1970, Patterson borrowed a rifle from an acquaintance and went to the residence of his father-in-law. There, he observed his wife through a window in a state of semiundress in the presence of John Northrup. He entered the house and killed Northrup by shooting him twice in the head.

Patterson was charged with second-degree murder. In New York there are two elements of this crime: (1) "intent to cause the death of another person"; and (2) "caus[ing] the death of such person or of a third person." N.Y.Penal Law § 125.25 (McKinney). Malice aforethought is not an element of the crime. In addition, the State permits a person accused of murder to raise an affirmative defense that he "acted under the influence of extreme emotional disturbance for which there was a reasonable explanation or excuse."

New York also recognizes the crime of manslaughter. A person is guilty of manslaughter if he intentionally kills another person "under circumstances which do not constitute murder because he acts under the influence of extreme emotional disturbance." Appellant confessed before trial to killing Northrup, but at trial he raised the defense of extreme emotional disturbance.

The jury was instructed as to the elements of the crime of murder. Focusing on the element of intent, the trial court charged,

> Before you, considering all of the evidence, can convict this defendant or any one of murder, you must believe and decide that the People have established beyond a reasonable doubt that he intended, in firing the gun, to kill either the victim himself or some other human being . . . .

The jury was further instructed, consistently with New York law, that the defendant had the burden of proving his affirmative defense by a preponderance of the evidence. The jury was told that if it found beyond a reasonable doubt that appellant had intentionally killed Northrup but that appellant had demonstrated by a preponderance of the evidence that he had acted under the influence of extreme emotional disturbance, it must find appellant guilty of manslaughter instead of murder.

The jury found appellant guilty of murder. Judgment was entered on the verdict, and the Appellate Division affirmed. While appeal to the New York Court of Appeals was pending, this Court decided Mullaney v. Wilbur, 421 U.S. 684, 95 S.Ct. 1881 (1975), in which the Court declared Maine's murder statute unconstitutional. Under the Maine statute, a person accused of murder could rebut the statutory presumption that he committed the offense with "malice aforethought" by proving that he acted in the heat of passion on sudden provocation. The Court held that this scheme improperly shifted the burden of persuasion from the prosecutor to the defendant and was therefore a violation of due process. In the Court of Appeals appellant urged that New York's murder statute is functionally equivalent to the one struck down in *Mullaney* and that therefore his conviction should be reversed.

The Court of Appeals rejected appellant's argument, holding that the New York murder statute is consistent with due process. . . . We affirm.

It goes without saying that preventing and dealing with crime is much more the business of the States than it is of the Federal Government, and that we should not lightly construe the Constitution so as to intrude upon the administration of justice by the individual States. . . .

In determining whether New York's allocation to the defendant of proving the mitigating circumstances of severe emotional disturbance is consistent with due process, it is therefore relevant to note that this defense is a considerably expanded version of the common law defense of heat of passion on sudden provocation and that at common law the burden of proving the latter, as well as other affirmative defenses—indeed, "all . . . circumstances of justification, excuse or alleviation"—rested on the defendant. This was the rule when the Fifth Amendment was adopted, and it was the American rule when the Fourteenth Amendment was ratified. Commonwealth v. York, 50 Mass. 93 (1845).

In 1895 the common law view was abandoned with respect to the insanity defense in federal prosecutions. Davis v. United States, 160 U.S. 469, 16 S.Ct. 353 (1895). This ruling had wide impact on the practice in the federal courts with respect to the burden of proving various affirmative defenses, and the prosecution in a majority of jurisdictions in this country sooner or later came to shoulder the burden of proving the sanity of the accused and of disproving the facts constituting other affirmative defenses, including provocation. *Davis* was not a constitutional ruling, however, as Leland v. Oregon, 343 U.S. 790, 72 S.Ct. 1002 (1952), made clear.

At issue in Leland v. Oregon was the constitutionality under the Due Process Clause of the Oregon rule that the defense of insanity must be proved by the defendant beyond a reasonable doubt. Noting that *Davis* "obviously established no constitutional doctrine," the Court refused to strike down the Oregon scheme, saying that the burden of proving all elements of the crime beyond reasonable doubt, including the elements of premeditation and deliberation, was placed on the State under Oregon procedures and remained there throughout the trial. To convict, the jury was required to find each element of the crime beyond reasonable doubt, based on all the evidence, including the evidence going to the issue of insanity. Only then was the jury "to consider separately the issue of legal sanity *per se*. . . ." This practice did not offend the Due Process Clause even though among the 20 States then placing the burden of proving his insanity on the defendant, Oregon was alone in requiring him to convince the jury beyond a reasonable doubt.

In 1970, the Court declared [in Winship] that the Due Process Clause "protects the accused against conviction except upon proof beyond a reasonable doubt of every fact necessary to constitute the crime with which he is charged." Five years later, in Mullaney v. Wilbur, supra, the Court further announced that under the Maine law of homicide, the burden could not constitutionally be placed on the defendant of proving by a preponderance of the evidence that the killing had occurred in the heat of passion on sudden provocation. The Chief Justice and Mr. Justice Rehnquist, concurring, expressed their understanding that the *Mullaney* decision did not call into question the ruling in Leland v. Oregon, supra, with respect to the proof of insanity.

* * *

We cannot conclude that Patterson's conviction under the New York law deprived him of due process of law. The crime of murder is defined by the statute, which represents a recent revision of the State criminal code, as causing the death of another person with intent to do so. The death, the intent to kill, and causation are the facts that the State is required to prove beyond reasonable doubt if a person is to be convicted of murder. No further facts are either presumed or inferred in order to constitute the crime. The statute does provide an affirmative defense— that the defendant acted under the influence of extreme emotional disturbance for which there was a reasonable explanation—which, if proved by a preponderance of the evidence, would reduce the crime to manslaughter, an offense defined in a separate section of the statute. It is plain enough that if the intentional killing is shown, the State intends to deal with the defendant as a murderer unless he demonstrates the mitigating circumstances.

* * *

We are unwilling to reconsider *Leland* . . . But even if we were to hold that a State must prove sanity to convict once that fact is put in issue, it would not necessarily follow that a State must prove beyond a reasonable doubt every fact, the existence or nonexistence of which it is willing to recognize as an exculpatory or mitigating circumstance affecting the degree of culpability or the severity of the punishment. Here, in revising its criminal code, New York provided the affirmative defense of extreme emotional disturbance, a substantially expanded version of the older heat of passion concept; but it was willing to do so only if the facts making out the defense were established by the defendant with sufficient certainty. The State was itself unwilling to undertake to establish the absence of those facts beyond reasonable doubt, perhaps fearing that proof would be too difficult and that too many persons deserving treatment as murderers would escape that punishment if the evidence need merely raise a reasonable doubt about the defendant's emotional state. It has been said that the new criminal code of New York contains some 25 affirmative defenses which exculpate or mitigate but which must be established by the defendant to be operative. The Due Process Clause, as we see it, does not put New York to the choice of abandoning those defenses or undertaking to disprove their existence in order to convict for a crime which otherwise is within its constitutional powers to sanction by substantial punishment.

The requirement of proof beyond reasonable doubt in a criminal case is "bottomed on a fundamental value determination of our society that it is far worse to convict an innocent man than to let a guilty man go free." The social cost of placing the burden on the prosecution to prove guilt beyond a reasonable doubt is thus an increased risk that the guilty will go free. While it is clear that our society has willingly chosen to bear a substantial burden in order to protect the innocent, it is equally clear that the risk it must bear is not without limits; and Justice Harlan's aphorism provides little guidance for determining what those limits are. Due process does not require that every conceivable step be taken, at whatever cost, to eliminate the possibility of convicting an innocent person. Punishment of those found guilty by a jury, for example, is not forbidden merely because there is a remote possibility in some instances that an innocent person might go to jail.

It is said that the common law rule permits a State to punish one as a murderer when it is as likely as not that he acted in the heat of passion or under severe emotional distress and when, if he did, he is guilty only of manslaughter. But this has always been the case in those jurisdictions adhering to the traditional rule. It is also very likely true that fewer convictions for murder would occur if New York were required to negative the affirmative defense at issue here. But in each instance of a murder conviction under the present law New York will have proved beyond reasonable doubt that the defendant has intentionally killed another person, an act which it is not disputed the State may constitutionally criminalize and punish. . . .

We thus decline to adopt as a constitutional imperative, operative country-wide, that a State must disprove beyond reasonable doubt every fact constituting any and all affirmative defenses related to the culpability of an accused. Traditionally, due process has required that only the most basic procedural safeguards be observed; more subtle balancing of society's interests against those of the accused have been left to the legislative branch. We therefore will not disturb the balance struck in previous cases holding that the Due Process Clause requires the prosecution to prove beyond reasonable doubt all of the elements included in the definition of the offense of which the defendant is charged. Proof of the nonexistence of all affirmative defenses has never been constitutionally required; and we perceive no reason to fashion such a rule in this case and apply it to the statutory defense at issue here.

This view may seem to permit state legislatures to reallocate burdens of proof by labeling as affirmative defenses at least some elements of the crimes now defined in their statutes. But there are obviously constitutional limits beyond which the States may not go in this regard. "[I]t is not within the province of a legislature to declare an individual guilty or presumptively guilty of a crime." The legislature cannot "validly command that the finding of an indictment, or mere proof of the identity of the accused, should create a presumption of the existence of all the facts essential to guilt." . . .

It is urged that Mullaney v. Wilbur necessarily invalidates Patterson's conviction. In *Mullaney* the charge was murder, which the Maine statute defined as the unlawful killing of a human being "with malice aforethought either express or implied." The trial court instructed the jury that the words "malice aforethought" were most important "because malice aforethought is an essential and indispensable element of the crime of murder." Malice, as the statute indicated and as the court instructed, could be implied and was to be implied from "any deliberate, cruel act committed by one person against another suddenly or without a considerable provocation," in which event an intentional killing was murder unless by a preponderance of the evidence it was shown that the act was committed "in the heat of passion upon sudden provocation." The instructions emphasized that " 'malice aforethought and heat of passion on sudden provocation are two inconsistent things'; thus, by proving the latter the defendant would negate the former."

Mullaney's conviction, which followed, was affirmed. The Maine Supreme Judicial Court held that murder and manslaughter were varying degrees of the crime of felonious homicide and that the presumption of malice arising from the unlawful killing was a mere policy presumption operating to cast on the defendant the burden of proving provocation if he was to be found guilty of manslaughter rather than murder—a burden which the Maine law had allocated to him at least since the mid-1800's.

The Court of Appeals for the First Circuit then ordered that a writ of habeas corpus issue, holding that the presumption unconstitutionally shifted to the defendant the burden of proof with respect to an essential element of the crime. The Maine Supreme Judicial Court disputed this interpretation of Maine law in State v. Lafferty, 309 A.2d 647 (1973), declaring that malice aforethought, in the sense of premeditation, was not an element of the crime of murder and that the federal court had erroneously equated the presumption of malice with a presumption of premeditation.

Maine law does not rely on a presumption of "premeditation" (as Wilbur v. Mullaney assumed) to prove an essential element of unlawful homicide punishable as murder. Proof beyond reasonable doubt of "malice aforethought" (in the sense of "premeditation") is not essential to conviction. . . . [T]he failure of the State to prove "premeditation" in this context is not fatal to such a prosecution because, by legal definition under Maine law, a killing becomes unlawful and punishable as "murder" on proof of "any deliberate cruel act, committed by one person against another, suddenly *without any, or without a considerable provocation.*" State v. Neal, 37 Me. 468, 470 (1854). *Neal* has been frequently cited with approval by our Court. State v. Lafferty, supra, at 664–665. (Emphasis added; footnote omitted.)

When the judgment of the First Circuit was vacated for reconsideration in the light of *Lafferty*, that court reaffirmed its view that Mullaney's conviction was unconstitutional. This Court, accepting the Maine court's interpretation of the Maine law, unanimously agreed with the Court of Appeals that Mullaney's due process rights had been invaded by the presumption casting upon him the burden of proving by preponderance of the evidence that he had acted in the heat of passion upon sudden provocation.

Mullaney's holding, it is argued, is that the State may not permit the blameworthiness of an act or the severity of punishment authorized for its commission to depend on the presence or absence of an identified fact without assuming the burden of proving the presence or absence of that fact, as the case may be, beyond reasonable doubt. In our view, the *Mullaney* holding should not be so broadly read.

Mullaney surely held that a State must prove every ingredient of an offense beyond a reasonable doubt, and that it may not shift the burden of proof to the defendant by presuming that ingredient upon proof of the other elements of the offense. This is true even though the State's practice, as in Maine, had been traditionally to the contrary. Such shifting of the burden of persuasion with respect to a fact which the State deems so important that it must be either proved or presumed is impermissible under the Due Process Clause.

It was unnecessary to go further in *Mullaney*. The Maine Supreme Court made it clear that malice aforethought, which was mentioned in the statutory definition of the crime, was not equivalent to premeditation and that the presumption of malice traditionally arising in intentional homicide cases carried no factual meaning insofar as premeditation was concerned. Even so, a killing became murder in Maine when it resulted from a deliberate, cruel act committed by one person against another, "suddenly, and without any, or without considerable, provocation." State v. Lafferty, supra. Premeditation was not within the definition of murder; but malice, in the sense of the absence of provocation, was part of the definition of that crime. Yet malice, i.e., lack of provocation, was presumed and could be rebutted by the defendant only by proving by a preponderance of the evidence that he acted with heat of passion upon sudden provocation. In *Mullaney* we held that however traditional this mode of proceeding might have been, it is contrary to the Due Process Clause as construed in *Winship*.

As we have explained, nothing was presumed or implied against Patterson; and his conviction is not invalid under any of our prior cases. The judgment of the New York Court of Appeals is

Affirmed.

■ MR. JUSTICE REHNQUIST took no part in the consideration or decision of this case.

■ MR. JUSTICE POWELL, with whom MR. JUSTICE BRENNAN and MR. JUSTICE MARSHALL join, dissenting.

In the name of preserving legislative flexibility, the Court today drains In re Winship, supra, of much of its vitality. Legislatures do require broad discretion in the drafting of criminal laws, but the Court surrenders to the legislative branch a significant part of its responsibility to protect the presumption of innocence. . . .

Maine's homicide laws embodied the common-law distinctions along with the colorful common-law language. Murder was defined in the statute as the unlawful killing of a human being "with malice aforethought, either express or implied." Manslaughter was a killing "in the heat of passion, on sudden provocation, without express or implied malice aforethought. . . ." And the Maine Supreme Judicial Court had held that instructions concerning express malice (in the sense of premeditation) were unnecessary. The only inquiry for the jury in deciding whether a homicide amounted to murder or manslaughter was the inquiry into heat of passion on sudden provocation.

Our holding in *Mullaney* found no constitutional defect in these statutory provisions. Rather, the defect in Maine practice lay in its allocation of the burden of persuasion with respect to the crucial factor distinguishing murder from manslaughter. In Maine, juries were instructed that if the prosecution proved that the homicide was both intentional and unlawful, the crime was to be considered murder unless the *defendant* proved by a preponderance of the evidence that he acted in the heat of passion on sudden provocation. Only if the defendant carried this burden would the offense be reduced to manslaughter.

New York's present homicide laws had their genesis in lingering dissatisfaction with certain aspects of the common-law framework that this Court confronted in *Mullaney*. Critics charged that the archaic language tended to obscure the factors of real importance in the jury's decision. Also, only a limited range of aggravations would lead to mitigation under the common-law formula, usually only those resulting from direct provocation by the victim himself. It was thought that actors whose emotions were stirred by other forms of outrageous conduct, even conduct by someone other than the ultimate victim, also should be punished as manslaughterers rather than murderers. Moreover, the common-law formula was generally applied with rather strict objectivity. Only provocations that might cause the hypothetical reasonable man to lose control could be considered. And even provocations of that sort were inadequate to reduce the crime to manslaughter if enough time had passed for the reasonable man's passions to cool, regardless of whether the actor's own thermometer had registered any decline.

The American Law Institute took the lead in moving to remedy these difficulties. As part of its commendable undertaking to prepare a Model Penal Code, it endeavored to bring modern insights to bear on the law of homicide. The result was a proposal to replace "heat of passion" with the moderately broader concept of "extreme mental or emotional disturbance. . . ."

At about this time the New York Legislature undertook the preparation of a new criminal code, . . . The new code adopted virtually word-for-word the ALI formula for distinguishing murder from manslaughter. . . . There is no mention of malice aforethought, no attempt to give a name to the state of mind that exists when extreme emotional disturbance is not present. . . .

Despite these changes, the major factor that distinguishes murder from manslaughter in New York—"extreme emotional disturbance"—is undeniably the modern equivalent of "heat of passion. . . ."

But in one important respect the New York drafters chose to parallel Maine's practice precisely, departing markedly from the ALI recommendation. Under the Model Penal Code the prosecution must prove the absence of emotional disturbance beyond a reasonable doubt once the issue is properly raised. In New York, however, extreme emotional disturbance constitutes an affirmative defense rather than a simple defense. Consequently the defendant bears not only the burden of production on this issue; he has the burden of persuasion as well.

Mullaney held invalid Maine's requirement that the defendant prove heat of passion. The Court today, without disavowing the unanimous holding of *Mullaney*, approves New York's requirement that the defendant prove extreme emotional disturbance. The Court manages to run a constitutional boundary line through the barely visible space that separates Maine's law from New York's. It does so on the basis of distinctions in language that are formalistic rather than substantive.

This result is achieved by a narrowly literal parsing of the holding in *Winship*: "the Due Process Clause protects the accused against conviction except upon proof beyond a reasonable doubt of every fact necessary to constitute the crime with which he is charged." The only "facts" necessary to constitute a crime are said to be those that appear on the face of the statute as a part of the definition of the crime. Maine's statute was invalid, the Court reasons, because it "defined [murder] as the unlawful killing of a human being 'with malice aforethought either express or implied.'" [M]alice," the Court reiterates, "in the sense of the absence of provocation, was part of the definition of that crime." *Winship* was violated only because this "fact"—malice—was "presumed" unless the defendant persuaded the jury otherwise by showing that he acted in the heat of passion. New York, in form presuming no affirmative "fact" against Patterson, and blessed with a statute drafted in the leaner language of the 20th century, escapes constitutional scrutiny unscathed even though the effect on the defendant of New York's placement of the burden of persuasion is exactly the same as Maine's.

This explanation of the *Mullaney* holding bears little resemblance to the basic rationale of that decision. But this is not the cause of greatest concern. The test the Court today establishes allows a legislature to shift, virtually at will, the burden of persuasion with respect to any factor in a criminal case, so long as it is careful not to mention the nonexistence of that factor in the statutory language that defines the crime * * *

. . . What *Winship* and *Mullaney* had sought to teach about the limits a free society places on its procedures to safeguard the liberty of its citizens becomes a rather simplistic lesson in statutory draftmanship. Nothing in the Court's opinion prevents a legislature from applying this new learning to many of the classical elements of the crimes it punishes. . . .

The Court understandably manifests some uneasiness that its formalistic approach will give legislatures too much latitude in shifting the burden of persuasion. And so it issues a warning that "there are obviously constitutional limits beyond which the States may not go in this regard." The Court thereby concedes that legislative abuses may occur and that they must be curbed by the judicial branch. But if the State is careful to conform to the drafting formulas articulated today, the constitutional limits are anything but "obvious." This decision simply leaves us without a conceptual framework for distinguishing abuses from legitimate legislative adjustments of the burden of persuasion in criminal cases.

It is unnecessary for the Court to retreat to a formalistic test for applying *Winship*. Careful attention to the *Mullaney* decision reveals the principles that should control in this and like cases. *Winship* held that the prosecution must bear the burden of proving beyond a reasonable doubt "the existence of every fact necessary to constitute the crime charged." In *Mullaney* we concluded that heat of passion was one of the "facts" described in *Winship*—that is, a factor as to which the prosecution must bear the burden of persuasion beyond a reasonable doubt. We reached that result only after making two careful inquiries. First, we noted that the presence or absence of heat of passion made a substantial difference in punishment of the offender and in the stigma associated with the conviction. Second, we reviewed the history, in England and this country, of the factor at issue. Central to the holding in *Mullaney* was our conclusion that heat of passion "has been, almost from the inception of the common law of homicide, the single most important factor in determining the degree of culpability attaching to an unlawful homicide."

Implicit in these two inquiries are the principles that should govern this case. The Due Process Clause requires that the prosecutor bear the burden of persuasion beyond a reasonable doubt only if the factor at issue makes a substantial difference in punishment and stigma. The requirement of course applies *a fortiori* if the factor makes the difference between guilt and innocence. But a substantial difference in punishment alone is not enough. It also must be shown that in the Anglo-American legal tradition the factor in question historically has held that level of importance. If either branch of the test is not met, then the legislature retains its traditional authority over matters of proof. But to permit a shift in the burden of persuasion when both branches of this test are satisfied would invite the undermining of the presumption of innocence, "that bedrock 'axiomatic and elementary' principles whose 'enforcement lies at the foundation of the administration of our criminal law.'"

I hardly need add that New York's provisions allocating the burden of persuasion as to "extreme emotional disturbance" are unconstitutional when judged by these standards. . . .

NOTES AND QUESTIONS

1. In *Patterson*, both Justice White's majority opinion and Justice Powell's dissenting opinion spend a good deal of time discussing and comparing the Court's earlier decision in *Mullaney*. Can you reconcile the two cases or is Justice Powell correct that New York's statutory scheme considered in *Patterson* is simply a modern version of the Maine scheme involved in *Mullaney*?

2. Consider how courts interpret *Mullaney* and *Patterson* with respect to the federal murder statute (18 U.S.C.A. § 1111), which requires proof of malice. In United States v. Lofton, 776 F.2d 918 (10th Cir. 1985), the defendant shot her husband in the aftermath of his sexual abuse of their daughter. In reversing a second-degree murder conviction, the court stated that *Mullaney* requires a clear and unambiguous statement, in the form of a jury instruction, that the Government must prove the absence of heat of passion beyond a reasonable doubt. Similarly, see United States v. Lesina, 833 F.2d 156 (9th Cir. 1987).

Contrast these cases with United States v. Molina-Uribe, 853 F.2d 1193 (5th Cir. 1988), *cert. denied*, 489 U.S. 1022, 109 S.Ct. 1145, 103 L.Ed.2d 205 (1989), *overruled on other grounds by* United States v. Bachynsky, 934 F.2d 1349 (5th Cir. 1991). Here the court held that not instructing the jury that the government must prove the defendant acted in the absence of heat of passion was not impermissibly burden-shifting. Can these cases be reconciled?

Dixon v. United States

Supreme Court of the United States, 2006.
548 U.S. 1, 126 S.Ct. 2437, 165 L.Ed.2d 299.

■ JUSTICE STEVENS delivered the opinion of the Court.

In January 2003, petitioner Keshia Dixon purchased multiple firearms at two gun shows, during the course of which she provided an incorrect address and falsely stated that she was not under indictment for a felony. As a result of these illegal acts, petitioner was indicted and convicted on one count of receiving a firearm while under indictment in violation of 18 U.S.C. § 922(n) and eight counts of making false statements in connection with the acquisition of a firearm in violation of § 922(a)(6). At trial, petitioner admitted that she knew she was under indictment when she made the purchases and that she knew doing so was a crime; her defense was that she acted under duress because her boyfriend threatened to kill her or hurt her daughters if she did not buy the guns for him.

Petitioner contends that the trial judge's instructions to the jury erroneously required her to prove duress by a preponderance of the evidence instead of requiring the Government to prove beyond a reasonable doubt that she did not act under duress. The Court of Appeals rejected petitioner's contention; given contrary treatment of the issue by other federal courts,[1] we granted certiorari.

I

* * *

Petitioner argues here, as she did in the District Court and the Court of Appeals, that federal law requires the Government to bear the burden of disproving her defense beyond a reasonable doubt and that the trial court's erroneous instruction on this point entitles her to a new trial. There are two aspects to petitioner's argument in support of her proposed instruction that merit separate discussion. First, petitioner contends that her defense "controverted the *mens rea* required for conviction" and therefore that the Due Process Clause requires the Government to retain the burden of persuasion on that element. Second, petitioner argues that Fifth Circuit's rule is "contrary to modern common law."

II

The crimes for which petitioner was convicted require that she have acted "knowingly," § 922(a)(6), or "willfully". As we have explained, "unless the text of the statute dictates a different result, the term 'knowingly' merely requires proof of knowledge of the facts that constitute the offense." And the term "willfully" in § 924(a)(1)(D) requires

---

[1] Cf., *e.g., United States v. Talbott*, 78 F.3d 1183, 1186 (C.A.7 1996) *(per curiam); United States v. Riffe*, 28 F.3d 565, 568, n. 2 (C.A.6 1994); *United States v. Simpson*, 979 F.2d 1282, 1287 (C.A.8 1992).

a defendant to have "acted with knowledge that his conduct was unlawful." In this case, then, the Government bore the burden of proving beyond a reasonable doubt that petitioner knew she was making false statements in connection with the acquisition of firearms and that she knew she was breaking the law when she acquired a firearm while under indictment. See *In re Winship*, 397 U.S. 358, 364, 90 S.Ct. 1068, 25 L.Ed.2d 368 (1970). Although the Government may have proved these elements in other ways, it clearly met its burden when petitioner testified that she knowingly committed certain acts—she put a false address on the forms she completed to purchase the firearms, falsely claimed that she was the actual buyer of the firearms, and falsely stated that she was not under indictment at the time of the purchase—and when she testified that she knew she was breaking the law when, as an individual under indictment at the time, she purchased a firearm.

Petitioner contends, however, that she cannot have formed the necessary *mens rea* for these crimes because she did not freely choose to commit the acts in question. But even if we assume that petitioner's will was overborne by the threats made against her and her daughters, she still *knew* that she was making false statements and *knew* that she was breaking the law by buying a firearm. The duress defense, like the defense of necessity that we considered in *United States v. Bailey*, 444 U.S. 394, 409–410, 100 S.Ct. 624, 62 L.Ed.2d 575 (1980), may excuse conduct that would otherwise be punishable, but the existence of duress normally does not controvert any of the elements of the offense itself.[4] As we explained in *Bailey*, "[c]riminal liability is normally based upon the concurrence of two factors, 'an evil-meaning mind [and] and evil-doing hand. . . .'" *Id.*, at 402, 100 S.Ct. 624 (quoting *Morissette v. United States*, 342 U.S. 246, 251, 72 S.Ct. 240, 96 L.Ed. 288 (1952)). Like the defense of necessity, the defense of duress does not negate a defendant's criminal state of mind when the applicable offense requires a defendant to have acted knowingly or willfully; instead, it allows the defendant to "avoid liability . . . because coercive conditions or necessity negates a conclusion of guilt even though the necessary *mens rea* was present." Bailey, 444 U.S., at 402, 100 S.Ct. 624.[5]

---

[4] As the Government recognized at oral argument, there may be crimes where the nature of the *mens rea* would require the Government to disprove the existence of duress beyond a reasonable doubt. See Tr. of Oral Arg. 26–27; see also, *e.g.*, 1 W. LaFave, Substantive Criminal Law § 5.1, p. 333 (2d ed.2003) (hereinafter LaFave) (explaining that some common-law crimes require that the crime be done " 'maliciously' "); Black's Law Dictionary 968 (7th ed.1999) (defining malice as "[t]he intent, without justification or excuse, to commit a wrongful act").

[5] Professor LaFave has explained the duress defense as follows:

"The rationale of the defense is not that the defendant, faced with the unnerving threat of harm unless he does an act which violates the literal language of the criminal law, somehow loses his mental capacity to commit the crime in question. Nor is it that the defendant has not engaged in a voluntary act. Rather it is that, even though he has done the act the crime requires and has the mental state which the crime requires, his conduct which violates the literal language of the criminal law is excused. . . ." 2 LaFave § 9.7(a), at 72 (footnote omitted).

The fact that petitioner's crimes are statutory offenses that have no counterpart in the common law also supports our conclusion that her duress defense in no way disproves an element of those crimes. We have observed that "[t]he definition of the elements of a criminal offense is entrusted to the legislature, particularly in the case of federal crimes, which are solely creatures of statute." Here, consistent with the movement away from the traditional dichotomy of general versus specific intent and toward a more specifically defined hierarchy of culpable mental states, Congress defined the crimes at issue to punish defendants who act "knowingly," § 922(a)(6), or "willfully," § 924(a)(1)(D). It is these specific mental states, rather than some vague "evil mind," or "criminal" intent, that the Government is required to prove beyond a reasonable doubt, see *Patterson v. New York*, 432 U.S. 197, 211, n. 12, 97 S.Ct. 2319, 53 L.Ed.2d 281 (1977) ("The applicability of the reasonable-doubt standard, however, has always been dependent on how a State defines the offense that is charged in any given case"). The jury instructions in this case were consistent with this requirement and, as such, did not run afoul of the Due Process Clause when they placed the burden on petitioner to establish the existence of duress by a preponderance of the evidence.

* * *

■ [Part III of JUSTICE STEVENS's opinion rejecting Petitioner's common law argument is omitted.]

IV

Congress can, if it chooses, enact a duress defense that places the burden on the Government to disprove duress beyond a reasonable doubt. In light of Congress' silence on the issue, however, it is up to the federal courts to effectuate the affirmative defense of duress as Congress "may have contemplated" it in an offense-specific context. *Oakland Cannabis Buyers' Cooperative*, 532 U.S., at 491, n. 3, 121 S.Ct. 1711. In the context of the firearms offenses at issue—as will usually be the case, given the long-established common-law rule—we presume that Congress intended the petitioner to bear the burden of proving the defense of duress by a preponderance of the evidence. Accordingly, the judgment of the Court of Appeals is affirmed.

* * *

■ [The concurring opinions of JUSTICE KENNEDY and ALITO, and the dissenting opinion of JUSTICE BREYER are omitted.]

NOTES AND QUESTIONS

1. Given that the statute with which the petitioner in *Dixon* was charged required the government to prove that she acted "knowingly" *or* "willfully," was Justice Stevens correct in his conclusion that the Government had to prove "that she knew she was breaking the law when she acquired a firearm while under indictment"?

2. In light of the opinions in *Patterson* and *Dixon*, constitutionally on whom should the burden of proof lie with respect to the claims of unconsciousness, self-defense, alibi, and insanity?

3. For an example of the defenses of duress and necessity, see in Chapter 10 State v. St. Clair, *infra* p. 1183; United States v. Bailey, *infra* p. 1189.

Ring v. Arizona

Supreme Court of the United States, 2002.
536 U.S. 584, 122 S.Ct. 2428, 153 L.Ed.2d 556.

■ JUSTICE GINSBURG delivered the opinion of the Court.

This case concerns the Sixth Amendment right to a jury trial in capital prosecutions. In Arizona, following a jury adjudication of a defendant's guilt of first-degree murder, the trial judge, sitting alone, determines the presence or absence of the aggravating factors required by Arizona law for imposition of the death penalty.

In *Walton v. Arizona*, 497 U.S. 639, 110 S.Ct. 3047, 111 L.Ed.2d 511 (1990), this Court held that Arizona's sentencing scheme was compatible with the Sixth Amendment because the additional facts found by the judge qualified as sentencing considerations, not as "element[s] of the offense of capital murder." . . . Ten years later, however, we decided *Apprendi v. New Jersey*, 530 U.S. 466, 120 S.Ct. 2348, 147 L.Ed.2d 435 (2000), which held that the Sixth Amendment does not permit a defendant to be "expose[d] . . . to a penalty *exceeding* the maximum he would receive if punished according to the facts reflected in the jury verdict alone." . . . This prescription governs, *Apprendi* determined, even if the State characterizes the additional findings made by the judge as "sentencing factor[s]." . . .

Apprendi's reasoning is irreconcilable with *Walton*'s holding in this regard, and today we overrule *Walton* in relevant part. Capital defendants, no less than non-capital defendants, we conclude, are entitled to a jury determination of any fact on which the legislature conditions an increase in their maximum punishment.

* * *

II

Based solely on the jury's verdict finding Ring guilty of first-degree felony murder, the maximum punishment he could have received was life imprisonment. . . . This was so because, in Arizona, a "death sentence may not legally be imposed . . . unless at least one aggravating factor is found to exist beyond a reasonable doubt." . . . The question presented is whether that aggravating factor may be found by the judge, as Arizona law specifies, or whether the Sixth Amendment's jury trial guarantee, made applicable to the States by the Fourteenth Amendment, requires that the aggravating factor determination be entrusted to the jury.

* * *

The defendant-petitioner in [*Apprendi v. New Jersey*] was convicted of, *inter alia*, second-degree possession of a firearm, an offense carrying a maximum penalty of ten years under New Jersey law. . . . On the prosecutor's motion, the sentencing judge found by a preponderance of the evidence that Apprendi's crime had been motivated by racial animus. That finding triggered application of New Jersey's "hate crime enhancement," which doubled Apprendi's maximum authorized sentence. The judge sentenced Apprendi to 12 years in prison, 2 years over the maximum that would have applied but for the enhancement.

We held that Apprendi's sentence violated his right to "a jury determination that [he] is guilty of every element of the crime with which he is charged, beyond a reasonable doubt." . . . That right attached not only to Apprendi's weapons offense but also to the "hate crime" aggravating circumstance. New Jersey, the Court observed, "threatened Apprendi with certain pains if he unlawfully possessed a weapon and with additional pains if he selected his victims with a purpose to intimidate them because of their race. . . . Merely using the label 'sentence enhancement' to describe the [second act] surely does not provide a principled basis for treating [the two acts] differently." . . . (citations omitted)

The dispositive question, we said, "is one not of form, but of effect." . . . If a State makes an increase in a defendant's authorized punishment contingent on the finding of a fact, that fact—no matter how the State labels it—must be found by a jury beyond a reasonable doubt. . . . A defendant may not be "expose[d] . . . to a penalty *exceeding* the maximum he would receive if punished according to the facts reflected in the jury verdict alone." (citations omitted)

* * *

In an effort to reconcile its capital sentencing system with the Sixth Amendment as interpreted by *Apprendi*, Arizona first restates the *Apprendi* majority's portrayal of Arizona's system: Ring was convicted of first-degree murder, for which Arizona law specifies "death or life imprisonment" as the only sentencing options, see Ariz.Rev.Stat. Ann. § 13–1105(C) (West 2001); Ring was therefore sentenced within the range of punishment authorized by the jury verdict. See Brief for Respondent 9–19. This argument overlooks *Apprendi*'s instruction that "the relevant inquiry is one not of form, but of effect." . . . In effect, "the required finding [of an aggravated circumstance] expose[d] [Ring] to a greater punishment than that authorized by the jury's guilty verdict." . . . The Arizona first-degree murder statute "authorizes a maximum penalty of death only in a formal sense," . . . for it explicitly cross-references the statutory provision requiring the finding of an aggravating circumstance before imposition of the death penalty. . . . If Arizona prevailed on its opening argument, *Apprendi* would be reduced to a "meaningless and formalistic" rule of statutory drafting. . . . (citations omitted)

* * *

Even if facts increasing punishment beyond the maximum authorized by a guilty verdict standing alone ordinarily must be found by a jury, Arizona further urges, aggravating circumstances necessary to trigger a death sentence may nonetheless be reserved for judicial determination. As Arizona's counsel maintained at oral argument, there is no doubt that "[d]eath is different." . . . States have constructed elaborate sentencing procedures in death cases, Arizona emphasizes, because of constraints we have said the Eighth Amendment places on capital sentencing. . . . (citations omitted)

Apart from the Eighth Amendment provenance of aggravating factors, Arizona presents "no specific reason for excepting capital defendants from the constitutional protections . . . extend[ed] to defendants generally, and none is readily apparent." . . . The notion "that the Eighth Amendment's restriction on a state legislature's ability to define capital crimes should be compensated for by permitting States more leeway under the Fifth and Sixth Amendments in proving an aggravating fact necessary to a capital sentence . . . is without precedent in our constitutional jurisprudence. . . .

* * *

Arizona suggests that judicial authority over the finding of aggravating factors "may . . . be a better way to guarantee against the arbitrary imposition of the death penalty." . . . The Sixth Amendment jury trial right, however, does not turn on the relative rationality, fairness, or efficiency of potential factfinders. Entrusting to a judge the finding of facts necessary to support a death sentence might be

> an admirably fair and efficient scheme of criminal justice designed for a society that is prepared to leave criminal justice to the State. . . . The founders of the American Republic were not prepared to leave it to the State, which is why the jury-trial guarantee was one of the least controversial provisions of the Bill of Rights. It has never been efficient; but it has always been free. *Apprendi*, 530 U.S., at 498, 120 S.Ct. 2348 (SCALIA, J., concurring).

In any event, the superiority of judicial factfinding in capital cases is far from evident. Unlike Arizona, the great majority of States responded to this Court's Eighth Amendment decisions requiring the presence of aggravating circumstances in capital cases by entrusting those determinations to the jury.[6]

Although " 'the doctrine of *stare decisis* is of fundamental importance to the rule of law[,]' . . . [o]ur precedents are not sacrosanct." *Patterson v. McLean Credit Union*, 491 U.S. 164, 172, 109 S.Ct. 2363, 105 L.Ed.2d 132 (1989) (quoting *Welch v. Texas Dept. of Highways and Public Transp.*, 483 U.S. 468, 494, 107 S.Ct. 2941, 97 L.Ed.2d 389 (1987)). "[W]e have overruled prior decisions where the necessity and propriety of doing so has been established." 491 U.S., at 172, 109 S.Ct. 2363. We are satisfied that this is such a case.

For the reasons stated, we hold that *Walton* and *Apprendi* are irreconcilable; our Sixth Amendment jurisprudence cannot be home to both. Accordingly, we overrule *Walton* to the extent that it allows a sentencing judge, sitting without a jury, to find an aggravating circumstance necessary for imposition of the death penalty. . . . Because Arizona's enumerated aggravating factors operate as "the functional equivalent of an element of a greater offense," . . . the Sixth Amendment requires that they be found by a jury.

* * *

The guarantees of jury trial in the Federal and State Constitutions reflect a profound judgment about the way in which law should be enforced and justice administered. . . . If the defendant preferred the common-sense judgment of a jury to the more tutored but perhaps less sympathetic reaction of the single judge, he was to have it. *Duncan v. Louisiana*, 391 U.S. 145, 155–156, 88 S.Ct. 1444, 20 L.Ed.2d 491 (1968).

The right to trial by jury guaranteed by the Sixth Amendment would be senselessly diminished if it encompassed the factfinding necessary to increase a defendant's sentence by two years, but not the factfinding necessary to put him to death. We hold that the Sixth Amendment applies to both. The judgment of the Arizona Supreme Court is therefore reversed, and the case is remanded for further proceedings not inconsistent with this opinion.

It is so ordered.

■ Concurring opinions of SCALIA, J., KENNEDY, J., and BREYER, J., omitted.

■ JUSTICE O'CONNOR, with whom THE CHIEF JUSTICE joins, dissenting.

I understand why the Court holds that the reasoning of *Apprendi v. New Jersey*, 530 U.S. 466, 120 S.Ct. 2348, 147 L.Ed.2d 435 (2000), is irreconcilable with *Walton v. Arizona*, 497 U.S. 639, 110 S.Ct. 3047, 111

---

[6] Of the 38 States with capital punishment, 29 generally commit sentencing decisions to juries.

L.Ed.2d 511 (1990). Yet in choosing which to overrule, I would choose *Apprendi*, not *Walton*.

I continue to believe, for the reasons I articulated in my dissent in *Apprendi*, that the decision in *Apprendi* was a serious mistake. As I argued in that dissent, *Apprendi*'s rule that any fact that increases the maximum penalty must be treated as an element of the crime is not required by the Constitution, by history, or by our prior cases. . . . Indeed, the rule directly contradicts several of our prior cases. . . . And it ignores the "significant history in this country of . . . discretionary sentencing by judges." 530 U.S., at 544, 120 S.Ct. 2348 (O'CONNOR, J., dissenting). The Court has failed, both in *Apprendi* and in the decision announced today, to "offer any meaningful justification for deviating from years of cases both suggesting and holding that application of the 'increase in the maximum penalty' rule is not required by the Constitution." . . . (citations omitted)

Not only was the decision in *Apprendi* unjustified in my view, but it has also had a severely destabilizing effect on our criminal justice system. I predicted in my dissent that the decision would "unleash a flood of petitions by convicted defendants seeking to invalidate their sentences in whole or in part on the authority of *[Apprendi]*." *Id.*, at 551, 120 S.Ct. 2348. As of May 31, 2002, less than two years after *Apprendi* was announced, the United States Courts of Appeals had decided approximately 1,802 criminal appeals in which defendants challenged their sentences, and in some cases even their convictions, under *Apprendi*. These federal appeals are likely only the tip of the iceberg, as federal criminal prosecutions represent a tiny fraction of the total number of criminal prosecutions nationwide. . . . The number of second or successive habeas corpus petitions filed in the federal courts also increased by 77% in 2001, a phenomenon the Administrative Office of the United States Courts attributes to prisoners bringing *Apprendi* claims. Administrative Office of the U.S. Courts, 2001 Judicial Business 17. This Court has been similarly overwhelmed by the aftershocks of *Apprendi*. A survey of the petitions for certiorari we received in the past year indicates that 18% raised *Apprendi*-related claims. It is simply beyond dispute that *Apprendi* threw countless criminal sentences into doubt and thereby caused an enormous increase in the workload of an already overburdened judiciary.

The decision today is only going to add to these already serious effects. The Court effectively declares five States' capital sentencing schemes unconstitutional. See *ante*, at 2441, n. 5 (identifying Colorado, Idaho, Montana, and Nebraska as having sentencing schemes like Arizona's). There are 168 prisoners on death row in these States, Criminal Justice Project of the NAACP Legal Defense and Educational Fund, Inc., Death Row U.S.A. (Spring 2002), each of whom is now likely to challenge his or her death sentence. I believe many of these challenges will ultimately be unsuccessful, either because the prisoners will be unable to satisfy the standards of harmless error or plain error review, or because, having completed their direct appeals, they will be barred from taking advantage of today's holding on federal collateral review. See 28 U.S.C. §§ 2244(b)(2)(A), 2254(d)(1); *Teague v. Lane*, 489 U.S. 288, 109 S.Ct. 1060, 103 L.Ed.2d 334 (1989). Nonetheless, the need to evaluate these claims will greatly burden the courts in these five States. In addition, I fear that the prisoners on death row in Alabama, Delaware, Florida, and Indiana, which the Court identifies as having hybrid sentencing schemes in which the jury renders an advisory verdict but the judge makes the ultimate sentencing determination, . . . may also seize on today's decision to challenge their sentences. There are 529 prisoners on death row in these States. Criminal Justice Project, *supra*.

By expanding on *Apprendi*, the Court today exacerbates the harm done in that case. Consistent with my dissent, I would overrule *Apprendi* rather than *Walton*.

NOTES

1. In Blakely v. Washington, 542 U.S. 296, 124 S.Ct. 2531, 159 L.Ed.2d 403 (2004), the Supreme Court clarified *Apprendi*'s holding that "any fact that increases the penalty for a crime beyond the prescribed statutory maximum must be submitted to a jury," *Apprendi*, 530 U.S. at 490, by noting that statutory maximum means "the maximum sentence a judge may impose *solely on the basis of the facts reflected in the jury verdict or admitted by the defendant* . . . not the maximum sentence a judge may impose after finding additional facts, but the maximum he may impose *without* any additional findings." *Blakely*, 542 U.S. at 303–04. In *Blakely*, the defendant pleaded guilty to second-degree kidnapping involving domestic violence and use of a firearm and admitted the elements establishing this crime, but no other relevant facts. Washington's sentencing guidelines established a standard range sentence of forty-nine to fifty-three months for Blakely's crimes. However, Washington's sentencing guidelines also permitted the sentencing judge to impose a sentence above the standard range upon finding substantial and compelling reasons, *other than those used in computing the standard range sentence*. Instead of sentencing Blakely to a term within the standard range, the sentencing judge imposed a ninety-month sentence, finding that Blakely acted with "deliberate cruelty," a finding not admitted by Blakely or proved beyond a reasonable doubt to a jury. On appeal, Blakely argued that Washington's sentencing procedure deprived him of the Sixth Amendment right to have a jury determine beyond a reasonable doubt all facts legally essential to his sentence. The Court agreed and invalidated Blakely's sentence and Washington's sentencing procedures under *Apprendi* because Washington law permitted the sentencing judge to consider facts not proved to the jury beyond a reasonable doubt or admitted by the defendant in violation of the Sixth Amendment.

2. In the combined cases of United States v. Booker and United States v. Fanfan, 543 U.S. 220, 125 S.Ct. 738, 160 L.Ed.2d 621 (2005), the Court applied *Apprendi* and *Blakely* to the Federal Sentencing Guidelines. In *Booker*, the jury's findings and Booker's criminal history mandated Booker receive a 210- to 262-month sentence, but the district court increased Booker's sentence to 360 months to life, as required by the Guidelines, based on the judge's finding that Booker had possessed additional drugs and was also guilty of obstruction of justice. The Court held that the Sixth Amendment required juries to find facts relevant to sentencing, not judges. The Court did not invalidate the Guidelines as a whole; instead, the Court found the provision making the Guidelines mandatory unconstitutional and void, but the remainder of the Guidelines valid. The practical effect of *Booker/Fanfan* is that the Guidelines are effectively advisory. The sentencing court must consider the Guidelines but "may tailor the sentence in light of other statutory concerns." 543 U.S. at 245–46.

Sandstrom v. Montana

Supreme Court of the United States, 1979.
442 U.S. 510, 99 S.Ct. 2450, 61 L.Ed.2d 39.

■ MR. JUSTICE BRENNAN delivered the opinion of the Court.

The question presented is whether, in a case in which intent is an element of the crime charged, the jury instruction, "the law presumes that a person intends the ordinary consequences of his voluntary acts," violates the Fourteenth Amendment's requirement that the State prove every element of a criminal offense beyond a reasonable doubt.

I

On November 22, 1976, 18-year-old David Sandstrom confessed to the slaying of Annie Jessen. Based upon the confession and corroborating evidence, petitioner was charged on December 2 with "deliberate homicide," Mont.Code Ann. § 45–5–102 (1978), in that he "purposely or knowingly caused the death of Annie Jessen."[1] At trial, Sandstrom's attorney informed the jury that, although his client admitted killing Jessen, he did not do so "purposely or knowingly," and was therefore not guilty of "deliberate homicide" but of a lesser crime. The basic support for this contention was the testimony of two court-appointed mental health experts, each of whom described for the jury petitioner's mental state at the time of the incident. Sandstrom's attorney argued that this testimony

---

[1] The statute provides:

"45–5–101. Criminal homicide. (1) A person commits the offense of criminal homicide if he purposely, knowingly, or negligently causes the death of another human being.

"(2) Criminal homicide is deliberate homicide, mitigated deliberate homicide, or negligent homicide.

"45–5–102. Deliberate homicide. (1) Except as provided in 45–5–103(1), criminal homicide constitutes deliberate homicide if:

"(a) it is committed purposely or knowingly. . . ."

demonstrated that petitioner, due to a personality disorder aggravated by alcohol consumption, did not kill Annie Jessen "purposely or knowingly."

The prosecution requested the trial judge to instruct the jury that "[t]he law presumes that a person intends the ordinary consequences of his voluntary acts." Petitioner's counsel objected, arguing that "the instruction has the effect of shifting the burden of proof on the issue of" purpose or knowledge to the defense, and that "that is impermissible under the Federal Constitution, due process of law." He offered to provide a number of federal decisions in support of the objection, including this Court's holding in Mullaney v. Wilbur (1975), but was told by the judge: "You can give those to the Supreme Court. The objection is overruled." The instruction was delivered, the jury found petitioner guilty of deliberate homicide, *id.*, at 38, and petitioner was sentenced to 100 years in prison.

Sandstrom appealed to the Supreme Court of Montana, again contending that the instruction shifted to the defendant the burden of disproving an element of the crime charged in violation of Mullaney v. Wilbur, In re Winship, and Patterson v. New York. The Montana court conceded that these cases did prohibit shifting the burden of proof to the defendant by means of a presumption, but held that the cases "do not prohibit allocation of *some* burden of proof to a defendant under certain circumstances." Since in the court's view, "[d]efendant's sole burden under instruction No. 5 was to produce *some* evidence that he did not intend the ordinary consequences of his voluntary acts, not to disprove that he acted 'purposely' or 'knowingly,' . . . the instruction does not violate due process standards as defined by the United States or Montana Constitution. . . ." (emphasis added.)

Both federal and state courts have held, under a variety of rationales, that the giving of an instruction similar to that challenged here is fatal to the validity of a criminal conviction. We granted certiorari, to decide the important question of the instruction's constitutionality. We reverse.

II

The threshold inquiry in ascertaining the constitutional analysis applicable to this kind of jury instruction is to determine the nature of the presumption it describes. That determination requires careful attention to the words actually spoken to the jury, for whether a defendant has been accorded his constitutional rights depends upon the way in which a reasonable juror could have interpreted the instruction.

Respondent argues, first, that the instruction merely described a permissive inference—that is, it allowed but did not require the jury to draw conclusions about defendant's intent from his actions—and that such inferences are constitutional. These arguments need not detain us long, for even respondent admits that "it's possible" that the jury believed they were required to apply the presumption. Sandstrom's jurors were told that "[t]he law presumes that a person intends the ordinary consequences of his voluntary acts." They were not told that they had a choice, or that they might infer that conclusion; they were told only that the law presumed it. It is clear that a reasonable juror could easily have viewed such an instruction as mandatory. . . .

In the alternative, respondent urges that, even if viewed as a mandatory presumption rather than as a permissive inference, the presumption did not conclusively establish intent but rather could be rebutted. On this view, the instruction required the jury, if satisfied as to the facts which trigger the presumption, to find intent *unless* the defendant offered evidence to the contrary. Moreover, according to the State, all the defendant had to do to rebut the presumption was produce "some" contrary evidence; he did not have to "prove" that he lacked the required mental state. Thus, "[a]t most, it placed a *burden of production* on the petitioner," but "did not shift to petitioner the *burden of persuasion* with respect to any element of the offense. . . ." (emphasis added). Again, respondent contends that presumptions with this limited effect pass constitutional muster.

We need not review respondent's constitutional argument on this point either, however, for we reject this characterization of the presumption as well. Respondent concedes there is a "risk" that the jury, once having found petitioner's act voluntary, would interpret the instruction as automatically directing a finding of intent. Moreover, the State also concedes that numerous courts "have differed as to the effect of the presumption when given as a jury instruction without further explanation as to its use by the jury," and that some have found it to shift more than the burden of production, and even to have conclusive effect. Nonetheless, the State contends that the only authoritative reading of the effect of the presumption resides in the Supreme Court of Montana. And the State argues that by holding that "[d]efendant's sole burden under instruction No. 5 was to produce *some* evidence that he did not intend the ordinary consequences of his voluntary acts, not to disprove that he acted 'purposely' or 'knowingly,' " (emphasis added), the Montana Supreme Court decisively established that the presumption at most affected only the burden of going forward with evidence of intent—that is, the burden of production.

The Supreme Court of Montana is, of course, the final authority on the legal weight to be given a presumption under Montana law, but it is not the final authority on the interpretation which a jury could have given the instruction. If Montana intended its presumption to have only the effect described by its Supreme Court, then we are convinced that a reasonable juror could well have been misled by the instruction given, and could have believed that the presumption was not limited to requiring the defendant to satisfy only a burden of production.

Petitioner's jury was told that *"[t]he law presumes* that a person intends the ordinary consequences of his voluntary acts." They were not told that the presumption could be rebutted, as the Montana Supreme Court held, by the defendant's simple presentation of "some" evidence; nor even that it could be rebutted at all. Given the common definition of "presume" as "to suppose to be true without proof," Webster's New Collegiate Dictionary 911 (1974), and given the lack of qualifying instructions as to the legal effect of the presumption, we cannot discount the possibility that the jury may have interpreted the instruction in either of two more stringent ways.

First, a reasonable jury could well have interpreted the presumption as "conclusive," that is, not technically as a presumption at all, but rather as an irrebuttable direction by the court to find intent once convinced of the facts triggering the presumption. Alternatively, the jury may have interpreted the instruction as a direction to find intent upon proof of the defendant's voluntary actions (and their "ordinary" consequences), unless *the defendant* proved the contrary by some quantum of proof which may well have been considerably greater than "some" evidence—thus effectively shifting the burden of persuasion on the element of intent. Numerous federal and state courts have warned that instructions of the type given here can be interpreted in just these ways. . . . And although the Montana Supreme Court held to the contrary in this case, Montana's own Rules of Evidence expressly state that the presumption at issue here may be overcome only "by a preponderance of evidence contrary to the presumption." Montana Rule of Evidence 301(b)(2). Such a requirement shifts not only the burden of production, but also the ultimate burden of persuasion on the issue of intent. . . .

III

In *Winship*, this Court stated:

Lest there remain any doubt about the constitutional stature of the reasonable-doubt standard, we explicitly hold that the Due Process Clause protects the accused against conviction except upon proof beyond a reasonable doubt *of every fact* necessary to constitute the crime with which he is charged. (emphasis added).

The petitioner here was charged with and convicted of deliberate homicide, committed purposely or knowingly, under Mont.Code Ann. § 45–5–102(a) (1978). It is clear that under Montana law, whether the crime was committed purposely or knowingly is a fact necessary to constitute the crime of deliberate homicide. Indeed, it was the lone element of the offense at issue in Sandstrom's trial, as he confessed to causing the death of the victim, told the jury that knowledge and purpose were the only questions he was controverting, and introduced evidence solely on those points. Moreover, it is conceded that proof of defendant's "intent" would be sufficient to establish this element. Thus, the question before this Court is whether the challenged jury instruction had the effect of relieving the State of the burden of proof enunciated in *Winship* on the critical question of petitioner's state of mind. We conclude that under either of the two possible interpretations of the instruction set out above, precisely that effect would result, and that the instruction therefore represents constitutional error.

We consider first the validity of a conclusive presumption. This Court has considered such a presumption on at least two prior occasions. In Morissette v. United States (1952), the defendant was charged with willful and knowing theft of Government property. Although his attorney argued that for his client to be found guilty, "the taking must have been with felonious intent," the trial judge ruled that "[t]hat is presumed by his own act." After first concluding that intent was in fact an element of the crime charged, and after declaring that "[w]here intent of the accused is an ingredient of the crime charged, its existence is . . . a jury issue," *Morissette* held:

> *It follows that the trial court may not withdraw or prejudge the issue by instruction that the law raises a presumption of intent from an act.* It often is tempting to cast in terms of a "presumption" a conclusion which a court thinks probable from given facts. . . . [But] [w]e think presumptive intent has no place in this case. *A conclusive presumption which testimony could not overthrow would effectively eliminate intent as an ingredient of the offense.* A presumption which would permit but not require the jury to assume intent from an isolated fact would prejudge a conclusion which the jury should reach of its own volition. A presumption which would permit the jury to make an assumption which all the evidence considered together does not logically establish would give to a proven fact an artificial and fictional effect. In either case, *this presumption would conflict with the overriding presumption of innocence with which the law endows the accused and which extends to every element of the crime.* (Emphasis added; footnote omitted.)

Just last Term, in United States v. United States Gypsum Co., 438 U.S. 422 (1978), we reaffirmed the holding of *Morissette*. In that case defendants, who were charged with criminal violations of the Sherman Act, challenged the following jury instruction:

> The law presumes that a person intends the necessary and natural consequences of his acts. Therefore, if the effect of the exchanges of pricing information was to raise, fix, maintain, and stabilize prices, then the parties to them are presumed, as a matter of law, to have intended that result.

After again determining that the offense included the element of intent, we held:

> [A] defendant's state of mind or *intent is an element of a criminal antitrust offense which . . . cannot be taken from the trier of fact through reliance on a legal presumption* of wrongful intent from proof of an effect on prices. . . .

> Although an effect on prices may well support an inference that the defendant had knowledge of the probability of such a consequence at the time he acted, the jury must remain free to consider additional evidence before accepting or rejecting the inference. . . . [U]ltimately the decision on the issue of intent must be left to the trier of fact alone. The instruction given invaded this factfinding function. (emphasis added.)

As in *Morissette* and *United States Gypsum Co.*, a conclusive presumption in this case would "conflict with the overriding presumption of innocence with which the law endows the accused and which extends to every element of the crime," and would "invade [the] factfinding function" which in a criminal case the law assigns solely to the jury. The instruction announced to David Sandstrom's jury may well have had exactly these consequences. Upon finding proof of one element of the crime (causing death), and of facts insufficient to establish the second (the voluntariness and "ordinary consequences" of defendant's action), Sandstrom's jurors could reasonably have concluded that they were directed to find against defendant on the element of intent. The State was thus not forced to prove "beyond a reasonable doubt . . . every fact necessary to constitute the crime . . . charged," and defendant was deprived of his constitutional rights as explicated in *Winship*.

A presumption which, although not conclusive, had the effect of shifting the burden of persuasion to the defendant, would have suffered from similar infirmities. If Sandstrom's jury interpreted the presumption in that manner, it could have concluded that upon proof by the State of the slaying, and of additional facts not themselves establishing the element of intent, the burden was shifted to the defendant to prove that he lacked the requisite mental state. Such a presumption was found constitutionally deficient in Mullaney v. Wilbur, 421 U.S. 684 (1975). In *Mullaney*, the charge was murder, which under Maine law required proof not only of intent but of malice. The trial court charged the jury that " 'malice aforethought is an essential and indispensable element of the crime of murder.' " However, it also instructed that if the prosecution established that the homicide was both intentional and unlawful, malice aforethought was to be implied unless the defendant proved by a fair preponderance of the evidence that he acted in the heat of passion on sudden provocation. Ibid. As we recounted just two Terms ago in Patterson v. New York, "[t]his Court . . . unanimously agreed with the Court of Appeals that Wilbur's due process rights had been invaded by the presumption casting upon him the burden of proving by a preponderance of the evidence that he had acted in the heat of passion upon sudden provocation." And *Patterson* reaffirmed that "a State must prove every ingredient of an offense beyond a reasonable doubt, and . . . may not shift the burden of proof to the defendant" by means of such a presumption.

Because David Sandstrom's jury may have interpreted the judge's instruction as constituting either a burden-shifting presumption like that in *Mullaney*, or a conclusive presumption like those in *Morissette* and *United States Gypsum Co.*, and because either interpretation would have deprived defendant of his right to the due process of law, we hold the instruction given in this case unconstitutional.

* * *

■ [The concurring opinion of MR. JUSTICE REHNQUIST, with whom THE CHIEF JUSTICE joins, is omitted.]

NOTES AND QUESTIONS

1. In Chapman v. California, 386 U.S. 18, 87 S.Ct. 824, 17 L.Ed.2d 705 (1967), the Court established the doctrine of "harmless error," which essentially provides that a conviction need not be reversed for errors, even constitutional ones, which are harmless beyond a reasonable doubt, that is, the government can "prove beyond a reasonable doubt that the error complained of did not contribute to the verdict obtained." *See also* Fed.R.Crim.P. 52(a) ("Any error, defect, irregularity or variance which does not affect substantial rights shall be disregarded."). Do you think the doctrine of harmless error could ever be applied to a *Sandstrom* violation? *See* Rose v. Clark, 478 U.S. 570, 106 S.Ct. 3101, 92 L.Ed.2d 460 (1986); Connecticut v. Johnson, 460 U.S. 73, 103 S.Ct. 969, 74 L.Ed.2d 823 (1983).

Problem 2–9. In Francis v. Franklin, 471 U.S. 307, 105 S.Ct. 1965, 85 L.Ed.2d 344 (1985), the defendant in a murder prosecution shot and killed a person in the neighborhood of a dentist's office where the defendant had obtained treatment. The killing occurred at the moment the victim, a resident in a nearby home, slammed the front door shut as defendant asked for the key to the victim's car. Defendant's pistol fired and a bullet pierced the door hitting the victim in the chest. Defendant argued that he lacked the intent to commit malice-murder and claimed that the killing was an accident. The trial court instructed the jury on the issue of intent as follows:

> The acts of a person of sound mind and discretion are presumed to be the product of a person's will, but the presumption may be rebutted. A person of sound mind and discretion is presumed to intend the natural and probable consequences of his acts, but the presumption may be rebutted. A person will not be presumed to act with criminal intention but the trier of facts . . . may find criminal intention upon a consideration of the words, conduct, demeanor,

motive and all of the circumstances connected with the act for which the accused is prosecuted.

The court also instructed the jury on the presumption of innocence and the state's burden of proof. Did the trial court's instruction to the jury overcome the concerns expressed in *Sandstrom*?

2. The issue of the validity of presumptions prevails, of course, in all types of criminal cases. A good illustration is Leary v. United States, 395 U.S. 6, 89 S.Ct. 1532, 23 L.Ed.2d 57 (1969), *remanded to* 431 F.2d 85 (5th Cir. 1970), which involved a prosecution for the violation of federal statutes governing traffic in marijuana. The defendant, Dr. Timothy Leary, and several other persons had been to Mexico. As they reentered the United States, Leary's car and the occupants were searched and small amounts of marijuana were found. The federal prosecution relied upon a statutory provision declaring that possession of marijuana was sufficient evidence that it had been illegally transported into the United States. Leary's conviction was reversed upon a Supreme Court finding that the presumption was invalid because of the fact that there were many other ways he might have acquired the marijuana other than by illegally transporting it into the country. In contrast, however, is the case of Turner v. United States, 396 U.S. 398, 90 S.Ct. 642, 24 L.Ed.2d 610 (1970), in which the Court held the presumption to be valid with respect to the possession of heroin, because of its unavailability except by importation. Nevertheless, in *Turner* the Court held that the presumption was not applicable to cocaine, because it is produced in the United States in sizeable quantity for medicinal purposes and therefore may be obtainable other than by importation.

County Court of Ulster County v. Allen

Supreme Court of the United States, 1979.
442 U.S. 140, 99 S.Ct. 2213, 60 L.Ed.2d 777.

■ MR. JUSTICE STEVENS delivered the opinion of the Court.

A New York statute provides that, with certain exceptions, the presence of a firearm in an automobile is presumptive evidence of its illegal possession by all persons then occupying the vehicle.[1] The United

---

[1] New York Penal Law § 265.15(3) (McKinney 1967):

The presence in an automobile, other than a stolen one or a public omnibus, of any firearm, defaced firearm, firearm silencer, bomb, bombshell, gravity knife, switchblade knife, dagger, dirk, stiletto, billy, blackjack, metal knuckles, sandbag, sandclub or slungshot is presumptive evidence of its possession by all persons occupying such automobile at the time such weapon, instrument or appliance is found, except under the following circumstances:

(a) if such weapon, instrument or appliance is found upon the person of one of the occupants therein; (b) if such weapon, instrument or appliance is found in an automobile which is being operated for hire by a duly licensed driver in the due, lawful and proper pursuit of his trade, then such presumption shall not apply to the driver; or (c) if the weapon so found is a pistol or revolver and one of the occupants, not present under duress, has in his possession a valid license to have and carry concealed the same.

In addition to the three exceptions delineated in §§ 265.15(3)(a)–(c) above as well as the stolen-vehicle and public-omnibus exception in § 265.15(3) itself, § 265.20

States Court of Appeals for the Second Circuit held that respondents may challenge the constitutionality of this statute in a federal habeas corpus proceeding and that the statute is "unconstitutional on its face." We granted certiorari to review these holdings and also to consider whether the statute is constitutional in its application to respondents.

Four persons, three adult males (respondents) and a 16-year-old girl (Jane Doe, who is not a respondent here), were jointly tried on charges that they possessed two loaded handguns, a loaded machine gun, and over a pound of heroin found in a Chevrolet in which they were riding when it was stopped for speeding on the New York Thruway shortly after noon on March 28, 1973. The two large-caliber handguns, which together with their ammunition weighed approximately six pounds, were seen through the window of the car by the investigating police officer. They were positioned crosswise in an open handbag on either the front floor or the front seat of the car on the passenger side where Jane Doe was sitting. Jane Doe admitted that the handbag was hers. The machine gun and the heroin were discovered in the trunk after the police pried it open. The car had been borrowed from the driver's brother earlier that day; the key to the trunk could not be found in the car or on the person of any of its occupants, although there was testimony that two of the occupants had placed something in the trunk before embarking in the borrowed car. The jury convicted all four of possession of the handguns and acquitted them of possession of the contents of the trunk.

Counsel for all four defendants objected to the introduction into evidence of the two handguns, the machine gun, and the drugs, arguing that the State had not adequately demonstrated a connection between their clients and the contraband. The trial court overruled the objection, relying on the presumption of possession created by the New York statute. Because that presumption does not apply if a weapon is found "upon the person" of one of the occupants of the car, see n. 1, supra, the three male defendants also moved to dismiss the charges relating to the handguns on the ground that the guns were found on the person of Jane Doe. Respondents made this motion both at the close of the prosecution's case and at the close of all evidence. The trial judge twice denied it, concluding that the applicability of the "upon the person" exception was a question of fact for the jury.

At the close of the trial, the judge instructed the jurors that they were entitled to infer possession from the defendants' presence in the car. He did not make any reference to the "upon the person" exception in his explanation of the statutory presumption, nor did any of the defendants object to this omission or request alternative or additional instructions on the subject.

---

contains various exceptions that apply when weapons are present in an automobile pursuant to certain military, law enforcement, recreational, and commercial endeavors.

Defendants filed a post-trial motion in which they challenged the constitutionality of the New York statute as applied in this case. The challenge was made in support of their argument that the evidence, apart from the presumption, was insufficient to sustain the convictions. The motion was denied, and the convictions were affirmed by the Appellate Division without opinion.

The New York Court of Appeals also affirmed. It rejected the argument that as a matter of law the guns were on Jane Doe's person because they were in her pocketbook. Although the court recognized that in some circumstances the evidence could only lead to the conclusion that the weapons were in one person's sole possession, it held that this record presented a jury question on that issue. Since the defendants had not asked the trial judge to submit the question to the jury, the Court of Appeals treated the case as though the jury had resolved this fact question in the prosecution's favor. It therefore concluded that the presumption did apply and that there was sufficient evidence to support the convictions. It also summarily rejected the argument that the presumption was unconstitutional as applied in this case.

Respondents filed a petition for a writ of habeas corpus in the United States District Court for the Southern District of New York contending that they were denied due process of law by the application of the statutory presumption of possession. The District Court issued the writ, holding . . . that the mere presence of two guns in a woman's handbag in a car could not reasonably give rise to the inference that they were in the possession of three other persons in the car.

The Court of Appeals for the Second Circuit affirmed, but for different reasons. First, the entire panel concluded that the New York Court of Appeals had decided respondents' constitutional claim on its merits rather than on any independent state procedural ground that might have barred collateral relief. Then, the majority of the court, without deciding whether the presumption was constitutional as applied in this case, concluded that the statute is unconstitutional on its face because the "presumption obviously sweeps within its compass (1) many occupants who may not know they are riding with a gun (which may be out of their sight), and (2) many who may be aware of the presence of the gun but not permitted access to it." . . .

* * *

Inferences and presumptions are a staple of our adversary system of factfinding. It is often necessary for the trier of fact to determine the existence of an element of the crime—that is, an "ultimate" or "elemental" fact—from the existence of one or more "evidentiary" or "basic" facts. The value of these evidentiary devices, and their validity under the Due Process Clause, vary from case to case, however, depending on the strength of the connection between the particular basic and elemental facts involved and on the degree to which the device curtails the factfinder's freedom to assess the evidence independently. Nonetheless, in criminal cases, the ultimate test of any device's constitutional validity in a given case remains constant: the device must not undermine the factfinder's responsibility at trial, based on evidence adduced by the State, to find the ultimate facts beyond a reasonable doubt.

The most common evidentiary device is the entirely permissive inference or presumption, which allows—but does not require—the trier of fact to infer the elemental fact from proof by the prosecutor of the basic one and which places no burden of any kind on the defendant. In that situation the basic fact may constitute prima facie evidence of the elemental fact. When reviewing this type of device, the Court has required the party challenging it to demonstrate its invalidity as applied to him. Because this permissive presumption leaves the trier of fact free to credit or reject the inference and does not shift the burden of proof, it affects the application of the "beyond a reasonable doubt" standard only if, under the facts of the case, there is no rational way the trier could make the connection permitted by the inference. For only in that situation is there any risk that an explanation of the permissible inference to a jury, or its use by a jury, has caused the presumptively rational factfinder to make an erroneous factual determination.

A mandatory presumption is a far more troublesome evidentiary device. For it may affect not only the strength of the "no reasonable doubt" burden but also the placement of that burden; it tells the trier that he or they *must* find the elemental fact upon proof of the basic fact, at least unless the defendant has come forward with some evidence to rebut the presumed connection between the two facts. In this situation, the Court has generally examined the presumption on its face to determine the extent to which the basic and elemental facts coincide. To the extent that the trier of fact is forced to abide by the presumption, and may not reject it based on an independent evaluation of the particular facts presented by the State, the analysis of the presumption's constitutional validity is logically divorced from those facts and based on the presumption's accuracy in the run of cases. . . .

Without determining whether the presumption in this case was mandatory, the Court of Appeals analyzed it on its face as if it were. In fact, it was not, as the New York Court of Appeals had earlier pointed out.

The trial judge's instructions make it clear that the presumption was merely a part of the prosecution's case,[19] that it gave rise to a permissive

---

[19] "It is your duty to consider all the testimony in this case, to weigh it carefully and to test the credit to be given to a witness by his apparent intention to speak the truth and by the accuracy of his memory to reconcile, if possible, conflicting statements as to material facts and in such ways to try and get at the truth and to reach a verdict upon the evidence." Tr. 739–740.

"To establish the unlawful possession of the weapons, again the People relied upon the presumption and, in addition thereto, the testimony of Anderson and Lemmons who testified in their case in chief." *Id.*, at 744.

inference available only in certain circumstances, rather than a mandatory conclusion of possession, and that it could be ignored by the jury even if there was no affirmative proof offered by defendants in rebuttal.[20] The judge explained that possession could be actual or constructive, but that constructive possession could not exist without the intent and ability to exercise control or dominion over the weapons. He also carefully instructed the jury that there is a mandatory presumption of innocence in favor of the defendants that controls unless it, as the exclusive trier of fact, is satisfied beyond a reasonable doubt that the defendants possessed the handguns in the manner described by the judge. In short, the instructions plainly directed the jury to consider all the circumstances tending to support or contradict the inference that all four occupants of the car had possession of the two loaded handguns and to decide the matter for itself without regard to how much evidence the defendants introduced.

Our cases considering the validity of permissive statutory presumptions such as the one involved here have rested on an evaluation of the presumption as applied to the record before the Court. None suggests that a court should pass on the constitutionality of this kind of statute "on its face." It was error for the Court of Appeals to make such a determination in this case.

As applied to the facts of this case, the presumption of possession is entirely rational. Notwithstanding the Court of Appeals' analysis, respondents were not "hitchhikers or other casual passengers," and the guns were neither "a few inches in length" nor "out of [respondents'] sight." The argument against possession by any of the respondents was predicated solely on the fact that the guns were in Jane Doe's pocketbook. But several circumstances—which, not surprisingly, her counsel repeatedly emphasized in his questions and his argument—made it highly improbable that she was the sole custodian of those weapons.

"Accordingly, you would be warranted in returning a verdict of guilt against the defendants or defendant if you find the defendants or defendant was in possession of a machine gun and the other weapons and that the fact of possession was proven to you by the People beyond a reasonable doubt, and an element of such proof is the reasonable presumption of illegal possession of a machine gun or the presumption of illegal possession of firearms, as I have just before explained to you." *Id.*, at 746.

[20] "Our Penal Law also provides that the presence in an automobile of any machine gun or of any handgun or firearm which is loaded is presumptive evidence of their unlawful possession.

"In other words, these presumptions or this latter presumption upon proof of the presence of the machine gun and the hand weapons, you may infer and draw a conclusion that such prohibited weapon was possessed by each of the defendants who occupied the automobile at the time when such instruments were found. The presumption or presumptions is effective only so long as there is no substantial evidence contradicting the conclusion flowing from the presumption, and the presumption is said to disappear when such contradictory evidence is adduced." *Id.*, at 743.

"The presumption or presumptions which I discussed with the jury relative to the drugs or weapons in this case need not be rebutted by affirmative proof or affirmative evidence but may be rebutted by any evidence or lack of evidence in the case." *Id.*, at 760.

Even if it was reasonable to conclude that she had placed the guns in her purse before the car was stopped by police, the facts strongly suggest that Jane Doe was not the only person able to exercise dominion over them. The two guns were too large to be concealed in her handbag. The bag was consequently open, and part of one of the guns was in plain view, within easy access of the driver of the car and even, perhaps, of the other two respondents who were riding in the rear seat.

Moreover, it is highly improbable that the loaded guns belonged to Jane Doe or that she was solely responsible for their being in her purse. As a 16-year-old girl in the company of three adult men she was the least likely of the four to be carrying one, let alone two, heavy handguns. It is far more probable that she relied on the pocketknife found in her brassiere for any necessary self-protection. Under these circumstances, it was not unreasonable for her counsel to argue and for the jury to infer that when the car was halted for speeding, the other passengers in the car anticipated the risk of a search and attempted to conceal their weapons in a pocketbook in the front seat. The inference is surely more likely than the notion that these weapons were the sole property of the 16-year-old girl.

Under these circumstances, the jury would have been entirely reasonable in rejecting the suggestion—which, incidentally, defense counsel did not even advance in their closing arguments to the jury—the handguns were in the sole possession of Jane Doe. Assuming that the jury did reject it, the case is tantamount to one in which the guns were lying on the floor or the seat of the car in the plain view of the three other occupants of the automobile. In such a case, it is surely rational to infer that each of the respondents was fully aware of the presence of the guns and had both the ability and the intent to exercise dominion and control over the weapons. The application of the statutory presumption in this case therefore comports with the standard laid down in *Tot v. United States*, 319 U.S., at 467, 63 S.Ct., at 1244, and restated in *Leary v. United States, supra*, 395 U.S., at 36, 89 S.Ct., at 1548. For there is a "rational connection" between the basic facts that the prosecution proved and the ultimate fact presumed, and the latter is "more likely than not to flow from" the former.

Respondents argue, however, that the validity of the New York presumption must be judged by a "reasonable doubt" test rather than the "more likely than not" standard employed in *Leary*. Under the more stringent test, it is argued that a statutory presumption must be rejected unless the evidence necessary to invoke the inference is sufficient for a rational jury to find the inferred fact beyond a reasonable doubt. See *Barnes v. United States*, 412 U.S., at 842–843, 93 S.Ct., at 2361–2362. Respondents' argument again overlooks the distinction between a permissive presumption on which the prosecution is entitled to rely as one not necessarily sufficient part of its proof and a mandatory presumption which the jury must accept even if it is the sole evidence of an element of the offense.

In the latter situation, since the prosecution bears the burden of establishing guilt, it may not rest its case entirely on a presumption unless the fact proved is sufficient to support the inference of guilt beyond a reasonable doubt. But in the former situation, the prosecution may rely on all of the evidence in the record to meet the reasonable-doubt standard. There is no more reason to require a permissive statutory presumption to meet a reasonable-doubt standard before it may be permitted to play any part in a trial than there is to require that degree of probative force for other relevant evidence before it may be admitted. As long as it is clear that the presumption is not the sole and sufficient basis for a finding of guilt, it need only satisfy the test described in *Leary*.

The permissive presumption, as used in this case, satisfied the *Leary* test. And, as already noted, the New York Court of Appeals has concluded that the record as a whole was sufficient to establish guilt beyond a reasonable doubt.

The judgment is reversed.

■ MR. CHIEF JUSTICE BURGER, concurring.

I join fully in the Court's opinion reversing the judgment under review. In the necessarily detailed step-by-step analysis of the legal issues, the central and controlling facts of a case often can become lost. The "underbrush" of finely tuned legal analysis of complex issues tends to bury the facts.

On this record, the jury could readily have reached the same result without benefit of the challenged statutory presumption; here it reached what was rather obviously a compromise verdict. Even without relying on evidence that two people had been seen placing something in the car trunk shortly before respondents occupied it, and that a machine gun and a package of heroin were soon after found in that trunk, the jury apparently decided that it was enough to hold the passengers to knowledge of the two handguns which were in such plain view that the officer could see them from outside the car. Reasonable jurors could reasonably find that what the officer could see from outside, the passengers within the car could hardly miss seeing. Courts have long held that in the practical business of deciding cases the factfinders, not unlike negotiators, are permitted the luxury of verdicts reached by compromise.

■ MR. JUSTICE POWELL, with whom MR. JUSTICE BRENNAN, MR. JUSTICE STEWART and MR. JUSTICE MARSHALL join, dissenting.

* * *

In sum, our decisions uniformly have recognized that due process requires more than merely that the prosecution be put to its proof. In addition, the Constitution restricts the court in its charge to the jury by requiring that, when particular factual inferences are recommended to the jury, those factual inferences be accurate reflections of what history, common sense, and experience tell us about the relations between events in our society. Generally, this due process rule has been articulated as requiring that the truth of the inferred fact be more likely than not whenever the premise for the inference is true. Thus, to be constitutional a presumption must be at least more likely than not true.

In the present case, the jury was told:

Our Penal Law also provides that the presence in an automobile of any machine gun or of any handgun or firearm which is loaded is presumptive evidence of their unlawful possession. In other words, [under] these presumptions or this latter presumption upon proof of the presence of the machine gun and the hand weapons, you may infer and draw a conclusion that such prohibited weapon was possessed by each of the defendants who occupied the automobile at the time when such instruments were found. The presumption or presumptions is effective only so long as there is no substantial evidence contradicting the conclusion flowing from the presumption, and the presumption is said to disappear when such contradictory evidence is adduced.

Undeniably, the presumption charged in this case encouraged the jury to draw a particular factual inference regardless of any other evidence presented: to infer that respondents possessed the weapons found in the automobile "upon proof of the presence of the machine gun and the hand weapon" and proof that respondents "occupied the automobile at the time such instruments were found." I believe that the presumption thus charged was unconstitutional because it did not fairly reflect what common sense and experience tell us about passengers in automobiles and the possession of handguns. People present in automobiles where there are weapons simply are not "more likely than not" the possessors of those weapons.

Under New York law, "to possess" is "to have physical possession or otherwise to exercise dominion or control over tangible property." N.Y.Penal Law § 10.00(8) (McKinney 1975). Plainly, the mere presence of an individual in an automobile—without more—does not indicate that he exercises "dominion or control over" everything within it. As the Court of Appeals noted, there are countless situations in which individuals are invited as guests into vehicles the contents of which they know nothing about, much less have control over. Similarly, those who invite others into their automobile do not generally search them to determine what they may have on their person; nor do they insist that any handguns be identified and placed within reach of the occupants of the automobile. Indeed, handguns are particularly susceptible to concealment and therefore are less likely than are other objects to be observed by those in an automobile.

In another context, this Court has been particularly hesitant to infer possession from mere presence in a location, noting that "[p]resence is relevant and admissible evidence in a trial on a possession charge; but absent some showing of the defendant's function at the [illegal] still, its connection with possession is too tenuous to permit a reasonable inference of guilt—'the inference of the one from proof of the other is arbitrary. . . .' *Tot v. United States*, 319 U.S. 463, 467, 63 S.Ct. 1241, 1245, 87 L.Ed. 1519." *United States v. Romano*, 382 U.S., at 141, 86 S.Ct., at 282. We should be even more hesitant to uphold the inference of possession of a handgun from mere presence in an automobile, in light of common experience concerning automobiles and handguns. Because the specific factual inference recommended to the jury in this case is not one that is supported by the general experience of our society, I cannot say that the presumption charged is "more likely than not" to be true. Accordingly, respondents' due process rights were violated by the presumption's use.

As I understand it, the Court today does not contend that in general those who are present in automobiles are more likely than not to possess any gun contained within their vehicles. It argues, however, that the nature of the presumption here involved requires that we look, not only to the immediate facts upon which the jury was encouraged to base its inference, but to the other facts "proved" by the prosecution as well. The Court suggests that this is the proper approach when reviewing what it calls "permissive" presumptions because the jury was urged "to consider all the circumstances tending to support or contradict the inference."

It seems to me that the Court mischaracterizes the function of the presumption charged in this case. As it acknowledges was the case in Romano, supra, the "instruction authorized conviction even if the jury disbelieved all of the testimony except the proof of presence" in the automobile.[7] The Court nevertheless relies on all of the evidence introduced by the prosecution and argues that the "permissive" presumption could not have prejudiced defendants. The possibility that the jury disbelieved all of this evidence, and relied on the presumption, is simply ignored.

---

[7] In commending the presumption to the jury, the court gave no instruction that would have required a finding of possession to be based on anything more than mere presence in the automobile. Thus, the jury was not instructed that it should infer that respondents possessed the handguns only if it found that the guns were too large to be concealed in Jane Doe's handbag, *ante*, at 2227–2228; that the guns accordingly were in the plain view of respondents, *ibid.*; that the weapons were within "easy access of the driver of the car and even, perhaps, of the other two respondents who were riding in the rear seat," *ibid.*; that it was unlikely that Jane Doe was solely responsible for the placement of the weapons in her purse, ibid.; or that the case was "tantamount to one in which the guns were lying on the floor or the seat of the car in the plain view of the three other occupants of the automobile."

I agree that the circumstances relied upon by the Court in determining the plausibility of the presumption charged in this case would have made it reasonable for the jury to "infer that each of the respondents was fully aware of the presence of the guns and had both the ability and the intent to exercise dominion and control over the weapons." But the jury was told that it could conclude that respondents possessed the weapons found therein from proof of the mere fact of respondents' presence in the automobile. For all we know, the jury rejected all of the prosecution's evidence concerning the location and origin of the guns, and based its conclusion that respondents possessed the weapons solely upon its belief that respondents had been present in the automobile.[8] For purposes of reviewing the constitutionality of the presumption at issue here, we must assume that this was the case.

* * *

In sum, it seems to me that the Court today ignores the teaching of our prior decisions. By speculating about what the jury may have done with the factual inference thrust upon it, the Court in effect assumes away the inference altogether, constructing a rule that permits the use of any inference—no matter how irrational in itself—provided that otherwise there is sufficient evidence in the record to support a finding of guilt. Applying this novel analysis to the present case, the Court upholds the use of a presumption that it makes no effort to defend in isolation. In substance, the Court—applying an unarticulated harmless-error standard—simply finds that the respondents were guilty as charged. They may well have been but rather than acknowledging this rationale, the Court seems to have made new law with respect to presumptions that could seriously jeopardize a defendant's right to a fair trial. Accordingly, I dissent.

NOTES AND QUESTIONS

1. Why does the Court view permissive presumptions differently than mandatory or rebuttable ones? Why does Justice Stevens conclude in *Allen* that a permissive presumption should be judged in light of the facts in the record?

2. Does Justice Powell's dissenting opinion disagree with the standard employed by the majority or the application of the standard?

---

[8] The Court is therefore mistaken in its conclusion that, because "respondents were not 'hitchhikers or other casual passengers,' and the guns were neither 'a few inches in length' nor 'out of [respondents'] sight,' " reference to these possibilities is inappropriate in considering the constitutionality of the presumption as charged in this case. *Ante,* at 2227. To be sure, respondents' challenge is to the presumption as charged to the jury in this case. But in assessing its application here, we are not free, as the Court apparently believes, to disregard the possibility that the jury may have disbelieved all other evidence supporting an inference of possession. The jury may have concluded that respondents—like hitchhikers—had only an incidental relationship to the auto in which they were traveling, or that, contrary to some of the testimony at trial, the weapons were indeed out of respondents' sight.

3. How does one determine into which category a particular presumption falls? Consider the following presumption:

If there was at the time [of the accident] an alcohol concentration of 0.10 or more, it shall be presumed that the person was under the influence of alcohol. Such a presumption is rebuttable . . .

"Presumption" or "presumed" means that the trier of fact must find the existence of the fact presumed unless and until evidence is introduced which would support a finding of its nonexistence.

See State v. Leverett, 245 Mont. 124, 799 P.2d 119 (1990).

CHAPTER 3

THE POWER TO CREATE CRIMES AND ITS LIMITATIONS

INTRODUCTION

In the broadest sense, both civil and criminal law are attempts to create and maintain "the good society." The law of torts, the law of contracts, and every other branch of civil law prohibit or require specific conduct within the social community. For example, tort law demands that citizens behave reasonably to avoid injuring others. Contract law commands citizens to honor the commitments pledged in contracts. Failure to live up to these requirements subjects the citizen to suit in the civil courts and to the imposition of civil sanctions, most commonly, paying money damages to an injured party. Thus, civil law governs the issues that arise between individual parties over private rights. In a typical civil case, suit is brought by the injured party for damage to that party's personal rights, person, or property. The injured party (the plaintiff) seeks some sort of compensation (usually monetary) for the injury to that party's person or property.

As civil law does, criminal law also prohibits or requires specified conduct. Some of the commands of the criminal law are expressed as affirmative requirements to "file your income tax return," or "take care of your children." But most criminal law commands are prohibitions of conduct—"Do not murder, rape, or rob." Criminal law thus encompasses principles of right and wrong as well as the principle that wrong will result in penalty. A criminal case is brought by the government for violation or injury to public rights, and an individual who violates criminal laws has damaged the rights of the public as a whole, regardless of the status of any individual victim.

Of course, those individual victims may pursue civil suits because a single act may give rise to both criminal and civil cases. The most famous example is the litigation surrounding O.J. Simpson. In criminal proceedings, Simpson was initially tried and acquitted of two charges of murder. The families of the victims then brought and prevailed in a civil suit against Simpson for wrongful death. (The constitutional prohibition against double jeopardy precludes multiple criminal prosecutions for the same offense, but has no application to civil suits.)

Thus, the most fundamental difference between the two branches of law is that civil law normally focuses on compelling a person to compensate an individual victim for any harm suffered, whereas criminal law uses punishment as a means of controlling the behavior of citizens. (Conviction of a crime carries a penalty of imprisonment or a fine paid to the government rather than to a particular victim.)

181

A. SOURCES OF THE CRIMINAL LAW

1. THE COMMON LAW

Penn: I desire you would let me know by what law it is you prosecute me, and upon what law you ground my indictment.

Rec.: Upon the common-law.

Penn: Where is that common law?

Rec.: You must not think that I am able to run up so many years, and over so many adjudged cases, which we call common law, to answer your curiosity.

Penn: This answer I am sure is very short of my question, for if it be common, it should not be so hard to produce.

Rec.: The question is, whether you are Guilty of this Indictment?

Penn: The question is not, whether I am Guilty of this Indictment, but whether this Indictment be legal. It is too general and imperfect an answer, to say it is the common law, unless we knew both where and what it is. For where there is no law, there is no transgression; and that law which is not in being, is so far from being common, that it is no law at all.

Rec.: You are an impertinent fellow, will you teach the court what the law is? It is "*Lex non scripta*," that which many have studied 30 or 40 years to know, and would you have me tell you in a moment?

Penn: Certainly, if the common law be so hard to understand it is far from being common.

Trial of William Penn, 6 How.St.Trials 951, 958 (1670).

———

Shaw v. Director of Public Prosecutions
2 House of Lords, 1961.
2 W.L.R. 897, 45 Cr.App.R. 113, 2 All E.R. 446.

[The appellant, Frederick Charles Shaw, pleaded not guilty at the Central Criminal Court, before Judge Maxwell Turner and a jury, on an indictment containing the following three counts: (1) "Conspiracy to corrupt public morals. Particulars of Offence. . . . conspired with certain persons who inserted advertisements in issues of a magazine entitled 'Ladies' Directory' numbered 7, 7 revised, 8, 9, 10 and a supplement thereto, and with certain other persons whose names are unknown, by means of the said magazine and the said advertisements to induce readers thereof to resort to the said advertisers for the purposes of fornication and of taking part in or witnessing other disgusting and immoral acts and exhibitions, with intent thereby to debauch and corrupt the morals as well of youth as of divers other liege subjects of Our Lady The Queen and to raise and create in their minds inordinate and lustful desires"; (2) living on the earnings of prostitution, contrary to section 30 of the Sexual Offences Act, 1956; and (3) publishing an obscene article, the Ladies' Directory, contrary to section 2 of the Obscene Publications Act, 1959.

The Ladies' Directory was a booklet of some 28 pages, most of which were taken up with the names and addresses of women who were prostitutes, together with a number of photographs of nude female figures, and the matter published left no doubt that the advertisers could be got in touch with at the telephone numbers given and were offering their services for sexual intercourse and, in some cases, for the practice of sexual perversions.

The appellant did not give evidence, but he had admitted publication and his avowed object in publishing was to assist prostitutes to ply their trade when, as a result of the Street Offences Act, 1959, they were no longer able to solicit in the streets. There was evidence that on October 22, 1959, prior to publication, he had taken advice as to whether publication would be legal, and had shown a police officer at Scotland Yard the first issue of the booklet and asked him if it would be all right to publish; apparently he had arranged that the Director of Public Prosecutions should see a copy. There was also evidence that he had assured the owner of a kiosk, whom he had asked to sell the booklet, that it would not be published unless it was legal. When later he was asked by a police officer if he was the Shaw who had published the Ladies' Directory he said: "Yes," and "I publish this and distribute it for 5s. each to help the prostitutes who advertise in it," but would not state how much he charged for advertisements, saying that he ran it as a business and that his solicitor thought it was all right. There was evidence that advertisers paid 25 guineas for the front cover, 15 guineas for the back cover, and inside, 10 guineas for a full-page advertisement, 8 guineas for a half-page photograph, and 2 guineas for a small printed advertisement; the amount paid by prostitutes advertising in issue No. 9 was calculated to be £250 19s., but there was no evidence as to how much of that was profit. The appellant charged 2s. 6d. to sellers for the booklet and it was sold to the public for 5s. Evidence was given by five prostitutes that they had paid for the advertisements out of their earnings as prostitutes, that the advertisements were good at bringing clients in and as to the ages of the persons resorting to them; they also gave evidence as to the meaning of certain abbreviations and about the sexual perversions referred to in their advertisements, and there was police evidence as to the objects found at their addresses.

After the close of the evidence for the prosecution, counsel for the appellant submitted that the conspiracy alleged in count 1 disclosed no offence. . . .

Judge Maxwell Turner ruled that a conspiracy to debauch and corrupt public morals was a common law misdemeanour and was indictable at common law and that the particulars of the offences set out in count 1 were particulars of such a conspiracy, if the jury found the facts alleged to be true.

The jury convicted the appellant on all three counts and he was sentenced to nine months' imprisonment.]

[*Opinion of the Court of Criminal Appeal*] The appellant appealed against his conviction on all three counts to the Court of Criminal Appeal. On count 1 it was contended, in effect, that there was no such offence at common law as a conspiracy to corrupt public morals unless the acts alleged were offences against the criminal law or amounted to a civil wrong and that, as the acts alleged in the indictment were not in either of those classes, the conspiracy alleged disclosed no offence. . . .

Conspiracy is an offence which takes many different forms but in the present appeal the matter was greatly simplified when Mr. Buzzard, on behalf of the prosecution, made it clear that the form of conspiracy, which he had alleged at the trial and to which he adhered, was a conspiracy to commit an unlawful act, and not a conspiracy to commit a lawful act by unlaw means. He reserved the right to contend, should it be necessary, that a conspiracy to corrupt the morals of a particular individual was an indictable offence by reason of the conspiracy, even if such corruption if done by one person would not be an offence. The unlawful act which he alleged was said to be a common law misdemeanour, namely, the corruption of public morals. His proposition was two-fold: at common law any act calculated or intended to corrupt the morals of the public or a portion thereof in general, as opposed to the morals of a particular individual or individuals, is indictable as a substantive offence. Secondly, an act calculated or intended to outrage public decency is also indictable as a substantive offence. Both parts of this proposition were naturally contested by Mr. Rees Davies and the main issue before us on this first count is whether the first of Mr. Buzzard's propositions is well-founded.

We were referred to a large number of cases, but before alluding to any of them in detail we may usefully refer to the speech of Lord Sumner in Bowman v. Secular Society Ltd. in which is set out an illuminating survey of this branch of the law from the beginning of the seventeenth century. He said: "The time of Charles II was one of notorious laxity both in faith and morals, and for a time it seemed as if the old safeguards were in abeyance or had been swept away. Immorality and irreligion were cognisable in the Ecclesiastical Courts, but spiritual censures had lost their sting and those civil courts were extinct, which had specially dealt with such matters viewed as offences against civil order. The Court of King's Bench stepped in to fill the gap."

The first reported occasion on which the Court of King's Bench thus stepped in appears to be Rex v. Sidley. Amongst other acts alleged against Sir Charles Sidley were his exposure of his naked body upon a balcony in Covent Garden before a large gathering of people and making water on the persons below. In addition he was said to have thrown down bottles upon such persons' heads. This latter conduct was plainly within the jurisdiction of the Court of King's Bench but there was evidently an issue whether the other conduct was such as could be dealt with in that court. In the short report of the case there appears the statement that "this court is custos morum of all the King's subjects and that it is high time to punish such profane conduct." In 1708, in Reg. v. Read, the court expressed a different view when considering a charge of publishing an obscene libel, but the judgment in the defendant's favour was only a "judgment nisi," that is, a provisional judgment. Not long afterwards the case of Rex v. Curl came before the Court of King's Bench, in which the charge against the accused was that of publishing an obscene libel. Reliance was naturally placed on *Read's* case by defending counsel, but the Attorney-General's argument to the contrary prevailed: "What I insist upon is, that this is an offence at common law, as it tends to corrupt the morals of the King's subjects, and is against the peace of the King. . . . I do not insist that every immoral act is indictable, such as telling a lie, or the like; but if it is destructive of morality in general, if it does, or may, affect all the King's subjects, it then is an offence of a public nature." Lord Raymond C.J., in giving judgment, said: ". . . if it reflects on religion, virtue, or morality, if it tends to disturb the civil order of society, I think it is a temporal offence." After the case had been adjourned the court "gave it as their unanimous opinion, that this was a temporal offence. They said it was plain that the force used in *Sidley's* case was but a small ingredient in the judgment of the court who fined him £2,000. And if the force was all they went upon there was no occasion to talk of the court's being censor morum of the King's subjects. They said that if *Read's* case was to be adjudged, they should rule it otherwise: and therefore in this case they gave judgment for the King." * * *

In our opinion, having regard to the long line of cases to which we have been referred, it is an established principle of common law that conduct calculated or intended to corrupt public morals (as opposed to the morals of a particular individual) is an indictable misdemeanour. As the reports show, the conduct to which that principle is applicable may vary considerably, but the principle itself does not, and in our view the facts of the present case fall plainly within it.

The contrary view put forward by Mr. Rees Davies may be summarised as follows: He accepted for the purposes of his argument the claim of the Court of King's Bench to be custos morum but he contended that acting in that role the court had, so to speak, from time to time declared particular conduct to be an offence, thereby creating an offence rather than applying existing law to particular facts. He went on to contend that Parliament in the last 100 years had concerned itself with legislation on issues of morality, decency and the like, that such legislation must be taken to be in effect a comprehensive code, and that there is no longer any occasion for the court to create new offences in its capacity as custos morum. We are unable to agree with this argument, which fails to give sufficient weight to the repeated statements of the established principle of common law to which we have already referred. The courts in the relevant cases were not creating new offences or making new law: they were applying existing law to new facts.

It is perhaps worth adding that the principle itself is not in any way affected or qualified by the fact that in the course of time public opinion as expressed in juries' verdicts may change in regard to matters of public decency and morality. This was emphasized by Lord Sumner in *Bowman's* case: "The fact that opinion grounded on experience has moved one way does not in law preclude the possibility of its moving on fresh experience in the other; nor does it bind succeeding generations, when conditions have again changed. After all, the question whether a given opinion is a danger to society is a question of the times and is a question of fact." * * *

In the present case the issue involved in this first count was fully argued in the absence of a jury, and the judge's ruling was in the following terms: "In my opinion a conspiracy to debauch and corrupt public morals is a common law misdemeanour and is indictable at common law." We agree with this ruling. If the principle to which we have referred is part of the common law of this country, it must follow that a conspiracy of the type alleged is an indictable offence.

■ [Opinion of the HOUSE OF LORDS.]

■ VISCOUNT SIMONDS. My Lords . . . the first count in the indictment is "Conspiracy to corrupt public morals," and the particulars of offence will have sufficiently appeared. I am concerned only to assert what was vigorously denied by counsel for the appellant, that such an offence is known to the common law, and that it was open to the jury to find on the facts of this case that the appellant was guilty of such an offence. I must say categorically that, if it were not so, Her Majesty's courts would strangely have failed in their duty as servants and guardians of the common law. Need I say, my Lords, that I am no advocate of the right of the judges to create new criminal offences? I will repeat well-known words: "Amongst many other points of happiness and freedom which your Majesty's subjects have enjoyed there is none which they have accounted more dear and precious than this, to be guided and governed by certain rules of law which giveth both to the head and members that which of right belongeth to them and not by any arbitrary or uncertain form of government." These words are as true today as they were in the seventeenth century and command the allegiance of us all. But I am at a loss to understand how it can be said either that the law does not recognise a conspiracy to corrupt public morals or that, though there may not be an exact precedent for such a conspiracy as this case reveals, it does not fall fairly within the general words by which it is described. I do not propose to examine all the relevant authorities. That will be done by my noble and learned friend. The fallacy in the argument that was addressed to us lay in the attempt to exclude from the scope of general words acts well calculated to corrupt public morals just because they had not been committed or had not been brought to the notice of the court before. It is not thus that the common law has developed. We are perhaps more accustomed to hear this matter discussed upon the question whether such and such a transaction is contrary to public policy. At once the controversy arises. On the one hand it is said that it is not possible in the twentieth century for the court to create a new head of public policy, on the other it is said that this is but a new example of a well-established head. In the sphere of criminal law I entertain no doubt that there remains in the courts of law a residual power to enforce the supreme and fundamental purpose of the law, to conserve not only the safety and order but also the moral welfare of the State, and that it is their duty to guard it against attacks which may be the more insidious because they are novel and unprepared for. That is the broad head (call it public policy if you wish) within which the present indictment falls. It matters little what label is given to the offending act. To one of your Lordships it may appear an affront to public decency, to another, considering that it may succeed in its obvious intention of provoking libidinous desires, it will seem a corruption of public morals. Yet others may deem it aptly described as the creation of a public mischief or the undermining of moral conduct. The same act will not in all ages be regarded in the same way. The law must be related to the changing standards of life, not yielding to every shifting impulse of the popular will but having regard to fundamental assessments of human values and the purposes of society. Today a denial of the fundamental Christian doctrine, which in past centuries would have been regarded by the ecclesiastical courts as heresy and by the common law as blasphemy, will no longer be an offence if the decencies of controversy are observed. When Lord Mansfield, speaking long after the Star Chamber had been abolished, said that the Court of King's Bench was the custos morum of the people and had the superintendency of offences contra bonos mores, he was asserting, as I now assert, that there is in that court a residual power, where no statute has yet intervened to supersede the common law, to superintend those offences which are prejudicial to the public welfare. Such occasions will be rare, for Parliament has not been slow to legislate when attention has been sufficiently aroused. But gaps remain and will always remain since no one can foresee every way in which the wickedness of man may disrupt the order of society. Let me take a single instance . . . Let it be supposed that at some future, perhaps, early date, homosexual practices between adult consenting males are no longer a crime. Would it not be an offence if even without obscenity, such practices were publicly advocated and encouraged by pamphlet and advertisement? Or must we wait until Parliament finds time to deal with such conduct? I say, my Lords, that if the common law is powerless in such an event, then we should no longer do her reverence. But I say that her hand is still powerful and that it is for Her Majesty's judges to play the part which Lord Mansfield pointed out to them.

I have so far paid little regard to the fact that the charge here is of conspiracy. But, if I have correctly described the conduct of the appellant, it is an irresistible inference that a conspiracy between him and others to do such acts is indictable. * * *

I will say a final word upon an aspect of the case which was urged by counsel. No one doubts—and I have put it in the forefront of this opinion—that certainty is a most desirable attribute of the criminal and civil law alike. Nevertheless there are matters which must ultimately depend on the opinion of a jury. In the civil law I will take an example which comes perhaps nearest to the criminal law—the tort of negligence. It is for a jury to decide not only whether the defendant has committed the act complained of but whether in doing it he has fallen short of the standard of care which the circumstances require. Till their verdict is given it is uncertain what the law requires. The same branch of the civil law supplies another interesting analogy. For, though in the Factory Acts and the regulations made under them, the measure of care required of an employer is defined in the greatest detail, no one supposes that he may not be guilty of negligence in a manner unforeseen and unprovided for. That will be a matter for the jury to decide. There are still, as has recently been said, "unravished remnants of the common law."

So in the case of a charge of conspiracy to corrupt public morals the uncertainty that necessarily arises from the vagueness of general words can only be resolved by the opinion of twelve chosen men and women. I am content to leave it to them.

The appeal on both counts should, in my opinion, be dismissed.

■ LORD REID [In dissent] * * *

In my opinion there is no such general offence known to the law as conspiracy to corrupt public morals. Undoubtedly there is an offence of criminal conspiracy and undoubtedly it is of fairly wide scope. In my view its scope cannot be determined without having regard first to the history of the matter and then to the broad general principles which have generally been thought to underlie our system of law and government and in particular our system of criminal law.

It appears to be generally accepted that the offence of criminal conspiracy was the creature of the Star Chamber. So far as I am able to judge the summary in Kenny's Outlines of Criminal Law, section 59, 17th ed., p. 88, is a fair one. There it is said that the criminal side of conspiracy was "emphasised by the Star Chamber which recognised its possibilities as an engine of government and moulded it into a substantive offence of wide scope whose attractions were such that its principles were gradually adopted by the common law courts. . . ." The Star Chamber perhaps had more merits than its detractors will admit but its methods and principles were superseded and what it did is of no authority today. The question is how far the common law courts in fact went in borrowing from it. * * *

There are two competing views. One is that conspiring to corrupt public morals is only one facet of a still more general offence, conspiracy to effect public mischief; and that, like the categories of negligence, the categories of public mischief are never closed. The other is that, whatever may have been done two or three centuries ago, we ought not now to extend the doctrine further than it has already been carried by the common law courts. Of course I do not mean that it should only be applied in circumstances precisely similar to those in some decided case. Decisions are always authority for other cases which are reasonably analogous and are not properly distinguishable. But we ought not to extend the doctrine to new fields.

I agree [with the viewpoint that]: "There appear to be great theoretical objections to any general rule that agreement may make punishable that which ought not to be punished in the absence of agreement." And I think, or at least I hope, that it is now established that the courts cannot create new offences by individuals. So far at least I have the authority of Lord Goddard C.J. in delivering the opinion of the court in *Newland*: "The dictum [in Rex v. Higgins] was that all offences of a public nature, that is, all such acts or attempts as tend to the prejudice of the public are indictable, but no other member of the court stated the law in such wide terms. It is the breadth of that dictum that was so strongly criticised by Sir Fitzjames Stephen in the passage in his History of the Criminal Law (vol. 3, p. 359) . . . and also by Dr. Stallybrass in the Law Quarterly Review, vol. 34, p. 183. In effect it would leave it to the judges to declare new crimes and enable them to hold anything which they considered prejudicial to the community to be a misdemeanour. However beneficial that might have been in days when Parliament met seldom, or at least only at long intervals it surely is now the province of the legislature and not of the judiciary to create new criminal offences." Every argument against creating new offences by an individual appears to me to be equally valid against creating new offences by a combination of individuals. * * *

Finally I must advert to the consequences of holding that this very general offence exists. It has always been thought to be of primary importance that our law, and particularly our criminal law, should be certain: that a man should be able to know what conduct is and what is not criminal, particularly when heavy penalties are involved. Some suggestion was made that it does not matter if this offence is very wide: no one would ever prosecute and if they did no jury would ever convict if the breach was venial. Indeed, the suggestion goes even further: that the meaning and application of the words "deprave" and "corrupt" (the traditional words in obscene libel now enacted in the 1959 Act) or the words "debauch" and "corrupt" in this indictment ought to be entirely for the jury, so that any conduct of this kind is criminal if in the end a jury think it so. In other words, you cannot tell what is criminal except by guessing what view a jury will take, and juries' views may vary and may change with the passing of time. Normally, the meaning of words is a question of law for the court. For example, it is not left to a jury to determine the meaning of negligence: they have to consider on evidence and on their own knowledge a much more specific question—Would a reasonable man have done what this man did? I know that in obscene libel the jury has great latitude but I think that it is an understatement to say that this has not been found wholly satisfactory. If the trial judge's charge in the present case was right, if a jury is entitled to water down the strong words "deprave," "corrupt" or "debauch" so as merely to mean lead astray morally, then it seems to me that the court has transferred to the jury the whole of its functions as censor morum, the law will be whatever any jury may happen to think it ought to be, and this branch of the law will have lost all the certainty which we rightly prize in other branches of our law.

■ [Opinions of LORDS TUCKER, MORRIS OF BORTH-Y-GEST, and HODSON omitted.]

Appeal dismissed.

NOTES

1. For an excellent analysis of the problems raised by the *Shaw* case, see Ian Brownlie & D.G.T. Williams, *Judicial Legislation In Criminal Law*, 42 Can. Bar Rev. 561 (1964). *See also* H.L.A. HART, LAW, LIBERTY, AND MORALITY (1963); G.H. Gordon, *Crimes Without Laws?*, 11 Jurid. Rev. 214 (1966). At one point *Shaw* stated that not "every immoral act is indictable, such as telling a lie, or the like; but if it is destructive of morality in general, if it does, or may affect all the King's subjects, it then is an offence of a public nature." Could government officials be prosecuted if they lied about weapons of mass destruction justifying a "pre-emptive war"?

2. Consider the following statute:

> If any person, with intent to coerce, intimidate, or harass any person, shall use a computer or computer network to communicate obscene, vulgar, profane, lewd, lascivious, or indecent language or make any suggestion or proposal of an obscene nature, or threaten any illegal or immoral act, he shall be guilty of a misdemeanor punishable by one year's confinement.

Va. Code. Ann. § 18.2–152.7:1.

> The statute was applied in Airhart v. Commonwealth, Rec. No. 1219–05–2, 2007 WL 88747 (Va. 2007), where a male and female college student corresponded by instant messaging on their

computers. In April 2004, the woman requested a study guide from the defendant, who responded: "If you fuck me, I'll give you your study guide." The woman was upset and frightened, but did not make a complaint to the police. In August 2004, the defendant sent an e-mail telling the woman to leave his roommate alone, and called her an "Italian whore." The defendant also repeatedly wrote "fuck you" in the message. The defendant was convicted of harassment by computer for the August communication. On appeal, the conviction was reversed because "while offensive and coarse, use of the words was a method to show his anger, contempt, or disgust with the victim." Thus the words failed to meet the definition of obscene, which requires an appeal to a prurient interest.

2. STATUTES AND JUDICIAL CONSTRUCTION

The judicial function is that of interpretation; it does not include the power of amendment under the guise of interpretation.

Justice Sutherland, in W. Coast Hotel Co. v. Parrish, 300 U.S. 379, 404, 57 S.Ct. 578, 81 L.Ed. 703 (1937).

Caminetti v. U.S.;
Diggs v. U.S.;
Hays v. U.S.

Supreme Court of the United States, 1916.
242 U.S. 470, 37 S.Ct. 192, 61 L.Ed. 442.

■ MR. JUSTICE DAY delivered the opinion of the court:

These three cases were argued together, and may be disposed of in a single opinion. In each of the cases there was a conviction and sentence for violation of the so-called White Slave Traffic Act of June 25, 1910 (36 Stat. at L. 825, chap. 395, Comp.Stat.1913, § 8813),[1] the judgments were

---

[1] The White Slave Traffic Act, U.S.C.A., Title 18, § 2421, currently provides as follows:

Whoever knowingly transports in interstate or foreign commerce, or in the District of Columbia or in any Territory or Possession of the United States, any woman or girl for the purpose of prostitution or debauchery, or for any other immoral purpose, or with the intent and purpose to induce, entice, or compel such woman or girl to become a prostitute or to give herself up to debauchery, or to engage in any other immoral practice; or

— Whoever knowingly procures or obtains any ticket or tickets, or any form of transportation or evidence of the right thereto, to be used by any woman or girl in interstate or foreign commerce, or in the District of Columbia or any Territory or Possession of the United States, in going to any place for the purpose of prostitution or debauchery, or for any other immoral purpose, or with the intent or purpose on the part of such person to induce, entice, or compel her to give herself up to the practice of prostitution, or to give herself up to debauchery, or any other immoral practice, whereby any such woman or girl shall be transported in interstate or foreign commerce, or in the District of Columbia or any Territory or Possession of the United States." [In 1986 the Mann Act was amended to read:

Whoever knowingly transports any individual in interstate or foreign commerce, or in any Territory or Possession of the United States, with intent that such individual engage in prostitution, or in any sexual activity for which any person can be charged

affirmed by the circuit courts of appeals, and writs of certiorari bring the cases here.

In the *Caminetti* Case, the petitioner was indicted in the United States district court for the northern district of California, upon the 6th day of May, 1913, for alleged violations of the act. The indictment was in four counts, the first of which charged him with transporting and causing to be transported, and aiding and assisting in obtaining transportation for a certain woman from Sacramento, California, to Reno, Nevada, in interstate commerce, for the purpose of debauchery, and for an immoral purpose, to wit, that the aforesaid woman should be and become his mistress and concubine. A verdict of not guilty was returned as to the other three counts of this indictment. As to the first count, defendant was found guilty and sentenced to imprisonment for eighteen months and to pay a fine of $1,500. Upon writ of error to the United States circuit court of appeals for the ninth circuit, that judgment was affirmed. . . .

Diggs was indicted at the same time as was Caminetti. . . . The first count charged the defendant with transporting and causing to be transported, and aiding and assisting in obtaining transportation for, a certain woman from Sacramento, California, to Reno, Nevada, for the purpose of debauchery, and for an immoral purpose, to wit, that the aforesaid woman should be and become his concubine and mistress. The second count charged him with a like offense as to another woman (the companion of Caminetti) in transportation, etc., from Sacramento to Reno, that she might become the mistress and concubine of Caminetti. The third count charged him (Diggs) with procuring a ticket for the first-mentioned woman from Sacramento to Reno in interstate commerce, with the intent that she should become his concubine and mistress. The fourth count made a like charge as to the girl companion of Caminetti. Upon trial and verdict of guilty on these four counts, he was sentenced to imprisonment for two years and to pay a fine of $2,000. As in the *Caminetti* Case, that judgment was affirmed by the circuit court of appeals. . . .

In the *Hays* Case, upon June 26th, 1914, an indictment was returned in the United States district court for the western district of Oklahoma against Hays and another, charging violations of the act. The first count charged the said defendants with having, on March 17th, 1914, persuaded, induced, enticed, and coerced a certain woman, unmarried and under the age of eighteen years, from Oklahoma City, Oklahoma, to the city of Wichita, Kansas, in interstate commerce and travel, for the purpose and with intent then and there to induce and coerce the said woman, and intending that she should be induced and coerced to engage in prostitution, debauchery, and other immoral practices, and did then and there, in furtherance of such purposes, procure and furnish a railway

---

with a criminal offense, shall be fined under this title or imprisoned not more than five years, or both.]

ticket entitling her to passage over the line of railway, to wit, the Atchison, Topeka & Santa Fe Railway, and did then and there and thereby, knowingly entice and cause the said women to go and to be carried and transported as a passenger in interstate commerce upon said line of railway. The second count charged that on the same date the defendants persuaded, induced, enticed, and coerced the same woman to be transported from Oklahoma City to Wichita, Kansas, with the purpose and intent to induce and coerce her to engage in prostitution, debauchery, and other immoral practices at and within the state of Kansas, and that they enticed her and caused her to go and be carried and transported as a passenger in interstate commerce from Oklahoma City, Oklahoma, to Wichita, Kansas, upon a line and route of a common carrier, to wit: The Atchison, Topeka & Santa Fe Railway. Defendants were found guilty by a jury upon both counts, and Hays was sentenced to imprisonment for eighteen months. Upon writ of error to the circuit court of appeals for the eighth circuit, judgment was affirmed. . . .

It is contended that the act of Congress is intended to reach only "commercialized vice," or the traffic in women for gain, and that the conduct for which the several petitioners were indicted and convicted, however, reprehensible in morals, is not within the purview of the statute when properly construed in the light of its history and the purposes intended to be accomplished by its enactment. In none of the cases was it charged or proved that the transportation was for gain or for the purpose of furnishing women for prostitution for hire, and it is insisted that, such being the case, the acts charged and proved, upon which conviction was had, do not come within the statute.

It is elementary that the meaning of a statute must, in the first instance, be sought in the language in which the act is framed, and if that is plain, and if the law is within the constitutional authority of the law-making body which passed it, the sole function of the courts is to enforce it according to its terms. . . .

Where the language is plain and admits of no more than one meaning, the duty of interpretation does not arise, and the rules which are to aid doubtful meanings need no discussion. . . . There is no ambiguity in the terms of this act. It is specifically made an offense to knowingly transport or cause to be transported, etc., in interstate commerce, any woman or girl for the purpose of prostitution or debauchery, or for "any other immoral purpose," or with the intent and purpose to induce any such woman or girl to become a prostitute or to give herself up to debauchery, or to engage in any other immoral practice.

Statutory words are uniformly presumed, unless the contrary appears, to be used in their ordinary and usual sense, and with the meaning commonly attributed to them. To cause a woman or girl to be transported for the purposes of debauchery, and for an immoral purpose, to wit, becoming a concubine or mistress, for which Caminetti and Diggs were convicted; or to transport an unmarried woman, under eighteen years of age, with the intent to induce her to engage in prostitution, debauchery, and other immoral practices, for which Hays was convicted, would seem by the very statement of the facts to embrace transportation for purposes denounced by the act, and therefore fairly within its meaning.

While such immoral purpose would be more culpable in morals and attributed to baser motives if accompanied with the expectation of pecuniary gain, such considerations do not prevent the lesser offense against morals of furnishing transportation in order that a woman may be debauched, or become a mistress or a concubine, from being the execution of purposes within the meaning of this law. To say the contrary would shock the common understanding of what constitutes an immoral purpose when those terms are applied, as here, to sexual relations.

In United States v. Bitty . . . , it was held that the act of Congress against the importation of alien women and girls for the purpose of prostitution "and any other immoral purpose" included the importation of an alien woman to live in concubinage with the person importing her. In that case this court said:

"All will admit that full effect must be given to the intention of Congress as gathered from the words of the statute. There can be no doubt as to what class was aimed at by the clause forbidding the importation of alien women for purposes of 'prostitution.' It refers to women who, for hire or without hire, offer their bodies to indiscriminate intercourse with men. The lives and example of such persons are in hostility to 'the idea of the family, as consisting in and springing from the union for life of one man and one woman in the holy estate of matrimony; the sure foundation of all that is stable and noble in our civilization; the best guaranty of that reverent morality which is the source of all beneficient progress in social and political improvement.' . . . Now the addition in the last statute of the words, 'or for any other immoral purpose,' after the word 'prostitution,' must have been made for some practical object. Those added words show beyond question that Congress had in view the protection of society against another class of alien women other than those who might be brought here merely for purposes of 'prostitution.' In forbidding the importation of alien women 'for any other immoral purpose,' Congress evidently thought that there were purposes in connection with the importations of alien women which, as in the case of importations for prostitution, were to be deemed immoral. It may be admitted that, in accordance with the familiar rule of *ejusdem generis*, the immoral purpose referred to by the words 'any other immoral purpose' must be one of the same general class or kind as the particular purpose of 'prostitution' specified in the same clause of the statute. 2 Lewis' Sutherland Stat.Constr. § 423, and authorities cited. But that rule cannot avail the accused in this case; for the immoral purpose charged in the indictment is of the same general class or kind as the one that controls in the importation of an alien woman for the purpose strictly of prostitution. The prostitute may, in the popular sense, be more degraded in character than the concubine, but the latter none the less must be held to lead an immoral life, if any regard whatever be had to the views that are almost universally held in this country as to the relations which may rightfully, from the standpoint of morality, exist between man and woman in the matter of sexual intercourse."

This definition of an immoral purpose was given prior to the enactment of the act now under consideration, and must be presumed to have been known to Congress when it enacted the law here involved. . . .

But it is contended that though the words are so plain that they cannot be misapprehended when given their usual and ordinary interpretation, and although the sections in which they appear do not in terms limit the offense defined and punished to acts of "commercialized vice," or the furnishing or procuring of transportation of women for debauchery, prostitution, or immoral practices for hire, such limited purpose is to be attributed to Congress and engrafted upon the act in view of the language of § 8 and the report which accompanied the law upon its introduction into and subsequent passage by the House of Representatives.

In this connection, it may be observed that while the title of an act cannot overcome the meaning of plain and unambiguous words used in its body . . . , the title of this act embraces the regulation of interstate commerce "by prohibiting the transportation therein for immoral purposes of women and girls, and for other purposes." It is true that § 8 of the act provides that it shall be known and referred to as the "White Slave Traffic Act," and the report accompanying the introduction of the same into the House of Representatives set forth the fact that a material portion of the legislation suggested was to meet conditions which had arisen in the past few years, and that the legislation was needed to put a stop to a villainous interstate and international traffic in women and girls. Still, the name given to an act by way of designation or description, or the report which accompanies it, cannot change the plain import of its words. If the words are plain, they give meaning to the act, and it is neither the duty nor the privilege of the courts to enter speculative fields in search of a different meaning.

Reports to Congress accompanying the introduction of proposed laws may aid the courts in reaching the true meaning of the legislature in cases of doubtful interpretation. . . . But, as we have already said, and it has been so often affirmed as to become a recognized rule, when words are free from doubt they must be taken as the final expression of the legislative intent, and are not to be added to or subtracted from by considerations drawn from titles or designating names or reports accompanying their introduction, or from any extraneous source. In other words, the language being plain, and not leading to absurd or wholly impracticable consequences, it is the sole evidence of the ultimate legislative intent. . . .

The fact, if it be so, that the act as it is written opens the door to blackmailing operations upon a large scale, is no reason why the courts should refuse to enforce it according to its terms, if within the constitutional authority of Congress. Such considerations are more appropriately addressed to the legislative branch of the government, which alone had authority to enact and may, if it sees fit, amend the law.

It is further insisted that a different construction of the act than is to be gathered from reading it is necessary in order to save it from constitutional objections, fatal to its validity. The act has its constitutional sanction in the power of Congress over interstate commerce. The broad character of that authority was declared once for all in the judgment pronounced by this court, speaking by Chief Justice Marshall, . . . and has since been steadily adhered to and applied to a variety of new conditions as they have arisen. . . .

The transportation of passengers in interstate commerce, it has long been settled, is within the regulatory power of Congress, under the commerce clause of the Constitution, and the authority of Congress to keep the channels of interstate commerce free from immoral and injurious uses has been frequently sustained, and is no longer open to question. . . .

The judgment in each of the cases is affirmed.

■ MR. JUSTICE MCKENNA, with whom concurred THE CHIEF JUSTICE and MR. JUSTICE CLARKE, dissenting:

Undoubtedly, in the investigation of the meaning of a statute we resort first to its words, and, when clear, they are decisive. The principle has attractive and seemingly disposing simplicity, but that it is not easy of application, or, at least, encounters other principles, many cases demonstrate. The words of a statute may be uncertain in their signification or in their application. If the words be ambiguous, the problem they present is to be resolved by their definition; the subject matter and the lexicons become our guides. But here, even, we are not exempt from putting ourselves in the place of the legislators. If the words be clear in meaning, but the objects to which they are addressed be uncertain, the problem then is to determine the uncertainty. And for this a realization of conditions that provoked the statute must inform our judgment. Let us apply these observations to the present case.

The transportation which is made unlawful is of a woman or girl "to become a prostitute or to give herself up to debauchery, or to engage in any other immoral practice." Our present concern is with the words "any other immoral practice," which, it is asserted, have a special office. The words are clear enough as general descriptions; they fail in particular designation; they are class words, not specifications. Are they controlled by those which precede them? If not, they are broader in generalization and include those that precede them, making them unnecessary and confusing. To what conclusion would this lead us? "Immoral" is a very comprehensive word. It means a dereliction of morals. In such sense it covers every form of vice, every form of conduct that is contrary to good order. It will hardly be contended that in this sweeping sense it is used in the statute. But, if not used in such sense, to what is it limited and by what limited? If it be admitted that it is limited at all, that ends the imperative effect assigned to it in the opinion of the court. But not insisting quite on that, we ask again, By what is it limited? By its context, necessarily, and the purpose of the statute.

For the context I must refer to the statute; of the purpose of the statute Congress itself has given us illumination. It devotes a section to the declaration that the "act shall be known and referred to as the 'White Slave Traffic Act.'" And its prominence gives it prevalence in the construction of the statute. It cannot be pushed aside or subordinated by indefinite words in other sentences, limited even there by the context. It is a peremptory rule of construction that all parts of a statute must be taken into account in ascertaining its meaning, and it cannot be said that § 8 has no object. Even if it gives only a title to the act, it has especial weight. . . . But it gives more than a title; it makes distinctive the purpose of the statute. The designation "white slave traffic" has the sufficiency of an axiom. If apprehended, there is no uncertainty as to the conduct it describes. It is commercialized vice, immoralities having a mercenary purpose, and this is confirmed by other circumstances.

The author of the bill was Mr. Mann, and in reporting it from the House committee on interstate and foreign commerce he declared for the committee that it was not the purpose of the bill to interfere with or usurp in any way the police power of the states, and further, that it was not the intention of the bill to regulate prostitution or the places where prostitution or immorality was practised, which were said to be matters wholly within the power of the states,[2] and over which the Federal

---

[2] State statutory coverage of prostitution and related activities is extensive. Although these statutes vary greatly in their wording, they are fairly uniform with respect to the specific matters dealt with. For purposes of illustration, the Wisconsin provisions, which are uncommonly succinct, are set forth below:

§ 944.30. *Prostitution.* Any female who intentionally does any of the following may be fined not more than $500 or imprisoned not more than one year or both:

(1) Has or offers to have non-marital sexual intercourse for money; or

(2) Commits or offers to commit an act of sexual perversion for money; or

(3) Is an inmate of a place of prostitution.

§ 944.31. *Patronizing Prostitutes.* Any male who enters or remains in any place of prostitution with intent to have non-marital sexual intercourse or to commit an act of sexual perversion may be fined not more than $100 or imprisoned not more than 3 months or both.

§ 944.32. *Soliciting Prostitutes.* Whoever intentionally solicits or causes any female to practice prostitution or establishes any female in a place of prostitution may

government had no jurisdiction. And further explaining the bill, it was said that the sections of the act had been "so drawn that they are limited to the cases in which there is an act of transportation in interstate commerce of women for the purposes of prostitution." and again:

"The White Slave Trade.—A material portion of the legislation suggested and proposed is necessary to meet conditions which have arisen within the past few years. The legislation is needed to put a stop to a villainous interstate and international traffic in women and girls. The legislation is not needed or intended as an aid to the states in the exercise of the police powers in the suppression or regulation of immorality in general. It does not attempt to regulate the practice of voluntary prostitution, but aims solely to prevent panderers and procurers from compelling thousands of women and girls against their will and desire to enter and continue in a life of prostitution." . . .

In other words, it is vice as a business at which the law is directed, using interstate commerce as a facility to procure or distribute its victims.

In 1912 the sense of the Department of Justice was taken of the act in a case where a woman of twenty-four years went from Illinois, where she lived, to Minnesota, at the solicitation and expense of a man. She was there met by him and engaged with him in immoral practices like those for which petitioners were convicted. The assistant district attorney forwarded her statement to the Attorney General, with the comment that the element of traffic was absent from the transaction and that therefore, in his opinion, it was not "within the spirit and intent of the Mann Act." Replying, the Attorney General expressed his concurrence in the view of his subordinate.

Of course, neither the declarations of the report of the committee on interstate commerce of the House nor the opinion of the Attorney General are conclusive of the meaning of the law, but they are highly persuasive.

---

be fined not more than $1,000 or imprisoned not more than 5 years or both. If the female is under the age of 18, the defendant may be fined not more than $2,000 or imprisoned not more than 10 years or both.

§ 944.33. *Pandering.* (1) Whoever does any of the following may be fined not more than $200 or imprisoned not more than 6 months or both:

(a) Solicits another to have non-marital sexual intercourse or to commit an act of sexual perversion with a female he knows is a prostitute; or

(b) With intent to facilitate another in having non-marital intercourse or committing an act of sexual perversion with a prostitute, directs or transports him to a prostitute or directs or transports a prostitute to him.

(2) If the accused received compensation from the earnings of the prostitute, he may be fined not more than $5,000 or imprisoned not more than 10 years or both. . . .

§ 944.34. *Keeping Place of Prostitution.* Whoever intentionally does any of the following may be fined not more than $5,000 or imprisoned not more than 5 years or both:

(1) Keeps a place of prostitution; or

(2) Grants the use or allows the continued use of a place as a place of prostitution. [Eds.]

The opinion was by one skilled in the rules and methods employed in the interpretation or construction of laws, and informed, besides, of the conditions to which the act was addressed. The report was by the committee charged with the duty of investigating the necessity for the act, and to inform the House of the results of that investigation, both of evil and remedy. The report of the committee has, therefore, a higher quality than debates on the floor of the House. The representations of the latter may indeed be ascribed to the exaggerations of advocacy or opposition. The report of a committee is the execution of a duty and has the sanction of duty. There is a presumption, therefore, that the measure it recommends has the purpose it declares and will accomplish it as declared.

This being the purpose, the words of the statute should be construed to execute it, and they may be so construed even if their literal meaning be otherwise. . . .

There is danger in extending a statute beyond its purpose, even if justified by a strict adherence to its words. The purpose is studied, all effects measured, not left at random,—one evil practice prevented, opportunity given to another. The present case warns against ascribing such improvidence to the statute under review. Blackmailers of both sexes have arisen, using the terrors of the construction now sanctioned by this court as a help—indeed, the means—for their brigandage. The result is grave and should give us pause. It certainly will not be denied that legal authority justifies the rejection of a construction which leads to mischievous consequences, if the statute be susceptible of another construction. . . .

NOTES AND QUESTIONS

Although the objective of the legislatures is to state precisely the meaning of the expressions contained in their codes and statutes, the courts are often required to attempt clarification in litigated cases. Following are several illustrations of the basic problem.

Problem 3–1. When a defendant transports two or more women in interstate commerce for immoral purposes and they are in the same vehicle on the same trip, how many crimes have occurred? Only one crime because it is the use of interstate commerce that is the essence of the offense. Thus, the charge would be brought in a single count of an indictment or information. When more than one alien is smuggled into the United States in a single trip, how many crimes have occurred?

1. A federal statute prohibits interstate travel with intent to carry on "extortion" in violation of the laws of the state in which it is committed. X and Y entered the state of Pennsylvania for the purpose of "shaking down" homosexuals, by getting wealthy persons with homosexual interests into compromising situations and threatening to expose them unless certain sums of money were given to X and Y.

In Pennsylvania an offense of this type is "blackmail"; a separate statute deals with "extortion," but its coverage is confined to activities involving public officials.

Does the Pennsylvania differentiation between "blackmail" and "extortion" render the federal statute inapplicable to X and Y?

In United States v. Nardello, 393 U.S. 286, 89 S.Ct. 534, 21 L.Ed.2d 487 (1969), the Supreme Court held that the federal statute was designed to be of material assistance to the States in combatting pernicious undertakings which cross state lines, and it was not Congress' intention to limit its coverage to state classifications. The Court pointed out that many states prohibit such conduct by various designations such as theft, coercion, and even robbery. In any event "extortion" covers "shakedown" activities as here involved.

2. In U.S. v. Jones, 471 F.3d 535 (4th Cir. 2006), the defendant was charged with violating a federal statute that provides:

> A person who knowingly transports an individual who has not attained the age of 18 years in interstate or foreign commerce, . . . with intent that the individual engage in prostitution, . . . shall be fined under this title and imprisoned not less than 5 years and not more than 30 years.

The defendant contented that "knowingly" applies to the clause "who has not attained the age of 18 years" and, thus, that the defendant's knowledge of the victim's minority was an element of the offense which the government must prove to convict. The court recognized that determining the mental state required for commission of a federal crime requires construction of the statute and inference of the intent of Congress. The court then found that it was clear from the grammatical structure of the statute that

> the adverb knowingly modifies the verb transports. Adverbs generally modify verbs, and the thought that they would typically modify the infinite hereafters of statutory sentences would cause grammarians to recoil. We see nothing on the face of this statute to suggest that the modifying force of 'knowingly' extends beyond the verb to other components of the offense." The court also noted that "our interpretation is the only one consistent with any reasonable inference of the intent of Congress. . . . It would be nonsensical to require proof of knowledge of the victim's age when the statute exists to provide special protection for all minors, including, if not especially, those who could too easily be mistaken for adults. 'Such minors are still minors, regardless of what they say or how they appear. For this reason, ignorance of the victim's age provides no safe harbor from the penalties in [the statute].

3. The Child Pornography Prevention Act of 1996 (CPPA), 18 U.S.C. § 2251 *et seq.*, prohibited: (1) "any visual depiction, including any photograph, film, video, picture, or computer or computer-generated image or picture" that "is, or appears to be, of a minor engaging in sexually explicit conduct"; and (2) any sexually explicit image that was "advertised, promoted, presented, described, or distributed in such a manner that conveys the impression" it depicts "a minor engaging in sexually explicit conduct." The prohibition on "any visual depiction" does not depend at all on how the image is produced. The section captures a range of depictions, sometimes called "virtual child pornography," which include computer-generated images, as well as images produced by more traditional means.

These images do not involve, let alone harm, any children in the production process; but Congress decided the materials threaten children in other, less direct, ways. Pedophiles might use the materials to encourage children to participate in sexual activity. "[A] child who is reluctant to engage in sexual activity with an adult, or to pose for sexually explicit photographs, can sometimes be convinced by viewing depictions of other children 'having fun' participating in such activity." Omnibus Consolidated Appropriations Act of 1997, Pub.L.No. 104–208, 110 Stat. 3009 (subsection 1(3) of Congress' findings regarding 18 U.S.C. § 2251). Furthermore, pedophiles might "whet their own sexual appetites" with the pornographic images, "thereby increasing the creation and distribution of child pornography and the sexual abuse and exploitation of actual children." *Id.* (subsection 1(4) of Congress' findings regarding 18 U.S.C. § 2251). Under these rationales, harm flows from the content of the images, not from the means of their production. In addition, Congress identified another problem created by computer-generated images: Their existence can make it harder to prosecute pornographers who do use real minors. See *id.* (subsection 1(6)(A) of Congress' findings regarding 18 U.S.C. § 2251). As imaging technology improves, Congress found, it becomes more difficult to prove that a particular picture was produced using actual children. To ensure that defendants possessing child pornography using real minors cannot evade prosecution, Congress extended the ban to virtual child pornography.

In Ashcroft v. The Free Speech Coalition, 535 U.S. 234, 122 S.Ct. 1389, 152 L.Ed.2d 403 (2002), the Court held as follows:

"The CPPA prohibits speech despite its serious literary, artistic, political, or scientific value. . . . For this reason, and the others we have noted, the CPPA cannot be read to prohibit obscenity, because it lacks the required link between its prohibitions and the affront to community standards prohibited by the definition of obscenity. The Government has shown no more than a remote connection between speech that might encourage thoughts or impulses and any resulting child abuse. Without a significantly stronger, more direct connection, the Government may not prohibit speech on the ground that it may encourage pedophiles to engage in illegal conduct."

4. With regard to the general principles governing the interpretation of criminal statutes, consider the views of Professor Livingston Hall in his article *Strict or Liberal Construction of Penal Statutes*:

I. Introduction

Doctrines of strict or liberal construction have a peculiarly important place in the interpretation of criminal statutes. The extraordinary vitality of the old common-law rule of strict construction, statutes in about a third of the states substituting more liberal rules of construction in place of the common-law rule, and the absence of other guides to the "intent of the legislature" in so many cases, unite to contribute to the influence of such doctrines at the present time. . . .

Undoubtedly precedent—the hundreds of cases stating and usually applying the common-law rule of strict construction of penal statutes—is one of the most powerful forces shaping the attitude of the courts today toward this problem. . . . [However,] the unrestrained application of this rule, particularly in regard to the extreme technicality invoked to find an "ambiguity" which would call for its application, led to the formulation . . . of a counter-irritant, thus stated by Chief Justice Marshall: ". . . though penal laws are to be construed strictly, they are not to be construed so strictly as to defeat the obvious intention of the legislature. . . . The intention of the legislature is to be collected from the words they employ. Where there is no ambiguity in the words, there is no room for construction." . . .

The numerous examples of legislative frustration which the common-law rule produced finally led to direct action by the legislatures of many states to overthrow, in whole or in part, the older rule. . . . Various types of statutes were tried. The most common . . . specifically abrogates the common-law rule of strict construction, providing instead that all penal statutes "are to be construed according to the fair import of their terms, with a view to effect their objects and to promote justice". . . . Another type of statute, without specifically abrogating the old rule, provides that statutes shall be "liberally construed", either to carry out "the true intent and meaning of the legislature" . . . or "with a view to effecting their objects and promoting justice". . . .

II. The Rationale of the Legal Rules

For Strict Construction. Potentially the most serious argument is that the rule is founded "on the plain principle that the power of punishment is vested in the legislative, not in the judicial department." For if this were true, a liberal construction statute would be an unconstitutional delegation of legislative power to the judiciary. But this objection is clearly unsound. Liberal construction does not involve going beyond the intention of the legislature. . . . Where liberal construction statutes have been passed, courts have never raised this objection to their enforcement. . . .

It has further been claimed that as the state makes the laws, they should be most strongly construed against it. But the contract analogy is weak, for the state is presumably acting in the public interest in enacting criminal statutes, and need not in every case be subjected to a rule of interpretation designed to secure justice between private parties. . . .

Obviously, the original reason for the growth of this rule, to mitigate the extension of capital felonies, no longer applies to all penal statutes; . . . this has often been recognized in states where the rule has been abrogated. . . .

There remains for consideration only Mr. Justice Holmes' statement in McBoyle v. United States[3] that it is "reasonable" for penal statutes to be construed to give "fair warning" of "what the law intends to do if a certain line is passed" in language "that the common world will understand". Why such a warning should be needed in murder and theft, two crimes as to which Mr. Justice Holmes himself admits that "it is not likely that a criminal will carefully consider the text of the law before he murders or steals," or especially in transporting stolen property, as in the McBoyle case itself, . . . is far from self-evident. Even if "fair warning" had been called for in the particular case, as it undoubtedly is in many crimes, it was unnecessary to lay down a general rule. Simply because a liberal construction might work injustice in some cases is no proper reason for inflicting on the people the rule of strict construction in all cases.

For Liberal Construction. The argument for liberal construction of non-penal statutes has been put forcibly by Dean Pound nearly 20 years ago in an article concluding: "The public cannot be relied upon permanently to tolerate judicial obstruction or nullification of the social policies to which more and more it is compelled to be committed."[4] This argument is equally applicable to penal statutes, except insofar as "political liberty requires clear and exact definition of the offense." The public is already impatient with the refined, and for practical purposes unnecessary, distinctions embodied in the penal codes. Strict construction of . . . statutes has completed the degradation of the substantive criminal law [in the mind of the average man]. . . . An attitude of liberal construction goes far, on the other hand, to make the law appear rational. . . .

III. Guides to Rational Construction

The conclusions which may be drawn from the foregoing are twofold: first, that there is no sound reason for a general doctrine

---

[3] 283 U.S. 25, 51 S.Ct. 340, 75 L.Ed. 816 (1931). The Court held that an airplane was not "an automobile, automobile truck, automobile wagon, motorcycle, or any other self-propelled vehicle not running on rails" and hence did not come under the National Motor Vehicle Theft Act, . . .

[4] Pound, Common Law and Legislation, 21 Harv.L.Rev. 383, 407 (1908).

of strict construction of penal statutes, and *prima facie* all such should have as liberal a construction as statutes generally, and second, that certain penal statutes should be strictly construed to avoid injustice. These exceptions range themselves into a few fairly well defined categories.

Effect of a Disproportionate Penalty. A statute imposing a penalty which the court regards as disproportionately heavy for the acts committed can hardly escape a strict construction. . . . [T]he history of the past four hundred years has amply proved that under such circumstances courts, juries, and even prosecutors will cooperate to defeat a clearly avowed "legislative will" by any available means . . .

It would serve only to perpetuate an unnecessary conflict between principle and decision to ignore this tendency; hence, a cautious modification of the rule of liberal construction here seems proper. . . .

Effect of Honest Attempt at Compliance. Where an honest attempt is commonly made by those to whom the law applies to ascertain the precise limits of the legal sanction imposed, particularly in the regulation of business practices for the social welfare, indefiniteness is usually fatal to the enforcement of the law. It is unfair to those affected to inflict punishment, which is *ex post facto* by nature, for acts whose criminality was not readily apparent before the commission of the crime, where the honest motives of the defendant cannot be questioned, as is true in many crimes. . . .

It is difficult to lay down a practical guide defining this class of crime. . . . The gist of this exception is the tendency of a liberal construction to mislead persons acting in good faith and honestly attempting to comply with the law, and a general exception in these terms should prove sufficient.

Effect of Changed Conditions. The spasmodic attempt to enforce old legislation which is inapplicable to changed social or economic conditions presents another instance in which the doctrine of strict construction provides some measure of needed protection against administrative tyranny. The dead hand of the past, where it bars rather than leads social progress, must be narrowly limited in scope until outright repeal becomes possible. . . .

IV. Reform of the Present Rules

If the foregoing argument is sound, there is urgent need of reform in the construction of penal statutes. . . .

Undoubtedly the most effective way to secure reform in this field, as in most others, is by new legislation. The whole problem of statutory interpretation calls for the finest exercise of judgment, and the standards to be applied are necessarily somewhat indefinite. . . .

The following form of statute is offered as a suggested model:

"Sec. 1. The rule of the common law that penal statutes shall be strictly construed shall not apply to any penal statute now in force or hereafter enacted in this state. All such statutes shall be construed liberally, without regard to any distinction between the construction of penal and nonpenal statutes, except as specifically provided in Section 2 of this Act.

"Sec. 2. A penal statute may be construed strictly where such construction is necessary (1) to make the words of the statute not misleading to persons acting in good faith and honestly attempting to comply with all provisions of the law regulating their conduct; or (2) to prevent the imposition of a penalty which is so disproportionate to other penalties imposed by law or which is so clearly inappropriate in view of changed social or economic conditions in the state that it is reasonable to believe that the legislature did not intend such a result."

Livingston Hall, Strict or Liberal Construction of Penal Statutes, 48 Harv.L.Rev. 748, 748–70 (1935).

3. ADMINISTRATIVE REGULATIONS

Hobbs v. Jones

Supreme Court of Arkansas, 2012.
412 S.W.3d 844.

■ JIM GUNTER, JUSTICE.

The Arkansas Department of Correction and its director, Ray Hobbs, and a group of several prisoners awaiting execution on Arkansas's death row, appeal an order of the Pulaski County Circuit Court granting in part and denying in part cross-motions for summary judgment. We have jurisdiction over this appeal as it involves issues pertaining to the interpretation or construction of the Arkansas Constitution. We affirm the circuit court's order to the extent it declared Ark.Code Ann. § 5–4–617 (Supp.2011), unconstitutional.

On March 8, 2010, Jack Harold Jones, a prisoner incarcerated on Arkansas's death row, filed suit against Ray Hobbs, in his official capacity as Director of the Arkansas Department of Correction, and the Arkansas Department of Correction (hereinafter collectively referred to as "ADC"). Jones asserted that the Method of Execution Act of 2009 ("MEA"), codified at Ark.Code Ann. § 5–4–617, violates the separation-of-powers doctrine in article 4 of the Arkansas Constitution. Jones asked the court to grant preliminary injunctive relief to stay his execution during the pendency of the case, to enter declaratory judgment that Jones's execution pursuant to the MEA was unconstitutional, and to grant permanent injunctive relief barring Jones's execution until passage of a new statute incorporating standards to satisfy the Arkansas Constitution.

On July 29, 2010, Jones filed an amended complaint, listing a total of six claims: (1) that the MEA was an unconstitutional violation of the separation-of-powers doctrine; (2) that his execution would violate the Federal Food, Drug & Cosmetic Act (FDCA), codified at 21 U.S.C. §§ 301 et seq., because the ADC lacked a valid prescription for the drugs it intended to use during Jones's execution; (3) that his execution would violate the FDCA because the drugs the ADC intended to use had not been approved by the Food and Drug Administration (FDA); (4) that his execution would violate the Federal Controlled Substances Act (CSA), codified at 21 U.S.C. §§ 801 et seq., because the ADC lacked a valid prescription for the drugs it intended to use during his execution; (5) that his execution would violate the CSA because the ADC staff were to administer controlled substances to Jones without proper registration; and (6) that his execution would violate the Nurse Practices Act (NPA), codified at Ark.Code Ann. § 17–87–101, because the ADC intended to use lay persons to administer the drugs during execution. Jones again sought declaratory and injunctive relief. With permission of the circuit court, nine other death-row inmates (hereinafter collectively referred to with Jones as "the prisoners"), subsequently filed complaints in intervention asserting substantially the same claims and requesting the same relief as Jones in his amended complaint.

The ADC contended that with regard to the facial challenge to the MEA on the basis of separation of powers, it was entitled to judgment as a matter of law because the statute could be applied constitutionally and provided sufficient guidance to executive officials in administering executions. The prisoners filed a cross-motion for summary judgment as to claim one regarding the constitutionality of the MEA on May 31, 2011, asserting that the MEA delegates policymaking discretion to the ADC director without setting forth reasonable standards for the exercise of that discretion in violation of the separation-of-powers clause of the Arkansas Constitution.

The court held a hearing on the motions on August 15, 2011, and found the MEA unconstitutional.

I. Constitutionality of Ark.Code Ann. § 5–4–617

For its first point on appeal, ADC maintains that the circuit court erred in finding that Ark.Code Ann. § 5–4–617 is facially unconstitutional and erred in striking a portion of the statute. It contends that because Ark.Code Ann. § 5–4–617 can be applied in a manner that fully comports with the prohibition on cruel and unusual punishment in both the federal and state constitutions, the prisoners' argument that the statute is unconstitutional on its face fails. Moreover, ADC argues that the doctrine of separation of powers is not violated where the legislature merely makes law and then confers authority or discretion with regard to execution of that law to the executive branch. The legislature can set forth general provisions and give power to the executive branch to complete the details. Additionally, where the Arkansas Constitution is silent on which branch of government possesses the power to determine the precise conditions to carry out a criminal sentence, the legislature may delegate that power to the executive branch. Here, ADC contends that the legislature did just that with the MEA and furthermore, although unnecessary, gave significant guidance to the executive branch in how to accomplish that general purpose.

The prisoners maintain, in their response on direct appeal and their argument on cross-appeal, that the circuit court was correct to find that the MEA violates the separation-of powers doctrine but that it erred in striking a portion of the MEA. The prisoners maintain that because the MEA provides no guidelines for the ADC in carrying out lethal-injection executions and allows the ADC unfettered discretion in determining the chemicals to be used and the policies and procedures for administering lethal injection, it is an unconstitutional delegation of legislative power. Additionally, the prisoners assert that as altered by the circuit court, the statute remains constitutionally infirm, and alternatively that it is not severable.

Statutes are presumed constitutional, and the burden of proving otherwise is on the challenger of the statute. If it is possible to construe a statute as constitutional, we must do so. Because statutes are presumed to be framed in accordance with the Constitution, they should not be held invalid for repugnance thereto unless such conflict is clear and unmistakable. Moreover, when interpreting statutes, we make a de novo review, as it is for this court to decide what a statute means. Thus, although we are not bound by the trial court's interpretation, in the absence of a showing that the trial court erred, its interpretation will be accepted as correct on appeal. The basic rule of statutory construction is to give effect to the intent of the legislature. Where the language of a statute is plain and unambiguous, we determine legislative intent from the ordinary meaning of the language used. In considering the meaning of a statute, we construe it just as it reads, giving the words their ordinary and usually accepted meaning in common language. We construe the statute so that no word is left void, superfluous or insignificant, and we give meaning and effect to every word in the statute, if possible.

Within our state constitution is a specific separation-of-powers provision, providing:

§ 1. The powers of the government of the State of Arkansas shall be divided into three distinct departments, each of them to be confided to a separate body of magistracy, to-wit: Those which are legislative, to one, those which are executive, to another, and those which are judicial, to another.

§ 2. No person or collection of persons, being of one of these departments, shall exercise any power belonging to either of the others, except in the instances hereinafter expressly directed or permitted.

In Department of Human Services v. Howard, 367 Ark. 55, 238 S.W.3d 1 (2006), we explained the specific powers delegated to each branch. The legislative branch of the state government has the power and responsibility to proclaim the law through statutory enactments. The judicial branch has the power and responsibility to interpret the legislative enactments. The executive branch has the power and responsibility to enforce the laws as enacted and interpreted by the other two branches. The doctrine of separation of powers is a basic principle upon which our government is founded, and should not be violated or abridged.

Although on many occasions we have noted that the legislature cannot delegate its power to proclaim the law to one of its sister branches of government, we have recognized that it can delegate discretionary authority to the other branches:

While it is a doctrine of universal application that the functions of the Legislature must be exercised by it alone and cannot be delegated, it is equally well settled that the Legislature may delegate to executive officers the power to determine certain facts, or the happening of a certain contingency, on which the operation of the statute is, by its terms, made to depend.

The true distinction is between the delegation of power to make the law, which necessarily involves the discretion as to what it shall be, and conferring authority or discretion as to its execution to be exercised under and in pursuance of the law. The first cannot be done. To the latter no valid objection can be made.

Consequently, this court has held that such discretionary power may be delegated by the legislature to a state agency as long as reasonable guidelines are provided. This guidance must include appropriate standards by which the administrative body is to exercise this power. A statute that, in effect, reposes an absolute, unregulated, and undefined discretion in an administrative agency bestows arbitrary powers and is an unlawful delegation of legislative powers.

Turning to the specific statute in this case, the current version of the MEA provides that,

(a) (1) The sentence of death is to be carried out by intravenous lethal injection of one (1) or more chemicals, as determined in kind and amount in the discretion of the Director of the Department of Correction.

(2) The chemical or chemicals injected may include one (1) or more of the following substances:

(A) One (1) or more ultra-short-acting barbiturates

(B) One (1) or more chemical paralytic agents;

(C) Potassium chloride; or

(D) Any other chemical or chemicals, including but not limited to saline solution.

(3) The condemned convict's death will be pronounced according to accepted standards of medical practice.

(4) The director shall determine in his or her discretion any and all policies and procedures to be applied in connection with carrying out the sentence of death, including but not limited to:

(A) Matters concerning logistics and personal correspondence concerning witnesses;

(B) Security;

(C) Injection preparations;

(D) Injection implementation; or

(E) Arrangements for disposition of the executed convict's body and personal property.

(5) (A) The policies and procedures for carrying out the sentence of death and any and all matters related to the policies and procedures for the sentence of death including but not limited to the director's determinations under this subsection are not subject to the Arkansas Administrative Procedure Act, § 25–15–201 et seq.

(B) The policies and procedures for carrying out the sentence of death and any and all matters related to the policies and procedures for the sentence of death are not subject to the Freedom of Information Act of 1967, § 25–19–101 et seq., except for the choice of chemical or chemicals that may be injected, including the quantity, method, and order of the administration of the chemical or chemicals.

(b) (1) If this section is held unconstitutional by an appellate court of competent jurisdiction, the sentence of death shall be carried out by electrocution in a manner determined by the director in his or her discretion.

(2) However, if the holding of the appellate court described in subdivision (b)(1) of this section is subsequently vacated, overturned, overruled, or reversed, the sentence of death shall be carried out by lethal injection as described in this section.

Our prior cases interpreting statutes in conflict with the doctrine of separation of powers focus on whether a statute gives "absolute, unregulated, and undefined discretion" to a government agency and whether reasonable guidelines have been provided by which the administrative body is to exercise its discretionary power. The MEA plainly gives absolute and exclusive discretion to the ADC to determine what chemicals are to be used. Although subsection (a)(2) attempts to provide a list of chemicals for use in lethal injection, the ADC has unfettered discretion to use chemicals from that list or chemicals not included on that list. It can hardly be said that the word "may" used in conjunction with a list of chemicals that itself is unlimited provides reasonable guidance. Although the General Assembly can delegate to the ADC the power to determine certain facts or the happening of a certain contingency, the current MEA gives the ADC the power to decide all the facts and all the contingencies with no reasonable guidance given absent the generally permissive use of one or more chemicals. Moreover, subsection (a)(4) expressly gives complete discretion to the ADC to determine all policies and procedures to administer the sentence of death, including injection preparations and implementation. The statute provides no guidance and no general policy with regard to the procedures for the ADC to implement lethal injections.

It is evident to this court that the legislature has abdicated its responsibility and passed to the executive branch, in this case the ADC, the unfettered discretion to determine all protocol and procedures, most notably the chemicals to be used, for a state execution. The MEA fails to provide reasonable guidelines for the selection of chemicals to be used during lethal injection and it fails to provide any general policy with regard to the lethal-injection procedure.

For these reasons, we declare the entirety of the MEA unconstitutional. Accordingly, we affirm the circuit court's ruling that the statute is unconstitutional and reverse its ruling striking specific language from subsection (a)(2)(D). We remand for entry of an order consistent with this opinion.

■ KAREN R. BAKER, JUSTICE, dissenting.

The majority holds that granting discretion to the Director of the Department of Correction to administer the death penalty is a violation of the separation-of-powers provision of our constitution. With this holding, Arkansas becomes the only state to find such a violation. In addition, Arkansas is left no method of carrying out the death penalty in cases where it has been lawfully imposed. Because there is no basis for holding that the MEA violates our state constitution's separation-of-powers doctrine, I dissent.

Here, the legislative delegation contained in the MEA is not the delegation of the authority to make the law, but rather is the delegation of the authority and discretion to carry out the law. The execution of this law is precisely the type of delegation of "details with which it is impracticable for the legislature to deal directly." Leathers v. Gulf Rice

Ark., Inc., 338 Ark. 425, 429, 994 S.W.2d 481, 483 (1999) (quoting Currin v. Wallace, 306 U.S. 1, 15, 59 S.Ct. 379, 83 L.Ed. 441 (1939)). The standards for applying the method of execution, although general, are capable of being reasonably applied where the General Assembly has (1) clearly defined the punishment, death by lethal injection; (2) made clear that the statute's purpose is to impose death; and (3) the methodology and chemicals are best left to the discretion of the Director because the ADC personnel are better qualified to make such determinations and the methodology and chemicals are details with which it is impracticable for the legislature to deal directly.

The majority, in contrast, does not allow for the legislature to grant the Director any discretion at all in determining the chemicals or procedures used in carrying out the lethal-injection procedure. They find the MEA constitutionally flawed because the guidance found in subsection (a)(2) is "not mandatory." However, a guideline is a recommended practice that allows discretion in its implementation rather than a "mandatory" directive. Guidance does not require a dictation of all terms, and such a construction is antithetical to our case law. See, e.g., Holloway v. Ark. State Bd. of Architects, 352 Ark. 427, 101 S.W.3d 805 (2003) (clearly rejecting the argument that a statute must spell out all details, leaving no discretion vested with the administrative body). While the current MEA does not give mandatory directives to the Director as to the chemicals and procedure used in carrying out lethal injection, it does provide guidance.

Further, appellants' discretion is not "unfettered" because they are at all times bound by the constraints of our federal and state constitutions against cruel and unusual punishment. We have noted that the failure of a statute to incorporate the terms of the constitution does not render the statute constitutionally deficient. In other words, it is not necessary to write the constitution into every legislative act. In addition, the Eighth Circuit Court of Appeals has specifically determined that Arkansas's lethal-injection protocol does not violate the Eighth Amendment prohibition against cruel and unusual punishment in a case brought by one of the appellees. In reviewing the protocol, the court noted that Arkansas uses the same three-drug protocol that at least thirty other states use, which had been developed "to cause as little pain as possible."

Based on the foregoing, I would reverse the circuit court's finding that the MEA is unconstitutional.

■ SPECIAL JUSTICE BYRON FREELAND joins.

NOTES

1. On the question of the construction of administrative regulations which define and punish a criminal offense, consider the following:

This delegation to the Price Administrator of the power to provide in detail against circumvention and evasion, as to which Congress has imposed criminal sanctions, creates a grave responsibility. In a very literal sense the liberties and fortunes of others may depend upon his definitions and specifications regarding evasion. Hence to these provisions must be applied the same strict rule of construction that is applied to statutes defining criminal action. In other words, the Administrator's provisions must be explicit and unambiguous in order to sustain a criminal prosecution; they must adequately inform those who are subject to their terms what conduct will be considered evasive so as to bring the criminal penalties of the Act into operation. . . . The dividing line between unlawful evasion and lawful action cannot be left to conjecture. The elements of evasive conduct should be so clearly expressed by the Administrator that the ordinary person can know in advance how to avoid an unlawful course of action . . . A prosecutor in framing an indictment, a court in interpreting the Administrator's regulations or a jury in judging guilt cannot supply that which the Administrator failed to do by express word or fair implication. Not even the Administrator's interpretation of his own regulations can cure an omission or add certainty and definiteness to otherwise vague language. The prohibited conduct must, for criminal purposes, be set forth with clarity in the regulations and orders which he is authorized by Congress to promulgate under the Act. Congress has warned the public to look to that source alone to discover what conduct is evasive and hence likely to create criminal liability.

M. Kraus & Bros., Inc. v. United States, 327 U.S. 614, 621–22, 66 S.Ct. 705, 707–08, 90 L.Ed. 894 (1946).

2. The Virginia Court of Appeals recently confronted "the unusual question of . . . the constitutionality of the participation of the judiciary in the executive clemency process." In *Montgomery v. Commonwealth*, 62 Va. App. 656, 751 S.E.2d 692 (2013) Montgomery petitioned the Court to grant a writ of actual innocence based on newly discovered non-biological evidence. Based on this evidence, the Governor granted a conditional pardon which would become a full pardon upon this Court's issuance of a writ of actual innocence.

The Constitution of Virginia declares the 'legislative, executive, and judicial departments shall be separate and distinct, so that none exercise the powers properly belonging to the others, nor any person exercise the power of more than one of them at the same time.' While the three branches should be "as separate and distinct from each other as practicable," logistically, no government could operate if an absolute and unqualified adherence was enforced. Therefore, 'the whole power of one of these departments should not be exercised by the same hands which possess the whole power of either of the other departments, but either department may exercise the powers of another to a limited extent.'

We therefore must determine whether the conditional pardon issued to Montgomery requires this Court to exercise the 'whole power' granted to the Governor to pardon Montgomery. Resolving this issue requires this Court determine whether the governmental branch constitutionally vested with authority retains the final decision-making power. Clearly, the judiciary has the constitutional authority to adjudicate criminal matters, and equally clearly, this Court has the statutory authority to vacate the conviction of someone who demonstrates their actual innocence. Unquestionably, the Governor has the constitutional authority to grant full or conditional pardons. The constitutional question is whether these otherwise separate but similar roles have been improperly consolidated in this case.

The Governor may not transfer or delegate his constitutional authority to pardon to another department of government nor does the judiciary have any proper constitutional role in a decision to grant executive clemency. Because it effectively transfers the final decision regarding clemency for Montgomery from the Governor to this Court, we therefore conclude that in this case, the condition of Montgomery's pardon requiring that he receive a writ of actual innocence from this Court is a condition that delegates the chief executive's 'whole clemency power' to the judiciary thereby transgressing the constitution.

4. THE FEDERAL-STATE DICHOTOMY

(A) THE CONSTITUTION AND FEDERAL "COMMON LAW"

* * *

ARTICLE I

Section 1. All legislative Powers herein granted shall be vested in a Congress of the United States, which shall consist of a Senate and House of Representatives.

* * *

Section 8. The Congress shall have Power To lay and collect Taxes, Duties, Imposts and Excises, to pay the Debts and provide for the common Defence and general Welfare of the United States; but all Duties, Imposts and Excises shall be uniform throughout the United States;

To borrow Money on the credit of the United States;

To regulate Commerce with foreign Nations, and among the several States, and with the Indian Tribes;

To establish an uniform Rule of Naturalization, and uniform Laws on the subject of Bankruptcies throughout the United States;

To coin Money, regulate the Value thereof, and of foreign Coin, and fix the Standard of Weights and Measures;

To provide for the Punishment of counterfeiting the Securities and current Coin of the United States;

To establish Post Offices and post Roads; * * *

To define and punish Piracies and Felonies committed on the high Seas, and Offences against the Law of Nations;

To declare War, grant Letters of Marque and Reprisal, and make Rules concerning Captures on Land and Water;

To raise and support Armies, but no Appropriation of Money to that Use shall be for a longer Term than two Years;

To provide and maintain a Navy;

To make Rules for the Government and Regulation of the land and naval Forces; * * *

To exercise exclusive Legislation in all Cases whatsoever, over such District (not exceeding ten Miles square) as may, by Cession of particular States, and the Acceptance of Congress, become the Seat of the Government of the United States, and to exercise like Authority over all Places purchased by the Consent of the Legislature of the State in which the Same shall be, for the Erection of Forts, Magazines, Arsenals, Dock-Yards, and other needful Buildings;—And

To make all Laws which shall be necessary and proper for carrying into Execution the foregoing Powers, and all other Powers vested by this Constitution in the Government of the United States, or in any Department or Officer thereof. * * *

ARTICLE [XIV]

Section 1. All persons born or naturalized in the United States, and subject to the jurisdiction thereof, are citizens of the United States and of the State wherein they reside. No State shall make or enforce any law which shall abridge the privileges or immunities of citizens of the United States; nor shall any State deprive any person of life, liberty, or property, without due process of law; nor deny to any person within its jurisdiction the equal protection of the laws.

* * *

Section 5. The Congress shall have power to enforce, by appropriate legislation, the provisions of this article.

The United States v. Hudson and Goodwin

Supreme Court of the United States, 1812.
11 U.S. (7 Cranch) 32, 3 L.Ed. 259.

This was a case certified from the Circuit Court for the District of *Connecticut*, in which, upon argument of a general demurrer to an *indictment* for a libel on the President and Congress of the United States, contained in the *Connecticut Courant*, of the 7th of May, 1806, charging them with having in secret voted two millions of dollars as a present to Bonaparte for leave to make a treaty with Spain, the judges of that Court were divided in opinion upon the question, *whether the Circuit Court of the United States had a common law jurisdiction in cases of libel.*

■ The Court having taken time to consider, the following opinion was delivered (on the last day of the term, all the judges being present) by JOHNSON, J.

The only question which this case presents is, whether the Circuit Courts of the United States can exercise a common law jurisdiction in criminal cases. We state it thus broadly because a decision on a case of libel will apply to every case in which jurisdiction is not vested in those courts by statute.

Although this question is brought up now for the first time to be decided by this Court, we consider it as having been long since settled in public opinion. In no other case for many years has this jurisdiction been asserted; and the general acquiescence of legal men shews the prevalence of opinion in favor of the negative of the proposition.

The course of reasoning which leads to this conclusion is simple, obvious, and admits of but little illustration. The powers of the general Government are made up of concessions from the several states— whatever is not expressly given to the former, the latter expressly reserve. The judicial power of the United States is a constituent part of those concessions—that power is to be exercised by Courts organized for the purpose, and brought into existence by an effort of the legislative power of the Union. Of all the Courts which the United States may, under their general powers, constitute, one only, the Supreme Court, possesses jurisdiction derived immediately from the Constitution, and of which the legislative power cannot deprive it. All other Courts created by the general Government possess no jurisdiction but what is given them by the power that creates them, and can be vested with none but what the power ceded to the general Government will authorize them to confer.

It is not necessary to inquire whether the general Government, in any and what extent, possesses the power of conferring on its Courts a jurisdiction in cases similar to the present; it is enough that such jurisdiction has not been conferred by any legislative act, if it does not result to those Courts as a consequence of their creation.

And such is the opinion of a majority of this court: For, the power which Congress possess to create Courts of inferior jurisdiction, necessarily implies the power to limit the jurisdiction of those Courts to particular objects; and when a Court is created, and its operations confined to certain specific objects, with what propriety can it assume to itself a jurisdiction—much more extended—in its nature very indefinite—applicable to a great variety of subjects—varying in every State in the Union—and with regard to which there exists no definite criterion of distribution between the district and Circuit Courts of the same district?

The only ground on which it has ever been contended that this jurisdiction could be maintained is, that, upon the formation of any political body, an implied power to preserve its own existence and promote the end and object of its creation, necessarily results to it. But, without examining how far this consideration is applicable to the peculiar character of our constitution, it may be remarked that it is a principle by no means peculiar to the common law. It is coeval, probably, with the first formation of a limited Government; belongs to a system of universal law, and may as well support the assumption of many other powers as those more peculiarly acknowledged by the common law of England.

But if admitted as applicable to the state of things in this country, the consequence would not result from it which is here contended for. If it may communicate certain implied powers to the general Government, it would not follow that the Courts of that Government are vested with jurisdiction over any particular act done by an individual in supposed violation of the peace and dignity of the sovereign power. The legislative authority of the Union must first make an act a crime, affix a punishment to it, and declare the Court that shall have jurisdiction of the offence.

Certain implied powers must necessarily result to our Courts of justice from the nature of their institution. But jurisdiction of crimes against the state is not among those powers. To fine for contempt—imprison for contumacy—inforce the observance of order, & c. are powers which cannot be dispensed with in a Court, because they are necessary to the exercise of all others: and so far our Courts no doubt possess powers not immediately derived from statute; but all exercise of criminal law cases we are of opinion is not within their implied powers.

(B) DIRECT FEDERAL INTEREST OFFENSES

Sonzinsky v. United States

Supreme Court of the United States, 1937.
300 U.S. 506, 57 S.Ct. 554, 81 L.Ed. 772.

■ MR. JUSTICE STONE delivered the opinion of the Court.

The question for decision is whether § 2 of the National Firearms Act of June 26, 1934, . . . 26 U.S.C.A., §§ 1132–1132q, which imposes a $200 annual license tax on dealers in firearms, is a constitutional exercise of the legislative power of Congress.

Petitioner was convicted by the District Court for Eastern Illinois on two counts of an indictment, the first charging him with violation of § 2, by dealing in firearms without payment of the tax. On appeal the Court of Appeals set aside the conviction on the second count and affirmed on the first. 86 F.2d 486. On petition of the accused we granted certiorari, limited to the question of the constitutional validity of the statute in its application under the first count in the indictment.

Section 2 of the National Firearms Act requires every dealer in firearms to register with the Collector of Internal Revenue in the district where he carries on business, and to pay a special excise tax of $200 a year. Importers or manufacturers are taxed $500 a year. Section 3 imposes a tax of $200 on each transfer of a firearm, payable by the transferor, and § 4 prescribes regulations for the identification of purchases. The term "firearm" is defined by § 1 as meaning a shotgun or a rifle having a barrel less than eighteen inches in length, or any other weapon, except a pistol or revolver, from which a shot is discharged by an explosive, if capable of being concealed on the person, or a machine gun, and includes a muffler or silencer for any firearm. * * *

In the exercise of its constitutional power to lay taxes, Congress may select the subjects of taxation, choosing some and omitting others. . . . Its power extends to the imposition of excise taxes upon the doing of business. . . . Petitioner does not deny that Congress may tax his business as a dealer in firearms. He insists that the present levy is not a true tax, but a penalty imposed for the purpose of suppressing traffic in a certain noxious type of firearms, the local regulation of which is reserved to the states because not granted to the national government. To establish its penal and prohibitive character, he relies on the amounts of the tax imposed by § 2 on dealers, manufacturers and importers, and of the tax imposed by § 3 on each transfer of a "firearm," payable by the transferor. The cumulative effect on the distribution of a limited class of firearms, of relatively small value, by the successive imposition of different taxes, one on the business of the importer or manufacturer, another on that of the dealer, and a third on the transfer to a buyer, is said to be prohibitive in effect and to disclose unmistakably the legislative purpose to regulate rather than to tax.

The case is not one where the statute contains regulatory provisions related to a purported tax in such a way as has enabled this Court to say in other cases that the latter is a penalty resorted to as a means of enforcing the regulations. . . . Nor is the subject of the tax described or treated as criminal by the taxing statute. . . . Here § 2 contains no regulation other than the mere registration provisions, which are obviously supportable as in aid of a revenue purpose. On its face it is only a taxing measure, and we are asked to say that the tax, by virtue of its deterrent effect on the activities taxed, operates as a regulation which is beyond the congressional power.

Every tax is in some measure regulatory. To some extent it interposes an economic impediment to the activity taxed as compared with others not taxed. But a tax is not any the less a tax because it has a regulatory effect, . . . and it has long been established that an Act of Congress which on its face purports to be an exercise of the taxing power is not any the less so because the tax is burdensome or tends to restrict or suppress the thing taxed. . . .

Inquiry into the hidden motives which may move Congress to exercise a power constitutionally conferred upon it is beyond the competency of courts. . . . They will not undertake, by collateral inquiry as to the measure of the regulatory effect of a tax, to ascribe to Congress an attempt, under the guise of taxation, to exercise another power denied by the Federal Constitution. . . .

Here the annual tax of $200 is productive of some revenue.[1] We are not free to speculate as to the motives which moved Congress to impose it, or as to the extent to which it may operate to restrict the activities taxed. As it is not attended by an offensive regulation, and since it operates as a tax, it is within the national taxing power. . . .

Affirmed.

NOTE

The judiciary has taken the position that, given the broad grant of constitutional power vested in Congress to collect taxes, it will not restrain an exercise of the taxing power because of the onerous and burdensome results to taxpayers. McCray v. United States, 195 U.S. 27, 24 S.Ct. 769, 49 L.Ed. 78 (1904). Congress, not the courts, has the right to select the objects of taxation and the measures for implementing the collection process. Thus, without inquiring into the reasons underlying Congress' decision to select a particular subject for taxation the courts will not limit any tax unless there are provisions in the tax statute extraneous to a constitutionally authorized

---

[1] The $200 tax was paid by 27 dealers in 1934, and by 22 dealers in 1935. Annual Report of the Commissioner of Internal Revenue, Fiscal Year Ended June 30, 1935, pp. 129–131; id., Fiscal Year Ended June 30, 1936, pp. 139–141.

taxing need. United States v. Kahriger, 345 U.S. 22, 73 S.Ct. 510, 97 L.Ed. 754 (1953).

In this manner, the courts have recognized Congress' power to collect taxes whether the business involved is lawful or unlawful, Wainer v. United States, 299 U.S. 92, 57 S.Ct. 79, 81 L.Ed. 58 (1936), although the method of reporting the income subject to taxation may generate Fifth Amendment self- incrimination problems. *See* Marchetti v. United States, 390 U.S. 39, 88 S.Ct. 697, 19 L.Ed.2d 889 (1968). Consequently, the taxing power has been upheld in a wide variety of situations. *E.g.*, United States v. Singer, 82 U.S. (15 Wall.) 111, 21 L.Ed. 49 (1872) (distilled spirits); United States v. Gullett, 322 F.Supp. 272 (D.Colo. 1971) (transfer of firearms); United States v. Gross, 313 F.Supp. 1330 (D.Ind. 1970), *aff'd*, 451 F.2d 1355 (7th Cir. 1971) (firearms dealers). *But see* Harper v. Va. St. Bd. of Elections, 383 U.S. 663, 86 S.Ct. 1079, 16 L.Ed.2d 169 (1966) (state poll tax unconstitutional).

United States v. Sharpnack

Supreme Court of the United States, 1958.
355 U.S. 286, 78 S.Ct. 291, 2 L.Ed.2d 282.

■ MR. JUSTICE BURTON delivered the opinion of the Court. The issue in this case is whether the Assimilative Crimes Act of 1948 ... is constitutional insofar as it makes applicable to a federal enclave a subsequently enacted criminal law of the State in which the enclave is situated. For the reasons hereafter stated, we hold that it is constitutional.

* * *

The 1948 Assimilative Crimes Act was enacted ... and reads as follows:

§ 13. Laws of States adopted for areas within Federal jurisdiction.

Whoever within or upon any of the places now existing or hereafter reserved or acquired ... is guilty of any act not made punishable by any enactment of Congress, would be punishable if committed or omitted within the jurisdiction of the State, Territory, Possession, or District in which such place is situated, by the laws thereof in force at the time of such act or omission, shall be guilty of a like offense and subject to a like punishment. . . .

In the absence of restriction in the cessions of the respective enclaves to the United States, the power of Congress to exercise legislative jurisdiction over them is clearly stated in Article I, § 8, cl. 17, and Article IV, § 3, cl. 2, of the Constitution.[4] . . . The first Federal Crimes Act,

---

4 "The Congress shall have Power to dispose of and make all needful Rules and Regulations respecting the Territory or other Property belonging to the United States; and

enacted in 1790, . . . defined a number of federal crimes and referred to federal enclaves. The need for dealing more extensively with criminal offenses in the enclaves was evident, and one natural solution was to adopt for each enclave the offenses made punishable by the State in which it was situated . . . .

* * *

The application of the Assimilative Crimes Act to subsequently adopted state legislation, under the limitations here prescribed, is a reasonable exercise of congressional legislative power and discretion.

[The majority's reasons in support of the decision and the opposing views of the dissent have been omitted. The differences only concerned the constitutionality of the law as it relates to subsequently enacted state legislation. In the casebook our only objective is to acquaint students with the existence of the Assimilative Crimes Act.]

(C) THE "NECESSARY AND PROPER" OFFENSES

In conjunction with the specific authority to create laws in a number of enumerated areas, the Necessary and Proper Clause of the Constitution, U.S. Const. Art. 1, § 8, cl. 18, provides Congress with the power to legislate in areas that will facilitate the execution of the powers vested in the federal government. In Logan v. United States, 144 U.S. 263, 12 S.Ct. 617, 36 L.Ed. 429 (1892), the Court recognized the applicability of this clause. There, taking cognizance of the propriety of the civil rights conspiracy statute, the Court upheld the right of federal authorities to protect prisoners in their custody:

> Among the powers which the Constitution expressly confers upon Congress is the power to make all laws necessary and proper for carrying into execution the powers specifically granted to it, and all other powers vested by the Constitution in the government of the United States, or in any department or officer thereof. In the exercise of this general power of legislation, Congress may use any means, appearing to it most eligible and appropriate, which are adapted to the end to be accomplished, and are consistent with the letter and the spirit of the Constitution.

> Although the Constitution contains no grant, general or specific, to Congress of the power to provide for the punishment of crimes, except piracies and felonies on the high seas, offences against the law of nations, treason, and counterfeiting the securities and current coin of the United States, no one doubts the power of Congress to provide for the punishment of all crimes and offences against the United States, whether

---

nothing in this Constitution shall be so construed as to Prejudice any Claims of the United States, or of any particular State." U.S. Const.

committed within one of the States of the Union, or within territory over which Congress has plenary and exclusive jurisdiction.

To accomplish this end, Congress has the right to enact laws for the arrest and commitment of those accused of any such crime or offence, and for holding them in safe custody until indictment and trial; and persons arrested and held pursuant to such laws are in the exclusive custody of the United States, and are not subject to the judicial process or executive warrant of any State. The United States, having the absolute right to hold such prisoners, have an equal duty to protect them, while so held, against assault or injury from any quarter. The existence of that duty on the part of the government necessarily implies a corresponding right of the prisoners to be so protected; and this right of the prisoners is a right secured to them by the Constitution and laws of the United States.

Therefore, notwithstanding the fact that the Constitution may not specifically grant Congress the power to regulate conduct in certain areas, where a given piece of legislation may be characterized as an incident of sovereignty which inheres in the government, it will be upheld under the Necessary and Proper Clause. Congress, thus, has the power to create, define, and punish offenses whenever it is necessary and proper, by law, to do so to effectuate the objects of government.

United States v. States

United States Court of Appeals, Eighth Circuit, 1973.
488 F.2d 761.

■ MATTHES, SENIOR CIRCUIT JUDGE. * * *

Before trial appellants moved to dismiss [their] indictment [under the mail fraud statute] asserting that it failed to allege that anyone had been defrauded of any money or property, and consequently failed to state an offense against the United States. . . . [After their motion was denied] appellants waived a jury and a bench trial resulted in their convictions. Their appeals challenge the court's action in entertaining the charge.

* * *

The indictment charges that the defendants devised a scheme to defraud the voters and residents of the third and nineteenth wards of the City of St. Louis and the Board of Election Commissioners of the City of St. Louis by the use of fraudulent voter registrations and applications for absentee ballots. It is alleged that the purpose of the scheme to defraud was to influence the outcome of the election of the Republican Committeeman for the nineteenth ward and the Democratic Committeeman for the third ward "for the purpose of securing and controlling said political offices and the political influence and financial benefits of said offices * * *." It is further alleged that as part of the scheme to defraud, the defendants submitted false and fraudulent voter registration affidavits bearing the names of false and fictitious persons with false addresses and caused the St. Louis Board of Election Commissioners to place absentee ballots for the fictitious persons in an authorized depository for mail matter.

* * *

At the outset of their claim for reversal the appellants submit that the very language of 18 U.S.C.A. § 1341 mandates a holding that there is an offense under the statute only if money or property is involved in the scheme to defraud. Appellants argue that the first phrase of § 1341, dealing with "any scheme or artifice to defraud," must be read in conjunction with the second phrase, concerning "obtaining money or property by means of false or fraudulent pretenses, representations, or promises," which was added to the statute by a subsequent amendment.[3] Appellants suggest that the second phrase was added to the predecessor of § 1341 because Congress believed that the "scheme to defraud" language included only frauds perpetrated without misrepresentations. They argue that the explicit "money or property" limitation in the added passage reveals that Congress believed that the first phrase in the original legislation dealt only with schemes to defraud of money or property.

But no case or legislative history is cited by the appellants supporting such an interpretation of legislative intent, nor does there appear to be any authority justifying such a construction of the statute. Moreover, not only does the appellants' conjunctive construction of the two phrases place a very strained and limited meaning on the broad wording of the first phrase, but a reading of the statute as a whole reveals that the two phrases in question are part of an uninterrupted listing of a series of obviously diverse schemes which result in criminal sanctions if the mails are used. The more natural construction of the wording in the statute is to view the two phrases independently, rather than complementary of one another. Indeed, numerous courts have construed

---

[3] § 1341. Frauds and swindles

Whoever, having devised or intending to devise any scheme or artifice to defraud, or for obtaining money or property by means of false or fraudulent pretenses, representations, or promises, or to sell, dispose of, loan, exchange, alter, give away, distribute, supply, or furnish or procure for unlawful use any counterfeit or spurious coin, obligation, security, or other article, or anything represented to be or intimated or held out to be such counterfeit or spurious article, for the purpose of executing such scheme or artifice or attempting to do so, places in any post office or authorized depository for mail matter, any matter or thing whatever to be sent or delivered by the Postal Service, or takes or receives therefrom, any such matter or thing, or knowingly causes to be delivered by mail according to the direction thereon, or at the place at which it is directed to be delivered by the person to whom it is addressed, any such matter or thing, shall be fined not more than $1,000 or imprisoned not more than five years, or both.

the "scheme or artifice to defraud" language of § 1341 without reference to the "obtaining money or property" phrase.

* * *

Consequently, we hold that the language of the statute on its face does not preclude a finding that a "scheme or artifice to defraud" need not concern money or property. Since the statutory wording itself does not conclusively resolve the issue presented by the appellants, and since the legislative history does not deal with the scope and meaning of the provision of the statute in issue, we examine judicial opinions construing § 1341 for assistance in definitely determining whether the statute should apply to the facts of this case.

Initially, it should be noted that the concept of fraud in § 1341 is to be construed very broadly. . . . In Blachly v. United States [380 F.2d 665 (5th Cir.1967)], the court observed:

> The crime of mail fraud is broad in scope. * * * The fraudulent aspect of the scheme to "defraud" is measured by a nontechnical standard. * * * Law puts its imprimatur on the accepted moral standards and condemns conduct which fails to match, the "reflection of moral uprightness, of fundamental honesty, fair play and right dealing in the general and business life of the members of society." This is indeed broad. For as Judge Holmes once observed, "[t]he law does not define fraud; it needs no definition. It is as old as falsehood and as versable as human ingenuity."

Likewise, the definition of fraud in § 1341 is to be broadly and liberally construed to further the purpose of the statute; namely, to prohibit the misuse of the mails to further fraudulent enterprises. Accordingly, many courts have construed the term "scheme or artifice to defraud" to include within its ambit widely diverse schemes. [For instance, a divorce mill granting decrees of questionable validity; bribery of public officials; bribery of an oil company employee to gain the company's geophysical maps; mailing an extortion note; and ballot tampering by election officials.] * * *

There are also cases concerning bribery schemes which support the view that money or tangible property need not be involved in the scheme to defraud in order for the mail fraud statute to be invoked. Beginning with Shushan v. United States, the term "scheme or artifice to defraud" [included] an operation to bribe and corrupt public officials in order to gain advantages and special treatment. In *Shushan* there is the implication that a scheme to gain personal favors from public officials is a scheme to defraud the public, although the interest lost by the public can be described no more concretely than as an intangible right to the proper and honest administration of government. "[T]here must be a purpose to do wrong which is inconsistent with moral uprightness." This concept, that a scheme to defraud of certain intangible rights is grounds for prosecution under § 1341 if the mails are used, is more explicitly stated in United States v. Faser . . . (1969). In *Faser*, the defendants were indicted under the mail fraud statute after they accepted bribes to deposit public funds in a certain bank. There, as here, the defendants contended the indictment failed to state an offense because it did not allege that someone was actually defrauded out of something tangible that can be measured in terms of money or property. In rejecting that argument the court specifically discussed whether a fraudulent scheme must entail money or property in order for there to be an offense under § 1341. As an alternative ground for overruling the motion to dismiss, the court stated:

> [I]t is further the opinion of this Court that the thing out of which it is charged that the State was defrauded need not necessarily be that which can be measured in terms of money or property. It is the opinion of this Court that it is a violation of the statute in question if a person defrauds the State out of the "loyal and faithful services of an employee." * * *

> Thus it seems quite clear that even if the thing out of which the State was allegedly defrauded was not susceptible of measurement in terms of money or physical property, a valid indictment may still result therefrom.

. . . In [a number of cases the courts have] upheld the mail fraud indictment on the ground that the mails had been used in a scheme to defraud a corporation of the "honest and faithful services" of one or more employees. . . . These cases serve as persuasive authority for the proposition that in a prosecution for use of the mails to further and execute a vote fraud scheme the indictment states an offense even though it does not contain allegations that anyone was defrauded of any property or money. Nevertheless, the appellants argue that the application of the mail fraud statute to the facts of this case will result in a "policing" of state election procedure, and that Congress has never explicitly authorized such widespread intervention into state affairs. The appellants' argument misinterprets the purpose of the mail fraud legislation. The focus of the statute is upon the misuse of the Postal Service, not the regulation of state affairs, and Congress clearly has the authority to regulate such misuse of the mails. [In Badders v. United States (1916), the court said:] "The overt act of putting a letter into the post office of the United States is a matter that Congress may regulate. * * * Whatever the limits to its power, it may forbid any such acts done in furtherance of a scheme it regards as contrary to public policy, whether it can forbid the scheme or not." The purpose of 18 U.S.C. § 1341 is to prevent the Postal Service from being used to carry out fraudulent schemes, regardless of what is the exact nature of the scheme and regardless of whether it happens to be forbidden by state law. . . .

"Congress definitely intends that the misuse of the mails shall be controlled even though it be its policy to leave the control of elections to the several States."

The appellants' argument presents no justification for refusing to apply the mail fraud statutes to the facts of this case. The prosecution of appellants in federal court for mail fraud does not interfere with the state's enforcement of its election laws. There are no grounds for dismissing the indictment under the principles of comity or the abstention doctrine or under any other principle of federalism.

* * *

Affirmed.

■ ROSS, CIRCUIT JUDGE (concurring).

I reluctantly concur. The law, as capably expressed by Judge Matthes, leaves us no other alternative.

However, I cannot believe that it was the original intent of Congress that the Federal Government should take over the prosecution of every state crime involving fraud just because the mails have been used in furtherance of that crime. The facts in this case show that this election fraud was purely a state matter. It should have been prosecuted in state court. [The federal government's decision to prosecute this case] relieved the state of its duty to police the violation of its local election laws and helped create a precedent which will encourage the same sort of unwarranted federal preemption in the future.

NOTE

United States v. Coates, 949 F.2d 104 (4th Cir. 1991) reversed a judgment of conviction where the government did not have an independent reason for using an interstate facility to provide federal jurisdiction. An undercover detective who lived in the same state as Coates crossed a state line to place a phone call to Coates just to gain federal jurisdiction. The circuit court reversed Coates' conviction, adopting the view that "federal jurisdiction in criminal prosecutions should not be recognized when patently contrived by means adopted *solely* for the purpose of creating a federal crime." *See also* United States v. Archer, 486 F.2d 670, 681 (2d Cir. 1973) ("Whatever Congress may have meant . . . it certainly did not intend to include a telephone call manufactured by the Government for the precise purpose of transforming a local bribery offense into a federal crime.").

(D)　THE COMMERCE CLAUSE OFFENSES

Gonzales v. Raich

Supreme Court of the United States, 2005.
545 U.S. 1, 125 S.Ct. 2195, 162 L.Ed.2d 1.

[Most footnotes have been omitted]

■ JUSTICE STEVENS delivered the opinion of the Court.

California is one of at least nine States that authorize the use of marijuana for medicinal purposes. The question presented in this case is whether the power vested in Congress by Article I, § 8, of the Constitution "[t]o make all Laws which shall be necessary and proper for carrying into Execution" its authority to "regulate Commerce with foreign Nations, and among the several States" includes the power to prohibit the local cultivation and use of marijuana in compliance with California law.

I

California has been a pioneer in the regulation of marijuana. In 1913, California was one of the first States to prohibit the sale and possession of marijuana, and at the end of the century, California became the first State to authorize limited use of the drug for medicinal purposes. In 1996, California voters passed Proposition 215, now codified as the Compassionate Use Act of 1996. The proposition was designed to ensure that "seriously ill" residents of the State have access to marijuana for medical purposes, and to encourage Federal and State Governments to take steps towards ensuring the safe and affordable distribution of the drug to patients in need. The act creates an exemption from criminal prosecution for physicians, as well as for patients and primary caregivers who possess or cultivate marijuana for medicinal purposes with the recommendation or approval of a physician. A "primary caregiver" is a person who has consistently assumed responsibility for the housing, health, or safety of the patient.

Respondents Angel Raich and Diane Monson are California residents who suffer from a variety of serious medical conditions and have sought to avail themselves of medical marijuana pursuant to the terms of the Compassionate Use Act. They are being treated by licensed, board-certified family practitioners, who have concluded, after prescribing a host of conventional medicines to treat respondents' conditions and to alleviate their associated symptoms, that marijuana is the only drug available that provides effective treatment. Both women have been using marijuana as a medication for several years pursuant to their doctors' recommendation, and both rely heavily on cannabis to function on a daily basis. Indeed, Raich's physician believes that forgoing cannabis treatments would certainly cause Raich excruciating pain and could very well prove fatal.

Respondent Monson cultivates her own marijuana, and ingests the drug in a variety of ways including smoking and using a vaporizer. Respondent Raich, by contrast, is unable to cultivate her own, and thus relies on two caregivers, litigating as "John Does," to provide her with locally grown marijuana at no charge. These caregivers also process the cannabis into hashish or keif, and Raich herself processes some of the marijuana into oils, balms, and foods for consumption.

On August 15, 2002, county deputy sheriffs and agents from the federal Drug Enforcement Administration (DEA) came to Monson's home. After a thorough investigation, the county officials concluded that her use of marijuana was entirely lawful as a matter of California law. Nevertheless, after a 3-hour standoff, the federal agents seized and destroyed all six of her cannabis plants.

Respondents thereafter brought this action against the Attorney General of the United States and the head of the DEA seeking injunctive and declaratory relief prohibiting the enforcement of the federal Controlled Substances Act (CSA), 21 U.S.C. § 801 *et seq.*, to the extent it prevents them from possessing, obtaining, or manufacturing cannabis for their personal medical use. . . . Respondents claimed that enforcing the CSA against them would violate the Commerce Clause, the Due Process Clause of the Fifth Amendment, the Ninth and Tenth Amendments of the Constitution, and the doctrine of medical necessity.

The District Court denied respondents' motion for a preliminary injunction. . . .

A divided panel of the Court of Appeals for the Ninth Circuit reversed and ordered the District Court to enter a preliminary injunction. The court found that respondents had demonstrated a strong likelihood of success on their claim that, as applied to them, the CSA is an unconstitutional exercise of Congress' Commerce Clause authority. . . .

The majority placed heavy reliance on our decisions in *United States v. Lopez*, 514 U.S. 549, 115 S.Ct. 1624, 131 L.Ed.2d 626 (1995), and *United States v. Morrison*, 529 U.S. 598, 120 S.Ct. 1740, 146 L.Ed.2d 658 (2000), as interpreted by recent Circuit precedent, to hold that this separate class of purely local activities was beyond the reach of federal power. . . .

The obvious importance of the case prompted our grant of certiorari. The case is made difficult by respondents' strong arguments that they will suffer irreparable harm because, despite a congressional finding to the contrary, marijuana does have valid therapeutic purposes. The question before us, however, is not whether it is wise to enforce the statute in these circumstances; rather, it is whether Congress' power to regulate interstate markets for medicinal substances encompasses the portions of those markets that are supplied with drugs produced and consumed locally. . . .

[Part II of the opinion, on the historical development of laws passed in the "national 'war on drugs'" and the criminalization of marijuana is omitted.]

III

Respondents in this case do not dispute that passage of the CSA, as part of the Comprehensive Drug Abuse Prevention and Control Act, was well within Congress' commerce power. Nor do they contend that any provision or section of the CSA amounts to an unconstitutional exercise of congressional authority. Rather, respondents' challenge is actually quite limited; they argue that the CSA's categorical prohibition of the manufacture and possession of marijuana as applied to the intrastate manufacture and possession of marijuana for medical purposes pursuant to California law exceeds Congress' authority under the Commerce Clause.

In assessing the validity of congressional regulation, none of our Commerce Clause cases can be viewed in isolation. As charted in considerable detail in *United States v. Lopez*, our understanding of the reach of the Commerce Clause, as well as Congress' assertion of authority thereunder, has evolved over time. . . . Then, in response to rapid industrial development and an increasingly interdependent national economy, Congress "ushered in a new era of federal regulation under the commerce power," beginning with the enactment of the Interstate Commerce Act in 1887, and the Sherman Antitrust Act in 1890, . . .

Cases decided during that "new era," which now spans more than a century, have identified three general categories of regulation in which Congress is authorized to engage under its commerce power. First, Congress can regulate the channels of interstate commerce. *Perez v. United States*, 402 U.S. 146, 150, 91 S.Ct. 1357, 28 L.Ed.2d 686 (1971). Second, Congress has authority to regulate and protect the instrumentalities of interstate commerce, and persons or things in interstate commerce. *Ibid.* Third, Congress has the power to regulate activities that substantially affect interstate commerce. *Ibid.*; *NLRB v. Jones & Laughlin Steel Corp.*, 301 U.S. 1, 37, 57 S.Ct. 615, 81 L.Ed. 893 (1937). Only the third category is implicated in the case at hand.

Our case law firmly establishes Congress' power to regulate purely local activities that are part of an economic "class of activities" that have a substantial effect on interstate commerce. See, *e.g.*, . . . *Wickard v. Filburn*, 317 U.S. 111, 128–129, 63 S.Ct. 82, 87 L.Ed. 122 (1942). As we stated in *Wickard*, "even if appellee's activity be local and though it may not be regarded as commerce, it may still, whatever its nature, be reached by Congress if it exerts a substantial economic effect on interstate commerce." . . . When Congress decides that the "total incidence" of a practice poses a threat to a national market, it may regulate the entire class. . . . In this vein, we have reiterated that when "a general regulatory statute bears a substantial relation to commerce, the *de minimis* character of individual instances arising under that statute is of no consequence." *E.g., Lopez*, 514 U.S., at 558, 115 S.Ct. 1624.

* * *

In assessing the scope of Congress' authority under the Commerce Clause, we stress that the task before us is a modest one. We need not determine whether respondents' activities, taken in the aggregate, substantially affect interstate commerce in fact, but only whether a "rational basis" exists for so concluding. *Lopez*, 514 U.S., at 557, 115 S.Ct. 1624; Given the enforcement difficulties that attend distinguishing between marijuana cultivated locally and marijuana grown elsewhere, and concerns about diversion into illicit channels, we have no difficulty concluding that Congress had a rational basis for believing that failure to regulate the intrastate manufacture and possession of marijuana would leave a gaping hole in the CSA. Thus, as in *Wickard*, when it enacted comprehensive legislation to regulate the interstate market in a fungible commodity, Congress was acting well within its authority to "make all Laws which shall be necessary and proper" to "regulate Commerce . . . among the several States." U.S. Const., Art. I, § 8. That the regulation ensnares some purely intrastate activity is of no moment. As we have done many times before, we refuse to excise individual components of that larger scheme.

IV

To support their contrary submission, respondents rely heavily on two of our more recent Commerce Clause cases. In their myopic focus, they overlook the larger context of modern-era Commerce Clause jurisprudence preserved by those cases. Moreover, even in the narrow prism of respondents' creation, they read those cases far too broadly. Those two cases, of course, are *Lopez*, 514 U.S. 549, 115 S.Ct. 1624, and *Morrison*, 529 U.S. 598, 120 S.Ct. 1740. As an initial matter, the statutory challenges at issue in those cases were markedly different from the challenge respondents pursue in the case at hand. Here, respondents ask us to excise individual applications of a concededly valid statutory scheme. In contrast, in both *Lopez* and *Morrison*, the parties asserted that a particular statute or provision fell outside Congress' commerce power in its entirety. This distinction is pivotal. . . .

At issue in Lopez was the validity of the Gun-Free School Zones Act of 1990, which was a brief, single-subject statute making it a crime for an individual to possess a gun in a school zone. 18 U.S.C. § 922(q)(1)(A). The Act did not regulate any economic activity and did not contain any requirement that the possession of a gun have any connection to past interstate activity or a predictable impact on future commercial activity. Distinguishing our earlier cases holding that comprehensive regulatory statutes may be validly applied to local conduct that does not, when viewed in isolation, have a significant impact on interstate commerce, we held the statute invalid. We explained:

"Section 922(q) is a criminal statute that by its terms has nothing to do with 'commerce' or any sort of economic enterprise, however broadly one might define those terms. Section 922(q) is not an essential part of a larger regulation of economic activity, in which the regulatory scheme could be undercut unless the intrastate activity were regulated. It cannot, therefore, be sustained under our cases upholding regulations of activities that arise out of or are connected with a commercial transaction, which viewed in the aggregate, substantially affects interstate commerce."

The statutory scheme that the Government is defending in this litigation is at the opposite end of the regulatory spectrum. As explained above, the CSA, enacted in 1970 as part of the Comprehensive Drug Abuse Prevention and Control Act, 84 Stat. 1242–1284, was a lengthy and detailed statute creating a comprehensive framework for regulating the production, distribution, and possession of five classes of "controlled substances." Most of those substances—those listed in Schedules II through V—"have a useful and legitimate medical purpose and are necessary to maintain the health and general welfare of the American people." 21 U.S.C. § 801(1). The regulatory scheme is designed to foster the beneficial use of those medications, to prevent their misuse, and to prohibit entirely the possession or use of substances listed in Schedule I, except as a part of a strictly controlled research project.

While the statute provided for the periodic updating of the five schedules, Congress itself made the initial classifications. It identified 42 opiates, 22 opium derivatives, and 17 hallucinogenic substances as Schedule I drugs. 84 Stat. 1248. Marijuana was listed as the 10th item in the 3d subcategory. That classification, unlike the discrete prohibition established by the Gun-Free School Zones Act of 1990, was merely one of many "essential part[s] of a larger regulation of economic activity, in which the regulatory scheme could be undercut unless the intrastate activity were regulated." Our opinion in *Lopez* casts no doubt on the validity of such a program.

Nor does this Court's holding in *Morrison*, 529 U.S. 598, 120 S.Ct. 1740. The Violence Against Women Act of 1994, 108 Stat.1902, created a federal civil remedy for the victims of gender-motivated crimes of violence. 42 U.S.C. § 13981. The remedy was enforceable in both state and federal courts, and generally depended on proof of the violation of a state law. Despite congressional findings that such crimes had an adverse impact on interstate commerce, we held the statute unconstitutional because, like the statute in *Lopez*, it did not regulate economic activity. We concluded that "the noneconomic, criminal nature of the conduct at issue was central to our decision" in *Lopez*, and that our prior cases had identified a clear pattern of analysis: "Where economic

relief, is broad enough to allow even the most scrupulous doctor to conclude that some recreational uses would be therapeutic.[39] . . .

The exemption for cultivation by patients and caregivers can only increase the supply of marijuana in the California market. The likelihood that all such production will promptly terminate when patients recover or will precisely match the patients' medical needs during their convalescence seems remote; whereas the danger that excesses will satisfy some of the admittedly enormous demand for recreational use seems obvious. Moreover, that the national and international narcotics trade has thrived in the face of vigorous criminal enforcement efforts suggests that no small number of unscrupulous people will make use of the California exemptions to serve their commercial ends whenever it is feasible to do so. Taking into account the fact that California is only one of at least nine States to have authorized the medical use of marijuana, . . . Congress could have rationally concluded that the aggregate impact on the national market of all the transactions exempted from federal supervision is unquestionably substantial.

* * *

V

. . . Respondents also raise a substantive due process claim and seek to avail themselves of the medical necessity defense. These theories of relief were set forth in their complaint but were not reached by the Court of Appeals. We therefore do not address the question whether judicial relief is available to respondents on these alternative bases. . . . Under the present state of the law, however, the judgment of the Court of Appeals must be vacated. The case is remanded for further proceedings consistent with this opinion.

It is so ordered.

■ [The opinion of JUSTICE SCALIA, concurring in the judgment, is omitted.]

■ JUSTICE O'CONNOR, with whom THE CHIEF JUSTICE and JUSTICE THOMAS join as to all but Part III, dissenting.

We enforce the "outer limits" of Congress' Commerce Clause authority not for their own sake, but to protect historic spheres of state sovereignty from excessive federal encroachment and thereby to maintain the distribution of power fundamental to our federalist system of government One of federalism's chief virtues, of course, is that it promotes innovation by allowing for the possibility that "a single courageous State may, if its citizens choose, serve as a laboratory; and

---

[39] California's Compassionate Use Act has since been amended, limiting the catchall category to "[a]ny other chronic or persistent medical symptom that either: . . . [s]ubstantially limits the ability of the person to conduct one or more major life activities as defined" in the Americans with Disabilities Act of 1990, or "[i]f not alleviated, may cause serious harm to the patient's safety or physical or mental health." Cal. Health & Safety Code Ann. §§ 11362.7(h)(12)(A), (B) (West Supp.2005).

try novel social and economic experiments without risk to the rest of the country." *New State Ice Co. v. Liebmann*, 285 U.S. 262, 311, 52 S.Ct. 371, 76 L.Ed. 747 (1932) (BRANDEIS, J., dissenting).

This case exemplifies the role of States as laboratories. The States' core police powers have always included authority to define criminal law and to protect the health, safety, and welfare of their citizens. Exercising those powers, California (by ballot initiative and then by legislative codification) has come to its own conclusion about the difficult and sensitive question of whether marijuana should be available to relieve severe pain and suffering. Today the Court sanctions an application of the federal Controlled Substances Act that extinguishes that experiment, without any proof that the personal cultivation, possession, and use of marijuana for medicinal purposes, if economic activity in the first place, has a substantial effect on interstate commerce and is therefore an appropriate subject of federal regulation. In so doing, the Court announces a rule that gives Congress a perverse incentive to legislate broadly pursuant to the Commerce Clause—nestling questionable assertions of its authority into comprehensive regulatory schemes—rather than with precision. That rule and the result it produces in this case are irreconcilable with our decisions in *Lopez*, *supra*, and *United States v. Morrison*, 529 U.S. 598, 120 S.Ct. 1740, 146 L.Ed.2d 658 (2000). Accordingly I dissent.

I

In *Lopez*, we considered the constitutionality of the Gun-Free School Zones Act of 1990, which made it a federal offense "for any individual knowingly to possess a firearm . . . at a place that the individual knows, or has reasonable cause to believe, is a school zone," We explained that "Congress' commerce authority includes the power to regulate those activities having a substantial relation to interstate commerce . . ., *i.e.*, those activities that substantially affect interstate commerce." This power derives from the conjunction of the Commerce Clause and the Necessary and Proper Clause. *Garcia v. San Antonio Metropolitan Transit Authority*, 469 U.S. 528, 585–586, 105 S.Ct. 1005, 83 L.Ed.2d 1016 (1985) (O'CONNOR, J., dissenting) (explaining that *United States v. Darby*, 312 U.S. 100, 61 S.Ct. 451, 85 L.Ed. 609 (1941), *United States v. Wrightwood Dairy Co.*, 315 U.S. 110, 62 S.Ct. 523, 86 L.Ed. 726 (1942), and *Wickard v. Filburn*, 317 U.S. 111, 63 S.Ct. 82, 87 L.Ed. 122 (1942), based their expansion of the commerce power on the Necessary and Proper Clause, and that "the reasoning of these cases underlies every recent decision concerning the reach of Congress to activities affecting interstate commerce"). We held in *Lopez* that the Gun-Free School Zones Act could not be sustained as an exercise of that power.

Our decision about whether gun possession in school zones substantially affected interstate commerce turned on four considerations. First, we observed that our "substantial effects" cases generally have upheld federal regulation of economic activity that affected interstate commerce, but that § 922(q) was a criminal statute having "nothing to do with 'commerce' or any sort of economic enterprise." *Lopez*, 514 U.S., at 561, 115 S.Ct. 1624. In this regard, we also noted that "[s]ection 922(q) is not an essential part of a larger regulation of economic activity, in which the regulatory scheme could be undercut unless the intrastate activity were regulated. It cannot, therefore, be sustained under our cases upholding regulations of activities that arise out of or are connected with a commercial transaction, which viewed in the aggregate, substantially affects interstate commerce." Second, we noted that the statute contained no express jurisdictional requirement establishing its connection to interstate commerce.

Third, we found telling the absence of legislative findings about the regulated conduct's impact on interstate commerce. We explained that while express legislative findings are neither required nor, when provided, dispositive, findings "enable us to evaluate the legislative judgment that the activity in question substantially affect[s] interstate commerce, even though no such substantial effect [is] visible to the naked eye." Finally, we rejected as too attenuated the Government's argument that firearm possession in school zones could result in violent crime which in turn could adversely affect the national economy. The Constitution, we said, does not tolerate reasoning that would convert congressional authority under the Commerce Clause to a general police power of the sort retained by the States. Later in *Morrison, supra*, we relied on the same four considerations to hold that § 40302 of the Violence Against Women Act of 1994, 42 U.S.C. § 13981, exceeded Congress' authority under the Commerce Clause.

In my view, the case before us is materially indistinguishable from *Lopez* and *Morrison* when the same considerations are taken into account.

II

A

What is the relevant conduct subject to Commerce Clause analysis in this case? The Court takes its cues from Congress, applying the above considerations to the activity regulated by the Controlled Substances Act (CSA) in general. The Court's decision rests on two facts about the CSA: (1) Congress chose to enact a single statute providing a comprehensive prohibition on the production, distribution, and possession of all controlled substances, and (2) Congress did not distinguish between various forms of intrastate noncommercial cultivation, possession, and use of marijuana. See 21 U.S.C. §§ 841(a)(1), 844(a). Today's decision suggests that the federal regulation of local activity is immune to Commerce Clause challenge because Congress chose to act with an ambitious, all-encompassing statute, rather than piecemeal. In my view, allowing Congress to set the terms of the constitutional debate in this way, *i.e.*, by packaging regulation of local activity in broader schemes, is tantamount to removing meaningful limits on the Commerce Clause.

The Court's principal means of distinguishing *Lopez* from this case is to observe that the Gun-Free School Zones Act of 1990 was a "brief, single-subject statute," whereas the CSA is "a lengthy and detailed statute creating a comprehensive framework for regulating the production, distribution, and possession of five classes of 'controlled substances,'" Thus, according to the Court, it was possible in *Lopez* to evaluate in isolation the constitutionality of criminalizing local activity (there gun possession in school zones), whereas the local activity that the CSA targets (in this case cultivation and possession of marijuana for personal medicinal use) cannot be separated from the general drug control scheme of which it is a part.

Today's decision allows Congress to regulate intrastate activity without check, so long as there is some implication by legislative design that regulating intrastate activity is essential (and the Court appears to equate "essential" with "necessary") to the interstate regulatory scheme. . . .

I cannot agree that our decision in *Lopez* contemplated such evasive or overbroad legislative strategies with approval. Until today, such arguments have been made only in dissent. . . . Likewise I did not understand our discussion of the role of courts in enforcing outer limits of the Commerce Clause for the sake of maintaining the federalist balance our Constitution requires, as a signal to Congress to enact legislation that is more extensive and more intrusive into the domain of state power. If the Court always defers to Congress as it does today, little may be left to the notion of enumerated powers.

The hard work for courts, then, is to identify objective markers for confining the analysis in Commerce Clause cases. . . .

A number of objective markers are available to confine the scope of constitutional review here. Both federal and state legislation—including the CSA itself, the California Compassionate Use Act, and other state medical marijuana legislation—recognize that medical and nonmedical (*i.e.*, recreational) uses of drugs are realistically distinct and can be segregated, and regulate them differently. Respondents challenge only the application of the CSA to medicinal use of marijuana. . . . Moreover, because fundamental structural concerns about dual sovereignty animate our Commerce Clause cases, it is relevant that this case involves the interplay of federal and state regulation in areas of criminal law and social policy, where States lay claim by right of history and expertise. California, like other States, has drawn on its reserved powers to distinguish the regulation of medicinal marijuana. To ascertain whether Congress' encroachment is constitutionally justified in this case, then, I would focus here on the personal cultivation, possession, and use of marijuana for medicinal purposes.

B

Having thus defined the relevant conduct, we must determine whether, under our precedents, the conduct is economic and, in the aggregate, substantially affects interstate commerce. Even if intrastate cultivation and possession of marijuana for one's own medicinal use can properly be characterized as economic, and I question whether it can, it has not been shown that such activity substantially affects interstate commerce. Similarly, it is neither self-evident nor demonstrated that regulating such activity is necessary to the interstate drug control scheme.

The Court's definition of economic activity is breathtaking. It defines as economic any activity involving the production, distribution, and consumption of commodities. And it appears to reason that when an interstate market for a commodity exists, regulating the intrastate manufacture or possession of that commodity is constitutional either because that intrastate activity is itself economic, or because regulating it is a rational part of regulating its market. Putting to one side the problem endemic to the Court's opinion—the shift in focus from the activity at issue in this case to the entirety of what the CSA regulates, the Court's definition of economic activity for purposes of Commerce Clause jurisprudence threatens to sweep all of productive human activity into federal regulatory reach.

. . . It will not do to say that Congress may regulate noncommercial activity simply because it may have an effect on the demand for commercial goods, or because the noncommercial endeavor can, in some sense, substitute for commercial activity. Most commercial goods or services have some sort of privately producible analogue. Home care substitutes for daycare. Charades games substitute for movie tickets. Backyard or windowsill gardening substitutes for going to the supermarket. To draw the line wherever private activity affects the demand for market goods is to draw no line at all, and to declare everything economic. We have already rejected the result that would follow—a federal police power. *Lopez, supra*, at 564, 115 S.Ct. 1624.

In *Lopez* and *Morrison*, we suggested that economic activity usually relates directly to commercial activity. . . . The homegrown cultivation and personal possession and use of marijuana for medicinal purposes has no apparent commercial character. Everyone agrees that the marijuana at issue in this case was never in the stream of commerce, and neither were the supplies for growing it. (Marijuana is highly unusual among the substances subject to the CSA in that it can be cultivated without any materials that have traveled in interstate commerce.) *Lopez* makes clear that possession is not itself commercial activity. And respondents have not come into possession by means of any commercial transaction; they have simply grown, in their own homes, marijuana for their own use, without acquiring, buying, selling, or bartering a thing of value. . . .

* * *

The Court suggests that *Wickard*, which we have identified as "perhaps the most far reaching example of Commerce Clause authority over intrastate activity," *Lopez, supra*, at 560, 115 S.Ct. 1624, established federal regulatory power over any home consumption of a commodity for which a national market exists. I disagree. *Wickard* involved a challenge to the Agricultural Adjustment Act of 1938(AAA), which directed the Secretary of Agriculture to set national quotas on wheat production, and penalties for excess production. 317 U.S., at 115–116, 63 S.Ct. 82. The AAA itself confirmed that Congress made an explicit choice not to reach—and thus the Court could not possibly have approved of federal control over-small-scale, noncommercial wheat farming. In contrast to the CSA's limitless assertion of power, Congress provided an exemption within the AAA for small producers. When Filburn planted the wheat at issue in *Wickard*, the statute exempted plantings less than 200 bushels (about six tons), and when he harvested his wheat it exempted plantings less than six acres. *Id.*, at 130, n. 30, 63 S.Ct. 82. *Wickard*, then, did not extend Commerce Clause authority to something as modest as the home cook's herb garden. This is not to say that Congress may never regulate small quantities of commodities possessed or produced for personal use, or to deny that it sometimes needs to enact a zero tolerance regime for such commodities. It is merely to say that *Wickard* did not hold or imply that small-scale production of commodities is always economic, and automatically within Congress' reach.

Even assuming that economic activity is at issue in this case, the Government has made no showing in fact that the possession and use of homegrown marijuana for medical purposes, in California or elsewhere, has a substantial effect on interstate commerce. Similarly, the Government has not shown that regulating such activity is necessary to an interstate regulatory scheme. Whatever the specific theory of "substantial effects" at issue (*i.e.*, whether the activity substantially affects interstate commerce, whether its regulation is necessary to an interstate regulatory scheme, or both), a concern for dual sovereignty requires that Congress' excursion into the traditional domain of States be justified.

* * *

There is simply no evidence that homegrown medicinal marijuana users constitute, in the aggregate, a sizable enough class to have a discernable, let alone substantial, impact on the national illicit drug market—or otherwise to threaten the CSA regime. Explicit evidence is helpful when substantial effect is not "visible to the naked eye." See *Lopez*, 514 U.S., at 563, 115 S.Ct. 1624. And here, in part because common sense suggests that medical marijuana users may be limited in number and that California's Compassionate Use Act and similar state legislation may well isolate activities relating to medicinal marijuana from the illicit market, the effect of those activities on interstate drug traffic is not self-evidently substantial.

* * *

In particular, the CSA's introductory declarations are too vague and unspecific to demonstrate that the federal statutory scheme will be undermined if Congress cannot exert power over individuals like respondents. The declarations are not even specific to marijuana. (Facts about substantial effects may be developed in litigation to compensate for the inadequacy of Congress' findings; in part because this case comes to us from the grant of a preliminary injunction, there has been no such development.) Because here California, like other States, has carved out a limited class of activity for distinct regulation, the inadequacy of the CSA's findings is especially glaring. . . . We generally assume States enforce their laws, and have no reason to think otherwise here.

The Government has not overcome empirical doubt that the number of Californians engaged in personal cultivation, possession, and use of medical marijuana, or the amount of marijuana they produce, is enough to threaten the federal regime. Nor has it shown that Compassionate Use Act marijuana users have been or are realistically likely to be responsible for the drug's seeping into the market in a significant way. The Government does cite one estimate that there were over 100,000 Compassionate Use Act users in California in 2004, but does not explain, in terms of proportions, what their presence means for the national illicit drug market. It also provides anecdotal evidence about the CSA's enforcement. The Court also offers some arguments about the effect of the Compassionate Use Act on the national market. It says that the California statute might be vulnerable to exploitation by unscrupulous physicians, that Compassionate Use Act patients may overproduce, and that the history of the narcotics trade shows the difficulty of cordoning off any drug use from the rest of the market. These arguments are plausible; if borne out in fact they could justify prosecuting Compassionate Use Act patients under the federal CSA. But, without substantiation, they add little to the CSA's conclusory statements about diversion, essentiality, and market effect. Piling assertion upon assertion does not, in my view, satisfy the substantiality test of *Lopez* and *Morrison*.

III

We would do well to recall how James Madison, the father of the Constitution, described our system of joint sovereignty to the people of New York: "The powers delegated by the proposed Constitution to the federal government are few and defined. Those which are to remain in the State governments are numerous and indefinite. . . . The powers reserved to the several States will extend to all the objects which, in the ordinary course of affairs, concern the lives, liberties, and properties of the people, and the internal order, improvement, and prosperity of the State." The Federalist No. 45, pp. 292–293 (C. Rossiter ed.1961).

Relying on Congress' abstract assertions, the Court has endorsed making it a federal crime to grow small amounts of marijuana in one's own home for one's own medicinal use. This overreaching stifles an express choice by some States, concerned for the lives and liberties of their people, to regulate medical marijuana differently. If I were a California citizen, I would not have voted for the medical marijuana ballot initiative; if I were a California legislator I would not have supported the Compassionate Use Act. But whatever the wisdom of California's experiment with medical marijuana, the federalism principles that have driven our Commerce Clause cases require that room for experiment be protected in this case. For these reasons I dissent.

■ JUSTICE THOMAS, dissenting.

Respondents Diane Monson and Angel Raich use marijuana that has never been bought or sold, that has never crossed state lines, and that has had no demonstrable effect on the national market for marijuana. If Congress can regulate this under the Commerce Clause, then it can regulate virtually anything—and the Federal Government is no longer one of limited and enumerated powers.

* * *

The majority prevents States like California from devising drug policies that they have concluded provide much-needed respite to the seriously ill. It does so without any serious inquiry into the necessity for federal regulation or the propriety of displacing state regulation in areas of traditional state concern. The majority's rush to embrace federal power "is especially unfortunate given the importance of showing respect for the sovereign States that comprise our Federal Union." *United States v. Oakland Cannabis Buyers' Cooperative*, 532 U.S. 483, 502, 121 S.Ct. 1711, 149 L.Ed.2d 722 (2001) (STEVENS, J., concurring in judgment). Our federalist system, properly understood, allows California and a growing number of other States to decide for themselves how to safeguard the health and welfare of their citizens. I would affirm the judgment of the Court of Appeals. I respectfully dissent.

NOTES

1. In Printz v. United States, 521 U.S. 898, 117 S.Ct. 2365, 138 L.Ed.2d 914 (1997), the Court found that the Constitution was violated by provisions of the Brady Handgun Violence Prevention Act, Pub.L. 103–159, 107 Stat. 1536, commanding state and local law enforcement officers to conduct background checks on prospective handgun purchasers and to perform certain related tasks. The Court stated that:

> It is incontestible that the Constitution established a system of "dual sovereignty." Although the States surrendered many of

their powers to the new Federal Government, they retained "a residuary and inviolable sovereignty." Residual state sovereignty was also implicit, of course, in the Constitution's conferral upon Congress of not all governmental powers, but only discrete, enumerated ones, Art. I, § 8, which implication was rendered express by the Tenth Amendment's assertion that "[t]he powers not delegated to the United States by the Constitution, nor prohibited by it to the States, are reserved to the States respectively, or to the people."

The Federal Government may neither issue directives requiring the States to address particular problems, nor command the States' officers, or those of their political subdivisions, to administer or enforce a federal regulatory program. It matters not whether policymaking is involved, and no case-by-case weighing of the burdens or benefits is necessary; such commands are fundamentally incompatible with our constitutional system of dual sovereignty.

2. 18 U.S.C. § 1951, commonly called the Hobbs Act, prohibits obstructing, delaying and affecting commerce and the movement of articles in commerce by extortion. Only a minimal connection between the extortion and interstate commerce is required under the Hobbs Act, noted the majority in United States v. Wright, 797 F.2d 245 (5th Cir. 1986). In *Wright*, a city attorney in Louisiana and a defense attorney who was formerly an assistant city attorney, operated a scheme of extortion whereby the clients of the defense attorney were not prosecuted for drunken driving. What is the interstate commerce nexus required for federal jurisdiction under the Hobbs Act? The court said:

> [T]he district court relied on the testimony of a government witness, Robert Voas, qualified as an expert in the field of alcohol and highway safety. Mr. Voas testified that the consumption of alcohol is "a major, perhaps the major factor causing highway accidents." His experience evaluating law enforcement techniques in the area of DWI led him to conclude that the more serious an automobile accident is, the more likely it is that a drinking driver is involved. . . . It was Voas' opinion that the higher risk can be reduced either by treating the drinking driver or by suspending or revoking his driving privileges. . . . Failure to prosecute cases where the evidence is sufficient to sustain a conviction has a demoralizing effect on police officers to the point that they tend to make fewer arrests. Finally Voas testified that alcoholism is a tremendous problem in the United States, costing the nation one hundred billion dollars per year in medical expenses and lost working time, and that people with drinking problems who finally do seek help often do so because they have been arrested and prosecuted on a charge of drunk driving.

> The district court, clearly acting within its prerogative, credited this testimony, and relied on it to find that the government

had proved the interstate commerce element of a Hobbs Act crime. . . . The district court's findings to support its conclusion on interstate commerce are not clearly erroneous, and we are powerless to disturb them.

The dissenting judge didn't believe that every case of small-town corruption was an appropriate target for cranking up the federal prosecution machinery, and while a minimal connection between the extortion and the effect on interstate commerce is undoubtedly sufficient, he did not think that the tenuous connection between local DWI prosecutions in Louisiana and interstate commerce amounted to a sufficient nexus.

3. Commerce may be affected either as a direct result of the extortionate transaction or by a depletion of the resources of a business operating in interstate commerce. The latter theory is predicated on the notion that the business would have been in a position to purchase more or better quality merchandise from out of state if the extortionate payment had not been made. For example, in United States v. Tropiano, 418 F.2d 1069 (2d Cir. 1969), *cert. denied*, 397 U.S. 1021, 90 S.Ct. 1258, 25 L.Ed.2d 530 (1970), defendants, engaged in the rubbish removal business, were charged with threatening to harm certain individuals engaged in the same business for soliciting accounts in the city in which defendants operated. At trial, the government's sole evidence in support of the interstate commerce aspect of the offense was the fact that the victim purchased refuse removal trucks from an out of state corporation. In response to defendants' claim that this proof was insufficient, the court said: "[The victim's] surrender of his right to solicit additional customers in [the city] automatically limited his future orders for receptacles for new customers and the trucks required to serve such customers."

4. For a case which appears to extend the Hobbs Act coverage to its outer limits, consider United States v. Staszcuk, 517 F.2d 53 (7th Cir. 1975), *cert. denied*, 423 U.S. 837, 96 S.Ct. 65, 46 L.Ed.2d 56 (1975). The defendant, a Chicago alderman, was convicted of extorting $9000 for a favorable zoning ruling with respect to the planned construction of an animal hospital. The commerce clause connection was based upon the fact that the building contractor needed various materials such as a furnace, plate glass, plumbing, and electrical fixtures which would be purchased from out-of-state suppliers.

5. Does the extraordinarily broad reading of the Hobbs Act trench upon state's rights? See Tracy W. Resch, Comment, *The Scope of Federal Criminal Jurisdiction Under the Commerce Clause*, 1972 U. Ill. L.F. 805, 822:

> [I]t should be noted that the use of the commerce clause as an expansive basis for federal intervention in the area of crime control has not been opposed by the states, though similar federal intervention in economic affairs faced heavy resistance. State acquiescence, if not encouragement, can be attributed to several factors: the federal government has not preempted state powers; federal intervention has helped states deal with problems serious enough to override the usual states' rights fears; and the federal government has entered this area gradually, reluctantly, and

primarily with programs aimed at organized crime, a problem generally felt to be incapable of solution by the states acting alone.

(E) CIVIL RIGHTS OFFENSES

A number of statutes, both federal and state, make it a criminal offense to deprive a person of his constitutional rights. Foremost are the following two federal enactments.

18 U.S.C. § 241 provides:

> If two or more persons conspire to injure, oppress, threaten, or intimidate any citizen in the free exercise or enjoyment of any right or privilege secured to him by the Constitution or laws of the United States, or because of his having so exercised the same: or

> If two or more persons go in disguise on the highway, or on the premises of another, with intent to prevent or hinder his free exercise or enjoyment of any right or privilege so secured—

> They shall be fined not more than $10,000 or imprisoned not more than ten years, or both; and if death results, they shall be subject to imprisonment for any term of years or for life.

A companion provision, 18 U.S.C. § 242, reads:

> Whoever, under color of any law, statute, ordinance, regulation, or custom, willfully subjects any inhabitant of any State, Territory, or District to the deprivation of any rights, privileges, or immunities secured or protected by the Constitution or laws of the United States, or to different punishments, pains, or penalties, on account of such inhabitant being an alien, or by reason of his color, or race, than are prescribed for the punishment of citizens, shall be fined not more than $1,000 or imprisoned not more than one year, or both; and if death results shall be subject to imprisonment for any term of years or for life.

There is also the Federal Civil Rights Act of 1871, 42 U.S.C. § 1983, under which a civil action may be brought by any person who has been deprived of his constitutional rights by a person who acts "under color of any statute, ordinance, regulation, custom, or usage of any State or territory." The language of the statute obviously confines its application to agents of state governments. However, the Court has held (in a 6–3 decision) that federal law enforcement officials may be subject to a civil action in the federal courts where such officials violate a person's Fourth Amendment protection against unreasonable searches and seizures. The dissenting justices were of the view that congressional authorization was needed for according such civil actions against federal officers. Bivens v. Six Unknown Named Agents of Federal Bureau of Narcotics, 403 U.S. 388, 91 S.Ct. 1999, 29 L.Ed.2d 619 (1971).

(F) FEDERAL PROSECUTORIAL DISCRETION AND STATE LAW ENFORCEMENT

The relationship of federal and state law enforcement authorities in acting upon offenses and offenders within a common sphere is a delicate and critical one. Apart from an early article—L.B. Schwartz, *Federal Criminal Jurisdiction and Prosecutorial Discretion*, 13 L. & Contemp. Prob. 64 (1948)—little has been written on the subject.

Two areas deserve focus. The first is the notion that primary and plenary law enforcement is the task of the states. The second is the growing reach of federal jurisdiction—by Congressional enactment and judicial construction—in areas where state jurisdiction has not been satisfactorily used (e.g., extortion, theft, bribery, especially in organized crime and official corruption cases).

In these circumstances, how does the federal prosecutor—newly armed with broadened jurisdictional powers, all-encompassing immunity statutes, and federal resources—define his area of activity and avoid federal-state tensions by supplanting, in whole or in part, the state prosecutor and police? Does vigorous federal prosecution of essentially local offenses weaken local law enforcement in the long run by encouraging lethargy or inactivity on the part of the local prosecutor who has other resource allocation problems, e.g., violent street crime, narcotics and the so-called "victimless" offenses in the area of gambling, prostitution and drunkenness?

What standards should a federal prosecutor employ to guide his prosecutorial discretion in the overlap area? Perhaps the threshold consideration for the federal prosecutor is to determine whether he has—or can obtain—the resources and manpower to broaden his prosecutorial base and, at the same time, continue to deter the commission of uniquely federal offenses. Assuming that he can, the question is reduced to whether he should branch out into the area of overlap between state and federal jurisdiction.

A key yardstick for measuring the degree to which the federal government should enter into this area is the quality of the local prosecutor's office. While some part of this evaluation may be subjective, factors such as community confidence in local authorities, as reflected by the media, the extent of local resources devoted to the prosecutor's office and the relationship between that office and local judges are relatively objective considerations in the overall determination. Moreover, where the same political party that controls a large part of the local government also controls the prosecutor's office, it is inconceivable, either because of purse-string control or political association, that local officials can always deal satisfactorily with the problems of official corruption. And where corruption appears in the local prosecutor's own investigative force—the community police—it is virtually impossible for him to take any extensive action because of the cohesion within the police fraternity. In instances such as this, an independent investigative agency, such as the FBI, is essential.

Thus, there may be some legitimate areas of prosecutorial concern in which the local officials are unwilling or unable to act. It is in these areas that the federal prosecutor must employ the existing federal statutes—and some degree of imagination—to combat and deter crime. But the decision to enter into this area depends upon a balancing of the factors outlined above in the particular circumstances of the jurisdiction over which the federal prosecutor presides. Are there any other factors that should be considered in reaching this ultimate decision?

Consider also the following case.

United States v. Jones

United States District Court, E.D. Virginia, 1999.
36 F.Supp.2d 304.

■ PER CURIAM.

This matter is before the Court on defendant's motion to dismiss the indictment. Defendant argues that his prosecution in federal, rather than state, court is an unconstitutional attempt to avoid a jury pool consisting of greater numbers of African-Americans. For the reasons stated below, the Court is compelled to DENY the motion.

I. FACTS

The defendant, Chad Ramon Jones ("Jones"), is an African-American. On May 31, 1998, he was operating his motor vehicle in the City of Richmond. He had two passengers in his vehicle. A Richmond Deputy Sheriff observed defendant proceed in the wrong direction on a one-way street. The police officer stopped defendant's vehicle and determined that defendant's driver's license was suspended. During a search of the vehicle subsequent to the stop, the police officer discovered marijuana, a nine-millimeter pistol, and drug paraphernalia.

The defendant was initially charged with violating statutes of the Commonwealth of Virginia and was slated for prosecution in state court. However, a program designated "Project Exile" resulted in the transfer of Jones' case for prosecution in this Court. On July 8, 1998, a federal grand jury issued a four-count indictment against Jones. The federal indictment covered precisely the same conduct originally prosecuted in the state proceedings.

Project Exile is a project jointly undertaken by the Commonwealth's Attorney for the City of Richmond and the United States Attorney for the Eastern District of Virginia. It was conceived in November 1996 and implemented in the City of Richmond in February 1997. The Program was later expanded to the City of Norfolk. Both cities suffer from high rates of violent crime. While Richmond possesses only three percent of the Commonwealth's population, it accounts for twenty-seven percent of its homicides.

The stated goal of Project Exile is to reduce violent crime by federally prosecuting firearm-related crimes whenever possible. Under Project Exile, local police review each firearm-related offense to determine whether the conduct alleged also constitutes a federal crime. In those cases in which the conduct alleged also constitutes a federal crime, local police refer the matter to the United States Attorney for the Eastern District of Virginia. If the United States Attorney obtains an indictment charging the defendant with federal firearm-related crimes, then the Commonwealth's Attorney drops the state charges, and the case proceeds in federal court.

Project Exile has resulted in the prosecution of several hundred defendants in federal court. To assist federal prosecutors with this additional workload, one Assistant Commonwealth's Attorney (of the thirty assigned to the office of the Commonwealth's Attorney for the City of Richmond) and one prosecutor from the Office of the Attorney General are assigned as a Special Assistant United States Attorneys ("Special AUSAs"). No additional resources are provided the federal judiciary, prosecutors, or law enforcement. Project Exile is widely publicized on television, radio, billboards, and buses. A professional advertising agency is responsible for this publicity. The advertising agency is paid with private funds donated by the "Project Exile Citizen Support Foundation."

The parties were unable to provide the Court precise empirical data concerning either the race of Project Exile defendants or the racial composition of the relevant jury pools. However, the parties agree to these general facts. Both Norfolk and Richmond have significant African-American populations. The vast majority, and perhaps as many as ninety percent of the defendants prosecuted under Project Exile are African-American. The jury pool for the Circuit Court for the City of Richmond is approximately seventy-five percent African-American. The jury pool for the Richmond Division of the Eastern District of Virginia is drawn from a broader geographic area. In contrast to the state jury pool, it is only about ten percent African-American. At a local Bench-Bar Conference discussing the issue, an Assistant United States Attorney ("AUSA") stated that one goal of Project Exile is to avoid "Richmond juries."

In addition to the racial differences between the relevant jury pools, there are several other relevant comparisons between prosecutions in the state and federal courts.

The state has no statute that prohibits possession of a firearm by a person who is an "unlawful user of or addicted to any controlled substance." *See* 18 U.S.C. 922(g)(3). However, the state targets the same general conduct by prohibiting a person who was twice convicted within the previous thirty-six months of a drug-related misdemeanor from possessing a firearm. The state does not prohibit the possession of a firearm by a person previously convicted of domestic abuse. *See* 18 U.S.C. § 922(g)(9). Again however, the state has an analogous statute prohibiting possession by one currently subject to a protective order. In the Court's experience, nearly all Project Exile defendants are prosecuted under one of the four federal statutes cited above.

In addition to the minor statutory differences cited above, the federal and state systems are governed by different sentencing provisions. In criminal cases, a state jury recommends a sentence. While the Circuit Court Judge is not bound by that recommendation, the recommendation imposes a ceiling, above which the judge may not sentence the defendant. Both the federal and state systems now have sentencing guidelines. The federal guidelines are mandatory. The state guidelines are discretionary. Both have abolished parole.

The basic statutes at issue impose different maximum penalties. The federal statute imposes a maximum penalty of ten years for most violations. This statutory maximum penalty is rarely imposed, however. The sentencing guidelines impose a base offense level of fourteen for possession of a firearm by a prohibited person. The sentencing guidelines call for a range of imprisonment varying from fifteen to forty-six months for this base offense level, depending upon a defendant's criminal history. The state statutes prohibiting possession of firearm by a felon or by a person in possession of controlled substances impose a sentence of one to five years. Each system has separate provisions to enhance the sentences of recidivists.

At the inception of Project Exile, the United States Attorney, the Commonwealth's Attorney and the Chief of Police asserted that federal prosecution was necessary because state court judges were unlikely to impose sentences sufficiently severe to serve as sufficient punishment for, or adequate deterrence of, narcotics related firearm offenses. However, that assertion was disproved by the empirical data for prosecution of cases involving narcotics and firearms offenses for 1993 through 1995 (the last period preceding the inception of Project Exile for which statistics are available). In particular, the data showed that few firearms offenses ever reached the state judiciary for sentencing. And, the same statistics suggested strongly that the paucity of firearms convictions was attributable to the failure to arrest or prosecute such offenses or to the disposition of those offenses by plea bargain.

II. LEGAL ANALYSIS

A. THE RACIAL COMPOSITION OF THE JURY

[The Court's discussion of whether Project Exile could violate Jones' guarantee of equal protection is omitted].

B. SELECTIVE PROSECUTION

The equal protection component of the Fifth Amendment's Due Process Clause also prohibits the selective federal prosecution based upon race. A prima facie case of selective prosecution contains two distinct elements. First, the defendant must establish that similarly situated individuals of a different race were not prosecuted. Second, he must establish that the differing treatment is "motivated by a discriminatory purpose," or was "invidious or in bad faith." The United States Supreme Court has repeatedly emphasized that a defendant's burden in establishing a prima facie case of selective prosecution is "a demanding one."

Project Exile would be vulnerable on selective prosecution grounds if African-American defendants were routinely diverted from state to federal prosecution while prosecutors allowed similarly situated Caucasian defendants to remain in state court. Both federal and state prosecutors deny that the decision to federally prosecute a Project Exile defendant is any way attributable to a defendant's race. However, the parties acknowledge that the vast majority, and perhaps as many as ninety percent, of Project Exile defendants are African-American. Although defendant suggests otherwise, he presents no evidence of Caucasian defendants similarly situated to defendant Jones evading diversion to federal court. A successful case of selective prosecution cannot be made absent a clear showing of racial animus and the defendant has not made a clear showing on that facet of his claim.

Despite the absence of direct evidence of selective prosecution, the Court takes this opportunity to express its concern about the discretion afforded individuals who divert cases from state to federal court for prosecution under Project Exile. Witnesses from the offices of both the Commonwealth's Attorney and the United States Attorney were unable to detail the specific process by which this review and diversion occur. A local police officer is apparently individually responsible for this task. That officer reviews the records of potential Project Exile defendants to determine whether their cases are appropriate for federal prosecution. A defendant's race is evident from these records. While cases referred for federal prosecution are reviewed to ensure that the alleged conduct constitutes a federal crime, witnesses identified no means of reviewing the cases retained for state prosecution. Absent more comprehensive scrutiny, there exists no means to ensure that this substantial discretion is constitutionally exercised.

If the process of diverting cases for federal prosecution is indeed independently accomplished by one unsupervised individual who is aware of the defendants' race, then Project Exile unnecessarily invites a substantial risk of selective prosecution. Indeed, if, as proponents of Project Exile maintain, there are disparities in the effectiveness of federal and state prosecutions, then those disparities only increase the potential for discriminatory diversions for federal prosecution absent some form of review.

Despite this unnecessary potential for constitutional infirmities, the defendant has produced no specific evidence that a similarly situated defendant of another race has evaded federal prosecution under Project Exile. While the Court recognizes the inherent risk of constitutional violations engendered by the absence of any institutional review of Project Exile diversions to federal Court, it is compelled to rule on this record that defendant Jones has failed to demonstrate a prima facie case of selective prosecution.

III. OTHER FACETS OF DEFENDANT'S MOTION

The defendant's motion presents several other questions which warrant assessment.

A. FEDERALISM

Project Exile raises serious questions respecting basic principles of federalism. The United States Constitution preserved for the states an "inviolable sovereignty." Historically, there may be no state that has more vehemently defended its sovereignty than has Virginia. This history of resolute opposition to federal incursion into state matters makes the local authorities' acquiescence to Project Exile all the more puzzling.

The purpose of Project Exile is, beyond question, laudable. However, the problems it targets are undeniably local in both nature and effect. As a comparative examination of the state and federal systems will indicate, local law enforcement authorities suffer from no inherent incapacity to redress the problems Project Exile targets. However, instead of bringing the resources of the Commonwealth to bear, local authorities have abdicated their responsibility to the federal government. Citizens of Richmond, Norfolk, and the Commonwealth of Virginia have the right to expect more from their elected officials. An abdication of responsibility lowers citizens' expectations of the Commonwealth's public servants, it insulates those officials from constructive criticism, and it dissipates political pressure that citizens might otherwise exert to improve the performance of local law enforcement.

Not only does Project Exile threaten to diminish local law enforcement, it also requires that citizens of the forty-nine other states subsidize local law enforcement activities. One Assistant Commonwealth's Attorney and one prosecutor from the Office of the Attorney General are assigned as a Special AUSAs to assist with Project Exile prosecutions. Additionally, the marketing effort publicizing Project Exile is privately funded. However, excepting these relatively insignificant items, federal taxpayers pay for every Project Exile prosecution, every resulting incarceration, and for the vast majority of criminal defense attorneys defending these prosecutions.

Not only does Project Exile force federal taxpayers to support local law enforcement, it does so at a significantly greater expense than would a comparable state prosecution. The rates that the federal government pays for court-appointed counsel and incarceration, for example, are both significantly more than that paid by the Commonwealth. The Commonwealth will pay no more than $305 to court-appointed counsel representing an indigent defendant accused of firearms-related felonies. In the federal system, the Criminal Justice Act ("CJA") allows payments of up to $3500, or more than ten times the amount the Commonwealth provides, for court-appointed counsel. In addition to benefiting by not incurring the expenses involved in incarcerating Project Exile defendants, the Commonwealth of Virginia actually leases prison space to the federal government to relieve overcrowding at federal facilities caused, at least in some part, by the federal prosecution of state crimes. Finally, it is important to note that the organizers of Project Exile have shifted this significant expense to federal taxpayers without the approval of any federally-elected official who is politically accountable for the expenditure.

B. EFFECT ON THE FEDERAL JUDICIARY

In addition to the deleterious effects noted above, Project Exile's potentially negative effect on the federal judiciary is readily apparent. In his year-end report on the federal judiciary to Congress, Chief Justice William Rehnquist warned that "[t]he trend to federalize crimes that traditionally have been handled in state courts . . . threatens to change entirely the nature of our federal system." Although these cases are typically not complex, their quantity alone is gradually making it more difficult to accord both civil and criminal cases possessing a greater federal interest the attention which they are due. For this and other reasons, Chief Justice Rehnquist counsels that the fundamental requisite for federal prosecution of such cases be "demonstrated state failure" to prosecute. *Id.* During the hearing on defendant's motion to dismiss, the Commonwealth's Attorney for the City of Richmond vehemently and, in the Court's opinion, correctly denied that his office lacked the resources to properly accomplish its assigned duties. In light of this capacity and the Chief Justice's warning, the imposition of the substantial burdens attendant to Project Exile on the federal judiciary is particularly unwarranted.

IV. CONCLUSION

Despite its laudable purpose, Project Exile represents a substantial federal incursion into a sovereign state's area of authority and responsibility. That the incursion has been acquiesced in, or invited by, state law enforcement officers makes it no less troublesome. Indeed, where, as here, the local authorities claim to have the capacity to address the problem, the invited federal incursion raises serious motivational concerns. An examination of the Commonwealth's statutes suggests that this incursion likely is not necessary. Despite these numerous and substantial objections, however, the judges of the Richmond Division of the Eastern District of Virginia are compelled to conclude that, on the record as made, Project Exile does not violate defendant's right to equal protection as guaranteed by the Fifth Amendment's Due Process Clause.

B. PROBLEMS IN DEFINING CRIMINAL CONDUCT

1. SUICIDE AND ASSISTED SUICIDE

Washington v. Glucksberg

Supreme Court of the United States, 1997.
521 U.S. 702, 117 S.Ct. 2258, 138 L.Ed.2d 772.

■ CHIEF JUSTICE REHNQUIST delivered the opinion of the Court.

The question presented in this case is whether Washington's prohibition against "caus[ing]" or "aid[ing]" a suicide offends the Fourteenth Amendment to the United States Constitution. We hold that it does not.

I

We begin, as we do in all due-process cases, by examining our Nation's history, legal traditions, and practices. In almost every State—indeed, in almost every western democracy—it is a crime to assist a suicide. The States' assisted-suicide bans are not innovations. Rather, they are longstanding expressions of the States' commitment to the protection and preservation of all human life.

Though deeply rooted, the States' assisted-suicide bans have in recent years been reexamined and, generally, reaffirmed. Because of advances in medicine and technology, Americans today are increasingly likely to die in institutions, from chronic illnesses. President's Comm'n for the Study of Ethical Problems in Medicine and Biomedical and Behavioral Research, Deciding to Forego Life-Sustaining Treatment 16–18 (1983). Public concern and democratic action are therefore sharply focused on how best to protect dignity and independence at the end of life, with the result that there have been many significant changes in state laws and in the attitudes these laws reflect. Many States, for example, now permit "living wills," surrogate health-care decisionmaking, and the withdrawal or refusal of life-sustaining medical treatment. At the same time, however, voters and legislators continue for the most part to reaffirm their States' prohibitions on assisting suicide.

The Washington statute at issue in this case, was enacted in 1975 as part of a revision of that State's criminal code. Four years later, Washington passed its Natural Death Act, which specifically stated that the "withholding or withdrawal of life-sustaining treatment . . . shall not, for any purpose, constitute a suicide" and that "[n]othing in this chapter shall be construed to condone, authorize, or approve mercy killing. . . ." In 1991, Washington voters rejected a ballot initiative which, had it passed, would have permitted a form of physician-assisted suicide. Washington then added a provision to the Natural Death Act expressly excluding physician-assisted suicide.

California voters rejected an assisted-suicide initiative similar to Washington's in 1993. On the other hand, in 1994, voters in Oregon enacted, also through ballot initiative, that State's "Death With Dignity Act," which legalized physician-assisted suicide for competent, terminally ill adults. Since the Oregon vote, many proposals to legalize assisted-suicide have been and continue to be introduced in the States' legislatures, but none has been enacted. And just last year, Iowa and Rhode Island joined the overwhelming majority of States explicitly prohibiting assisted suicide. See Iowa Code Ann. ss 707A.2, 707A.3 (Supp.1997); R.I. Gen. Laws ss 11–60–1, 11–60–3 (Supp.1996). Also, on April 30, 1997, President Clinton signed the Federal Assisted Suicide Funding Restriction Act of 1997, which prohibits the use of federal funds in support of physician-assisted suicide. Pub.L. 105–12, 111 Stat. 23 (codified at 42 U.S.C. § 14401 et seq.).

Thus, the States are currently engaged in serious, thoughtful examinations of physician-assisted suicide and other similar issues. For example, New York State's Task Force on Life and the Law—an ongoing, blue-ribbon commission composed of doctors, ethicists, lawyers, religious leaders, and interested laymen—was convened in 1984 and commissioned with "a broad mandate to recommend public policy on issues raised by medical advances." Over the past decade, the Task Force has recommended laws relating to end-of-life decisions, surrogate pregnancy, and organ donation. After studying physician-assisted suicide, however, the Task Force unanimously concluded that "[l]egalizing assisted suicide and euthanasia would pose profound risks to many individuals who are ill and vulnerable. . . . [T]he potential dangers of this dramatic change in public policy would outweigh any benefit that might be achieved."

Attitudes toward suicide itself have changed, but our laws have consistently condemned, and continue to prohibit, assisting suicide. Despite changes in medical technology and notwithstanding an increased emphasis on the importance of end-of-life decisionmaking, we have not retreated from this prohibition. Against this backdrop of history, tradition, and practice, we now turn to respondents' constitutional claim.

II

The Due Process Clause guarantees more than fair process, and the "liberty" it protects includes more than the absence of physical restraint. . . . The Clause also provides heightened protection against government interference with certain fundamental rights and liberty interests. In a long line of cases, we have held that, in addition to the specific freedoms protected by the Bill of Rights, the "liberty" specially protected by the Due Process Clause includes the rights to marry, Loving

v. Virginia, 388 U.S. 1, 87 S.Ct. 1817, 18 L.Ed.2d 1010 (1967); to have children, Skinner v. Oklahoma ex rel. Williamson, 316 U.S. 535, 62 S.Ct. 1110, 86 L.Ed. 1655 (1942); to direct the education and upbringing of one's children, Meyer v. Nebraska, 262 U.S. 390, 43 S.Ct. 625, 67 L.Ed. 1042 (1923); Pierce v. Society of Sisters, 268 U.S. 510, 45 S.Ct. 571, 69 L.Ed. 1070 (1925); to marital privacy, Griswold v. Connecticut, 381 U.S. 479, 85 S.Ct. 1678, 14 L.Ed.2d 510 (1965); to use contraception, ibid.; Eisenstadt v. Baird, 405 U.S. 438, 92 S.Ct. 1029, 31 L.Ed.2d 349 (1972); to bodily integrity, Rochin v. California, 342 U.S. 165, 72 S.Ct. 205, 96 L.Ed. 183 (1952), and to abortion. We have also assumed, and strongly suggested, that the Due Process Clause protects the traditional right to refuse unwanted lifesaving medical treatment. Cruzan v. Director, Missouri Department of Health, 497 U.S. 261, 110 S.Ct. 2841, 111 L.Ed.2d 224 (1990).

But we have always been reluctant to expand the concept of substantive due process because guideposts for responsible decisionmaking in this unchartered area are scarce and open-ended. By extending constitutional protection to an asserted right or liberty interest, we, to a great extent, place the matter outside the arena of public debate and legislative action. We must therefore exercise the utmost care whenever we are asked to break new ground in this field, lest the liberty protected by the Due Process Clause be subtly transformed into the policy preferences of the members of this Court.

Our established method of substantive-due-process analysis has two primary features: First, we have regularly observed that the Due Process Clause specially protects those fundamental rights and liberties which are, objectively, deeply rooted in this Nation's history and tradition. Second, we have required in substantive-due-process cases a careful description of the asserted fundamental liberty interest. Our Nation's history, legal traditions, and practices thus provide the crucial guideposts for responsible decisionmaking, that direct and restrain our exposition of the Due Process Clause. As we stated recently . . ., the Fourteenth Amendment forbids the government to infringe fundamental liberty interests at all, no matter what process is provided, unless the infringement is narrowly tailored to serve a compelling state interest.

Justice Souter, relying on Justice Harlan's dissenting opinion in Poe v. Ullman, would largely abandon this restrained methodology, and instead ask whether Washington's statute sets up one of those "arbitrary impositions" or "purposeless restraints" at odds with the Due Process Clause of the Fourteenth Amendment. In our view, however, the development of this Court's substantive-due-process jurisprudence, described briefly above, has been a process whereby the outlines of the "liberty" specially protected by the Fourteenth Amendment—never fully clarified, to be sure, and perhaps not capable of being fully clarified— have at least been carefully refined by concrete examples involving fundamental rights found to be deeply rooted in our legal tradition. This approach tends to rein in the subjective elements that are necessarily present in due-process judicial review. In addition, by establishing a threshold requirement—that a challenged state action implicate a fundamental right—before requiring more than a reasonable relation to a legitimate state interest to justify the action, it avoids the need for complex balancing of competing interests in every case.

Turning to the claim at issue here, the Court of Appeals stated that "[p]roperly analyzed, the first issue to be resolved is whether there is a liberty interest in determining the time and manner of one's death," or, in other words, "[i]s there a right to die?." Similarly, respondents assert a "liberty to choose how to die" and a right to "control of one's final days," and describe the asserted liberty as "the right to choose a humane, dignified death," and "the liberty to shape death." As noted above, we have a tradition of carefully formulating the interest at stake in substantive-due-process cases. For example, although Cruzan is often described as a "right to die" case, we were, in fact, more precise: we assumed that the Constitution granted competent persons a constitutionally protected right to refuse lifesaving hydration and nutrition. The Washington statute at issue in this case prohibits "aid[ing] another person to attempt suicide," and, thus, the question before us is whether the "liberty" specially protected by the Due Process Clause includes a right to commit suicide which itself includes a right to assistance in doing so.

We now inquire whether this asserted right has any place in our Nation's traditions. Here, as discussed above, we are confronted with a consistent and almost universal tradition that has long rejected the asserted right, and continues explicitly to reject it today, even for terminally ill, mentally competent adults. To hold for respondents, we would have to reverse centuries of legal doctrine and practice, and strike down the considered policy choice of almost every State.

Respondents contend, however, that the liberty interest they assert is consistent with this Court's substantive-due-process line of cases, if not with this Nation's history and practice. Pointing to Casey and Cruzan, respondents read our jurisprudence in this area as reflecting a general tradition of "self-sovereignty," and as teaching that the "liberty" protected by the Due Process Clause includes "basic and intimate exercises of personal autonomy." According to respondents, our liberty jurisprudence, and the broad, individualistic principles it reflects, protects the "liberty of competent, terminally ill adults to make end-of-life decisions free of undue government interference." The question presented in this case, however, is whether the protections of the Due Process Clause include a right to commit suicide with another's assistance. With this "careful description" of respondents' claim in mind, we turn to Casey and Cruzan.

In Cruzan, we considered whether Nancy Beth Cruzan, who had been severely injured in an automobile accident and was in a persistive vegetative state, "ha[d] a right under the United States Constitution which would require the hospital to withdraw life-sustaining treatment" at her parents' request. We began with the observation that "[a]t common law, even the touching of one person by another without consent and without legal justification was a battery." Ibid. We then discussed the related rule that "informed consent is generally required for medical treatment." After reviewing a long line of relevant state cases, we concluded that "the common-law doctrine of informed consent is viewed as generally encompassing the right of a competent individual to refuse medical treatment." Next, we reviewed our own cases on the subject, and stated that "[t]he principle that a competent person has a constitutionally protected liberty interest in refusing unwanted medical treatment may be inferred from our prior decisions." Therefore, "for purposes of [that] case, we assume[d] that the United States Constitution would grant a competent person a constitutionally protected right to refuse lifesaving hydration and nutrition." We concluded that, notwithstanding this right, the Constitution permitted Missouri to require clear and convincing evidence of an incompetent patient's wishes concerning the withdrawal of life-sustaining treatment.

Respondents contend that in Cruzan we "acknowledged that competent, dying persons have the right to direct the removal of life-sustaining medical treatment and thus hasten death," and that "the constitutional principle behind recognizing the patient's liberty to direct the withdrawal of artificial life support applies at least as strongly to the choice to hasten impending death by consuming lethal medication," Similarly, the Court of Appeals concluded that "Cruzan, by recognizing a liberty interest that includes the refusal of artificial provision of life-sustaining food and water, necessarily recognize[d] a liberty interest in hastening one's own death."

The right assumed in Cruzan, however, was not simply deduced from abstract concepts of personal autonomy. Given the common-law rule that forced medication was a battery, and the long legal tradition protecting the decision to refuse unwanted medical treatment, our assumption was entirely consistent with this Nation's history and constitutional traditions. The decision to commit suicide with the assistance of another may be just as personal and profound as the decision to refuse unwanted medical treatment, but it has never enjoyed similar legal protection. Indeed, the two acts are widely and reasonably regarded as quite distinct. In Cruzan itself, we recognized that most States outlawed assisted suicide—and even more do today—and we certainly gave no intimation that the right to refuse unwanted medical treatment could be somehow transmuted into a right to assistance in committing suicide.

Respondents also rely on Casey. There, the Court's opinion concluded that "the essential holding of Roe v. Wade should be retained and once again reaffirmed." We held, first, that a woman has a right, before her fetus is viable, to an abortion "without undue interference from the State"; second, that States may restrict post-viability abortions, so long as exceptions are made to protect a woman's life and health; and third, that the State has legitimate interests throughout a pregnancy in protecting the health of the woman and the life of the unborn child. In reaching this conclusion, the opinion discussed in some detail this Court's substantive-due-process tradition of interpreting the Due Process Clause to protect certain fundamental rights and "personal decisions relating to marriage, procreation, contraception, family relationships, child rearing, and education," and noted that many of those rights and liberties "involv[e] the most intimate and personal choices a person may make in a lifetime."

The Court of Appeals, like the District Court, found Casey " 'highly instructive' " and " 'almost prescriptive' " for determining " 'what liberty interest may inhere in a terminally ill person's choice to commit suicide' ": "Like the decision of whether or not to have an abortion, the decision how and when to die is one of 'the most intimate and personal choices a person may make in a lifetime,' a choice 'central to personal dignity and autonomy.' " Similarly, respondents emphasize the statement in Casey that: "At the heart of liberty is the right to define one's own concept of existence, of meaning, of the universe, and of the mystery of human life. Beliefs about these matters could not define the attributes of personhood were they formed under compulsion of the State." By choosing this language, the Court's opinion in Casey described, in a general way and in light of our prior cases, those personal activities and decisions that this Court has identified as so deeply rooted in our history and traditions, or so fundamental to our concept of constitutionally ordered liberty, that they are protected by the Fourteenth Amendment. The opinion moved from the recognition that liberty necessarily includes freedom of conscience and belief about ultimate considerations to the observation that "though the abortion decision may originate within the zone of conscience and belief, it is more than a philosophic exercise." That many of the rights and liberties protected by the Due Process Clause sound in personal autonomy does not warrant the sweeping conclusion that any and all important, intimate, and personal decisions are so protected, and Casey did not suggest otherwise.

The history of the law's treatment of assisted suicide in this country has been and continues to be one of the rejection of nearly all efforts to permit it. That being the case, our decisions lead us to conclude that the asserted "right" to assistance in committing suicide is not a fundamental liberty interest protected by the Due Process Clause. The Constitution also requires, however, that Washington's assisted-suicide ban be rationally related to legitimate government interests. . . . As the court below recognized, Washington's assisted-suicide ban implicates a number of state interests.

First, Washington has an unqualified interest in the preservation of human life. The State's prohibition on assisted suicide, like all homicide laws, both reflects and advances its commitment to this interest. . . . This interest is symbolic and aspirational as well as practical:

While suicide is no longer prohibited or penalized, the ban against assisted suicide and euthanasia shores up the notion of limits in human relationships. It reflects the gravity with which we view the decision to take one's own life or the life of another, and our reluctance to encourage or promote these decisions.

. . . The Court of Appeals . . . recognized Washington's interest in protecting life, but held that the weight of this interest depends on the "medical condition and the wishes of the person whose life is at stake." Washington, however, has rejected this sliding-scale approach and, through its assisted-suicide ban, insists that all persons' lives, from beginning to end, regardless of physical or mental condition, are under the full protection of the law. As we have previously affirmed, the States may properly decline to make judgments about the "quality" of life that a particular individual may enjoy. This remains true, as Cruzan makes clear, even for those who are near death.

Relatedly, all admit that suicide is a serious public-health problem, especially among persons in otherwise vulnerable groups. See Washington State Dept. of Health, Annual Summary of Vital Statistics 1991, pp. 29–30 (Oct.1992) (suicide is a leading cause of death in Washington of those between the ages of 14 and 54); New York Task Force 10, 23–33 (suicide rate in the general population is about one percent, and suicide is especially prevalent among the young and the elderly). The State has an interest in preventing suicide, and in studying, identifying, and treating its causes.

Those who attempt suicide—terminally ill or not—often suffer from depression or other mental disorders. See New York Task Force 13–22, 126–128 (more than 95% of those who commit suicide had a major psychiatric illness at the time of death; among the terminally ill, uncontrolled pain is a "risk factor" because it contributes to depression); Physician-Assisted Suicide and Euthanasia in the Netherlands: A Report of Chairman Charles T. Canady to the Subcommittee on the Constitution of the House Committee on the Judiciary, 104th Cong., 2d Sess., 10–11 (Comm. Print 1996); cf. Back, Wallace, Starks, & Pearlman, Physician-Assisted Suicide and Euthanasia in Washington State, 275 JAMA 919, 924 (1996) ("[I]ntolerable physical symptoms are not the reason most patients request physician-assisted suicide or euthanasia"). Research indicates, however, that many people who request physician-assisted suicide withdraw that request if their depression and pain are treated.

H. Hendin, Seduced by Death: Doctors, Patients and the Dutch Cure 24–25 (1997) (suicidal, terminally ill patients "usually respond well to treatment for depressive illness and pain medication and are then grateful to be alive"). The New York Task Force, however, expressed its concern that, because depression is difficult to diagnose, physicians and medical professionals often fail to respond adequately to seriously ill patients' needs. Thus, legal physician-assisted suicide could make it more difficult for the State to protect depressed or mentally ill persons, or those who are suffering from untreated pain, from suicidal impulses.

The State also has an interest in protecting the integrity and ethics of the medical profession. In contrast to the Court of Appeals' conclusion that "the integrity of the medical profession would [not] be threatened in any way by [physician-assisted suicide]," the American Medical Association, like many other medical and physicians' groups, has concluded that "[p]hysician-assisted suicide is fundamentally incompatible with the physician's role as healer." And physician-assisted suicide could, it is argued, undermine the trust that is essential to the doctor-patient relationship by blurring the time-honored line between healing and harming.

Next, the State has an interest in protecting vulnerable groups—including the poor, the elderly, and disabled persons—from abuse, neglect, and mistakes. The Court of Appeals dismissed the State's concern that disadvantaged persons might be pressured into physician-assisted suicide as ludicrous on its face. We have recognized, however, the real risk of subtle coercion and undue influence in end-of-life situations. . . . If physician-assisted suicide were permitted, many might resort to it to spare their families the substantial financial burden of end-of-life health-care costs.

The State's interest here goes beyond protecting the vulnerable from coercion; it extends to protecting disabled and terminally ill people from prejudice, negative and inaccurate stereotypes, and "societal indifference." The State's assisted-suicide ban reflects and reinforces its policy that the lives of terminally ill, disabled, and elderly people must be no less valued than the lives of the young and healthy, and that a seriously disabled person's suicidal impulses should be interpreted and treated the same way as anyone else's. . . .

Finally, the State may fear that permitting assisted suicide will start it down the path to voluntary and perhaps even involuntary euthanasia. The Court of Appeals struck down Washington's assisted-suicide ban only as applied to competent, terminally ill adults who wish to hasten their deaths by obtaining medication prescribed by their doctors. Washington insists, however, that the impact of the court's decision will not and cannot be so limited. If suicide is protected as a matter of constitutional right, it is argued, every man and woman in the United States must enjoy it. The Court of Appeals' decision, and its expansive reasoning, provide ample support for the State's concerns. The court noted, for example, that the "decision of a duly appointed surrogate decision maker is for all legal purposes the decision of the patient himself,"; that "in some instances, the patient may be unable to self-administer the drugs and . . . administration by the physician . . . may be the only way the patient may be able to receive them," and that not only physicians, but also family members and loved ones, will inevitably participate in assisting suicide. Thus, it turns out that what is couched as a limited right to "physician-assisted suicide" is likely, in effect, a much broader license, which could prove extremely difficult to police and contain. Washington's ban on assisting suicide prevents such erosion.

This concern is further supported by evidence about the practice of euthanasia in the Netherlands. The Dutch government's own study revealed that in 1990, there were 2,300 cases of voluntary euthanasia (defined as "the deliberate termination of another's life at his request"), 400 cases of assisted suicide, and more than 1,000 cases of euthanasia without an explicit request. In addition to these latter 1,000 cases, the study found an additional 4,941 cases where physicians administered lethal morphine overdoses without the patients' explicit consent. This study suggests that, despite the existence of various reporting procedures, euthanasia in the Netherlands has not been limited to competent, terminally ill adults who are enduring physical suffering, and that regulation of the practice may not have prevented abuses in cases involving vulnerable persons, including severely disabled neonates and elderly persons suffering from dementia. The New York Task Force, citing the Dutch experience, observed that "assisted suicide and euthanasia are closely linked," and concluded that the "risk of . . . abuse is neither speculative nor distant." Washington, like most other States, reasonably ensures against this risk by banning, rather than regulating, assisting suicide.

We need not weigh exactingly the relative strengths of these various interests. They are unquestionably important and legitimate, and Washington's ban on assisted suicide is at least reasonably related to their promotion and protection. We therefore hold that Wash. Rev.Code section 9A.36.060(1) (1994) does not violate the Fourteenth Amendment, either on its face or "as applied to competent, terminally ill adults who wish to hasten their deaths by obtaining medication prescribed by their doctors."

* * *

Throughout the Nation, Americans are engaged in an earnest and profound debate about the morality, legality, and practicality of physician-assisted suicide. Our holding permits this debate to continue, as it should in a democratic society. The decision of the en banc Court of Appeals is reversed, and the case is remanded for further proceedings consistent with this opinion.

It is so ordered.

NOTES

1. Vacco v. Quill, 521 U.S. 793, 117 S.Ct. 2293, 138 L.Ed.2d 834 (1997) reversed the Second Circuit, holding that New York's prohibition on assisting suicide violate the Equal Protection Clause of the Fourteenth Amendment. The Second Circuit had held that "some terminally ill people—those who are on life-support systems—are treated differently than those who are not, in that the former may 'hasten death' by ending treatment, but the latter may not 'hasten death' through physician-assisted suicide. This conclusion depends on the submission that ending or refusing lifesaving medical treatment 'is nothing more nor less than assisted suicide.' "

The Court held that:

Unlike the Court of Appeals, we think the distinction between assisting suicide and withdrawing life-sustaining treatment, a distinction widely recognized and endorsed in the medical profession and in our legal traditions, is both important and logical; it is certainly rational.

New York's reasons for recognizing and acting on this distinction—including prohibiting intentional killing and preserving life; preventing suicide; maintaining physicians' role as their patients' healers; protecting vulnerable people from indifference, prejudice, and psychological and financial pressure to end their lives; and avoiding a possible slide towards euthanasia—are discussed in greater detail in our opinion in Glucksberg. These valid and important public interests easily satisfy the constitutional requirement that a legislative classification bear a rational relation to some legitimate end.

2. In Oregon, "the earnest and profound debate about the morality, legality, and practicality of physician-assisted suicide" resulted in the Oregon Death with Dignity Act recognizing the right to physician-assisted suicide. In Gonzales v. Oregon, 546 U.S. 243, 126 S.Ct. 904, 163 L.Ed.2d 748 (2006), the Court noted that:

On November 9, 2001, without consulting Oregon or apparently anyone outside his Department, the [U.S.] Attorney General issued an Interpretive Rule announcing his intent to restrict the use of controlled substances for physician-assisted suicide.... [T]he Attorney General ruled: 'assisting suicide is not a legitimate medical purpose', and that prescribing, dispensing, or administering federally controlled substances to assist suicide violates the Controlled Substances Act. Such conduct by a physician registered to dispense controlled substances" may subject the physician to revocation of his license and to criminal punishment. The Court ruled against the Attorney General because the Controlled Substance Act was not intended to allow "a single Executive Officer the power to effect a radical shift of authority from the States to the Federal Government [by defining] general standards of medical practice in every locality."

3. In some cultures committing suicide for a "higher cause" is considered praiseworthy. For example, kamikaze pilots in World War II and the suicide bombers utilized by many terrorist groups are viewed by some as martyr heroes. Even in these cultures, however, if a person commits suicide for a personal motive the act of committing suicide brings great shame and humiliation upon his family. It may even expose the deceased's family to punishment in the form of fines if the suicide also causes damage or loss to society.

2. DEFINING "DANGEROUS" AND "DEADLY"

The desire to punish dangerous behavior furnishes serious drafting challenges to a legislator. Dangerous conduct requires that we spell out, with some degree of precision and clarity, the type of act (conduct) that is prohibited, while at the same time also incorporating the mental state required for criminality. In view of the many offenses which seek to punish certain "dangerous" behavior or the use of "deadly" or "dangerous" weapons, definitional problems abound. Even when the statute contains definitions, courts still face problems of construction. But the problems are greatly magnified when a statute defining a crime uses general characterizations without definitional legislative assistance. Sometimes, the uncertainty as to what conduct is prohibited may impair the validity of the statute on constitutional grounds (see, in the next chapter, discussions on vagueness and overbreadth). Here, however, we deal not with the unconstitutional failure to define clearly what is prohibited; rather, we explore the difficulties encountered in seeking to spell out what conduct is criminal.

Commonwealth v. Davis
Appeals Court of Massachusetts, Hampden, 1980.
10 Mass.App.Ct. 190, 406 N.E.2d 417.

■ GREANEY, JUSTICE.

On December 16, 1978, the defendant and the victim quarrelled at the "Diamond Mine" Lounge in Holyoke. An encounter ensued, in the course of which the defendant bit off a piece of the victim's left ear. The defendant was indicted for the crimes of mayhem (G.L. c. 265, § 14), and assault and battery by means of a dangerous weapon "to wit, [t]eeth" (G.L. c. 265, § 15A). A Superior Court jury convicted him on both indictments, and he has appealed, assigning as error: . . .; and (2) the denial of his motion for a directed verdict on so much of indictment no. 79–705 as charged the use of a dangerous weapon, contending that human teeth cannot constitute a dangerous weapon. We hold that . . . the motion for a directed verdict should have been allowed as to that portion of the assault and battery indictment that charged the use of teeth as a dangerous weapon.

* * *

2. We turn now to the question whether human teeth or parts of the body should be excluded from consideration by the fact finder as instrumentalities which can be used as dangerous weapons in indictments framed under G.L. c. 265, § 15A. . . . Section 15A punishes assaults and batteries committed by "means of a dangerous weapon" but does not expressly define the term "dangerous weapon." Instead, the meaning of the term was evolved through case law. Recently in Commonwealth v. Appleby, 380 Mass. 296, 402 N.E.2d 1051 (1980) the Supreme Judicial Court stated that the concept of a dangerous weapon as used in § 15A embraces two classes of objects—"dangerous weapons per se" (those specially designed and constructed to produce death or great bodily harm;) and objects which are not dangerous per se but which can be used in a dangerous fashion to inflict serious harm. A wide variety of objects have been held to fall within the latter category. See Commonwealth v. Farrell, 322 Mass. 606, 615, 78 N.E.2d 697 (1948) (lighted cigarette); Commonwealth v. Tarrant, 2 Mass.App. 483, 486–487, 314 N.E.2d 448 (1974), Id., 367 Mass. 411, 326 N.E.2d 710 (1975) ("kitchen-type" knife and German shepherd dog); Commonwealth v. LeBlanc, 3 Mass.App. 780, 334 N.E.2d 647 (1975) (automobile door used to strike police officer); United States v. Johnson, 324 F.2d 264, 266 (4th Cir.1963) (chair brought down upon victim's head); United States v. Loman, 551 F.2d 164, 169 (7th Cir.), cert. denied, 433 U.S. 912, 97 S.Ct. 2982, 53 L.Ed.2d 1097 (1977) (walking stick used with enough force to break it); People v. White, 212 Cal.App.2d 464, 465, 28 Cal.Rptr. 67 (1963) (a rock); Commonwealth v. Branham, 71 Ky. (8 Bush.) 387, 388 (1871) (a chisel used for stabbing); Bennett v. State, 237 Md. 212, 216, 205 A.2d 393 (1964) (microphone cord tied around victim's neck); People v. Buford, 69 Mich.App. 27, 30, 244 N.W.2d 351 (1976) (dictum) (automobile, broomstick, flashlight and lighter fluid all may be dangerous as used); State v. Howard, 125 N.J.Super. 39, 45, 308 A.2d 366 (App.Div.1973) (straight razor); State v. Martinez, 57 N.M. 174, 176, 256 P.2d 791 (1953) (a knife with a blade two inches long); Regan v. State, 46 Wis. 256, 258, 50 N.W. 287 (1879) (large stones). We recognize that our cases have held that questions as to whether instrumentalities which are not dangerous per se have been used in a dangerous fashion are generally reserved to the fact finder to be decided on the basis of the circumstances surrounding the crime, the nature, size and shape of the object, and the manner in which it is handled or controlled. However, for the reasons now discussed we think that human teeth and other parts of the human body should be removed from consideration as dangerous weapons in § 15A indictments, even on a case-by-case basis.

First, all the Massachusetts cases which have considered the use of neutral objects as potential weapons in the commission of assault crimes have considered instrumentalities apart from the defendant's person. The *Farrell, Tarrant* and *Appleby* decisions considered a lighted cigarette, an attack dog, and a riding crop, respectively. Even when the act of "kicking" underlies the charge of assault with a "dangerous weapon," the shoe or boot, not the foot, is the object which is considered as the "weapon" subjecting the assailant to a charge of aggravated assault. . . . Since the adoption of § 15A, there has been no decision reported in this State which holds that human hands, feet or teeth alone can constitute a dangerous weapon. This suggests that for over fifty years prosecutors have not considered assault cases involving the use of hands, feet, fingers or teeth as incidents where "dangerous weapons" were employed. It also suggests that prosecutors have been reluctant to read our judicial precedent on the subject as inviting indictments pressing factual contentions that parts of the body can be used as weapons. Rather, where serious or disabling injuries are inflicted, and the requisite intent is present, district attorneys typically bring indictments under § 14 (mayhem) or § 15 (assault with intent to maim or disfigure) of c. 265; otherwise § 13A (assault and battery) is used as the prosecutorial tool to vindicate society's interest. Thus in the context of the practical application of the statute the concept of neutral objects used as dangerous weapons has been confined to independent nonhuman instrumentalities. These considerations, in light of the fact that fifty-three years have elapsed since the Legislature enacted § 15A, call, in our view, for the exercise of judicial restraint in expanding the concept beyond its traditional scope.

Second, the notion that parts of the body may be used as dangerous weapons has not been generally accepted elsewhere. The clear weight of authority is to the effect that bodily parts alone cannot constitute a dangerous weapon for the purpose of an aggravated assault based on the alleged use of such a weapon. This is so, irrespective of the degree of harm inflicted. See Ransom v. State, 460 P.2d at 172; Dickson v. State, 230 Ark. 491, 492, 323 S.W.2d 432 (1959); Reed v. Commonwealth, 248 S.W.2d 911, 914 (Ky.1952); State v. Calvin, 209 La. 257, 265–266, 24 So.2d 467 (1945); People v. VanDiver, 80 Mich.App. 352, 356–357, 263 N.W.2d 370 (1977); People v. Vollmer, 299 N.Y. 347, 350, 87 N.E.2d 291 (1949); Bean v. State, 77 Okl.Cr. 73, 81–84, 138 P.2d 563 (1943); State v. Wier, 22 Or.App. 549, 540 P.2d 394 (1975); State v. Hariott, 210 S.C. 290, 299–300, 42 S.E.2d 385 (1947).

State v. Calvin, supra, the sole reported decision dealing with the question whether teeth may constitute a dangerous weapon, is particularly instructive. In that case there was evidence that the defendant had bitten the victim, and the trial judge had charged the jury that since "a person's bare fist could be classed and used as a dangerous weapon, . . . a person's teeth could be classed as a dangerous weapon."

The Supreme Court of Louisiana, applying a definition of "dangerous weapon" ("any . . . instrumentality, which, in the manner used, is calculated or likely to produce death or great bodily harm") virtually identical to that set forth in *Commonwealth v. Farrell*, supra, held that charge to be error: . . .

Third, in the absence of reconsideration by the Legislature of the term "dangerous weapon" or of the gist of the crime defined in § 15A, we see no compelling reason to stretch the term "weapon" to allow prosecution under § 15A of actions that are ordinarily prosecuted in other ways. Almost every attack which involves the use of a part of the body to inflict serious injury has been and remains punishable under one or the other of the felonious assault statutes apart from § 15A. Thus, an attack such as an attempt to strangle falls under G.L. c. 265, § 15 (assault with intent to murder), or under § 29 of the same chapter (assault with intent to commit a felony, i.e., to kill). Attacks without weapons which result in injuries to particular parts of the body or which cause disabling or disfiguring injuries are prosecuted under the first portion of G.L. c. 265, § 14, as mayhem, or under § 15, as assault with intent to maim. If weapons, chemicals, or substances are used to maim or disfigure, the indictment is brought under the second portion of § 14 which "allows conviction of mayhem for a more general range of injury." The mental state required for conviction of mayhem or assault with intent to maim is satisfied by direct or inferential proof that the assault was intentional, unjustified, and made with the reasonable appreciation on the assailant's part that a disabling or disfiguring injury would result. Bending § 15A to include an assault of the type that occurred in the present case would result in needless duplicity and would frustrate what we perceive to be the legislative intent in separating felonious assaults. On similar analysis, the Court of Appeals of Michigan has held, in a well-reasoned opinion based on the intent of the Legislature in that State, that "the term 'dangerous weapon' cannot be construed to include the bare hands." People v. Van Diver, 80 Mich.App. at 357, 263 N.W.2d at 373.

* * *

We think, essentially for the reasons of public policy stated, that a broadening of the definition of a dangerous weapon in the context discussed should occur, if it occurs, through deliberative legislative action.

. . . The judgment on indictment no. 79–705 is reversed, and so much of the verdict is set aside as found the defendant guilty of the use of a dangerous weapon. The case is remanded to the Superior Court for the defendant's resentencing on indictment no. 79–705 as if for assault and battery.

So ordered.

United States v. Moore

United States Court of Appeals, Eighth Circuit, 1988.
846 F.2d 1163.

■ TIMBERS, CIRCUIT JUDGE.

Appellant James Vernell Moore appeals from a judgment entered September 25, 1987 . . . , following Moore's conviction by a jury on June 24, 1987 of two counts of assault with a deadly and[1] dangerous weapon upon federal correctional officers engaged in their official duties, in violation of 18 U.S.C. §§ 111 (1982) and 1114 (Supp. IV 1986). . . .

Moore had tested positive for antibodies for the Human Immunodeficiency Virus ("HIV virus") which are considered to be indicative of the presence of Acquired Immune Deficiency Syndrome ("AIDS"). After learning that he had tested positive for the HIV virus, Moore bit two correctional officers during a struggle. The indictment charged that the deadly and dangerous weapon Moore used was his own mouth and teeth.

On appeal, Moore claims, first, that the evidence at trial was insufficient to sustain a finding that Moore's mouth and teeth were a deadly and dangerous weapon; . . .

We hold that the evidence at trial was sufficient to sustain a finding that Moore's mouth and teeth were a deadly and dangerous weapon because that evidence supported a finding that Moore used his teeth in a manner likely to inflict serious bodily harm—even if he had not been infected with the HIV virus. . . .

We affirm.

I.

We shall summarize only those facts and prior proceedings believed necessary to an understanding of the issues raised on appeal.

At the time of the incident which is the subject of this appeal, Moore was an inmate at the Federal Medical Center ("FMC") in Rochester, Minnesota. On November 25 and December 3, 1986, Dr. Clifford Gastineau had Moore tested for the HIV virus because his long time heroin addiction placed him in a risk category for AIDS. In mid-December, Dr. Gastineau advised Moore that the tests were positive and that the disease could be fatal. He told Moore that the disease could be transmitted by way of blood or semen and counseled him to avoid unprotected intercourse and not to share needles, razor blades or toothbrushes.

---

1 It should be noted that, although the statutory language is in the disjunctive—"deadly *or* dangerous weapon", the indictment charged in the conjunctive—"deadly *and* dangerous weapon" (emphasis added). In this opinion we shall use the conjunctive language adopted by the parties.

On January 7, 1987, Lieutenant Ronald E. McCullough, a correctional officer at the FMC, called Moore to his office as part of his investigation of a report that Moore had been smoking in a non-smoking area in the FMC's medical surgical unit. Moore refused to answer questions. When McCullough told Moore he would have to be placed in seclusion and administrative detention, Moore refused to move. McCullough called for assistance. Correctional officer Timothy Voigt arrived. He told Moore to stand so that he could be handcuffed. Moore said "I won't be cuffed." McCullough called two additional correctional officers who arrived and attempted to lift Moore from his chair. Moore reacted violently.

In the ensuing struggle, Moore kneed McCullough in the groin twice, attempted to bite him on the hand, and did bite him on the left knee and hip without breaking the skin. Moore held his mouth over the bite on the leg for several seconds. He also bit Voigt on the right leg, holding his mouth against the bite from five to seven seconds. Dr. Gastineau testified that during the struggle a mild abrasion appeared at the point on Voigt's thigh where Moore had bitten him. This abrasion apparently resulted from friction with the fabric of Voigt's pants.[2] The abrasion may have come into contact with a wet patch on Voigt's pants which possibly was made by Moore's saliva. During the struggle, Moore threatened to kill the officers.

On January 10, 1987, Moore told Debra Alberts, a nurse at the FMC, that he had "wanted to hurt them bad, wanted to kill the bastards." He also said that he "hopes the wounds that he inflicted on the officers when he bit them were bad enough that they get the disease that he has."

On April 9, 1987, Moore was indicted. The indictment charged that Moore willfully had assaulted McCullough and Voigt, federal correctional officers engaged in their official duties, by means of a deadly and dangerous weapon, i.e., Moore's mouth and teeth. The indictment specifically charged that Moore was "a person then having been tested positively for the [HIV] antibody". Although Moore also had tested positive for hepatitis, the indictment did not refer to this disease.

At trial, Dr. Gastineau testified that the medical profession knew of no "well-proven instances in which a human bite has resulted in transmission of the [HIV] virus to the bitten person." He agreed with a medical manual that stated there is no evidence that AIDS can be transmitted through any contact that does not involve the exchange of bodily fluids and that, while the virus has appeared in minute amounts

---

[2] The parties dispute whether this bite punctured Voigt's skin. Moore, citing Dr. Gastineau's testimony, asserts that the bite failed to penetrate the fabric of Voigt's pants. The government, citing Voigt's testimony, asserts that Moore bit deeply into Voigt's thigh, puncturing Voigt's skin in three places. Voigt's subsequent testimony indicates, however, that the bleeding at the site of this wound was due to an abrasion caused by the friction of his pants rubbing against his legs. Thus the "puncture" wounds he describes apparently were indentations that in themselves did not cause bleeding.

in saliva, it has never been shown to have been spread through contact with saliva. He said that theoretically "one cannot exclude the possibility" of transmission through biting. Later he added, however, "it seems that in medicine everything is conceivable or possible." He testified about a case of a person who had been bitten deeply by a person with AIDS and had tested negative 18 months later.

Dr. Gastineau also testified that, apart from the matter of AIDS, a human bite can be dangerous. He said that when a human bite is of a more damaging nature than the ones inflicted by Moore and "where the skin is really broken to greater depths", it can be "much more dangerous than a dog bite." He also said that "there are probably 30 to 50 variet[ies] of germs in the human mouth that together, all of them acting in concert, could cause serious infection." He characterized a human bite as "a very dangerous form of aggression" and "one of the most dangerous of all forms of bites".

On June 24, 1987, the jury found Moore guilty on both counts of the indictment. The jury had been instructed on the lesser included offense of assaulting a federal officer. The court declined to instruct the jury that the government was required to prove that AIDS could be transmitted by way of a bite in order to prove that Moore's mouth and teeth were a deadly and dangerous weapon. Moore was sentenced to concurrent five-year prison terms, which were to run consecutively to the seven-year federal prison sentence he was serving at the time of the incident.

II.

In reviewing the sufficiency of the evidence to determine whether it supports the conviction, we must view the evidence in the light most favorable to the government, grant the government the benefit of all inferences that reasonably may be drawn from the evidence, and uphold the conviction if there is substantial evidence to support it.

The question of what constitutes a "deadly and dangerous weapon" is a question of fact for the jury. We previously have defined a "deadly and dangerous weapon" as an object "used in a manner likely to endanger life or inflict serious bodily harm." United States v. Hollow, 747 F.2d 481, 482 (8th Cir.1984). "Serious bodily harm" has been defined as something more than minor injury, but not necessarily injury creating a substantial likelihood of death. See United States v. Webster, 620 F.2d 640, 641–42 (7th Cir.1980); United States v. Johnson, 324 F.2d 264, 267 (4th Cir.1963). In *Webster*, a case arising under 18 U.S.C. § 113 (1982), the court stated that the phrase contains "words in general use by laymen" and that "[t]here is no indication that Congress in adopting such commonly used terms intended to include only the very highest degree of serious bodily injury."

As a practical matter, it often is difficult to determine whether a particular object is a deadly and dangerous weapon. Almost any weapon, as used or attempted to be used, may endanger life or inflict great bodily harm; as such, in appropriate circumstances, it may be a dangerous and deadly weapon. Moreover, the object need not be inherently dangerous, or a "weapon" by definition, such as a gun or a knife, to be found to be a dangerous and deadly weapon. Courts frequently have considered various kinds of objects to be deadly and dangerous, including such normally innocuous objects as (1) a chair; (2) a walking stick; (3) a broken beer bottle and pool cue; (4) an automobile; and (5) mop handles. In short, what constitutes a dangerous weapon depends not on the nature of the object itself but on its capacity, given the manner of its use, to . . . endanger life or inflict great bodily harm.

As a corollary, it is not necessary that the object, as used by a defendant, actually cause great bodily harm, as long as it has the capacity to inflict such harm in the way it was used. . . .

Courts also have held that in appropriate circumstances a part of the body may be a dangerous weapon. United States v. Parman, 461 F.2d 1203, 1204 n. 1 (D.C.Cir.1971) (indictment charged assault with a deadly weapon, the deadly weapon being "biting with teeth"); State v. Born, 280 Minn. 306, 159 N.W.2d 283 (1968) (fists or feet in certain circumstances may be dangerous weapons when used to inflict injury).

III.

In light of the law on what may be considered a deadly and dangerous weapon, we conclude that the evidence in the instant case was sufficient to support the jury's finding that Moore used his mouth and teeth as a deadly and dangerous weapon. As stated above, Dr. Gastineau testified that a human bite is potentially "more dangerous than a dog bite"; that it is capable of causing "serious infection"; and that it can be "a very dangerous form of aggression". We reaffirm that this potential for "serious infection" is a form of "serious bodily harm" . . . especially since we use the term in its general lay meaning and do not limit it to only the highest degree of injury. We therefore hold that Dr. Gastineau's testimony, viewed in the light most favorable to the government, was substantial evidence supporting the jury's finding that Moore used his mouth and teeth in a manner likely to inflict serious bodily harm.

It is true that Dr. Gastineau testified that he was describing a bite "more damaging" than those actually inflicted by Moore. As stated above, however, it is the *capacity* for harm in the weapon and its use that is significant, not the *actual* harm inflicted. It may be that Moore did not transmit any of the "30 to 50" varieties of germs he might have transmitted to the officers. He nevertheless used his mouth and teeth in a way that *could* have transmitted disease. It was only a fortuity that he did not do so. The instant case is similar to *Johnson*, where it was only fortuity which prevented the defendant from causing serious bodily injury when he struck the victim in the head with a chair. Since a human bite has the capacity to inflict serious bodily harm, we hold that the human mouth and teeth are a deadly and dangerous weapon in circumstances like those in the instant case, even if the harm actually inflicted was not severe.

The gravamen of Moore's claim is that on the evidence the only way the government could establish that his mouth and teeth were used as a deadly and dangerous weapon was for it to establish that AIDS can be transmitted by biting. As Moore points out, Dr. Gastineau's testimony, which was the only evidence on the transmissibility of the HIV virus, established only a remote or theoretical possibility that the virus could be transmitted through biting. He asserts that the government did not try the case on the theory that *any* human bite—regardless of the presence of the HIV virus—was a deadly and dangerous weapon. His assertion rests on the facts that the indictment charged that Moore, "a person then having been tested positively for the [HIV] antibody, did willfully and forcibly assault" the two officers "by means of a deadly and dangerous weapon, namely, his mouth and teeth"; that the indictment failed to make any similar charge with respect to his hepatitis infection; and that the government introduced a substantial amount of evidence at trial concerning the transmissibility of AIDS by way of biting.

We reject Moore's massive emphasis on the AIDS aspect of this case. As stated above, the record, viewed in the light most favorable to the government, contained sufficient evidence to allow the jury to find that Moore's mouth and teeth were used as a deadly and dangerous weapon, even if Moore was *not* infected with AIDS. As the district court correctly held, moreover, the reference to AIDS in the indictment was mere surplusage and did not limit the government to one theory of the case at trial.

Although there is sufficient evidence in the record that the human mouth and teeth may be used as a deadly and dangerous weapon, we nevertheless wish to emphasize that the medical evidence in the record was insufficient to establish that AIDS may be transmitted by a bite. The evidence established that there are no well-proven cases of AIDS transmission by way of a bite; that contact with saliva has never been shown to transmit the disease; and that in one case a person who had been deeply bitten by a person with AIDS tested negative several months later. Indeed, a recent study has indicated that saliva actually may contain substances that *protect* the body from AIDS. New York Times, May 6, 1988, at A 16, col. 4. While Dr. Gastineau testified "in medicine everything is conceivable", in a legal context the possibility of AIDS transmission by means of a bite is too remote to support a finding that the mouth and teeth may be considered a deadly and dangerous weapon in this respect.

In short, we hold that the evidence was sufficient to support the finding that Moore's mouth and teeth were a deadly and dangerous weapon, regardless of the presence or absence of AIDS.

* * *

NOTE

For an analysis of "dangerous" weapons and the use of teeth, see also, Commonwealth v. Sexton, 425 Mass. 146, 680 N.E.2d 23 (1997) (concrete pavement as a dangerous weapon).

CHAPTER 4

CONSTITUTIONAL LIMITATIONS ON DEFINING CRIMINAL CONDUCT

A. DUE PROCESS, VAGUENESS, OVERBREADTH AND THE FIRST AMENDMENT

Papachristou v. City of Jacksonville
Supreme Court of the United States, 1972.
405 U.S. 156, 92 S.Ct. 839, 31 L.Ed.2d 110.

■ MR. JUSTICE DOUGLAS delivered the opinion of the Court.

This case involves eight defendants who were convicted in a Florida municipal court of violating a Jacksonville, Florida, vagrancy ordinance.[1] Their convictions, entailing fines and jail sentences (some of which were suspended), were affirmed by the Florida Circuit Court in a consolidated appeal, and their petition for certiorari was denied by the District Court of Appeals, . . . The case is here on a petition for certiorari, which we granted. . . . For reasons which will appear, we reverse.[4]

---

[1] Jacksonville Ordinance Code § 26–57 provided at the time of these arrests and convictions as follows:

> Rogues and vagabonds, or dissolute persons who go about begging, common gamblers, persons who use juggling or unlawful games or plays, common drunkards, common night walkers, thieves, pilferers or pickpockets, traders in stolen property, lewd, wanton and lascivious persons, keepers of gambling places, common railers and brawlers, persons wandering or strolling around from place to place without any lawful purpose or object, habitual loafers, disorderly persons, persons neglecting all lawful business and habitually spending their time by frequenting houses of ill fame, gaming houses, or places where alcoholic beverages are sold or served, persons able to work but habitually living upon the earnings of their wives or minor children shall be deemed vagrants and, upon conviction in the Municipal Court shall be punished [90 days imprisonment, $500 fine, or both.]

We are advised that at present the Jacksonville vagrancy ordinance is § 330.107 and identical with the earlier one except that "juggling" has been eliminated.

[4] Florida also has a vagrancy statute . . . which reads quite closely on the Jacksonville ordinance. . . . [It] makes the commission of any Florida misdemeanor a Class D offense against the City of Jacksonville. In 1971 Florida made minor amendments to its statute.

[The statute] was declared unconstitutionally overbroad in Lazarus v. Faircloth, D.C., 301 F.Supp. 266. The Court said: "All loitering, loafing, or idling on the streets and highways of a city, even though habitual, is not necessarily detrimental to the public welfare nor is it under all circumstances an interference with travel upon them. It may be and often is entirely innocuous. The statute draws no distinction between conduct that is calculated to harm and that which is essentially innocent." See also Smith v. Florida, 405 U.S. 172, 92 S.Ct. 848, 31 L.Ed.2d 122 (1972).

The Florida disorderly conduct ordinance, covering "loitering about any hotel, block, barroom, dramshop, gambling house or disorderly house, or wandering about

271

At issue are five consolidated cases. Margaret Papachristou, Betty Calloway, Eugene Eddie Melton, and Leonard Johnson were all arrested early on a Sunday morning, and charged with vagrancy—"prowling by auto."

Jimmy Lee Smith and Milton Henry were charged with vagrancy—"vagabonds."

Henry Edward Heath and a co-defendant were arrested for vagrancy—"loitering" and "common thief."

Thomas Owen Campbell was charged with vagrancy—"common thief."

Hugh Brown was charged with vagrancy—"disorderly loitering on street" and "disorderly conduct—resisting arrest with violence."

The facts are stipulated. Papachristou and Calloway are white females. Melton and Johnson are black males. Papachristou was enrolled in a job-training program sponsored by the State Employment Service at Florida Junior College in Jacksonville. Calloway was a typing and shorthand teacher at a state mental institution located near Jacksonville. She was the owner of the automobile in which the four defendants were arrested. Melton was a Vietnam war veteran who had been released from the Navy after nine months in a veterans' hospital. On the date of his arrest he was a part-time computer helper while attending college as a full-time student in Jacksonville. Johnson was a tow-motor operator in a grocery chain warehouse and was a lifelong resident of Jacksonville.

At the time of their arrest the four of them were riding in Calloway's car on the main thoroughfare in Jacksonville. They had left a restaurant owned by Johnson's uncle where they had eaten and were on their way to a night club. The arresting officers denied that the racial mixture in the car played any part in the decision to make the arrest. The arrest they said, was made because the defendants had stopped near a used-car lot which had been broken into several times. There was, however, no evidence of any breaking and entering on the night in question.

Of these four charged with "prowling by auto" none had been previously arrested except Papachristou who had once been convicted of a municipal offense.

Jimmy Lee Smith and Milton Henry (who is not a petitioner) were arrested between 9 and 10 a.m. on a weekday in downtown Jacksonville, while waiting for a friend who was to lend them a car so they could apply for a job at a produce company. Smith was a part-time produce worker and part-time organizer for a Negro political group. He had a common-

---

the streets either by night or by day without any known lawful means of support or without being able to give a satisfactory account of themselves" has also been held void for "excessive broadness and vagueness" by the Florida Supreme Court, Headley v. Selkowitz, 171 So.2d 368, 370.

law wife and three children supported by him and his wife. He had been arrested several times but convicted only once. Smith's companion, Henry, was an 18-year-old high school student with no previous record of arrest.

This morning it was cold, and Smith had no jacket, so they went briefly into a dry cleaning shop to wait, but left when requested to do so. They thereafter walked back and forth two or three times over a two-block stretch looking for their friend. The store owners, who apparently were wary of Smith and his companion, summoned two police officers who searched the men and found neither had a weapon. But they were arrested because the officers said they had no identification and because the officers did not believe their story.

Heath and a codefendant were arrested for "loitering" and for "common thief." Both were residents of Jacksonville, Heath having lived there all his life and being employed at an automobile and body shop. Heath had previously been arrested but his codefendant had no arrest record. Heath and his companion were arrested when they drove up to a residence shared by Heath's girlfriend and some other girls. Some police officers were already there in the process of arresting another man. When Heath and his companion started backing out of the driveway, the officers signaled to them to stop and asked them to get out of the car, which they did. Thereupon they and the automobile were searched. Although no contraband or incriminating evidence was found, they were both arrested, Heath being charged with being a "common thief" because he was reputed to be a thief. The codefendant was charged with "loitering" because he was standing in the driveway, an act which the officers admitted was done only at their command.

Campbell was arrested as he reached his home very early one morning and was charged with "common thief." He was stopped by officers because he was traveling at a high rate of speed, yet no speeding charge was placed against him.

Brown was arrested when he was observed leaving a downtown, Jacksonville, hotel by a police officer seated in a cruiser. The police testified he was reputed to be a thief, narcotics pusher, and generally opprobrious character. The officer called Brown over to the car, intending at that time to arrest him unless he had a good explanation for being on the street. Brown walked over to the police cruiser, as commanded, and the officer began to search him, apparently preparatory to placing him in the car. In the process of the search he came on two small packets which were later found to contain heroin. When the officer touched the pocket where the packets were, Brown began to resist. He was charged with "disorderly loitering on the street" and "disorderly conduct—resisting arrest with violence." While he was also charged with a narcotics violation, that charge was *nolled*.

Jacksonville's ordinance and Florida's statute were "derived from early English law," . . . and employ "archaic language" in their definitions of vagrants. The history is an often-told tale. The breakup of feudal estates in England led to labor shortages which in turn resulted in the Statutes of Laborers, designed to stabilize the labor force by prohibiting increases in wages and prohibiting the movement of workers from their home areas in search of improved conditions. Later vagrancy laws became criminal aspects of the poor laws. The series of laws passed in England on the subject became increasingly severe. But "the theory of the Elizabethan poor laws no longer fits the facts," . . . The conditions which spawned these laws may be gone, but the archaic classifications remain.

This ordinance is void-for-vagueness, both in the sense that it "fails to give a person of ordinary intelligence fair notice that his contemplated conduct is forbidden by the statute," . . . and because it encourages arbitrary and erratic arrests and convictions . . .

Living under a rule of law entails various suppositions, one of which is that "All [persons] are entitled to be informed as to what the State commands or forbids." Lanzetta v. New Jersey, . . .

Lanzetta is one of a well-recognized group of cases insisting that the law give fair notice of the offending conduct. . . . In the field of regulatory statutes governing business activities, where the acts limited are in a narrow category, greater leeway is allowed. . . .

The poor among us, the minorities, the average householder are not in business and not alerted to the regulatory schemes of vagrancy laws; and we assume they would have no understanding of their meaning and impact if they read them. Nor are they protected from being caught in the vagrancy net by the necessity of having a specific intent to commit an unlawful act. . . .

The Jacksonville ordinance makes criminal activities which by modern standards are normally innocent. "Nightwalking" is one. Florida construes the ordinance not to make criminal one night's wandering, . . . only the "habitual" wanderer or as the ordinance describes it "common night walkers." We know, however, from experience that sleepless people often walk at night, perhaps hopeful that sleep-inducing relaxation will result.

Luis Munoz-Marin, former Governor of Puerto Rico, commented once that "loafing" was a national virtue in his Commonwealth and that it should be encouraged. It is, however, a crime in Jacksonville.

"Persons able to work but habitually living on the earnings of their wives or minor children"—like habitually living "without visible means of support"—might implicate unemployed pillars of the community who have married rich wives.

"Persons able to work but habitually living on the earnings of their wives or minor children" may also embrace unemployed people out of the labor market, by reason of a recession or disemployed by reason of technological or so-called structural displacements.

Persons "wandering or strolling" from place to place have been extolled by Walt Whitman and Vachel Lindsay. The qualification "without any lawful purpose or object" may be a trap for innocent acts. Persons "neglecting all lawful business and habitually spending their time by frequenting . . . places where alcoholic beverages are sold or served" would literally embrace many members of golf clubs and city clubs.

Walkers and strollers and wanderers may be going to or coming from a burglary. Loafers or loiterers may be "casing" a place for a holdup. Letting one's wife support him is an intra-family matter, and normally of no concern to the police. Yet it may, of course, be the setting for numerous crimes.

The difficulty is that these activities are historically part of the amenities of life as we have known it. They are not mentioned in the Constitution or in the Bill of Rights. These unwritten amenities have been in part responsible for giving our people the feeling of independence and self-confidence, the feeling of creativity. These amenities have dignified the right of dissent and have honored the right to be nonconformists and the right to defy submissiveness. They have encouraged lives of high spirits rather than hushed, suffocating silence.

They are embedded in Walt Whitman's writings especially in his Song of the Open Road. They are reflected too, in the spirit of Vachel Lindsay's I Want to go Wandering and by Henry D. Thoreau.

This aspect of the vagrancy ordinance before us is suggested by what this Court said in 1875 about a broad criminal statute enacted by Congress: "It would certainly be dangerous if the legislature could set a net large enough to catch all possible offenders, and leave it to the courts to step inside and say who could be rightfully detained, and who should be set at large." . . .

While that was a federal case, the due process implications are equally applicable to the States and to this vagrancy ordinance. Here the net cast is large, not to give the courts the power to pick and choose but to increase the arsenal of the police. . . .

* * *

Where the list of crimes is so all-inclusive and generalized as that one in this ordinance, those convicted may be punished for no more than vindicating affronts to police authority: . . .

Another aspect of the ordinance's vagueness appears when we focus, not on the lack of notice given a potential offender, but on the effect of the unfettered discretion it places in the hands of the Jacksonville police.

Caleb Foote, an early student of this subject, has called the vagrancy-type law as offering "punishment by analogy." Such crimes, though long common in Russia, are not compatible with our constitutional system. We allow our police to make arrests only on "probable cause," a Fourth and Fourteenth Amendment standard applicable to the States as well as to the Federal Government. Arresting a person on suspicion, like arresting a person for investigation, is foreign to our system, even when the arrest is for past criminality. Future criminality, however, is the common justification for the presence of vagrancy statutes. . . . Florida has indeed construed her vagrancy statute "as necessary regulations," *inter alia*, "to deter vagabondage and prevent crimes." . . .

A direction by a legislature to the police to arrest all "suspicious" persons would not pass constitutional muster. A vagrancy prosecution may be merely the cloak for a conviction which could not be obtained on the real but undisclosed grounds for the arrest. . . .

Those generally implicated by the imprecise terms of the ordinance—poor people, nonconformists, dissenters, idlers—may be required to comport themselves according to the life-style deemed appropriate by the Jacksonville police and the courts. Where, as here, there are no standards governing the exercise of the discretion granted by the ordinance, the scheme permits and encourages an arbitrary and discriminatory enforcement of the law. It furnishes a convenient tool for "harsh and discriminatory enforcement by prosecuting officials, against particular groups deemed to merit their displeasure." . . . It results in a regime in which the poor and the unpopular are permitted to "stand on a public sidewalk . . . only at the whim of any police officer." . . .

A presumption that people who might walk or loaf or loiter or stroll or frequent houses where liquor is sold, or who are supported by their wives or who look suspicious to the police are to become future criminals is too precarious for a rule of law. The implicit presumption in these generalized vagrancy standards—that crime is being nipped in the bud—is too extravagant to deserve extended treatment. Of course, vagrancy statutes are useful to the police. Of course they are nets making easy the round-up of so-called undesirables. But the rule of law implies equality and justice in its application. Vagrancy laws of the Jacksonville type teach that the scales of justice are so tipped that even-handed administration of the law is not possible. The rule of law, evenly applied to minorities as well as majorities, to the poor as well as the rich, is the great mucilage that holds society together.

City of Chicago v. Morales

Supreme Court of the United States, 1999.
527 U.S. 41, 119 S.Ct. 1849, 144 L.Ed.2d 67.

■ JUSTICE STEVENS.

In 1992, the Chicago City Council enacted the Gang Congregation Ordinance, which prohibits "criminal street gang members" from "loitering" with one another or with other persons in any public place. The question presented is whether the Supreme Court of Illinois correctly held that the ordinance violates the Due Process Clause of the Fourteenth Amendment to the Federal Constitution.

I

Before the ordinance was adopted, the city council's Committee on Police and Fire conducted hearings to explore the problems created by the city's street gangs, and more particularly, the consequences of public loitering by gang members. Witnesses included residents of the neighborhoods where gang members are most active, as well as some of the aldermen who represent those areas. Based on that evidence, the council made a series of findings that are included in the text of the ordinance and explain the reasons for its enactment

The council found that a continuing increase in criminal street gang activity was largely responsible for the city's rising murder rate, as well as an escalation of violent and drug related crimes. It noted that in many neighborhoods throughout the city, " 'the burgeoning presence of street gang members in public places has intimidated many law abiding citizens.' " Furthermore, the council stated that gang members " 'establish control over identifiable areas . . . by loitering in those areas and intimidating others from entering those areas; and . . . [m]embers of criminal street gangs avoid arrest by committing no offense punishable under existing laws when they know the police are present. . . .' " It further found that " 'loitering in public places by criminal street gang members creates a justifiable fear for the safety of persons and property in the area' " and that " '[a]ggressive action is necessary to preserve the city's streets and other public places so that the public may use such places without fear.' " Moreover, the council concluded that the city " 'has an interest in discouraging all persons from loitering in public places with criminal gang members.' "

The ordinance creates a criminal offense punishable by a fine of up to $500, imprisonment for not more than six months, and a requirement to perform up to 120 hours of community service. Commission of the offense involves four predicates. First, the police officer must reasonably believe that at least one of the two or more persons present in a " 'public place' " is a " 'criminal street gang membe[r].' " Second, the persons must be " 'loitering,' " which the ordinance defines as "remain[ing] in any one place with no apparent purpose." Third, the officer must then order

" 'all' " of the persons to disperse and remove themselves " 'from the area.' " Fourth, a person must disobey the officer's order. If any person, whether a gang member or not, disobeys the officer's order, that person is guilty of violating the ordinance.

During the three years of its enforcement, the police issued over 89,000 dispersal orders and arrested over 42,000 people for violating the ordinance. In the ensuing enforcement proceedings, 2 trial judges upheld the constitutionality of the ordinance, but 11 others ruled that it was invalid . . .

The Illinois Supreme Court held "that the gang loitering ordinance violates due process of law in that it is impermissibly vague on its face and an arbitrary restriction on personal liberties."

In support of its vagueness holding, the court pointed out that the definition of "loitering" in the ordinance drew no distinction between innocent conduct and conduct calculated to cause harm. "Moreover, the definition of 'loiter' provided by the ordinance does not assist in clearly articulating the proscriptions of the ordinance." Furthermore, it concluded that the ordinance was "not reasonably susceptible to a limiting construction which would affirm its validity."

We granted certiorari, and now affirm. Like the Illinois Supreme Court, we conclude that the ordinance enacted by the city of Chicago is unconstitutionally vague.

Vagueness may invalidate a criminal law for either of two independent reasons. First, it may fail to provide the kind of notice that will enable ordinary people to understand what conduct it prohibits; second, it may authorize and even encourage arbitrary and discriminatory enforcement. Accordingly, we first consider whether the ordinance provides fair notice to the citizen and then discuss its potential for arbitrary enforcement.

"It is established that a law fails to meet the requirements of the Due Process Clause if it is so vague and standardless that it leaves the public uncertain as to the conduct it prohibits. . . ." *Giaccio v. Pennsylvania*, 382 U.S. 399, 402–403, 86 S.Ct. 518, 15 L.Ed.2d 447 (1966). The Illinois Supreme Court recognized that the term "loiter" may have a common and accepted meaning, but the definition of that term in this ordinance—"to remain in any one place with no apparent purpose"—does not. It is difficult to imagine how any citizen of the city of Chicago standing in a public place with a group of people would know if he or she had an "apparent purpose." If she were talking to another person, would she have an apparent purpose? If she were frequently checking her watch and looking expectantly down the street, would she have an apparent purpose?

Since the city cannot conceivably have meant to criminalize each instance a citizen stands in public with a gang member, the vagueness that dooms this ordinance is not the product of uncertainty about the normal meaning of "loitering," but rather about what loitering is covered by the ordinance and what is not. The Illinois Supreme Court emphasized the law's failure to distinguish between innocent conduct and conduct threatening harm. Its decision followed the precedent set by a number of state courts that have upheld ordinances that criminalize loitering combined with some other overt act or evidence of criminal intent. However, state courts have uniformly invalidated laws that do not join the term "loitering" with a second specific element of the crime.

The city's principal response to this concern about adequate notice is that loiterers are not subject to sanction until after they have failed to comply with an officer's order to disperse. "[W]hatever problem is created by a law that criminalizes conduct people normally believe to be innocent is solved when persons receive actual notice from a police order of what they are expected to do."

Second, the terms of the dispersal order compound the inadequacy of the notice afforded by the ordinance. It provides that the officer "shall order all such persons to disperse and remove themselves from the area." App. to Pet. for Cert. 61a. This vague phrasing raises a host of questions. After such an order issues, how long must the loiterers remain apart? How far must they move? If each loiterer walks around the block and they meet again at the same location, are they subject to arrest or merely to being ordered to disperse again.

Lack of clarity in the description of the loiterer's duty to obey a dispersal order might not render the ordinance unconstitutionally vague if the definition of the forbidden conduct were clear, but it does buttress our conclusion that the entire ordinance fails to give the ordinary citizen adequate notice of what is forbidden and what is permitted. The Constitution does not permit a legislature to "set a net large enough to catch all possible offenders, and leave it to the courts to step inside and say who could be rightfully detained, and who should be set at large." This ordinance is therefore vague "not in the sense that it requires a person to conform his conduct to an imprecise but comprehensible normative standard, but rather in the sense that no standard of conduct is specified at all."

The broad sweep of the ordinance also violates " 'the requirement that a legislature establish minimal guidelines to govern law enforcement.' " There are no such guidelines in the ordinance. In any public place in the city of Chicago, persons who stand or sit in the company of a gang member may be ordered to disperse unless their purpose is apparent. The mandatory language in the enactment directs the police to issue an order without first making any inquiry about their possible purposes. It matters not whether the reason that a gang member and his father, for example, might loiter near Wrigley Field is to rob an unsuspecting fan or just to get a glimpse of Sammy Sosa leaving the ballpark; in either event, if their purpose is not apparent to a nearby police officer, she may—indeed, she "shall"—order them to disperse.

Recognizing that the ordinance does reach a substantial amount of innocent conduct, we turn, then, to its language to determine if it "necessarily entrusts lawmaking to the moment-to-moment judgment of the policeman on his beat." As we discussed in the context of fair notice, this page, the principal source of the vast discretion conferred on the police in this case is the definition of loitering as "to remain in any one place with no apparent purpose."

As the Illinois Supreme Court interprets that definition, it "provides absolute discretion to police officers to decide what activities constitute loitering." We have no authority to construe the language of a state statute more narrowly than the construction given by that State's highest court. "The power to determine the meaning of a statute carries with it the power to prescribe its extent and limitations as well as the method by which they shall be determined."

Nevertheless, the city disputes the Illinois Supreme Court's interpretation, arguing that the text of the ordinance limits the officer's discretion in three ways. First, it does not permit the officer to issue a dispersal order to anyone who is moving along or who has an apparent purpose. Second, it does not permit an arrest if individuals obey a dispersal order. Third, no order can issue unless the officer reasonably believes that one of the loiterers is a member of a criminal street gang.

Even putting to one side our duty to defer to a state court's construction of the scope of a local enactment, we find each of these limitations insufficient. That the ordinance does not apply to people who are moving—that is, to activity that would not constitute loitering under any possible definition of the term—does not even address the question of how much discretion the police enjoy in deciding which stationary persons to disperse under the ordinance. Similarly, that the ordinance does not permit an arrest until after a dispersal order has been disobeyed does not provide any guidance to the officer deciding whether such an order should issue. The "no apparent purpose" standard for making that decision is inherently subjective because its application depends on whether some purpose is "apparent" to the officer on the scene.

Presumably an officer would have discretion to treat some purposes—perhaps a purpose to engage in idle conversation or simply to enjoy a cool breeze on a warm evening—as too frivolous to be apparent if he suspected a different ulterior motive. Moreover, an officer conscious of the city council's reasons for enacting the ordinance might well ignore its text and issue a dispersal order, even though an illicit purpose is actually apparent.

It is true, as the city argues, that the requirement that the officer reasonably believe that a group of loiterers contains a gang member does place a limit on the authority to order dispersal. That limitation would no doubt be sufficient if the ordinance only applied to loitering that had an apparently harmful purpose or effect, or possibly if it only applied to loitering by persons reasonably believed to be criminal gang members. But this ordinance, for reasons that are not explained in the findings of the city council, requires no harmful purpose and applies to nongang members as well as suspected gang members. It applies to everyone in the city who may remain in one place with one suspected gang member as long as their purpose is not apparent to an officer observing them. Friends, relatives, teachers, counselors, or even total strangers might unwittingly engage in forbidden loitering if they happen to engage in idle conversation with a gang member.

Ironically, the definition of loitering in the Chicago ordinance not only extends its scope to encompass harmless conduct, but also has the perverse consequence of excluding from its coverage much of the intimidating conduct that motivated its enactment. As the city council's findings demonstrate, the most harmful gang loitering is motivated either by an apparent purpose to publicize the gang's dominance of certain territory, thereby intimidating nonmembers, or by an equally apparent purpose to conceal ongoing commerce in illegal drugs. As the Illinois Supreme Court has not placed any limiting construction on the language in the ordinance, we must assume that the ordinance means what it says and that it has no application to loiterers whose purpose is apparent. The relative importance of its application to harmless loitering is magnified by its inapplicability to loitering that has an obviously threatening or illicit purpose.

Finally, in its opinion striking down the ordinance, the Illinois Supreme Court refused to accept the general order issued by the police department as a sufficient limitation on the "vast amount of discretion" granted to the police in its enforcement. We agree. That the police have adopted internal rules limiting their enforcement to certain designated areas in the city would not provide a defense to a loiterer who might be arrested elsewhere. Nor could a person who knowingly loitered with a well-known gang member anywhere in the city safely assume that they would not be ordered to disperse no matter how innocent and harmless their loitering might be.

In our judgment, the Illinois Supreme Court correctly concluded that the ordinance does not provide sufficiently specific limits on the enforcement discretion of the police "to meet constitutional standards for definiteness and clarity."

We recognize the serious and difficult problems testified to by the citizens of Chicago that led to the enactment of this ordinance. "We are mindful that the preservation of liberty depends in part on the maintenance of social order." However, in this instance the city has enacted an ordinance that affords too much discretion to the police and too little notice to citizens who wish to use the public streets.

Accordingly, the judgment of the Supreme Court of Illinois is *Affirmed.*

■ JUSTICE SCALIA, dissenting.

The citizens of Chicago were once free to drive about the city at whatever speed they wished. At some point Chicagoans (or perhaps Illinoisans) decided this would not do, and imposed prophylactic speed limits designed to assure safe operation by the average (or perhaps even subaverage) driver with the average (or perhaps even subaverage) vehicle. This infringed upon the "freedom" of all citizens, but was not unconstitutional.

Similarly, the citizens of Chicago were once free to stand around and gawk at the scene of an accident. At some point Chicagoans discovered that this obstructed traffic and caused more accidents. They did not make the practice unlawful, but they did authorize police officers to order the crowd to disperse, and imposed penalties for refusal to obey such an order. Again, this prophylactic measure infringed upon the "freedom" of all citizens, but was not unconstitutional.

Until the ordinance that is before us today was adopted, the citizens of Chicago were free to stand about in public places with no apparent purpose—to engage, that is, in conduct that appeared to be loitering. In recent years, however, the city has been afflicted with criminal street gangs. As reflected in the record before us, these gangs congregated in public places to deal in drugs, and to terrorize the neighborhoods by demonstrating control over their "turf." Many residents of the inner city felt that they were prisoners in their own homes. Once again, Chicagoans decided that to eliminate the problem it was worth restricting some of the freedom that they once enjoyed. The means they took was similar to the second, and more mild, example given above rather than the first: Loitering was not made unlawful, but when a group of people occupied a public place without an apparent purpose and in the company of a known gang member, police officers were authorized to order them to disperse, and the failure to obey such an order was made unlawful. See Chicago Municipal Code § 8–4–015 (1992). The minor limitation upon the free state of nature that this prophylactic arrangement imposed upon all Chicagoans seemed to them (and it seems to me) a small price to pay for liberation of their streets.

The majority today invalidates this perfectly reasonable measure by ignoring our rules governing facial challenges, by elevating loitering to a constitutionally guaranteed right, and by discerning vagueness where, according to our usual standards, none exists.

I

Respondents' consolidated appeal presents a facial challenge to the Chicago ordinance on vagueness grounds. When a facial challenge is successful, the law in question is declared to be unenforceable in *all* its applications, and not just in its particular application to the party in suit. To tell the truth, it is highly questionable whether federal courts have any business making such a declaration. The rationale for our power to review federal legislation for constitutionality, expressed in *Marbury v. Madison*, 1 Cranch 137, 2 L.Ed. 60 (1803), was that we *had* to do so in order to decide the case before us. But that rationale only extends so far as to require us to determine that the statute is unconstitutional as applied to *this* party, in the circumstances of *this* case.

That limitation was fully grasped by Tocqueville, in his famous chapter on the power of the judiciary in American society:

> The second characteristic of judicial power is, that it pronounces on special cases, and not upon general principles. If a judge, in deciding a particular point, destroys a general principle by passing a judgment which tends to reject all the inferences from that principle, and consequently to annul it, he remains within the ordinary limits of his functions. But if he directly attacks a general principle without having a particular case in view, he leaves the circle in which all nations have agreed to confine his authority; he assumes a more important, and perhaps a more useful influence, than that of the magistrate; but he ceases to represent the judicial power.

It seems to me fundamentally incompatible with this system for the Court not to be content to find that a statute is unconstitutional as applied to the person before it, but to go further and pronounce that the statute is unconstitutional in *all* applications. Its reasoning may well suggest as much, but to pronounce a *holding* on that point seems to me no more than an advisory opinion—which a federal court should never issue at all, and *especially* should not issue with regard to a constitutional question, as to which we seek to avoid even *non* advisory opinions, I think it quite improper, in short, to ask the constitutional claimant before us: Do you just want us to say that this statute cannot constitutionally be applied to you in this case, or do you want to go for broke and try to get the statute pronounced void in all its applications?

I must acknowledge, however, that for some of the present century we have done just this. But until recently, at least, we have—except in free-speech cases subject to the doctrine of overbreadth,—*required* the facial challenge to *be* a go-for-broke proposition. That is to say, before declaring a statute to be void in all its applications (something we should not be doing in the first place), we have at least imposed upon the litigant the eminently reasonable requirement that he establish that the statute was *unconstitutional* in all its applications. I say that is an eminently reasonable requirement, not only because we should not be holding a statute void in all its applications unless it is unconstitutional in all its applications, but also because *unless* it is unconstitutional in all its applications we do not even know, without conducting an as-applied analysis, whether it is void with regard to the very litigant *before* us— whose case, after all, was the occasion for undertaking this inquiry in the first place.

As we said in *United States v. Salerno*, 481 U.S. 739, 745, 107 S.Ct. 2095, 95 L.Ed.2d 697 (1987):

> "A facial challenge to a legislative Act is, of course, the most difficult challenge to mount successfully, since the *challenger must establish that no set of circumstances exists under which the Act would be valid.* The fact that [a legislative Act] might operate unconstitutionally under some conceivable set of circumstances is insufficient to render it wholly invalid, since we have not recognized an 'overbreadth' doctrine outside the limited context of the First Amendment." (Emphasis added.).

I am aware, of course, that in some recent facial-challenge cases the Court has, without any attempt at explanation, created entirely irrational exceptions to the "unconstitutional in every conceivable application" rule, when the statutes at issue concerned hot-button social issues on which "informed opinion" was zealously united. But the present case does not even lend itself to such a "political correctness" exception— which, though illogical, is at least predictable. It is not *à la mode* to favor gang members and associated loiterers over the beleaguered law-abiding residents of the inner city.

When our normal criteria for facial challenges are applied, it is clear that the Justices in the majority have transposed the burden of proof. Instead of requiring respondents, who are challenging the ordinance, to show that it is invalid in all its applications, they have required petitioner to show that it is valid in all its applications. Both the plurality opinion and the concurrences display a lively imagination, creating hypothetical situations in which the law's application would (in their view) be ambiguous. But that creative role has been usurped from petitioner, who can defeat respondents' facial challenge by conjuring up *a single valid application* of the law. My contribution would go something like this:[5] Tony, a member of the Jets criminal street gang, is standing alongside and chatting with fellow gang members while staking out their turf at Promontory Point on the South Side of Chicago; the group is flashing gang signs and displaying their distinctive tattoos to passersby. Officer Krupke, applying the ordinance at issue here, orders the group to disperse. After some speculative discussion (probably irrelevant here) over whether the Jets are depraved because they are deprived, Tony and the other gang members break off further conversation with the statement—not entirely coherent, but evidently intended to be rude— "Gee, Officer Krupke, krup you." A tense standoff ensues until Officer Krupke arrests the group for failing to obey his dispersal order. Even

---

[5] With apologies for taking creative license with the work of Messrs. Bernstein, Sondheim, and Laurents. West Side Story, copyright 1959.

assuming (as the Justices in the majority do, but I do not) that a law requiring obedience to a dispersal order is impermissibly vague unless it is clear to the objects of the order, before its issuance, that their conduct justifies it, I find it hard to believe that the Jets would not have known they had it coming. That should settle the matter of respondents' facial challenge to the ordinance's vagueness.

Of course respondents would still be able to claim that the ordinance was vague as applied to them. But the ultimate demonstration of the inappropriateness of the Court's holding of *facial* invalidity is the fact that it is doubtful whether some of these respondents could even sustain an *as-applied* challenge on the basis of the majority's own criteria. For instance, respondent Jose Renteria—who admitted that he was a member of the Satan Disciples gang—was observed by the arresting officer loitering on a street corner with other gang members. The officer issued a dispersal order, but when she returned to the same corner 15 to 20 minutes later, Renteria was still there with his friends, whereupon he was arrested. In another example, respondent Daniel Washington and several others—who admitted they were members of the Vice Lords gang—were observed by the arresting officer loitering in the street, yelling at passing vehicles, stopping traffic, and preventing pedestrians from using the sidewalks. The arresting officer issued a dispersal order, issued *another* dispersal order later when the group did not move, and finally arrested the group when they were found loitering in the same place still later. Finally, respondent Gregorio Gutierrez—who had previously admitted to the arresting officer his membership in the Latin Kings gang—was observed loitering with two other men. The officer issued a dispersal order, drove around the block, and arrested the men after finding them in the same place upon his return. See Brief for Petitioner 7, n. 5; Brief for United States as *Amicus Curiae* 16, n. 11. Even on the majority's assumption that to avoid vagueness it must be clear to the object of the dispersal order *ex ante* that his conduct is covered by the ordinance, it seems most improbable that any of these as-applied challenges would be sustained. Much less is it possible to say that the ordinance is invalid in *all* its applications.

The fact is that the present ordinance is entirely clear in its application, cannot be violated except with full knowledge and intent, and vests no more discretion in the police than innumerable other measures authorizing police orders to preserve the public peace and safety. As suggested by their tortured analyses, and by their suggested solutions that bear no relation to the identified constitutional problem, the majority's real quarrel with the Chicago ordinance is simply that it permits (or indeed requires) too much harmless conduct by innocent citizens to be proscribed. As Justice O'CONNOR's concurrence says with disapprobation, "the ordinance applies to hundreds of thousands of persons who are *not* gang members, standing on any sidewalk or in any park, coffee shop, bar, or other location open to the public."

But in our democratic system, how much harmless conduct to proscribe is not a judgment to be made by the courts. So long as constitutionally guaranteed rights are not affected, and so long as the proscription has a rational basis, *all sorts* of perfectly harmless activity by millions of perfectly innocent people can be forbidden—riding a motorcycle without a safety helmet, for example, starting a campfire in a national forest, or selling a safe and effective drug not yet approved by the Food and Drug Administration. All of these acts are entirely innocent and harmless in themselves, but because of the *risk* of harm that they entail, the freedom to engage in them has been abridged. The citizens of Chicago have decided that depriving themselves of the freedom to "hang out" with a gang member is necessary to eliminate pervasive gang crime and intimidation—and that the elimination of the one is worth the deprivation of the other. This Court has no business second-guessing either the degree of necessity or the fairness of the trade.

I dissent from the judgment of the Court.

———

Considerable case law exists on inhibitions that the First Amendment places upon the power of the states to create and define criminal conduct. There also are important other United States Supreme Court cases in this area of the law that trace how the right to freedom of speech and the press impacts crime creation in the areas of obscenity, the exercise of religious practices, the freedom of association, and the like. A study of these cases is typically undertaken in courses of constitutional law or specialized courses and seminars dealing with the Bill of Rights, or even just the First Amendment alone. For that reason, no comprehensive treatment of that broad subject is attempted in this casebook.

For classes where the subject is incorporated into the Criminal Law course, the following cases are but examples of the difficulties in drafting criminal statutes that regulate speech or speech-related activities without running afoul of the First Amendment or the related constitutional prohibition against vague and overbroad statutes, especially as it applies to free speech concerns.

———

Gooding, Warden v. Wilson

Supreme Court of the United States, 1972.
405 U.S. 518, 92 S.Ct. 1103, 31 L.Ed.2d 408.

■ MR. JUSTICE BRENNAN delivered the opinion of the Court.

Appellee was convicted in Superior Court, Fulton County, Georgia, on two counts of using opprobrious words and abusive language in violation of Georgia Code § 26–6303, which provides: "Any person who shall, without provocation, use to or of another, and in his presence . . . opprobrious words or abusive language, tending to cause a breach of the peace . . . shall be guilty of a misdemeanor."

* * *

Section 26–6303 punishes only spoken words. It can therefore withstand appellee's attack upon its facial constitutionality only if, as authoritatively construed by the Georgia courts, it is not susceptible of application to speech, although vulgar or offensive, that is protected by the First and Fourteenth Amendments, . . . Only the Georgia courts can supply the requisite construction, since of course "we lack jurisdiction authoritatively to construe state legislation." . . . It matters not that the words appellee used might have been constitutionally prohibited under a narrowly and precisely drawn statute. At least when statutes regulate or proscribe speech and when "no readily apparent construction suggests itself as a vehicle for rehabilitating the statutes in a single prosecution," . . . the transcendent value to all society of constitutionally protected expression is deemed to justify allowing "attacks on overly broad statutes with no requirement that the person making the attack demonstrate that his own conduct could not be regulated by a statute drawn with the requisite narrow specificity," . . . this is deemed necessary because persons whose expression is constitutionally protected may well refrain from exercising their rights for fear of criminal sanctions provided by a statute susceptible of application to protected expression.

* * *

The constitutional guarantees of freedom of speech forbid the States from punishing the use of words or language not within "narrowly limited classes of speech." Chaplinsky v. New Hampshire, . . . Even as to such a class, however, because "the line between speech unconditionally guaranteed and speech which may legitimately be regulated, suppressed, or punished is finely drawn," . . . "[i]n every case the power to regulate must be so exercised as not, in attaining a permissible end, unduly to infringe the protected freedom,". . . . In other words, the statute must be carefully drawn or be authoritatively construed to punish only unprotected speech and not be susceptible of application to protected expression. "Because First Amendment freedoms need breathing space to survive, government may regulate in the area only with narrow specificity." . . .

Appellant does not challenge these principles but contends that the Georgia statute is narrowly drawn to apply only to a constitutionally unprotected class of words—"fighting" words—"those which by their very utterance inflict injury or tend to incite an immediate breach of the peace." . . . In *Chaplinsky*, we sustained a conviction under Chapter 378, § 2, of the Public Laws of New Hampshire, which provided: "No person shall address any offensive, derisive or annoying word to any other person who is lawfully in any street or other public place, nor call him by any offensive or derisive name. . . ." Chaplinsky was convicted for addressing to another on a public sidewalk the words, "You are a God damned racketeer," and "a damned Fascist and the whole government of Rochester are Fascists or agents of Fascists." Chaplinsky challenged the constitutionality of the statute as inhibiting freedom of expression because it was vague and indefinite. The Supreme Court of New Hampshire, however, "long before the words for which Chaplinsky was convicted," sharply limited the statutory language "offensive, derisive or annoying word" to "fighting" words . . .

* * *

Appellant argues that the Georgia appellate courts have by construction limited the proscription of § 26–6303 to "fighting" words, as the New Hampshire Supreme Court limited the New Hampshire statute. . . . We have however, made our own examination of the Georgia cases, both those cited and others discovered in research. That examination brings us to the conclusion, in agreement with the courts below, that the Georgia appellate decisions have not construed § 26–6303 to be limited in application, as in *Chaplinsky*, to words that "have a direct tendency to cause acts of violence by the person to whom, individually, the remark is addressed."

The dictionary definitions of "opprobrious" and "abusive" give them greater reach than "fighting" words. . . .

* * *

■ MR. JUSTICE POWELL and MR. JUSTICE REHNQUIST, took no part in the consideration or decision of this case.

■ MR. CHIEF JUSTICE BURGER, dissenting.

I fully join in Mr. Justice Blackmun's dissent against the bizarre result reached by the Court. It is not merely odd, it is nothing less than remarkable that a court can find a state statute void on its face, not because of its language—which is the traditional test—but because of the way courts of that State have applied the statute in a few isolated cases, decided as long ago as 1905 and generally long before this Court's decision in Chaplinsky v. New Hampshire, . . . Even if all of those cases had been decided yesterday, they do nothing to demonstrate that the narrow language of the Georgia statute has any significant potential for sweeping application to suppress or deter important protected speech.

In part the Court's decision appears to stem from its assumption that a statute should be regarded in the same light as its most vague clause, without regard to any of its other language. . . . The statute at bar, however, does not prohibit language "tending to cause a breach of the peace." Nor does it prohibit the use of "opprobrious words or abusive language" without more. Rather, it prohibits use "to or of another, and in his presence opprobrious words or abusive language, tending to cause a breach of the peace." If words are to bear their common meaning, and are to be considered in context, rather than dissected with surgical precision using a semantical scalpel, this statute has little potential for application outside the realm of "fighting words" which this Court held beyond the protection of the First Amendment in *Chaplinsky*. Indeed, the language used by the *Chaplinsky* Court to describe words properly subject to regulation bears a striking resemblance to that of the Georgia statute, which was enacted many, many years before *Chaplinsky* was decided. And, if the early Georgia cases cited by the majority establish any proposition, it is that the statute, as its language so clearly indicates, is aimed at preventing precisely that type of personal, face-to-face abusive and insulting language likely to provoke a violent retaliation—self help, as we euphemistically call it—which the *Chaplinsky* case recognized could be validly prohibited. The facts of the case now before the Court demonstrate that the Georgia statute is serving that valid and entirely proper purpose. There is no persuasive reason to wipe the statute from the books, unless we want to encourage victims of such verbal assaults to seek their own private redress.

* * *

■ MR. JUSTICE BLACKMUN, with whom THE CHIEF JUSTICE joins, dissenting.

It seems strange indeed that in this day a man may say to a police officer, who is attempting to restore access to a public building, "White son of a bitch, I'll kill you" and "You son of a bitch, I'll choke you to death," and say to an accompanying officer, "You son of a bitch, if you ever put your hands on me again, I'll cut you all to pieces," and yet constitutionally cannot be prosecuted and convicted under a state statute which makes it a misdemeanor to "use to or of another, and in his presence, opprobrious words or abusive language, tending to cause a breach of the peace. . . ." This, however, is precisely what the Court pronounces as the law today.

The Supreme Court of Georgia, when the conviction was appealed, unanimously held the other way. . . . Surely any adult who can read—and I do not exclude this appellee-defendant from that category—should reasonably expect no other conclusion. The words of Georgia Code § 26–6303 are clear. They are also concise. They are not, in my view, overbroad or incapable of being understood. Except perhaps for the "big" word "opprobrious"—and no point is made of its bigness—any Georgia schoolboy would expect that his defendant's fighting and provocative words to the officers were covered by § 26–6303. Common sense permits no other conclusion. This is demonstrated by the fact that the appellee, and this Court, attacks the statute not as it applies to the appellee, but as it conceivably might apply to others who might utter other words.

The Court reaches its result by saying that the Georgia statute has been interpreted by the State's courts so as to be applicable in practice to otherwise constitutionally protected speech. It follows, says the Court, that the statute is overbroad and therefore is facially unconstitutional and to be struck down in its entirety. Thus Georgia apparently is to be left with no valid statute on its books to meet Wilson's bullying tactic. This result, achieved by what is indeed a very strict construction, will be totally incomprehensible to the State of Georgia, to its courts, and to its citizens.

The Court would justify its conclusion by unearthing a 66-year-old decision, . . . , of the Supreme Court of Georgia, and two intermediate appellate court cases over 55 years old, . . . broadly applying the statute in those less permissive days, and by additional reference to (a) a 1956 Georgia intermediate appellate court decision, . . . which, were it the first and only Georgia case, would surely not support today's decision, and (b) another intermediate appellate court decision . . . (1961), relating not to § 26–6303, but to another statute.

This Court appears to have developed its overbreadth rationale in the years since these early Georgia cases. The State's statute, therefore, is condemned because the State's courts have not had an opportunity to adjust to this Court's modern theories of overbreadth.

I wonder, now that § 26–6303 is voided, just what Georgia can do if it seeks to proscribe what the Court says it still may constitutionally proscribe. The natural thing would be to enact a new statute reading just as § 26–6303 reads. But it, too, presumably would be overbroad unless the legislature would add words to the effect that it means only what this Court says it may mean and no more.

* * *

For me, Chaplinsky v. New Hampshire . . . was good law when it was decided and deserves to remain as good law now. A unanimous Court, including among its members Chief Justice Stone and Justices Black, Reed, Douglas and Murphy, obviously thought it was good law. But I feel that by decisions such as this one . . . , despite its protestations to the contrary, is merely paying lip service to *Chaplinsky*. As the appellee states in a footnote to his brief, p. 14, "Although there is no doubt that the state can punish 'fighting words' this appears to be about all that is left of the decision in *Chaplinsky*." If this is what the overbreadth doctrine means, and if this is what it produces, it urgently needs reexamination. The Court has painted itself into a corner from which it, and the States, can extricate themselves only with difficulty.

R.A.V. v. City of St. Paul, Minnesota

Supreme Court of the United States, 1992.
505 U.S. 377, 112 S.Ct. 2538, 120 L.Ed.2d 305.

■ JUSTICE SCALIA delivered the opinion of the Court.

In the predawn hours of June 21, 1990, petitioner and several other teenagers allegedly assembled a crudely made cross by taping together broken chair legs. They then allegedly burned the cross inside the fenced yard of a black family that lived across the street from the house where petitioner was staying. Although this conduct could have been punished under any of a number of laws,[1] one of the two provisions under which respondent city of St. Paul chose to charge petitioner (then a juvenile) was the St. Paul Bias-Motivated Crime Ordinance, St. Paul, Minn., Legis.Code § 292.02 (1990), which provides:

> Whoever places on public or private property a symbol, object, appellation, characterization or graffiti, including, but not limited to, a burning cross or Nazi swastika, which one knows or has reasonable grounds to know arouses anger, alarm or resentment in others on the basis of race, color, creed, religion or gender commits disorderly conduct and shall be guilty of a misdemeanor.

Petitioner moved to dismiss this count on the ground that the St. Paul ordinance was substantially overbroad and impermissibly content based and therefore facially invalid under the First Amendment. The trial court granted this motion, but the Minnesota Supreme Court reversed. . . . We granted certiorari.

$$* \ * \ *$$

The First Amendment generally prevents government from proscribing speech, or even expressive conduct, because of disapproval of the ideas expressed. Content-based regulations are presumptively invalid. From 1791 to the present, however, our society, like other free but civilized societies, has permitted restrictions upon the content of speech in a few limited areas, which are of such slight social value as a step to truth that any benefit that may be derived from them is clearly outweighed by the social interest in order and morality. We have recognized that the freedom of speech referred to by the First Amendment does not include a freedom to disregard these traditional limitations. . . .

We have sometimes said that these categories of expression are not within the area of constitutionally protected speech, or that the protection of the First Amendment does not extend to them. Such statements must be taken in context, however, and are no more literally true than is the occasionally repeated shorthand characterizing obscenity "as not being speech at all," Sunstein, Pornography and the First Amendment, 1986 Duke L.J. 589, 615, n. 146. What they mean is that these areas of speech can, consistently with the First Amendment, be regulated *because of their constitutionally proscribable content*

---

1   The conduct might have violated Minnesota statutes carrying significant penalties. See, *e.g.*, Minn. Stat. § 609.713(1) (1987) (providing for up to five years in prison for terroristic threats); § 609.563 (arson) (providing for up to five years and a $10,000 fine, depending on the value of the property intended to be damaged); § 609.595 (Supp.1992) (criminal damage to property) (providing for up to one year and a $3,000 fine, depending upon the extent of the damage to the property).

(obscenity, defamation, etc.)—not that they are categories of speech entirely invisible to the Constitution, so that they may be made the vehicles for content discrimination unrelated to their distinctively proscribable content. Thus, the government may proscribe libel; but it may not make the further content discrimination of proscribing only libel critical of the government. . . .

* * *

The proposition that a particular instance of speech can be proscribable on the basis of one feature (*e.g.*, obscenity) but not on the basis of another (*e.g.*, opposition to the city government) is commonplace and has found application in many contexts. We have long held, for example, that nonverbal expressive activity can be banned because of the action it entails, but not because of the ideas it expresses—so that burning a flag in violation of an ordinance against outdoor fires could be punishable, whereas burning a flag in violation of an ordinance against dishonoring the flag is not. Similarly, we have upheld reasonable "time, place, or manner" restrictions, but only if they are justified without reference to the content of the regulated speech. And just as the power to proscribe particular speech on the basis of a noncontent element (*e.g.*, noise) does not entail the power to proscribe the same speech on the basis of a content element; so also, the power to proscribe it on the basis of *one* content element (*e.g.*, obscenity) does not entail the power to proscribe it on the basis of *other* content elements.

In other words, the exclusion of "fighting words" from the scope of the First Amendment simply means that, for purposes of that Amendment, the unprotected features of the words are, despite their verbal character, essentially a "nonspeech" element of communication. Fighting words are thus analogous to a noisy sound truck: Each is, as Justice Frankfurter recognized, a "mode of speech," *Niemotko v. Maryland*, 340 U.S. 268, 282, 71 S.Ct. 325, 333, 95 L.Ed. 267 (1951) (opinion concurring in result); both can be used to convey an idea; but neither has, in and of itself, a claim upon the First Amendment. As with the sound truck, however, so also with fighting words: The government may not regulate use based on hostility—or favoritism—towards the underlying message expressed. Compare *Frisby v. Schultz*, 487 U.S. 474, 108 S.Ct. 2495, 101 L.Ed.2d 420 (1988) (upholding, against facial challenge, a content-neutral ban on targeted residential picketing), with *Carey v. Brown*, 447 U.S. 455, 100 S.Ct. 2286, 65 L.Ed.2d 263 (1980) (invalidating a ban on residential picketing that exempted labor picketing).

* * *

Applying these principles to the St. Paul ordinance, we conclude that, even as narrowly construed by the Minnesota Supreme Court, the ordinance is facially unconstitutional. Although the phrase in the ordinance, "arouses anger, alarm or resentment in others," has been limited by the Minnesota Supreme Court's construction to reach only those symbols or displays that amount to "fighting words," the remaining, unmodified terms make clear that the ordinance applies only to "fighting words" that insult, or provoke violence, "on the basis of race, color, creed, religion or gender." Displays containing abusive invective, no matter how vicious or severe, are permissible unless they are addressed to one of the specified disfavored topics. Those who wish to use "fighting words" in connection with other ideas—to express hostility, for example, on the basis of political affiliation, union membership, or homosexuality—are not covered. The First Amendment does not permit St. Paul to impose special prohibitions on those speakers who express views on disfavored subjects.

In its practical operation, moreover, the ordinance goes even beyond mere content discrimination, to actual viewpoint discrimination. Displays containing some words—odious racial epithets, for example— would be prohibited to proponents of all views. But "fighting words" that do not themselves invoke race, color, creed, religion, or gender— aspersions upon a person's mother, for example—would seemingly be usable *ad libitum* in the placards of those arguing *in favor* of racial, color, etc., tolerance and equality, but could not be used by those speakers' opponents. One could hold up a sign saying, for example, that all "anti-Catholic bigots" are misbegotten; but not that all "papists" are, for that would insult and provoke violence "on the basis of religion." St. Paul has no such authority to license one side of a debate to fight freestyle, while requiring the other to follow Marquis of Queensberry rules.

* * *

. . . What makes the anger, fear, sense of dishonor, etc., produced by violation of this ordinance distinct from the anger, fear, sense of dishonor, etc., produced by other fighting words is nothing other than the fact that it is caused by a distinctive idea, conveyed by a distinctive message. The First Amendment cannot be evaded that easily. It is obvious that the symbols which will arouse "anger, alarm or resentment in others on the basis of race, color, creed, religion or gender" are those symbols that communicate a message of hostility based on one of these characteristics. St. Paul concedes in its brief that the ordinance applies only to "racial, religious, or gender-specific symbols" such as "a burning cross, Nazi swastika or other instrumentality of like import." Indeed, St. Paul argued in the Juvenile Court that "[t]he burning of a cross does express a message and it is, in fact, the content of that message which the St. Paul Ordinance attempts to legislate."

. . . [T]he reason why fighting words are categorically excluded from the protection of the First Amendment is not that their content communicates any particular idea, but that their content embodies a particularly intolerable (and socially unnecessary) mode of expressing whatever idea the speaker wishes to convey. St. Paul has not singled out an especially offensive mode of expression—it has not, for example, selected for prohibition only those fighting words that communicate ideas in a threatening (as opposed to a merely obnoxious) manner. Rather, it has proscribed fighting words of whatever manner that communicate messages of racial, gender, or religious intolerance. Selectivity of this sort creates the possibility that the city is seeking to handicap the expression of particular ideas. That possibility would alone be enough to render the ordinance presumptively invalid, but St. Paul's comments and concessions in this case elevate the possibility to a certainty.

* * *

Finally, St. Paul and its *amici* defend the conclusion of the Minnesota Supreme Court that, even if the ordinance regulates expression based on hostility towards its protected ideological content, this discrimination is nonetheless justified because it is narrowly tailored to serve compelling state interests. Specifically, they assert that the ordinance helps to ensure the basic human rights of members of groups that have historically been subjected to discrimination, including the right of such group members to live in peace where they wish. We do not doubt that these interests are compelling, and that the ordinance can be said to promote them. But the "danger of censorship" presented by a facially content-based statute requires that that weapon be employed only where it is "*necessary* to serve the asserted [compelling] interest." The existence of adequate content-neutral alternatives thus "undercut[s] significantly" any defense of such a statute, casting considerable doubt on the government's protestations that "the asserted justification is in fact an accurate description of the purpose and effect of the law." The dispositive question in this case, therefore, is whether content discrimination is reasonably necessary to achieve St. Paul's compelling interests; it plainly is not. An ordinance not limited to the favored topics, for example, would have precisely the same beneficial effect. In fact the only interest distinctively served by the content limitation is that of displaying the city council's special hostility towards the particular biases thus singled out. That is precisely what the First Amendment forbids. The politicians of St. Paul are entitled to express that hostility— but not through the means of imposing unique limitations upon speakers who (however benightedly) disagree.

* * *

Let there be no mistake about our belief that burning a cross in someone's front yard is reprehensible. But St. Paul has sufficient means at its disposal to prevent such behavior without adding the First Amendment to the fire.

The judgment of the Minnesota Supreme Court is reversed, and the case is remanded for proceedings not inconsistent with this opinion.

It is so ordered.

■ JUSTICE WHITE, with whom JUSTICE BLACKMUN and JUSTICE O'CONNOR join, and with whom JUSTICE STEVENS joins except as to Part I-A, concurring in the judgment.

* * *

II

Although I disagree with the Court's analysis, I do agree with its conclusion: The St. Paul ordinance is unconstitutional. However, I would decide the case on overbreadth grounds.

We have emphasized time and again that overbreadth doctrine is an exception to the established principle that a person to whom a statute may constitutionally be applied will not be heard to challenge that statute on the ground that it may conceivably be applied unconstitutionally to others, in other situations not before the Court. A defendant being prosecuted for speech or expressive conduct may challenge the law on its face if it reaches protected expression, even when that person's activities are not protected by the First Amendment. This is because "the possible harm to society in permitting some unprotected speech to go unpunished is outweighed by the possibility that protected speech of others may be muted" . . .

* * *

I agree with petitioner that the ordinance is invalid on its face. Although the ordinance as construed reaches categories of speech that are constitutionally unprotected, it also criminalizes a substantial amount of expression that—however repugnant—is shielded by the First Amendment.

In attempting to narrow the scope of the St. Paul antibias ordinance, the Minnesota Supreme Court relied upon two of the categories of speech and expressive conduct that fall outside the First Amendment's protective sphere: words that incite imminent lawless action, and "fighting" words. The Minnesota Supreme Court erred in its application of the *Chaplinsky* fighting words test and consequently interpreted the St. Paul ordinance in a fashion that rendered the ordinance facially overbroad.

In construing the St. Paul ordinance, the Minnesota Supreme Court drew upon the definition of fighting words that appears in *Chaplinsky*— words "which by their very utterance inflict injury or tend to incite an immediate breach of the peace." *Id.*, at 572, 62 S.Ct., at 769. However, the Minnesota court was far from clear in identifying the "injur[ies]" inflicted by the expression that St. Paul sought to regulate. Indeed, the Minnesota court emphasized (tracking the language of the ordinance) that "the ordinance censors only those displays that one knows or should know will create anger, alarm or resentment based on racial, ethnic, gender or religious bias." I therefore understand the court to have ruled that St. Paul may constitutionally prohibit expression that "by its very utterance" causes "anger, alarm or resentment."

Our fighting words cases have made clear, however, that such generalized reactions are not sufficient to strip expression of its constitutional protection. The mere fact that expressive activity causes hurt feelings, offense, or resentment does not render the expression unprotected. . . .

In the First Amendment context, "[c]riminal statutes must be scrutinized with particular care; those that make unlawful a substantial amount of constitutionally protected conduct may be held facially invalid even if they also have legitimate application." The St. Paul antibias ordinance is such a law. Although the ordinance reaches conduct that is unprotected, it also makes criminal expressive conduct that causes only hurt feelings, offense, or resentment, and is protected by the First Amendment. The ordinance is therefore fatally overbroad and invalid on its face.

* * *

NOTES AND QUESTIONS

1. According to Justice Scalia's majority opinion, exactly what is the First Amendment difficulty with the St. Paul Bias-Motivated Crime Ordinance? Is not the policy and prohibition of the St. Paul ordinance a laudable one? Would it be possible to draft such a criminal provision to avoid the Constitutional problems cited in both the majority and concurring opinions?

Problem 4–1. Instead of including the bias motivated conduct in the definition of the crime, would it be permissible to consider exactly the same conduct as that included in the St. Paul ordinance at the sentencing stage?

In Wisconsin v. Mitchell, 508 U.S. 476, 113 S.Ct. 2194, 124 L.Ed.2d 436 (1993), after viewing the film *Mississippi Burning* (which depicts a white man beating a young black who is praying), Mitchell, who is black, urged a group of blacks to beat a young white boy who happened to walk by. The group, including Mitchell, beat the white boy severely. Mitchell was convicted of aggravated battery, which normally carries a maximum sentence of two years' imprisonment. But because the jury found that Mitchell had intentionally selected his victim because of race, the maximum sentence for his offense was increased to seven years under the State's hate-crime penalty enhancement statute, which enhances the maximum penalty for an offense whenever the defendant "intentionally selects a person against whom the crime . . . is committed . . . because of the race, religion, color, disability, sexual orientation, national origin or ancestry of that person."

In light of *R.A.V.* and what you know of the operation of the criminal justice system, is the hate-crime penalty enhancement statute constitutional?

2. Surely the First Amendment protection of free speech cannot act as a shield to all criminal law enforcement. When is speech or communication sufficiently threatening that it can be proscribed by the criminal law irrespective of the fact that it amounts to a restraint on speech? Note the situations mentioned by the majority and concurring opinions in *R.A.V.* and, in particular, Chaplinsky v. New Hampshire, 315 U.S. 568, 62 S.Ct. 766, 86 L.Ed. 1031 (1942) ("fighting" words); Brandenburg v. Ohio, 395 U.S. 444, 89 S.Ct. 1827, 23 L.Ed.2d 430 (1969) (incitement to imminent lawless action); Roth v. United States, 354 U.S. 476, 77 S.Ct. 1304, 1 L.Ed.2d 1498 (1957) (obscenity).

Reno v. American Civil Liberties Union

Supreme Court of the United States, 1997.
521 U.S. 844, 117 S.Ct. 2329, 138 L.Ed.2d 874.

■ JUSTICE STEVENS delivered the opinion of the Court.

At issue is the constitutionality of two statutory provisions enacted to protect minors from "indecent" and "patently offensive" communications on the Internet. Notwithstanding the legitimacy and importance of the congressional goal of protecting children from harmful materials, we agree with the three-judge District Court that the statute abridges "the freedom of speech" protected by the First Amendment.

* * *

II

. . . [T]he "Communications Decency Act of 1996" (CDA) . . . contains . . . the two statutory provisions challenged in this case. They are informally described as the "indecent transmission" provision and the "patently offensive display" provision.

The first, 47 U.S.C.A. § 223(a) (Supp.1997), prohibits the knowing transmission of obscene or indecent messages to any recipient under 18 years of age. It provides in pertinent part:

(a) Whoever—

(1) in interstate or foreign communications—

. . .

(B) by means of a telecommunications device knowingly—

(i) makes, creates, or solicits, and

(ii) initiates the transmission of,

any comment, request, suggestion, proposal, image, or other communication which is obscene or indecent, knowing that the recipient of the communication is under 18 years of age, regardless of whether the maker of such communication placed the call or initiated the communication;

. . .

(2) knowingly permits any telecommunications facility under his control to be used for any activity prohibited by paragraph (1) with the intent that it be used for such activity,

shall be fined under Title 18, or imprisoned not more than two years, or both.

The second provision, § 223(d), prohibits the knowing sending or displaying of patently offensive messages in a manner that is available to a person under 18 years of age. It provides:

(d) Whoever—

(1) in interstate or foreign communications knowingly—

(A) uses an interactive computer service to send to a specific person or persons under 18 years of age, or

(B) uses any interactive computer service to display in a manner available to a person under 18 years of age,

any comment, request, suggestion, proposal, image, or other communication that, in context, depicts or describes, in terms patently offensive as measured by contemporary community standards, sexual or excretory activities or organs, regardless of whether the user of such service placed the call or initiated the communication; or

(2) knowingly permits any telecommunications facility under such person's control to be used for an activity prohibited by paragraph (1) with the intent that it be used for such activity,

shall be fined under Title 18, or imprisoned not more than two years, or both.

The breadth of these prohibitions is qualified by two affirmative defenses. See § 223(e)(5). One covers those who take "good faith, reasonable, effective, and appropriate actions" to restrict access by minors to the prohibited communications. § 223(e)(5)(A). The other covers those who restrict access to covered material by requiring certain designated forms of age proof, such as a verified credit card or an adult identification number or code. § 223(e)(5)(B).

III

* * *

The judgment of the District Court enjoins the Government from enforcing the prohibitions in § 223(a)(1)(B) insofar as they relate to "indecent" communications, but expressly preserves the Government's right to investigate and prosecute the obscenity or child pornography activities prohibited therein. The injunction against enforcement of §§ 223(d)(1) and (2) is unqualified because those provisions contain no separate reference to obscenity or child pornography.

The Government appealed under the Act's special review provisions, § 561, 110 Stat. 142–143, and we noted probable jurisdiction. In its appeal, the Government argues that the District Court erred in holding that the CDA violated both the First Amendment because it is overbroad and the Fifth Amendment because it is vague. While we discuss the vagueness of the CDA because of its relevance to the First Amendment overbreadth inquiry, we conclude that the judgment should be affirmed without reaching the Fifth Amendment issue. . . .

* * *

V

In *Southeastern Promotions, Ltd. v. Conrad* (1975), we observed that "[e]ach medium of expression . . . may present its own problems." Thus, some of our cases have recognized special justifications for regulation of the broadcast media that are not applicable to other speakers, see *Red Lion Broadcasting Co. v. FCC* (1969); *FCC v. Pacifica Foundation* (1978). In these cases, the Court relied on the history of extensive government regulation of the broadcast medium, the scarcity of available frequencies at its inception, and its "invasive" nature.

Those factors are not present in cyberspace. Neither before nor after the enactment of the CDA have the vast democratic fora of the Internet been subject to the type of government supervision and regulation that has attended the broadcast industry. Moreover, the Internet is not as "invasive" as radio or television. The District Court specifically found that "[c]ommunications over the Internet do not 'invade' an individual's home or appear on one's computer screen unbidden. Users seldom encounter content 'by accident.'" It also found that "[a]lmost all sexually explicit images are preceded by warnings as to the content," and cited testimony that "'odds are slim' that a user would come across a sexually explicit sight by accident."

We distinguished *Pacifica* in *Sable* on just this basis. In *Sable Communications of Cal., Inc.* (1989), a company engaged in the business of offering sexually oriented prerecorded telephone messages (popularly known as "dial-a-porn") challenged the constitutionality of an amendment to the Communications Act that imposed a blanket prohibition on indecent as well as obscene interstate commercial telephone messages. We held that the statute was constitutional insofar as it applied to obscene messages but invalid as applied to indecent messages. In attempting to justify the complete ban and criminalization of indecent commercial telephone messages, the Government relied on *Pacifica*, arguing that the ban was necessary to prevent children from gaining access to such messages. We agreed that "there is a compelling interest in protecting the physical and psychological well-being of minors" which extended to shielding them from indecent messages that are not obscene by adult standards, but distinguished our "emphatically narrow holding" in *Pacifica* because it did not involve a complete ban and because it involved a different medium of communication. We explained that "the dial-it medium requires the listener to take affirmative steps to receive the communication." "Placing a telephone call," we continued, "is not the same as turning on a radio and being taken by surprise by an indecent message."

Finally, unlike the conditions that prevailed when Congress first authorized regulation of the broadcast spectrum, the Internet can hardly be considered a "scarce" expressive commodity. It provides relatively unlimited, low-cost capacity for communication of all kinds. The Government estimates that "[a]s many as 40 million people use the Internet today, and that figure is expected to grow to 200 million by 1999." This dynamic, multifaceted category of communication includes not only traditional print and news services, but also audio, video, and still images, as well as interactive, real-time dialogue. Through the use of chat rooms, any person with a phone line can become a town crier with a voice that resonates farther than it could from any soapbox. Through the use of Web pages, mail exploders, and news groups, the same individual can become a pamphleteer. As the District Court found, "the content on the Internet is as diverse as human thought." We agree with its conclusion that our cases provide no basis for qualifying the level of First Amendment scrutiny that should be applied to this medium.

VI

Regardless of whether the CDA is so vague that it violates the Fifth Amendment, the many ambiguities concerning the scope of its coverage render it problematic for purposes of the First Amendment. For instance, each of the two parts of the CDA uses a different linguistic form. The first uses the word "indecent," 47 U.S.C.A. § 223(a) (Supp.1997), while the second speaks of material that "in context, depicts or describes, in terms patently offensive as measured by contemporary community standards, sexual or excretory activities or organs," § 223(d). Given the absence of a definition of either term,[35] this difference in language will provoke uncertainty among speakers about how the two standards relate to each other and just what they mean.[37] Could a speaker confidently assume

---

[35] "Indecent" does not benefit from any textual embellishment at all. "Patently offensive" is qualified only to the extent that it involves "sexual or excretory activities or organs" taken "in context" and "measured by contemporary community standards."

[37] The statute does not indicate whether the "patently offensive" and "indecent" determinations should be made with respect to minors or the population as a whole. The Government asserts that the appropriate standard is "what is suitable material for minors." But the Conferees expressly rejected amendments that would have imposed such a "harmful to minors" standard. The Conferees also rejected amendments that would have limited the

that a serious discussion about birth control practices, homosexuality, . . . or the consequences of prison rape would not violate the CDA? This uncertainty undermines the likelihood that the CDA has been carefully tailored to the congressional goal of protecting minors from potentially harmful materials.

The vagueness of the CDA is a matter of special concern for two reasons. First, the CDA is a content-based regulation of speech. The vagueness of such a regulation raises special First Amendment concerns because of its obvious chilling effect on free speech. Second, the CDA is a criminal statute. In addition to the opprobrium and stigma of a criminal conviction, the CDA threatens violators with penalties including up to two years in prison for each act of violation. The severity of criminal sanctions may well cause speakers to remain silent rather than communicate even arguably unlawful words, ideas, and images. . . .

* * *

VII

We are persuaded that the CDA lacks the precision that the First Amendment requires when a statute regulates the content of speech. In order to deny minors access to potentially harmful speech, the CDA effectively suppresses a large amount of speech that adults have a constitutional right to receive and to address to one another. That burden on adult speech is unacceptable if less restrictive alternatives would be at least as effective in achieving the legitimate purpose that the statute was enacted to serve.

In evaluating the free speech rights of adults, we have made it perfectly clear that sexual expression which is indecent but not obscene is protected by the First Amendment. . . . See also *Carey v. Population Services Int'l* (1977) ("[W]here obscenity is not involved, we have consistently held that the fact that protected speech may be offensive to some does not justify its suppression"). Indeed, *Pacifica* itself admonished that the fact that society may find speech offensive is not a sufficient reason for suppressing it.

It is true that we have repeatedly recognized the governmental interest in protecting children from harmful materials. But that interest does not justify an unnecessarily broad suppression of speech addressed to adults. As we have explained, the Government may not "reduc[e] the adult population . . . to . . . only what is fit for children." . . .

The District Court was correct to conclude that the CDA effectively resembles the ban on "dial-a-porn" invalidated in *Sable*. In *Sable*, this Court rejected the argument that we should defer to the congressional judgment that nothing less than a total ban would be effective in preventing enterprising youngsters from gaining access to indecent

---

proscribed materials to those lacking redeeming value. See S. Conf. Rep., at 189, 142 Cong. Rec. H1165–1166 (Feb. 1, 1996).

communications. *Sable* thus made clear that the mere fact that a statutory regulation of speech was enacted for the important purpose of protecting children from exposure to sexually explicit material does not foreclose inquiry into its validity. As we pointed out last Term, that inquiry embodies an "over-arching commitment" to make sure that Congress has designed its statute to accomplish its purpose "without imposing an unnecessarily great restriction on speech."

In arguing that the CDA does not so diminish adult communication, the Government relies on the incorrect factual premise that prohibiting a transmission whenever it is known that one of its recipients is a minor would not interfere with adult-to-adult communication. The findings of the District Court make clear that this premise is untenable. Given the size of the potential audience for most messages, in the absence of a viable age verification process, the sender must be charged with knowing that one or more minors will likely view it. Knowledge that, for instance, one or more members of a 100-person chat group will be minor—and therefore that it would be a crime to send the group an indecent message—would surely burden communication among adults.

The District Court found that at the time of trial existing technology did not include any effective method for a sender to prevent minors from obtaining access to its communications on the Internet without also denying access to adults. The Court found no effective way to determine the age of a user who is accessing material through e-mail, mail exploders, news groups, or chat rooms. As a practical matter, the Court also found that it would be prohibitively expensive for noncommercial—as well as some commercial—speakers who have Web sites to verify that their users are adults. These limitations must inevitably curtail a significant amount of adult communication on the Internet. By contrast, the District Court found that "[d]espite its limitations, currently available *user-based* software suggests that a reasonably effective method by which *parents* can prevent their children from accessing sexually explicit and other material which *parents* may believe is inappropriate for their children will soon be widely available."

The breadth of the CDA's coverage is wholly unprecedented. Unlike the regulations upheld in . . . *Pacifica*, the scope of the CDA is not limited to commercial speech or commercial entities. Its open-ended prohibitions embrace all nonprofit entities and individuals posting indecent messages or displaying them on their own computers in the presence of minors. The general, undefined terms "indecent" and "patently offensive" cover large amounts of nonpornographic material with serious educational or other value. Moreover, the "community standards" criterion as applied to the Internet means that any communication available to a nation-wide audience will be judged by the standards of the community most likely to be offended by the message. The regulated subject matter includes any of the seven "dirty words" used in the Pacifica monologue, the use of which the Government's expert acknowledged could constitute a felony. It may also extend to discussions about prison rape or safe sexual practices, artistic images that include nude subjects, and arguably the card catalogue of the Carnegie Library.

* * *

The breadth of this content-based restriction of speech imposes an especially heavy burden on the Government to explain why a less restrictive provision would not be as effective as the CDA. It has not done so. The arguments in this Court have referred to possible alternatives such as requiring that indecent material be "tagged" in a way that facilitates parental control of material coming into their homes, making exceptions for messages with artistic or educational value, providing some tolerance for parental choice, and regulating some portions of the Internet—such as commercial web sites—differently than others, such as chat rooms. Particularly in the light of the absence of any detailed findings by the Congress, or even hearings addressing the special problems of the CDA, we are persuaded that the CDA is not narrowly tailored if that requirement has any meaning at all.

* * *

For the foregoing reasons, the judgment of the district court is affirmed.

It is so ordered.

■ JUSTICE O'CONNOR, with whom THE CHIEF JUSTICE joins, concurring in the judgment in part and dissenting in part.

I write separately to explain why I view the Communications Decency Act of 1996 (CDA) as little more than an attempt by Congress to create "adult zones" on the Internet. Our precedent indicates that the creation of such zones can be constitutionally sound. Despite the soundness of its purpose, however, portions of the CDA are unconstitutional because they stray from the blueprint our prior cases have developed for constructing a "zoning law" that passes constitutional muster.

Appellees bring a facial challenge to three provisions of the CDA. The first, which the Court describes as the "indecency transmission" provision, makes it a crime to knowingly transmit an obscene or indecent message or image to a person the sender knows is under 18 years old. 47 U.S.C.A. § 223(a)(1)(B) (May 1996 Supp.). What the Court classifies as a single "'patently offensive display'" provision, see *ante*, at 2338, is in reality two separate provisions. The first of these makes it a crime to knowingly send a patently offensive message or image to a specific person under the age of 18 ("specific person" provision). § 223(d)(1)(A). The second criminalizes the display of patently offensive messages or images "in a[ny] manner available" to minors ("display" provision). § 223(d)(1)(B). None of these provisions purports to keep indecent (or patently offensive) material away from adults, who have a First Amendment right to obtain this speech. *Sable Communications of Cal., Inc. v. FCC* (1989) ("Sexual expression which is indecent but not obscene is protected by the First Amendment"). Thus, the undeniable purpose of the CDA is to segregate indecent material on the Internet into certain areas that minors cannot access. See S. Conf. Rep. No. 104–230, p. 189 (1996) (CDA imposes "access restrictions . . . to protect minors from exposure to indecent material").

The creation of "adult zones" is by no means a novel concept. States have long denied minors access to certain establishments frequented by adults. States have also denied minors access to speech deemed to be "harmful to minors." The Court has previously sustained such zoning laws, but only if they respect the First Amendment rights of adults and minors. That is to say, a zoning law is valid if (i) it does not unduly restrict adult access to the material; and (ii) minors have no First Amendment right to read or view the banned material. As applied to the Internet as it exists in 1997, the "display" provision and some applications of the "indecency transmission" and "specific person" provisions fail to adhere to the first of these limiting principles by restricting adults' access to protected materials in certain circumstances. Unlike the Court, however, I would invalidate the provisions only in those circumstances.

* * *

. . . [T]he constitutionality of the CDA as a zoning law hinges on the extent to which it substantially interferes with the First Amendment rights of adults. Because the rights of adults are infringed only by the "display" provision and by the "indecency transmission" and "specific person" provisions as applied to communications involving more than one adult, I would invalidate the CDA only to that extent. Insofar as the "indecency transmission" and "specific person" provisions prohibit the use of indecent speech in communications between an adult and one or more minors, however, they can and should be sustained. The Court reaches a contrary conclusion, and from that holding that I respectfully dissent.

NOTES AND QUESTIONS

1. Should the permissible regulation of speech vary depending on the medium? For example, what is Justice Stevens referring to in *Reno* when he suggests that the broadcast media have presented special problems? Doesn't the Internet present its own special justifications for regulations?

2. In light of *Reno*, is it possible for Congress to regulate communication in cyberspace? In this regard, see Miller v. California, 413 U.S. 15, 93 S.Ct. 2607, 37 L.Ed.2d 419 (1973), where the Supreme Court defined obscenity in the following way:

The basic guidelines for the trier of fact must be: (a) whether "the average person, applying contemporary community standards" would find that the work, taken as a whole, appeals to the prurient interest, (b) whether the work depicts or describes, in a patently offensive way, sexual conduct specifically defined by the applicable state law, and (c) whether the work, taken as a whole, lacks serious literary, artistic, political, or scientific value. 413 U.S. at 24, 93 S.Ct. at 2615.

See also The Child Protection Act of 1984, Pub. L. 98–292, 98 Stat. 204, which criminalizes the knowing receipt through the mails of a "visual depiction [that] involves the use of a minor engaging in sexually explicit conduct." 18 U.S.C. § 2252(a)(2)(A).

3. After the Supreme Court's decision in *Reno*, Congress attempted to address the Court's concerns by passing the Child Online Protection Act ("COPA"). Unlike the Communications Decency Act invalidated in *Reno*, COPA applies only to material displayed on the World Wide Web, covers only communications made for commercial purposes, and restricts only "material that is harmful to minors." 47 U.S.C. § 231(a)(1). "Material that is harmful to minors" is defined by reference to the three-part obscenity test from *Miller* (above), requiring jurors to apply "contemporary community standards" in evaluating challenged material. 47 U.S.C. § 231(e)(6)(A). The United States Court of Appeals for the Third Circuit held this use of "contemporary community standards" to be overbroad in the context of the Internet where dissemination could not be limited to a particular geographic region, thus forcing all speakers on the Web to abide by the "most puritan" community standards.

In Ashcroft v. American Civil Liberties Union, 535 U.S. 564, 122 S.Ct. 1700, 152 L.Ed.2d 771 (2002), the Supreme Court disagreed, holding that since COPA, unlike the statute in *Reno*, defined the "harmful to minors" material restricted by the statute in a manner parallel to the *Miller* definition of obscenity, requiring a speaker disseminating material to a national audience to observe varying community standards did not violate the First Amendment. However, because the Third Circuit did not rule on whether COPA suffers from substantial overbreadth for reasons other than its use of community standards, whether the statute is unconstitutionally vague, or whether it would otherwise withstand the strict scrutiny standard of review, the case was remanded to the Court of Appeals for consideration of these issues.

Problem 4–2. The Child Pornography Protection Act of 1996 ("CPPA") expanded the federal prohibition on child pornography to include "any visual depiction, including any photograph, film, video, picture, or computer or computer-generated image or picture" that "is, or appears to be, of a minor engaging in sexually explicit conduct," and any sexually explicit image that is "advertised, promoted, presented, described, or distributed in such a manner that conveys the impression" that it depicts "a minor engaging in sexually explicit conduct." This ban is directed at what has been called "virtual child pornography," sexually explicit images that were produced without real children by using youthful-looking actors or computer-imaging technology. Although pornography can be banned only if it satisfies the definition of obscenity provided in *Miller* (above), child pornography can be banned regardless of whether it is obscene because of the governmental interest in protecting children from sexual exploitation. Is the CPPA nevertheless overbroad and vague, chilling production of material protected by the First Amendment? *See* Ashcroft v. Free Speech Coalition, 535 U.S. 234, 122 S.Ct. 1389, 152 L.Ed.2d 403 (2002).

4. Is the criminal law the appropriate vehicle for restricting harmful speech? Is there any other regulatory device readily available? Is this generally the conundrum faced by the criminal law when it steps beyond the prohibition of basic street crime or crimes generally regarded as *mala in se*?

B. THE RIGHT TO PRIVACY AND TO EQUAL PROTECTION

1. ORIGIN OF THE RIGHT OF PRIVACY

Griswold v. Connecticut

Supreme Court of the United States, 1965.
381 U.S. 479, 85 S.Ct. 1678, 14 L.Ed.2d 510.

■ MR. JUSTICE DOUGLAS delivered the opinion of the Court.

Appellant Griswold is Executive Director of the Planned Parenthood League of Connecticut. Appellant Buxton is a licensed physician and a professor at the Yale Medical School who served as Medical Director for the League at its Center in New Haven—a center open and operating from November 1 to November 10, 1961, when appellants were arrested.

They gave information, instruction, and medical advice to *married persons* as to the means of preventing conception. They examined the wife and prescribed the best contraceptive device or material for her use. Fees were usually charged, although some couples were serviced free.

The statutes whose constitutionality is involved in this appeal are §§ 53–32 and 54–196 of the General Statutes of Connecticut (1958 rev.). The former provides:

> Any person who uses any drug, medicinal article or instrument for the purpose of preventing conception shall be fined not less than fifty dollars or imprisoned not less than sixty days nor more than one year or be both fined and imprisoned.

Section 54–196 provides:

> Any person who assists, abets, counsels, causes, hires or commands another to commit any offense may be prosecuted and punished as if he were the principal offender.

The appellants were found guilty as accessories and fined $100 each, against the claim that the accessory statute as so applied violated the Fourteenth Amendment. . . .

* * *

Coming to the merits, we are met with a wide range of questions that implicate the Due Process Clause of the Fourteenth Amendment. . . . We do not sit as a super-legislature to determine the wisdom, need, and propriety of laws that touch economic problems, business affairs, or social conditions. This law, however, operates directly on an intimate relation of husband and wife and their physician's role in one aspect of that relation.

The association of people is not mentioned in the Constitution nor in the Bill of Rights. The right to educate a child in a school of the parents' choice—whether public or private or parochial—is also not mentioned. Nor is the right to study any particular subject or any foreign language. Yet the First Amendment has been construed to include certain of those rights.

. . . Without those peripheral rights the specific rights would be less secure. . . .

* * *

[The] specific guarantees in the Bill of Rights have penumbras, formed by emanations from those guarantees that help give them life and substance. . . . Various guarantees create zones of privacy. The right of association contained in the penumbra of the First Amendment is one, The Third Amendment in its prohibition against the quartering of soldiers "in any house" in time of peace without the consent of the owner is another facet of that privacy. The Fourth Amendment explicitly affirms the "right of the people to be secure in their persons, houses, papers, and effects, against unreasonable searches and seizures." The Fifth Amendment in its Self-Incrimination Clause enables the citizen to create a zone of privacy which government may not force him to surrender to his detriment. The Ninth Amendment provides: "The enumeration in the Constitution, of certain rights, shall not be construed to deny or disparage others retained by the people."

The present case, then, concerns a relationship lying within the zone of privacy created by several fundamental constitutional guarantees. And it concerns a law which, in forbidding the *use* of contraceptives rather than regulating their manufacture or sale, seeks to achieve its goals by means having a maximum destructive impact upon that relationship. Such a law cannot stand in light of the familiar principle, so often applied by this Court, that a "governmental purpose to control or prevent activities constitutionally subject to state regulation may not be achieved by means which sweep unnecessarily broadly and thereby invade the area of protected freedoms."

. . . Would we allow the police to search the sacred precincts of marital bedrooms for telltale signs of the use of contraceptives? The very idea is repulsive to the notions of privacy surrounding the marriage relationship.

We deal with a right of privacy older than the Bill of Rights—older than our political parties, older than our school system. Marriage is a coming together for better or for worse, hopefully enduring, and intimate to the degree of being sacred. It is an association that promotes a way of life, not causes; a harmony in living, not political faiths; a bilateral loyalty, not commercial or social projects. Yet it is an association for as noble a purpose as any involved in our prior decisions.

Reversed.

■ MR. JUSTICE GOLDBERG, whom, THE CHIEF JUSTICE and MR. JUSTICE BRENNAN join, concurring.

I agree with the Court that Connecticut's birth-control law unconstitutionally intrudes upon the right of marital privacy, and I join in its opinion and judgment. Although I have not accepted the view that "due process" as used in the Fourteenth Amendment includes all of the first eight Amendments . . . , I do agree that the concept of liberty protects those personal rights that are fundamental, and is not confined to the specific terms of the Bill of Rights. My conclusion that the concept of liberty is not so restricted and that it embraces the right of marital privacy though that right is not mentioned explicitly in the Constitution is supported both by numerous decisions of this Court, . . . and by the language and history of the Ninth Amendment. In reaching the conclusion that the right of marital privacy is protected, as being within the protected penumbra of specific guarantees of the Bill of Rights, the Court refers to the Ninth Amendment. I add these words to emphasize the relevance of that Amendment to the Court's holding.

* * *

. . . The language and history of the Ninth Amendment reveal that the Framers of the Constitution believed that there are additional fundamental rights, protected from governmental infringement, which exist alongside those fundamental rights specifically mentioned in the first eight constitutional amendments.

The Ninth Amendment reads, "The enumeration in the Constitution, of certain rights, shall not be construed to deny or disparage others retained by the people." The Amendment is almost entirely the work of James Madison. It was introduced in Congress by him and passed the House and Senate with little or no debate and virtually no change in language. It was proffered to quiet expressed fears that a bill of specifically enumerated rights could not be sufficiently broad to cover all essential rights and that the specific mention of certain rights would be interpreted as a denial that others were protected.[4]

* * *

In presenting the proposed Amendment, Madison said:

It has been objected also against a bill of rights, that, by enumerating particular exceptions to the grant of power, it would disparage those rights which were not placed in that enumeration; and it might follow by implication, that those rights which were not singled out, were intended to be assigned into the hands of the General Government, and were consequently insecure. This is one of the most plausible arguments I have ever heard urged against the admission of a bill of rights into this system; but, I conceive, that it may be guarded against. I have attempted it, as gentlemen may see by turning to the last clause of the fourth resolution [the Ninth Amendment]. I Annals of Congress 439 (Gales and Seaton ed. 1834).

Mr. Justice Story wrote of this argument against a bill of rights and the meaning of the Ninth Amendment:

In regard to * * * [a] suggestion, that the affirmance of certain rights might disparage others, or might lead to argumentative implications in favor of other powers, it might be sufficient to say that such a course of reasoning could never be sustained upon any solid basis * * *. But a conclusive answer is, that such an attempt may be interdicted (as it has been) by a positive declaration in such a bill of rights that the enumeration of certain rights shall not be construed to deny or disparage others retained by the people. II Story, Commentaries on the Constitution of the United States 626–627 (5th ed. 1891).

---

[4] Alexander Hamilton was opposed to a bill of rights on the ground that it was unnecessary because the Federal Government was a government of delegated powers and it was not granted the power to intrude upon fundamental personal rights. The Federalist, No. 84 (Cooke ed. 1961), at 578–579.

He also argued,

"I go further, and affirm that bills of rights, in the sense and in the extent in which they are contended for, are not only unnecessary in the proposed constitution, but would even be dangerous. They would contain various exceptions to powers which are not granted; and on this very account, would afford a colourable pretext to claim more than were granted. For why declare that things shall not be done which there is no power to do? Why for instance, should it be said, that the liberty of the press shall not be restrained, when no power is given by which restrictions may be imposed? I will not contend that such a provision would confer a regulating power; but it is evident that it would furnish, to men disposed to usurp, a plausible pretence for claiming that power." The Ninth Amendment and the Tenth Amendment, which provides, "The powers not delegated to the United States by the Constitution, nor prohibited by it to the States, are reserved to the States respectively, or to the people," were apparently also designed in part to meet the above-quoted argument of Hamilton.

He further stated, referring to the Ninth Amendment:

> This clause was manifestly introduced to prevent any perverse or ingenious misapplication of the well-known maxim, that an affirmation in particular cases implies a negation in all others; and, *e converso*, that a negation in particular cases implies an affirmation in all others.

These statements of Madison and Story make clear that the Framers did not intend that the first eight amendments be construed to exhaust the basic and fundamental rights which the Constitution guaranteed to the people.

While this Court has had little occasion to interpret the Ninth Amendment, ... "[i]t cannot be presumed that any clause in the constitution is intended to be without effect." ... In interpreting the Constitution, "real effect should be given to all the words it uses." ... The Ninth Amendment to the Constitution may be regarded by some as a recent discovery but since 1791 it has been a basic part of the Constitution which we are sworn to uphold. To hold that a right so basic and fundamental and so deep-rooted in our society as the right of privacy in marriage may be infringed because that right is not guaranteed in so many words by the first eight amendments to the Constitution is to ignore the Ninth Amendment and to give it no effect whatsoever. Moreover, a judicial construction that this fundamental right is not protected by the Constitution because it is not mentioned in explicit terms by one of the first eight amendments or elsewhere in the Constitution would violate the Ninth Amendment, which specifically states that "[t]he enumeration in the Constitution, of certain rights shall not be *construed* to deny or disparage others retained by the people." (Emphasis added.)

A dissenting opinion suggests that my interpretation of the Ninth Amendment somehow "broaden[s] the powers of this Court." ... With all due respect, I believe that it misses the import of what I am saying. ... [The] Ninth Amendment shows a belief of the Constitution's authors that fundamental rights exist that are not expressly enumerated in the first eight amendments and an intent that the list of rights included there not be deemed exhaustive. As any student of this Court's opinions knows, this Court has held, often unanimously, that the Fifth and Fourteenth Amendments protect certain fundamental personal liberties from abridgment by the Federal Government or the States. ... The Ninth Amendment simply shows the intent of the Constitution's authors that other fundamental personal rights should not be denied such protection or disparaged in any other way simply because they are not specifically listed in the first eight constitutional amendments. I do not see how this broadens the authority of the Court; rather it serves to support what this Court has been doing in protecting fundamental rights.

Nor am I turning somersaults with history in arguing that the Ninth Amendment is relevant in a case dealing with a *State's* infringement of a fundamental right. While the Ninth Amendment—and indeed the entire Bill of Rights—originally concerned restrictions upon *federal* power, the subsequently enacted Fourteenth Amendment prohibits the States as well from abridging fundamental personal liberties. And, the Ninth Amendment, in indicating that not all such liberties are specifically mentioned in the first eight amendments, is surely relevant in showing the existence of other fundamental personal rights, now protected from state, as well as federal, infringement. In sum, the Ninth Amendment simply lends strong support to the view that the "liberty" protected by the Fifth and Fourteenth Amendments from infringement by the Federal Government or the States is not restricted to rights specifically mentioned in the first eight amendments. * * *

The entire fabric of the Constitution and the purposes that clearly underlie its specific guarantees demonstrate that the rights to marital privacy and to marry and raise a family are of similar order and magnitude as the fundamental rights specifically protected.

Although the Constitution, does not speak in so many words of the right of privacy in marriage, I cannot believe that it offers these fundamental rights no protection. The fact that no particular provision of the Constitution explicitly forbids the State from disrupting the traditional relation of the family—a relation as old and as fundamental as our entire civilization—surely does not show that the Government was meant to have the power to do so. Rather, as the Ninth Amendment expressly recognizes, there are fundamental personal rights such as this one, which are protected from abridgment by the Government though not specifically mentioned in the Constitution. * * *

Although the Connecticut birth-control law obviously encroaches upon a fundamental personal liberty, the State does not show that the law serves any "subordinating [state] interest which is compelling" or that it is "necessary . . . to the accomplishment of a permissible state policy." The State, at most, argues that there is some rational relation between this statute and what is admittedly a legitimate subject of state concern—the discouraging of extra-marital relations. It says that preventing the use of birth-control devices by married persons helps prevent the indulgence by some in such extra-marital relations. The rationality of this justification is dubious, particularly in light of the admitted widespread availability to all persons in the State of Connecticut, unmarried as well as married, of birth-control devices for the prevention of disease, as distinguished from the prevention of conception, . . . But, in any event, it is clear that the state interest in safeguarding marital fidelity can be served by a more discriminately tailored statute, which does not, like the present one, sweep unnecessarily broadly, reaching far beyond the evil sought to be dealt with and intruding upon the privacy of all married couples. . . . The State of Connecticut does have statutes, the constitutionality of which is beyond doubt, which prohibit adultery and fornication. . . . These statutes demonstrate that means for achieving the same basic purpose of protecting marital fidelity are available to Connecticut without the need to "invade the area of protected freedoms." . . .

In sum, I believe that the right of privacy in the marital relation is fundamental and basic—a personal right "retained by the people" within the meaning of the Ninth Amendment. Connecticut cannot constitutionally abridge this fundamental right, which is protected by the Fourteenth Amendment from infringement by the States. I agree with the Court that petitioners' convictions must therefore be reversed.

* * *

■ [JUSTICE HARLAN's concurring opinion is omitted. He expressed the view that the decision should rest upon the due process clause of the Fourteenth Amendment because he considered the statute violative of the basic values "implicit in the concept of ordered liberty".]

■ [JUSTICE WHITE's concurring opinion is also omitted. He, too, thought that the basis for the decision should be in violation of due process.]

■ [JUSTICE BLACK's dissenting opinion, in which JUSTICE STEWART concurred, is omitted too.]

* * *

■ MR. JUSTICE STEWART, whom MR. JUSTICE BLACK joins, dissenting.

Since 1879 Connecticut has had on its books a law which forbids the use of contraceptives by anyone. I think this is an uncommonly silly law. As a practical matter, the law is obviously unenforceable, except in the oblique context of the present case. As a philosophical matter, I believe the use of contraceptives in the relationship of marriage should be left to personal and private choice, based upon each individual's moral, ethical, and religious beliefs. As a matter of social policy, I think professional counsel about methods of birth control should be available to all, so that each individual's choice can be meaningfully made. But we are not asked in this case to say whether we think this law is unwise, or even asinine. We are asked to hold that it violates the United States Constitution. And that I cannot do.

In the course of its opinion the Court refers to no less than six Amendments to the Constitution: the First, the Third, the Fourth, the Fifth, the Ninth, and the Fourteenth. But the Court does not say which of these Amendments, if any, it thinks is infringed by this Connecticut law.

We *are* told that the Due Process Clause of the Fourteenth Amendment is not, as such, the "guide" in this case. With that much I agree. There is no claim that this law, duly enacted by the Connecticut

Legislature, is unconstitutionally vague. There is no claim that the appellants were denied any of the elements of procedural due process at their trial, so as to make their convictions constitutionally invalid. And, as the Court says, the day has long passed since the Due Process Clause was regarded as a proper instrument for determining "the wisdom, need, and propriety" of state laws. . . .

As to the First, Third, Fourth, and Fifth Amendments, I can find nothing in any of them to invalidate this Connecticut law, even assuming that all those Amendments are fully applicable against the States. It has not even been argued that this is a law "respecting an establishment of religion, or prohibiting the free exercise thereof." And surely, unless the solemn process of constitutional adjudication is to descend to the level of a play on words, there is not involved here any abridgment of "the freedom of speech, or of the press; or the right of the people peaceably to assemble, and to petition the Government for a redress of grievances." No soldier has been quartered in any house. There has been no search, and no seizure. Nobody has been compelled to be a witness against himself.

The Court, also quotes the Ninth Amendment, and my Brother Goldberg's concurring opinion relies heavily upon it. But to say that the Ninth Amendment has anything to do with this case is to turn somersaults with history. The Ninth Amendment, like its companion, the Tenth, which this Court held "states but a truism that all is retained which has not been surrendered" . . . was framed by James Madison and adopted by the States simply to make clear that the adoption of the Bill of Rights did not alter the plan that the *Federal* Government was to be a government of express and limited powers, and that all rights and powers not delegated to it were retained by the people and the individual States. Until today no member of this Court has ever suggested that the Ninth Amendment meant anything else, and the idea that a federal court could ever use the Ninth Amendment to annul a law passed by the elected representatives of the people of the State of Connecticut would have caused James Madison no little wonder.

What provision of the Constitution, then, does make this state law invalid? The Court says it is the right of privacy "created by several fundamental constitutional guarantees." With all deference, I can find no such general right of privacy in the Bill of Rights, in any other part of the Constitution, or in any case ever before decided by this Court.

At the oral argument in this case we were told that the Connecticut law does not "conform to current community standards." But it is not the function of this Court to decide cases on the basis of community standards. We are here to decide cases "agreeably to the Constitution and laws of the United States." It is the essence of judicial duty to subordinate our own personal views, our own ideas of what legislation is wise and what is not. If, as I should surely hope, the law before us does not reflect the standards of the people of Connecticut, the people of Connecticut can freely exercise their true Ninth and Tenth Amendment rights to persuade their elected representatives to repeal it. That is the constitutional way to take this law off the books.

NOTES AND QUESTIONS

1. Would or should the outcome in *Griswold* be different if the relevant statute prohibited providing contraceptive information or devices to *unmarried* persons? Is there something more special or sacrosanct about the marital relationship that makes it more amenable to Justice Douglas' "right to privacy"? *Cf.* Roe v. Wade, *infra* p. 316; Eisenstadt v. Baird, 405 U.S. 438, 92 S.Ct. 1029, 31 L.Ed.2d 349 (1972).

2. In City of Chicago v. Wilson, 75 Ill.2d 525, 27 Ill.Dec. 458, 389 N.E.2d 522 (1978), defendant was arrested for violating a section of the Chicago Municipal Code prohibiting a person from wearing clothing of the opposite sex with the intent to conceal his or her sex. He was a transsexual preparing for a sex-reassignment operation and preoperative therapy required that he cross-dress. The Illinois Supreme Court reversed the conviction, holding that the ordinance was unconstitutional as applied to the defendant. The court recognized that there exist unspecified constitutionally protected freedoms, which include the freedom to choose one's appearance. The ability of the state to regulate one's appearance uncontrolled by constitutional restraints "is fundamentally inconsistent with values of privacy, self-identity, autonomy and personal integrity that . . . the constitution was designed to protect." Although the state may infringe upon a person's right of privacy, the court asserted that the state's justification for intrusion must be stronger in the context of regulation which "controls the dress of the citizens at large," as opposed to regulation "in the context of an organized government activity." When these principles are applied to the defendant, the court found little justification against cross-dressing. We cannot "assume that individuals who cross-dress . . . as a means of . . . therapy are prone to commit crimes," the court said. It also found no evidence that this preoperative therapy violates public morals.

What would the result be if the defendant were a transvestite rather than a transsexual? Are a transvestite's constitutional rights to cross-dress less worthy of protection than a transsexual's?

3. A person lives in a home with her son and two grandsons in a neighborhood zoned for single family dwellings. A housing ordinance defines "family" in such a way that the grandsons do not qualify. If the person refuses to remove her grandsons from the home, can she be convicted of violating the ordinance over her claim that her constitutional right of privacy is infringed? The Supreme Court said "no" in Moore v. City of East Cleveland, Ohio, 431 U.S. 494, 97 S.Ct. 1932, 52 L.Ed.2d 531 (1977). The majority opinion held the ordinance unconstitutional because it had, at best, only a tenuous relationship to the objectives cited by the city: avoiding overcrowding, traffic congestion, and undue financial burdens on the school system. Considering the strong constitutional protection of the sanctity of the family which it had established in numerous previous decisions, the Court's plurality opinion felt this also included the family choice involved in this case. "Family," the Court said, is not confined within an arbitrary boundary drawn at the limits of the nuclear family.

4. A state statute makes it mandatory for physicians who prescribe, and pharmacists who dispense, certain controlled legitimate dangerous drugs to use an official form, a copy of which has to be filed with the State Health Department, where pertinent data, including names of the doctors, pharmacists, and patients, are recorded on tapes for computer processing. In such situations, is the "doctor-patient relationship" one of the zones of privacy accorded constitutional protection? Is the statute an unconstitutional impairment of the physician's right to practice medicine free from unwarranted state interference? Answering both questions in the negative, a unanimous Supreme Court, in Whalen v. Roe, 429 U.S. 589, 97 S.Ct. 869, 51 L.Ed.2d 64 (1977), reversed a District Court decision that had held the statute unconstitutional. At the conclusion of the opinion, the Court stated:

> We are not unaware of the threat to privacy implicit in the accumulation of vast amounts of personal information in computerized data banks or other massive government files. The collection of taxes, the distribution of welfare and social security benefits, the supervision of public health, the direction of our Armed Forces, and the enforcement of the criminal laws all require the orderly preservation of great quantities of information, much of which is personal in character and potentially embarrassing or harmful if disclosed. The right to collect and use such data for public purposes is typically accompanied by a concomitant statutory or regulatory duty to avoid unwarranted disclosures. Recognizing that in some circumstances that duty arguably has its roots in the Constitution, nevertheless New York's statutory scheme, and its implementing administrative procedures, evidence a proper concern with, and protection of, the individual's interest in privacy. We therefore need not, and do not, decide any question which might be presented by the unwarranted disclosure of accumulated private data—whether intentional or unintentional— or by a system that did not contain comparable security provisions. We simply hold that this record does not establish an invasion of any right or liberty protected by the Fourteenth Amendment.

5. In Stanley v. Georgia, 394 U.S. 557, 89 S.Ct. 1243, 22 L.Ed.2d 542 (1969), the Court held that the mere private possession of obscene matter cannot constitutionally be made a crime. Although obscene matter is not protected by the First Amendment freedom of the press guarantee, the Court said that, when this obscene matter is located in the privacy of one's own home, the "right takes on an added dimension." The Court held that, even though the states are free to regulate, or even ban, obscenity, "that power simply does not extend to mere possession by the individual in the privacy of his own home."

In light of *Stanley*, is it constitutionally permissible for a statute to provide criminal penalties for the simple possession of marijuana in one's home? *See, e.g.*, People v. Shepard, 50 N.Y.2d 640, 431 N.Y.S.2d 363, 409 N.E.2d 840 (1980).

6. Is it an invasion of one's privacy for male officers to search a female or for male inmates to be subjected to body searches by female guards? *See* Sterling v. Cupp, 290 Or. 611, 625 P.2d 123 (1981).

2. ABORTION AS A PRIVACY RIGHT

Roe v. Wade

Supreme Court of the United States, 1973.
410 U.S. 113, 93 S.Ct. 705, 35 L.Ed.2d 147.

[The majority and minority opinions in this case occupied sixty-four pages in the official U.S. reporter, so they obviously had to be condensed extensively for casebook usage. Although the following excerpts deal primarily with the right of privacy issue, we have retained certain tangentially related ones, for the reason that the subject of abortion is not treated elsewhere in the casebook. Students with a greater interest in the subject than is here presented will have access, of course, to the unabridged opinions themselves.]

■ MR. JUSTICE BLACKMUN delivered the opinion of the Court.

* * *

The Texas statutes that concern us here ... make it a crime to "procure an abortion," as therein defined, or to attempt one, except with respect to "an abortion procured or attempted by medical advice for the purpose of saving the life of the mother." Similar statutes are in existence in a majority of the States. . . .

* * *

Jane Roe, a single woman who was residing in Dallas County, Texas, instituted this federal action in March 1970 against the District Attorney of the county. She sought a declaratory judgment that the Texas criminal abortion statutes were unconstitutional on their face, and an injunction restraining the defendant from enforcing the statutes.

Roe alleged that she was unmarried and pregnant; that she wished to terminate her pregnancy by an abortion "performed by a competent, licensed physician, under safe, clinical conditions"; that she was unable to get a "legal" abortion in Texas because her life did not appear to be threatened by the continuation of her pregnancy; and that she could not afford to travel to another jurisdiction in order to secure a legal abortion under safe conditions. She claimed that the Texas statutes were unconstitutionally vague and that they abridged her right of personal privacy, protected by the First, Fourth, Fifth, Ninth, and Fourteenth

Amendments. By an amendment to her complaint Roe purported to sue "on behalf of herself and all other women" similarly situated.

* * *

The principal thrust of appellant's attack on the Texas statutes is that they improperly invade a right, said to be possessed by the pregnant woman, to choose to terminate her pregnancy. Appellant would discover this right in the concept of personal "liberty" embodied in the Fourteenth Amendment's Due Process Clause; or in personal, marital, familial, and sexual privacy said to be protected by the Bill of Rights or its penumbras, . . . Before addressing this claim, we feel it desirable briefly to survey, in several aspects, the history of abortion, for such insight as that history may afford us, and then to examine the state purposes and interests behind the criminal abortion laws.

It perhaps is not generally appreciated that the restrictive criminal abortion laws in effect in a majority of States today are of relatively recent vintage. Those laws, generally proscribing abortion or its attempt at any time during pregnancy except when necessary to preserve the pregnant woman's life, are not of ancient or even of common law origin. Instead, they derive from statutory changes effected, for the most part, in the latter half of the 19th century.

1. *Ancient Attitudes.* These are not capable of precise determination. We are told that at the time of the Persian Empire abortifacients were known and that criminal abortions were severely punished. We are also told, however, that abortion was practiced in Greek times as well as in the Roman Era, and that "it was resorted to without scruple." The Ephesian, Soranos, often described as the greatest of the ancient gynecologists, appears to have been generally opposed to Rome's prevailing pre-abortion practices. He found it necessary to think first of the life of the mother, and he resorted to abortion when, upon this standard, he felt the procedure advisable. Greek and Roman law afforded little protection to the unborn. If abortion was prosecuted in some places, it seems to have been based on a concept of a violation of the father's right to his offspring. Ancient religion did not bar abortion.

2. *The Hippocratic Oath.* What then of the famous Oath that has stood so long as the ethical guide of the medical profession and that bears the name of the great Greek (460 (?)–377 (?) B.C.), who has been described as the Father of Medicine, the "wisest and the greatest practitioner of his art," and the "most important and most complete medical personality of antiquity," who dominated the medical schools of this time, and who typified the sum of the medical knowledge of the past? The Oath varies somewhat according to the particular translation, but in any translation the content is clear: "I will give no deadly medicine to anyone if asked, nor suggest any such counsel; and in like manner I will not give to a woman a pessary to produce abortion," or "I will neither give

a deadly drug to anybody if asked for it, nor will I make a suggestion to this effect. Similarly, I will not give to a woman an abortive remedy."

Although the Oath is not mentioned in any of the principal briefs in this case, . . . it represents the apex of the development of strict ethical concepts in medicine, and its influence endures to this day. Why did not the authority of Hippocrates dissuade abortion practice in his time and that of Rome? The late Dr. Edelstein provides us with a theory: . . . The Oath was not uncontested even in Hippocrates' day; only the Pythagorean school of philosophers frowned upon the related act of suicide. Most Greek thinkers, on the other hand, commended abortion, at least prior to viability. . . . For the Pythagoreans, however, it was a matter of dogma. For them the embryo was animate from the moment of conception, and abortion meant destruction of a living being. The abortion clause of the Oath, therefore, "echoes Pythagorean doctrines," and "[i]n no other stratum of Greek opinion were such views held or proposed in the same spirit of uncompromising austerity."

Edelstein then concludes that the Oath originated in a group representing only a small segment of Greek opinion and that it certainly was not accepted by all ancient physicians. He points out that medical writings down to Galen (130–200 A.D.) "give evidence of the violation of almost every one of its injunctions." But with the end of antiquity a decided change took place. Resistance against suicide and against abortion became common. The Oath came to be popular. The emerging teachings of Christianity were in agreement with the Pythagorean ethic. The Oath "became the nucleus of all medical ethics" and "was applauded as the embodiment of truth." Thus, suggests Dr. Edelstein, it is "a Pythagorean manifesto and not the expression of an absolute standard of medical conduct."

This, it seems to us, is a satisfactory and acceptable explanation of the Hippocratic Oath's apparent rigidity. It enables us to understand, in historical context, a long accepted and revered statement of medical ethics.

3. *The Common Law.* It is undisputed that at the common law, abortion performed *before* "quickening"—the first recognizable movement of the fetus *in utero*, appearing usually from the 16th to the 18th week of pregnancy—was not an indictable offense. The absence of a common law crime for pre-quickening abortion appears to have developed from a confluence of earlier philosophical, theological, and civil and canon law concepts of when life begins. These disciplines variously approached the question in terms of the point at which the embryo or fetus became "formed" or recognizably human, or in terms of when a "person" came into being, that is, infused with a "soul" or "animated." A loose consensus evolved in early English law that these events occurred at some point between conception and live birth. This was "mediate animation." Although Christian theology and the canon law came to fix the point of

animation at 40 days for a male and 80 days for a female, a view that persisted until the 19th century, there was otherwise little agreement about the precise time of formation or animation. There was agreement, however, that prior to this point the fetus was to be regarded as part of the mother and its destruction, therefore, was not homicide. Due to continued uncertainty about the precise time when animation occurred, to the lack of any empirical basis for the 40–80 day view, and perhaps to Acquinas' definition of movement as one of the two first principles of life, Bracton focused upon quickening as the critical point. The significance of quickening was echoed by later common law scholars and found its way into the received common law in this country.

Whether abortion of a *quick* fetus was a felony at common law, or even a lesser crime, is still disputed. Bracton, writing early in the 13th century, thought it homicide. But the later and predominant view, following the great common law scholars, has been that it was at most a lesser offense. In a frequently cited passage, Coke took the position that abortion of a woman "quick with childe" is "a great misprision and no murder." Blackstone followed, saying that while abortion after quickening had once been considered manslaughter (though not murder), "modern law" took a less severe view. A recent review of the common law precedents argues, however, that those precedents contradict Coke and that even post-quickening abortion was never established as a common law crime. This is of some importance because while most American courts ruled, in holding or dictum, that abortion of an unquickened fetus was not criminal under their received common law, others followed Coke in stating that abortion of a quick fetus was a "misprision," a term they translated to mean "misdemeanor." That their reliance on Coke on this aspect of the law was uncritical and, apparently in all the reported cases, dictum (due probably to the paucity of common law prosecutions for post-quickening abortion), makes it now appear doubtful that abortion was ever firmly established as a common law crime even with respect to the destruction of a quick fetus.

4. *The English Statutory Law.* England's first criminal abortion statute . . . came in 1803. It made abortion of a quick fetus, § 1, a capital crime, but in § 2 it provided lesser penalties for the felony of abortion before quickening, and thus preserved the quickening distinction. This contrast was continued in the general revision of 1828 . . . It disappeared, however, together with the death penalty, in 1837 . . . and did not reappear in the Offenses Against the Person Act of 1861 . . . that formed the core of English anti-abortion law until the liberalizing reforms of 1967. * * *

[The 1967 Abortion Act] permits a licensed physician to perform an abortion where two other licensed physicians agree (a) "that the continuance of the pregnancy would involve risk to the life of the pregnant woman, or of injury to the physical or mental health of the pregnant woman or any existing children of her family, greater than if the pregnancy were terminated," or (b) "that there is a substantial risk that if the child were born it would suffer from such physical or mental abnormalities as to be seriously handicapped." The Act also provides that, in making this determination, "account may be taken of the pregnant woman's actual or reasonably foreseeable environment." It also permits a physician, without the concurrence of others, to terminate a pregnancy where he is of the good faith opinion that the abortion "is immediately necessary to save the life or to prevent grave permanent injury to the physical or mental health of the pregnant woman."

5. *The American Law.* In this country the law in effect in all but a few States until mid-19th century was the pre-existing English common law. Connecticut, the first State to enact abortion legislation, adopted in 1821 that part of [the early English act] that related to a woman "quick with child." The death penalty was not imposed. Abortion before quickening was made a crime in that State only in 1860. In 1828 New York enacted legislation that, in two respects, was to serve as a model for early anti-abortion statutes. First, while barring destruction of an unquickened fetus as well as a quick fetus, it made the former only a misdemeanor, but the latter second-degree manslaughter. Second, it incorporated a concept of therapeutic abortion by providing that an abortion was excused if it "shall have been necessary to preserve the life of such mother, or shall have been advised by two physicians to be necessary for such purpose." By 1840, when Texas had received the common law, only eight American States had statutes dealing with abortion. It was not until after the War Between the States that legislation began generally to replace the common law. Most of these initial statutes dealt severely with abortion after quickening but were lenient with it before quickening. Most punished attempts equally with completed abortions. While many statutes included the exception for an abortion thought by one or more physicians to be necessary to save the mother's life, that provision soon disappeared and the typical law required that the procedure actually be necessary for that purpose.

Gradually, in the middle and late 19th century the quickening distinction disappeared from the statutory law of most States and the degree of the offense and the penalties were increased. By the end of the 1950's a large majority of the States banned abortion, however and whenever performed, unless done to save or preserve the life of the mother. The exceptions, Alabama and the District of Columbia, permitted abortion to preserve the mother's health. Three other States permitted abortions that were not "unlawfully" performed or that were not "without lawful justification," leaving interpretation of those standards to the courts. In the past several years, however, a trend toward liberalization of abortion statutes has resulted in adoption, by about one-third of the States, of less stringent laws, most of them patterned after the ALI Model Penal Code, . . .

It is thus apparent that at common law, at the time of the adoption of our Constitution, and throughout the major portion of the 19th century, abortion was viewed with less disfavor than under most American statutes currently in effect. Phrasing it another way, a woman enjoyed a substantially broader right to terminate a pregnancy than she does in most States today. At least with respect to the early stage of pregnancy, and very possibly without such a limitation, the opportunity to make this choice was present in this country well into the 19th century. Even later, the law continued for some time to treat less punitively an abortion procured in early pregnancy.

6. *The Position of the American Medical Association.* The anti-abortion mood prevalent in this country in the late 19th century was shared by the medical profession. Indeed, the attitude of the profession may have played a significant role in the enactment of stringent criminal abortion legislation during that period. * * *

. . . [In 1967 the AMA's] Committee on Human Reproduction urged the adoption of a stated policy of opposition to induced abortion except when there is "documented medical evidence" of a threat to the health or life of the mother, or that the child "may be born with incapacitating physical deformity or mental deficiency," or that a pregnancy "resulting from legally established statutory or forcible rape or incest may constitute a threat to the mental or physical health of the patient," and two other physicians "chosen because of their recognized professional competency have examined the patient and have concurred in writing," and the procedure "is performed in a hospital accredited by the Joint Commission on Accreditation of Hospitals." The providing of medical information by physicians to state legislatures in their consideration of legislation regarding therapeutic abortion was "to be considered consistent with the principles of ethics of the American Medical Association." This recommendation was adopted by the House of Delegates. . . .

In 1970, after the introduction of a variety of proposed resolutions, and of a report from its Board of Trustees, a reference committee noted "polarization of the medical profession on this controversial issue"; division among those who had testified; a difference of opinion among AMA councils and committees; "the remarkable shift in testimony" in six months, felt to be influenced "by the rapid changes in state laws and by the judicial decisions which tend to make abortion more freely available;" and a feeling "that this trend will continue." On June 25, 1970, the House of Delegates adopted preambles and most of the resolutions proposed by the reference committee. The preambles emphasized "the best interests of the patient," "sound clinical judgment," and "informed patient consent," in contrast to "mere acquiescence to the patient's demand." The resolutions asserted that abortion is a medical procedure that should be performed by a licensed physician in an accredited hospital only after consultation with two other physicians and in conformity with state law, and that no party to the procedure should be required to violate personally held moral principles. . . . The AMA Judicial Council rendered a complementary opinion. * * *

[Omitted here are the reported position of the American Public Health Association, and that of the American Bar Association. The latter organization's House of Delegates in 1972 approved the Uniform Abortion Act drafted by the Conference of Commissioners on Uniform State Laws. It appears in footnote 40 of the court's opinion.] * * *

Three reasons have been advanced to explain historically the enactment of criminal abortion laws in the 19th century and to justify their continued existence.

It has been argued occasionally that these laws were the product of a Victorian social concern to discourage illicit sexual conduct. Texas, however, does not advance this justification in the present case, and it appears that no court or commentator has taken the argument seriously. . . .

A second reason is concerned with abortion as a medical procedure. When most criminal abortion laws were first enacted, the procedure was a hazardous one for the woman. This was particularly true prior to the development of antisepsis. Antiseptic techniques, of course, were based on discoveries by Lister, Pasteur, and others first announced in 1867, but were not generally accepted and employed until about the turn of the century. Abortion mortality was high. Even after 1900, and perhaps until as late as the development of antibiotics in the 1940's, standard modern techniques such as dilation and curettage were not nearly so safe as they are today. Thus it has been argued that a State's real concern in enacting a criminal abortion law was to protect the pregnant woman, that is, to restrain her from submitting to a procedure that placed her life in serious jeopardy.

Modern medical techniques have altered this situation. Appellants and various *amici* refer to medical data indicating that abortion in early pregnancy, that is, prior to the end of first trimester, although not without its risk, is now relatively safe. Mortality rates for women undergoing early abortions, where the procedure is legal, appear to be as low as or lower than the rates for normal childbirth. Consequently, any interest of the State in protecting the woman from an inherently hazardous procedure, except when it would be equally dangerous for her to forgo it, has largely disappeared. Of course, important state interests in the area of health and medical standards do remain. The State has a legitimate interest in seeing to it that abortion, like any other medical procedure, is performed under circumstances that insure maximum safety for the patient. . . . The prevalence of high mortality rates at illegal "abortion mills" strengthens, rather than weakens, the State's interest in regulating the conditions under which abortions are performed.

Moreover, the risk to the woman increases as her pregnancy continues. Thus the State retains a definite interest in protecting the woman's own health and safety when an abortion is proposed at a late stage of pregnancy.

The third reason is the State's interest—some phrase it in terms of duty—in protecting prenatal life. Some of the argument for this justification rests on the theory that a new human life is present from the moment of conception. The State's interest and general obligation to protect life then extends, it is argued, to prenatal life. Only when the life of the pregnant mother herself is at stake, balanced against the life she carries within her, should the interest of the embryo or fetus not prevail. Logically, of course, a legitimate state interest in this area need not stand or fall on acceptance of the belief that life begins at conception or at some other point prior to live birth. In assessing the State's interest, recognition may be given to the less rigid claim that as long as at least *potential* life is involved, the State may assert interests beyond the protection of the pregnant woman alone.

Parties challenging state abortion laws have sharply disputed in some courts the contention that a purpose of these laws, when enacted, was to protect prenatal life. Pointing to the absence of legislative history to support the contention, they claim that most state laws were designed solely to protect the woman. . . . Proponents of this view point out that in many States, including Texas, by statute or judicial interpretation, the pregnant woman herself could not be prosecuted for self-abortion or for cooperating in an abortion performed upon her by another. They claim that adoption of the "quickening" distinction through received common law and state statutes tacitly recognizes the greater health hazards inherent in late abortion and impliedly repudiates the theory that life begins at conception.

It is with these interests, and the weight to be attached to them, that this case is concerned.

The Constitution does not explicitly mention any right of privacy. In a line of decisions, however, going back perhaps as far as [1891] . . . , the Court has recognized that a right of personal privacy, or a guarantee of certain areas or zones of privacy, does exist under the Constitution. In varying contexts the Court or individual Justices have indeed found at least the roots of that right in the First Amendment, . . . ; in the Fourth and Fifth Amendments, . . . ; in the penumbras of the Bill of Rights, . . . ; in the Ninth Amendment, . . . ; or in the concept of liberty guaranteed by the first section of the Fourteenth Amendment, . . . These decisions make it clear that only personal rights that can be deemed "fundamental" or "implicit in the concept of ordered liberty," . . . are included in this guarantee of personal privacy. They also make it clear that the right has some extension to activities relating to marriage, . . . procreation, . . .

contraception, ... family relationships, ... and child rearing and education, ...

This right of privacy, whether it be founded in the Fourteenth Amendment's concept of personal liberty and restrictions upon state action, as we feel it is, or, as the District Court determined, in the Ninth Amendment's reservation of rights to the people, is broad enough to encompass a woman's decision whether or not to terminate her pregnancy. The detriment that the State would impose upon the pregnant woman by denying this choice altogether is apparent. Specific and direct harm medically diagnosable even in early pregnancy may be involved. Maternity, or additional offspring, may force upon the woman a distressful life and future. Psychological harm may be imminent. Mental and physical health may be taxed by child care. There is also the distress, for all concerned, associated with the unwanted child, and there is the problem of bringing a child into a family already unable, psychologically and otherwise, to care for it. In other cases, as in this one, the additional difficulties and continuing stigma of unwed motherhood may be involved. All these are factors the woman and her responsible physician necessarily will consider in consultation.

On the basis of elements such as these, appellants and some *amici* argue that the woman's right is absolute and that she is entitled to terminate her pregnancy at whatever time, in whatever way, and for whatever reason she alone chooses. With this we do not agree. Appellants' arguments that Texas either has no valid interest at all in regulating the abortion decision, or no interest strong enough to support any limitation upon the woman's sole determination, is unpersuasive. The Court's decisions recognizing a right of privacy also acknowledge that some state regulation in areas protected by that right is appropriate. As noted above, a state may properly assert important interests in safeguarding health, in maintaining medical standards, and in protecting potential life. At some point in pregnancy, these respective interests become sufficiently compelling to sustain regulation of the factors that govern the abortion decision. The privacy right involved, therefore, cannot be said to be absolute. . . .

The appellee and certain *amici* argue that the fetus is a "person" within the language and meaning of the Fourteenth Amendment. In support of this they outline at length and in detail the well-known facts of fetal development. If this suggestion of personhood is established, the appellant's case, of course, collapses, for the fetus' right to life is then guaranteed specifically by the Amendment. The appellant conceded as much on reargument. On the other hand, the appellee conceded on reargument that no case could be cited that holds that a fetus is a person within the meaning of the Fourteenth Amendment.

The Constitution does not define "person" in so many words. Section 1 of the Fourteenth Amendment contains three references to "person."

The first, in defining "citizens," speaks of "persons born or naturalized in the United States." The word also appears both in the Due Process Clause and in the Equal Protection Clause. "Person" is used in other places in the Constitution: in the listing of qualifications for representatives and senators [etc.], and in the Fifth, Twelfth, and Twenty-second Amendments as well as in §§ 2 and 3 of the Fourteenth Amendment. But in nearly all these instances, the use of the word is such that it has application only postnatally. None indicates, with any assurance, that it has any possible pre-natal application.

All this, together with our observation, supra, that throughout the major portion of the 19th century prevailing legal abortion practices were far freer than they are today, persuades us that the word "person," as used in the Fourteenth Amendment, does not include the unborn. . . .

This conclusion, however, does not of itself fully answer the contentions raised by Texas, and we pass on to other considerations.

The pregnant woman cannot be isolated in her privacy. She carries an embryo, and, later, a fetus, if one accepts the medical definitions of the developing young in the human uterus. The situation therefore is inherently different from marital intimacy, or bedroom possession of obscene material, or marriage, or procreation, or education. . . . As we have intimated above, it is reasonable and appropriate for a State to decide that at some point in time another interest, that of health of the mother or that of potential human life, becomes significantly involved. The woman's privacy is no longer sole and any right of privacy she possesses must be measured accordingly.

[At this point Justice Blackmun discusses the issue of when life begins, a portion of which is included in Note 1 on pp. 465–466, following the case of Keeler v. Superior Court *infra* Chapter 5.]

* * *

In view of all this, we do not agree that, by adopting one theory of life, Texas may override the rights of the pregnant woman that are at stake. We repeat, however, that the State does have an important and legitimate interest in preserving and protecting the health of the pregnant woman, whether she be a resident of the State or a nonresident who seeks medical consultation and treatment there, and that it has still *another* important and legitimate interest in protecting the potentiality of human life. These interests are separate and distinct. Each grows in substantiality as the woman approaches term and, at a point during pregnancy, each becomes "compelling."

With respect to the State's important and legitimate interest in the health of the mother, the "compelling" point, in the light of present medical knowledge, is at approximately the end of the first trimester. This is so because of the now established medical fact, referred to above that until the end of the first trimester mortality in abortion is less than mortality in normal childbirth. It follows that, from and after this point, a State may regulate the abortion procedure to the extent that the regulation reasonably relates to the preservation and protection of maternal health. Examples of permissible state regulation in this area are requirements as to the qualifications of the person who is to perform the abortion; as to the licensure of that person; as to the facility in which the procedure is to be performed, that is, whether it must be a hospital or may be a clinic or some other place of less-than-hospital status; as to the licensing of the facility; and the like.

This means, on the other hand, that, for the period of pregnancy prior to this "compelling" point, the attending physician, in consultation with his patient, is free to determine, without regulation by the State, that in his medical judgment the patient's pregnancy should be terminated. If that decision is reached, the judgment may be effectuated by any abortion free of interference by the State.

With respect to the State's important and legitimate interest in potential life, the "compelling" point is at viability. This is so because the fetus then presumably has the capability of meaningful life outside the mother's womb. State regulation protective of fetal life after viability thus has both logical and biological justifications. If the State is interested in protecting fetal life after viability, it may go so far as to proscribe abortion during that period except when it is necessary to preserve the life or health of the mother.

Measured against these standards, the Texas Penal Code, in restricting legal abortions to those "procured or attempted by medical advice for the purpose of saving the life of the mother," sweeps too broadly. The statute makes no distinction between abortions performed early in pregnancy and those performed later, and it limits to a single reason, "saving" the mother's life, the legal justification for the procedure. The statute, therefore, cannot survive the constitutional attack made upon it here. * * *

To summarize and to repeat:

1. A state criminal abortion statute of the current Texas type, that excepts from criminality only a *life saving* procedure on behalf of the mother, without regard to pregnancy stage and without recognition of the other interests involved, is violative of the Due Process Clause of the Fourteenth Amendment.

(a) For the stage prior to approximately the end of the first trimester, the abortion decision and its effectuation must be left to the medical judgment of the pregnant woman's attending physician.

(b) For the stage subsequent to approximately the end of the first trimester, the State, in promoting its interest in the health of the mother, may, if it chooses, regulate the abortion procedure in ways that are reasonably related to maternal health.

(c) For the stage subsequent to viability the State, in promoting its interest in the potentiality of human life, may, if it chooses, regulate, and even proscribe, abortion except where it is necessary, in appropriate medical judgment, for the preservation of the life or health of the mother.

2. The State may define the term "physician" . . . to mean only a physician currently licensed by the State, and may proscribe any abortion by a person who is not a physician as so defined. * * *

■ [The concurring opinions of CHIEF JUSTICE BURGER and of JUSTICES DOUGLAS and STEWART are omitted.]

■ MR. JUSTICE REHNQUIST, dissenting.

The Court's opinion brings to the decision of this troubling question both extensive historical fact and a wealth of legal scholarship. While its opinion thus commands my respect, I find myself nonetheless in fundamental disagreement with those parts of it which invalidate the Texas statute in question, and therefore dissent.

The Court's opinion decides that a State may impose virtually no restriction on the performance of abortions during the first trimester of pregnancy. Our previous decisions indicate that a necessary predicate for such an opinion is a plaintiff who was in her first trimester of pregnancy at some time during the pendency of her law suit. While a party may vindicate his own constitutional rights, he may not seek vindication for the rights of others. . . . The Court's statement of facts in this case makes clear, however, that the record in no way indicates the presence of such a plaintiff. . . .

* * *

Even if there were a plaintiff in this case capable of litigating the issue which the Court decides, I would reach a conclusion opposite to that reached by the Court. I have difficulty in concluding as the Court does, that the right of "privacy" is involved in this case. Texas by the statute here challenged bars the performance of a medical abortion by a licensed physician on a plaintiff such as Roe. A transaction resulting in an operation such as this is not "private" in the ordinary usage of that word. Nor is the "privacy" which the Court finds here even a distant relative of the freedom from searches and seizures protected by the Fourth Amendment to the Constitution which the Court has referred to as embodying a right to privacy. . . .

If the Court means by the term "privacy" no more than that the claim of a person to be free from unwanted state regulation of consensual transactions may be a form of "liberty" protected by the Fourteenth Amendment, there is no doubt that similar claims have been upheld in our earlier decisions on the basis of that liberty. I agree with the statement of Mr. Justice Stewart in his concurring opinion that the "liberty," against deprivation of which without due process the Fourteenth Amendment protects, embraces more than the rights found in the Bill of Rights. But that liberty is not guaranteed absolutely against deprivation, but only against deprivation without due process of law. The test traditionally applied in the area of social and economic legislation is whether or not a law such as that challenged has a rational relation to a valid state objective. . . . The Due Process Clause of the Fourteenth Amendment undoubtedly does place a limit on legislative power to enact laws such as this, albeit a broad one. If the Texas statute were to prohibit an abortion even where the mother's life is in jeopardy, I have little doubt that such a statute would lack a rational relation to a valid state objective. . . . But the Court's sweeping invalidation of any restrictions on abortion during the first trimester is impossible to justify under that standard, and the conscious weighing of competing factors which the Court's opinion apparently substitutes for the established test is far more appropriate to a legislative judgment than to a judicial one. * * *

The fact that a majority of the States, reflecting after all the majority sentiment in those States, have had restrictions on abortions for at least a century seems to me as strong an indication there is that the asserted right to an abortion is not "so rooted in the traditions and conscience of our people as to be ranked as fundamental." . . . Even today, when society's views on abortion are changing, the very existence of the debate is evidence that the "right" to an abortion is not so universally accepted as the appellants would have us believe.

To reach its result the Court necessarily has had to find within the Scope of the Fourteenth Amendment a right that was apparently completely unknown to the drafters of the Amendment. As early as 1821, the first state law dealing directly with abortion was enacted by the Connecticut legislature. . . . By the time of the adoption of the Fourteenth Amendment in 1868 there were at least 36 laws enacted by state or territorial legislatures limiting abortion. While many States have amended or updated their laws, 21 of the laws on the books in 1868 remain in effect today. Indeed, the Texas statute struck down today was, as the majority notes, first enacted in 1857 and "has remained substantially unchanged to the present time."

There apparently was no question concerning the validity of this provision or of any of the other state statutes when the Fourteenth Amendment was adopted. The only conclusion possible from this history is that the drafters did not intend to have the Fourteenth Amendment withdraw from the States the power to legislate with respect to this matter.

* * *

■ MR. JUSTICE WHITE, with whom MR. JUSTICE REHNQUIST joins, dissenting.

At the heart of the controversy in these cases are those recurring pregnancies that pose no danger whatsoever to the life or health of the mother but are nevertheless unwanted for any one or more of a variety of reasons—convenience, family planning, economics, dislike of children, the embarrassment of illegitimacy, etc. The common claim before us is that for any one of such reasons, or for no reason at all, and without asserting or claiming any threat to life or health, any woman is entitled to an abortion at her request if she is able to find a medical advisor willing to undertake the procedure.

The Court for the most part sustains this position: During the period prior to the time the fetus becomes viable, the Constitution of the United States values the convenience, whim or caprice of the putative mother more than the life or potential life of the fetus; the Constitution, therefore, guarantees the right to an abortion as against any state law or policy seeking to protect the fetus from an abortion not prompted by more compelling reasons of the mother.

With all due respect, I dissent. I find nothing in the language or history of the Constitution to support the Court's judgment. The Court simply fashions and announces a new constitutional right for pregnant mothers and with scarcely any reason or authority for its action, invests that right with sufficient substance to override most existing state abortion statutes. The upshot is that the people and the legislatures of the 50 States are constitutionally disentitled to weigh the relative importance of the continued existence and development of the fetus on the one hand against a spectrum of possible impacts on the mother on the other hand. As an exercise of raw judicial power, the Court perhaps has authority to do what it does today; but in my view its judgment is an improvident and extravagant exercise of the power of judicial review which the Constitution extends to this Court.

The Court apparently values the convenience of the pregnant mother more than the continued existence and development of the life or potential life which she carries. Whether or not I might agree with that marshaling of values, I can in no event join the Court's judgment because I find no constitutional warrant for imposing such an order of priorities on the people and legislatures of the States. In a sensitive area such as this, involving as it does issues over which reasonable men may easily and heatedly differ, I cannot accept the Court's exercise of its clear power of choice by interposing a constitutional barrier to state efforts to protect human life and by investing mothers and doctors with the constitutionally protected right to exterminate it. This issue, for the most part, should be left with the people and to the political processes the people have devised to govern their affairs.

It is my view, therefore, that the Texas statute is not constitutionally infirm because it denies abortions to those who seek to serve only their convenience rather than to protect their life or health. Nor is this plaintiff, who claims no threat to her mental or physical health, entitled to assert the possible rights of those women whose pregnancy assertedly implicates their health. . . .

NOTES AND QUESTIONS

1. In the companion case of Doe v. Bolton, 410 U.S. 179, 93 S.Ct. 739, 35 L.Ed.2d 201 (1973), not only did a majority of the court re-affirm what had been decided in *Roe*, but it also declared unconstitutional a 1968 Georgia "therapeutic abortion" statute because the Court found invalid certain conditions that were attached to the performance of the abortions authorized by the statute. The conditions prescribed in the statute were: (1) that the abortion be performed in a hospital accredited by a "Joint Commission on Accreditation of Hospitals"; (2) that the procedure be approved by the hospital staff abortion committee; (3) that the performing physician's judgment be confirmed by the independent examination of two other licensed physicians; and (4) that the woman be a resident of Georgia. The Court found the statute (1) objectionable because Georgia placed no restriction on the performance of nonabortion surgery in hospitals without the commission's accreditation and there was no showing that there was a particular need for it in abortion cases; (2) was "unduly restrictive of the patient's rights and needs"; (3) had no rational connection with a patient's needs and unduly infringed upon the physician's right to practice; and (4) was not based upon any policy of preserving state-supported facilities for Georgia's residents, since the restriction also applied to private hospitals and to privately retained physicians.

2. The Supreme Court has dealt with issues relating to financial assistance and Medicaid support of desired nontherapeutic abortions in Beal v. Doe, 432 U.S. 438, 97 S.Ct. 2366, 53 L.Ed.2d 464 (1977); Maher v. Roe, 432 U.S. 464, 97 S.Ct. 2376, 53 L.Ed.2d 484 (1977); and Poelker v. Doe, 432 U.S. 519, 97 S.Ct. 2391, 53 L.Ed.2d 528 (1977), all decided the same day.

The foregoing line of cases held that public funds could not be required to perform abortions. However, Nyberg v. Virginia, 667 F.2d 754 (8th Cir. 1982), held that willing staff physicians had a right to perform abortions in a publicly funded hospital. *Nyberg* emphasized the difference between direct funding of abortions and allowing qualified doctors to voluntarily perform abortions at a publicly owned hospital.

3. In Webster v. Reproductive Health Services, 492 U.S. 490, 109 S.Ct. 3040, 106 L.Ed.2d 410 (1989), a five-member majority of the Court stopped short of overruling *Roe v. Wade*, but indicated a willingness to uphold a wide range of state laws restricting abortion. Only Justice Scalia indicated he would have voted to overturn *Roe v. Wade*. In *Webster*, the Court upheld a Missouri statute that imposes significant restrictions on the availability of abortions by prohibiting the use of public facilities and public employees to perform or assist in the performance of abortions. This holding is consistent with other holdings, said Chief Justice Rehnquist, that teach that the state has no obligation to commit any resources to facilitate abortions. On the issue of fetal viability testing, which the statute required, he stated that the statute only required such tests to be done as are necessary in accordance with the exercise of the physician's professional judgment. The Chief Justice also criticized the trimester framework set out in Roe as "overly rigid" and unworkable. With respect to the preamble of the Missouri statute, which states that life begins at conception, the Court's majority noted that this only sets forth the value judgment made by the Missouri legislature, but does not actually regulate abortion.

The court, in equally splintered opinions, has generally upheld parental consent or notification requirements provided the statute includes a judicial bypass provision that meets four criteria: (1) allow the minor to bypass the consent requirement if she establishes that she is mature enough and well informed to make the abortion decision independently; (2) allow the minor to bypass the consent requirement if she establishes that the abortion or bypass of notification would be in her best interests; (3) ensure the minor's anonymity; and (4) provide for expeditious bypass procedures. *See* Bellotti v. Baird, 443 U.S. 622, 99 S.Ct. 3035, 61 L.Ed.2d 797 (1979); Hodgson v. Minnesota, 497 U.S. 417, 110 S.Ct. 2926, 111 L.Ed.2d 344 (1990); Ohio v. Akron Center for Reproductive Health, 497 U.S. 502, 110 S.Ct. 2972, 111 L.Ed.2d 405 (1990); Lambert v. Wicklund, 520 U.S. 292, 117 S.Ct. 1169, 137 L.Ed.2d 464 (1997).

Thereafter, in Planned Parenthood of Southeastern Pennsylvania v. Casey, 505 U.S. 833, 112 S.Ct. 2791, 120 L.Ed.2d 674 (1992), another fractured opinion, the Court upheld provisions of the Pennsylvania statute requiring that a woman seeking an abortion give her prior informed consent, specifying that she be provided with certain information at least twenty-four hours before the abortion is performed; a parental consent requirement for a young woman under eighteen; and certain reporting requirements on facilities that perform abortion services. Struck down, however, as a substantial obstacle to a woman's choice to undergo an abortion, was a provision that required a married woman seeking an abortion to provide a signed statement indicating that she has notified her husband of her intended abortion. Notably, for members of the Court, Chief Justice Rehnquist and Justices White, Scalia, and Thomas, indicated that they would overrule *Roe v. Wade*.

However, in Stenberg v. Carhart, 530 U.S. 914, 120 S.Ct. 2597, 147 L.Ed.2d 743 (2000), the Court continued to follow *Roe v. Wade* in declaring Nebraska's "partial birth abortion" statute unconstitutional. The Nebraska law defined "partial birth abortion" as a procedure in which the doctor "partially delivers vaginally a living unborn child before killing the . . . child" and further defines this to mean "intentionally delivering into the vagina a living unborn child, or a substantial portion thereof, for the purpose of performing a procedure that the person performing such procedure knows will kill the unborn child and does kill the unborn child." A majority of the Justices invalidated the statute both because its application to the "dilation and extraction" abortion procedure and its potential application to the "dilation and evacuation" procedure imposed an "undue burden" on a woman's ability to choose an abortion, and because the statute lacked the requisite exception "for the preservation of the . . . health of the mother."

Following *Stenberg*, Congressed passed the Partial-Birth Abortion Ban Act of 2003, which provides, in part, as follows:

Any physician who, in or affecting interstate commerce, knowingly performs a partial-birth abortion and thereby kills a human fetus shall be fined under this title or imprisoned not more than 2 years, or both. This subsection does not apply to a partial-birth abortion that is necessary to save the life of a mother whose life is endangered by a physical disorder, physical illness, or physical injury, including a life-endangering physical condition caused by or arising from the pregnancy itself.

18 U.S.C. § 1531(a).

Shortly following the enactment of the Act, two groups challenged the constitutionality of the act on its face—a challenge in the Eighth Circuit was brought by physicians, and a challenge in the Ninth Circuit was brought by abortion advocacy groups. The Supreme Court entertained both challenges in Gonzales v. Carhart, 550 U.S. 124, 127 S.Ct. 1610, 167 L.Ed.2d 480 (2007). First, Justice Kennedy, writing for the five-member majority of the Court, distinguished the Act from the statute at issue and deemed unconstitutional in *Stenberg*. For example, where the language at issue in *Stenberg* failed to provide guidance regarding what constituted a "substantial portion" of a "living unborn child," the Act provided express "anatomical landmarks . . . clarify[ing] that the removal of a small portion of the fetus is not prohibited . . . [and] requir[ing] the fetus to be delivered so that it is partially 'outside the body of the mother.'" *See* 18 U.S.C. 1531(b)(1)(A). In short, where the language in *Stenberg* lacked guidelines, "the Act defines the line between potentially criminal conduct on the one hand and lawful abortion on the other." Thus, Justice Kennedy, writing for the five-member majority of the Court, found that the Act was immune to a facial challenge because it was not void for vagueness and because it did not "impose[ ] an undue burden on a woman's right to abortion based on its overbreadth or lack of a health exception." Discussing whether the Act created a "substantial obstacle to late-term, but previability, abortions," Justice Kennedy noted that the government has a substantial interest "in regulating the medical profession in order to promote respect for life." He continued, finding that, with the Act, Congress only intended to ban partial-birth abortions as defined in the Act, *see* 18 U.S.C. § 1531(b)(1) (2006), and did not address other forms of abortion. As "[a]lternatives are available to the prohibited procedure," the Act did not impose an undue burden when considered as a facial challenge. Nonetheless, Justice Kennedy noted that "[t]he Act is open to a proper as-applied challenge in a discrete case."

4. In Tatro v. State, 372 So.2d 283 (Miss. 1979), a majority of the Mississippi Supreme Court held unconstitutional, on equal protection grounds, a state law criminalizing conduct by a "male person" who handles, touches, or rubs any child under the age of 14 for the purpose of gratifying his sexual desires. The court found no valid reason for this "patent discrimination against males," inasmuch as women clearly could perform the same acts. The court also noted that the state failed to show "that such unequal treatment serves any traditional, governmental or public policy or is based upon a rational distinction based upon sex." The dissenting opinion argued that the majority should have saved the statute by striking the word "male" so as to make the statute sex-neutral. Should courts use that approach?

5. See Garnett v. State, *infra* p. 647, for an example of how a state court dealt with the issue of mistake as to the age of a victim of a "statutory rape" as a matter of construction of its own statutes.

6. Are prostitution statutes unconstitutionally invalid because they discriminate against women? *See, e.g.,* State v. Gaither, 236 Ga. 497, 224 S.E.2d 378 (1976); State v. Butler, 331 So.2d 425 (La. 1976); Commonwealth v. King, 374 Mass. 5, 372 N.E.2d 196 (1977); State v. Mertes, 60 Wis.2d 414, 210 N.W.2d 741 (1973). On the constitutionality of assault and battery laws that provide protection to females only or provide greater penalties for males than for females, see Anno., 5 A.L.R. 4th 708.

7. The conviction of a woman for being "a common scold" was voided in State v. Palendrano, 120 N.J.Super. 336, 293 A.2d 747 (1972). Among the grounds for the decision was the element of unequal protection, since only a woman, and not a man, could be subject to prosecution, whereas a man might be just as "troublesome and angry" by "wrangling" among his neighbors.

Is there an equal protection violation in a regulation that requires a woman visitor to an all-male prison to wear a brassiere? See Holdman v. Olim, 59 Hawai'i 346, 581 P.2d 1164 (1978).

8. For the United States Supreme Court's view on the effect of constitutional protections on the criminalization of consensual acts of sodomy by the states as deviate sexual conduct, see Lawrence v. Texas, *infra* p. 334.

3. CONSENSUAL SODOMY

At common law, same-sex sexual conduct and various proscribed opposite-sex consensual sexual conduct were prosecutable as sodomy, though the statutes employed other colorful euphemisms.[1] Statutes prohibiting sodomy and various other forms of sexual conduct have remained on the books in many American jurisdictions well up into the twenty-first century, a practice that the Supreme Court had held constitutional in Bowers v. Hardwick, 478 U.S. 186, 106 S.Ct. 2841, 92 L.Ed.2d 140 (1986). The Supreme Court's approach to the problem a mere decade and a half later is illustrated in the following case.

---

[1] E.g., the "crime against nature," or the "abominable and detestable crime against nature." *See Rose v. Locke,* 423 U.S. 48, 96 S.Ct. 243, 46 L.Ed.2d 185 (1975) (determining what is includable under the term "crime against nature").

Lawrence v. Texas

Supreme Court of the United States, 2003.
539 U.S. 558, 123 S.Ct. 2472, 156 L.Ed.2d 508.

■ KENNEDY, J.:

Liberty protects the person from unwarranted government intrusions into a dwelling or other private places. In our tradition the State is not omnipresent in the home. And there are other spheres of our lives and existence, outside the home, where the State should not be a dominant presence. Freedom extends beyond spatial bounds. Liberty presumes an autonomy of self that includes freedom of thought, belief, expression, and certain intimate conduct. The instant case involves liberty of the person both in its spatial and more transcendent dimensions.

I

The question before the Court is the validity of a Texas statute making it a crime for two persons of the same sex to engage in certain intimate sexual conduct.

In Houston, Texas, officers of the Harris County Police Department were dispatched to a private residence in response to a reported weapons disturbance. They entered an apartment where one of the petitioners, John Geddes Lawrence, resided. The right of the police to enter does not seem to have been questioned. The officers observed Lawrence and another man, Tyron Garner, engaging in a sexual act. The two petitioners were arrested, held in custody over night, and charged and convicted before a Justice of the Peace.

The complaints described their crime as "deviate sexual intercourse, namely anal sex, with a member of the same sex (man)." The applicable state law is Tex. Penal Code Ann. § 21.06(a) (2003). It provides: "A person commits an offense if he engages in deviate sexual intercourse with another individual of the same sex." The statute defines "[d]eviate sexual intercourse" as follows:

(A) any contact between any part of the genitals of one person and the mouth or anus of another person; or

(B) the penetration of the genitals or the anus of another person with an object. § 21.01(1).

The petitioners exercised their right to a trial *de novo* in Harris County Criminal Court. They challenged the statute as a violation of the Equal Protection Clause of the Fourteenth Amendment and of a like provision of the Texas Constitution. Those contentions were rejected. The petitioners, having entered a plea of *nolo contendere*, were each fined $200 and assessed court costs . . .

The Court of Appeals for the Texas Fourteenth District considered the petitioners' federal constitutional arguments under both the Equal

Protection and Due Process Clauses of the Fourteenth Amendment. After hearing the case *en banc*, the court, in a divided opinion, rejected the constitutional arguments and affirmed the convictions. The majority opinion indicates that the Court of Appeals considered our decision in *Bowers v. Hardwick*, to be controlling on the federal due process aspect of the case. *Bowers* then being authoritative, this was proper.

We granted *certiorari* to consider three questions:

1. Whether Petitioners' criminal convictions under the Texas "Homosexual Conduct" law—which criminalizes sexual intimacy by same-sex couples, but not identical behavior by different-sex couples—violate the Fourteenth Amendment guarantee of equal protection of laws?

2. Whether Petitioners' criminal convictions for adult consensual sexual intimacy in the home violate their vital interests in liberty and privacy protected by the Due Process Clause of the Fourteenth Amendment?

3. Whether Bowers v. Hardwick should be overruled?

The petitioners were adults at the time of the alleged offense. Their conduct was in private and consensual.

II

We conclude the case should be resolved by determining whether the petitioners were free as adults to engage in the private conduct in the exercise of their liberty under the Due Process Clause of the Fourteenth Amendment to the Constitution. For this inquiry we deem it necessary to reconsider the Court's holding in *Bowers*.

There are broad statements of the substantive reach of liberty under the Due Process Clause in earlier cases, including *Pierce v. Society of Sisters*, 268 U.S. 510 (1925), and *Meyer v. Nebraska*, 262 U.S. 390 (1923); but the most pertinent beginning point is our decision in *Griswold v. Connecticut*, 381 U.S. 479 (1965).

In *Griswold* the Court invalidated a state law prohibiting the use of drugs or devices of contraception and counseling or aiding and abetting the use of contraceptives. The Court described the protected interest as a right to privacy and placed emphasis on the marriage relation and the protected space of the marital bedroom.

After *Griswold* it was established that the right to make certain decisions regarding sexual conduct extends beyond the marital relationship. In *Eisenstadt v. Baird*, 405 U.S. 438 (1972), the Court invalidated a law prohibiting the distribution of contraceptives to unmarried persons. The case was decided under the Equal Protection Clause, but with respect to unmarried persons, the Court went on to state the fundamental proposition that the law impaired the exercise of their personal rights. It quoted from the statement of the Court of Appeals finding the law to be in conflict with fundamental human rights, and it followed with this statement of its own:

It is true that in *Griswold* the right of privacy in question inhered in the marital relationship. . . . If the right of privacy means anything, it is the right of the *individual*, married or single, to be free from unwarranted governmental intrusion into matters so fundamentally affecting a person as the decision whether to bear or beget a child.

The opinions in *Griswold* and *Eisenstadt* were part of the background for the decision in *Roe v. Wade*, 410 U.S. 113 (1973). As is well known, the case involved a challenge to the Texas law prohibiting abortions, but the laws of other States were affected as well. Although the Court held the woman's rights were not absolute, her right to elect an abortion did have real and substantial protection as an exercise of her liberty under the Due Process Clause. The Court cited cases that protect spatial freedom and cases that go well beyond it. *Roe* recognized the right of a woman to make certain fundamental decisions affecting her destiny and confirmed once more that the protection of liberty under the Due Process Clause has a substantive dimension of fundamental significance in defining the rights of the person.

In *Carey v. Population Services Int'l*, 431 U.S. 678 (1977), the Court confronted a New York law forbidding sale or distribution of contraceptive devices to persons under 16 years of age. Although there was no single opinion for the Court, the law was invalidated. Both *Eisenstadt* and *Carey*, as well as the holding and rationale in *Roe*, confirmed that the reasoning of *Griswold* could not be confined to the protection of rights of married adults. This was the state of the law with respect to some of the most relevant cases when the Court considered *Bowers v. Hardwick*.

The facts in *Bowers* had some similarities to the instant case. A police officer, whose right to enter seems not to have been in question, observed Hardwick, in his own bedroom, engaging in intimate sexual conduct with another adult male. The conduct was in violation of a Georgia statute making it a criminal offense to engage in sodomy. One difference between the two cases is that the Georgia statute prohibited the conduct whether or not the participants were of the same sex, while the Texas statute, as we have seen, applies only to participants of the same sex. Hardwick was not prosecuted, but he brought an action in federal court to declare the state statute invalid. He alleged he was a practicing homosexual and that the criminal prohibition violated rights guaranteed to him by the Constitution. The Court, in an opinion by Justice White, sustained the Georgia law. Chief Justice Burger and Justice Powell joined the opinion of the Court and filed separate, concurring opinions. Four Justices dissented. 478 U.S., at 199 (opinion of

Blackmun, J., joined by Brennan, Marshall, and Stevens, JJ.); *id.*, at 214 (opinion of Stevens, J., joined by Brennan and Marshall, JJ.).

The Court began its substantive discussion in *Bowers* as follows: "The issue presented is whether the Federal Constitution confers a fundamental right upon homosexuals to engage in sodomy and hence invalidates the laws of the many States that still make such conduct illegal and have done so for a very long time." That statement, we now conclude, discloses the Court's own failure to appreciate the extent of the liberty at stake. To say that the issue in *Bowers* was simply the right to engage in certain sexual conduct demeans the claim the individual put forward, just as it would demean a married couple were it to be said marriage is simply about the right to have sexual intercourse. The laws involved in *Bowers* and here are, to be sure, statutes that purport to do no more than prohibit a particular sexual act. Their penalties and purposes, though, have more far-reaching consequences, touching upon the most private human conduct, sexual behavior, and in the most private of places, the home. The statutes do seek to control a personal relationship that, whether or not entitled to formal recognition in the law, is within the liberty of persons to choose without being punished as criminals.

This, as a general rule, should counsel against attempts by the State, or a court, to define the meaning of the relationship or to set its boundaries absent injury to a person or abuse of an institution the law protects. It suffices for us to acknowledge that adults may choose to enter upon this relationship in the confines of their homes and their own private lives and still retain their dignity as free persons. When sexuality finds overt expression in intimate conduct with another person, the conduct can be but one element in a personal bond that is more enduring. The liberty protected by the Constitution allows homosexual persons the right to make this choice.

Having misapprehended the claim of liberty there presented to it, and thus stating the claim to be whether there is a fundamental right to engage in consensual sodomy, the *Bowers* Court said: "Proscriptions against that conduct have ancient roots." In academic writings, and in many of the scholarly *amicus* briefs filed to assist the Court in this case, there are fundamental criticisms of the historical premises relied upon by the majority and concurring opinions in *Bowers*. . . . We need not enter this debate in the attempt to reach a definitive historical judgment, but the following considerations counsel against adopting the definitive conclusions upon which *Bowers* placed such reliance.

At the outset it should be noted that there is no longstanding history in this country of laws directed at homosexual conduct as a distinct matter. Beginning in colonial times there were prohibitions of sodomy derived from the English criminal laws passed in the first instance by the Reformation Parliament of 1533. The English prohibition was understood to include relations between men and women as well as relations between men and men. Nineteenth-century commentators similarly read American sodomy, buggery, and crime-against-nature statutes as criminalizing certain relations between men and women and between men and men. The absence of legal prohibitions focusing on homosexual conduct may be explained in part by noting that according to some scholars the concept of the homosexual as a distinct category of person did not emerge until the late 19th century. Thus early American sodomy laws were not directed at homosexuals as such but instead sought to prohibit nonprocreative sexual activity more generally. This does not suggest approval of homosexual conduct. It does tend to show that this particular form of conduct was not thought of as a separate category from like conduct between heterosexual persons.

Laws prohibiting sodomy do not seem to have been enforced against consenting adults acting in private.... Thus the model sodomy indictments presented in a 19th-century treatise addressed the predatory acts of an adult man against a minor girl or minor boy. Instead of targeting relations between consenting adults in private, 19th-century sodomy prosecutions typically involved relations between men and minor girls or minor boys, relations between adults involving force, relations between adults implicating disparity in status, or relations between men and animals.

* * *

The policy of punishing consenting adults for private acts was not much discussed in the early legal literature. We can infer that one reason for this was the very private nature of the conduct. Despite the absence of prosecutions, there may have been periods in which there was public criticism of homosexuals as such and an insistence that the criminal laws be enforced to discourage their practices. But far from possessing "ancient roots," American laws targeting same-sex couples did not develop until the last third of the 20th century....

It was not until the 1970s that any State singled out same-sex relations for criminal prosecution, and only nine States have done so.... Post-*Bowers* even some of these States did not adhere to the policy of suppressing homosexual conduct. Over the course of the last decades, States with same-sex prohibitions have moved toward abolishing them.

In summary, the historical grounds relied upon in *Bowers* are more complex than the majority opinion and the concurring opinion by Chief Justice Burger indicate. Their historical premises are not without doubt and, at the very least, are overstated.

It must be acknowledged, of course, that the Court in *Bowers* was making the broader point that for centuries there have been powerful voices to condemn homosexual conduct as immoral. The condemnation has been shaped by religious beliefs, conceptions of right and acceptable behavior, and respect for the traditional family. For many persons these are not trivial concerns but profound and deep convictions accepted as ethical and moral principles to which they aspire and which thus determine the course of their lives. These considerations do not answer the question before us, however. The issue is whether the majority may use the power of the State to enforce these views on the whole society through operation of the criminal law. "Our obligation is to define the liberty of all, not to mandate our own moral code." *Planned Parenthood of Southeastern Pa. v. Casey*, 505 U.S. 833, 850 (1992).

Chief Justice Burger joined the opinion for the Court in *Bowers* and further explained his views as follows: "Decisions of individuals relating to homosexual conduct have been subject to state intervention throughout the history of Western civilization. Condemnation of those practices is firmly rooted in Judeo-Christian moral and ethical standards." As with Justice White's assumptions about history, scholarship casts some doubt on the sweeping nature of the statement by Chief Justice Burger as it pertains to private homosexual conduct between consenting adults. In all events we think that our laws and traditions in the past half century are of most relevance here. These references show an emerging awareness that liberty gives substantial protection to adult persons in deciding how to conduct their private lives in matters pertaining to sex. "[H]istory and tradition are the starting point but not in all cases the ending point of the substantive due process inquiry."

This emerging recognition should have been apparent when *Bowers* was decided. In 1955 the American Law Institute promulgated the Model Penal Code and made clear that it did not recommend or provide for "criminal penalties for consensual sexual relations conducted in private." ALI, Model Penal Code § 213.2, Comment 2, p. 372 (1980). . . .

* * *

The sweeping references by Chief Justice Burger to the history of Western civilization and to Judeo-Christian moral and ethical standards did not take account of other authorities pointing in an opposite direction. . . .

Of even more importance, almost five years before *Bowers* was decided the European Court of Human Rights considered a case with parallels to *Bowers* and to today's case. An adult male resident in Northern Ireland alleged he was a practicing homosexual who desired to engage in consensual homosexual conduct. The laws of Northern Ireland forbade him that right. He alleged that he had been questioned, his home had been searched, and he feared criminal prosecution. The court held that the laws proscribing the conduct were invalid under the European Convention on Human Rights. *Dudgeon v. United Kingdom*, 45 Eur. Ct. H.R. (1981) & ¶ 52. Authoritative in all countries that are members of the Council of Europe (21 nations then, 45 nations now), the decision is at odds with the premise in *Bowers* that the claim put forward was insubstantial in our Western civilization.

* * *

As an alternative argument in this case, counsel for the petitioners and some *amici* contend that *Romer v. Evans*, 517 U.S. 620 (1996), provides the basis for declaring the Texas statute invalid under the Equal Protection Clause. That is a tenable argument, but we conclude the instant case requires us to address whether *Bowers* itself has continuing validity. Were we to hold the statute invalid under the Equal Protection Clause some might question whether a prohibition would be valid if drawn differently, say, to prohibit the conduct both between same-sex and different-sex participants.

Equality of treatment and the due process right to demand respect for conduct protected by the substantive guarantee of liberty are linked in important respects, and a decision on the latter point advances both interests. If protected conduct is made criminal and the law which does so remains unexamined for its substantive validity, its stigma might remain even if it were not enforceable as drawn for equal protection reasons. When homosexual conduct is made criminal by the law of the State, that declaration in and of itself is an invitation to subject homosexual persons to discrimination both in the public and in the private spheres. The central holding of *Bowers* has been brought in question by this case, and it should be addressed. Its continuance as precedent demeans the lives of homosexual persons.

The stigma this criminal statute imposes, moreover, is not trivial. The offense, to be sure, is but a class C misdemeanor, a minor offense in the Texas legal system. Still, it remains a criminal offense with all that imports for the dignity of the persons charged. The petitioners will bear on their record the history of their criminal convictions. Just this Term we rejected various challenges to state laws requiring the registration of sex offenders. We are advised that if Texas convicted an adult for private, consensual homosexual conduct under the statute here in question the convicted person would come within the registration laws of a least four States were he or she to be subject to their jurisdiction. This underscores the consequential nature of the punishment and the state-sponsored condemnation attendant to the criminal prohibition. Furthermore, the Texas criminal conviction carries with it the other collateral consequences always following a conviction, such as notations on job application forms, to mention but one example.

* * *

The rationale of *Bowers* does not withstand careful analysis. In his dissenting opinion in *Bowers* Justice Stevens came to these conclusions:

> Our prior cases make two propositions abundantly clear. First, the fact that the governing majority in a State has traditionally

viewed a particular practice as immoral is not a sufficient reason for upholding a law prohibiting the practice; neither history nor tradition could save a law prohibiting miscegenation from constitutional attack. Second, individual decisions by married persons, concerning the intimacies of their physical relationship, even when not intended to produce offspring, are a form of "liberty" protected by the Due Process Clause of the Fourteenth Amendment. Moreover, this protection extends to intimate choices by unmarried as well as married persons.

Justice Stevens' analysis, in our view, should have been controlling in *Bowers* and should control here.

Bowers was not correct when it was decided, and it is not correct today. It ought not to remain binding precedent. *Bowers v. Hardwick* should be and now is overruled.

The present case does not involve minors. It does not involve persons who might be injured or coerced or who are situated in relationships where consent might not easily be refused. It does not involve public conduct or prostitution. It does not involve whether the government must give formal recognition to any relationship that homosexual persons seek to enter. The case does involve two adults who, with full and mutual consent from each other, engaged in sexual practices common to a homosexual lifestyle. The petitioners are entitled to respect for their private lives. The State cannot demean their existence or control their destiny by making their private sexual conduct a crime. Their right to liberty under the Due Process Clause gives them the full right to engage in their conduct without intervention of the government. "It is a promise of the Constitution that there is a realm of personal liberty which the government may not enter." The Texas statute furthers no legitimate state interest which can justify its intrusion into the personal and private life of the individual.

Had those who drew and ratified the Due Process Clauses of the Fifth Amendment or the Fourteenth Amendment known the components of liberty in its manifold possibilities, they might have been more specific. They did not presume to have this insight. They knew times can blind us to certain truths and later generations can see that laws once thought necessary and proper in fact serve only to oppress. As the Constitution endures, persons in every generation can invoke its principles in their own search for greater freedom.

The judgment of the Court of Appeals for the Texas Fourteenth District is reversed, and the case is remanded for further proceedings not inconsistent with this opinion.

It is so ordered.

■ JUSTICE O'CONNOR, concurring in the judgment.

The Court today overrules *Bowers v. Hardwick*. I joined *Bowers*, and do not join the Court in overruling it. Nevertheless, I agree with the Court that Texas' statute banning same-sex sodomy is unconstitutional. Rather than relying on the substantive component of the Fourteenth Amendment's Due Process Clause, as the Court does, I base my conclusion on the Fourteenth Amendment's Equal Protection Clause.

The Equal Protection Clause of the Fourteenth Amendment "is essentially a direction that all persons similarly situated should be treated alike." ... Under our rational basis standard of review, "legislation is presumed to be valid and will be sustained if the classification drawn by the statute is rationally related to a legitimate state interest."

* * *

The statute at issue here makes sodomy a crime only if a person "engages in deviate sexual intercourse with another individual of the same sex." Sodomy between opposite-sex partners, however, is not a crime in Texas. That is, Texas treats the same conduct differently based solely on the participants. Those harmed by this law are people who have a same-sex sexual orientation and thus are more likely to engage in behavior prohibited by § 21.06.

The Texas statute makes homosexuals unequal in the eyes of the law by making particular conduct—and only that conduct—subject to criminal sanction. It appears that prosecutions under Texas' sodomy law are rare. This case shows, however, that prosecutions under § 21.06 *do* occur. And while the penalty imposed on petitioners in this case was relatively minor, the consequences of conviction are not. . . .

* * *

This case raises a different issue than *Bowers*: whether, under the Equal Protection Clause, moral disapproval is a legitimate state interest to justify by itself a statute that bans homosexual sodomy, but not heterosexual sodomy. It is not. Moral disapproval of this group, like a bare desire to harm the group, is an interest that is insufficient to satisfy rational basis review under the Equal Protection Clause. Indeed, we have never held that moral disapproval, without any other asserted state interest, is a sufficient rationale under the Equal Protection Clause to justify a law that discriminates among groups of persons.

Moral disapproval of a group cannot be a legitimate governmental interest under the Equal Protection Clause because legal classifications must not be "drawn for the purpose of disadvantaging the group burdened by the law." Texas' invocation of moral disapproval as a legitimate state interest proves nothing more than Texas' desire to criminalize homosexual sodomy. But the Equal Protection Clause prevents a State from creating "a classification of persons undertaken for its own sake." And because Texas so rarely enforces its sodomy law as applied to private, consensual acts, the law serves more as a statement of dislike and disapproval against homosexuals than as a tool to stop criminal behavior. The Texas sodomy law "raise[s] the inevitable inference that the disadvantage imposed is born of animosity toward the class of persons affected."

* * *

A law branding one class of persons as criminal solely based on the State's moral disapproval of that class and the conduct associated with that class runs contrary to the values of the Constitution and the Equal Protection Clause, under any standard of review. I therefore concur in the Court's judgment that Texas' sodomy law banning "deviate sexual intercourse" between consenting adults of the same sex, but not between consenting adults of different sexes, is unconstitutional.

■ SCALIA, J., with whom THE CHIEF JUSTICE and THOMAS, J. join, dissenting. . . .

* * *

II

Having decided that it need not adhere to *stare decisis*, the Court still must establish that *Bowers* was wrongly decided and that the Texas statute, as applied to petitioners, is unconstitutional.

Texas Penal Code Ann. § 21.06(a) (2003) undoubtedly imposes constraints on liberty. So do laws prohibiting prostitution, recreational use of heroin, and, for that matter, working more than 60 hours per week in a bakery. But there is no right to "liberty" under the Due Process Clause, though today's opinion repeatedly makes that claim. . . . The Fourteenth Amendment *expressly allows* States to deprive their citizens of "liberty," *so long as "due process of law" is provided*: "No state shall . . . deprive any person of life, liberty, or property, *without due process of law*." Amdt. 14 (emphasis added).

* * *

. . . We have held repeatedly, in cases the Court today does not overrule, that *only* fundamental rights qualify for this so-called "heightened scrutiny" protection—that is, rights which are " 'deeply rooted in this Nation's history and tradition,' " All other liberty interests may be abridged or abrogated pursuant to a validly enacted state law if that law is rationally related to a legitimate state interest.

Bowers held, first, that criminal prohibitions of homosexual sodomy are not subject to heightened scrutiny because they do not implicate a "fundamental right" under the Due Process Clause . . . *Bowers* concluded that a right to engage in homosexual sodomy was not " 'deeply rooted in this Nation's history and tradition,' "

The Court today does not overrule this holding. Not once does it describe homosexual sodomy as a "fundamental right" or a "fundamental liberty interest," nor does it subject the Texas statute to strict scrutiny. Instead, having failed to establish that the right to homosexual sodomy is "'deeply rooted in this Nation's history and tradition,'" the Court concludes that the application of Texas's statute to petitioners' conduct fails the rational-basis test, and overrules *Bowers*' holding to the contrary. . . .

III

The Court's description of "the state of the law" at the time of *Bowers* only confirms that *Bowers* was right. The Court points to *Griswold v. Connecticut.* But that case *expressly disclaimed* any reliance on the doctrine of "substantive due process," and grounded the so-called "right to privacy" in penumbras of constitutional provisions *other than* the Due Process Clause. Eisenstadt v. Baird likewise had nothing to do with "substantive due process"; it invalidated a Massachusetts law prohibiting the distribution of contraceptives to unmarried persons solely on the basis of the Equal Protection Clause. Of course *Eisenstadt* contains well known dictum relating to the "right to privacy," but this referred to the right recognized in *Griswold*—a right penumbral to the *specific* guarantees in the Bill of Rights, and not a "substantive due process" right.

Roe v. Wade recognized that the right to abort an unborn child was a "fundamental right" protected by the Due Process Clause. The *Roe* Court, however, made no attempt to establish that this right was "'deeply rooted in this Nation's history and tradition'"; instead, it based its conclusion that "the Fourteenth Amendment's concept of personal liberty . . . is broad enough to encompass a woman's decision whether or not to terminate her pregnancy" on its own normative judgment that anti-abortion laws were undesirable. We have since rejected *Roe*'s holding that regulations of abortion must be narrowly tailored to serve a compelling state interest. . . .

IV

I turn now to the ground on which the Court squarely rests its holding: the contention that there is no rational basis for the law here under attack. This proposition is so out of accord with our jurisprudence—indeed, with the jurisprudence of *any* society we know— that it requires little discussion. . . .

The Texas statute undeniably seeks to further the belief of its citizens that certain forms of sexual behavior are "immoral and unacceptable,"—the same interest furthered by criminal laws against fornication, bigamy, adultery, adult incest, bestiality, and obscenity. *Bowers* held that this *was* a legitimate state interest. The Court today reaches the opposite conclusion. The Texas statute, it says, "furthers *no legitimate state interest* which can justify its intrusion into the personal and private life of the individual," (emphasis added). The Court embraces instead Justice Stevens' declaration in his *Bowers* dissent, that "the fact that the governing majority in a State has traditionally viewed a particular practice as immoral is not a sufficient reason for upholding a law prohibiting the practice." This effectively decrees the end of all morals legislation. If, as the Court asserts, the promotion of majoritarian sexual morality is not even a *legitimate* state interest, none of the above-mentioned laws can survive rational-basis review.

V

* * *

Today's opinion is the product of a Court, which is the product of a law-profession culture, that has largely signed on to the so-called homosexual agenda, by which I mean the agenda promoted by some homosexual activists directed at eliminating the moral opprobrium that has traditionally attached to homosexual conduct. I noted in an earlier opinion the fact that the American Association of Law Schools (to which any reputable law school *must* seek to belong) excludes from membership any school that refuses to ban from its job-interview facilities a law firm (no matter how small) that does not wish to hire as a prospective partner a person who openly engages in homosexual conduct.

One of the most revealing statements in today's opinion is the Court's grim warning that the criminalization of homosexual conduct is "an invitation to subject homosexual persons to discrimination both in the public and in the private spheres." It is clear from this that the Court has taken sides in the culture war, departing from its role of assuring, as neutral observer, that the democratic rules of engagement are observed. Many Americans do not want persons who openly engage in homosexual conduct as partners in their business, as scoutmasters for their children, as teachers in their children's schools, or as boarders in their home. They view this as protecting themselves and their families from a lifestyle that they believe to be immoral and destructive. The Court views it as "discrimination" which it is the function of our judgments to deter. . . .

Let me be clear that I have nothing against homosexuals, or any other group, promoting their agenda through normal democratic means. Social perceptions of sexual and other morality change over time, and every group has the right to persuade its fellow citizens that its view of such matters is the best. That homosexuals have achieved some success in that enterprise is attested to by the fact that Texas is one of the few remaining States that criminalize private, consensual homosexual acts. But persuading one's fellow citizens is one thing, and imposing one's views in absence of democratic majority will is something else. I would no more *require* a State to criminalize homosexual acts—or, for that matter, display *any* moral disapprobation of them—than I would *forbid* it to do so. . . .

■ [The brief dissenting opinion of JUSTICE THOMAS, who also joined in JUSTICE SCALIA's dissent, is omitted.]

NOTES

1. *Lawrence* did not address and does not affect laws prohibiting forcible sodomy. See, for example, The American Law Institute's Model Penal Code, which does not proscribe unconventional sexual conduct between consenting adults, either heterosexual or homosexual. Its relevant provisions are as follows:

§ 213.2 Deviate Sexual Intercourse by Force or Imposition

(1) *By Force or Its Equivalent.* A person who engages in deviate sexual intercourse with another person, or who causes another to engage in deviate sexual intercourse, commits a felony of the second degree if:

> (a) he compels the other person to participate by force or by threat of imminent death, serious bodily injury, extreme pain or kidnapping, to be inflicted on anyone; or

> (b) he has substantially impaired the other person's power to appraise or control his conduct, by administering or employing without the knowledge of the other person drugs, intoxicants or other means for the purpose of preventing resistance; or

> (c) the other person is unconscious; or

> (d) the other person is less than 10 years old.

(2) *By Other Imposition.* A person who engages in deviate sexual intercourse with another person, or who causes another to engage in deviate sexual intercourse, commits a felony of the third degree if:

> (a) he compels the other person to participate by any threat that would prevent resistance by a person of ordinary resolution; or

> (b) he knows that the other person suffers from a mental disease or defect which renders him incapable of appraising the nature of his conduct; or

> (c) he knows that the other person submits because he is unaware that a sexual act is being committed upon him.

2. According to the pathfinding research by Dr. Kinsey et al., human sexuality is a continuum, with most persons falling somewhere between exclusively heterosexual and exclusively homosexual. Although Kinsey's studies have been criticized, his statistics on human sexuality have been substantiated by more recent studies discussed in *Susan J. Becker, Many Are Chilled, but Few Are Frozen: How Transformative Learning in Popular CultEventual Demise of Legally Sanctioned Discrimination Against Sexual Minorities in the United States,* 14 Am. U.J. Gender Soc. Pol'y & L. 177, 199 n.119 (2006); *see also* Benedict Carey, *Long After Kinsey, Only the Brave Study Sex,* N.Y. TIMES, Nov. 9, 2004, at F-1 (ambivalence about the scientific study of sexuality has remained constant since Kinsey's work in the 1940s; religious conservatives have been especially vocal critics of studying sexuality). Catharine MacKinnon posits that sexual minorities are "among the most stigmatized, persecuted, and denigrated people on earth."[2]

3. In 2008, the Supreme Court of California determined that, "the California Constitution properly must be interpreted to guarantee [the right to marry] to *all* individuals and couples, without regard to their sexual orientation." In re Marriage Cases, 43 Cal.4th 757, 76 Cal.Rptr.3d 683 (Cal. 2008). In response to the California Court's ruling, California voters adopted Proposition 8 amending the State's constitution to deny same-sex couples the right to marry. *See* CAL. FAM. CODE § 300(a). In response to the California court's ruling, California voters adopted Proposition 8, denying same-sex couples the right to marry again in the 2008 election. Shortly after Proposition 8 was adopted by the voters, two California couples challenged the constitutionality—on due process and equal protection grounds—of Proposition 8 in Perry v. Schwarzenegger, 704 F.Supp.2d 921 (N.D. Cal. 2010). First, with regard to the due process challenge, the district court found the right to marry—whether involving different-sex or same-sex partners— was a fundamental right and the government's restriction could not withstand strict scrutiny. The court did not elaborate on the strict scrutiny issue because it found, in its equal protection analysis, that the restriction did not withstand even a rational basis review. Second, with regard to the equal protection challenge, the court did not address "whether laws classifying on the basis of sexual orientation should be subject to a heightened standard of review" because Proposition 8 was unconstitutional under any standard of review. The court swept away each of the government's purported interest, finding that "what remains . . . is an inference . . . that Proposition 8 was premised on the belief that same-sex couples are not as good as opposite sex couples." This, the court found, was an impermissible ground on which to legislate. Thus, the court deemed Proposition 8 unconstitutional on both grounds. The United States Court of Appeals for the 9th Circuit largely affirmed this ruling and the United States Supreme Court granted review. The decision should be out by the end of June, 2013.

4. As of June 2012, same-sex couples were able to obtain marriage licenses in the District of Columbia and six states—Massachusetts, Connecticut, Iowa, Vermont, New Hampshire, and New York. Additionally, by February 2012, Washington and Maryland had passed legislation allowing same-sex marriages, but those laws had not gone into effect as of June 2012. Five states—Delaware, Hawaii, Illinoi, New Jersey, and Rhode Island—allowed same-sex couples to enter into civil unions. *See Defining Marriage: Defense of Marriage Acts and Same-Sex Marriage Laws*, NAT'L CONF. ST. LEGISLATURES, http://www.ncsl.org/issues-research/human-services/same-sex-marriage-over view.aspx (last updated June 2012).

---

[2] CATHARINE A. MACKINNON, SEX EQUALITY 1057 (2003); *see also* KAISER FAMILY FOUNDATION, Views on Issues and Policies Related to Sexual Orientation Survey (2000), *available at* http://www.lgbtdata.com/uploads/1/0/8/8/10884149/ds020_ksso_report.pdf (identifying in a nationwide survey that adults viewed gay men and lesbian women as suffering the most prejudice and discrimination in this country, followed by Blacks, Hispanics, and the disabled).

5. The Defense of Marriage Act (DOMA), Pub. L. No. 104–199, 110 Stat. 2419 (1996) (codified at 1 U.S.C. § 7, 28 U.S.C. § 1738C), provides that marriage "means only a legal union between one man and one woman as husband and wife." For purposes of federal law, regulations and rulings, including federal tax law, this meant that only heterosexual marriages were recognized as falling within the term "marriage." After two United States Courts of Appeal struck down DOMA on equal protection grounds the United States Supreme Court granted review in *United States v. Windsor*, 570 U.S. ___, 133 S. Ct. 2675, 186 L.Ed.2d 808 (2013), and affirmed. The challenger in Windsor had been legally married to a same-sex partner in New York, state law recognizing same-sex marriages, but had been denied federal estate tax benefits on the death of her spouse. Justice Kennedy's majority opinion held since state law governed domestic relations and the definition of marriage, the federal law violated both equal protection and due process in states that recognized same-sex marriage. Four Justices dissented in three separate opinions.

6. Although the Supreme Court in *Windsor* did not invalidate all bans on same-sex marriage, the Court took up this issue two years later in *Obergefell v. Hodges*, 576 U.S. ___, 135 S. Ct. 2584, 192 L.Ed.2d 609 (2015). In *Obergefell*, the Court, in another opinion by Justice Kennedy, held that bans on same-sex marriage again violated both the Due Process and Equal Protection Clauses of the Fourteenth Amendment. Justice Kennedy's opinion surveyed both the historical evolution of marriage and the treatment of homosexuality, and the trend toward the legalization of gay marriage. He mentioned four principles that demonstrate that the fundamental right to marriage applies with equal force to same-sex couples. First, he stated that the Court's relevant precedents demonstrate that "the right to personal choice regarding marriage is inherent in the concept of individual autonomy." Second, Justice Kennedy concluded "that the right to marry is fundamental because it supports a two-person union unlike any other in its importance to the committed individuals." Third, the right to marry "safeguards children and families and thus draws meaning from related rights of childrearing, procreation, and education." Lastly, he stated that "this Court's cases and the Nation's traditions make clear that marriage is a keystone of our social order." From this the majority opinion concluded "that the right to marry is a fundamental right inherent in the liberty of the person, and under the Due Process and Equal Protection Clauses of the Fourteenth Amendment couples of the same-sex may not be deprived of that right."

Four separate dissents were filed by Justice Scalia, Chief Justice Roberts, and Justices Thomas and Alito.

C. THE PROHIBITION AGAINST CRUEL AND UNUSUAL PUNISHMENT

1. PUNISHMENT FOR NARCOTIC ADDICTION AND ALCOHOLISM

Robinson v. California

Supreme Court of the United States, 1962.
370 U.S. 660, 82 S.Ct. 1417, 8 L.Ed.2d 758.

■ MR. JUSTICE STEWART delivered the opinion of the Court.

A California statute makes it a criminal offense for a person to "be addicted to the use of narcotics."[1] This appeal draws into question the constitutionality of that provision of the state law, as construed by the California courts in the present case.

The appellant was convicted after a jury trial in the Municipal Court of Los Angeles. The evidence against him was given by two Los Angeles police officers. Officer Brown testified that he had had occasion to examine the appellant's arms one evening on a street in Los Angeles some four months before the trial. The officer testified that at that time he had observed "scar tissue and discoloration on the inside" of the appellant's right arm, and "what appeared to be numerous needle marks and a scab which was approximately three inches below the crook of the elbow" on the appellant's left arm. The officer also testified that the appellant under questioning had admitted to the occasional use of narcotics.

Officer Lindquist testified that he had examined the appellant the following morning in the Central Jail in Los Angeles. The officer stated that at that time he had observed discolorations and scabs on the appellant's arms, and he identified photographs which had been taken of the appellant's arms shortly after his arrest the night before. Based upon more than ten years of experience as a member of the Narcotic Division of the Los Angeles Police Department, the witness gave his opinion that "these marks and the discoloration were the result of the injection of hypodermic needles into the tissue into the vein that was not sterile." He

---

[1] The statute is § 11721 of the California Health and Safety Code. It provides:

No person shall use, or be under the influence of, or be addicted to the use of narcotics, excepting when administered by or under the direction of a person licensed by the State to prescribe and administer narcotics. It shall be the burden of the defense to show that it comes within the exception. Any person convicted of violating any provision of this section is guilty of a misdemeanor and shall be sentenced to serve a term of not less than 90 days nor more than one year in the county jail. The court may place a person convicted hereunder on probation for a period not to exceed five years and shall in all cases in which probation is granted require as a condition thereof that such person be confined in the county jail for at least 90 days. In no event does the court have the power to absolve a person who violates this section from the obligation of spending at least 90 days in confinement in the county jail.

stated that the scabs were several days old at the time of his examination, and that the appellant was neither under the influence of narcotics nor suffering withdrawal symptoms at the time he saw him. This witness also testified that the appellant had admitted using narcotics in the past.

The appellant testified in his own behalf, denying the alleged conversations with the police officers and denying that he had ever used narcotics or been addicted to their use. He explained the marks on his arms as resulting from an allergic condition contracted during his military service. His testimony was corroborated by two witnesses.

The trial judge instructed the jury that the statute made it a misdemeanor for a person "either to use narcotics, or to be addicted to the use of narcotics * * * That portion of the statute referring to the 'use' of narcotics is based upon the 'act' of using. That portion of the statute referring to 'addicted to the use' of narcotics is based upon a condition or status. They are not identical. * * * To be addicted to the use of narcotics is said to be a status or condition and not an act. It is a continuing offense and differs from most other offenses in the fact that [it] is chronic rather than acute; that it continues after it is complete and subjects the offender to arrest at any time before he reforms. The existence of such a chronic condition may be ascertained from a single examination, if the characteristic reactions of that condition be found present."

The judge further instructed the jury that the appellant could be convicted under a general verdict if the jury agreed *either* that he was of the "status" *or* had committed the "act" denounced by the statute. "All that the People must show is either that the defendant did use a narcotic in Los Angeles County, or that while in the City of Los Angeles he was addicted to the use of narcotics * * *."

Under these instructions the jury returned a verdict finding the appellant "guilty of the offense charged." An appeal was taken to the Appellate Department of the Los Angeles County Superior Court, "the highest court of a State in which a decision could be had" in this case. . . . Although expressing some doubt as to the constitutionality of "the crime of being a narcotic addict," the reviewing court in an unreported opinion affirmed the judgment of conviction, citing two of its own previous unreported decisions which had upheld the constitutionality of the statute. We noted probable jurisdiction of this appeal . . . because it squarely presents the issue whether the statute as construed by the California courts in this case is repugnant to the Fourteenth Amendment of the Constitution.

The broad power of a State to regulate the narcotic drugs traffic within its borders is not here in issue. More than forty years ago, in Whipple v. Martinson, 256 U.S. 41, 41 S.Ct. 425, 65 L.Ed. 819, this Court explicitly recognized the validity of that power: "There can be no question of the authority of the state in the exercise of its police power to regulate the administration, sale, prescription and use of dangerous and habit-forming drugs * * *. The right to exercise this power is so manifest in the interest of the public health and welfare, that it is unnecessary to enter upon a discussion of it beyond saying that it is too firmly established to be successfully called in question." . . .

Such regulation, it can be assumed, could take a variety of valid forms. A State might impose criminal sanctions, for example, against the unauthorized manufacture, prescription, sale, purchase, or possession of narcotics within its borders. In the interest of discouraging the violation of such laws, or in the interest of the general health or welfare of its inhabitants, a State might establish a program of compulsory treatment for those addicted to narcotics.[7] Such a program of treatment might require periods of involuntary confinement. And penal sanctions might be imposed for failure to comply with established compulsory treatment procedures. . . . Or a State might choose to attack the evils of narcotics traffic on broader fronts also—through public health education, for example, or by efforts to ameliorate the economic and social conditions under which those evils might be thought to flourish. In short, the range of valid choice which a State might make in this area is undoubtedly a wide one, and the wisdom of any particular choice within the allowable spectrum is not for us to decide. Upon that premise we turn to the California law in issue here.

It would be possible to construe the statute under which the appellant was convicted as one which is operative only upon proof of the actual use of narcotics within the State's jurisdiction. But the California courts have not so construed this law. Although there was evidence in the present case that the appellant had used narcotics in Los Angeles, the jury were instructed that they could convict him even if they disbelieved that evidence. The appellant could be convicted, they were told, if they found simply that the appellant's "status" or "chronic condition" was that of being "addicted to the use of narcotics." And it is impossible to know from the jury's verdict that the defendant was not convicted upon precisely such a finding.

The instructions of the trial court, implicitly approved on appeal, amounted to "a ruling on a question of state law that is as binding on us as though the precise words had been written" into the statute. Terminiello v. Chicago, 337 U.S. 1, 4, 69 S.Ct. 894, 895, 93 L.Ed. 1131. "We can only take the statute as the state courts read it." Id., at 6, 69 S.Ct. at 896. Indeed, in their brief in this Court counsel for the State have emphasized that it is "the proof of addiction by circumstantial evidence * * * by the tell-tale track of needle marks and scabs over the veins of his arms, that remains the gist of the section."

---

[7] California appears to have established just such a program in §§ 5350–5361 of its Welfare and Institutions Code. The record contains no explanation of why the civil procedures authorized by this legislation were not utilized in the present case.

This statute, therefore, is not one which punishes a person for the use of narcotics, for their purchase, sale or possession, or for antisocial or disorderly behavior resulting from their administration. It is not a law which even purports to provide or require medical treatment. Rather, we deal with a statute which makes the "status" of narcotic addiction a criminal offense, for which the offender may be prosecuted "at any time before he reforms". California has said that a person can be continuously guilty of this offense, whether or not he has ever used or possessed any narcotics within the State, and whether or not he has been guilty of any antisocial behavior there.

It is unlikely that any State at this moment in history would attempt to make it a criminal offense for a person to be mentally ill, or a leper, or to be afflicted with a venereal disease. A State might determine that the general health and welfare require that the victims of these and other human afflictions be dealt with by compulsory treatment, involving quarantine, confinement, or sequestration. But, in the light of contemporary human knowledge, a law which made a criminal offense of such a disease would doubtless be universally thought to be an infliction of cruel and unusual punishment in violation of the Eighth and Fourteenth Amendments. . . .

We cannot but consider the statute before us as of the same category. In this Court counsel for the State recognized that narcotic addiction is an illness. Indeed, it is apparently an illness which may be contracted innocently or involuntarily.[9] We hold that a state law which imprisons a person thus afflicted as a criminal, even though he has never touched any narcotic drug within the State or been guilty of any irregular behavior there, inflicts a cruel and unusual punishment in violation of the Fourteenth Amendment. To be sure, imprisonment for ninety days is not, in the abstract, a punishment which is either cruel or unusual. But the question cannot be considered in the abstract. Even one day in prison would be a cruel and unusual punishment for the "crime" of having a common cold.

We are not unmindful that the vicious evils of the narcotics traffic have occasioned the grave concern of government. There are, as we have said, countless fronts on which those evils may be legitimately attacked. We deal in this case only with an individual provision of a particularized local law as it has so far been interpreted by the California courts.

Reversed.

■ [MR. JUSTICE FRANKFURTER took no part in the case. MR. JUSTICE DOUGLAS' concurring opinion is omitted.]

---

[9] Not only may addiction innocently result from the use of medically prescribed narcotics, but a person may even be a narcotics addict from the moment of his birth. [citation here to many supporting authorities.]

■ MR. JUSTICE HARLAN, concurring. I am not prepared to hold that on the present state of medical knowledge it is completely irrational and hence unconstitutional for a State to conclude that narcotics addiction is something other than an illness nor that it amounts to cruel and unusual punishment for the State to subject narcotics addicts to its criminal law. Insofar as addiction may be identified with the use or possession of narcotics within the State (or, I would suppose, without the State), in violation of local statutes prohibiting such acts, it may surely be reached by the State's criminal law. But in this case the trial court's instructions permitted the jury to find the appellant guilty on no more proof than that he was present in California while he was addicted to narcotics. Since addiction alone cannot reasonably be thought to amount to more than a compelling propensity to use narcotics, the effect of this instruction was to authorize criminal punishment for a bare desire to commit a criminal act.

If the California statute reaches this type of conduct, and for present purposes we must accept the trial court's construction as binding, . . . it is an arbitrary imposition which exceeds the power that a State may exercise in enacting its criminal law. Accordingly, I agree that the application of the California statute was unconstitutional in this case and join the judgment of reversal.

■ MR. JUSTICE CLARK, dissenting. The Court finds § 11721 of California's Health and Safety Code, making it an offense to "be addicted to the use of narcotics," violative of due process as "a cruel and unusual punishment." I cannot agree.

The statute must first be placed in perspective. California has a comprehensive and enlightened program for the control of narcotism based on the overriding policy of prevention and cure. It is the product of an extensive investigation made in the mid-Fifties by a committee of distinguished scientists, doctors, law enforcement officers and laymen appointed by the then Attorney General, now Governor, of California. The committee filed a detailed study entitled "Report on Narcotic Addiction" which was given considerable attention. No recommendation was made therein for the repeal of § 11721, and the State Legislature in its discretion continued the policy of that section.

Apart from prohibiting specific acts such as the purchase, possession and sale of narcotics, California has taken certain legislative steps in regard to the status of being a narcotic addict—a condition commonly recognized as a threat to the State and to the individual. The Code deals with this problem in realistic stages. At its incipiency narcotic addiction is handled under § 11721 of the Health and Safety Code which is at issue here. It provides that a person found to be addicted to the use of narcotics shall serve a term in the county jail of not less than 90 days nor more than one year, with the minimum 90-day confinement applying in all cases without exception. Provision is made for parole with periodic tests to detect readdiction.

The trial court defined "addicted to narcotics" as used in § 11721 in the following charge to the jury:

> The word "addicted" means, strongly disposed to some taste or practice or habituated, especially to drugs. In order to inquire as to whether a person is addicted to the use of narcotics is in effect an inquiry as to his habit in that regard. Does he use them habitually? To use them often or daily is, according to the ordinary acceptance of those words, to use them habitually.

There was no suggestion that the term "narcotic addict" as here used included a person who acted without volition or who had lost the power of self-control. Although the section is penal in appearance—perhaps a carry-over from a less sophisticated approach—its present provisions are quite similar to those for civil commitment and treatment of addicts who have lost the power of self-control, and its present purpose is reflected in a statement which closely follows § 11721: "The rehabilitation of narcotic addicts and the prevention of continued addiction to narcotics is a matter of statewide concern." California Health and Safety Code, § 11728.

Where narcotic addiction has progressed beyond the incipient, volitional stage, California provides for commitment of three months to two years in a state hospital. California Welfare and Institutions Code, § 5355. For the purposes of this provision, a narcotic addict is defined as

> any person who habitually takes or otherwise uses *to the extent of having lost the power of self-control* any opium, morphine, cocaine, or other narcotic drug as defined in Article 1 of Chapter 1 of Division 10 of the Health and Safety Code. California Welfare and Institutions Code, § 5350. (Emphasis supplied.)

This proceeding is clearly civil in nature with a purpose of rehabilitation and cure. Significantly, if it is found that a person committed under § 5355 will not receive substantial benefit from further hospital treatment and is not dangerous to society, he may be discharged—but only after a minimum confinement of three months, § 5355.1.

Thus, the "criminal" provision applies to the incipient narcotic addict who retains self-control, requiring confinement of three months to one year and parole with frequent tests to detect renewed use of drugs. Its overriding purpose is to cure the less seriously addicted person by preventing further use. On the other hand, the "civil" commitment provision deals with addicts who have lost the power of self-control, requiring hospitalization up to two years. Each deals with a different type of addict but with a common purpose. This is most apparent when the sections overlap: if after civil commitment of an addict it is found that hospital treatment will not be helpful, the addict is confined for a minimum period of three months in the same manner as is the volitional addict under the "criminal" provision.

In the instant case the proceedings against the petitioner were brought under the volitional-addict section. There was testimony that he had been using drugs only four months with three to four relatively mild doses a week. At arrest and trial he appeared normal. His testimony was clear and concise, being simply that he had never used drugs. The scabs and pocks on his arms and body were caused, he said, by "overseas shots" administered during army service preparatory to foreign assignment. He was very articulate in his testimony but the jury did not believe him, apparently because he had told the clinical expert while being examined after arrest that he had been using drugs, as I have stated above. The officer who arrested him also testified to like statements and to scabs—some 10 or 15 days old—showing narcotic injections. There was no evidence in the record of withdrawal symptoms. Obviously he could not have been committed under § 5355 as one who had completely "lost the power of self-control." The jury was instructed that narcotic "addiction" as used in § 11721 meant strongly disposed to a taste or practice or habit of its use, indicated by the use of narcotics often or daily. A general verdict was returned against petitioner, and he was ordered confined for 90 days to be followed by a two-year parole during which he was required to take periodic Nalline tests.

The majority strikes down the conviction primarily on the grounds that petitioner was denied due process by the imposition of criminal penalties for nothing more than being in a status. This viewpoint is premised upon the theme that § 11721 is a "criminal" provision authorizing a punishment, for the majority admits that "a State might establish a program of compulsory treatment for those addicted to narcotics" which "might require periods of involuntary confinement." I submit that California has done exactly that. The majority's error is in instructing the California Legislature that hospitalization is the *only treatment* for narcotics addiction—that anything less is a punishment denying due process. California has found otherwise after a study which I suggest was more extensive than that conducted by the Court. Even in California's program for hospital commitment of nonvolitional narcotic addicts—which the majority approves—it is recognized that some addicts will not respond to or do not need hospital treatment. As to these persons its provisions are identical to those of § 11721—confinement for a period of not less than 90 days. Section 11721 provides this confinement as treatment for the volitional addicts to whom its provisions apply, in addition to parole with frequent tests to detect and prevent further use of drugs. The fact that § 11721 might be labeled "criminal" seems irrelevant,* not only to the majority's own "treatment" test but to the

---

* Any reliance upon the "stigma" of a misdemeanor conviction in this context is misplaced, as it would hardly be different from the stigma of a civil commitment for narcotics addiction.

"concept of ordered liberty" to which the States must attain under the Fourteenth Amendment. The test is the overall purpose and effect of a State's act, and I submit that California's program relative to narcotic addicts—including both the "criminal" and "civil" provisions—is inherently one of treatment and lies well within the power of a State.

However, the case in support of the judgment below need not rest solely on this reading of California law. For even if the overall statutory scheme is ignored and a purpose and effect of punishment is attached to § 11721, that provision still does not violate the Fourteenth Amendment. The majority acknowledges, as it must, that a State can punish persons who purchase, possess or use narcotics. Although none of these acts are harmful to society *in themselves*, the State constitutionally may attempt to deter and prevent them through punishment because of the grave threat of future harmful conduct which they pose. Narcotics addiction—including the incipient, volitional addiction to which this provision speaks—is no different. California courts have taken judicial notice that "the inordinate use of a narcotic drug tends to create an irresistible craving and forms a habit for its continued use until one becomes an addict, and he respects no convention or obligation and will lie, steal, or use any other base means to gratify his passion for the drug, being lost to all considerations of duty or social position." . . . Can this Court deny the legislative and judicial judgment of California that incipient, volitional narcotic addiction poses a threat of serious crime similar to the threat inherent in the purchase or possession of narcotics? And if such a threat is inherent in addiction, can this Court say that California is powerless to deter it by punishment?

It is no answer to suggest that we are dealing with an involuntary status and thus penal sanctions will be ineffective and unfair. The section at issue applies only to persons who use narcotics often or even daily but not to the point of losing self-control. When dealing with involuntary addicts California moves only through § 5355 of its Welfare and Institutions Code which clearly is not penal. Even if it could be argued that § 11721 may not be limited to volitional addicts, the petitioner in the instant case undeniably retained the power of self-control and thus to him the statute would be constitutional. Moreover, "status" offenses have long been known and recognized in the criminal law. A ready example is drunkenness, which plainly is as involuntary after addiction to alcohol as is the taking of drugs.

Nor is the conjecture relevant that petitioner may have acquired his habit under lawful circumstances. There was no suggestion by him to this effect at trial, and surely the State need not rebut all possible lawful sources of addiction as part of its prima facie case.

The argument that the statute constitutes a cruel and unusual punishment is governed by the discussion above. Properly construed, the statute provides a treatment rather than a punishment. But even if interpreted as penal, the sanction of incarceration for 3 to 12 months is not unreasonable when applied to a person who has voluntarily placed himself in a condition posing a serious threat to the State. Under either theory, its provisions for 3 to 12 months' confinement can hardly be deemed unreasonable when compared to the provisions for 3 to 24 months' confinement under § 5355 which the majority approves.

I would affirm the judgment.

■ MR. JUSTICE WHITE, dissenting. If appellant's conviction rested upon sheer status, condition or illness or if he was convicted for being an addict who had lost his power of self-control, I would have other thoughts about this case. But this record presents neither situation. And I believe the Court has departed from its wise rule of not deciding constitutional questions except where necessary and from its equally sound practice of construing state statutes, where possible, in a manner saving their constitutionality.

I am not at all ready to place the use of narcotics beyond the reach of the States' criminal laws. I do not consider appellant's conviction to be a punishment for having an illness or for simply being in some status or condition, but rather a conviction for the regular, repeated or habitual use of narcotics immediately prior to his arrest and in violation of the California law. As defined by the trial court, addiction *is* the regular use of narcotics and can be proved only by evidence of such use. To find addiction in this case the jury had to believe that appellant had frequently used narcotics in the recent past.[3] California is entitled to have its statute and the record so read, particularly where the State's only purpose in allowing prosecutions for addiction was to supersede its own venue requirements applicable to prosecutions for the use of narcotics and in effect to allow convictions for use where there is no precise evidence of the county where the use took place.

Nor do I find any indications in this record that California would apply to § 11721 to the case of the helpless addict. I agree with my Brother Clark that there was no evidence at all that appellant had lost the power to control his acts. There was no evidence of any use within 3 days prior to appellant's arrest. The most recent marks might have been 3 days old or they might have been 10 days old. The appellant admitted before trial that he had last used narcotics 8 days before his arrest. At the trial he denied having taken narcotics at all. The uncontroverted

---

3   This is not a case where a defendant is convicted "even though he has never touched any narcotic drug within the State or been guilty of any irregular behavior there." The evidence was that appellant lived and worked in Los Angeles. He admitted before trial that he had used narcotics for three or four months, three or four times a week, usually at his place with his friends. He stated to the police that he had last used narcotics at 54th and Central in the City of Los Angeles on January 27, 8 days before his arrest. According to the State's expert, no needle mark or scab found on appellant's arms was newer than 3 days old and the most recent mark might have been as old as 10 days, which was consistent with appellant's own pretrial admissions. The State's evidence was that appellant had used narcotics at least 7 times in the 15 days immediately preceding his arrest.

evidence was that appellant was not under the influence of narcotics at the time of his arrest nor did he have withdrawal symptoms. He was an incipient addict, a redeemable user, and the State chose to send him to jail for 90 days rather than to attempt to confine him by civil proceedings under another statute which requires a finding that the addict has lost the power of self-control. In my opinion, on this record, it was within the power of the State of California to confine him by criminal proceedings for the use of narcotics or for regular use amounting to habitual use.[5]

The Court clearly does not rest its decision upon the narrow ground that the jury was not expressly instructed not to convict if it believed appellant's use of narcotics was beyond his control. The Court recognizes no degrees of addiction. The Fourteenth Amendment is today held to bar any prosecution for addiction regardless of the degree or frequency of use, and the Court's opinion bristles with indications of further consequences. If it is "cruel and unusual punishment" to convict appellant for addiction, it is difficult to understand why it would be any less offensive to the Fourteenth Amendment to convict him for use on the same evidence of use which proved he was an addict. It is significant that in purporting to reaffirm the power of the States to deal with the narcotics traffic, the Court does not include among the obvious powers of the State the power to punish for the use of narcotics. I cannot think that the omission was inadvertent.

The Court has not merely tidied up California's law by removing some irritating vestige of an outmoded approach to the control of narcotics. At the very least, it has effectively removed California's power to deal effectively with the recurring case under the statute where there is ample evidence of use but no evidence of the precise location of use. Beyond this it has cast serious doubt upon the power of any State to forbid the use of narcotics under threat of criminal punishment. I cannot believe that the Court would forbid the application of the criminal laws to the use of narcotics under any circumstances. But the States, as well as the Federal Government, are now on notice. They will have to await a final answer in another case.

Finally, I deem this application of "cruel and unusual punishment" so novel that I suspect the Court was hard put to find a way to ascribe to the Framers of the Constitution the result reached today rather than to its own notions of ordered liberty. If this case involved economic regulation, the present Court's allergy to substantive due process would surely save the statute and prevent the Court from imposing its own philosophical predilections upon state legislatures or Congress. I fail to see why the Court deems it more appropriate to write into the Constitution its own abstract notions of how best to handle the narcotics

---

[5] Health and Safety Code § 11391 expressly permits and contemplates the medical treatment of narcotics addicts confined to jail.

problem, for it obviously cannot match either the States or Congress in expert understanding.

I respectfully dissent.

NOTE

Presumably if addiction cannot be made a crime, neither can alcoholism. Would it nevertheless be permissible, in light of *Robinson*, to punish an addict for being under the influence of drugs or an alcoholic for public intoxication? This issue is explored in Chapter 10 at the end of Section B.3. dealing with addiction.

2. THE DEATH PENALTY

Gregg v. Georgia

Supreme Court of the United States, 1976.
428 U.S. 153, 96 S.Ct. 2909, 49 L.Ed.2d 859.

■ Judgment of the Court, and opinion of MR. JUSTICE STEWART, MR. JUSTICE POWELL, and MR. JUSTICE STEVENS, announced by MR. JUSTICE STEWART.

The issue in this case is whether the imposition of the sentence of death for the crime of murder under the law of Georgia violates the Eighth and Fourteenth Amendments.

I

The petitioner, Troy Gregg, was charged with committing armed robbery and murder. In accordance with Georgia procedure in capital cases, the trial was in two stages, a guilt stage and a sentencing stage. The evidence at the guilt trial established that on November 21, 1973, the petitioner and a traveling companion, Floyd Allen, while hitchhiking north in Florida were picked up by Fred Simmons and Bob Moore. Their car broke down, but they continued north after Simmons purchased another vehicle with some of the cash he was carrying. While still in Florida, they picked up another hitchhiker, Dennis Weaver, who rode with them to Atlanta, where he was let out about 11 p.m. A short time later the four men interrupted their journey for a rest stop along the highway. The next morning the bodies of Simmons and Moore were discovered in a ditch nearby.

On November 23, after reading about the shootings in an Atlanta newspaper, Weaver communicated with the Gwinnett County police and related information concerning the journey with the victims, including a description of the car. The next afternoon, the petitioner and Allen, while in Simmons' car, were arrested in Asheville, N.C. In the search incident to the arrest a .25 caliber pistol, later shown to be that used to kill Simmons and Moore, was found in the petitioner's pocket. After receiving the warnings required by Miranda v. Arizona, 384 U.S. 436, 86 S.Ct. 1602

(1966), and signing a written waiver of his rights, the petitioner signed a statement in which he admitted shooting, then robbing Simmons and Moore. He justified the slayings on grounds of self-defense. The next day, while being transferred to Lawrenceville, Ga., the petitioner and Allen were taken to the scene of the shootings. Upon arriving there, Allen recounted the events leading to the slayings. His version of these events was as follows: After Simmons and Moore left the car, the petitioner stated that he intended to rob them. The petitioner then took his pistol in hand and positioned himself on the car to improve his aim. As Simmons and Moore came up an embankment toward the car, the petitioner fired three shots and the two men fell near a ditch. The petitioner, at close range, then fired a shot into the head of each. He robbed them of valuables and drove away with Allen.

A medical examiner testified that Simmons died from a bullet wound in the eye and that Moore died from bullet wounds in the cheek and in the back of the head. He further testified that both men had several bruises and abrasions about the face and head which probably were sustained either from the fall into the ditch or from being dragged or pushed along the embankment. Although Allen did not testify, a police detective recounted the substance of Allen's statements about the slayings and indicated that directly after Allen had made these statements the petitioner had admitted that Allen's account was accurate. The petitioner testified in his own defense. He confirmed that Allen had made the statements described by the detective, but denied their truth or ever having admitted to their accuracy. He indicated that he had shot Simmons and Moore because of fear and in self-defense, testifying they had attacked Allen and him, one wielding a pipe and the other a knife.

The trial judge submitted the murder charges to the jury on both felony-murder and nonfelony-murder theories. He also instructed on the issue of self-defense but declined to instruct on manslaughter. He submitted the robbery case to the jury on both an armed-robbery theory and on the lesser included offense of robbery by intimidation. The jury found the petitioner guilty of two counts of armed robbery and two counts of murder.

At the penalty stage, which took place before the same jury, neither the prosecutor nor the petitioner's lawyer offered any additional evidence. Both counsel, however, made lengthy arguments dealing generally with the propriety of capital punishment under the circumstances and with the weight of the evidence of guilt. The trial judge instructed the jury that it could recommend either a death sentence or a life prison sentence on each count. The judge further charged the jury that in determining what sentence was appropriate the jury was free to consider the facts and circumstances, if any, presented by the parties in mitigation or aggravation.

Finally, the judge instructed the jury that it "would not be authorized to consider [imposing] the penalty of death" unless it first found beyond a reasonable doubt one of these aggravating circumstances:

One—That the offense of murder was committed while the offender was engaged in the commission of two other capital felonies, to-wit the armed robbery of [Simmons and Moore].

Two—That the offender committed the offense of murder for the purpose of receiving money and the automobile described in the indictment.

Three—The offense of murder was outrageously and wantonly vile, horrible and inhuman, in that they [*sic*] involved the depravity of [the] mind of the defendant.

Finding the first and second of these circumstances, the jury returned verdicts of death on each count.

The Supreme Court of Georgia affirmed the convictions and the imposition of the death sentences for murder. After reviewing the trial transcript and the record, including the evidence, and comparing the evidence and sentence in similar cases in accordance with the requirements of Georgia law, the court concluded that, considering the nature of the crime and the defendant, the sentences of death had not resulted from prejudice or any other arbitrary factor and were not excessive or disproportionate to the penalty applied in similar cases. The death sentences imposed for armed robbery, however, were vacated on the grounds that the death penalty had rarely been imposed in Georgia for that offense and that the jury improperly considered the murders as aggravating circumstances for the robberies after having considered the armed robberies as aggravating circumstances for the murders. * * *

II

Before considering the issues presented it is necessary to understand the Georgia statutory scheme for the imposition of the death penalty. The Georgia statute, as amended after our decision in Furman v. Georgia, 408 U.S. 238, 92 S.Ct. 2726 (1972), retains the death penalty for six categories of crime: murder, kidnaping for ransom or where the victim is harmed, armed robbery, rape, treason, and aircraft hijacking. The capital defendant's guilt or innocence is determined in the traditional manner, either by a trial judge or a jury, in the first stage of a bifurcated trial.

If trial is by jury, the trial judge is required to charge lesser included offenses when they are supported by any view of the evidence. After a verdict, finding, or plea of guilty to a capital crime, a presentence hearing is conducted before whoever made the determination of guilt. The sentencing procedures are essentially the same in both bench and jury trials. At the hearing:

[T]he judge [or jury] shall hear additional evidence in extenuation, mitigation and aggravation of punishment,

> including the record of any prior criminal convictions and pleas of guilty or pleas of nolo contendere of the defendant, or the absence of any prior conviction and pleas: Provided, however, that only such evidence in aggravation as the State has made known to the defendant prior to his trial shall be admissible. The judge [or jury] shall also hear argument by the defendant or his counsel and the prosecuting attorney ... regarding the punishment to be imposed.

The defendant is accorded substantial latitude as to the types of evidence that he may introduce. Evidence considered during the guilt stage may be considered during the sentencing stage without being resubmitted.

In the assessment of the appropriate sentence to be imposed the judge is also required to consider or to include in his instructions to the jury "any mitigating circumstances or aggravating circumstances otherwise authorized by law and any of [10] statutory aggravating circumstances which may be supported by the evidence. . . ." The scope of the nonstatutory aggravating or mitigating circumstances is not delineated in the statute. Before a convicted defendant may be sentenced to death, however, except in cases of treason or aircraft hijacking, the jury, or the trial judge in cases tried without a jury, must find beyond a reasonable doubt one of the 10 aggravating circumstances specified in the statute.[9] The sentence of death may be imposed only if the jury (or

---

[9] The statute provides in part:

(a) The death penalty may be imposed for the offenses of aircraft hijacking or treason, in any case.

(b) In all cases of other offenses for which the death penalty may be authorized, the judge shall consider, or he shall include in his instructions to the jury for it to consider, any mitigating circumstances or aggravating circumstances otherwise authorized by law and any of the following statutory aggravating circumstances which may be supported by the evidence:

(1) The offense of murder, rape, armed robbery, or kidnaping was committed by a person with a prior record of conviction for a capital felony, or the offense of murder was committed by a person who has a substantial history of serious assaultive criminal convictions.

(2) The offense of murder, rape, armed robbery, or kidnaping was committed while the offender was engaged in the commission of another capital felony, or aggravated battery, or the offense of murder was committed while the offender was engaged in the commission of burglary or arson in the first degree.

(3) The offender by his act of murder, armed robbery, or kidnaping knowingly created a great risk of death to more than one person in a public place by means of a weapon or device which would normally be hazardous to the lives of more than one person.

(4) The offender committed the offense of murder for himself or another, for the purpose of receiving money or any other thing of monetary value.

(5) The murder of a judicial officer, former judicial officer, district attorney or solicitor or former district attorney or solicitor during or because of the exercise of his official duty.

(6) The offender caused or directed another to commit murder or committed murder as an agent or employee of another person.

(7) The offense of murder, rape, armed robbery, or kidnaping was outrageously or wantonly vile, horrible or inhuman in that it involved torture, depravity of mind, or an aggravated battery to the victim.

judge) finds one of the statutory aggravating circumstances and then elects to impose that sentence. If the verdict is death, the jury or judge must specify the aggravating circumstance(s) found. In jury cases, the trial judge is bound by the jury's recommended sentence.

In addition to the conventional appellate process available in all criminal cases, provision is made for special expedited direct review by the Supreme Court of Georgia of the appropriateness of imposing the sentence of death in the particular case. The court is directed to consider "the punishment as well as any errors enumerated by way of appeal," and to determine:

(1) Whether the sentence of death was imposed under the influence of passion, prejudice, or any other arbitrary factor, and

(2) Whether, in cases other than treason or aircraft hijacking, the evidence supports the jury's or judge's finding of a statutory aggravating circumstance as enumerated in section 27.2534.1(b), and

(3) Whether the sentence of death is excessive or disproportionate to the penalty imposed in similar cases, considering both the crime and the defendant.

If the court affirms a death sentence, it is required to include in its decision reference to similar cases that it has taken into consideration.

A transcript and complete record of the trial, as well as a separate report by the trial judge, are transmitted to the court for its use in reviewing the sentence. The report is in the form of a 6 1/2-page questionnaire, designed to elicit information about the defendant, the crime, and the circumstances of the trial. It requires the trial judge to characterize the trial in several ways designed to test for arbitrariness and disproportionality of sentence. Included in the report are responses to detailed questions concerning the quality of the defendant's representation, whether race played a role in the trial, and, whether, in the trial court's judgment, there was any doubt about the defendant's guilt or the appropriateness of the sentence. A copy of the report is served

---

(8) The offense of murder was committed against any peace officer, corrections employee or fireman while engaged in the performance of his official duties.

(9) The offense of murder was committed by a person in, or who has escaped from, the lawful custody of a peace officer or place of lawful confinement.

(10) The murder was committed for the purpose of avoiding, interfering with, or preventing a lawful arrest or custody in a place of lawful confinement, of himself or another.

(c) The statutory instructions as determined by the trial judge to be warranted by the evidence shall be given in charge and in writing to the jury for its deliberation. The jury, if its verdict be a recommendation of death, shall designate in writing, signed by the foreman of the jury, the aggravating circumstance or circumstances which it found beyond a reasonable doubt. In non-jury cases the judge shall make such designation. Except in cases of treason or aircraft hijacking, unless at least one of the statutory aggravating circumstances enumerated in section 27–2534.1(b) is so found, the death penalty shall not be imposed. § 27–2534.1 (Supp.1975).

upon defense counsel. Under its special review authority, the court may either affirm the death sentence or remand the case for resentencing. In cases in which the death sentence is affirmed there remains the possibility of executive clemency.

III

We address initially the basic contention that the punishment of death for the crime of murder is, under all circumstances, "cruel and unusual" in violation of the Eighth and Fourteenth Amendments of the Constitution. . . .

The Court on a number of occasions has both assumed and asserted the constitutionality of capital punishment. In several cases that assumption provided a necessary foundation for the decision, as the Court was asked to decide whether a particular method of carrying out a capital sentence would be allowed to stand under the Eighth Amendment. But until Furman v. Georgia (1972) the Court never confronted squarely the fundamental claim that the punishment of death always, regardless of the enormity of the offense or the procedure followed in imposing the sentence, is cruel and unusual punishment in violation of the Constitution. Although this issue was presented and addressed in *Furman*, it was not resolved by the Court. Four Justices would have held that capital punishment is not unconstitutional *per se*; two Justices would have reached the opposite conclusion; and three Justices, while agreeing that the statutes then before the Court were invalid as applied, left open the question whether such punishment may ever be imposed. We now hold that the punishment of death does not invariably violate the Constitution. * * *

The imposition of the death penalty for the crime of murder has a long history of acceptance both in the United States and in England.

Four years ago, the petitioners in *Furman* and its companion cases predicated their argument primarily upon the asserted proposition that standards of decency had evolved to the point where capital punishment no longer could be tolerated. The petitioners in those cases said, in effect, that the evolutionary process had come to an end, and that standards of decency required that the Eighth Amendment be construed finally as prohibiting capital punishment for any crime regardless of its depravity and impact on society. This view was accepted by two Justices. Three other Justices were unwilling to go so far; focusing on the procedures by which convicted defendants were selected for the death penalty rather than on the actual punishment inflicted, they joined in the conclusion that the statutes before the Court were constitutionally invalid.

The petitioners in the capital cases before the Court today renew the "standards of decency" argument, but developments during the four years since *Furman* have undercut substantially the assumptions upon which their argument rested. Despite the continuing debate, dating back to the 19th century, over the morality and utility of capital punishment, it is now evident that a large proportion of American society continues to regard it as an appropriate and necessary criminal sanction.

The most marked indication of society's endorsement of the death penalty for murder is the legislative response to *Furman*. The legislatures of at least 35 States have enacted new statutes that provide for the death penalty for at least some crimes that result in the death of another person. And the Congress of the United States, in 1974, enacted a statute providing the death penalty for aircraft piracy that results in death. . . .

In the only statewide referendum occurring since *Furman* and brought to our attention, the people of California adopted a constitutional amendment that authorized capital punishment, in effect negating a prior ruling by the Supreme Court of California in People v. Anderson, 6 Cal.3d 628, 493 P.2d 880, cert. denied, 406 U.S. 958, 92 S.Ct. 2060 (1972), that the death penalty violated the California Constitution.

The jury also is a significant and reliable objective index of contemporary values because it is so directly involved. The Court has said that "one of the most important functions any jury can perform in making . . . a selection [between life imprisonment and death for a defendant convicted in a capital case] is to maintain a link between contemporary community values and the penal system." Witherspoon v. Illinois, 391 U.S. 510, 519 n. 15, 88 S.Ct. 1770, 1775 (1968). It may be true that evolving standards have influenced juries in recent decades to be more discriminating in imposing the sentence of death. But the relative infrequency of jury verdicts imposing the death sentence does not indicate rejection of capital punishment *per se*. . . . Indeed, the actions of juries in many States since *Furman* are fully compatible with the legislative judgments, reflected in the new statutes, as to the continued utility and necessity of capital punishment in appropriate cases. At the close of 1974 at least 254 persons had been sentenced to death since *Furman*, and by the end of March 1976, more than 460 persons were subject to death sentences.

As we have seen, however, the Eighth Amendment demands more than that a challenged punishment be acceptable to contemporary society. The Court also must ask whether it comports with the basic concept of human dignity at the core of the Amendment. Trop v. Dulles, 356 U.S., at 100, 78 S.Ct., at 597 (plurality opinion). Although we cannot "invalidate a category of penalties because we deem less severe penalties adequate to serve the ends of penology," Furman v. Georgia, supra, 408 U.S., at 451, 92 S.Ct., at 2834 (POWELL, J., dissenting), the sanction imposed cannot be so totally without penological justification that it results in the gratuitous infliction of suffering.

The death penalty is said to serve two principal social purposes: retribution and deterrence of capital crimes by prospective offenders.

In part, capital punishment is an expression of society's moral outrage at particularly offensive conduct. This function may be unappealing to many, but it is essential in an ordered society that asks its citizens to rely on legal processes rather than self-help to vindicate their wrongs. . . . "Retribution is no longer the dominant objective of the criminal law," Williams v. New York, 337 U.S. 241, 248, 69 S.Ct. 1079, 1084 (1949), but neither is it a forbidden objective nor one inconsistent with our respect for the dignity of men. Indeed, the decision that capital punishment may be the appropriate sanction in extreme cases is an expression of the community's belief that certain crimes are themselves so grievous an affront to humanity that the only adequate response may be the penalty of death.

Statistical attempts to evaluate the worth of the death penalty as a deterrent to crimes by potential offenders have occasioned a great deal of debate. The results simply have been inconclusive. . . .

In sum, we cannot say that the judgment of the Georgia Legislature that capital punishment may be necessary in some cases is clearly wrong. Considerations of federalism, as well as respect for the ability of a legislature to evaluate, in terms of its particular State, the moral consensus concerning the death penalty and its social utility as a sanction, require us to conclude, in the absence of more convincing evidence that the infliction of death as a punishment for murder is not without justification and thus is not unconstitutionally severe.

Finally, we must consider whether the punishment of death is disproportionate in relation to the crime for which it is imposed. There is no question that death as a punishment is unique in its severity and irrevocability. When a defendant's life is at stake, the Court has been particularly sensitive to insure that every safeguard is observed. But we are concerned here only with the imposition of capital punishment for the crime of murder, and when a life has been taken deliberately by the offender,[35] we cannot say that the punishment is invariably disproportionate to the crime. It is an extreme sanction, suitable to the most extreme of crimes.

We hold that the death penalty is not a form of punishment that may never be imposed, regardless of the circumstances of the offense, regardless of the character of the offender, and regardless of the procedure followed in reaching the decision to impose it.

IV

We now consider whether Georgia may impose the death penalty on the petitioner in this case.

---

[35] We do not address here the question whether the taking of the criminal's life is a proportionate sanction where no victim has been deprived of life—for example, when capital punishment is imposed for rape, kidnaping, or armed robbery that does not result in the death of any human being.

A

While *Furman* did not hold that the infliction of the death penalty *per se* violates the Constitution's ban on cruel and unusual punishments, it did recognize that the penalty of death is different in kind from any other punishment imposed under our system of criminal justice. Because of the uniqueness of the death penalty, *Furman* held that it could not be imposed under sentencing procedures that created a substantial risk that it would be inflicted in an arbitrary and capricious manner. . . .

While some have suggested that standards to guide a capital jury's sentencing deliberations are impossible to formulate, the fact is that such standards have been developed. When the drafters of the Model Penal Code faced this problem, they concluded "that it is within the realm of possibility to point to the main circumstances of aggravation and of mitigation that should be weighed *and weighed against each other* when they are presented in a concrete case." ALI, Model Penal Code § 201.6, Comment 3, p. 71 (Tent.Draft No. 9, 1959) (emphasis in original). While such standards are by necessity somewhat general, they do provide guidance to the sentencing authority and thereby reduce the likelihood that it will impose a sentence that fairly can be called capricious or arbitrary. Where the sentencing authority is required to specify the factors it relied upon in reaching its decision, the further safeguard of meaningful appellate review is available to ensure that death sentences are not imposed capriciously or in a freakish manner.

In summary, the concerns expressed in *Furman* that the penalty of death not be imposed in an arbitrary or capricious manner can be met by a carefully drafted statute that ensures that the sentencing authority is given adequate information and guidance. As a general proposition these concerns are best met by a system that provides for a bifurcated proceeding at which the sentencing authority is apprised of the information relevant to the imposition of sentence and provided with standards to guide its use of the information.

We do not intend to suggest that only the above-described procedures would be permissible under *Furman* or that any sentencing system constructed along these general lines would inevitably satisfy the concerns of *Furman*, for each distinct system must be examined on an individual basis. Rather, we have embarked upon this general exposition to make clear that it is possible to construct capital-sentencing systems capable of meeting *Furman's* constitutional concerns.

B

We now turn to consideration of the constitutionality of Georgia's capital-sentencing procedures. In the wake of *Furman*, Georgia amended its capital punishment statute, but chose not to narrow the scope of its murder provisions. See Part II, supra. Thus, now as before *Furman*, in Georgia "[a] person commits murder when he unlawfully and with malice aforethought, either express or implied, causes the death of another human being." All persons convicted of murder "shall be punished by death or by imprisonment for life."

Georgia did act, however, to narrow the class of murderers subject to capital punishment by specifying 10 statutory aggravating circumstances, one of which must be found by the jury to exist beyond a reasonable doubt before a death sentence can ever be imposed. In addition, the jury is authorized to consider any other appropriate aggravating or mitigating circumstances. The jury is not required to find any mitigating circumstance in order to make a recommendation of mercy that is binding on the trial court, but it must find a *statutory* aggravating circumstance before recommending a sentence of death. * * *

In short, Georgia's new sentencing procedures require as a prerequisite to the imposition of the death penalty, specific jury findings as to the circumstances of the crime or the character of the defendant. Moreover, to guard further against a situation comparable to that presented in *Furman*, the Supreme Court of Georgia compares each death sentence with the sentences imposed on similarly situated defendants to ensure that the sentence of death in a particular case is not disproportionate. On their face these procedures seem to satisfy the concerns of *Furman*. . . .

The petitioner contends, however, that the changes in the Georgia sentencing procedures are only cosmetic, that the arbitrariness and capriciousness condemned by *Furman* continue to exist in Georgia—both in traditional practices that still remain and in the new sentencing procedures adopted in response to *Furman*.

1

First, the petitioner focuses on the opportunities for discretionary action that are inherent in the processing of any murder case under Georgia law. He notes that the state prosecutor has unfettered authority to select those persons whom he wishes to prosecute for a capital offense and to plea bargain with them. Further, at the trial the jury may choose to convict a defendant of a lesser included offense rather than find him guilty of a crime punishable by death, even if the evidence would support a capital verdict. And finally, a defendant who is convicted and sentenced to die may have his sentence commuted by the Governor of the State and the Georgia Board of Pardons and Paroles.

The existence of these discretionary stages is not determinative of the issues before us. . . .

2

The petitioner further contends that the capital-sentencing procedures adopted by Georgia in response to *Furman* do not eliminate the dangers of arbitrariness and caprice in jury sentencing that were held in *Furman* to be violative of the Eighth and Fourteenth Amendments. He claims that the statute is so broad and vague as to leave juries free to act as arbitrarily and capriciously as they wish in deciding whether to impose the death penalty. . . .

. . . We think that the Georgia court wisely has chosen not to impose unnecessary restrictions on the evidence that can be offered at such a hearing and to approve open and far-ranging argument. So long as the evidence introduced and the arguments made at the pre-sentence hearing do not prejudice a defendant, it is preferable not to impose restrictions. We think it desirable for the jury to have as much information before it as possible when it makes the sentencing decision.

3

Finally, the Georgia statute has an additional provision designed to assure that the death penalty will not be imposed on a capriciously selected group of convicted defendants. The new sentencing procedures require that the State Supreme Court review every death sentence to determine whether it was imposed under the influence of passion, prejudice, or any other arbitrary factor, whether the evidence supports the findings of a statutory aggravating circumstance, and "[w]hether the sentence of death is excessive or disproportionate to the penalty imposed in similar cases, considering both the crime and the defendant." In performing its sentence-review function, the Georgia court has held that "if the death penalty is only rarely imposed for an act or it is substantially out of line with sentences imposed for other acts it will be set aside as excessive." . . .

It is apparent that the Supreme Court of Georgia has taken its review responsibilities seriously. . . .

The provision for appellate review in the Georgia capital-sentencing system serves as a check against the random or arbitrary imposition of the death penalty. In particular, the proportionality review substantially eliminates the possibility that a person will be sentenced to die by the action of an aberrant jury. If a time comes when juries generally do not impose the death sentence in a certain kind of murder case, the appellate review procedures assure that no defendant convicted under such circumstances will suffer a sentence of death.

V

The basic concern of *Furman* centered on those defendants who were being condemned to death capriciously and arbitrarily. Under the procedures before the Court in that case, sentencing authorities were not directed to give attention to the nature or circumstances of the crime committed or to the character or record of the defendant. Left unguided, juries imposed the death sentence in a way that could only be called freakish. The new Georgia sentencing procedures, by contrast, focus the jury's attention on the particularized nature of the crime and the particularized characteristics of the individual defendant. While the jury is permitted to consider any aggravating or mitigating circumstances, it must find and identify at least one statutory aggravating factor before it may impose a penalty of death. In this way the jury's discretion is channeled. No longer can a jury wantonly and freakishly impose the death sentence; it is always circumscribed by the legislative guidelines. In addition, the review function of the Supreme Court of Georgia affords additional assurance that the concerns that prompted our decision in *Furman* are not present to any significant degree in the Georgia procedure applied here.

For the reasons expressed in this opinion, we hold that the statutory system under which Gregg was sentenced to death does not violate the Constitution. Accordingly, the judgment of the Georgia Supreme Court is affirmed.

■ [The concurring opinion of MR. JUSTICE WHITE, with whom the CHIEF JUSTICE and MR. JUSTICE REHNQUIST join, is omitted. The statements of the CHIEF JUSTICE and MR. JUSTICE REHNQUIST, as well as the brief concurrence by MR. JUSTICE BLACKMUN, are also omitted.]

■ MR. JUSTICE BRENNAN, dissenting.

The Cruel and Unusual Punishments Clause "must draw its meaning from the evolving standards of decency that mark the progress of a maturing society." The opinions of Mr. Justice Stewart, Mr. Justice Powell, and Mr. Justice Stevens today hold that "evolving standards of decency" require focus not on the essence of the death penalty itself but primarily upon the procedures employed by the State to single out persons to suffer the penalty of death. Those opinions hold further that, so viewed, the Clause invalidates the mandatory infliction of the death penalty but not its infliction under sentencing procedures that Mr. Justice Stewart, Mr. Justice Powell, and Mr. Justice Stevens conclude adequately safeguard against the risk that the death penalty was imposed in an arbitrary and capricious manner.

In Furman v. Georgia (concurring opinion), I read "evolving standards of decency" as requiring focus upon the essence of the death penalty itself and not primarily or solely upon the procedures under which the determination to inflict the penalty upon a particular person was made. . . . That continues to be my view. For the Clause forbidding cruel and unusual punishments under our constitutional system of government embodies in unique degree moral principles restraining the punishments that our civilized society may impose on those persons who transgress its laws. Thus, I too say: "For myself, I do not hesitate to assert the proposition that the only way the law has progressed from the days of the rack, the screw and the wheel is the development of moral concepts, or, as stated by the Supreme Court . . . the application of 'evolving standards of decency'. . . ."

This Court inescapably has the duty, as the ultimate arbiter of the meaning of our Constitution, to say whether, when individuals condemned to death stand before our Bar, "moral concepts" require us to hold that the law has progressed to the point where we should declare that the punishment of death, like punishments on the rack, the screw, and the wheel, is no longer morally tolerable in our civilized society. My opinion in Furman v. Georgia concluded that our civilization and the law had progressed to this point and that therefore the punishment of death, for whatever crime and under all circumstances, is "cruel and unusual" in violation of the Eighth and Fourteenth Amendments of the Constitution. I shall not again canvass the reasons that led to that conclusion. I emphasize only that foremost among the "moral concepts" recognized in our cases and inherent in the Clause is the primary moral principle that the State, even as it punishes, must treat its citizens in a manner consistent with their intrinsic worth as human beings—a punishment must not be so severe as to be degrading to human dignity. . . .

* * *

The fatal constitutional infirmity in the punishment of death is that it treats "members of the human race as nonhumans, as objects to be toyed with and discarded. [It is] thus inconsistent with the fundamental premise of the Clause that even the vilest criminal remains a human being possessed of common human dignity." As such it is a penalty that "subjects the individual to a fate forbidden by the principle of civilized treatment guaranteed by the [Clause]." I therefore would hold, on that ground alone, that death is today a cruel and unusual punishment prohibited by the Clause. "Justice of this kind is obviously no less shocking than the crime itself, and the new 'official' murder, far from offering redress for the offense committed against society, adds instead a second defilement to the first." * * *

■ MR. JUSTICE MARSHALL, dissenting.

In Furman v. Georgia (concurring opinion), I set forth at some length my views on the basic issue presented to the Court in these cases. The death penalty, I concluded, is a cruel and unusual punishment prohibited by the Eighth and Fourteenth Amendments. That continues to be my view.

I have no intention of retracing the "long and tedious journey," that led to my conclusion in *Furman*. My sole purposes here are to consider the suggestion that my conclusion in *Furman* has been undercut by developments since then. . . .

Since the decision in *Furman*, the legislatures of 35 States have enacted new statutes authorizing the imposition of the death sentence for certain crimes, and Congress has enacted a law providing the death penalty for air piracy resulting in death. I would be less than candid if I did not acknowledge that these developments have a significant bearing on a realistic assessment of the moral acceptability of the death penalty to the American people. But if the constitutionality of the death penalty turns, as I have urged, on the opinion of an *informed* citizenry, then even the enactment of new death statutes cannot be viewed as conclusive. In *Furman*, I observed that the American people are largely unaware of the information critical to a judgment on the morality of the death penalty, and concluded that if they were better informed they would consider it shocking, unjust, and unacceptable. A recent study, conducted after the enactment of the post-*Furman* statutes, has confirmed that the American people know little about the death penalty, and that the opinions of an informed public would differ significantly from those of a public unaware of the consequences and effects of the death penalty.

* * *

The contentions [presented in the majority opinion]—that society's expression of moral outrage through the imposition of the death penalty pre-empts the citizenry from taking the law into its own hands and reinforces moral values—are not retributive in the purest sense. They are essentially utilitarian in that they portray the death penalty as valuable because of its beneficial results. These justifications for the death penalty are inadequate because the penalty is, quite clearly I think, not necessary to the accomplishment of those results.

There remains for consideration, however, what might be termed the purely retributive justification for the death penalty—that the death penalty is appropriate, not because of its beneficial effect on society, but because the taking of the murderer's life is itself morally good. Some of the language of the opinion of my Brothers Stewart, Powell, and Stevens . . . appears positively to embrace this notion of retribution for its own sake as a justification for capital punishment. They state:

> "[T]he decision that capital punishment may be the appropriate sanction in extreme cases is an expression of the community's belief that certain crimes are themselves so grievous an affront to humanity that the only adequate response may be the penalty of death."

* * *

Of course, it may be that these statements are intended as no more than observations as to the popular demands that it is thought must be responded to in order to prevent anarchy. But the implication of the statements appears to me to be quite different—namely, that society's judgment that the murderer "deserves" death must be respected not simply because the preservation of order requires it, but because it is appropriate that society make the judgment and carry it out. It is this latter notion, in particular, that I consider to be fundamentally at odds with the Eighth Amendment. The mere fact that the community demands the murderer's life in return for the evil he has done cannot sustain the death penalty, for as Justices Stewart, Powell, and Stevens remind us, "the Eighth Amendment demands more than that a challenged punishment be acceptable to contemporary society." To be sustained under the Eighth Amendment, the death penalty must "compor[t] with the basic concept of human dignity at the core of the Amendment," ibid.; the objective in imposing it must be "[consistent] with our respect for the dignity of [other] men." Under these standards, the taking of life "because the wrongdoer deserves it" surely must fall, for such a punishment has as its very basis the total denial of the wrongdoer's dignity and worth.

The death penalty, unnecessary to promote the goal of deterrence or to further any legitimate notion of retribution, is an excessive penalty forbidden by the Eighth and Fourteenth Amendments. I respectfully dissent from the Court's judgment upholding the sentences of death imposed upon the petitioners in these cases.

NOTES

1. *Gregg* was one of a series of cases handed down the same day. In Proffitt v. Florida, 428 U.S. 242, 96 S.Ct. 2960, 49 L.Ed.2d 913 (1976), the Court sustained imposition of the death penalty under a Florida capital crimes scheme similar to Georgia's except that the jury role on sentencing is advisory. Justice Powell, writing the Court's plurality opinion, distinguished the two schemes thusly:

> On their face these procedures, like those used in Georgia appear to meet the constitutional deficiencies identified in *Furman*. The sentencing authority in Florida, the trial judge, is directed to weigh eight aggravating factors against seven mitigating factors to determine whether the death penalty shall be imposed. This determination requires the trial judge to focus on the circumstances of the crime and the character of the individual defendant. He must, *inter alia*, consider whether the defendant has a prior criminal record, whether the defendant acted under duress or under the influence of extreme mental or emotional disturbance, whether the defendant's role in the crime was that of a minor accomplice, and whether the defendant's youth argues in favor of a more lenient sentence than might otherwise be imposed. The trial judge must also determine whether the crime was committed in the course of one of several enumerated felonies, whether it was committed for pecuniary gain, whether it was committed to assist in an escape from custody or to prevent a lawful arrest, and whether the crime was especially heinous, atrocious, or cruel. To answer these questions, which are not unlike those considered by a Georgia sentencing jury, . . . the sentencing judge must focus on the individual circumstances of each homicide and each defendant.
>
> The basic difference between the Florida system and the Georgia system is that in Florida the sentence is determined by the trial judge rather than by the jury. This Court has pointed out that jury sentencing in a capital case can perform an important societal

function, Witherspoon v. Illinois, 391 U.S. 510, 519 n. 15, 88 S.Ct. 1770, 1775, but it has never suggested that jury sentencing is constitutionally required. And it would appear that judicial sentencing should lead, if anything, to even greater consistency in the imposition at the trial court level of capital punishment, since a trial judge is more experienced in sentencing than a jury, and therefore is better able to impose sentences similar to those imposed in analogous cases.

The Florida capital-sentencing procedures thus seek to assure that the death penalty will not be imposed in an arbitrary or capricious manner. Moreover, to the extent that any risk to the contrary exists, it is minimized by Florida's appellate review system, under which the evidence of the aggravating and mitigating circumstances is reviewed and reweighed by the Supreme Court of Florida "to determine independently whether the imposition of the ultimate penalty is warranted." Songer v. State, 322 So.2d 481, 484 (1975). . . . The Supreme Court of Florida, like that of Georgia, has not hesitated to vacate a death sentence when it has determined that the sentence should not have been imposed. Indeed, it has vacated eight of the 21 death sentences that it has reviewed to date.

Under Florida's capital-sentencing procedures, in sum, trial judges are given specific and detailed guidance to assist them in deciding whether to impose a death penalty or imprisonment for life. Moreover, their decisions are reviewed to ensure that they are consistent with other sentences imposed in similar circumstances. Thus, in Florida, as in Georgia, it is no longer true that there is "no meaningful basis for distinguishing the few cases in which [the death penalty] is imposed from the many cases where it is not." On its face the Florida system thus satisfies the constitutional deficiencies identified in *Furman*.

The Court also sustained the Texas death penalty statute procedures in Jurek v. Texas, 428 U.S. 262, 96 S.Ct. 2950, 49 L.Ed.2d 929 (1976), finding, in part:

While Texas has not adopted a list of statutory aggravating circumstances the existence of which can justify the imposition of the death penalty as have Georgia and Florida, its action in narrowing the categories of murders for which a death sentence may never be imposed serves much the same purpose. In fact, each of the five classes of murders made capital by the Texas statute is encompassed in Georgia and Florida by one or more of their statutory aggravating circumstances. For example, the Texas statute requires the jury at the guilt determining stage to consider whether the crime was committed in the course of a particular felony, whether it was committed for hire, or whether the defendant was an inmate of a penal institution at the time of its commission. Thus, in essence, the Texas statute requires that the jury find the existence of a statutory aggravating circumstance before the death penalty may be imposed. So far as consideration of aggravating circumstances is concerned, therefore, the principal difference between Texas and the other two States is that the death penalty is an available sentencing option—even potentially—for a smaller class of murders in Texas. Otherwise the statutes are similar. Each requires the sentencing authority to focus on the particularized nature of the crime.

* * *

We conclude that Texas' capital-sentencing procedures, like those of Georgia and Florida, do not violate the Eighth and Fourteenth Amendments. By narrowing its definition of capital murder, Texas has essentially said that there must be at least one statutory aggravating circumstance in a first-degree murder case before a death sentence may even be considered. By authorizing the defense to bring before the jury at the separate sentencing hearing whatever mitigating circumstances relating to the individual defendant can be adduced, Texas has ensured that the sentencing jury will have adequate guidance to enable it to perform its sentencing function. By providing prompt judicial review of the jury's decision in a court with statewide jurisdiction, Texas has provided a means to promote the evenhanded, rational, and consistent imposition of death sentences under law. Because this system serves to assure that sentences of death will not be "wantonly" or "freakishly" imposed, it does not violate the Constitution.

2. In Woodson v. North Carolina, 428 U.S. 280, 96 S.Ct. 2978, 49 L.Ed.2d 944 (1976), however, the Court struck down the North Carolina capital punishment scheme. The State had previously provided that the jury could, in its unbridled discretion, impose the death penalty for certain crimes, but subsequent to *Furman* had changed its statute to make the death penalty mandatory in first-degree murder cases. Petitioners' convictions under this new statutory scheme were reversed. The court said, in part:

Although it seems beyond dispute that, at the time of the *Furman* decision in 1972, mandatory death penalty statutes had been renounced by American juries and legislatures, there remains the question whether the mandatory statutes adopted by North Carolina and a number of other States following *Furman* evince a sudden reversal of societal values regarding the imposition of capital punishment. In view of the persistent and unswerving legislative rejection of mandatory death penalty statutes beginning in 1838 and continuing for more than 130 years until *Furman*, it seems evident that the post-*Furman* enactments reflect attempts by the States to retain the death penalty in a form consistent with the Constitution, rather than a renewed societal acceptance of mandatory death sentencing.

* * *

[O]ne of the most significant developments in our society's treatment of capital punishment has been the rejection of the common-law practice of inexorably imposing a death sentence upon every person convicted of a specified offense. North Carolina's mandatory death penalty statute for first-degree murder departs markedly from contemporary standards respecting the imposition of the punishment of death and thus cannot be applied consistently with the Eighth and Fourteenth Amendments' requirement that the State's power to punish "be exercised within the limits of civilized standards."

A separate deficiency of North Carolina's mandatory death sentence statute is its failure to provide a constitutionally tolerable response to *Furman's* rejection of unbridled jury discretion in the imposition of capital sentences. Central to the limited holding in *Furman* was the conviction that the vesting of standardless sentencing power in the jury violated the Eighth and Fourteenth Amendments. It is argued that North Carolina has remedied the inadequacies of the death penalty statutes held unconstitutional in *Furman* by withdrawing all sentencing discretion from juries in capital cases. But when one considers the long and consistent American experience with the death penalty in first-degree murder cases, it becomes evident that mandatory statutes enacted in response to *Furman* have simply papered over the problem of unguided and unchecked jury discretion.

* * *

A third constitutional shortcoming of the North Carolina statute is its failure to allow the particularized consideration of relevant aspects of the character and record of each convicted defendant before the imposition upon him of a sentence of death. . . . A process that accords no significance to relevant facets of the character and record of the individual offender or the circumstances of the particular offense excludes from consideration in fixing the ultimate punishment of death the possibility of compassionate or mitigating factors stemming from the diverse frailties of humankind. It treats all persons convicted of a designated offense not as uniquely individual human beings, but as members of a faceless, undifferentiated mass to be subjected to the blind infliction of the penalty of death.

Louisiana's death penalty statute, enacted in the wake of *Furman*, was also invalidated by the Court in Roberts v. Louisiana, 428 U.S. 325, 96 S.Ct. 3001, 49 L.Ed.2d 974 (1976). The Louisiana statute required imposition of the death penalty for five different types of homicide, if the jury should find that the defendant specifically intended to kill or do great bodily harm. The *Roberts* homicide was a felony-murder (killing during the commission of an armed robbery). Despite the narrower definition of murder than under the North Carolina scheme reviewed in *Woodson*, the plurality opinion identified these reasons for the statute's invalidity:

The constitutional vice of mandatory death sentence statutes—lack of focus on the circumstances of the particular offense and the character and propensities of the offender—is not resolved by Louisiana's limitation of first-degree murder to various categories of killings. The diversity of circumstances presented in cases falling within the single category of killings during the commission of a specified felony, as well as the variety of possible offenders involved in such crimes, underscores the rigidity of Louisiana's enactment and its similarity to the North Carolina statute. Even the other more narrowly drawn categories of first-degree murder in the Louisiana law afford no meaningful opportunity for consideration of mitigating factors presented by the circumstances of the particular crime or by the attributes of the individual offender.

3. In Coker v. Georgia, 433 U.S. 584, 97 S.Ct. 2861, 53 L.Ed.2d 982 (1977), the Supreme Court struck down a death sentence for the crime of rape as grossly disproportionate and excessive punishment forbidden by the Eighth Amendment. The rape and armed robbery had been committed by an escaped felon and the death sentence had been imposed because of that aggravated factor. Justice White, authoring the plurality opinion, stressed that the Eighth Amendment bars not only those punishments that are barbaric, but also those that are excessive in relation to the crime committed. A punishment is excessive and therefore unconstitutional if it "(1) makes no measurable contribution to acceptable goals of punishment and hence is nothing more than a purposeless and needless imposition of pain and suffering; or (2) is grossly out of proportion to the severity of the crime."

While rape is deserving of serious punishment, the Court's opinion suggested that the imposition of the death sentence for the rape, even though committed by a person with prior felony convictions, was excessive where, under Georgia law, a deliberate killer cannot be sentenced to death absent aggravating circumstances. It seemed incongruous to the Court that a rapist who does not take life should be punished more severely than a deliberate killer.

4. See also Lockett v. Ohio, 438 U.S. 586, 98 S.Ct. 2954, 57 L.Ed.2d 973 (1978), where a plurality of the Court held state law provisions unconstitutional because the provisions did not permit a defendant to argue that he was only a minor participant in a homicide and that he had no prior criminal record. The Court said that "the Eighth and Fourteenth Amendments require that the sentencer, in all but the rarest of capital cases, not be precluded from considering *as a mitigating factor*, any aspect of a defendant's character or record and any of the circumstances of the offense that the defendant proffers as a basis for a sentence less than death." See also, in this regard, Bell v. Ohio, 438 U.S. 637, 98 S.Ct. 2977, 57 L.Ed.2d 1010 (1978).

5. The Supreme Court denies certiorari in a great number of petitions from state convictions imposing capital punishment. In Coleman v. Balkcom, 451 U.S. 949, 101 S.Ct. 2994, 68 L.Ed.2d 334 (1981), Justice Rehnquist dissented from the denial of certiorari. He said the Court should grant review in a greater number of death row cases, not to free more inmates from the imposition of the death penalty, but to insulate death sentences from further attack. He said that while hundreds of defendants have been condemned to death since the *Gregg v. Georgia* decision in 1976, only one defendant who did not want to die (John Spenkelink) was actually executed. Justice Rehnquist characterized this as "a mockery of our criminal justice system" in which the Supreme Court participates by sending a "signal to the lower state and federal courts that the actual imposition of the death sentence is to be avoided at all costs." Such a state of affairs frustrates the purposes of retribution and deterrence, he said. Justice Stevens concurred in the majority's denial of certiorari and criticized Justice Rehnquist's proposal as one that might result in an improper allocation of the Supreme Court's limited resources because the Court could easily spend half its time with capital cases if it were to grant the many certiorari petitions of death row inmates. But even if the Court were to take that step, Justice Stevens said that would still not achieve Justice Rehnquist's purpose "(b)ecause this Court is not equipped to process all of these cases as expeditiously as the several district courts." It would therefore be "most unlikely that this innovative proposal would dramatically accelerate the execution of the persons on death row."

6. In Godfrey v. Georgia, 446 U.S. 420, 100 S.Ct. 1759, 64 L.Ed.2d 398 (1980), the Supreme Court dealt again with the Georgia death statute under which a person convicted of murder may be sentenced to death if it is found beyond a reasonable doubt that the offense was "outrageously or wantonly vile, horrible or inhuman in that it involved torture, depravity of mind, or an aggravated battery to the victim." This provision was held to be unconstitutionally vague as applied to a murder that did not involve torture nor an aggravated battery and in which the defendant's mental state was not shown to be more depraved than that of any person guilty of murder.

7. In Mills v. Maryland, 486 U.S. 367, 108 S.Ct. 1860, 100 L.Ed.2d 384 (1988), the Court held, in a 5–4 decision, that Maryland's statutory scheme was unconstitutional in requiring that the jurors unanimously find specific mitigating circumstances present in the case, before an individual juror could consider that circumstance in deciding whether to impose the death penalty. And in McKoy v. North Carolina, 494 U.S. 433, 110 S.Ct. 1227, 108 L.Ed.2d 369 (1990), it was held that individual jurors cannot be limited to considering those mitigating factors which the jury unanimously determines to exist.

McCleskey v. Kemp

Supreme Court of the United States, 1987.
481 U.S. 279, 107 S.Ct. 1756, 95 L.Ed.2d 262.

■ JUSTICE POWELL delivered the opinion of the Court.

This case presents the question whether a complex statistical study that indicates a risk that racial considerations enter into capital sentencing determinations proves that petitioner McCleskey's capital sentence is unconstitutional under the Eighth or Fourteenth Amendment.

I

McCleskey, a black man, was convicted of two counts of armed robbery and one count of murder in the Superior Court of Fulton County, Georgia, on October 12, 1978. McCleskey's convictions arose out of the robbery of a furniture store and the killing of a white police officer during the course of the robbery. The evidence at trial indicated that McCleskey and three accomplices planned and carried out the robbery. All four were armed. McCleskey entered the front of the store while the other three entered the rear. McCleskey secured the front of the store by rounding up the customers and forcing them to lie face down on the floor. The other three rounded up the employees in the rear and tied them up with tape. The manager was forced at gunpoint to turn over the store receipts, his watch, and $6. During the course of the robbery, a police officer, answering a silent alarm, entered the store through the front door. As he was walking down the center aisle of the store, two shots were fired. Both struck the officer. One hit him in the face and killed him.

Several weeks later, McCleskey was arrested in connection with an unrelated offense. He confessed that he had participated in the furniture store robbery, but denied that he had shot the police officer. At trial, the State introduced evidence that at least one of the bullets that struck the officer was fired from a .38 caliber Rossi revolver. This description matched the description of the gun that McCleskey had carried during the robbery. The State also introduced the testimony of two witnesses who had heard McCleskey admit to the shooting.

The jury convicted McCleskey of murder. At the penalty hearing, the jury heard arguments as to the appropriate sentence. Under Georgia law, the jury could not consider imposing the death penalty unless it found beyond a reasonable doubt that the murder was accompanied by one of the statutory aggravating circumstances. The jury in this case found two aggravating circumstances to exist beyond a reasonable doubt: the murder was committed during the course of an armed robbery, and the murder was committed upon a peace officer engaged in the performance of his duties, . . . The jury recommended that he be sentenced to death on the murder charge and to consecutive life sentences on the armed robbery charges. . . .

On appeal, the Supreme Court of Georgia affirmed the convictions and the sentences. . . .

McCleskey next filed a petition for a writ of habeas corpus in the Federal District Court for the Northern District of Georgia. His petition raised 18 claims, one of which was that the Georgia capital sentencing process is administered in a racially discriminatory manner in violation of the Eighth and Fourteenth Amendments to the United States

Constitution. In support of his claim, McCleskey proffered a statistical study performed by Professors David C. Baldus, Charles Pulaski, and George Woodworth, and (the Baldus study) that purports to show a disparity in the imposition of the death sentence in Georgia based on the race of the murder victim and, to a lesser extent, the race of the defendant. . . .

Baldus subjected his data to an extensive analysis, taking account of 230 variables that could have explained the disparities on nonracial grounds. One of his models concludes that, even after taking account of 39 nonracial variables, defendants charged with killing white victims were 4.3 times as likely to receive a death sentence as defendants charged with killing blacks. According to this model, black defendants were 1.1 times as likely to receive a death sentence as other defendants. Thus, the Baldus study indicates that black defendants, such as McCleskey, who kill white victims have the greatest likelihood of receiving the death penalty.

The District Court . . . found that the methodology of the Baldus study was flawed in several respects. Because of these defects, the court held that the Baldus study "fail[ed] to contribute anything of value" to McCleskey's claim. Accordingly, the court denied the petition insofar as it was based upon the Baldus study.

The Court of Appeals for the Eleventh Circuit, sitting en banc, carefully reviewed the District Court's decision on McCleskey's claim. It assumed the validity of the study itself and addressed the merits of McCleskey's Eighth and Fourteenth Amendment claims. That is, the court assumed that the study "showed that systematic and substantial disparities existed in the penalties imposed upon homicide defendants in Georgia based on race of the homicide victim, that the disparities existed at a less substantial rate in death sentencing based on race of defendants, and that the factors of race of the victim and defendant were at work in Fulton County." Even assuming the study's validity, the Court of Appeals found the statistics "insufficient to demonstrate discriminatory intent or unconstitutional discrimination in the Fourteenth Amendment context, [and] insufficient to show irrationality, arbitrariness and capriciousness under any kind of Eighth Amendment analysis." The court noted:

> The very exercise of discretion means that persons exercising discretion may reach different results from exact duplicates. Assuming each result is within the range of discretion, all are correct in the eyes of the law. It would not make sense for the system to require the exercise of discretion in order to be facially constitutional, and at the same time hold a system unconstitutional in application where that discretion achieved different results for what appear to be exact duplicates, absent the state showing the reasons for the difference. . . .

The Baldus approach would take the cases with different results on what are contended to be duplicate facts, where the differences could not be otherwise explained, and conclude that the different result was based on race alone. . . . This approach ignores the realities. . . . There are, in fact, no exact duplicates in capital crimes and capital defendants. The type of research submitted here tends to show which of the directed factors were effective, but is of restricted use in showing what undirected factors control the exercise of constitutionally required discretion.

The court concluded:

Viewed broadly, it would seem that the statistical evidence presented here, assuming its validity, confirms rather than condemns the system. . . . The marginal disparity based on the race of the victim tends to support the state's contention that the system is working far differently from the one which *Furman* [v. Georgia (1972)] condemned. In pre-*Furman* days, there was no rhyme or reason as to who got the death penalty and who did not. But now, in the vast majority of cases, the reasons for a difference are well documented. That they are not so clear in a small percentage of the cases is no reason to declare the entire system unconstitutional.

The Court of Appeals affirmed the denial by the District Court of McCleskey's petition for a writ of habeas corpus insofar as the petition was based upon the Baldus study, with three judges dissenting as to McCleskey's claims based on the Baldus study. We granted certiorari, and now affirm.

II

McCleskey's first claim is that the Georgia capital punishment statute violates the Equal Protection Clause of the Fourteenth Amendment.[7] He argues that race has infected the administration of Georgia's statute in two ways: persons who murder whites are more likely to be sentenced to death than persons who murder blacks, and black murderers are more likely to be sentenced to death than white murderers. As a black defendant who killed a white victim, McCleskey claims that the Baldus study demonstrates that he was discriminated against because of his race and because of the race of his victim. . . . We agree with the Court of Appeals, and every other court that has considered such a challenge, that this claim must fail.

A

Our analysis begins with the basic principle that a defendant who alleges an equal protection violation has the burden of proving "the

---

[7] Although the District Court rejected the findings of the Baldus study as flawed, the Court of Appeals assumed that the study is valid and reached the constitutional issues. . . .

existence of purposeful discrimination." A corollary to this principle is that a criminal defendant must prove that the purposeful discrimination "had a discriminatory effect" on him. Thus, to prevail under the Equal Protection Clause, McCleskey must prove that the decisionmakers in his case acted with discriminatory purpose. He offers no evidence specific to his own case that would support an inference that racial considerations played a part in his sentence. Instead, he relies solely on the Baldus study. McCleskey argues that the Baldus study compels an inference that his sentence rests on purposeful discrimination. McCleskey's claim that these statistics are sufficient proof of discrimination, without regard to the facts of a particular case, would extend to all capital cases in Georgia, at least where the victim was white and the defendant black.

The Court has accepted statistics as proof of intent to discriminate in certain limited contexts. First, this Court has accepted statistical disparities as proof of an equal protection violation in the selection of the jury venire in a particular district. . . . Second, this Court has accepted statistics in the form of multiple-regression analysis to prove statutory violations under Title VII of the Civil Rights Act of 1964.

But the nature of the capital sentencing decision, and the relationship of the statistics to that decision, are fundamentally different from the corresponding elements in the venire-selection or Title VII cases. . . . Each jury is unique in its composition, and the Constitution requires that its decision rest on consideration of innumerable factors that vary according to the characteristics of the individual defendant and the facts of the particular capital offense. Thus, the application of an inference drawn from the general statistics to a specific decision in a trial and sentencing simply is not comparable to the application of an inference drawn from general statistics to a specific venire-selection or Title VII case. In those cases, the statistics relate to fewer entities, and fewer variables are relevant to the challenged decisions.

Another important difference between the cases in which we have accepted statistics as proof of discriminatory intent and this case is that, in the venire-selection and Title VII contexts, the decision maker has an opportunity to explain the statistical disparity. Here, the State has no practical opportunity to rebut the Baldus study. "[C]ontrolling considerations of . . . public policy," McDonald v. Pless (1915), dictate that jurors "cannot be called to testify to the motives and influences that led to their verdict." Chicago, B. & Q.R. Co. v. Babcock (1907). Similarly, the policy considerations behind a prosecutor's traditionally "wide discretion" suggest the impropriety of our requiring prosecutors to defend their decisions to seek death penalties, "often years after they were made." See Imbler v. Pachtman (1976). Moreover, absent far stronger proof, it is unnecessary to seek such a rebuttal, because a legitimate and unchallenged explanation for the decision is apparent from the record:

McCleskey committed an act for which the United States Constitution and Georgia laws permit imposition of the death penalty.

Finally, [b]ecause discretion is essential to the criminal justice process, we would demand exceptionally clear proof before we would infer that the discretion has been abused. The unique nature of the decisions at issue in this case also counsels against adopting such an inference from the disparities indicated by the Baldus study. Accordingly, we hold that the Baldus study is clearly insufficient to support an inference that any of the decision makers in McCleskey's case acted with discriminatory purpose.

B

McCleskey also suggests that the Baldus study proves that the State as a whole has acted with a discriminatory purpose. He appears to argue that the State has violated the Equal Protection Clause by adopting the capital punishment statute and allowing it to remain in force despite its allegedly discriminatory application. . . . For this claim to prevail, McCleskey would have to prove that the Georgia Legislature enacted or maintained the death penalty statute because of an anticipated racially discriminatory effect. In Gregg v. Georgia, supra, this Court found that the Georgia capital sentencing system could operate in a fair and neutral manner. There was no evidence then, and there is none now, that the Georgia Legislature enacted the capital punishment statute to further a racially discriminatory purpose.[20]

Nor has McCleskey demonstrated that the legislature maintains the capital punishment statute because of the racially disproportionate impact suggested by the Baldus study. As legislatures necessarily have wide discretion in the choice of criminal laws and penalties, and as there were legitimate reasons for the Georgia Legislature to adopt and maintain capital punishment, we will not infer a discriminatory purpose on the part of the State of Georgia. Accordingly, we reject McCleskey's equal protection claims.

* * *

IV

A

In light of our precedents under the Eighth Amendment, McCleskey cannot argue successfully that his sentence is "disproportionate to the crime in the traditional sense." He does not deny that he committed a murder in the course of a planned robbery, a crime for which this Court

---

[20] McCleskey relies on "historical evidence" to support his claim of purposeful discrimination by the State. This evidence focuses on Georgia laws in force during and just after the Civil War. Of course, the historical background of the decision is one evidentiary source for proof of intentional discrimination. But unless historical evidence is reasonably contemporaneous with the challenged decision, it has little probative value. Although the history of racial discrimination in this country is undeniable, we cannot accept official actions taken long ago as evidence of current intent.

has determined that the death penalty constitutionally may be imposed. His disproportionality claim "is of a different sort." McCleskey argues that the sentence in his case is disproportionate to the sentences in other murder cases.

On the one hand, he cannot base a constitutional claim on an argument that his case differs from other cases in which defendants *did* receive the death penalty. On automatic appeal, the Georgia Supreme Court found that McCleskey's death sentence was not disproportionate to other death sentences imposed in the State. The court supported this conclusion with an appendix containing citations to 13 cases involving generally similar murders. Moreover, where the statutory procedures adequately channel the sentencer's discretion, such proportionality review is not constitutionally required.

On the other hand, absent a showing that the Georgia capital punishment system operates in an arbitrary and capricious manner, McCleskey cannot prove a constitutional violation by demonstrating that other defendants who may be similarly situated did not receive the death penalty. . . .

Because McCleskey's sentence was imposed under Georgia sentencing procedures that focus discretion "on the particularized nature of the crime and the particularized characteristics of the individual defendant," we lawfully may presume that McCleskey's death sentence was not "wantonly and freakishly" imposed, and thus that the sentence is not disproportionate within any recognized meaning under the Eighth Amendment.

B

. . . [McCleskey] . . . further contends that the Georgia capital punishment system is arbitrary and capricious in *application*, and therefore his sentence is excessive, because racial considerations may influence capital sentencing decisions in Georgia. We now address this claim.

To evaluate McCleskey's challenge, we must examine exactly what the Baldus study may show. Even Professor Baldus does not content that his statistics *prove* that race enters into any capital sentencing decisions or that race was a factor in McCleskey's particular case. Statistics at most may show only a likelihood that a particular factor entered into some decisions. There is, of course, some risk of racial prejudice influencing a jury's decision in a criminal case. There are similar risks that other kinds of prejudice will influence other criminal trials. The question is at what point that risk becomes constitutionally unacceptable. McCleskey asks us to accept the likelihood allegedly shown by the Baldus study as the constitutional measure of an unacceptable risk of racial prejudice influencing capital sentencing decisions. This we decline to do.

* * *

Individual jurors bring to their deliberations qualities of human nature and varieties of human experience, the range of which is unknown and perhaps unknowable. The capital sentencing decision requires the individual jurors to focus their collective judgment on the unique characteristics of a particular criminal defendant. It is not surprising that such collective judgments often are difficult to explain. But the inherent lack of predictability of jury decisions does not justify their condemnation. On the contrary, it is the jury's function to make the difficult and uniquely human judgments that defy codification and that "buil[d] discretion, equity, and flexibility into a legal system." H. KALVEN & H. ZEISEL, THE AMERICAN JURY 498 (1966).

McCleskey's argument that the Constitution condemns the discretion allowed decision makers in the Georgia capital sentencing system is antithetical to the fundamental role of discretion in our criminal justice system. . . .

C

. . . Despite these imperfections, our consistent rule has been that constitutional guarantees are met when the mode for determining guilt or punishment itself has been surrounded with safeguards to make it as fair as possible. Where the discretion that is fundamental to our criminal process is involved, we decline to assume that what is unexplained is invidious. In light of the safeguards designed to minimize racial bias in the process, the fundamental value of jury trial in our criminal justice system, and the benefits that discretion provides to criminal defendants, we hold that the Baldus study does not demonstrate a constitutionally significant risk of racial bias affecting the Georgia capital sentencing process.

V

Two additional concerns inform our decision in this case. First, McCleskey's claim, taken to its logical conclusion, throws into serious question the principles that underlie our entire criminal justice system. The Eighth Amendment is not limited in application to capital punishment, but applies to all penalties. Thus, if we accepted McCleskey's claim that racial bias has impermissibly tainted the capital sentencing decision, we could soon be faced with similar claims as to other types of penalty.[38] Moreover, the claim that his sentence rests on the irrelevant factor of race easily could be extended to apply to claims based on unexplained discrepancies that correlate to membership in other minority groups, and even to gender. . . .

Second, McCleskey's arguments are best presented to the legislative bodies. It is not the responsibility—or indeed even the right—of this

---

[38] Studies already exist that allegedly demonstrate a racial disparity in the length of prison sentences. See, e.g., Spohn, Gruhl, & Welch, *The Effect of Race on Sentencing: A Reexamination of an Unsettled Question*, 16 LAW & SOC. REV. 71 (1981–1982); Unnever, Frazier, & Henretta, *Race Differences in Criminal Sentencing*, 21 SOCIOLOGICAL Q. 197 (1980).

Court to determine the appropriate punishment for particular crimes. It is the legislatures, the elected representatives of he people, that are constituted to respond to the will and consequently the moral values of the people. Legislatures also are better qualified to weigh and "evaluate the results of statistical studies in terms of their own local conditions and with a flexibility of approach that is not available to the courts." . . .

VI

Accordingly, we affirm the judgment of the Court of Appeals for the Eleventh Circuit.

It is so ordered.

■ JUSTICE BRENNAN, with whom JUSTICE MARSHALL joins, and with whom JUSTICE BLACKMUN and JUSTICE STEVENS join in all but Part I, dissenting.

I

Adhering to my view that the death penalty is in all circumstances cruel and unusual punishment forbidden by the Eighth and Fourteenth Amendments, I would vacate the decision below insofar as it left undisturbed the death sentence imposed in this case. The Court observes that "[t]he Gregg-type statute imposes unprecedented safeguards in the special context of capital punishment," which "ensure a degree of care in the imposition of the death penalty that can be described only as unique." Notwithstanding these efforts, murder defendants in Georgia with white victims are more than four times as likely to receive the death sentence as are defendants with black victims. Nothing could convey more powerfully the intractable reality of the death penalty: that the effort to eliminate arbitrariness in the infliction of that ultimate sanction is so plainly doomed to failure that it—and the death penalty—must be abandoned altogether.

Even if I did not hold this position, however, I would reverse the Court of Appeals, for petitioner McCleskey has clearly demonstrated that his death sentence was imposed in violation of the Eighth and Fourteenth Amendments. While I join Parts I through IV-A of JUSTICE BLACKMUN'S dissenting opinion discussing petitioner's Fourteenth Amendment claim, I write separately to emphasize how conclusively McCleskey has also demonstrated precisely the type of risk of irrationality in sentencing that we have consistently condemned in our Eighth Amendment jurisprudence.

II

At some point in this case, Warren McCleskey doubtless asked his lawyer whether a jury was likely to sentence him to die. A candid reply to this question would have been disturbing. First, counsel would have to tell McCleskey that few of the details of the crime or of McCleskey's past criminal conduct were more important than the fact that his victim was white. Furthermore, counsel would feel bound to tell McCleskey that defendants charged with killing white victims in Georgia are 4.3 times as likely to be sentenced to death as defendants charged with killing blacks. Petitioner's Exhibit DB 82. In addition, frankness would compel the disclosure that it was more likely than not that the race of McCleskey's victim would determine whether he received a death sentence: 6 of every 11 defendants convicted of killing a white person would not have received the death penalty if their victims had been black, Supp. Exh. 51, while, among defendants with aggravating and mitigating factors comparable to McCleskey's, 20 of every 34 would not have been sentenced to die if their victims had been black. Finally, the assessment would not be complete without the information that cases involving black defendants and white victims are more likely to result in a death sentence than cases featuring any other racial combination of defendant and victim. The story could be told in a variety of ways, but McCleskey could not fail to grasp its essential narrative line: there was a significant chance that race would play a prominent role in determining if he lived or died.

The Court today holds that Warren McCleskey's sentence was constitutionally imposed. It finds no fault in a system in which lawyers must tell their clients that race casts a large shadow on the capital sentencing process. The Court arrives at this conclusion by stating that the Baldus study cannot "*prove* that race enters into any capital sentencing decisions or that race was a factor in McCleskey's particular case." Since, according to Professor Baldus, we cannot say "to a moral certainty" that race influenced a decision, we can identify only "a likelihood that a particular factor entered into some decisions," and "a discrepancy that appears to correlate with race." This "likelihood" and "discrepancy," holds the Court, is insufficient to establish a constitutional violation. The Court reaches this conclusion by placing four factors on the scales opposite McCleskey's evidence: the desire to encourage sentencing discretion, the existence of "statutory safeguards" in the Georgia scheme, the fear of encouraging widespread challenges to other sentencing decisions, and the limits of the judicial role. The Court's evaluation of the significance of petitioner's evidence is fundamentally at odds with our consistent concern for rationality in capital sentencing, and the considerations that the majority invokes to discount that evidence cannot justify ignoring its force.

* * *

■ JUSTICE BLACKMUN, with whom JUSTICE MARSHALL and JUSTICE STEVENS join, and with whom JUSTICE BRENNAN joins in all but Part IV-B, dissenting.

* * *

. . . McCleskey's case raises concerns that are central not only to the principles underlying the Eighth Amendment, but also to the principles underlying the Fourteenth Amendment. Analysis of his case in terms of the Fourteenth Amendment is consistent with this Court's recognition that racial discrimination is fundamentally at odds with our constitutional guarantee of equal protection. The protections afforded by the Fourteenth Amendment are not left at the courtroom door. Nor is equal protection denied to persons convicted of crimes. The court in the past has found that racial discrimination within the criminal justice system is particularly abhorrent: "Discrimination on the basis of race, odious in all aspects, is especially pernicious in the administration of justice." Rose v. Mitchell (1979). Disparate enforcement of criminal sanctions "destroys the appearance of justice and thereby casts doubt on the integrity of the judicial process." And only last Term JUSTICE POWELL, writing for the Court, noted: "Discrimination within the judicial system is most pernicious because it is 'a stimulant to that race prejudice which is an impediment to securing to [black citizens] that equal justice which the law aims to secure it all other.' " Batson v. Kentucky (1986), quoting Strauder v. West Virginia (1880).

Moreover, the legislative history of the Fourteenth Amendment reminds us that discriminatory enforcement of States' criminal laws was a matter of great concern for the drafters. In the introductory remarks to its Report to Congress, the Joint Committee on Reconstruction, which reported out the Joint Resolution proposing the Fourteenth Amendment, specifically noted: "This deep-seated prejudice against color . . . leads to acts of cruelty, oppression, and murder, which the local authorities are at no pains to prevent or punish." H.R. Joint Comm. Rep. No. 30, 39th Cong., 1st Sess., p. XVII (1866). Witnesses who testified before the Committee presented accounts of criminal acts of violence against black persons that were not prosecuted despite evidence as to the identity of the perpetrators.

The Court today seems to give a new meaning to our recognition that death is different. Rather than requiring "a correspondingly greater degree of scrutiny of the capital sentencing determination," California v. Ramos (1983), the Court relies on the very fact that this is a case involving capital punishment to apply a lesser standard of scrutiny under the Equal Protection Clause. The Court concludes that "legitimate" explanations outweigh McCleskey's claim that his death sentence reflected a constitutionally impermissible risk of racial discrimination. The Court explains that McCleskey's evidence is too weak to require rebuttal "because a legitimate and unchallenged explanation for the decision is apparent from the record: McCleskey committed an act for which the United States Constitution and Georgia laws permit imposition of the death penalty." The court states that it will not infer a discriminatory purpose on the part of the state legislature because "there were legitimate reasons for the Georgia Legislature to adopt and maintain capital punishment."

The Court's assertion that the fact of McCleskey's conviction undermines his constitutional claim is inconsistent with a long and unbroken line of this Court's case law. The Court on numerous occasions during the past century has recognized that an otherwise legitimate basis for a conviction does not outweigh an equal protection violation. In cases where racial discrimination in the administration of the criminal justice system is established, it has held that setting aside the conviction is the appropriate remedy. . . .

* * *

NOTES AND QUESTIONS

1. Exactly why does a majority of the Court in *McCleskey* choose to ignore the statistical results of the Baldus study? Because, as Justice Powell admits, if the Court has relied on statistics in other cases as proof of intent to discriminate, why not with respect to capital sentencing? How could a petitioner show that a state legislature enacted the statute to further a racially-discriminatory purpose or maintained the statute because of a racially-disproportionate impact? How could a petitioner establish that the death penalty in his particular case was racially motivated?

2. Does the majority have some lurking, underlying concern regarding the consequences of accepting McCleskey's claim? Is it well-founded?

3. How would you respond to Justice Brennan's point that McCleskey's lawyer would have to tell him that his chances of receiving the death penalty were 4.3 times greater because his victim was white and that he was more likely to receive a death sentence because he was black and his victim was white?

4. Are you troubled by the fact that blacks make up only fourteen percent of the population but comprise over sixty percent of the prison population? To what do you attribute this discrepancy? Would it surprise you to hear that in some metropolitan areas, over three-quarters of the black male population between the ages of eighteen and forty have had some contact with the criminal justice system?

Problem 4–3. Prior to being amended, a person had to possess 100 times more powder cocaine to receive a sentence equivalent to that for the possession of crack cocaine under the Federal Sentencing Guidelines. Do you think that this results in sentencing disparity between white and black defendants convicted of these drug crimes? If so, do you think it is justified? Would you change your mind if you were told that when the Federal Sentencing Commission first recommended to Congress that this disparity be abolished, Congress retained it in any event? The U.S. Sentencing Commission in May 2002 again made a recommendation to Congress on this disparity, but this time recommended a reduction in the disparity to a ratio of 20–1. In asking Congress for the change, the Commission pointed out that the "overwhelming majority" (eighty-five percent) of persons subjected to heightened penalties for crack offenses are black. Finally, in 2010, Congress passed bipartisan legislation changing the ratio to 18–1.

Atkins v. Virginia

Supreme Court of the United States, 2002.
536 U.S. 304, 122 S.Ct. 2242, 153 L.Ed.2d 335.

■ JUSTICE STEVENS delivered the opinion of the Court.

Those mentally retarded persons who meet the law's requirements for criminal responsibility should be tried and punished when they commit crimes. Because of their disabilities in areas of reasoning, judgment, and control of their impulses, however, they do not act with the level of moral culpability that characterizes the most serious adult criminal conduct. Moreover, their impairments can jeopardize the reliability and fairness of capital proceedings against mentally retarded defendants. Presumably for these reasons, in the 13 years since we decided *Penry* v. *Lynaugh*, 492 U.S. 302, 109 S.Ct. 2934, 106 L.Ed.2d 256 (1989), the American public, legislators, scholars, and judges have deliberated over the question whether the death penalty should ever be imposed on a mentally retarded criminal. The consensus reflected in those deliberations informs our answer to the question presented by this case: whether such executions are "cruel and unusual punishments" prohibited by the Eighth Amendment to the Federal Constitution.

I

Petitioner, Daryl Renard Atkins, was convicted of abduction, armed robbery, and capital murder, and sentenced to death. At approximately midnight on August 16, 1996, Atkins and William Jones, armed with a semiautomatic handgun, abducted Eric Nesbitt, robbed him of the money on his person, drove him to an automated teller machine in his pickup truck where cameras recorded their withdrawal of additional cash, then took him to an isolated location where he was shot eight times and killed.

Jones and Atkins both testified in the guilt phase of Atkins' trial. Each confirmed most of the details in the other's account of the incident, with the important exception that each stated that the other had actually shot and killed Nesbitt. Jones' testimony, which was both more coherent and credible than Atkins', was obviously credited by the jury and was sufficient to establish Atkins' guilt. At the penalty phase of the trial, the State introduced victim impact evidence and proved two aggravating circumstances: future dangerousness and "vileness of the offense." To prove future dangerousness, the State relied on Atkins' prior felony convictions as well as the testimony of four victims of earlier robberies and assaults. To prove the second aggravator, the prosecution relied upon the trial record, including pictures of the deceased's body and the autopsy report.

In the penalty phase, the defense relied on one witness, Dr. Evan Nelson, a forensic psychologist who had evaluated Atkins before trial and concluded that he was "mildly mentally retarded." His conclusion was based on interviews with people who knew Atkins, a review of school and court records, and the administration of a standard intelligence test which indicated that Atkins had a full scale IQ of 59.

The jury sentenced Atkins to death, but the Virginia Supreme Court ordered a second sentencing hearing because the trial court had used a misleading verdict form. At the resentencing, Dr. Nelson again testified. The State presented an expert rebuttal witness, Dr. Stanton Samenow, who expressed the opinion that Atkins was not mentally retarded, but rather was of "average intelligence, at least," and diagnosable as having antisocial personality disorder. The jury again sentenced Atkins to death.

The Supreme Court of Virginia affirmed the imposition of the death penalty. Atkins did not argue before the Virginia Supreme Court that his sentence was disproportionate to penalties imposed for similar crimes in Virginia, but he did contend "that he is mentally retarded and thus cannot be sentenced to death." The majority of the state court rejected this contention, relying on our holding in *Penry*. The court was "not willing to commute Atkins' sentence of death to life imprisonment merely because of his IQ score."

Justice Hassell and Justice Koontz dissented. They rejected Dr. Samenow's opinion that Atkins possesses average intelligence as "incredulous as a matter of law," and concluded that "the imposition of the sentence of death upon a criminal defendant who has the mental age of a child between the ages of 9 and 12 is excessive." In their opinion, "it is indefensible to conclude that individuals who are mentally retarded are not to some degree less culpable for their criminal acts. By definition, such individuals have substantial limitations not shared by the general population. A moral and civilized society diminishes itself if its system of justice does not afford recognition and consideration of those limitations in a meaningful way."

Because of the gravity of the concerns expressed by the dissenters, and in light of the dramatic shift in the state legislative landscape that has occurred in the past 13 years, we granted certiorari to revisit the issue that we first addressed in the *Penry* case.

II

The Eighth Amendment succinctly prohibits "[e]xcessive" sanctions. It provides: "Excessive bail shall not be required, nor excessive fines imposed, nor cruel and unusual punishments inflicted." In *Weems v. United States*, 217 U.S. 349, 30 S.Ct. 544, 54 L.Ed. 793 (1910), we held that a punishment of 12 years jailed in irons at hard and painful labor for the crime of falsifying records was excessive. We explained "that it is a precept of justice that punishment for crime should be graduated and proportioned to [the] offense." We have repeatedly applied this proportionality precept in later cases interpreting the Eighth Amendment. Thus, even though "imprisonment for ninety days is not, in the abstract, a punishment which is either cruel or unusual," it may not be imposed as a penalty for "the 'status' of narcotic addiction," *Robinson v. California*, 370 U.S. 660, 666–667, 82 S.Ct. 1417, 8 L.Ed.2d 758 (1962), because such a sanction would be excessive. As Justice Stewart explained in *Robinson*: "Even one day in prison would be a cruel and unusual punishment for the 'crime' of having a common cold."

A claim that punishment is excessive is judged not by the standards that prevailed in 1685 when Lord Jeffreys presided over the "Bloody Assizes" or when the Bill of Rights was adopted, but rather by those that currently prevail. As Chief Justice Warren explained in his opinion in *Trop v. Dulles*, 356 U.S. 86, 78 S.Ct. 590, 2 L.Ed.2d 630 (1958): "The basic concept underlying the Eighth Amendment is nothing less than the dignity of man. . . . The Amendment must draw its meaning from the evolving standards of decency that mark the progress of a maturing society."

Proportionality review under those evolving standards should be informed by " 'objective factors to the maximum possible extent,' " see *Harmelin*, 501 U.S., at 1000, 111 S.Ct. 2680. We have pinpointed that the clearest and most reliable objective evidence of contemporary values is the legislation enacted by the country's legislatures. Relying in part on such legislative evidence, we have held that death is an impermissibly excessive punishment for the rape of an adult woman, *Coker v. Georgia*, 433 U.S. 584, 593–596, 97 S.Ct. 2861, 53 L.Ed.2d 982 (1977), or for a defendant who neither took life, attempted to take life, nor intended to take life, *Enmund v. Florida*, 458 U.S. 782, 789–793, 102 S.Ct. 3368, 73 L.Ed.2d 1140 (1982). In *Coker*, we focused primarily on the then-recent legislation that had been enacted in response to our decision 10 years earlier in *Furman v. Georgia*, 408 U.S. 238, 92 S.Ct. 2726, 33 L.Ed.2d 346 (1972) *(per curiam)*, to support the conclusion that the "current judgment," though "not wholly unanimous," weighed very heavily on the side of rejecting capital punishment as a "suitable penalty" for raping an adult woman. The "current legislative judgment" relevant to our decision in *Enmund* was less clear than in *Coker* but "nevertheless weigh[ed] on the side of rejecting capital punishment for the crime at issue."

We also acknowledged in *Coker* that the objective evidence, though of great importance, did not "wholly determine" the controversy, "for the Constitution contemplates that in the end our own judgment will be brought to bear on the question of the acceptability of the death penalty under the Eighth Amendment." For example, in *Enmund*, we concluded by expressing our own judgment about the issue:

> "For purposes of imposing the death penalty, Enmund's criminal *culpability* must be limited to his participation in the robbery, and his punishment must be tailored to his personal responsibility and moral guilt. Putting Enmund to death to avenge two killings that he did not commit and had no intention of committing or causing does not measurably contribute to the retributive end of ensuring that the criminal gets his just

deserts. This is the judgment of most of *the legislatures that have recently addressed the matter, and we have no reason to disagree with that judgment* for purposes of construing and applying the Eighth Amendment."

Thus, in cases involving a consensus, our own judgment is "brought to bear," by asking whether there is reason to disagree with the judgment reached by the citizenry and its legislators.

Guided by our approach in these cases, we shall first review the judgment of legislatures that have addressed the suitability of imposing the death penalty on the mentally retarded and then consider reasons for agreeing or disagreeing with their judgment.

III

The parties have not called our attention to any state legislative consideration of the suitability of imposing the death penalty on mentally retarded offenders prior to 1986. In that year, the public reaction to the execution of a mentally retarded murderer in Georgia apparently led to the enactment of the first state statute prohibiting such executions. In 1988, when Congress enacted legislation reinstating the federal death penalty, it expressly provided that a "sentence of death shall not be carried out upon a person who is mentally retarded." In 1989, Maryland enacted a similar prohibition. It was in that year that we decided *Penry*, and concluded that those two state enactments, "even when added to the 14 States that have rejected capital punishment completely, do not provide sufficient evidence at present of a national consensus."

Much has changed since then. Responding to the national attention received by the Bowden execution and our decision in *Penry*, state legislatures across the country began to address the issue. In 1990, Kentucky and Tennessee enacted statutes similar to those in Georgia and Maryland, as did New Mexico in 1991, and Arkansas, Colorado, Washington, Indiana, and Kansas in 1993 and 1994. In 1995, when New York reinstated its death penalty, it emulated the Federal Government by expressly exempting the mentally retarded. Nebraska followed suit in 1998. There appear to have been no similar enactments during the next two years, but in 2000 and 2001 six more States—South Dakota, Arizona, Connecticut, Florida, Missouri, and North Carolina—joined the procession. The Texas Legislature unanimously adopted a similar bill, and bills have passed at least one house in other States, including Virginia and Nevada.

It is not so much the number of these States that is significant, but the consistency of the direction of change. Given the well-known fact that anticrime legislation is far more popular than legislation providing protections for persons guilty of violent crime, the large number of States prohibiting the execution of mentally retarded persons (and the complete absence of States passing legislation reinstating the power to conduct such executions) provides powerful evidence that today our society views mentally retarded offenders as categorically less culpable than the average criminal. The evidence carries even greater force when it is noted that the legislatures that have addressed the issue have voted overwhelmingly in favor of the prohibition. Moreover, even in those States that allow the execution of mentally retarded offenders, the practice is uncommon. Some States, for example New Hampshire and New Jersey, continue to authorize executions, but none have been carried out in decades. Thus there is little need to pursue legislation barring the execution of the mentally retarded in those States. And it appears that even among those States that regularly execute offenders and that have no prohibition with regard to the mentally retarded, only five have executed offenders possessing a known IQ less than 70 since we decided *Penry*. The practice, therefore, has become truly unusual, and it is fair to say that a national consensus has developed against it.

To the extent there is serious disagreement about the execution of mentally retarded offenders, it is in determining which offenders are in fact retarded. In this case, for instance, the Commonwealth of Virginia disputes that Atkins suffers from mental retardation. Not all people who claim to be mentally retarded will be so impaired as to fall within the range of mentally retarded offenders about whom there is a national consensus. As was our approach in *Ford v. Wainwright*, 477 U.S. 399, 106 S.Ct. 2595, 91 L.Ed.2d 335 (1986), with regard to insanity, "we leave to the State[s] the task of developing appropriate ways to enforce the constitutional restriction upon [their] execution of sentences."

IV

This consensus unquestionably reflects widespread judgment about the relative culpability of mentally retarded offenders, and the relationship between mental retardation and the penological purposes served by the death penalty. Additionally, it suggests that some characteristics of mental retardation undermine the strength of the procedural protections that our capital jurisprudence steadfastly guards.

As discussed above, clinical definitions of mental retardation require not only subaverage intellectual functioning, but also significant limitations in adaptive skills such as communication, self-care, and self-direction that became manifest before age 18. Mentally retarded persons frequently know the difference between right and wrong and are competent to stand trial. Because of their impairments, however, by definition they have diminished capacities to understand and process information, to communicate, to abstract from mistakes and learn from experience, to engage in logical reasoning, to control impulses, and to understand the reactions of others. There is no evidence that they are more likely to engage in criminal conduct than others, but there is abundant evidence that they often act on impulse rather than pursuant to a premeditated plan, and that in group settings they are followers

and unusual primarily because 18 States recently have passed laws limiting the death eligibility of certain defendants based on mental retardation alone, despite the fact that the laws of 19 other States besides Virginia continue to leave the question of proper punishment to the individuated consideration of sentencing judges or juries familiar with the particular offender and his or her crime.

I agree with JUSTICE SCALIA (dissenting opinion), that the Court's assessment of the current legislative judgment regarding the execution of defendants like petitioner more resembles a *post hoc* rationalization for the majority's subjectively preferred result rather than any objective effort to ascertain the content of an evolving standard of decency. I write separately, however, to call attention to the defects in the Court's decision to place weight on foreign laws, the views of professional and religious organizations, and opinion polls in reaching its conclusion. The Court's suggestion that these sources are relevant to the constitutional question finds little support in our precedents and, in my view, is antithetical to considerations of federalism, which instruct that any "permanent prohibition upon all units of democratic government must [be apparent] in the operative acts (laws and the application of laws) that the people have approved." The Court's uncritical acceptance of the opinion poll data brought to our attention, moreover, warrants additional comment, because we lack sufficient information to conclude that the surveys were conducted in accordance with generally accepted scientific principles or are capable of supporting valid empirical inferences about the issue before us.

In making determinations about whether a punishment is "cruel and unusual" under the evolving standards of decency embraced by the Eighth Amendment, we have emphasized that legislation is the "clearest and most reliable objective evidence of contemporary values. The reason we ascribe primacy to legislative enactments follows from the constitutional role legislatures play in expressing policy of a State." "[I]n a democratic society legislatures, not courts, are constituted to respond to the will and consequently the moral values of the people." And because the specifications of punishments are "peculiarly questions of legislative policy," our cases have cautioned against using "the aegis of the Cruel and Unusual Punishment Clause" to cut off the normal democratic processes.

Our opinions have also recognized that data concerning the actions of sentencing juries, though entitled to less weight than legislative judgments, " 'is a significant and reliable objective index of contemporary values,' " because of the jury's intimate involvement in the case and its function of " 'maintain[ing] a link between contemporary community values and the penal system.' " In *Coker, supra*, at 596–597, 97 S.Ct. 2861, for example, we credited data showing that "at least 9 out of 10" juries in Georgia did not impose the death sentence for rape convictions.

And in *Enmund v. Florida*, 458 U.S. 782, 793–794, 102 S.Ct. 3368, 73 L.Ed.2d 1140 (1982), where evidence of the current legislative judgment was not as "compelling" as that in *Coker* (but more so than that here), we were persuaded by "overwhelming [evidence] that American juries . . . repudiated imposition of the death penalty" for a defendant who neither took life nor attempted or intended to take life.

In my view, these two sources—the work product of legislatures and sentencing jury determinations—ought to be the sole indicators by which courts ascertain the contemporary American conceptions of decency for purposes of the Eighth Amendment. They are the only objective indicia of contemporary values firmly supported by our precedents. More importantly, however, they can be reconciled with the undeniable precepts that the democratic branches of government and individual sentencing juries are, by design, better suited than courts to evaluating and giving effect to the complex societal and moral considerations that inform the selection of publicly acceptable criminal punishments.

In reaching its conclusion today, the Court does not take notice of the fact that neither petitioner nor his *amici* have adduced any comprehensive statistics that would conclusively prove (or disprove) whether juries routinely consider death a disproportionate punishment for mentally retarded offenders like petitioner. Instead, it adverts to the fact that other countries have disapproved imposition of the death penalty for crimes committed by mentally retarded offenders. I fail to see, however, how the views of other countries regarding the punishment of their citizens provide any support for the Court's ultimate determination. While it is true that some of our prior opinions have looked to "the climate of international opinion," to reinforce a conclusion regarding evolving standards of decency, we have since explicitly rejected the idea that the sentencing practices of other countries could "serve to establish the first Eighth Amendment prerequisite, that [a] practice is accepted among our people." For if it is evidence of a *national* consensus for which we are looking, then the viewpoints of other countries simply are not relevant. And nothing in *Thompson, Enmund, Coker*, or *Trop* suggests otherwise.

To further buttress its appraisal of contemporary societal values, the Court marshals public opinion poll results and evidence that several professional organizations and religious groups have adopted official positions opposing the imposition of the death penalty upon mentally retarded offenders. In my view, none should be accorded any weight on the Eighth Amendment scale when the elected representatives of a State's populace have not deemed them persuasive enough to prompt legislative action.

Even if I were to accept the legitimacy of the Court's decision to reach beyond the product of legislatures and practices of sentencing juries to discern a national standard of decency, I would take issue with the blind-faith credence it accords the opinion polls brought to our attention. An extensive body of social science literature describes how methodological and other errors can affect the reliability and validity of estimates about the opinions and attitudes of a population derived from various sampling techniques. Everything from variations in the survey methodology, such as the choice of the target population, the sampling design used, the questions asked, and the statistical analyses used to interpret the data can skew the results.

* * *

There are strong reasons for limiting our inquiry into what constitutes an evolving standard of decency under the Eighth Amendment to the laws passed by legislatures and the practices of sentencing juries in America. Here, the Court goes beyond these well-established objective indicators of contemporary values. It finds "further support to [its] conclusion" that a national consensus has developed against imposing the death penalty on all mentally retarded defendants in international opinion, the views of professional and religious organizations, and opinion polls not demonstrated to be reliable. Believing this view to be seriously mistaken, I dissent.

■ JUSTICE SCALIA, with whom THE CHIEF JUSTICE and JUSTICE THOMAS join, dissenting.

Today's decision is the pinnacle of our Eighth Amendment death-is-different jurisprudence. Not only does it, like all of that jurisprudence, find no support in the text or history of the Eighth Amendment; it does not even have support in current social attitudes regarding the conditions that render an otherwise just death penalty inappropriate. Seldom has an opinion of this Court rested so obviously upon nothing but the personal views of its Members.

Under our Eighth Amendment jurisprudence, a punishment is "cruel and unusual" if it falls within one of two categories: "those modes or acts of punishment that had been considered cruel and unusual at the time that the Bill of Rights was adopted," *Ford v. Wainwright*, 477 U.S. 399, 405, 106 S.Ct. 2595, 91 L.Ed.2d 335 (1986), and modes of punishment that are inconsistent with modern " 'standards of decency,' " as evinced by objective indicia, the most important of which is "legislation enacted by the country's legislatures," *Penry v. Lynaugh*, 492 U.S. 302, 330–331, 109 S.Ct. 2934, 106 L.Ed.2d 256 (1989).

The Court makes no pretense that execution of the mildly mentally retarded would have been considered "cruel and unusual" in 1791. Only the *severely* or *profoundly* mentally retarded, commonly known as "idiots," enjoyed any special status under the law at that time. They, like lunatics, suffered a "deficiency in will" rendering them unable to tell right from wrong. 4 W. Blackstone, Commentaries on the Laws of England 24 (1769) (hereinafter Blackstone).

The Court is left to argue, therefore, that execution of the mildly retarded is inconsistent with the "evolving standards of decency that mark the progress of a maturing society." Before today, our opinions consistently emphasized that Eighth Amendment judgments regarding the existence of social "standards" "should be informed by objective factors to the maximum possible extent" and "should not be, or appear to be, merely the subjective views of individual Justices." "First" among these objective factors are the "statutes passed by society's elected representatives," because it "will rarely if ever be the case that the Members of this Court will have a better sense of the evolution in views of the American people than do their elected representatives.

The Court pays lipservice to these precedents as it miraculously extracts a "national consensus" forbidding execution of the mentally retarded, from the fact that 18 States—less than *half* (47%) of the 38 States that permit capital punishment (for whom the issue exists)—have very recently enacted legislation barring execution of the mentally retarded. Even that 47% figure is a distorted one. If one is to say, as the Court does today, that *all* executions of the mentally retarded are so morally repugnant as to violate our national "standards of decency," surely the "consensus" it points to must be one that has set its righteous face against *all* such executions. Not 18 States, but only 7—18% of death penalty jurisdictions—have legislation of that scope. Eleven of those that the Court counts enacted statutes prohibiting execution of mentally retarded defendants *convicted after, or convicted of crimes committed after, the effective date* of the legislation; those already on death row, or consigned there before the statute's effective date, or even (in those States using the date of the crime as the criterion of retroactivity) tried in the future for murders committed many years ago, could be put to death. That is not a statement of absolute moral repugnance, but one of current preference between two tolerable approaches. Two of these States permit execution of the mentally retarded in other situations as well: Kansas apparently permits execution of all except the *severely* mentally retarded; New York permits execution of the mentally retarded who commit murder in a correctional facility.

But let us accept, for the sake of argument, the Court's faulty count. That bare number of States alone—*18*—should be enough to convince any reasonable person that no "national consensus" exists. How is it possible that agreement among 47% of the death penalty jurisdictions amounts to "consensus"? Our prior cases have generally required a much higher degree of agreement before finding a punishment cruel and unusual on "evolving standards" grounds. In *Coker*, we proscribed the death penalty for rape of an adult woman after finding that only one jurisdiction, Georgia, authorized such a punishment. In *Enmund, supra*, at 789, 102 S.Ct. 3368, we invalidated the death penalty for mere participation in a robbery in which an accomplice took a life, a punishment not permitted in 28 of the death penalty States (78%). In *Ford*, 477 U.S., at 408, 106

S.Ct. 2595, we supported the common-law prohibition of execution of the insane with the observation that "[t]his ancestral legacy has not outlived its time," since not a single State authorizes such punishment. In *Solem v. Helm*, 463 U.S. 277, 300, 103 S.Ct. 3001, 77 L.Ed.2d 637 (1983), we invalidated a life sentence without parole under a recidivist statute by which the criminal "was treated more severely than he would have been in any other State." What the Court calls evidence of "consensus" in the present case (a fudged 47%) more closely resembles evidence that we found *inadequate* to establish consensus in earlier cases. *Tison v. Arizona*, 481 U.S. 137, 154, 158, 107 S.Ct. 1676, 95 L.Ed.2d 127 (1987), upheld a state law authorizing capital punishment for major participation in a felony with reckless indifference to life where only 11 of the 37 death penalty States (30%) prohibited such punishment. *Stanford*, 492 U.S., at 372, 109 S.Ct. 2969, upheld a state law permitting execution of defendants who committed a capital crime at age 16 where only 15 of the 36 death penalty States (42%) prohibited death for such offenders.

Moreover, a major factor that the Court entirely disregards is that the legislation of all 18 States it relies on is still in its infancy. The oldest of the statutes is only 14 years old; five were enacted last year; over half were enacted within the past eight years. Few, if any, of the States have had sufficient experience with these laws to know whether they are sensible in the long term. It is "myopic to base sweeping constitutional principles upon the narrow experience of [a few] years."

The Court attempts to bolster its embarrassingly feeble evidence of "consensus" with the following: "It is not so much the number of these States that is significant, but the *consistency* of the direction of change." But in what *other* direction *could we possibly* see change? Given that 14 years ago *all* the death penalty statutes included the mentally retarded, *any* change (except precipitate undoing of what had just been done) was *bound to be* in the one direction the Court finds significant enough to overcome the lack of real consensus. That is to say, to be accurate the Court's "*consistency*-of-the-direction-of-change" point should be recast into the following unimpressive observation: "No State has yet undone its exemption of the mentally retarded, one for as long as 14 whole years." In any event, reliance upon "trends," even those of much longer duration than a mere 14 years, is a perilous basis for constitutional adjudication.

The Court's thrashing about for evidence of "consensus" includes reliance upon the *margins* by which state legislatures have enacted bans on execution of the retarded. Presumably, in applying our Eighth Amendment "evolving-standards-of-decency" jurisprudence, we will henceforth weigh not only how many States have agreed, but how many States have agreed *by how much*. Of course if the percentage of legislators voting for the bill is significant, surely the number of people *represented* by the legislators voting for the bill is also significant: the fact that 49% of the legislators in a State with a population of 60 million voted *against* the bill should be more impressive than the fact that 90% of the legislators in a State with a population of 2 million voted *for* it. (By the way, the population of the death penalty States that exclude the mentally retarded is only 44% of the population of all death penalty States.) This is quite absurd. What we have looked for in the past to "evolve" the Eighth Amendment is a consensus of the same sort as the consensus that *adopted* the Eighth Amendment: a consensus of the sovereign States that form the Union, not a nose count of Americans for and against.

Even less compelling (if possible) is the Court's argument, that evidence of "national consensus" is to be found in the infrequency with which retarded persons are executed in States that do not bar their execution. To begin with, what the Court takes as true is in fact quite doubtful. It is not at all clear that execution of the mentally retarded is "uncommon," as even the sources cited by the Court suggest, then surely the explanation is that mental retardation is a constitutionally mandated mitigating factor at sentencing. For that reason, even if there were uniform national sentiment in *favor* of executing the retarded in appropriate cases, one would still expect execution of the mentally retarded to be "uncommon." To adapt to the present case what the Court itself said in Stanford,: "[I]t is not only possible, but overwhelmingly probable, that the very considerations which induce [today's majority] to believe that death should *never* be imposed on [mentally retarded] offenders . . . cause prosecutors and juries to believe that it should *rarely* be imposed."

But the Prize for the Court's Most Feeble Effort to fabricate "national consensus" must go to its appeal (deservedly relegated to a footnote) to the views of assorted professional and religious organizations, members of the so-called "world community," and respondents to opinion polls. I agree with THE CHIEF JUSTICE, that the views of professional and religious organizations and the results of opinion polls are irrelevant. Equally irrelevant are the practices of the "world community," whose notions of justice are (thankfully) not always those of our people. "We must never forget that it is a Constitution for the United States of America that we are expounding. . . . [W]here there is not first a settled consensus among our own people, the views of other nations, however enlightened the Justices of this Court may think them to be, cannot be imposed upon Americans through the Constitution."

III

Beyond the empty talk of a "national consensus," the Court gives us a brief glimpse of what really underlies today's decision: pretension to a power confined *neither* by the moral sentiments originally enshrined in the Eighth Amendment (its original meaning) *nor even* by the current moral sentiments of the American people. " '[T]he Constitution,' the

Court says, 'contemplates that in the end *our own judgment* will be brought to bear on the question of the acceptability of the death penalty under the Eighth Amendment.'" (The unexpressed reason for this unexpressed "contemplation" of the Constitution is presumably that really good lawyers have moral sentiments superior to those of the common herd, whether in 1791 or today.) The arrogance of this assumption of power takes one's breath away. And it explains, of course, why the Court can be so cavalier about the evidence of consensus. It is just a game, after all. " '[I]n the end,'" it is the *feelings* and *intuition* of a majority of the Justices that count—"the perceptions of decency, or of penology, or of mercy, entertained . . . by a majority of the small and unrepresentative segment of our society that sits on this Court."

The genuinely operative portion of the opinion, then, is the Court's statement of the reasons why it agrees with the contrived consensus it has found, that the "diminished capacities" of the mentally retarded render the death penalty excessive. The Court's analysis rests on two fundamental assumptions: (1) that the Eighth Amendment prohibits excessive punishments, and (2) that sentencing juries or judges are unable to account properly for the "diminished capacities" of the retarded. The first assumption is wrong, as I explained at length in *Harmelin v. Michigan*, 501 U.S. 957, 966–990, 111 S.Ct. 2680, 115 L.Ed.2d 836 (1991) (opinion of SCALIA, J.). The Eighth Amendment is addressed to always-and-everywhere "cruel" punishments, such as the rack and the thumbscrew. But where the punishment is in itself permissible, "[t]he Eighth Amendment is not a ratchet, whereby a temporary consensus on leniency for a particular crime fixes a permanent constitutional maximum, disabling the States from giving effect to altered beliefs and responding to changed social conditions." The second assumption—inability of judges or juries to take proper account of mental retardation—is not only unsubstantiated, but contradicts the immemorial belief, here and in England, that they play an *indispensable* role in such matters:

> "[I]t is very difficult to define the indivisible line that divides perfect and partial insanity; but it must rest upon circumstances duly to be weighed and considered both by the judge and jury, lest on the one side there be a kind of inhumanity towards the defects of human nature, or on the other side too great an indulgence given to great crimes. . . ." 1 Hale, Pleas of the Crown, at 30.

Proceeding from these faulty assumptions, the Court gives two reasons why the death penalty is an excessive punishment for all mentally retarded offenders. First, the "diminished capacities" of the mentally retarded raise a "serious question" whether their execution contributes to the "social purposes" of the death penalty, viz., retribution and deterrence. But never mind; its discussion of even the other two does not bear analysis. Retribution is not advanced, the argument goes, because the mentally retarded are *no more culpable* than the average murderer, whom we have already held lacks sufficient culpability to warrant the death penalty. Who says so? Is there an established correlation between mental acuity and the ability to conform one's conduct to the law in such a rudimentary matter as murder? Are the mentally retarded really more disposed (and hence more likely) to commit willfully cruel and serious crime than others? In my experience, the opposite is true: being childlike generally suggests innocence rather than brutality.

Assuming, however, that there is a direct connection between diminished intelligence and the inability to refrain from murder, what scientific analysis can possibly show that a mildly retarded individual who commits an exquisite torture-killing is "no more culpable" than the "average" murderer in a holdup-gone-wrong or a domestic dispute? Or a moderately retarded individual who commits a series of 20 exquisite torture-killings? Surely culpability, and deservedness of the most severe retribution, depends not merely (if at all) upon the mental capacity of the criminal (above the level where he is able to distinguish right from wrong) but also upon the depravity of the crime—which is precisely why this sort of question has traditionally been thought answerable not by a categorical rule of the sort the Court today imposes upon all trials, but rather by the sentencer's weighing of the circumstances (both degree of retardation and depravity of crime) in the particular case. The fact that juries continue to sentence mentally retarded offenders to death for extreme crimes shows that society's moral outrage sometimes demands execution of retarded offenders. By what principle of law, science, or logic can the Court pronounce that this is wrong? There is none. Once the Court admits (as it does) that mental retardation does not render the offender morally blameless,, there is no basis for saying that the death penalty is *never* appropriate retribution, no matter *how* heinous the crime. As long as a mentally retarded offender knows "the difference between right and wrong," only the sentencer can assess whether his retardation reduces his culpability enough to exempt him from the death penalty for the particular murder in question.

As for the other social purpose of the death penalty that the Court discusses, deterrence: That is not advanced, the Court tells us, because the mentally retarded are "less likely" than their non-retarded counterparts to "process the information of the possibility of execution as a penalty and . . . control their conduct based upon that information." Of course this leads to the same conclusion discussed earlier—that the mentally retarded (because they are less deterred) are more likely to kill—which neither I nor the society at large believes. In any event, even the Court does not say that *all* mentally retarded individuals cannot "process the information of the possibility of execution as a penalty and . . . control their conduct based upon that information"; it merely asserts that they are "less likely" to be able to do so. But surely the deterrent effect of a penalty is adequately vindicated if it successfully deters many, but not all, of the target class. Virginia's death penalty, for example, does not fail of its deterrent effect simply because *some* criminals are unaware that Virginia *has* the death penalty. In other words, the supposed fact that *some* retarded criminals cannot fully appreciate the death penalty has nothing to do with the deterrence rationale, but is simply an echo of the arguments denying a retribution rationale, discussed and rejected above. I am not sure that a murderer is somehow less blameworthy if (though he knew his act was wrong) he did not fully appreciate that he could die for it; but if so, we should treat a mentally retarded murderer the way we treat an offender who may be "less likely" to respond to the death penalty because he was abused as a child. We do not hold him immune from capital punishment, but require his background to be considered by the sentencer as a mitigating factor.

The Court throws one last factor into its grab bag of reasons why execution of the retarded is "excessive" in all cases: Mentally retarded offenders "face a special risk of wrongful execution" because they are less able "to make a persuasive showing of mitigation," "to give meaningful assistance to their counsel," and to be effective witnesses. "Special risk" is pretty flabby language (even flabbier than "less likely")—and I suppose a similar "special risk" could be said to exist for just plain stupid people, inarticulate people, even ugly people. If this unsupported claim has any substance to it (which I doubt), it might support a due process claim in all criminal prosecutions of the mentally retarded; but it is hard to see how it has anything to do with an *Eighth Amendment* claim that execution of the mentally retarded is cruel and unusual. We have never before held it to be cruel and unusual punishment to impose a sentence in violation of some *other* constitutional imperative.

* * *

Nothing has changed the accuracy of Matthew Hale's endorsement of the common law's traditional method for taking account of guilt-reducing factors, written over three centuries ago:

> [Determination of a person's incapacity] is a matter of great difficulty, partly from the easiness of counterfeiting this disability . . . and partly from the variety of the degrees of this infirmity, whereof some are sufficient, and some are insufficient to excuse persons in capital offenses. . . .

> Yet the law of England hath afforded the best method of trial, that is possible, of this and all other matters of fact, namely, by a jury of twelve men all concurring in the same judgment, by the testimony of witnesses . . . , and by the inspection and direction of the judge. 1 Pleas of the Crown, at 32–33.

I respectfully dissent.

Roper v. Simmons

United States Supreme Court, 2005.
543 U.S. 551, 125 S.Ct. 1183, 161 L.Ed.2d 1.

■ JUSTICE KENNEDY delivered the opinion of the Court.

This case requires us to address, for the second time in a decade and a half, whether it is permissible under the Eighth and Fourteenth Amendments to the Constitution of the United States to execute a juvenile offender who was older than 15 but younger than 18 when he committed a capital crime. In *Stanford v. Kentucky*, 492 U.S. 361, 109 S.Ct. 2969, 106 L.Ed.2d 306 (1989), a divided Court rejected the proposition that the Constitution bars capital punishment for juvenile offenders in this age group. We reconsider the question.

I

At the age of 17, when he was still a junior in high school, Christopher Simmons, the respondent here, committed murder. About nine months later, after he had turned 18, he was tried and sentenced to death. There is little doubt that Simmons was the instigator of the crime. Before its commission Simmons said he wanted to murder someone. In chilling, callous terms he talked about his plan, discussing it for the most part with two friends, Charles Benjamin and John Tessmer, then aged 15 and 16 respectively. Simmons proposed to commit burglary and murder by breaking and entering, tying up a victim, and throwing the victim off a bridge. Simmons assured his friends they could "get away with it" because they were minors.

The three met at about 2 a.m. on the night of the murder, but Tessmer left before the other two set out. (The State later charged Tessmer with conspiracy, but dropped the charge in exchange for his testimony against Simmons.) Simmons and Benjamin entered the home of the victim, Shirley Crook, after reaching through an open window and unlocking the back door. Simmons turned on a hallway light. Awakened, Mrs. Crook called out, "Who's there?" In response Simmons entered Mrs. Crook's bedroom, where he recognized her from a previous car accident involving them both. Simmons later admitted this confirmed his resolve to murder her.

Using duct tape to cover her eyes and mouth and bind her hands, the two perpetrators put Mrs. Crook in her minivan and drove to a state park. They reinforced the bindings, covered her head with a towel, and walked her to a railroad trestle spanning the Meramec River. There they tied her hands and feet together with electrical wire, wrapped her whole face in duct tape and threw her from the bridge, drowning her in the waters below.

By the afternoon of September 9, Steven Crook had returned home from an overnight trip, found his bedroom in disarray, and reported his wife missing. On the same afternoon fishermen recovered the victim's body from the river. Simmons, meanwhile, was bragging about the killing, telling friends he had killed a woman "because the bitch seen my face."

The next day, after receiving information of Simmons' involvement, police arrested him at his high school and took him to the police station in Fenton, Missouri. They read him his *Miranda* rights. Simmons waived his right to an attorney and agreed to answer questions. After less than two hours of interrogation, Simmons confessed to the murder and agreed to perform a videotaped reenactment at the crime scene.

The State charged Simmons with burglary, kidnaping, stealing, and murder in the first degree. As Simmons was 17 at the time of the crime, he was outside the criminal jurisdiction of Missouri's juvenile court system. He was tried as an adult. At trial the State introduced Simmons' confession and the videotaped reenactment of the crime, along with testimony that Simmons discussed the crime in advance and bragged about it later. The defense called no witnesses in the guilt phase. The jury having returned a verdict of murder, the trial proceeded to the penalty phase.

The State sought the death penalty. As aggravating factors, the State submitted that the murder was committed for the purpose of receiving money; was committed for the purpose of avoiding, interfering with, or preventing lawful arrest of the defendant; and involved depravity of mind and was outrageously and wantonly vile, horrible, and inhuman. The State called Shirley Crook's husband, daughter, and two sisters, who presented moving evidence of the devastation her death had brought to their lives.

In mitigation Simmons' attorneys first called an officer of the Missouri juvenile justice system, who testified that Simmons had no prior convictions and that no previous charges had been filed against him. Simmons' mother, father, two younger half brothers, a neighbor, and a friend took the stand to tell the jurors of the close relationships they had formed with Simmons and to plead for mercy on his behalf. Simmons' mother, in particular, testified to the responsibility Simmons demonstrated in taking care of his two younger half brothers and of his grandmother and to his capacity to show love for them.

During closing arguments, both the prosecutor and defense counsel addressed Simmons' age, which the trial judge had instructed the jurors they could consider as a mitigating factor. Defense counsel reminded the jurors that juveniles of Simmons' age cannot drink, serve on juries, or even see certain movies, because "the legislatures have wisely decided that individuals of a certain age aren't responsible enough." Defense counsel argued that Simmons' age should make "a huge difference to [the jurors] in deciding just exactly what sort of punishment to make." In rebuttal, the prosecutor gave the following response: "Age, he says. Think about age. Seventeen years old. Isn't that scary? Doesn't that scare you? Mitigating? Quite the contrary I submit. Quite the contrary."

The jury recommended the death penalty after finding the State had proved each of the three aggravating factors submitted to it. Accepting the jury's recommendation, the trial judge imposed the death penalty.

After these proceedings in Simmons' case had run their course, this Court held that the Eighth and Fourteenth Amendments prohibit the execution of a mentally retarded person. *Atkins v. Virginia*, 536 U.S. 304, 122 S.Ct. 2242, 153 L.Ed.2d 335 (2002). Simmons filed a new petition for state postconviction relief, arguing that the reasoning of *Atkins* established that the Constitution prohibits the execution of a juvenile who was under 18 when the crime was committed.

The Missouri Supreme Court agreed. It held that since *Stanford*,

"a national consensus has developed against the execution of juvenile offenders, as demonstrated by the fact that eighteen states now bar such executions for juveniles, that twelve other states bar executions altogether, that no state has lowered its age of execution below 18 since *Stanford*, that five states have legislatively or by case law raised or established the minimum age at 18, and that the imposition of the juvenile death penalty has become truly unusual over the last decade."

On this reasoning it set aside Simmons' death sentence and resentenced him to "life imprisonment without eligibility for probation, parole, or release except by act of the Governor."

We granted certiorari, and now affirm.

II

The Eighth Amendment provides: "Excessive bail shall not be required, nor excessive fines imposed, nor cruel and unusual punishments inflicted." As the Court explained in *Atkins*, the Eighth Amendment guarantees individuals the right not to be subjected to excessive sanctions. The right flows from the basic "precept of justice that punishment for crime should be graduated and proportioned to [the] offense." By protecting even those convicted of heinous crimes, the Eighth Amendment reaffirms the duty of the government to respect the dignity of all persons.

The prohibition against "cruel and unusual punishments," like other expansive language in the Constitution, must be interpreted according to its text, by considering history, tradition, and precedent, and with due regard for its purpose and function in the constitutional design. To implement this framework we have established the propriety and affirmed the necessity of referring to "the evolving standards of decency that mark the progress of a maturing society" to determine which punishments are so disproportionate as to be cruel and unusual

In *Thompson v. Oklahoma*, 487 U.S. 815, 108 S.Ct. 2687, 101 L.Ed.2d 702 (1988), a plurality of the Court determined that our standards of decency do not permit the execution of any offender under the age of 16 at the time of the crime. The plurality opinion explained that no death penalty State that had given express consideration to a minimum age for the death penalty had set the age lower than 16. The plurality also observed that "[t]he conclusion that it would offend civilized standards of decency to execute a person who was less than 16 years old at the time of his or her offense is consistent with the views that have been expressed by respected professional organizations, by other nations that share our Anglo-American heritage, and by the leading members of the Western European community." The opinion further noted that juries imposed the death penalty on offenders under 16 with exceeding rarity; the last execution of an offender for a crime committed under the age of 16 had been carried out in 1948, 40 years prior.

Bringing its independent judgment to bear on the permissibility of the death penalty for a 15-year-old offender, the *Thompson* plurality stressed that "[t]he reasons why juveniles are not trusted with the privileges and responsibilities of an adult also explain why their irresponsible conduct is not as morally reprehensible as that of an adult." According to the plurality, the lesser culpability of offenders under 16 made the death penalty inappropriate as a form of retribution, while the low likelihood that offenders under 16 engaged in "the kind of cost-benefit analysis that attaches any weight to the possibility of execution" made the death penalty ineffective as a means of deterrence. With JUSTICE O'CONNOR concurring in the judgment on narrower grounds, the Court set aside the death sentence that had been imposed on the 15-year-old offender.

The next year, in *Stanford v. Kentucky*, 492 U.S. 361, 109 S.Ct. 2969, 106 L.Ed.2d 306 (1989), the Court, over a dissenting opinion joined by four Justices, referred to contemporary standards of decency in this country and concluded the Eighth and Fourteenth Amendments did not proscribe the execution of juvenile offenders over 15 but under 18. The Court noted that 22 of the 37 death penalty States permitted the death penalty for 16-year-old offenders, and, among these 37 States, 25 permitted it for 17-year-old offenders. These numbers, in the Court's view, indicated there was no national consensus "sufficient to label a particular punishment cruel and unusual." A plurality of the Court also "emphatically reject[ed]" the suggestion that the Court should bring its own judgment to bear on the acceptability of the juvenile death penalty.

The same day the Court decided *Stanford*, it held that the Eighth Amendment did not mandate a categorical exemption from the death penalty for the mentally retarded. *Penry v. Lynaugh*, 492 U.S. 302, 109 S.Ct. 2934, 106 L.Ed.2d 256 (1989). In reaching this conclusion it stressed that only two States had enacted laws banning the imposition of the death penalty on a mentally retarded person convicted of a capital offense. According to the Court, "the two state statutes prohibiting execution of the mentally retarded, even when added to the 14 States that have rejected capital punishment completely, [did] not provide sufficient evidence at present of a national consensus."

Just as the *Atkins* Court reconsidered the issue decided in *Penry*, we now reconsider the issue decided in *Stanford*. The beginning point is a review of objective indicia of consensus, as expressed in particular by the enactments of legislatures that have addressed the question. These data give us essential instruction. We then must determine, in the exercise of our own independent judgment, whether the death penalty is a disproportionate punishment for juveniles.

III

A

The evidence of national consensus against the death penalty for juveniles is similar, and in some respects parallel, to the evidence *Atkins* held sufficient to demonstrate a national consensus against the death penalty for the mentally retarded. When *Atkins* was decided, 30 States prohibited the death penalty for the mentally retarded. This number comprised 12 that had abandoned the death penalty altogether, and 18 that maintained it but excluded the mentally retarded from its reach. By a similar calculation in this case, 30 States prohibit the juvenile death penalty, comprising 12 that have rejected the death penalty altogether and 18 that maintain it but, by express provision or judicial interpretation, exclude juveniles from its reach. *Atkins* emphasized that even in the 20 States without formal prohibition, the practice of executing the mentally retarded was infrequent. Since *Penry*, only five States had executed offenders known to have an IQ under 70. In the present case, too, even in the 20 States without a formal prohibition on executing juveniles, the practice is infrequent. Since *Stanford*, six States have executed prisoners for crimes committed as juveniles. In the past 10 years, only three have done so: Oklahoma, Texas, and Virginia. In December 2003 the Governor of Kentucky decided to spare the life of Kevin Stanford, and commuted his sentence to one of life imprisonment without parole, with the declaration that " '[w]e ought not be executing people who, legally, were children.' " By this act the Governor ensured Kentucky would not add itself to the list of States that have executed juveniles within the last 10 years even by the execution of the very defendant whose death sentence the Court had upheld in *Stanford v. Kentucky.*

There is, to be sure, at least one difference between the evidence of consensus in *Atkins* and in this case. Impressive in *Atkins* was the rate of abolition of the death penalty for the mentally retarded. Sixteen States that permitted the execution of the mentally retarded at the time of *Penry* had prohibited the practice by the time we heard *Atkins*. By contrast, the rate of change in reducing the incidence of the juvenile death penalty, or in taking specific steps to abolish it, has been slower. Five States that allowed the juvenile death penalty at the time of *Stanford* have abandoned it in the intervening 15 years—four through legislative enactments and one through judicial decision.

Though less dramatic than the change from *Penry* to *Atkins* ("telling," to borrow the word *Atkins* used to describe this difference,) we still consider the change from *Stanford* to this case to be significant. As noted in *Atkins*, with respect to the States that had abandoned the death penalty for the mentally retarded since *Penry*, "[i]t is not so much the number of these States that is significant, but the consistency of the direction of change." In particular we found it significant that, in the wake of *Penry*, no State that had already prohibited the execution of the mentally retarded had passed legislation to reinstate the penalty. The number of States that have abandoned capital punishment for juvenile offenders since *Stanford* is smaller than the number of States that abandoned capital punishment for the mentally retarded after *Penry*; yet we think the same consistency of direction of change has been demonstrated. Since *Stanford*, no State that previously prohibited capital punishment for juveniles has reinstated it. This fact, coupled with the trend toward abolition of the juvenile death penalty, carries special force in light of the general popularity of anticrime legislation, and in light of the particular trend in recent years toward cracking down on juvenile crime in other respects. Any difference between this case and *Atkins* with respect to the pace of abolition is thus counterbalanced by the consistent direction of the change.

The slower pace of abolition of the juvenile death penalty over the past 15 years, moreover, may have a simple explanation. When we heard *Penry*, only two death penalty States had already prohibited the execution of the mentally retarded. When we heard *Stanford*, by contrast, 12 death penalty States had already prohibited the execution of any juvenile under 18, and 15 had prohibited the execution of any juvenile under 17. If anything, this shows that the impropriety of executing juveniles between 16 and 18 years of age gained wide recognition earlier than the impropriety of executing the mentally retarded.

As in *Atkins*, the objective indicia of consensus in this case—the rejection of the juvenile death penalty in the majority of States; the infrequency of its use even where it remains on the books; and the consistency in the trend toward abolition of the practice—provide sufficient evidence that today our society views juveniles, in the words *Atkins* used respecting the mentally retarded, as "categorically less culpable than the average criminal."

B

A majority of States have rejected the imposition of the death penalty on juvenile offenders under 18, and we now hold this is required by the Eighth Amendment.

Because the death penalty is the most severe punishment, the Eighth Amendment applies to it with special force. Capital punishment must be limited to those offenders who commit "a narrow category of the most serious crimes" and whose extreme culpability makes them "the most deserving of execution." This principle is implemented throughout the capital sentencing process. States must give narrow and precise definition to the aggravating factors that can result in a capital sentence. In any capital case a defendant has wide latitude to raise as a mitigating factor "any aspect of [his or her] character or record and any of the circumstances of the offense that the defendant proffers as a basis for a sentence less than death." There are a number of crimes that beyond question are severe in absolute terms, yet the death penalty may not be imposed for their commission. The death penalty may not be imposed on certain classes of offenders, such as juveniles under 16, the insane, and the mentally retarded, no matter how heinous the crime. These rules vindicate the underlying principle that the death penalty is reserved for a narrow category of crimes and offenders.

Three general differences between juveniles under 18 and adults demonstrate that juvenile offenders cannot with reliability be classified among the worst offenders. First, as any parent knows and as the scientific and sociological studies respondent and his *amici* cite tend to confirm, "[a] lack of maturity and an underdeveloped sense of responsibility are found in youth more often than in adults and are more understandable among the young. These qualities often result in impetuous and ill-considered actions and decisions." It has been noted that "adolescents are overrepresented statistically in virtually every category of reckless behavior." In recognition of the comparative immaturity and irresponsibility of juveniles, almost every State prohibits those under 18 years of age from voting, serving on juries, or marrying without parental consent.

The second area of difference is that juveniles are more vulnerable or susceptible to negative influences and outside pressures, including peer pressure . . . This is explained in part by the prevailing circumstance that juveniles have less control, or less experience with control, over their own environment.

The third broad difference is that the character of a juvenile is not as well formed as that of an adult. The personality traits of juveniles are more transitory, less fixed.

These differences render suspect any conclusion that a juvenile falls among the worst offenders. The susceptibility of juveniles to immature and irresponsible behavior means "their irresponsible conduct is not as morally reprehensible as that of an adult." Their own vulnerability and comparative lack of control over their immediate surroundings mean juveniles have a greater claim than adults to be forgiven for failing to escape negative influences in their whole environment. The reality that juveniles still struggle to define their identity means it is less supportable to conclude that even a heinous crime committed by a juvenile is evidence of irretrievably depraved character. From a moral standpoint it would be misguided to equate the failings of a minor with those of an adult, for a greater possibility exists that a minor's character deficiencies will be reformed. Indeed, "[t]he relevance of youth as a mitigating factor derives from the fact that the signature qualities of youth are transient; as individuals mature, the impetuousness and recklessness that may dominate in younger years can subside."

In *Thompson*, a plurality of the Court recognized the import of these characteristics with respect to juveniles under 16, and relied on them to hold that the Eighth Amendment prohibited the imposition of the death penalty on juveniles below that age. We conclude the same reasoning applies to all juvenile offenders under 18.

Once the diminished culpability of juveniles is recognized, it is evident that the penological justifications for the death penalty apply to them with lesser force than to adults. We have held there are two distinct social purposes served by the death penalty: " 'retribution and deterrence of capital crimes by prospective offenders.' " As for retribution, we remarked in *Atkins* that "[i]f the culpability of the average murderer is insufficient to justify the most extreme sanction available to the State, the lesser culpability of the mentally retarded offender surely does not merit that form of retribution." The same conclusions follow from the lesser culpability of the juvenile offender. Whether viewed as an attempt to express the community's moral outrage or as an attempt to right the balance for the wrong to the victim, the case for retribution is not as strong with a minor as with an adult. Retribution is not proportional if the law's most severe penalty is imposed on one whose culpability or blameworthiness is diminished, to a substantial degree, by reason of youth and immaturity.

As for deterrence, it is unclear whether the death penalty has a significant or even measurable deterrent effect on juveniles, as counsel for the petitioner acknowledged at oral argument. In general we leave to legislatures the assessment of the efficacy of various criminal penalty schemes. Here, however, the absence of evidence of deterrent effect is of special concern because the same characteristics that render juveniles less culpable than adults suggest as well that juveniles will be less susceptible to deterrence. In particular, as the plurality observed in "[t]he likelihood that the teenage offender has made the kind of cost-benefit analysis that attaches any weight to the possibility of execution is so remote as to be virtually nonexistent." To the extent the juvenile death penalty might have residual deterrent effect, it is worth noting that the punishment of life imprisonment without the possibility of parole is itself a severe sanction, in particular for a young person.

In concluding that neither retribution nor deterrence provides adequate justification for imposing the death penalty on juvenile offenders, we cannot deny or overlook the brutal crimes too many juvenile offenders have committed. Certainly it can be argued, although we by no means concede the point, that a rare case might arise in which a juvenile offender has sufficient psychological maturity, and at the same time demonstrates sufficient depravity, to merit a sentence of death. Indeed, this possibility is the linchpin of one contention pressed by petitioner and his *amici*. They assert that even assuming the truth of the observations we have made about juveniles' diminished culpability in general, jurors nonetheless should be allowed to consider mitigating arguments related to youth on a case-by-case basis, and in some cases to impose the death penalty if justified. A central feature of death penalty sentencing is a particular assessment of the circumstances of the crime and the characteristics of the offender. The system is designed to consider both aggravating and mitigating circumstances, including youth, in every case. Given this Court's own insistence on individualized consideration, petitioner maintains that it is both arbitrary and unnecessary to adopt a categorical rule barring imposition of the death penalty on any offender under 18 years of age.

We disagree. The differences between juvenile and adult offenders are too marked and well understood to risk allowing a youthful person to receive the death penalty despite insufficient culpability. An unacceptable likelihood exists that the brutality or cold-blooded nature of any particular crime would overpower mitigating arguments based on youth as a matter of course, even where the juvenile offender's objective immaturity, vulnerability, and lack of true depravity should require a sentence less severe than death. In some cases a defendant's youth may even be counted against him. In this very case, as we noted above, the prosecutor argued Simmons' youth was aggravating rather than mitigating. While this sort of overreaching could be corrected by a particular rule to ensure that the mitigating force of youth is not overlooked, that would not address our larger concerns.

It is difficult even for expert psychologists to differentiate between the juvenile offender whose crime reflects unfortunate yet transient immaturity, and the rare juvenile offender whose crime reflects irreparable corruption. See Steinberg & Scott 1014–1016. As we understand it, this difficulty underlies the rule forbidding psychiatrists from diagnosing any patient under 18 as having antisocial personality disorder, a disorder also referred to as psychopathy or sociopathy, and which is characterized by callousness, cynicism, and contempt for the feelings, rights, and suffering of others. If trained psychiatrists with the advantage of clinical testing and observation refrain, despite diagnostic expertise, from assessing any juvenile under 18 as having antisocial personality disorder, we conclude that States should refrain from asking jurors to issue a far graver condemnation—that a juvenile offender merits the death penalty. When a juvenile offender commits a heinous crime, the State can exact forfeiture of some of the most basic liberties, but the State cannot extinguish his life and his potential to attain a mature understanding of his own humanity.

Drawing the line at 18 years of age is subject, of course, to the objections always raised against categorical rules. The qualities that distinguish juveniles from adults do not disappear when an individual turns 18. By the same token, some under 18 have already attained a level of maturity some adults will never reach. For the reasons we have discussed, however, a line must be drawn. The plurality opinion in *Thompson* drew the line at 16. In the intervening years the *Thompson* plurality's conclusion that offenders under 16 may not be executed has not been challenged. The logic of *Thompson* extends to those who are under 18. The age of 18 is the point where society draws the line for many purposes between childhood and adulthood. It is, we conclude, the age at which the line for death eligibility ought to rest.

IV

Our determination that the death penalty is disproportionate punishment for offenders under 18 finds confirmation in the stark reality that the United States is the only country in the world that continues to give official sanction to the juvenile death penalty. This reality does not become controlling, for the task of interpreting the Eighth Amendment remains our responsibility. Yet at least from the time of the Court's decision in *Trop*, the Court has referred to the laws of other countries and to international authorities as instructive for its interpretation of the Eighth Amendment's prohibition of "cruel and unusual punishments."

As respondent and a number of *amici* emphasize, Article 37 of the United Nations Convention on the Rights of the Child, which every country in the world has ratified save for the United States and Somalia, contains an express prohibition on capital punishment for crimes committed by juveniles under 18. No ratifying country has entered a reservation to the provision prohibiting the execution of juvenile offenders. Parallel prohibitions are contained in other significant international covenants.

Respondent and his *amici* have submitted, and petitioner does not contest, that only seven countries other than the United States have executed juvenile offenders since 1990: Iran, Pakistan, Saudi Arabia, Yemen, Nigeria, the Democratic Republic of Congo, and China. Since then each of these countries has either abolished capital punishment for juveniles or made public disavowal of the practice. In sum, it is fair to say that the United States now stands alone in a world that has turned its face against the juvenile death penalty.

It is proper that we acknowledge the overwhelming weight of international opinion against the juvenile death penalty, resting in large part on the understanding that the instability and emotional imbalance of young people may often be a factor in the crime. The opinion of the world community, while not controlling our outcome, does provide respected and significant confirmation for our own conclusions.

Over time, from one generation to the next, the Constitution has come to earn the high respect and even, as Madison dared to hope, the veneration of the American people. See The Federalist No. 49, p. 314 (C. Rossiter ed.1961). The document sets forth, and rests upon, innovative principles original to the American experience, such as federalism; a proven balance in political mechanisms through separation of powers; specific guarantees for the accused in criminal cases; and broad provisions to secure individual freedom and preserve human dignity. These doctrines and guarantees are central to the American experience and remain essential to our present-day self-definition and national identity. Not the least of the reasons we honor the Constitution, then, is because we know it to be our own. It does not lessen our fidelity to the Constitution or our pride in its origins to acknowledge that the express affirmation of certain fundamental rights by other nations and peoples simply underscores the centrality of those same rights within our own heritage of freedom.

* * *

The Eighth and Fourteenth Amendments forbid imposition of the death penalty on offenders who were under the age of 18 when their crimes were committed. The judgment of the Missouri Supreme Court setting aside the sentence of death imposed upon Christopher Simmons is affirmed.

It is so ordered.

■ JUSTICE STEVENS, with whom JUSTICE GINSBURG joins, concurring.

Perhaps even more important than our specific holding today is our reaffirmation of the basic principle that informs the Court's interpretation of the Eighth Amendment. If the meaning of that Amendment had been frozen when it was originally drafted, it would impose no impediment to the execution of 7-year-old children today. See *Stanford v. Kentucky*, 492 U.S. 361, 368, 109 S.Ct. 2969, 106 L.Ed.2d 306 (1989) (describing the common law at the time of the Amendment's adoption). The evolving standards of decency that have driven our construction of this critically important part of the Bill of Rights foreclose any such reading of the Amendment. In the best tradition of the common law, the pace of that evolution is a matter for continuing debate; but that our understanding of the Constitution does change from time to time has been settled since John Marshall breathed life into its text. If great lawyers of his day—Alexander Hamilton, for example—were sitting with us today, I would expect them to join Justice KENNEDY's opinion for the Court. In all events, I do so without hesitation.

■ JUSTICE O'CONNOR, dissenting.

The Court's decision today establishes a categorical rule forbidding the execution of any offender for any crime committed before his 18th birthday, no matter how deliberate, wanton, or cruel the offense. Neither the objective evidence of contemporary societal values, nor the Court's moral proportionality analysis, nor the two in tandem suffice to justify this ruling.

Although the Court finds support for its decision in the fact that a majority of the States now disallow capital punishment of 17-year-old offenders, it refrains from asserting that its holding is compelled by a genuine national consensus. Indeed, the evidence before us fails to demonstrate conclusively that any such consensus has emerged in the brief period since we upheld the constitutionality of this practice in Stanford v. Kentucky,.

Instead, the rule decreed by the Court rests, ultimately, on its independent moral judgment that death is a disproportionately severe punishment for any 17-year-old offender. I do not subscribe to this judgment. Adolescents *as a class* are undoubtedly less mature, and therefore less culpable for their misconduct, than adults. But the Court has adduced no evidence impeaching the seemingly reasonable conclusion reached by many state legislatures: that at least *some* 17-year-old murderers are sufficiently mature to deserve the death penalty in an appropriate case. Nor has it been shown that capital sentencing juries are incapable of accurately assessing a youthful defendant's maturity or of giving due weight to the mitigating characteristics associated with youth.

On this record—and especially in light of the fact that so little has changed since our recent decision in *Stanford*—I would not substitute our judgment about the moral propriety of capital punishment for 17-year-old murderers for the judgments of the Nation's legislatures. Rather, I would demand a clearer showing that our society truly has set its face against this practice before reading the Eighth Amendment categorically to forbid it.

■ JUSTICE SCALIA, with whom THE CHIEF JUSTICE and JUSTICE THOMAS join, dissenting.

In urging approval of a constitution that gave life-tenured judges the power to nullify laws enacted by the people's representatives, Alexander Hamilton assured the citizens of New York that there was little risk in this, since "[t]he judiciary . . . ha[s] neither FORCE nor WILL but merely judgment." The Federalist No. 78, p. 465 (C. Rossiter ed.1961). But

Hamilton had in mind a traditional judiciary, "bound down by strict rules and precedents which serve to define and point out their duty in every particular case that comes before them." Bound down, indeed. What a mockery today's opinion makes of Hamilton's expectation, announcing the Court's conclusion that the meaning of our Constitution has changed over the past 15 years—not, mind you, that this Court's decision 15 years ago was *wrong*, but that the Constitution *has changed*. The Court reaches this implausible result by purporting to advert, not to the original meaning of the Eighth Amendment, but to "the evolving standards of decency," of our national society. It then finds, on the flimsiest of grounds, that a national consensus which could not be perceived in our people's laws barely 15 years ago now solidly exists. Worse still, the Court says in so many words that what our people's laws say about the issue does not, in the last analysis, matter: "[I]n the end our own judgment will be brought to bear on the question of the acceptability of the death penalty under the Eighth Amendment." The Court thus proclaims itself sole arbiter of our Nation's moral standards—and in the course of discharging that awesome responsibility purports to take guidance from the views of foreign courts and legislatures. Because I do not believe that the meaning of our Eighth Amendment, any more than the meaning of other provisions of our Constitution, should be determined by the subjective views of five Members of this Court and like-minded foreigners, I dissent.

II

Of course, the real force driving today's decision is not the actions of four state legislatures, but the Court's "own judgment" that murderers younger than 18 can never be as morally culpable as older counterparts. The Court claims that this usurpation of the role of moral arbiter is simply a "retur[n] to the rul[e] established in decisions predating *Stanford*," That supposed rule—which is reflected solely in dicta and never once in a *holding* that purports to supplant the consensus of the American people with the Justices' views—was repudiated in *Stanford* for the very good reason that it has no foundation in law or logic. If the Eighth Amendment set forth an ordinary rule of law, it would indeed be the role of this Court to say what the law is. But the Court having pronounced that the Eighth Amendment is an ever-changing reflection of "the evolving standards of decency" of our society, it makes no sense for the Justices then to *prescribe* those standards rather than discern them from the practices of our people. On the evolving-standards hypothesis, the only legitimate function of this Court is to identify a moral consensus of the American people. By what conceivable warrant can nine lawyers presume to be the authoritative conscience of the Nation?

We need not look far to find studies contradicting the Court's conclusions. As petitioner points out, the American Psychological Association (APA), which claims in this case that scientific evidence shows persons under 18 lack the ability to take moral responsibility for their decisions, has previously taken precisely the opposite position before this very Court. In its brief in *Hodgson v. Minnesota*, 497 U.S. 417, 110 S.Ct. 2926, 111 L.Ed.2d 344 (1990), the APA found a "rich body of research" showing that juveniles are mature enough to decide whether to obtain an abortion without parental involvement. The APA brief, citing psychology treatises and studies too numerous to list here, asserted: "[B]y middle adolescence (age 14–15) young people develop abilities similar to adults in reasoning about moral dilemmas, understanding social rules and laws, [and] reasoning about interpersonal relationships and interpersonal problems." Given the nuances of scientific methodology and conflicting views, courts—which can only consider the limited evidence on the record before them—are ill equipped to determine which view of science is the right one. Legislatures "are better qualified to weigh and 'evaluate the results of statistical studies in terms of their own local conditions and with a flexibility of approach that is not available to the courts.' "

Even putting aside questions of methodology, the studies cited by the Court offer scant support for a categorical prohibition of the death penalty for murderers under 18. At most, these studies conclude that, *on average*, or *in most cases*, persons under 18 are unable to take moral responsibility for their actions. Not one of the cited studies opines that all individuals under 18 are unable to appreciate the nature of their crimes.

The Court concludes, however, that juries cannot be trusted with the delicate task of weighing a defendant's youth along with the other mitigating and aggravating factors of his crime. This startling conclusion undermines the very foundations of our capital sentencing system, which entrusts juries with "mak[ing] the difficult and uniquely human judgments that defy codification and that 'buil[d] discretion, equity, and flexibility into a legal system.' " . . . The Court says, *ante*, at 1196–1197, that juries will be unable to appreciate the significance of a defendant's youth when faced with details of a brutal crime. This assertion is based on no evidence; to the contrary, the Court itself acknowledges that the execution of under-18 offenders is "infrequent" even in the States "without a formal prohibition on executing juveniles," *ante*, at 1192, suggesting that juries take seriously their responsibility to weigh youth as a mitigating factor.

III

Though the views of our own citizens are essentially irrelevant to the Court's decision today, the views of other countries and the so-called international community take center stage.

More fundamentally, however, the basic premise of the Court's argument—that American law should conform to the laws of the rest of the world—ought to be rejected out of hand. In fact the Court itself does not believe it. In many significant respects the laws of most other countries differ from our law—including not only such explicit provisions of our Constitution as the right to jury trial and grand jury indictment, but even many interpretations of the Constitution prescribed by this Court itself. The Court-pronounced exclusionary rule, for example, is distinctively American. When we adopted that rule in *Mapp v. Ohio*, 367 U.S. 643, 655, 81 S.Ct. 1684, 6 L.Ed.2d 1081 (1961), it was "unique to American jurisprudence." *Bivens v. Six Unknown Fed. Narcotics Agents*, 403 U.S. 388, 415, 91 S.Ct. 1999, 29 L.Ed.2d 619 (1971) (BURGER, C.J., dissenting). Since then a categorical exclusionary rule has been "universally rejected" by other countries, including those with rules prohibiting illegal searches and police misconduct, despite the fact that none of these countries "appears to have any alternative form of discipline for police that is effective in preventing search violations."

The Court has been oblivious to the views of other countries when deciding how to interpret our Constitution's requirement that "Congress shall make no law respecting an establishment of religion. . . ." Amdt. 1. Most other countries—including those committed to religious neutrality—do not insist on the degree of separation between church and state that this Court requires. For example, whereas "we have recognized special Establishment Clause dangers where the government makes direct money payments to sectarian institutions," *Rosenberger v. Rector and Visitors of Univ. of Va.*, 515 U.S. 819, 842, 115 S.Ct. 2510, 132 L.Ed.2d 700 (1995) (citing cases), countries such as the Netherlands, Germany, and Australia allow direct government funding of religious schools on the ground that "the state can only be truly neutral between secular and religious perspectives if it does not dominate the provision of so key a service as education, and makes it possible for people to exercise their right of religious expression within the context of public funding."

And let us not forget the Court's abortion jurisprudence, which makes us one of only six countries that allow abortion on demand until the point of viability. Though the Government and *amici* in cases following *Roe v. Wade*, 410 U.S. 113, 93 S.Ct. 705, 35 L.Ed.2d 147 (1973), urged the Court to follow the international community's lead, these arguments fell on deaf ears.

The Court should either profess its willingness to reconsider all these matters in light of the views of foreigners, or else it should cease putting forth foreigners' views as part of the *reasoned basis* of its decisions. To invoke alien law when it agrees with one's own thinking, and ignore it otherwise, is not reasoned decisionmaking, but sophistry.

The Court responds that "[i]t does not lessen our fidelity to the Constitution or our pride in its origins to acknowledge that the express affirmation of certain fundamental rights by other nations and peoples simply underscores the centrality of those same rights within our own heritage of freedom." *Ante*, at 1200. To begin with, I do not believe that approval by "other nations and peoples" should buttress our commitment to American principles any more than (what should logically follow) disapproval by "other nations and peoples" should weaken that commitment. More importantly, however, the Court's statement flatly misdescribes what is going on here. Foreign sources are cited today, *not* to underscore our "fidelity" to the Constitution, our "pride in its origins," and "our own [American] heritage." To the contrary, they are cited *to set aside* the centuries-old American practice—a practice still engaged in by a large majority of the relevant States—of letting a jury of 12 citizens decide whether, in the particular case, youth should be the basis for withholding the death penalty. What these foreign sources "affirm," rather than repudiate, is the Justices' own notion of how the world ought to be, and their dicta that it shall be so henceforth in America. The Court's parting attempt to downplay the significance of its extensive discussion of foreign law is unconvincing. "Acknowledgment" of foreign approval has no place in the legal opinion of this Court *unless it is part of the basis for the Court's judgment*—which is surely what it parades as today.

IV

We must disregard the new reality that, to the extent our Eighth Amendment decisions constitute something more than a show of hands on the current Justices' current personal views about penology, they purport to be nothing more than a snapshot of American public opinion at a particular point in time (with the timeframes now shortened to a mere 15 years). We must treat these decisions just as though they represented *real* law, *real* prescriptions democratically adopted by the American people, as conclusively (rather than sequentially) construed by this Court. Allowing lower courts to reinterpret the Eighth Amendment whenever they decide enough time has passed for a new snapshot leaves this Court's decisions without any force—especially since the "evolution" of our Eighth Amendment is no longer determined by objective criteria. To allow lower courts to behave as we do, "updating" the Eighth Amendment as needed, destroys stability and makes our case law an unreliable basis for the designing of laws by citizens and their representatives, and for action by public officials. The result will be to crown arbitrariness with chaos.

NOTES

1. Five years after the Supreme Court decided *Roper*, it was faced with determining the constitutionality of imposing a life without parole ("LWOP") sentence on a juvenile for a non-homicide offence. In Graham v. Florida, 560 U.S. 48, 130 S.Ct. 2011, 176 L.Ed.2d. 825 (2010), the Court held, relying in part on *Roper*, that juveniles must be afforded "some meaningful opportunity to obtain release based on demonstrated maturity and rehabilitation." The Court found that an LWOP sentence for a non-homicide offence was in conflict with this principle and, therefore, found such sentences unconstitutional. Two years later, in Miller v. Alabama, 567 U.S. 460, 132 S.Ct. 2455, 183 L.Ed.2d 407 (2012), the Court further extended its juvenile sentencing jurisprudence to prohibit mandatory life sentences imposed on juveniles convicted of homicide.

2. Despite the *Roper-Graham-Miller* trilogy, there is still a lack of clarity with regard to constitutional sentencing and juveniles. Consider the following circumstances. A fifteen-year-old defendant is convicted of four counts of rape, one count of kidnapping, and one count of battery, all of which are non-homicide offenses. At the defendant's sentencing hearing, the judge determines that the defendant's sentences will run consecutively, imprisoning the defendant for eighty-five years. Additionally, the judge determines that the defendant is not entitled to parole for any of the sentences. Would this constitute an unconstitutional sentence under the *Roper-Graham-Miller* trilogy? *Compare* Bunch v. Smith, 685 F.3d 546 (6th Cir. 2012), *with* People v. Caballero, 55 Cal.4th 262, 145 Cal.Rptr.3d 286 (2012).

3. DISPROPORTIONALITY OF SENTENCES

Rummel v. Estelle, Corrections Director

Supreme Court of the United States, 1980.
445 U.S. 263, 100 S.Ct. 1133, 63 L.Ed.2d 382.

■ MR. JUSTICE REHNQUIST delivered the opinion of the Court.

Petitioner William James Rummel is presently serving a life sentence imposed by the State of Texas in 1973 under its "recidivist statute," formerly Art. 63 of its Penal Code, which provided that "[w]hoever shall have been three times convicted of a felony less than capital shall on such third conviction be imprisoned for life in the penitentiary." . . .

I

In 1964 the State of Texas charged Rummel with fraudulent use of a credit card to obtain $80 worth of goods or services. Because the amount in question was greater than $50, the charged offense was a felony punishable by a minimum of 2 years and a maximum of 10 years in the Texas Department of Corrections. Rummel eventually pleaded guilty to the charge and was sentenced to three years' confinement in a state penitentiary.

In 1969 the State of Texas charged Rummel with passing a forged check in the amount of $28.36, a crime punishable by imprisonment in a penitentiary for not less than two nor more than five years. Rummel pleaded guilty to this offense and was sentenced to four years' imprisonment.

In 1973 Rummel was charged with obtaining $120.75 by false pretenses. Because the amount obtained was greater than $50, the charged offense was designated "felony theft," which, by itself, was punishable by confinement in a penitentiary for not less than 2 nor more than 10 years. The prosecution chose, however, to proceed against Rummel under Texas' recidivist statute, and cited in the indictment his 1964 and 1969 convictions as requiring imposition of a life sentence if Rummel were convicted of the charged offense. A jury convicted Rummel of felony theft and also found as true the allegation that he had been convicted of two prior felonies. As a result, on April 26, 1973, the trial court imposed upon Rummel the life sentence mandated by Art. 63.

The Texas appellate courts rejected Rummel's direct appeal as well as his subsequent collateral attacks on his imprisonment. Rummel then filed a petition for a writ of habeas corpus in the United States District Court for the Western District of Texas. In that petition, he claimed, *inter alia*, that his life sentence was so disproportionate to the crimes he had committed as to constitute cruel and unusual punishment. The District Court rejected this claim, . . .

A divided panel of the Court of Appeals reversed. The majority relied upon this Court's decision in Weems v. United States, 217 U.S. 349 (1910), and a decision of the United States Court of Appeals for the Fourth Circuit, Hart v. Coiner, 483 F.2d 136 (1973), cert. denied, 415 U.S. 983 (1974), in holding that Rummel's life sentence was "so grossly disproportionate" to his offenses as to constitute cruel and unusual punishment.

Rummel's case was reheard by the Court of Appeals sitting en banc. That court vacated the panel opinion and affirmed the District Court's denial of habeas corpus relief on Rummel's Eighth Amendment claim. Of particular importance to the majority of the Court of Appeals en banc was the probability that Rummel would be eligible for parole within 12 years of his initial confinement. Six members of the Court of Appeals dissented, arguing that Rummel had no enforceable right to parole and that *Weems* and *Hart* compelled a finding that Rummel's life sentence was unconstitutional.

II

Initially, we believe it important to set forth two propositions that Rummel does not contest. First, Rummel does not challenge the constitutionality of Texas' recidivist statute as a general proposition. . . .

Second, Rummel does not challenge Texas' authority to punish each of his offenses as felonies, that is, by imprisoning him in a state penitentiary. . . . Rummel's challenge thus focuses only on the State's authority to impose a sentence of life imprisonment, as opposed to a substantial term of years, for his third felony.

This Court has on occasion stated that the Eighth Amendment prohibits imposition of a sentence that is grossly disproportionate to the severity of the crime. In recent years this proposition has appeared most frequently in opinions dealing with the death penalty. Rummel cites these latter opinions dealing with capital punishment as compelling the conclusion that his sentence is disproportionate to his offenses. But as Mr. Justice Stewart noted in *Furman*:

> "The penalty of death differs from all other forms of criminal punishment, not in degree but in kind. It is unique in its total irrevocability. It is unique in its rejection of rehabilitation of the convict as a basic purpose of criminal justice. And it is unique, finally, in its absolute renunciation of all that is embodied in our concept of humanity."

This theme, the unique nature of the death penalty for purposes of Eighth Amendment analysis, has been repeated time and time again in our opinions. . . . Because a sentence of death differs in kind from any sentence of imprisonment, no matter how long, our decisions applying the prohibition of cruel and unusual punishments to capital cases are of limited assistance in deciding the constitutionality of the punishment meted out to Rummel.

Outside the context of capital punishment, successful challenges to the proportionality of particular sentences have been exceedingly rare. In Weems v. United States, supra, a case coming to this Court from the Supreme Court of the Philippine Islands, petitioner successfully attacked the imposition of a punishment known as *"cadena temporal"* for the crime of falsifying a public record. Although the Court in *Weems* invalidated the sentence after weighing "the mischief and the remedy," its finding of disproportionality cannot be wrenched from the extreme facts of that case. As for the "mischief," Weems was convicted of falsifying a public document, a crime apparently complete upon the knowing entry of a single item of false information in a public record, "though there be no one injured, though there be no fraud or purpose of it, no gain or desire of it." The mandatory "remedy" for this offense was *cadena temporal*, a punishment described graphically by the Court:

> Its minimum degree is confinement in a penal institution for twelve years and one day, a chain at the ankle and wrist of the offender, hard and painful labor, no assistance from friend or relative, no marital authority or parental rights or rights of property, no participation even in the family council. These parts of his penalty endure for the term of imprisonment. From other parts there is no intermission. His prison bars and chains are removed, it is true, after twelve years, but he goes from them to a perpetual limitation of his liberty. He is forever kept under the shadow of his crime, forever kept within voice and view of the criminal magistrate, not being able to change his domicil without giving notice to the "authority immediately in charge of his surveillance," and without permission in writing.

Although Rummel argues that the length of Weems' imprisonment was, by itself, a basis for the Court's decision, the Court's opinion does not support such a simple conclusion. The opinion consistently referred jointly to the length of imprisonment and its "accessories" or "accompaniments." Indeed, the Court expressly rejected an argument made on behalf of the United States that "the provision for imprisonment in the Philippine Code is separable from the accessory punishment, and that the latter may be declared illegal, leaving the former to have application." According to the Court, "[t]he Philippine Code unites the penalties of *cadena temporal*, principal and accessory, and it is not in our power to separate them. . . ." Thus, we do not believe that *Weems* can be applied without regard to its peculiar facts: the triviality of the charged offense, the impressive length of the minimum term of imprisonment, and the extraordinary nature of the "accessories" included within the punishment of *cadena temporal*.

Given the unique nature of the punishments considered in *Weems* and in the death penalty cases, one could argue without fear of contradiction by any decision of this Court that for crimes concededly classified and classifiable as felonies, that is, as punishable by significant terms of imprisonment in a state penitentiary, the length of the sentence actually imposed is purely a matter of legislative prerogative.[11] Only six years after *Weems*, for example, Mr. Justice Holmes wrote for a unanimous Court in brushing aside a proportionality challenge to concurrent sentences of five years' imprisonment and cumulative fines of $1,000 on each of seven counts of mail fraud. See Badders v. United States, 240 U.S. 391 (1916). According to the Court, there was simply "no ground for declaring the punishment unconstitutional."

Such reluctance to review legislatively mandated terms of imprisonment is implicit in our more recent decisions as well. . . .

In an attempt to provide us with objective criteria against which we might measure the proportionality of his life sentence, Rummel points to certain characteristics of his offenses that allegedly render them "petty." He cites, for example, the absence of violence in his crimes. But the presence or absence of violence does not always affect the strength of society's interest in deterring a particular crime or in punishing a particular criminal. A high official in a large corporation can commit undeniably serious crimes in the area of antitrust, bribery, or clean air or water standards without coming close to engaging in any "violent" or short-term "life-threatening" behavior. Additionally, Rummel cites the "small" amount of money taken in each of his crimes. But to recognize that the State of Texas could have imprisoned Rummel for life if he had stolen $5,000, $50,000, or $500,000, rather than the $120.75 that a jury

---

[11] This is not to say that a proportionality principle would not come into play in the extreme example mentioned by the dissent, if a legislature made overtime parking a felony punishable by life imprisonment.

convicted him of stealing, is virtually to concede that the lines to be drawn are indeed "subjective," and therefore properly within the province of legislatures, not courts. Moreover, if Rummel had attempted to defraud his victim of $50,000, but had failed, no money whatsoever would have changed hands; yet Rummel would be no less blameworthy, only less skillful, than if he had succeeded.

* * *

Nearly 70 years ago, and only 2 years after *Weems*, this Court rejected an Eighth Amendment claim that seems factually indistinguishable from that advanced by Rummel in the present case. In Graham v. West Virginia, 224 U.S. 616 (1912), this Court considered the case of an apparently incorrigible horse thief who was sentenced to life imprisonment under West Virginia's recidivist statute. In 1898 Graham had been convicted of stealing "one bay mare" valued at $50; in 1901 he had been convicted of "feloniously and burglariously" entering a stable in order to steal "one brown horse, named Harry, of the value of $100"; finally, in 1907 he was convicted of stealing "one red roan horse" valued at $75 and various tack and accessories valued at $85. Upon conviction of this last crime, Graham received the life sentence mandated by West Virginia's recidivist statute. This Court did not tarry long on Graham's Eighth Amendment claim, noting only that it could not be maintained "that cruel and unusual punishment [had] been inflicted."

Undaunted by earlier cases like *Graham* and *Badders*, Rummel attempts to ground his proportionality attack on an alleged "nationwide" trend away from mandatory life sentences and toward "lighter, discretionary sentences." According to Rummel, "[n]o jurisdiction in the United States or the Free World punishes habitual offenders as harshly as Texas." In support of this proposition, Rummel offers detailed charts and tables documenting the history of recidivist statutes in the United States since 1776.

* * *

Rummel's charts and tables do appear to indicate that he might have received more lenient treatment in almost any State other than Texas, West Virginia, or Washington. The distinctions, however, are subtle rather than gross. A number of States impose a mandatory life sentence upon conviction of four felonies rather than three. Other States require one or more of the felonies to be "violent" to support a life sentence. Still other States leave the imposition of a life sentence after three felonies within the discretion of a judge or jury. It is one thing for a court to compare those States that impose capital punishment for a specific offense with those States that do not. It is quite another thing for a court to attempt to evaluate the position of any particular recidivist scheme within Rummel's complex matrix.

Nor do Rummel's extensive charts even begin to reflect the complexity of the comparison he asks this Court to make. Texas, we are told, has a relatively liberal policy of granting "good time" credits to its prisoners, a policy that historically has allowed a prisoner serving a life sentence to become eligible for parole in as little as 12 years. We agree with Rummel that his inability to enforce any "right" to parole precludes us from treating his life sentence as if it were equivalent to a sentence of 12 years. Nevertheless, because parole is "an established variation on imprisonment of convicted criminals," a proper assessment of Texas' treatment of Rummel could hardly ignore the possibility that he will not actually be imprisoned for the rest of his life. If nothing else, the possibility of parole, however slim, serves to distinguish Rummel from a person sentenced under a recidivist statute like Mississippi's, which provides for a sentence of life without parole upon conviction of three felonies including at least one violent felony.

* * *

III

The most casual review of the various criminal justice systems now in force in the 50 States of the Union shows that the line dividing felony theft from petty larceny, a line usually based on the value of the property taken, varies markedly from one State to another. We believe that Texas is entitled to make its own judgment as to where such lines lie, subject only to those strictures of the Eighth Amendment that can be informed by objective factors. Moreover, given Rummel's record, Texas was not required to treat him in the same manner as it might treat him were this his first "petty property offense." Having twice imprisoned him for felonies, Texas was entitled to place upon Rummel the onus of one who is simply unable to bring his conduct within the social norms prescribed by the criminal law of the State.

The purpose of a recidivist statute such as that involved here is not to simplify the task of prosecutors, judges, or juries. Its primary goals are to deter repeat offenders and, at some point in the life of one who repeatedly commits criminal offenses serious enough to be punished as felonies, to segregate that person from the rest of society for an extended period of time. This segregation and its duration are based not merely on that person's most recent offense but also on the propensities he has demonstrated over a period of time during which he has been convicted of and sentenced for other crimes. Like the line dividing felony theft from petty larceny, the point at which a recidivist will be deemed to have demonstrated the necessary propensities and the amount of time that the recidivist will be isolated from society are matters largely within the discretion of the punishing jurisdiction.

We therefore hold that the mandatory life sentence imposed upon this petitioner does not constitute cruel and unusual punishment under the Eighth and Fourteenth Amendments. The judgment of the Court of Appeals will be

Affirmed.

■ The opinion of JUSTICE STEWART, concurring, is omitted.

■ MR. JUSTICE POWELL, with whom MR. JUSTICE BRENNAN, MR. JUSTICE MARSHALL, and MR. JUSTICE STEVENS join, dissenting.

The question in this case is whether petitioner was subjected to cruel and unusual punishment in contravention of the Eighth Amendment, made applicable to the States by the Fourteenth Amendment, when he received a mandatory life sentence upon his conviction for a third property-related felony. Today, the Court holds that petitioner has not been punished unconstitutionally. I dissent.

I

* * *

This Court today affirms the Fifth Circuit's decision. I dissent because I believe that (i) the penalty for a noncapital offense may be unconstitutionally disproportionate, (ii) the possibility of parole should not be considered in assessing the nature of the punishment, (iii) a mandatory life sentence is grossly disproportionate as applied to petitioner, and (iv) the conclusion that this petitioner has suffered a violation of his Eighth Amendment rights is compatible with principles of judicial restraint and federalism.

II

A

The Eighth Amendment prohibits "cruel and unusual punishments." That language came from Art. I, § 9, of the Virginia Declaration of Rights, which provided that "excessive bail ought not to be required, nor excessive fines imposed, nor cruel and unusual punishment inflicted." The words of the Virginia Declaration were taken from the English Bill of Rights of 1689. See Granucci, "Nor Cruel and Unusual Punishments Inflicted": The Original Meaning, 57 Calif.L.Rev. 839, 840 (1969).

Although the legislative history of the Eighth Amendment is not extensive, we can be certain that the Framers intended to proscribe inhumane methods of punishment. When the Virginia delegates met to consider the Federal Constitution, for example, Patrick Henry specifically noted the absence of the provisions contained within the Virginia Declaration. Henry feared that without a "cruel and unusual punishments" clause, Congress "may introduce the practice . . . of torturing, to extort a confession of the crime." Indeed, during debate in the First Congress on the adoption of the Bill of Rights, one Congressman objected to adoption of the Eighth Amendment precisely because "villains often deserve whipping, and perhaps having their ears cut off."

In two 19th-century cases, the Court considered constitutional challenges to forms of capital punishment. In Wilkerson v. Utah, 99 U.S. 130, 135 (1879), the Court held that death by shooting did not constitute cruel and unusual punishment. The Court emphasized, however, that torturous methods of execution, such as burning a live offender, would violate the Eighth Amendment. In re Kemmler, 136 U.S. 436 (1890), provided the Court with its second opportunity to review methods of carrying out a death penalty. That case involved a constitutional challenge to New York's use of electrocution. Although the Court did not apply the Eighth Amendment to state action, it did conclude that electrocution would not deprive the petitioner of due process of law. See also Louisiana ex rel. Francis v. Resweber, 329 U.S. 459, 464 (1947).

B

The scope of the Cruel and Unusual Punishments Clause extends not only to barbarous methods of punishment, but also to punishments that are grossly disproportionate. Disproportionality analysis measures the relationship between the nature and number of offenses committed and the severity of the punishment inflicted upon the offender. The inquiry focuses on whether a person deserves such punishment, not simply on whether punishment would serve a utilitarian goal. A statute that levied a mandatory life sentence for overtime parking might well deter vehicular lawlessness, but it would offend our felt sense of justice. The Court concedes today that the principle of disproportionality plays a role in the review of sentences imposing the death penalty, but suggests that the principle may be less applicable when a noncapital sentence is challenged. Such a limitation finds no support in the history of Eighth Amendment jurisprudence.

The principle of disproportionality is rooted deeply in English constitutional law. The Magna Carta of 1215 insured that "[a] free man shall not be [fined] for a trivial offence, except in accordance with the degree of the offence; and for a serious offence he shall be [fined] according to its gravity." By 1400, the English common law had embraced the principle, not always followed in practice, that punishment should not be excessive either in severity or length. One commentator's survey of English law demonstrates that the "cruel and unusual punishments" clause of the English Bill of Rights of 1689 "was first, an objection to the imposition of punishments which were unauthorized by statute and outside the jurisdiction of the sentencing court, and second, a reiteration of the English policy against disproportionate penalties." Granucci, supra, at 860.

In Weems v. United States (1910), a public official convicted for falsifying a public record claimed that he suffered cruel and unusual punishment when he was sentenced to serve 15 years' imprisonment in hard labor with chains.[5] The sentence also subjected Weems to loss of civil rights and perpetual surveillance after his release. This Court agreed that the punishment was cruel and unusual. The Court was attentive to the methods of the punishment, but its conclusion did not rest solely upon the nature of punishment. The Court relied explicitly upon the relationship between the crime committed and the punishment imposed:

> Such penalties for such offenses amaze those who have formed their conception of the relation of a state to even its offending citizens from the practice of the American commonwealths, and believe that it is a precept of justice that punishment for crime should be graduated and proportioned to offense.

In both capital and noncapital cases this Court has recognized that the decision in Weems v. United States "proscribes punishment grossly disproportionate to the severity of the crime."

In order to resolve the constitutional issue, the *Weems* Court measured the relationship between the punishment and the offense. The Court noted that Weems had been punished more severely than persons in the same jurisdiction who committed more serious crimes, or persons who committed a similar crime in other American jurisdictions.

Robinson v. California (1962), established that the Cruel and Unusual Punishments Clause applies to the States through the operation of the Fourteenth Amendment. The Court held that imprisonment for the crime of being a drug addict was cruel and unusual. The Court based its holding not upon the method of punishment, but on the nature of the "crime." Because drug addiction is an illness which may be contracted involuntarily, the Court said that "imprisonment for ninety days is not, in the abstract, a punishment which is either cruel or unusual. But the question cannot be considered in the abstract. Even one day in prison would be a cruel and unusual punishment for the 'crime' of having a common cold."

In Furman v. Georgia (1972), the Court held that the death penalty may constitute cruel and unusual punishment in some circumstances. The special relevance of *Furman* to this case lies in the general acceptance by Members of the Court of two basic principles. First, the Eighth Amendment prohibits grossly excessive punishment. Second, the

---

[5] The principle that grossly disproportionate sentences violate the Eighth Amendment was first enunciated in this Court by Mr. Justice Field in O'Neil v. Vermont, 144 U.S. 323 (1892). In that case, a defendant convicted of 307 offenses for selling alcoholic beverages in Vermont had been sentenced to more than 54 years in prison. The Court did not reach the question whether the sentence violated the Eighth Amendment because the issue had not been raised properly, and because the Eighth Amendment had yet to be applied against the States. But Mr. Justice Field dissented, asserting that the "cruel and unusual punishment" Clause was directed "against all punishments which by their excessive length or severity are greatly disproportionate to the offences charged."

scope of the Eighth Amendment is to be measured by "evolving standards of decency."

* * *

In sum, a few basic principles emerge from the history of the Eighth Amendment. Both barbarous forms of punishment and grossly excessive punishments are cruel and unusual. A sentence may be excessive if it serves no acceptable social purpose, or is grossly disproportionate to the seriousness of the crime. The principle of disproportionality has been acknowledged to apply to both capital and noncapital sentences.

* * *

III

* * *

IV

The Eighth Amendment commands this Court to enforce the constitutional limitation of the Cruel and Unusual Punishments Clause. In discharging this responsibility, we should minimize the risk of constitutionalizing the personal predilections of federal judges by relying upon certain objective factors. Among these are (i) the nature of the offense; (ii) the sentence imposed for commission of the same crime in other jurisdictions; and (iii) the sentence imposed upon other criminals in the same jurisdiction.

A

Each of the crimes that underlies the petitioner's conviction as a habitual offender involves the use of fraud to obtain small sums of money ranging from $28.36 to $120.75. In total, the three crimes involved slightly less than $230. None of the crimes involved injury to one's person, threat of injury to one's person, violence, the threat of violence, or the use of a weapon. Nor does the commission of any such crimes ordinarily involve a threat of violent action against another person or his property. It is difficult to imagine felonies that pose less danger to the peace and good order of a civilized society than the three crimes committed by the petitioner. Indeed, the state legislature's recodification of its criminal law supports this conclusion. Since the petitioner was convicted as a habitual offender, the State has reclassified his third offense, theft by false pretext, as a misdemeanor.

B

Apparently, only 12 States have ever enacted habitual offender statutes imposing a mandatory life sentence for the commission of two or three nonviolent felonies and only 3, Texas, Washington, and West Virginia, have retained such a statute. Thus, three-fourths of the States that experimented with the Texas scheme appear to have decided that the imposition of a mandatory life sentence upon some persons who have committed three felonies represents excess punishment. Kentucky, for example, replaced the mandatory life sentence with a more flexible scheme "because of a judgment that under some circumstances life imprisonment for an habitual criminal is not justified. An example would be an offender who has committed three Class D felonies, none involving injury to person." Commentary following Criminal Law of Kentucky Annotated, Penal Code § 532.080, p. 790 (1978). The State of Kansas abolished its statute mandating a life sentence for the commission of three felonies after a state legislative commission concluded that "[t]he legislative policy as expressed in the habitual criminal law bears no particular resemblance to the enforcement policy of prosecutors and judges." Kansas Legislative Council, The Operation of the Kansas Habitual Criminal Law, Pub. No. 47, p. 4 (1936). In the eight years following enactment of the Kansas statute, only 96 of the 733 defendants who committed their third felony were sentenced to life imprisonment. This statistic strongly supports the belief that prosecutors and judges thought the habitual offender statute too severe. In Washington, which retains the Texas rule, the State Supreme Court has suggested that application of its statute to persons like the petitioner might constitute cruel and unusual punishment.

More than three-quarters of American jurisdictions have never adopted a habitual offender statute that would commit the petitioner to mandatory life imprisonment. The jurisdictions that currently employ habitual offender statutes either (i) require the commission of more than three offenses, (ii) require the commission of at least one violent crime, (iii) limit a mandatory penalty to less than life, or (iv) grant discretion to the sentencing authority. In none of the jurisdictions could the petitioner have received a mandatory life sentence merely upon the showing that he committed three nonviolent property-related offenses.

The federal habitual offender statute also differs materially from the Texas statute. Title 18 U.S.C. § 3575 provides increased sentences for "dangerous special offenders" who have been convicted of a felony. A defendant is a "dangerous special offender" if he has committed two or more previous felonies, one of them within the last five years, if the current felony arose from a pattern of conduct "which constituted a substantial source of his income, and in which he manifested special skill or expertise," or if the felony involved a criminal conspiracy in which the defendant played a supervisory role. Federal courts may sentence such persons "to imprisonment for an appropriate term not to exceed twenty-five years and not disproportionate in severity to the maximum term otherwise authorized by law for such felony." Thus, Congress and an overwhelming number of state legislatures have not adopted the Texas scheme. These legislative decisions lend credence to the view that a mandatory life sentence for the commission of three nonviolent felonies is unconstitutionally disproportionate.[21]

* * *

C

* * *

V

The Court today agrees with the State's arguments that a decision in petitioner's favor would violate principles of federalism and, because of difficulty in formulating standards to guide the decision of the federal courts, would lead to excessive interference with state sentencing decisions. Neither contention is convincing.

Each State has sovereign responsibilities to promulgate and enforce its criminal law. In our federal system we should never forget that the Constitution "recognizes and preserves the autonomy and independence of the States—independence in their legislative and independence in their judicial departments." But even as the Constitution recognizes a sphere of state activity free from federal interference, it explicitly compels the States to follow certain constitutional commands. When we apply the Cruel and Unusual Punishments Clause against the States, we merely enforce an obligation that the Constitution has created. As Mr. Justice Rehnquist has stated, "[c]ourts are exercising no more than the judicial function conferred upon them by Art. III of the Constitution when they assess, in a case before them, whether or not a particular legislative enactment is within the authority granted by the Constitution to the enacting body, and whether it runs afoul of some limitation placed by the Constitution on the authority of that body."

Because the State believes that the federal courts can formulate no practicable standard to identify grossly disproportionate sentences, it fears that the courts would intervene into state criminal justice systems at will. Such a "floodgates" argument can be easy to make and difficult to rebut. But in this case we can identify and apply objective criteria that reflect constitutional standards of punishment and minimize the risk of judicial subjectivity. Moreover, we can rely upon the experience of the

---

[21] The American Law Institute proposes that a felon be sentenced to an extended term of punishment only if he is a persistent offender, professional criminal, dangerous mentally abnormal person whose extended commitment is necessary for the protection of the public, or "a multiple offender whose criminality was so extensive that a sentence of imprisonment for an extended term is warranted." ALI, Model Penal Code § 7.03 (Prop.Off.Draft 1962). The term for a multiple offender may not exceed the longest sentences of imprisonment authorized for each of the offender's crimes if they ran consecutively. Under this proposal the petitioner could have been sentenced up to 25 years.

The American Bar Association has proposed that habitual offenders be sentenced to no more than 25 years and that "[a]ny increased term which can be imposed because of prior criminality should be related in severity to the sentence otherwise provided for the new offense." The choice of sentence would be left to the discretion of the sentencing court. ABA Project on Standards for Criminal Justice, Sentencing Alternatives and Procedures § 3.3 (App.Draft 1968).

United States Court of Appeals for the Fourth Circuit in applying criteria similar to those that I believe should govern this case.

In 1974, the Fourth Circuit considered the claim of a West Virginia prisoner who alleged that the imposition of a mandatory life sentence for three nonviolent crimes violated the Eighth Amendment. In Hart v. Coiner, 483 F.2d 136 (1973), cert. denied, 415 U.S. 983 (1974), the court held that the mandatory sentence was unconstitutional as applied to the prisoner. The court noted that none of the offenses involved violence or the danger of violence, that only a few States would apply such a sentence, and that West Virginia gave less severe sentences to first- and second-time offenders who committed more serious offenses. The holding in Hart v. Coiner is the holding that the State contends will undercut the ability of the States to exercise independent sentencing authority. Yet the Fourth Circuit subsequently has found only twice that noncapital sentences violate the Eighth Amendment. In Davis v. Davis, 601 F.2d 153 (1979) (en banc), the court held that a 40-year sentence for possession and distribution of less than nine ounces of marihuana was cruel and unusual. In Roberts v. Collins, 544 F.2d 168 (1976), the court held that a person could not receive a longer sentence for a lesser included offense (assault) than he could have received for the greater offense (assault with intent to murder).

More significant are those cases in which the Fourth Circuit held that the principles of Hart v. Coiner were inapplicable. In a case decided the same day as Hart v. Coiner, the Court of Appeals held that a 10-year sentence given for two obscene telephone calls did not violate the Cruel and Unusual Punishments Clause. The court stated that "[w]hatever may be our subjective view of the matter, we fail to discern here objective factors establishing disproportionality in violation of the eighth amendment." Wood v. South Carolina, 483 F.2d 149, 150 (1973). In Griffin v. Warden, 517 F.2d 756 (1975), the court refused to hold that the West Virginia statute was unconstitutionally applied to a person who had been convicted of breaking and entering a gasoline and grocery store, burglary of a residence, and grand larceny. The court distinguished Hart v. Coiner on the ground that Griffin's offenses "clearly involve the potentiality of violence and danger to life as well as property." Similarly, the Fourth Circuit turned aside an Eighth Amendment challenge to the imposition of a 10- to 20-year sentence for statutory rape of a 13-year-old female. Hall v. McKenzie, 537 F.2d 1232, 1235–1236 (1976). The court emphasized that the sentence was less severe than a mandatory life sentence, that the petitioner would have received a similar sentence in 17 other American jurisdictions, and that the crime involved violation of personal integrity and the potential of physical injury. The Fourth Circuit also has rejected Eighth Amendment challenges brought by persons sentenced to 12 years for possession and distribution of heroin, United States v. Atkinson, 513 F.2d 38, 42 (1975), 2 years for unlawful possession of a firearm, United States v. Wooten, 503 F.2d 65, 67 (1974),

15 years for assault with intent to commit murder, Robinson v. Warden, 455 F.2d 1172 (1972), and 40 years for kidnaping, United States v. Martell, 335 F.2d 764 (1964).

I do not suggest that each of the decisions in which the Court of Appeals for the Fourth Circuit applied Hart v. Coiner is necessarily correct. But I do believe that the body of Eighth Amendment law that has developed in that Circuit constitutes impressive empirical evidence that the federal courts are capable of applying the Eighth Amendment to disproportionate noncapital sentences with a high degree of sensitivity to principles of federalism and state autonomy.

VI

I recognize that the difference between the petitioner's grossly disproportionate sentence and other prisoners' constitutionally valid sentences is not separated by the clear distinction that separates capital from noncapital punishment. "But the fact that a line has to be drawn somewhere does not justify its being drawn anywhere." The Court has, in my view, chosen the easiest line rather than the best.

* * *

We are construing a living Constitution. The sentence imposed upon the petitioner would be viewed as grossly unjust by virtually every layman and lawyer. In my view, objective criteria clearly establish that a mandatory life sentence for defrauding persons of about $230 crosses any rationally drawn line separating punishment that lawfully may be imposed from that which is proscribed by the Eighth Amendment. I would reverse the decision of the Court of Appeals.

NOTES AND QUESTIONS

1. In Hutto v. Davis, 454 U.S. 370, 102 S.Ct. 703, 70 L.Ed.2d 556 (1982) (per curiam), the Court upheld, on the basis of *Rummel*, a forty-year sentence for two marijuana convictions. Yet, in Solem v. Helm, 463 U.S. 277, 103 S.Ct. 3001, 77 L.Ed.2d 637 (1983), the Supreme Court concluded that *Rummel* and *Hutto* did not preclude a "disproportionality" inquiry into the sentence imposed by a state court. Helm, an alcoholic, had a record of several non-violent felonies, including third-degree burglary, drunk driving, grand larceny, and obtaining money under false pretenses. When he pleaded guilty to the offense of uttering a "no account" check, he was sentenced to life imprisonment under the habitual offender statute. The Supreme Court held that the life sentence with ineligibility for parole constituted cruel and unusual punishment.

However, eight years later in Harmelin v. Michigan, 501 U.S. 957, 111 S.Ct. 2680, 115 L.Ed.2d 836 (1991), a badly fractured Court again drastically limited federal court proportionality review of state sentences under the cruel and unusual punishment clause of the Eighth Amendment. In *Harmelin*, the Court upheld a mandatory term of life in prison without parole for the possession of 672 grams of cocaine. Is it possible to reconcile *Harmelin* and *Solem*? After *Harmelin*, where has the Supreme Court left proportionality analysis under the cruel and unusual punishment clause?

2. The Court upheld two convictions under California's "three strikes" sentencing law in 2003. Both cases involved the imposition of lengthy sentences for relatively minor property crimes on offenders whose records for prior, more serious offenses made them eligible for sentencing under the California statute. *See* Lockyer v. Andrade, 538 U.S. 63, 123 S.Ct. 1166, 155 L.Ed.2d 144 (2003); Ewing v. California, 538 U.S. 11, 123 S.Ct. 1179, 155 L.Ed.2d 108 (2003). In *Andrade*, the petitioner had been convicted of petty theft for shoplifting nine video tapes from K-Mart, which under California law was enhanced to a felony because of prior, albeit nonviolent, offenses. Then because Andrade had committed prior felony offenses, such as burglary and transportation of marijuana, he was sentenced under California's "three strikes" law to life in prison with no possibility of parole for fifty years. The United States Court of Appeals for the Ninth Circuit had reversed his conviction, holding that the sentence was grossly disproportionate to the crimes and therefore violated the constitutional prohibition against cruel and unusual punishment. In *Ewing*, the petitioner was sentenced to twenty-five years to life under California's "three strikes" law for the theft of three golf clubs. His criminal record, however, dated back to 1984 and included numerous misdemeanor and felony convictions for theft, battery, firearms possession, robbery, and burglary, at least two of which were violent and involved the use of weapons. The various opinions in the cases indicated that the Court would continue to follow the principle that a noncapital sentence violates the Eighth Amendment's Cruel and Unusual Punishment Clause when it is "grossly disproportionate" to the gravity of the crime. A majority of the Court in both cases, however, found this principle not to have been violated.

3. Would giving a convicted rapist a choice between surgical castration and a lengthy prison sentence be constitutional? In State v. Brown, 284 S.C. 407, 326 S.E.2d 410 (1985), the South Carolina Supreme Court ruled that castration of convicted rapists would be cruel and unusual punishment.

4. In Ingraham v. Wright, 430 U.S. 651, 97 S.Ct. 1401, 51 L.Ed.2d 711 (1977), a civil case, the Court had to deal with the issue of corporal punishment of children in public schools. In a 5–4 decision, the Court concluded that such punishment, which dates back to the colonial period and which has survived the transformation of early private instruction to our present system of compulsory education, is not cruel and unusual punishment.

D. EXCLUSION OF EVIDENCE FROM CRIMINAL TRIALS

Mapp v. Ohio

Supreme Court of the United States, 1961.
367 U.S. 643, 81 S.Ct. 1684, 6 L.Ed.2d 1081.

■ MR. JUSTICE CLARK delivered the opinion of the Court.

Appellant stands convicted of knowingly having had in her possession and under her control certain lewd and lascivious books, pictures, and photographs in violation of § 2905.34 of Ohio's Revised Code. As officially stated in the syllabus to its opinion, the Supreme Court of Ohio found that her conviction was valid though "based primarily upon the introduction in evidence of lewd and lascivious books and pictures unlawfully seized during an unlawful search of defendant's home . . ."

On May 23, 1957, three Cleveland police officers arrived at appellant's residence in that city pursuant to information that "a person [was] hiding out in the home, who was wanted for questioning in connection with a recent bombing, and that there was a large amount of policy paraphernalia being hidden in the home." Miss Mapp and her daughter by a former marriage lived on the top floor of the two-family dwelling. Upon their arrival at that house, the officers knocked on the door and demanded entrance but appellant, after telephoning her attorney, refused to admit them without a search warrant. They advised their headquarters of the situation and undertook a surveillance of the house.

The officers again sought entrance some three hours later when four or more additional officers arrived on the scene. When Miss Mapp did not come to the door immediately, at least one of the several doors to the house was forcibly opened and the policemen gained admittance. Meanwhile Miss Mapp's attorney arrived, but the officers, having secured their own entry, and continuing in their defiance of the law, would permit him neither to see Miss Mapp nor to enter the house. It appears that Miss Mapp was halfway down the stairs from the upper floor to the front door when the officers, in this highhanded manner, broke into the hall. She demanded to see the search warrant. A paper, claimed to be a warrant, was held up by one of the officers. She grabbed the "warrant" and placed it in her bosom. A struggle ensued in which the officers recovered the piece of paper and as a result of which they handcuffed appellant because she had been "belligerent" in resisting their official rescue of the "warrant" from her person. Running roughshod over appellant, a policeman "grabbed" her, "twisted [her] hand," and she "yelled [and] pleaded with him" because "it was hurting." Appellant, in handcuffs, was then forcibly taken upstairs to her bedroom where the officers searched a dresser, a chest of drawers, a closet and some suitcases. They also looked into a photo album and through personal papers belonging to the appellant. The search spread to the rest of the second floor including the child's bedroom, the living room, the kitchen and a dinette. The basement of the building and a trunk found therein were also searched. The obscene materials for possession of which she was ultimately convicted were discovered in the course of that widespread search.

At the trial no search warrant was produced by the prosecution, nor was the failure to produce one explained or accounted for. At best, "There is, in the record, considerable doubt as to whether there ever was any warrant for the search of defendant's home." . . .

The State says that even if the search were made without authority, or otherwise unreasonably, it is not prevented from using the unconstitutionally seized evidence at trial, citing Wolf v. People of State of Colorado (1949), in which this Court did indeed hold "that in a prosecution in a State court for a State crime the Fourteenth Amendment does not forbid the admission of evidence obtained by an unreasonable search and seizure." On this appeal, of which we have noted probable jurisdiction, it is urged once again that we review that holding.

* * *

. . . [T]his Court, in *Weeks v. United States* (1914) stated that "the Fourth Amendment . . . put the courts of the United States and Federal officials, in the exercise of their power and authority, under limitations and restraints [and] . . . forever secure[d] the people, their persons, houses, papers, and effects, against all unreasonable searches and seizures under the guise of law . . . and the duty of giving to it force and effect is obligatory upon all entrusted under our Federal system with the enforcement of the laws."

Specifically dealing with the use of the evidence unconstitutionally seized, the Court concluded:

> If letters and private documents can thus be seized and held and used in evidence against a citizen accused of an offense, the protection of the Fourth Amendment declaring his right to be secure against such searches and seizures is of no value, and, so far as those thus placed are concerned, might as well be stricken from the Constitution. The efforts of the courts and their officials to bring the guilty to punishment, praiseworthy as they are, are not to be aided by the sacrifice of those great principles established by years of endeavor and suffering which have resulted in their embodiment in the fundamental law of the land.

Finally, the Court in that case clearly stated that use of the seized evidence involved "a denial of the constitutional rights of the accused." Thus, in the year 1914, in the *Weeks* case, this Court "for the first time" held that "in a federal prosecution the Fourth Amendment barred the use of evidence secured through an illegal search and seizure." This Court has ever since required of federal law officers a strict adherence to that command which this Court has held to be a clear, specific, and constitutionally required—even if judicially implied—deterrent safeguard without insistence upon which the Fourth Amendment would have been reduced to "a form of words." . . .

* * *

In 1949, 35 years after *Weeks* was announced, this Court, in Wolf v. Colorado, again for the first time, discussed the effect of the Fourth Amendment upon the States through the operation of the Due Process Clause of the Fourteenth Amendment. It said:

> (W)e have no hesitation in saying that were a State affirmatively to sanction such police incursion into privacy it would run counter to the guaranty of the Fourteenth Amendment.

Nevertheless, after declaring that the "security of one's privacy against arbitrary intrusion by the police" is "implicit in 'the concept of ordered liberty' and as such enforceable against the States through the Due Process Clause," and announcing that it "stoutly adhere[d]" to the *Weeks* decision, the Court decided that the *Weeks* exclusionary rule would not then be imposed upon the States as "an essential ingredient of the right." The Court's reasons for not considering essential to the right to privacy, as a curb imposed upon the States by the Due Process Clause, that which decades before had been posited as part and parcel of the Fourth Amendment's limitations upon federal encroachment of individual privacy, were bottomed on factual considerations.

While they are not basically relevant to a decision that the exclusionary rule is an essential ingredient of the Fourth Amendment as the right it embodies is vouchsafed against the States by the Due Process Clause, we will consider the current validity of the factual grounds upon which *Wolf* was based.

The Court in *Wolf* first stated that "[t]he contrariety of views of the States" on the adoption of the exclusionary rule of *Weeks* was "particularly impressive"; and, in this connection that it could not "brush aside the experience of States which deem the incidence of such conduct by the police too slight to call for a deterrent remedy . . . by overriding the (States') relevant rules of evidence." While in 1949, prior to the *Wolf* case, almost two-thirds of the States were opposed to the use of the exclusionary rule, now, despite the *Wolf* case, more than half of those since passing upon it, by their own legislative or judicial decision, have wholly or partly adopted or adhered to the *Weeks* rule. Significantly, among those now following the rule is California, which, according to its highest court, was "compelled to reach that conclusion because other remedies have completely failed to secure compliance with the constitutional provisions . . ." *People v. Cahan* (1955). In connection with this California case, we note that the second basis elaborated in *Wolf* in support of its failure to enforce the exclusionary doctrine against the States was that "other means of protection" have been afforded "the right to privacy." The experience of California that such other remedies have been worthless and futile is buttressed by the experience of other States. The obvious futility of relegating the Fourth Amendment to the protection of other remedies has, moreover, been recognized by this Court since *Wolf*. See *Irvine v. People of State of California* (1954).

* * *

It, therefore, plainly appears that the factual considerations supporting the failure of the *Wolf* Court to include the *Weeks* exclusionary rule when it recognized the enforceability of the right to privacy against the States in 1949, while not basically relevant to the constitutional consideration, could not, in any analysis, now be deemed controlling.

* * *

. . . Today we once again examine *Wolf's* constitutional documentation of the right to privacy free from unreasonable state intrusion, and, after its dozen years on our books, are led by it to close the only courtroom door remaining open to evidence secured by official lawlessness in flagrant abuse of that basic right, reserved to all persons as a specific guarantee against that very same unlawful conduct. We hold that all evidence obtained by searches and seizures in violation of the Constitution is, by that same authority, inadmissible in a state court.

* * *

There are those who say, as did JUSTICE (then Judge) CARDOZO, that under our constitutional exclusionary doctrine "[t]he criminal is to go free because the constable has blundered." *People v. Defore*, 242 N.Y. at page 21, 150 N.E. at page 587. In some cases this will undoubtedly be the result. But, as was said in *Elkins*, "there is another consideration—the imperative of judicial integrity." 364 U.S. at page 222, 80 S.Ct. at page 1447. The criminal goes free, if he must, but it is the law that sets him free. Nothing can destroy a government more quickly than its failure to observe its own laws, or worse, its disregard of the charter of its own existence. As MR. JUSTICE BRANDEIS, dissenting, said in *Olmstead v. United States* (1928): "Our government is the potent, the omnipresent teacher. For good or for ill, it teaches the whole people by its example. . . . If the government becomes a lawbreaker, it breeds contempt for law; it invites every man to become a law unto himself; it invites anarchy." Nor can it lightly be assumed that, as a practical matter, adoption of the exclusionary rule fetters law enforcement. Only last year this Court expressly considered that contention and found that "pragmatic evidence of a sort" to the contrary was not wanting. *(Elkins v. United States.)* The Court noted that

> The federal courts themselves have operated under the exclusionary rule of *Weeks* for almost half a century; yet it has not been suggested either that the Federal Bureau of Investigation has thereby been rendered ineffective, or that the administration of criminal justice in the federal courts has thereby been disrupted. Moreover, the experience of the states is impressive. . . . The movement towards the rule of exclusion has been halting but seemingly inexorable.

The ignoble shortcut to conviction left open to the State tends to destroy the entire system of constitutional restraints on which the liberties of the people rest. Having once recognized that the right to privacy embodied in the Fourth Amendment is enforceable against the States, and that the right to be secure against rude invasions of privacy by state officers is, therefore, constitutional in origin, we can no longer permit that right to remain an empty promise. Because it is enforceable in the same manner and to like effect as other basic rights secured by the Due Process Clause, we can no longer permit it to be revocable at the whim of any police officer who, in the name of law enforcement itself, chooses to suspend its enjoyment. Our decision, founded on reason and truth, gives to the individual no more than that which the Constitution guarantees him, to the police officer no less than that to which honest law enforcement is entitled, and, to the courts, that judicial integrity so necessary in the true administration of justice.

The judgment of the Supreme Court of Ohio is reversed and the cause remanded for further proceedings not inconsistent with this opinion.

Reversed and remanded.

* * *

■ MR. JUSTICE HARLAN, whom MR. JUSTICE FRANKFURTER and MR. JUSTICE WHITTAKER join, dissenting.

* * *

I would not impose upon the States this federal exclusionary remedy. The reasons given by the majority for now suddenly turning its back on *Wolf* seem to me notably unconvincing.

First, it is said that "the factual grounds upon which *Wolf* was based" have since changed, in that more States now follow the *Weeks* exclusionary rule than was so at the time *Wolf* was decided. While that is true, a recent survey indicates that at present one-half of the States still adhere to the common-law non-exclusionary rule, and one, Maryland, retains the rule as to felonies. Berman and Oberst, *Admissibility of Evidence Obtained by an Unconstitutional Search and*

Seizure, 55 N.W. L. REV. 525, 532–533. But in any case surely all this is beside the point, as the majority itself indeed seems to recognize. Our concern here, as it was in *Wolf*, is not with the desirability of that rule but only with the question whether the States are Constitutionally free to follow it or not as they may themselves determine, and the relevance of the disparity of views among the States on this point lies simply in the fact that the judgment involved is a debatable one. Moreover, the very fact on which the majority relies, instead of lending support to what is now being done, points away from the need of replacing voluntary state action with federal compulsion.

The preservation of a proper balance between state and federal responsibility in the administration of criminal justice demands patience on the part of those who might like to see things move faster among the States in this respect. Problems of criminal law enforcement vary widely from State to State. One State, in considering the totality of its legal picture, may conclude that the need for embracing the *Weeks* rule is pressing because other remedies are unavailable or inadequate to secure compliance with the substantive Constitutional principle involved. Another, though equally solicitous of Constitutional rights, may choose to pursue one purpose at a time, allowing all evidence relevant to guilt to be brought into a criminal trial, and dealing with Constitutional infractions by other means. Still another may consider the exclusionary rule too rough-and-ready a remedy, in that it reaches only unconstitutional intrusions which eventuate in criminal prosecution of the victims. Further, a State after experimenting with the *Weeks* rule for a time may, because of unsatisfactory experience with it, decide to revert to a non-exclusionary rule. And so on. From the standpoint of Constitutional permissibility in pointing a State in one direction or another, I do not see at all why "time has set its face against" the considerations which led MR. JUSTICE CARDOZO, then chief judge of the New York Court of Appeals, to reject for New York in *People v. Defore*, 242 N.Y. 13, 150 N.E. 585, the *Weeks* exclusionary rule. For us the question remains, as it has always been, one of state power, not one of passing judgment on the wisdom of one state course or another. In my view this Court should continue to forbear from fettering the States with an adamant rule which may embarrass them in coping with their own peculiar problems in criminal law enforcement.

* * *

NOTES AND QUESTIONS

1. The exclusionary rule is one that is ordinarily studied in great detail in a separate course dealing with criminal procedure. Indeed, the many ramifications of its application call for an extensive and detailed study in a context different from one devoted primarily to substantive rights. It is useful, however, to consider it here as well, and to use it to ponder certain principles that relate to the chapter of constitutional limitations on the power of the states to define crimes and punish for their commission. Where in the Constitution does Justice Clark find the authority to exclude illegally seized evidence from a criminal trial?

2. What interest(s) does the Court think will be served by excluding evidence obtained in violation of the Constitution? Is such exclusion too high a price for the criminal justice system to pay to correct its own abuses? What other remedies might be available, in lieu of the exclusion of evidence, for Constitutional violations?

3. The Court also has applied the exclusionary rule to out-of-court statements made by defendants in response to overly coercive interrogation practices that the Court concludes violate the Fifth Amendment privilege against self-incrimination. Should out-of-court statements obtained in violation of the Fifth Amendment be treated differently than physical evidence obtained in violation of the Fourth Amendment?

4. In United States v. Leon, 468 U.S. 897, 104 S.Ct. 3405, 82 L.Ed.2d 677 (1984), the Supreme Court, per Justice White, held that evidence seized on the basis of objectively reasonable, good faith reliance on a regularly executed search warrant was not subject to suppression even if the warrant was later declared invalid. On what basis do you think the Court adopted this "good faith exception" to the exclusionary rule?

5. Most recently, Hudson v. Michigan, 547 U.S. 586, 126 S.Ct. 2159, 165 L.Ed.2d 56 (2006), refused to apply the exclusionary rule to violations of the Fourth Amendment's knock and notice requirement. The Court noted that the exclusionary rule carries "substantial social costs" and will only apply when its benefits outweigh those costs.

PART 2

CRIMES

CHAPTER 5

HOMICIDES

A. MURDER

1. WHEN DOES DEATH OCCUR?

Some states hold that death occurs when the end of life is confirmed by the cessation of all electrical impulses in the brain—the "flat EEG." Other states still adhere to the common law view that death occurs only when there is a cessation of breathing and a stopping of the heart.

For an example of a modern "definition of death" statute, see Va. Code Ann. § 54.1–2972, which reads as follows:

A person shall be medically and legally dead if:

1. In the opinion of a physician duly authorized to practice medicine in this Commonwealth, based on the ordinary standards of medical practice, there is the absence of spontaneous respiratory and spontaneous cardiac functions and, because of the disease or condition which directly or indirectly caused these functions to cease, or because of the passage of time since these functions ceased, attempts at resuscitation would not, in the opinion of such physician, be successful in restoring spontaneous life-sustaining functions, and, in such event, death shall be deemed to have occurred at the time these functions ceased; or

2. In the opinion of a physician, who shall be duly licensed and a specialist in the field of neurology, neurosurgery, or electroencephalography, when based on the ordinary standards of medical practice, there is the absence of spontaneous brain functions and spontaneous respiratory functions and, in the opinion of another physician and such neurospecialist, based on the ordinary standards of medical practice and considering the absence of spontaneous brain functions and spontaneous respiratory functions and the patient's medical record, further attempts at resuscitation or continued supportive maintenance would not be successful in restoring such spontaneous functions, and, in such event, death shall be deemed to have occurred at the time when these conditions first coincide.

Death, as defined in subdivision 2 hereof, shall be pronounced by one of the two physicians and recorded in the patient's medical record and attested by the other physician. One of two physicians pronouncing or attesting to brain death

447

may be the attending physician regardless of his specialty so long as at least one of the physicians is a neurospecialist.

Either of these alternative definitions of death may be utilized for all purposes in the Commonwealth, including the trial of civil and criminal cases.

For a commentary on the foregoing statute, see A. Christian Compton, Telling the Time of Human Death by Statute: An Essential and Progressive Trend, 31 Wash. & Lee L. Rev. 521 (1974). *See also* W.F. Gorman, *Medical Diagnosis Versus Legal Determination of Death*, 30 J. For. Sci. 150 (1985).

(A) PROVING DEATH—THE "CORPUS DELICTI"

State v. Grissom

Supreme Court of Kansas, 1992.
251 Kan. 851, 840 P.2d 1142.

[The facts in the case showed that three women, in their early twenties, and living in Overland Park, Kansas, disappeared in June, 1989. The women, Joan Butler, Chrisine Rusch, and Teresa Brown, were not heard from since. No remains were found. The defendant owned and operated a business that cleaned and painted apartments in the Kansas City area. Evidence showed that defendant had "pass keys" for all three women's apartments and that the defendant was seen operating a car rented by one of the missing women after her own car had been totaled in an accident. Blood, matched by DNA from another of the women was found in the car. Additional evidence showed large transactions on the women's bank accounts from ATMs and drive-through lanes, where tellers later described a man fitting the description of the defendant as a passenger in the vehicle. Other circumstantial evidence, including hair samples, tied the defendant to the women.]

■ ABBOTT, JUSTICE:

This is a direct appeal by Richard Grissom, Jr., from his convictions of three counts of first degree murder, one count of aggravated kidnapping, four counts of robbery, two counts of aggravated burglary, and one count of misdemeanor theft.

* * *

After a jury trial in the fall of 1990, Grissom was convicted of three counts of first-degree murder, one count of aggravated kidnapping, four counts of robbery, two counts of aggravated burglary, and one count of misdemeanor theft. . . .

I.   CORPUS DELICTI

Grissom argues that the State failed to establish the corpus delicti for homicide. Much of his argument is based upon the fact that bodies have not been found, that the exact events leading up to the deaths of the three women are not known, and that the State's case rests upon circumstantial evidence.

In homicide cases the corpus delicti is established by proof of two facts: that one person was killed, and that another person killed him. The corpus delicti may be proved by direct testimony, by indirect or circumstantial evidence, or by a combination of both. Circumstantial evidence is evidence that tends to prove a fact in issue by proving other events or circumstances which, according to the common experience of mankind, are usually or always attended by the fact in issue, and therefore affords a basis for a reasonable inference by the jury or court of the occurrence of the fact in issue.

Grissom [argues] . . . that in order to prove corpus delicti, all evidence must be consistent with the defendant's guilt and inconsistent with the defendant's innocence. . . . Grissom, however, does not argue that the deaths of the three women were due to natural causes or suicide. More importantly, Grissom does not mention that subsequent decisions have . . . rejected the theory that the prosecution is under an affirmative duty to rule out every hypothesis except that of guilt beyond a reasonable doubt.

* * *

Grissom argues that the State failed to make a prima facie showing of the corpus delicti for the homicide for each of the three murder charges. The essence of Grissom's argument is that the circumstantial evidence presented is insufficient to link him to the deaths of the three women. Grissom primarily is arguing sufficiency of the evidence, not corpus delicti.

Although evidence establishing the corpus delicti often is intertwined with evidence establishing the identity of the killer, it is not necessary to establish the killer's identity in order to establish the corpus delicti. Here, in order to establish the corpus delicti, the State only needed to prove that Butler, Rusch, and Brown were killed by criminal means, not that Grissom was the killer. Grissom's claim that the State failed to link him to the deaths of the three women will be discussed shortly.

The deaths of Butler, Rusch, and Brown by criminal means are established in part by the fact that family and friends never heard from Butler after June 18, 1989, and from Rusch or Brown after June 26, 1989, and that such behavior was atypical. Circumstances unique to the disappearance of each is discussed below; however, there is also much similarity among the women and their lifestyles. All three women were single and lived in apartments in Johnson County. Each woman had maintained close contact with her family prior to her disappearance. Each woman was considered reliable and responsible. All three had discussed future plans with family and friends. There was no indication any of the women were depressed or would be inclined to leave the area without word to anyone. There was no indication Butler, Rusch, or Brown suddenly had moved. For example, the kitchens in both apartments were stocked with food and there was no indication anything had been taken from either apartment. Neither Butler's apartment nor Rusch and Brown's apartment showed signs of a struggle or forced entry; however, keys to both apartments were found in Grissom's car. There is evidence Grissom previously had used a master key to enter Rusch and Brown's apartment under false pretenses.

There are additional facts supporting the State's theory that Butler's death was by criminal means. When Butler left Becker's apartment at 4 a.m. on Sunday, June 18, Butler told Becker she was going home to go to bed. The clothes Butler had been wearing when she left Becker's were found in the bedroom of Butler's apartment. Around the time that Butler would have arrived home or shortly thereafter, Butler's neighbor, who lived in the apartment below Butler, was awakened by a loud thump noise coming from above her. All of the money from Butler's checking account was withdrawn at unusual hours over a three-day period in the maximum allowed increments. The first withdrawal occurred within two hours of when Butler left Becker's apartment. Butler did not show up for work or call in the following Monday. Butler's rental car was stolen. Traces of blood, which were linked to Butler through reverse style paternity testing, were found in the trunk of the rental car.

There are additional facts supporting the State's theory that Rusch's death was by criminal means. When Rusch left a club, where she had spent the evening with friends, after midnight on June 26, she told a friend she was going home to bed because she had to go to work the next day. Rusch withdrew $2,400 from her money market account in four withdrawals between 7:58 and 8:43 a.m. on June 26. Another bank customer, who was in the drive-up lane at approximately the same time as when Rusch made her first withdrawal, said he noticed a car with a white woman driver and a black male passenger. Shortly after making the last transaction, Rusch called in sick to work on the morning of June 26. Neither Rusch nor her roommate, who supposedly also was ill, answered their door or telephone on June 26 and thereafter. Rusch's car was not parked in her apartment complex parking lot. On the evening of June 26, Rusch was photographed using Brown's ATM card and looking grim and disheveled. In the background of the photograph and behind Rusch, part of a car could be seen with its lights on.

When Rusch's father entered her apartment on Tuesday morning, June 27, he found no one in the apartment, but noticed a curling iron was turned on in one of the bathrooms. When the apartment was searched later, a pubic hair consistent with Grissom's pubic hair was found in Rusch's bedding. Also on Tuesday, credit cards and personal papers belonging to Rusch were found in a ditch in southern Johnson County, and Rusch's driver's license was found near I-435 in southern Kansas City. On June 28, when Grissom's car was searched, the police found a credit card in Rusch's name, several keys to her apartment, and a key to her parents' house. Three of her rings were discovered in the glove compartment. Rusch's car was located June 28 in a motel parking lot near the complex where she had lived. The car had a new dent with blue paint in it. The blue paint was matched to the Mini Warehouse in Raytown, a location to which Grissom was linked. Several hair fragments, which displayed the same characteristics as Grissom's hair, were found in Rusch's car. A pair of sunglasses found in a South Metcalf Mini Storage locker, which Grissom had rented, was identified as belonging to Rusch. Hair found on a carpet, which had been found in that locker, was indistinguishable from hair taken from a hairbrush found in Rusch's bathroom.

There are additional facts supporting the State's theory that Brown's death was by criminal means. Brown had a serious, romantic relationship with Mike Raunig. Raunig never heard from nor saw Brown again after she left his place about 6 a.m. on June 26 to return to her apartment and get ready for work. The T-shirts she was wearing when she left Raunig's house were found in her apartment on her bedroom floor. The manager of the Mini Warehouse in Raytown testified that the woman who signed a rental agreement as Christine Rusch on June 26 looked much like the photograph of Brown. The manager said the woman seemed distressed and looked to the man who was accompanying her for assistance in completing the form.

Brown also did not show up for work on June 26. A woman, who identified herself as Brown's roommate, called and said Brown was sick. Brown did not show up for lunch at her sister's house or call her. Despite repeated attempts to contact Brown, neither Brown nor Rusch, who supposedly also was ill, answered their door or telephone on June 26 or thereafter. Brown's car, however, was continually parked in front of her apartment building. When the apartment was searched later, a pubic hair consistent with Grissom's pubic hair was found in Brown's bedding. When Grissom's car was searched, a credit card in Brown's name and keys to Rusch and Brown's apartment were discovered.

Once the State established a prima facie showing of the corpus delicti for homicide on each murder count, which the State did here, the State then could introduce evidence of any admission by Grissom. Although Grissom never admitted to injuring or killing the three women, he did indicate during his statement in Texas on July 7, 1989, that the women probably were dead by now and that their bodies were buried. This supports the conclusion that each of the women had been killed by criminal means.

The corpus delicti for homicide on each of the three counts of murder was established.

Identifying the killer is not required to establish the corpus delicti for homicide . . .

[The discussion of the evidence that allowed the jury to find the defendant guilty of the murders is omitted.]

* * *

A jury could rationally link Grissom to Rusch's murder. . . .

* * *

It is not necessary that every fact point directly and independently to Grissom's guilt. It is enough if the jury's conclusion is warranted by combined and cumulative force of all incriminating circumstances.

* * *

[Discussion of the many remaining procedural issues is omitted.]

NOTES

1. The origin of the corpus delicti rule can be traced back at least as far as seventeenth century England. In 1660, John Perry was subjected to continuous and repeated questioning as to the disappearance of his master, William Harrison. After initially denying all wrongdoing, Perry finally confessed that he, his mother, and his brother had together robbed and murdered Harrison. Although a body was never found, and Perry's mother and brother denied all wrongdoing, all three suspects were convicted and executed on the strength of Perry's confession. Several years later, however, Harrison returned home, claiming to have been kidnapped and sold into slavery in Turkey. In short, Perry had admitted to a falsehood resulting in the execution of himself, his mother, and his brother. *See Perry's Case* (1660), 14 Howell St. Tr. 1312, 1312–24 (Eng.).

The injustice of *Perry's Case* and similar cases triggered the creation of the corpus delicti rule, although the corpus delicti rule is not uniformly applied as part of the English common law. In the United States, the corpus delicti rule took root after the Boorn trial in Vermont, which replicated the false confession scenario of *Perry's Case,* was widely publicized. *See Trial of Stephen and Jesse Boorn,* 6 Am. St. Tr. 73, 73–95 (1819). Today, the corpus delicti rule has received near-universal adoption by the states. *Allen v. Commonwealth*, 287 Va 68 (2014).

2. For other murder cases in which the corpus delicti was established by circumstantial evidence alone, consider the following:

(a) In People v. Scott, 176 Cal.App.2d 458, 1 Cal.Rptr. 600 (1959), the defendant's wife, a woman in excellent health, disappeared. Although her glasses and dentures were found in a trash pile, no traces of her body were ever found. Before his arrest the defendant had told his friends a number of conflicting stories and lies by way of trying to explain his wife's disappearance. He also forged her name on checks and had obtained large sums of her money. The affirmance of his murder conviction was disapproved in 34 Tul.L.Rev. 820 (1960).

(b) Among the numerous crimes and atrocities of which Charles Manson was convicted in California was the murder of one person whose body was never found. In upholding the conviction, the court said:

> The fact that Shea's body was never recovered would justify an inference by the jury that death was caused by a criminal agency. It is highly unlikely that a person who dies from natural causes will successfully dispose of his own body. Although such a result may be a theoretical possibility, it is contrary to the normal course of human affairs.

People v. Manson, 71 Cal.App.3d 1, 139 Cal.Rptr. 275 (1977), *cert. denied*, 435 U.S. 953, 98 S.Ct. 1582, 55 L.Ed.2d 803 (1978).

Also, for an account of case convictions for murders where no killings had ever occurred, see EDWIN MONTEFIORE BORCHAND, CONVICTING THE INNOCENT: SIXTY-FIVE ACTUAL ERRORS OF CRIMINAL JUSTICE (1932). For another case involving the corpus delicti issue, see Commonwealth v. Burns, 409 Pa. 619, 187 A.2d 552 (1963).

3. In the United States, there is disagreement among the courts as to what constitutes the *corpus delicti*. Some courts require only that the particular loss or injury involved in the case be proved. Other courts—probably a majority—also require proof that the loss or injury was caused by a criminal act. Some courts go even further and require a third element—proof that the accused himself committed the crime involved.

The courts are also in disagreement as to what degree of proof is required to establish the elements which comprise the *corpus delicti*. A majority of the courts hold that the *corpus delicti* need not be proven beyond a reasonable doubt. *But see, e.g.*, Smith v. Commonwealth, 62 Va. (21 Gratt.) 809, 820 (1871): "(T)he fact of the death must be established by clear and unequivocal proof, either by direct testimony or by presumptive evidence of the most cogent and irresistible kind." On the other hand, in State v. Kelley, 308 A.2d 877 (Me. 1973), the court said the *corpus delicti* should be proved by "credible evidence which, if believed, would create in the mind of a reasonable man, not a mere surmise or suspicion but rather a really substantial belief" that the crime has occurred. Does "a really substantial belief" require a greater or a lesser quantum of proof than "evidence of the most cogent and irresistible kind"?

4. A majority of courts hold that the *corpus delicti* cannot be established solely by the extra-judicial confession of an accused. Some independent corroboration is required. Opper v. United States, 348 U.S. 84, 75 S.Ct. 158, 99 L.Ed. 101 (1954).

5. Contrary to a prevailing misconception, proof of *corpus delicti* is a requirement of all criminal cases and not merely in homicide cases. In Commonwealth v. Leslie, 424 Pa. 331, 227 A.2d 900 (1967), the defendant confessed that he had started the fire that destroyed a summer cottage.

While the police had suspected as much, they could not uncover any evidence that the fire had been started deliberately. In reversing the conviction, the Supreme Court of Pennsylvania, while recognizing that the *corpus delicti* could be proved by circumstantial evidence, found that the state had relied on the confession alone to prove the *corpus delicti* and held that this was insufficient. Proof of *corpus delicti* is one of the most difficult tasks facing the prosecution in arson cases. *See* Comment, *Proof of* Corpus Delicti *in Arson Cases*, 45 J. Crim. L. Criminology & Police Sci. 185 (1954). For *corpus delicti* issues in other crimes, see People v. Call, 176 Ill.App.3d 571, 126 Ill.Dec. 156, 531 N.E.2d 451 (1988) [Driving under the influence of alcohol or drugs].

2. WHEN DOES LIFE BEGIN?

Keeler v. Superior Court

Supreme Court of California, 1970.
2 Cal.3d 619, 87 Cal.Rptr. 481, 470 P.2d 617.

■ MOSK, JUSTICE.

In this proceeding for writ of prohibition we are called upon to decide whether an unborn but viable fetus is a "human being" within the meaning of the California statute defining murder (Pen.Code, § 187). We conclude that the Legislature did not intend such a meaning, and that for us to construe the statute to the contrary and apply it to this petitioner would exceed our judicial power and deny petitioner due process of law.

The evidence received at the preliminary examination may be summarized as follows: Petitioner and Teresa Keeler obtained an interlocutory decree of divorce on September 27, 1968. They had been married for 16 years. Unknown to petitioner, Mrs. Keeler was then pregnant by one Ernest Vogt, whom she had met earlier that summer. She subsequently began living with Vogt in Stockton, but concealed the fact from petitioner. Petitioner was given custody of their two daughters, aged 12 and 13 years, and under the decree Mrs. Keeler had the right to take the girls on alternate weekends.

On February 23, 1969, Mrs. Keeler was driving on a narrow mountain road in Amador County after delivering the girls to their home. She met petitioner driving in the opposite direction; he blocked the road with his car, and she pulled over to the side. He walked to her vehicle and began speaking to her. He seemed calm, and she rolled down her window to hear him. He said, "I hear you're pregnant. If you are you had better stay away from the girls and from here." She did not reply, and he opened the car door; as she later testified, "He assisted me out of the car. * * * [I]t wasn't roughly at this time." Petitioner then looked at her abdomen and became "extremely upset." He said, "You sure are. I'm going to stomp it out of you." He pushed her against the car, shoved his knee into her abdomen, and struck her in the face with several blows. She fainted, and when she regained consciousness petitioner had departed.

Mrs. Keeler drove back to Stockton, and the police and medical assistance were summoned. . . . A Caesarian section was performed and the fetus was examined *in utero*. Its head was found to be severely fractured, and it was delivered stillborn. The pathologist gave as his opinion that the cause of death was skull fracture with consequent cerebral hemorrhaging, that death would have been immediate, and that the injury could have been the result of force applied to the mother's abdomen. There was no air in the fetus' lungs, and the umbilical cord was intact.

Upon delivery the fetus weighed five pounds and was 18 inches in length. Both Mrs. Keeler and her obstetrician testified that fetal movements had been observed prior to February 23, 1969. The evidence was in conflict as to the estimated age of the fetus; the expert testimony on the point, however, concluded "with reasonable medical certainty" that the fetus had developed to the stage of viability, i.e., that in the event of premature birth on the date in question it would have had a 75 percent to 96 percent chance of survival.

An information was filed charging petitioner, in Count I, with committing the crime of murder (Pen.Code, § 187) in that he did "unlawfully kill a human being, to wit Baby Girl VOGT, with malice aforethought." . . . His motion to set aside the information for lack of probable cause (Pen.Code, § 995) was denied, and he now seeks a writ of prohibition; . . .

I

Penal Code section 187 provides: "Murder is the unlawful killing of a human being, with malice aforethought." The dispositive question is whether the fetus which petitioner is accused of killing was, on February 23, 1969, a "human being" within the meaning of this statute. If it was not, petitioner cannot be charged with its "murder" and prohibition will lie.

Section 187 was enacted as part of the Penal Code of 1872. Inasmuch as the provision has not been amended since that date, we must determine the intent of the Legislature at the time of its enactment. But section 187 was, in turn, taken verbatim from the first California statute defining murder, part of the Crimes and Punishments Act of 1850. (Stats.1850, ch. 99, § 19, p. 231.) Penal Code section 5 (also enacted in 1872) declares: "The provisions of this Code, so far as they are substantially the same as existing statutes, must be construed as continuations thereof, and not as new enactments." We begin, accordingly, by inquiring into the intent of the Legislature in 1850 when it first defined murder as the unlawful and malicious killing of a "human being."

It will be presumed, of course, that in enacting a statute the Legislature was familiar with the relevant rules of the common law, and, when it couches its enactment in common law language, that its intent was to continue those rules in statutory form. This is particularly appropriate in considering the work of the first session of our Legislature: its precedents were necessarily drawn from the common law, as modified in certain respects by the Constitution and by legislation of our sister states.

We therefore undertake a brief review of the origins and development of the common law of abortional homicide. . . . From that inquiry it appears that by the year 1850—the date with which we are concerned—an infant could not be the subject of homicide at common law unless it had been born alive. Perhaps the most influential statement of the "born alive" rule is that of Coke, in mid-17th century: "If a woman be quick with childe, and by a potion or otherwise killeth it in her wombe, or if a man beat her, whereby the childe dyeth in her body, and she is delivered of a dead childe, this is a great misprision [i.e., misdemeanor], and no murder; but if the childe be born alive and dyeth of the potion, battery, or other cause, this is murder; for in law it is accounted a reasonable creature, in rerum natura, when it is born alive." (3 Coke, Institutes *58 (1648).) In short, "By Coke's time, the common law regarded abortion as murder only if the foetus is (1) quickened, (2) born alive, (3) lives for a brief interval, and (4) then dies." Whatever intrinsic defects there may have been in Coke's work, the common law accepted his views as authoritative. . . .

* * *

By the year 1850 this rule of the common law had long been accepted in the United States. . . .

While it was thus "well settled" in American case law that the killing of an unborn child was not homicide, a number of state legislatures in the first half of the 19th century undertook to modify the common law in this respect. The movement began when New York abandoned the common law of abortion in 1830. The revisers' notes on that legislation recognized the existing rule, but nevertheless proposed a special feticide statute which, as enacted, provided that "The wilful killing of an unborn quick child, by any injury to the mother of such child, which would be murder if it resulted in the death of such mother, shall be deemed manslaughter in the first degree." (N.Y.Rev.Stat.1829, pt. IV, ch. 1, tit. 2, § 8.) At the same time the New York Legislature enacted a companion section (§ 9) which, although punishing a violation thereof as second degree manslaughter, was in essence an "abortion law" similar to those in force in most states today.

In the years between 1830 and 1850 at least five other states followed New York and enacted, as companion provisions, (1) a statute declaring feticide to be a crime, punishable as manslaughter, and (2) a statute prohibiting abortion. In California, however, the pattern was not repeated. Much of the Crimes and Punishments Act of 1850 was based on existing New York statute law; but although a section proscribing abortion was included in the new Act (§ 45), the Legislature declined to adopt any provision defining and punishing a special crime of feticide.

We conclude that in declaring murder to be the unlawful and malicious killing of a "human being" the Legislature of 1850 intended that term to have the settled common law meaning of a person who had been born alive, and did not intend the act of feticide—as distinguished from abortion—to be an offense under the laws of California.

Nothing occurred between the years 1850 and 1872 to suggest that in adopting the new Penal Code on the latter date the Legislature entertained any different intent. The case law of our sister states, for example, remained consonant with the common law. . . .

Any lingering doubt on this subject must be laid to rest by a consideration of the legislative history of the Penal Code of 1872. The Act establishing the California Code Commission (Stats.1870, ch. 516, § 2, p. 774) required the commissioners to revise all statutes then in force, correct errors and omissions, and "recommend all such enactments as shall, in the judgment of the Commission, be necessary to supply the defects of and give completeness to the existing legislation of the State * * *." In discharging this duty the statutory schemes of our sister states were carefully examined, and we must assume the commissioners had knowledge of the feticide laws noted hereinabove. Yet the commissioners proposed no such law for California, and none has been adopted to this day.

That such an omission was not an oversight clearly appears, moreover, from the commissioners' explanatory notes to Penal Code section 187. After quoting the definitions of murder given by Coke, Blackstone, and Hawkins, the commissioners conclude: "A child within its mother's womb is not a 'human being' within the meaning of that term as used in defining murder. The rule is that it must be born.—" Rex vs. Brain, 6 Car. & P., p. 349. That every part of it must have come from the mother before the killing of it will constitute a felonious homicide. . . .

* * *

It is the policy of this state to construe a penal statute as favorably to the defendant as its language and the circumstances of its application may reasonably permit; just as in the case of a question of fact, the defendant is entitled to the benefit of every reasonable doubt as to the true interpretation of words or the construction of language used in a statute. We hold that in adopting the definition of murder in Penal Code section 187 the Legislature intended to exclude from its reach the act of killing an unborn fetus.

II

The People urge, however, that the sciences of obstetrics and pediatrics have greatly progressed since 1872, to the point where with proper medical care a normally developed fetus prematurely born at 28 weeks or more has an excellent chance of survival, i.e., is "viable"; that the common law requirement of live birth to prove the fetus had become a "human being" who may be the victim of murder is no longer in accord with scientific fact, since an unborn but viable fetus is now fully capable of independent life; and that one who unlawfully and maliciously terminates such a life should therefore be liable to prosecution for murder under section 187. We may grant the premises of this argument; indeed, we neither deny nor denigrate the vast progress of medicine in the century since the enactment of the Penal Code. But we cannot join in the conclusion sought to be deduced: we cannot hold this petitioner to answer for murder by reason of his alleged act of killing an unborn—even thought viable—fetus. To such a charge there are two insuperable obstacles, one "jurisdictional" and the other constitutional.

Penal Code section 6 declares in relevant part that "No act or omission" accomplished after the code has taken effect "is criminal or punishable, except as prescribed or authorized by this Code, or by some of the statutes which it specifies as continuing in force and as not affected by its provisions, or by some ordinance, municipal, county, or township regulation * * *." This section embodies a fundamental principle of our tripartite form of government, i.e., that subject to the constitutional prohibition against cruel and unusual punishment, the power to define crimes and fix penalties is vested exclusively in the legislative branch. Stated differently, there are no common law crimes in California. In order that a public offense be committed, some statute, ordinance or regulation prior in time to the commission of the act must denounce it; likewise with excuses or justifications—if no statutory excuse or justification apply as to the commission of the particular offense, neither the common law nor the so-called "unwritten law" may legally supply it.

* * *

Applying these rules to the case at bar, we would undoubtedly act in excess of the judicial power if we were to adopt the People's proposed construction of section 187. As we have shown, the Legislature has defined the crime of murder in California to apply only to the unlawful and malicious killing of one who has been born alive. We recognize that the killing of an unborn but viable fetus may be deemed by some to be an offense of similar nature and gravity; but as Chief Justice Marshall warned long ago, "It would be dangerous, indeed, to carry the principle, that a case which is within the reason or mischief of a statute, is within its provisions, so far as to punish a crime not enumerated in the statute, because it is of equal atrocity, or of kindred character, with those which are enumerated." (United States v. Wiltberger (1820) 18 U.S. (5 Wheat.)

76, 96, 5 L.Ed. 37.) Whether to thus extend liability for murder in California is a determination solely within the province of the Legislature. For a court to simply declare, by judicial fiat, that the time has now come to prosecute under section 187 one who kills an unborn but viable fetus would indeed be to rewrite the statute under the guise of construing it. . . .

The second obstacle to the proposed judicial enlargement of section 187 is the guarantee of due process of law. Assuming *arguendo* that we have the power to adopt the new construction of this statute as the law of California, such a ruling, by constitutional command, could operate only prospectively, and thus could not in any event reach the conduct of petitioner on February 23, 1969.

The first essential of due process is fair warning of the act which is made punishable as a crime. "That the terms of a penal statute creating a new offense must be sufficiently explicit to inform those who are subject to it what conduct on their part will render them liable to its penalties, is a well-recognized requirement, consonant alike with ordinary notions of fair play and the settled rules of law." (Connally v. General Constr. Co. (1926) 269 U.S. 385, 391, 46 S.Ct. 126, 127, 70 L.Ed. 322.) "No one may be required at peril of life, liberty or property to speculate as to the meaning of penal statutes. All are entitled to be informed as to what the State commands or forbids." (Lanzetta v. New Jersey (1939) 306 U.S. 451, 453, 59 S.Ct. 618, 619, 83 L.Ed. 888.) The law of California is in full accord.

This requirement of fair warning is reflected in the constitutional prohibition against the enactment of ex post facto laws (U.S. Const., art. I, §§ 9, 10; Cal. Const., art. I, § 16). When a new penal statute is applied retrospectively to make punishable an act which was not criminal at the time it was performed, the defendant has been given no advance notice consistent with due process. And precisely the same effect occurs when such an act is made punishable under a preexisting statute but by means of an unforeseeable *judicial* enlargement thereof. . . .

* * *

. . . In the present case, it will be remembered, petitioner's avowed goal was not primarily to kill the fetus while it was inside his wife's body, but rather to "stomp it out of" her; although one presumably cannot be done without the other, petitioner's choice of words is significant and strongly implies an "intent thereby to procure the miscarriage" of his wife in violation of section 274.

Turning to the case law, we find no reported decision of the California courts which should have given petitioner notice that the killing of an unborn but viable fetus was prohibited by section 187. . . .

Properly understood, the often cited case of People v. Chavez (1947) 77 Cal.App.2d 621, 176 P.2d 92, does not derogate from this rule. There the defendant was charged with the murder of her newborn child, and convicted of manslaughter. She testified that the baby dropped from her womb into the toilet bowl; that she picked it up two or three minutes later, and cut but did not tie the umbilical cord; that the baby was limp and made no cry; and that after 15 minutes she wrapped it in a newspaper and concealed it, where it was found dead the next day. The autopsy surgeon testified that the baby was a full-term, nine-month child, weighing six and one-half pounds and appearing normal in every respect; that the body had very little blood in it, indicating the child had bled to death through the untied umbilical cord; that such a process would have taken about an hour; and that in his opinion "the child was born alive, based on conditions he found and the fact that the lungs contained air and the blood was extravasated or pushed back into the tissues, indicating heart action."

On appeal, the defendant emphasized that a doctor called by the defense had suggested other tests which the autopsy surgeon could have performed to determine the matter of live birth; on this basis, it was contended that the question of whether the infant was born alive "rests entirely on pure speculation." The Court of Appeal found only an insignificant conflict in that regard and focused its attention instead on testimony of the autopsy surgeon admitting the possibility that the evidence of heart and lung action could have resulted from the child's breathing "after presentation of the head but before the birth was completed".

The court cited the mid-19th century English infanticide cases mentioned hereinabove, and noted that the decisions had not reached uniformity on whether breathing, heart action, severance of the umbilical cord, or some combination of these or other factors established the status of "human being" for purposes of the law of homicide. The court then adverted to the state of modern medical knowledge, discussed the phenomenon of viability, and held that "a viable child *in the process of being born* is a human being within the meaning of the homicide statutes, whether or not the process has been fully completed. It should at least be considered a human being where it is a living baby and where in the natural course of events *a birth which is already started* would naturally be successfully completed." (Italics added.) Since the testimony of the autopsy surgeon left no doubt in that case that a live birth had at least begun, the court found "the evidence is sufficient here to support the implied finding of the jury that this child *was born alive and became a human being within the meaning of the homicide statutes.*" (Italics added.)

Chavez thus stands for the proposition—to which we adhere—that a viable fetus "in the process of being born" is a human being within the meaning of the homicide statutes. But it stands for no more; in particular it does not hold that a fetus, however viable, which is *not* "in the process of being born" is nevertheless a "human being" in the law of homicide. On the contrary, the opinion is replete with references to the common law requirement that the child be "born alive," however that term is defined, and must accordingly be deemed to reaffirm that requirement as part of the law of California.

* * *

We conclude that the judicial enlargement of section 187 now urged upon us by the People would not have been foreseeable to this petitioner, and hence that its adoption at this time would deny him due process of law.

Let a peremptory writ of prohibition issue restraining respondent court from taking any further proceedings on Count I of the information, charging petitioner with the crime of murder.

■ McCOMB, PETERS, and TOBRINER, JJ., and PEEK, J. pro tem., concur.

■ BURKE, ACTING CHIEF JUSTICE (dissenting).

The majority hold that "Baby Girl" Vogt, who, according to medical testimony, had reached the 35th week of development, had a 96 percent chance of survival, and was "definitely" alive and viable at the time of her death, nevertheless was not a "human being" under California's homicide statutes. In my view, in so holding, the majority ignore significant common law precedents, frustrate the express intent of the Legislature, and defy reason, logic and common sense.

* * *

The majority cast a passing glance at the common law concept of quickening, but fail to explain the significance of that concept: At common law, the quickened fetus *was* considered to be a human being, a second life separate and apart from its mother. . . .

Modern scholars have confirmed this aspect of common law jurisprudence. As Means observes, "The common law itself prohibited abortion after quickening and hanging a pregnant felon after quickening, *because the life of a second human being would thereby be taken*, although it did not call the offense murder or manslaughter." (Italics added; Means, The Law of New York Concerning Abortion and the Status of the Foetus, 1664–1968: A Case of Cessation of Constitutionality (1968) 14 N.Y.L.F. 411, 504.)

This reasoning explains why the killing of a quickened child was considered "a great misprision," although the killing of an unquickened child was no crime at all at common law (Means, *supra*, at p. 420). Moreover, although the common law did not apply the labels of "murder" or "manslaughter" to the killing of a quickened fetus, it appears that at common law this "great misprision" was severely punished. . . .

In my view, we cannot assume that the Legislature intended a person such as defendant charged with the malicious slaying of a fully viable child, to suffer only the mild penalties imposed upon common abortionists who, ordinarily, procure only the miscarriage of a nonviable fetus or embryo. To do so would completely ignore the important common law distinction between the quickened and unquickened child.

Of course, I do not suggest that we should interpret the term "human being" in our homicide statutes in terms of the common law concept of quickening. At one time, that concept had a value in differentiating, as accurately as was then scientifically possible, between life and nonlife. The analogous concept of viability is clearly more satisfactory, for it has a well defined and medically determinable meaning denoting the ability of the fetus to live or survive apart from its mother.

The majority opinion suggests that we are confined to common law concepts, and to the common law definition of murder or manslaughter. However, the Legislature, in Penal Code sections 187 and 192, has defined those offenses for us: homicide is the unlawful killing of a "human being." Those words need not be frozen in place as of any particular time, but must be fairly and reasonably interpreted by this court to promote justice and to carry out the evident purposes of the Legislature in adopting a homicide statute. . . .

". . . The true doctrine is that the common law by its own principles adapts itself to varying conditions, and modifies its own rules so as to serve the ends of justice under the different circumstances, a principle adopted into our code by section 3510 of the Civ.Code: 'When the reason of a rule ceases, so should the rule itself.' "

. . . Consequently, nothing should prevent this court from holding that Baby Girl Vogt was a human ("belonging or relating to ban; characteristic of man") being ("existence, as opp. to nonexistence; specif. life") under California's homicide statutes.

We commonly conceive of human existence as a spectrum stretching from birth to death. However, if this court properly might expand the definition of "human being" at one end of that spectrum, we may do so at the other end. Consider the following example: All would agree that "Shooting or otherwise damaging a corpse is not homicide. * * *" (Perkins, Criminal Law (2d ed. 1969) ch. 2, § 1, p. 31.) In other words, a corpse is not considered to be a "human being" and thus cannot be the subject of a "killing" as those terms are used in homicide statutes. However, it is readily apparent that our concepts of what constitutes a "corpse" have been and are being continually modified by advances in the field of medicine, including new techniques for life revival, restoration and resuscitation such as artificial respiration, open heart massage, transfusions, transplants and a variety of life-restoring stimulants, drugs and new surgical methods. Would this court ignore these developments and exonerate the killer of an apparently "drowned" child merely because that child would have been pronounced dead in 1648 or 1850? Obviously not. Whether a homicide occurred in that case would be determined by medical testimony regarding the capability of the child to have survived prior to the defendant's act. And that is precisely the test which this court should adopt in the instant case.

The common law reluctance to characterize the killing of a quickened fetus as a homicide was based solely upon a presumption that the fetus would have been born dead. This presumption seems to have persisted in this country at least as late as 1876. Based upon the state of the medical art in the 17th, 18th and 19th centuries, that presumption may have been well-founded. However, as we approach the 21st century, it has become apparent that "This presumption is not only contrary to common experience and the ordinary course of nature, but it is contrary to the usual rule with respect to presumptions followed in this state."

There are no accurate statistics disclosing fetal death rates in "common law England," although the foregoing presumption of death indicates a significantly high death experience. On the other hand, in California the fetal death rate in 1968 is estimated to be 12 deaths in 1,000, a ratio which would have given Baby Girl Vogt a 98.8 percent chance of survival. (California Statistical Abstract (1969) Table E-3, p. 65.) If, as I have contended, the term "human being" in our homicide statutes is a fluid concept to be defined in accordance with present conditions, then there can be no question that the term should include the fully viable fetus.

The majority suggest that to do so would improperly create some new offense. However, the offense of murder is no new offense. Contrary to the majority opinion, the Legislature has not "defined the crime of murder in California to apply only to the unlawful and malicious killing one who has been born alive." Instead, the Legislature simply used the broad term "human being" and directed the courts to construe that term according to its "fair import" with a view to effect the objects of the homicide statutes and promote justice. (Pen.Code, § 4.) What justice will be promoted, what objects effectuated, by construing "human being" as excluding Baby Girl Vogt and her unfortunate successors? Was defendant's brutal act of stomping her to death any less an act of homicide than the murder of a newly born baby? No one doubts that the term "human being" would include the elderly or dying persons whose potential for life has nearly lapsed; their proximity to death is deemed immaterial. There is no sound reason for denying the viable fetus, with its unbounded potential for life, the same status.

The majority also suggest that such an interpretation of our homicide statutes would deny defendant "fair warning" that his act was punishable as a crime. Aside from the absurdity of the underlying premise that defendant consulted Coke, Blackstone or Hale before kicking Baby Girl Vogt to death, it is clear that defendant had adequate notice that his act could constitute homicide. Due process only precludes prosecution under a new statute insufficiently explicit regarding the specific conduct proscribed, or under a pre-existing statute "by means of an unforeseeable *judicial* enlargement thereof."

Our homicide statutes have been in effect in this state since 1850. The fact that the California courts have not been called upon to determine the precise question before us does not render "unforeseeable" a decision which determines that a viable fetus is a "human being" under those statutes. Can defendant really claim surprise that a 5-pound, 18-inch, 34-week-old, living, viable child is considered to be a human being?

The fact is that the foregoing construction of our homicide statutes easily could have been anticipated from strong dicta in People v. Chavez, wherein the court reviewed common law precedents but disapproved their requirement that the child be born alive and completely separated from its mother. The court in *Chavez* held that a viable child killed during, but prior to completion of, the birth process, was a human being under the homicide statutes. However, the court did not hold that partial birth was a prerequisite, for the court expressly set forth its holding "Without drawing a line of distinction applicable to all cases * * *." In dicta, the court discussed the question when an unborn infant becomes a human being under the homicide statutes, as follows: "There is not much change in the child itself between a moment before and a moment after its expulsion from the body of its mother, and normally, while still dependent upon its mother, the child for some time before it is born, has not only the possibility but a strong probability of an ability to live an independent life. * * * While before birth or removal it is in a sense dependent upon its mother for life, there is another sense in which it has started an independent existence after it has reached a state of development where it is capable of living and where it will, in the normal course of nature and with ordinary care, continue to live and grow as a separate being. While it may not be possible to draw an exact line applicable to all cases, the rules of law should recognize and make some attempt to follow the natural and scientific facts to which they relate. * * * [I]t would be a mere fiction to hold that a child is not a human being because the process of birth has not been fully completed, when it has reached that state of viability when the destruction of the life of its mother would not end its existence and when, if separated from the mother naturally or by artificial means, it will live and grow in the normal manner."

* * *

The trial court's denial of defendant's motion to set aside the information was proper, and the peremptory writ of prohibition should be denied.

■ SULLIVAN, J., concurs.

■ Rehearing denied; BURKE and SULLIVAN, JJ., dissenting.

NOTES

1. Consider the following excerpt of Justice Blackmun's opinion for the Court in Roe v. Wade, 410 U.S. 113, 93 S.Ct. 705, 35 L.Ed.2d 147 (1973), which has been discussed more fully in Chapter 4 in the Section on The Right of Privacy. After concluding that the definition of "person" does not include the unborn, Justice Blackmun's opinion states this in connection with when life begins:

> Texas urges that, apart from the Fourteenth Amendment, life begins at conception and is present throughout pregnancy, and that, therefore, the State has a compelling interest in protecting that life from and after conception. We need not resolve the difficult question of when life begins. When those trained in the respective disciplines of medicine, philosophy, and theology are unable to arrive at any consensus, the judiciary, at this point in the development of man's knowledge, is not in a position to speculate as to the answer.
>
> It should be sufficient to note briefly the wide divergence of thinking on this most sensitive and difficult question. There has always been strong support for the view that life does not begin until live birth. This was the belief of the Stoics. It appears to be the predominant, though not the unanimous, attitude of the Jewish faith. It may be taken to represent also the position of a large segment of the Protestant community, insofar as that can be ascertained; organized groups that have taken a formal position on the abortion issue have generally regarded abortion as a matter for the conscience of the individual and her family. As we have noted, the common law found greater significance in quickening. Physicians and their scientific colleagues have regarded that event with less interest and have tended to focus either upon conception or upon live birth or upon the interim point at which the fetus becomes "viable," that is, potentially able to live outside the mother's womb, albeit with artificial aid. Viability is usually placed at about seven months (28 weeks) but may occur earlier, even at 24 weeks. The Aristotelian theory of "mediate animation," that held sway throughout the Middle Ages and the Renaissance in Europe, continued to be official Roman Catholic dogma until the 19th century, despite opposition to this "ensoulment" theory from those in the Church who would recognize the existence of life from the moment of conception. The latter is now, of course, the official belief of the Catholic Church. As one of the briefs *amicus* discloses, this is a view strongly held by many non-Catholics as well, and by many physicians. Substantial problems for precise definition of this view are posed, however, by new embryological data that purport to indicate that conception is a "process" over time, rather than an event, and by new medical techniques such as menstrual extraction, the "morning-after" pill, implantation of embryos, artificial insemination, and even artificial wombs.

In areas other than criminal abortion the law has been reluctant to endorse any theory that life, as we recognize it, begins before live birth or to accord legal rights to the unborn except in narrowly defined situations and except when the rights are contingent upon live birth. For example, the traditional rule of tort law had denied recovery for prenatal injuries even though the child was born alive. That rule has been changed in almost every jurisdiction. In most States recovery is said to be permitted only if the fetus was viable, or at least quick, when the injuries were sustained, though few courts have squarely so held. In a recent development, generally opposed by the commentators, some States permit the parents of a stillborn child to maintain an action for wrongful death because of prenatal injuries. Such an action, however, would appear to be one to vindicate the parents' interest and is thus consistent with the view that the fetus, at most, represents only the potentiality of life. Similarly, unborn children have been recognized as acquiring rights or interests by way of inheritance or other devolution of property, and have been represented by guardians *ad litem*. Perfection of the interests involved, again, has generally been contingent upon live birth. In short, the unborn have never been recognized in the law as persons in the whole sense.

2. The New York Penal Code provides, in § 125.05 where definitions applicable to homicide prosecutions are contained, that " '[p]erson,' when referring to the victim of a homicide, means a human being who has been born and is alive."

3. For a court's holding that a viable fetus is not a "human being" for purposes of Kansas' aggravated vehicular homicide statute, see State v. Trudell, 243 Kan. 29, 755 P.2d 511 (1988). While the State's wrongful death statute had been interpreted liberally to give parents of a viable fetus a right to maintain a wrongful death action despite any specific statutory language in the act, the Kansas Supreme Court said that criminal statutes, with their punitive effects, must be construed more narrowly. If the common law rule, requiring a live birth, is to be changed, the legislative branch is the proper forum to resolve such an issue. *See also* Commonwealth v. Booth, 564 Pa. 228, 766 A.2d 843 (2001) (holding that the prosecution may not rely upon the death of an unborn child as the predicate for the crime of homicide by vehicle while driving under the influence); Johnson v. State, 602 So.2d 1288 (Fla. 1992) (holding that a pregnant woman cannot be held criminally liable for passing cocaine in utero to her fetus).

4. The *Keeler* case probably still represents the prevailing view among the states. *Accord* Jones v. Commonwealth, 830 S.W.2d 877 (Ky.1992). For a rejection of the common law "born alive" rule, see Hughes v. State, 868 P.2d 730 (Okl.Crim.App. 1994). In People v. Davis, 7 Cal.4th 797, 30 Cal.Rptr.2d 50, 872 P.2d 591 (1994), the California Supreme Court held that California's murder statute, Cal. Penal Code § 187, which applies to the killing of a "human being" or a "fetus" with malice aforethought, can be applied to the killing of a non-viable fetus.

Texas follows the "born-alive" rule. In such a jurisdiction, where the victim of the offense was a fetus at the time of the defendant's assaultive behavior, and, therefore, not an "individual" within the legal meaning of that term, could the defendant nevertheless be held responsible of a statutory involuntary manslaughter (during DUI) offense if the victim is thereafter born alive but dies from the from the injuries sustained before birth? *See* Cuellar v. State, 957 S.W.2d 134 (Tex.App. 1997).

3. THE MALICE FACTOR

Commonwealth v. Webster

Supreme Judicial Court of Massachusetts, 1850.
59 Mass. (5 Cush.) 295, 386.

The defendant, professor of chemistry, in the medical college, in Boston, attached to the university at Cambridge, was indicted in the municipal court at the January term, 1850, for the murder of Dr. George Parkman, at Boston, on the 23d of November, 1849. . . .

The government introduced evidence, that George Parkman, quite peculiar in person and manners, and very well known to most persons in the city of Boston, left his home in Walnut Street in Boston in the forenoon of the 23d of November, 1849, in good health and spirits; and that he was traced through various streets of the city until about a quarter before two o'clock of that day, when he was seen going towards and about to enter the medical college: That he did not return to his home: That on the next day a very active, particular, and extended search was commenced in Boston and the neighboring towns and cities, and continued until the 30th of November; and that large rewards were offered for information about Dr. Parkman: That on the 30th of November certain parts of a human body were discovered, in and about the defendant's laboratory in the medical college; and a great number of fragments of human bones and certain blocks of mineral teeth, imbedded in slag and cinders, together with small quantities of gold, which had been melted, were found in an assay furnace of the laboratory: That in consequence of some of these discoveries the defendant was arrested on the evening of the 30th of November: That the parts of a human body so found resembled in every respect the corresponding portions of the body of Dr. Parkman, and that among them all there were no duplicate parts; and that they were not the remains of a body which had been dissected: That the artificial teeth found in the furnace were made for Dr. Parkman by a dentist in Boston in 1846, and refitted in his mouth by the same dentist a fortnight before his disappearance: That the defendant was indebted to Dr. Parkman on certain notes, and was pressed by him for payment; that the defendant has said that on the 23d of November, about nine o'clock in the morning, he left word at Dr. Parkman's house, that if he would come to the medical college at half past one o'clock on that day, he would pay him; and that, as he said, he accordingly had an interview with Dr. Parkman at half past one o'clock on that day, at his laboratory in the medical college: That the defendant then had no means of paying, and that the notes were afterwards found in his possession. . . .

[The defendant was tried before the Chief Justice, and Justices Wilde, Dewey and Metcalf. The opinion of the court on the law of the case was given in the charge to the jury as follows:]

■ SHAW, C.J. Homicide, of which murder is the highest and most criminal species, is of various degrees, according to circumstances. The term, in its largest sense, is generic, embracing every mode by which the life of one man is taken by the act of another. Homicide may be lawful or unlawful; it is lawful when done in lawful war upon an enemy in battle, it is lawful when done by an officer in the execution of justice upon a criminal, pursuant to a proper warrant. It may also be justifiable, and of course lawful, in necessary self-defence. But it is not necessary to dwell on these distinctions; it will be sufficient to ask attention to the two species of criminal homicide, familiarly known as murder and manslaughter.

In seeking for the sources of our law upon this subject, it is proper to say, that whilst the statute law of the commonwealth declares that "Every person who shall commit the crime of murder shall suffer the punishment of death for the same;" yet it nowhere defines the crimes of murder or manslaughter, with all their minute and carefully-considered distinctions and qualifications. For these, we resort to that great repository of rules, principles, and forms, the common law. This we commonly designate as the common law of England; but it might now be properly called the common law of Massachusetts. It was adopted when our ancestors first settled here, by general consent. It was adopted and confirmed by an early act of the provincial government, and was formally confirmed by the provision of the constitution declaring that all the laws which had theretofore been adopted, used, and approved, in the province or state of Massachusetts bay, and usually practiced on in the courts of law, should still remain and be in full force until altered or repealed by the legislature. So far, therefore, as the rules and principles of the common law are applicable to the administration of criminal law, and have not been altered and modified by acts of the colonial or provincial government or by the state legislature, they have the same force and effect as laws formally enacted.

By the existing law, as adopted and practiced on, unlawful homicide is distinguished into murder and manslaughter.

Murder, in the sense in which it is now understood, is the killing of any person in the peace of the commonwealth, with *malice aforethought*, either express or implied by law. Malice in this definition, is used in a technical sense, <u>including not only anger, hatred, and revenge, but every</u> <u>other unlawful and unjustifiable motive.</u> It is not confined to ill-will towards one or more individual persons, but is intended to denote an action flowing from any wicked and corrupt motive, a thing done *malo animo*, where the fact has been attended with such circumstances as carry in them the plain indications of a heart regardless of social duty, and fatally bent on mischief. And therefore <u>malice is implied from any</u> <u>deliberate or cruel act against another, however sudden.</u>

Manslaughter is the unlaw<u>ful killing of another without malice</u>; and may be either <u>voluntary</u>, as when the act is committed with a real design and purpose to kill, but through the violence of sudden passion, occasioned by some great provocation, which in tenderness for the frailty of human nature the law considers sufficient to palliate the criminality of the offence; or <u>involuntary</u>, as when the death of another is caused by some unlawful act not accompanied by any intention to take life.

From these two definitions, it will be at once perceived, that the characteristic distinction between murder and manslaughter is malice, express or implied. It therefore becomes necessary, in every case of homicide proved, and in order to an intelligent inquiry into the legal character of the act, to ascertain with some precision the <u>nature of legal</u> <u>malice, and what evidence is requisite to establish its existence.</u>

Upon this subject, the rule as deduced from the authorities is, that the implication of <u>malice arises in every case of intentional homicide</u>; and, the fact of killing being first proved, all the circumstances of accident, necessity, or infirmity, are to be satisfactorily established by the party charged, unless they arise out of the evidence produced against him to prove the homicide, and the circumstances attending it. If there are, in fact, circumstances of justification, excuse, or palliation, such proof will naturally indicate them. But where the fact of killing is proved by satisfactory evidence, and there are no circumstances disclosed, tending to show justification or excuse, there is nothing to rebut the natural presumption of malice. This rule is founded on the plain and obvious principle, <u>that a person must be presumed to intend to do that</u> <u>which he voluntarily and willfully does in fact do,</u> and that he must intend all the natural, probable, and usual consequences of his own acts. Therefore, when one person assails another violently with a dangerous weapon likely to kill and which does in fact destroy the life of the party assailed, the natural presumption is, that he intended death or other great bodily harm; and, as there can be no presumption of any proper motive or legal excuse for such a cruel act, the consequence follows, that, in the absence of all proof to the contrary, there is nothing to rebut the presumption of malice. On the other hand, if death, though wilfully intended, was inflicted immediately after provocation given by the deceased, supposing that such provocation consisted of a blow or an assault, or other provocation on his part, which the law deems adequate to excite sudden and angry passion and create heat of blood, this fact rebuts the presumption of malice; but still, the homicide being unlawful, because a man is bound to curb his passions, is criminal, and is manslaughter.

[handwritten margin note: Provocation (not just words)]

In considering what is regarded as such adequate provocation, it is a settled rule of law, that no provocation by words only, however opprobrious, will mitigate an intentional homicide, so as to reduce it to manslaughter. Therefore, if, upon provoking language given, the party immediately revenges himself by the use of a dangerous and deadly weapon likely to cause death, such as a pistol discharged at the person, a heavy bludgeon, an axe, or a knife; if death ensues, it is a homicide not mitigated to manslaughter by the circumstances, and so is homicide by malice aforethought, within the true definition of murder. It is not the less malice aforethought, within the meaning of the law, because the act is done suddenly after the intention to commit the homicide is formed; it is sufficient that the malicious intention precedes and accompanies the act of homicide. It is manifest, therefore, that the words "malice aforethought," in the description of murder, do not imply deliberation, or the lapse of considerable time between the malicious intent to take life and the actual execution of that intent, but rather denote purpose and design, in contradistinction to accident and mischance.

[handwritten margin note: if no intent but uses deadly force, still homicide]

In speaking of the use of a dangerous weapon, and the mode of using it upon the person of another, I have spoken of it as indicating an intention to kill him, or do him great bodily harm. The reason is this. Where a man, without justification or excuse, causes the death of another by the intentional use of a dangerous weapon likely to destroy life, he is responsible for the consequences, upon the principle already stated, that he is liable for the natural and probable consequences of his act. Suppose, therefore, for the purpose of revenge, one fires a pistol at another, regardless of consequences, intending to kill, maim, or grievously wound him, as the case may be, without any definite intention to take his life; yet, if that is the result, the law attributes the same consequences to homicide so committed, as if done under an actual and declared purpose to take the life of the party assailed. . . .

The true nature of manslaughter is, that it is homicide mitigated out of tenderness to the frailty of human nature. Every man, when assailed with violence or great rudeness, is inspired with a sudden impulse of anger, which puts him upon resistance before time for cool reflection; and if, during that period, he attacks his assailant with a weapon likely to endanger life, and death ensues, it is regarded as done through heat of blood or violence of anger, and not through malice, or that cold-blooded desire of revenge which more properly constitutes the feeling, emotion or passion of malice.

The same rule applies to homicide in mutual combat, which is attributed to sudden and violent anger occasioned by the combat, and not to malice. When two meet, not intending to quarrel, and angry words suddenly arise, and a conflict springs up in which blows are given on both sides, without much regard to who is the assailant, it is mutual combat. And if no unfair advantage is taken in the outset, and the occasion is not sought for the purpose of gratifying malice, and one seizes a weapon and strikes a deadly blow, it is regarded as homicide in heat of blood; and though not excusable, because a man is bound to control his angry passions, yet it is not the higher offence of murder.

[handwritten margin note: manslaughter]

We have stated these distinctions, not because there is much evidence in the present case which calls for their application, but that the jury may have a clear and distinct view of the leading principles in the law of homicide. There seems to have been little evidence in the present case that the parties had a contest. There is some evidence tending to show the previous existence of angry feelings; but unless these feelings resulted in angry words, and words were followed by blows, there would be no proof of heat of blood in mutual combat, or under provocation of an assault, on the one side or the other; and the proof of the defendant's declarations, as to the circumstances under which the parties met and parted, as far as they go, repel the supposition of such a contest.

With these views of the law of homicide, we will proceed to the further consideration of the present case. The prisoner at the bar is charged with the wilful murder of Dr. George Parkman. This charge divides itself into two principal questions, to be resolved by the proof: first, whether the party alleged to have been murdered came to his death by an act of violence inflicted by any person; and if so, secondly, whether the act was committed by the accused. . . .

[handwritten margin note: issue]

This case is to be proved, if proved at all, by circumstantial evidence; because it is not suggested that any direct evidence can be given, or that any witness can be called to give direct testimony, upon the main fact of the killing. It becomes important, therefore, to state what circumstantial evidence is; to point out the distinction between that and positive or direct evidence.

The distinction, then, between direct and circumstantial evidence, is this. Direct or positive evidence is when a witness can be called to testify to the precise fact which is the subject of the issue on trial; that is, in a case of homicide, that the party accused did cause the death of the deceased. Whatever may be the kind of force of the evidence, that is the fact to be proved. But suppose no person was present on the occasion of the death, and of course that no one can be called to testify to it; is it wholly unsusceptible of legal proof? Experience has shown that circumstantial evidence may be offered in such a case; that is, that a body of facts may be proved of so conclusive a character, as to warrant a firm belief of the fact, quite as strong and certain as that on which discreet men are accustomed to act, in relation to their most important concerns. It would be injurious to the best interests of society, if such proof could not avail in judicial proceedings. If it was necessary always to have positive evidence how many criminal acts committed in the community, destructive of its peace and subversive of its order and security, would go wholly undetected and unpunished?

The necessity, therefore, of resorting to circumstantial evidence, if it is a safe and reliable proceeding, is obvious and absolute. Crimes are secret. Most men, conscious of criminal purposes, and about the execution of criminal acts, seek the security of secrecy and darkness. It is therefore necessary to use all modes of evidence besides that of direct testimony, provided such proofs may be relied on as leading to safe and satisfactory conclusions; and, thanks to a beneficent providence, the laws of nature and the relations of things to each other are so linked and combined together, that a medium of proof is often thereby furnished, leading to inferences and conclusions as strong as those arising from direct testimony. . . . The evidence must establish the *corpus delicti*, as it is termed, or the offence committed as charged; and, in case of homicide, must not only prove a death by violence, but must, to a reasonable extent, exclude the hypothesis of suicide, and a death by the act of any other person. This is to be proved beyond reasonable doubt.

Then, what is reasonable doubt? It is a term often used, probably pretty well understood, but not easily defined. It is not mere possible doubt; because every thing relating to human affairs, and depending on moral evidence, is open to some possible or imaginary doubt. It is that state of the case, which, after the entire comparison and consideration of all the evidence, leaves the minds of the jurors in that condition and they cannot say they feel an abiding conviction, to a moral certainty, of the truth of the charge. The burden of proof is upon the prosecutor. All the presumptions of law independent of evidence are in favor of innocence; and every person is presumed to be innocent until he is proved guilty. If upon such proof there is reasonable doubt remaining, the accused is entitled to the benefit of it by an acquittal. For it is not sufficient to establish a probability, though a strong one arising from the doctrine of chances, that the fact charged is more likely to be true than the contrary; but the evidence must establish the truth of the fact to a reasonable and moral certainty; a certainty that convinces and directs the understanding, and satisfies the reason and judgment of those who are bound to act conscientiously upon it. This we take to be proof beyond reasonable doubt; because if the law, which mostly depends upon considerations of a moral nature, should go further than this, and require absolute certainty, it would exclude circumstantial evidence altogether. . . .

[The jury returned a verdict of guilty, and the defendant's sentence of death by hanging was sustained by the Supreme Judicial Court of Massachusetts. Subsequently, Dr. Webster confessed:

On Tuesday the 20th of November, I sent the note to Dr. Parkman. . . . It was to ask Dr. Parkman to call at my rooms on Friday the 23d, after my lecture. . . . My purpose was, if he should accede to the proposed interview, to state to him my embarrassments and utter inability to pay him at present, to apologize for those things in my conduct which had offended him, to throw myself upon his mercy, to beg for further time and indulgence for the sake of my family, if not for my own, and to make as good promises to him as I could have any hope of keeping. . . .

Dr. Parkman agreed to call on me as I proposed.

He came, accordingly, between half-past one and two. . . . He immediately addressed me with great energy: "Are you ready for me, sir? Have you got the money?" I replied, "No, Dr. Parkman"; and was then beginning to state my condition and make my appeal to him. He would not listen to me, but interrupted me with much vehemence. He called me "scoundrel" and "liar," and went on heaping upon me the most bitter taunts and opprobrious epithets. . . . I cannot tell how long the torrent of threats and invectives continued, and I can now recall to memory but a small portion of what he said. At first I kept interposing, trying to pacify him, so that I might obtain the object for which I had sought the interview. But I could not stop him, and soon my own temper was up. I forgot everything. I felt nothing but the sting of his words. I was excited to the highest degree of passion; and while he was speaking and gesticulating in the most violent and menacing manner, thrusting the letter and his fist into my face, in my fury I seized whatever was the handiest,—it was a stick of wood,—and dealt him an instantaneous blow with all the force that passion could give it. I did not know, nor think, nor care where I should hit him, nor how hard nor what the effect would be. It was on the side of his head, and there was nothing to break the force of the blow. He fell instantly upon the pavement. . . . Perhaps I spent ten minutes in attempts to resuscitate him; but I found that he was absolutely dead. . . .

My next move was to get the body into the sink which stands in the small private room. By setting the body partially erect against the corner, and getting up into the sink myself, I succeeded in drawing it up. There it was entirely dismembered. . . .

There was a fire burning in the furnace of the lower laboratory. . . . The head and viscera were put into that furnace that day. . . .

When the body had been thus all disposed of, I cleared away all traces of what had been done. I took up the stick with which the fatal blow had been struck. It proved to be the stump of a large grape vine, say two inches in diameter, and two feet long. . . . I had carried it in from Cambridge . . . for the purpose of showing the effect of certain chemical fluids in coloring wood. . . . I put it into the fire. . . .

The full confession appears in George Bemis, Report of the Case of John W. Webster 564–71 (1850).

Had the above story been told at the trial, and believed, should the jury, in light of the judge's charge, have convicted Dr. Webster of murder or manslaughter?][1]

NOTES: "MALICE AFORETHOUGHT"

1. As Chief Justice Shaw noted in his charge to the jury in the Webster case, supra, "[T]he characteristic distinction between murder and manslaughter is malice, express or implied."

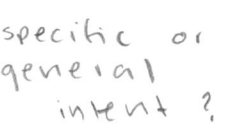

"Malice aforethought" is the mental state required for murder. Is this the equivalent of specific intent? Or is it general intent? Refer to materials on "mental states" in Chapter 2, supra.

With respect to the meaning and significance of the term "malice," consider the following:

The meaning of "malice aforethought," which is the distinguishing criterion of murder, is certainly not beyond the range of controversy. The first thing that must be said about it is that neither of the two words is used in its ordinary sense. . . . "It is now only an arbitrary symbol. For the 'malice' may have in it nothing really malicious; and need never be really 'aforethought,' except in the sense that every desire must necessarily come before—though perhaps only an instant before—the act which is desired. The word 'aforethought,' in the definition, has thus become either false or else superfluous. The word 'malice' is neither; but it is apt to be misleading, for it is not employed in its original (and its popular) meaning." "Malice aforethought" is simply a comprehensive name for a number of different mental attitudes which have been variously defined at different stages in the development of the law, the presence of any one of which in the accused has been held by the courts to render a homicide particularly heinous and therefore to make it murder. . . . As

---

[1]   For an interesting account of the trial of Dr. Webster, see Robert Sullivan, *The Murder Trial of Dr. Webster, Boston, 1850*, 51 Mass. L. Quarterly 367 (1966); 52 *ibid.*, 67 (1967). Also see the same author's book, Robert Sullivan, The Disappearance of Dr. Parkman (1971), in which he states that the "charge to the jury" by Justice Shaw was not the one actually delivered, but rather an extensively rewritten and moderated third draft, partly composed after Webster's execution. *See also* Albert I. Borowitz, The Janitor's Story: An Ethical Dilemma in the Harvard Murder Case, 66 A.B.A.J. 1540 (1980) (suggesting that the confession was a "hoax" and was viewed by the press as a last-ditch effort by Webster to save his life).

Stephen put it ". . . when a particular state of mind came under their notice the Judges called it malice or not according to their view of the propriety of hanging particular people. . . .' "

REPORT OF THE ROYAL COMMISSION ON CAPITAL PUNISHMENT, 1949–1953, at 26–28 (1953).

2. Consider, with respect to the present English concept, the case of Hyam v. Director of Public Prosecutions, 2 All E.R. 41 (1974), the defendant was a woman who had been abandoned by her lover in favor of another woman. She set fire to the house where her rival lived, supposedly to frighten her into leaving town, but the fire killed two of the occupant's infants. The jury was instructed that it could convict if it found that "when the accused set fire to the house she knew that it was highly probable that this would cause . . . serious bodily harm." The House of Lords ultimately affirmed the conviction by a three to two vote. The various opinions of the Lords deserve careful analysis for any extensive discussion of the effect of the mental state on the concept of malice in murder.

The statement was made in the *Hyam* case that despite the wording of the English Homicide Act of 1957 which abolished "constructive malice," "malice aforethought" was retained without declaring what it meant. The conclusion was reached that the law actually remained the same as it was before.

3. The following definition of "malice aforethought" is deserving of consideration: "an unjustifiable, inexcusable and unmitigated man-endangering-state-of-mind." ROLLIN M. PERKINS, PERKINS ON CRIMINAL LAW 40 (1957).

A good example within Professor Perkins' definition is the early case of Banks v. State, 85 Tex.Cr.R. 165, 211 S.W. 217 (1919), which involved the firing of shots into a moving train and resulted in the death of one of the crew, and where the court said:

One who deliberately used a deadly weapon in such reckless manner as to evince a heart regardless of social duty and fatally bent on mischief, as is shown by firing into a moving train upon which human beings necessarily are, cannot shield himself from the consequences of his acts by disclaiming malice. Malice may be toward a group of persons as well as toward an individual. It may exist without former grudges or antecedent menaces. The intentional doing of any wrongful act in such manner and under such circumstances as that the death of a human being may result therefrom is malice.

Another example is Commonwealth v. Ashburn, 459 Pa. 625, 331 A.2d 167 (1975), where the defendant was convicted of murder for killing a friend in a game of Russian Roulette. Only one chamber of the revolver had been loaded with live ammunition. When defendant argued there was only one chance in six that the victim would be killed and that such odds do not make it highly foreseeable that death would result, the Pennsylvania Supreme Court stated that the finding of malice does not depend on any precise mathematical calculation of the probable consequences of defendant's acts. A somewhat similar case is Commonwealth v. Malone, 354 Pa. 180, 47 A.2d 445 (1946), in which the defendant's conviction for murder was affirmed when it was shown he had placed a gun against the decedent and pulled the trigger three times. He erroneously believed that he had placed the bullet in such a manner that the gun would not fire.

For other Russian Roulette cases, see *infra* the materials on involuntary manslaughter.

4. Consider the following interesting definition of malice in Cal. Penal Code § 188 (enacted in 1872):

> Malice may be express or implied. It is express when there is manifested a deliberate intention unlawfully to take away the life of a fellow creature. It is implied, when no considerable provocation appears, or when the circumstances attending the killing show an abandoned and malignant heart.

In 1981, the California legislature added a new paragraph to the statute:

> When it is shown that the killing resulted from the intentional doing of an act with express or implied malice as defined above, no other mental state need be shown to establish the mental state of malice aforethought. Neither an awareness of the obligation to act within the general body of laws regulating society nor acting despite such awareness is included within the definition of malice.

Also consider Kasieta v. State, 62 Wis.2d 564, 215 N.W.2d 412 (1974), in which the defendant was convicted of the murder of his girlfriend whom he had discovered in bed with another man. The victim had Hodgkins' disease, a condition of which the defendant was aware. He had hit the victim and caused several bruises about her face as well as a superficial wound over the left eye, a wound on the scalp, and a fractured nose which caused bleeding. The doctor testified that due to the Hodgkins' disease, as well as some other factors such as intoxication by alcohol and drugs, she had been unable to cough up or expel the blood as a result of which the blood filled her diseased lungs. The Supreme Court of Wisconsin held that the jury could find that the striking of someone in the nose, while not imminently dangerous in ordinary cases, was dangerous in the instant case because of the fact the victim was seriously ill, and that the blows struck by defendant under such circumstances evinced a depraved mind regardless of human life.

———

At the common law there were no degrees of murder. Any homicide, committed with malice aforethought, express or implied, constituted murder. The penalty for murder under the common law was death.

In order to lessen the penalty attaching to certain forms of murder not thought to warrant the punishment of death, many states have statutorily divided the crime of murder into various degrees, with a sliding scale of penalties deemed appropriate to the various degrees.

State v. Guthrie

Supreme Court of Appeals of West Virginia, 1995.
194 W.Va. 657, 461 S.E.2d 163.

■ CLECKLEY, JUSTICE.

It is undisputed that on the evening of February 12, 1993, the defendant removed a knife from his pocket and stabbed his co-worker, Steven Todd Farley, in the neck and killed him. The two men worked together as dishwashers at Danny's Rib House in Nitro and got along well together before this incident. On the night of the killing, the victim, his brother, Tracy Farley, and James Gibson were joking around while working in the kitchen of the restaurant. The victim was poking fun at the defendant who appeared to be in a bad mood. He told the defendant to "lighten up" and snapped him with a dishtowel several times. Apparently, the victim had no idea he was upsetting the defendant very much. The dishtowel flipped the defendant on the nose and he became enraged. The defendant removed his gloves and started toward the victim. Mr. Farley, still teasing, said: "Ooo, he's taking his gloves off." The defendant then pulled a knife from his pocket and stabbed the victim in the neck. He also stabbed Mr. Farley in the arm as he fell to the floor. Mr. Farley looked up and cried: "Man, I was just kidding around." The defendant responded: "Well, man, you should have never hit me in my face." The police arrived at the restaurant and arrested the defendant. He was given his Miranda rights. The defendant made a statement at the police station and confessed to the killing. The police officers described him as calm and willing to cooperate.

It is also undisputed that the defendant suffers from a host of psychiatric problems. He experiences up to two panic attacks daily and had received treatment for them at the Veterans Administration Hospital in Huntington for more than a year preceding the killing. He suffers from chronic depression (dysthymic disorder), an obsession with his nose (body dysmorphic disorder), and borderline personality disorder. The defendant's father shed some light on his nose fixation. He stated that dozens of times a day the defendant stared in the mirror and turned his head back and forth to look at his nose. His father estimated that 50 percent of the time he observed his son he was looking at his nose. The defendant repeatedly asked for assurances that his nose was not too big. This obsession began when he was approximately seventeen years old. The defendant was twenty-nine years old at the time of trial. The defendant testified he suffered a panic attack immediately preceding the stabbing. He described the attack as "intense"; he felt a lot of pressure and his heart beat rapidly. In contrast to the boisterous atmosphere in the kitchen that evening, the defendant was quiet and kept to himself. He stated that Mr. Farley kept irritating him that night. The defendant could not understand why Mr. Farley was picking on him because he had never done that before. Even at trial, the defendant did not comprehend his utter overreaction to the situation. In hindsight, the defendant believed the better decision would have been to punch out on his time card and quit over the incident. However, all the witnesses related that the defendant was in no way attacked, as he perceived it, but that Mr. Farley was playing around. The defendant could not bring himself to tell the other workers to leave him alone or inform them about his panic attacks. In contrast to his written statement, the defendant testified he was unable to recall stabbing the victim. After he was struck in the nose, he stated that he "lost it" and, when he came to himself, he was holding the knife in his hand and Mr. Farley was sinking to the floor.

A psychiatrist, Dr. Sidney Lerfald, testified on behalf of the defendant. He diagnosed the various disorders discussed above. Dr. Lerfald felt the defendant's diagnoses "may have affected his perception somewhat." Nevertheless, it was his opinion the defendant was sane at the time of the offense because he was able to distinguish between right and wrong and could have conformed his actions accordingly. It was the State's position that the facts supported a first degree murder conviction. At the close of the State's case-in-chief, the defense moved for a directed verdict contending the State failed to present evidence of malice and premeditation. This motion was denied. The defense argued the facts of the case supported voluntary manslaughter or, at worse, second degree murder. The jury returned a verdict finding the defendant guilty of first degree murder with a recommendation of mercy.

A.   SUFFICIENCY OF THE EVIDENCE

In his appeal, the defendant raises several assignments of error. First, the defendant strives to persuade us that the record in this case does not support the verdict of guilty of first degree murder beyond a reasonable doubt. We begin by emphasizing that our review is conducted from a cold appellate transcript and record. For that reason, we must assume that the jury credited all witnesses whose testimony supports the verdict. . . .

There is no doubt what inferences and findings of fact the jury had to draw in order to convict the defendant of first degree murder. The jury must have believed that: (1) The "horseplay" provocation was not sufficient to justify a deadly attack; (2) the defendant was under no real fear of his own from being attacked; (3) the stabbing was intentional; and (4) the time it took the defendant to open his knife and inflict the mortal wound was sufficient to establish premeditation. The difficult factual question must have been the mental state of the defendant at the time of the stabbing.

After reviewing the record, this Court has some doubt as to whether this is a first degree murder case; but, at this point, . . . it makes absolutely no difference whether we on the appellate bench as jurors would have voted to convict the defendant of a lesser-included offense or whether we would have thought there was some reasonable doubt. To the contrary, the question is whether any rational jury could on the evidence presented think the defendant premeditated and intentionally killed the victim. We do not find the evidence so weak as to render the verdict irrational. A rational jury may well have found the defendant guilty of some lesser-included crime without violating its oath; but, drawing all favorable inferences in favor of the prosecution, a rational jury could also convict. We end by suggesting that variations in human experience suggest it is not unexpected to see a considerable range of reasonable verdicts or estimates about what is likely or unlikely. Thus, we find the evidence sufficient.

B. ADEQUACY OF JURY INSTRUCTIONS AS TO THE ELEMENTS OF FIRST DEGREE MURDER

The principal question before us under this assignment of error is whether our instructions on murder when given together deprive a criminal defendant of due process or are otherwise wrong and confusing. Because the instructions given in this case conform to what we have already approved in this area, the essence of what the defendant asks us to decide is whether our previously approved instructions in first degree murder cases are legally correct. In concluding his presentation, the defendant asks us "to write an opinion which clearly and specifically defines (1) the term wilful, (2) the term deliberate, and (3) the term premeditated."

The defendant asserts the trial court's instructions regarding the elements of first degree murder were improper because the terms wilful, deliberate, and premeditated were equated with a mere intent to kill. The jury was instructed that in order to find the defendant guilty of murder it had to find five elements beyond a reasonable doubt: "The Court further instructs the jury that murder in the first degree is when one person kills another person unlawfully, willfully, maliciously, deliberately and premeditatedly." In its effort to define these terms, the trial court gave three instructions.

State's Instruction No. 8, commonly referred to as the *Clifford* instruction, stated:

The Court instructs the jury that to constitute a willful, deliberate and premeditated killing, it is not necessary that the intention to kill should exist for any particular length of time prior to the actual killing; it is only necessary that such intention should have come into existence for the first time at the time of such killing, or at any time previously. See State v. Clifford, 59 W.Va. 1, 52 S.E. 981 (1906).

State's Instruction No. 10 stated: "The Court instructs the jury that in order to constitute a 'premeditated' murder an intent to kill need exist only for an instant." State's Instruction No. 12 stated: "The Court instructs the jury that what is meant by the language willful, deliberate and premeditated is that the killing be intentional." State's Instruction

Nos. 10 and 12 are commonly referred to as *Schrader* instructions. See State v. Schrader, 172 W.Va. 1, 302 S.E.2d 70 (1982).

The linchpin of the problems that flow from these instructions is the failure adequately to inform the jury of the difference between first and second degree murder. Of particular concern is the lack of guidance to the jury as to what constitutes premeditation and the manner in which the instructions infuse premeditation with the intent to kill. At common law, murder was defined as the unlawful killing of another human being with "malice aforethought." Because the common law definition of "malice aforethought" was extremely flexible, "it became over time an 'arbitrary symbol' used by trial judges to signify any of the number of mental states deemed sufficient to support liability for murder." Nevertheless, most American jurisdictions maintained a law of murder built around common law classifications. Pertinent to this case, the most significant departure from the common law came on April 22, 1794, when the Pennsylvania Legislature enacted a statute dividing murder into degrees. It decreed that the death penalty would be inflicted only for first degree murder. West Virginia, like most other states, followed the Pennsylvania practice. Indeed, the 1794 Pennsylvania statute is nearly identical to W.Va.Code, 61–2–1 (1991), our murder statute.

The West Virginia Legislature chose not to define the term "premeditated" in W.Va.Code, 61–2–1. As a result, this Court consistently has resorted to the common law. In State v. Dodds, 54 W.Va. 289, 297–98, 46 S.E. 228, 231 (1903), we said: " 'The next ingredient of the crime is that it must be deliberate. To deliberate is to reflect, with a view to make a choice. If a person reflects, though but for a moment before he acts, it is unquestionably a sufficient deliberation within the meaning of the statute. The last requisite is that the killing must be premeditated. To premeditate is to think of a matter before it is executed. The word, premeditated, would seem to imply something more than deliberate, and may mean that the party not only deliberated, but had formed in his mind the plan of destruction.' "

In State v. Hatfield, 169 W.Va. 191, 286 S.E.2d 402 (1982), we made an effort to distinguish the degrees of murder by indicating that the elements that separate first degree murder and second degree murder are deliberation and premeditation in addition to the formation of the specific intent to kill. Deliberation and premeditation mean to reflect upon the intent to kill and make a deliberate choice to carry it out. Although no particular amount of time is required, there must be at least a sufficient period to permit the accused to actually consider in his or her mind the plan to kill. In this sense, murder in the first degree is a calculated killing as opposed to a spontaneous event. After noting the above language in *Dodds*, Justice Miller stated in *Hatfield*: "The terms 'deliberate' and 'premeditated' have not often been defined in our cases but do carry a certain degree of definitional overlap."

Although we approved the jury instruction from *Clifford* that "it is only necessary that the intention to kill should have come into existence for the first time at the time of the killing" in Hatfield, Justice Miller explained this instruction was merely intended to convey the notion that it is possible for deliberation and premeditation to precede the formation of the actual intent to kill. Justice Miller further stated: "Here, the *Clifford* instruction refers primarily to the intention to kill not existing for any particular time and arising at the moment of the killing. This means the specific intent to kill and is to be distinguished from the elements of deliberation and premeditation which are the state of mind conveying the characteristics of reflection." This is the meaning of the so-called *Clifford* instruction and, when it is given, its significance should be explained to the jury. The source of the problem in the present case stems from language in State v. Schrader (1982). While this Court elaborated on the meaning of premeditation, we gave it a different definition than that approved in *Hatfield* and *Dodds*. In *Schrader*, we stated: "Hence, when the West Virginia Legislature adopted the Virginia murder statute in 1868, the meaning of 'premeditated' as used in the statute was essentially 'knowing' and 'intentional.' Since then, courts have consistently recognized that the mental process necessary to constitute 'willful, deliberate and premeditated' murder can be accomplished very quickly or even in the proverbial 'twinkling of an eye.' . . . The achievement of a mental state contemplated in a statute such as ours can immediately precede the act of killing. Hence, what is really meant by the language 'willful, deliberate and premeditated' in W.Va.Code, 61–2–1 [1923] is that the killing be intentional." The language emphasized above supplied the legal authority and basis for State's Instruction Nos. 10 and 12.

While many jurisdictions do not favor the distinction between first and second degree murder,[22] given the doctrine of separation of powers, we do not have the judicial prerogative to abolish the distinction between first and second degree murder and rewrite the law of homicide for West Virginia; unless, of course, we were to declare this classification a violation of due process and force the Legislature to rewrite the law—a bold stroke that we refuse to do. On the other hand, we believe within the parameters of our current homicide statutes the *Schrader* definition of premeditation and deliberation is confusing, if not meaningless. To

---

[22] The Model Penal Code and many of the modern state criminal codes abolish the first and second degree murder distinction in favor of classifications based on more meaningful criteria. Interestingly, defining premeditation in such a way that the formation of the intent to kill and the killing can result from successive impulses, see *Schrader* (intent equals premeditation formula), grants the jury complete discretion to find more ruthless killers guilty of first degree murder regardless of actual premeditation. History teaches that such unbridled discretion is not always carefully and thoughtfully employed, and this case may be an example. In 1994, the Legislature raised the penalty for second degree murder to ten-to-forty years (from five-to-eighteen years), making it less important to give juries the unguided discretion to find the aggravated form of murder in the case of more ruthless killings, irrespective of actual premeditation. The penalties are now comparable.

allow the State to prove premeditation and deliberation by only showing that the intention came "into existence for the first time at the time of such killing" completely eliminates the distinction between the two degrees of murder. Hence, we feel compelled in this case to attempt to make the dichotomy meaningful by making some modifications to our homicide common law.

Premeditation and deliberation should be defined in a more careful, but still general way to give juries both guidance and reasonable discretion. Although premeditation and deliberation are not measured by any particular period of time, there must be some period between the formation of the intent to kill and the actual killing, which indicates the killing is by prior calculation and design. As suggested by the dissenting opinion in Green v. State, 1 Tenn.Crim.App. 719, 735, 450 S.W.2d 27, 34 (1969): "True, it is not necessary to prove premeditation existed for any definite period of time. But it is necessary to prove that it did exist." This means there must be an opportunity for some reflection on the intention to kill after it is formed. The accused must kill purposely after contemplating the intent to kill. Although an elaborate plan or scheme to take life is not required, our *Schrader*'s notion of instantaneous premeditation and momentary deliberation is not satisfactory for proof of first degree murder. In Bullock v. United States, 74 App.D.C. 220, 221, 122 F.2d 213, 214 (1941), cert. denied, 317 U.S. 627, 63 S.Ct. 39, 87 L.Ed. 507 (1942), the court discussed the need to have some appreciable time elapse between the intent to kill and the killing: "To speak of premeditation and deliberation which are instantaneous, or which take no appreciable time, is a contradiction in terms. It deprives the statutory requirement of all meaning and destroys the statutory distinction between first and second degree murder. At common law there were no degrees of murder. If the accused had no overwhelming provocation to kill, he was equally guilty whether he carried out his murderous intent at once or after mature reflection. Statutes like ours, which distinguish deliberate and premeditated murder from other murder, reflect a belief that one who meditates an intent to kill and then deliberately executes it is more dangerous, more culpable or less capable of reformation than one who kills on sudden impulse; or that the prospect of the death penalty is more likely to deter men from deliberate than from impulsive murder. The deliberate killer is guilty of first degree murder; the impulsive killer is not. The quoted part of the charge was therefore erroneous. Thus, there must be some evidence that the defendant considered and weighed his decision to kill in order for the State to establish premeditation and deliberation under our first degree murder statute.[23] This is what is

---

[23] In the absence of statements by the accused which indicate the killing was by prior calculation and design, a jury must consider the circumstances in which the killing occurred to determine whether it fits into the first degree category. Relevant factors include the relationship of the accused and the victim and its condition at the time of the homicide; whether plan or preparation existed either in terms of the type of weapon utilized or the place where the killing occurred; and the presence of a reason or motive to deliberately take life. No one factor is

meant by a ruthless, cold-blooded, calculating killing. Any other intentional killing, by its spontaneous and nonreflective nature, is second degree murder."[24]

We are asked to overrule the language appearing in *Schrader*, as reflected in State's Instruction No. 8 and, particularly, the language of State's Instruction Nos. 10 and 12, so that there might be some clarity and coherence to the law of homicide. We naturally are reluctant to overrule prior decisions of this Court. No court likes to acknowledge a mistake, and adherence to precedent is based on deeper reasons than amour propre; rather, it is in fact a cornerstone of Anglo-American adjudication. Additionally, the more recent a precedent, the more authoritative it is because there is less likelihood of significantly changed circumstances that would provide a "special justification" for reassessing the soundness of the precedent. Nevertheless, the circumstances of this case are different, and we agree with the defendant that the language in our opinion in *Schrader* virtually eliminates the distinction in this State between first and second degree murder, equating as it does premeditation with the formation of the intent to kill. We have tried to clarify the difference between the degrees of murder in the preceding paragraphs. We find that *Schrader* wrongly equated premeditation with intent to kill and in so doing undermined the more meaningful language of *Hatfield* and *Dodds*. To the extent that the *Schrader* opinion is inconsistent with our holding today, it is overruled. In overruling *Schrader*, we do not take lightly the policy underlying stare decisis. However, we believe: "Remaining true to an 'intrinsically sounder' doctrine established in prior cases better serves the values of stare decisis than would following a more recently decided case inconsistent with the decisions that came before it; the latter course would simply compound the recent error and would likely make the unjustified break from previously established doctrine complete. In such a situation 'special justification' exists to depart from the recently decided case." Adarand Constr., Inc. v. Pena, 515 U.S. 200, 115 S.Ct. 2097, 2115, 132 L.Ed.2d 158, 185 (1995). Overturning precedent with a long standing in the law that has become an integrated fabric in the law is different. Therefore, we leave in tact the *Clifford* rule as amplified by *Hatfield*. So by refusing to follow *Schrader* but continuing *Clifford* and *Hatfield*, "we do not depart from the fabric of the law; we restore it." Finally, we feel obligated to

---

controlling. Any one or all taken together may indicate actual reflection on the decision to kill. This is what our statute means by "willful, deliberate and premeditated killing."

[24] As examples of what type of evidence supports a finding of first degree murder, we identify three categories: (1) "planning" activity—facts regarding the defendant's behavior prior to the killing which might indicate a design to take life; (2) facts about the defendant's prior relationship or behavior with the victim which might indicate a motive to kill; and (3) evidence regarding the nature or manner of the killing which indicate a deliberate intention to kill according to a preconceived design. The California courts evidently require evidence of all three categories or at least extremely strong evidence of planning activity or evidence of category (2) in conjunction with either (1) or (3). See People v. Anderson, 70 Cal.2d 15, 73 Cal.Rptr. 550, 447 P.2d 942 (1968). These examples are illustrative only and are not intended to be exhaustive.

discuss what instruction defining premeditation is now acceptable. What came about as a mere suggestion in *Hatfield*, we now approve as a proper instruction under today's decision. Note 7 of *Hatfield*, states: "A more appropriate instruction for first degree murder, is: 'The jury is instructed that murder in the first degree consists of an intentional, deliberate and premeditated killing which means that the killing is done after a period of time for prior consideration. The duration of that period cannot be arbitrarily fixed. The time in which to form a deliberate and premeditated design varies as the minds and temperaments of people differ, and according to the circumstances in which they may be placed. Any interval of time between the forming of the intent to kill and the execution of that intent, which is of sufficient duration for the accused to be fully conscious of what he intended, is sufficient to support a conviction for first degree murder.' "

Having approved a new instruction in the area of homicide law, we do not believe today's decision should be applied retroactively. Applying the test articulated in Teague v. Lane, 489 U.S. 288, 109 S.Ct. 1060, 103 L.Ed.2d 334 (1989), a "new rule" should not be given retroactive effect. Nevertheless, we need not apply the "new rule" to the defendant's case on this appeal because this case is being reversed on other grounds. The defendant is entitled, however, to the benefit of this decision on remand.

■ WORKMAN, JUSTICE, concurring:

I concur with the holding of the majority, but write this separate opinion to reiterate that the duration of the time period required for premeditation cannot be arbitrarily fixed. Neither the jury instruction approved by the majority, created from our past decisions in *Clifford*, and *Hatfield*, nor the new instruction approved in the majority opinion affix any specific amount of time which must pass between the formation of the intent to kill and the actual killing for first degree murder cases. Given the majority's recognition that these concepts are necessarily incapable of being reduced formulaically, I am concerned that some of the language in the opinion may indirectly suggest that some appreciable length of time must pass before premeditation can occur.

I agree with the majority in its conclusion that our decision in, *Schrader* incorrectly equated premeditation with intent to kill. However, I must point out that the majority's suggested basis for defining premeditation and deliberation in terms of requiring some "appreciable time elapse between the intent to kill and the killing" and "some period between the formation of the intent to kill and the actual killing which indicates that the killing is by prior calculation and design" may create confusion in suggesting that premeditation must be the deeply thoughtful enterprise typically associated with the words reflection and contemplation. The majority's interpretation may create ambiguity, if not clarified, by adding arguably contradictory factors to the law enunciated by the majority in the approved instruction, as well as the language in the *Hatfield* and *Dodds* cases that the majority upholds.

Accordingly, it is necessary to make abundantly clear that premeditation is sufficiently demonstrated as long as "any interval of time, no matter how short that interval is, lapses between the forming of the intent to kill and the execution of that intent."

Midgett v. State

Supreme Court of Arkansas, 1987.
292 Ark. 278, 729 S.W.2d 410.

■ NEWBERN, JUSTICE.

This child abuse case resulted in the appellant's conviction of first degree murder. The sole issue on appeal is whether the state's evidence was sufficient to sustain the conviction. We hold there was no evidence of the ". . . premeditated and deliberated purpose of causing the death of another person . . ." required for conviction of first degree murder by Ark.Stat.Ann. § 41–1502(1)(b) (Repl.1977). However, we find the evidence was sufficient to sustain a conviction of second degree murder, described in Ark.Stat.Ann. § 41–1503(1)(c) (Repl.1977), as the appellant was shown to have caused his son's death by delivering a blow to his abdomen or chest ". . . with the purpose of causing serious physical injury. . . ." The conviction is thus modified from one of first degree murder to one of second degree murder and affirmed.

The facts of this case are as heart-rending as any we are likely to see. The appellant is six feet two inches tall and weighs 300 pounds. His son, Ronnie Midgett, Jr., was eight years old and weighed between thirty-eight and forty-five pounds. The evidence showed that Ronnie Jr. had been abused by brutal beating over a substantial period of time. Typically, as in other child abuse cases, the bruises had been noticed by school personnel, and a school counselor as well as a SCAN worker had gone to the Midgett home to inquire. Ronnie Jr. would not say how he had obtained the bruises or why he was so lethargic at school except to blame it all, vaguely, on a rough playing little brother. He did not even complain to his siblings about the treatment he was receiving from the appellant. His mother, the wife of the appellant, was not living in the home. The other children apparently were not being physically abused by the appellant.

Ronnie Jr.'s sister, Sherry, aged ten, testified that on the Saturday preceding the Wednesday of Ronnie Jr.'s death their father, the appellant, was drinking whiskey (two to three quarts that day) and beating on Ronnie Jr. She testified that the appellant would "bundle up his fist" and hit Ronnie Jr. in the stomach and in the back. On direct examination she said that she had not previously seen the appellant beat Ronnie Jr., but she had seen the appellant choke him for no particular reason on Sunday nights after she and Ronnie Jr. returned from church. On cross-examination, Sherry testified that Ronnie Jr. had lied and her father was, on that Saturday, trying to get him to tell the truth. She said the bruises on Ronnie Jr.'s body noticed over the preceding six months had been caused by the appellant. She said the beating administered on the Saturday in question consisted of four blows, two to the stomach and two to the back.

On the Wednesday Ronnie Jr. died, the appellant appeared at a hospital carrying the body. He told hospital personnel something was wrong with the child. An autopsy was performed, and it showed Ronnie Jr. was a very poorly nourished and under-developed eight-year-old. There were recently caused bruises on the lips, center of the chest plate, and forehead as well as on the back part of the lateral chest wall, the soft tissue near the spine, and the buttocks. There was discoloration of the abdominal wall and prominent bruising on the palms of the hands. Older bruises were found on the right temple, under the chin, and on the left mandible. Recent as well as older, healed, rib fractures were found.

The conclusion of the medical examiner who performed the autopsy was that Ronnie Jr. died as the result of intra-abdominal hemorrhage caused by a blunt force trauma consistent with having been delivered by a human fist. The appellant argues that in spite of all this evidence of child abuse, there is no evidence that he killed Ronnie Jr. having premeditated and deliberated causing his death. We must agree.

It is true that premeditation and deliberation may be found on the basis of circumstantial evidence. That was the holding in House v. State, 230 Ark. 622, 324 S.W.2d 112 (1959), where the evidence showed a twenty-four-year-old man killed a nineteen-year-old woman with whom he was attempting to have sexual intercourse. The evidence showed a protracted fight after which the appellant dumped the body in a water-filled ditch not knowing, according to House's testimony, whether she was dead or alive. Although it is not spelled out, presumably the rationale of the opinion was that House had time to premeditate during the fight and there was substantial evidence he intended the death of the victim when he left her in the water. Our only citation of authority on the point of showing premeditation and deliberation by circumstantial evidence in that case was Weldon v. State, 168 Ark. 534, 270 S.W. 968 (1925), where we said:

> The very manner in which the deadly weapons were used was sufficient to justify the jury in finding that whoever killed Jones used the weapons with a deliberate purpose to kill. Jones' body was perforated three times through the center with bullets from a pistol or rifle, and was also horribly mutilated with a knife. The manner, therefore, in which these deadly weapons were used tended to show that the death of Jones was the result of premeditation and deliberation.

While a fist may be a deadly weapon, the evidence of the use of the fist in this case is not comparable to the evidence in *House v. State*, supra, and *Weldon v. State*, supra, where there was some substantial evidence consisting of other circumstances that the appellant who dumped the apparently immobile body in the water and walked away and the appellant who wielded the deadly weapons intended and premeditated that death occur. Nor do we have in this case evidence of any remark made or other demonstration that the appellant was abusing his son in the hope that he eventually would die.

The annotation at 89 A.L.R.2d 396 (1963) deals with the subject of crimes resulting from excessive punishment of children. While some of the cases cited are ones in which a parent or stepparent flew into a one-time rage and killed the child, others are plain child abuse syndrome cases like the one before us now. None of them, with one exception, resulted in affirmance of a first degree murder conviction. Several were decisions in which first degree murder convictions were set aside for lack of evidence of premeditation and deliberation. . . . The case cited in the annotation in which a first degree murder conviction was affirmed is Morris v. State, 270 Ind. 245, 384 N.E.2d 1022 (1979). There the appellant was left alone for about fifteen minutes with his five-month-old baby. When the child's mother returned to their home she found the baby had been burned severely on one side. About a month later, the appellant and his wife were engaged in an argument when the baby began to whine. The appellant laid the baby on the floor, began hitting the baby in the face and then hit the baby's head on the floor, causing the baby's death. At the time of the offense, the Indiana law required malice, purpose, and premeditation to convict of first degree murder. In discussing the premeditation requirement, the court said only:

> Premeditation which also may be inferred from the facts and circumstances surrounding the killing, need not long be deliberated upon, but may occur merely an instant before the act. [Citation omitted.] It is clear from the facts adduced at trial regarding the burning and beating of the child that the jury could well have inferred that his killing was perpetrated purposely and with premeditated malice.

No explanation is given for the quantum leap from "the facts," horrible as they were, to the inference of premeditation. We made the same error in Burnett v. State, 287 Ark. 158, 697 S.W.2d 95 (1985), another child abuse case in which the facts were particularly repugnant, where we said:

> Premeditation, deliberation and intent may be inferred from the circumstances of the case, such as the weapon used and the nature, extent and location of the wounds inflicted. . . . [T]he weapon used was a fist which struck the abdomen with such force as to rupture the colon. The child sustained fingernail

scratches, four broken ribs, and other internal damage, as well as numerous bruises due to blows with a fist all over his body. The required mental state for first degree murder can be inferred from the evidence of abuse, which is substantial.

The problem with these cases is that they give no reason, like the reasons found in *House v. State*, supra, and *Weldon v. State*, supra, to make the inference of premeditation and deliberation.

. . . The appellant argues, and we must agree, that in a case of child abuse of long duration the jury could well infer that the perpetrator comes not to expect death of the child from his action, but rather that the child will live so that the abuse may be administered again and again. Had the appellant planned his son's death, he could have accomplished it in a previous beating.

In this case the evidence might possibly support the inference that the blows which proved fatal to Ronnie Jr. could have been struck with the intent to cause his death developed in a drunken, misguided, and overheated attempt at disciplining him for not having told the truth. Even if we were to conclude there was substantial evidence from which the jury could fairly have found the appellant intended to cause Ronnie Jr.'s death in a drunken disciplinary beating on that Saturday, there would still be no evidence whatever of a premeditated and deliberated killing.

In Ford v. State, 276 Ark. 98, 633 S.W.2d 3, cert. den. 459 U.S. 1022, 103 S.Ct. 389, 74 L.Ed.2d 519 (1982), we held that to show the appellant acted with a premeditated and deliberated purpose, the state must prove that he (1) had the conscious object to cause death, (2) formed that intention before acting, and (3) weighed in his mind the consequences of a course of conduct, as distinguished from acting upon sudden impulse without the exercise of reasoning power. Viewing the evidence most favorable to the appellee, the circumstances of this case are not substantial evidence the appellant did (2) and (3), as opposed to acting on impulse or with no conscious object of causing death. The jury was thus forced to resort to speculation on these important elements.

A clear exposition of the premeditation and deliberation requirement which separates first degree from second degree murder is found in 2 W. LaFave and A. Scott, Jr., Substantive Criminal Law § 7.7 (1986):

Almost all American jurisdictions which divide murder into degrees include the following two murder situations in the category of first degree murder: (1) intent-to-kill murder where there exists (in addition to the intent to kill) the elements of premeditation and deliberation, and (2) felony murder where the felony in question is one of five or six listed felonies, generally including rape, robbery, kidnaping, arson and burglary. Some states instead or in addition have other kinds of first degree murder.

(a) Premeditated, Deliberate, Intentional Killing. To be guilty of this form of first degree murder the defendant must not only intend to kill but in addition he must premeditate the killing and deliberate about it. It is not easy to give a meaningful definition of the words "premeditate" and "deliberate" as they are used in connection with first degree murder. Perhaps the best that can be said of "deliberation" is that it requires a cool mind that is capable of reflection, and of "premeditation" that it requires that the one with the cool mind did in fact reflect, at least for a short period of time before his act of killing.

It is often said that premeditation and deliberation require only a "brief moment of thought" or a "matter of seconds," and convictions for first degree murder have frequently been affirmed where such short periods of time were involved. The better view, however, is that to "speak of premeditation and deliberation which are instantaneous, or which take no appreciable time, . . . destroys the statutory distinction between first and second degree murder," and (in much the same fashion that the felony-murder rule is being increasingly limited) this view is growing in popularity. This is not to say, however, that premeditation and deliberation cannot exist when the act of killing follows immediately after the formation of the intent. The intention may be finally formed only as a conclusion of prior premeditation and deliberation, while in other cases the intention may be formed without prior thought so that premeditation and deliberation occurs only with the passage of additional time for "further thought, and a turning over in the mind." [Footnotes omitted.]

The evidence in this case supports only the conclusion that the appellant intended not to kill his son but to further abuse him or that his intent, if it was to kill the child, was developed in a drunken, heated, rage while disciplining the child. Neither of those supports a finding of premeditation or deliberation.

Perhaps because they wish to punish more severely child abusers who kill their children, other states' legislatures have created laws permitting them to go beyond second degree murder. For example, Illinois has made aggravated battery one of the felonies qualifying for "felony murder," and a child abuser can be convicted of murder if the child dies as a result of aggravated battery. See People v. Ray, 80 Ill.App.3d 151, 35 Ill.Dec. 688, 399 N.E.2d 977 (1979). Georgia makes "cruelty to children" a felony, and homicide in the course of cruelty to children is "felony murder." See Bethea v. State, 251 Ga. 328, 304 S.E.2d 713 (1983). Idaho has made murder by torture a first degree offense, regardless of intent of the perpetrator to kill the victim, and the offense is punishable by the death penalty. See State v. Stuart, 110 Idaho 163,

715 P.2d 833 (1985). California has also adopted a murder by torture statute making the offense murder in the first degree without regard to the intent to kill. See People v. Demond, 59 Cal.App.3d 574, 130 Cal.Rptr. 590 (1976). Cf. People v. Steger, 16 Cal.3d 539, 128 Cal.Rptr. 161, 546 P.2d 665 (1976), in which the California Supreme Court held that the person accused of torture murder in the first degree must be shown to have had a premeditated intent to inflict extreme and prolonged pain in order to be convicted.

All of this goes to show that there remains a difference between first and second degree murder, not only under our statute, but generally. Unless our law is changed to permit conviction of first degree murder for something like child abuse or torture resulting in death, our duty is to give those accused of first degree murder the benefit of the requirement that they be shown by substantial evidence to have premeditated and deliberated the killing, no matter how heinous the facts may otherwise be. We understand and appreciate the state's citation of *Burnett v. State*, supra, but, to the extent it is inconsistent with this opinion, we must overrule it.

The dissenting opinion begins by stating the majority concludes that one who starves and beats a child to death cannot be convicted of murder. That is not so, as we are affirming the conviction of murder; we are, however, reducing it to second degree murder. The dissenting opinion's conclusion that the appellant starved Ronnie Jr., must be based solely on the child's underdeveloped condition which could, presumably, have been caused by any number of physical malfunctions. There is no evidence the appellant starved the child. The dissenting opinion says it is for the jury to determine the degree of murder of which the appellant is guilty. That is true so long as there is substantial evidence to support the jury's choice. The point of this opinion is to note that there was no evidence of premeditation or deliberation which are required elements of the crime of first degree murder. . . .

In this case we have no difficulty with reducing the sentence to the maximum for second degree murder. Dixon v. State, 260 Ark. 857, 545 S.W.2d 606 (1977). The jury gave the appellant a sentence of forty years imprisonment which was the maximum for first degree murder, and we reduce that to twenty years which is the maximum imprisonment for second degree murder. Just as walking away from the victim in the water-filled ditch in *House v. State*, supra, after a protracted fight, and the "overkill" and mutilation of the body in *Weldon v. State*, supra, were circumstances creating substantial evidence of premeditation and deliberation, the obvious effect the beatings were having on Ronnie Jr. and his emaciated condition when the final beating occurred are circumstances constituting substantial evidence that the appellant's purpose was to cause serious physical injury, and that he caused his death in the process. That is second degree murder, § 41–1503(1)(c).

Therefore, we reduce the appellant's sentence to imprisonment for twenty years.

Affirmed as modified.

■ HICKMAN, HAYS and GLAZE, JJ., dissent.

■ HICKMAN, JUSTICE, dissenting.

Simply put, if a parent deliberately starves and beats a child to death, he cannot be convicted of the child's murder. In reaching this decision, the majority overrules a previous unanimous decision and substitutes its judgment for that of the jury. The majority has decided it cannot come to grips with the question of the battered child who dies as a result of deliberate, methodical, intentional and severe abuse. A death caused by such acts is murder by any legal standard, and that fact cannot be changed—not even by the majority. The degree of murder committed is for the jury to decide—not us.

Convictions for murder resulting from child abuse have become more common in our courts. That is probably because such cases are being reported more often and prosecutors are more apt to seek retribution.

The decision of what charge to file in a homicide case rests with the prosecuting attorney. He has the duty to prove the charge. The decision of whether the state has proved the crime rests with the jury. Our role is only to determine if substantial evidence exists to support the verdict.

Sometimes the facts may warrant a charge of second degree murder. We have affirmed convictions for second degree murder in two such cases.

Whether the particular acts of child abuse amount to first degree murder depend on the particular facts and circumstances in each case. Just as in any other murder case, the state must prove each element of the crime. For a first degree murder conviction, the state must prove premeditation and deliberation.

We have never held motive relevant to murder, nor do we even try to look into the warped minds that commit murder to make their acts rational. Consequently, circumstantial evidence usually plays a strong part in determining intent in any murder case.

In this case the majority, with clairvoyance, decides that this parent did not intend to kill his child, but rather to keep him alive for further abuse. This is not a child neglect case. The state proved Midgett starved the boy, choked him, and struck him several times in the stomach and back. The jury could easily conclude that such repeated treatment was intended to kill the child.

In *Burnett*, supra, the state chose to seek a first degree murder conviction. The child was killed in an extremely horrible way. He was malnourished and dehydrated, bruises on his face and upper and lower extremities, four broken ribs, a ruptured colon, and abrasions. His life was made intolerable and insufferable until at last a blow killed him. The parents, who could not have been unaware or innocent, were found guilty of killing him, which they did. We unanimously upheld that jury verdict. It was no "quantum leap" on our part (whatever that means), just a decision based on the facts and the law. The majority unanimously joined in the *Burnett* decision.

The facts in this case are substantial to support a first degree murder conviction. The defendant was in charge of three small children. The victim was eight years old and had been starved; he weighed only 38 pounds at the time of his death. He had multiple bruises and abrasions. The cause of death was an internal hemorrhage due to blunt force trauma. His body was black and blue from repeated blows. The victim's sister testified she saw the defendant, a 30 year old man, 6′2″ tall, weighing 300 pounds, repeatedly strike the victim in the stomach and back with his fist. One time he choked the child.

The majority is saying that as a matter of law a parent cannot be guilty of intentionally killing a child by such deliberate acts. Why not? Is it because it is inconceivable to rational people that a parent would intend to kill his own child? Evidently, this is the majority's conclusion, because they hold the intention of Midgett was to keep him alive for further abuse, not to kill him. How does the majority know that? How do we ever know the actual or subliminal intent of a defendant? "If the *act* appellant intended was criminal, then the law holds him accountable, even though such *result* was not intended." Hankins v. State, 206 Ark. 881, 178 S.W.2d 56 (1944). There is no difference so far as the law is concerned in this case than in any other murder case. It is simply a question of proof. This parent killed his own child, and the majority cannot accept the fact that he intended to do just that.

Undoubtedly, the majority could accept it if the child were murdered with a bullet or a knife; but they cannot accept the fact, and it is a fact, that this defendant beat and starved his own child to death. His course of conduct could not have been negligent or unintentional.

Other states have not hesitated to uphold a conviction for first degree murder in such cases. The fact that some states (California and Idaho) have passed a murder by torture statute is irrelevant. Those statutes may make it easier to prosecute child murderers, but they do not replace or intend to replace the law of murder. Whether murder exists is a question of the facts—not the method. The majority spends a good deal of effort laboring over the words "premeditation and deliberation," ignoring what the defendant did. Oliver Wendell Holmes said: "We must think things not words . . ." Holmes, "Law in Science and Science in Law," Collected Legal Papers, p. 238 (1921). If what Midgett did was deliberate and intentional, and that is not disputed, and he killed the child, a jury can find first degree murder.

I cannot fathom how this father could have done what he did; but it is not my place to sit in judgment of his mental state, nor allow my human feelings to color my judgment of his accountability to the law. The law has an objective standard of accountability for all who take human life. If one does certain acts and the result is murder, one must pay. The jury found Midgett guilty and, according to the law, there is substantial evidence to support that verdict. That should end the matter for us. He is guilty of first degree murder in the eyes of the law. His moral crime as a father is another matter, and it is not for us to speculate why he did it.

I would affirm the judgment.

■ HAYS and GLAZE, JJ., join in the dissent.

NOTES

1. Consider, in the light of the dissent's statement that motive is not relevant to murder, Samuel H. Pillsbury, Evil and the Law of Murder, 24 U.C. Davis L. Rev. 437, 447 (1990), who states that "Anglo-American criminal law, with its emphasis upon mental states, clearly concerns itself with the 'why' of criminal acts and so makes a basic inquiry into moral disposition." He adds that "where culpability distinctions are of great importance, as in murder, motivation analysis provides a critical means of judging culpability. There is no substitute."

2. Under one modern type of statute, the common law definition of murder is retained. However, certain types of common law murder are denominated as being capital murder (punishable by death or imprisonment for life) or of the first degree, with all other kinds classified as murder in the second degree. For example, the Code of Virginia provides:

§ 18.2–31. **Capital murder defined; punishment.**—The following offenses shall constitute capital murder, punishable as a Class 1 felony:

1. The willful, deliberate, and premeditated killing of any person in the commission of abduction, as defined in § 18.2–48, when such abduction was committed with the intent to extort money or a pecuniary benefit or with the intent to defile the victim of such abduction;

2. The willful, deliberate, and premeditated killing of any person by another for hire;

3. The willful, deliberate, and premeditated killing of any person by a prisoner confined in a state or local correctional facility as defined in § 53.1–1, or while in the custody of an employee thereof;

4. The willful, deliberate, and premeditated killing of any person in the commission of robbery or attempted robbery;

5. The willful, deliberate, and premeditated killing of any person in the commission of, or subsequent to, rape or attempted rape, forcible sodomy or attempted forcible sodomy or object sexual penetration;

6. The willful, deliberate, and premeditated killing of a law-enforcement officer as defined in § 9–169(9) or any law-enforcement officer of another state or the United States having the power to arrest for a felony under the laws of such state or the United States, when such killing is for the purpose of interfering with the performance of his official duties;

7. The willful, deliberate, and premeditated killing of more than one person as a part of the same act or transaction;

8. The willful, deliberate and premeditated killing of more than one person within a three-year period;

9. The willful, deliberate, and premeditated killing of any person in the commission of or attempted commission of a violation of § 18.2–248, involving a Schedule I or II controlled substance, when such killing is for the purpose of furthering the commission or attempted commission of such violation.

10. The willful, deliberate, and premeditated killing of any person by another pursuant to the direction or order of one who is engaged in a continuing criminal enterprise as defined in subsection I of § 18.2–248.

11. The willful, deliberate, and premeditated killing of a pregnant woman by one who knows that the woman is pregnant and has the intent to cause the involuntary termination of the woman's pregnancy without a live birth.

12. The willful, deliberate, and premeditated killing of a person under the age of fourteen by a person age twenty-one or older.

13. The willful, deliberate, and premeditated killing of any person by another in the commission of or attempted commission of an act of terrorism as defined in § 18.2–46.4.

14. The willful, deliberate, and premeditated killing of a justice of the Supreme court, a judge of the Court of Appeals, a judge of a circuit court or district court, a retired judge sitting by designation or under temporary recall, or a substitute judge . . . when the killing is for the purpose of interfering with his official duties as a judge.

15. The willful, deliberate, and premeditated killing of any witness in a criminal case after a subpoena has been issued for such witness . . . when the killing is for the purpose of interfering with the person's duties in such case.

§ 18.2–32. First and second degree murder defined; punishment.—Murder, other than capital murder, by poison, lying in wait, imprisonment, starving, or by any willful, deliberate, and premeditated killing, or in the commission of, or attempt to commit, arson, rape, forcible sodomy, inanimate object sexual penetration, robbery, burglary or abduction, except as provided in

§ 18.2–31, is murder of the first degree, punishable as a Class 2 felony.

All murder other than capital murder and murder in the first degree is murder of the second degree and is punishable as a Class 3 felony.

The Virginia Supreme Court originally stated that "we take the expression 'lying in wait,' not merely to mean his concealing himself in the path of his intended victim for the purpose of killing him, but the deliberately, and premeditatedly seeking an occasion to effect the deadly purpose." Burgess v. Commonwealth, 4 Va. 488 (1825). What change caused the recent holding in *Tisdale v. Commonwealth*, 65 Va. App. 478, 778 S.E.2d 554 (2015): "First-degree murder by lying in wait is an enumerated type of murder, listed disjunctively from those killings that are willful, deliberate, and premeditated. Murder by lying in wait does not require proof of premeditation. . . . Therefore, evidence of voluntary intoxication as a defense to premeditation is irrelevant to a charge of murder by lying in wait because the Commonwealth was not required to prove premeditation."

3. Can the *mens rea* needed for proof of first-degree murder be affected by terror and panic? In a case of first impression in its state, the Pennsylvania Supreme Court, in Commonwealth v. Stewart, 461 Pa. 274, 336 A.2d 282 (1975), stated:

> Although our research on this issue reveals no Pennsylvania case specifically holding that terror stricken panic may negate the *mens rea* element of murder in the first degree, we are convinced that it may do so. Strong emotions have previously been found to prevent the formulation of the intent required for first degree murder. . . . We hold that in excluding evidence of gang activity in appellant's neighborhood, the trial court withheld from the jury evidence of vital probative value to a determination of the defendant's state of mind. . . . In the context of gang violence, the violent nature not only of the deceased, but also of the gang of which he was a member may be relevant to the inquiry into the defendant's state of mind, for his state of mind is related to the threat presented by group violence.

4. Consider the "Talk Show Murder." In a taped episode of "The Jenny Jones Show" one guest, Jonathan Schmitz, was surprised to find another guest had a homosexual attraction to him. A few days later, Schmitz shot and killed the other man. Schmitz was tried for first degree murder. The jury found Schmitz guilty of second-degree murder. In weighing the evidence, the jury questioned whether Schmitz had the required premeditation or deliberation to convict for first degree murder. The jury found that Schmitz's mental state, combined with drinking and using marijuana the night before the murder, "led us to question whether he was in his right mind." Keith Bradsher, *Talk Show Guest is Guilty of Second Degree Murder*, N.Y.TIMES, Nov. 13, 1996, at A-8.

Langford v. State

Supreme Court of Alabama, 1977.
354 So.2d 313.

■ JONES, JUSTICE.

* * *

On June 24, 1975, Heflin Mack Langford, Petitioner, was involved in an automobile collision which resulted in the death of sixteen-year-old Randall Holt. Langford's automobile struck a mileage marker on the right side of a four-lane highway in Montgomery County, swerved to the left and crossed the median. It collided with Holt's automobile which was traveling in the opposite direction, and killed Holt instantly.

The extent to which Langford had been drinking was in dispute. Several witnesses stated that alcohol could be smelled on his breath; and it was shown that his blood-alcohol level was 0.25 per cent. Furthermore, witnesses testified that they had seen Langford's car traveling in excess of 90 miles per hour immediately preceding the collision.

In response to this evidence, Langford stated that he had consumed only "two beers" and was not intoxicated. He stated that mechanical steering problems had caused his loss of control of the vehicle.

The jury was charged as to the law involved, and no exceptions or objections were taken, except for an adverse ruling to Langford's motion for directed verdict at the close of the evidence. The jury found Langford guilty of murder in the first degree and he was sentenced to life imprisonment. It was in this posture, then, that the Court of Criminal Appeals addressed the merits of the defendant's contention that the evidence was insufficient to support a conviction of murder in the first degree. That Court affirmed, holding:

> Although a case of first impression, and while a very close question of whether Langford's gross and wanton misconduct rises to the degree necessary to show universal malice by evidencing a "depraved mind regardless of human life," . . . the evidence was sufficient to present a jury question in that regard.

Our grant of the petition for writ of certiorari was limited to a review of that holding.

Langford contends that an individual cannot be convicted of murder in the first degree where the facts show only that he determined to, and did, drive an automobile which was involved in a collision which caused the death of an individual, even though the driver had knowledge of his own intoxication. . . .

The applicable statute, Tit. 14, § 314, Code, provides:

> Every homicide, perpetrated by poison lying in wait, or any other kind of wilful deliberate, malicious and premeditated killing; or committed in the perpetration of, or the attempt to

perpetrate, any arson, rape, robbery, or burglary; or perpetrated from a premeditated design unlawfully and maliciously to effect the death of any human being other than him who is killed; *or perpetrated by any act greatly dangerous to the lives of others, and evidencing a depraved mind regardless of human life, although without any preconceived purpose to deprive any particular person of life, is murder in the first degree . . .* (Emphasis added.)

Langford was charged and convicted of the fourth type of first-degree murder (the emphasized segment).

It is settled that, in appropriate circumstances, a homicide committed by an intoxicated driver of an automobile may be murder. This, however, does not satisfy the inquiry before us; and this for the reason that this State has two degrees of murder, and a determination that a conviction of murder may be appropriate does not necessarily assure the appropriateness of a conviction of murder in the first degree.

Justice Stone, in Mitchell v. State, 60 Ala. 26 (1877), stated:

. . . the legislature, in this [fourth] clause, intended to raise to the high grade of murder in the first degree those homicides which are the result of what is called "universal malice." By universal malice we do not mean a malicious purpose to take the life of all persons. It is that depravity of the human heart which *determines* to take life upon slight or insufficient provocation, without knowing or caring who may be the victim. (Emphasis added.)

The word "determines" presupposes that some mental operation has taken place; the reasoning faculty must be called into play. State v. Massey, 20 Ala.App. 56, 100 So. 625 (1924).

If one *knowingly* and *consciously* drives a high-powered automobile . . . at an excessive rate of speed into a railroad train moving over a street crossing, *knowing* that the train is moving over the crossing, and *that the automobile will strike the train*, and that death will probably result to one or more occupants of the car, although without any preconceived purpose to deprive any particular person of life, but with a reckless disregard of human life, and death results from such act, the driver of the automobile may be guilty of murder in the first degree under the fourth division . . . If he *did not know that he was driving the automobile into the train and he did not determine to drive it into the train regardless of consequences*, but if the act of so driving it was purely accidental, but while in the commission of an unlawful act, such as driving along a public highway at a reckless rate of speed, or exceeding the speed limit, the offense would be manslaughter. (Emphasis added.)

As Langford has correctly pointed out, in the instant case, the defendant *determined* only to drive upon the highway after drinking. There is no showing that he *determined* to have a collision; nor is there any evidence that he realized the likelihood of a collision; and the consequent taking of human life, and proceeded in the face of such probabilities.

The State has cited various cases where an intoxicated driver was found guilty of murder. It should be noted, however, that no case has been cited, or found, wherein an intoxicated automobile driver was found guilty of murder in the first degree.

The classic examples of universal malice include shooting into an occupied house, and driving an automobile into a crowd. While these examples are not exhaustive, they do illustrate the parameter of the type factual situation wherein such malice may be found or implied. We do not believe that the facts before us are within the ambit of the degree of malice exemplified by the above-stated circumstances.

We hold that the trial court erred in not granting the motion for directed verdict as to the charge of murder in the first degree. As to all lesser included offenses, however, the evidence was sufficient for submission to the jury. The judgment of the Court of Criminal Appeals is reversed with instructions to remand the cause for a new trial not inconsistent with this opinion.

Reversed and remanded.

■ TORBERT, C.J., and BLOODWORTH, FAULKNER, ALMON, SHORES and EMBRY, JJ., concur.

■ MADDOX and BEATTY, JJ., dissent.

■ MADDOX, JUSTICE (dissenting).

I think the Court of Criminal Appeals was absolutely correct in this case by upholding a *jury's determination* that the defendant was guilty of murder in the first degree. As Judge Bookout points out in his special concurrence, there have been several cases where drivers of automobiles have been indicted for murder in the first degree and the *jury* has convicted for *second degree*, but this is the first time that this Court has held as a *matter of law*, that a jury could not find a person guilty of murder in the first degree when he had done what Langford did here. I think the majority has erred.

The law of this case is contained in Reed v. State, 25 Ala.App. 18, 142 So. 441 (1932), certiorari denied, 225 Ala. 219, 142 So. 442 (1932). Reed was indicted for *first degree* murder. The jury found him guilty of *second degree* murder. From the opinion is the following:

> The court delivered an able and explicit charge to the jury covering every phase of the law applicable to this case. No exception was reserved to this charge, nor was it subject to

objection and exception. Among other things, the court charged the jury: * * * If a person driving an automobile along the public highway knew that he was intoxicated, and, with that knowledge and the knowledge of other persons present on the highway, should proceed to drive the car in a highly reckless manner and operate the car in such manner as to be greatly dangerous to the lives of others and thus evidencing a depraved mind and regardless of human life, then you might consider that fact in determining whether or not the operator of the car was guilty of murder. * * *

In Nixon v. State, 268 Ala. 101, 105 So.2d 349 (1958), this Court, commenting on the earlier *Reed* case, stated:

The earliest case which we have found in this jurisdiction in which a conviction for murder in the second degree caused by an automobile was affirmed is Reed v. State, 25 Ala.App. 18, 142 So. 441, 442, certiorari denied, 225 Ala. 219, 142 So. 442. The indictment was for murder in the first degree. As to the oral charge of the trial court in that case, the Court of Appeals said:

The court delivered an able and explicit charge to the jury covering every phase of the law applicable to this case. No exception was reserved to this charge, nor was it subject to objection and exception. * * *

While the charge in the *Reed* case does not comply strictly with the statutory definition in that the charge characterizes the act as having been done without intention to deprive "the deceased" of life, where the statute employs the term "any particular person," *both charge and statute declare that the facts hypothesized constitute murder in the first, not in the second, degree.*

The jury here was sufficiently charged on the fourth class of murder in the first degree. It was a *jury question* whether Langford drove an automobile along a public highway knowing he was highly intoxicated— the evidence was conflicting. It was a *jury question* whether he knew other persons were present on the highway. It was a *jury question* whether he proceeded to drive the car in a highly reckless manner and operated it in such a manner as to be greatly dangerous to the lives of others. It was a *jury question* whether he had a depraved mind and did this without regard to human life.

The majority has substituted its determination of the facts for that of the jury by holding as a *matter of law* that first degree murder was not proved. Consequently, I dissent.

■ BEATTY, J., concurs.

NOTES

1. As in the *Langford* case, the defendant in Essex v. Commonwealth, 228 Va. 273, 322 S.E.2d 216 (1984), was driving an automobile while under the influence of alcohol, and caused a collision as a result of which three people died. He was charged and convicted of three counts of second-degree murder. The Virginia Supreme Court reversed, holding that if the killing resulted from negligence, however gross or culpable, and the killing was contrary to the defendant's intention, malice cannot be implied. The court continued:

> In order to elevate the crime to second-degree murder, the defendant must be shown to have willfully or purposefully, rather than negligently, embarked upon a course of wrongful conduct likely to cause death or great bodily harm.
>
> A motor vehicle, wrongfully used, can be a weapon as deadly as a gun or a knife. . . . [T]he premeditated use of an automobile to kill can be first-degree murder. . . . A killing in sudden heat of passion, upon reasonable provocation, by the use of a motor vehicle, could be voluntary manslaughter. Killings caused by the grossly negligent operation of motor vehicles, showing a reckless disregard of human life, have frequently resulted in convictions of involuntary manslaughter.
>
> We have not, heretofore, had occasion to review a second-degree murder conviction based upon the use of an automobile, but the governing principles are the same as those which apply to any other kind of second-degree murder: the victim must be shown to have died as a result of the defendant's conduct, and the defendant's conduct must be shown to be malicious. In the absence of express malice, this element may only be implied from conduct likely to cause death or great bodily harm, wilfully or purposefully undertaken. Thus, for example, one who deliberately drives a car into a crowd of people at high speed, not intending to kill or injure any particular person, but rather seeking the perverse thrill of terrifying them and causing them to scatter, might be convicted of second-degree murder if death results. *One who accomplishes the same result inadvertently, because of grossly negligent driving, causing him to lose control of his car, could be convicted only of involuntary manslaughter.* [emphasis added]

2. For a contrary view, see Pears v. State, 672 P.2d 903 (Alaska App. 1983), affirming a two-count conviction of second degree murder of a driver involved in an accident which caused two deaths. The court opined that under the Alaska statutes, "where a driver's recklessness manifests an extreme indifference to human life he can be charged with murder even though the instrument by which he causes death is an automobile." The Alaska Supreme Court remanded by a divided court. Pears v. State, 698 P.2d 1198 (1985). *See also* Commonwealth v. Scales, 437 Pa.Super. 14, 648 A.2d 1205 (1994) ("[H]e drove his car as though it were a guided missile which predictably would result in loss of life or serious injury to innocent persons.").

4. EUTHANASIA—"MERCY KILLINGS"

Malice may be present even though the motive for a killing is of the highest order. Thus, a "mercy killing" is usually murder, inasmuch as it constitutes an intentional taking of life without provocation or other mitigation, and without legal justification or excuse. The present state of the law concerning euthanasia is well summarized in the following excerpt from GLANVILLE LLEWELYN WILLIAMS, THE SANCTITY OF LIFE AND THE CRIMINAL LAW 318–26 (1957):

> Under the present law, voluntary euthanasia would, except in certain narrow circumstances, be regarded as suicide, in the patient who consents and murder in the doctor who administers; even on a lenient view, most lawyers would say that it could not be less than manslaughter in the doctor, the punishment for which, according to the jurisdiction and the degree of manslaughter, can be anything up to imprisonment for life.

More specifically, the following principles may be stated:

> (a) If the doctor gives the patient a fatal injection with the intention of killing him, and the patient dies in consequence, the doctor is a common murderer because it is his hand that caused the death. Neither the consent of the patient, nor the extremity of his suffering, nor the imminence of death by natural causes, nor all of these factors taken together, is a defence. . . .

> (b) If the doctor furnishes poison (for example, an overdose of sleeping tablets) for the purpose of enabling the patient to commit suicide, and the patient takes it accordingly and dies, this is suicide and a kind of self-murder in the patient, and the doctor, as an abettor, again becomes guilty of murder. So, at any rate, is it in strict legal theory. . . .

> (c) A case that may be thought to be distinguishable from both of those already considered is that of the administration of a fatal dose of a drug where this dose is in fact the minimum necessary to deaden pain. Where a patient is suffering from an incurable and agonizing disease, and ordinary quantities of a drug fail to render the pain tolerable, many doctors will give the minimum dose necessary to kill the pain, knowing that this minimum is at the same time an amount that is likely to kill the patient. In other words, with the choice of either doing nothing, or killing both the pain and the patient, the doctor chooses the latter course. . . . Thus a point is reached at which, proceeding upon the same principles as he has followed heretofore, and which have so far been lawful, the doctor is led to give what he knows is likely to be an immediately fatal dose. It would be extremely artificial to say that this last dose, which is administered upon the same principle as all the previous ones,

is alone unlawful. . . . [The physician's] legal excuse . . . rests upon the doctrine of necessity, there being at this junction no way of relieving pain without ending life. In this limited form the excuse of necessity would be likely to be accepted by a judge, and to this extent it may be held that euthanasia is permitted under the existing law. . . .

(d) We come, finally, to the problem of killing by inaction. "Mercy-killing" by omission to use medical means to prolong life is probably lawful. Although a physician is normally under a duty to use reasonable care to conserve his patient's life, he is probably exempted from that duty if life has become a burden to the patient.

NOTES

1. Attitudes regarding legislative change in the law concerning euthanasia include (1) the view that the status quo has sufficient flexibility, through such factors as the jury system and the pardoning power, to afford just treatment in each case according to its merits; (2) the position that the penalty for a killing motivated by mercy should be reduced; and (3) the view that euthanasia should be legalized within certain narrow bounds and placed under state supervision and control. These positions are ably discussed and evaluated in Helen Silving, *Euthanasia: A Study in Comparative Criminal Law, 103 U. Pa. L. Rev. 350 (1954). See also* William H. Baugham et al., Survey, *Euthanasia: Criminal, Tort, Constitutional and Legislative Considerations,* 48 Notre Dame L. Rev. 1202 (1973); Yale Kamisar, *Some Non-Religious Views Against Proposed "Mercy-Killing" Legislation, 42 Minn. L. Rev. 969 (1958)*; A.A. Levinsohn, *Voluntary Mercy Deaths,* 8 J. For. Med. 57 (1961); O.R. Russell, *Moral and Legal Aspects of Euthanasia,* 34 Humanist 22 (1974); Joseph Sanders, *Euthanasia: None Dare Call It Murder,* 60 J. Crim. L. Criminology & Police Sci. 351 (1969); Glanville Williams, *"Mercy-Killing" Legislation—A Rejoinder, 43 Minn. L. Rev. 1 (1958).*

2. For modern views regarding euthanasia and "aiding suicide," reconsider *Washington v. Glucksberg,* in Chapter 3, supra on p. 251.

3. In 2000, the Dutch Lower House became the first legislative body in the world to approve a bill legalizing euthanasia and permitting doctors to help suffering patients end their lives. The bill passed by a 104 to 40 vote. Under the bill, patients seeking aid in terminating their lives must be "undergoing unremitting and unbearable suffering," though not necessarily suffering from a terminal disease. The law requires consultations on all medical options and the obtaining of a second opinion. The reporting on the passage of this legislation, an Associated Press report filed on November 28, 2000, pointed out that "the bill does not stipulate that the patient's suffering must be physical, leaving room for unbearable mental suffering to be sufficient case." Before medical aid in dying can be received, a committee of no less than three individuals, including a physician, a lawyer, and an expert in medical ethics must review the request to ensure that the legal requirements are satisfied. In April, 2001, the Senate of the Netherlands (Upper House) backed the legislation in a 46 to 28 vote, and the law went into effect.

People v. Kevorkian

Supreme Court of Michigan, 1994.
447 Mich. 436, 527 N.W.2d 714.

■ MEMORANDUM OPINION.

This memorandum opinion is signed by the seven justices. There are separate concurring and dissenting opinions. However, at least four justices concur in every holding, statement, and disposition of this memorandum opinion.

■ MICHAEL F. CAVAHAGH, CHIEF JUSTICE, and BRICKLEY and ROBERT P. GRIFFIN, JUSTICES.

We conclude: (1) the provisions of the assisted suicide statute were validly enacted and do not violate the Michigan Constitution; (2) the United States Constitution does not prohibit a state from imposing criminal penalties on one who assists another in committing suicide; (3) in the murder case, the motion to quash must be reconsidered by the circuit court to determine if the evidence produced at the preliminary examination was sufficient to bind the defendant over for trial.

* * *

Finally, we turn to the issue presented in the Oakland County case involving the deaths of Sherry Miller and Marjorie Wantz. Their deaths occurred before the enactment of Michigan's ban on assisted suicide, and the question is whether defendant Kevorkian can be prosecuted for his role in the deaths.

Each woman was said to be suffering from a condition that caused her great pain or was severely disabling. Each separately had sought defendant Kevorkian's assistance in ending her life. The women and several friends and relatives met the defendant at a cabin in Oakland County on October 23, 1991.

According to the testimony presented at the defendant's preliminary examination, the plan was to use his "suicide machine." The device consisted of a board to which one's arm is strapped to prevent movement, a needle to be inserted into a blood vessel and attached to IV tubing, and containers of various chemicals that are to be released through the needle into the bloodstream. Strings are tied to two of the fingers of the person who intends to die. The strings are attached to clips on the IV tubing that control the flow of the chemicals. As explained by one witness, the person raises that hand, releasing a drug called methohexital, which was described by expert witnesses as a fast-acting barbiturate that is used under controlled circumstances to administer anesthesia rapidly. When the person falls asleep, the hand drops, pulling the other string, which releases another clip and allows potassium chloride to flow into the body in concentrations sufficient to cause death.

The defendant tried several times, without success, to insert the suicide-machine needle into Ms. Miller's arm and hand. He then left the cabin, returning several hours later with a cylinder of carbon monoxide gas and a mask apparatus. He attached a screw driver to the cylinder, and showed Ms. Miller how to use the tool as a lever to open the gas valve.

The defendant then turned his attention to Ms. Wantz. He was successful in inserting the suicide-machine needle into her arm. The defendant explained to Ms. Wantz how to activate the device so as to allow the drugs to enter her bloodstream. The device was activated,[62] and Ms. Wantz died.

* * *

The defendant then placed the mask apparatus on Ms. Miller. The only witness at the preliminary examination who was present at the time said that Ms. Miller opened the gas valve by pulling on the screw driver. The cause of her death was determined to be carbon-monoxide poisoning.

The defendant was indicted on two counts of open murder. He was bound over for trial following a preliminary examination. However, in circuit court, the defendant moved to quash the information and dismiss the charges, and the court granted the motion.

B

A divided Court of Appeals reversed. People v. *Kevorkian No. 1*, 205 Mich.App. 180, 517 N.W.2d 293 (1994). The Court of Appeals majority relied principally on *People v. Roberts*, 211 Mich. 187, 178 N.W. 690 (1920).

In *Roberts*, the defendant's wife was suffering from advanced multiple sclerosis and in great pain. She previously had attempted suicide and, according to the defendant's statements at the plea proceeding, requested that he provide her with poison. He agreed, and

---

[62] No one who testified at the preliminary examination actually witnessed the activation of the device. The only persons in the cabin at that time were the decedents, the defendant, and the defendant's sister, who since has died. Ms. Wantz' husband was walking away from the cabin. He testified as follows:

Q. You don't know who pulled the string?

A. I have no idea. She knew that she had to pull the string when I left.

Q. You don't know if she tried to pull the string and it didn't work and Kevorkian pushed her hand at all, do you?

A. I can say this, when I left the room she was in the process of trying to pull the string.

Q. You don't know who pulled the string? That's what you're telling me?

A. I can tell you she was in the process of trying to pull the string when I left the room, but I did not see her pull the string. The only thing I can take and tell you is once I left the room, Dr. Kevorkian did—I heard Dr. Kevorkian say, "Marj, you have to hold your hand up," and that is the only thing I know.

placed a glass of poison within her reach. She drank the mixture and died. The defendant was charged with murder. He pleaded guilty, and the trial court determined the crime to be murder in the first degree.

The defendant appealed. He argued, among other things, that because suicide is not a crime in Michigan, and his wife thus committed no offense, he committed none in acting as an accessory before the fact. The Court rejected that argument, explaining:

> If we were living in a purely common-law atmosphere with a strictly common-law practice, and defendant were charged with being guilty as an accessory of the offense of suicide, counsel's argument would be more persuasive than it is. But defendant is not charged with that offense. He is charged with murder and the theory of the people was that he committed the crime by means of poison. He has come into court and confessed that he mixed poison with water and placed it within her reach, but at her request. The important question, therefore, arises as to whether what defendant did constitutes murder by means of poison.

After discussing a similar Ohio case, *Blackburn v. State*, 23 Ohio. St. 146 (1872), the *Roberts* Court concluded:

> We are of the opinion that when defendant mixed the paris green with water and placed it within reach of his wife to enable her to put an end to her suffering by putting an end to her life, he was guilty of murder by means of poison within the meaning of the statute, even though she requested him to do so. By this act he deliberately placed within her reach the means of taking her own life, which she could have obtained in no other way by reason of her helpless condition.

In the instant case, defendant Kevorkian had argued that the discussion of this issue in *Roberts* was dicta because the defendant in that case had pleaded guilty of murder, and thus the controlling authority was *People v. Campbell*, 124 Mich.App. 333, 335 N.W.2d 27 (1983).[64] The Court of Appeals majority rejected that view and said that *Roberts* controlled the issue presented in the instant case.

---

[64] In *Campbell*, the decedent and the defendant had been drinking heavily at the decedent's home. The decedent had been talking about suicide, and the fact that he did not have a gun. The defendant offered to sell the decedent a gun. At first, the decedent did not accept the offer. However, defendant Campbell persisted in alternately encouraging and ridiculing him. Eventually, the defendant provided the decedent with a gun and five shells. The defendant and the decedent's girlfriend left, and some time later, the decedent shot himself. The defendant was charged with open murder.

Although the defendant failed to persuade the circuit court to quash the information, the Court of Appeals reversed. Among other things, the Court said that more recent Supreme Court decisions had "cast doubt" that *Roberts* remained good law. The Court also noted that the trial judge in *Roberts* had "assumed that a murder had occurred and considered only the degree of that crime." The *Campbell* panel further found that the defendant did not have the required

C

We agree with the Court of Appeals that the holding in *Roberts* was not dicta. While it is true that defendant Roberts pleaded guilty of placing a poisonous mixture at the bedside of his sick wife, knowing that she intended to use it to commit suicide, nothing in the opinion indicates that this Court based its affirmance of the conviction of first-degree murder on the fact that the conviction stemmed from a guilty plea.

However, it is not sufficient in the instant case to decide simply that the holding in *Roberts* was not dicta. We must determine further whether *Roberts* remains viable, because, as noted in *People v. Stevenson*, 416 Mich. 383, 390, 331 N.W.2d 143 (1982): This Court has often recognized its authority, and indeed its duty, to change the common law when change is required.

The crime of murder has been classified and categorized by the Legislature, but the definition of murder has been left to the common law. Unless abrogated by the constitution, the Legislature, or this Court, the common law applies.

Under the common-law definition, " '[m]urder is where a person of sound memory and discretion unlawfully kills any reasonable creature in being, in peace of the state, with malice prepense or aforethought, either express or implied.' " Implicit in this definition is a finding that the defendant performed an act that caused the death of another. To convict a defendant of criminal homicide, it must be proven that death occurred as a direct and natural result of the defendant's act.

Early decisions indicate that a murder conviction may be based on merely providing the means by which another commits suicide. However, few jurisdictions, if any, have retained the early common-law view that assisting in a suicide is murder. The modern statutory scheme in the majority of states treats assisted suicide as a separate crime, with penalties less onerous than those for murder.

Recent decisions draw a distinction between active participation in a suicide and involvement in the events leading up to the suicide, such as providing the means. Frequently, these cases arise in the context of a claim by the defendant that the prosecution should have been brought under an assisted suicide statute. The courts generally have held that a person may be prosecuted for murder if the person's acts went beyond the conduct that the assisted suicide statute was intended to cover.

For example, in *People v. Cleaves*, 229 Cal.App.3d 367, 280 Cal.Rptr. 146 (1991), the defendant was charged with first-degree murder in the strangulation death of another man. The trial court had refused a defense request to instruct the jury on the statutory offense of aiding and abetting a suicide, and the jury convicted him of second-degree murder.

"present intention to kill." He only "hoped" that the decedent would kill himself, and "hope" is not the degree of intent required to sustain a charge of murder.

In deciding whether an instruction on the statutory offense of aiding and abetting suicide should have been given, the appellate court accepted the defendant's detailed version of the events. The decedent in *Cleaves* was suffering from AIDS and wanted the defendant's assistance in strangling himself. With the defendant's help, the decedent trussed his body in an arched position, with his face down on a pillow. The defendant's role, when the decedent "pulled down" on the truss to effect strangulation, was to put his hand on the decedent's back to steady him. At one point, when the sash slipped from the decedent's neck, the defendant rewrapped it at the decedent's request and retied it to the decedent's hands. By straightening out his body with his feet, the decedent was in sole control of how tight the sash was around his neck. In holding that the trial judge properly refused to instruct the jury under the assisted suicide statute, the appeals court said:

> [The statute] provides: "Every person who deliberately aids, or advises, or encourages another to commit suicide, is guilty of a felony." As explained by our Supreme Court, the "key to distinguishing between the crimes of murder and of assisting suicide is the active or passive role of the defendant in the suicide. If the defendant merely furnishes the means, he is guilty of aiding a suicide; if he actively participates in the death of the suicide victim, he is guilty of murder." [*In re Joseph G.*, 34 Cal.3d 429, 436, 194 Cal.Rptr. 163, 667 P.2d 1176, 40 A.L.R.4th 690 (1983)]. The statute providing for a crime less than murder " 'does not contemplate active participation by one in the overt act directly causing death. It contemplates some participation in the events leading up to the commission of the final overt act, such as furnishing the means for bringing about death, the gun, the knife, the poison, or providing the water, for the use of the person who himself commits the act of self-murder. But where a person actually performs, or actively assists in performing, the overt act resulting in death, such as shooting or stabbing the victim, administering the poison, or holding one under water until death takes place by drowning, his act constitutes murder, and it is wholly immaterial whether this act is committed pursuant to an agreement with the victim. . . .' "

In *Cleaves*, viewing the evidence most favorably for the defense, the court said there were no facts to support the requested instruction on aiding and abetting an assisted suicide. Although the defendant may not have applied pressure to the ligature itself, he admitted that his act of holding the decedent to keep him from falling off the bed was designed to assist the decedent in completing an act of strangulation. "This factual scenario indisputably shows active assistance in the overt act of strangulation," the court said.

[handwritten margin note: Sexson • Active participant • guilty of 2nd degree]

Similarly, in *State v. Sexson*, 117 N.M. 113, 869 P.2d 301 (N.M.App., 1994) the defendant was charged with first-degree murder in connection with the fatal shooting of his wife. He was convicted of second-degree murder following a bench trial, and argued on appeal that he should have been prosecuted under the state's assisted suicide statute.

The only fact in dispute in *Sexson* was whether it was the defendant or the decedent who actually pulled the trigger of the rifle that killed her. It was not disputed that there was a suicide agreement between the two, and that the pact was genuine. The defendant claimed simply to have held the rifle in position while the decedent pulled the trigger, and that he had failed to then kill himself because he "freaked out" when the decedent continued to breathe after being shot.

The appellate court rejected the defendant's argument that he could not be prosecuted under the more general murder statute because of the specific assisted suicide statute. In so doing, the court emphasized that the two statutes proscribed different conduct:

> The wrongful act triggering criminal liability for the offense of assisting suicide is "aiding another" in the taking of his or her own life. It is well accepted that "aiding," in the context of determining whether one is criminally liable for their involvement in the suicide of another, is intended to mean providing the means to commit suicide, not actively performing the act which results in death. . . .

[handwritten margin note: Passive = providing the means]

> There are three different views about the criminal liability of one who, whether pursuant to a suicide pact or not, solicits (by talk) or aids (as by providing the means of self-destruction) another to commit suicide. Occasionally aiding or soliciting suicide has been held to be no crime at all on the ground that suicide is not criminal. That view is most certainly unsound. At one time many jurisdictions held it to be murder, but a great many states now deal specifically with causing or aiding suicide by statute, treating it either as a form of manslaughter or as a separate crime. Such statutes typically do "not contemplate active participation by one in the overt act directly causing death," and thus their existence is not barrier to a murder conviction in such circumstances.

> In contrast, the wrongful act triggering criminal liability for second degree murder is "kill[ing]" or "caus[ing] the death" of another. In the context of the instant case, the second degree murder statute is aimed at preventing an individual from actively causing the death of someone contemplating suicide, whereas the assisting suicide statute is aimed at preventing an individual from providing someone contemplating suicide with the means to commit suicide. Thus, the two statutes do not condemn the same offense. . . .

Turning to the evidence presented in *Sexson*, the court reiterated that the distinction accepted in other jurisdictions between murder and aiding suicide "generally hinges upon whether the defendant actively participates in the overt act directly causing death, or whether he merely provides the means of committing suicide." This distinction applies even where the decedent has given consent or requested that actual assistance be provided. In *Sexson*, the defendant admitted holding the rifle in a position calculated to assure the decedent's death. The court concluded: "That action transcends merely providing Victim a means to kill herself and becomes active participation in the death of another."

In the years since 1920, when *Roberts* was decided, interpretation of causation in criminal cases has evolved in Michigan to require a closer nexus between an act and a death than was required in *Roberts*. See, e.g., *People v. Flenon, supra; People v. Scott*, 29 Mich.App. 549, 558, 185 N.W.2d 576 (1971). The United States Supreme Court also has addressed the importance of relating culpability to criminal liability. See *Tison v. Arizona*, 481 U.S. 137, 107 S.Ct. 1676, 95 L.Ed.2d 127 (1987); Mullaney v. Wilbur, 421 U.S. 684, 697–698, 95 S.Ct. 1881, 1888–1889, 44 L.Ed.2d 508 (1975).

In the context of participation in a suicide, the distinction recognized in *In re Joseph G, supra*, constitutes the view most consistent with the overwhelming trend of modern authority. There, the California Supreme Court explained that a conviction of murder is proper if a defendant participates in the final overt act that causes death, such as firing a gun or pushing the plunger on a hypodermic needle. However, where a defendant is involved merely "in the events leading up to the commission of the final overt act, such as furnishing the means . . . ," a conviction of assisted suicide is proper.

As noted, this Court has modified the common law when it perceives a need to tailor culpability to fit the crime more precisely than is achieved through application of existing interpretations of the common law. For the reasons given, we perceive such a need here. Accordingly, we would overrule *Roberts* to the extent that it can be read to support the view that the common-law definition of murder encompasses the act of intentionally providing the means by which a person commits suicide. Only where there is probable cause to believe that death was the direct and natural result of a defendant's act can the defendant be properly bound over on a charge of murder.[70] Where a defendant merely is involved in the events leading up to the death, such as providing the means, the proper charge is assisting in a suicide.

---

[70] However, there may be circumstances where one who recklessly or negligently provides the means by which another commits suicide could be found guilty of a lesser offense, such as involuntary manslaughter. There are a number of cases in which providing a gun to a person known to the defendant to be intoxicated and despondent or agitated has constituted sufficient recklessness to support such a conviction. For example, see *People v. Duffy*, 79 N.Y.2d 611, 79 N.Y.2d 611, 613, 595 N.E.2d 814 (1992),

The decision regarding whether an examining magistrate erred in binding a defendant over for trial is one that should be made in the first instance by the trial court. In this case, the lower courts did not have the benefit of the analysis set forth in this opinion for evaluating the degree of participation by defendant Kevorkian in the events leading to the deaths of Ms. Wantz and Ms. Miller. Accordingly, we remand this matter to the circuit court for reconsideration of the defendant's motion to quash in light of the principles discussed in this opinion.

■ BOYLE, JUSTICE (concurring in part and dissenting in part).

The lead opinion would hold that where one "only" plans and participates in a death the actor can claim was "suicide," he may not be charged as a matter of law with criminal homicide. No jurisdiction in the history of this country has so held and for obvious reasons. We have no way of assuring that redefining the line that constitutes causation will distinguish between terminally ill or desperately suffering people and those who think they are, no way of deciding in advance that the act of suicide is that of a rational person who chose death with dignity or that of a severely depressed person who would not have chosen death had help been available. Most significantly, the lead opinion's unwillingness to allow a jury to dispense mercy by determining the degree of culpability for a result clearly intended and caused in fact by a defendant is a sea change in the fundamental value we have assigned to the preservation of human life as one of the last great faiths that unites us.

The question whether the definition of murder should be changed so as to exclude one who participates in all events leading up to the death, save for the final act, is a matter of compelling public interest, demanding a balancing of legitimate interests that this Court is institutionally unsuited to perform. Although the Legislature passed a temporary assisted suicide law that included participation, it has not indicated that it intends to redefine murder, and every jurisdiction that has adopted a specific law covering assisted suicide has permitted prosecution for murder where the participation goes "too far." No issue is more deserving of continued legislative debate and public study regarding whether, when, and how persons can maximize personal autonomy without running the risk of creating a societal quicksand for irreversible error.

The decision to stay our hand in this matter is not simply a matter of adhering to the rule of law. It reflects the wisdom in recognizing that if we choose not to intervene, we have left the pressure for change in this rapidly developing and exceedingly complex field in the forum where it is best addressed. To choose to intervene is to remove the pressure to decide that assisting suicide can be found by a jury to be murder, and to add the Court's imprimatur to the voices of those who argue for an expansive right to self-determination that would decriminalize assisted suicide.

The profound questions that must be debated and the regulatory decisions that must be made are uniquely suited for legislative resolution. There is no principled method by which the Court can amend the common-law definition of murder, included in the statutes of this state.

■ RILEY, J., concurs.

■ LEVIN, JUSTICE (concurring in part and dissenting in part). *[handwritten: Justice Levin]*

Dr. Kevorkian is not a murderer. The evidence in the cases, in contrast with the record in *People v. Roberts*, which depended substantially on the possibly self-serving testimony of the defendant, who had pleaded guilty, establishes that Dr. Kevorkian did no more than provide the physical means by which the decedents took their own lives. That evidence establishes no more than criminal assistance of suicide or a common-law assisted suicide offense for which no provision is made by statute.

I agree with the lead opinion that *Roberts* should be overruled insofar as it can be read as holding that a person who does no more than assist another in committing suicide has acted with the requisite malice to establish that element of the crime of murder.

Because the evidence adduced in the murder prosecutions showed no more than criminal assistance to suicide or such a common-law assisted suicide offense, I see no need for a remand to determine whether Dr. Kevorkian should be bound over on a charge of murder. I join in part VI of the lead opinion to join in overruling *Roberts* to the extent that it can be read to support the view that the common-law definition of murder encompasses intentionally providing the means by which a person commits suicide.

The lead opinion contends that withdrawal of life support can be distinguished from assisted suicide. I generally agree.

A rule allowing a person to have his respirator disconnected, but to take no other steps to end his life, condemns him to choke to death on his own sputum. Similarly, if the law bars a person who can only take nourishment through a feeding tube from taking steps in addition to ordering the tube removed to end his life, he is required to suffer death by starvation and dehydration. Barring such persons from taking other steps to end their lives would, I think, constitute an undue burden on the right implicitly recognized in *Cruzan*. *Cruzan* should not be read as *[handwritten: Cruzan]* limiting a person to a half step when that would result in greater suffering.

The legitimate concerns about involuntary euthanasia apply with at least as much force to the withdrawal of life support where the person is incompetent, yet the United States Supreme Court in *Cruzan* held that a state statute permitting the withdrawal of life support on proof of the incompetent's wishes by clear and convincing evidence was consistent with due process.

In *Cruzan*, the Court struck a balance between the state's interest in life and preventing euthanasia, and the incompetent person's interest in being free of unwelcome bodily intrusions. The Court found that a "clear and convincing" evidentiary standard provided a permissible balance of the competing interests.

In the suicide context, legitimate state interests generally outweigh a person's interest in ending his life. The vast majority of suicides are "irrational" efforts by the depressed or mentally disturbed. Society can reasonably assume that a person's mental problems have clouded his perception. Where an otherwise healthy person is depressed or mentally disturbed, the personal liberty interest is weak, and the state has a strong interest in protecting the person's interests in life.

In contrast, where the person involved is competent, terminally ill, and facing imminent, agonizing death, the interest of the state in preserving life is weak, and the interest of the terminally ill person in ending suffering is strong.

■ MALLETT, JUSTICE (concurring in part and dissenting in part).

Because the lead opinion would find that there is no constitutional right, in any situation, to hasten one's death through physician-prescribed medications, I dissent.

The statute at issue should be deemed facially invalid because it bans all assisted suicides. A terminally ill individual who is suffering from great pain and who has made a competent decision should have a constitutional due process right to hasten his death. Because plaintiffs are in a position to now make a choice that I believe should survive any challenge from the state, I would hold that the statute represents an undue burden on that right.

The assumption that the recognition of this right would be problematic in its administration is not an appropriate consideration when determining the existence of a fundamental right. Indeed, constitutional litigation often creates the necessity to draw abstract lines that in practice are not easily workable. Nevertheless, the recognition of fundamental rights requires choices in these areas that are not readily ascribable to any particular administrative device.

We need only look to the development of the living will as an example of guidelines in the death and dying area that work effectively and remain constitutional. A competent person already has the right to document the desire to refuse lifesaving medical treatment. While such documentation provides us with the right to refuse life-sustaining treatment, our laws currently do not permit us to choose to end our suffering as we near death through physician-prescribed medications. If we were allowed such an opportunity, our own reasoned judgment would prevail in each case.

There is no adequate distinction between the right of a terminally ill person to refuse unwanted medical treatment and the right to physician-assisted suicide. There is no sense in disallowing the competent choice to have a physician intervene to relieve intolerable suffering at the end of one's life. Furthermore, such a result conflicts with what many of us would desire when faced with severe pain and an inevitable death.

Many citizens of this state are disturbed by defendant Kevorkian's crusade and, at the same time, wish to see a resolution of the difficulties facing the terminally ill. Perhaps even more troubling is that, under this law, an individual is forbidden from consulting with a private, trusted physician about such matters. The recognition of a right to make such private decisions with a trusted physician would allow open and honest discussion with the patient of all options and consequences.

Substantive due process cases invariably address those rights that are considered so fundamental that they cannot be unduly burdened by the state. Here, it is fundamentally wrong not to allow a competent, terminally ill person who is suffering from great pain the opportunity to die with some dignity.

Therefore, I would hold that the plaintiffs may assert a constitutional right to physician-assisted suicide if it can be shown that they have made a competent decision and are suffering from great pain. I would further allow, consistent with *Cruzan*, that the state may require proof of such a competent decision by clear and convincing evidence if it chooses to so legislate.

I would reverse the judgment of the Court of Appeals and allow plaintiffs to document their intent to receive physician-prescribed medications should their terminal illnesses progress to the point of great pain.

■ LEVIN, J., concurs.

5. FELONY MURDER

Commonwealth v. Almeida

Supreme Court of Pennsylvania, 1949.
362 Pa. 596, 68 A.2d 595.

[During an exchange of shots between robbers and police, Ingling, a police officer, was killed. The prosecution claimed that one of the felons killed Ingling; the defense, on the other hand, contended that Ingling was shot by a fellow officer. The defendant was convicted of first degree murder committed in the course of the robbery and sentenced to death.]

■ MAXEY, CHIEF JUSTICE. . . . The defendant's thirteenth point for charge which the trial judge correctly rejected was in effect a request that the court instruct the jury that in order to convict the defendant of the death of Officer Ingling, the jury would have to find that the fatal shot was fired by one of the three robbers . . .

. . . The *legal* question presented [is] . . . when men who are feloniously shot at by robbers return their fire in self-defense and a third person is killed by a shot fired by the defenders, are the robbers whose felonious action caused the shooting guilty of murder? . . .

[In] the instant case, we have a band of robbers engaged in an exchange of shots with city policemen *whose duty it is to subdue the bandits if possible*. In the course of the exchange of deadly bullets Officer Ingling is slain. The policemen cannot be charged with any wrongdoing because their participation in the exchange of bullets with the bandits was both in justifiable self-defense and *in the performance of their duty*. The felonious acts of the robbers in firing shots at the policemen, well knowing that their fire would be returned, as it should have been, was the proximate cause of Officer Ingling's death . . .

. . . Their acts were "the cause of the cause" of the murder. They "set in motion the physical power" which resulted in Ingling's death and they are criminally responsible for that result. Whether the fatal bullet was fired by one of the bandits or by one of the policemen who were performing their duty in repelling the bandit's assault and defending themselves and endeavoring to prevent the escape of the felons is immaterial. Whoever fired the fatal shot, the killing of Officer Ingling had its genesis in the robbing by the defendant and his confederates . . . and in their firing upon the police officers who in the performance of their duty were attempting to take them into custody . . .

There can be no doubt about the "justice" of holding that felon guilty of murder in the first degree who engages in a robbery or burglary and thereby inevitably calls into action defensive forces against him, the activity of which forces result in the death of a human being. Neither can there be any doubt about the "general utility" of a ruling which holds this defendant Almeida guilty of the murder of Officer Ingling, even if it had been established that the bullet which killed that officer was fired by one of the police officers who were returning the fire of Almeida and his confederates and were attempting to prevent their escape . . .

A knave who feloniously and maliciously starts "a chain reaction" of acts dangerous to human life must be held responsible for the natural fatal results of such acts. This is the doctrine enunciated by the textbook writers on criminal law, and which has been applied by the courts.

When men engaged in a scheme of robbery arm themselves with loaded revolvers they show that they expect to encounter forcible opposition and that to overcome it they are prepared to kill anyone who stands in their way. If in the course of their felonious enterprise they open deadly fire upon policemen or others and if in self-defense and to vindicate the law the fire is returned and someone is killed by a bullet fired in the exchange of shots, who can challenge the conclusion that the *proximate cause* of the killing was the malicious criminal action of the felons? No *other* genesis can justly be assigned to the homicide. The felons should be adjudged guilty of murder in the perpetration of a robbery, that is, murder in the first degree . . .

The judgment is affirmed and the record is remitted to the court below so that the sentence imposed may be carried out. * * *

■ JONES, JUSTICE (dissenting). I would reverse the judgment and remand the case for a retrial because of fundamental error in the trial court's charge to the jury. The case was submitted on the felony murder theory, yet, the trial judge charged in effect that, even though the fatal shot was not fired by one of the felons but by someone attempting to frustrate the robbery, all the jury would need find in order to hold the defendant guilty of murder was that he was engaged in a robbery at the time of the killing. That instruction inadequately stated the law applicable to the circumstances.

On proof of no more than the perpetration of a felony and an incidental killing, liability for murder can be visited upon the participating felons *only* where the causation of the homicide is direct, i.e., where one of the felons or one acting in furtherance of the felonious design inflicted the fatal wound . . . [E]ven though a felon or one acting in his aid does not fire the fatal bullet, his conduct may have initiated such a causative chain of events as to render him legally chargeable with having been the causa causans of the homicide. . . . In such circumstances, the felony murder theory supplies the malice necessary to make the killing murder while the proximate (although indirect) causation of the death is capable of fastening on the felon responsibility for the homicide. Sufficiency of the evidence to support a finding of the "chain of events" is, of course, a question of law for a court, but whether the "chain of events" existed unbroken and was the proximate cause of the homicide are questions of fact that only *a jury* can properly resolve. . . . Those important factual inquiries were not submitted in the instant case. Causation was assumed by the learned trial judge and all that was left to the jury to determine, in order to hold the defendant guilty of murder, was that he was engaged in a "holdup" at the time of the killing notwithstanding there was evidence that someone other than the felons had fired the fatal bullet . . .

. . . Whether the acts of Almeida and his confederates *were sufficient* to constitute the proximate cause of the killing was a question of law but whether they *did constitute* the proximate cause was a question of fact for the jury . . .

The jury should have been instructed that, in order to find the defendant guilty of murder, it was not only necessary for them to find the killing to have been coincidental with the perpetration of a felony in which the defendant was at the time participating but that they would also have to find that the fatal shot was fired by one of the felons or, if not fired by one of them, that the conduct of the defendant or his accomplices set in motion a chain of events among whose reasonably foreseeable consequences was a killing such as actually occurred. The only way that the question of the defendant's guilt can any longer be properly adjudicated upon adequate instructions to the jury is by the medium of a new trial . . .

NOTES

1. Subsequent to the *Almeida* case, the Pennsylvania Supreme Court was required to rule on the following fact situation, in Commonwealth v. Thomas, 382 Pa. 639, 117 A.2d 204 (1955). Thomas and a confederate committed a robbery. While fleeing from the scene, the confederate was shot and killed by the store owner. Thomas was indicted for murder of his co-felon. However, the trial court sustained Thomas' demurrer to the commonwealth's evidence and the decision was appealed. The Pennsylvania Supreme Court, with three justices dissenting, reversed the judgment of the lower court. In so doing, the court stated:

> The sole question is whether defendant can be convicted of murder under this state of facts. That is, can a co-felon be found guilty of murder where the victim of an armed robbery justifiably kills the other felon as they flee from the scene of the crime? . . . If the defendant sets in motion the physical power of another, he is liable for its result. . . . Commonwealth v. Almeida. . . . As has been said many times, such a rule is equally consistent with reason and sound public policy, and is essential to the protection of human life. The felon's robbery set in motion a chain of events which were or should have been within his contemplation when the motion was initiated. He therefore should be held responsible for *any death* which by direct and almost inevitable sequence results from the initial criminal act. . . . We can see no sound reason for distinction merely because the one killed was a co-felon.

Following the above action of the Pennsylvania Supreme Court in the *Thomas* case, the District Attorney of Philadelphia moved the trial court for entry of a *nolle prosequi* on the murder indictment, and the court approved the motion. At the same time, Thomas pleaded guilty to an indictment charging him with armed robbery and was sentenced to the penitentiary. The Pennsylvania penalty for armed robbery is a fine not exceeding ten thousand dollars, imprisonment in solitary confinement at labor for not exceeding twenty years, or both.

2. A few years later, the Pennsylvania Supreme Court again found it necessary to struggle with the felony-murder concept. The occasion was the case of Commonwealth v. Redline, 391 Pa. 486, 137 A.2d 472 (1958), where the defendant and his accomplice perpetrated a robbery and, while fleeing from the scene, engaged in a gun battle with the police. The accomplice was killed by a policeman, and defendant was indicted for and convicted of the murder of the accomplice. Here, the Supreme Court changed its mind and overruled *Thomas*, holding that felony-murder applies only if the killing is done by one of the felons, and not if the killing is done by a police officer or a bystander. The court did not overrule *Almeida*, although it expressed its dissatisfaction with that case, because the two cases could be distinguished on the basis that in *Almeida* the victim of the killing was a police officer, while in *Redline*, the victim was one of the felons.

3. On the same day that the Supreme Court of Pennsylvania decided the *Redline* case, it handed down a decision in Commonwealth v. Bolish, 391 Pa. 550, 138 A.2d 447 (1958). Bolish and one Flynn planned an arson, and in carrying out the plan Flynn was fatally injured by an explosion which occurred when he placed a jar of gasoline on an electric hot plate. Bolish was convicted of first degree murder and sentenced to life imprisonment. The judgment was affirmed on appeal, the court rejecting the defendant's contention that the felony-murder doctrine does not apply to the death of an accomplice resulting from the accomplice's own act. The court stated that the defendant

> was actively participating in the felony which resulted in death. The element of malice, present in the design of defendant, necessarily must be imputed to the resulting killing, and made him responsible for the death. . . . The fact that the victim was an accomplice does not alter the situation, since his own act which caused his death was in furtherance of the felony.

Two justices dissented.

Is the *Bolish* case distinguishable from *Redline*?

Was the majority holding in *Bolish* correct in view of the wording of the Pennsylvania statute which provides, in part, as follows: "All murder which shall be . . . committed in the perpetration of . . . arson . . . shall be murder in the first degree"?

4. The conviction in the *Almeida* case was set aside by a federal district court, upon a habeas corpus hearing, because of the fact that the prosecution had suppressed evidence establishing that the fatal bullet was actually fired by a police officer and not by one of the felons. United States ex rel. Almeida v. Baldi, 104 F.Supp. 321 (E.D.Pa.1951), *aff'd*, 195 F.2d 815 (3d Cir. 1952). Almeida was retried. He pled guilty and received a life sentence.

After the court's decision in *Redline*, Almeida appealed on the basis that under the new (*Redline*) rule he was not guilty of murder. The Pennsylvania Supreme Court held that the *Redline* decision was not relevant because the legality of Almeida's conviction must be governed by the law as it existed at that time. Commonwealth ex rel. Almeida v. Rundle, 409 Pa. 460, 187 A.2d 266 (1963). To the same effect, see United States ex rel. Almeida v. Rundle, 383 F.2d 421 (3d Cir. 1967).

Commonwealth ex rel. Smith v. Myers

Supreme Court of Pennsylvania, 1970.
438 Pa. 218, 261 A.2d 550.

■ O'BRIEN, JUSTICE. This is an appeal from the order of the Court of Common Pleas of Philadelphia County, denying James Smith's petition for a writ of habeas corpus. The facts upon which the convictions of appellant and his co-felons, Almeida and Hough, rest are well known to this Court and to the federal courts. In addition to vexing the courts, these cases have perplexed a generation of law students, both within and without the Commonwealth, and along with their progeny, have spawned reams of critical commentary.[3]

Briefly, the facts of the crime are these. On January 30, 1947, Smith, along with Edward Hough and David Almeida, engaged in an armed robbery of a supermarket in the City of Philadelphia. An off-duty policeman, who happened to be in the area, was shot and killed while attempting to thwart the escape of the felons. Although the evidence as to who fired the fatal shot was conflicting in appellant's 1948 trial, the court charged the jury that it was irrelevant who fired the fatal bullet:

> Even if you should find from the evidence that Ingling was killed by a bullet from the gun of one of the policemen, that policeman having shot at the felons in an attempt to prevent the robbery or the escape of the robbers, or to protect Ingling, the felons would be guilty of murder, or if they did that in returning the fire of the felons that was directed toward them.

To this part of the charge appellant took a specific exception.

The jury convicted Smith of first degree murder, with punishment fixed at life imprisonment. He filed no post-trial motions, and took no appeal. Nor did Smith initiate any post-conviction proceedings until the instant case, despite the litigious propensities of his co-felons.

On February 4, 1966, appellant filed the present petition for a writ of habeas corpus. * * *

. . . The court below held that appellant had knowingly waived his right to appeal, and although the opinion does not discuss the question, the denial of relief necessarily manifested a belief by the court below that appellant was aware of his right to counsel on appeal. The other issues raised by appellant were not mentioned by the court, apparently of the view that they were cognizable only if it appeared that appellant had been denied his right to appeal, and was entitled to an appeal nunc pro tunc.

---

[3] It would be virtually impossible to catalogue all of the articles on these cases which have been published in the learned journals. Some of the more enlightening include Morris, The Felon's Responsibility for the Lethal Acts of Others, 105 U.Pa.L.Rev. 50 (1956); Ludwig, Foreseeable Death in Felony Murder, 18 U.Pitt.L.Rev. 51 (1956); and Case Notes, 71 Harv.L.Rev. 1565 (1958), and 106 U.Pa.L.Rev. 1176 (1958).

We reverse, grant the writ, allow an appeal nunc pro tunc, and grant a new trial. * * *

verdict

Appellant urges that he was denied due process by virtue of the trial court's charge that it was irrelevant who fired the fatal bullet. Such a charge was consistent with the dictum of this Court in Commonwealth v. Moyer and Byron, 357 Pa. 181, 53 A.2d 736 (1947), and with the holding shortly thereafter in the appeal of appellant's co-felon, David Almeida, in Commonwealth v. Almeida, . . . (1949). In the latter case, by a stretch of the felony-murder rule, we held that Almeida could indeed be found guilty of murder even though the fatal bullet was fired by another officer acting in opposition to the felony. We adopted a proximate cause theory of murder: "[H]e whose felonious act is the *proximate* cause of another's death is *criminally* responsible for that death and must answer to society for it exactly as he who is *negligently* the *proximate cause* of another's death is civilly responsible for that death and must answer in damages for it. . . ."

Holding of Almeida (overruled)

The proximate cause theory was taken a millimeter further by this Court in Commonwealth v. Thomas, . . . (1955). In that case the victim of an armed robbery shot and killed one of the felons, Jackson; the other felon, Thomas, was convicted of the murder.

Thomas was repudiated by this Court in Commonwealth v. Redline,. . . (1958). The facts there were virtually identical to those of *Thomas;* a policeman shot one fleeing felon and the other was convicted of murder. In a famous opinion by the late Chief Justice Charles Alvin Jones, this Court interred *Thomas* and dealt a fatal blow to *Almeida.* At the outset of this Court's opinion in *Redline*, we stated: "The decision in the Almeida case was a radical departure from common law criminal jurisprudence." The thorough documentation which followed in this lengthy opinion proved beyond a shadow of a doubt that *Almeida* and *Thomas* constituted aberrations in the annals of Anglo-American adjudicature.

Almeida was wrong

Redline began with a rather general review of the entire felony-murder theory. If we may presume to elaborate a bit on that review, we should point out that the felony-murder rule really has two separate branches in Pennsylvania. The first, and the easier concept, is statutory. The Act of June 24, 1939 provides, *inter alia:* "All murder which shall * * * be committed in the perpetration of, or attempting to perpetrate any arson, rape, robbery, burglary, or kidnaping, shall be murder in the first degree. All other kinds of murder shall be murder in the second degree." Clearly this statutory felony-murder rule merely serves to raise the degree of certain murders to first degree; it gives no aid to the determination of what constitutes murder in the first place. *Redline,* pointing out that except for one isolated situation there is no statutory crime of murder, directed us to the common law for a determination of what constitutes murder. It is here that the other branch of the felony-

Felony murder statute

[margin note: common law det murder ·need malice]

murder rule, the common law branch, comes into play. Citing Commonwealth v. Drum, 58 Pa. 9 (1868), the early leading case on murder in the Commonwealth, and Blackstone, Commentaries, *Redline* reaffirmed that the distinguishing criterion of murder is malice. The common law felony-murder rule is a means of imputing malice where it may not exist expressly. Under this rule, the malice necessary to make a killing, even an accidental one, murder, is constructively inferred from the malice incident to the perpetration of the initial felony.

The common law felony-murder rule as thus explicated has been subjected to some harsh criticism, most of it thoroughly warranted. * * *

[margin note: F-murder rule not needed]

In fact, not only is the felony-murder rule non-essential, but it is very doubtful that it has the deterrent effect its proponents assert.[9] On the contrary, it appears that juries rebel against convictions, adopting a homemade rule against fortuities, where a conviction must result in life imprisonment. . . . To similar effect, Justice Oliver Wendell Holmes, in The Common Law, argued that the wise policy is not to punish the fortuity, but rather to impose severe penalties on those types of criminal activity which experience has demonstrated carry a high degree of risk to human life . . .

We have gone into this lengthy discussion of the felony-murder rule not for the purpose of hereby abolishing it. That is hardly necessary in the instant case. But we do want to make clear how shaky are the basic premises on which it rests. With so weak a foundation, it behooves us not to extend it further and indeed, to restrain it within the bounds it has always known. As stated above, *Redline* . . . demolished the extension to the felony-murder rule made in *Almeida:* "In adjudging a felony-murder, it is to be remembered at all times that the thing which is imputed to a felon for a killing incidental to his felony is *malice* and *not the act of killing*. . . . '*The malice of the initial* offense attaches to whatever else the *criminal* may do in connection therewith.' * * * And so, until the decision of this court in Commonwealth v. Almeida, supra, in 1949, the rule which was uniformly followed, whether by express statement or by implication, was that in order to convict for felony-murder, *the killing must have been done by the defendant or by an accomplice or confederate or by one acting in furtherance of the felonious undertaking*." [citing a long line of cases.]

"Until the Almeida case there was no reported instance in this State of a jury ever having been instructed on the trial of an indictment for

---

[9]   See, e.g. the dissenting opinion of Justice (now Chief Justice) Bell in Commonwealth v. Redline, supra, where he stated: "The brutal crime wave which is sweeping and appalling our Country can be halted only if the Courts stop coddling, and stop freeing murderers, communists and criminals on technicalities made of straw." To similar effect is the statement in Commonwealth v. Kelly, 333 Pa. 280, 287, 4 A.2d 805 (1939): "To this Commonwealth one must answer as a malicious criminal for any fatal injury he here causes a human being by anything done by him intentionally or unintentionally during the commission or attempted commission of any of the specified felonies, for malice is the mainspring of his outlawed enterprise and his every act within the latter's ambit is imputable to that base quality. *Such a rule is essential to the protection of human life*." (Emphasis added).

murder for a killing occurring contemporaneously with the perpetration of a felony that the defendant was guilty of murder regardless of the fact that the fatal shot was fired by a third person acting in hostility and resistance to the felon and in deliberate opposition to the success of the felon's criminal undertaking." (Emphasis in original).

Redline proceeded to discuss the cases, both within and without Pennsylvania, which establish the rule that murder is not present where the fatal shot is fired by a third person acting in opposition to the felon. . . .

We then proceeded to distinguish the cases relied upon in *Almeida*. Chief among those cases was Commonwealth v. Moyer and Byron, . . . We referred to the statement in that case to the effect that a felon can be convicted of murder if the shot is fired by the intended victim as "a palpable gratuity," since the court below had charged that the defendant was entitled to an acquittal unless the Commonwealth proved beyond a reasonable doubt that one of the felons had fired the fatal bullet. We further distinguished the cases, cited in *Almeida*, in which the death-dealing act was committed by one participating in the initial felony . . .

Finally, we distinguished the *express* malice cases. These included the so-called "shield" cases, where a felon used the interposition of the body of an innocent person to escape harm in flight from the scene of the crime. . . . These cases were not based on the felony-murder rule and imputed malice, but on the express malice found in the use of an innocent person as a shield or breastwork against hostile bullets . . .

This lengthy review of *Redline* should have made it clear that the cases on which *Almeida* was based did not support the result reached therein, nor do the later cases. However, *Redline*, was not limited merely to a factual explication of the cases on which *Almeida* relied. *Redline*, . . . rejected the proximate cause tort analogy which Almeida found so appealing: "As we have already seen, the 'causation' requirement for responsibility in a felony-murder is that the homicide stem from the commission of the felony. Obviously, the assumed analogy between that concept and the tort-liability requirement of proximate cause is not conclusive. If it were, then the doctrine of supervening cause, which, for centuries courts have recognized and rendered operative on questions of proximate cause, would have to be considered and passed upon by the jury. But, that qualification, the Almeida case entirely disregarded."

The issue of the application of tort proximate cause principles to homicide prosecutions again arose a few years after *Redline* in *Commonwealth v. Root*. In that case the defendant was engaged in a drag race on a public highway with another person who swerved to the left side of the road, crashed head-on into an on-coming truck, and was killed. This Court reversed Root's conviction for involuntary manslaughter, and rejected utterly the tort concept of proximate cause in criminal homicide prosecutions:

"While precedent is to be found for application of the tort law concept of 'proximate cause' in fixing responsibility for criminal homicide, the want of any rational basis for its use in determining criminal liability can no longer be properly disregarded. When proximate cause was first borrowed from the field of tort law and applied to homicide prosecutions in Pennsylvania, the concept connoted a much more direct causal relation in producing the alleged culpable result than it does today. Proximate cause, as an essential element of a tort founded in negligence, has undergone in recent times, and is still undergoing, a marked extension. More specifically, this area of civil law has been progressively liberalized in favor of claims for damages for personal injuries to which careless conduct of others can in some way be associated. To persist in applying the tort liability concept of proximate cause to prosecutions for criminal homicide after the marked expansion of *civil* liability of defendants in tort actions for negligence would be to extend possible *criminal* liability to persons chargeable with unlawful or reckless conduct in circumstances not generally considered to present the likelihood of a resultant death."
* * *

After this review of *Redline*, the uninitiated might be surprised to learn that *Redline* did not specifically overrule *Almeida*. This Court did overrule *Thomas*, holding that no conviction was possible for a *justifiable* homicide where a policeman shot a felon, but "distinguished" *Almeida* on the ground that the homicide there, where an innocent third party was killed by a policeman, was only *excusable*.

The "distinction" *Redline* half-heartedly tries to draw has not escaped criticism from the commentators. While the result reached in *Redline* and most of its reasoning have met with almost unanimous approval, the *deus ex machina* ending has been condemned. One learned journal has commented:

"It seems, however, that Almeida cannot validly be distinguished from [Redline]. The probability that a felon will be killed seems at least as great as the probability that the victim will be an innocent bystander. Any distinction based on the fact that the killing of a felon by a policeman is sanctioned by the law and therefore justifiable, while the killing of an innocent bystander is merely excusable, seems unwarranted. No criminal sanctions now attach to either in other areas of criminal law, and any distinction here would seem anomalous. Indeed, to make the result hinge on the character of the victim is, in many instances, to make it hinge on the marksmanship of resisters. Any attempt to distinguish between the cases on the theory that the cofelon assumes the risk of being killed would also be improper since this tort doctrine has no place in the criminal law in which the wrong to be redressed is a public one—a killing with the victim's consent is nevertheless murder. It is very doubtful that public desire for vengeance should alone justify a conviction of felony murder for the death of an innocent bystander when no criminal responsibility will attach for the death of a cofelon." * * *

Appellant is therefore in no way precluded from asserting his claim that *Almeida* should be overruled. We thus give *Almeida* burial, taking it out of its limbo, and plunging it downward into the bowels of the earth.[17]

Almeida is overruled

The order of the court below is reversed, an appeal is allowed *nunc pro tunc*, and a new trial is granted.

■ EAGEN, J., concurs in the result.

■ BELL, C.J., files a dissenting opinion.

Dissent

This is the age of Crime and Criminals, and the peace-loving citizen is the forgotten man. Murder, robbery and rape are rampant, and this tidal wave of ruthless crime, violence and widespread lawlessness which too often goes unpunished is due in considerable part to recent procriminal decisions of the highest Courts in our State and Country. No matter how guilty a convicted criminal undoubtedly is, no matter how terrible his crime was, or how many crimes he has previously committed, the highest Courts of our Country (1) have in recent years extended and continue to *expand* the so-called rights of criminals, and (2) are completely oblivious of the rights, the security, the safety and the welfare of the law-abiding public. * * *

The Majority specifically hold that if a killing occurs during the commission or attempted perpetration of robbery or other major felony, or during the attempted escape of one of the robbers or any of the dangerous co-felons, none of the robbers and *none of the co-felons is guilty of murder—if the fatal shot was fired by the holdup victim or by a policeman* or other law enforcement officer, or by a person attempting to prevent the robbery or the robber's (or felon's) escape, *or by anyone except one of the robbers or a co-felon.* This decision, which is so disastrous to Society, is reached by unrealistic, and at times far-fetched reasoning which together with its predecessor, Commonwealth v. Redline, . . . which it expands, will produce the most harmful damage to law-abiding citizens ever inflicted sua sponte by the Supreme Court of Pennsylvania. * * *

For ages, it has been the well-settled and wisely-established law that when a person intentionally commits or joins or conspires with another to commit a felonious act, or sets or joins another in setting in motion a chain of circumstances the natural and probable or reasonably foreseeable result of which will be death or serious bodily harm to some person, he and his co-felons are guilty of the crime which was a product

---

[17] See fn #14, . . . of the Dissenting Opinion in *Redline*, where Justice (now Chief Justice) Bell laments: "In the majority opinion, Commonwealth v. Almeida, like Mohammed's coffin, is suspended between Heaven and earth. However, unlike Mohammed's coffin, which is headed upward toward Heaven, the coffin containing Commonwealth v. Almeida is pointed downward in preparation for a speedy flight into the bowels of the earth."

All the felons should be guilty of the result of their actions

or result of the aforesaid criminal act or chain of circumstances. If the felon or co-felons possessed legal malice, and death resulted, all the felons who participated in the felonious act or in the aforesaid chain of circumstances would be guilty of murder.

In the leading case of Commonwealth v. Moyer and Commonwealth v. Byron, 357 Pa. 181, 53 A.2d 736, the Court unanimously held that every person who committed or attempted to commit a felony such as robbery, or feloniously participated therein, was guilty of murder in the first degree, even though the fatal bullet is fired by the intended victim in repelling the robbery. Chief Justice Maxey, speaking for a unanimous Court, relevantly and wisely said (pages 190–191, 53 A.2d page 741–742):

"The doctrine that when malice is the mainspring of a criminal act the actor will be held responsible for any consequence of his act though it was not the one intended was recognized centuries ago when it was held that, quoting from Blackstone, Book IV, page 1599, Sec. 201, 'if one shoots at A and misses him, but kills B, this is murder, because of the previous felonious intent, *which the law transfers from one to the other*.' (Italics supplied.) It is equally consistent with reason and sound public policy to hold that when a felon's attempt to commit robbery or burglary sets in motion a chain of events which were or should have been within his contemplation when the motion was initiated, he should be held responsible for any death which by direct and almost inevitable sequence results from the initial criminal act. For any individual forcibly to defend himself or his family or his property from criminal aggression is a primal human instinct. It is the right and duty of both individuals and nations to meet criminal aggression with effective countermeasures. Every robber or burglar knows when he attempts to commit his crime that he is inviting dangerous resistance. Any robber or burglar who carries deadly weapons (as most of them do and as these robbers did) thereby reveals that he expects to meet and overcome forcible opposition. . . . Every robber or burglar knows that a likely later act in the chain of events he inaugurates will be the use of deadly force against him on the part of the selected victim. For whatever results follow from that natural and legal use of retaliating force, the felon must be held responsible. For Earl Shank, the proprietor of a gas station in Ridley Township, Delaware County, which at 11 P.M. on July 13, 1946, was being attacked by armed robbers, to return the fire of these robbers with a pistol which he had at hand was as proper and as inevitable as it was for the American forces at Pearl Harbor on the morning of December 7, 1941, to return the fire of the Japanese invaders. The Japanese felonious invasion of the Hawaiian Islands on that date was in law and morals the proximate cause of all the resultant fatalities. The Moyer-Byron felonious invasion of the Shank gas station on July 13, 1946, was likewise the proximate cause of the resultant fatality. . . ."

In Commonwealth v. Lowry, . . . we held that the driver of the alleged get-away car was guilty of first-degree murder, and in an unanimous Opinion said: "Where a killing occurs in the course of a robbery, all who participate in the robbery including the driver of the get-away car are equally guilty of murder in the first degree even though someone other than the defendant fired the fatal shot. . . ."

In Commonwealth v. Robb, the defendant was indicted and convicted of murder. He was a lookout and had nothing to do with the burglary or the murder. The Court said: "If defendants 'combine to commit a felony or make an assault, and, in carrying out the common purpose, another is killed, the one who enters into the combination but does not personally commit the wrongful act is equally responsible for the homicide with the one who directly causes it.' " . . .

MR. JUSTICE CARDOZO in The Nature of the Judicial Process, wisely said: "When they [judges] are called upon to say how far existing rules are to be extended or restricted, they must let the welfare of society fix the path, its direction and its distance * * * The final cause of law is the welfare of society. * * *"

Blackstone, . . .: "If a man, however, does such an act of which the probable consequences may be, and eventually is, death; such killing may be murder, although no stroke be struck by himself and no killing primarily intended."

All of the aforesaid cases were actually or in practical effect overruled when there was a change of personnel in the Supreme Court of Pennsylvania, at which time they ignored all the reasoning and the principles and the prior decisions of this Court and changed the law and decided Commonwealth v. Redline, 391 Pa. 486, 137 A.2d 472. This was until today, I repeat, the most damaging blow to the protection and safety of Society ever delivered by the Supreme Court of Pennsylvania.

For all of the reasons hereinabove mentioned, I very vigorously dissent.

The decision of the Majority giving Smith a new trial—Smith never took any kind of appeal or any post-conviction petition until the present appeal—is inexcusably unfair and unjust to Almeida and Hough, whose repeated petitions for a new trial and their appeals from the judgment of sentence of murder were rejected and dismissed by this Court.

It has often been said that "Justice is blind," meaning thereby that Justice is absolutely fair to each and every one and is not subject to any outside influence whatsoever. In this case, Justice is certainly blind, but its blindness is real and realistic and not figurative blindness, and what it erroneously terms "Justice" is "gross injustice."

NOTES

1. The *Redline* rationale was adopted in People v. Morris, 1 Ill.App.3d 566, 274 N.E.2d 898 (1971), holding that the felony-murder doctrine is not applicable to convict the surviving felon when his accomplice was justifiably killed during the commission of a forcible felony. However, in People v. Hickman, 59 Ill.2d 89, 319 N.E.2d 511 (1974), the Illinois Supreme Court specifically rejected the approach of *Redline* and Commonwealth ex rel. Smith v. Myers as well as that reached in Taylor v. Superior Court of Alameda County, 3 Cal.3d 578, 91 Cal.Rptr. 275, 477 p.2d 131 (1970), and held that a felony murder conviction is possible for fleeing perpetrators of a forcible felony when a pursuing police officer is shot by a fellow officer. In discussing the cases cited above, the court stated, "Our statutory and case law, however, dictate a different, and we believe preferable, result."

Among the state courts holding that their felony-murder statutes should apply only when an innocent person is killed, and not when the deceased is one of the felons, is State v. Williams, 254 So.2d 548 (Fla.App.1971). Other similar holdings noted include People v. Austin, 370 Mich. 12, 120 N.W.2d 766 (1963); People v. Wood, 8 N.Y.2d 48, 201 N.Y.S.2d 328, 167 N.E.2d 736 (1960); State v. Schwensen, 237 Or. 506, 392 P.2d 328 (1964).

2. In People v. Washington, 62 Cal.2d 777, 44 Cal.Rptr. 442, 402 P.2d 130 (1965), the defendant was convicted of murder for participating in a robbery in which his accomplice was killed by the victim of the robbery. Upon his appeal he urged the court to confine a felon's homicide responsibility to situations where the victim was an *innocent* person. Here, of course, the person killed was one of the felons. Although ultimately reversing the defendant's conviction the majority of the California Supreme Court, per Chief Justice Traynor, expressed the view that a distinction based upon a consideration of the person killed would make the defendant's criminal liability turn upon the marksmanship of the police and the victims of the felony during which the killing occurred. The court preferred to face up to the basic issue as to whether a felon can be convicted of murder for the killing of *any* person by another who is resisting the robbery; and it held that there could be no conviction in such instances. It interpreted the language of the California felony-murder statute to mean that for a killing to occur in the "perpetration," or in an "attempt to perpetrate" a felony, it had to be done by one of the felons; in other words, in furtherance of the felony. The court rejected the causation theory upon which the opposite result would have been reached. Also, as regards the prosecution's contention that responsibility for any death would serve to prevent dangerous felonies, the court said:

> Neither the common-law rationale of the rule nor the Penal Code supports this contention. In every robbery there is a possibility that the victim will resist and kill. The robber has little control over such a killing once the robbery is undertaken as this case demonstrates. To impose an additional penalty for the killing would discriminate between robbers, not on the basis of any difference in their own conduct, but solely on the basis of the

response by others that the robber's conduct happened to induce. ✗
An additional penalty for a homicide committed by the victim would
deter robbery haphazardly at best.

Two justices dissented; they expressed the view that the rule adopted
by the court contained the following implicit advice to would-be felons:

> Henceforth in committing certain crimes, including robbery,
> rape and burglary, you are free to arm yourselves with a gun and
> brandish it in the faces of your victims without fear of a murder
> conviction unless you or your accomplice pulls the trigger. If the
> menacing effect of your gun causes a victim or policeman to fire and
> kill an innocent person or a cofelon, you are absolved of
> responsibility for such killing unless you shoot first.

They added the following: "Obviously this advance judicial absolution
removes one of the most meaningful deterrents to the commission of armed
felonies."

3. On the other hand, in Taylor v. Superior Court, 3 Cal.3d 578, 91 Cal.Rptr.
275, 477 P.2d 131 (1970), a sharply divided California Supreme Court upheld
the conviction of murder of the driver of a getaway car where one of his
accomplices, who were engaged in a robbery and assault with a deadly
weapon, was shot and killed by the robbery victim. The court cited with
approval the following language from its earlier case of *People v. Gilbert*:

> When the defendant or his accomplice, with a conscious
> disregard for life, intentionally commits an act that is likely to
> cause death, and his victim or a police officer kills in reasonable
> response to such act, the defendant is guilty of murder. In such a
> case, the killing is attributable, not merely to the commission of a
> felony, but to the intentional act of the defendant or his accomplice
> committed with conscious disregard for life.

4. Where an offender seizes hostages to be used as shields, and one of the
hostages is killed by a policeman or other victim of the crime, the felony-
murder rule applies. Thus, in Johnson v. State, 252 Ark. 1113, 482 S.W.2d
600 (1972), a burglar who had been discovered seized the daughter of the
householder as a shield. A struggle ensued in the course of which the
householder shot his daughter. The murder conviction was upheld because
the defendant had placed the deceased in the perilous position.

5. What felonies are "inherently or potentially dangerous to human life"?

> Some states list or define, in their statutes, the felonies which
> trigger the applicability of the felony-murder rule. Cal. Penal Code
> § 189 includes among its first degree murders killings occurring
> during the commission or attempted commission of "arson, rape,
> robbery, burglary, mayhem, or any act punishable under Section 288
> [lewd or lascivious acts, willfully and lewdly committed upon
> children under 14]." Pennsylvania, on the other hand, views felony-
> murder in a broader context and considers such acts essentially
> murders in the second degree. 18 Penn. Cons. Stat. Ann. § 2502(b)
> provides: "Murder of the second degree.—A criminal homicide

constitutes murder of the second degree when it is committed while defendant was engaged as a principal or an accomplice in the perpetration of a felony."

Muhammad v. Commonwealth

Supreme Court of Virginia, 2005.
269 Va. 451, 611 S.E.2d 537.

■ JUSTICE LEMMONS delivered the majority opinion.

In these appeals, we consider two capital murder convictions and two death sentences imposed upon John Allen Muhammad ("Muhammad"). This prosecution arose from the investigation of a series of sixteen shootings, including ten murders that occurred in Alabama, Louisiana, Maryland, Washington, D.C., and Virginia over a 47-day period from September 5 to October 22, 2002. For the reasons discussed herein, the judgment of the trial court and the sentences of death will be affirmed.

A. Facts

On the morning of Wednesday, October 9, 2002, Dean H. Meyers ("Meyers") was shot and killed while fueling his car at the Sunoco gas station on Sudley Road in Manassas, Virginia. Meyers was shot in the head by a single bullet. Evidence at trial established that the bullet came from the .223 caliber Bushmaster rifle Muhammad possessed when he was arrested. Meyers was killed during a 47-day period, from September 5 to October 22, 2002, in which ten others were murdered and six more suffered gunshot wounds as a result of the acts of Muhammad and Lee Boyd Malvo ("Malvo") in concert. The murder of Meyers was the twelfth of these sixteen shootings.

The fifteenth shooting occurred in Ashland, Virginia on October 19, 2002. Jeffrey Hopper ("Hopper") and his wife stopped in Ashland to fuel their car and eat dinner. They left the restaurant and were walking to their car when Hopper was shot in the abdomen. Hopper survived the shooting, but underwent five surgeries to repair his pancreas, stomach, kidneys, liver, diaphragm, and intestines. In the woods near the shooting, police found a hunting-type blind similar to the one found at the Brown shooting. At the blind, police found a shell casing, a plastic sandwich bag attached to a tree with a thumbtack at eye level that was decorated with Halloween characters and self-adhesive stars, and a candy wrapper. Tests determined that the shell casing and bullet fragments recovered from the Hopper shooting came from the Bushmaster rifle possessed by Muhammad when he was arrested. Surveillance videotapes identified Muhammad in a Big Lots Store on October 19, 2002 near the shooting from which the plastic sandwich bag and decorations were likely obtained. The candy wrapper contained both Malvo's and Muhammad's DNA.

Police also found a handwritten message in the plastic sandwich bag that read:

For you Mr. Police. "Call me God." Do not release to the Press.

We have tried to contact you to start negotiation . . . These people took our call for a Hoax or Joke, so your failure to respond has cost you five lives.

If stopping the killing is more important than catching us now, then you will accept our demand which are non-negotiable.

(i)   You will place ten million dollar in Bank of america account . . . We will have unlimited withdrawl at any atm worldwide. You will activate the bank account, credit card, and pin number. We will contact you at Ponderosa Buffet, Ashland, Virginia, tel. # . . . 6:00 am Sunday Morning. You have until 9:00 a.m. Monday morning to complete transaction. "Try to catch us withdrawing at least you will have less body bags."

(ii)   If trying to catch us now more important then prepare you body bags.

If we give you our word that is what takes place.

"Word is Bond."

P.S. Your children are not safe anywhere at anytime.

The note was not found until after the deadline had passed. The day after Hopper was shot at the Ponderosa, an FBI agent operating the "Sniper Tip Line" received a call from a young male who said, "Don't talk. Just listen. Call me God. I left a message for you at the Ponderosa. I am trying to reach you at the Ponderosa. Be there to take a call in ten minutes."

On October 21, 2002, an FBI agent received a call to the FBI negotiations team which had been re-routed from the Ponderosa telephone number referenced in the note left after the Hopper shooting. A recorded voice stated:

Don't say anything. Just listen. Dearest police, Call me God. Do not release to the press. Five red stars. You have our terms. They are non-negotiable. If you choose Option 1, you will hold a press conference stating to the media that you believe you have caught the sniper like a duck in a noose. Repeat every word exactly as you heard it. If you choose Option 2, be sure to remember we will not deviate. P.S.—Your children are not safe.

Muhammad and Malvo were captured and arrested on October 24, 2002, by agents of the FBI at a rest area in Frederick County, Maryland. They were asleep in a Chevrolet Caprice (Caprice) at the time of their capture. Inside the Caprice, police found a loaded .223 caliber Bushmaster rifle behind the rear seat. Tests determined that the DNA on the Bushmaster rifle matched the DNA of both Malvo and

Muhammad. The only fingerprints found on the Bushmaster rifle were those of Malvo.

The Caprice had been modified after Muhammad purchased it. The windows were heavily tinted. The rear seat was hinged, providing easy access to the trunk from the passenger compartment. The trunk was spray-painted blue. A hole had been cut into the trunk lid, just above the license plate. The hole was blocked by a right-handed brown glove that matched the left-handed glove found in the woods near the Johnson shooting. The trunk also had a rubber seal that crossed over the hole. Inside the Caprice, police found slip of paper containing the Sniper Task Force phone number, and a list of schools in the Baltimore area.

B.   Proceedings Below

Subsequent to his arrest on October 24, 2002, Muhammad was indicted by a grand jury on October 28, 2002, for the capital murder of Meyers in the commission of an act of terrorism, Code §§ 18.2–31(13) and 18.2–46.4; capital murder of Meyers and at least one other person within a three-year period, Code § 18.2–31(8); conspiracy to commit capital murder, Code §§ 18.2–22 and 18.2–32; and illegal use of a firearm in the commission of capital murder, Code § 18.2–53.1.

From October 20 through November 17, 2003, Muhammad was tried before a jury in the Circuit Court of the City of Virginia Beach. The jury convicted Muhammad of all charges in the grand jury indictments. In a separate sentencing proceeding from November 17 through November 24, 2003, the jury sentenced Muhammad to two death sentences for the capital murder convictions, finding both the future dangerousness and vileness aggravating factors. The jury also sentenced Muhammad to 13 years in prison upon the remaining convictions.

Among the challenges made, Muhammad argues that the trial court erred in permitting a legally flawed "triggerman" theory to be presented to the jury as a result of various rulings and instructions. Muhammad further argues that, even under the Commonwealth's theory, the evidence was insufficient to prove that he was the so-called "triggerman." Also, Muhammad challenges the sufficiency of the evidence to support his capital murder conviction based upon acts of terrorism.

1.   Capital Murder Conviction Based Upon Murder of More Than One Person in Three Years

(a)   Sniper Team Theory

The Commonwealth introduced the testimony of Sergeant Major Mark Spicer ("Spicer") of the British Armed Forces as an expert in sniper methodology. Spicer testified that "sniping is the ability of two men to go out and inflict injuries or kill people and more importantly spread terror across a much larger force." While acknowledging that a sniper can act alone or in a team of three, he stated, "the basic unit for a sniper team . . . is . . . a two-man unit." Spicer testified at length about the distinct responsibilities of each member of a two-man sniper unit. Essentially, one member of the team is the long-range shooter occupying an obscured position with the opportunity to shoot a particular victim. Because of the intensity and discipline required to take advantage of the narrow window of opportunity to take the long-range shot, the other member of the team, the "spotter," informs the long-range shooter by radio that the victim is coming within the zone of potential fire and that other circumstances are ripe for the shot. The "spotter" may ultimately give the order to shoot.

Spicer connected the evidence found by police investigators in this case to the tools and methods ordinarily used by a sniper team. The .223 caliber Bushmaster rifle used in at least ten of the shootings, including Dean Meyers, is equivalent to the M4 rifle used by military snipers. Additionally, sniper teams use tools such as those found in the Caprice: a bipod support system for support of the rifle; holographic and telescopic scopes to aid sighting; GPS equipment to locate and relocate a vantage point for the long-range shot; "walkie-talkie" handheld radio sets for communication; pocket recording equipment for recording data in the dark, bungee cords for easy "break down" of the rifle for transportation; maps; silencers.

Spicer also testified about the methodology of a sniper team which was supported by the evidence in this case. Spicer emphasized the constant training with the rifle to maintain skills, the creation of a camouflaged location for firing, the use of existing traffic to facilitate escape, and the "team" approach with a "spotter" who is armed with a handgun and may additionally participate in the assault by firing from close range.

With regard to the Caprice, Spicer testified about the alterations made to it to facilitate the methodology of the sniper team. The rear firewall had been removed from the Caprice to provide entry into the trunk from the passenger compartment. The trunk compartment had been spray-painted a dark color to minimize contrast and shadow to avoid detection in the event the trunk was opened.

Finally, Spicer gave particular significance to the peculiar hole placed in the back of the trunk lid that enlarged the field of vision while minimizing the ability to see the person in the trunk. He referred to this special process as implementing the "castle principle" making reference to ancient methods of protecting the castle while minimizing danger to the shooter and maximizing the range of fire.

The Commonwealth presented compelling evidence that such a sniper team methodology was used by Muhammad and Malvo in multiple shootings prior to and after the murder of Dean Myers. Perhaps no one or two incidents could reasonably confirm the use of this methodology by the two perpetrators of this unique criminal enterprise. But in its entirety, the weight of the direct and circumstantial evidence in the case is sufficient to prove that Muhammad and Malvo acted together as a sniper team.

(b)   Jury Instructions on Multiple Homicide
Theory of Capital Murder

Muhammad was convicted under Code § 18.2–31(8), of the willful, deliberate, and premeditated killing of Dean Meyers and others within a three-year period. He maintains, "Only the immediate perpetrator of a homicide, the one who fired the fatal shot, and not an accessory before the fact or a principal in the second degree, may be convicted of capital murder." He claims that under the Commonwealth's theory of the case, Muhammad could never be the "triggerman" as defined in our cases.

It is well-established that in felony cases:

A principal in the first degree is the actual perpetrator of the crime. A principal in the second degree, or an aider or abettor as he is sometimes termed, is one who is present, actually or constructively, assisting the perpetrator in the commission of the crime. In order to make a person a principal in the second degree actual participation in the commission of the crime is not necessary. The test is whether or not he was encouraging, inciting, or in some manner offering aid in the commission of the crime. If he was present lending countenance, or otherwise aiding while another did the act, he is an aider and abettor or principal in the second degree. A principal in the second degree "must share the criminal intent of the actual perpetrator or be guilty of some overt act." *Hall v. Commonwealth*, 225 Va. 533, 536, 303 S.E.2d 903, 904 (1983). That there may be more than one principal in the first degree for a particular offense is beyond dispute:

Where two people engage in criminal conduct together, as where they participate in striking and killing another, each participant is a principal in the first degree in the homicide. Likewise, where part of a crime is committed in one place and another part is committed in a different place, the author of each part is a principal in the first degree.

1 Wharton's Criminal Law § 30 (15th ed.1993).

Generally in Virginia, a principal in the second degree is subject to the same punishment as the principal in the first degree. However, with certain exceptions "an accessory before the fact or principal in the second degree to a capital murder shall be indicted, tried, convicted and punished as though the offense were murder in the first degree." Code § 18.2–18. Accordingly, pursuant to the charge of capital murder based upon killing of two or more persons within a three-year period, the Commonwealth must prove that Muhammad was a principal in the first degree.

The euphemism, "triggerman," is inadequate to describe the breadth of criminal responsibility subject to the death penalty in Virginia. Immediately and obviously, capital murder cases are not confined to murders completed by the instrumentality of a firearm. Recognizing this inadequacy, our capital murder cases routinely use the term "immediate perpetrator" as the appropriate descriptive term.

In *Strickler v. Commonwealth*, 241 Va. 482, 404 S.E.2d 227, we reviewed a capital murder conviction wherein the "Commonwealth's theory of the case was that Strickler and Henderson had acted jointly to accomplish the actual killing" of the victim by crushing her skull with a 69-pound rock. The evidence was consistent with the Commonwealth's argument that one of the two men held the victim immobile while the other dropped or threw the rock on her head. We held that a defendant who "jointly participated in [a] fatal beating" was subject to conviction and punishment for capital murder, we restated the rule of culpability for capital murder as follows: We adhere to the view that where two or more persons take a direct part in inflicting fatal injuries, each joint participant is an "immediate perpetrator" for the purposes of the capital murder statutes.

Similarly, we must consider the evidence in support of the Commonwealth's theory of how Muhammad and Malvo acted together in the murder of Dean Meyers. Spicer's expert testimony, the evidence recovered from the Caprice, the evidence from the 16 shootings, and the additional evidence concerning Malvo and Muhammad's relationship and activities support the Commonwealth's theory of the case. Muhammad and Malvo and the Caprice were identified in the immediate vicinity of Dean Meyers' murder approximately one hour before it occurred. Immediately after the murder, Muhammad was identified in the parking lot across the street from where Meyers was shot. Muhammad was driving the Caprice in which he and Malvo were later arrested. Ballistics tests determined that the bullet that killed Meyers was shot from the .223 caliber Bushmaster rifle found in the Caprice with Muhammad and Malvo when they were arrested. The Caprice was located in a position providing a direct line of fire to accomplish the murder. Significantly, the shot from the parking lot had to cross nine lanes of traffic on a heavily traveled highway at approximately 8:15 p.m. on a weekday evening. With the relatively small portal offered by the hole in the trunk of the Caprice and the obstacle presented by nine traffic lanes, the evidence supports the Commonwealth's theory of a "shooter" and a "spotter" and the direction by the spotter to shoot at the opportune time. As in *Strickler*, we review the evidence in the light most favorable to the Commonwealth to determine if it is sufficient to support the Commonwealth's theory. Upon review of that evidence, we cannot say that the trial court was plainly wrong or without evidence to support its judgment.

The theory of the Commonwealth concerning multiple immediate perpetrators acting as principals in the first degree accurately encompasses Virginia law.

2.   Capital Murder in the Commission of an Act of Terrorism

(a) Sufficiency of Evidence. Muhammad was also convicted of capital murder pursuant to Code § 18.2–31(13) for the willful, deliberate, and premeditated killing of Dean Meyers in the commission of an act of terrorism as defined in Code § 18.2–46.4.

Code § 18.2–46.4 defines an "act of terrorism" as an act of violence as defined in clause (i) of subdivision A of § 19.2–297.1 committed with the intent to (i) intimidate the civilian population at large; or (ii) influence the conduct or activities of the government of the United States, a state or locality through intimidation. Code § 19.2–297.1 includes, among the acts of violence the offenses of first and second degree murder, voluntary manslaughter, malicious wounding, and robbery. Additionally, Code § 18.2–18 provides that a person convicted of capital murder under Code § 18.2–31(13) is not required to be a principal in the first degree to the murder if the killing was "pursuant to the direction or order of the one who is engaged in the commission of . . . an act of terrorism."

Significantly, Muhammad does not contest the sufficiency of evidence to support the charge that acts of violence committed by him and Malvo were done with the intent to "intimidate the civilian population at large" or to "influence the conduct or activities of the government of the United States, a state or locality through intimidation." Rather, he challenges his conviction for capital murder based upon the terrorism predicate by attacking the validity of the statute, constitutionally and otherwise, and by challenging the sufficiency of the evidence that he "directed" or "ordered" Malvo with respect to the killing of Dean Meyers.

The Commonwealth argues that the evidence is sufficient to support two separate evidentiary theories upon which Muhammad's conviction for capital murder in the commission of an act of terrorism is based. One theory is based upon Muhammad committing the murder of Dean Meyers as a principal in the first degree because he is an immediate perpetrator of the crime. The second evidentiary theory is based upon Muhammad giving a direction or order to Malvo to kill Dean Meyers. Either or both theories are sufficient to sustain the proof necessary to affirm Muhammad's conviction for capital murder in the commission of an act of terrorism.

As stated above, the proof is sufficient to establish beyond a reasonable doubt that Muhammad acted as a principal in the first degree, as an immediate perpetrator, in the death of Dean Meyers. The "sniper theory" advanced by the Commonwealth is supported through Spicer's expert testimony, the ample evidence of such a methodology, and our prior decisions. As an immediate perpetrator of the death of Dean Meyers in a murder that qualifies as an act of violence under Code § 19.2–297.1, Muhammad was a principal in the first degree in the "willful, deliberate, and premeditated killing of [a] person . . . in the commission . . . of an act of terrorism." Code § 18.2–31(13).

Additionally, the combined weight of direct and circumstantial evidence is sufficient to sustain Muhammad's conviction even if he is considered to have been a criminal actor in the second degree who gave an order or direction to Malvo to kill Dean Meyers. Malvo and Muhammad were seen in the Caprice in the vicinity of Meyers' shooting approximately one hour beforehand. The Caprice was the same vehicle in which Muhammad and Malvo were arrested. It was altered to provide access to the trunk from the inside and a portal for firing a rifle through the trunk lid. Muhammad was interviewed by police immediately after the shooting in a parking lot across the street from where Meyers was shot. Malvo was not seen at the parking lot. There was a direct line of fire between the parking lot and the Sunoco station where Meyers was shot. Between the parking lot and the site where Meyers was shot were nine traffic lanes. The evidence shows that Malvo and Muhammad possessed the .223 caliber Bushmaster rifle, mittens with open fingers, a GPS receiver, earplugs, maps, rifle scopes, "walkie-talkies," a voice recorder, an electronic organizer, and other evidence previously described. The evidence proves that the bullet that killed Dean Meyers came from the .223 caliber Bushmaster rifle in the possession of Muhammad and Malvo when they were arrested. The evidence also contains direct or circumstantial proof of instances where the two men committed similar crimes together.

Furthermore, the record is replete with evidence that Muhammad directed and ordered Malvo in the entire criminal enterprise. As the Commonwealth argued based upon evidence presented:

> It was Muhammad who brought Malvo to this country from Jamaica. It was Muhammad who had the military background in shooting and snipering skills and who trained Malvo. It was Muhammad who provided the weapons. It was Muhammad who was determined to terrorize his ex-wife's area of the country. It was Muhammad who was the "father" and Malvo who was the "son." All the evidence about their relationship—from the Lighthouse Mission and friends in Washington state to Muhammad's cousin in Baton Rouge and the YMCA personnel in Maryland—consistently showed Muhammad directing and ordering Malvo's conduct. Everyone who saw them together observed that Malvo was extremely obedient to Muhammad, not the other way around.

On this issue, the trial court held that there was "overwhelming circumstantial evidence regarding [Muhammad's] direction and ordering of Mr. Malvo." Upon review of the evidence, we cannot say that the trial court was clearly wrong or without evidence to support this conclusion.

We hold that Muhammad was an immediate perpetrator and as such was a principal in the first degree in the commission of capital murder during the commission of an act of terrorism. We further hold that the evidence proves that Muhammad gave a direction or order sufficient to satisfy the requirements of Code § 18.2–18 such that even if he were a criminal actor ordinarily demonstrating culpability as a principal in the second degree, he is nonetheless guilty of capital murder under Code §§ 18.2–31(13) and 18.2–18.

The Death Penalty

Muhammad's crimes cannot be compared to any other case in the Commonwealth. The evidence of vileness and future dangerousness in support of the jury's verdict justifies its sanction of death.

Muhammad with his sniper team partner, Malvo, randomly selected innocent victims. With calculation, extensive planning, premeditation, and ruthless disregard for life, Muhammad carried out his cruel scheme of terror. He did so by employing stealth and secrecy using a sniper methodology that put his victims at great risk while reducing his own. He employed a weapon with truly awesome power to inflict massive injury upon his victims. Muhammad recruited a younger boy, Malvo, and carefully trained and guided him in this murderous enterprise.

His victims came from all walks of life who were engaged in everyday pursuits when their lives were tragically ended or altered. Paul LaRuffa, Muhammad Rashid, Hong Im Ballenger, Claudine Parker, and Kelly Adams were closing and leaving their places of business. Sarah Ramos was sitting on a bench in front of a store. Lori Lewis-Rivera was vacuuming her car at a gas station. Paschal Charlot was crossing an intersection as a pedestrian. Caroline Seawell and Linda Franklin were putting packages in their respective automobiles. Iran Brown was walking to school. Dean Meyers, Kenneth Bridges, and Premkumar Walekar were putting fuel in their vehicles at gasoline stations. Jeffrey Hopper was leaving a restaurant after a meal. Conrad Johnson, a bus driver, was standing in the doorway of his bus. Muhammad inflicted death or massive injury upon these victims as he pursued his mission of terror.

Muhammad's threats to those within the communities he stalked including the warning, "Your children are not safe anywhere at anytime." He communicated his desire to extort money from the government through the demand to deposit ten million dollars in an account connected to a card for accessing the account through automated teller machines. Whatever else may have been his intentions, he certainly intended to intimidate the civilian population and to influence the conduct and activities of government. He did so with breathtaking cruelty. If society's ultimate penalty should be reserved for the most heinous offenses, accompanied by proof of vileness or future dangerousness, then surely, this case qualifies.

Conclusion

Upon review of the record and upon consideration of the arguments presented, we find no reversible error in the judgment of the trial court. Further, we find no reason to commute or set aside the sentences of death. We will affirm the judgment of the trial court.

Affirmed.

■ JUSTICE AGEE, with whom JUSTICE LACY and JUSTICE KOONTZ join, dissenting in part and concurring in part.

The common law classification of criminal perpetrators that distinguished between principals in the first and second degree has become of limited significance in modern times. Nearly all jurisdictions have enacted provisions similar to Virginia Code § 18.2–18, which erase the distinction between principals of the first and second degree by treating both categories of criminal actors as principals in the first degree for purposes of indictment, trial, conviction, and punishment.

However, the common law distinction between principals of the first and second degrees remains of significant importance in a case of capital murder in Virginia because the General Assembly has specifically provided in Code § 18.2–18 that a "principal in the second degree to a capital murder shall be indicted, tried, convicted and punished as though the offense were murder in the first degree." Thus, unless the Commonwealth proved beyond a reasonable doubt that John Allen Muhammad was a principal in the first degree to the murder of Dean Meyers under Code § 18.2–31(8), the plain language of Code § 18.2–18 bars conviction and punishment of Muhammad for capital murder.

At common law, a principal in the first degree is a person who engages in criminal conduct by his own hand—he fires the gun that kills, he takes and carries away the property of another.

At common law, a principal in the second degree is a person who is present at the scene of a crime, but does not engage in the criminal conduct; he merely aids and abets the principal in the first degree in committing the crime. He may be actually present, assisting the principal in the first degree, standing ready to assist if needed, or commanding, counseling, or otherwise encouraging the principal in the first degree to commit the crime; or, although at a distance from the scene of the crime, he may be deemed present when he is acting as a driver of the getaway car or as a lookout with instructions to warn the principal in the first degree if anyone approaches.

Based on the record in this case, the Commonwealth did not prove that Muhammad was a principal in the first degree to the capital murder of Dean Meyers under Code § 18.2–31(8). Under established law, Muhammad may be a principal in the first degree to the Meyers murder in two circumstances: (1) if he actually shot Meyers or (2) if he and Lee Boyd Malvo are found to be joint principals, with each acting as an "immediate perpetrator" in the killing. The record does not establish that the Commonwealth proved either circumstance.

Our decision in *Rogers v. Commonwealth*, 242 Va. 307, 410 S.E.2d 621 (1991), precludes finding that Muhammad is a principal in the first degree as the actual shooter of Meyers under the facts of this case. In *Rogers*, we reversed a defendant's capital murder conviction because the evidence placed the defendant and another man in the victim's house at the time of the murder and the Commonwealth failed to present "any evidence . . . which places the murder weapon in defendant's hands." "Stated differently, the Commonwealth . . . failed to exclude [the second man] as the perpetrator."

Following *Rogers*, Muhammad cannot be a principal in the first degree as the actual shooter of Meyers because the Commonwealth has not excluded Malvo as that person, and it presented no evidence that Muhammad was the actual shooter. "Because the circumstances of defendant's conduct do not exclude the reasonable hypothesis that [the second man (Malvo)] killed the victim, the capital murder prosecution fails." Therefore, Muhammad may not be convicted of Meyers' capital murder upon this record if the Commonwealth's position is Muhammad actually shot Meyers.

The Commonwealth primarily relies, however, on an expansive reading of the concept of "immediate perpetrator" based on Sergeant Spicer's theory of how a sniper team should operate. The majority opinion adopts this theory and concludes both Malvo and Muhammad are culpable as principals in the first degree because "actual participation together in a unified act" renders each an immediate perpetrator. In doing so, the Commonwealth and the majority opinion reach beyond any precedent of this court and ignore clear foundations of the criminal law that have long defined the distinction between principals of the first and second degree. Our precedent establishes that co-actors in a capital murder can only be immediate perpetrators when each actor undertook a direct act "in the immediate presence of the victim's body when the fatal blows were struck and, hence, had jointly participated in the killing."

All of the prior cases involve direct, contemporaneous acts on the part of the co-perpetrators that combined to proximately inflict the injury on the victim. In each case, both perpetrators were physically present and personally participated by a direct act against the victim to accomplish the murder. In the case at bar, however, there is no such evidence of a similar direct act by Muhammad.

Assuming Muhammad acted as hypothesized by the Commonwealth's witness, Mark Spicer, in positioning the Caprice in the Bob Evans parking lot to face the gas station and communicating to Malvo that the coast was clear to fire at Meyers, that is not the act of a principal in the first degree under Virginia law. Such conduct is the quintessence of activity by a principal in the second degree: "encouraging, inciting, or in some manner offering aid in the commission of the crime . . . lending countenance, or otherwise aiding while another did the act."

In that regard, Muhammad's actions were of the same character as those of a lookout or wheelman in a robbery. Such a person may provide the means and direction for the commission of the robbery by driving the actual perpetrators to the scene and keeping watch while the others directly commit the crime. Like Muhammad, the wheelman may communicate by walkie-talkie or cell phone to the actual perpetrators instructing them as to when to commit the robbery and then exit the premises in heavy traffic. Undoubtedly these acts accord the actual perpetrators, who take the immediate and direct action to effectuate the robbery, an easier task with an increased likelihood of escape. Nevertheless, no serious argument can be made such a wheelman is a principal in the first degree under our jurisprudence.

That is because the wheelman takes an indirect role, not a direct role, in the crime of robbery. He is present, keeping watch and offering his counsel and direction to commit the crime to the actual perpetrators, which is Muhammad's role under the Commonwealth's theory of the case. The wheelman is an actual participant in the unified act of disparate persons culminating in a robbery, just as Muhammad was an actual participant in an act with Malvo that resulted in Meyers' murder. Neither the wheelman, nor Muhammad, in the given circumstances, can be deemed an immediate perpetrator and thus a principal in the first degree under Virginia law.

Assuming that the events occurred as the Commonwealth theorizes, it was nonetheless, Malvo, not Muhammad, who finally sighted the rifle to its target and made the ultimate decision to pull the trigger. Malvo could have picked any target and decided at any time to fire or not. While the range of Malvo's vision was more restricted than Muhammad's, the record reflects that Malvo was not "blind" and dependent on Muhammad in order to shoot Meyers. Spicer's own testimony confirms the shooter had "a very large field of view by slightly moving [his] head left or right while still maintaining a very small outward chance of . . . being seen." The prosecutor even argued this point to the jury, noting that the shooter had "a much wider field of vision and a much narrower exposure." Obviously, Muhammad's advice and direction to Malvo of the traffic flow along the multiple lane highway made Malvo's choice easier and more likely to succeed. But in the end, it was Malvo who had to make the final decision to shoot and performed the direct act of firing the rifle.

Put simply, there is a failure of proof to establish Muhammad as a principal in the first degree so as to sustain his conviction under Code § 18.2–31(8). The evidence in this record, viewed in the light most favorable to the Commonwealth and indulging all the inferences from its theory of the case, establishes Muhammad's actions as those of a principal in the second degree, "actually present, assisting the principal in the first degree [Malvo], standing ready to assist if needed, or commanding, counseling, or otherwise encouraging the principal in the first degree to commit the crime," Conversely, this same evidence of Muhammad commanding and directing Malvo's actions effectively proves the requisite conduct for the conviction under Code § 18.2–31(13) for "a killing pursuant to . . . direction and order." Code § 18.2–18.

Virginia law is clear that "a principal in the second degree, may [not] be convicted of capital murder under the provisions of [the] Code," unless one of the enumerated exceptions applies. Thus, we have noted that

> [o]nly the actual perpetrator of the crime may be convicted of capital murder . . . Thus, neither an accessory before the fact nor a principal in the second degree may be so convicted. . . . The Commonwealth has the burden of proving beyond a reasonable doubt that one accused of capital murder was the actual perpetrator of the crime. Suspicion of guilt, however strong, or even a probability of guilt is insufficient to support a conviction.

The General Assembly has specifically limited a capital murder conviction under Code § 18.2–31(8) by its enactment of Code § 18.2–18. In doing so, the General Assembly has mandated that a principal in the second degree cannot be convicted of capital murder, but his conviction is limited to murder in the first degree. This statutory mandate is binding on the judiciary until altered by the General Assembly.

For the forgoing reasons, Muhammad's conviction and sentence for the capital murder of Dean Meyers under Code § 18.2–31(8) should be reversed and remanded according to the statutory directive of Code § 18.2–18. Accordingly, I respectfully dissent from section II(B)(1) of the majority opinion regarding the conviction and sentence under Code § 18.2–31(8). To the extent the conviction under Code § 18.2–31(13) is based upon a principal in the first-degree analysis, I respectfully dissent from section II(B)(2), but I concur in the alternative ground in section II(B)(2) and would thus affirm the conviction and sentence of death under Code § 18.2–31(13). Otherwise, I concur in the majority opinion.

NOTES

1. If defendant sells drugs to a user who then dies from an overdose, can defendant be convicted of felony-murder?

See Sheriff, Clark County v. Morris, 99 Nev. 109, 659 P.2d 852 (1983), wherein a majority of the Nevada Supreme Court held that a drug dealer could be convicted of second-degree felony-murder where he is involved in helping the recipient consume the drugs or is present when he does so. The court was careful to point out that it did not intend to hold that all deaths resulting from sales of dangerous drugs would be felony murder, but only when there is a direct and causal relationship between the defendant's act and the decedent's death.

2. Must the intent to commit the underlying felony precede the death? For a thoughtful analysis of the cases wherein the predicate intent was formed subsequent to the death of the victim, see Dana K. Cole, *Expanding Felony-Murder in Ohio: Felony-Murder or Murder-Felony?*, 63 Ohio St. L.J. 15 (2002).

People v. Salas

Supreme Court of California, 1972.
7 Cal.3d 812, 103 Cal.Rptr. 431, 500 P.2d 7.

■ WRIGHT, CHIEF JUSTICE.

* * *

On the morning of June 7, 1968, five or ten minutes after midnight, defendant entered the Hub Bar in Sacramento and asked the bartender, George Finnegan, for a six-pack of beer. After Finnegan reached into the cooler for the beer he saw that defendant was pointing a pistol directly at him. David Wright, a customer, and Richard Schwab, an insurance salesman who entered the bar at this moment, were ordered to lie down on the floor at the back of the barroom. Defendant then ordered Finnegan to deliver all the money in the bar's cash register.

The cash register had two drawers and after Finnegan had emptied the contents of one of them (amounting to about $150) into a cloth bank bag, defendant asked, "How about the other drawer on the register?" Upon being satisfied that the second drawer was empty defendant took the bank bag, ordered Finnegan to lie down near the other men, told them not to move or he would shoot them and backed out of the front door.

Defendant had been driven to the bar by Arlin Damion, a friend who remained in the car during the robbery. When defendant emerged from the bar and entered the vehicle on the passenger's side of the front seat, Damion drove away.

Shortly after midnight Deputy Sheriff George O'Neal received a radio broadcast advising that the Hub Bar had just been robbed. He immediately drove his patrol car three-tenths of a mile to an intersection 1.2 miles from the bar. He knew that this intersection was on a route frequently used by robbers in making escapes from the general area. Just as he reached the intersection he saw an approaching car with two men who appeared to be of Mexican descent. The car approached from the direction of the bar and was the only vehicle in sight. The deputy followed the car and was then advised by radio that the suspect was a "male Mexican." After further radio communication the deputy activated the red light and siren of the police vehicle and the suspects eventually stopped their vehicle.

The deputy halted his patrol car about 15 to 18 feet behind the suspects' car, stepped out and shouted to the two men to put their hands out of the car windows. Neither suspect responded to the demand; the deputy thereupon reached for his shotgun. Damion opened the door on the driver's side of his car and fled on foot into an open field. Defendant, however, did not respond to the officer's further demands.

A second deputy sheriff, Kenneth B. Royal, arrived in his patrol car. Royal drew his service revolver and walked toward the suspects' car on the driver's side. O'Neal heard shots fired and saw Royal fall to the ground. Defendant emerged from the car on the passenger's side with a gun in his hand. O'Neal fired his shotgun at defendant. Defendant fell to the ground and then arose. Royal fired his revolver, and O'Neal fired his shotgun a second time. Defendant again fell to the ground, but once more got up and continued down the road away from the deputies. Defendant fell to the ground again and was then apprehended by another officer who had arrived at the scene. Royal died of a single gunshot wound in the neck.

* * *

We deal next with defendant's contention that, as a matter of law, the robbery had been completed prior to the time of and at a different place than the killing; that the homicide therefore could not have been committed in the course of the robbery within the felony-murder rule and that the trial court erred in instructing the jury on such rule. Defendant further contends that, even assuming that instructions on the felony-murder rule were appropriate, it was error for the court to refuse to define the term "scrambling possession" as applied to the proceeds of the robbery wen requested to do so by the jury.

Section 189, which establishes the limits of the felony-first-degree-murder rule, provides that all "murder . . . which is committed in the perpetration of, or attempt to perpetrate . . . robbery . . . is murder of the first degree. . . ." Our particular concern is whether the killing of the deputy after defendant had been stopped while fleeing from the scene of the robbery, was a killing in the "perpetration" of the robbery. The trial court gave four instructions which we have numbered and set forth in the margin concerning the time within which a robbery is still in progress for purposes of application of the felony-murder rule.[5]

---

[5]   (1) A robbery is still in commission while the perpetrator is being pursued immediately after the commission of the act of taking the property of another by force or fear with the fruits of the crime in his possession so long as the culprit has not won his way even momentarily to a place of temporary safety and the possession of the plunder is nothing more than a scrambling possession.

(2) A robbery is still in commission during the continuous, integrated attempt to successfully leave with the loot.

(3) If the robbery has been completed and terminated prior to the killing, then the robbery may not be used to find the defendant guilty of murder of the first degree. Whether the killing was committed during the perpetration of the robbery must be decided by the jury.

After retiring to deliberate, the jury returned to the court requesting further instructions on . . . the law applying to "zone of danger," that is, how long a felony continues in progress. Included in the instructions read by the court pursuant to the request were the four instructions heretofore quoted. Some of them, after questions by the jurors, were read more than once. Two jurors requested that the court define "scrambling." The court, after saying that the dictionary definition would not help and that the jurors should consider the word in the context of a person fleeing from the scene of a robbery with the plunder. Approximately two hours later, the jury again returned and a juror asked the court to reread the instructions in connection with whether the robbery was in progress. The court read the instructions designated as (1) through (4) in footnote [1] several times enabling the jurors to write them down. The jury deliberated for a little more than an hour before retiring for the night and returned its verdict shortly after reconvening the following morning.

zone of danger — jury instructions

Instructions (1) and (3) appear to require that the jury find *both* that the robber did not win his way to a "place of temporary safety" *and* that his possession of the plunder was no more than a "scrambling possession" before it could find that the robbery was still in progress. Instruction (1) further requires pursuit "immediately" after the physical taking of the property. Instructions (2) and (4), on the other hand, appear to require that the jury find only that the robber did not win his way to a "place of temporary safety"—that is, that the robber was still attempting to escape—to find that the robbery was still in progress.

jury instructions

The phrases "place of temporary safety" and "scrambling possession" are derived from the landmark case of People v. Boss (1930) 210 Cal. 245, 290 P. 881. In that case two defendants robbed a store and ran into the street; an employee immediately pursued them and was shot by Boss a moment later when the furthermost defendant was no more than 125 feet from the store. We held that the trial court properly instructed the jury as to first degree felony murder as the homicide was committed in the

---

A robbery is still being committed, no matter how far from the scene of the robbery, nor how long afterward, if the robber has not won his way even momentarily to a place of temporary safety and the possession of the plunder is nothing more than a scrambling possession. (This instruction was given at defendant's request.)

(4) If the robbery has been completed and terminated prior to the killing then the robbery may not be used to find the defendant guilty of the murder of the first degree. On the other hand, the unlawful killing of a human being which is committed in the perpetration or attempt to perpetrate robbery, the commission of which crime itself must be proved beyond a reasonable doubt, is murder of the first degree whether the killing was intentional, unintentional or even accidental.

Whether the killing was committed during the perpetration of robbery must be decided by the jury.

A robbery is still being committed no matter how far from the scene of the robbery nor how long afterward if the robber has not won his way, even momentarily, to a place of temporary safety. That is to say, that a robbery is not completed at the moment the robber obtains possession of the stolen property, but is still in progress during the robber's attempt to escape with the loot. In other words, the escape of the robbers with the loot is a part of the robbery itself. (This instruction was given at the request of the prosecution.)

perpetration of a robbery and we stated: "It is a sound principle of law which inheres in common reason that where two or more persons engaged in a conspiracy to commit robbery and an officer or citizen is murdered while in immediate pursuit of one of their number who is fleeing from the scene of the crime with the fruits thereof in his possession, or in the possession of a coconspirator, the crime is not complete in the purview of the law, inasmuch as said conspirators have not won their way even momentarily to a place of temporary safety and the possession of the plunder is nothing more than a scrambling possession. In such a case the continuation of the use of arms which was necessary to aid the felon in reducing the property to possession is necessary to protect him in its possession and in making good his escape. Robbery, unlike burglary, is not confined to a fixed *locus*, but is frequently spread over considerable distance and varying periods of time. The escape of the robbers with the loot, by means of arms, necessarily is as important to the execution of the plan as gaining possession of the property. Without revolvers to terrify, or, if occasion requires, to kill any person, who attempts to apprehend them at the time of or immediately upon gaining possession of said property, their plan would be childlike. The defense of felonious possession which is challenged immediately upon the forcible taking is a part of the plan of robbery, or, as the books express it, it is *res gestae* of the crime."

* * *

The great majority of felony-murder rule cases involving robbery as the underlying felony decided by this court since *Boss* involve fact situations with both elements, continuous flight (lack of a "place of temporary safety") and continuous challenging pursuit ("scrambling possession") and generally set forth the language of *Boss* without further analysis. Thus these cases do little to clarify the question whether *both* elements are required for a robbery to be considered continuing for purposes of the felony-murder rule.

In People v. Kendrick (1961) 56 Cal.2d 71, 14 Cal.Rptr. 13, 363 P.2d 13, however, the element of "scrambling possession" was clearly missing. It was nevertheless held in that case that instructions on the felony-murder rule were properly given when the killing occurred about 48 minutes after the robbery victim had first been accosted by the defendant and when the police officer who was fatally shot by the defendant had apparently stopped him for a traffic violation and had no information about the robbery. We ignored the language in *Boss* concerning "place of temporary safety" and "scrambling possession" and quoted that part of *Boss* which stresses the importance of "[t]he escape . . . with the loot . . . to the execution of the plan," . . . Although not expressly so described, the "rule" as applied in *Kendrick* required only the element of the defendant's failure to have reached a "place of temporary safety."

People v. Ketchel (1963) 59 Cal.2d 503, 30 Cal.Rptr. 538, 381 P.2d 394 involved a fact situation with both elements present: "place of temporary safety" and "scrambling possession." Defendants attempted to bring themselves within *Boss* and relied upon the language in that case which spoke of both "a place of temporary safety" and "scrambling possession." In rejecting their contention we relied only upon facts which established that the defendants had not reached a place of temporary safety and ignored the element of scrambling possession. That case like *Kendrick* must stand for the proposition that a fleeing robber's failure to reach a place of temporary safety is alone sufficient to establish the continuity of the robbery within the felony-murder rule.

In the present case as in *Ketchel*, the homicide was committed before defendant had reached a place of safety while he "was in hot flight with the stolen property and in the belief that the officer was about to arrest him for the robbery." Deputy O'Neal commenced to follow defendant's vehicle within three minutes of the time defendant left the bar and the killing occurred within six or seven minutes of that time. Thus the robbery was still in the escape stage, as conceded by defendant at trial. Defendant testified not only that he was caught while attempting to escape with the loot, but also that he did not know whether he would split the loot with Damion as they had had no opportunity to make that determination.

Under the circumstances here present and even if the killing were accidental or unintentional as contended by defendant, it occurred while the robbery continued in progress and constituted first degree murder under the felony-murder rule. Although the introduction in the instructions to the jury of concepts of immediate pursuit together with scrambling possession and the court's refusal to define "scrambling possession" may have been erroneous, no prejudice resulted to defendant as in any event the jurors were compelled to find that the homicide was committed before defendant had reached a place of safety. The introduction of the pursuit and scrambling concepts did in fact confer benefits to which defendant was not entitled . . .

The judgment, insofar as it provides for the penalty of death, is modified to provide in place of the death penalty a punishment of life imprisonment and as so modified is affirmed in all other respects.

■ TOBRINER, MOSK, BURKE, and SULLIVAN, JJ., concur.

■ PETERS, J., dissenting.

I dissent.

The majority have extended the felony-murder rule and repudiated in part the landmark decision in People v. Boss (1930) 210 Cal. 245, 290 P. 881. I would adhere to the decision in *Boss*, and when this is done, it is clear that prejudicial error occurred in instructing the jury on the felony-murder doctrine thus requiring reversal of the judgment.

Section 189 of the Penal Code, which establishes the felony-first-degree-murder rule, provides that all "murder . . . which is committed in the perpetration of, or attempt to perpetrate . . . robbery . . . is murder of the first degree; . . ."

Section 211 of the Penal Code defines robbery as "the felonious taking of personal property in the possession of another, from his person or immediate presence, and against his will, accomplished by means of force or fear."

A literal reading of the sections, in light of the requirement of commission in the perpetration of the robbery and in light of the definition of robbery, would mean that the homicide must occur during the taking of the property and prior to the termination of the force and fear by which the taking was accomplished.

However, this court rejected a literal construction of the two statutes in People v. Boss, supra, and established a broader rule for determining whether a homicide occurred in the perpetration of the robbery or after its termination. In expanding the operation of the felony-murder rule in the robbery situation, the court in *Boss* established two limitations on the continuation of the robbery. Today, the majority repudiate one of the limitations and to that extent overrule *Boss*. I cannot agree with the further expansion of the felony-murder doctrine.

* * *

The court [in *Boss*] thus established two requirements to establish that the robbery was not complete. First, there must be "immediate pursuit" which means that the possession is merely a "scrambling possession." This limitation finds some support in the language of the robbery statute because, so long as there is "immediate pursuit" and a mere "scrambling possession," it can be argued that the "taking" of the property is not complete because it is being physically disputed. Second, the robbers must not have reached "a place of temporary safety."

The majority today recognize but repudiate the first limitation, holding that the sole test is a place of temporary safety. In doing so, the majority rely upon People v. Ketchel, 59 Cal.2d 503, 30 Cal.Rptr. 538, 381 P.2d 394, and People v. Kendrick, 56 Cal.2d 71, 14 Cal.Rptr. 13, 363 P.2d 13. *Ketchel*, however, on its facts involved a homicide which occurred within both limitations. There was immediate pursuit with the resulting mere scrambling possession, and the robbers had not reached a place of temporary safety. Although the court spoke only of the failure to reach a place of temporary safety in connection with the defendants' contention, this was because the defendants' contention was based on the temporary-safety language in *Boss*. There was no intent to depart from the immediate pursuit and scrambling possession limitation; the court in fact quoted that limitation from *Boss*.

It is true that in *Kendrick* there was no immediate pursuit or scrambling possession and that the court, although citing and relying upon *Boss*, merely relied upon the failure of the robber to reach a point of temporary safety in upholding instructions on the felony-murder rule. However, I do not believe that *Kendrick* may be viewed as substantial authority warranting repudiation of the limitation of immediate pursuit and scrambling possession and of *Boss* and the numerous cases which have followed it. The defendant in that case urged that the homicide was too distant in time and place to classify it as having occurred during perpetration of the robbery. So far as appears, the defendant did not rely on the limitation of immediate pursuit and scrambling possession, and in answering the specific contention of defendant, it was proper to point out that *Boss* had established a rule which meant that it was not determinative that the homicide occurred some distance from the robbery and sometime later. Under the circumstances, it seems improper to hold that the court intended to repudiate one of the requirements of *Boss*, the case which was quoted from and principally relied upon.

Apart from their reliance on *Ketchel* and *Kendrick*, the majority give no reason to repudiate the first limitation of *Boss*, and in my view, those cases provide a weak foundation for the majority's action . . .

The felony-murder doctrine ascribes malice aforethought to the felon who kills in the perpetration of an inherently dangerous felony and classifies the offense as murder of the first degree in homicides which are the direct result of those six felonies enumerated in section 189 of the Penal Code . . .

"The felony-murder rule has been criticized on the grounds that in almost all cases in which it is applied it is unnecessary and that it erodes the relation between criminal liability and moral culpability." The rule has been abolished in England where it had its origin (English Homicide Act, § 1, 1957, 5 & 6 Eliz. II, ch. 11.) We have recently pointed out that the rule "expresses a highly artificial concept that deserves no extension beyond its required application." (People v. Phillips, 64 Cal.2d 574, 582, 51 Cal.Rptr. 225, 232, 414 P.2d 353, 360.) Although the rule remains the law in this state, I do not believe we should extend its applicability by broadly defining the term robbery; instead in furtherance of the policy to equate criminal liability with culpability we should strictly limit the meaning of the term robbery as used in section 189.

To extend the felony-murder rule until the robber has reached a place of temporary safety, without regard to whether the decedent is a victim or witness of the crime and without regard to whether there has been a break in the pursuit, would mean that the death of victims of automobile collisions or of pedestrians occurring accidentally during an escape may constitute first degree murder. In the absence of a direct pursuit by victims or witnesses, such a broad application of the first degree felony-murder rule to accidental killings is not in accord with the purpose of the rule or the language of the statutes.

Once we depart from the literal definition of robbery in section 211 of the Penal Code, any test that might be used to determine whether a robbery is complete for purposes of the felony-murder rule is necessarily arbitrary. The place of temporary safety, or continuous flight, test is not directly related either to the increased foreseeable danger caused by the robbery or to the robber's motive in seeking to escape detection. The increased risk of a killing occurring due to the commission of the robbery continues long after the robber reaches a place of temporary safety for he will continue to have the motive to kill to escape apprehension. In other words, the risk of injury or death to investigating officers seeking to apprehend the criminal may relate to whether the robber has the loot, is armed, or anticipates conviction, but it bears little relationship to whether the robber has reached a place of temporary safety.

A test based solely on place of temporary safety makes the *length* of the escape route the decisive consideration. If the robber leaves the scene of the robbery and reaches his hideout or home near the scene, the felony-murder rule is inapplicable under the place-of-temporary-safety test whether he is armed or still in possession of the loot, but if he must cross the city to his hideout and the homicide occurs prior to his doing so, the test would make the felony-murder rule applicable although the robber was not armed, he had lost or disposed of the loot, a pedestrian was killed, and the homicide occurred a substantial time after the taking of the property and the termination of the force and fear incident to it.

On the other hand, the limitation to immediate pursuit and scrambling possession, as we have seen, finds some support in the definition of robbery in section 211 of the Penal Code. Although this court may refuse to adhere to the literal wording of the statute as was done in *Boss* and the case following it, we should not ignore the terms of the statute entirely. Where there is immediate pursuit by victims or witnesses of the taking or of the force and fear used in the robbery, the risk of injury or death is greatly increased, and it is not the same risk as exists with regard to apprehension occurring subsequent to the taking.

* * *

Accordingly, I would not repudiate either of the limitations established in *Boss* and the cases which have followed it.

As the majority point out, the evidence in the instant case is sufficient to warrant a finding of first degree murder on a theory of premeditation. . . . The felony-murder instructions, however, permitted a finding of first degree murder even if the shooting was inadvertent or unintentional, and in view of the jury's express concern with the felony-murder instructions, the error must be held prejudicial.

I would reverse the judgment.

NOTES

1. Compare the principal case with Commonwealth v. Doris, 287 Pa. 547, 135 A. 313 (1926). Doris and three companions robbed the occupants of a bank car transporting funds. In the course of the robbery, Doris was captured; however, his companions fled from the scene. In the chase that followed, one of the pursuing policemen was shot and killed by the felons, who were captured a short time thereafter. Doris was separately tried, convicted of first degree murder committed "in the perpetration of . . . robbery", and sentenced to death. The Pennsylvania Supreme Court affirmed.

> The proof of the common purpose to take, by force, the money of the bank, carrying it away, and make a safe escape, may be inferred from the attending circumstances. Whether such a criminal intent existed was a question for the jury, and the evidence warranted their conclusion. . . . It is urged that the escape and flight are not to be considered as part of the perpetration of the robbery, which, it is claimed, had been completed . . . and thereafter no responsibility attached to any individual for the act of the other. . . . Whether the act of departing is a continuous part of the attempted or accomplished crime is for the jury.

2. The felony-murder doctrine was applied in Commonwealth v. De Moss, 401 Pa. 395, 165 A.2d 14 (1960), to convict for murder a robbery conspirator who was in another state at the time of the robbery-murder.

3. For a general discussion of the subject matter in the foregoing cases, see What Constitutes Termination of Felony for Purpose of the Felony-Murder Rule, 58 A.L.R.3d 851.

————

NOTE: THE LINDBERGH-HAUPTMANN CASE

During the evening of March 1, 1932, between the hours of eight and ten o'clock, little Charles A. Lindbergh, Jr., disappeared from the home of his parents at East Amwell, New Jersey. In the baby's room was left a letter, demanding $50,000 in ransom, and stating that later instructions as to the method of payment and the return of the child would be forthcoming. Immediately negotiations were begun by the child's father, through one Dr. J.F. Condon, with supposed agents of the child's abductors, during the course of which the baby's sleeping suit was sent by mail to Condon as evidence that the family was 'dealing with the right parties.' Subsequently, on April 2, the ransom was paid, in marked money, to a man who met Condon in a cemetery in the Bronx, New York. The baby was never returned. On May 12 his body was found in the adjoining county of Mercer, several miles from the home of his parents. An autopsy disclosed that the child had suffered three violent fractures of the skull, and that death had been instantaneous.

As a result of investigations covering many months, the defendant was arrested on October 8, 1934, and indicted for first-degree murder. The indictment charged the killing of a human being during the commission of a burglary. On this charge he was convicted and sentenced to death. Held: on appeal, affirmed. There was adequate evidence to establish common-law burglary and a killing resulting therefrom: State v. Hauptmann, 115 N.J.L. 412, 180 A. 809 (1935)"[1]

The burglary with which the defendant was charged in the indictment was breaking and entering the Lindbergh home, in the nighttime, with intent to steal *the sleeping suit of the child*. Legally, Hauptmann was electrocuted because he caused the death of a child in the course of stealing its sleeping suit.

Why did the result in the Hauptmann case rest upon such a technicality? Although any child kidnaping case attracts a great deal of public attention, there was an added factor here: the victim was the son of the famous Charles A. Lindbergh, the first person to fly the Atlantic Ocean alone, and his flight was only six years old in the public memory. Accordingly, the public demanded a death penalty. In this regard, however, the prosecution was faced with several difficulties. Kidnaping itself was only a "high misdemeanor" in New Jersey and not punishable with death. The death penalty could be awarded only for premeditated murder, common law felony murder, and statutory felony murder—the killing of another during the commission of (or attempt to commit) arson, burglary, rape, robbery or sodomy. Because the state had no evidence that Hauptmann had a preconceived intent to kill the child, and accordingly could not proceed on the theory of premeditated murder, the prosecution was forced to seek a conviction of felony murder, either at common law or under the statute. Since kidnaping was not among the crimes enumerated in the felony murder statute, and inasmuch as it was not a felony under the common law, a killing arising out of a kidnaping would not sustain a death penalty sentence. Accordingly, the prosecution's only possible course lay in charging that the killing occurred during the commission of a burglary, although the only thing which Hauptmann took in addition to the child (who, under the common law, could not be a subject of larceny) was the sleeping suit it wore.

The defense contended that the evidence did not show the commission of a burglary. It was argued that there was no evidence of the required intent to steal the sleeping garment, since it was surrendered by the defendant of his own volition. It was held, however, that the evidence showed the commission of a burglary, in that the jury could find that the defendant took the sleeping suit for his own advantage in furthering the plan of extortion, and that he would not have returned the sleeping suit had the preliminaries of the extortion been unsuccessful.

Thus the felony murder doctrine, possibly stretched to the utmost limits of application, was employed to obtain the result desired by the prosecution and demanded by public sentiment. The case affords an interesting study of the effect a heinous offense may have upon judicial reasoning and the criminal law generally.

---

[1]   Comment, *Recent Criminal Cases*, 26 J. Am. Inst. Crim. L. & Criminology 759 (1935).

———

NOTE

Modern kidnaping statutes typically are felonies, thereby avoiding the dilemma created for the prosecution in the *Hauptmann* case.

NOTE: ELIMINATION OF THE FELONY-MURDER RULE

In People v. Aaron, 409 Mich. 672, 299 N.W.2d 304 (1980) the Supreme Court of Michigan stated:

> Whatever reasons can be gleaned from the dubious origin of the felony-murder rule to explain its existence, those reasons no longer exist today. Indeed, most states, including our own, have recognized the harshness and inequity of the rule as is evidenced by the numerous restrictions placed on it. . . . Today we exercise our role in the development of the common law by abrogating the common-law felony-murder rule.

The Court suggested that, as a practical matter, the felony-murder rule is not needed because in most traditional "felony murder" situations, the existence of implied malice can be proved by other evidence than that of the underlying felony (i.e. use of deadly weapon; doing an act creating a great probability of death or great bodily harm, etc.).

Much of this Casebook's material has been devoted to a discussion of decisions that limit the common law felony murder rule. Some opinions have been critical of the rule, like *Aaron*, and condemn it as an anachronistic and unnecessary part of the criminal law. As was noted in Justice Peters' dissent in *People v. Salas*, the United Kingdom abolished the rule when it revised the English Homicide Act of 1957. Yet, most legislatures that have amended criminal statutes have chosen to retain the rule in the face of scorn and criticism heaped upon the felony murder doctrine by scholars and some courts. This raises the question whether there are legitimate contemporary purposes served by a retention of the concept of punishing as murder conduct that does not exhibit the "malice" blameworthiness traditionally associated with that crime.

Virginia, apart from its first degree murder statute, which incorporates specific felonies, also has a separate offense called Felony Homicide, which is defined as "[t]he killing of one accidentally, contrary to the intention of the parties, while in the prosecution of some felonious act other than those specified in §§ 18.2–31 [capital murders] and 18.2–32 [first degree murders]." Va.Code Ann. § 18.2–33.

B. VOLUNTARY MANSLAUGHTER

Consider the discussions on the distinction between two types of intentional killings—murder and voluntary manslaughter—in the case of *Commonwealth v. Webster, supra* p. 467.

At common law, manslaughter was considered to be a form of mitigated murder which deserved a lesser sentence than murder—a killing with "malice aforethought." The fact finder confronted with evidence of the circumstances under which a killing occurred may consider an intentional killing to be voluntary manslaughter if the act occurred in the heat of passion after the victim had "provoked" the killer.

Assume a victim taunts a defendant in a manner that causes defendant to lose control over his passions, and he thereafter kills that person. Does it matter that the killing took place three days after the provocation for it occurred? Cases dealing with the issue suggest that in order for voluntary manslaughter to be an appropriate fact finding, the killing must occur reasonably soon after the provocation occurred and before the defendant's "blood had cooled." How soon is that?

What is considered either "reasonable" or "lawful" provocation? Is the jury permitted to take into account particular characteristics of a defendant that may make him more susceptible to loss of control over his emotions? Or does the "reasonable person" test apply?

The case in this section, and the Notes following, explore these issues.

While voluntary manslaughter has traditionally been defined as a "heat of passion" killing, many courts also recognize, as voluntary manslaughter, those killings which result from mutual quarrel or combat, as well as those which occur when a defendant kills the victim while unreasonably believing he is using justifiable deadly force. See, Part C of this Chapter *infra*.

In 1987, Illinois did away with its offense of voluntary manslaughter and renamed it murder in the second degree. For an extensive analysis of what prompted the change and the anticipated difficulties flowing from it, see James B. Haddad, *Second Degree Murder Replaces Voluntary Manslaughter in Illinois: Problems Solved, Problems Created*, 19 Loyola U. Chi. L.J. 995 (1988).

Director of Public Prosecutions Appellant v. Camplin

House of Lords, 1978.
2 W.L.R. 679.

APPEAL from the Court of Appeal.

* * *

■ LORD DIPLOCK.

My Lords, for the purpose of answering the question of law upon which this appeal will turn only a brief account is needed of the facts that have given rise to it. The respondent, Camplin, who was 15 years of age, killed a middle-aged Pakistani, Mohammed Lal Khan, by splitting his skull with a chapati pan, a heavy kitchen utensil like a rimless frying pan. At the time, the two of them were alone together in Khan's flat. At Camplin's trial for murder . . . his only defence was that of provocation so as to reduce the offence to manslaughter. According to the story that he told in the witness box . . . Khan had buggered him in spite of his resistance and had then laughed at him. Whereupon Camplin had lost his self-control and attacked Khan fatally with the chapati pan.

In his address to the jury on the defence of provocation . . . counsel for Camplin, had suggested to them that when they addressed their minds to the question whether the provocation relied on was enough to make a reasonable man do as Camplin had done, what they ought to consider was not the reaction of a reasonable adult but the reaction of a reasonable boy of Camplin's age. The judge thought that this was wrong in law. So in his summing up he took pains to instruct the jury that they must consider whether:

> ". . . the provocation was sufficient to make a reasonable man in like circumstances act as the defendant did. Not a reasonable boy, as [Camplin's counsel] would have it, or a reasonable lad; it is an objective test—a reasonable man."

The jury found Camplin guilty of murder. On appeal the Court of Appeal (Criminal Division) allowed the appeal and substituted a conviction for manslaughter upon the ground that the passage I have cited from the summing up was a misdirection. The court held that

> ". . . the proper direction to the jury is to invite the jury to consider whether the provocation was enough to have made a reasonable person of the same age as the defendant in the same circumstances do as he did."

The point of law of general public importance involved in the case has been certified as being:

> Whether on the prosecution for murder of a boy of 15, where the issue of provocation arises, the jury should be directed to consider the question . . . whether the provocation was enough to make a reasonable man do as he did by reference to a "reasonable adult" or by reference to a "reasonable boy of 15."

My Lords, the doctrine of provocation in crimes of homicide has always represented an anomaly in English law. In crimes of violence which result in injury short of death, the fact that the act of violence was committed under provocation which had caused the accused to lose his self-control does not affect the nature of the offence of which he is guilty. It is merely a matter to be taken into consideration in determining the penalty which it is appropriate to impose. . . .

The doctrine of provocation has a long history of evolution at common law. . . .

For my part I find it instructive to approach this question by a brief survey of the historical development of the doctrine of provocation at common law. Its origin at a period when the penalty for murder was death is to be found . . . in Rex v. Hayward (1833) 6 C. & P. 157, 159, in "the law's compassion to human infirmity." The human infirmity upon which the law first took compassion in a violent age when men bore weapons for their own protection when going about their business appears to have been chance medley or a sudden falling out at which both parties have recourse to their weapons and fight on equal terms. . . .

The "reasonable man" was a comparatively late arrival in the law of provocation. As the law of negligence emerged in the first half of the 19th century he became the anthropomorphic embodiment of the standard of care required by the law. It would appear that [an 1869 case] was the first to make use of the reasonable man as the embodiment of the standard of self-control required by the criminal law of persons exposed to provocation; . . .

*　*　*

My Lords, this was the state of law when Bedder v. Director of Public Prosecutions [1954] 1 W.L.R. 1119 fell to be considered by this House. The accused had killed a prostitute. He was sexually impotent. According to his evidence he had tried to have sexual intercourse with her and failed. She taunted him with his failure and tried to get away from his grasp. In the course of her attempts to do so she slapped him in the face, punched him in the stomach and kicked him in the groin; whereupon he took a knife out of his pocket and stabbed her twice and caused her death. The struggle which led to her death thus started because the deceased taunted the accused with his physical infirmity; but in the state of the law as it then was taunts unaccompanied by any physical violence did not constitute provocation. The taunts were followed by violence on the part of the deceased in the course of her attempt to get away from the accused, and it may be that this subsequent violence would have a greater effect upon the self-control of an impotent man already enraged by the taunts than it would have had upon a person conscious of possessing normal physical attributes. So there might have been some justification for the judge to instruct the jury to ignore the fact that the accused was impotent when they were considering whether the deceased's conduct amounted to such provocation as would cause a reasonable or ordinary person to lose his self-control. This indeed appears to have been the ground on which the Court of Criminal Appeal had approved the summing up when they said:

> "no distinction is to be made in the case of a person who, though it may not be a matter of temperament, is physically impotent, is conscious of that impotence, and therefore mentally liable to be more excited unduly if he is 'twitted' or attacked on the subject of that particular infirmity."

This statement, for which I have myself supplied the emphasis, was approved by Lord Simonds L.C. speaking on behalf of all the members of this House who sat on the appeal; but he also went on to lay down the broader proposition that

> "It would be plainly illogical not to recognise an unusually excitable or pugnacious temperament in the accused as a matter to be taken into account but yet to recognise for that purpose some unusual physical characteristic, be it impotence or another."

Section 3 of the Act of 1957 is in the following terms:

> "Where on a charge of murder there is evidence on which the jury can find that the person charged was provoked (whether by things done or by things said or by both together) to lose his self-control the question whether the provocation was enough to make a reasonable man do as he did shall be left to be determined by the jury; and in determining that question the jury shall take into account everything both done and said according to the effect which, in their opinion, it would have on a reasonable man."

My Lords, this section was intended to mitigate in some degree the harshness of the common law of provocation as it had been developed . . . It recognises and retains the dual test: the provocation must not only have caused the accused to lose his self-control but must also be such as might cause a reasonable man to react to it as the accused did. Nevertheless it brings about two important changes in the law. The first is: it abolishes all previous rules of law as to what can or cannot amount to provocation and in particular the rule of law that, save in the two exceptional cases I have mentioned, words unaccompanied by violence could not do so. Secondly it makes it clear that if there was any evidence that the accused himself at the time of the act which caused the death in fact lost his self-control in consequence of some provocation however slight it might appear to the judge, he was bound to leave to the jury the question, which is one of opinion not of law: whether a reasonable man might have reacted to that provocation as the accused did.

* * *

Although it is now for the jury to apply the "reasonable man" test, it still remains for the judge to direct them what, in the new context of the section, is the meaning of this apparently inapt expression, since powers of ratiocination bear no obvious relationship to powers of self-control. . . .

As I have already pointed out, for the purposes of the law of provocation the "reasonable man" has never been confined to the adult male. It means an ordinary person of either sex, not exceptionally excitable or pugnacious, but possessed of such powers of self-control as everyone is entitled to expect that his fellow citizens will exercise in society as it is today. A crucial factor in the defence of provocation from earliest times has been the relationship between the gravity of provocation and the way in which the accused retaliated, both being judged by the social standards of the day. When Hale was writing in the seventeenth century, pulling a man's nose was thought to justify retaliation with a sword; when Mancini v. Director of Public Prosecutions, [1942] A.C. 1, was decided by this House, a blow with a fist would not justify retaliation with a deadly weapon. But so long as words unaccompanied by violence could not in law amount to provocation the relevant proportionality between provocation and retaliation was primarily one of degrees of violence. Words spoken to the accused before the violence started were not normally to be included in the proportion sum. But now that the law has been changed so as to permit of words being treated as provocation even though unaccompanied by any other acts, the gravity of verbal provocation may well depend upon the particular characteristics or circumstances of the person to whom a taunt or insult is addressed. To taunt a person because of his race, his physical infirmities or some shameful incident in his past may well be considered by the jury to be more offensive to the person addressed, however equable his temperament, if the facts on which the taunt is founded are true than it would be if they were not. It would stultify much of the mitigation of the previous harshness of the common law in ruling out verbal provocation as capable of reducing murder to manslaughter if the jury could not take into consideration all those factors which in their opinion would affect the gravity of taunts or insults when applied to the person whom they are addressed. So to this extent at any rate the unqualified proposition accepted by this House in *Bedder* that for the purposes of the "reasonable man" test any unusual physical characteristics of the accused must be ignored requires revision as a result of the passing of the Act of 1957.

That he was only 15 years of age at the time of the killing is the relevant characteristic of the accused in the instant case. It is a characteristic which may have its effects on temperament as well as physique. If the jury think that the same power of self-control is not to be expected in an ordinary, average or normal boy of 15 as in an older person, are they to treat the lesser powers of self-control possessed by an ordinary, average or normal boy of 15 as the standard of self-control with which the conduct of the accused is to be compared?

It may be conceded that in strict logic there is a transition between treating age as a characteristic that may be taken into account in assessing the gravity of the provocation addressed to the accused and treating it as a characteristic to be taken into account in determining what is the degree of self-control to be expected of the ordinary person with whom the accused's conduct is to be compared. But to require old heads upon young shoulders is inconsistent with the law's compassion to human infirmity to which Sir Michael Foster ascribed the doctrine of provocation more than two centuries ago. The distinction as to the purposes for which it is legitimate to take the age of the accused into account involves considerations of too great nicety to warrant a place in deciding a matter of opinion, which is no longer one to be decided by a judge trained in logical reasoning but is to be decided by a jury drawing on their experience of how ordinary human beings behave in real life.

* * *

I accordingly agree with the Court of Appeal that the judge ought *[handwritten: Affirmed]* not to have instructed the jury to pay no account to the age of the accused even though they themselves might be of opinion that the degree of self-control to be expected in a boy of that age was less than in an adult. So to direct them was to impose a fetter on the right and duty of the jury which the Act accords to them to act upon their own opinion on the matter.

I would dismiss this appeal.

* * *

[All other Lords voted to dismiss the appeal. Their statements are omitted.]

———————

NOTE

Subsequently, the House of Lords, in Regina v. Smith, [2001] AC 1466, ruled 3-to-2 that the trial judge erred when he instructed the jury that they should ignore psychiatric evidence that the defendant suffered from clinical depression which made him susceptible to erupt "with violence" and lose control over his reactions in considering whether defendant was provoked. The opinion by Lord Hoffmann suggested the evidence should have been presented to the jury, which was the ultimate arbiter of whether provocation existed. In considering the evidence, "The jury must think that the circumstances were such as to make the loss of self-control sufficiently *excusable* to reduce the gravity of the offence from murder to manslaughter."

NOTE: WHAT CONSTITUTES PROVOCATION

In situations where a homicide is committed in the heat of passion brought on by provoking circumstances, several types of provocation have traditionally been recognized as legally sufficient to reduce the grade of the homicide from murder to voluntary manslaughter. The cases listed are representative of the wide array of approaches taken by various courts.

(a) *Assault and Battery*. The law takes account of the possibility that *[handwritten: Assault & battery]* an assault and battery may so provoke a "reasonable man" that he may lose his powers of reason and judgment and kill as a consequence. The states are not uniform, however, in their treatment of this type of provocation.

Some jurisdictions follow a flexible rule and regard assault alone as legally adequate provocation where the particular circumstances appear sufficient to excite the passions of a reasonable man. Thus, in Beasley v. State, 64 Miss. 518, 8 So. 234 (1886), adequate provocation was held to exist where the defendant shot the deceased after the latter had first fired at the defendant and then turned to run.

Other jurisdictions, notably Missouri, require an actual battery, as a matter of law, before sufficient provocation is deemed to exist. Under this rule, it was held, for example, that where the deceased had chased the defendant with an axe and then broke into the latter's house, threatening to kill him, the defendant, who shot the deceased, had no right to an instruction on voluntary manslaughter, since there had been no actual battery. State v. Kizer, 360 Mo. 744, 230 S.W.2d 690 (1950).

Ordinarily, a battery that is no more than "technical" is regarded as too slight to qualify as legal incitement to homicide. Commonwealth v. Cisneros, 381 Pa. 447, 113 A.2d 293 (1955). Moreover, a battery that is somewhat more than "technical" may occasionally be held insufficient as a matter of law where the court concludes that the provocation was insufficient under the circumstances to cause a reasonable person to kill. In Commonwealth v. Webb, 252 Pa. 187, 97 A. 189 (1916), the defendant's wife (5'7"; 200+ lbs.) hit the defendant (6'; 165 lbs.) with a fifteen-inch poker. He retaliated with five mortal razor slashes. The Supreme Court of Pennsylvania, after discussing the comparative sizes of defendant and his wife, and noting that the defendant was not left with a mark on his head from the blow he received, concluded that there was not adequate provocation for the homicide. Normally such considerations would probably be left to the jury; the court apparently felt, however, that the defendant's brutality was out of all proportion to the nature of the provocation.

(b) *Adultery.* Adultery, under common law principles, constituted sufficient provocation where a husband discovered his wife in the act of intercourse and kills either her or her paramour. Sheppard v. State, 243 Ala. 498, 10 So.2d 822 (1942). It had also been held that adequate provocation exists where a mistake of fact could lead to the homicide, as in the case of the husband finding his wife in suspicious circumstances and having a reasonable belief that she has committed adultery. State v. Yanz, 74 Conn. 177, 50 A. 37 (1901).

In marked contrast to the common law, under which paramour killings are manslaughter at least, several states had statutes, now repealed, which provided that such killings were *justifiable*. The following provision was contained in Article 1220 of the Texas Penal Code:

> Homicide is justifiable when committed by the husband upon one taken in the act of adultery with the wife, provided the killing takes place before the parties to the act have separated. Such circumstances cannot justify a homicide when it appears that there has been on the part of the husband, any connivance in or assent to the adulterous connection.

As interpreted in Price v. State, 18 Tex.App. 474 (1885), the above statement "taken in the act of adultery" did not mean that the husband must be an actual eyewitness to the physical act. "It is sufficient if he sees them in bed together, or leaving that position, or in such a position as indicates with reasonable certainty to a rational mind that they have just then committed the adulterous act, or were then about to commit it."

Although a husband in Texas, under this earlier law, was justified in killing his wife's paramour, there was no privilege to use a razor merely to maim and torture. Sensobaugh v. State, 92 Tex.Crim.R. 417, 244 S.W. 379 (1922); *see also* Shaw v. State, 510 S.W.2d 926 (Tex. Crim. App.1974). Similar statutes were in effect in New Mexico and Utah, but they, along with the Texas statute, have been repealed.

Apart from other considerations behind the repeal of such adultery killing statutes, it will be observed that they accorded such "open season" privileges only to the husband; the wife was not accorded the same privilege as regards her adulterous husband. Clearly, this blatantly sexist approach, once so pervasive in the development of the criminal law, has no place in modern jurisprudence.

In today's society, ought the partial "heat of passion" defense, which reduces an intentional killing from murder to voluntary manslaughter upon reasonable provocation, also be extended to cover infidelity in connection with a long-standing romantic relationship in which the parties are not married? Equivocating on the issue, without resolving it is People v. McCarthy, 132 Ill.2d 331, 341, 138 Ill.Dec. 292, 302, 547 N.E.2d 459 (1989). Consider also the following thought-provoking articles: Joshua Dressler, *Men Kill "Homosexual" Men: Reflections on Provocation Law, Sexual Advances, and the "Reasonable Man" Standard*, 85 J. Crim. L. & Criminology 726 (1995); Timothy Macklen & John Gardner, *Provocation and Pluralism*, 64 Modern L. Rev. 815 (2001); Robert B. Mison, *Homophobia in Manslaughter: The Homosexual Advance as Insufficient Provocation*, 80 Cal. L. Rev. 133 (1992; James J. Sing, *Culture as Sameness: Toward a Synthetic View of Provocation and Culture in the Criminal Law*, 108 Yale L.J. 1845 (1999).

(c) *Trespass*. By one view, trespass constitutes legally sufficient provocation for a homicide committed in the heat of passion. Pearce v. State, 154 Fla. 656, 18 So.2d 754 (1944). Under another view, however, trespass is regarded as too minor an incident to qualify as legal incitement. People v. Free, 37 Ill.App.3d 1050, 347 N.E.2d 505 (1976).

(d) *Acts Against Third Persons*. It is generally held that certain acts committed by one against a close relative of the slayer constitute sufficient provocation. *See, e.g.*, People v. Rice, 351 Ill. 604, 184 N.E. 894 (1933) (murder or felonious injury); State v. Flory, 40 Wyo. 184, 276 P. 458 (1929) (rape); Toler v. State, 152 Tenn. 1, 260 S.W. 134 (1924) (seduction); State v. Burnett, 354 Mo. 45, 188 S.W.2d 51 (1945) (illegal arrest). In Commonwealth v. Paese, 220 Pa. 371, 69 A. 891 (1908), a severe beating of a friend was held to be insufficient as a matter of law, inasmuch as there was no family relationship between the slayer and the victim of the beating.

(e)   *Words and Gestures.* Strongly entrenched in the United States is the almost uniform rule that words or gestures, alone, are never sufficient provocation for an intentional homicide. A few legislatures have altered this doctrine. *See, e.g.,* People v. Valentine, 28 Cal.2d 121, 169 P.2d 1 (1946); Elsmore v. State, 132 Tex.Crim.R. 261, 104 S.W.2d 493 (1937) (interpreting legislative omission of former codification of the rule as abolishing it). For the most part, however, the states have firmly adhered to the rule, and the courts have rigidly applied it, often with harsh results. *See, e.g.,* Freddo v. State, 127 Tenn. 376, 155 S.W. 170 (1913) (deceased intentionally and continuously used epithets which he knew were highly upsetting to the defendant); Commonwealth v. Cisneros, 381 Pa. 447, 113 A.2d 293 (1955) (deceased, defendant's estranged wife, refused reconciliation, explaining in strongly insulting terms that she would not live with or have children by one who was half-Mexican and half-Puerto Rican). Occasionally sufficient provocation is held to exist where the words or gestures are accompanied by a technical battery or other minor incident. *See* Lamp v. State, 38 Ga.App. 36, 142 S.E. 202 (1928); State v. Davis, 34 S.W.2d 133 (Mo.1930). Such additional aggravations, however, are not always permitted to alter the rule. *See* Commonwealth v. Cisneros, 381 Pa. 447, 113 A.2d 293 (1955).

Under one view, informational language, as opposed to words which in themselves constitute the incitement, may qualify as adequate provocation where the fact communicated would be sufficient, and where the slayer has not previously known of the matter revealed. *See* Commonwealth v. Berry, 461 Pa. 233, 336 A.2d 262 (1975); People v. Rice, 351 Ill. 604, 184 N.E. 894 (1933). Another view, however, does not admit of this exception. *See* Humphreys v. State, 175 Ga. 705, 165 S.E. 733 (1932).

NOTE: COOLING OF BLOOD

Consider the following comments of the court in Ex parte Fraley, 3 Okl.Crim. 719, 109 P. 295 (1910), and compare them with the statements of the court on this subject in *State v. Flory, supra* p. 559:

> [I]t was stated by counsel for the petitioner . . . that the deceased, some nine or ten months previously, had shot and killed the son of the petitioner . . . and it is urged here that when the petitioner saw the deceased . . . the recollection of that event must have engendered in him a passion which overcame him; that the killing was committed in the heat of such passion, was without premeditation, and therefore was not murder. To this we cannot assent. . . . In Ragland v. State . . . four hours intervening between the provocation and the killing was held as a matter of law to be sufficient cooling time to preclude the reduction of a homicide to manslaughter. Perry v. State . . . and Rockmore v. State . . . each hold three days as a matter of law sufficient cooling time. Commonwealth v. Aiello . . . holds from one to two hours sufficient, and State v. Williams. . . holds fifteen minutes sufficient. And the authorities are all agreed that the question is not alone whether the defendant's passion in fact cooled, but also was there sufficient

time in which the passion of a reasonable man would cool. If in fact the defendant's passion did cool, which may be shown by circumstances, such as the transaction of other business in the meantime, rational conversations upon other subjects, evidence of preparation for the killing, etc., then the length of time intervening is immaterial. But if in fact it did not cool yet if such time intervened between the provocation and the killing that the passion of the average man would have cooled and his reason have resumed its sway, then still there is not reduction of the homicide to manslaughter. . . . If the fatal wound be inflicted immediately following a sufficient provocation given, then the question as to whether the defendant's passion thereby aroused had in fact cooled, or as to whether or not such time had elapsed that the passion of a reasonable man would have cooled, is a question of fact to be determined upon a consideration of all the facts and circumstances in evidence; but when an unreasonable period of time has elapsed between the provocation and the killing, then the court is authorized to say as a matter of law that the cooling time was sufficient.

See also Farr v. State, 54 Ala.App. 80, 304 So.2d 898 (1974).

With regard to the application of the "reasonable man" test in this area, compare the following statement of the court in State v. Hazlett, 16 N.D. 426, 113 N.W. 374 (1907):

> Where the evidence shows that a homicide was committed, in the heat of passion and with provocation, we think the jury, in determining whether there was sufficient cooling time for the passion to subside and reason to resume its sway, should be governed, not by the standard of an ideal, reasonable man, but they should determine such question from the standpoint of the defendant in the light of all the facts and circumstances disclosed by the evidence. . . . We are aware that some courts have held to the contrary, but we are convinced that the rule as above announced is the more reasonable and just one.

NOTE: THE SOURCE AND TARGET OF "KILLING RAGE"

1. Suppose a particularly vicious "Islamic terrorist" attack kills 10 people at the Pentagon. An outraged citizen in New York heads to the nearest mosque and kills the first Muslim he encounters. Does the citizen meet the requirements for voluntary manslaughter?

2. Suppose a citizen escapes from a painful "choke hold" placed on him by a police officer. The citizen retrieves a gun from his vehicle and shoots the arresting officer. The still enraged citizen then shoots two other police officers when they arrive as "backup" for the first officer. Does this citizen meet the requirements for voluntary manslaughter?

Commonwealth v. LeClair

Supreme Judicial Court of Massachusetts, Worcester, 2006.
445 Mass. 734.

The defendant was indicted for murder in the first degree in connection with the stabbing death of his wife. A jury in the Superior Court convicted him of murder in the second degree. On this appeal, he argues his request for a voluntary manslaughter instruction was improperly denied because he had acted in heat of passion caused by a third person, his wife's brother. We granted the defendant's application for direct appellate review and affirm his conviction.

The jury could have found the following facts. The victim returned home on the morning of January 4, 1998. The victim's brother arrived shortly thereafter and found the victim and the defendant talking in the kitchen. On her brother's arrival, the victim went outside on the back deck to smoke a cigarette. The defendant was irritated to see his brother-in-law and said, "She's not dead yet." The victim's brother then joined his sister on the deck. After about five minutes, they both went back inside the house, and the victim told the defendant that she was going to leave him. The defendant became upset. The defendant and the victim then asked her brother to go outside and wait while they finished their conversation. While outside, the victim's brother could not discern what was being said indoors, but could hear that the conversation in the kitchen was "getting loud." At some point, the victim grabbed her cigarettes, lighter, and keys, and rejoined her brother on the deck. The defendant, now visibly upset, followed. He pointed inches from his brother-in-law's face and said, "I don't want you on my fucking property." The victim's brother responded, "[A]fter everything that I heard that's going on, you don't want to mess with me." The defendant then swung at the victim's brother but missed. The two men wrestled, and the victim's brother eventually pinned the defendant to the ground. Her brother yelled to the victim to telephone the police. The victim, who had gone into the house to telephone the police, ran back outside to urge her brother to let the defendant go.

The victim's brother, who had planned to hold the defendant until the police arrived, released him when the defendant said, "Just lay off, I'm not going to do anything. I'm not going to do anything." Once released, the defendant went quickly into the kitchen and picked up a knife. The victim, who was in the kitchen on the telephone with the police, screamed, "Oh my God, he's got a knife . . . . Oh my God, he's going to stab me." The defendant grabbed the victim and, while her brother and sons looked on, raised the knife and brought it straight down into her upper arm. He then held the knife to the victim's throat and dragged her down the hallway. As the two boys ran to a neighbor's house, the defendant went toward his brother-in-law with the knife and said, "I'll fucking kill her if you don't get out of the house." The victim's brother then ran outside to wait for the police. When the police arrived, they found the defendant kneeling on the floor beside the victim, a cocked revolver at his temple. One officer told him to put the weapon down, and the defendant complied. The defendant was handcuffed and placed in the back of a police cruiser. A sergeant of the Charlton police department advised him of his Miranda rights. The defendant told the sergeant that he and the victim's brother had argued; that the victim stood between them during the argument; and that he (the defendant) had grabbed a knife and stabbed her. The victim was pronounced dead that afternoon at a hospital.

The defendant argues that he was entitled to a voluntary manslaughter instruction because he had been provoked to a point where the jury reasonably could find manslaughter by reason of his fight with the victim's brother. In support of that argument, the defendant points to language in the American Law Institute's Model Penal Code § 210.3 (1980) that would appear to support such a principle and a decision by the Supreme Court of Minnesota holding that the defense of "heat of passion" may be based on conduct of a third party and need not be caused by the victim. See *State v. Stewart,* 624 N.W.2d 585, 589 (Minn.2001). We reject the defendant's arguments and reaffirm our well-established rule that evidence of provocation by a third party, rather than the victim of a homicide, is insufficient to warrant a voluntary manslaughter instruction.

Our case law has consistently held that provocation sufficient to support an instruction of voluntary manslaughter must come from the victim. The Model Penal Code provides that a criminal homicide constitutes manslaughter when it is committed "under the influence of extreme mental or emotional disturbance for which there is reasonable explanation or excuse. The reasonableness of such explanation or excuse shall be determined from the viewpoint of a person in the actor's situation under the circumstances as he believes them to be." Model Penal Code, *supra* at § 210.3(b). According to the commentary, this provision does not require that the defendant's emotional distress arise from some "injury, affront, or other provocative act perpetrated upon him by the deceased. Under the Code, mitigation may be appropriate where the [defendant] believes that the deceased is responsible for some injustice to another or even where he strikes out in a blinding rage and kills an innocent bystander." Model Penal Code and Commentaries § 210.3 comment 5, at 61 (1980). Evidence of extreme mental or emotional disturbance is left to the jury to determine whether, in the circumstances, there is a reasonable "explanation or excuse for the [defendant's] mental condition." *Id.* We have not adopted the Model Penal Code and now decline to join its drafters in accepting the principle that reasonable provocation should not have to come from the victim.

As noted, the highest court of at least one State has applied the reasoning of the Model Penal Code to a murder case involving assertions of provocation by a third party. In *State v. Stewart*, 624 N.W.2d 585 (Minn.2001), the court was called to interpret statutory language defining the crime of manslaughter as "intentionally caus[ing] the death of another person in the heat of passion provoked by such words or acts of another as would provoke a person of ordinary self-control under like circumstances." The defendant in that case was indicted and tried on counts of murder in the first and second degrees for the stabbing deaths of a woman, their two year old son, and her unborn child, in a fit of rage after the victim disclosed to the defendant that she was HIV positive. Although the trial judge had instructed the jury as to manslaughter in connection with the deaths of the woman and the unborn child, he refused to so instruct the jury in connection with the death of the two year old, on the ground that the boy was not involved in the provocation. The fundamental question presented to the Minnesota Supreme Court thus was whether the Legislature intended that the statutory designations of "another person" (in reference to the victim) and "another" (in reference to the provocateur) must be the same person. The court concluded that "[t]he plain wording of the statute suggests that the [L]egislature did not intend them to be the same person." *Id.* at 589. Turning to the legislative history of § 609.20, the court noted that the statute was adopted as part of Minnesota's revised criminal code soon after the American Law Institute adopted the Model Penal Code. *Id.* (noting comment on § 609.20 by advisory committee on criminal law revision stated approval of Model Penal Code). The court recognized, as we have recognized above, that § 210.3 of the Model Penal Code focuses almost exclusively on the extreme mental state of the defendant and not on the source of the provocation. The defendant argues that we should join the debate concerning the nature of provocation adequate to justify a manslaughter instruction and adopt the modern view that a defendant should not be precluded, as a matter of law, from receiving a voluntary manslaughter instruction, simply because the source of the defendant's provocation is a third party rather than the victim. We have previously rejected similar requests. We reject this one as well.

Our position reaffirms our case law and follows the prevailing view of other States that have considered this subject. It is also the view subscribed to by authoritative commentators on criminal law. According to one such commentator, "[t]he courts have quite consistently held that the killing of [one known to be an innocent bystander] does not qualify as manslaughter, apparently upon the assumption that a reasonable man would never be so greatly provoked as to strike out in blind anger at an innocent person." 2 W.R. LaFave, Substantive Criminal Law § 15.2(g), at 511 (2d ed.2003). To hold otherwise would open up the law of voluntary manslaughter to far-reaching claims of heat of passion and provocation that are well beyond its common-law antecedents.

Here, the victim went inside to call for help on the telephone when her husband confronted her brother outside. After her brother had restrained the defendant, she asked her brother to let him go. She then returned to the kitchen to telephone the police. The defendant ran directly into the kitchen, picked up a knife, grabbed the victim from behind and stabbed her. Clearly, the moments leading up the killing were emotionally charged. Just as clearly, however, there is no view of the evidence that would permit a determination that the victim played even an inconsequential role in provoking her own death. The judge correctly refused to instruct the jury on voluntary manslaughter.

C. JUSTIFIABLE USE OF DEADLY FORCE

1. SELF DEFENSE

People v. Goetz
Court of Appeals of New York, 1986.
68 N.Y.2d 96, 506 N.Y.S.2d 18, 497 N.E.2d 41.

■ CHIEF JUDGE WACHTLER.

A Grand Jury has indicted defendant on attempted murder, assault, and other charges for having shot and wounded four youths on a New York City subway train after one or two of the youths approached him and asked for $5. The lower courts, concluding that the prosecutor's charge to the Grand Jury on the defense of justification was erroneous, have dismissed the attempted murder, assault and weapons possession charges. We now reverse and reinstate all counts of the indictment.

I.

The precise circumstances of the incident giving rise to the charges against defendant are disputed, and ultimately it will be for a trial jury to determine what occurred. We feel it necessary, however, to provide some factual background to properly frame the legal issues before us. Accordingly, we have summarized the facts as they appear from the evidence before the Grand Jury. We stress, however, that we do not purport to reach any conclusions or holding as to exactly what transpired or whether defendant is blameworthy. The credibility of witnesses and the reasonableness of defendant's conduct are to be resolved by the trial jury.

On Saturday afternoon, December 22, 1984, Troy Canty, Darryl Cabey, James Ramseur, and Barry Allen boarded an IRT express subway train in The Bronx and headed south toward lower Manhattan. The four youths rode together in the rear portion of the seventh car of the train. Two of the four, Ramseur and Cabey, had screwdrivers inside their coats, which they said were to be used to break into the coin boxes of video machines.

Defendant Bernhard Goetz boarded this subway train at 14th Street in Manhattan and sat down on a bench towards the rear section of the same car occupied by the four youths. Goetz was carrying an unlicensed .38 caliber pistol loaded with five rounds of ammunition in a waistband holster. The train left the 14th Street station and headed towards Chambers Street.

It appears from the evidence before the Grand Jury that Canty approached Goetz, possibly with Allen beside him, and stated "give me five dollars". Neither Canty nor any of the other youths displayed a weapon. Goetz responded by standing up, pulling out his handgun and firing four shots in rapid succession. The first shot hit Canty in the chest; the second struck Allen in the back; the third went through Ramseur's arm and into his left side; the fourth was fired at Cabey, who apparently was then standing in the corner of the car, but missed, deflecting instead off of a wall of the conductor's cab. After Goetz briefly surveyed the scene around him, he fired another shot at Cabey, who then was sitting on the end bench of the car. The bullet entered the rear of Cabey's side and severed his spinal cord.

All but two of the other passengers fled the car when, or immediately after, the shots were fired. The conductor, who had been in the next car, heard the shots and instructed the motorman to radio for emergency assistance. The conductor then went into the car where the shooting occurred and saw Goetz sitting on a bench, the injured youths lying on the floor or slumped against a seat, and two women who had apparently taken cover, also lying on the floor. Goetz told the conductor that the four youths had tried to rob him.

While the conductor was aiding the youths, Goetz headed towards the front of the car. The train had stopped just before the Chambers Street station and Goetz went between two of the cars, jumped onto the tracks and fled. Police and ambulance crews arrived at the scene shortly thereafter. Ramseur and Canty, initially listed in critical condition, have fully recovered. Cabey remains paralyzed, and has suffered some degree of brain damage.

On December 31, 1984, Goetz surrendered to police in Concord, New Hampshire, identifying himself as the gunman being sought for the subway shootings in New York nine days earlier. Later that day, after receiving *Miranda* warnings, he made two lengthy statements, both of which were tape recorded with his permission. In the statements, which are substantially similar, Goetz admitted that he had been illegally carrying a handgun in New York City for three years. He stated that he had first purchased a gun in 1981 after he had been injured in a mugging. Goetz also revealed that twice between 1981 and 1984 he had successfully warded off assailants simply by displaying the pistol.

According to Goetz's statement, the first contact he had with the four youths came when Canty, sitting or lying on the bench across from him, asked "how are you," to which he replied "fine". Shortly thereafter, Canty, followed by one of the other youths, walked over to the defendant and stood to his left, while the other two youths remained to his right, in the corner of the subway car. Canty then said "give me five dollars". Goetz stated that he knew from the smile on Canty's face that they wanted to "play with me". Although he was certain that none of the youths had a gun, he had a fear, based on prior experiences, of being "maimed".

Goetz then established "a pattern of fire," deciding specifically to fire from left to right. His stated intention at that point was to "murder [the four youths], to hurt them, to make them suffer as much as possible". When Canty again requested money, Goetz stood up, drew his weapon, and began firing, aiming for the center of the body of each of the four. Goetz recalled that the first two he shot "tried to run through the crowd [but] they had nowhere to run". Goetz then turned to his right to "go after the other two". One of these two "tried to run through the wall of the train, but * * * he had nowhere to go". The other youth (Cabey) "tried pretending that he wasn't with [the others]" by standing still, holding on to one of the subway hand straps, and not looking at Goetz. Goetz nonetheless fired his fourth shot at him. He then ran back to the first two youths to make sure they had been "taken care of". Seeing that they had both been shot, he spun back to check on the latter two. Goetz noticed that the youth who had been standing still was now sitting on a bench and seemed unhurt. As Goetz told the police, "I said '[y]ou seem to be all right, here's another' ", and he then fired the shot which severed Cabey's spinal cord. Goetz added that "if I was a little more under self-control * * * I would have put the barrel against his forehead and fired." He also admitted that "if I had had more [bullets], I would have shot them again, and again, and again."

II.

After waiving extradition, Goetz was brought back to New York and arraigned on a felony complaint charging him with attempted murder and criminal possession of a weapon. The matter was presented to a Grand Jury in January 1985, with the prosecutor seeking an indictment for attempted murder, assault, reckless endangerment, and criminal possession of a weapon. . . . On January 25, 1985, the Grand Jury indicted defendant on one count of criminal possession of a weapon in the *charges* third degree for possessing the gun used in the subway shootings, and two counts of criminal possession of a weapon in the fourth degree for possessing two other guns in his apartment building. It dismissed, however, the attempted murder and other charges stemming from the shootings themselves.

Several weeks after the Grand Jury's action, the People, asserting that they had newly available evidence, moved for an order authorizing them to resubmit the dismissed charges to a second Grand Jury. . . . Presentation of the case to the second Grand Jury began on March 14,

1985. Two of the four youths, Canty and Ramseur, testified. Among the other witnesses were four passengers from the seventh car of the subway who had seen some portions of the incident. Goetz again chose not to testify, though the tapes of his two statements were played for the grand jurors, as had been done with the first Grand Jury.

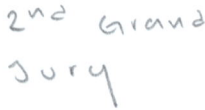

On March 27, 1985, the second Grand Jury filed a 10-count indictment, containing four charges of attempted murder, four charges of assault in the first degree, one charge of reckless endangerment in the first degree, and one charge of criminal possession of a weapon in the second degree [possession of loaded firearm with intent to use it unlawfully against another] . . .

On October 14, 1985, Goetz moved to dismiss the charges contained in the second indictment . . .

On November 25, 1985, while the motion to dismiss was pending before Criminal Term, a column appeared in the New York Daily News containing an interview which the columnist had conducted with Darryl Cabey the previous day in Cabey's hospital room. The columnist claimed that Cabey had told him in this interview that the other three youths had all approached Goetz with the intention of robbing him. The day after the column was published, a New York City police officer informed the prosecutor that he had been one of the first police officers to enter the subway car after the shootings, and that Canty had said to him "we were going to rob [Goetz]". The prosecutor immediately disclosed this information to the court and to defense counsel, adding that this was the first time his office had been told of this alleged statement and that none of the police reports filed on the incident contained any such information . . .

In an order dated January 21, 1986, Criminal Term granted Goetz's motion to the extent that it dismissed all counts of the second indictment, other than the reckless endangerment charge, . . .

* * *

On appeal by the People, a divided Appellate Division affirmed Criminal Term's dismissal of the charges . . .

* * *

Justice Asch granted the People leave to appeal to this court . . .

III.

Penal Law article 35 recognizes the defense of justification, which "permits the use of force under certain circumstances". One such set of circumstances pertains to the use of force in defense of a person, encompassing both self-defense and defense of a third person. Penal Law § 35.15(1) sets forth the general principles governing all such uses of force: "[a] person may * * * use physical force upon another person when and to the extent he *reasonably believes* such to be necessary to defend himself or a third person from what he *reasonably believes* to be the use or imminent use of unlawful physical force by such other person" (emphasis added).

[handwritten margin note: physical force can be used if reasonable]

Section 35.15(2) sets forth further limitations on these general principles with respect to the use of "deadly physical force": "A person may not use deadly physical force upon another person under circumstances specified in subdivision one unless (a) He *reasonably believes* that such other person is using or about to use deadly physical force * * * or (b) He *reasonably believes* that such other person is committing or attempting to commit a kidnapping, forcible rape, forcible sodomy or robbery" (emphasis added).

Thus, consistent with most justification provisions, Penal Law § 35.15 permits the use of deadly physical force only where requirements as to triggering conditions and the necessity of a particular response are met. As to the triggering conditions, the statute requires that the actor "reasonably believes" that another person either is using or about to use deadly physical force or is committing or attempting to commit one of certain enumerated felonies, including robbery. As to the need for the use of deadly physical force as a response, the statute requires that the actor "reasonably believes" that such force is necessary to avert the perceived threat.

Because the evidence before the second Grand Jury included statements by Goetz that he acted to protect himself from being maimed or to avert a robbery, the prosecutor correctly chose to charge the justification defense in section 35.15 to the Grand Jury. The prosecutor properly instructed the grand jurors to consider whether the use of deadly physical force was justified to prevent either serious physical injury or a robbery, and, in doing so, to separately analyze the defense with respect to each of the charges. He elaborated upon the prerequisites for the use of deadly physical force essentially by reading or paraphrasing the language in Penal Law § 35.15. The defense does not contend that he committed any error in this portion of the charge.

When the prosecutor had completed his charge, one of the grand jurors asked for clarification of the term "reasonably believes". The prosecutor responded by instructing the grand jurors that they were to consider the circumstances of the incident and determine "whether the defendant's conduct was that of a reasonable man in the defendant's situation". It is this response by the prosecutor—and specifically his use of "a reasonable man"—which is the basis for the dismissal of the charges by the lower courts. As expressed repeatedly in the Appellate Division's plurality opinion, because section 35.15 uses the term "*he* reasonably believes", the appropriate test, according to that court, is whether a defendant's beliefs and reactions were "reasonable to *him*". Under that reading of the statute, a jury which believed a defendant's testimony that he felt that his own actions were warranted and were reasonable would have to acquit him, regardless of what anyone else in defendant's situation might have concluded. Such an interpretation defies the ordinary meaning and significance of the term "reasonably" in a statute, and misconstrues the clear intent of the Legislature, in enacting section 35.15, to retain an objective element as part of any provision authorizing the use of deadly physical force. . . .

* * *

Goetz also argues that the introduction of an objective element will preclude a jury from considering factors such as the prior experiences of a given actor and thus, require it to make a determination of "reasonableness" without regard to the actual circumstances of a particular incident. This argument, however, falsely presupposes that an objective standard means that the background and other relevant characteristics of a particular actor must be ignored. To the contrary, we have frequently noted that a determination of reasonableness must be based on the "circumstances" facing a defendant or his "situation". Such terms encompass more than the physical movements of the potential assailant. As just discussed, these terms include any relevant knowledge the defendant had about that person. They also necessarily bring in the physical attributes of all persons involved, including the defendant. Furthermore, the defendant's circumstances encompass any prior experiences he had which could provide a reasonable basis for a belief that another person's intentions were to injure or rob him or that the use of deadly force was necessary under the circumstances.

Accordingly, a jury should be instructed to consider this type of evidence in weighing the defendant's actions. The jury must first determine whether the defendant had the requisite beliefs . . . , that is, whether he believed deadly force was necessary to avert the imminent use of deadly force or the commission of one of the felonies enumerated therein. If the People do not prove beyond a reasonable doubt that he did not have such beliefs, then the jury must also consider whether these beliefs were reasonable. The jury would have to determine, in light of all the "circumstances", as explicated above, if a reasonable person could have had these beliefs.

* * *

Accordingly, the order of the Appellate Division should be reversed, and the dismissed counts of the indictment reinstated.

■ MEYER, SIMONS, KAYE, ALEXANDER, TITONE and HANCOCK, JJ., concur.

Order reversed, etc.

NOTES

1. For a comment on the principal case, see, Note, *The Proper Standard for Self-Defense In New York: "Should* People v. Goetz *Be Viewed As Judicial Legislation or Judicial Restraint?",* 39 Syracuse L. Rev. 845 (1988). After one of Goetz's "victims" filed a civil law suit and won a verdict for forty-three million dollars against Goetz, the latter filed for bankruptcy on April 22, 1996.

2. Despite the fact that the statutory defense of self-defense did not explicitly include an element of imminency of the perceived danger, such imminence is required both at common law and under the applicable statute, according to the Court of Appeals of Alaska in Xi Van Ha v. State, 892 P.2d 184 (Alaska App. 1995). In this case, the defendant reasonably believed that he was in danger at some future time, that there was no escape from the person who had beaten and threatened him, and also that according to his culture (Vietnamese) no help can be expected from police because he was taught that "all police are corrupt." The majority stated the following:

> When the law states that the reasonableness of self-defense must be evaluated from the point of view of the defendant, this does not mean from the point of the mentally ill defendant. The reasonableness of a defendant's perceptions and actions must be evaluated from the point of view of a reasonable person in the defendant's situation, not a person suffering mental dysfunction.

3. Does a person who justifiably uses deadly force in self-defense by wounding the "victim" lose the benefit of the defense by failing to summon medical help? For a case exploring this issue, see State ex rel. Kuntz v. Montana Thirteenth Judicial Dist., Yellowstone Cnty., 298 Mont. 146, 995 P.2d 951 (2000). Consider, in this regard, the "American bystander rule," discussed in Chapter 2, which provides that no one has a legal duty to rescue or summon aid for another person who is at risk and the rule's exceptions.

NOTE: THE "RETREAT RULE" OR "CASTLE DOCTRINE"

The use of force to defend one's self is an undisputed right. It is only with respect to the manner in which he does it, or the circumstances under which it occurs, that there are differences and uncertainties in the law. For instance, when a person who is free from fault is faced with a threat of great bodily danger, may he stand his ground and kill his assailant, or is he under an obligation to retreat?

Model Penal Code § 3.04 (Tentative Draft No. 8) provides that:

> The use of deadly force is not justifiable . . . if the actor knows . . . that he can avoid the necessity of using such force with complete safety by retreating or by surrendering possession of a thing to a person asserting a claim of right thereto or by complying with a demand that he abstain from any action which he has no duty to take, except that:
>
> (1) the actor is not obliged to retreat from his dwelling or place of work, unless he was the initial aggressor . . .

In adopting the "retreat to the wall" doctrine the drafters of the Model Penal Code, in their commentary, offer the following justification:

There is a sense in which a duty to retreat may be regarded as a logical derivative of the underlying justifying principle of self-defense, belief in the necessity of the protective action; the actor who knows he can retreat with safety also knows that the necessity can be avoided in that way. The logic of this position never has been accepted when moderate force is used in self-defense; here all agree that the actor may stand his ground and estimate necessity upon that basis. When the resort is to deadly force, however, Beale argued that the common law was otherwise, that the law of homicide demanded that the estimation of necessity take account of the possibility of safe retreat. . . . Perkins has challenged this conclusion in the case of actors free from fault in bringing on the struggle, urging that it was only true with respect to aggressors or cases of mutual combat. . . . American jurisdictions have divided on the question, no less in crime than tort, with the preponderant position favoring the right to stand one's ground. . . . In a famous opinion Justice Holmes advanced what seems to be a median position: "Rationally the failure to retreat is a circumstance to be considered with all the others in order to determine whether the defendant went farther than he was justified in doing; not a categorical proof of guilt." . . . This would apparently remit the issue to the jury, without a legal mandate on the point . . .

The Institute has deemed considerations of this kind decisive with respect to torts and it is clear that they apply with equal force to penal law."

Id. p. 23.

In rejecting the rationale of the retreat rule, Mr. Justice Holmes said this in an early case:

Rationally, the failure to retreat is a circumstance to be considered with all the others in order to determine whether the defendant went farther than he was justified in doing; not a categorical proof of guilt. The law has grown, and even if historical mistakes have contributed to its growth, it has tended in the direction of rules consistent with human nature. Many respectable writers agree that if a man reasonably believes that he is in immediate danger of death or grievous bodily harm from his assailant, he may stand his ground, and that if he kills him, he has not exceeded the bounds of lawful self-defense. That has been the decision of this court. . . . Detached reflection cannot be demanded in the presence of an uplifted knife. Therefore, in this court, at least, it is not a condition of immunity that one in that situation should pause to consider whether a reasonable man might not think it possible to fly with safety, or to disable his assailant rather than to kill him.[2]

---

[2]   Brown v. United States, 256 U.S. 335, 343, 41 S.Ct. 501, 502, 65 L.Ed. 961 (1921).

The majority of states permit one to stand his own ground and meet force with force, as long as the defender is not the original aggressor.[3] In State v. Walton, 615 A.2d 469 (R.I.1992), the defendant was found to have no duty to retreat when attacked in his dwelling by a victim who initially entered as a social guest but became a trespasser by remaining after being ordered to leave. See also, State v. Thomas, 77 Ohio St.3d 323, 673 N.E.2d 1339 (1997) (no duty to retreat before using lethal force in self-defense against cohabitant with equal right to be in home); State v. Glowacki, 630 N.W.2d 392 (Minn. 2001) (no duty to retreat for a battered wife from an assailant (e.g., battering husband) in one's own home even when the assailant is a co-resident).

Even in those jurisdictions following the so-called "true man" rule that permits a self-defender to stand his ground, a person who "brings on the difficulty" will find that his self-defense right becomes an "imperfect" one. He may then be required to retreat before he can excusably kill, even though he used non-deadly force at the outset; and under some circumstances he is completely foreclosed and must settle, as a minimum, for a manslaughter conviction.[4]

NOTE: THE "IMPERFECT" SELF-DEFENSE

What if a defendant acted with an "imperfect" self-defense? That is, she acted under a subjective belief that the use of deadly force was necessary to prevent death or great bodily harm from occurring, but that belief was not objectively reasonable?

In Faulkner v. State, 54 Md.App. 113, 458 A.2d 81 (1983), it was said that this defense

> requires no more than a subjective honest belief on the part of the killer that his actions were necessary for his safety, even though, on an objective appraisal by a reasonable man, they would not be found to be so. If established, the killer remains culpable and his actions are excused only to the extent that mitigation is invoked. The mitigating effect of imperfect self-defense is to negate malice. It therefore serves not only to reduce murder to manslaughter in the case of a felonious homicide but applies also to the felony of assault with intent to murder.

In dissent, Judge Lowe concluded that "[t]he criminal law as an instrument of societal control cannot allow violence to be excused solely upon the whims of the perpetrator."

In a carefully reasoned opinion, and after examining all of the cases and statutes of other jurisdictions, the Maryland Court of Appeals came to the

---

[3]   WAYNE R. LAFAVE & AUSTIN WAKEMAN SCOTT, HANDBOOK ON CRIMINAL LAW 395 (1972).

The early history of the "retreat to the wall" concept is traced in Fred E. Inbau, *Firearms and Legal Doctrine*, 7 Tulane L. Rev. 529, 531–36 (1933).

[4]   For a general discussion of the "perfect" as well as the "imperfect" right to self-defense, consult Rollin M. Perkins, *Self-Defense Re-Examined*, 1 U.C.L.A.L. Rev. 133, 154–159 (1954).

same conclusion as did the majority of the Court of Special Appeals, permitting the imperfect self-defense to be used as a defense to murder to achieve, as the result, a conviction of manslaughter instead. *See* State v. Faulkner, 301 Md. 482, 483 A.2d 759 (1984).

Commonwealth v. Cary

Supreme Court of Virginia, 2006.
271 Va. 87, 623 S.E.2d 906.

■ KOONTZ, JUSTICE.

In an unpublished opinion, the Court of Appeals of Virginia vacated Rebecca Scarlett Cary's convictions in a jury trial for the first-degree murder of Mark Beekman, Code § 18.2–32, and the use of a firearm in the commission of that crime, Code § 18.2–53.1. The Court of Appeals reversed the convictions on the ground that the trial court erred in excluding evidence of Beekman's prior threats and acts of violence against Cary and in failing to grant her proffered jury instructions on self-defense, right-to-arm, and voluntary manslaughter based upon a "heat of passion" theory. We awarded the Commonwealth an appeal from the judgment of the Court of Appeals.

BACKGROUND

Because the principal issue we consider in this appeal is whether the trial court erred in refusing to grant a proper instruction of law proffered by the accused, we view the facts relevant to the determination of that issue in the light most favorable to Cary. When so viewed, the evidence at trial showed that Cary and Beekman were involved in a tumultuous relationship for more than 15 years during which time Beekman fathered three of Cary's four children. Although the two had cohabited in the past, they were not living together in 2002. They habitually argued violently regarding Beekman's failure to provide child support for his children.

On May 23, 2002, Cary purchased a handgun "to protect me and my children and our home" because she lived in a "bad neighborhood." In August 2002, Cary allegedly told Beekman's sister that she had purchased the handgun and threatened to kill Beekman because he continued to fail to provide child support. Cary allegedly made a similar statement to Tracy Tabron the day before Beekman was killed. Cary denied making these statements.

On the evening of September 6, 2002, Beekman went to Cary's apartment in the City of Norfolk. Cary detected the odor of alcohol on Beekman's person and knew from past experience that Beekman became violent when intoxicated. Post-mortem tests subsequently confirmed that Beekman had a highly-elevated blood alcohol level and also that he had recently used cocaine. The couple immediately began to quarrel over Beekman's failure to provide Cary with child support, and Beekman called Cary vulgar names and attacked her, grabbing her by the hair and hitting her in the "face and sides." Beekman refused to leave the apartment despite Cary's request that he do so.

Cary testified that when Beekman went to use the bathroom in the apartment, she decided to retrieve the handgun from where she kept it, but found that Darron, her teenage son, had already done so. Cary took the handgun from Darron and removed its ammunition clip, intending to use the apparently unloaded weapon to frighten Beekman into leaving the apartment.

When Beekman came out of the bathroom, Cary was sitting on a couch in the living room. Beekman again refused to leave the home and "was still verbally assaulting" Cary, threatening that he would "smack" her, " 'F' [her] up," and "break [her] up." As Beekman "was getting ready to come into the living room," Cary pointed the handgun at Beekman, and it discharged. The bullet struck Beekman in the chest. Cary could not "remember doing anything [to make the handgun] go off" and "believe[d] it was on safety" and unloaded. Cary subsequently testified that she thought Beekman intended to resume his physical assault on her.

Cary instructed her son to call 911 and proceeded to apply pressure to the wound in Beekman's chest. Cary pulled Beekman's body outside of the home, later explaining that she did so because "the ambulance could get to him a whole lot faster . . . instead of them having to come all through the house." Emergency medical technicians arrived and attempted to revive Beekman, but were unsuccessful.

When police arrived following the shooting, Cary first claimed that an unknown assailant had shot Beekman outside the home and that Beekman had come to the home's door "holding his chest and gasping for air." Cary repeated versions of this fabrication to the police several times that night.

she lied

When the police subsequently interviewed Cary two days after the shooting, she claimed to be unable to remember what had happened but that her memory "was starting to come back." However, she denied having a handgun in the home and when asked if she had shot Beekman, Cary responded, "I don't think so." As the interview progressed, Cary ultimately admitted to police that she had shot Beekman, but maintained that she had only intended to frighten him into leaving the home and that the handgun had discharged accidentally. Cary also told police that after the shooting, she gave the handgun to her son to give to his uncle, who disposed of it. The handgun was never recovered.

On December 4, 2002, a grand jury indicted Cary for the first-degree murder of Beekman and use of a firearm in the commission of a felony. On April 7, 2003, a jury trial commenced in the Circuit Court of the City of Norfolk (trial court) with the Commonwealth presenting evidence in accord with the above-recited facts.

Relevant to the issues raised in this appeal, during her direct testimony in her defense Cary sought to introduce evidence of Beekman's prior threats and acts of violence against her. The Commonwealth objected to the introduction of such evidence, contending that "a defendant cannot introduce evidence of a victim's reputation for violence or evidence of specific facts of violence unless the defendant first adduces evidence of self-defense." The Commonwealth asserted that because Cary was claiming the shooting occurred accidentally, she could not also claim self-defense. The Commonwealth asserted further that, in any case, there had been no evidence of any overt act by Beekman at the time of the shooting that would have placed Cary in reasonable fear for her life or safety. The Commonwealth contended that, when Beekman went to the bathroom, he had effectively ended his assault on Cary and did nothing afterwards to place her in fear.

Cary responded that she was entitled to assert concurrent claims of accident and self-defense and that these claims were not mutually exclusive. Cary contended that the evidence did show an overt act sufficient to put Cary in fear for her life or safety. Cary maintained that Beekman's uninvited presence in the home, his verbal and physical abuse of her, and his refusal to leave after repeated requests, were part of a pattern of behavior that she could have reasonably believed would continue when Beekman returned from the bathroom, given his continued verbal abuse and refusal to leave the home. Moreover, Cary maintained that the space of time between the actual assault on her and the shooting was sufficient to permit the jury to find that Cary remained in imminent danger. At this point in the proceeding, however, Cary did not assert the argument that Beekman was actually advancing toward her when the gun discharged.

Before ruling on the admissibility of the anticipated evidence of Beekman's prior acts of violence, the trial court asked Cary's counsel if she had "presented all the evidence that . . . supports the establishment of [a] prima facie case [for] self-defense . . . including overt acts in support of that particular defense." Counsel responded that the series of actions by Beekman that preceded the shooting constituted the overt act necessary to establish an apprehension of imminent harm and that it was for the jury to determine whether Cary's fear was reasonable.

The trial court then ruled that Beekman's assault on Cary prior to the shooting was not an overt act sufficient to support a claim of self-defense, agreeing with the Commonwealth that when Beekman stopped the attack to go to the bathroom, Cary was no longer in imminent danger. The trial court reasoned that Cary's presence of mind in retrieving the handgun and of removing the ammunition clip showed that she was no longer in fear. The trial court further reasoned that at the time of the shooting, Cary did not claim that she was "using that weapon to repel any act or prevent any act by [Beekman] at that moment in time."

Accordingly, the trial court ruled that Cary would not be entitled to present evidence of Beekman's prior threats and acts of violence against her and that she could not assert a defense of self-defense.

After the trial court made this ruling, Cary continued her testimony. During redirect examination, Cary testified that immediately prior to shooting Beekman, "[h]e was coming back. I am not sure whether he was walking or running." After this evidence was received, Cary did not request the trial court to reconsider its prior ruling that there was no evidence of an overt act by Beekman after he returned from the bathroom that would have caused Cary to be in reasonable fear for her life or safety.

Outside the presence of the jury, however, the trial court permitted Cary to proffer evidence of Beekman's prior threats and acts of violence against her. That evidence, presented by Cary and her son, established that Beekman had raped Cary when they first met and that he had physically abused her and her children throughout their relationship. On one occasion, Beekman cut her face with a glass, allegedly resulting in "75 stitches," and on another he broke her jaw. Beekman was particularly prone to violence when he was intoxicated.

Cary proffered instructions on the defenses of self-defense and heat of passion and further requested that the jury be instructed on the right-to-arm. Cary also sought an instruction on the lesser-included offense of voluntary manslaughter. The trial court refused these instructions.

The jury convicted Cary of both charged offenses and sentenced her to 20 years imprisonment for the first-degree murder of Beekman and three years imprisonment for the firearm offense. In an order dated September 17, 2003, the trial court imposed sentence in accord with the jury's verdicts.

Cary noted an appeal in the trial court and filed a petition for appeal in the Court of Appeals. In opposing Cary's petition, relevant to her claim that the trial court erred in not instructing the jury on self-defense, the Commonwealth did not assert a procedural bar with respect to this issue. Instead, the Commonwealth argued that the trial court correctly found that the record did not support a finding that Cary was acting in self-defense.

After Cary's petition for appeal was granted in part by the Court of Appeals, the Commonwealth raised for the first time the issue whether Cary's assertion that the trial court erred in not instructing the jury on self-defense was procedurally barred. The Commonwealth asserted that Cary had not expressly "argued to the trial court that Beekman was advancing on Cary at the time she shot him" when the self-defense instruction was proffered. The Commonwealth further maintained that Cary's assertion that she should have been permitted to introduce evidence of Beekman's prior threats and acts of violence against her was also procedurally barred because at the time she sought to introduce such evidence she had not yet testified that Beekman was either "walking or running" toward her when the gun discharged and did not reassert the issue once that evidence was presented.

In reversing Cary's convictions, the Court of Appeals did not expressly address the Commonwealth's assertion of a procedural bar. However, the Court of Appeals expressly found that with regard to Beekman's actions immediately prior to the shooting, Cary "testified without equivocation that 'he was coming back' and she was 'not sure whether he was walking or running.'" Accordingly, the Court of Appeals held that "[t]his evidence, viewed in the light most favorable to [Cary], established an overt act of sufficient imminence to entitle her to a self-defense instruction because it supported a finding that the victim, although still over ten feet away, was advancing toward her in a threatening fashion to resume the attack he had stopped only moments earlier."

In reaching this conclusion, the Court of Appeals distinguished *Sands*, the principal case relied upon by the Commonwealth, stating that facts in the present case stood "in marked contrast to those in *Sands*, in which the victim had at least temporarily ceased his repeated attacks on the defendant and was watching television in another room when she retrieved a gun and 'shot him five times while he reclined on the bed.'" The Court of Appeals further held that although Beekman, like the victim in *Sands*, "appeared [to be] unarmed [that fact] does not defeat the threat. The victim had beaten [Cary] with his fists on numerous prior occasions and, on one occasion, broke a glass in her face. [Cary] testified that, prior to the night on which she shot the victim, he had beaten her as recently as the previous weekend."

The Court of Appeals further noted that Cary's claim that the killing "was an accident does not prevent her from asserting a legal claim of self-defense." Accordingly, the Court of Appeals held that the trial court erred in failing to instruct the jury on self-defense.

The Court of Appeals reasoned that because the record would have supported giving an instruction on self-defense, "at least some of [Cary's] evidence about the victim's prior threats and abuse was admissible to show 'the reasonable apprehensions of [appellant] for [her] life and safety,' immediately prior to the shooting." The Court did not address the Commonwealth's assertion that at the time she first sought to introduce the evidence of Beekman's prior threats and acts of violence she had not yet introduced evidence that Beekman was advancing on her when the gun discharged.

The Court of Appeals further held that because Cary's claim of right-to-arm would have been supported by the evidence of Beekman's prior threats and acts of violence and, thus, would potentially rebut the Commonwealth's assertion that her purchase of the handgun showed premeditation, the trial court erred in refusing Cary's instruction on right-to-arm. Addressing Cary's assertion that she was entitled to a heat of passion instruction and further that this would have warranted the trial court instructing the jury on the lesser-included offense of voluntary manslaughter, the Court of Appeals held that Cary's "testimony of the victim's prior conduct that evening and her testimony that he was coming back into the living room, where she feared he would assault her further and perhaps kill her, created a jury issue on whether there had been a cooling off period sufficient to preclude a finding that [Cary] acted in the heat of passion."

The Court of Appeals recognized that "[w]hen a jury is instructed on first-degree murder and second-degree murder and convicts the defendant of first-degree murder, such a verdict 'compels the conclusion that [the jury] would never have reached a voluntary manslaughter verdict.'" However, the Court of Appeals concluded that the trial court's failure to instruct the jury on self-defense and right-to-arm might have impacted the jury's consideration of the evidence in favor of finding first-degree murder and, thus, it was not clear that a properly instructed jury would not have considered the lesser offense of voluntary manslaughter in the heat of passion. Accordingly, the Court of Appeals held that the trial court erred in failing to instruct the jury on that offense.

DISCUSSION

The Commonwealth maintains that in offering the self-defense instruction, Cary "never articulated for the court what overt act the victim had committed." . . .

* * *

We now consider whether the Court of Appeals correctly concluded that the evidence was sufficient to warrant the jury being instructed on the defense of self-defense. The Commonwealth contends that in determining that the trial court erred in failing to grant Cary's self-defense instruction, "[t]he Court of Appeals ... stitch[ed] together unconnected threads from various portions of Cary's testimony to create the impression of an overt act." The Commonwealth further contends that although these "unconnected threads" of evidence were before the trial court when it rejected Cary's proffered self-defense instruction, the evidence was not unequivocal, and when viewed in the context of Cary's full testimony established nothing more than that Beekman was returning to the living room from the bathroom, and not that he was advancing upon Cary in a threatening manner.

Cary responds that the Commonwealth's argument fails to apply the proper standard for reviewing the refusal of a correct instruction of law. Because that standard requires that the evidence be viewed in the light favorable to Cary, as the proponent of the instruction, Cary contends that the Court of Appeals properly focused its attention on those elements of her testimony that the jury could have found supported her claim of self-defense.

Both parties rely extensively upon the rationale underlying the holding in *Sands* to support their respective positions. Certainly, that case provides the most recent, succinct, and comprehensive survey of the law of self-defense as it has developed in this Commonwealth:

> The principles governing a plea of self-defense are well-established. Self-defense is an affirmative defense to a charge of murder, and in making such a plea, a "defendant implicitly admits the killing was intentional and assumes the burden of introducing evidence of justification or excuse that raises a reasonable doubt in the minds of the jurors." The "bare fear" of serious bodily injury, or even death, however well-grounded, will not justify the taking of human life. "There must [also] be some overt act indicative of imminent danger at the time." In other words, a defendant "must wait till some overt act is done[,] ... till the danger becomes imminent." In the context of a self-defense plea, "imminent danger" is defined as "an immediate, real threat to one's safety. . . ." Black's Law Dictionary 399 (7th ed.1999). "There must be . . . some act menacing present peril . . . [and] the act . . . must be of such a character as to afford a reasonable ground for believing there is a design . . . to do some serious bodily harm, and imminent danger of carrying such design into immediate execution."

Moreover, in *Sands*, this Court reiterated the well-established rule that, as with any proffered instruction that is otherwise a correct statement of law, an instruction on the defense of self-defense "is proper only if supported by more than a scintilla of evidence" and "it is not error to refuse an instruction when there is *no evidence* to support it."

Except that the victim and the defendant in *Sands* were married, the underlying history of their relationship is materially indistinguishable from that of the tumultuous relationship between Beekman and Cary. In both instances, the couples had a long history of acts of violence committed by the male upon the female that were frequently occasioned by the excessive use by the male of alcohol and illicit drugs. In both instances, the male had made repeated threats to kill the female, and the female had a subjective belief that the male would eventually carry out that threat.

In *Sands*, on the evening of the killing, the victim had savagely beaten the defendant. However, the evidence showed that subsequent to that assault, the defendant's sister-in-law had arrived at the couple's home and offered assistance to the defendant. Meanwhile, the victim "was lying in bed, watching television." The defendant, who was in the bathroom with her sister-in-law, suddenly became frantic, went to the kitchen where she retrieved a gun, and then went to the bedroom. The victim merely asked the defendant what she was "doing," and then the defendant shot the victim five times, killing him.

This Court concluded that there was no evidence to support the defendant's proffered self-defense instruction because the record did not "reveal any overt act by her husband that presented an imminent danger at the time of the shooting." This Court specifically noted that while less than an hour had elapsed between the victim ending his assault on the defendant and the shooting, "sufficient time elapsed for [the sister-in-law] to arrive at the couple's home, and for the defendant to view the extent of her injuries while in the bathroom with [the sister-in-law], walk from the bathroom to the living room door, turn around and proceed back into the kitchen, retrieve a gun from a cabinet, and walk back into the bedroom where her husband was reclining on the bed, watching television."

In the present case, when considered in the light most favorable to Cary, the evidence is sufficient to establish Cary's genuine fear for her life in view of the atrocities inflicted upon her by Beekman. Thus, as before, we are concerned only with whether the record would provide the trier-of-fact with more than a scintilla of evidence to support a finding that there was an overt act of sufficient imminence on the part of Beekman that would warrant Cary to act upon that genuine fear to use deadly force in self-defense.

The Commonwealth asserts, and we agree, that Cary cannot rely solely on the initial assault upon her as the "overt act" that occasioned her resort to self-defense. However, contrary to the apparent view of the Commonwealth, neither may we disregard that evidence entirely, merely because "Beekman retired to the bathroom" for approximately five minutes. Rather, we consider Beekman's subsequent actions in light of that assault.

According to Cary's testimony, Beekman did not simply emerge from the bathroom and make his way to the living room. Rather, she confronted Beekman as he returned to the living room and repeated her demand that he leave the home. Beekman refused this demand and threatened to "smack" her and commit other acts of violence upon her. It was in this context that Cary testified that Beekman was "walking or running" toward her. And that fact must be viewed in the context that Beekman's assault on Cary, which had ended only five minutes before, had been occasioned by the same demand that he leave the home, his refusal, and a vile verbal assault. When so viewed, the trier-of-fact could reasonably conclude that Beekman, although 11 to 18 feet away from Cary at the time of the shooting, was nonetheless advancing toward her with the intent to resume his physical assault upon her. Such act constituted an overt act of sufficient imminence on the part of Beekman to warrant Cary to respond in her defense. Accordingly, we hold that the Court of Appeals did not err in finding that there was sufficient evidence in the record to warrant the trial court instructing the jury on Cary's claim of self-defense and, thus, that the trial court erred in not giving the proffered self-defense instruction.

CONCLUSION

For these reasons, we will affirm the judgment of the Court of Appeals vacating Cary's convictions and remanding the case to the trial court for a new trial, if the Commonwealth be so advised.

Affirmed.

■ JUSTICE AGEE, with whom JUSTICE KINSER joins, dissenting.

I.   THE SELF-DEFENSE CLAIMS

The majority opinion correctly recites from our holding in *Sands* that in order for the affirmative defense of self-defense to apply "[t]here must [also] be some overt act indicative of imminent danger at the time" made against the defendant. That overt act must be "some act menacing present peril" and "of such a character as to afford a reasonable ground for believing there is a design . . . to do some serious bodily harm, and imminent danger of carrying such design into immediate execution." On appeal, at least in this Court, Cary has posited the overt act justifying her claims of self-defense to be that Beekman advanced at her in the apartment in such a way as to constitute an "imminent danger" about to be carried "into immediate execution" when she shot him. This is a position *never* argued in the trial court and only implied before the Court of Appeals.

The overt act of imminent danger is crucial because it is the foundation without which Cary is not entitled to a jury instruction on self-defense. Furthermore, and just as importantly, the overt act justifying self-defense is an absolute condition precedent to Cary's claim for an instruction on accidental self-defense,, or to the admission into evidence of the victim's character for violence or aggression. Thus, if the record fails to support Cary's claim that she argued Beekman's advance on her as the overt act justifying self-defense in the trial court, then all of her related claims of trial court error, as found by the Court of Appeals, fail.

A.   The Overt Act Argued in the Trial Court

Before determining that Cary had not set forth a prima facie case of self-defense and therefore could not present evidence of Beekman's prior violent acts, the trial court specifically questioned Cary's trial counsel: "[D]o you represent to the Court that you have presented all of the evidence that you claim supports the establishment of your prima facie . . . self-defense defense including overt acts in support of that particular defense. . . ?" Counsel's response is unequivocal:

Your Honor, I believe that with the testimony of Ms. Cary as to the actions of the victim, Mark Beekman, on the evening in question where he had proceeded to assault her, make verbal threats towards her and

[by] other means terrorize her that evening, that that does constitute the overt act. And as I had previously said, the issue of imminence, I believe, is an issue for the jury.

The overt act in Ms. Cary's mind at the time put her or would have put her in a position to fear, as she stated, future violence against her and that at the time her son had brought the gun from the room, she was still under that fear.

Although the overt act may not have coincided or occurred concomitantly at the exact same moment as the possession of the weapon, it was fresh enough in her mind the actions that Mr. Beekman had taken against her as well as the verbal threats that he had made as to constitute an overt act for purposes [of a] self-defense defense.

(Emphasis added). The Court immediately asked, "So then is the answer to my question yes?" Cary's attorney replied, "Yes."

Cary's trial counsel never mentions in this direct exchange or anywhere else in the record that Beekman advancing toward Cary immediately prior to the shooting was the overt act of immediate peril creating an imminent danger to Cary that supports self-defense. Cary never made any argument regarding the self-defense or accidental self-defense instructions that differed from this argument. Indeed, counsel's statement here not only omits any contention that the decedent was moving toward Cary immediately prior to the shooting, but it actually negates that argument by admitting the alleged overt act "may not have coincided or occurred concomitantly" with the possession and firing of the gun. From this text, Cary's trial court argument of an overt act justifying self-defense does not include even a passing reference to Beekman's movement toward Cary immediately prior to the shooting. To the contrary, Cary's trial court argument is based on the totality of the decedent's prior acts both earlier that evening and on previous occasions.

Indeed, when defense counsel contended that Cary was entitled to instructions on self-defense and accidental self-defense, she did so because:

> while [Cary] was holding the gun in self-defense of herself, the victim returns to the room, is continuing to make threats to her which, *based on her prior experience that evening*, the assault coupled with the threats, she at that time believed herself to be in reasonable danger.

> So I would submit *the overt act, even though it did not occur concomitantly with the gun going off, occurred in a reasonable time* which the jury could determine led Ms. Cary to believe that she was in imminent danger. (Emphasis added).

Once again, in arguing to the trial court that a sufficient overt act existed, Cary never argued that Beekman advanced toward her immediately prior to the shooting. Instead, Cary again represented that the opposite occurred because the overt act "did *not occur concomitantly with* the gun going off." (Emphasis added).

In addition to defense counsel's own statements, which contradict the argument now made on appeal, the trial court transcripts reflect several instances in which the trial court attempted to clarify Cary's position and explain the basis for its holdings. For example, in reviewing the facts in the light most favorable to Cary on self-defense and accidental self-defense, the trial court summarized her testimony:

> [Cary] says that more conversation takes place, and then the gun goes off accidentally, clearly the gun goes off accidentally. She does not testify, does not suggest that she was using that weapon to repel any act or to prevent any act by the defendant at that moment in time. She was simply holding a gun that she believed to be empty, and that it accidentally discharged and struck him in the chest which ultimately resulted in his death.
>
> . . . .
>
> There is no claim that there was some struggle, that he was assaulting her, that she was repelling that force and that in the context of that this gun accidentally went off.

(Emphasis added).

Similarly, after hearing Cary's later proffer of testimony, the trial court stated:

> [N]otwithstanding anything that's been said at this stage through the proffer is that the defendant clearly did not set forth any overt act on [the day of the shooting] or any basis upon which a viable case of self-defense could reasonably or rationally be considered in this case. . . . at the time of the event the defendant's and her son's testimony clearly state that there was no act of overt threat or violence toward the defendant at the time.

At no time during or after these statements from the bench did Cary object to the characterization of her arguments or contend to the trial court that the decedent's movements immediately prior to the shooting established the existence of an overt act justifying self-defense. Instead, the sole basis argued to the trial court at any time was that the overt act of imminent danger to Cary was the decedent's prior physical and verbal assaults.

The arguments now made by Cary, and adopted by the Court of Appeals and the majority opinion, were simply never made at trial. For example, nothing in Cary's proffered testimony supports the claim that the decedent committed the overt act she now argues justifies the self-defense claims. Her proffered testimony focuses on the decedent's prior acts against Cary, and date back to 1984, nearly twenty years prior to the shooting. After detailing these prior events, Cary's trial counsel asked

Cary what she was "afraid of" when Beekman physically assaulted her earlier on the evening of the shooting. Cary's response was, "I was afraid that one day he would just take me out of this world because that almost like took me out of here being busted in the face and the glass and near the jugular vein." The events Cary recounts here as to what precipitated her fear on the evening of the shooting were all events that occurred on previous occasions. None of the proffered testimony contends Beekman was moving toward Cary to attack her immediately prior to the shooting, so as to put Cary in immediate fear of an imminent danger of bodily injury or death.[2]

Because the record clearly shows that Cary did not argue to the trial court that the decedent's alleged movement toward her immediately prior to the shooting was the overt act that placed her in imminent danger of immediate harm, Rule 5:25 bars Cary from making this argument on appeal as an after-the-fact basis to justify the self-defense claims. Based on the record, the trial court correctly held that Cary failed to establish the existence of an overt act under *Sands*, and therefore no basis existed to warrant any of the self-defense claims. As such, the trial court properly denied Cary's request to introduce evidence of Beekman's past violent conduct and properly refused Cary's proposed jury instructions relating to self-defense and accidental self-defense. The Court of Appeals erred in holding to the contrary.

III. CONCLUSION

Because Cary never argued to the trial court that the overt act justifying the self-defense claims was that an advancing Beekman forced her to act in self-defense, I respectfully dissent from the majority opinion and would reverse the judgment of the Court of Appeals and affirm the judgment of the trial court.

NOTES

1. For penetrating comments on the battered spouse syndrome defense, see Linda L. Ammons, *What's God Got to Do with It? Church and State Collaboration in the Subordination of Women and Domestic Violence,* 51 Rutgers L. Rev. 1207 (1999) (in which Professor Ammons explores the role of Judeo-Christian institutions, ideology, and doctrine in promoting women's subordination and in condoning domestic violence).

Professor Linda Mills takes the position that the feminist view, which advocates a vigorous prosecution and mandatory intervention in domestic violence cases, may not serve the best interests of all battered women. Whenever there is mandatory intervention by state agents, prosecution and

---

[2] The record shows that prior to the shooting, Beekman used the bathroom, which was through the kitchen and down a hall away from the living room. The only entry or exit from the apartment was a single door in the living room where Cary was sitting. Thus, Beekman had to re-enter the living room where Cary was sitting at the time of the shooting in order to exit the apartment. Beekman could not have fulfilled Cary's request to leave without re-entering the living room in order to reach the apartment's only door.

punishment of the guilty party is the paramount objective. Professor Mills argues that this overlooks the clinical concerns for "healing," an approach that relies on clinical methods that engage the battered woman, foster her healing, and promote her safety. *See* Linda G. Mills, *Killing Her Softly: Intimate Abuse and the Violence of State Intervention,* 113 Harv. L. Rev. 551 (1999); *see also* Denise Bricker, *Fatal Defense: An Analysis of Battered Woman's Syndrome Expert Testimony for Gay Men and Lesbians Who Kill Abusive Partners,* 58 Brook. L. Rev. 1379 (1993); Charles Patrick Ewing, *Psychological Self-Defense—A Proposed Justification for Battered Women Who Kill,* 14 L. & Human Behav. 579 (1990) (suggesting that traditional self-defense concepts rarely apply comfortably to battered spouses but arguing that current law be expanded); Christine A. Gardner, Note, *Postpartum Depression Defense: Are Mothers Getting Away with Murder?,* 24 New Eng. L. Rev. 953 (1990); Stephen J. Morse, *The Misbegotten Marriage of Soft Psychology and Bad Law: Psychological Self-Defense as a Justification for Homicide,* 14 L. & Hum. Behav. 595 (1990) (arguing that a recognition of a battered spouses defense rests on an insecure scientific foundation, that an expansion of self-defense would create substantial administrative problems and would facilitate adoption or expansion of related undesirable doctrines); Laura E. Reece, *Mothers Who Kill: Postpartum Disorders and Criminal Infanticide,* 38 U.C.L.A.L. Rev. 699 (1991); Cathryn Jo Rosen, *The Excuse of Self-Defense: Correcting a Historical Accident on Behalf of Battered Women Who Kill,* 36 Am. U.L. Rev. 11 (1986).

For other views on domestic violence and use of a battered spouse defense, see, for example, Mary Beeker, *Access to Justice for Battered Women,* 12 WASH. U.J.L. & POL'Y 63 (2003); Alafair S. Burke, *Rational Actors, Self-Defense, and Duress: Making Sense, Not Syndromes, Out of Battered Women,* 81 N.C.L. REV. 211 (2002); Joshua Dressler, *Battered Women and Sleeping Abusers: Some Reflections,* 3 OHIO ST. J. CRIM. L. 457 (2006); Kit Kinports, *So Much Activity, So Little Change: A Reply to Critics of Battered Women's Self Defense,* 23 ST. LOUIS U. PUB. L. REV. 155 (2004); Joan H. Krause, *Distorted Reflections of Battered Women Who Kill: A Response to Professor Dressler,* 4 OHIO ST. J. CRIM. L. 555 (2007).

2. Applying an analogous issue of self-defense by a battered child, defending a patricide, see Jahnke v. State, 682 P.2d 991 (Wyo.1984), where a defendant charged with the first degree murder of his father sought to show, through expert testimony that he was a battered child who believed that he was in imminent danger of his life when he shot his father. The proffered expert testimony was excluded and the defendant was convicted of voluntary manslaughter. In upholding the conviction, the majority of the Wyoming Supreme Court, over vigorous dissent, said, in part: "Although many people, and the public media, seem to be prepared to espouse the notion that a victim of abuse is entitled to kill the abuser, that special justification defense is antithetical to the mores of modern civilized society. . . ." *See also* State v. Mapp, 45 N.C.App. 574, 264 S.E.2d 348 (1980). *See* Diana J. Ensign, Note, *Links Between the Battered Woman Syndrome and the Battered Child Syndrome: An Argument for Consistent Standards in the Admissibility of Expert Testimony in Family Abuse Cases,* 36 Wayne L. Rev. 1619 (1990).

2. DEFENSE OF OTHERS

The law recognizes the right of a person to kill in defense of not only his own life but also that of another. Two doctrines bear upon this privilege to defend others: (1) the rule that one may defend a close relative, and (2) the rule that one may take life if necessary to prevent a dangerous or forcible felony. In application to specific situations, these principles are frequently cumulative. Thus, if one kills the assailant of a near relative, he may invoke his specific right to defend a member of his family, as well as his general privilege to interfere to prevent a felonious assault.

Cases involving defense of a party who, at the time of the killing, was engaged in an affray brought on by his own misconduct have resulted in disagreement among the courts as to whether the "assistant" must "stand in the shoes" of the wrongdoer, or instead be judged according to the reasonableness of his own conduct in interfering to protect one whose life seemed to be unlawfully endangered.

It is a matter of speculation as to which view is the more socially tolerable. In other words, will a person who sees a close relative in great and immediate danger pause to determine whether the relative was himself free from fault?

State v. Beeley

Supreme Court of Rhode Island, 1995.
653 A.2d 722.

In this appeal Beeley avers that the trial justice erred in denying his motions requesting judgment of acquittal and a new trial. We sustain the appeal.

Defendant Beeley drove John Perry to 80 Evergreen Drive in East Providence where, John testified, he lived in an apartment with his wife, Julie Perry (Julie). By then it was approximately four o'clock in the morning. John invited Beeley to spend the night at the apartment since it was so late. Beeley dropped off John at the entrance to the apartment building and then went to park his car. The testimony in the record is contradictory as to what occurred next. John testified that upon entering the apartment, he walked toward the bedroom and came face-to-face with his wife, Julie, in the hallway. Julie turned on the hallway light and John observed a man sleeping in the bed. John began screaming at Julie and asked her "Who was in the bed?" Julie responded "You know who it is." John recognized the man as Robert Harding (Harding). Harding was not wearing any clothes. The two men began wrestling and moved toward the door of the apartment. Harding attempted to force John out of the apartment through the door. John yelled out to Beeley who was waiting outside the apartment. Beeley entered through the doorway and pulled John out of the apartment. John testified that he waited outside of the apartment with Beeley for the police to arrive who had been called by Julie.

Julie and Harding offered a different version of the events. Julie testified that on May 20, 1991, Harding was sleeping on the couch in the living room of the apartment. At approximately four o'clock in the morning she was awakened by "noise." From her bedroom she observed John standing in the hallway. Julie and John began arguing and Harding woke up. John kicked Harding in the face several times as he sat on the couch. As the two men struggled Julie called the police. John hollered to Beeley "somebody is in here" and then unlocked the door. Beeley entered the apartment, punched Harding in the face, and then left with John.

Harding corroborated Julie's testimony and indicated that as he was locked in combat with John, both tried to open the door. Harding testified that as he attempted to push John out the door, John unlocked the door. Initially Harding testified that John had opened the door, but later on cross-examination he recalled that he opened the door after John had unlocked it. John then called out to Beeley and Beeley entered and hit Harding in the face. Harding indicated that this was the first time he had ever met Beeley. Harding sustained facial injuries; however, it is unclear from the record whether Harding's injuries were caused by the single punch executed by Beeley or by the altercation with John.

Beeley testified that as he waited outside the apartment he could hear John and Julie yelling. He walked to the door and banged on it but did not attempt to open it. The door opened and then slammed shut. When the door opened again Beeley could see Harding who was naked grabbing John by the waist. Beeley did not know Harding and did not know what Harding was doing in the apartment. John was crying, and he yelled to Beeley, "This is the guy." Beeley hit Harding once to break his hold on John. Beeley observed Julie on the telephone, talking to the police. He then grabbed John and pulled him out of the apartment. Beeley and John waited outside for the police to arrive.

We consider Beeley's contention that he is entitled to a new trial on the charge of simple assault. Beeley contends that the trial justice erred in instructing the jury that one acting to defend another has only a derivative right of self-defense, and that his or her actions are not judged by the reasonableness of his or her own conduct and perceptions.

It is undisputed that Beeley hit Harding as Beeley entered the apartment. Beeley's defense to the charge of simple assault upon Harding was that when he entered the apartment, he saw John being held by a naked man (Harding) and speculated that the latter was an intruder who may have raped Julie. Beeley, in an attempt to break Harding's hold on John, executed a single punch at Harding. Beeley contends that he was therefore justified in assaulting Harding.

The trial justice instructed the jury with respect to defense of another and explained that

> one who comes to the aid of another person must do so at his own peril and should be excused only when that other person would be justified in defending himself. Thus, if you find that Mr. Perry was not the aggressor and was justified in defending himself from the acts of Mr. Harding, then Mr. Beeley is then excused from any criminal responsibility for coming to the aid of Mr. Perry if Mr. Beeley in so doing did not use excessive force. However, if you find that Mr. Perry was in fact the aggressor and was not justified in his actions and was inflicting punches and kicks on Mr. Harding, then Mr. Beeley acted at his own peril and his actions would not be justified. In short, if Mr. Perry was justified in his actions, then so was Mr. Beeley in coming to his assistance. If Mr. Perry was not justified in his actions, then neither was Mr. Beeley. Our Supreme Court has said on repeated occasions, an intervening person stands in the shoes of the person that he is aiding.

The issue before us is whether an intervenor in an altercation between private individuals should be judged by his or her own reasonable perceptions or whether he or she stands in the shoes of the person that he or she is defending. A review of the relevant authorities reveals that there are two rules followed by American jurisdictions. The first rule, adopted by the trial justice in the instant case, is sometimes referred to as the "alter ego" rule, and it holds that the right to defend another is coextensive with the other's right to defend himself or herself. The other view, which follows the Model Penal Code, is that as long as the defendant-intervenor reasonably believes that the other is being unlawfully attacked, he or she is justified in using reasonable force to defend him or her.

The Model Penal Code § 3.05, entitled "Use of Force for the Protection of Other Persons," provides in pertinent part as follows. "(1) Subject to the provisions of this Section and of Section 3.09, the use of force upon or toward the person of another is justifiable to protect a third person when: (a) the actor would be justified under Section 3.04 in using such force to protect himself against the injury he believes to be threatened to the person whom he seeks to protect; and (b) under the circumstances as the actor believes them to be, the person whom he seeks to protect would be justified in using such protective force; and (c) the actor believes that his intervention is necessary for the protection of such other person." Model Penal Code § 3.05(1) (Adopted 1962).

Under this section in order for the defense to be raised successfully, three conditions must be met. First, the force must be such as the actor could use in defending himself or herself from the harm that he or she believes to be threatened to the third person. In other words, the actor may use the same amount of force that he or she could use to protect himself or herself. Second, the third person must be justified in using such protective force in the circumstances as the actor believes them to be. Thus, if the third person was resisting an arrest by a known police officer, he or she would have no defense and, if the circumstances were known to the actor, the actor would have no defense either. Finally, the actor must believe that his or her intervention is necessary for the protection of the third party.

This view, which has been adopted in the new state criminal codes, is in our opinion the better view. We favor the doctrine which judges a defendant upon his or her own reasonable perceptions as he or she comes to the aid of the apparent victim. The justification should, of course, be based upon what a reasonable person might consider to be the imminence of serious bodily harm. As one court expressed it, not only as a matter of justice should one "not be convicted of a crime if he selflessly attempts to protect the victim of an apparently unjustified assault, but how else can we encourage bystanders to go to the aid of another who is being subjected to assault?" State v. Fair, 45 N.J. 77, 93, 211 A.2d 359, 368 (1965). Moreover, to impose liability upon the defendant-intervenor in these circumstances is to impose liability upon him or her without fault.

In sum it seems to this court preferable to predicate the justification on the actor's own reasonable beliefs. We are of the opinion that an intervenor is justified in using reasonable force to defend another as long as the intervenor reasonably believes that the other is being unlawfully attacked. This rule is "predicated on the social desirability of encouraging people to go to the aid of third parties who are in danger of harm as a result of unlawful actions of others" and there is an "important social goal of crime prevention, a duty of every citizen."

Applying the foregoing to the instant case, we conclude that the trial justice incorrectly instructed the jury with respect to the charge of assault against Beeley. The rule that we adopted in Gelinas, supra, applied to a defendant-intervenor in an arrest situation. The trial justice's application of the Gelinas rule in his instructions to the jury in the instant case was therefore incorrect. Accordingly we vacate Beeley's conviction on the assault charge.

NOTES

1. Consider the following from State v. Westlund, 13 Wash.App. 460, 536 P.2d 20 (1975):

> We hold that a bystander may not come to the aid of one being lawfully or unlawfully arrested by a uniformed police officer or one known or who should have been known to the bystander to be a police officer unless the arrestee was in actual danger of serious physical injury. Several elements, therefore, must be present before such a third person's assault of a police officer can be justified on

the basis of defense of another. First, a third party may never intervene when the only threat to the arrestee is deprivation of his liberty by an arrest which has no legal justification. Aid is justified only if serious physical injury or death is threatened or inflicted. Second, the serious physical danger threatened or inflicted must be actual. A reasonable but mistaken belief that the arrestee was about to be seriously injured or that the arrestee was entitled to protect himself from such danger is insufficient. The third party acts at his own peril and if it is subsequently determined that the arrestee was not about to be seriously injured, the third party's assault is not justifiable. Third, the physical injury must be serious, the police actions of the type which shock the conscience. Fourth, only force reasonable and necessary to protect the arrestee may be used against the officer

2. Nebraska enacted a statute which read in part as follows:

No person in this state shall be placed in legal jeopardy of any kind whatsoever for protecting, by any means necessary, himself, his family, or his real or personal property, or when coming to the aid of another who is in imminent danger of or the victim of aggravated assault, armed robbery, holdup, rape, murder, or other heinous crime.

The statute was held unconstitutional on the ground that the legislature could not delegate to private citizens the power to fix and execute punishment. State v. Goodseal, 186 Neb. 359, 183 N.W.2d 258 (1971).

3. DEFENSE OF HABITATION

People v. McNeese
Supreme Court of Colorado, 1995.
892 P.2d 304.

The defendant, Robert Earl McNeese, was charged with first-degree murder, attempted first-degree murder, and first-degree assault. After a preliminary hearing, the county court bound the defendant over for trial on two counts of second-degree murder. The defendant was also bound over for trial on the attempted first-degree murder and first-degree assault charges arising out of the stabbing of Vivian Daniels. Defendant pleaded not guilty and filed a motion to dismiss in the district court, alleging that he was immune from prosecution under the "make-my-day" statute, section 18–1–704.5, 8B C.R.S. (1986). Section 18–1–704.5 provides:

Use of deadly physical force against an intruder.

(1) The general assembly hereby recognizes that the citizens of Colorado have a right to expect absolute safety within their own homes.

(2) Notwithstanding the provisions of section 18–1–704, any occupant of a dwelling is justified in using any degree of

physical force, including deadly physical force, against another person when that other person has made an unlawful entry into the dwelling, and when the occupant has a reasonable belief that such other person has committed a crime in the dwelling in addition to the uninvited entry, or is committing or intends to commit a crime against a person or property in addition to the uninvited entry, and when the occupant reasonably believes that such other person might use any physical force, no matter how slight, against any occupant.

(3) Any occupant of a dwelling using physical force, including deadly physical force, in accordance with the provisions of subsection (2) of this section shall be immune from criminal prosecution for the use of such force.

(4) Any occupant of a dwelling using physical force, including deadly physical force, in accordance with the provisions of subsection (2) of this section shall be immune from any civil liability for injuries or death resulting from the use of such force.

Following a pretrial hearing, the trial judge granted the defendant's motion to dismiss the second-degree murder charge for the stabbing death of John Daniels. The defendant's motion to dismiss the charges of second-degree murder of Wessels and attempted first-degree murder and first-degree assault of Vivian Daniels was denied.

I

Vivian Daniels testified that she was not getting along with John Daniels, her common-law husband, and was looking for a place to stay. She contacted the defendant and asked whether she could stay in his apartment and sleep on his couch. The apartment contained a small bedroom, a bathroom, and a combined living room and kitchen. Vivian Daniels moved into the defendant's apartment after agreeing to pay rent and on the condition that John Daniels was not to enter or come into the apartment under any circumstances. The defendant is an African-American, and the testimony established that John Daniels had a reputation for not liking African-Americans and was prone to violence, especially after he had been drinking. Vivian Daniels told the defendant that John Daniels had killed another man. John Daniels knew that the defendant did not want him in the apartment.

Vivian Daniels agreed to pay the defendant $50 a month for rent and to contribute funds for her share of the food. The defendant gave her a key shortly after she moved in, and she kept her clothes, television, art work, bedding, fan, and cat in the apartment. John Daniels never entered the apartment and would wave from across the street or knock on the window when he wanted to see his wife.

On November 15, 1991, approximately three months after moving into the apartment, Vivian Daniels and the defendant spent the day drinking at various bars. When they returned to the apartment, the defendant made sexual advances and Vivian Daniels decided to move. The defendant agreed that she should move out. She left the defendant's apartment at 11:30 p.m. on a cold, snowy night without a coat or any of her belongings. She went to John Daniels' apartment, which was about six blocks away.

Keith Tollefson, who shared the apartment with John Daniels, let her in, and she slept on a couch until John Daniels returned. John Daniels and David Wessels had both been drinking heavily at a number of bars and, when they returned to the apartment, they were told of the sexual advances made by the defendant. They decided to get Vivian Daniels' clothes and possessions from the defendant's apartment. John Daniels told Vivian Daniels there would be no violence. However, a defense witness testified he overheard John Daniels say to Wessels, in the presence of Vivian Daniels just before they left to go to the defendant's apartment, "let's go kill that fuckin' nigger." Vivian Daniels denied that John Daniels made such a statement to David Wessels. John Daniels had a blood alcohol level of .349, and Wessels had a blood alcohol level of .188. Vivian Daniels admitted that she was drunk. At approximately 2:30 a.m., John Daniels, Vivian Daniels, and Wessels entered the defendant's apartment using Vivian Daniels' key.

The defendant was in his bedroom asleep. When John Daniels went to get his wife's clothes out of the closet located immediately outside of the bedroom, he opened the defendant's door and talked to the defendant from the doorway. After Vivian Daniels asked her husband to help her collect her belongings, he returned to the living room and the defendant followed. Vivian Daniels went to the defendant's bedroom to get her pillow, and, when she returned to the living room, John Daniels was on the couch with his arm around the defendant's throat applying a choke hold and threatening to kill the defendant if he harmed Vivian Daniels.

The altercation ended after approximately two or three minutes. Vivian Daniels testified that neither the defendant nor John Daniels was hurt, and they were not arguing.

Vivian Daniels was gathering her possessions when she saw Wessels lying on the floor by the front door and John Daniels on the floor near the kitchen. The defendant confronted Vivian Daniels and stabbed her in the head. She ran from the apartment and called the police. Vivian Daniels could not recall anything else. She testified that she did not see, hear, or know what occurred when John Daniels and David Wessels were stabbed to death.

II

The trial judge centered his analysis on the oral lease agreement between the defendant and Vivian Daniels, and concluded that, since

Vivian Daniels was entitled to a three-day notice of eviction, she was authorized to return to the apartment on November 16, 1991. The trial judge also held that she had the right to invite David Wessels into the apartment. However, allowing John Daniels to enter the apartment violated the oral lease agreement between Vivian Daniels and the defendant and made John Daniels' entry into the apartment unlawful.

The trial judge held John Daniels inflicted a third-degree assault on the defendant, and that the assault satisfied the requirement that John Daniel had committed or intended to commit a crime on the premises. See s 18–1–704.5(2) & (3). Also, because the physical contact may not have been over, the trial court held that the defendant was justified in fearing that John Daniels might use further physical force against him. The trial court found that the defendant established immunity from prosecution because he met the requirements of the "make-my-day" statute.

The prosecution appealed the trial judge's order of dismissal. The court of appeals affirmed the trial judge and concluded that the terms "unlawful" and "uninvited" in section 18–1–704.5 were used interchangeably by the General Assembly. Judge Tursi, writing for a divided court, concluded that John Daniels' entry was both uninvited and unlawful because Vivian Daniels' oral lease with the defendant denied her authority to invite John Daniels into the defendant's apartment. The court of appeals held that the trial judge did not err in finding that John Daniels inflicted a third-degree assault on the defendant or in finding that the defendant reasonably believed John Daniels might use further physical force against him.

Judge Taubman, in his dissent, asserted the statutory terms "unlawful" and "uninvited" were not interchangeable, and that section 18–1–704.5 required a finding that the entry was both unlawful and uninvited. Judge Taubman concluded that John Daniels' entry was unlawful because it violated the terms of Vivian Daniels' tenancy, but was not uninvited since Vivian Daniels "clearly invited the decedent into the apartment, albeit that she was not authorized to make such an invitation." Judge Taubman would have vacated the order of dismissal and would have reinstated the murder charge against the defendant for the stabbing death of John Daniels.

The findings of fact and conclusions of law of the trial judge were based on an erroneous interpretation of the elements that must be proven to obtain immunity under section 18–1–704.5. Accordingly, the findings and conclusions were erroneous as a matter of law and are not binding on this court.

The court of appeals also erred in its analysis of the "make-my-day" statute. The General Assembly did not intend that the occupant of a dwelling be granted immunity from prosecution for the appearance of an unlawful entry by an intruder. The fact that John Daniels' entry may have been uninvited because the entry violated an oral agreement, does not establish that the entry was a knowing violation of the criminal law. John Daniels' entry does not satisfy the unlawful entry element in the "make-my-day" statute.

Section 18–1–704.5 contains two separate elements. In order to be granted immunity the defendant must first prove by a preponderance of the evidence that there was an unlawful entry. The second statutory requirement involves a determination of whether the occupant had a reasonable belief that the intruder intended to commit or committed a crime in the dwelling. When the legislature enacted 18–1–704.5 as part of the criminal code it did not define all of the terms used in the statute. We are guided by other provisions in the criminal code in determining the definition of unlawful entry and the elements that must be proven by a preponderance of the evidence.

III

Section 18–1–704.5 is part of the criminal code (Title 18). Article 1 of the criminal code includes "Provisions Applicable to Offenses Generally." The article contains part 7, labeled "Justification and Exemptions from Criminal Responsibility." Part 7 includes statutes justifying the use of physical force against a person, use of physical force in defense of premises, and use of physical force in defense of property. The "make-my-day" statute lies in the criminal code along side these statutes. Section 18–1–704.5 is similar to self-defense and extends the justifications and exemptions formulated in part 7. The "make-my-day" statute justifies "deadly physical force," not just "physical force." However, the statute is not a license to commit homicide. The occupant of a dwelling is granted immunity from criminal prosecution for homicide, so safeguards must be imposed. Because the statute readily grants immunity for the taking of a life, the "knowingly" *mens rea* is required to carry out the principles of self-defense.

The specific provisions of the "make-my-day" statute permit an occupant of a dwelling to use physical force, including deadly physical force, against an intruder. Immunity from criminal prosecution is granted for acts and conduct that would be criminal but for the statute. Immunity may be determined by the court in a Crim.P. 12 motion to dismiss or as an affirmative defense at the time of trial. When section 18–1–704.5(3) is invoked prior to trial, the burden is on the defendant to establish by a preponderance of evidence, that:

> (1) another person made an unlawful entry into the defendant's dwelling; (2) the defendant had a reasonable belief that such other person had committed a crime in the dwelling in addition to the uninvited entry, or was committing or intended to commit a crime against a person or property in addition to the uninvited entry; (3) the defendant reasonably believed that such other person might use physical force, no

matter how slight, against any occupant of the dwelling; and (4) the defendant used force against the person who actually made the unlawful entry into the dwelling.

In the House and Senate debates on the original "make-my-day" bill, the sponsors bill referred to the bill as a "homeowner's protection bill." In describing the function of the bill, the House and Senate sponsors repeatedly alluded to the bill's protection of homeowners from "intruders" and people who "break[ ] and enter[ ]" into homes "illegally."

The sponsors pointed out the bill's potential for deterring criminals from breaking into homes. The typical scenario discussed in the debates and hearings involved an illegal entry into a home by a stranger in the middle of the night. The legislative history indicates that the General Assembly intended the "make-my-day" statute to apply in situations where an intruder illegally enters a dwelling. The hearings and debates also demonstrate that the bill was meant to deter criminals from breaking into a home to commit a crime. The legislative history supports the conclusion that an unlawful entry means a knowing, criminal entry into a dwelling.

IV

The most vexing question under the "make-my-day" statute is the proper definition of "unlawful entry." For purposes of section 18–1–704.5, the "unlawful entry" element requires an entry in knowing violation of the criminal law. The statutory language justifies an occupant's use of physical force against another person when the other person is knowingly engaging in criminal conduct. The statute provides that the occupant of the dwelling must reasonably believe that a crime has been, is being, or will be committed in addition to the threshold requirement of proof of an unlawful entry. By providing both objective and subjective elements, the structure of section 18–1–704.5 contemplates that an unlawful entry means a knowing, criminal entry.

The statute was enacted to immunize the occupant of a dwelling from prosecution for using physical force against another person who has committed, is committing, or intends to commit criminal acts in the dwelling. Immunity from criminal prosecution provides protection to the occupant of a dwelling who uses force against an intruder who has knowingly and unlawfully entered the dwelling to commit a crime. The immunity was not intended to justify use of physical force against persons who enter a dwelling accidently or in good faith.

Requiring a knowing, criminal entry reconciles two competing interests. First, the General Assembly recognized that an occupant of a dwelling should be able to use force against an intruder who knowingly and unlawfully enters the dwelling. Second, the General Assembly did not want to encourage the use of physical force in response to otherwise benign situations. The knowing, criminal entry requirement affords the occupant of a dwelling sufficient protection from criminal prosecution, while discouraging random violence.

V

In addition to an unlawful entry, the "make-my-day" statute requires that the occupant have a reasonable belief that the intruder has committed, or intends to commit, a crime in the dwelling. Analysis of the subjective belief requirement is only undertaken after the threshold unlawful entry requirement has been satisfied.

The prosecution contends that the defendant failed to establish by a preponderance of the evidence that he had a reasonable belief that John Daniels committed or intended to commit a crime against a person or property in the dwelling in addition to an unlawful entry. We agree.

To be immune from prosecution under the "make-my-day" statute, a defendant must establish by a preponderance of the evidence that he "had a reasonable belief that such other person had committed a crime in the dwelling in addition to the uninvited entry, or was committing or intended to commit a crime against a person or property in addition to the uninvited entry. . . . "The inquiry for the second requirement focuses on the reasonable belief of the occupant. It does not center on the actual conduct of the intruder. The defendant failed to prove by a preponderance of the evidence that he had a reasonable belief that John Daniels committed or intended to commit a crime in the apartment. Vivian Daniels' testimony regarding the confrontation between John Daniels and the defendant in the apartment was insufficient to establish the second requirement of section 18–1–704.5.

Accordingly, we return this case to the court of appeals with directions to remand to the district court to make findings of facts and conclusions of law consistent with this opinion or for a further or new hearing on the defendant's motion to dismiss.

NOTES

1. The leading case interprets Colorado's so-called make-my-day statute (a reference to a movie wherein Clint Eastwood taunts a thug to make threatening moves toward him so that he will be legally justified in killing the thug). The statute, and similar ones like it enacted in a few other states, were passed because of some celebrated civil cases in which homeowners who shot—but failed to kill—intruders then lost their home and all their belongings in defending damage suits brought by the intruders. In some cases, homeowners were convicted of manslaughter for killings under circumstances where the threats were not deemed serious enough to permit the use of deadly force. Make-my-day statutes do not represent the general view in the United States.

2. Defense of the habitation against a dangerous intruder is a right which stems from the law's early view that a man's home is his "fortress" or "castle." This privilege permits one to take the life of an intending trespasser, if the dweller reasonably believes that the threatened entry is for the purpose of committing a felony or inflicting great bodily harm upon an occupant of the house.[5] The rule is even broader in some jurisdictions, allowing the occupant to prevent an intrusion the apparent purpose of which is an assault or other violence non-felonious in nature.[6] The right to defend the habitation permits one to use non-deadly force to prevent a mere civil trespass, although it does not countenance the use of deadly force for that purpose.[7] Where deadly force is inflicted upon a trespasser, however, aggravating circumstances of the trespass may constitute such provocation as to make the killing manslaughter, rather than murder.[8]

The rule allows defense of the habitation by guests or servants of the household, where the occupant himself would be justified in making a defense.[9] It has also been held to encompass the protection of one's place of business, in addition to his dwelling.[10]

One is not bound to retreat from his own house, even if he may do so with safety, in order to avoid taking the life of an assailant. He may stand his ground and kill the aggressor if it becomes necessary.[11]

The use of spring guns or traps for the protection of property or dwellings, resulting in the death of an intruder, may expose the owner of the property to liability for homicide,[12] although some cases have suggested that where the landowner would have been entitled to use similar force if he had been present, the use of the device was lawful.[13]

4.   DEFENSE OF PROPERTY OTHER THAN A DWELLING

Ordinarily, deadly force cannot be used to protect property or to preserve a lawful right of possession. Use of such force, to be justified,

---

[5]   52 A.L.R.2d 1458.

[6]   *See, e.g.,* 720 Ill. Comp. Stat. 5/7–2 (permitting the use of deadly force if the entry into a dwelling is made in a "violent, riotous, or tumultuous manner, and he reasonably believes that such force is necessary to prevent an assault upon, or offer personal violence to him or another then in the dwelling"); Hayner v. People, 213 Ill. 142, 72 N.E. 792 (1904); *see also* Rex v. Hussey, 18 Cr.App.R. 160 (1924) (criticized in Note, *Notes on Recent Cases*, 2 Cambridge L. Quarterly 215, 231 (1925), as carrying the defense of one in his home to an "extreme limit").

[7]   State v. Hibler, 79 S.C. 170, 60 S.E. 438 (1908).

[8]   State v. Adams, 78 Iowa 292, 43 N.W. 194 (1889); State v. Welch, 37 N.M. 549, 25 P.2d 211 (1933).

[9]   Davis v. Commonwealth, 252 S.W.2d 9 (Ky. 1952).

[10]   Suell v. Derricott, 161 Ala. 259, 49 So. 895 (1909). Commonwealth v. Johnston, 438 Pa. 485, 263 A.2d 376 (1970). *See also* 41 A.L.R.3d 584.

[11]   Jones v. State, 76 Ala. 8 (1884). *But see* Cooper v. United States, 512 A.2d 1002 (D.C. App. 1986) (holding that a defendant who sought to prove that he acted in self-defense in killing his brother in their home was not entitled to a jury instruction that he had no duty whatsoever to retreat in his own home). The "castle doctrine" does not apply where a defendant claims self-defense in response to an attack in his home by a co-occupant.

[12]   State v. Childers, 133 Ohio St. 508, 14 N.E.2d 767 (1938); Pierce v. Commonwealth, 135 Va. 635, 115 S.E. 686 (1923); Katko v. Briney, 183 N.W.2d 657 (Iowa 1971); People v. Ceballos, 12 Cal.3d 470, 116 Cal.Rptr. 233, 526 P.2d 241 (1974).

[13]   State v. Beckham, 306 Mo. 566, 267 S.W. 817 (1924); State v. Barr, 11 Wash. 481, 39 P. 1080 (1895). However, in State v. Marfaudille, 48 Wash. 117, 92 P. 939 (1907), the court indicated that use of a device could be sanctioned only to prevent atrocious and violent felonies creating danger to human life.

must be sanctioned under a different principle, such as that of self-defense, defense of dwelling, or preventing a felony.

Consider the following provision of the Illinois Criminal Code (S.H.A. ch. 38):

§ 7–3. Use of Force in Defense of Other Property.

A person is justified in the use of force against another when and to the extent that he reasonably believes that such conduct is necessary to prevent or terminate such other's trespass on or other tortious or criminal interference with either real property (other than a dwelling) or personal property, lawfully in his possession or in the possession of another who is a member of his immediate family or household or of a person whose property he has a legal duty to protect. However, he is justified in the use of force which is intended or likely to cause death or great bodily harm only if he reasonably believes that such force is necessary to prevent the commission of a forcible felony.

5. PREVENTION OF FELONY AND APPREHENSION OF DANGEROUS FELONS

The right to take life to prevent the commission of a felony is confined to the prevention of a *dangerous* felony. A corollary of this principle is the rule that homicide is not justifiable when committed for the protection of mere property rights or interests, although the punishment for such killings is usually of the manslaughter grade rather than murder.[14]

---

[14] *See* State v. Green, 118 S.C. 279, 110 S.E. 145, 19 A.L.R. 1431 (1921) ("spring gun" killing). Thus a burglar or robber—but not a larcenist or trespasser—may be killed, if such a measure reasonably seems necessary to frustrate the criminal. In Commonwealth v. Beverly, 237 Ky. 35, 34 S.W.2d 941 (1931), which involved the shooting of chicken thieves, the court said:

The law does not justify the taking of human life to prevent a mere trespass without felonious intention, nor to prevent a felony not involving the security of the person or the home or in which violence is not a constituent part.

The right to kill to prevent a felony applies at any stage prior to completion of the crime. In Viliborghi v. State, 45 Ariz. 275, 291, 43 P.2d 210, 217 (1935), the court stated:

. . . [T]he owner of the premises burglarized may, at any stage of a burglary, kill the burglar if it be reasonably necessary to prevent the final completion of his felonious purpose, regardless at what stage of the crime the shooting occurs. He may, even after the burglary has been completed, and the burglar is withdrawing from the scene of his crime, if the latter attempts to resist or flee from arrest, use such force as is reasonably necessary for the apprehension of the offender, even to the taking of life.

An individual not only has a right but also an obligation to prevent the commission of a felony in his presence. "According to the common law, it is the duty of everyone, seeing any felony attempted, by force to prevent it, if need be, by the extinguishment of the felon's existence. This is a public duty, and the discharge of it is regarded as promotive of justice. Anyone who fails to discharge it is guilty of an indictable misdemeanor, called misprision of felony." Carpenter v. State, 62 Ark. 286, 308, 36 S.W. 900, 906 (1896).

6. DEADLY FORCE BY POLICE OFFICERS

Tennessee v. Garner

Supreme Court of United States, 1985.
471 U.S. 1, 105 S.Ct. 1694, 85 L.Ed.2d 1.

■ JUSTICE WHITE delivered the opinion of the Court.

* * *

I

At about 10:45 p.m. on October 3, 1974, Memphis Police Officers Elton Hymon and Leslie Wright were dispatched to answer a "prowler inside call." Upon arriving at the scene they saw a woman standing on her porch and gesturing toward the adjacent house. She told them she had heard glass breaking and that "they" or "someone" was breaking in next door. While Wright radioed the dispatcher to say that they were on the scene, Hymon went behind the house. He heard a door slam and saw someone run across the backyard. The fleeing suspect, who was appellee-respondent's decedent, Edward Garner, stopped at a 6-feet-high chain link fence at the edge of the yard. With the aid of a flashlight, Hymon was able to see Garner's face and hands. He saw no sign of a weapon, and, though not certain, was "reasonably sure" and "figured" that Garner was unarmed. He thought Garner was 17 or 18 years old and about 5'5" or 5'7" tall. While Garner was crouched at the base of the fence, Hymon called out "police, halt" and took a few steps toward him. Garner then began to climb over the fence. Convinced that if Garner made it over the fence he would elude capture, Hymon shot him. The bullet hit Garner in the back of the head. Garner was taken by ambulance to a hospital, where he died on the operating table. Ten dollars and a purse taken from the house were found on his body.

In using deadly force to prevent the escape, Hymon was acting under the authority of a Tennessee statute and pursuant to Police Department policy. The statute provides that "[i]f, after notice of the intention to arrest the defendant, he either flee or forcibly resist, the officer may use all the necessary means to effect the arrest." Tenn.Code Ann. § 40–7–108 (1982). The Department policy was slightly more restrictive than the statute, but still allowed the use of deadly force in cases of burglary. The incident was reviewed by the Memphis Police Firearm's Review Board and presented to a grand jury. Neither took any action.

Garner's father then brought this action in the Federal District Court for the Western District of Tennessee, seeking damages under 42 U.S.C. § 1983 for asserted violations of Garner's constitutional rights. . . . [T]he District Court entered judgment for all defendants. It dismissed the claims against the Mayor and the Director for lack of evidence . . .

* * *

. . . The Court of Appeals reversed and remanded. It reasoned that the killing of a fleeing suspect is a "seizure" under the Fourth Amendment, and is therefore constitutional only if "reasonable." . . . The State of Tennessee, which had intervened to defend the statute, appealed to this Court . . .

II

Whenever an officer restrains the freedom of a person to walk away, he has seized that person. While it is not always clear just when minimal police interference becomes a seizure, there can be no question that apprehension by the use of deadly force is a seizure subject to the reasonableness requirement of the Fourth Amendment.

A police officer may arrest a person if he has probable cause to believe that person has committed a crime. Petitioners and appellant argue that if this requirement is satisfied the Fourth Amendment has nothing to say about *how* that seizure is made. This submission ignores the many cases in which this Court, by balancing the extent of the intrusion against the need for it, has examined the reasonableness of the manner in which a search and seizure is conducted. . . . We have described the balancing of competing interests as the key principle of the Fourth Amendment. Because one of the factors is the extent of the intrusion, it is plain that reasonableness depends on not only when a seizure is made, but also how it is carried out.

* * *

The same balancing process applied in the cases cited above demonstrates that, notwithstanding probable cause to seize a suspect, an officer may not always do so by killing him. The intrusiveness of a seizure by means of deadly force is unmatched. The suspect's fundamental interest in his own life need not be elaborated upon. The use of deadly force also frustrates the interests of the individual, and of society, in judicial determination of guilt and punishment. Against these interests are ranged governmental interests in effective law enforcement. It is argued that overall violence will be reduced by encouraging the peaceful submission of suspects who know that they may be shot if they flee. Effectiveness in making arrests requires the resort to deadly force, or at least the meaningful threat thereof . . .

Without in any way disparaging the importance of these goals, we are not convinced that the use of deadly force is a sufficiently productive means of accomplishing them to justify the killing of nonviolent suspects. The use of deadly force is a self-defeating way of apprehending a suspect and so setting the criminal justice mechanism in motion. If successful, it guarantees that that mechanism will not be set in motion. And while the meaningful threat of deadly force might be thought to lead to the arrest of more live suspects by discouraging escape attempts, the presently available evidence does not support this thesis. The fact is that a majority of police departments in this country have forbidden the use of deadly force against nonviolent suspects. If those charged with the enforcement of the criminal law have adjured the use of deadly force in arresting nondangerous felons, there is a substantial basis for doubting that the use of such force is an essential attribute of the arrest power in all felony cases. Petitioners and appellant have not persuaded us that shooting nondangerous fleeing suspects is so vital as to outweigh the suspect's interest in his own life.

The use of deadly force to prevent the escape of all felony suspects, whatever the circumstances, is constitutionally unreasonable. It is not better that all felony suspects die than that they escape. Where the suspect poses no immediate threat to the officer and no threat to others, the harm resulting from failing to apprehend him does not justify the use of deadly force to do so. It is no doubt unfortunate when a suspect who is in sight escapes, but the fact that the police arrive a little late or are a little slower afoot does not always justify killing the suspect. A police officer may not seize an unarmed, nondangerous suspect by shooting him dead. The Tennessee statute is unconstitutional insofar as it authorizes the use of deadly force against such fleeing suspects.

Tennessee statute unconst. in some cases

It is not, however, unconstitutional on its face. Where the officer has probable cause to believe that the suspect poses a threat of serious physical harm, either to the officer or to others, it is not constitutionally unreasonable to prevent escape by using deadly force. Thus, if the suspect threatens the officer with a weapon or there is probable cause to believe that he has committed a crime involving the infliction or threatened infliction of serious physical harm, deadly force may be used if necessary to prevent escape, and if, where feasible, some warning has been given . . .

III

It is insisted that the Fourth Amendment must be construed in light of the common-law rule, which allowed the use of whatever force was necessary to effect the arrest of a fleeing felon, though not a misdemeanant . . .

The State and city argue that because this was the prevailing rule at the time of the adoption of the Fourth Amendment and for some time thereafter, and is still in force in some States, use of deadly force against a fleeing felon must be "reasonable." It is true that this Court has often looked to the common law in evaluating the reasonableness, for Fourth Amendment purposes, of police activity. On the other hand, it has not simply frozen into constitutional law those law enforcement practices that existed at the time of the Fourth Amendment's passage. Because of sweeping change in the legal and technological context, reliance on the common-law rule in this case would be a mistaken literalism that ignores the purposes of an historical inquiry.

It has been pointed out many times that the common-law rule is best understood in light of the fact that it arose at a time when virtually all felonies were punishable by death. "Though effected without the protections and formalities of an orderly trial and conviction, the killing of a resisting or fleeing felon resulted in no greater consequences than those authorized for punishment of the felony of which the individual was charged or suspected." American Law Institute, Model Penal Code § 3.07, Comment 3, p. 56 (Tentative Draft No. 8, 1958) (hereinafter Model Penal Code Comment). Courts have also justified the common-law rule by emphasizing the relative dangerousness of felons.

Neither of these justifications makes sense today. Almost all crimes formerly punishable by death no longer are or can be. And while in earlier times "the gulf between the felonies and the minor offences was broad and deep," today the distinction is minor and often arbitrary. Many crimes classified as misdemeanors, or nonexistent, at common law are now felonies. These changes have undermined the concept, which was questionable to begin with, that use of deadly force against a fleeing felon is merely a speedier execution of someone who has already forfeited his life. They have also made the assumption that a "felon" is more dangerous than a misdemeanant untenable. Indeed, numerous misdemeanors involve conduct more dangerous than many felonies.

There is an additional reason why the common-law rule cannot be directly translated to the present day. The common-law rule developed at a time when weapons were rudimentary. Deadly force could be inflicted almost solely in a hand-to-hand struggle during which, necessarily, the safety of the arresting officer was at risk. Handguns were not carried by police officers until the latter half of the last century. Only then did it become possible to use deadly force from a distance as a means of apprehension. As a practical matter, the use of deadly force under the standard articulation of the common-law rule has an altogether different meaning—and harsher consequences—now than in past centuries.

One other aspect of the common-law rule bears emphasis. It forbids the use of deadly force to apprehend a misdemeanant, condemning such action as disproportionately severe.

In short, though the common law pedigree of Tennessee's rule is pure on its face, changes in the legal and technological context mean the rule is distorted almost beyond recognition when literally applied.

In evaluating the reasonableness of police procedures under the Fourth Amendment, we have also looked to prevailing rules in individual jurisdictions. The rules in the States are varied. Some 19 States have codified the common-law rule, though in two of these the courts have significantly limited the statute.[15] Four States, though without a

---

[15] In California, the police may use deadly force to arrest only if the crime for which the arrest is sought was "a forcible and atrocious one which threatens death or serious bodily harm," or there is a substantial risk that the person whose arrest is sought will cause death or serious

relevant statute, apparently retain the common-law rule. Two States have adopted the Model Penal Code's provision verbatim. Eighteen others allow, in slightly varying language, the use of deadly force only if the suspect has committed a felony involving the use or threat of physical or deadly force, or is escaping with a deadly weapon, or is likely to endanger life or inflict serious physical injury if not arrested. Louisiana and Vermont, though without statutes or case-law on point, do forbid the use of deadly force to prevent any but violent felonies. The remaining States either have no relevant statute or case-law, or have positions that are unclear.

It cannot be said that there is a constant or overwhelming trend away from the common-law rule. In recent years, some States have reviewed their laws and expressly rejected abandonment of the common-law rule.[21] Nonetheless, the long-term movement has been away from the rule that deadly force may be used against any fleeing felon, and that remains the rule in less than half the States.

This trend is more evident and impressive when viewed in light of the policies adopted by the police departments themselves. Overwhelmingly, these are more restrictive than the common-law rule. The Federal Bureau of Investigation and the New York City Police Department, for example, both forbid the use of firearms except when necessary to prevent death or grievous bodily harm. For accreditation by the Commission on Accreditation for Law Enforcement Agencies, a department must restrict the use of deadly force to situations where "the officer reasonably believes that the action is in defense of human life . . . or in defense of any person in immediate danger of serious physical injury." . . . Overall, only 7.5% of departmental and municipal policies explicitly permit the use of deadly force against any felon; 86.8% explicitly do not. In light of the rules adopted by those who must actually administer them, the older and fading common-law view is a dubious indicium of the constitutionality of the Tennessee statute now before us.

Actual departmental policies are important for an additional reason. We would hesitate to declare a police practice of longstanding "unreasonable" if doing so would severely hamper effective law enforcement. But the indications are to the contrary. There has been no suggestion that crime has worsened in any way in jurisdictions that have

---

bodily harm if apprehension is delayed. Kortum v. Alkire, 69 Cal.App.3d 325, 333, 138 Cal.Rptr. 26, 30–31 (1977). See also Long Beach Police Officers Assn. v. Long Beach, 61 Cal.App.3d 364, 373–374, 132 Cal.Rptr. 348, 353–354 (1976). In Indiana, deadly force may be used only to prevent injury, the imminent danger of injury or force, or the threat of force. It is not permitted simply to prevent escape. Rose v. State, 431 N.E.2d 521 (Ind.App.1982).

[21] In adopting its current statute in 1979, for example, Alabama expressly chose the common-law rule over more restrictive provisions. Ala.Code §§ 67–68 (1982). Missouri likewise considered but rejected a proposal akin to the Model Penal Code rule. See Mattis v. Schnarr, 547 F.2d 1007, 1022 (C.A.8 1976) (GIBSON, C.J., dissenting), vacated as moot sub nom. Ashcroft v. Mattis, 431 U.S. 171, 97 S.Ct. 1739, 52 L.Ed.2d 219 (1977). Idaho, whose current statute codifies the common-law rule, adopted the Model Penal Code in 1971, but abandoned it in 1972.

adopted, by legislation or departmental policy, rules similar to that announced today. *Amici* noted that "[a]fter extensive research and consideration, [they] have concluded that laws permitting police officers to use deadly force to apprehend unarmed, non-violent fleeing felony suspects actually do not protect citizens or law enforcement officers, do not deter crime or alleviate problems caused by crime, and do not improve the crime-fighting ability of law enforcement agencies." The submission is that the obvious state interests in apprehension are not sufficiently served to warrant the use of lethal weapons against all fleeing felons.

* * *

V

. . . We hold that the statute is invalid insofar as it purported to give Hymon the authority to act as he did. As for the policy of the Police Department, the absence of any discussion of this issue by the courts below, and the uncertain state of the record, preclude any consideration of its validity.

The judgment of the Court of Appeals is affirmed, and the case is remanded for further proceedings consistent with this opinion.

So ordered.

■ JUSTICE O'CONNOR, with whom THE CHIEF JUSTICE, and JUSTICE REHNQUIST join, dissenting.

The Court today holds that the Fourth Amendment prohibits a police officer from using deadly force as a last resort to apprehend a criminal suspect who refuses to halt when fleeing the scene of a nighttime burglary. This conclusion rests on the majority's balancing of the interests of the suspect and the public interest in effective law enforcement. Notwithstanding the venerable common-law rule authorizing the use of deadly force if necessary to apprehend a fleeing felon, and continued acceptance of this rule by nearly half the States, the majority concludes that Tennessee's statute is unconstitutional inasmuch as it allows the use of such force to apprehend a burglary suspect who is not obviously armed or otherwise dangerous. Although the circumstances of this case are unquestionably tragic and unfortunate, our constitutional holdings must be sensitive both to the history of the Fourth Amendment and to the general implications of the Court's reasoning. By disregarding the serious and dangerous nature of residential burglaries and the longstanding practice of many States, the Court effectively creates a Fourth Amendment right allowing a burglary suspect to flee unimpeded from a police officer who has probable cause to arrest, who has ordered the suspect to halt, and who has no means short of firing his weapon to prevent escape. I do not believe that the Fourth Amendment supports such a right, and I accordingly dissent.

* * *

The public interest involved in the use of deadly force as a last resort to apprehend a fleeing burglary suspect relates primarily to the serious nature of the crime. Household burglaries represent not only the illegal entry into a person's home, but also "pos[e] real risk of serious harm to others." . . . According to recent Department of Justice statistics, "[t]hree-fifths of all rapes in the home, three-fifths of all home robberies, and about a third of home aggravated and simple assaults are committed by burglars." During the period 1973–1982, 2.8 million such violent crimes were committed in the course of burglaries. Victims of a forcible intrusion into their home by a nighttime prowler will find little consolation in the majority's confident assertion that "burglaries only rarely involve physical violence." Moreover, even if a particular burglary, when viewed in retrospect, does not involve physical harm to others, the "harsh potentialities for violence" inherent in the forced entry into a home preclude characterization of the crime as "innocuous, inconsequential, minor, or 'nonviolent.' " . . .

Because burglary is a serious and dangerous felony, the public interest in the prevention and detection of the crime is of compelling importance. Where a police officer has probable cause to arrest a suspected burglar, the use of deadly force as a last resort might well be the only means of apprehending the suspect. With respect to a particular burglary, subsequent investigation simply cannot represent a substitute for immediate apprehension of the criminal suspect at the scene. Indeed, the Captain of the Memphis Police Department testified that in his city, if apprehension is not immediate, it is likely that the suspect will not be caught. Although some law enforcement agencies may choose to assume the risk that a criminal will remain at large, the Tennessee statute reflects a legislative determination that the use of deadly force in prescribed circumstances will serve generally to protect the public. Such statutes assist the police in apprehending suspected perpetrators of serious crimes and provide notice that a lawful police order to stop and submit to arrest may not be ignored with impunity.

The Court unconvincingly dismisses the general deterrence effects by stating that "the presently available evidence does not support [the] thesis" that the threat of force discourages escape and that "there is a substantial basis for doubting that the use of such force is an essential attribute to the arrest power in all felony cases." There is no question that the effectiveness of police use of deadly force is arguable and that many States or individual police departments have decided not to authorize it in circumstances similar to those presented here. But it should go without saying that the effectiveness or popularity of a particular police practice does not determine its constitutionality. . . . Moreover, the fact that police conduct pursuant to a state statute is challenged on constitutional grounds does not impose a burden on the State to produce social science statistics or to dispel any possible doubts about the necessity of the conduct. This observation, I believe, has particular force where the challenged practice both predates enactment of the Bill of Rights and continues to be accepted by a substantial number of the States.

Against the strong public interests justifying the conduct at issue here must be weighed the individual interests implicated in the use of deadly force by police officers. The majority declares that "[t]he suspect's fundamental interest in his own life need not be elaborated upon." This blithe assertion hardly provides an adequate substitute for the majority's failure to acknowledge the distinctive manner in which the suspect's interest in his life is even exposed to risk. For purposes of this case, we must recall that the police officer, in the course of investigating a nighttime burglary, had reasonable cause to arrest the suspect and ordered him to halt. The officer's use of force resulted because the suspected burglar refused to heed this command and the officer reasonably believed that there was no means short of firing his weapon to apprehend the suspect. Without questioning the importance of a person's interest in his life, I do not think this interest encompasses a right to flee unimpeded from the scene of a burglary. . . . The legitimate interests of the suspect in these circumstances are adequately accommodated by the Tennessee statute: to avoid the use of deadly force and the consequent risk to his life, the suspect need merely obey the valid order to halt.

A proper balancing of the interests involved suggests that use of deadly force as a last resort to apprehend a criminal suspect fleeing from the scene of a nighttime burglary is not unreasonable within the meaning of the Fourth Amendment. . . .

* * *

III

The Court's silence on critical factors in the decision to use deadly force simply invites second-guessing of difficult police decisions that must be made quickly in the most trying of circumstances. Police are given no guidance for determining which objects, among an array of potentially lethal weapons ranging from guns to knives to baseball bats to rope, will justify the use of deadly force. The Court also declines to outline the additional factors necessary to provide "probable cause" for believing that a suspect "poses a significant threat of death or serious physical injury," when the officer has probable cause to arrest and the suspect refuses to obey an order to halt. But even if it were appropriate in this case to limit the use of deadly force to that ambiguous class of suspects, I believe the class should include nighttime residential burglars who resist arrest by attempting to flee the scene of the crime. We can expect an escalating volume of litigation as the lower courts struggle to determine if a police officer's split-second decision to shoot was justified by the danger posed by a particular object and other facts related to the crime.

IV

The Court's opinion sweeps broadly to adopt an entirely new standard for the constitutionality of the use of deadly force to apprehend fleeing felons. Thus, the Court lightly brushe[s] aside a long-standing police practice that predates the Fourth Amendment and continues to receive the approval of nearly half of the state legislatures. I cannot accept the majority's creation of a constitutional right to flight for burglary suspects seeking to avoid capture at the scene of the crime. Whatever the constitutional limits on police use of deadly force in order to apprehend a fleeing felon, I do not believe they are exceeded in a case in which a police officer has probable cause to arrest a suspect at the scene of a residential burglary, orders the suspect to halt, and then fires his weapon as a last resort to prevent the suspect's escape into the night. I respectfully dissent.

NOTES

1. *Tennessee v. Garner* was applied by the Minnesota Supreme Court in Mumm v. Mornson, 708 N.W.2d 475 (2006), a case where police use of deadly force—the intentional ramming of a reckless woman's car with a police vehicle—resulted in injury and a fatality. Officers had gone to Mornson's therapist's office to transport the Mornson to a hospital after being informed she was potentially suicidal. While driving her car away from the therapist's office, Mornson noticed she was being pursued by police she began driving recklessly. Rather than calling of the pursuit, the officers decided to ram the plaintiff's car, which action resulted in injuries and a fatality. She brought a 42 U.S.C. § 1983 civil rights action, claiming the use of excessive police force. The court stated:

> The fact that a person suffering from a mental disturbance or mental illness drives recklessly to evade police does not automatically signal to police that the individual poses a significant threat of serious injury to others . . . Given that the Mornson's only crimes were traffic violations and her refusal to stop for police and given the evidence that Mornson did not overtly seek to injure anyone either before or during the chase, it would have been clear to a reasonable officer that he did not have probable cause to believe that Mornson posed a significant risk of serious injury to the officer or others.

What about the threat to the reckless driver himself? In Phelps v. Commonwealth, 639 S.E.2d 689 (Va. App. 2007), "the uncontested facts show[ed] that defendant, while driving at a high rate of speed in an attempt to elude police, crossed over the oncoming lane of traffic, drove into a ditch, struck a culvert, and flipped his own vehicle." Defendant was convicted of driving a motor vehicle in such a way as to endanger "a person." Although the car chase occurred late at night on an isolated country road, and threatened no one other than defendant, the defendant was deemed "a person" within the meaning of the statute. Could the police have used force to prevent the defendant from endangering himself?

2. With respect to the listing of Illinois among the various states in leading case's footnote 6, consider the wording of 720 Ill. Comp. Stat. 5/7–5, and particularly subsection (a)(2):

> **§ 7–5 Peace Officer's Use of Force in Making Arrest.** (a) A peace officer, or any person whom he has summoned or directed to assist him, need not retreat or desist from efforts to make a lawful arrest because of resistance or threatened resistance to the arrest. He is justified in the use of any force which he reasonably believes to be necessary to effect the arrest and of any force which he reasonably believes to be necessary to defend himself or another from bodily harm while making the arrest. However, he is justified in using force likely to cause death or great bodily harm only when he reasonably believes that such force is necessary to prevent death or great bodily harm to himself or such other person, or when he reasonably believes both that:
>
> > (1) Such force is necessary to prevent the arrest from being defeated by resistance or escape; and
> >
> > (2) The person to be arrested has committed or attempted a forcible felony or is attempting to escape by use of a deadly weapon, or otherwise indicates that he will endanger human life or inflict great bodily harm unless arrested without delay.
>
> > (b) A peace officer making an arrest pursuant to an invalid warrant is justified in the use of any force which he would be justified in using if the warrant were valid, unless he knows that the warrant is invalid.

3. In Saucier v. Katz, 533 U.S. 194, 121 S.Ct. 2151, 150 L.Ed.2d 272 (2001), the Court

> cautioned against the '20/20 vision of hindsight' in favor of deference to the judgment of reasonable officers on the scene. Factors relevant to the merits of the constitutional excessive force claim, 'require careful attention to the facts and circumstances of each particular case, including the severity of the crime at issue, whether the suspect poses an immediate threat to the safety of the officers or others, and whether he is actively resisting arrest or attempting to evade arrest by flight.' If an officer reasonably, but mistakenly, believed that a suspect was likely to fight back, for instance, the officer would be justified in using more force than in fact was needed.

4. In Robles v. Prince George's Cnty., 308 F.3d 437 (4th Cir. 2002), the court noted that

> [t]he Fourth Amendment "governs claims of excessive force during the course of an arrest, investigatory stop, or other seizure of a person." However, this court has rejected any concept of a continuing seizure rule, noting that the "Fourth Amendment . . .

applies to the initial decision to detain an accused, not to the conditions of confinement after that decision has been made." Once the single act of detaining an individual has been accomplished, the Amendment ceases to apply. [The Due Process clause governs the conditions of continuing restraint.]

7. FORCIBLY RESISTING ARREST

Commonwealth v. Hill
Supreme Court of Virginia, 2002.
264 Va. 541, 570 S.E.2d 805.

■ Opinion by JUSTICE BARBARA MILANO KEENAN.

In this appeal, we consider whether the Court of Appeals erred in reversing a defendant's conviction and dismissing an indictment on the ground that the common law right to use reasonable force to resist an illegal arrest also confers a right to use reasonable force to resist an illegal detention.

John H. Hill, Jr., was indicted for assault and battery of a law enforcement officer, in violation of Code § 18.2–57(C). Hill was accused of striking Officer K.I. Fromme of the City of Suffolk Police Department while Fromme was attempting to conduct a "pat down" search of Hill to determine whether he was carrying a weapon. Hill was convicted of the offense in the Circuit Court of the City of Suffolk. The court sentenced him to a term of three years' imprisonment and suspended two and one-half years of that sentence.

Hill appealed from his conviction to the Court of Appeals, which reversed the trial court's judgment and dismissed the indictment. The Court of Appeals concluded, among other things, that Hill's physical resistance "to an illegal detention and search was reasonable and proportionate to the conduct of the police." The Commonwealth appeals the Court of Appeals' judgment.

The evidence showed that on July 9, 1999, at 1:21 a.m., Officer Fromme received a dispatch report, which was based on an anonymous telephone call, stating that two black males were "possibly dealing firearms" in front of a green house in the 400 block of Briggs Street. Fromme was familiar with that part of Briggs Street as "an area where drugs are bought and sold." A few minutes later, he arrived at the scene and was met shortly thereafter by two other police officers.

At that time, Officer Fromme saw Hill sitting in the driver's seat of a car, which had the driver's side door opened and was parked in front of a green house in the 400 block of Briggs Street. The officers did not observe any suspicious activity as they approached the car. Hill and his companion did not attempt to run away and Hill complied with the officers' request that he get out of the car.

Officer Fromme explained to the two men that he had received a complaint about two suspects "possibly dealing weapons," and that, for reasons concerning safety, he wanted to "pat them down" to determine whether they carried any firearms. Fromme "patted down" Hill's left side without encountering any resistance from Hill. However, as Fromme attempted to "pat down" Hill's right side, Fromme noticed a bulge in the right pocket of Hill's pants. Hill pushed Fromme's hand away in an attempt to prevent him from "patting down" that pocket.

Officer Fromme again told Hill that he only wanted to determine whether Hill carried any weapons. As Fromme reached toward the right pocket of Hill's pants, Hill placed his hand in that pocket. When Fromme grabbed Hill's hand and removed it from the pocket, Hill turned and tried to run away.

As Hill turned away from Officer Fromme, he struck the officer in the mouth with his open hand, splitting Fromme's lip. Hill was able to run a short distance before all three officers struggled with him in an attempt to force him to the ground and restrain him. During the struggle, Hill struck Fromme "a couple of times" before the officers were able to place Hill in handcuffs.

Officer Fromme searched the right pocket of Hill's pants and discovered "a corner of a plastic baggie" concealed inside of a black pen cap. The plastic baggie contained about 0.17 grams of cocaine. In Hill's right hand, Officer Fromme discovered a film canister containing five "rocks" of crack cocaine, which weighed a total of 5.01 grams. The officers did not find any weapons on Hill's person or in the vehicle he had occupied.

Before trial, Hill filed a motion to suppress the seized evidence on the ground that his detention was illegal because Officer Fromme did not have reasonable suspicion that Hill was armed and dangerous or was involved in any criminal activity. At a hearing that was later made part of the trial record, Hill testified that he consented to a "pat down" search for weapons, and that he did not resist Fromme's actions until Fromme tried to reach into Hill's pocket. Hill also testified that he "accidentally hit" Fromme while attempting to run away.

The trial court denied Hill's motion. The court concluded that given the nature of the dispatch report, Officer Fromme "made a reasonable pat down or attempt at a pat down for officer safety. And it was the [resistance to] that pat down that led to . . . the arrest."

In a bench trial, the court found Hill guilty of the felonious assault charge. After this conviction, but before Hill's sentencing, the United States Supreme Court published *Florida v. J.L.*, 529 U.S. 266, 120 S.Ct. 1375, 146 L.Ed.2d 254 (2000).

In *J.L.*, the Court considered the issue "whether an anonymous tip that a person is carrying a gun is, without more, sufficient to justify a police officer's stop and frisk of that person." The Court concluded that "reasonable suspicion . . . requires that a tip be reliable in its assertion of illegality, not just in its tendency to identify a determinate person." The Court held that "an anonymous tip lacking indicia of reliability . . . does not justify a stop and frisk whenever and however it alleges the illegal possession of a firearm."

Before his sentencing hearing, Hill filed a motion to set aside his conviction, relying on the Supreme Court's holding in *J.L.* The trial court concluded that under the decision in *J.L.*, Hill was unlawfully detained. However, the court held that Hill's actions were unlawful because his resistance was disproportionate to Officer Fromme's attempt to remove Hill's hand from his pocket. On this basis, the court denied the motion to set aside the conviction.

In his appeal to the Court of Appeals, Hill argued that his conviction should be reversed "because he used reasonable force to repel an illegal arrest." The Court of Appeals concluded that Hill was the subject of an illegal detention, not an illegal arrest. However, the Court held that the common law doctrine allowing an individual to use reasonable force to resist an illegal arrest applies also to a detainee's efforts to resist an illegal detention.

The Court further concluded that Hill did not use excessive force to resist the detention because he struck Officer Fromme with an "open hand," he "did not aggressively pursue or attack" Fromme, and he only struck Fromme in attempting "to get away from the officer's assault." Based on this holding, the Court reversed Hill's conviction and dismissed the indictment.

On appeal to this Court, the Commonwealth argues that the Court of Appeals erred in extending the common law right to use reasonable force to resist an unlawful arrest to an incident involving only an unlawful detention. The Commonwealth asserts that there is a significant distinction between a detention and an arrest because a detention involves only a temporary deprivation of the detainee's liberty, while an arrest is the initial stage of a criminal prosecution that restricts the arrested person's freedom for an extended period of time. The Commonwealth contends that a rule permitting a detainee to resist an illegal detention would escalate the danger of violence to law enforcement officers engaged in the reasonable performance of their duties. Thus, the Commonwealth maintains that the determination whether a detention is legal "should be left solely to the courts, not the fist of the suspect."

In response, Hill argues that the "pat down" search conducted by Officer Fromme was unlawful because he did not have a basis for concluding that Hill may have been armed and dangerous or engaged in criminal activity. Hill contends that Fromme's actions gave Hill the right to use reasonable force to resist the unlawful detention and search. We disagree with Hill's arguments.

We first observe that the trial court held that Officer Fromme acted illegally when he detained Hill based on an anonymous tip. The Commonwealth did not challenge this ruling either in the trial court or in the Court of Appeals. Therefore, we do not consider that issue and restrict our analysis to the question whether the common law right to use reasonable force to resist an illegal arrest is applicable to the use of such force to resist an illegal detention.

This issue presents a pure question of law. Thus, we do not give deference to the trial court's conclusions on the subject, and we are permitted the same opportunity as the trial court to consider that question of law.

Under the common law, a citizen generally is permitted to use reasonable force to resist an illegal arrest. The underlying rationale supporting this common law right is the "provocation" of an illegal arrest, which operates to excuse an assault directed at thwarting the unlawful arrest. An unlawful arrest was considered a great provocation at common law because of the dire consequences, including incarceration of extreme duration, which often resulted before an accused was permitted a trial for the charged offense.

This historical impetus underlying the common law right to resist an illegal arrest does not raise corresponding concerns in the context of a contemporary investigative detention. In our present justice system, the different consequences that attend an arrest and an investigative detention are manifest. As the Supreme Court stated in *Terry v. Ohio*, 392 U.S. 1, 88 S.Ct. 1868, 20 L.Ed.2d 889 (1968):

> An arrest is a wholly different kind of intrusion upon individual freedom from a limited search for weapons, and the interests each is designed to serve are likewise quite different. An arrest is the initial stage of a criminal prosecution. It is intended to vindicate society's interest in having its laws obeyed, and it is inevitably accompanied by future interference with the individual's freedom of movement, whether or not trial or conviction ultimately follows.

After an arrest, a citizen's liberty is completely constrained, at a minimum, until a judicial officer has determined the issue of bail. Police and court records permanently record the event of an arrest, which becomes an indelible part of a citizen's history unless a court order later is issued expunging those arrest records.

In contrast, a protective search for weapons or other investigative detention constitutes a brief, though not inconsequential, restriction on an individual's freedom of movement. Such detentions are informal encounters that generally are not the subject of any public record.

Because a detention is, by its nature, a brief intrusion on an individual's liberty, the provocation resulting from an illegal detention is far less significant than the provocation that attends an illegal arrest. Thus, recognition of a right to resist an unlawful detention would not advance the rationale supporting the common law right to use reasonable force to resist an unlawful arrest, but would only serve to increase the danger of violence inherent in such detentions.[2] "Close questions as to whether an officer possesses articulable suspicion must be resolved in the courtroom and not fought out on the streets."

Accordingly, we hold that a person in this Commonwealth does not have the right to use force to resist an unlawful detention or "pat down" search. Thus, in the present case, Hill did not have the right to use force to resist the challenged detention and "pat down" search by Officer Fromme, and the Court of Appeals erred in reaching a contrary conclusion.

For these reasons, we will reverse the judgment of the Court of Appeals, and we will reinstate Hill's conviction in accordance with the trial court's judgment order because the trial court reached the correct result in this case, although for the wrong reason.

Reversed and final judgment.

D. INVOLUNTARY MANSLAUGHTER

State v. Horton

Supreme Court of North Carolina, 1905.
139 N.C. 588, 51 S.E. 945.

[The defendant, Horton, in violation of a statute, was hunting turkeys on the land of another without the written consent of the owner of the land or his lawful agent. While hunting, Horton unintentionally killed one Hunt, mistaking him for a wild turkey. Horton was indicted for manslaughter, convicted and sentenced to four months in the county jail. Thereupon, the defendant appealed.]

■ HOKE, JUSTICE. It will be noted that the finding of the jury declares that the act of the defendant was not in itself dangerous to human life, and excludes every element of criminal negligence, and rests the guilt or innocence of the defendant on the fact alone that at the time of the homicide the defendant was hunting on another's land without written permission from the owner. The act . . . makes the conduct a misdemeanor, and imposes a punishment on conviction of not less than $5 nor more than $10. The statement sometimes appears in works of approved excellence to the effect that an unintentional homicide is a criminal offense when occasioned by a person engaged at the time in an unlawful act. In nearly every instance, however, will be found the

---

[2]   We note that the overall trend in a majority of states has been toward abrogation of the common law right to use reasonable force to resist an unlawful arrest. *See Valentine*, 935 P.2d at 1302; *Hobson*, 577 N.W.2d at 834–35. That issue is not before us here.

qualification that if the act in question is free from negligence, and not in itself of dangerous tendency, and the criminality must arise, if at all, entirely from the fact that it is unlawful, in such case, the unlawful act must be one that is "malum in se," and not merely "malum prohibitum," and this we hold to be the correct doctrine . . .

. . . Bishop, in his work entitled New Criminal Law (volume 1, § 332), treats of the matter as follows: "In these cases of an unintended evil result, the intent whence the act accidentally sprang must probably be, if specific, to do a thing which is malum in se, and not merely malum prohibitum." Thus Archbold says: "When a man in the execution of one act, by misfortune or chance, and not designedly, does another act, for which, if he had willfully committed it, he would be liable to be punished, in that case, if the act he were doing were lawful, or merely malum prohibitum, he shall not be punishable for the act arising from misfortune or chance; but, if it be malum in se, it is otherwise. To illustrate: Since it is malum prohibitum, not malum in se, for an unauthorized person to kill game in England contrary to the statutes, if, in unlawfully shooting at game, he accidentally kills a man, it is no more criminal in him than if he were authorized. But to shoot at another's fowls, wantonly or in sport, an act which is malum in se, though a civil trespass, and thereby accidentally to kill a human being, is manslaughter. If the intent in the shooting were to commit larceny of the fowls, we have seen that it would be murder." To same effect is Estell v. State, 51 N.J.L. 182, 17 A. 118; Com. v. Adams, 114 Mass. 323, 19 Am.Rep. 362. An offense malum in se is properly defined as one which is naturally evil as adjudged by the sense of a civilized community, whereas an act malum prohibitum is wrong only because made so by statute. For the reason that acts malum in se have, as a rule, become criminal offenses by the course and development of the common law, an impression has sometimes obtained that only acts can be so classified which the common law makes criminal; but this is not at all the test. An act can be, and frequently is, malum in se, when it amounts only to a civil trespass, provided it has a malicious element or manifests an evil nature or wrongful disposition to harm or injure another in his person or property. The distinction between the two classes of acts is well stated in 19 Am. & Eng.Enc. (2d Ed.), at page 705: "An offense malum in se is one which is naturally evil, as murder, theft, and the like. Offenses at common law are generally malum in se. An offense malum prohibitum, on the contrary, is not naturally an evil, but becomes so in consequence of being forbidden."

We do not hesitate to declare that the offense of the defendant in hunting on the land without written permission of the owner was malum prohibitum, and, the special verdict having found that the act in which the defendant was engaged was not in itself dangerous to human life and negatived all idea of negligence, we hold that the case is one of excusable homicide, and the defendant should be declared not guilty . . .

. . . [I]t has been called to our attention that courts of the highest authority have declared that the distinction between malum prohibitum and malum in se is unsound, and has now entirely disappeared. Our own court so held in Sharp v. Farmer, 20 N.C. 255, and decisions to the same effect have been made several times since. Said Ruffin, C.J., in Sharp v. Farmer: "The distinction between an act malum in se and one malum prohibitum was never sound, and is entirely disregarded; for the law would be false to itself if it allowed a party through its tribunals to derive advantage from a contract made against the intent and express provisions of the law." It will be noted that this decision was on a case involving the validity of a contract, and the principle there established is undoubtedly correct. The fact, however, that the judge who delivered the opinion uses the words "was never sound," and that other opinions to the same effect use the words "has disappeared," shows that the distinction has existed; and it existed, too, at a time when this feature in the law of homicide was established. And we are well assured that because the courts, in administering the law on the civil side of the docket, have come to the conclusion that a principle once established is unsound and should be rejected, this should not have the effect of changing the character of an act from innocence to guilt, which had its status fixed when the distinction was recognized and enforced . . .

There was error in holding the defendant guilty, and, on the facts declared, a verdict of not guilty should be directed, and the defendant discharged.

Reversed.

NOTE

Compare the following statement of the court in State v. Brown, 205 S.C. 514, 519, 32 S.E.2d 825, 827 (1945):

> The responsibility for a death is sometimes made to depend on whether the unlawful act is malum in se or malum prohibitum. The authorities agree, however, without regard to this distinction, that if the act is a violation of a statute intended and designated to prevent injury to the person, and is itself dangerous, and death ensues, the person violating the statute is guilty of manslaughter at least.

People v. Marshall

Supreme Court of Michigan, 1961.
362 Mich. 170, 106 N.W.2d 842.

■ SMITH, JUSTICE. At approximately 3:00 a.m. on the morning of February 4, 1958, a car driven by Neal McClary, traveling in the wrong direction on the Edsel Ford Expressway, crashed head-on into another vehicle driven by James Coldiron. The drivers of both cars were killed.

Defendant William Marshall has been found guilty of involuntary manslaughter of Coldiron. At the time that the fatal accident took place, he, the defendant William Marshall, was in bed at his place of residence. His connection with it was that he owned the car driven by McClary, and as the evidence tended to prove, he voluntarily gave his keys to the car to McClary, with knowledge that McClary was drunk.

The principal issue in the case is whether, upon these facts, the defendant may be found guilty of involuntary manslaughter. It is axiomatic that "criminal guilt under our law is personal fault." . . . As Sayre . . . puts the doctrine "it is of the very essence of our deeprooted notions of criminal liability that guilt be personal and individual." This was not always true in our law, nor is it universally true in all countries even today, but for us it is settled doctrine.

The State relies on a case, Story v. United States, . . . in which the owner, driving with a drunk, permitted him to take the wheel, and was held liable for aiding and abetting him "in his criminal negligence." The owner, said the court, sat by his side and permitted him "without protest so recklessly and negligently to operate the car as to cause the death of another." . . . If defendant Marshall had been by McClary's side an entirely different case would be presented, but on the facts before us Marshall, as we noted, was at home in bed. The State also points out that although it is only a misdemeanor to drive while drunk, yet convictions for manslaughter arising out of drunk driving have often been sustained. It argues from these cases that although it was only a misdemeanor for an owner to turn his keys over to a drunk driver, nevertheless a conviction for manslaughter may be sustained if such driver kills another. This does not follow from such cases as Story, supra. In the case before us death resulted from the misconduct of driver. The accountability of the owner must rest as a matter of general principle, upon his complicity in such misconduct. In turning his keys over, he was guilty of a specific offense, for which he incurred a specific penalty. Upon these facts he cannot be held a principal with respect to the fatal accident: the killing of Coldiron was not counselled by him, accomplished by another acting jointly with him, nor did it occur in the attempted achievement of some common enterprise.

This is not to say that defendant is guilty of nothing. He was properly found guilty of violation of paragraph (b) of section 625 of the Michigan vehicle code which makes it punishable for the owner of an automobile knowingly to permit it to be driven by a person "who is under the influence of intoxicating liquor." The State urges that this is not enough, that its manslaughter theory, above outlined, "was born of necessity," and that the urgency of the drunk-driver problem "has made it incumbent upon responsible and concerned law enforcement officials to seek new approaches to a new problem within the limits of our law." What the State actually seeks from us is an interpretation that the manslaughter statute imposes an open-end criminal liability. That is to say, whether the owner may ultimately go to prison for manslaughter or some lesser offense will depend upon whatever unlawful act the driver commits while in the car. Such a theory may be defensible as a matter of civil liability but [in his American Rights, 85, 86] Gellhorn's language in another criminal context is equally applicable here: "It is a basic proposition in a constitutional society that crimes should be defined in advance, and not after action has been taken." We are not unaware of the magnitude of the problem presented, but the new approaches demanded for its solution rest with the legislature, not the courts.

The view we have taken of the case renders it unnecessary to pass upon other allegations of error. The verdict and sentence on that count of the information dealing with involuntary manslaughter are set aside and the case remanded to the circuit court for sentencing on the verdict of the jury respecting the violation, as charged, of section 625(b) of the Michigan Vehicle Code, discussed hereinabove.

Commonwealth v. Feinberg

Superior Court of Pennsylvania, 1967.
211 Pa.Super. 100, 234 A.2d 913, affirmed 433 Pa. 558, 253 A.2d 636 (1969).

■ MONTGOMERY, JUDGE. These appeals are from judgments of sentence imposed following appellant's conviction on five charges of involuntary manslaughter. They arose by reason of the deaths of five individuals from methyl alcohol (methanol) poisoning due to their consumption of Sterno, a jelly-like substance prepared and intended for heating purposes. It is solidified alcohol popularly called "canned heat" but has additives specified by the United States government to render it unfit for drinking purposes.

Appellant Max Feinberg was the owner of a cigar store handling tobacco, candy, etc., in the skid-row section of Philadelphia and sold to residents of that area Sterno in two types of containers, one for home use and one for institutional use. Such sales were made under circumstances from which it could be reasonably concluded that appellant knew the purchasers were intending to use it for drinking purposes by diluting it with water or other beverages, and not for its intended use. Prior to December, 1963, there had been no known fatal consequences resulting from this practice, presumably for the reason that the product then sold by appellant contained only four per cent methyl alcohol (methanol). However, on December 21, 1963 appellant bought from the Richter Paper Company ten additional cases of institutional Sterno containing seventy-two cans each, unaware that it contained fifty-four per cent methanol, although the lid of each container was marked "Institutional Sterno. Danger. Poison; Not for home use. For commercial and industrial use only", and had a skull and crossbones imprinted thereon. Nevertheless appellant ignored this warning and sold part of this supply in the same manner he had previously dispensed his other supply of the product. The containers of the regular Sterno and the institutional type previously sold contained no such warning and were merely marked "Caution. Flammable. For use only as a fuel." The only difference in the containers previously sold was that the institutional type was so marked but had no wrap-around label as was affixed to the container intended for regular use. Both containers were the same size, as were the containers sold after December 21st which did not contain wrap-around labels. Between December 23 and December 30, 1963, thirty-one persons died in this area as a result of methyl alcohol poisoning. After hearing of their deaths, appellant, on December 28, 1963 returned to the Richter Paper Company four cases and forty-two cans which remained unsold from the ten cases he had purchased on December 21, 1963, at which time he remarked about the change in markings on the cans. Appellant was the only purchaser in the Philadelphia area of this new institutional product from the Richter Company. The methanol content of institutional Sterno had been increased by the manufacturer from four per cent to fifty-four per cent in September, 1963 but the new product was not marketed until December, 1963. Richter received the first shipment of it on December 11, and another on December 17, 1963. The chemical contents of the new institutional product were not stated on the container; nor was the appellant informed otherwise of any change in the contents of that product except by the notice of its dangerous contents for home use, as previously recited.

It is the contention of the appellant that his convictions on the charges of involuntary manslaughter cannot be sustained . . . as a result of any criminal negligence on his part. * * *

There remains the question of whether the Commonwealth has established that the deaths under consideration were due to the criminal negligence of the appellant. Involuntary manslaughter consists of the killing of another person without malice and unintentionally, but in doing some unlawful act not amounting to a felony, or in doing some lawful act in an unlawful way. Where the act in itself is not unlawful, to make it criminal the negligence must be of such a departure from prudent conduct as to evidence a disregard of human life or an indifference to consequences . . .

We are satisfied that the record clearly establishes that appellant, in the operation of his small store with part-time help, knew that he was selling Sterno in substantial quantities to a clientele that was misusing it; that in order to profit more from such sales he induced Richter Paper Company to procure for him a supply of the institutional product because the cost of same was less than the regular type with labels; that he was aware of the "poison" notice and warning of harmful effects of the new shipment received on December 21, 1963 but nevertheless placed it in stock for general sale by himself and his employees; and thereafter sold several hundred cans of it; and that he dispensed it without warning his purchasers of the harmful effect it would have if misused for drinking purposes, and without directing their attention to the warning on the containers.

If the deaths of these five persons were the result of appellant's actions, it justifies his conviction for involuntary manslaughter. Although a more culpable degree of negligence is required to establish a criminal homicide than is required in a civil action for damages, we find the appellant's actions as fully meeting the definition and requirement of proof set forth in Commonwealth v. Aurick, 342 Pa. 282, 19 A.2d 920 (1941). In the light of the recognized weaknesses of the purchasers of the product, the appellant's greater concern for profit than with the results of his actions, he was grossly negligent and demonstrated a wanton and reckless disregard for the welfare of those whom he might reasonably have expected to use the product for drinking purposes. * * *

We find no merit in appellant's argument that there is no evidence to prove he ever sold a can of the new institutional Sterno. The evidence clearly shows that he was in full charge of the operation of the store when the bulk of the new product was sold. Harold was only a part-time employe coming in after school and on Saturdays, and during this period appellant's wife and family were in Florida, which left appellant as the one who made the bulk of the sales.

Nor do we find any merit in his argument that he was unaware of the warning on the cans. He must have handled many of them during the course of events when almost four hundred cans were sold. The circumstances established by the evidence sufficiently supports a finding that he did know of the change in markings but disregarded it. As far as instructing anyone else to sell the product, the fact that it was available for sale in an opened carton under the counter is sufficient to indicate an implied authorization.

The facts in this case do not indicate the prosecution of a person for acts done by another without his knowledge or consent. Appellant was the active participant with full knowledge. He, personally, and through his part-time employe, acting under his orders, committed the crimes . . .

The judgments of sentence, therefore, are affirmed in the cases of Lynwood Scott; John Streich; James Newsome; and Juanita Williams; and the judgment is reversed and appellant discharged in the case of Edward Harrell.

■ HOFFMAN, J., files a dissenting opinion.

* * *

NOTES

1. When death is caused through an overdose of drugs or excessive use of liquor, the courts generally require that the person furnishing the drugs or liquor be shown to have unlawfully furnished the substances. Also, it must be established that the unlawful furnishing is the proximate cause of the death. In Coyle v. Commonwealth, 653 S.E.2d 291 (Va. App. 2007), the court held that a victim's voluntary ingestion of a potentially lethal substance does not break the causal link between the provider's criminally negligent act in supplying the known dangerous substance and the victim's death. Thus defendant's "criminally negligent conduct was a proximate cause of the victim's death."

Depending upon the degree of foreseeability of death under the circumstances of a case, the charge could properly be murder. In Ureta v. Superior Court, 199 Cal.App.2d 672, 18 Cal.Rptr. 873 (1962), a murder prosecution for a death produced by morphine poisoning, the court stated it made no difference whether the decedent or the defendant who furnished the drug actually injected it.

2. If, during a legal abortion, a doctor fails to take steps to keep an aborted fetus alive, can the doctor be convicted of involuntary manslaughter? A Massachusetts jury answered affirmatively in the 1975 trial of Dr. Kenneth C. Edelin, chief resident in surgery in a Boston hospital, who aborted a fetus during a legal hysterotomy performed on a woman between twenty-two and twenty-four weeks pregnant. Superior Court Judge James P. McGuire sentenced Dr. Edelin to one year's probation, but stayed the sentence pending an appeal. The Massachusetts Supreme Judicial Court reversed the conviction and ordered that a judgment of acquittal be entered. Commonwealth v. Edelin, 371 Mass. 497, 359 N.E.2d 4 (1976); *see also* Commonwealth v. Cass, 392 Mass. 799, 467 N.E.2d 1324 (1984).

3. In People v. Nelson, 309 N.Y. 231, 128 N.E.2d 391 (1955), the owner of an apartment building which was in violation of the New York Multiple Dwelling Law and constituted a fire hazard was convicted of manslaughter when two tenants died in a fire. The court held that failure to comply with various building codes regarding fire safety constituted conduct of such a nature that human life was endangered.

4. In State v. Strobel, 130 Mont. 442, 304 P.2d 606 (1956), the defendant, while driving to the left of the centerline of the highway, collided with a gasoline truck driven by one Little. The truck overturned and exploded causing Little's death. The defendant was convicted of manslaughter and appealed. In reversing the judgment and ordering a new trial, the court stated:

> Instruction No. 7, submitting the question of driving on the wrong side of the road in violation of the statutes, was apparently intended to present to the jury the issue of defendant's guilt in the unlawful killing of a human being "in the commission of an unlawful act, not amounting to felony." . . .

> The driving of an automobile to the left of the centerline of the highway appears to be an act merely *malum prohibitum*. . . . In some jurisdictions it is held that when one commits an act expressly prohibited by law which results in the death of a human being he

is thereby guilty of manslaughter and that in such a case an instruction on criminal negligence is neither necessary nor proper. . . . [That] rule . . . has not been followed in Montana. . . . This court has committed itself to the rule that the unlawful killing of a human being, "in the commission of an unlawful act, not amounting to felony," does not constitute involuntary manslaughter unless the element of criminal negligence is also present . . .

It is not incumbent upon us to go further and determine the character of the unlawful act, *aside from such criminal negligence,* which makes a person guilty of manslaughter should death ensue. Irrespective of the character of the unlawful act, whether *malum in se* or merely *malum prohibitum,* the criminality of the act resulting in death is established if that act was done negligently in such a manner as to evince a disregard for human life or an indifference to consequences. Negligence of this character is culpable in itself. Hence it is wholly unnecessary in involuntary manslaughter cases to superimpose upon the requirement of the element of criminal negligence the further requirement that a determination must be made as to whether the act resulting in death might ordinarily be classified as *malum in se* or *malum prohibitum,* for, if that act is done in a manner which is criminally negligent, it thereby becomes *malum in se* and thereby includes the element of *mens rea* . . .

Applying the foregoing discussion to the case at bar, we hold that Instruction No. 7 . . . was erroneous in advising the jury that they might find the defendant guilty if she was driving on the wrong side of the road in violation of the statutes and if she thereby caused the death of Gerald Little. . . .

5. In State v. Pankow, 134 Mont. 519, 333 P.2d 1017 (1958), an involuntary manslaughter prosecution against a motorist arising out of the deaths of his three passengers when his automobile passed two preceding automobiles near a curve and skidded and ran over the left edge of the road and tumbled to its side in a creek below, the court had this to say about *Strobel*:

"Much confusion has been caused . . . by this court's discussion of criminal negligence in an involuntary manslaughter case in State v. Strobel. Insofar as that case would seem to add the requirement of a willful or evil intent as an element of involuntary manslaughter, we hereby overrule the holding on that point in that case."

6. Deaths resulting from traffic offenses are viewed as possible involuntary manslaughter offenses if the degree of foreseeability of death was fairly high, but not if the causal connection is less obvious. Thus, in Beck v. Commonwealth, 216 Va. 1, 216 S.E.2d 8 (1975), the court affirmed a conviction of involuntary manslaughter where the defendant had consumed "around seven beers" in a very short period of time, was unsteady on his feet and had difficulty closing his car door, failed to see seven young men with his lights on and after striking something in "a blur" was reported by other witnesses to have departed at high speed. The finding of driving while intoxicated was deemed to be the proximate cause of the resulting homicide which occurred during the performance of an unlawful act. On the other hand, in King v. Commonwealth, 217 Va. 601, 231 S.E.2d 312 (1977), the defendant was operating a motor vehicle without headlights at night, in violation of a state statute, as a result of which a death occurred and she was convicted of involuntary manslaughter. The Virginia Supreme Court reversed, stating that the operation of an automobile without headlights in violation of law amounted only to ordinary negligence and was therefore an insufficient predicate for a conviction of involuntary manslaughter. The court said:

> In the operation of motor vehicles violation of a safety statute amounting to mere negligence proximately causing an accidental death is not sufficient to support a conviction of involuntary manslaughter. Likewise, the improper performance of a lawful act proximately causing an accidental killing is also insufficient unless that improper performance constitutes criminal negligence.

crim vs. civil ng.———

CHAPTER 6

"SEX" OFFENSES AND RELATED PROBLEMS

A. RAPE (CRIMINAL SEXUAL ASSAULT)

The crime of rape, at common law, was the unlawful carnal knowledge of a woman, not married to the defendant, forcibly and against her will. Many jurisdictions retain something very close to this language; other jurisdictions have adopted statutes such as the Model Penal Code definition, discussed *infra.*, which is generally gender-neutral, and encompasses acts that would not have been rape at common law.

1. THE PREVALENCE OF THE PROBLEM

Centers for Disease Control and Prevention, The National Intimate Partner and Sexual Violence Survey 2010 Summary Report (2011)
pp. 18–19, 21, 23–27 & 42–43.

* * *

Rape

Nearly 1 in 5 women in the United States has been raped in her lifetime (18.3%). This translates to almost 22 million women in the United States. The most common form of rape victimization experienced by women was completed forced penetration, experienced by 12.3% of women in the United States. About 5% of women (5.2%) experienced attempted forced penetration, and 8.0% experienced alcohol/drug-facilitated completed forced penetration. One percent, or approximately 1.3 million women, reported some type of rape victimization in the 12 months prior to taking the survey.

Approximately 1 in 71 men in the United States (1.4%) reported having been raped in his lifetime, which translates to almost 1.6 million men in the United States. Too few men reported rape in the 12 months prior to taking the survey to produce a reliable 12 month prevalence estimate.

Sexual Violence Other than Rape

Nearly 1 in 2 women (44.6%) and 1 in 5 men (22.2%) experienced sexual violence victimization other than rape at some point in their lives. This equates to more than 53 million women and more than 25 million men in the United States. Approximately 1 in 20 women (5.6%) and men

(5.3%) experienced sexual violence victimization other than rape in the 12 months prior to taking the survey.

* * *

Unwanted Sexual Contact

More than one-quarter of women (27.2%) have experienced some form of unwanted sexual contact in their lifetime. This equates to over 32 million women in the United States. The 12 month prevalence of unwanted sexual contact reported by women was 2.2%. Approximately 1 in 9 men (11.7%) reported experiencing unwanted sexual contact in his lifetime, which translates to an estimated 13 million men in the United States. The 12 month prevalence of unwanted sexual contact reported by men was 2.3%.

* * *

Type of Perpetrator in Lifetime Reports of Sexual Violence

Rape

The majority of both female and male victims of rape knew their perpetrators. More than half of female victims of rape (51.1%) reported that at least one perpetrator was a current or former intimate partner. Four out of 10 of female victims (40.8%) reported being raped by an acquaintance. Approximately 1 in 8 female victims (12.5%) reported being raped by a family member, and 2.5% by a person in a position of authority. About 1 in 7 female victims (13.8%) reported being raped by a stranger. In terms of lifetime alcohol/drug-facilitated rape, half of female victims (50.4%) were raped by an acquaintance, while 43.0% were raped by an intimate partner.

* * *

Number of Perpetrators in Lifetime Reports of Sexual Violence

Among sexual violence victims, the majority of both women and men reported one perpetrator in their lifetime. Almost three-quarters of female rape victims (71.2%) reported being raped by one perpetrator. For female rape victims, 1 in 6 (16.4%) reported two perpetrators and 1 in 8 (12.4%) reported three or more perpetrators in their lifetime.

Almost half of female victims (45.8%) of lifetime sexual violence other than rape reported one perpetrator, approximately one-quarter (23.4%) reported two perpetrators, and just under one-third (30.8%) reported three or more perpetrators. For male victims of rape and sexual violence other than rape, the large majority (86.6% and 92.1%, respectively) reported one perpetrator in their lifetime . . . .

Sex of Perpetrator in Lifetime Reports of Sexual Violence

Most perpetrators of all forms of sexual violence against women were male. For female rape victims, 98.1% reported only male perpetrators. Additionally, 92.5% of female victims of sexual violence other than rape reported only male perpetrators. For male victims, the sex of the perpetrator varied by the type of sexual violence experienced. The majority of male rape victims (93.3%) reported only male perpetrators . . . .

Age at the Time of First Completed Rape

More than three-quarters of female victims of completed rape (79.6%) were first raped before their 25th birthday, with 42.2% experiencing their first completed rape before the age of 18 (29.9% between 11–17 years old and 12.3% at or before age 10). Approximately 1 in 7 female victims (14.2%) experienced their first completed rape between 25–34 years of age.

More than one-quarter of male victims of completed rape (27.8%) were first raped when they were 10 years old or younger. With the exception of the youngest age category (i.e. age 10 or younger), the estimates for age at first completed rape for male victims in the other age groups were based upon numbers too small to calculate a reliable estimate and therefore not reported.

Rape Victimization as a Minor and Subsequent Rape Victimization

More than one-third (35.2%) of the women who reported a completed rape before the age of 18 also experienced a completed rape as an adult, compared to 14.2% of the women who did not report being raped prior to age 18. Thus, the percentage of women who were raped as children or adolescents and also raped as adults was more than two times higher than the percentage among women without an early rape history.

Too few men reported rape victimization in adulthood to examine rape victimization as a minor and subsequent rape victimization in adulthood.

* * *

Sexual Violence by an Intimate Partner

Prevalence Among Women

Nearly 1 out of 10 women in the United States (9.4% or approximately 11.1 million) has been raped by an intimate partner in her lifetime. More specifically, 6.6% of women reported completed forced penetration by an intimate partner, 2.5% reported attempted forced penetration, and 3.4% reported alcohol/drug-facilitated rape. Approximately 1 in 6 women (16.9% or nearly 19 million) has experienced sexual violence other than rape by an intimate partner in her lifetime; this includes sexual coercion (9.8%), unwanted sexual contact (6.4%) and non-contact unwanted sexual experiences (7.8%).

In the 12 months prior to taking the survey, 0.6% or an estimated 686,000 women in the United States indicated that they were raped by an intimate partner, and 2.3% or an estimated 2.7 million women experienced other forms of sexual violence by an intimate partner.

* * *

Physical Violence by an Intimate Partner

Prevalence Among Women

Nearly 1 in 3 women (30.3%) in the United States has been slapped, pushed or shoved by an intimate partner at some point in her lifetime. This translates to approximately 36.2 million women in the United States. An estimated 3.6%, or approximately 4.3 million women, reported experiencing these behaviors in the 12 months prior to taking the survey.

Approximately 1 in 4 women in the United States (24.3%) has experienced severe physical violence by an intimate partner in her lifetime, translating to nearly 29 million women. An estimated 17.2% of women have been slammed against something by a partner, 14.2% have been hit with a fist or something hard, and 11.2% reported that they have been beaten by an intimate partner in their lifetime. An estimated 2.7%, or approximately 3.2 million women, reported experiencing severe physical violence by an intimate partner in the 12 months prior to taking the survey.

* * *

————

NOTES

1. The reporting rate for rape is extremely low. By some estimates, more than 80% of women who are sexually assaulted do not report it to the police. *See* Michelle J. Anderson, *Women Do Not Report the Violence They Suffer: Violence Against Women and the State Action Doctrine*, 46 VILL. L. REV. 907 (2001). Professor Anderson contends that the low rate is in part due to police discouraging complaints by labeling them unfounded or pressuring women to withdraw their complaints. *See id.* at 928–932.

2. Professor Anderson also documents the high dismissal rate of rape cases by prosecutors. *See id.* at 932–933. Why might prosecutors choose to dismiss criminal charges when victims stand by their complaints? For a thorough discussion of the reasons prosecutors dismiss charges, as well as the difficulties of convicting in acquaintance rape trials, see David P. Bryden & Sonja Lengnick, *Rape in the Criminal Justice System*, 87 J. CRIM. L. & CRIMINOLOGY 36 (1997). Jurors are far less likely to convict in acquaintance-rape trials than in stranger-rape trials. *See* HARRY KALVEN, JR. & HANS ZEISEL, THE AMERICAN JURY 253 (1966) (reviewing thousands of criminal jury trials of various crimes and finding that juries convicted in only 3 of the 42 acquaintance rape cases that went to trial).

3. Were you surprised that the study found that 1 in 71 men were rape victims? According to a survey by the Bureau of Justice Statistics, 8.7% of former state prisoners said they had been sexually assaulted during their most recent period of incarceration. *See* ALLEN BECK, BUREAU OF JUSTICE STATISTICS, SEXUAL VICTIMIZATION REPORTED BY FORMER STATE PRISONERS,

2008 (2012), at 15. Another Bureau of Justice Statistics study found that more than 36,000 males age twelve and over were victims of completed rape or attempted rape during 2008 alone and that one in thirty-three men in the United States has been the victim of rape or attempted rape. *See* MICHAEL RAND, BUREAU OF JUSTICE STATISTICS, CRIME VICTIMIZATION 2008 (2009). For a review of the statistics and an argument that society has inappropriately minimized male on male rape, see Bennett Capers, *Real Rape Too*, 99 CAL. L. REV. 1259 (2011).

4. What percentage of rape accusations are false? Anecdotal evidence suggests false accusations of rape are not uncommon, but there appear to be no reliable data on the frequency with which false rape claims are made. According to Professor Michelle Anderson, "[f]alse accusations of sexual assault are estimated to occur at the low rate of two percent—similar to the rate of false accusations for other violent crimes." Michelle J. Anderson, *The Legacy of the Prompt Complaint Requirement, Corroboration Requirement, and Cautionary Instructions on Campus Sexual Assault*, 84 B.U. L. REV. 945, 985 (2004).

2. THE *ACTUS REUS* OF RAPE AND SEXUAL ASSAULT: THE ISSUES OF FORCE AND CONSENT

Rape is a general intent crime in which the only *mens rea* is the intent to do the act. It can loosely be divided into forcible rape and "statutory" rape, in which consent is irrelevant because the victim is underage or incompetent. The *actus reus* of forcible rape (or sexual assault) is some form of sexual contact (penetration, for rape) by force, and without the victim's consent. Over time, the line between proof of force and proof of non-consent has become blurred. This section addresses issues of force and consent together for that reason, including the issue of what constitutes consent, who is competent to give it, and whether it can be effectively withdrawn.

(A) UNCONSCIOUS OR IMPAIRED VICTIMS

If a person is completely unconscious, she is incapacitated and unable to give consent. The issue is more complex when it comes to partial incapacitation. If a person is intoxicated, does it follow as a matter of law that she is unable to give consent? If not, what degree of intoxication must be shown before capacity to consent becomes an issue? How does this affect the issue of force?

Commonwealth v. Urban

Appeals Court of Massachusetts, 2006.
67 Mass. App. Ct. 301, 853 N.E.2d 594.
further review granted 448 Mass. 1101, 859 N.E.2d 432 (2006).

■ BROWN, J.

The defendant was convicted by a Superior Court jury of rape (two counts).... On appeal, he alleges that the trial judge erred by (1) misstating the law in her charge on the relationship between intoxication and consent; (2) failing to give an instruction on mistake of fact; ... We agree that the judge's charge on consent was fatally flawed and reverse on that basis....

The chief disputed issue at trial was whether the complainant had consented to engage in sexual intercourse with the defendant; more specifically, whether the complainant, due to intoxication, had the mental capacity to consent. The Commonwealth took the position that the complainant, at the time of the alleged rape, was sufficiently under the influence of drugs and alcohol as to be incapable of consent.... For his part, the defendant maintained that, while the complainant had indeed used drugs or alcohol on the evening in question, she was nonetheless sober enough to consent to intercourse and had, in fact, done so.

The conflict surrounding this point was the subject matter of numerous discussions between the parties and the trial judge concerning the precise contents of the judge's charge on the relationship between intoxication and consent. During the initial charge conference, which *preceded* closing argument (the relevance of which will become clear presently) the following exchange occurred:

DEFENSE COUNSEL: "Are you charging, Judge, that by reason of a person being intoxicated they can't give consent?"

THE COURT: "No. It's a fact [the jury] can consider in determining whether or not a person was able to give consent. They have to make that determination. That's a question of fact, whether she—obviously there's different degrees of drunkenness."

DEFENSE COUNSEL: "That's the point."

THE COURT: "And there are, there are. And if a person is so drunk that they're not capable of consenting, then the jury can consider that on the issue. But they have to make that finding as to whether she was drunk and, if so, what degree of drunkenness or stupefaction or helplessness there was. That's solely for them. I'm just going to tell them what the law is."

DEFENSE COUNSEL: "What you just said now, is that how you will tell them?"

THE COURT: "Basically."

The judge, at least up to this point, had correctly articulated the governing law as it has existed in Massachusetts for more than 130 years. In determining whether a person is "incapable of consenting" to sexual intercourse as a result of intoxication, the inquiry focuses on whether that person is "wholly insensible . . . in a state of utter stupefaction . . . *caused* by drunkenness . . . or drugs" (emphasis supplied), a formulation derived from *Commonwealth v. Burke*, 105 Mass. 376, 380–381 (1870). That is to say, the question is not merely whether a person is intoxicated, but whether *due to intoxication*, a person has been rendered physically or mentally "incapable of consenting." Where such a finding is made, a conviction for rape lawfully may be premised on proof only of such force as was necessary to effect the purpose. In conducting this inquiry, a jury necessarily must assess the degree of the complainant's intoxication for the purpose of determining whether the high standard . . . has been met.

We recently confirmed the continuing vitality of this approach in *Commonwealth v. Molle*, 56 Mass. App. Ct. 621, 626–627, 779 N.E.2d 658 (2002). In *Molle*, relying on Burke, we noted that where, due to intoxication, the question of a rape victim's capacity to consent is legitimately in dispute, a judge should instruct the jury to determine whether the victim was "wholly insensible so as to be unable [to] consent[ ] . . . [by] consider[ing] what *state* of intoxication, if any, [the victim] was in at the time of the incident alleged" . . . .

[D]efense counsel readily conceded in his closing that the complainant had been drinking: "There's no question that that night [the complainant] was drunk." However, defense counsel then devoted virtually the entire balance of his closing to a meticulous rebuttal of the government's suggestion that the complainant was so impaired as to be deemed "wholly insensible." By way of example, defense counsel argued:

> "[The government] would have you believe that at this point in time [the complainant] was out on her feet, she's dead drunk and whatever. On the ride over to Sison and Urban's home, what do you hear? You hear out the window of Dr. Urban's car, on the right-hand side, [the complainant] yells over to Cookie Faris . . . 'Hey, Cookie, you shouldn't be driving. You haven't got a license.' Now what does that tell you . . . about the mental acuity of [the complainant]? What does it tell you about whether or not she's awake or asleep? What does it tell you about how drunk she is . . . ?"

Defense counsel continued in the same vein for much of the remainder of his argument, citing many specific examples from the evidence tending to suggest that the complainant, while intoxicated, was by no means "wholly insensible."

However, when the judge thereafter instructed the jury on the relationship between intoxication and consent, she departed significantly from her earlier proposed instruction, stating simply: "If, by reason of sleep, or intoxication, or drunkenness, or stupefication [*sic*], or unconsciousness, or helplessness, a person is incapable of consenting, an act of sexual intercourse occurring with that person during such incapacity, is without the valid consent of the incapacitated person."

The defendant objected to the judge's instruction:

DEFENSE COUNSEL: . . . I guess this is my objection to the charge that you gave, that you didn't specify that the level of intoxication is for [the jury] to determine . . . .

THE COURT: "Okay, I'll say that [the jury has] to determine the level of intoxication, because some people could be drunk and still be capable of consenting."

The judge subsequently gave a supplemental charge, but failed to augment her instruction on the crucial issue of consent as promised. Indeed, the judge said nothing about the disputed point. Again, defense counsel objected. The trial judge simply stated: "I'm not going to further instruct on the levels of intoxication, I think it was covered." This was error.

The judge correctly responded to defense counsel's initial objection: "the jury has to determine the level of intoxication, *because some people could be drunk and still be capable of consenting*" (emphasis supplied). Unfortunately, the judge's actual charge easily could have been interpreted to convey the opposite meaning; *i.e.*, that whenever a person is intoxicated, that person, as matter of law, is incapable of consenting to sexual intercourse. In the first instance, by listing intoxication and drunkenness alongside sleep, stupefaction, unconsciousness, and helplessness as potential bases for a finding of incapacity, the judge created the risk that jurors would equate these conditions, at least as they bear on the question of consent. Needless to say, the latter forms of impairment—sleep, stupefaction, unconsciousness, and helplessness—ordinarily would altogether preclude any possibility of voluntary consent. The jury might have improperly assumed that the law, at least, takes the same view of drunkenness and intoxication.

Finally, and perhaps most important, the judge's charge was defective insofar as it lacked any reference to the "wholly insensible" language derived from *Burke*, 105 Mass. at 380 . . . . Thus, even if the jury understood that they were required to assess the degree of the complainant's intoxication in determining her capacity to consent—a dubious assumption as we have indicated already—we are not confident that the jury also appreciated the high degree of intoxication required to negate the capacity to consent; *i.e.*, that the complainant must be "wholly insensible." For all of the foregoing reasons, the disputed charge amounts to error . . . .

* * *

Further, to the extent that the error in the charge might have relieved the Commonwealth of at least a portion of its burden of proof, the misstep implicates due process concerns. Proof of lack of consent is an element of rape, and a finding of incapacity satisfies that element as matter of law. To the extent that the jury might have misunderstood the judge's charge to indicate that mere proof of intoxication, or proof of intoxication short of impairment that renders the complainant "wholly insensible," satisfies the government's burden in this regard, the instruction essentially redefined the crime of rape. Where an error in a jury charge eliminates a requisite element of an offense, at least where that element is contested, the conviction cannot stand . . . .

Judgments reversed. Verdicts set aside.

_____

NOTES

1. Alcohol is often a precursor to sexual assault cases. "Researchers have determined that approximately half of all sexual-assault victims and half of all sexual-assault perpetrators drink alcohol before an offense occurs." Valerie M. Ryan, Comment, *Intoxicating Encounters: Allocating Responsibility in the Law of Rape*, 40 CAL. W. L. REV. 407, 411 (2004). In a world where alcohol fuels sexual encounters—most voluntary, but some nonconsensual—is a test that asks whether someone is "wholly insensible" the right standard? If a person is too intoxicated to drive a car—for instance, she has a blood alcohol level of .16, which is twice the legal limit—is she capable of giving consent? What if her blood alcohol level is .24? What if a woman meets a man at a college party and agrees to go back to his apartment to have sex. On the walk to the apartment, the woman falls down three times and nearly walks into oncoming traffic. What if, in addition, she throws up in the stairwell of the apartment and has to lie down as soon as she gets inside? Under these circumstances is she "wholly insensible" or not?

2. Ordinarily, we allow consent to be inferred from body language without an express "yes." Should consent have to be more explicit when one of the parties has been drinking? *See* Christine Chambers Goodman, *Protecting the Party Girl: A New Approach for Evaluating Intoxicated Consent*, 2009 B.Y.U. L. REV. 57 (2009). How would we enforce such a rule? Would your answer differ if both parties were drinking?

3. In some states, a man who did not facilitate the intoxication is not guilty of rape simply because he had sex with an extremely intoxicated woman. As Professor Patricia Falk has explained, "a considerable number of jurisdictions punish only instances in which the defendant administers the intoxicant, leaving unprotected victims who have voluntarily ingested intoxicants unless they fall within alternative categories such as unconsciousness." Patricia J. Falk, *Rape by Drugs: A Statutory Overview and Proposals for Reform*, 44 ARIZ. L. REV. 131, 138 (2002). Should it matter whether the defendant "administered the intoxicant" if he knowingly had sex with an extremely drunk woman?

———————

(B) DEVELOPMENTALLY DISABLED VICTIMS

A different set of force and consent issues arises when the charge of rape or sexual assault concerns the consent of a person with developmental or psychiatric disabilities. When, if ever, is a person with such disabilities able to give valid consent?

People v. Thompson

Court of Appeal, Fourth District, Division 2, California, 2006.
142 Cal.App.4th 1426, 48 Cal.Rptr.3d 803.

■ ICHLI, JUSTICE.

It is a felony to have sex—including intercourse, oral sex, sodomy and digital penetration—with a person who is so developmentally disabled as to be "incapable . . . of giving legal consent," provided "this is known or reasonably should be known to the person committing the act." Pen. Code, §§ 261, subd. (a)(1), 286, subds. (g), (h), 288a, subd. (d), 289, subds. (b), (c). This is true even if the victim purports to consent. Obviously, it is the proper business of the state to stop sexual predators from taking advantage of developmentally disabled people. Less obviously, however, in doing so, the state has restricted the ability of developmentally disabled people to have consensual sex.

Here, a group home for the developmentally disabled hired defendant Jason Markeith Thompson to help care for its residents, including victim Renee R. Defendant betrayed this trust by sexually violating her. Renee, who is trusting and docile, did not resist; instead, she dissociated—at trial, she was able to describe everything defendant did to her, yet she insisted that she had been "in a deep sleep." Thus, while the record leaves no doubt that she did not consent, there was some question as to whether defendant *knew* that she did not consent, and also as to whether he used force.

For this reason, the People chose to prosecute defendant on the *sole* theory that Renee was incapable of giving legal consent. Indeed, as defendant admitted performing the charged sex acts, this was the key disputed issue at trial. Renee did have some notion, albeit childlike and confused, of what sex was; in fact, she testified that she had once had sex with her developmentally disabled boyfriend, John E., and that it "[m]ade [her] feel good inside."

In this appeal, defendant contends there was insufficient evidence that Renee was incapable of giving legal consent. He also argues that, if the evidence in this case is sufficient, then the statutes involved are unconstitutionally vague. We will hold, however, that there was sufficient evidence that, at the time and under the circumstances, Renee's mental impairment, and particularly her impaired understanding of the sex acts involved, rendered her incapable of giving legal consent. This does not necessarily mean that she could never have consensual sex. Moreover, given the requirement that the defendant either must know or should know that the victim is incapable of giving legal consent, the statutes are not unconstitutionally vague.

FACTUAL AND PROCEDURAL BACKGROUND

A.   *The Commission of the Crimes.*

Victim Renee R. was born with Down Syndrome. As a result, she suffers from a cluster of physical deformities and disabilities, as well as mental retardation. She was living at a group home for developmentally disabled adults in La Quinta. May 7–8, 2004, was defendant's first day on the job as a staff member at Renee's group home.

Renee testified that at 2:00 a.m., defendant came into her bedroom while she was asleep. He took off his clothes, then got on top of her. She was wearing a nightgown but no underwear. She testified: "I felt his fingers to open my vagina and put his penis inside of me." Then he put his penis in her mouth. She did not move or say anything because she was "sound asleep."

At 3:00 a.m., defendant left. At 3:15 a.m., however, he came back and said, "Don't tell nobody about this." Renee's vagina hurt; she was "in a lot of pain." She cried "[f]or a long time."

The next morning, Renee phoned her mother and told her that defendant had "raped" and "molested" her. She sounded very upset. Her mother took her to a hospital, where Nurse Vicki Dippner-Robertson performed a sexual assault examination. . . .

In a physical examination, Dippner-Robertson found a small tear in Renee's posterior fourchette. Dippner-Robertson testified that this is where 70 percent of sexual assault injuries occur; it indicates a forced entry. No semen was found in Renee's vagina. Some semen was found on a sleeping bag on Renee's bed. The DNA profile of the semen matched defendant's DNA profile, which would be found in less than one out of 70 trillion people.

On May 8, defendant was arrested and interviewed. At first, he said he had been asleep from 1:00 to 9:00 a.m. After the police asked him why his semen had been found on Renee's sleeping bag, however, he admitted that he went into Renee's room while on his nightly rounds. When he saw that she was not wearing any underwear, he began to "massage[ ]" her vagina while masturbating. He put one finger into her vagina, then three fingers. He straddled her, on his knees. He rubbed his penis against her vagina, but he denied penetrating her. He ejaculated onto the bedclothes.

Defendant claimed he could not tell whether Renee was awake or not; she never said anything.

B.　*Evidence Regarding the Victim's Ability to Consent.*

Renee was three or four when she learned to speak, four or five when she learned to feed herself, and six or seven when she learned to dress herself. She had attended special education classes. She could read out loud at approximately a second-grade level but did not always understand what she read. She had gone to high school, but she had received a certificate of completion rather than a diploma.

At the time of crimes, Renee was 34 years old. She had lived with her mother until she was 26, when she chose to move into a group home. She worked in sheltered workshops for the developmentally disabled. Her tasks included stuffing envelopes, painting ceramics, hanging up clothing and sorting books. She was paid less than minimum wage. In addition, she received Social Security disability benefits, based on her permanent mental retardation.

Despite receiving training on using public transportation, Renee could not use it on her own. She could not get a driver's license because she was unable to pass the written test or to drive without supervision. She had taken a driver's education class and had driven under supervision, but her mother characterized her driving as "[v]ery nerve[-w]racking." She was not able to cross a street at a crosswalk safely until she was about 30.

Renee could carry on a conversation, but it would be immediately apparent to her interlocutor that she was mentally impaired. Nurse Dippner-Robertson had been able to communicate with her by talking to her at the level of a 9- or 10-year-old child. Her mother described her as "naïve" and "very trusting."

Renee could add but had trouble subtracting and could not divide. She could not make change. She could not carry out banking transactions unaided. She did not understand the concept of a credit card.

Renee could not cook a meal, except for scrambling eggs, microwaving bacon, or boiling water for spaghetti. If she was left in the kitchen unsupervised for more than 15 minutes, there was a risk that "the kitchen might burn down." She had to be reminded to use soap and shampoo while taking a shower and to wear underwear. She voted, but only by copying her mother's ballot. When she needed medical care, her mother signed any necessary consent forms.

At trial, when asked what had happened to her on May 8, Renee answered, "I been raped." She defined that as "[w]hen a man wants to have sex" but she "wasn't ready to have sex" with him.

When asked what sex is, Renee kept calling it "special love." She also answered that sex is when you "fall in love, get married, have sex, get somebody pregnant and have a baby." She added that, a couple of weeks after the honeymoon, the couple can "faint" or "pass out" and get pregnant. She testified:

Q. Do people's bodies do anything to have sex?

A. The man's sperm, the woman's sperm, they can drop the egg and make the baby grow. And they can do childbirth.

Q. How does the man's sperm get to the woman's sperm?

A. It connects to the egg.

Q. How does it get there? How does it get from the boy to the girl?

A. The man's penis from the woman's vagina, you get his sperm inside me, it can get pregnant.

Renee was unaware of any diseases you can get from having sex. She had heard of AIDS; when asked how one gets AIDS, she answered, "When a man goes with another woman and gets somebody pregnant, it goes to somebody's wife."

Renee had a boyfriend named John E., who was also developmentally disabled. She testified that she had once had sex with John. When asked what they did that was sex, she said John "liked to touch" her "butt," and it "[m]ade [her] feel good inside." . . .

If a resident of the group home was having sex, his or her parents would be notified. Renee's mother knew she was having sex with John and had consented to their relationship.

Defense expert Dr. Morton Kurland, a psychiatrist, opined that Renee had the ability to give legal consent. He relied primarily on the fact that she had been asked to sign—and had signed—consent forms for searching her room, for keeping her full name confidential, and for conducting the sexual assault examination . . . .

II

INCAPABLE . . . OF GIVING LEGAL CONSENT

As noted, defendant contends there was insufficient evidence that Renee was incapable of giving legal consent . . . .

Defendant was convicted . . . on the theory that the victim was "at the time incapable, because of a mental disorder or developmental or physical disability, of giving legal consent . . ." Pen. Code, §§ 288a, subd. (g), 289, subd. (b). This was the only theory alleged in the information and the only theory on which the jury was instructed. Consent, in this context, means "positive cooperation in act or attitude pursuant to an exercise of free will. The person must act freely and voluntarily and have knowledge of the nature of the act or transaction involved." (Pen. Code, § 261.6.) Again, the jury was so instructed.

The principle that rape may be committed by having sex with a person so mentally incapacitated as to be incapable of consenting is hardly novel. "Under English common law this situation was considered no different from intercourse with an unconscious person . . ." 2 LaFave, SUBSTANTIVE CRIMINAL LAW (2d ed. 2003) § 17.4(b), p. 645, fn. omitted. In California law, the phrase "incapable . . . of giving legal consent" dates back at least as far as the original Penal Code of 1872, which defined rape so as to include "an act of sexual intercourse accomplished with a female, not the wife of the perpetrator, . . . [w]here she is incapable, through lunacy or other unsoundness of mind, whether temporary or permanent, of giving legal consent . . . ."

* * *

. . . [T]here was substantial evidence that Renee was incapable of giving legal consent . . . Renee could not cook, use a bus, or do simple arithmetic . . . [S]he could not hold down a real job, handle money, or cast an independent vote. She conversed at the level of a 9 or 10 year old and read at the level of a 7 or 8 year old. Although she had attended high school, she . . . was not really qualified for a diploma.

. . . Renee had some idea of what sexual intercourse was, including that it could result in pregnancy. However, her understanding was on the same level as the children's rhyme, "First comes love, then comes marriage, then comes a baby in a baby carriage." She did not understand that sex could result in disease. Although she had had some kind of sexual experience with John, the group home required that her mother be notified, and it had occurred with her mother's knowledge and consent. The "sex" apparently did not consist of intercourse, as John was unable to get an erection. Renee testified that John touched her buttocks; however, she drew a distinction between a "butt" and a "vagina." Thus, the "sex" apparently did not consist of digital penetration or masturbation, either. The jury could therefore reasonably find that Renee was unequipped to consent to sexual penetration . . . .

Defendant points out that Renee understood the concept of rape, which she defined as "[w]hen a man wants to have sex" but she "wasn't ready to have sex" with him. The fact that she knew what consent (or lack of consent) was, however, did not conclusively prove that she was able to give it.

Similarly, defendant notes that he was found guilty of sexual battery, which requires a sexual touching "against the will of the person touched. . ." Pen. Code, § 243.4, subd. (a). He argues that a person who can have the "will" *not* to be sexually touched cannot be viewed as being incapable of giving consent to be sexually touched. We disagree. Even a severely disabled person may object to a sexual touching because he or she finds it unpleasant—a "bad touch;" this does not necessarily mean he or she could give legal consent . . .

* * *

Defendant argues . . . that if Renee was incapable of giving legal consent, then it must be a crime not only for defendant, but for anyone (including John) to have sex of any kind with her. At trial, when the prosecutor was confronted with this argument, she replied that John was probably too developmentally disabled to have the necessary *mens rea*. That is not at all clear from the record, which indicates that John functioned at a somewhat higher level than Renee did. The argument, in any event, goes beyond just John.

We do not agree, however, that Renee's incapacity to consent in this case necessarily debars her from all future consensual sexual activity. The relevant statutes require proof that the victim was "*at the time* incapable . . . of giving legal consent . . ." Pen. Code, §§ 288a, subd. (g), 289, subd. (b) (italics added). "It is important to distinguish between a person's *general* ability to understand the nature and consequences of sexual intercourse and that person's ability to understand the nature and consequences at a given time and in a given situation." *State v. Ortega-Martinez* (1994) 124 Wash.2d 702, 716, 881 P.2d 231 . . . . Here, it is relevant that defendant was one of Renee's caretakers and that he exploited her vulnerability, the very type of harm the statute seeks to guard against. It is also relevant that she was, in fact, unable to express either consent or refusal; instead, she convinced herself that she was asleep. Finally, we note that, even assuming Renee would be incapable of giving legal consent under any circumstances, that fact would not render the statute vague in any way.

We therefore conclude that there was sufficient evidence that Renee was incapable of giving legal consent. We further conclude that the requirement that the victim must be "incapable . . . of giving legal consent" is not unconstitutionally vague.

III

The judgment is affirmed.

■ HOLLENHORST, ACTING P.J., and KING, J., concur.

————

NOTES: IMPAIRED OR DEVELOPMENTALLY DISABLED VICTIMS

1. In Commonwealth v. Helfant, 398 Mass. 214, 496 N.E.2d 433 (1986) defendant Helfant, a fifty-one year-old neurosurgeon, practiced medicine at the hospital, where the complainant worked as a radiologic technologist. The defendant and the complainant had dated in the past but had broken off their relationship two years before the rape. The complainant injured her back, and made an appointment with Helfant for treatment, but before the appointment the defendant telephoned and suggested that he examine her at her apartment instead. Helfant examined the complainant on her bed. He told her that she had a muscle spasm and injected her with five to ten milligrams of Valium. The complainant testified that immediately after the injection she became virtually unconscious, did not feel the needle being removed, and felt "[v]ery groggy. Very out of it. Very heavy. . . . Like I couldn't move my arm or my legs." During the next several hours, she answered the phone several times, sounding "slow, slurred, and groggy" to her callers. She could not remember the conversations later. At some point she noticed that the defendant was lying naked beside her, that her clothes had been removed, and that the defendant was "handling" her crotch. She "blacked out again" and later reawoke to find the defendant on top of her, having intercourse with her. Her mind was "in a fog . . . like it wasn't real . . . Like I was in like a Twilight Zone." She lost consciousness and reawoke to find the defendant having intercourse with her again. She later reawoke and heard water running in the bathroom. At the defendant's request, she got out of bed to let him out of the apartment. Her legs were "[l]ike rubber" and she felt like she had "about ten drinks." The complainant reported her allegation of rape to a series of people throughout the rest of the day and the next morning.

Helfant, was convicted of rape and of drugging a person for unlawful sexual intercourse, and appealed, arguing that where the complainant is possessed of her faculties, the amount of actual force required to sustain proof of rape must exceed that which is necessary to accomplish mere intercourse, and arguing that the complainant had not resisted. Rejecting his argument, the court said,

> There was ample evidence from which a jury could have found beyond a reasonable doubt that the complainant was incapable of consent. She was injected with Valium and rendered unconscious. She awoke from her stupor only when jarred by noises such as a ringing telephone and by the motion of the defendant's body on top of her own. Her speech was barely coherent. There was also evidence that intravenous Valium is used in hospitals to lessen patients' capacity to resist or protest invasive procedures. . . . [S]uch force as was necessary to accomplish the purpose, was rape.
> *Id.* at 380–381.

2. Rape of unconscious or helpless victims can also occur without the defendant having administered the drugs. Consider State v. Luckabaugh, 327 S.C. 495, 489 S.E.2d 657 (App. 1997) in which a male nurse was convicted of raping hospital patients rendered helpless by their injuries. Luckabaugh was later involuntarily committed as a sexually violent predator. *See* In re Treatment and Care of Luckabaugh, 351 S.C. 122, 568 S.E.2d 338 (2002).

3. The Model Penal Code observes:

> Hypothetically, at least, it might be possible to condemn as rape intercourse with any female who lacks substantial capacity to appraise or control her conduct. At a wholly conceptual level, that position would accord with the underlying premise that the law of rape and related offenses should protect against non-consensual intimacy.

Model Penal Code § 213.1 cmt. at 315 (1980). Elsewhere the commentators write: "The unifying principle among this diversity of conduct is the idea of meaningful consent." *Id.* at 301. The writers then go on to argue that such a rule would be unsatisfactory because of the role that alcohol and drugs play in normal courtship activities. *See id.* at 315, 318.

(C) FRAUD IN THE INDUCEMENT AND FRAUD IN THE FACTUM

People lie about all kinds of things. Some lies—such as perjured testimony under oath or wire fraud—are illegal. Other lies—such as claiming to sell the "world's greatest cup of coffee"—are obviously not illegal. What about lying to procure sex? Can any lies or exaggerations to convince a person to have sex be grounds for criminal charges?

Boro v. Superior Court

Court of Appeal, First District, Division 1, California, 1985.
163 Cal.App.3rd 1224, 210 Cal.Rptr.122.

■ NEWSOM, ASSOCIATE JUSTICE.

By timely petition filed with this court, petitioner Daniel Boro seeks a writ of prohibition to restrain further prosecution of Count II of the information . . . charging him with a violation of Penal Code section 261, subdivision (4), rape: "an act of sexual intercourse accomplished with a person not the spouse of the perpetrator, under any of the following circumstances: . . . (4) Where a person is at the time unconscious of the nature of the act, and this is known to the accused."

Petitioner contends that his motion to dismiss should have been granted with regard to Count II because the evidence at the preliminary hearing proved that the prosecutrix, Ms. R., was aware of the "nature of the act" within the meaning of section 261, subdivision (4). The Attorney General contends the opposite, arguing that the victim's agreement to intercourse was predicated on a belief—fraudulently induced by petitioner—that the sex act was necessary to save her life, and that she was hence unconscious of the *nature* of the act within the meaning of the statute.

In relevant part the factual background may be summarized as follows. Ms. R., the rape victim, was employed as a clerk at the Holiday Inn in South San Francisco when, on March 30, 1984, at about 8:45 a.m., she received a telephone call from a person who identified himself as "Dr. Stevens" and said that he worked at Peninsula Hospital.

"Dr. Stevens" told Ms. R. that he had the results of her blood test and that she had contracted a dangerous, highly infectious and perhaps fatal disease; that she could be sued as a result; that the disease came from using public toilets; and that she would have to tell him the identity of all her friends who would then have to be contacted in the interest of controlling the spread of the disease.

"Dr. Stevens" further explained that there were only two ways to treat the disease. The first was a painful surgical procedure—graphically described—costing $9,000, and requiring her uninsured hospitalization for six weeks. A second alternative, "Dr. Stevens" explained, was to have sexual intercourse with an anonymous donor who had been injected with a serum which would cure the disease. The latter, non-surgical procedure would only cost $4,500. When the victim replied that she lacked sufficient funds the "doctor" suggested that $1,000 would suffice as a down payment. The victim thereupon agreed to the non-surgical alternative and consented to intercourse with the mysterious donor, believing "it was the only choice I had."

After discussing her intentions with her work supervisor, the victim proceeded to the Hyatt Hotel in Burlingame as instructed, and contacted "Dr. Stevens" by telephone. The latter became furious when he learned Ms. R. had informed her employer of the plan, and threatened to terminate his treatment, finally instructing her to inform her employer she had decided not to go through with the treatment. Ms. R. did so, then went to her bank, withdrew $1,000 and, as instructed, checked into another hotel and called "Dr. Stevens" to give him her room number.

About a half hour later the defendant "donor" arrived at her room. When Ms. R. had undressed, the "donor," petitioner, after urging her to relax, had sexual intercourse with her.

At the time of penetration, it was Ms. R.'s belief that she would die unless she consented to sexual intercourse with the defendant: as she testified, "My life felt threatened, and for that reason and that reason alone did I do it."

Petitioner was apprehended when the police arrived at the hotel room, having been called by Ms. R.'s supervisor. Petitioner was identified as "Dr. Stevens" at a police voice lineup by another potential victim of the same scheme.

Upon the basis of the evidence just recounted, petitioner was charged with five crimes, as follows: Count I: section 261, subdivision (2)—rape: accomplished against a person's will by means of force or fear of immediate and unlawful bodily injury on the person or another. Count II: section 261, subdivision (4)—rape "[w]here a person is at the time unconscious of the nature of the act, and this is known to the accused. Count III: section 266—procuring a female to have illicit carnal connection with a man "by any false pretenses, false representation, or other fraudulent means, . . ." Count IV: section 664/487—attempted grand theft. Count V: section 459—burglary (entry into the hotel room with intent to commit theft).

A . . . motion to set aside the information was granted as to Counts I and III—the latter by concession of the district attorney. Petitioner's sole challenge is to denial of the motion to dismiss Count II.

The People's position is stated concisely: "We contend, quite simply, that at the time of the intercourse Ms. R., the victim, was 'unconscious of the nature of the act': because of [petitioner's] misrepresentation she believed it was in the nature of a medical treatment and not a simple, ordinary act of sexual intercourse." Petitioner, on the other hand, stresses that the victim was plainly aware of the *nature* of the act in which she voluntarily engaged, so that her motivation in doing so (since it did not fall within the proscription of section 261, subdivision (2)) is irrelevant.

Our research discloses sparse California authority on the subject. A victim need not be totally and physically unconscious in order that section 261, subdivision (4) apply. In *People v. Minkowski* (1962) 204 Cal.App.2d 832, 23 Cal.Rptr. 92, the defendant was a physician who "treated" several victims for menstrual cramps. Each victim testified that she was treated in a position with her back to the doctor, bent over a table, with feet apart, in a dressing gown. And in each case the "treatment" consisted of the defendant first inserting a metal instrument, then substituting an instrument which "felt different"—the victims not realizing that the second instrument was in fact the doctor's penis. The precise issue before us was never tendered in *People v. Minkowski* because the petitioner there *conceded* the sufficiency of evidence to support the element of consciousness.

The decision is useful to this analysis, however, because it exactly illustrates certain traditional rules in the area of our inquiry. Thus, as a leading authority has written, "if deception causes a misunderstanding as to the fact itself (fraud in the *factum*) there is no legally-recognized consent because what happened is not that for which consent was given; whereas consent induced by fraud is as effective as any other consent, so far as direct and immediate legal consequences are concerned, if the deception relates not to the thing done but merely to some collateral matter (fraud in the inducement)." (Perkins & Boyce, Criminal Law (3d ed. 1982) ch. 9, § 3, p. 1079.)

The victims in *Minkowski* consented, not to sexual intercourse, but to an act of an altogether different nature, penetration by medical instrument. The consent was to a pathological, and not a carnal, act, and the mistake was, therefore, in the *factum* and not merely in the inducement.

Another relatively common situation in the literature on this subject . . . is the fraudulent obtaining of intercourse by impersonating a spouse. As Professor Perkins observes, the courts are not in accord as to whether . . . the crime of rape is thereby committed. "[T]he disagreement is not in regard to the underlying principle but only as to its application. Some courts have taken the position that such a misdeed is fraud in the inducement on the theory that the woman consents to exactly what is done (sexual intercourse) and hence there is no rape; other courts, with better reason it would seem, hold such a misdeed to be rape on the theory that it involves fraud in the *factum* since the woman's consent is to an innocent act of marital intercourse while what is actually perpetrated upon her is an act of adultery. Her innocence seems never to have been questioned in such a case and the reason she is not guilty of adultery is because she did not consent to adulterous intercourse . . . .

In California, of course, we have by statute[3] adopted the majority view that such fraud is in the *factum,* not the inducement, and have thus held it to vitiate consent. It is otherwise, however, with respect to the conceptually much murkier statutory offense with which we here deal, and the language of which has remained essentially unchanged since its enactment (as section 261, subdivision (5), now subd. (4)) in 1872).

The language itself could not be plainer. It defines rape to be "an act of sexual intercourse" with a non-spouse, accomplished where the victim is "at the time unconscious of the nature of the act . . ." Nor, as we have just seen, can we entertain the slightest doubt that the Legislature well understood how to draft a statute to encompass fraud in the *factum* and how to specify certain fraud in the inducement as vitiating consent . . . .

* * *

If the Legislature at that time had desired to correct the apparent oversight [that allowed this type of case not to be covered by the statute][5] it could certainly have done so . . . .

. . . [T]here is not a shred of evidence on the record before us to suggest that as the result of mental retardation Ms. R. lacked the capacity to appreciate the nature of the sex act in which she engaged. On the contrary, her testimony was clear that she precisely understood the "nature of the act," but, motivated by a fear of disease, and death, succumbed to petitioner's fraudulent blandishments.

To so conclude is not to vitiate the heartless cruelty of petitioner's scheme, but to say that it comprised crimes of a different order than a violation of section 261, subdivision (4).

* * *

———

NOTES: FRAUD AND RAPE

1. The *Boro* decision cites a 1962 decision, *People v. Minkowski*, 204 Cal.App.2d 832, 23 Cal.Rptr. 92, in which a patient expected to receive a

---

[3] Section 261, subdivision (5) reads as follows: "Where a person submits under the belief that the person committing the act is the victim's spouse, and this belief is induced by any artifice, pretense, or concealment practiced by the accused, with intent to induce the belief."

[5] It is not difficult to conceive of reasons why the Legislature may have consciously wished to leave the matter where it lies. Thus, as a matter of degree, where consent to intercourse is obtained by promises of travel, fame, celebrity and the like—ought the liar and seducer to be chargeable as a rapist? Where is the line to be drawn?

medical procedure but instead was subjected to sexual intercourse by the doctor. The court explained that because the victims consented to only a medical procedure, with no expectation of sexual relations, the act amounted to fraud in the factum and was therefore rape. Sadly, there are other cases like *Minkowski*. For instance, in People v. Ogunmola, 193 Cal.App.3d 274, 238 Cal.Rptr. 300, 304 (1987) two patients who consented to gynecological examinations were in fact subjected to a sex act by Dr. Ogunmola. In McNair v. State, 108 Nev. 53, 825 P.2d 571 (1992), a doctor who had graduated from the prestigious Stanford Medical School was convicted of six counts of sexual assault and sentenced to four consecutive terms of life imprisonment after engaging in sexual relations with patients who thought they were being subjected to a medical examination. For other cases involving doctors engaged in fraud in the factum, *see* Jay M. Zitter, *Annot., "Conviction of Rape or Related Sexual Offenses on Basis of Intercourse Accomplished Under the Pretext of, or in the Course of, Medical Treatment,"* 65 A.L.R.4th 1064 (1988) (2007 update).

2. Consider the following hypotheticals:

A. Victim meets Johnny Jerk in a bar. Jerk tells Victim he is a talent scout and that he can get her a spot on the popular television show, *The Bachelor*. In reality, though, Jerk is just an intern and has no connections in the entertainment industry. Victim has sex with Jerk before learning his true identity.

B. Victim is in Hollywood, California for a business meeting and goes to Starbucks for a cup of coffee. While standing in line, Victim notices that the man in back of her looks exactly like the actor, George Clooney. Slightly embarrassed, Victim asks the man "Are you George Clooney?" to which the man replies "Yes, I am." Victim and Clooney strike up a conversation about Clooney's best movie roles, and Clooney invites Victim to dinner. After dinner, Victim and Clooney have sex. Unfortunately, for Victim, she has just spent the evening with a George Clooney impersonator, not the real actor.

C. The *Animal House* Scenario: Otter and his friends have developed a scheme to trick college students into having sex with them. After reading a young woman's obituary, Otter shows up at the sorority house where the deceased woman lived and claims that he was her fiancé. When the deceased woman's friends inform Otter about the woman's death, Otter pretends to be devastated. The roommates attempt to comfort Otter, and he eventually convinces one of them to have sex with him to ease his pain.

D. Victim comes to her spiritual leader—a minister, a priest, or a rabbi—to ask for guidance. Victim is distraught because her life is not going well. Victim has lost her job and her husband has just left her for another woman. Victim says she wants to become closer to God in order to begin rebuilding her life. The spiritual leader tells Victim that simple prayer is not enough. He explains that the only way to truly become close to God is to have sex with him because he communicates with God and can help God to listen to her. (This, of course, is totally counter to the religious teachings of the minister's, priest's, or rabbi's religion. He is simply lying to her.) Victim has sex with the spiritual leader.

Which scenario—A, B, C, or D—is the worst conduct? Which scenarios, if any, do you think should be criminalized? Can legislatures competently draft statutes that would criminalize the worst types of fraud while not making other "white lies" illegal?

3. Consider another hypothetical: Victim is walking at an outdoor shopping mall and sees a kiosk advertising "Great Concert Tickets, at Best Prices." Victim stops and notices a poster for "The Voice—A Concert Featuring Adam Levine of Maroon 5, Alicia Keys, Blake Shelton, and Miley Cyrus From the Hit Television Show." Although the tickets are expensive at $200 per seat, Victim loves all the musicians and decides to buy tickets for herself and her boyfriend. When Victim attends the concert however, she discovers that the real stars of The Voice are not performing, but instead that it is impersonators. Extremely upset that she wasted $400 on tickets, Victim goes to the police station to file a criminal complaint against the person who sold her the tickets. Should the police take criminal charges?

4. Consider one last hypothetical: Victim recently married the love of her life, Harry Husband. Harry is a wonderful man, although he has kept a few details about his family from Victim because he is ashamed of his family. In particular, Harry never told Victim that he has an identical twin brother (Barry) who is in prison for grand theft and aggravated assault. One day, Victim comes home from work and finds her husband in the living room watching television. Husband suggests that he and Victim have sex before going out to dinner and Victim readily agrees. Later that evening, Victim learns that she did not actually have sex with Harry Husband. Rather, Barry had recently been paroled from prison, snuck into Victim's house, and pretended to be Harry in order to have sexual relations with Victim. As the *Boro* decision makes clear, Barry has engaged in fraud in the factum, not fraud in the inducement, and is therefore guilty of rape. *See also* Anne M. Coughlin, *Sex and Guilt*, 84 VA. L. REV. 1, 19 (1998). Can you distinguish Barry's misconduct from the hypothetical in note 2B? Does it make sense to say that Barry has engaged in rape, but "George Clooney" has not?

5. Some state legislatures have adopted statutes that reject the common law rule and allow conviction for various types of rape by fraud. For instance, the crime of sexual battery in Tennessee includes situations in which "[t]he sexual contact is accomplished by fraud." Tenn. Code Ann. § 39–13–505(a)(4). The definition section of the statute explains that "[f]raud" means as used in normal parlance and includes, but is not limited to, deceit, trickery, misrepresentation and subterfuge, and shall be broadly construed to accomplish the purposes of this title[.]" Tenn. Code Ann. § 39–11–106(a)(13). Do you feel confident that you understand the difference between illegal fraud to procure sex and white lies in Tennessee? For a discussion of other state statutes criminalizing fraud in the inducement and an argument that criminalizing rape by fraud is long overdue, see Patricia J. Falk, *Rape by Fraud and Rape by Coercion*, 64 BROOKLYN L. REV. 39 (1998).

———

(D) "STATUTORY" RAPE

The statutory rape cases make an interesting contrast with the cases concerning incompetent or incapacitated victims, in that the consent of the victim is deemed irrelevant, rendering the sexual intercourse automatically non-consensual. Should a reasonable mistake as to the victim's age be a defense?

Garnett v. State

Court of Appeals of Maryland, 1993.
332 Md. 571, 632 A.2d 797.

■ MURPHY, CHIEF JUDGE.

Maryland's "statutory rape" law prohibiting sexual intercourse with an underage person is codified in Maryland Code (1957, 1992 Repl. Vol.) Art. 27, § 463, which reads in full:

Second degree rape.

(a) *What constitutes.*—A person is guilty of rape in the second degree if the person engages in vaginal intercourse with another person:

(1) By force or threat of force against the will and without the consent of the other person; or

(2) Who is mentally defective, mentally incapacitated, or physically helpless, and the person performing the act knows or should reasonably know the other person is mentally defective, mentally incapacitated, or physically helpless; or

(3) Who is under 14 years of age and the person performing the act is at least four years older than the victim.

(b) *Penalty.*—Any person violating the provisions of this section is guilty of a felony and upon conviction is subject to imprisonment for a period of not more than 20 years."

Now we consider whether under the present . . . statute, the State must prove that a defendant knew the complaining witness was younger than 14 and, in a related question, whether it was error at trial to exclude evidence that he had been told, and believed, that she was 16 years old.

I

Raymond Lennard Garnett is a young retarded man. At the time of the incident in question he was 20 years old. He has an I.Q. of 52. His guidance counselor from the Montgomery County public school system, Cynthia Parker, described him as a mildly retarded person who read on the third-grade level, did arithmetic on the 5th-grade level, and interacted with others socially at school at the level of someone 11 or 12 years of age. Ms. Parker added that Raymond attended special education classes and for at least one period of time was educated at home when he was afraid to return to school due to his classmates' taunting. Because he could not understand the duties of the jobs given him, he failed to complete vocational assignments; he sometimes lost his way to work. As Raymond was unable to pass any of the State's functional tests required for graduation, he received only a certificate of attendance rather than a high-school diploma.

In November or December 1990, a friend introduced Raymond to Erica Frazier, then aged 13; the two subsequently talked occasionally by telephone. On February 28, 1991, Raymond, apparently wishing to call for a ride home, approached the girl's house at about nine o'clock in the evening. Erica opened her bedroom window, through which Raymond entered; he testified that "she just told me to get a ladder and climb up her window." The two talked, and later engaged in sexual intercourse. Raymond left at about 4:30 a.m. the following morning. On November 19, 1991, Erica gave birth to a baby, of which Raymond is the biological father.

Raymond was tried before the Circuit Court for Montgomery County (Miller, J.) on one count of second degree rape under § 463(a)(3) . . . At trial, the defense twice proffered evidence to the effect that Erica herself and her friends had previously told Raymond that she was 16 years old, and that he had acted with that belief. The trial court excluded such evidence as immaterial, explaining:

> Under 463, the only two requirements as relate to this case are that there was vaginal intercourse, [and] that . . . Ms. Frazier was under 14 years of age and that . . . Mr. Garnett was at least four years older than she.

> In the Court's opinion, consent is no defense to this charge. The victim's representation as to her age and the defendant's belief, if it existed, that she was not under age, what amounts to what otherwise might be termed a good faith defense, is in fact no defense to what amount[s] to statutory rape.

> It is, in the Court's opinion, a strict liability offense.

> The court found Raymond guilty . . . .

II

* * *

Section 463(a)(3) does not expressly set forth a requirement . . . that the accused have acted with a criminal state of mind, or *mens rea*. The State insists that the statute, by design, defines a strict liability offense, and that its essential elements were met in the instant case when Raymond, age 20, engaged in vaginal intercourse with Erica, a girl under 14 and more than 4 years his junior. Raymond replies that the criminal law exists to assess and punish morally culpable behavior. He says such culpability was absent here. He asks us either to engraft onto subsection (a)(3) an implicit *mens rea* requirement, or to recognize an affirmative defense of reasonable mistake as to the complainant's age. . . .

III

Raymond asserts that the events of this case were inconsistent with the criminal sexual exploitation of a minor by an adult. As earlier observed, Raymond entered Erica's bedroom at the girl's invitation; she directed him to use a ladder to reach her window. They engaged voluntarily in sexual intercourse. They remained together in the room for more than seven hours before Raymond departed at dawn. With an I.Q. of 52, Raymond functioned at approximately the same level as the 13-year-old Erica; he was mentally an adolescent in an adult's body. Arguably, had Raymond's chronological age, 20, matched his socio-intellectual age, about 12, he and Erica would have fallen . . . well within the four-year age difference obviating a violation of the statute, and Raymond would not have been charged with any crime at all . . . .

The precise legal issue here rests on Raymond's unsuccessful efforts to introduce into evidence testimony that Erica and her friends had told him she was 16 years old, the age of consent to sexual relations, and that he believed them. Thus the trial court did not permit him to raise a defense of reasonable mistake of Erica's age, by which defense Raymond would have asserted that he acted innocently without a criminal design . . . .

* * *

IV

The legislatures of 17 states have enacted laws permitting a mistake of age defense in some form in cases of sexual offenses with underage persons. In Kentucky, the accused may prove in exculpation that he did not know the facts or conditions relevant to the complainant's age. Ky. Rev. Stat. Ann. § 510.030 (1992). In Washington, the defendant may assert that he reasonably believed the complainant to be of a certain age based on the alleged victim's own declarations. Wash. Rev. Code Ann. § 9A.44.030 (1988, 1993 Cum. Supp.) In some states, the defense is available in instances where the complainant's age rises above a statutorily prescribed level, but is not available when the complainant falls below the defining age. In other states, the availability of the defense depends on the severity of the sex offense charged to the accused.

In addition, the highest appellate courts of four states have determined that statutory rape laws by implication required an element of *mens rea* as to the complainant's age . . . .

V

We think it sufficiently clear, however, that Maryland's second degree rape statute defines a strict liability offense that does not require the State to prove *mens rea*; it makes no allowance for a mistake-of-age defense. The plain language of § 463, viewed in its entirety, and the legislative history of its creation lead to this conclusion . . . .

While penal statutes are to be strictly construed in favor of the defendant, the construction must ultimately depend upon discerning the intention of the Legislature when it drafted and enacted the law in question. To that end, the Court may appropriately look at the larger context, including external manifestations of the legislative purpose, within which statutory language appears.

Section 463(a)(3) prohibiting sexual intercourse with underage persons makes no reference to the actor's knowledge, belief, or other state of mind. As we see it, this silence as to *mens rea* results from legislative design. First, subsection (a)(3) stands in stark contrast to the provision immediately before it, subsection (a)(2) prohibiting vaginal intercourse with incapacitated or helpless persons. In subsection (a)(2), the Legislature expressly provided as an element of the offense that "the person performing the act *knows or should reasonably know* the other person is mentally defective, mentally incapacitated, or physically helpless." Code, § 463(a)(2) (emphasis added). In drafting this subsection, the Legislature showed itself perfectly capable of recognizing and allowing for a defense that obviates criminal intent; if the defendant objectively did not understand that the sex partner was impaired, there is no crime. That it chose not to include similar language in subsection (a)(3) indicates that the Legislature aimed to make statutory rape with underage persons a more severe prohibition based on strict criminal liability.

Second, an examination of the drafting history of § 463 during the 1976 revision of Maryland's sexual offense laws reveals that the statute was viewed as one of strict liability from its inception and throughout the amendment process . . . . Amendment #16 then added a provision defining a sexual offense in the second degree as a sex act with another "under 14 years of age, which age the person performing the sexual act knows or should know." 1976 Senate Journal, at 1364. These initial amendments suggest that, at the very earliest stages of the bill's life, the Legislature distinguished between some form of strict criminal liability, applicable to offenses where the victim was age 12 or under, and a lesser offense with a *mens rea* requirement when the victim was between the ages of 12 and 14.

Senate Bill 358 in its amended form was passed by the Senate on March 11, . . . 1976. 1976 Senate Journal, at 1566. The House of Delegates' Judiciary Committee, however, then proposed changes of its own. It rejected the Senate amendments, and defined an offense of rape, without a *mens rea* requirement, for sexual acts performed with someone under the age of 14 . . . . The Senate concurred in the House amendments and S.B. 358 became law. 1976 House Journal, at 3761; 1976 Senate Journal, at 3429; 1976 Acts of Maryland, at 1536. Thus the Legislature explicitly raised, considered, and then explicitly jettisoned any notion of a *mens rea* element with respect to the complainant's age in enacting the law that formed the basis of current § 463(a)(3). In the light of such legislative action, we must inevitably conclude that the current law imposes strict liability on its violators.

This interpretation is consistent with the traditional view of statutory . . . rape as a strict liability crime designed to protect young persons from the dangers of sexual exploitation by adults, loss of chastity, physical injury, and, in the case of girls, pregnancy. The majority of states retain statutes which impose strict liability for sexual acts with underage complainants. We observe again, as earlier, that even among those states providing for a mistake-of-age defense in some instances, the defense often is not available where the sex partner is 14 years old or less; the complaining witness in the instant case was only 13 . . . .

VI

Maryland's second degree rape statute is by nature a creature of legislation. Any new provision introducing an element of *mens rea*, or permitting a defense of reasonable mistake of age, with respect to the offense of sexual intercourse with a person less than 14, should properly result from an act of the . . . Legislature itself, rather than judicial fiat. Until then, defendants in extraordinary cases, like Raymond, will rely upon the tempering discretion of the trial court at sentencing.

JUDGMENT AFFIRMED, WITH COSTS.

■ [The dissenting opinions of JUDGE ELDRIDGE and JUDGE BELL are omitted.]

NOTES ON STATUTORY RAPE

1. In very early common law, consensual intercourse with an underage female was not classified as rape, but that rule was changed by the Statute of Westminster 1, 1275, 3 Edw. 1, c.13, criminalizing as rape what had previously been non-criminal behavior. *See generally* Stephen Lease, 75 C.J.S. *Rape* § 12, Rape. (2002, updated Dec. 2007).

2. In the not-too-distant past, statutory rape laws were gendered, meaning that only men could be convicted of the crime. *See, e.g.,* Michael M. v. Superior Court of Sonoma County, 450 U.S. 464, 101 S.Ct. 1200, 67 L.Ed.2d 437 (1981) (holding that a California law which allowed only men to be guilty of statutory rape did not violate the Equal Protection Clause). In recent decades, states have amended their statutory rape laws to also criminalize female perpetrators. S*ee* Kay L. Levine, *No Penis, No Problem*, in *Special Feature: Women as Perpetrators of Crime* 33 FORDHAM URB. L.J. 357, 368 (2006). Nevertheless, the general public still tends to look at statutory rape as an exclusively male problem, even though there are numerous female perpetrators as well. *See id.* at 380–388 (documenting female perpetration of statutory rape).

3. The Model Penal Code contemplates the availability of a defense of reasonable mistake of age. The Commentary observes,

> [A] girl of [fifteen] may appear to be [eighteen] or even older. A man who engages in consensual intercourse in the reasonable belief that his partner has reached her eighteenth birthday evidences no abnormality, no willingness to take advantage of immaturity, no propensity to corruption of minors. In short, he has demonstrated neither intent nor inclination to violate any of the interests that the law of statutory rape seeks to protect. . . . Whether he should be punished at all depends on a judgment about continuing fornication as a criminal offense, but at least he should not be subject to felony sanctions for statutory rape. Model Penal Code § 213.6, Comment 2 at 415.

4. A large percentage of teenagers who give birth and drop out of school do so in relationships with men in their twenties or older, which creates a burden not only on the immediate family, but on society to care for the child mother and her offspring. For a thoughtful examination of some of the problems with using criminal law to address this social problem, *see* Elizabeth Hollenberg, *The Criminalization of Teenage Sex: Statutory Rape and the Politics of Teenage Motherhood*, 10 STAN. L. & POL'Y REV. 267 (1999).

5. In *Garnett*, why did the prosecutor not bring charges against Erica Frazier for violating Maryland Code (1957, 1992 Repl. Vol.) Art. 27, § 463(a)(2)? Did the prosecutor wisely exercise his or her prosecutorial discretion in this case?

6. Think back to the fraudulent rape materials covered in the last section. As the *Garnett* court notes, "the defense twice proffered evidence to the effect that Erica herself and her friends had previously told Raymond that she was 16 years old . . ." In other words, Erica lied to a man with a low I.Q. by telling him that she was 16 years old (and therefore of legal age to consent) when in fact she was only 13 years old. Is this fraud in the factum or fraud in the inducement? Irrespective of the Maryland statute, should Erica's lie make her guilty of rape by fraud? Should the lie excuse Garnett from criminal liability? *See* Russell L. Christopher & Kathryn H. Christopher, *Adult Impersonation: Rape by Fraud as a Defense to Statutory Rape*, 101 NW. U. L. REV. 75 (2007) (arguing that when a minor induces an adult to participate in statutory rape by falsely representing his or her age, there should be a defense to statutory rape).

7. When asked for an example of a strict liability crime, almost everyone responds "statutory rape." As *Garnett* demonstrates, strict liability for statutory rape is the majority rule in the United States. However as *Garnett* also mentions, a considerable minority of states allow for at least some type of mistake of fact defense. Professor Carpenter has explained that "[w]hile thirty jurisdictions, including the District of Columbia, treat statutory rape as a strict liability offense, three states allow a good faith mistake-of-age defense in all cases, and eighteen states that employ strict liability provide a limited mistake-of-age defense where the victim is close to the age of consent as prescribed by statute." Catherine L. Carpenter, *The Constitutionality of Strict Liability in Sex Offender Registration Laws*, 86 B.U. L. REV. 295, 317 (2006).

8. In 1994, Megan Kanka was raped and murdered by a neighbor who, unbeknownst to Megan's family, had prior convictions for sexually assaulting children. As a result of this and other cases, states enacted "Megan's Laws" that required the registration of sex offenders. Defendants convicted of statutory rape as a strict liability crime are often required to register for lengthy periods. As Professor Carpenter has explained, "[m]any states call for registration for a set term of years, with lengths varying from between ten and twenty years, but a sizeable minority require the statutory rapist to register for life. Carpenter, *The Constitutionality of Strict Liability in Sex Offender Registration Laws*, 86 B.U. L. REV. at 334–335. Is it sound public policy to impose the stigma of sex offender registration on statutory rapists, possibly for the rest of their lives?

————

(E) ACQUAINTANCE RAPE: DOES ACQUIESCENCE EQUAL CONSENT?

The issues of force and consent become more difficult when the victim is conscious and acquiesces because of fear or intimidation, rather than truly consenting. Consent issues of this sort are often raised when the accuser is acquainted with the defendant. The law seems to take for granted that a rapist will be a stranger to the victim, but more often than not, that is not the case. In cases of "acquaintance rape," it often appears that the victim is on trial as much as the defendant. Consider the conflicting opinions in the following case:

State v. Rusk

Court of Appeals of Maryland, 1981.
289 Md. 230, 424 A.2d 720.

■ MURPHY, CHIEF JUDGE.

Edward Rusk was found guilty by a jury in the Criminal Court of Baltimore (Karwacki, J. presiding) of second degree rape in violation of Maryland Code . . . Art. 27, § 463(a)(1), which provides in pertinent part:

> A person is guilty of rape in the second degree if the person engages in vaginal intercourse with another person:

> (1) By force or threat of force against the will and without the consent of the other person; . . . .

On appeal, the Court of Special Appeals, sitting *en banc*, reversed the conviction; it concluded by an 8–5 majority that in view of the prevailing law as set forth in *Hazel v. State*, 221 Md. 464, 157 A.2d 922 (1960), insufficient evidence of Rusk's guilt had been adduced at the trial to permit the case to go to the jury. We granted *certiorari* to consider whether the Court of Special Appeals properly applied the principles of *Hazel* in determining that insufficient evidence had been produced to support Rusk's conviction.

At the trial, the 21-year-old prosecuting witness, Pat, testified that on the evening of September 21, 1977, she attended a high school alumnae meeting where she met a girl friend, Terry. After the meeting, Terry and Pat agreed to drive in their respective cars to Fells Point to have a few drinks. On the way, Pat stopped to telephone her mother, who was baby sitting for Pat's two-year-old son; she told her mother that she was going with Terry to Fells Point and would not be late in arriving home.

The women arrived in Fells Point about 9:45 p.m. They went to a bar where each had one drink. After staying approximately one hour, Pat and Terry walked several blocks to a second bar, where each of them had another drink. After about thirty minutes, they walked two blocks to a third bar known as E.J. Buggs. The bar was crowded and a band was playing in the back. Pat ordered another drink and as she and Terry were leaning against the wall, Rusk approached and said "hello" to Terry. Terry, who was then conversing with another individual, momentarily interrupted her conversation and said "Hi, Eddie." Rusk then began talking with Pat, and during their conversation both of them acknowledged being separated from their respective spouses and having a child. Pat told Rusk that she had to go home because it was a week night and she had to wake up with her baby early in the morning.

Rusk asked Pat the direction in which she was driving and after she responded, Rusk requested a ride to his apartment. Although Pat did not know Rusk, she thought that Terry knew him. She thereafter agreed to give him a ride. Pat cautioned Rusk on the way to the car that "I'm just giving a ride home, you know, as a friend, not anything to be, you know, thought of other than a ride;" and he said, "Oh, okay." They left the bar between 12:00 and 12:20 a.m.

Pat testified that on the way to Rusk's apartment, they continued the general conversation that they had started in the bar. After a twenty-minute drive, they arrived at Rusk's apartment in the 3100 block of Guilford Avenue. Pat testified that she was totally unfamiliar with the neighborhood. She parked the car at the curb on the opposite side of the street from Rusk's apartment but left the engine running. Rusk asked Pat to come in, but she refused. He invited her again, and she again declined. She told Rusk that she could not go into his apartment even if she wanted to because she was separated from her husband and a detective could be observing her movements. Pat said that Rusk was fully aware that she did not want to accompany him to his room. Notwithstanding her repeated refusals, Pat testified that Rusk reached over and turned off the ignition to her car and took her car keys. He got out of the car, walked over to her side, opened the door and said, "Now, will you come up?" Pat explained her subsequent actions:

> At that point, because I was scared, because he had my car keys. I didn't know what to do. I was someplace I didn't even know where I was. It was in the city. I didn't know whether to run. I really didn't think at that point, what to do.

> Now, I know that I should have blown the horn. I should have run. There were a million things I could have done. I was scared, at that point, and I didn't do any of them.

Pat testified that at this moment she feared that Rusk would rape her. She said: "[I]t was the way he looked at me, and said 'Come on up, come on up;' and when he took the keys, I knew that was wrong."

It was then about 1 a.m. Pat accompanied Rusk across the street into a totally dark house. She followed him up two flights of stairs. She neither saw nor heard anyone in the building. Once they ascended the stairs, Rusk unlocked the door to his one-room apartment, and turned on the light. According to Pat, he told her to sit down. She sat in a chair beside the bed. Rusk sat on the bed. After Rusk talked for a few minutes, he left the room for about one to five minutes. Pat remained seated in the chair. She made no noise and did not attempt to leave. She said that she did not notice a telephone in the room. When Rusk returned, he turned off the light and sat down on the bed. Pat asked if she could leave; she told him that she wanted to go home and "didn't want to come up." She said, "Now, [that] I came up, can I go?" Rusk, who was still in possession of her car keys, said he wanted her to stay.

Rusk then asked Pat to get on the bed with him. He pulled her by the arms to the bed and began to undress her, removing her blouse and bra. He unzipped her slacks and she took them off after he told her to do so. Pat removed the rest of her clothing, and then removed Rusk's pants because "he asked me to do it." After they were both undressed Rusk started kissing Pat as she was lying on her back. Pat explained what happened next:

> I was still begging him to please let, you know, let me leave. I said, "you can get a lot of other girls down there, for what you want," and he just kept saying, "no"; and then I was really scared, because I can't describe, you know, what was said. It was more the look in his eyes; and I said, at that point—I didn't know what to say; and I said, "If I do what you want, will you let me go without killing me?" Because I didn't know, at that point, what he was going to do; and I started to cry; and when I did, he put his hands on my throat, and started lightly to choke me; and I said, "If I do what you want, will you let me go?" And he said, yes, and at that time, I proceeded to do what he wanted me to.

Pat testified that Rusk made her perform oral sex and then vaginal intercourse.

Immediately after the intercourse, Pat asked if she could leave. She testified that Rusk said, "Yes," after which she got up and got dressed and Rusk returned her car keys. She said that Rusk then "walked me to my car, and asked if he could see me again; and I said, 'Yes;' and he asked me for my telephone number; and I said, 'No, I'll see you down Fells Point sometime,' just so I could leave." Pat testified that she "had no intention of meeting him again." She asked him for directions out of the neighborhood and left.

On her way home, Pat stopped at a gas station, went to the ladies room, and then drove "pretty much straight home and pulled up and parked the car." At first she was not going to say anything about the incident. She explained her initial reaction not to report the incident: "I didn't want to go through what I'm going through now [at the trial]." As she sat in her car reflecting on the incident, Pat said she began to "wonder what would happen if I hadn't of done what he wanted me to do. So I thought the right thing to do was to go report it, and I went from there to Hillendale to find a police car." She reported the incident to the police at about 3:15 a.m. Subsequently, Pat took the police to Rusk's apartment, which she located without any great difficulty.

Pat's girlfriend Terry corroborated her testimony concerning the events which occurred up to the time that Pat left the bar with Rusk. Questioned about Pat's alcohol consumption, Terry said she was drinking screwdrivers that night but normally did not finish a drink. Terry testified about her acquaintanceship with Rusk: "I knew his face, and his first name, but I honestly couldn't tell you—apparently I ran into him sometime before. I couldn't tell you how I know him. I don't know him very well at all."

Officer Hammett of the Baltimore City Police Department acknowledged receiving Pat's rape complaint at 3:15 a.m. on September 22, 1977. He accompanied her to the 3100 block of Guilford Avenue where it took Pat several minutes to locate Rusk's apartment. Officer Hammett entered Rusk's multi-dwelling apartment house, which contained at least six apartments, and arrested Rusk in a room on the second floor.

Hammett testified that Pat was sober, and she was taken to City Hospital for an examination. The examination disclosed that seminal fluid and spermatozoa were detected in Pat's vagina, on her underpants, and on the bed sheets recovered from Rusk's bed.

At the close of the State's case-in-chief, Rusk moved for a judgment of acquittal. In denying the motion, the trial court said:

> There is evidence that there is a taking of automobile keys
> forcibly, a request that the prosecuting witness accompany the

Defendant to the upstairs apartment. She described a look in his eye which put her in fear.

Now, you are absolutely correct that there was no weapon, no physical threatening testified to. However, while she was seated on a chair next to the bed, the Defendant excused himself, and came back in five minutes; and then she testifies, he pulled her on to the bed by reaching over and grabbing her wrists, and/or had her or requested, that she disrobe, and assist him in disrobing.

Again, she said she was scared, and then she testified to something to the effect that she said to him, she was begging him to let her leave. She was scared. She started to cry. He started to strangle her softly she said. She asked the Defendant, that if she would submit, would he not kill her, at which point he indicated that he would not; and she performed oral sex on him, and then had intercourse.

Rusk and two of his friends, Michael Trip and David Carroll, testified on his behalf. According to Trimp, they went in Carroll's car to Buggs' bar to dance, drink and "tr[y] to pick up some ladies." Rusk stayed at the bar, while the others went to get something to eat.

Trimp and Carroll next saw Rusk walking down the street arm-in-arm with a lady whom Trip was unable to identify. Trimp asked Rusk if he needed a ride home. Rusk responded that the woman he was with was going to drive him home. Trimp testified that at about 2:00–2:30 a.m. he returned to the room he rented with Rusk on Guilford Avenue and found Rusk to be the only person present. Trimp said that as many as twelve people lived in the entire building and that the room he rented with Rusk was referred to as their "pit stop." Both Rusk and Trimp actually resided at places other than the Guilford Avenue room. Trip testified that there was a telephone in the apartment.

Carroll's testimony corroborated Trimp's. He saw Rusk walking down the street arm-in-arm with a woman. He said "[s]he was kind of like, you know, snuggling up to him like. . . . She was hanging all over him then." Carroll was fairly certain that Pat was the woman who was with Rusk.

Rusk, the 31-year-old defendant, testified that he was in the Buggs Tavern for about thirty minutes when he noticed Pat standing at the bar. Rusk said: "She looked at me, and she smiled. I walked over and said, hi, and started talking to her." He did not remember either knowing or speaking to Terry. When Pat mentioned that she was about to leave, Rusk asked her if she wanted to go home with him. In response, Pat said that she would like to, but could not because she had her car. Rusk then suggested that they take her car. Pat agreed and they left the bar arm-in-arm.

Rusk testified that during the drive to her apartment, he discussed with Pat their similar marital situations and talked about their children. He said that Pat asked him if he was going to rape her. When he inquired why she was asking, Pat said that she had been raped once before. Rusk expressed his sympathy for her. Pat then asked him if he planned to beat her. He inquired why she was asking and Pat explained that her husband used to beat her. Rusk again expressed his sympathy. He testified that at no time did Pat express a fear that she was being followed by her separated husband.

According to Rusk, when they arrived in front of his apartment Pat parked the car and turned the engine off. They sat for several minutes "petting each other." Rusk denied switching off the ignition and removing the keys. He said that they walked to the apartment house and proceeded up the stairs to his room. Rusk testified that Pat came willingly to his room and that at no time did he make threatening facial expressions. Once inside his room, Rusk left Pat alone for several minutes while he used the bathroom down the hall. Upon his return, he switched the light on but immediately turned it off because Pat, who was seated in the dark in a chair next to the bed, complained it was too bright. Rusk said that he sat on the bed across from Pat and reached out

> and started to put my arms around her, and started kissing her; and we fell back into the bed, and she—we were petting, kissing, and she stuck her hand down in my pants and started playing with me; and I undid her blouse, and took off her bra; and then I sat up and I said "Lets take our clothes off;" and she said, "Okay;" and I took my clothes off, and she took her clothes off; and then we proceeded to have intercourse.

Rusk explained that after the intercourse, Pat "got uptight."

> Well, she started to cry. She said that—she said, "You guys are all alike," she says, "just out for," you know, "one thing."

> She started talking about—I don't know, she was crying and all. I tried to calm her down and all; and I said, "What's the matter?" And she said, that she just wanted to leave; and I said, "Well, okay;" and she walked out to the car. I walked out to the car. She got in the car and left.

Rusk denied placing his hands on Pat's throat or attempting to strangle her. He also denied using force or threats of force to get Pat to have intercourse with him.

In reversing Rusk's second degree rape conviction, the Court of Special Appeals, quoting from *Hazel*, noted that:

> Force is an essential element of the crime [of rape] and to justify a conviction, the evidence must warrant a conclusion either that the victim resisted and her resistance was overcome by force or that she was prevented from resisting by threats to her safety.

Writing for the majority, Judge Thompson said:

In all of the victim's testimony we have been unable to see any resistance on her part to the sex acts and certainly can we see no fear as would overcome her attempt to resist or escape as required by *Hazel*. Possession of the keys by the accused may have deterred her vehicular escape but hardly a departure seeking help in the rooming house or in the street. We must say that "the way he looked" fails utterly to support the fear required by *Hazel*.

The Court of Special Appeals interpreted *Hazel* as requiring a showing of a reasonable apprehension of fear in instances where the prosecutrix did not resist. It concluded:

we find the evidence legally insufficient to warrant a conclusion that appellant's words or actions created in the mind of the victim a reasonable fear that if she resisted, he would have harmed her, or that faced with such resistance, he would have used force to overcome it. The prosecutrix stated that she was afraid, and submitted because of "the look in his eyes." After both were undressed and in the bed, and she pleaded to him that she wanted to leave, he started to lightly choke her. At oral argument it was brought out that the "lightly choking" could have been a heavy caress. We do not believe that "lightly choking" along with all the facts and circumstances in the case, were sufficient to cause a reasonable fear which overcame her ability to resist. In the absence of any other evidence showing force used by appellant, we find that the evidence was insufficient to convict appellant of rape. *Id.* at 484, 406 A.2d 624.

In argument before us on the merits of the case, the parties agreed that the issue was whether, in light of the principles of *Hazel*, there was evidence before the jury legally sufficient to prove beyond a reasonable doubt that the intercourse was "[b]y force or threat of force against the will and without the consent" of the victim in violation of Art. 27, § 463(a)(1). Of course, due process requirements mandate that a criminal conviction not be obtained if the evidence does not reasonably support a finding of guilt beyond a reasonable doubt. However, as the Supreme Court made clear in *Jackson v. Virginia*, 443 U.S. 307 (1979), the reviewing court does not ask itself whether *it* believes that the evidence established guilt beyond a reasonable doubt; rather, the applicable standard is "whether, after viewing the evidence in the light most favorable to the prosecution, *any* rational trier of fact could have found the essential elements of the crime beyond a reasonable doubt." (emphasis in original).

The vaginal intercourse once being established, the remaining elements of rape in the second degree under § 463(a)(1) are, as in a prosecution for common law rape (1) force—actual or constructive, and (2) lack of consent. The terms in § 463 (a)(1)—"force," "threat of force," "against the will" and "without the consent"—are not defined in the statute, but are to be afforded their "judicially determined meaning" as applied in cases involving common law rape. In this regard, it is well settled that the terms "against the will" and "without the consent" are synonymous in the law of rape.

Hazel, which was decided in 1960, long before the enactment of § 463(a)(1), involved a prosecution for common law rape, there defined as "the act of a man having unlawful carnal knowledge of a female over the age of ten years by force without the consent and against the will of the victim." The evidence in that case disclosed that Hazel followed the prosecutrix into her home while she was unloading groceries from her car. He put his arm around her neck, said he had a gun, and threatened to shoot her baby if she moved. Although the prosecutrix never saw a gun, Hazel kept one hand in his pocket and repeatedly stated that he had a gun. He robbed the prosecutrix, tied her hands, gagged her, and took her into the cellar. The prosecutrix complied with Hazel's commands to lie on the floor and to raise her legs. Hazel proceeded to have intercourse with her while her hands were still tied. The victim testified that she did not struggle because she was afraid for her life. There was evidence that she told the police that Hazel did not use force at any time and was extremely gentle. Hazel claimed that the intercourse was consensual and that he never made any threats. The Court said that the issue before it was whether "the evidence was insufficient to sustain the conviction of rape because the conduct of the prosecutrix was such as to render her failure to resist consent in law." It was in the context of this evidentiary background that the Court set forth the principles of law which controlled the disposition of the case. It recognized that force and lack of consent are distinct elements of the crime of rape. It said:

> Force is an essential element of the crime and to justify a conviction, the evidence must warrant a conclusion either that the victim resisted and her resistance was overcome by force or that she was prevented from resisting by threats to her safety. But no particular amount of force, either actual or constructive, is required to constitute rape. Necessarily, that fact must depend upon the prevailing circumstances. As in this case force may exist without violence. If the acts and threats of the defendant were reasonably calculated to create in the mind of the victim—having regard to the circumstances in which she was placed—a real apprehension, due to fear, of imminent bodily harm, serious enough to impair or overcome her will to resist, then such acts and threats are the equivalent of force.

As to the element of lack of consent, the Court said in *Hazel*:

> [I]t is true, of course, that however reluctantly given, consent to the act at any time prior to penetration deprives the subsequent intercourse of its criminal character. There is, however, a wide

difference between consent and a submission to the act. Consent may involve submission, but submission does not necessarily imply consent. Furthermore, submission to a compelling force, or as a result of being put in fear, is not consent.

The Court noted that lack of consent is generally established through proof of resistance or by proof that the victim failed to resist because of fear. The degree of fear necessary to obviate the need to prove resistance, and thereby establish lack of consent, was defined in the following manner:

> The kind of fear which would render resistance by a woman unnecessary to support a conviction of rape includes, but is not necessarily limited to, a fear of death or serious bodily harm, or a fear so extreme as to preclude resistance, or a fear which would well nigh render her mind incapable of continuing to resist, or a fear that so overpowers her that she does not dare resist.

Hazel thus made it clear that lack of consent could be established through proof that the victim submitted as a result of fear of imminent death or serious bodily harm. In addition, if the actions and conduct of the defendant were reasonably calculated to induce this fear in the victim's mind, then the element of force is present. *Hazel* recognized, therefore, that the same kind of evidence may be used in establishing both force and non-consent, particularly when a threat rather than actual force is involved.

The Court noted in *Hazel* that the judges who heard the evidence, and who sat as the trier of fact in Hazel's non-jury case, had concluded that, in light of the defendant's acts of violence and threats of serious harm, there existed a genuine and continuing fear of such harm on the victim's part, so that the ensuing act of sexual intercourse under this fear "amounted to a felonious and forcible act of the defendant against the will and consent of the prosecuting witness." In finding the evidence sufficient to sustain the conviction, the Court observed that "[t]he issue of whether the intercourse was accomplished by force and against the will and consent of the victim was one of credibility, properly to be resolved by the trial court."

Hazel did not expressly determine whether the victim's fear must be "reasonable." Its only reference to reasonableness related to whether "the acts and threats of the defendant were reasonably calculated to create in the mind of the victim . . . a real apprehension, due to fear, of imminent bodily harm . . ." Manifestly, the Court was there referring to the calculations of the accused, not to the fear of the victim. While *Hazel* made it clear that the victim's fear had to be genuine, it did not pass upon whether a real but unreasonable fear of imminent death or serious bodily harm would suffice. The vast majority of jurisdictions have required that the victim's fear be reasonably grounded in order to obviate the need for either proof of actual force on the part of the assailant or physical resistance on the part of the victim. . . . We think that, generally, this is the correct standard.

As earlier indicated, the Court of Special Appeals held that a showing of a reasonable apprehension of fear was essential under *Hazel* to establish the elements of the offense where the victim did not resist. The Court did not believe, however, that the evidence was legally sufficient to demonstrate the existence of "a reasonable fear" which overcame Pat's ability to resist. In support of the Court's conclusion, Rusk maintains that the evidence showed that Pat voluntarily entered his apartment without being subjected to a "single threat nor a scintilla of force"; that she made no effort to run away nor did she scream for help; that she never exhibited a will to resist; and that her subjective reaction of fear to the situation in which she had voluntarily placed herself was unreasonable and exaggerated. Rusk claims that his acts were not reasonably calculated to overcome a will to resist; that Pat's verbal resistance was not resistance within the contemplation of *Hazel*; that his alleged menacing look did not constitute a threat of force; and that even had he pulled Pat to the bed, and lightly choked her, as she claimed, these actions, viewed in the context of the entire incident—no prior threats having been made—would be insufficient to constitute force or a threat of force or render the intercourse non-consensual.

We think the reversal of Rusk's conviction by the Court of Special Appeals was in error for the fundamental reason so well expressed in the dissenting opinion by Judge Wilner when he observed that the majority had "trampled upon the first principle of appellate restraint . . . [because it had] substituted [its] own view of the evidence (and the inferences that may fairly be drawn from it) for that of the judge and jury . . . [and had thereby] improperly invaded the province allotted to those tribunals." In view of the evidence adduced at the trial, the reasonableness of Pat's apprehension of fear was plainly a question of fact for the jury to determine. . . . Quite obviously, the jury disbelieved Rusk and believed Pat's testimony. From her testimony, the jury could have reasonably concluded that the taking of her car keys was intended by Rusk to immobilize her alone, late at night, in a neighborhood with which she was not familiar; that after Pat had repeatedly refused to enter his apartment, Rusk commanded in firm tones that she do so; that Pat was badly frightened and feared that Rusk intended to rape her; that unable to think clearly and believing that she had no other choice in the circumstances, Pat entered Rusk's apartment; that once inside Pat asked permission to leave but Rusk told her to stay; that he then pulled Pat by the arms to the bed and undressed her; that Pat was afraid that Rusk would kill her unless she submitted; that she began to cry and Rusk then put his hands on her throat and began "lightly to choke" her; that Pat asked him if he would let her go without killing her if she complied with his demands; that Rusk gave an affirmative response, after which she finally submitted.

Just where persuasion ends and force begins in cases like the present is essentially a factual issue, to be resolved in light of the controlling legal precepts. That threats of force need not be made in any particular manner in order to put a person in fear of bodily harm is well established. Indeed, conduct, rather than words, may convey the threat. That a victim did not scream out for help or attempt to escape, while bearing on the question of consent, is unnecessary where she is restrained by fear of violence.

Considering all of the evidence in the case, with particular focus upon the actual force applied by Rusk to Pat's neck, we conclude that the jury could rationally find that the essential elements of second degree rape had been established and that Rusk was guilty of that offense beyond a reasonable doubt.

Judgment of the Court of Special Appeals reversed; case remanded to that court with directions that it affirm the judgment of the Criminal Court of Baltimore; costs to be paid by the appellee.

■ COLE, JUDGE, dissenting.

I agree with the Court of Special Appeals that the evidence adduced at the trial of Edward Salvatore Rusk was insufficient to convict him of rape. I, therefore, respectfully dissent.

The standard of appellate review in deciding a question of sufficiency, as the majority correctly notes, is whether, after viewing the evidence in the light most favorable to the prosecution, *any* rational trier of fact could have found the essential elements of the crime beyond a reasonable doubt. However, it is equally well settled that when one of the essential elements of a crime is not sustained by the evidence, the conviction of the defendant cannot stand as a matter of law.

The majority, in applying this standard, concludes that "[i]n view of the evidence adduced at the trial, the reasonableness of Pat's apprehension of fear was plainly a question of fact for the jury to determine." In so concluding, the majority has skipped over the crucial issue. It seems to me that whether the prosecutrix's fear is reasonable becomes a question only after the court determines that the defendant's conduct under the circumstances was reasonably calculated to give rise to a fear on her part to the extent that she was unable to resist. In other words, the fear must stem from his articulable conduct, and equally, if not more importantly, cannot be inconsistent with her own contemporaneous reaction to that conduct. The conduct of the defendant, in and of itself, must clearly indicate force or the threat of force such as to overpower the prosecutrix's ability to resist or will to resist. In my view, there is no evidence to support the majority's conclusion that the prosecutrix was forced to submit to sexual intercourse, certainly not fellatio.

* * *

In *State v. Hoffman*, 280 N.W. 357 (Wis.1938), the complaining witness entered the defendant's car under friendly circumstances and was driven out into the country without protest. When the defendant made his advances she shouted she was going home, pulled away from him and ran. He caught up with her and there was a tussle; she fell and tried to kick him. Again she ran and he caught her and said "if you run again I will choke you and throw you in the ditch . . ." After that she walked with him back to the car. He did not order her to get in, but begged her. No force was used thereafter. Finally, she consented and acquiesced in the events which followed. At trial the complainant testified she was terribly frightened. Nevertheless the court concluded:

. . . .

> From the testimony of the complaining witness, it appears that she was fully cognizant of everything that was going on, fully able to relate every detail thereof and that she was in no reasonable sense dominated by that fear which excused the "utmost resistance" within her power.

> While the evidence is well calculated to arouse keen indignation against the defendant who so persistently and importunately pursued the complaining witness, who at that time was a virgin, it falls short, in our opinion, of proving a case of rape . . . .

* * *

. . . *Hazel* intended to require clear and cognizable evidence of force or the threat of force sufficient to overcome or prevent resistance by the female before there would arise a jury question of whether the prosecutrix had a reasonable apprehension of harm. The majority today departs from this requirement and places its imprimatur on the female's conclusory statements that she was in fear, as sufficient to support a conviction of rape.

It is significant to note that in each of the fourteen reported rape cases decided since *Hazel*, in which sufficiency of the evidence was the issue, the appellate courts of this State have adhered to the requirement that evidence of force or the threat of force overcoming or preventing resistance by the female must be demonstrated on the record to sustain a conviction. In two of those cases the convictions were reversed by the Court of Special Appeals. *Goldberg* [*v. State*, 41 Md. App. 58, 395 A.2d 1213 (1979)] concerned a student, professing to be a talent agent, who lured a young woman to an apartment upon the pretext of offering her a modeling job. She freely accompanied him, and though she protested verbally, she did not physically resist his advances. The Court of Special Appeals held: . . . "Without proof of force, actual or constructive, evidenced by words or conduct of the defendant or those acting in consort with him, sexual intercourse is not rape . . . ."

Of the other twelve cases, four from this Court, not one contains the paucity of evidence regarding force or threat of force which exists in the case *sub judice*. In *Johnson v. State*, 232 Md. 199, 192 A.2d 506 (1963), the court stated that although there was some evidence tending to indicate consent, which, standing alone, might have justified a judgment of acquittal, there was also evidence of violent acts and verbal threats on the part of the appellant, which, if believed, would have been the equivalent of such force as was reasonably calculated to create the apprehension of imminent bodily harm which could have impaired or overcome the victim's will to resist . . . .

In each of the above 12 cases there was either physical violence or specific threatening words or conduct which were calculated to create a very real and specific fear of *immediate* physical injury to the victim if she did not comply, coupled with the apparent power to execute those threats in the event of non-submission. While courts no longer require a female to resist to the utmost or to resist where resistance would be foolhardy, they do require her acquiescence in the act of intercourse to stem from fear generated by something of substance. She may not simply say, "I was really scared," and thereby transform consent or mere unwillingness into submission by force. These words do not transform a seducer into a rapist . . . .

Here we have a full grown married woman who meets the defendant in a bar under friendly circumstances. They drink and talk together. She agrees to give him a ride home in her car. When they arrive at his house, located in an area with which she was unfamiliar but which was certainly not isolated, he invites her to come up to his apartment and she refuses. According to her testimony he takes her keys, walks around to her side of the car, and says "Now will you come up?" She answers, "yes." The majority suggests that "from her testimony the jury could have reasonably concluded that the taking of her keys was intended by Rusk to immobilize her alone, late at night, in a neighborhood with which she was unfamiliar . . . ." But on what facts does the majority so conclude? There is no evidence descriptive of the tone of his voice; her testimony indicates only the bare statement quoted above. How can the majority extract from this conduct a threat reasonably calculated to create a fear of imminent bodily harm? There was no weapon, no threat to inflict physical injury.

She also testified that she was afraid of "the way he looked," and afraid of his statement, "come on up, come on up." But what can the majority conclude from this statement coupled with a "look" that remained undescribed? There is no evidence whatsoever to suggest that this was anything other than a pattern of conduct consistent with the ordinary seduction of a female acquaintance who at first suggests her disinclination. After reaching the room she described what occurred as follows:

> I was still begging him to please let, you know, let me leave. I said, "you can get a lot of other girls down there, for what you want," and he just kept saying, "no," and then I was really scared, because I can't describe, you know, what was said. It was more the look in his eyes; and I said, at that point—I didn't know what to say; and I said, "If I do what you want, will you let me go without killing me?" Because I didn't know, at that point, what he was going to do; and I started to cry; and when I did, he put his hands on my throat and started lightly to choke me; and I said "If I do what you want, will you let me go?" And he said, yes, and at that time. I proceeded to do what he wanted me to.

The majority relies on the trial court's statement that the defendant responded affirmatively to her question "If I do what you want, will you let me go without killing me?" The majority further suggests that the jury could infer the defendant's affirmative response. The facts belie such inference since by the prosecutrix's own testimony the defendant made *no* response. *He said nothing!*

She then testified that she started to cry and he "started lightly to choke" her, whatever that means. Obviously, the choking was not of any persuasive significance. During this "choking" she was able to talk. She said "If I do what you want will you let me go?" It was at this point that the defendant said yes. I find it incredible for the majority to conclude that on these facts, without more, a woman was *forced* to commit oral sex upon the defendant and then to engage in vaginal intercourse. In the absence of any verbal threat to do her grievous bodily harm or the display of any weapon and threat to use it, I find it difficult to understand how a victim could participate in these sexual activities and not be willing.

* * *

As the defendant well knew, this was not a child. This was a married woman with children, a woman familiar with the social setting in which these two actors met. It was an ordinary city street, not an isolated spot. He had not forced his way into her car; he had not taken advantage of a difference in years or any state of intoxication or mental or physical incapacity on her part. He did not grapple with her. She got out of the car, *walked with him* across the street and *followed* him up the stairs to his room. She certainly had to realize that they were not going upstairs to play *Scrabble*.

Once in the room she waited while he went to the bathroom where he stayed for five minutes. In his absence, the room was lighted but she did not seek a means of escape. She did not even "try the door" to determine if it was locked. She waited. Upon his return, he turned off the lights and pulled her on the bed. There is no suggestion or inference to be drawn from her testimony that he yanked her on the bed or in any manner physically abused her by this conduct. As a matter of fact there is no suggestion by her that he bruised or hurt her in any manner, or that the "choking" was intended to be disabling.

He then proceeded to unbutton her blouse and her bra. He did not rip her clothes off or use any greater force than was necessary to unfasten her garments. He did not even complete this procedure but requested that she do it, which she did "because he asked me to." However, she not only removed her clothing but took his clothes off, too. Then for a while they lay together on the bed kissing, though she says she did not return his kisses. However, without protest she then proceeded to perform oral sex and later submitted to vaginal intercourse. After these activities were completed, she asked to leave. They dressed and he walked her to her car and asked to see her again. She indicated that perhaps they might meet at Fells Point. He gave her directions home and returned to his apartment where the police found him later that morning.

The record does not disclose the basis for this young woman's misgivings about her experience with the defendant . . . . In my judgment the State failed to prove the essential element of force beyond a reasonable doubt and, therefore, the judgment of conviction should be reversed.

Judges Smith and Digges have authorized me to state that they concur in the views expressed herein.

————

NOTES

1. If you agree that Rusk was guilty of rape, you must conclude that Rusk utilized force or threat of force to engage in sex with the victim. Which one—force, or threat of force—did Rusk use? Is it possible to separate the two terms? If you can't specifically identify what particular force or threat of force Rusk used, does that mean the majority is incorrect?

2. As noted in the opinions, the lower court—the Court of Special Appeals—initially overruled Rusk's conviction. Although the Fifth Amendment's double jeopardy clause ordinarily prevents prosecutors from appealing, there is an exception when a case is reversed on appeal and there is a higher court that could overturn the intermediate court's decision. Prosecutors used that avenue to the Court of Appeals of Maryland, the highest court in Maryland, which subsequently reinstated Rusk's conviction.

3. In his dissenting opinion, Judge Cole contended that:

> [The victim] must follow the natural instinct of every proud female to resist, by more than mere words, the violation of her person by a stranger or an unwelcomed friend. She must make it plain that she regards such sexual acts as abhorrent and repugnant to her natural sense of pride. She must resist unless the defendant has objectively

manifested his intent to use physical force to accomplish his purpose.

State v. Rusk, 424 A.2d 720, 733 (1981) (Cole, J. dissenting). Besides protecting her "natural sense of pride" what does a victim's physical resistance demonstrate that would be valuable evidence in a criminal prosecution?

4. Judge Cole's dissenting opinion also remarked that Pat "certainly had to realize that they were not going upstairs to play *Scrabble*." What is your reaction to this statement? What if Pat testified that she intended to engage in some types of intimate activity, but not necessarily sexual intercourse, when she went upstairs? What would be the significance of that testimony?

5. In the Court of Special Appeals, Judge Wilner dissented from the court's decision to reverse Rusk's conviction. Judge Wilner explained that if the victim had given "her wallet instead of her body, there would be no question about appellant's guilt of robbery . . . . No one would seriously contend that because she failed to raise a hue and a cry she had consented to the theft of her money." The comparison between rape and robbery is common in critiques of rape jurisprudence. For example, consider the following explanation:

> The attitude of the law and society toward rape victims stands in sharp contrast to the attitude expressed toward the victims of any other crime. For instance, it would be difficult to seriously imagine the following cross-examination of a robbery victim, asserted by Connie K. Borkinhagen in an effort to convince the House of Delegates of the American Bar Association to redefine rape: "Mr. Smith, you were held up at gunpoint on the corner of First and Main?" "Yes." "Did you struggle with the robber?" "No." "Why not?" "He was armed." "Then you made a conscious decision to comply with his demands rather than resist?" "Yes." "Did you scream? Cry out?" "No. I was afraid." "I see. Have you ever been held up before?" "No." "Have you ever given money away?" "Yes, of course." "And you did so willingly?" "What are you getting at?" "Well, let's put it like this, Mr. Smith. You've given money away in the past. In fact, you have quite a reputation for philanthropy. How can we be sure that you weren't contriving to have your money taken from you by force?" "Listen, if I wanted . . ." "Never mind. What time did this holdup take place, Mr. Smith?" "About 11:00 p.m." "You were out on the street at 11:00 p.m.? Doing what?" "Just walking." "Just walking?" You know that it's dangerous being out on the street that late at night. Weren't you aware that you could have been held up?" "I hadn't thought about it." "What were you wearing at the time, Mr. Smith?" "Let's see . . . a suit. Yes, a suit." "An expensive suit?" "Well-yes. I'm a successful lawyer, you know." "In other words, Mr. Smith, you were walking around the streets late at night in a suit that practically advertised the fact that you might be a good target for some easy money, isn't that so? I mean, if we didn't know better,

Mr. Smith, we might even think you were asking for this to happen, mightn't we?"

John Dwight Ingram, *Date Rape: It's Time for "No" to Really Mean "No,"* 21 AM. J. CRIM. L. 3, 7–8 (1993). Does this mock cross-examination demonstrate a fatal flaw in requiring victims to prove resistance? Or does it prove too much? In other words, is there something very different about the question of whether you've been robbed as opposed to being raped? If so, what is the difference?

6. The eight judges who formed the majority in the Court of Special Appeals decision and the three judges who dissented from the Court of Appeals reinstatement of Rusk's conviction believed that a reasonable person would have engaged in more resistance. Did those judges consider the matter from the perspective of a reasonable woman? Consider Professor Susan Estrich's view:

> In a very real sense, the "reasonable" woman under the view of the eleven judges who would reverse Mr. Rusk's conviction is not a woman at all. Their version of a reasonable person is one who does not scare easily, one who does not feel vulnerability, one who is not passive, one who fights back, not cries. The reasonable woman, it seems, is not a schoolboy "sissy." She is a real man.

Susan Estrich, *Rape*, 95 YALE L.J. 1087, 1114 (1986).

Commonwealth v. Berkowitz

Superior Court of Pennsylvania, 1992.
415 Pa. Super. 505, 609 A.2d 1338.

OPINION

■ PER CURIAM:

* * *

I. FACTS AND PROCEDURAL HISTORY

In the spring of 1988, appellant and the victim were both college sophomores at East Stroudsburg State University, ages twenty and nineteen years old, respectively. They had mutual friends and acquaintances. On April nineteenth of that year, the victim went to appellant's dormitory room. What transpired in that dorm room between appellant and the victim thereafter is the subject of the instant appeal.

During a one day jury trial held on September 14, 1988, the victim gave the following account during direct examination by the Commonwealth. At roughly 2:00 on the afternoon of April 19, 1988, after attending two morning classes, the victim returned to her dormitory room. There, she drank a martini to "loosen up a little bit" before going to meet her boyfriend, with whom she had argued the night before. Roughly ten minutes later she walked to her boyfriend's dormitory lounge to meet him. He had not yet arrived.

Having nothing else to do while she waited for her boyfriend, the victim walked up to appellant's room to look for Earl Hassel, appellant's roommate. She knocked on the door several times but received no answer. She therefore wrote a note to Mr. Hassel, which read, "Hi Earl, I'm drunk. That's not why I came to see you. I haven't seen you in a while. I'll talk to you later, [victim's name]." She did so, although she had not felt any intoxicating effects from the martini, "for a laugh."

After the victim had knocked again, she tried the knob on the appellant's door. Finding it open, she walked in. She saw someone lying on the bed with a pillow over his head, whom she thought to be Earl Hassel. After lifting the pillow from his head, she realized it was appellant. She asked appellant which dresser was his roommate's. He told her, and the victim left the note.

Before the victim could leave appellant's room, however, appellant asked her to stay and "hang out for a while." She complied because she "had time to kill" and because she didn't really know appellant and wanted to give him "a fair chance." Appellant asked her to give him a back rub but she declined, explaining that she did not "trust" him. Appellant then asked her to have a seat on his bed. Instead, she found a seat on the floor, and conversed for a while about a mutual friend.[1] No physical contact between the two had, to this point, taken place.

Thereafter, however, appellant moved off the bed and down on the floor, and "kind of pushed [the victim] back with his body. It wasn't a shove, it was just kind of a leaning-type of thing." Next appellant "straddled" and started kissing the victim. The victim responded by saying, "Look, I gotta go. I'm going to meet [my boyfriend]." Then appellant lifted up her shirt and bra and began fondling her. The victim then said "no."

After roughly thirty seconds of kissing and fondling, appellant "undid his pants and he kind of moved his body up a little bit." The victim was still saying "no" but "really couldn't move because [appellant] was shifting at [her] body so he was over [her]." Appellant then tried to put his penis in her mouth. The victim did not physically resist, but rather continued to verbally protest, saying "No, I gotta go, let me go," in a "scolding" manner.

Ten or fifteen more seconds passed before the two rose to their feet. Appellant disregarded the victim's continual complaints that she "had to go," and instead walked two feet away to the door and locked it so that no one from the outside could enter.[2]

Then, in the victim's words, "[appellant] put me down on the bed. It was kind of like-he didn't throw me on the bed. It's hard to explain. It

---

[1] On cross-examination, the victim testified that during this conversation she had explained she was having problems with her boyfriend.

[2] The victim testified that she realized at the time that the lock was not of a type that could lock people inside the room.

was kind of like a push but no . . ." She did not bounce off the bed. "It wasn't slow like a romantic kind of thing, but it wasn't a fast shove either. It was kind of in the middle."

Once the victim was on the bed, appellant began "straddling" her again while he undid the knot in her sweatpants. He then removed her sweatpants and underwear from one of her legs. The victim did not physically resist in any way while on the bed because appellant was on top of her, and she "couldn't like go anywhere." She did not scream out at anytime because, "[i]t was like a dream was happening or something."

Appellant then used one of his hands to "guide" his penis into her vagina. At that point, after appellant was inside her, the victim began saying "no, no to him softly in a moaning kind of way . . . because it was just so scary." After about thirty seconds, appellant pulled out his penis and ejaculated onto the victim's stomach.

Immediately thereafter, appellant got off the victim and said, "Wow, I guess we just got carried away." To this the victim retorted, "No, we didn't get carried away, you got carried away." The victim then quickly dressed, grabbed her school books and raced downstairs to her boyfriend who was by then waiting for her in the lounge.

Once there, the victim began crying. Her boyfriend and she went up to his dorm room where, after watching the victim clean off appellant's semen from her stomach, he called the police.

Defense counsel's cross-examination elicited more details regarding the contact between appellant and the victim before the incident in question. The victim testified that roughly two weeks prior to the incident, she had attended a school seminar entitled, "Does 'no' sometimes means 'yes'?" Among other things, the lecturer at this seminar had discussed the average length and circumference of human penises. After the seminar, the victim and several of her friends had discussed the subject matter of the seminar over a speaker-telephone with appellant and his roommate Earl Hassel. The victim testified that during that telephone conversation, she had asked appellant the size of his penis. According to the victim, appellant responded by suggesting that the victim "come over and find out." She declined.

When questioned further regarding her communications with appellant prior to the April 19, 1988 incident, the victim testified that on two other occasions, she had stopped by appellant's room while intoxicated. During one of those times, she had laid down on his bed. When asked whether she had asked appellant again at that time what his penis size was, the victim testified that she did not remember.

Appellant took the stand in his own defense and offered an account of the incident and the events leading up to it which differed only as to the consent involved. According to appellant, the victim had begun communication with him after the school seminar by asking him of the size of his penis and of whether he would show it to her. Appellant had suspected that the victim wanted to pursue a sexual relationship with him because she had stopped by his room twice after the phone call while intoxicated, laying down on his bed with her legs spread and again asking to see his penis. He believed that his suspicions were confirmed when she initiated the April 19, 1988 encounter by stopping by his room (again after drinking), and waking him up.

Appellant testified that, on the day in question, he did initiate the first physical contact, but added that the victim warmly responded to his advances by passionately returning his kisses. He conceded that she was continually "whispering . . . no's," but claimed that she did so while "amorously . . . passionately" moaning. In effect, he took such protests to be thinly veiled acts of encouragement. When asked why he locked the door, he explained that "that's not something you want somebody to just walk in on you [doing.]"

According to appellant, the two then laid down on the bed, the victim helped him take her clothing off, and he entered her. He agreed that the victim continued to say "no" while on the bed, but carefully qualified his agreement, explaining that the statements were "moaned passionately." According to appellant, when he saw a "blank look on her face," he immediately withdrew and asked "is anything wrong, is something the matter, is anything wrong." He ejaculated on her stomach thereafter because he could no longer "control" himself. Appellant testified that after this, the victim "saw that it was over and then she made her move. She gets right off the bed . . . she just swings her legs over and then she puts her clothes back on." Then, in wholly corroborating an aspect of the victim's account, he testified that he remarked, "Well, I guess we got carried away," to which she rebuked, "No, we didn't get carried, you got carried away.'"

After hearing both accounts, the jury convicted appellant of rape and indecent assault . . . . Appellant was then sentenced to serve a term of imprisonment of one to four years for rape and a concurrent term of six to twelve months for indecent assault . . . .

* * *

II. SUFFICIENCY OF THE EVIDENCE

Appellant's argument in this regard was well summarized by appellant's counsel in his brief.

The issues on appeal are real. At sentencing, they were recognized by the trial court as being on the cutting edge of the criminal jurisprudence of this Commonwealth . . .

Mr. Berkowitz prays that this Court overturns his rape conviction. He asks that this Court define the parameters between what may have been unacceptable social conduct and the criminal conduct necessary to support the charge for forcible rape.

We contend that upon review, the facts show no more than what legal scholars refer to as "reluctant submission." The complainant herself admits that she was neither hurt nor threatened at any time during the encounter. She admits she never screamed or attempted to summon help. The incident occurred in a college dormitory in the middle of the afternoon.

There has never been an affirmed conviction for forcible rape under similar circumstances. Not one factor which this Court has considered significant in prior cases, exists here. The uncontroverted evidence fails to establish forcible compulsion.

The Commonwealth counters:

Viewing the evidence and its inferences in the light most favorable to the Commonwealth, the jury's conclusion that the Defendant's forcible conduct overcame [the victim's] will is reasonable. The assault was rapid and the victim was physically overcome. Because she was acquainted with the Defendant, [the victim] had no reason to be fearful or suspicious of him and her resorting to verbal resistance only is understandable. More importantly, perhaps, it is only her lack of consent that is truly relevant. It is entirely reasonable to believe that the Defendant sat on her, pushed her on the bed and penetrated her before she had time to fully realize her plight and raise a hue and cry. If the law required active resistance, rather the simple absence of consent, speedy penetration would immunize the most violent attacks and the goal-oriented rapist would reap an absurd reward. Certainly a victim must communicate her objections. But, contrary to the Defendant's arguments, Pennsylvania law says she can "just say no." [The victim] said "no." She said it repeatedly, clearly and sternly. She was rapidly, forcibly raped and deserves the protection of the law.

With the Commonwealth's position, the trial court agreed. We cannot.

In viewing the evidence, we remain mindful that credibility determinations were a matter solely for the fact finder below. On appeal, we must examine the evidence in the light most favorable to the Commonwealth drawing all reasonable inferences therefrom. If a jury could have reasonably determined from the evidence adduced that all of the necessary elements of the crime were established, then the evidence will be deemed sufficient to support the verdict.

In Pennsylvania, the crime of rape is defined by statute as follows:

A person commits a felony of the first degree when he engages in sexual intercourse with another person not his spouse:

(1) by forcible compulsion;

(2) by threat of forcible compulsion that would prevent resistance by a person of reasonable resolution;

(3) who is unconscious; or

(4) who is so mentally deranged or deficient that such person is incapable of consent.

18 Pa.C.S.A. § 3121. A statutory caveat to this rule may be found in section 3107 of title 18.

Resistance Not Required

The alleged victim need not resist the actor in prosecution under this chapter: Provided, however, that nothing in this section shall be construed to prohibit a defendant from introducing evidence that the alleged victim consented to the conduct in question.

The contours of Pennsylvania's rape statute, however, are not immediately apparent. As our Supreme Court explained in the landmark case, *Commonwealth v. Rhodes,* 510 Pa. 537, 510 A.2d 1217 (1986):

"[F]orcible compulsion" as used in section 3121(1) includes not only physical force or violence but also moral, psychological or intellectual force used to compel a person to engage in sexual intercourse against that person's will.

Closely related to section 3121(1) is section 3121(2) which applies to the situation where "forcible compulsion" is not actually used but is threatened. That section uses the phrase "by threat of forcible compulsion that would prevent resistance by a person of reasonable resolution." The Model Penal Code used the terminology "compels her to submit by any threat that would prevent resistance by a woman of ordinary resolution" and graded that offense as gross sexual imposition, a felony of the third degree. The Pennsylvania legislature rejected the concept that sexual intercourse compelled by "gross imposition" should be graded as a less serious offense and, therefore, enacted section 3121(2). By use of the phrase "person of reasonable resolution," the legislature introduced an objective standard regarding the use of *threats* of forcible compulsion to prevent resistance (as opposed to actual application of "forcible compulsion.")

The determination of whether there is sufficient evidence to demonstrate beyond a reasonable doubt that an accused engaged in sexual intercourse by forcible compulsion (which we have defined to include "not only physical force or violence, but also moral, psychological or intellectual force used to compel a person to engage in sexual intercourse against that person's will," or by the threat of such forcible compulsion that would prevent resistance by a person of reasonable resolution *is, of course, a determination that will be made in each case based upon the totality of the circumstances that have been presented to the fact finder.* Significant factors to be weighed in that determination would include the respective ages of the victim and the accused, the respective mental and physical conditions of the victim and the accused, the atmosphere and physical setting in which the incident was alleged to have taken place, the extent to which the accused may have been in a position of authority, domination or custodial control over the victim, and whether the victim was under duress. This list of possible factors is by no means exclusive.

Before us is not a case of mental coercion. There existed no significant disparity between the ages of appellant and the victim. They were both college sophomores at the time of the incident. Appellant was age twenty; the victim was nineteen. The record is devoid of any evidence suggesting that the physical or mental condition of one party differed from the other in any material way. Moreover, the atmosphere and physical setting in which the incident took place was in no way coercive. The victim walked freely into appellant's dorm room in the middle of the afternoon on a school day and stayed to talk of her own volition. There was no evidence to suggest that appellant was in any position of authority, domination or custodial control over the victim. Finally, no record evidence indicates that the victim was under duress. Indeed, nothing in the record manifests any intent of appellant to impose "moral, psychological or intellectual" coercion upon the victim.

Nor is this a case of a threat of forcible compulsion. When asked by defense counsel at trial whether appellant had at any point threatened her in any manner, the victim responded, "No, he didn't." Moreover, careful review of the record fails to reveal any express or even implied threat that could be viewed as one which, by the objective standard applicable herein, "would prevent resistance by a person of reasonable resolution."

Rather, the Commonwealth contends that the instant rape conviction is supported by the evidence of actual physical force used to complete the act of intercourse. Essentially, the Commonwealth maintains that, viewed in the light most favorable to it, the record establishes that the victim did not consent to engage in the intercourse, and thus, any force used to complete the act of intercourse thereafter constituted "forcible compulsion."

In response, appellant urges that the victim's testimony itself precludes a finding of "forcible compulsion." Appellant essentially argues that the indisputable lack of physical injuries and physical resistance proves that the evidence was insufficient to establish rape.

In beginning our review of these arguments, it is clear that any reliance on the victim's absence of physical injuries or physical resistance is misplaced. Although it is true that the instant victim testified that she was not "physically hurt in any fashion," and that it was "possible that [she] took no physical action to discourage [appellant]," such facts are insignificant in a sufficiency determination. As our Supreme Court has made clear, " 'rape . . . is defined, not in terms of the physical injury to the victim, but in terms of the effect it has on the victim's volition.' " *Commonwealth v. Rhodes, supra,* 510 Pa. at 555, 510 A.2d at 1226. Similarly, our legislature has expressly commanded that the "victim *need not resist* the actor in prosecutions under." 18 Pa.C.S.A. § 3107 (emphasis added). As the *Rhodes* Court observed, this legislative mandate was intended to make it clear that "lack of consent is not synonymous with lack of resistance." *Commonwealth v. Rhodes, supra,* 510 Pa. at 557, 510 A.2d at 1227 n. 14. Thus, while the *presence* of actual injury or physical resistance might well indicate "forcible compulsion," we are compelled to conclude that the absence of either or both is not fatal to the Commonwealth's case.

* * *

What is comparatively uncertain, however, in the absence of either an injury or resistance requirement, is the precise degree of actual physical force necessary to prove "forcible compulsion." As the *Rhodes* Court has made clear, no precise definition of the term "forcible compulsion" may be found.

* * *

Here, the victim testified that the physical aspects of the encounter began when appellant "kind of pushed me back with his body. It wasn't a shove, it was just kind of a leaning-type thing." She did not testify that appellant "pinned" her to the floor with his hands thereafter; she testified that he "started kissing me . . . [and] lift[ing] my shirt [and] bra . . . straddling me kind of . . . shifting at my body so that he was over me." When he attempted to have oral sex with her, appellant "knelt up straight . . . [and] tried to put his penis in my mouth . . . and after he obviously couldn't . . . he, we got up." Although appellant then locked the door, his act cannot be seen as an attempt to imprison the victim since she knew and testified that the type of lock on the door of appellant's dorm room simply prevented those on the outside from entering but could be opened from the inside without hindrance. Appellant did not push, shove or throw the victim to his bed; he "put" her on the bed, not in a "romantic" way, but not with a "fast shove either." Once on the bed, appellant did not try to restrain the victim with his hands in any fashion. Rather, while she was "just kind of laying there," he "straddled" her, "quick[ly] undid" the knot in her sweatpants, "took off" her sweatpants and underwear, placed the "weight of his body" on top of her and "guided" his penis inside her vagina.

Even in the light most favorable to the Commonwealth, the victim's testimony as to the physical aspects of the encounter cannot serve as a basis to prove "forcible compulsion." The cold record is utterly devoid of any evidence regarding the respective sizes of either appellant or the victim. As such, we are left only to speculate as to the coercive effect of such acts as "leaning" against the victim or placing the "weight of his body" on top of her. This we may not do. Moreover, even if the record indicated some disparity in the respective weights or strength of the parties, such acts are not themselves inconsistent with consensual relations. Except for the fact that appellant was on top of the victim before and during intercourse, there is no evidence that the victim, if she had wanted to do so, could not have removed herself from appellant's bed and walked out of the room without any risk of harm or danger to herself whatsoever. These circumstances simply cannot be bootstrapped into sexual intercourse by forcible compulsion.

Similarly inconclusive is the fact that the victim testified that the act occurred in a relatively brief period of time. The short time frame might, without more, indicate that the victim desired the sexual encounter as easily as it might that she didn't, given the fact that no threats or mental coercion were alleged. At most, therefore, the physical aspects of the encounter establishes that appellant's sexual advances may have been unusually rapid, persistent and virtually uninterrupted. However inappropriate, undesirable or unacceptable such conduct may be seen to be, it does not, standing alone, prove that the victim was "forced to engage in sexual intercourse against her will."

The only evidence which remains to be considered is the fact that both the victim and appellant testified that throughout the encounter, the victim repeatedly and continually said "no."[6] Unfortunately for the Commonwealth, under the existing statutes, this evidence alone cannot suffice to support a finding of "forcible compulsion."

Evidence of verbal resistance is unquestionably relevant in a determination of "forcible compulsion." At least twice previously this Court has given weight to the failure to heed the victim's oral admonitions. In each such case, however, evidence of verbal resistance was only found sufficient where coupled with a sufficient threat of forcible compulsion, mental coercion, or actual physical force of a type inherently inconsistent with consensual sexual intercourse. Thus, although evidence of verbal protestations may be relevant to prove that the intercourse was against the victim's will, it is not dispositive or sufficient evidence of "forcible compulsion."

If the legislature had intended to define rape, a felony of the first degree, as non-consensual intercourse, it could have done so. It did not do this. It defined rape as sexual intercourse by "forcible compulsion." If

---

[6]   The accounts differed in this respect only as to the tone in which the word was spoken. Appellant claimed it was whispered "passionately." The victim testified that she voiced her objections *before* the intercourse in a "scolding" manner. At trial, it was peculiarly for the jury to determine the credibility of the parties. On appeal, we must view the record in the light most favorable to the Commonwealth. Viewed in this way, we must consider the victim's admonitions *before* the intercourse to be sincere protests. . . .

the legislature means what it said, then where as here no evidence was adduced by the Commonwealth which established either that mental coercion, or a threat, or force inherently inconsistent with consensual intercourse was used to complete the act of intercourse, the evidence is insufficient to support a rape conviction.[7] Accordingly, we hold that the trial court erred in determining that the evidence adduced by the Commonwealth was sufficient to convict appellant of rape.

* * *

IV. CONCLUSION

For the foregoing reasons, we conclude that the evidence adduced by the Commonwealth was insufficient to convict appellant of rape, and that a new trial is warranted on the indecent assault charge. . . . Accordingly, we *discharge* appellant as to the rape conviction and *reverse* and *remand* for a new trial in accordance with this opinion.

———

NOTES

1. Do you believe the court was wrong to overturn Berkowitz's conviction? Do you think the victim consented to sex? Did Berkowitz use force to engage in sex with the victim?

2. The Pennsylvania Supreme Court affirmed the reversal of Berkowitz's rape conviction but reinstated the guilty verdict on the charge of indecent assault. *See* Commonwealth v. Berkowitz, 537 Pa. 143, 641 A.2d 1161 (1994). Does it make logical sense to uphold the assault conviction but overturn the rape conviction?

3. Is it possible that the victim and Berkowitz were both telling the truth? Put differently, could the victim have really meant "no" when she said it, while Berkowitz heard an amorous moan that he interpreted as encouragement? If the victim meant one thing and Berkowitz heard another thing, what should the jury do? Should it matter whether Berkowitz was reasonable in interpreting the "no" as amorous encouragement?

4. Assume that Berkowitz honestly and reasonably believed that the victim consented. Should that be a valid defense? The general rule is that a mistake

---

[7] It may be argued that our conclusion requires the victim, whose *verbal* resistance did not deter the sexual advances, to *physically* resist, in violation of the "no resistance requirement." In this regard, we note the following. Although the "no resistance requirement" does not, on its face, in any way restrict the situations to which it may apply, it appears that the statute must have limits. Section 3121(2) of title 18, which describes the threat element of rape, states that rape occurs when a person "engages in sexual intercourse with another . . . by threat of forcible compulsion *that would prevent resistance* by a person of reasonable resolution" (emphasis added). If the "no resistance requirement" were applied in that setting, the description of the type of threat which is sufficient would be rendered wholly meaningless. To be consistent, therefore, the "no resistance requirement" must be applied only to prevent any *adverse inference* to be drawn against the person who, *while* being "forcibly compelled" to engage in intercourse, chooses not to physically resist. Since there is no evidence that the instant victim was at any time "forcibly compelled" to engage in sexual intercourse, our conclusion is not at odds with the "no resistance requirement."

of fact is a valid defense, but this is not true everywhere. In Commonwealth v. Lopez, 433 Mass. 722, 745 N.E.2d 961 (2001), the defendant was convicted of rape and indecent assault and battery upon a person over the age of fourteen. The victim claimed she resisted the defendant's advances but was threatened and forcibly raped. Medical testimony tended to corroborate the use of force. Lopez contended, however, that the victim had consented. The defense proposed the following jury instruction on mistake of fact as to consent:

> If the Commonwealth has not proved beyond a reasonable doubt that the defendant was not motivated by a reasonable and honest belief that the complaining witness consented to sexual intercourse, you must find the defendant not guilty.

The trial judge refused to give the instruction. On appeal, the Massachusetts Supreme Judicial Court affirmed on the ground that Massachusetts does not require proof of the defendant's knowledge of the victim's lack of consent. The court further explained that

> [T]he mistake of fact defense would tend to eviscerate the long-standing rule in this Commonwealth that victims need not use any force to resist an attack. A shift in focus from the victim's to the defendant's state of mind might require victims to use physical force in order to communicate an unqualified lack of consent to defeat any honest and reasonable belief as to consent. The mistake of fact defense is incompatible with the evolution of our jurisprudence with respect to the crime of rape.

Do you find this explanation convincing? For a thoughtful analysis of the mistake issue, see Rosanna Cavallaro, *A Big Mistake: Eroding the Defense of Mistake of Fact About Consent in Rape*, 86 J. CRIM. L. & CRIMINOLOGY 815 (1996). Most other states reject the Massachusetts rationale and allow for the defendant to claim an honest and reasonable mistake of fact as to consent.

State of New Jersey In the Interest of M.T.S.

Supreme Court of New Jersey, 1992.
129 N.J. 422, 609 A.2d 1266.

■ HANDLER, J.

Under New Jersey law a person who commits an act of sexual penetration using physical force or coercion is guilty of second-degree sexual assault. The sexual assault statute does not define the words "physical force." The question posed by this appeal is whether the element of "physical force" is met simply by an act of non-consensual penetration involving no more force than necessary to accomplish that result.

That issue is presented in the context of what is often referred to as "acquaintance rape." The record in the case discloses that the juvenile, a seventeen-year-old boy, engaged in consensual kissing and heavy petting with a fifteen-year-old girl and thereafter engaged in actual sexual penetration of the girl to which she had not consented. There was no evidence or suggestion that the juvenile used any unusual or extra force or threats to accomplish the act of penetration.

The trial court determined that the juvenile was delinquent for committing a sexual assault. The Appellate Division reversed the disposition of delinquency, concluding that non-consensual penetration does not constitute sexual assault unless it is accompanied by some level of force more than that necessary to accomplish the penetration. We granted the State's petition for certification.

I

* * *

On Monday, May 21, 1990, fifteen-year-old C.G. was living with her mother, her three siblings, and several other people, including M.T.S. and his girlfriend. A total of ten people resided in the three-bedroom town-home at the time of the incident. M.T.S., then age seventeen, was temporarily residing at the home with the permission of C.G.'s mother; he slept downstairs on a couch. C.G. had her own room on the second floor. At approximately 11:30 p.m. on May 21, C.G. went upstairs to sleep after having watched television with her mother, M.T.S., and his girlfriend. When C.G. went to bed, she was wearing underpants, a bra, shorts, and a shirt. At trial, C.G. and M.T.S. offered very different accounts concerning the nature of their relationship and the events that occurred after C.G. had gone upstairs. The trial court did not credit fully either teenager's testimony.

C.G. stated that earlier in the day, M.T.S. had told her three or four times that he "was going to make a surprise visit up in [her] bedroom." She said that she had not taken M.T.S. seriously and considered his comments a joke because he frequently teased her. She testified that M.T.S. had attempted to kiss her on numerous other occasions and at least once had attempted to put his hands inside of her pants, but that she had rejected all of his previous advances.

C.G. testified that on May 22, at approximately 1:30 a.m., she awoke to use the bathroom. As she was getting out of bed, she said, she saw M.T.S., fully clothed, standing in her doorway. According to C.G., M.T.S. then said that "he was going to tease [her] a little bit." C.G. testified that she "didn't think anything of it"; she walked past him, used the bathroom, and then returned to bed, falling into a "heavy" sleep within fifteen minutes. The next event C.G. claimed to recall of that morning was waking up with M.T.S. on top of her, her underpants and shorts removed. She said "his penis was into [her] vagina." As soon as C.G. realized what had happened, she said, she immediately slapped M.T.S. once in the face, then "told him to get off [her], and get out." She did not scream or cry out. She testified that M.T.S. complied in less than one minute after being struck; according to C.G., "he jumped right off of [her]." She said she did not know how long M.T.S. had been inside of her before she awoke.

C.G. said that after M.T.S. left the room, she "fell asleep crying" because "[she] couldn't believe that he did what he did to [her]." She explained that she did not immediately tell her mother or anyone else in the house of the events of that morning because she was "scared and in shock." According to C.G., M.T.S. engaged in intercourse with her "without [her] wanting it or telling him to come up [to her bedroom]." By her own account, C.G. was not otherwise harmed by M.T.S.

At about 7:00 a.m., C.G. went downstairs and told her mother about her encounter with M.T.S. earlier in the morning and said that they would have to "get [him] out of the house." While M.T.S. was out on an errand, C.G.'s mother gathered his clothes and put them outside in his car; when he returned, he was told that "[he] better not even get near the house." C.G. and her mother then filed a complaint with the police.

According to M.T.S., he and C.G. had been good friends for a long time, and their relationship "kept leading on to more and more." He had been living at C.G.'s home for about five days before the incident occurred; he testified that during the three days preceding the incident they had been "kissing and necking" and had discussed having sexual intercourse. The first time M.T.S. kissed C.G., he said, she "didn't want him to, but she did after that." He said C.G. repeatedly had encouraged him to "make a surprise visit up in her room."

M.T.S. testified that at exactly 1:15 a.m. on May 22, he entered C.G.'s bedroom as she was walking to the bathroom. He said C.G. soon returned from the bathroom, and the two began "kissing and all," eventually moving to the bed. Once they were in bed, he said, they undressed each other and continued to kiss and touch for about five minutes. M.T.S. and C.G. proceeded to engage in sexual intercourse. According to M.T.S., who was on top of C.G., he "stuck it in" and "did it [thrust] three times, and then the fourth time [he] stuck it in, that's when [she] pulled [him] off of her." M.T.S. said that as C.G. pushed him off, she said "stop, get off," and he "hopped off right away."

According to M.T.S., after about one minute, he asked C.G. what was wrong; she replied with a back-hand to his face. He recalled asking C.G. what was wrong a second time, and her replying, "how can you take advantage of me or something like that." M.T.S. said that he proceeded to get dressed and told C.G. to calm down, but that she then told him to get away from her and began to cry. Before leaving the room, he told C.G., "I'm leaving . . . I'm going with my real girlfriend, don't talk to me . . . I don't want nothing to do with you or anything, stay out of my life . . . don't tell anybody about this . . . it would just screw everything up." He then walked downstairs and went to sleep.

On May 23, 1990, M.T.S. was charged with conduct that if engaged in by an adult would constitute second-degree sexual assault of the victim, contrary to *N.J.S.A.* 2C:14–2c(1) . . .

Following a two-day trial on the sexual assault charge, M.T.S. was adjudicated delinquent. After reviewing the testimony, the court concluded that the victim had consented to a session of kissing and heavy petting with M.T.S. The trial court did not find that C.G. had been sleeping at the time of penetration, but nevertheless found that she had not consented to the actual sexual act. Accordingly, the court concluded that the State had proven second-degree sexual assault beyond a reasonable doubt. On appeal, following the imposition of suspended sentences on the sexual assault and the other remaining charges, the Appellate Division determined that the absence of force beyond that involved in the act of sexual penetration precluded a finding of second-degree sexual assault. It therefore reversed the juvenile's adjudication of delinquency for that offense.

II

The New Jersey Code of Criminal Justice, *N.J.S.A.* 2C:14–2c(1), defines "sexual assault" as the commission "of sexual penetration" "with another person" with the use of "physical force or coercion."[1] An unconstrained reading of the statutory language indicates that both the act of "sexual penetration" and the use of "physical force or coercion" are separate and distinct elements of the offense. Neither the definitions section of *N.J.S.A.* 2C:14–1 to –8, nor the remainder of the Code of Criminal Justice provides assistance in interpreting the words "physical force." The initial inquiry is, therefore, whether the statutory words are unambiguous on their face and can be understood and applied in accordance with their plain meaning . . . .

The parties offer two alternative understandings of the concept of "physical force" as it is used in the statute. The State would read "physical force" to entail any amount of sexual touching brought about involuntarily. A showing of sexual penetration coupled with a lack of consent would satisfy the elements of the statute. The Public Defender urges an interpretation of "physical force" to mean force "used to overcome lack of consent." That definition equates force with violence and leads to the conclusion that sexual assault requires the application of some amount of force in addition to the act of penetration.

Current judicial practice suggests an understanding of "physical force" to mean "any degree of physical power or strength used against the victim, even though it entails no injury and leaves no mark." *Model Jury*

---

[1] The sexual assault statute, *N.J.S.A.:* 2C:14–2c(1), reads as follows:

c. An actor is guilty of sexual assault if he commits an act of sexual penetration with another person under any one of the following circumstances:

(1) The actor *uses physical force or coercion,* but the victim does not sustain severe personal injury. . . .

Charges, Criminal 3 (revised Mar. 27, 1989). Resort to common experience or understanding does not yield a conclusive meaning. The dictionary provides several definitions of "force," among which are the following: (1) "power, violence, compulsion, or constraint exerted upon or against a person or thing," (2) "a general term for exercise of strength or power, esp. physical, to overcome resistance," or (3) "strength or power of any degree that is exercised without justification or contrary to law upon a person or thing." *Webster's Third New International Dictionary* 887 (1961).

Thus, as evidenced by the disagreements among the lower courts and the parties, and the variety of possible usages, the statutory words "physical force" do not evoke a single meaning that is obvious and plain . . .

The provisions proscribing sexual offenses found in the Code of Criminal Justice, *N.J.S.A.* 2C:14–2c(1), became effective in 1979, and were written against almost two hundred years of rape law in New Jersey. The origin of the rape statute that the current statutory offense of sexual assault replaced can be traced to the English common law. Under the common law, rape was defined as "carnal knowledge of a woman against her will." American jurisdictions generally adopted the English view, but over time states added the requirement that the carnal knowledge have been forcible, apparently in order to prove that the act was against the victim's will. As of 1796, New Jersey statutory law defined rape as "carnal knowledge of a woman, forcibly and against her will." Those three elements of rape-carnal knowledge, forcibly, and against her will-remained the essential elements of the crime until 1979.

Under traditional rape law, in order to prove that a rape had occurred, the state had to show both that force had been used and that the penetration had been against the woman's will. Force was identified and determined not as an independent factor but in relation to the response of the victim, which in turn implicated the victim's own state of mind. "Thus, the perpetrator's use of force became criminal only if the victim's state of mind met the statutory requirement. The perpetrator could use all the force imaginable and no crime would be committed if the state could not prove additionally that the victim did not consent." National Institute of Law Enforcement and Criminal Justice, *Forcible Rape—An Analysis of Legal Issues* 5 (March 1978). Although the terms "non-consent" and "against her will" were often treated as equivalent, under the traditional definition of rape, both formulations squarely placed on the victim the burden of proof and of action. Effectively, a woman who was above the age of consent had actively and affirmatively to withdraw that consent for the intercourse to be against her will. As a Delaware court stated, "If sexual intercourse is obtained by milder means, or with the consent or silent submission of the female, it cannot constitute the crime of rape." *State v. Brown,* 83 *A.* 1083, 1084 (O.T.1912); 75 *C.J.S. Rape* § 11–12 (1952).

* * *

The judicial interpretation of the pre-reform rape law in New Jersey, with its insistence on resistance by the victim, greatly minimized the importance of the forcible and assaultive aspect of the defendant's conduct. Rape prosecutions turned then not so much on the forcible or assaultive character of the defendant's actions as on the nature of the victim's response . . . . That the law put the rape victim on trial was clear.

The resistance requirement had another untoward influence on traditional rape law. Resistance was necessary not only to prove non-consent but also to demonstrate that the force used by the defendant had been sufficient to overcome the victim's will. The amount of force used by the defendant was assessed in relation to the resistance of the victim . . . . Resistance, often demonstrated by torn clothing and blood, was a sign that the defendant had used significant force to accomplish the sexual intercourse. Thus, if the defendant forced himself on a woman, it was her responsibility to fight back, because force was measured in relation to the resistance she put forward. Only if she resisted, causing him to use more force than was necessary to achieve penetration, would his conduct be criminalized . . . .

* * *

To refute the misguided belief that rape was not real unless the victim fought back, reformers emphasized empirical research indicating that women who resisted forcible intercourse often suffered far more serious injury as a result. That research discredited the assumption that resistance to the utmost or to the best of a woman's ability was the most reasonable or rational response to a rape.

* * *

Critics of rape law agreed that the focus of the crime should be shifted from the victim's behavior to the defendant's conduct, and particularly to its forceful and assaultive, rather than sexual, character. Reformers also shared the goals of facilitating rape prosecutions and of sparing victims much of the degradation involved in bringing and trying a charge of rape. There were, however, differences over the best way to redefine the crime. Some reformers advocated a standard that defined rape as unconsented-to sexual intercourse; others urged the elimination of any reference to consent from the definition of rape. Nonetheless, all proponents of reform shared a central premise: that the burden of showing non-consent should not fall on the victim of the crime. In dealing with the problem of consent the reform goal was not so much to purge the entire concept of consent from the law as to eliminate the burden that had been placed on victims to prove they had not consented.

Similarly, with regard to force, rape law reform sought to give independent significance to the forceful or assaultive conduct of the defendant and to avoid a definition of force that depended on the reaction of the victim. Traditional interpretations of force were strongly criticized for failing to acknowledge that force may be understood simply as the invasion of "bodily integrity." In urging that the "resistance" requirement be abandoned, reformers sought to break the connection between force and resistance.

III

The history of traditional rape law sheds clearer light on the factors that became most influential in the enactment of current law dealing with sexual offenses. The circumstances surrounding the actual passage of the current law reveal that it was conceived as a reform measure reconstituting the law to address a widely-sensed evil and to effectuate an important public policy. Those circumstances are highly relevant in understanding legislative intent and in determining the objectives of the current law.

In October 1971, the New Jersey Criminal Law Revision Commission promulgated a Final Report and Commentary on its proposed New Jersey Penal Code. The proposed Code substantially followed the American Law Institute's Model Penal Code (MPC) with respect to sexual offenses . . . The comments to the MPC, on which the proposed Code was based, state that "[c]ompulsion plainly implies non-consent," and that the words "compels to submit" require more than "a token initial resistance." A.L.I., *MPC*, § 213.1, comments at 306 (revised commentary 1980).

The Legislature did not endorse the Model Penal Code approach to rape. Rather, it passed a fundamentally different proposal in 1978 when it adopted the Code of Criminal Justice. The new statutory provisions covering rape were formulated by a coalition of feminist groups assisted by the National Organization of Women (NOW) National Task Force on Rape. Both houses of the Legislature adopted the NOW bill, as it was called, without major changes and Governor Byrne signed it into law on August 10, 1978. The NOW bill had been modeled after the 1976 Philadelphia Center for Rape Concern Model Sex Offense Statute . . . The stated intent of the drafters of the Philadelphia Center's Model Statute had been to remove all features found to be contrary to the interests of rape victims . . .

Since the 1978 reform, the Code has referred to the crime that was once known as "rape" as "sexual assault." The crime now requires "penetration," not "sexual intercourse." It requires "force" or "coercion," not "submission" or "resistance." It makes no reference to the victim's state of mind or attitude, or conduct in response to the assault. It eliminates the spousal exception based on implied consent. It emphasizes the assaultive character of the offense by defining sexual penetration to encompass a wide range of sexual contacts, going well beyond traditional "carnal knowledge." Consistent with the assaultive character, as opposed to the traditional sexual character, of the offense, the statute also renders the crime gender-neutral: both males and females can be actors or victims.

* * *

The Legislature's concept of sexual assault and the role of force was significantly colored by its understanding of the law of assault and battery . . . [B]y eliminating all references to the victim's state of mind and conduct, and by broadening the definition of penetration to cover not only sexual intercourse between a man and a woman but a range of acts that invade another's body or compel intimate contact, the Legislature emphasized the affinity between sexual assault and other forms of assault and battery.

* * *

The understanding of sexual assault as a criminal battery, albeit one with especially serious consequences, follows necessarily from the Legislature's decision to eliminate non-consent and resistance from the substantive definition of the offense. Under the new law, the victim no longer is required to resist and therefore need not have said or done anything in order for the sexual penetration to be unlawful. The alleged victim is not put on trial, and his or her responsive or defensive behavior is rendered immaterial. We are thus satisfied that an interpretation of the statutory crime of sexual assault to require physical force in addition to that entailed in an act of involuntary or unwanted sexual penetration would be fundamentally inconsistent with the legislative purpose to eliminate any consideration of whether the victim resisted or expressed non-consent.

* * *

Because the statute eschews any reference to the victim's will or resistance, the standard defining the role of force in sexual penetration must prevent the possibility that the establishment of the crime will turn on the alleged victim's state of mind or responsive behavior. We conclude, therefore, that any act of sexual penetration engaged in by the defendant without the affirmative and freely-given permission of the victim to the specific act of penetration constitutes the offense of sexual assault. Therefore, physical force in excess of that inherent in the act of sexual penetration is not required for such penetration to be unlawful. The definition of "physical force" is satisfied under *N.J.S.A.* 2C:14–2c(1) if the defendant applies any amount of force against another person in the absence of what a reasonable person would believe to be affirmative and freely-given permission to the act of sexual penetration.

Under the reformed statute, permission to engage in sexual penetration must be affirmative and it must be given freely, but that permission may be inferred either from acts or statements reasonably viewed in light of the surrounding circumstances. Persons need not, of course, expressly announce their consent to engage in intercourse for there to be affirmative permission. Permission to engage in an act of sexual penetration can be and indeed often is indicated through physical actions rather than words. Permission is demonstrated when the evidence, in whatever form, is sufficient to demonstrate that a reasonable person would have believed that the alleged victim had affirmatively and freely given authorization to the act.

* * *

IV

In a case such as this one, in which the State does not allege violence or force extrinsic to the act of penetration, the factfinder must decide whether the defendant's act of penetration was undertaken in circumstances that led the defendant reasonably to believe that the alleged victim had freely given affirmative permission to the specific act of sexual penetration. Such permission can be indicated either through words or through actions that, when viewed in the light of all the surrounding circumstances, would demonstrate to a reasonable person affirmative and freely-given authorization for the specific act of sexual penetration.

In applying that standard to the facts in these cases, the focus of attention must be on the nature of the defendant's actions. The role of the factfinder is not to decide whether reasonable people may engage in acts of penetration without the permission of others. The Legislature answered that question when it enacted the reformed sexual assault statute: reasonable people do not engage in acts of penetration without permission, and it is unlawful to do so. The role of the factfinder is to decide not whether engaging in an act of penetration without permission of another person is reasonable, but only whether the defendant's belief that the alleged victim had freely given affirmative permission was reasonable.

In these cases neither the alleged victim's subjective state of mind nor the reasonableness of the alleged victim's actions can be deemed relevant to the offense. The alleged victim may be questioned about what he or she did or said only to determine whether the defendant was reasonable in believing that affirmative permission had been freely given. To repeat, the law places no burden on the alleged victim to have expressed non-consent or to have denied permission, and no inquiry is made into what he or she thought or desired or why he or she did not resist or protest.

* * *

We acknowledge that cases such as this are inherently fact sensitive and depend on the reasoned judgment and common sense of judges and juries. The trial court concluded that the victim had not expressed consent to the act of intercourse, either through her words or actions. We conclude that the record provides reasonable support for the trial court's disposition.

Accordingly, we reverse the judgment of the Appellate Division and reinstate the disposition of juvenile delinquency for the commission of second-degree sexual assault.

————

NOTES

1. The *M.T.S.* decision offers a robust historical analysis of why extrinsic force—that is, force beyond that necessary to achieve penetration—is not necessary to prove rape. Does the court jump the gun however in analyzing legislative history? Shouldn't the court rely only on the plain text of the New Jersey statute if the statute is clear? Which raises the question: Does the text of the New Jersey sexual assault statute require extrinsic force? Review footnote 1 of the *M.T.S.* opinion.

2. After *M.T.S.*, sexual assault in New Jersey is based on permission, not force. What does permission mean though? Consider the explanation offered by the court:

> Under the reformed statute, permission to engage in sexual penetration must be affirmative and it must be given freely, but that permission may be inferred either from acts or statements reasonably viewed in light of the surrounding circumstances. Persons need not, of course, expressly announce their consent to engage in intercourse for there to be affirmative permission.

Why shouldn't the court require "express" permission? Wouldn't express permission be the simplest way to eliminate confusion and mistaken beliefs that the other partner has consented? And couldn't express permission be conveyed quickly? For instance, in the lead-up to sexual relations, couldn't the participants simply take a moment to ask each other: "Do you want to have sex?" Should the value of spontaneity outweigh the risk of mistaken consent?

3. Does eliminating the extrinsic force requirement also eliminate an important distinction between violent rapists and men who engaged in nonconsensual but not forcible rape? Professor Meredith Duncan has observed:

> In jurisdictions that have not already done so, rape law should redefine forcible rape as distinct from nonconsensual sex. That misconduct may occur between parties who are acquainted with one another and that these situations may make proof of forcible rape difficult (or sometimes disappointingly impossible) is an insufficient reason to unfairly neglect the rights of the criminally accused and abandon well-established principles of criminal law. Moreover, it is important that society be able to tell from one's

conviction whether one is a forcible rapist or another type of sexual offender, such as one who has engaged in nonconsensual sex. As the law currently is applied in too many jurisdictions, it is difficult (if not impossible) to distinguish between the two with reference to the offense of conviction. To alleviate this problem, it is important for jurisdictions to give each offense a distinct label, thereby clearly indicating nonconsensual sexual intercourse as a lesser criminal offense than forcible rape.

Meredith J. Duncan, *Sex Crimes and Sexual Miscues: The Need for a Clearer Line Between Forcible Rape and Nonconsensual Sex*, 42 WAKE FOREST L. REV. 1087, 1123 (2007). Do you agree?

4. The New Jersey statute in *M.T.S.* criminalizes "sexual assault" whereas the statute in many other jurisdictions labels the term "rape." Should the terminology matter? Does the phrase "sexual assault" better describe the crime because the victim is quite literally being assaulted? Or does being a convicted "rapist" carry much greater stigma than the term "sexual assault" such that we should retain the earlier term? For instance, after Jerry Sandusky was arrested for engaging in sexual relations with underage boys, the *New York Times* struggled with whether to describe the conduct as rape or sexual assault, explaining that "[r]ape is a word in flux." Arthur S. Brisbane, The Public Editor, *Confusing Sex and Rape*, N.Y. TIMES, Nov. 20, 2011, at 12.

5. The *M.T.S.* decision amounts to a dramatic reform of rape law. Only two other states—Wisconsin and Washington—have adopted a similar approach. *See* Richard Klein, *An Analysis of Thirty-Five Years of Rape Reform: A Frustrating Search for Fundamental Fairness*, 41 AKRON L. REV. 981, 1007 (2008). Moreover, while there has been a considerable amount of rape reform law (for instance, decreased focus on the victim's resistance, as well as rape shield laws that we will discuss later in this chapter), the reform movement has proved somewhat disappointing. Two researchers found that reform laws "have generally had little or no effect on the outcomes of rape cases, or the proportions of rapists who are prosecuted and convicted." David Bryden & Sonya Lengnick, *Rape in the Criminal Justice System*, 87 J. CRIM. L. & CRIMINOLOGY 1194, 1199 (1997). More recently, see Ilene Seidman & Susan Vickers, *The Second Wave: An Agenda for the Next Thirty Years of Rape Law Reform*, 38 SUFFOLK U. L. REV. 467, 467–68 (2005) ("Few commentators can point to any data suggesting that criminal rape reform laws have deterred the commission of rape, increased its prosecution, or increased conviction rates."). What explains the ineffectiveness of legal change? The answer might be that in areas like rape, the law is less important than social norms. As Professor Dan Kahan has explained:

> The failure of rape law reform fits the profile of a self-defeating "hard shove." There is genuine societal ambivalence about the "no sometimes means yes" norm. Empirical studies suggest that a substantial percentage of men and women behave consistently with the norm, either because they perceive that women who consent too readily will be deemed "promiscuous" or because they believe that

their partners view a certain degree of sexual aggression as alluring. Accordingly, decisionmakers balk in the face of a legal directive to impose the degree of condemnation associated with a rape conviction on the man who fails to take "no" at face value. Jurors either nullify or more likely conclude that the woman who failed to engage in physical resistance actually did consent. Because they know that juries are reluctant to convict, moreover, prosecutors are unlikely to charge men with rape when their victims did not engage in physical resistance. And the conspicuous failure of prosecutors to charge and juries to convict reinforces the public perception that men who follow the "no sometimes means yes" norm aren't engaged in rape after all—at which point jurors become even less likely to convict and prosecutors to charge.

Dan M. Kahan, *Gentle Nudges vs. Hard Shoves: Solving the Sticky Norms Problem*, 67 U. CHI. L. REV. 607, 623–624 (2000). Are you persuaded by this analysis? Do you think rape law reform is actually advancing faster than public opinion?

6. Would it make more sense for states to require affirmative consent prior to sexual intercourse? Rather than reading body language or interpreting whether "no" really meant "yes" or "maybe," should sexual partners each be obligated to say "yes" before engaging in sexual intercourse? In 2015, the American Law Institute circulated draft revisions to the Model Penal Code that would have required affirmative consent. Reaction among criminal law professors was swift and negative. *See* Judith Shulevitz, *Regulating Sex*, N.Y. TIMES, June 27, 2015. Critics suggested that the proposed revision would allow conviction of those who were negligent, a *mens rea* inconsistent with the Model Penal Code's approach generally. *See* Kevin Cole, *Better Sex Through Criminal Law: Proxy Crimes, Covert Negligence, and Other Difficulties of "Affirmative Consent" in the ALI's Draft Sexual Assault Provisions,* 53 SAN DIEGO L. REV. 507 (2016). The American Law Institute eventually rejected the affirmative consent revisions. Should states adopt affirmative consent statutes? What are the benefits and dangers of requiring affirmative consent?

7. Although affirmative consent is not required as a matter of criminal law, an increasing number of universities have adopted it as campus policy. *See* Deborah Tuerkheimer, *Rape On and Off Campus*, 65 EMORY L.J. 1, 9–12 (2015). Should colleges and universities follow the criminal law model and provide the same criminal procedure protections that a defendant would be afforded in a court of law?

———

(F) WITHDRAWN CONSENT

Cases considering the issues of force and consent most commonly consider what was said and done before penetration. What if a person gives consent to intercourse, but changes her mind after penetration has occurred? If the defendant persists, does the consensual sexual contact become rape?

State v. Bunyard

Supreme Court of Kansas, 2006.
281 Kan. 392, 133 P.3d 14.

■ The opinion of the court was delivered by DAVIS, J.:

Josiah R. Bunyard petitions this court for review of the Court of Appeals' decision affirming his conviction of rape . . . .

* * *

The defendant was 21 years old when he met E.N. at a pool party at the home of a mutual friend. E.N., who was 17 years old, flirted with the defendant. She thought the defendant was "cool" so she invited him to a party at her friend's house the following night.

The defendant and friends attended the party the next night. After talking with E.N. for awhile, the defendant invited her to watch a movie in his car with another one of his friends. The defendant drove a Chrysler Sebring two-door convertible with a DVD player built in the dash. The defendant put the car's convertible top up before they began watching the movie.

After the defendant's friend left the car, the defendant and E.N. began kissing. E.N. did not object when the defendant removed her clothing. Likewise, she did not object when the defendant removed his clothing and placed a condom on his penis. However, after the defendant laid E.N. back in the seat and penetrated her vagina with his penis, E.N. said, "I don't want to do this." The defendant did not stop, replying, "Just a little bit longer." E.N. again stated that she did not "want to do this," but the defendant did not stop. E.N. testified that she unsuccessfully tried to sit up and roll over on her stomach to get away from the defendant. After 5 or 10 minutes had passed, E.N. began to cry, and the defendant stopped having sexual intercourse with her. The defendant told her she had given him "blue balls," and E.N. declined his request for her to perform oral sex.

The defendant testified that E.N. was on top of him during consensual intercourse and they were talking. E.N. asked him if he wanted a relationship and if he planned on calling her the next day. When the defendant said he was not interested in a relationship, E.N. became upset, got off of him, and told him about how she had been hurt by other guys in the past. E.N. wanted to continue kissing and wanted him to stay in the car and hold her, but the defendant did not stay in the car and told her to get dressed.

E.N. went back into the house visibly upset and told K.B. that she had been taken advantage of, that the defendant had gotten inside of her, and that she had said "no" more than once. M.B. also spoke with E.N., who was crying. M.B. testified that E.N. said, "I was raped. We had sex. I said no." E.N. did not want to report the incident to the police at that time because she did not want her parents to find out that she had been drinking.

Four days later, E.N. reported the incident to the police, and she was examined at the local hospital. The sexual assault examiner detected a cluster of abrasions consistent with blunt force trauma in E.N.'s vagina. The examiner testified that the location of the abrasions was consistent with mounting injuries. Although consensual sex could not be ruled out, the examiner testified that mounting injuries are more commonly found after nonconsensual sexual intercourse.

* * *

Withdrawal of Consent After Consensual Penetration

. . . During its deliberations, the jury posed the following question: "If someone allows penetration, but then says no and he does not stop, does that fit the legal definition of rape? Please elaborate on the law. If there is any [to] elaborate." Outside the presence of the jury, the trial court discussed its answer with defense counsel and the State. The State asked the court to answer "yes," and defense counsel stated he would like for the answer to be "no." The court advised defense counsel that responding with a "no" would be absolutely wrong and that if its choice were between "yes" and "no," then "yes" would be the answer.

The trial court, with approval of the defense counsel, responded to the jury's question as follows: "The definition of rape is contained in instructions numbered 6, 7, 8, & 9. I cannot elaborate any further. Please reread the instructions."

. . . [The relevant instructions] stated:

"In Count Two (2) the defendant, Josiah R. Bunyard, is charged with the crime of rape. The defendant pleads not guilty.

"To establish this charge, each of the following claims must be proved:

      1.   That the defendant, Josiah R. Bunyard, had sexual intercourse with E.N.;

      2.   That the act of sexual intercourse was committed without the consent of E.N. under circumstances when she was overcome by force or fear; and

      3.   That this act occurred on or about August 25, 2000, in Sedgwick County, Kansas."

"As used in these instructions, sexual intercourse means any penetration of the sex organ by the male sex organ. Any penetration, however slight, is sufficient to constitute sexual intercourse."

* * *

The defendant argues that the Kansas rape statute does not include circumstances where consent is revoked after intercourse has begun. The defendant interprets the rape statute to apply only to the initial entry into the vagina and argues that if the woman consents to the initial entry, there can be no rape even if consent is withdrawn before the act of coitus is completed. According to the defendant, the sexual battery statutes, K.S.A. 21–3517 for sexual battery or K.S.A. 21–3518 for aggravated sexual battery, or another criminal statute should apply if intercourse is continued after the woman revokes her consent, but the rape statute is not violated.

* * *

Penal statutes are to be construed strictly in favor of the accused. Ordinary words are given their ordinary meanings. A court should not read a statute to add something that is not found in the language of the statute or to delete something that is clearly found in the language of the statute.

K.S.A.2004 Supp. 21–3502(a)(1)(A) defines rape as "[s]exual intercourse with a person who does not consent to the sexual intercourse . . . [w]hen the victim is overcome by force or fear." " 'Sexual intercourse' means any penetration of the female sex organ by a finger, the male sex organ or any object. Any penetration, however slight, is sufficient to constitute sexual intercourse." K.S.A. 21–3501(1).

The defendant focuses on the phrase "[a]ny penetration, however slight, is sufficient to constitute sexual intercourse," claiming that the statute limits penetration to the initial entry of the penis or other object into the woman's vagina. While we disagree with the defendant's narrow definition of penetration, he finds support in at least two states.

Maryland and North Carolina have concluded that consent may only be withdrawn prior to the initial penetration. If consent is withdrawn after the initial penetration, the defendant cannot be convicted of rape even if the sexual acts are continued against the victim's will by force or fear. Neither of these courts provide any analysis or citation to authority to support their conclusions. We decline to follow Maryland and North Carolina.

The defendant's narrow definition of penetration fails to comport with the ordinary meaning and understanding of sexual intercourse, which includes the entire sexual act. Under the defendant's definition of penetration, intercourse begins and ends at the same time. Rather than limiting the definition of intercourse, the phrase "[a]ny penetration, however slight, is sufficient to constitute sexual intercourse" establishes the threshold of evidence necessary to prove that intercourse has occurred. When K.S.A.2004 Supp. 21–3502(a)(1)(A) is construed in accordance with the ordinary meanings of its words, the defendant's argument fails. K.S.A.2004 Supp. 21–3502(a)(1)(A) proscribes *all* nonconsensual sexual intercourse that is accomplished by force or fear, not just the initial penetration. Thus, a person may be convicted of rape if consent is withdrawn after the initial penetration but intercourse is continued by the use of force or fear.

Our conclusion that rape may occur after the initial penetration is aligned with the majority of states that have addressed the issue of post-penetration rape.

A Reasonable Time to Withdraw

The defendant contends that even if rape can occur after consensual penetration, the State failed to prove that he did not cease sexual intercourse within a reasonable time after E.N. withdrew her consent . . . .

* * *

In the case of consensual intercourse and withdrawn consent . . . the defendant should be entitled to a reasonable time in which to act after consent is withdrawn and communicated to the defendant. However, we conclude that the jury should determine whether the time between withdrawal of consent and the interruption of intercourse was reasonable. This determination must be based upon the particular facts of each case, taking into account the manner in which consent was withdrawn. We believe this conclusion balances our rejection of the primal urge theory per se with our recognition of the unique facts and circumstances of each individual case.

While the facts of this case may establish that the defendant's continuation of intercourse by placing the victim in fear or by forcing the victim to continue for 5 to 10 minutes was well beyond a reasonable time, we reiterate that this is a jury determination and not for the trial court or the appellate courts to decide. We, thus, conclude that the trial court had a duty to instruct the jury that post-penetration rape can occur under Kansas law and that the defendant has a "reasonable time" to respond to the withdrawal of consent.

* * *

Judgment of the Court of Appeals affirming the district court is reversed [on other grounds]. The district court is reversed, and the case is remanded for a new trial.

■ [The opinion of CHIEF JUSTICE MCFARLAND dissenting in part and concurring in part is omitted.]

■ LUCKERT, J., dissenting in part and concurring in part:

. . . [A]lthough I concur in the majority's holding that rape can occur post-penetration, I dissent from the majority's conclusion that a defendant who is charged with rape under K.S.A.2004 Supp. 21–

3502(a)(1)(A) "is entitled to a reasonable time in which to act after consent is withdrawn."

The majority does not explain how a jury should interpret "reasonable time" when a defendant is charged with rape under K.S.A.2004 Supp. 21–3502(a)(1)(A), which requires the State to prove the victim was overcome by force or fear. There are two possible readings of the majority holding. The presence of an ambiguity is, in itself, troubling. Additionally, both of the potential interpretations are problematic.

Under one interpretation, the majority, by allowing a reasonable time to act, may be implicitly recognizing that persistence is sufficient to satisfy the requirement of force after penetration has occurred . . . .

The alternative reading is even more troubling. If the majority opinion is read to require more force than mere persistence, the effect of the ruling is to grant a defendant a safe harbor of "reasonable time" during which the defendant may exert this higher degree of force or strike fear in the victim.

I would hold that a defendant has committed rape if, after consent is withdrawn, the act of intercourse continues as the result of force or fear. This holding is consistent with the elements defined by K.S.A.2004 Supp. 21–3502(a)(1)(A). The court should not judicially add a defense allowing a reasonable time in which to commit rape.

———

NOTES ON WITHDRAWAL OF CONSENT

1. The *Bunyard* majority noted that only Maryland and North Carolina rejected the concept of post-penetration rape. Two years after *Bunyard*, Maryland's highest court reversed course and held that a woman may withdraw consent after penetration has occurred. *See* State v. Baby, 946 A.2d 463, 486 (Md. 2008).

2. Although Bunyard's actions seem morally wrongful to most observers, is it clear that they are criminal under K.S.A. 21–3501(1)? Immediately after quoting the Kansas statute, the court notes that "[p]enal statutes are to be construed strictly in favor of the accused . . . . A court should not read a statute to add something that is not found in the language of the statute . . ." Did the court follow its own rules of statutory interpretation?

3. In dissent, Justice Luckert accuses the majority of "add[ing] a defense allowing a reasonable time in which to commit rape." Is this what the majority has done? What do you think the majority means by its off-handed reference to a man's "primal urge?" The majority claims that it has "reject[ed] . . . the primal urge theory per se" and instead required looking to "the unique facts and circumstances of each individual case." After *Bunyard*, do you have a clear idea of how long a man has to desist from sexual activity following the revocation of consent? What is reasonable time under Kansas law?

4. As the *Bunyard* decision explains, a number of other courts have held that rape *may* occur after initial consensual penetration, *see* McGill v. State, 18 P.3d 77, 82–84 (Alaska App. 2001); In re John Z., 29 Cal.4th 756, 761–63 (2003) (overruling prior contrary holding); State v. Robinson, 496 A.2d 1067, 1069–71 (Me. 1985) (analyzing a definition for sexual intercourse like K.S.A. 21–3501[1]); State v. Crims, 540 N.W.2d 860, 865 (Minn. App. 1995) (rejecting a legal impossibility theory when the victim initially consents to penetration); State v. Jones, 521 N.W.2d 662, 672 (S.D.1994). At the same time, state statutes addressing post-penetration rape are almost nonexistent. For a rare example, see Ill. Comp. Stat. ch. 720 5/11.170© (2011) ("A person who initially consents to sexual penetration or sexual conduct is not deemed to have consented to any sexual penetration or conduct that occurs after he or she withdraws consent during the course of that sexual penetration or sexual conduct."). In fact, up until the Illinois statute was enacted in 2003, not a single state had legislation on the books that specifically criminalized continued sexual intercourse after the revocation of consent. *See* Erin G. Palmer, *Antiquated Notions of Womanhood and the Myth of the Unstoppable Male: Why Post-penetration Rape Should Be a Crime in North Carolina*, 82 N.C. L. REV. 1258, 1259 n.19 (2004). The revocation of consent is a serious issue that happens frequently. Why have legislatures abdicated their role for clarifying the relevant standards? Should courts be stepping in to fill the breach in the absence of clear legislation criminalizing continued sexual activity after the revocation of consent?

5. Should continued sexual intercourse after the woman revokes consent be labeled as rape or should it be placed in a different category with a less pejorative name? *See Note, Acquaintance Rape and Degrees of Consent: "No" Means "No," But What Does "Yes" Mean?*, 117 HARV. L. REV. 2341, 2364 (2004) (arguing that "postpenetration rape can be recognized as an act of rape, but perhaps not of forcible rape").

———

2. "UNLAWFUL" CARNAL KNOWLEDGE: THE SPOUSAL EXCEPTION

As a society, we are often conditioned to think of rape as a violent encounter perpetrated by a stranger. In recent decades, reformers have tried to bring attention to the more prevalent problem of acquaintance rape. There is a third type of problem, however, which often receives the least attention: unwanted sexual intercourse perpetrated by one spouse against another.

People v. Liberta

Court of Appeals of New York, 1984.
64 N.Y.2d 152, 474 N.E.2d 567.

■ WACHTLER, JUDGE.

* * *

I

Defendant Mario Liberta and Denise Liberta were married in 1978. Shortly after the birth of their son, in October of that year, Mario began to beat Denise. In early 1980 Denise brought a proceeding in the Family Court in Erie County seeking protection from the defendant. On April 30, 1980 a temporary order of protection was issued to her by the Family Court. Under this order, the defendant was to move out and remain away from the family home, and stay away from Denise. The order provided that the defendant could visit with his son once each weekend.

On the weekend of March 21, 1981, Mario, who was then living in a motel, did not visit his son. On Tuesday, March 24, 1981 he called Denise to ask if he could visit his son on that day. Denise would not allow the defendant to come to her house, but she did agree to allow him to pick up their son and her and take them both back to his motel after being assured that a friend of his would be with them at all times. The defendant and his friend picked up Denise and their son and the four of them drove to defendant's motel.

When they arrived at the motel the friend left. As soon as only Mario, Denise, and their son were alone in the motel room, Mario attacked Denise, threatened to kill her, and forced her to perform fellatio on him and to engage in sexual intercourse with him. The son was in the room during the entire episode, and the defendant forced Denise to tell their son to watch what the defendant was doing to her.

The defendant allowed Denise and their son to leave shortly after the incident. Denise, after going to her parents' home, went to a hospital to be treated for scratches on her neck and bruises on her head and back, all inflicted by her husband. She also went to the police station, and on the next day she swore out a felony complaint against the defendant. On July 15, 1981 the defendant was indicted for rape in the first degree and sodomy in the first degree.

II

Section 130.35 of the Penal Law provides in relevant part that "A male is guilty of rape in the first degree when he engages in sexual intercourse with a female * * * by forcible compulsion". "Female", for purposes of the rape statute, is defined as "any female person who is not married to the actor" (Penal Law, § 130.00, subd. 4). Section 130.50 of the Penal Law provides in relevant part that "a person is guilty of sodomy in the first degree when he engages in deviate sexual intercourse with another person * * * by forcible compulsion". "Deviate sexual intercourse" is defined as "sexual conduct between persons not married to each other consisting of contact between the penis and the anus, the mouth and penis, or the mouth and the vulva" (Penal Law, § 130.00, subd. 2). Thus, due to the "not married" language in the definitions of "female" and "deviate sexual intercourse", there is a "marital exemption" for both forcible rape and forcible sodomy. The marital exemption itself, however, has certain exceptions. For purposes of the rape and sodomy statutes, a husband and wife are considered to be "not married" if at the time of the sexual assault they "are living apart * * * pursuant to a valid and effective: (i) order issued by a court of competent jurisdiction which by its terms or in its effect requires such living apart, or (ii) decree or judgment of separation, or (iii) written agreement of separation" (Penal Law, § 130.00, subd. 4).

[margin note: "not married" exceptions]

Defendant moved to dismiss the indictment, asserting that because he and Denise were still married at the time of the incident he came within the "marital exemption" to both rape and sodomy. The People opposed the motion, contending that the temporary order of protection required Mario and Denise to live apart, and they in fact were living apart, and thus were "not married" for purposes of the statutes. The trial court granted the defendant's motion and dismissed the indictment, concluding that the temporary order of protection did not require Mario and Denise to live apart from each other, but instead required only that he remain away from her, and that therefore the "marital exemption" applied.

On appeal by the People, the Appellate Division . . . reversed the trial court, reinstated the indictment, and remanded the case for trial. The Appellate Division held that a Family Court order of protection is within the scope of "[an] order * * * which by its terms or in its effect requires such living apart" even though it is directed only at a husband, and thus found that Mario and Denise were "not married" for purposes of the statute at the time of the incident.

The defendant was then convicted of rape in the first degree and sodomy in the first degree and the conviction was affirmed . . .

* * *

. . . [U]nder the Penal Law a married man ordinarily cannot be convicted of forcibly raping or sodomizing his wife. This is the so-called marital exemption for rape. Although a marital exemption was not explicit in earlier rape statutes, an 1852 treatise stated that a man could not be guilty of raping his wife (Barbour, Criminal Law of State of New York [2d ed.], p. 69). The assumption, even before the marital exemption was codified, that a man could not be guilty of raping his wife, is traceable to a statement made by the 17th century English jurist Lord Hale, who wrote: "[T]he husband cannot be guilty of a rape committed by himself upon his lawful wife, for by their mutual matrimonial consent and contract the wife hath given up herself in this kind unto her husband, which she cannot retract" (1 Hale, History of Pleas of the Crown, p. 629). Although Hale cited no authority for his statement it was relied on by State Legislatures which enacted rape statutes with a marital exemption and by courts which established a common-law exemption for husbands.

The first American case to recognize the marital exemption was decided in 1857 by the Supreme Judicial Court of Massachusetts, which stated in dictum that it would always be a defense to rape to show marriage to the victim (*Commonwealth v. Fogerty,* 74 Mass. 489). Decisions to the same effect by other courts followed, usually with no rationale or authority cited other than Hale's implied consent view. In New York, a 1922 decision noted the marital exemption in the Penal Law and stated that it existed "on account of the matrimonial consent which [the wife] has given, and which she cannot retract" (*People v. Meli,* 193 N.Y.S. 365, 366 [Sup.Ct.]).

Presently, over 40 States still retain some form of marital exemption for rape . . . .

We find that there is no rational basis for distinguishing between marital rape and nonmarital rape. The various rationales which have been asserted in defense of the exemption are either based upon archaic notions about the consent and property rights incident to marriage or are simply unable to withstand even the slightest scrutiny. We therefore declare the marital exemption for rape in the New York statute to be unconstitutional.

Lord Hale's notion of an irrevocable implied consent by a married woman to sexual intercourse has been cited most frequently in support of the marital exemption. Any argument based on a supposed consent, however, is untenable. Rape is not simply a sexual act to which one party does not consent. Rather, it is a degrading, violent act which violates the bodily integrity of the victim and frequently causes severe, long-lasting physical and psychic harm. To ever imply consent to such an act is irrational and absurd. Other than in the context of rape statutes, marriage has never been viewed as giving a husband the right to coerced intercourse on demand. Certainly, then, a marriage license should not be viewed as a license for a husband to forcibly rape his wife with impunity. A married woman has the same right to control her own body as does an unmarried woman. If a husband feels "aggrieved" by his wife's refusal to engage in sexual intercourse, he should seek relief in the courts governing domestic relations, not in "violent or forceful self-help" (*State v. Smith,* 85 N.J. 193, 206, 426 A.2d 38).

The other traditional justifications for the marital exemption were the common-law doctrines that a woman was the property of her husband and that the legal existence of the woman was "incorporated and consolidated into that of the husband." Both these doctrines, of course, have long been rejected in this State. Indeed, "[n]owhere in the common-law world—[or] in any modern society—is a woman regarded as chattel or demeaned by denial of a separate legal identity and the dignity associated with recognition as a whole human being" (*Trammel v. United States,* 445 U.S. 40, 52, 100 S.Ct. 906, 913, 63 L.Ed.2d 186).

* * *

Another rationale sometimes advanced in support of the marital exemption is that marital rape would be a difficult crime to prove. A related argument is that allowing such prosecutions could lead to fabricated complaints by "vindictive" wives. The difficulty of proof argument is based on the problem of showing lack of consent. Proving lack of consent, however, is often the most difficult part of any rape prosecution, particularly where the rapist and the victim had a prior relationship. Similarly, the possibility that married women will fabricate complaints would seem to be no greater than the possibility of unmarried women doing so. The criminal justice system, with all of its built-in safeguards, is presumed to be capable of handling any false complaints. Indeed, if the possibility of fabricated complaints were a basis for not criminalizing behavior which would otherwise be sanctioned, virtually all crimes other than homicides would go unpunished.

* * *

Moreover, there is no evidence to support the argument that marital rape has less severe consequences than other rape. On the contrary, numerous studies have shown that marital rape is frequently quite violent and generally has *more* severe, traumatic effects on the victim than other rape.

Among the recent decisions in this country addressing the maritalexemption, only one court has concluded that there is a rational basis forit (see *People v. Brown*, 632 P.2d 1025 [Col.]). We agree with the other courts which have analyzed the exemption, which have been unable tofind any present justification for it . . .

* * *

Accordingly, the . . . [conviction] should be affirmed.

———————

NOTES ON MARITAL RAPE

1. For a more detailed analysis of the history of marital rape and immunity from prosecution, see Jill Elaine Hasday, *Contest and Consent: A Legal History of Marital Rape*, 88 CAL. L. REV. 1373 (2000).

2. The *Liberta* case is the most famous decision to reject the marital rape exception. During the 1970s, 1980s, and early 1990s other courts and legislatures took similar steps, leading one observer to note that "by 1993, spousal rape, just like nonmarital rape, was a crime in all fifty states and the District of Columbia." Jessica Klarfeld, Note, *A Striking Disconnect:*

Marital Rape Law's Failure To Keep Up With Domestic Violence Law, 48 AM. CRIM. L. REV. 1819 (2011). Yet, the law has not changed as much as it some might assume. As one leading expert has explained

> Many people believe that reformers won the battle against the marital rape exemption. This belief is, unfortunately, incorrect. The good news is that twenty-four states and the District of Columbia have abolished marital immunity for sexual offenses. The bad news is that twenty-six states retain marital immunity in one form or another. Although in some of these twenty-six states marital immunity for the specific crime of forcible rape is dead, immunity for other sexual offenses thrives. For example, twenty states grant marital immunity for sex with a wife who is incapacitated or unconscious and cannot consent. Fifteen states grant marital immunity for sexual offenses unless requirements such as prompt complaint, extra force, separation, or divorce are met.

Michelle J. Anderson, *Marital Immunity, Intimate Relationships, and Improper Inferences: A New Look on Sexual Offenses Against Intimates*, 54 HASTINGS L.J. 1465–1468–72 (2003).

3. *Reporting Restrictions*: Some states impose a shorter deadline for married women to report rape by their husbands. In South Carolina, "[t]he offending spouse's conduct must be reported to appropriate law enforcement authorities within thirty days in order for that spouse to be prosecuted for this offense." S.C. Code § 16–3–615(B). By contrast, a rape victim who is not married to the accused faces no deadline in South Carolina. *See* S.C. Code § 16–3–652.

[handwritten: shorter deadline]

4. *Punishment Differences*: A few states impose lower punishment ranges for marital rape cases. The most stark, once again, may be South Carolina which punishes ordinary rape with up to thirty years' incarceration, while authorizing a maximum of ten years for marital rape. *Compare* S.C. Code § 16–3–652 with S.C. Code § 16–3–615(B). For additional examples of differential treatment in Arizona, Tennessee, and Virginia, see Anderson, *Marital Immunity*, 54 HASTINGS L.J. at 1490–91. Is there any possible reason for punishing men who rape their wives less severely than men who rape strangers or acquaintances? Is there a plausible argument for punishing marital rape *more* severely?

[handwritten: lower punishment]

B. SPECIAL ISSUES OF PROOF IN RAPE CASES

Some of the issues of proof in rape and other sex assault cases are arguably beyond the scope of substantive criminal law courses, but at least a basic introduction to these special issues of proof is often essential to assessing the elements of the substantive crime.

1. "RAPE SHIELD" STATUTES

Rape trials, historically, have reflected the stated or unstated assumption that if the victim of rape or other sex assault were "unchaste," she had likely consented, and there was therefore no rape. "Rape Shield" statutes have sought to limit evidence of past sexual conduct by the complaining witness to matters that are truly relevant, such as, for example, a consensual relationship with the accused. Mere evidence of unchastity, or even of promiscuity, is not admissible as a general rule, and sexual orientation is likewise not admissible unless it is actually relevant to an issue in the case. Consider, in this context, the following case.

State v. Johnson

Supreme Court of New Mexico, 1997.
123 N.M. 640, 944 P.2d 869.

■ MINZNER, J.

. . . A jury convicted Defendant of two accounts each of aggravated assault and second degree criminal penetration, and one count of false imprisonment . . . .

I. FACTS AND PROCEDURE

The charges of which Defendant was convicted stem from two separate incidents, each occurring on Central Avenue in Albuquerque. The State contended that on or about August 25, 1991, Defendant enticed T.A. to enter his car by indicating that he was a law enforcement officer and needed to speak to her; and that on or about October 11, 1992, he offered T.S. a ride, which she accepted. After each woman entered his car, he drove her to a secluded area where he assaulted and raped her.

Defense counsel told the jury during opening statement that Defendant approached each woman believing her to be a prostitute, that each incident was "a commercial relationship, not forced sex," and that during the course of "these acts for which [Defendant] was paying money, he did things which annoyed, angered and, in some ways, frightened these women." Counsel for the State and for Defendant each told the jury the issue was whether Defendant used force to overcome each victim's will or whether each had consented.

Defense counsel filed a motion in limine . . . asking the court to consider the "admissibility of evidence of the prior sexual conduct of the alleged victims." . . . [T]he State opposed his motion . . . .

A few days before trial, Defendant and the State each made legal arguments to the court in support of their respective motions. The court ruled it would hold the in camera hearing after selecting the jury and before opening statements. Subsequently, at the in camera hearing, the court heard testimony from Detective Jeff Arbogast and arguments by the State and the Defendant. Detective Arbogast had investigated the case and interviewed the victim-witnesses, T.A. and T.S. Detective Arbogast testified that both T.A. and Defendant Johnson told him that, on that night, T.A. was not acting as a prostitute. Defendant elicited from

Detective Arbogast evidence that T.A. told him she had not been working as a prostitute when she got into the car with Defendant, but on occasions in the past she had engaged in acts of prostitution in order to pay her rent. Defendant argued that this admission went "to a central issue" and also "to her credibility." At the close of the hearing, the trial court denied Defendant's request and granted the State's motion.

At trial Defendant attempted to cross-examine T.S. on whether she was frightened while she was with Defendant; he also attempted to ask her whether she had stopped entering cars of strangers. The court sustained the State's objection. Defendant testified in his own defense. He admitted that he engaged in acts of sexual intercourse with each woman. He testified that they consented to some acts but not to others. The jury acquitted Defendant on a number of counts, including one that charged him with kidnapping and one that charged him with impersonating a police officer. The jury convicted Johnson of aggravated assault, second degree criminal penetration and false imprisonment.

The Court of Appeals reversed Defendant's conviction and remanded the case for a new trial on grounds that the evidence in question should have been admitted for the purpose of showing possible motive to fabricate . . . The Court of Appeals reasoned that Defendant's proffer of evidence "went beyond an attempt to show that the sexual acts were consensual," and "went to the issue of whether the victims had reason to fabricate the rape to avenge Defendant's failure or refusal to pay them." The Court of Appeals also stated in its analysis that the rape shield statute does not prevent the public disclosure of the acts of individuals who make themselves available for commercial sex.

We granted certiorari to review the trial court's exclusion of evidence of the victims' prior sexual activity. The central question is whether our rape shield law permits the introduction of such evidence when the evidence tends to prove that the alleged victim acted as a prostitute on the occasion, consented to sex, and subsequently fabricated a claim of rape. We conclude it does. However, this case also raises another question, which is whether a defendant must make a showing that there is evidence to support a theory of fabrication before being allowed to introduce evidence of prior acts of prostitution. We conclude the answer to this question is yes. We also conclude that Defendant did not make an adequate showing.

II. DISCUSSION

* * *

A. *History of Rape Shield Laws Generally*

Prior to the development of rape shield laws, evidence of a rape victim's past sexual experience was offered as evidence on various theories of relevance. If the rape victim had had prior sexual experience, this might be offered to impeach her credibility or to show her consent to the sexual act in question. At that time, some believed that evidence of consent to a previous act of sexual intercourse was relevant and material in a criminal trial to a subsequent charge of rape, based on the reasoning that someone who had consented previously would have been more likely to have consented on the particular occasion at issue. Evidentiary use of the complainant's prior sexual conduct, pursuant to various theories of relevance, appeared to have deterred victims of sexual assault from making formal complaints . . .

The rape shield laws and evidentiary rules enacted and adopted in recent years address the problem of underreporting and reluctance to testify. "Reformers have argued that inquiries into the sexual history of the rape complainant [chill] her willingness to testify. Moreover, reputation evidence is only marginally, if at all, probative of consent." *Commonwealth v. Joyce*, 415 N.E.2d 181, 186 (Mass. 1981). Rape shield laws, evidentiary rules, and case law generally limit the admission of prior sexual conduct evidence into trials of charges of criminal sexual penetration or other such criminal sexual contact, such as this case, unless such evidence can be demonstrated to be material to the defendant's theory and the trial court is persuaded that the probative nature of the evidence equals or outweighs its prejudicial effect. However, statutes, rules, and cases vary.

Some jurisdictions have chosen to make such evidence admissible only on a particular issue or issues. For example, in the State of Washington, such evidence is admissible to prove the victim's consent only "when the perpetrator and the victim have engaged in sexual intercourse with each other in the past." Wash.Rev.Code § 9A.44.020 (1996). In *Winfield v. Commonwealth*, 225 Va. 211, 301 S.E.2d 15, 19 (1983), the Virginia Supreme Court distinguished its statute from others. "Most of these [rape shield laws] limit or prohibit the admission of general reputation evidence as to the prior unchastity of the complaining witness but some, like ours, permit the introduction of evidence of specific acts of sexual conduct between the complaining witness and third persons in carefully limited circumstances." *Id.*

In *State v. Herndon,* 145 Wis.2d 91, 426 N.W.2d 347, 352 (App.1988), *overruled on other grounds sub nom. State v. Pulizzano,* 155 Wis.2d 633, 456 N.W.2d 325, 330–31 (1990), the Wisconsin Court of Appeals characterizes Wisconsin as following the approach Professor Galvin identifies as "the Michigan approach." Harriett R. Galvin, *Shielding Rape Victims in the State and Federal Courts: A Proposal for the Second Decade,* 70 Minn. L. Rev. 763, 907 (1986). *Herndon* describes "[t]he rape shield laws which follow the Michigan approach [as] general prohibitions on prior sexual conduct or reputation evidence [that] have highly specific exceptions allowing for this evidence in those circumstances in which it is highly relevant and material to the presentation of a defense and therefore constitutionally required." *Id.* 426 N.W.2d at 352–53. Professor

Galvin lists twenty-five states as following "the Michigan approach," including Virginia and Wisconsin. *Id.* at 907, tbl. 1(A). In these states, "statutes have stripped courts of their discretion to determine the relevancy of sexual conduct evidence on a case-by-case basis." Galvin, *supra,* at 773.

The Federal Rules of Evidence generally prohibit admission of evidence of a victim's past sexual behavior, except (a) when evidence of specific instances of sexual behavior by the alleged victim is offered to prove that a person other than the accused was the source of semen, injury, or other physical evidence; (b) when evidence of specific instances of sexual behavior between the victim and the defendant is offered to prove consent or offered by the prosecution; or (c) when exclusion of such evidence would violate the constitutional rights of the defendant. Fed.R.Evid. 412. Some states have modeled their statutes on the federal rule. Professor Galvin lists Connecticut, Hawaii, Iowa, New York and Oregon.

Other states' laws do not have such specific limitations. These statutes restrict the admission of prior sexual conduct for any purpose. New Mexico's statute falls in this group. In such states, the trial court usually conducts a pre-trial hearing in which the parties offer evidence and argument on the probative value and the material nature of the evidence. Under some statutes, the trial court must then balance probative value against prejudicial effect to decide whether to allow the admission of the evidence ... [Professor Galvin] characterizes such statutes as following the "Texas approach," under which the trial court has broad discretion to admit or exclude evidence of prior sexual conduct based on a pre-trial or in camera hearing at which the judge considers an offer of proof and weighs probative value against prejudicial effect. She characterizes this group as providing trial court judges "nearly unfettered discretion to admit sexual conduct evidence merely upon a showing of relevancy under traditional standards, that is, when probative value outweighs prejudicial effect." *Id.*

Professor Galvin identifies a fourth approach as "the California approach." *Id.* at 775. "Under the California approach, sexual conduct evidence is separated into two broad categories depending on the purpose for which it is offered. Evidence is categorized as either substantive evidence, which is offered to prove consent by the complainant, or credibility evidence, offered to attack her credibility." *Id.* . . .

B. *New Mexico's Statute, Rule and Cases*

Our Legislature first enacted a rape shield law in 1975. 1975 NM Laws, ch. 109, § 7. In its present form, it states in pertinent part:

> As a matter of substantive right, in prosecutions pursuant to the provisions of Section 30–9–11 through 30–9–15 NMSA 1978, evidence of the victim's past sexual conduct, opinion evidence of the victim's past sexual conduct or of reputation for past sexual

conduct, shall not be admitted unless, and only to the extent that the court finds that, the evidence is material to the case and that its inflammatory or prejudicial nature does not outweigh its probative value.

Section 30–9–16(A) . . . .

. . . Nothing in our statute or rule, however, limits the reasons a court might find evidence material and of sufficient probative value to justify admission. In particular, nothing in the statute or the rule precludes the introduction of relevant evidence of prostitution when the probative value of that evidence equals or outweighs its prejudicial effect.

In contrast to those jurisdictions in which statutes contain specific limitations or exceptions, *see, e.g.,* Wash.Rev.Code § 9A.44.020; *see also* Fed.R.Evid. 412, our statute, rule, and cases rely on the trial court judge to identify theories of relevance as well as to exercise discretion, balance prejudicial effect against probative value, and thus determine admissibility on a case by case basis. Our statute and rule provide for an in camera hearing to determine admissibility. The in camera hearing provides a formal opportunity to inform the trial court of the relevant facts and circumstances, make the arguments of relevancy, and explain the respective positions on balancing. In conducting that inquiry, the trial judge must depend on the moving party or parties to offer proof and argument in support of the ruling sought. In turn, the moving party must depend on our cases and, where appropriate, those of other jurisdictions to provide the trial judge with persuasive arguments and supporting proof. Our cases have not provided trial court judges particular direction in determining admissibility.

Our cases *have* held that trial courts should remove from the jury the temptation to pass judgment upon rape victims whenever possible. *See State v. Fish,* 101 N.M. 329, 332–33, 681 P.2d 1106, 1109–10 (1984) (upholding exclusion of prior sexual conduct evidence in the absence of substantial similarity between alleged prior rape and present case); *State v. Romero,* 94 N.M. 22, 27, 606 P.2d 1116, 1121 (Ct.App.1980) (recognizing the rape shield statute reflects "the strong public policy in this state to prevent unwarranted intrusions into the private affairs of victims of sex crimes") . . . .

* * *

3. The Admissibility of Evidence of Prior Acts of Prostitution as Evidence of Motive to Fabricate

In this case, Defendant sought to offer evidence of a prior act or acts in which the victims were alleged to have engaged with others who were not identified. This is not enough to implicate Defendant's constitutional right of confrontation. Motive to fabricate is a theory of relevance that does implicate the right of confrontation. A trial court would be entitled to determine that the prejudicial effect of prior sexual conduct evidence, such as evidence of prostitution, would not outweigh the probative value of evidence of a motive to fabricate. Nevertheless, evidence of prior acts of prostitution is not sufficient in itself to show a motive to fabricate.

* * *

. . . [W]e hold that when a defendant characterizes an alleged rape or other criminal sexual contact as an act of prostitution, evidence of prior acts of prostitution is not necessarily material and probative. A defendant must "specify the issue or issues the evidence is intended to address and demonstrate how the evidence is truly probative on those issues . . ." For example, a defendant may show that a victim has engaged in "a distinctive pattern of past sexual conduct, involving the extortion of money by threat after acts of prostitution, of which her alleged conduct in [a particular case] is but an example." *Winfield,* 301 S.E.2d at 20. Simply showing that the victim engaged in an act or acts of prostitution is not sufficient to show a motive to fabricate.

D. *Application of Law to Facts*

Defendant did not specify any valid reason why the sexual histories of the victim-witnesses were relevant. Defendant's written motion in limine to the trial court stated:

> Defendant has reason to believe that the alleged victims in this matter had engaged in sexual conduct prior to the incidents alleged in the indictment, which conduct is material and essential to the defense against those charges . . . The probative value of the conduct outweighs the inflammatory or prejudicial nature of its revelation.

Nowhere in his motion did Defendant state that he wished to proffer this evidence to show that the victim-witnesses had a motive to fabricate.

Prior to trial, Defendant asked the court to hold an in camera hearing at which he would show evidence of the victim-witnesses prior sexual conduct and its relevance to his defense. The trial court asked Defendant why he believed he was entitled to have this evidence admitted. Defense counsel told the court:

> The evidence which we would seek to elicit by questioning first the women themselves and then from other witnesses, as well, is the fact that at least two of the women-one woman is known to the police as a prostitute and, in fact, been arrested as a prostitute. Another woman admitted to the detective investigating the case that she had engaged in prostitution at the time this occurred, was in the habit of, if not gaining her income, at least supplementing it by prostitution. That is essentially the nature of the evidence which we want to go into.

Defense counsel further stated that he would distinguish between "amateurs" and "professionals and patrons" (apparently of prostitutes) and that such a distinction would be highly relevant and admissible.

In its opinion, the Court of Appeals noted that "defense counsel did not use the phrase 'motive to lie' when he argued to the trial court in favor of admission of corroborating evidence that the women were 'prostitutes.'" However, the Court of Appeals "believe[d] that his arguments that the participants had a difference of opinion as to remuneration for the sexual services performed pursuant to their 'contract' were adequate to alert the trial court to the basis for Defendant's proffer." We disagree. We have reviewed the transcript record of the hearing on the motion in limine and of cross-examination during trial. We conclude that Defendant never expressed his intention to use the prior sexual conduct evidence to expose the victims' motives to lie or as a basis for a theory of relevance other than propensity.

The possibility that T.A. and T.S. had engaged in prostitution either before or after the incidents in question does not support an inference that they had a reason to fabricate an accusation of rape. Defendant sought to introduce testimony that T.A. had admitted to the police that she had occasionally sold sex for money to pay the rent. Defendant also sought to introduce evidence that T.S. had been arrested on a prostitution charge subsequent to his arrest for sexual assault. This evidence does not show that either would retaliate against those who failed to pay her by fabricating false charges.

From the record, we are not certain that Defendant had a theory of relevance other than one based on propensity. Defendant indicated that he wanted to bring in evidence of prior acts of prostitution to show it was more likely than not that each woman got into his car willingly on the two occasions at issue, since "that's the nature of the business." He may have believed that, by entering his car, each woman had consented to anything he demanded. The law is otherwise. Defendant may have *believed* that the victims' apparent initial willingness to engage in a particular sexual act was a defense to his actions in insisting on a different kind of sexual act. That is not the law in this state.

For these reasons, we are not persuaded that Defendant showed the trial court that the evidence was relevant, other than as an attempt to show the likelihood that the victims had consented on this occasion because they had consented on other occasions. That theory is essentially a theory the rape shield law and the consistent rule of evidence were designed to restrict . . .

III. CONCLUSION

The New Mexico Legislature intended to prevent the disclosure of prior sexual conduct of victim-witnesses, including prior acts of prostitution. The resulting statute, the corresponding evidentiary rule, and subsequent cases advance the goal of protecting rape victims by prohibiting the admission of intimate details of their past sexual behavior . . . We conclude that the trial court did not abuse its discretion in rejecting the evidence Defendant proffered . . .

NOTES

1. Is the New Mexico Supreme Court saying that a victim's prior prostitution is never admissible under the state's rape shield law, or is the court making a more limited pronouncement?

2. Some states clearly authorize the admission of past evidence of prostitution. A New York statute specifically states that "evidence of a victim's sexual conduct shall not be admissible . . . unless such evidence . . . proves or tends to prove that the victim has been convicted of an offense [of prostitution] within three years prior to the sex offense which is the subject of the prosecution." N.Y. Crim. Proc. Law § 60.42(2) (McKinney 2003). Other states have reached the same conclusion by judicial decision. *See, e.g.,* Commonwealth v. Harris, 825 N.E.2d 58 (Mass. 2005) ("hold[ing] that a judge has discretion to allow impeachment of a sexual assault complainant by prior convictions of sexual offenses [in this case prostitution], but that in exercising that discretion, the purposes of the rape-shield statute should be considered."). Finally, some states appear to take the position that prior acts of prostitution can never be admissible under the state's rape shield laws. *See* Williams v. State, 681 N.E.2d 195, 200 (Ind. 1997) ("The trial court also properly excluded the friend's testimony that on prior occasions the victim had committed acts of prostitution in exchange for money or cocaine."). The majority of states have exceptions in their rape shield laws to allow prostitution evidence in at least some circumstances. *See* Karin S. Portlock, Note, *Status on Trial: The Racial Ramifications of Admitting Prostitution Evidence Under State Rape-Shield Legislation,* 107 COLUM. L. REV. 1404, 1415 (2007) (arguing for rape shield approach that would presumptively bar evidence of prostitution with third parties). Which approach is correct: (1) the New Mexico version that prior prostitution is admissible if there is evidence in the case at hand that it created a motive to fabricate; (2) the New York and Massachusetts approach in which prior prostitution convictions would be admissible in a wider array of cases; or (3) the Indiana approach in which evidence of prior prostitution is apparently never admissible?

3. According to one expert, "rape is not an exceptional experience for women who are prostituted. A study of prostitutes in San Francisco found that 68% of them had been raped while working as prostitutes. Forty-eight percent of those prostitutes who were raped had been raped more than five times." Michelle J. Anderson, *From Chastity Requirement to Sexuality License: Sexual Consent and a New Rape Shield Law,* 70 GEO. WASH. L. REV. 51, 113–114 (2002). Does this information affect your answer to the question posed in note 2?

4. One common exception to rape shield statutes is evidence that tends to show a motive to fabricate the accusation. In People v. Golden, 140 P.3d 1 (Colo.App.2005), Golden was convicted of sexual assault after the trial court barred him from cross-examining the accuser as to whether she was in a "committed relationship," with one of her female roommates. Golden claimed that she had fabricated the accusation against him to avoid trouble with her roommate. Agreeing, the Colorado Court of Appeals reversed, finding that being in a "committed relationship" was not evidence of past sexual behavior excludable under the rape shield statute; the Confrontation Clause required that he be permitted to present evidence to show why the charges against him might have been fabricated. Rape shield statutes also do not generally bar evidence that a victim had made prior rape accusations which proved to be unfounded. *See, e.g.*, State v. Wyrick, 62 S.W.3d 751 (Tenn. Crim. App.2001) (reversing conviction because trial court excluded evidence that alleged victim had, three years earlier, falsely claimed to have been raped to explain why she came home late).

5. The New Mexico Supreme Court describes the different categories of rape shield laws that have been identified by Professor Galvin. The most prevalent—the Michigan Approach—prohibits sexual conduct evidence except for "certain enumerated exceptions. According to Professor Galvin:

> The statutory exceptions are highly specific, reflecting legislative efforts to anticipate precisely those circumstances in which sexual conduct evidence will be critical to the presentation of a defense. In effect, these statutes have stripped courts of their discretion to determine the relevancy of sexual conduct evidence on a case-by-case basis. Although these statutes are highly protective of the interests of the complainant and the state, they do not accommodate sufficiently the needs of the accused to prevent relevant evidence in his behalf.

Harriet R. Galvin, *Shielding Rape Victims in the State and Federal Courts: A Proposal for the Second Decade*, 70 MINN. L. REV. 763, 773 (1986). Would it be better, as some states do, to provide judges with much greater discretion? Or are the dangers of discretion too great in the area of prior sexual conduct? Are judges well-situated to make judgment calls about the significance of prior sexual behavior? Consider the comments of noted judge and scholar Richard Posner: "[J]udges know next to nothing about [sex] beyond their own personal experience, which is limited, perhaps more so than average, because people with irregular sex lives are pretty much . . . screened out of the judiciary." RICHARD A. POSNER, SEX AND REASON 1 (1992).

State v. Colbath

Supreme Court of New Hampshire, 1988.
130 N.H. 316, 540 A.2d 1212.

■ SOUTER, JUSTICE.

In this appeal from his conviction on a charge of aggravated felonious sexual assault, the defendant argues that . . . [the trial judge incorrectly] barred the jury from considering evidence of the complainant's public behavior with men other than the defendant in the hours preceding the incident, as bearing on the defense of consent. . . . [W]e reverse and remand for a new trial.

During the noon hour of June 28, 1985, the defendant, Richard Colbath, went with some companions to the Smokey Lantern tavern in Farmington, where he became acquainted with the female complainant. There was evidence that she directed sexually provocative attention toward several men in the bar, with whom she associated during the ensuing afternoon, the defendant among them. He testified that he had engaged in "feeling [the complainant's] breasts [and] bottom [and that she had been] rubbing his crotch" before the two of them eventually left the tavern and went to the defendant's trailer. It is undisputed that sexual intercourse followed; forcible according to the complainant, consensual according to the defendant. In any case, before they left the trailer the two of them were joined unexpectedly by a young woman who lived with the defendant, who came home at an unusual hour suspecting that the defendant was indulging in faithless behavior. With her suspicion confirmed, she became enraged, kicked the trailer door open and went for the complainant, whom she assaulted violently and dragged outside by the hair. It took the intervention of the defendant and a third woman to bring the melee to an end.

As soon as the complainant returned to town she accused the defendant of rape, and the police promptly arrested and charged him accordingly. During the initial investigation on the evening of June 28, Candice Lepene, the daughter of the tavern's owner, told the police that she had seen the complainant leave the tavern with the defendant during the afternoon. In a subsequent written statement, however, she said that she did not know whether the complainant had left with a companion or alone, but she described the complainant prior to her departure as "a girl with dark hair hanging all over everyone and making out with Richard Colbath and a few others." . . . .

. . . . The trial itself focused on the defense of consent, which the defendant addressed by his own testimony about the complainant's behavior with him at the bar and at the trailer, and by seeking to elicit exculpatory evidence that the complainant had appeared to invite sexual advances from other men as well as from himself in the hours preceding the incident. Some of this evidence was excluded and some admitted. During the charge, however, the judge instructed the jury, subject to the defendant's objection, that evidence of the complainant's behavior with other men was irrelevant to the issues before them. This appeal followed the verdict of guilty.

* * *

The trial judge first allowed the defense to elicit testimony from the complainant that at one point during the afternoon she had been sitting in the lap of one of the defendant's companions named Gillis. Shortly after that testimony, and before the defendant had called any witnesses, the State moved for a ruling *in limine* to prohibit defense witnesses from testifying about the complainant's behavior in the tavern with any other men than the defendant . . . The court . . . grant[ed] the prosecution's motion . . .

This ruling did not end the matter, however. Although the court had ordered defense counsel not to ask his own witnesses about the complainant's behavior with third parties, further evidence of such activity did come in through the State's next witness, Candice Lepene. She testified on direct examination that the complainant had left the tavern in the company of various men several times during the afternoon, and the court admitted her statement to the police, quoted above, that she had seen "a girl with dark hair hanging all over everyone and making out with Richard Colbath and a few others." On cross-examination Lepene was permitted to testify further about her earlier statement.

When it came time for jury instructions, however, the court's charge reflected its earlier ruling on the motion *in limine*. First, the judge reminded the jurors that he had received evidence of the complainant's public activities with various men on the afternoon of the 28th, including her own admission that she had engaged in close physical contact with at least one man besides the defendant. Then the judge explained that he had allowed the jury to hear this testimony only to provide background information, and he went on to instruct the jurors plainly that the complainant's "conduct with other individuals is not relevant on the issue of whether or not she gave consent to sexual intercourse."

That part of the charge was tantamount to an instruction that the jury could not consider the evidence in question as bearing on guilt or innocence, and we therefore treat it as equivalent to an order striking the testimony about the complainant's openly observed behavior with other men during the course of the afternoon. The defendant made a timely objection to this instruction.

* * *

The defendant has suggested that we address this issue simply as one of statutory construction, by holding that the shield law's mandate to exclude evidence of "consensual sexual activity" with others can have no application to overt sexual activity of the complainant in a bar open to the public. This was, indeed, the position taken by defendant's trial counsel, who relied on prior construction of the act as intended to honor the complainant's interest in preserving the privacy of intimate activity.

While we do not reject this argument, we are not disposed to rule on it here. The State did not address the argument's merits at all in its brief, and we prefer not to rule on a legal position so little remarked upon by one side of the case when, as here, existing precedent provides a clear conceptual framework for the resolution of the issue before us.

That framework began to emerge in the first appeal to question the applicability of the shield law after its enactment in 1975. Despite the absolute terms of the shield law's prohibition, our cases have consistently reflected the common recognition that such a statute's reach has to be limited by a defendant's State and national constitutional rights to confront the witnesses against him and to present his own exculpatory evidence. Thus, this court has held that a rape defendant must be given an opportunity to demonstrate that the "probative value [of the statutorily inadmissible evidence] in the context of that particular case outweighs its prejudicial effect on the prosecutrix." *State v. Howard, supra* 121 N.H. at 59, 426 A.2d at 461.

* * *

. . . [It is] apparent that the public character of the complainant's behavior is significant. On the one hand, describing a complainant's open, sexually suggestive conduct in the presence of patrons of a public bar obviously has far less potential for damaging the sensibilities than revealing what the same person may have done in the company of another behind a closed door. On the other hand, evidence of public displays of general interest in sexual activity can be taken to indicate a contemporaneous receptiveness to sexual advances that cannot be inferred from evidence of private behavior with chosen sex partners.

In this case, for example, the jury could have taken evidence of the complainant's openly sexually provocative behavior toward a group of men as evidence of her probable attitude toward an individual within the group. Evidence that the publicly inviting acts occurred closely in time to the alleged sexual assault by one such man could have been viewed as indicating the complainant's likely attitude at the time of the sexual activity in question. It would, in fact, understate the importance of such evidence in this case to speak of it merely as relevant. We should recall that the fact of intercourse was not denied, and that the evidence of assault was subject to the explanation that the defendant's jealous living companion had inflicted the visible injuries. The companion's furious behavior had a further bearing on the case, as well, for the jury could have regarded her attack as a reason for the complainant to regret a voluntary liaison with the defendant, and as a motive for the complainant to allege rape as a way to explain her injuries and excuse her undignified predicament. With the sex act thus admitted, with the evidence of violence subject to exculpatory explanation, and with a motive for the complainant to make a false accusation, the outcome of the prosecution could well have turned on a very close judgment about the complainant's attitude of resistance or consent.

Because little significance can be assigned here either to the privacy interest or to a fear of misleading the jury, the trial court was bound to recognize the defendant's interest in presenting probably crucial evidence of the complainant's behavior closely preceding the alleged rape. Thus, the facts of this case well illustrate the . . . observation that the sexual activities of a complainant immediately prior to an alleged rape may well be subject to a defendant's constitutional right to present evidence. The demand of the Constitutions is all the clearer when those activities were carried on in a public setting. Because the jury instruction effectively excluded the evidence in question, the conviction must be reversed and the case remanded for a new trial.

Reversed and remanded.

———

NOTES

1. The opinion in *Colbath* was authored by New Hampshire Supreme Court Justice David Souter in 1988. Less than two years later, President Bush nominated Souter to a seat on the United States Court of Appeals for the First Circuit. During his confirmation hearings, Senator Ted Kennedy raised concerns about the *Colbath* decision to which Justice Souter responded that there is an "obvious tension between, on the one hand, the laudable policy of barring a rape prosecution of the complaining witness through embarrassing cross examination, and on the other hand the undoubted right of defendants to confront their accusers and present favorable evidence to their defense." TINSLEY E. YARBROUGH, DAVID HACKETT SOUTER: TRADITIONAL REPUBLICAN ON THE REHNQUIST COURT 98 (2005). Despite Senator Kennedy's concern about the *Colbath* decision, Souter was confirmed unanimously to the First Circuit. Only a few months later, President Bush nominated Judge Souter to the Supreme Court of the United States to fill the seat of retiring Justice William Brennan. Justice Souter's nomination came only a few years after an extremely contentious Supreme Court confirmation hearing in which Judge Robert Bork's nomination was rejected with 58 senators voting against him. *See* STEPHEN L. CARTER, THE CONFIRMATION MESS (1994). Justice Souter's confirmation hearing, by contrast, was not very contentious. Indeed, the *Colbath* decision was one of only two of Souter's cases that generated noticeable controversy at his confirmation hearing. *See* Linda Greenhouse, *An Intellectual Mind: David Hackett Souter*, N.Y. TIMES, July 24, 1990, at A1. Justice Souter was confirmed by a vote of 90 to 9. Given the growing political fighting over the direction of the Supreme Court, do you find it surprising that the *Colbath* case was not more of a lightning rod? Is the lack of controversy a function of the earlier time-period? Would the *Colbath* case be a more controversial matter if Justice Souter's confirmation hearing were held today, rather than in 1990?

2. Did Justice Souter and his colleagues on the New Hampshire Supreme Court reach the right decision in *Colbath*? The New Hampshire rape shield statute provided "[p]rior consensual sexual activity between the victim and any person other than the actor shall not be admitted into evidence in any prosecution under this chapter." N.H. Rev. Stat. Ann. § 632–A:6(II). Doesn't the plain language of the statute require exclusion of the very testimony the *Colbath* court admitted? Is there something that can trump the statute?

3. Although the New Hampshire statute does not list an explicit exception for sexual conduct with third parties, some rape shield statutes do authorize the admission of such evidence if the judge finds it more probative than prejudicial. *See, e.g.*, Minn. Stat. Ann. § 609.347 (Subd. 3).

4. Many rape shield statutes provide an exception for prior sexual conduct between the defendant and the victim. *See* Michelle J. Anderson, *From Chastity Requirement to Sexuality License: Sexual Consent and a New Rape Shield Law*, 70 GEO. WASH. L. REV. 51, 97 n.242 (2002) (identifying nearly two dozen state statutes). In the remaining states—those where judges have wide discretion to determine the admissibility of past sexual conduct—it is common to admit evidence of prior behavior involving the suspect and the complainant. *See id.* at 118. Does this ubiquitous exception make sense? Professor Anderson believes it is bad policy:

> Of all rapes that occur, acquaintance rape actually outpaces stranger rape by four to one. Rape occurs in violent dating, cohabiting, and married relationships. Rape is a serious form of battering in a society in which domestic violence between intimates is widespread. Friends and acquaintances commit 53% of all rapes and sexual assaults. Intimates—husbands, boyfriends, former husbands, and former boyfriends—commit an additional 26% of all rapes and sexual assaults. The categorical admission of prior sexual conduct between the complainant and the defendant is, therefore, not a narrow exception.
>
> . . . [T]he argument [for admitting prior sexual conduct] assumes that prior sexual intimacies between the defendant and the complainant were consensual. A complaint of rape to authorities, however, may not reflect the first episode of rape in a relationship. Approximately twenty percent of women have been forced to have intercourse against their will at some point in their lives, and 75% of rapes occur between those who are acquaintances or previous intimates. Therefore, it is inappropriate to assume that all prior sexual experiences between the defendant and the complainant have been consensual.
>
> . . . [T]he argument that a history of intimacies with the accused bolsters a claim of consent to another sexual encounter assumes that sex between two people is an interaction that does not meaningfully change character in different contexts: that a second, fifteenth, or eightieth experience of sexual intercourse is "yet another" similar sexual encounter. Sexual intercourse, however, can vary dramatically in terms of how it is experienced by the same couple. It can be at one time an expression of intimacy and concern and at another time an expression of dominance and abuse. For those couples engaged in a battering relationship, particularly, violent rape is often a part of the abusive phase in an ongoing cycle of cruelty, while (temporarily) tender sexual intimacy can be part of the reconciliation phase, which is itself simply a precursor to further abusive episodes. It is not obvious, therefore, that even gentle and consensual prior sexual acts between the defendant and

the complainant bolster a claim of consent to a later sexual act claimed to be rape.

Id. at 119, 121–122. Are you persuaded by Professor Anderson's argument? Does a complete prohibition on prior sexual activity between the defendant and the victim (even if there is no allegation that the prior activity was nonconsensual) seem like a step too far? Or is the percentage of intimate partner rape simply so high that we need to make more dramatic changes to how we handle rape trials?

5. Should rape shield laws prevent testimony about the victim's sexual orientation? In People v. Murphy, 919 P.2d 191 (Colo. 1996), Michael Murphy invited a male acquaintance over for a beer. Murphy handcuffed the victim and then "perpetrated sadistic homosexual acts" without consent. Murphy sought to introduce evidence of the victim's sexual orientation, including previous homosexual acts he had engaged in. Colorado's rape shield statute bars evidence of the victim's prior sexual conduct, but makes no mention of testimony about sexual orientation. The Colorado Supreme Court held that the rape shield statute's "prohibition against evidence of a rape victim's past sexual conduct also precludes evidence of sexual orientation." Does this make sense as a matter of rape shield law? Would questions like the one in *Murphy* be better handled by evidentiary rules of relevance? Is a person's sexual orientation ever relevant to the question of whether they consented to a particular sexual encounter? If evidence of heterosexuality is not determinative of whether a person consented to *e.g.*, sex with someone they barely knew (as in *Rusk*, for example), can evidence of a person's attraction to same-sex partners be relevant to whether they consented? For an exploration of some of these issues, *see*, Peter Nicolas, *"They Say He's Gay": The Admissibility of Evidence of Sexual Orientation*, 37 GA. L. REV. 793 (2003).

6. Rape shield statutes are designed to eliminate irrelevant information that could unfairly influence the jury. Consider the somewhat related issue of testimony about rape trauma syndrome. Rape Trauma Syndrome, or RTS, is a form of post-traumatic stress disorder that may be displayed by victims of rape and other sex assault and abuse. Expert testimony on RTS is often introduced to explain victim behavior that may seem inconsistent to a lay person on the jury. For example, RTS has been introduced in trials to explain why a victim might wash away evidence, deny having been assaulted, delay reporting, or behave in other ways that a layperson might not expect of a victim in the circumstances. Is such testimony a legitimate way to explain puzzling behavior, or does it cross the line by improperly bolstering the accuser's testimony? Some courts take the latter position. *See, e.g.,* Commonwealth v. Garcia, 403 Pa.Super. 280, 588 A.2d 951 (1991) (holding that to admit expert testimony that it is not uncommon for young sexual assault victims to delay reporting the abuse is error, because it improperly bolsters the credibility of complainants and invites the jurors to abdicate their responsibility in assessing the credibility of victim-witnesses). An additional problem that judges must grapple with is whether the experts in RTS are qualified to testify. *See* Andre A. Moenssens, *et al.*, SCIENTIFIC

EVIDENCE IN CIVIL AND CRIMINAL CASES 1345–1346 (5th ed. 2007) ("RTS is an area in which many of the so-called expert witnesses are not clinical psychologists or psychiatrists, but social workers, investigators for public agencies, or other skilled witnesses who have attended some workshops and training seminars on RTS but may lack the educational requirements expected of scientific examiners. Some of these "experts" are undoubtedly qualified; there is, however, a great risk that well-meaning but insufficiently trained investigators may be permitted to qualify to give opinion testimony.").

———

2. CHARGING ISSUES

A sexual assault case can raise challenging constitutional issues as to the number of charges that can legitimately be brought without violating Double Jeopardy. If an assailant grabs or fondles multiple parts of the victim's body within a few seconds, is that one assault, or several? Consider the conflicting views of the justices in the following case:

State v. Rummer
Supreme Court of Appeals of West Virginia, 1993.
189 W.Va. 369, 432 S.E.2d 39.

■ MILLER, JUSTICE:

This is an appeal from the final order of the Circuit Court of Wood County, entered September 13, 1991, sentencing the defendant, Ronald Dean Rummer, to two concurrent terms of imprisonment upon his conviction by a jury of two counts of sexual abuse in the first degree. The defendant contends that both sentences arose from the same transaction and that they therefore constitute unconstitutional double jeopardy. . . . Because we find no error below, the judgment of the trial court is affirmed.

The charges against the defendant arose from an incident that occurred in the early morning hours of June 21, 1991. C.D., . . . a twenty-one-year-old woman, had spent the earlier part of the evening riding around Parkersburg with friends in a friend's car. At approximately 1:00 a.m., as C.D. and her friends neared C.D.'s home, C.D. informed her friends that she wanted to go home. This led to a minor argument with her friends because they desired to continue driving. Therefore, C.D. was let out of the car approximately eight blocks from her home.

After taking leave of her friends, C.D. began to walk home. As she was walking, she became aware of a vehicle following her at a very slow rate of speed. C.D. noticed that the driver of the vehicle was hunched over as he drove and appeared to be balding. Gradually, the vehicle passed C.D. and turned the corner. Shortly thereafter, C.D. became aware of a man following her on foot. She became concerned and increased her pace, but the man followed even faster. As C.D. turned towards the man again, he caught her and roughly grabbed her. C.D. yelled and told him to leave her alone. He put one hand between her legs and began rubbing roughly. He attempted to put his other hand up C.D.'s shirt, and then grabbed her breasts through her shirt. C.D. tried to escape, but fell to the ground. The man fell on top of her and again roughly fondled her breasts through her shirt with both hands. She finally pushed him off of her and got up and ran to a nearby pay phone.

Upon reaching the pay phone, C.D. first dialed 9-1-1 and informed the police of the attack and her location, and a policeman was immediately dispatched to take her statement. She then phoned her mother, who lived nearby, and her mother drove to meet her.

C.D.'s mother arrived within minutes, and, as C.D. and her mother waited for the police to arrive, C.D. noticed the vehicle that had earlier followed her pass by. Shortly thereafter, a policeman, Officer Parsons, arrived. Officer Parsons asked C.D. if she wanted to file a complaint, and she agreed to do so. . . . She told him that the man who assaulted her was wearing white pants and a white shirt with red or pink stripes.

While she was sitting in the police car giving her statement to Officer Parsons, C.D. noticed the car that had earlier followed her again pass by. When she told this to Officer Parsons, he gave chase to the car. After pursuing it for several blocks, he was able to stop the car. He then asked C.D. to advise him if the driver, the lone occupant of the car, was the man who attacked her. After approaching the car, C.D. identified the man as her attacker.

* * *

At trial, the defendant testified that he had, in fact, followed C.D. in his car and later approached her on foot and asked her to go out with him. Although he admitted putting his arm around her waist, the defendant denied touching her breasts or sex organ. He asserted that he left her upon her request that he do so. He contended that he was familiar with C.D., whom he suggested was a prostitute. He also asserted that he had "picked up" C.D. several weeks before the incident, and that they had had sexual intercourse at that time. C.D. testified in rebuttal that she did not know the defendant and had never seen the defendant socially. She testified that the only time she may have seen the defendant was several years before the incident when she worked in a drive-through store. . . .

At the conclusion of the trial, the defendant was found guilty by the jury of two counts of sexual abuse in the first degree. . . .

I.   *Double Jeopardy*

With regard to the defendant's double jeopardy claim, he contends that his two convictions for first degree sexual abuse were improper because only one offense was committed. This conclusion is based upon the premise that the touching of the victim's breasts and her sex organ occurred within a brief period of time and should be considered one act. The defendant asserts that, under these circumstances, he is receiving multiple punishments for the same offense, a situation prohibited under the Double Jeopardy Clause of both our State and the federal constitutions.

Our double jeopardy principles have been patterned after the United States Supreme Court's interpretation of the Double Jeopardy Clause found in the Fifth Amendment to the United States Constitution.[3] Our general pronouncement of the scope of our Double Jeopardy Clause, contained in § 5 of Article III of the West Virginia Constitution, is set out in Syllabus Point 1 of *Conner v. Griffith*, 160 W.Va. 680, 238 S.E.2d 529 (1977):

> The Double Jeopardy Clause in Article III, § 5 . . . provides immunity from further prosecution where a court having jurisdiction has acquitted the accused. It protects against a second prosecution for the same offense after conviction. It also prohibits multiple punishments for the same offense. . . .

In *State v. Zaccagnini*, 172 W.Va. 491, 308 S.E.2d 131 (1983), we discussed in detail those cases decided by the United States Supreme Court which dealt with criminal statutes that were claimed to violate double jeopardy principles through the imposition of multiple punishments for the same offense. We pointed out in *Zaccagnini* that the beginning point for such an analysis is the test set out in *Blockburger v. United States*, 284 U.S. 299, 52 S.Ct. 180, 76 L.Ed. 306 (1932). We summarized the *Blockburger* test in Syllabus Point 8 of *Zaccagnini*:

> Where the same act or transaction constitutes a violation of two distinct statutory provisions, the test to be applied to determine whether there are two offenses or only one is whether each provision requires proof of an additional fact which the other does not.

We further recognized in *Zaccagnini* that the *Blockburger* test was not only a rule of statutory construction, but was also recognized by the United States Supreme Court to be a means of identifying legislative intent where such intent is unclear. We cited the following statement from *Albernaz v. United States*, 450 U.S. 333, 340 (1981), in *Zaccagnini*: "The *Blockburger* test is a 'rule of statutory construction,' and because it serves as a means of discerning congressional purpose the rule should not be controlling where, for example, there is a clear indication of contrary legislative intent." . . .

The Supreme Court in *Albernaz* elaborated on the *Blockburger* test's role in determining legislative intent in a double jeopardy analysis when

---

[3] The applicable provision of the Fifth Amendment states: "Nor shall any person be subject for the same offense to be twice put in jeopardy of life or limb."

it quoted this language from note 17 of *Iannelli v. United States*, 420 U.S. 770, 785 (1975):

> The test articulated in *Blockburger* . . . serves a generally similar function of identifying congressional intent to impose separate sanctions for multiple offenses arising in the course of a single act or transaction. In determining whether separate punishment might be imposed, *Blockburger* requires that courts examine the offenses to ascertain "whether each provision requires proof of a fact which the other does not." . . .

In *Missouri v. Hunter*, 459 U.S. 359, 103 S.Ct. 673, 74 L.Ed.2d 535 (1983), the Supreme Court considered the aspect of double jeopardy relating to multiple punishments for the same offense in regard to two Missouri statutes. One statute related to the felony of robbery with the use of a deadly weapon. The other statute provided that any person who committed any felony with the use of a deadly weapon was guilty of armed criminal action. The latter crime provided for a penalty of not less than three years, in addition to any punishment provided by law for the underlying felony committed by the use of a deadly weapon.

The Missouri Court of Appeals . . . concluded that, under these statutes, the imposition of two sentences upon a defendant who had committed the crime of armed robbery violated the double jeopardy prohibition against multiple sentences for the same offense. After granting *certiorari*, the United States Supreme Court established that the Missouri Court of Appeal's legal interpretation of the Double Jeopardy Clause was not binding upon it and concluded:

> [S]imply because two criminal statutes may be construed to proscribe the same conduct under the *Blockburger* test does not mean that the Double Jeopardy Clause precludes the imposition, in a single trial, of cumulative punishments pursuant to those statutes. The rule of statutory construction noted in *Whalen* . . . is not a constitutional rule requiring courts to negate clearly expressed legislative intent.

We have recently discussed and applied these double jeopardy principles in *State v. Gill*, 187 W.Va. 136, 416 S.E.2d 253 (1992), where we upheld separate convictions under both our sexual offense statute and W.Va.Code, 61–8D–5(a) (1991), where the same conduct formed the basis for both convictions. In *Gill*, the child's custodian had committed several sex acts on her in violation of W.Va.Code, 61–8B–3(a)(2) (1984), our first degree sexual assault statute. The State also charged and convicted the defendant under W.Va.Code, 61–8D–5(a), which relates to sexual offenses committed by a parent, guardian, or custodian of a child. The defendant claimed that he was being punished twice for the same act.

In *Gill*, . . . we also discussed *Missouri v. Hunter, supra*, and the later case of *Garrett v. United States*, 471 U.S. 773 (1985). In those cases, the Supreme Court expressly recognized that where the legislature intended to make the same conduct the subject of two criminal acts and, therefore, separately punishable, this could be done even though under the *Blockburger* test, the crimes would constitute the same offense:

> Where the same conduct violates two statutory provisions, the first step in the double jeopardy analysis is to determine whether the legislature—in this case Congress—intended that each violation be a separate offense. . . .

> We have recently indicated that the *Blockburger* rule is not controlling when the legislative intent is clear from the face of the statute or the legislative history. . . .

* * *

Our conclusion in *Gill* was that the language in W.Va.Code, 61–8D–5(a), stating that "[i]n addition to any other offenses set forth in this code, the Legislature hereby declares a separate and distinct offense under this subsection," was sufficiently explicit to demonstrate that the legislature intended to create a separate parent-custodial sexual misconduct offense in addition to our general sexual offense statutes. . . . Thus, two separate punishments were permissible under double jeopardy principles even though they arose from the same act. . . .

We have also discussed double jeopardy considerations in relation to sexual offenses in several other cases. In *State v. Carter*, 168 W.Va. 90, 282 S.E.2d 277 (1981), the defendant had been convicted of two counts of first degree sexual assault. The first count related to oral intercourse and the second to anal intercourse. We reviewed the definition of "sexual intercourse" contained in W.Va.Code, 61–8B–1(7) (1986), which provided, in relevant part, "penetration, however slight, of the female sex organ by the male sex organ, or involving contact between the sex organs of one person and the mouth or anus of another person," and came to this conclusion:

> The use of the word "or," which is a conjunction, expresses the legislative intent that sexual intercourse can be committed in each of the various alternative ways, with each type of prohibited contact constituting a separate offense. From this, it is apparent that the Legislature chose to broadly define the term "sexual intercourse" so that it would cover a variety of sexual encounters.

In *Carter*, although we did not utilize the *Blockburger-Zaccagnini* test, the same result would have been reached under it as interpreted by the United States Supreme Court and accepted by us in *Gill*. Under the *Blockburger-Zaccagnini* test, we would have analyzed legislative intent by determining if there was any clear expression of such intent. In the absence of any clear expression of such intent, we would have applied the *Blockburger-Zaccagnini* test to the elements of the crimes. It is clear that the offense of first degree sexual assault as set out in W.Va.Code, 61–8B–

3(a) (1991),[11] does not, on its face, contain any clear statement of legislative intent with regard to separate punishments, as was the case in *Gill*. However, applying a *Blockburger-Zaccagnini* analysis to W.Va.Code, 61–8B–3(a), we note that among the components of first degree sexual assault is the term "sexual intercourse." "Sexual intercourse" is defined in W.Va.Code, 61–8B–1(7), and consists of three alternative acts: (1) "penetration, however slight, of the female sex organ by the male sex organ," or (2) "contact between the sex organs of one person and the mouth . . . of another person," or (3) "contact between the sex organs of one person and . . . the anus of another person."

Clearly, by statutory definition, the elements of the crime of first degree sexual assault through sexual intercourse can be committed by three distinct acts or methods.[12] Under the *Blockburger-Zaccagnini* test, each of the crimes "requires proof of an additional fact which the other does not." . . . In the context of "sexual intercourse," the female sex organs, the mouth, and the anus are each distinct and separate matters of proof, any one of which is sufficient to prove the crime. If a defendant commits both unlawful oral and anal intercourse, as occurred in *Carter*, the defendant has committed two separate offenses. . . .

Although this is the first occasion we have had to discuss the double jeopardy aspect of "sexual contact," we find that its statutory pattern is substantially similar to that of "sexual intercourse," which we discussed in regard to double jeopardy principles in *State v. Carter, supra*. Applying the *Blockburger-Zaccagnini* test to the instant case, we find that the principal element of W.Va.Code, 61–8B–7, which defines sexual abuse in the first degree, involves "sexual contact" with another person. The term "sexual contact" is defined in W.Va.Code, 61–8B–1(6), and identifies several different acts which constitute sexual contact. Each act requires proof of a fact which the other does not. Consequently, a defendant who commits two or more of the separate acts of sexual contact on a victim may be convicted of each separate act without violation of double jeopardy principles.

When we look to other jurisdictions that have dealt with double jeopardy challenges to their sexual contact statute, we find that they have reached a result similar to the one we reach today. The Court of

---

[11] W.Va.Code, 61–8B–3(a), provides:

A person is guilty of sexual assault in the first degree when:

(1) Such person engages in sexual intercourse or sexual intrusion with another person and, in so doing:

    (i)   Inflicts serious bodily injury upon anyone; or

    (ii) Employs a deadly weapon in the commission of the act; or

(2) Such person, being fourteen years old or more, engages in sexual intercourse or sexual intrusion with another person who is eleven years old or less.

[12] The Supreme Court of California reached the same result in *People v. Perez*, 23 Cal.3d 545, 553, 153 Cal.Rptr. 40, 44, 591 P.2d 63, 68 (1979), where it concluded: "A defendant who attempts to achieve sexual gratification by committing a number of base criminal acts on his victim is substantially more culpable than a defendant who commits only one such act."

Appeals of New Mexico addressed facts almost identical to those presented here in *State v. Williams*, 105 N.M. 214, 730 P.2d 1196 (1986). In that case, the defendant was convicted of two counts of criminal sexual contact. The convictions resulted from unlawfully touching his victim's breasts and genital area during a time span of less than five minutes. The relevant statute stated that "[c]riminal sexual contact is intentionally touching or applying force without consent to the unclothed intimate parts of another who has reached his eighteenth birthday . . . For purposes of this section 'intimate parts' means the primary genital area, groin, buttocks, anus or breast." 105 N.M. at 216, 730 P.2d at 1198. . . . The Court of Appeals held that the intent of the New Mexico legislature was to protect the victim from intrusions to each enumerated part, and, therefore, that "[s]eparate punishments are sustainable where evidence shows distinctly separate touchings to the different parts." 105 N.M. at 217, 730 P.2d at 1199.

Although State v. Williams, did not involve any lengthy analysis of United States Supreme Court double jeopardy decisions, such an analysis was recently undertaken by the New Mexico Supreme Court in *Swafford v. State*, 112 N.M. 3, 810 P.2d 1223 (1991). In *Swafford*, the New Mexico court recognized some confusion in its double jeopardy decisions, reviewed recent United States Supreme Court cases that had construed *Blockburger*, and came to this conclusion:

> Taking as our cue the repeated admonitions of the Supreme Court that the sole limitation on multiple punishments is legislative intent, *Grady v. Corbin*, [495 U.S. 508, 517, 110 S.Ct. 2084, 2091, 109 L.Ed.2d 548, 561 (1990)]; . . . we adopt today a two-part test for determining legislative intent to punish. The first part of our inquiry asks the question that Supreme Court precedents assume to be true: whether the conduct underlying the offenses is unitary, *i.e.*, whether the same conduct violates both statutes. The second part focuses on the statutes at issue to determine whether the legislature intended to create separately punishable offenses. Only if the first part of the test is answered in the affirmative, and the second in the negative, will the double jeopardy clause prohibit multiple punishment in the same trial. . . .

The Court of Appeals of Utah in *State v. Suarez*, 736 P.2d 1040 (Utah App.1987), was also faced with a situation like the one in this case. There, the defendant was charged with two counts of forcible sexual abuse in violation of Utah Code Ann. § 76–5–404 (1982). The defendant had placed his mouth on the victim's breasts and touched her genitals in the same transaction. The applicable statute, Utah Code Ann. § 76–5–404(1) stated:

> (1) A person commits forcible sexual abuse if, under circumstances not amounting to rape or sodomy, or attempted

rape or sodomy, the actor touches the anus or any part of the genitals of another, *or otherwise* takes indecent liberties with another, or causes another to take indecent liberties with the actor or another, with intent to cause substantial emotional or bodily pain to any person or with the intent to arouse or gratify the sexual desire of any person, without the consent of the other, regardless of the sex of any participant. . . .

Although both charges were defined in the same section, the Court of Appeals emphasized that the charges were separated by the conjunctive "or," just as they are in the instant case. Therefore, the Utah court found that the "[d]efendant's argument is flawed in that he first placed his mouth on the victim's breasts, the taking of indecent liberties, and then placed his hand on her vagina. These are separate acts requiring proof of different elements and constitute separate offenses." 736 P.2d at 1042.

The Court of Appeals of Maryland in *State v. Boozer*, 304 Md. 98, 497 A.2d 1129 (1985), was confronted with an appeal by the State from a trial court's dismissal of a fourth degree sexual assault charge against a defendant. The State had previously charged the defendant with unlawfully engaging in a sexual act with a person age fourteen and four or more years younger than he. The State subsequently entered a *nolle prosequi* to that charge and issued a new statement of charges alleging that the defendant had unlawfully attempted to have vaginal intercourse with the fourteen-year-old victim. Both charges were based upon the same incident, and both charges were based upon the same statute describing fourth degree sexual assaults. Md.Ann.Code art. 27, § 464C. However, a separate article of the Maryland Code provided definitions for "sexual act" and "vaginal intercourse," and the Court of Appeals held that, because the two were separately defined, they constituted separate crimes and were not the same for double jeopardy purposes. . . .

The Supreme Court of Kentucky in *Hampton v. Commonwealth*, 666 S.W.2d 737 (Ky. 1984), dealt with a situation where a defendant was charged with first degree sodomy and first degree sexual abuse. The charges arose from an incident where the defendant performed fellatio on the victim and caused the victim to perform the same act on him either simultaneously or continuously. The Supreme Court of Kentucky held that "the separate charge of sexual abuse is based not on incidental contact, but on a separate act of sexual gratification. The fact that the two sexual acts occurred either simultaneously or nearly so is irrelevant." . . . Therefore, both charges stemming from the same transaction did not violate double jeopardy principles.

Other courts have held that charges of sexual assault in the first degree and sexual assault in the third degree may be brought for conduct occurring in the same transaction because they require proof of facts independent of each other . . .

Finally, we find unpersuasive the argument that first degree sexual abuse under W.Va. Code, 61–8B–7(a), should be considered like a battery since it involves an unlawful touching of various parts of the body. Our battery statute, W.Va.Code, 61–2–9(c) (1978), makes no attempt to delineate the crime either by the portions of the body touched, as does our sexual abuse statute, or by the number of blows struck. Consequently, the traditional double jeopardy analysis of a battery through legislative intent would fail to reveal any intention to create a separate crime based upon separate blows. . . . As we have pointed out, our sexual abuse statute, through its specific enumeration of the different ways in which sexual abuse can be accomplished, shows a legislative intent to separately punish sexual abuse to different parts of the body.

Courts that have discussed the battery question have not attempted a double jeopardy analysis based upon legislative intent. Instead, they conclude without any detailed analysis that multiple blows struck during the same battery are not separate crimes. . . .

It is clear from the foregoing cases that most jurisdictions that have addressed whether a legislature intended to distinguish separate sexual crimes by listing different methods of sexual assault or abuse have found that the legislature did intend to so distinguish. We also conclude that the West Virginia legislature, in establishing the crime of sexual abuse in the first degree under W.Va.Code, 61–8B–7(a), intended to make separate offenses of each of the various methods to commit the crime outlined in W.Va.Code, 61–8B–1(b). Therefore, the defendant was not subjected to unconstitutional double jeopardy when he was convicted of two counts of sexual abuse in the first degree for separately and unlawfully touching his victim's breasts and sex organ in a single criminal episode. . . .

For the foregoing reasons, the judgment of the Circuit Court of Wood County is affirmed.

■ [The opinion of WORKMAN, CHIEF JUSTICE, concurring is omitted.]

■ NEELY, JUSTICE, dissenting:

I dissent to the majority's holding in this case because it is contrary to the general law on double jeopardy and has led to an unjust result *for future cases.* Thus, I take the time to write this dissent in a case where no harm is done to the defendant (he is to serve his two sentences concurrently) because I believe that the majority's opinion is aiding and abetting a growing trend in American law to abolish civil rights and destroy citizens' right to trial by jury . . . .

* * *

Part I

THE HISTORY

[In this portion of the dissent, Justice Neely comments extensively on "the crime problem" and how courts have reacted to it.]

Part II

THE BENDING OF THE LAW FOR FASHIONABLE ENDS

On 21 June 1990, C.D. was walking along Seventh Street in Parkersburg when she was accosted by the appellant, Ronald Dean Rummer. A few moments earlier, Ms. D. had spotted Mr. Rummer following her slowly in his car while she walked. After circling the block, Mr. Rummer parked his car, got out and chased Ms. D. until he caught up with her. Appellant then stuck one hand between the victim's legs and his other hand up the victim's blouse and said "Baby, I want to screw you." In the process, the victim tripped and both the victim and Mr. Rummer tumbled to the ground. The victim then broke free, ran down the street, and called the police.[2]

Appellant was charged with two counts of first-degree sexual abuse under *W.Va. Code* 61–8B–7 [1984]; one count for touching Ms. D.'s breasts, and one count for touching her sex organ. The jury convicted him on both counts, and the circuit court sentenced him to concurrent terms

---

[2]   I note that the majority, in its recital of the facts, interpreted the facts to include a second sexual incident when Mr. Rummer fell on top of the victim and he "again roughly fondled her breasts through her shirt with both hands." Slip op. 2. However, the majority's description of an alleged second sexual incident is not based on the testimony of the victim who testified to the following description of the entire incident:

Q   Now, you—what did he first do to you?

A   Well, like I was saying, whenever I went to turn the next time he grabbed me. And he had—just kind of like—he put his arm up in between my legs. And, you know, I was telling him to stop and, you know, I was telling him to get away from me and yelling at him and all. And—. . .

A   Well, he grabbed me and he started like hunching up against my body. And—

[H]e was saying, you know—he was trying to get up my shirt and stuff. And he didn't get up my shirt because I was pushing his arms away. . . .

A   And like I had said, whenever he grabbed me from behind, you know, he was rubbing in between my legs real hard. And I was trying to get away from him. And so that's when he started hunching and saying, you know, "Baby, I want to screw you." And he said it a couple times. And—

Q   Did you stay standing up or what happened?

A   No. Somehow we got—I—it was like we got tripped to the ground. I can't recall exactly how it happened, if I tripped him or he tripped me. But we fell, and he—. . .

Q   How did you land? Who was on top?

A   He was.

Q   Were you face to face, back to back or side to side or what?

A   No, like face to face because—but—

Q   Did you look up in his face at that point?

A   Yes.

Q   And how long did you stay in that position when you were looking up to his face?

. . .

A   A few seconds.

of one to five years in prison. I dissent because the conviction on both counts of first—degree sexual abuse violates double jeopardy provisions of both the West Virginia and United States Constitutions.

A.

Appellant's main assignment of error is that his conviction on two counts of first-degree sexual abuse under *W.Va.Code* 61–8B–7 [1984] violates constitutional protections against double jeopardy. . . . The fact that the multiple convictions resulted in concurrent sentences does not render the double jeopardy issue moot. . . .

In Syl. pt. 8 of *State v. Zaccagnini*, 172 W.Va. 491, 308 S.E.2d 131 (1983), we adopted the *Blockburger* test . . . for determining whether multiple convictions arising from the same transaction violate double jeopardy protections:

> Where the same act or transaction constitutes a violation of two distinct statutory provisions, the test to be applied to determine whether there are two offenses or only one is whether each provision requires proof of an additional fact the other does not.

However, this test is not necessarily dispositive of the issue of multiple punishments for the same offense. In *State v. Miller*, 175 W.Va. 616, 336 S.E.2d 910 (1985), we noted that even though the *Blockburger* test is technically met by separate convictions for kidnapping and first-degree sexual assault (each requires proof of a different fact), if the kidnapping is merely incidental to the sexual assault, then double jeopardy would bar conviction and punishment for both offenses. . . .

A comparison of *Fortner* and *Reed* shows the intricacies of double jeopardy protections that the *Blockburger* test cannot adequately handle. In *Fortner*, the defendant was charged with ten counts of second-degree sexual assault, ten counts of first-degree sexual abuse, two counts of conspiracy, and one count each of kidnapping and abduction with intent to defile; *Reed* involved a situation where the defendant was charged with separate counts of sexual assault, sexual abuse and sexual misconduct. Although the circumstances in both *Reed* and *Fortner* passed the *Blockburger* test, we found a double jeopardy violation for the convictions for acts incident to the sexual assault, but we did not find any error in *Fortner* for separate convictions involving separate acts in different locations at different times. . . .

Such *ad hoc* departures from the *Blockburger* test show that in the area of sexually assaultive behavior, the test fails to clarify when a conviction on multiple counts for essentially the same offense violates double jeopardy protections. It has become easier for courts to cite the *Blockburger* test and then use it as a pretext for their decisions than to determine whether multiple convictions in a given instance violate double jeopardy principles. Reliance on this type of jurisprudence gives us only anecdotal comparisons to prior cases; it does not give us a framework with which to determine whether the double jeopardy protections have been violated in this case. . . .

* * *

B

1. NATURE OF THE ACT

It is clear that in cases where there are multiple penetrations the victim's different orifices, whether of mouth, vagina, or anus, a separate conviction is valid for each penetration. . . . Where a defendant commits separate acts of our statutorily defined term "sexual intercourse" in different ways, each act may be prosecuted and punished as a separate offense.

However, a close examination of the act in this case shows us that the analysis used in the penetration cases . . . does not fit. Appellant committed one grope in which he made contact with victim's breast and sex organ, but he did not repeatedly choose to violate the victim's body at different identifiable times. Indeed, first-degree sexual abuse is an aggravated form of battery that has heightened penalties due to the sexual overlay. This case is more akin to battery cases than to penetration cases. . . . The double jeopardy limitations on multiple battery convictions is clear: Each blow by a single defendant upon a single victim in one contemporaneous transaction cannot serve as a basis for multiple convictions for battery.

When examining the nature of the act here—one grope that was over in a few seconds—the appellant's conduct is much closer to battery than penetration. Accordingly, the unitary nature of the appellant's act militates against multiple convictions of first-degree sexual abuse. Although the nature of the act is perhaps the strongest factor for determining unitary conduct, this factor is not necessarily dispositive and, therefore, I examine the next most important factors, time and place. . . .

2. TIME AND PLACE

In *Harrell*, 88 Wis.2d 546, 572–573, 277 N.W.2d 462, 478 (App.1979), the court described the appropriate method for evaluating the time element of sexually assaultive behavior:

> The greater the interval of time between acts constituting an episode of sexually assaultive behavior, the greater the likelihood of separate offenses. That the interval is merely minutes or even seconds, as with the other elements and factors discussed, cannot be a solely determinative factor. . . . An episode of sexually assaultive behavior can and usually does involve multiple invasions of the intimate parts of the victim's body. Whether such invasions are a single offense or separate offenses can sometimes be placed in perspective by the time interval between specific acts.

The place element is strongly related to time. If a defendant grabs a woman in a parking garage by the breasts and says "Baby, I want to screw you," drags her into a nearby stairwell and puts his hand between her legs and rubs before she can run away, then the different places (garage for one contact and stairwell for the other contact) would be a significant factor that would support two separate convictions. An interruption in contact, either in time or space, followed by a resumption indicates the occurrence of two offenses.

However, no such interruption of either time or space occurred here. The entire episode lasted, according to the victim's testimony, only "a few seconds." . . . Furthermore, contact with both the victim's breasts and sex organ happened simultaneously. Similarly, all contact took place in one place, on Seventh Street in Parkersburg. No interruption in either time or place occurred (even under the majority's statement of facts), further indicating that only one conviction for first-degree sexual abuse is appropriate. . . .

3. INTENT, MUSCULAR CONTRACTION AND NUMBER OF VICTIMS

"The defendant's intent, as evidenced by his conduct and utterances, to sexually abuse or obtain sexual gratification from his victim may demonstrate his desire for differing and separate means or acts of abuse or gratification." *Harrell*, 88 Wis.2d at 574, 277 N.W.2d at 473. Obviously the passing of time between events may be an indication of intent; the moving of a victim and renewal of an assault may also indicate intent. Furthermore, a defendant by his statements or separate concentration (e.g., starting his contact on the breasts and after a time shifting focus to the sex organ) may show that he intends to commit multiple offenses. This is why the multiple penetration cases are treated differently from battery cases: each penetration is *prima facie* evidence of a new intent to invade the victim's body. . . .

Another way of viewing the multiple penetration distinction from battery is on the "muscular contraction" principle: If a defendant consciously chooses to commit a separate act (e.g., pulling the trigger on a gun twice) he must have intended to commit two acts. In penetration cases, the fact that a defendant consciously moved his sex organ to insert it into a second or third orifice is further evidence of intent to commit two crimes. . . .

However, the appellant did not separately attack different parts of Ms. D.'s body; he did not express any intent separately to abuse various parts of Ms. D.'s body; rather, he committed one "few second" grope that simultaneously made contact with the victim's breasts and sex organ. Although the appellant intended to cause "sexual contact" with the victim, he did not intend to cause multiple contacts. This lack of intent makes the appellant's dual convictions for sexual abuse violate his constitutional protections against double jeopardy.

* * *

C.

Until today this Court had not squarely addressed the issue of whether conviction on multiple counts of sexual abuse stemming from one incident that lasted a few seconds violates double jeopardy. Unfortunately, in deciding this issue, the majority forgot its obligation to read statutes "with the saving grace of common sense." . . . In *Reed, supra,* we found it unreasonable to divide one act of rape into its component elements; it seems even more unreasonable that the Legislature wanted the courts to stand as a referee in a wrestling match counting the number of contacts to various body parts in a single incident that lasts a few seconds.

The State maintains (and the majority agrees) that the convictions in this case are not multiple convictions for the same offense, but rather that the statutory definition of "sexual contact" in *W.Va.Code* 61–8B–1(6) [1986] actually defines three different offenses: unwanted contact with the anus, unwanted contact with the breasts, and unwanted contact with the sex organ. As support, the State points to our rule permitting two convictions in situations where a defendant penetrated both the mouth and anus of the victim. The majority ignored the "saving grace of common sense" by not noticing the difference between this case and the penetration cases. The majority has yielded to popular blood lust for those who commit a crime of fashion: If a crime has "sexual" in its title, defendants automatically lose all rights. As I pointed out above, the multiple convictions upheld in the penetration cases rested on the fact that each penetration was a separate and independent act, . . . *State v. Gill,* 187 W.Va. 136, 416 S.E.2d 253 (1992). The majority quickly abandons this requirement of legislative clarity for a murky, divorced-from-reality analysis of the word "or." A brief review of this "analysis" will clearly reveal its absurdity.

The majority's "analysis" starts with a quote from *State v. Carter* saying that the use of the word "or" makes it "apparent that the Legislature chose to broadly define the term 'sexual intercourse' so that it would cover a variety of sexual encounters." The majority goes on to state that the use of 'or' is "clearly designed to separate the various acts that may constitute 'sexual contact.' " . . . That makes sense: The Legislature wanted broadly to define *the conduct* that would violate the statute. But then, the majority loses all coherence by concluding that the Legislature's intent to define the crime broadly led the Legislature in fact *to define three different crimes*, rather than three different ways of committing the same crime.

This Court rejected the majority's argument in this very regard in *Pyles v. Boles,* 148 W.Va. 465, 135 S.E.2d 692 (1964). In *Pyles,* the question was whether *W.Va.Code* 61–2–14a . . . defined several discrete offenses or one offense of kidnapping. In *Pyles,* this Court held that "it is clear that the statute . . . creates a single capital offense and not . . . three separate and distinct offenses." *Pyles*, 148 W.Va. at 476, 135 S.E.2d at 699. What would the majority be holding today if the defendant were appealing his conviction because the indictment charged him with "sexual contact" without picking either the breasts, anus or sex organ? Would they be freeing the defendant, or would they be concluding that the code defines one offense? I believe that Mr. Rummer would remain convicted! The majority is being disingenuous in its reliance on the argument that the Legislature's use of "or" defines separate offenses.

* * *

The reasoning of *Pyles* . . . is far more persuasive and applicable to the present case than the majority's tortured abuse of the word "or". Appellant was convicted of two charges of sexual abuse . . . which consists of subjecting "another person to sexual contact without their consent, and the lack of consent results from forcible compulsion." The fact that "sexual contact" may arise from contact with either the breasts, the anus or the sex organ does not mean that a defendant has committed three offenses if he happens to have touched all three. The definition of "sexual contact" in *W.Va.Code* 61–8B–1(6) [1986] gives the State three ways of proving first-degree sexual assault; it does not define three different offenses.

The legislative intent analysis, therefore, leads to the same conclusion as did the conduct analysis: Appellant in this case may properly be convicted of only one count of first-degree sexual abuse. Both prongs of the *Swafford* test being satisfied, I must conclude that the circuit court erred in convicting appellant on two counts of first-degree sexual abuse.

Part III

REPERCUSSIONS OF THE MAJORITY'S DECISION ON CIVIL RIGHTS

The majority, with its decision today, has joined in the national trend of arming prosecutors with tools that will obtain more convictions, but the increase in convictions will come with total disregard for whether the accused actually committed the crime. Although the "war on drugs" has become fashionable, the "war" has done little to stop drugs and the violence associated with them! Indeed, the main casualties of this "war" have been justice and civil liberties. In this Court, it seems to me that when a defendant is accused of the current crime of fashion (any crime with the word "sexual" in it), his constitutional rights cease to exist. . . .

The majority should recall the recent case of Glenn Dale Woodall, and the way that the police and prosecutors manufactured the case against him, to realize that prosecutors do not behave as if they are seeking justice, but try to maximize convictions. *See State v. Woodall*, 182 W.Va. 15, 385 S.E.2d 253 (1989) (Neely, J., affirming in part, reversing in part the initial conviction due to errors at trial. Subsequent DNA evidence revealed that the prosecution and police manufactured a large part of their case against Mr. Woodall, and the State settled Mr. Woodall's lawsuit for wrongful imprisonment for $1 million). Moreover, the Woodall case stands out not because it is rare, but because the prosecutor and the police got caught manufacturing a case against an innocent defendant. . . .

* * *

It is time, then, for us to take a stand on this frontal assault on our civil liberties; it is time for the courts to reassert their proper role in the administration of justice. I regret that the majority, in its yielding to hysteria over a crime that has the word "sexual" attached to it, has failed to see the consequences of its ruling today.

NOTES: MULTIPLE CHARGES IN SEX ASSAULT CASES

1. Jurisdictions vary as to whether they consider multiple acts in a given episode to be separate offenses, punishable by separate sentences, or whether they consider them to be part of a "single impulse" or a single *res gestae* which happens to involve touching the victim more than once. For cases finding that multiple contacts during one assaultive episode constitute a single assault *see, e.g.,* Cullen v. United States, 886 A.2d 870 (D.C. App. 2005) (remanding with orders to vacate one of two convictions for two acts of kissing victim's thighs separated by a short interval of time; separate punishments for multiple acts of sexual abuse committed in single course of conduct violated prohibition against double jeopardy); Woellhaf v. People, 105 P.3d 209 (Colo. 2005) (reversing conviction where four types of prohibited conduct occurred in one incident of sexual assault, finding multiple punishments violate state and federal double jeopardy protections); People v. Watkins, 300 A.D.2d 1070, 752 N.Y.S.2d 500, 501 (N.Y. App.Div. 2002) (two penetrations of the victim, at knifepoint, was "part and parcel" of the continuous conduct "that constituted one act of rape" even though the rapist left the house briefly between penetrations); State v. Johnson, 53 S.W.3d 628, 632 (Tenn. 2001) (finding one sexual assault, during which a customer touched the breast and inner legs of a taxi driver in a single episode).

2. For cases finding multiple offenses on similar facts, under reasoning similar to that in *Rummer, see* Quintano v. People, 105 P.3d 585 (Colo.2005) (separate touchings constituted separate sexual assault violations when each touching was separated by time and place); State v. Garrison, No. 2003 CA 67, 2004 WL 1506125 (Ohio Ct. App.2004) (sustaining conviction of two counts of gross sexual imposition for acts that were part of one course of conduct, because the touching of the victim's breast and the attempted touching of her pubic area were distinct acts under the statute); State v. Soonalole, 99 Wash.App. 207, 992 P.2d 541, 543 (2000) (finding clear legislative intent to punish "each separate invasion of a protected area"); State v. Williams, 105 N.M. 214, 730 P.2d 1196, 1199 (1986) ("[s]eparate punishments are sustainable where evidence shows distinctly separate touchings to the different [enumerated body] parts" listed in the statute).

3. Does it make sense to charge Rummer with multiple offenses? What should we do with dangerous rapists who randomly target vulnerable women? Many states have responded to the problem by passing laws to confine or control persons deemed to be "sexually dangerous." In some instances, these laws allow the indefinite detention of individuals even after they have completed their sentences. In Kansas v. Hendricks, 521 U.S. 346 (1997), the Supreme Court upheld the detention of sex offenders on the ground that they were being civilly committed. The Court explained that it was permissible for states "in certain narrow circumstances [to] provide for the forcible civil detainment of people who are unable to control their behavior and who thereby pose a danger to the public health and safety." *Id.* at 357. In Kansas v. Crane, 534 U.S. 407 (2002) the Court further clarified that states need not show that the individual was "totally incapable of controlling his behavior." Rather, the state need only show proof "of serious difficulty in controlling behavior" and that "the severity of the mental abnormality itself, must be sufficient to distinguish the dangerous sexual offender . . . from the dangerous but typical, recidivist convicted in an ordinary criminal case. *Id.* at 870. Are preventive detention statutes for sexually dangerous persons a good idea? Is it fair to say that they are civil commitment decisions rather than double-punishment?

———

CHAPTER 7

MISAPPROPRIATION AND RELATED PROPERTY OFFENSES

INTRODUCTION: MISAPPROPRIATION AND RELATED PROPERTY OFFENSES

The cases in this chapter begin with larceny and theft[1] in their various forms, and continue into crimes such as robbery and burglary, which are not strictly property offenses, since they involve crimes against the person as well as against property.

A. THE PIGEON HOLE PROBLEM AT COMMON LAW

This chapter explores a variety of property related offenses. The first few—larceny, embezzlement, larceny by trick, and false pretenses—are what most people think of today as simply theft or stealing. But under traditional common law rules, there were important distinctions between the different crimes. And the distinctions were nuanced and often unclear. This posed a major problem for prosecutors, who were obligated to charge defendants correctly at the outset of a criminal case. Before proceeding to the elements of each of the major common law offenses, it is worth observing the importance of proper charging.

Weldon v. State
Court of Appeals of Alabama, 1919.
17 Ala. App. 68, 81 So. 846.

■ SAMFORD, J.

The defendant was the city clerk and tax collector for the city of Talladega. As such, it was his duty to collect all money due the city, and make a record thereof, and also to act as clerk and collect all moneys due the Talladega light and water commission. The money when collected was to be deposited in the bank. During the period covered by the indictment there was a shortage between the amount collected for the light and water commission and the amount deposited of about $2,300. Under an arrangement between the city and other parties in interest, the city of Talladega had a special property interest in the money collected

---

[1] The word "theft" has general and broad connotations, covering any criminal appropriation of another's property to the taker's use, unlike "larceny," a technical term of art with narrowly defined meaning. *See, e.g., Henson v. State*, 136 Ga.App. 868, 222 S.E.2d 685 (1975).

for the light and water commission, and therefore the ownership of the money was properly laid in the city of Talladega. There was evidence tending to prove the conversion of the $2,300 by the defendant before it was deposited in the banks to the credit of the city or to the light and water commission.

The question of importance in this case is: Can the defendant be convicted of larceny under the facts as presented? The defendant was admittedly the agent of the city and the light and water commission to collect the money and to deposit it. If the defendant had the right to collect the money and did collect it as such agent, then there was no element of a felonious taking from the possession of his principal, which was necessary to a conviction where the ownership of the property is laid in the principal. If the collection was made and the money taken from the debtor to the city, in such manner and under such circumstances as to have constituted larceny, then the trespass would have been against the possession of the debtor, and in that event the ownership would have been laid in the debtor, and not the city. In either of these events, the defendant would have been entitled to the affirmative charge on the larceny count.

In efforts to maintain and uphold judgments of courts in cases of dishonesty, the appellate courts have clouded, rather than elucidated, the distinction between embezzlement and larceny. But one thing remains clear, and that is that in larceny there must be a trespass and a trespass is a wrong to the possession. In order to render the offense larceny, where there is an appropriation by a servant who is already in possession, it must appear that the property was at the time in the constructive possession of the master. In order for property to be in the constructive possession of the master, the property must once have been in his possession, and have been delivered by him to the servant. But, if the money comes to the possession of the servant from a third person and has never been in the possession of the master, and the servant converts it, it may be embezzlement, but not larceny . . . .

In this case it does not appear from the testimony of the state that the money collected by the defendant was ever placed in the depositary provided by the city; but, on the contrary, it was claimed, and the state's evidence tended to show, that the money was collected and not deposited . . . There is, however, in the testimony of the defendant a casual allusion to a cash drawer in which Osborn, one of the collectors for the city, after collecting the money due the city or the water company, would put it; and, when there was a sufficient amount, defendant would deposit it in the bank. If this cash drawer was a depositary provided by the city for the deposit of its funds as collected from the various sources of its revenue, and this money was so deposited, and afterwards was taken and converted by the defendant with the felonious intent, it would be larceny; but, under the facts as here presented, it does not so appear . . . Under the facts as presented, the defendant could not be convicted of larceny, and the court erred in refusing to give to the jury the general affirmative charge as to the larceny count.

The judgment is reversed, and the cause remanded.

Reversed and remanded.

————

NOTES

1. In determining the difference between larceny, embezzlement, and false pretenses, Professor Wayne LaFave has explained that:

> the borderlines between the three crimes are thin and often difficult to draw, [giving] rise to a favorite indoor sport played for high stakes in our appellate courts: A defendant convicted of one of the three crimes, claimed on appeal that, though he is guilty of a crime, his crime is one of the other two. Sometimes, this pleasant game was carried to extremes: A defendant, charged with larceny, is acquitted by the trial court (generally on the defendant's motion for a directed verdict of acquittal) on the ground that the evidence shows him guilty of embezzlement. Subsequently tried for embezzlement, he is convicted; but he appeals on the ground that the evidence proves larceny rather than embezzlement. The appellate court agrees and reverses the conviction.

WAYNE R. LAFAVE, CRIMINAL LAW § 19.8 (5th ed. 2010). For an example of this turn of events, see Commonwealth v. O'Malley, 97 Mass. 584 (1867).

2. As you will see by the end of this chapter, most states have abandoned the formal distinctions that separate larceny from embezzlement and other crimes and simplified their criminal codes by creating a single offense of theft. But not all states. As one commentator has explained, Virginia's efforts to fix the problem with a procedural device, rather than a substantive change to the law, has left matters just as confusing. *See* John G. Douglass, *Rethinking Theft Crimes in Virginia*, 38 U. RICH. L. REV. 13 (2003).

3. Is there a valid reason to put so much pressure on prosecutors to select the correct charge? In the modern American criminal justice system, prosecutors can bring multi-count indictments that charge multiple crimes and assert multiple theories of criminal liability. For instance, a prosecutor can invite a jury to find the defendant guilty of murder or the lesser offense of manslaughter. The prosecutor can suggest that a defendant is guilty of murder under a depraved heart theory or based on a felony murder rationale. If that does not work, the prosecutor can suggest to the jury that it can find the defendant guilty of the lesser offense of involuntary manslaughter or, in some jurisdictions, negligent homicide. Does this approach make sense, or does it provide prosecutors with too much power? Would a fairer system require the prosecutor to charge the correct crime and the correct theory and provide the jury with the option to accept or reject that charge?

B. LARCENY

Larceny, generally speaking, is the crime of stealing. Larceny is the oldest form of theft criminally punished under the early common law, and has traditionally been regarded as one of the "infamous" crimes.[2] Larceny not only invaded the individual victim's property rights, it stirred a sense of insecurity in the whole community and aroused public demand for harsh penalties: the penalty for grand larceny was death. Because of the severity of the punishment and the stigma attached to larceny, the bench construed the elements very narrowly, relying on technical distinctions to acquit in many cases.[3]

At the time when the common law was developing, the social and economic community was less complex than our modern economic and financial systems. Ordinary prudence was deemed adequate protection from most sorts of deception; it was no crime to "make a fool of another" by deliberately delivering fewer goods than were ordered, for example.[4] The remedy for this kind of commercial knavery was a civil action; criminal law would intervene only if the fraud was one which common care could not prevent, such as the use of false weights and measures.

1.   ELEMENTS OF LARCENY

At common law, larceny consisted of:

a.   a taking and

b.   a carrying away

c.   of the personal property (of any value)

d.   of another

e.   with intent to steal (to deprive permanently).

The essence of larceny is trespass against possession, and the concept of trespass is implied in the word "taking" when used in connection with larceny and theft.

---

[2] "Infamous" crimes, in English common law, (the source of the phrase in the Fifth Amendment) were analogous to *infamia* in Roman law, in that a person convicted of such a crime experienced "civil death," *see, e.g.* Virginia E. Hench, *The Death of Voting Rights: The Legal Disenfranchisement of Minority Voters*, 48 CASE W. RES. L. REV. 727 (1998) (exploring racial disparities in felon disenfranchisement upon conviction of crimes).

[3] For a thorough and thought-provoking exploration of the evolution of larceny and related offenses in the common law, *see, e.g.,* Bruce P. Smith, *The Presumption of Guilt and the English Law of Theft, 1750–1850,* in *Forum, Presuming Guilt in English Law, 1750–1859: Variation or Theme?,* 23 L. HIST. R. 133, (Spring 2005) Professor Smith notes that "the rules surrounding proof of simple larceny covered nearly 150 pages" of Edward Hyde East's A TREATISE OF THE PLEAS OF THE CROWN 2:553 (London: A. Strahan, 1803); *also citing* William Hawkins, PLEAS OF THE CROWN 1716–1721 (1716; reprint, ed. P. R. Glazebrook [London: Professional Books, 1973]); Jerome Hall, THEFT, LAW AND SOCIETY (Boston: Little, Brown, 1935) and George P. Fletcher, *The Metamorphosis of Larceny*, 89 HARV. L. REV. 469 1976). Smith, *supra* this note, at nn. 11 & 42 and accompanying text. For an equally thorough treatment of the Model Penal Code, including all misappropriation offenses, *see* Markus D. Dubber, CRIMINAL LAW: MODEL PENAL CODE, 400 (Foundation Press, 2002).

[4] *Rex v. Wheatly*, 97 E.R. 746 (1761).

The strict application of these elements created gaps in the law, which were filled by a complex array of new, statutorily created crimes, including embezzlement and false pretenses. In an effort to simplify the law in this area, many states have abolished the separate offenses of larceny, embezzlement, etc., and combined them in new comprehensive theft statutes. These modern statutes often retain the language of larceny, redefining elements to bring in behavior that would not have been considered larceny at common law.[5] Others follow the American Law Institute's Model Penal Code, replacing the term "larceny" with "theft." Under either model, the modern comprehensive statutes frequently encompass a wide range of misappropriation offenses within one statute, but these modern statutes still carry their common law history within them.[6] Consider the following cases in connection with the *mens rea* of larceny:

(A) *MENS REA*: INTENT TO DEPRIVE

The *mens rea* element of larceny has two parts: the specific intent to deprive the owner or possessor of the property, and the general intent to take and carry the property away. Under modern statutes, however, the intent need not necessarily be to deprive permanently: one may commit theft by taking possession of goods with the intent to appropriate the property to one's own use without paying, or to deprive the owner of the possession of the property, or to deprive the owner of the value of it.

The "intent to deprive" element can be especially difficult in shoplifting cases, because determining the person's intent requires an assessment not only of the conduct, but of all the surrounding circumstances. In *Hugo v. City of Fairbanks*, for example, there was conduct which appeared to support the existence of an intent to deprive, but a full inquiry into the circumstances tended to raise reasonable doubt as to the defendant's actual intent. How do we determine whether the defendant had the intent to deprive? Often, this can only be determined by examining the circumstances surrounding the taking (or retention) of the property . . .

Hugo v. City of Fairbanks
Alaska Court of Appeals, 1983.
658 P.2d 155.

■ Opinion, COATS, J.

Ellen M. Hugo was convicted of shoplifting, in violation of Fairbanks General Code Ordinance (FGCO) § 6.303(a) . . . . The trial court construed the ordinance as not requiring an intent to permanently deprive. Hugo appeals her conviction on the basis that the ordinance

---

[5] *E.g.*, the taking of wild animals.

[6] *See, e.g., Morissette v. United States, supra* at 67.

requires such an intent. We agree and reverse the conviction. [The statute in question provides:]

> A person commits the offense of shoplifting if he takes possession of any goods offered for sale by a wholesale or retail business establishment with the intent to deprive the seller of such goods without paying their purchase price . . . .

Hugo is an elderly Eskimo woman from Anaktuvuk Pass. Sometime during the first two weeks of December, 1981, she flew to Fairbanks to be with her hospitalized husband. Hugo had visited Fairbanks occasionally and had often shopped in Fairbanks stores.

On December 18, 1981, Hugo went to a Fairbanks shopping mall to shop for Christmas presents. At about 7:30 p.m. she entered the mall's Pay 'N' Save store, where she was watched by store security agent Mary Clarke. Clarke testified that Hugo carried a purse, a small tote bag, and a paper sack. The paper sack contained a pair of shoes which Hugo apparently had already purchased elsewhere in the mall. Clarke saw Hugo place two pairs of suede gloves in the paper sack, then go to another aisle and place four pairs of boys' socks in the paper sack. Hugo then went to another aisle and removed a plastic shopping bag. She took it to the pharmacy checkout stand where she paid for it. Hugo then put the paper sack and its contents (shoes, gloves, and socks) in the plastic bag. She did not pay for the gloves and socks when she paid for the plastic shopping bag, although she could have done so. After purchasing the plastic bag, Hugo returned to the aisle where she had been before and removed two more pairs of gloves which she then placed in the tote bag.

Clarke testified that Hugo then left Pay 'N' Save by exiting through a closed checkout stand. Adjacent checkout stands were open. Hugo entered the mall and stopped by a refreshment stand nearby but outside the Pay 'N' Save entrance. Clarke apprehended Hugo in front of the stand. Hugo explained that she left the store to get a Coke at the refreshment stand. Clarke took Hugo to the store's security office where she gave Hugo a Coke and proceeded to document the incident in accordance with Pay 'N' Save's shoplifter apprehension procedures. . . . On March 31, 1982, Hugo was tried by the court on a charge of shoplifting, a violation of FGCO 6.303(a). At trial, Hugo testified that she knew she had the unpurchased socks and gloves when she left the store but that she was thirsty and wanted to buy a Coke and then resume shopping.

Defense witness Dr. Peter Marshall, a friend of the Hugo family since June 1980, and a physician who provided medical care for the residents of Anaktuvuk Pass, testified that he had visited Anaktuvuk Pass several times. He described the one store in Anaktuvuk Pass and the shopping methods he had observed there. He testified that the store has a table at the front with a cash register on it. Shoppers bring their purchases to the table, carrying them in whatever manner they can manage. Customers frequently carry items to the front, drop them off, and resume shopping. Marshall also testified that Hugo may have been under his care for a cold during her visit to Fairbanks. He stated that he commonly prescribed Actifed for his patients with colds. Actifed can cause thirst. Hugo testified that she had taken Actifed on the day she was apprehended outside of Pay 'N' Save. Marshall further testified that Hugo does not have a good command of English. She understands only simple statements . . . .

The trial court . . . determined that Hugo placed the gloves and socks into her bags in order to carry them in a manner like that commonly followed at the store in Anaktuvuk Pass, and not with the purpose of concealing them. The court noted that Hugo's paying for the plastic shopping bag demonstrated her honesty. The other findings of the court apply to the court's interpretation of the Fairbanks shoplifting ordinance and Hugo's conviction under the ordinance. The court concluded that Hugo left the store knowing that the goods were in her possession and with the intent of leaving without paying for them. The court indicated that it could not determine, on the basis of the evidence presented at trial, whether Hugo intended to return to Pay 'N' Save and pay for the goods at some future time.

The court further indicated that whether or not Hugo intended to return to pay for the items was immaterial. The court concluded that Hugo violated the Fairbanks shoplifting ordinance by leaving the store without intending to pay for the items before exiting the store. In short, the court ruled that any determination as to Hugo's intent to permanently deprive Pay 'N' Save of its merchandise was immaterial because conviction under the ordinance does not require such an intent. The court concluded that the statute required only an intent to leave the store with merchandise without paying for it, and found Hugo guilty of this offense . . . .

Hugo contends that the shoplifting ordinance under which she was convicted establishes an offense an element of which is an intent to permanently deprive a store of its merchandise . . . . Because the trial court did not find that she had such an intent, Hugo argues that this court cannot uphold her conviction. The city takes the position that the ordinance . . . . does not require an "intent to permanently deprive" as one of its elements. Since such an intent is not required, and since the trial court concluded that Hugo intended to deprive Pay 'N' Save of merchandise within this meaning of the ordinance, the city urges this court to affirm Hugo's conviction . . . .

This court has recently decided three cases concerning the extent to which a statute or ordinance dispenses with the common law larceny requirement of an intent to permanently deprive an owner of property. *Morris v. Municipality of Anchorage*, 652 P.2d 503 (Alaska App.1982) . . . In *Nell v. State*, [642 P.2d 1361 (Alaska App.1982)], the defendant was convicted of first-degree robbery. . . . Nell argued that the trial court erred in giving jury instructions that did not require the jurors to find, as an element of the offense under the statute, an intent to permanently deprive the robbery victim of his property. AS 11.41.510 states in relevant part:

> *Robbery in the Second Degree.* (a) A person commits the crime of robbery in the second degree if, in the course of taking or attempting to take property from the immediate presence and control of a person, he uses or threatens the immediate use of force upon any person with intent to
>
> (1) prevent or overcome resistance to his taking the property or his retention of the property after taking; or
>
> (2) compel any person to deliver the property or engage in other conduct which might aid in the taking of the property.

In holding that the statute did not require an intent to permanently deprive, this court stated:

> The plain language of the statute itself does not indicate that an intent to permanently deprive the victim of the property is an essential element of the offense. In fact, we note that the statute does not even require that property actually be taken from the victim. From the face of the statute it is clear that the legislature, in passing this robbery statute, intended to emphasize the fact that robbery is a crime against the person and de-emphasize the theft aspects of the offense. We see no reason to add to the statute an intent to permanently deprive another of the property. The instruction which the trial court gave basically sets forth the offense as it is described in the statute. We have reviewed the instruction and find no error.

642 P.2d at 1365–66 . . . . Thus, in determining whether an ordinance or statute requires an intent to permanently deprive, the "plain language" statutory consideration rule should be applied. *See* 2A C. SANDS, STATUTES AND STATUTORY CONSTRUCTION § 46.04, at 54 (4th ed. 1973). We must also take the probable intent of the legislature into account.

Both *Morris* and *Smith* involved ordinances designed to combat shoplifting. Smith was convicted under an Anchorage ordinance prohibiting shoppers from concealing merchandise on their person while shopping. *Morris* is more relevant to Hugo's case. Morris was convicted of shoplifting in violation of an Anchorage shoplifting ordinance that prohibited the removal of merchandise. In both of these cases, the defendants argued that their convictions could not stand because they could not be convicted absent an intent to "permanently deprive" a store of its merchandise. This court rejected those arguments.

The defendant in *Smith* made several arguments to support his position that the Anchorage ordinance prohibiting the concealment of merchandise required a specific intent to permanently deprive a store of property as an element of the offense. Smith argued that the Anchorage ordinance was derived from current and former Alaska statutes that also made it a crime to conceal merchandise. Those statutes required a specific intent to permanently deprive as an element. We rejected this argument, since it was clear that the ordinance was not derived from those statutes.

Smith next argued that because shoplifting is a common law, larceny-type offense, specific intent to permanently deprive must be required by implication. Although Smith did not question the constitutionality of the ordinance, this court addressed that issue, since the danger of unconstitutionality is a relevant concern in determining whether to construe intent into the regulation. We rejected Smith's argument on the basis of the history of shoplifting regulation. Anti-shoplifting ordinances and regulations were enacted in the 1950's and 1960's when it became apparent that traditional larceny statutes were inadequate to control shoplifting (citing) . . . *Comment, Legislation-Survey and Analysis of Criminal and Tort Aspects of Shoplifting Statutes*, 58 MICH. L. REV. 429, 432 (1960). . . . We quoted a portion of the Michigan Law Review comment to show that shoplifting laws were designed to permit conviction for the offense without requiring the state to prove an intent to permanently deprive. We further held that a shoplifting ordinance that prohibited the concealment of merchandise and defined the crime of shoplifting in a manner not requiring an intent to permanently deprive was not unconstitutional. Interpreting the ordinance as requiring only an intent to conceal satisfied the constitutional requirement that a person not be convicted . . . where he had no criminal intent. Thus, states and municipalities may constitutionally pass laws that define the offense of shoplifting without requiring an intent to permanently deprive.

Morris was convicted of violating Anch. Mun. Code § 8.05.505(A) which prohibits the removal of merchandise:

> *Removal of merchandise.* It is unlawful for any person to take or remove any merchandise or thing of value from the premises where such merchandise or thing of value is kept for purposes of sale, barter, or storage without the consent of the owner or person lawfully entitled to its possession.

Morris argued that conviction under the ordinance required a specific intent to permanently deprive. This court rejected that argument, and held that only an "intent to remove" was required. This court noted that [t]he Anchorage shoplifting ordinance, of which removal of merchandise is a part, is not a common law offense requiring a specific intent to deprive. Rejecting another line of argument, this court held that the ordinance's requirement that an actor have a specific intent to remove was adequate to ensure that a person convicted under the ordinance was aware of the wrongfulness of his conduct. [S]ee *Speidel v. State*, 460 P.2d 77 (Alaska 1969). Moreover, we concluded that there were:

> no substantive due process problems with the ordinance because almost all people are aware that removal of merchandise is a type of activity that will arouse suspicion and possibly result in allegations of criminal conduct . . . In addition, removal of an unpurchased item from the store is reasonably related to the legitimate purpose of preventing theft. To render the ordinance constitutional, it is necessary only to infer a requirement of an intent to remove.

(citation omitted). Thus, it is clear that a shoplifting ordinance that forbids the removal of merchandise from a store need not require an intent to permanently deprive in order to be constitutional.

Although the ordinance in *Morris* is similar to the ordinance in this case, the two provisions are sufficiently different so that *Morris* does not control this case. Comparison of the two ordinances is useful. AMC 8.05.550(A) provides:

> *Removal of merchandise.* It is unlawful for any person to take or remove any merchandise or thing of value from the premises where such merchandise or thing of value is kept for purposes of sale, barter, or storage without the consent of the owner or person lawfully entitled to its possession.

FGCO 6.303(a) states: "A person commits the offense of shoplifting if he takes possession of any goods offered for sale by a wholesale or retail business establishment with the intent to deprive the seller of such goods without paying their purchase price."

The Anchorage ordinance does not use any language reminiscent of common law larceny requirements. The Fairbanks ordinance, on the other hand, explicitly requires an "intent to deprive." The plain language of the Fairbanks ordinance does not permit the conclusion that its drafters wanted to dispense with the common law larceny requirement of an intent to permanently deprive, as was the case in *Nell v. State*. Rather, the question is whether, by using the term "intent to deprive" the lawmakers who passed the Fairbanks ordinance meant to establish an "intent to permanently deprive" as an element of the offense. The city and Hugo contest the significance of the inclusion of the words "intent to deprive." The city argues that intent to deprive "does not mean intent to permanently deprive." Since the ordinance does not use the word permanently, the city contends the ordinance requires not an intent to permanently deprive but only an intent to deprive.

We must decide whether "deprive" as used in FGCO 6.303(a) has a common law meaning. At common law, larceny required an intent to permanently deprive an owner of his property. *See* W. LaFave & A.

SCOTT, CRIMINAL LAW § 88, at 637 (1972). The term deprive, "used in a larceny statute, is generally defined to mean permanently deprive." LAFAVE AND SCOTT note that:

> Model Penal Code § 223.0(1) defines the word "deprive" (theft requires a purpose to deprive) as
>
> (a) to withhold property of another permanently or for so extended a period as to appropriate a major portion of its economic value, or with intent to restore only upon payment of reward or other compensation: or (b) to dispose of the property so as to make it unlikely that the owner will recover it.

Ill. Rev. Stat. ch. 38, §§ 15–3, 16–1 treats the matter in a similar way. Wis. Stat. Ann. § 943.20 is less specific, requiring merely an intent to deprive the owner permanently of possession of such property. *Id.* at 637 n. 2. The general provisions section of the Alaska criminal code also defines "deprive" in terms of deprivation of a permanent nature. AS 11.46.990(B)(2) states:

> (2) "deprive" or "deprive another of property" means to
>
> (A) withhold property of another or cause property of another to be withheld from him permanently or for so extended a period or under such circumstances that the major portion of its economic value or benefit is lost to him;
>
> (B) dispose of the property in such a manner or under such circumstances as to make it unlikely that the owner will recover the property;
>
> (C) retain the property of another with intent to restore it to him only if he pays a reward or other compensation for its return;
>
> (D) sell, give, pledge or otherwise transfer any interest in the property of another; or
>
> (E) subject the property of another to the claim of a person other than the owner.

Both the statutes referred to by LAFAVE AND SCOTT and the Alaska statutory definition of deprive "demonstrate that the term deprive," when used in a statute or ordinance to define larceny or a larceny-type offense, means to permanently deprive. If "deprive" is to mean something aside from permanent deprivation, it will be modified with an appropriate adverb. To interpret FGCO 6.303(a) as requiring an intent other than an intent to permanently deprive requires the conclusion that the drafters of the Fairbanks shoplifting ordinance used a common law term with the purpose of having it mean something aside from what it has traditionally meant. It could be that the use of "deprive" was inadvertent, and that in fact the drafters of the shoplifting ordinance did mean something less than an intent to permanently deprive. However, in the absence of any legislative history or other evidence that the drafters did intend to ascribe a lesser standard than an intent to permanently deprive in their use of the term "deprive," the only permissible conclusion is that they meant "deprive" to have its common law meaning.

Other rules apply to this case and militate in favor of Hugo's argument. "[A]mbiguities in penal statutes must be narrowly read and construed strictly against the government . . . ." *Cassell v. State*, 645 P.2d 219, 222 (Alaska App.1982); . . . . Statutes or ordinances that establish rights or exact penalties that are in derogation of the common law are construed in a manner that effects the least change possible in the common law. If a statute is intended to change the common law, then the legislative purpose to do so must be clearly and plainly expressed. Moreover:

> Words and phrases having well-defined meanings in the common law are interpreted to have the same meanings when used in statutes dealing with the same or similar subject matter as that with which they were associated at common law. . . . Although a statute may define the way in which a particular word is used, the common-law background and origin of the word may, in cases of reasonable doubt, be useful to a proper understanding of the statute.

2A C. Sands, [STATUTES AND STATUTORY CONSTRUCTIONS], § 50.03, at 277–78 . . . . Shoplifting is essentially larceny. We must therefore interpret the term "deprive," when used in a larceny-type statute, in accordance with its common law meaning. We hold that to violate FGCO 6.303(a) a defendant must have intended to permanently deprive a business establishment of its merchandise.

In this case the trial court specifically stated in its findings of fact and law that on the basis of the evidence presented at trial, it could not determine whether Hugo had an intent to permanently deprive Pay 'N' Save of property. The trial judge found that she did not know whether Hugo intended to return to the store to pay for the property. Given this finding, it is clear that under the proper interpretation of the municipal ordinance, the trial court erred in finding Hugo guilty.

The judgment of conviction is Reversed. The trial court is ordered to enter a judgment of acquittal.

————

United States v. Donato-Morales

United States Court of Appeals, First Circuit, 2004.
382 F.3d 42.

■ LYNCH, CIRCUIT JUDGE.

* * *

I.

On January 4, 2003, Donato went to the [Army and Air Force Exchange Service, the AAFES] to buy a VCR. He testified that he needed a VCR with an S-video input, so that he could transfer his daughter's wedding video from his brother's video camera onto tape. S-video is a technology for transferring video images between video cameras, game consoles, televisions, computer monitors, and the like; when images are to be displayed on a television screen, those transferred using S-video will be sharper . . . .

Mark Montalvo, a store employee, testified that, at a time before the events shown in the surveillance video, he opened a box containing a Mitsubishi VCR for Donato and showed Donato the S-video input jack in the back of the VCR. Donato, Montalvo testified, seemed "pleased" with what he saw, and their conversation ended. Although Montalvo could not remember the precise model number of the Mitsubishi VCR he showed Donato, he identified it as the one that Donato ultimately selected, *i.e.*, the 746. Montalvo further testified that he had said "[n]othing" to Donato concerning the opening of boxes and that store policy required a sales associate to be present when customers opened merchandise.

Donato's testimony contradicted Montalvo's. Donato denied that Montalvo showed him a VCR with an S-video input and also claimed that Montalvo gave him permission to open VCR boxes on his own to check for S-video inputs.

After speaking to Montalvo, Donato continued shopping and put a different VCR, a Sony N88 that Montalvo testified cost approximately $99, in his shopping cart. Donato's next moves were captured on surveillance video. Donato removed a Mitsubishi HS–U445 VCR, which did not have an S-video input, from its box and packaging, inspected it, and left the VCR unit on the display shelf. The 445 box (which was admitted in evidence) had both a $129 price sticker and a $99 price sticker on it. Donato put the 445 VCR box, with the foam packaging still inside, on the floor, leaving the VCR itself on the shelf. Donato then pulled the Mitsubishi HS–U746 VCR box from the bottom shelf and placed it onto the floor just next to the 445 box; he then sliced opened the 746 box. The 746 VCR, which cost $189, . . . did not have a price sticker on it. At this point, the 746 and 445 VCR boxes were next to each other; the 445 box had only foam packaging inside and the 746 box still had its VCR in it. Donato paused for several seconds, looking back and forth between the two boxes, and then removed the foam packaging from the 445 box, leaving it completely empty.

Donato next removed the 746 VCR from its box with its foam packaging and wrapper intact. The wrapper, which was semi-opaque, covered the entire VCR. At no point did Donato remove the wrapper to examine the VCR or attempt to look at the VCR through the wrapper. Instead, Donato briefly examined the cover of the 746 manual. That cover did not expressly indicate that the VCR had an S-video input . . . . Donato also examined a plastic bag with the cables and controls of the 746 for approximately three seconds. The controls of the 445 and 746 look identical, as do three of the four cables included with each VCR. The end of the black cable for the 746, though, is slightly different from its counterpart in the 445: the end of the 746 cable is about half a centimeter longer and has more pins inside it. Donato then put the 746 VCR, still unexamined and intact in its foam packaging and wrapper, into the 445 box, picked up that box, and put it into his shopping cart. The entire process of switching the two VCRs was completed in just over three minutes. Donato then gathered up the foam packaging, manual, controls, and cables for the 445 VCR, put them in the 746 box, and returned that box to the shelf. He put the Sony VCR that had been in his shopping cart on the shelf as well and began pushing his cart down the aisle.

The 445 VCR box, with the 746 VCR inside it, was sitting open in his shopping cart with the 746 manual lying face-up on top. "Model HS–U746" is printed in approximately 30 point font in the center of the 746 manual cover. When Donato first opened the 746 box, the manual had been lying flat on top. Montalvo confirmed in his trial testimony that this is the typical placement of the manual in most VCRs. In the video, Donato is shown folding the 746 manual and stuffing it down the side of the box, where its cover was no longer visible, before leaving the area. . . .

Once outside the aisle, Donato is shown speaking for two or three seconds to Mark Montalvo. Donato testified that he asked Montalvo if it was a problem that the box was open, and that Montalvo closed the box and said that it was not a problem because the cashier at the checkout counter was "going to check the box anyway." Donato is then shown pushing the cart away, pressing on the top of the box to keep it closed.

After wandering around the store for another ten minutes and picking up some other items, Donato proceeded to check out at the jewelry counter. At no point in the video did Donato place the VCR on the checkout counter or otherwise hand it to the cashier. During the entire checkout process, he kept the VCR in the shopping cart, and until he signed the credit card receipt, he kept his arm draped over the top of the box, holding it closed. Donato ultimately paid $99 for the VCR. He testified that the cashier told him that the VCR was discounted by $30 from its $129 price, but that he had not been aware of the discount until then. On cross-examination, Donato said that he had "turned the box around" so the cashier could "look[ ] at the price." The surveillance video shows that when Donato first approached the checkout counter, the $129 price faced the cashier, but he later turned the box so that the side with the $99 price faced the cashier instead.

Donato was apprehended at the exit by AAFES security officer Nelson Colón, who had been observing Donato on the surveillance video. . . . Colón testified that when he confronted Donato about the fact that Donato had switched the VCRs and that the wrong VCR was in the box, Donato "said it was probably a mistake." Colón further testified that he "asked [Donato] if he had a chance to switch the VCRs and the boxes" and that Donato said "no." The video shows that this was plainly untrue.

* * *

Donato was later interviewed by Ricardo Seija, a military police officer. Seija testified that when he informed Donato that Donato was suspected of shoplifting, Donato showed surprise and "said he didn't know what it was about." Donato confirmed at trial that when Seija told him that he was going to be given a citation for shoplifting, Donato said, "[W]hat? Shoplifting what? What do you mean?" Donato testified, "I told him, listen, that must have been a mistake."

On March 12, 2003, the government charged Donato with federal larceny under 18 U.S.C. § 641. A bench trial was held on April 1, 2003. Donato moved . . . for a judgment of acquittal at the close of the government's case, arguing that no specific intent had been shown. The court denied the motion. Donato then testified in his own defense. On cross-examination, he stated, "I didn't realize that [I had switched the VCRs] until I saw that in the video." He repeated, "I didn't realize I made a mistake." At the close of all evidence, Donato renewed his Rule 29 motion, which the court again denied.

Two days later, the court found Donato guilty . . . .

Donato timely appealed, challenging the sufficiency of evidence supporting his conviction.

II.

Donato's claims of insufficiency of the evidence as a whole and insufficiency on the issue of intent are reviewed *de novo*. . . . Donato argues more specifically that the evidence at trial was not sufficient to support a finding of specific intent. The statute under which Donato was convicted, 18 U.S.C. § 641, provides that:

> Whoever embezzles, steals, purloins, or knowingly converts to his use or the use of another, or without authority, sells, conveys or disposes of any record, voucher, money, or thing of value of the United States . . . [s]hall be fined under this title or imprisoned not more than ten years, or both. . . .

Although § 641 does not expressly require specific intent, the Supreme Court has held that Congress, in codifying the common law crimes described in § 641, intended to incorporate the common law requirement of specific intent as an element of the crime. *Morissette v. United States*, 342 U.S. 246, 72 S.Ct. 240, 96 L.Ed. 288 (1952).

The evidence here was sufficient to allow a rational factfinder to conclude beyond a reasonable doubt that Donato had specific intent to "steal . . . a thing of value" from the United States. Direct evidence of specific intent is seldom available, and this case is no exception. But specific intent, like any other element, . . . can be established through circumstantial evidence. We conclude that it has been here. . . .

From viewing the video, the district court could easily infer that Donato deliberately swapped the VCRs and that the video is inconsistent with Donato's claim of innocence. In addition to a visual depiction of Donato's deliberate movements, it is reasonable to conclude that there was no reason for Donato to remove the foam packaging from one empty box (which was the 445 box), other than to make room for the VCR taken from the other box (which was the 746 VCR). At that point, Donato had already taken the first VCR (the 445 VCR) out of its box, checked the back for an S-video input, and set it aside on the shelf. This inference is reinforced by the fact that, immediately before Donato removed the foam, he is shown on the surveillance video looking back and forth between the empty 445 box and the 746 VCR in its open box.

* * *

The conclusion that the switch was deliberate is further supported by what the court could have reasonably viewed as Donato's attempt to cover up the switch. *See United States v. Llinas*, 373 F.3d 26, 32–33 (1st Cir. 2004) (jury could reasonably find that the defendant lied and rely on that finding, in combination with other circumstantial evidence, to support an inference of criminal knowledge and intent); *United States v. Hadfield*, 918 F.2d 987, 999 (1st Cir. 1990) (defendant's attempt to cover up by telling a "tall tale" supports inference of guilt).

Donato is shown in the surveillance video stuffing the 746 manual, which stated the model number in large letters, and would thus give away that he had the wrong VCR in the 445 box, down the side of the box, where it would no longer be visible. Donato is also shown during checkout with his arm draped over the box, holding it closed, even though he testified that store associate Mark Montalvo had earlier informed him that the cashier was supposed to check the opened box. Moreover, according to the uncontroverted testimony of AAFES security officer Nelson Colón, Donato told Colón that he did not have a "chance to switch the VCRs," a statement that was plainly false.

In addition, a rational factfinder could conclude that Donato repeatedly lied in his trial testimony. Donato testified that the 746 manual was at the top of the box in plain view when he left the aisle and that he had not stuck it down the side of the box, a statement flatly contradicted by the surveillance footage. Donato testified that Montalvo had not shown him a VCR with an S-video input and that Montalvo gave him permission to open VCR boxes on his own. Montalvo contradicted both statements in his trial testimony. The court could reasonably find that Montalvo was telling the truth and Donato was lying. Also, Donato testified that he had not seen a price tag on the box he took to the cash register, when the video shows him turning the box at checkout so that the cashier could see the $99 price tag, rather than the $129 price tag. Indeed, at sentencing, the trial judge said that as a trier of fact he found Donato's testimony was not credible. . . .

This court has repeatedly noted that a defendant's materially false testimony can be powerful evidence of criminal intent, at least when supported by other circumstantial evidence. Here, given the strong evidence showing that the switch of the VCRs was deliberate, a rational factfinder could conclude that Donato lied to the AAFES security officer, again to the military police officer, and again to the trial judge when he claimed that the switch was a "mistake." A factfinder could further conclude that Donato lied again when he told the AAFES security officer that he had not had a chance to switch the VCRs and then repeatedly perjured himself in his trial testimony.

It is easy to infer from the evidence that Donato knew to a high degree of probability he was taking something of value belonging to the government. He did so by getting the benefit of a more expensive VCR for the less expensive price of the model 445 (or by getting a non-sale item at a sale price to the detriment to the government, or both). At a minimum, defendant knew his actions were highly probably to result in taking something of value, as indeed happened. . . . When knowledge of the existence of a particular fact is an element of an offense, such knowledge is established if a person is aware of a high probability of its existence, unless he actually believes that it does not exist. . . .

* * *

Here the evidence, while not direct, was strong, and certainly adequate to support the verdict. A rational trier of fact could have found the essential elements of a case beyond a reasonable doubt. We affirm the conviction.

■ TORRUELLA, CIRCUIT JUDGE (Dissenting).

Like anyone charged with a crime, appellant is entitled to put the government to the test to prove each and every element of the crime alleged by proof beyond a reasonable doubt. *In re Winship*, 397 U.S. 358, 361–62 (1970) (this requirement "dates at least from our early years as a Nation"). Because I am firmly convinced that the government has failed to meet this burden by failing to prove that appellant had the specific intent to steal a "thing of value" from the United States, as required by *Morissette v. United States*, 342 U.S. 246 (1952), I respectfully dissent.

The house of cards upon which the government bases its case is anchored on the theory that appellant intended to steal something of value because he switched the contents of two VCR boxes, in order to pay less for certain merchandise displayed at the Camp Buchanan PX than this merchandise was worth.[1] Crucially, the government has failed to establish criminal intent because there is *no proof*, direct *or circumstantial* that prior to his being stopped by security personnel as he left the store, appellant was aware of the difference in price between the two VCRs in question, Models 445 and 746. The uncontradicted evidence is that: (1) only the lower priced model (445) had a price tag, (2) the video introduced in evidence clearly shows that the place for the price on the 746 was blank, (3) the two models were next to each other on contiguous shelves without different pricing being displayed in the shelving (or for that matter, *anywhere* in the store) apprising prospective buyers of a difference in price, (4) the boxes on both models are practically indistinguishable, and (5) the two VCR models are also indistinguishable except for the end of the connecting cable in the 746 model, which is "about half a centimeter longer and has more pins inside it" than in the 445. . . .

With this record, it is impossible to supply the missing indispensable link establishing proof of appellant's intent to pay less. Less than what? Unless it was clearly apparent to the appellant, *at the time of the exchange*, that there was a difference in value and thus that appellant was taking "something of value," the proof of the appellant's criminal intent is missing. This proof cannot be supplied after the fact as has been done here. Appellant's alleged lack of credibility does not supply the missing element, as it cannot be claimed that he was lying about the price of the merchandise or any other matter establishing the price difference. Neither can one extract circumstantial evidence of guilt from appellant's demeanor in switching boxes which were practically identical and showed no price difference.

What we have here is a situation similar to one in which both VCR models are in fact equally priced. Clearly appellant could not be convicted of taking something of value from the United States under those circumstances. The government thus was required to show that, at the time of the alleged taking, appellant was aware that the merchandise had different prices. This has not happened.

The flaw in the majority's reasoning, and thus in its faulty conclusion, is highlighted when it states that "Donato *knew to a high*

---

[1]   Although the amount paid by appellant for the merchandise in question was only $99, the price tag actually on the VCR's box was for $129. The evidence does not show that appellant learned of the lower price before he paid for the VCR at the cash register and was informed by the cashier that this VCR was on sale at the lower price.

degree of probability he was taking *something of value* [because he was] getting the benefit of a *more expensive* VCR for the *less expensive price* of the model 445 (or by getting a *non-sale item* at a sale price to the detriment to the government, or both.)" . . . (emphasis supplied). There is no basis in the record for these assumptions which are key to finding appellant guilty. There is no evidence that appellant knew, or could have known, that one VCR was more expensive than the other.

* * *

I respectfully dissent.

———

NOTES ON INTENT TO DEPRIVE

1. In United States v. Stearns, 550 F.2d 1167 (9th Cir.1977) Stephanie Stearns and her boyfriend, Buck Walker had sailed to Palmyra atoll from Honolulu, a distance of approximately one thousand miles, on the *Iola*, a 30-foot vessel, with a broken motor. Walker, using the alias "Roy Allen," was wanted in Honolulu, and the pair apparently intended to remain on Palmyra indefinitely, partly living off the land, and partly supplied by friends who were expected to arrive with provisions. The expected provisions never arrived, and Stearns and Walker proved ill-adapted to live on fish and coconuts, which were the main supplies available at Palmyra. They had nearly exhausted their meager provisions when Mac and Elenor Graham arrived aboard the *Sea Wind*—a 37½ foot ketch with auxiliary engines, fitted with a complete tool shop, and stocked with abundant food and stores sufficient for a trip around the world which the Grahams had been planning for two years. In late August 1974, all other vessels had departed from Palmyra, and only the *Iola* and the *Sea Wind* remained. The Grahams had a prearranged pattern of radio contact with an operator in Hawai'i. The operator's last radio conversation with Mr. Graham took place on August 28, 1974. All attempts to make further radio contact with the *Sea Wind* proved unsuccessful. The Grahams had mysteriously disappeared.

Three months later, Stearns and Walker were caught aboard the *Sea Wind* in a Honolulu yacht harbor. The *Sea Wind* had been reregistered under another name and had been partially repainted. Stearns and Walker were charged with theft of the *Sea Wind*, theft of the Grahams' personal property aboard the *Sea Wind*, and transportation of stolen property in interstate commerce. Stearns contended that the Grahams disappeared while the *Sea Wind* was anchored in Palmyra harbor, and that she and Walker had found the Grahams' empty Zodiac® overturned on a beach of the lagoon. She said that she and Walker had sailed the *Sea Wind* to Hawai'i in order to protect it from vandalism, and because they were out of supplies and the *Iola* had become unseaworthy. Stearns claimed that she and Walker had tried to tow the *Iola* behind the *Sea Wind*, but that the *Iola* stranded on a reef and sank as it left the narrow channel leading from the lagoon to the ocean. She also said that she intended to contact a relative of the Grahams to deliver possession of the *Sea Wind*.

At common law it would have been impossible to prove that Stearns and Walker had had the larcenous intent at the time of taking the *Sea Wind*, since their stated purpose, to return to Honolulu and return it to the Grahams' next-of-kin, was at least plausible. Under the federal theft statute, however, it was not necessary to prove that the intent existed at the time of the taking, although the government offered photographs taken by Stearns (showing the *Iola* under full sail—seen from the *Sea Wind*) that tended to cast doubt on their story. The reregistration of the boat, changes in rigging, and the fact that Stearns and Walker never made any attempt to turn in the *Sea Wind* were sufficient evidence that the taking was done with intent to deprive the rightful owners.

Mr. Graham has never been found, but some years later Mrs. Graham's skeletal remains, crammed in a metal storage box and showing signs of violence, washed up on shore in the lagoon at Palmyra. The theft of the *Sea Wind*, of which both Stearns and Walker were convicted, became the predicate felony for a felony murder prosecution. Stearns was acquitted of the murder and Walker convicted. For an interesting view of the case by Stearns' defense counsel, Vincent Bugliosi, the prosecutor of the Manson Family for the Tate-LaBianca murders, *see* Bugliosi, *And the Sea Will Tell* (W.W. Norton & Co., 1991).

2. In State v. Hauptmann, 115 N.J.L. 412, 180 A. 809 (1935), the defendant contended that there was no proof of an intent to steal the sleeping clothes of the kidnapped Lindbergh child. (The defendant was convicted of felony-murder, and the felony charged was breaking and entering the Lindbergh home in the nighttime with intent to commit larceny by taking the sleeping suit of the child.) (For an account of the reasons why the prosecution proceeded on this charge, see earlier discussion of the *Hauptmann* case in the Homicide chapter, *supra*, at 491–92). The court noted that the evidence tended to show that the defendant had the sleeping suit in his possession, and that, in the course of the ransom negotiations; he sent the sleeping suit to the negotiator for the Lindberghs in order to prove that he was the actual kidnapper. The defendant argued that the return of the suit established that there was no intent permanently to deprive the owner of the property. In rejecting this argument, the court stated:

> [T]he intent to return should be unconditional; and, where there is an element of coercion or of reward, as a condition of return, larceny is inferable. . . . In the present case the evidence pointed to use of the sleeping suit to further the purposes of defendant and assist him in extorting many thousand dollars from the rightful owner. True, it was surrendered without payment; but, on the other hand, it was an initial and probably essential step in the intended extortion of money. . . . It was well within the province of the jury to infer that, if Condon had refused to go on with the preliminaries, the sleeping suit would never have been delivered. In that situation, the larceny was established.

3. Is larceny committed by one who takes property and converts it to his own use under the mistaken belief that the property is abandoned? Does his intent to take the property under such circumstances meet the requirement of felonious intent? *See* Morissette v. United States, 342 U.S. 246, 72 S.Ct. 240, 96 L.Ed. 288 (1952), *supra* in Chapter 2.

4. In shoplifting situations, many merchants are under the impression that the "intent to steal" cannot be established until the goods are taken out of the store. But the intent to steal is provable by other factors, such as the carrying of goods from one floor to another. *See* People v. Baker, 365 Ill. 328, 6 N.E.2d 665 (1936). In other words, conduct on the part of the accused that is clearly inconsistent with the ordinary behavior of customers can be used as evidence of intent to steal. According to this test, therefore, a person should not be arrested while he is carrying an unconcealed piece of merchandise in the direction of clerks whom he could conceivably be approaching for an inquiry about the merchandise or where it conceivably appears that he is taking it to a better lighted place for closer inspection. In such instances the accused could reasonably offer such explanations as evidence of no intent to steal.

PROBLEMS: INTENT TO DEPRIVE

Problem 7–1. Suppose that a customer removes a lipstick from its package, leaves the empty package with the price tag, walks through the store for at least 20 minutes with the lipstick in her hand, and leaves the store, passing a service desk, and discarding the tube in a handbag on a rack where no employee would be likely to discover the lipstick and return it to its original package?

Problem 7–2. What if the customer is seen stuffing two packages of meat into the waist of his trousers and pulling his shirt down over them, but the customer returns the meat to the display case after the store security guard and store manager started watching his actions and following him?

Problem 7–3. What if the defendant was seen removing two small medicinal items and retaining them for a period of time inside the store, but the items cannot be found on the defendant when she is stopped?

––––––

(B) *ACTUS REUS*: TAKING AND CARRYING AWAY

The *actus reus* of larceny has two parts: The "taking" (caption) of the property, and the "carrying away" (asportation) of the property. The taking and carrying away need not be done by the defendant's own hands: the *actus reus* can be achieved by a mechanical or electronic device, a trained animal, or an innocent agent, including a person who is deceived by the use of altered, switched, or forged price tags,[7] claim checks, or other documents into delivering another person's property to the defendant. The taking and carrying away are historically distinct elements, but in practice they often overlap; under some modern statutes

–––––––––

[7]   *See generally* Peter G. Guthrie, *Annot., Changing of Price Tags by Patron in Self-Service Store as Criminal Offense*, 60 ALR.3d 1293 (1993) (2006 supp.).

these elements are sometimes replaced with an *actus reus* of exerting "unauthorized control" over property of another. Proving Asportation (or unauthorized control) can be difficult in shoplifting cases, in which the defendant may have been stopped before having completely removed the property from the premises. The cases and notes that follow will consider the *actus reus* elements of larceny and theft, and in particular, the issue of "trespass," and "unauthorized control" which involves some form of interference with possession that is adverse to the rightful possessor's interests. As a starting question, how much interference with possession is necessary? Is it possible to "steal" something without actually moving it?

State v. Donaldson

Supreme Court of Iowa, 2003.
663 N.W.2d 882.

■ STREIT, J.

Is a person guilty of theft if he breaks into another's car and engages the entire electrical system, save the engine? Specifically, the question on appeal is whether Dean Lester Donaldson possessed or controlled another's van when he broke into it, dismantled the steering column, and manipulated the ignition switch, turning on the radio and lighting the "check engine" sign on the dashboard. After a trial, Donaldson was convicted of second-degree theft. The district court overruled Donaldson's motion for a judgment of acquittal. Donaldson argues there were insufficient facts to show he possessed the van to support the charge of theft. Because we find Donaldson took possession or control of another's property with the intent to steal, we affirm.

I.   Facts and Background

At 1:50 a.m., a Sioux City police officer saw a van parked in front of Combined Pool & Spa with its sliding door partially open. The officer illuminated the van. As he walked towards the van, the brake lights flashed. Two men hotfooted across Highway 75. The officer gave chase, but was unable to find them. Upon returning to his squad car, the officer saw the steering column in the van had been forcibly removed and there were wires protruding from it. The radio was on and the "check engine" sign was lit on the console. Later, one of the men was found and identified as Dean Lester Donaldson. . . .

Prior to the trial, Donaldson filed a motion to adjudicate law points arguing the facts did not support a charge of theft. Donaldson asserted because he never possessed the van, he could not be convicted of theft. Donaldson argued, at most, the facts supported a charge of attempted theft. However, Iowa does not recognize a separate crime of attempted theft. The State asserted Donaldson took possession of the van when he hot-wired it. The district court agreed with the State and denied Donaldson's motion . . . .

II.   The Merits

This appeal is limited to one main issue. We must determine whether the district court properly denied Donaldson's motion for judgment of acquittal challenging the sufficiency of the facts to support a conviction of second-degree theft. The question is whether Donaldson possessed or controlled another's van when he broke into it, dismantled the steering column, and manipulated the ignition switch turning the radio on, lighting the "check engine" sign, and causing the brake lights to flash. Our review is for correction of errors of law.

The Iowa theft statute is modeled after the Model Penal Code, with slight variation. Model Penal Code § 223.2 cmt. 2, at 165 (1980). Our terms "possession or control" of another's property replace the common law larceny requirements of "caption" and "asportation." "Caption," or taking, occurred when the actor secured dominion over the property of another. The element of "asportation," or carrying away, was satisfied with even the most slight change in position of the stolen object. At common law, to prove a theft, the State had to show a defendant took the property of another, *i.e.*, secured dominion over it, and carried the property away.

The asportation requirement was important at common law because if a defendant's actions fell short of causing the object of the theft to move, the defendant was guilty of attempt only. Because a completed larceny was generally a felony whereas attempt was a misdemeanor, significant differences in "procedure and punishment turned on the criminologically insignificant fact of slight movement of the object of theft." In modern criminal law, however, the penal consequences between attempt and a completed theft are so minimal that it has become less important to draw a bright line between the two actions. As such, the element of asportation is no longer necessary.

Iowa, like many other states following the Model Penal Code, has abandoned the common law asportation requirement.[2] Our definition of "theft" under Iowa Code § 714.1 is based on the Model Penal Code. We now define theft as the possession or control of another's property with intent to deprive the owner thereof. The key to our statute is the words "possession or control." In determining the meaning of "possession" and "control," we look to the Model Penal Code for guidance as our statute is modeled after it. The Model Penal Code contemplates "control" of the object to begin when the defendant "use[s] it in a manner beyond his

---

[2]   Other jurisdictions following the Model Penal Code are Alabama, Arizona, Arkansas, Colorado, Delaware, Hawai'i, Illinois, Indiana, Kansas, Kentucky, Maine, Minnesota, Missouri, Montana, Nebraska, New Hampshire, New Jersey, North Dakota, Ohio, Oregon, Pennsylvania, Texas, Utah, Washington, Wisconsin, Michigan, Oklahoma, and West Virginia. See Model Penal Code § 223.2 cmt. 2, n. 3, at 165.

authority." The method of exerting control over the object of the theft is important only insofar as it "sheds light on the authority of the actor to behave as he did." Our statute replaces the common law element of "taking" with "possession." The Model Penal Code provides a person commits theft if he or she "unlawfully takes, or exercises unlawful control over" the property of another. A taking in this sense concerns whether the offender exerted control over the object "adverse to or usurpatory of the owner's dominion." That is, one possesses an object if he or she secures dominion over it. To summarize the above concepts, "possession or control" begins and a theft is completed when the actor secures dominion over the object or uses it in a manner beyond his authority.

Donaldson argues his conduct, at most, is sufficient to prove attempted theft, not a completed theft. We acknowledge the issue before us is complicated because "all theft partakes of the character of attempt." The line between attempt and a completed theft is a thin one. The thief proposes to make the property his own more or less permanently; but he is nonetheless a thief if, shortly after he exerts his dominion over the property of another, he is prevented from making off with it. It is not necessary that the actor have gone far enough to gain unhindered control.

The question before us concerns whether the defendant possessed or controlled the object of the theft. The critical issue, as the statute dictates, is *not* whether the defendant used or operated the object of the theft. As to Donaldson's conduct, we must determine whether he exercised wrongful dominion or unauthorized control of the van. The judge instructed the jury on "possession" using the Iowa Criminal Jury Instructions.... Bearing in mind the definitions of "control" and "possession" as contemplated by the Model Penal Code, we turn to the facts.

The undisputed facts of the case are the following. At approximately 1:30 a.m., Donaldson entered a van owned by Combined Pool & Spa. The owner of the van did not give Donaldson authority or permission to take possession or control of the van. The officer spotted the van located in the parking lot of Combined Pool & Spa and noticed the van's sliding door was partially open. As the officer walked toward the van, he saw the brake lights flash suggesting someone was inside the van. As the officer approached, Donaldson got out of the driver's side and ran away. The officer called after Donaldson, identified himself as a police officer, and ordered him to stop. Donaldson kept running. When the officer checked the van, he saw the steering column had been forcibly dismantled; there were wires hanging from the column. The ignition switch had been removed. The radio was operating. The "check engine" sign on the dashboard was lit. At trial, one of the officers testified Donaldson had engaged all of the electric systems. After turning on the electric accessory systems in the car, according to the officer, all Donaldson had left to do was engage the starter.

There is no evidence in the record to suggest Donaldson's tearing apart the steering column was intended for any purpose other than to deprive the owner of her possession of the van. Donaldson argues he did not possess or control the van because he did not have the "ability to readily move or remove" it. This, however, is not the test for possession or control. Because we have abandoned the common law asportation requirement, movement or motion of the car is not essential to finding a defendant had possession or control of the car. Our theft statute does not state possession or control is tantamount to "operation" of the object of the theft. To interpret our statute in this manner is to restrict the definition of theft more narrowly than the legislature intended. Given a strict interpretation of the statute, the State only had to show Donaldson had control of the van, *i.e.*, he had dominion over it in a manner inconsistent with his authority. We are unwilling to imply an "operation" requirement for certain kinds of property that are normally operated by its possessor.

The mere fact that Donaldson was interrupted by the police officer before he engaged the starter motor does not remove this case from the realm of a completed theft. It is not necessary that the engine was running and the van could have been moved. *Alamo*, 358 N.Y.S.2d at 380, 315 N.E.2d at 450. That is, technical operation of the van is not necessary to find Donaldson exercised wrongful dominion or unauthorized control over the van.

Donaldson's acts were sufficient to set into motion the steps necessary to power the van. It was not necessary that the engine was actually running. Rather, at the moment Donaldson began to manipulate the electrical wires for the purpose of starting the engine, he exerted complete control over the vehicle.

In sum, the facts before us show Donaldson was using the van owned by another person. He had the power and intention at the given time to exercise unfettered dominion over the van. Donaldson was in a position to exclude all others from the van, for example, by locking it. No one else could have hot-wired the van or started it with a key while Donaldson had control over it. Moreover, he used the van without the owner's consent and in a manner beyond his authority. Donaldson entered the company's van around 1:30 in the morning. He tore apart the steering column. The ignition switch had been removed; wires protruded from the ignition. The brake lights flashed. The radio worked. The "check engine" sign was lit. When the officer approached the van, Donaldson got out of the driver's side and ran away. All of these facts together are sufficient to show Donaldson controlled the van within the meaning of Iowa Code section 714.1(1). As such, the trial court properly denied Donaldson's motion for judgment of acquittal. . . . We affirm.

IV. Conclusion . . .

The jury could have found from all the facts and circumstances of this case that Donaldson exercised unauthorized control over the van. He tampered with the steering column such that the radio was on, the check engine sign was lit, and the brake lights flashed. Under a plain reading of our theft statute, such conduct surpasses an attempt and accomplishes a completed theft offense. Donaldson's theft of the van was complete when he exerted control over the van, to the exclusion of all others, for the purpose of stealing it. . . . [W]e affirm.

AFFIRMED.

If a person can steal a car without moving it, can a defendant steal from a store if he never leaves the store with the goods?

Lee v. State

Court of Special Appeals of Maryland, 1984.
59 Md.App. 28, 474 A.2d 537.

■ BELL, JUDGE.

Appellant, Joe William Lee, Jr. (Lee) was convicted by the Circuit Court for Baltimore County of two separate charges of theft under $300.00 and sentenced to the Division of Correction for two consecutive one year sentences. . . .

Lee urges this Court to decide that his concealment of a bottle of liquor in his trousers while shopping in a self-service liquor store does not constitute evidence sufficient to convict him of theft. Since Lee was accosted with the merchandise in the store, abandoned it and then departed from the premises, this case poses a substantial question regarding the law of theft which has never specifically been resolved in this state: May a person be convicted of theft for shoplifting in a self-service store if he does not remove the goods from the premises of that store? . . .

[A]n employee of a pharmacy-liquor store observed Lee displacing two $16.47 bottles of cognac. Lee concealed one of the bottles in his pants and held the other in his hand. When approached by the employee, Lee returned both bottles to the shelf and fled the store. He was chased by the employee who flagged down a passing police cruiser. Subsequently, Lee was arrested and convicted. For the reasons set forth in our discussion, we uphold the theft conviction despite the fact Lee was accused and "returned" the merchandise before he left the store.

To resolve the question of whether the evidence in the second case is sufficient to satisfy the elements of larceny as defined by the theft statute, Md. Code (1954 Repl. Vol.1982) Art. 27 § 342, the development of the common law of larceny and its evolution into modern statutory form must be briefly addressed.

Common Law

Distinctions among larceny, embezzlement, obtaining by false pretenses, extortion, and the other closely related theft offenses, including shoplifting, can be explained by a brief exposition of the historical role criminal law played in protecting property. The history of these theft related offenses commenced with the common law courts' concern for crimes of violence (*e.g.* robbery) and for protecting society against breaches of peace; then expanded by means of the ancient quasi-criminal writ of trespass to cover all taking of another's property from his possession without his consent, even though no force was used. This latter misconduct was punished as larceny. Fletcher, *Metamorphosis of Larceny*, 89 HARV. L. REV. 469 (1976). Larceny at common law was defined as the trespassory taking and carrying away of personal property of another with intent to steal the same. . . . The requirement of a trespassory taking made larceny an offense against "possession;" and thus, a person such as a bailee who had rightfully obtained possession of property from its owner could not be guilty of larceny even if he used the property in a manner inconsistent with the owner's expectations.

Because of this narrow interpretation of larceny, the courts gradually broadened the offense by manipulating the concept of possession to embrace misappropriation by a person who with the consent of the owner already had physical control over the property. MPC § 223.1. First the common law courts distinguished "legal possession" from "physical possession", or actual control, in that a shopowner retained "legal possession" until the actual sale was made, regardless of who had physical possession. In *Chisser*, 83 Eng. Rep. 142 (1678), for example, the defendant bolted from a store without paying for two cravats the shopkeeper had handed him for inspection. The Exchequer found the taking to be felonious, despite the handing over of the cravats, in that the owner retained legal possession and was therefore protected until the actual sale.

In an effort to delineate further the contours of possession, the courts began to distinguish "possession" from "custody," thereby enabling an employer to temporarily entrust his merchandise to an employee or a customer while still retaining "possession" over the goods until a sale was consummated. *See People v. Olivo*, 420 N.E.2d at 42, citing 3 HOLDSWORTH, A HISTORY OF ENGLISH LAW [3d ed. 1923], at 365. These distinctions and delineations, which ultimately laid the foundation for the statutory offense of theft as it exists today, provided the courts with the judicial machinery with which to sustain a larceny conviction when the customer who had rightful "custody" or "physical possession" converted the property to his own use and thereby performed, albeit subjectively, the requisite "trespassory taking."

As the expansion of the offense continued, the intent element increased in importance while the "trespassory taking" element became less significant. In *King v. Pear*, 1 Leach 212, 168 Eng. Rep. 208 (1779), a case involving the fraudulent hiring of a horse, "larceny by trick" was born when the judges faced the problem of whether intent to steal was sufficient to overcome the immunity provided by rightfully acquiring possession. In *Pear's* case the judges reasoned that if Pear's intention was fraudulent at the outset, then he never acquired legal possession. Thus the conversion of the horse (presumably at the time of the sale) became equivalent to the taking and carrying away under common law larceny. Apparently, the courts began to realize that the actor's wrong typically had little to do with the act of acquiring physical control over the object, but, rather revolved around the intent behind the acquisition. Accordingly, later cases often ignored the fact that a defendant had obtained possession lawfully. Instead they focused upon the intent of the actor as evidenced by his unauthorized exercise of control over the property; thus the "trespassory taking" element became a subjective rather than objective element. . . . Most modern statutes have incorporated these developments under a unified definition of theft which tends to focus upon the perpetrator's intent and his "exercise of dominion and control over the property."

In Maryland, before the passage of the theft law which became effective on July 1, 1979 (Md. Code (1954 Repl.Vol.1982), Art. 27 §§ 340–344) the law of larceny was sprinkled throughout Art. 27. Several separate offenses, each involving some sort of taking and carrying away of property with an intent to deprive the owner, were consolidated under Art. 27 § 342. These offenses included larceny, larceny by trick, larceny after trust, embezzlement, false pretenses, shoplifting, and receiving stolen property. The legislature consolidated these offenses in an effort to eliminate the technical and absurd distinctions that have plagued the larceny related offenses and produced a plethora of special provisions in the criminal law. Under § 342 are the primary elements of theft: willfully and knowingly; obtaining unauthorized control over the property or services of another; by deception or otherwise; with intent to deprive the owner of his property; by using, concealing, or abandoning it in such a manner that it probably will not be returned to the owner.

The evolution of theft law is particularly relevant to thefts occurring in modern self-service stores where customers are impliedly invited to examine, try on, and carry about the merchandise on display. In a self-service store, the owner has, in a sense, consented to the customer's possession of the goods for a limited purpose. . . . Under common law principles of theft, a person could not have been convicted if apprehended while still in the store because the perpetrator would have rightful possession (albeit temporarily) and thus could not perform the element of trespassory taking until he left the store without paying (at which point it might be too late). Under the present law, the fact that the owner temporarily consents to possession does not preclude a conviction for larceny if the customer exercises dominion and control over the property by using or concealing it in an unauthorized manner. Such conduct would satisfy the element of trespassory taking as it could provide the basis for the inference of the intent to deprive the owner of the property. . . .

From this perusal of cases [in other jurisdictions], we conclude that several factors should be assessed to determine whether the accused intended to deprive the owner of property. First, concealment of goods inconsistent with the store owner's rights should be considered. "Concealment" is conduct which is not generally expected in a self-service store and may in many cases be deemed "obtaining unauthorized control over the property in a manner likely to deprive the owner of the property." Other furtive or unusual behavior on the part of the defendant should also be weighed. For instance, if a customer suspiciously surveys an area while secreting the merchandise this may evince larcenous behavior. Likewise, if the accused flees the scene upon being questioned or accosted about the merchandise, as in the instant case, an intent to steal may be inferred. The customer's proximity to the store's exits is also relevant. Additionally, possession by the customer of a shoplifting device with which to conceal merchandise would suggest a larcenous intent. One of these factors or any act on the part of the customer which would be inconsistent with the owner's property rights may be taken into account as relevant in determining whether there was a larcenous intent.

Legislative Intent

An examination of the legislative history relating to the law of theft leads this Court to conclude that the law in Maryland is intended to be no different than the above cited jurisdictions. Shoplifting in a self-service store constitutes theft by virtue of Md. Code Art. 27 § 342(a):

> (a) *Obtaining or exerting unauthorized control*—A person commits the offense of theft when he willfully or knowingly obtains control which is unauthorized or exerts control which is unauthorized over property of the owner, and:
>
> (1) Has the purpose of depriving the owner of the property; or
>
> (2) Willfully or knowingly uses, conceals, or abandons the property in such manner as to deprive the owner of the property; or
>
> (3) Uses, conceals, or abandons the property knowing the use, concealment or abandonment will deprive the owner of the property.

This subsection requires two primary elements to constitute the offense of theft. They are (1) a knowing exertion or obtainment of control (inadvertent or negligent exertion of control is not punished); and (2) a purpose to "deprive" (the mental element prevalent in most thefts). Subcommittee, *supra* at p. 31. *See generally* State of Md. Commission on

Criminal Law, REPORT AND PART I OF THE PROPOSED CRIMINAL CODE, 1 § 55 (June 1, 1972).

Most of the activities which previously constituted shoplifting will now be a theft offense through a violation of this subsection. The Subcommittee was of the opinion that shoplifting had become a crime that was not regarded seriously by many persons and was achieving an almost socially acceptable status. It was therefore decided that the sterile label of shoplifting would be purged from the Code and that the activities constituting shoplifting would be denominated as "theft." A perpetrator of these activities would then be known as a "thief"—a designation which properly reflects the character of "his crime and the class of offender with whom he should be categorized."

To illustrate that Lee's act of concealing a bottle of liquor in his trousers amounts to shoplifting and thus may be considered theft, we will apply the facts of this case to each element of the statute.

Lee knowingly obtained unauthorized control over the property of another when he consciously picked up the bottle of cognac and "concealed the bottle in his pants." A person acts knowingly when he is practically certain that the result will be caused by his conduct. When knowledge of the existence of a particular fact is an element of an offense, that knowledge is established if a person is practically certain of its existence.

"Obtain" is defined in § 340(f) as "bring[ing] about a transfer of interest or possession." The word "obtain" applies to instances where there is constructive acquisition of the property. "Property" means anything of value. Md. Code (1954 Repl. Vol. 1982) Art. 27 § 340(h). In this case when Lee placed the bottle of liquor in his pants, there is no question that he acted knowingly. It would be most difficult to negligently hide a bottle of liquor in such a manner. Lee obtained control over the property when he hid it from the owner's view.

The latter portion of the statute requires proof of mental state—did Lee have the purpose to deprive the owner of the bottle of liquor? The requisite mental state is usually inferred from the offender's disposition of the property. Section 342(a)(1) provides for proof of a "purpose to deprive" in general terms. To cover those instances where the purpose to deprive is more difficult to ascertain however, paragraphs (a)(2) and (a)(3) were added to the new theft statute. The most appropriate section to apply to the facts of this case would be (a)(2) where intent can be inferred if the accused "willfully or knowingly use[s] conceal[s] or abandon[s] property in such a manner as to deprive the owner of the property." "Conceal" is not specifically defined in the theft statute, but since the general rule of construction is that words are given their ordinary meaning unless stated otherwise, we refer to BLACK'S LAW DICTIONARY, which defines "conceal" as: "to hide, secrete, or withhold from the knowledge of others. To withdraw from observation . . . , to cover or keep from sight; or prevent discovery of." BLACK'S LAW DICTIONARY 261 (rev. 5th ed. 1979). "Deprive means to 'withhold property of another;' Permanently; or for such a period as to appropriate a portion of its value; or with the purpose to restore it only upon payment of reward or other compensation; or to dispose of the property and use or deal with the property so as to make it unlikely that the owner will recover it." *See* Md. Code (1954 Repl. Vol. 1982) Art. 27 § 340(c).

The requisite mental state of having an intent to deprive is most frequently proved by the defendant's handling of the property.

In the instant case, Lee knowingly removed the bottle of liquor from the shelf and secreted it under his clothing. This act in itself meets the requirement of concealment. The fact that this concealment was brief or that Lee was detected before the goods were removed from the owner's premises is immaterial. The intent to deprive the owner of his property can be inferred from his furtive handling of the property. Lee not only placed the bottle in the waistband of his pants, but did so in a particularly suspicious manner by concealing the bottle such that it was hidden from the shopowner's view. It cannot be so as a matter of law that these circumstances failed to establish the elements of theft. Once a customer goes beyond the mere removal of goods from a shelf and crosses the threshold into the realm of behavior inconsistent with the owner's expectations, the circumstances may be such that a larcenous intent can be inferred.

Judgments Affirmed.

NOTES

1. After reading the *Lee* case, do you feel confident that you can separate the case of a customer legitimately trying on merchandise and someone like Lee who is in the process of stealing it? If a customer tries on a sweater and walks around the store in it, should that constitute larceny? What if the store has dressing rooms and the customer did not use them? Would it make a difference if the store were a Marshalls as opposed to a Nordstrom?

2. The *Lee* decision turns on the fact that putting the bottle down his pants was not rightful possession. But what if property was originally taken rightfully, but the person in possession later formed a wrongful intent to deprive? Consider this hypothetical: A student who is studying criminal law comes by the professor's office and asks to borrow a study guide. The professor agrees to loan the study guide as long as the student returns it at the end of that day. The student agrees, plans to return it, and uses the study guide an hour later. Finding the study guide to be really great, the student then at that moment decides to keep it permanently. The student does not return the study guide. Is the student guilty of larceny? At common law, the answer was "no" because there was no concurrence of the *actus reus* and *mens rea* elements. At the time the student took the property, she did not do it with wrongful *mens rea*. The wrongful *mens rea* to permanently deprive was formed only after the taking. With no concurrence of the elements, the student could not be guilty of larceny.

3. Now consider a slightly different version of the hypothetical from Note 2. The criminal law student comes by the professor's office to ask to borrow a study guide. The professor is not there, but the door is open and the study guide is sitting on the professor's desk in plain view. The student takes the study guide intending to use it for a couple of hours and then bring it back. The student does not at that moment intend to permanently keep the study guide. After using it however and finding it to be excellent, the student later decides to keep it permanently and never returns it. Is the student guilty of larceny now? Even though the student only took the study guide with the intent to keep it temporarily (rather than to permanently deprive) the student is guilty of larceny in this scenario. The reason is that the initial taking of the study guide was without permission and thus wrongful. While wrongfully in possession of the study guide, the student formed the intent to permanently deprive. At common law, courts got around the concurrence of the elements problem by calling this situation a "continuing trespass." *See* 3 WHARTON'S CRIMINAL LAW § 350 (15th ed. 2016) ("Under the doctrine of continuing trespass, the trespassory nature of the initial taking continues throughout the time of defendant's possession.").

————

PROBLEMS: "TAKING AND CARRYING AWAY"

Problem 7–4. Danny Doofus entered a Macy's department store carrying a Macy's shopping bag. He went to the men's department and took a shirt from its hanger. Doofus carried the shirt into another department on the other side of the store. There he placed the shirt on a sales counter and told cashier Carrie that he had bought it for his father but it didn't fit and he wanted to return it. Carrie asked him whether he had the receipt, and he replied that he did not because "it was a gift." Carrie informed him that if the value of a returned item is more than $20 and there is no receipt, the store policy is not to make a cash refund but to issue a store credit voucher. Doofus agreed, but signed the voucher with a false name. Doofus was confronted by store security as he left the counter with the voucher, and he offered to pay for the shirt. Has he committed larceny? Theft? Attempted theft? Explain.

Problem 7–5. Johnny G. was acquainted with Toni D., a clerk at a store where he often shopped. One day when Johnny G. was shopping at the store, Toni D. undercharged Johnny G. for a camera valued at $279.00, a bottle of "Red" perfume valued at $42.00, and assorted clothing items "because he . . . didn't have enough money and wanted to give it to his wife for a present." Johnny G. paid with a twenty-dollar bill, received change, and left. Johnny G. claimed later that he just took advantage of the cashier's mistake, and that he "really wasn't paying any attention to her ringing me up. She told me what I needed to pay, and I was shocked or stunned. I didn't say anything. I just paid her what she asked for." Has Johnny G. satisfied the "taking" element to satisfy a charge of larceny?

(C) PROPERTY OF ANOTHER

Even if a defendant had the *mens rea* and *actus reus*, larceny still could not exist unless the property in question were "property of another." This element also has two dimensions: the subject matter of the larceny must be something that qualifies as "property" and it must belong "to another."

(1) What Is "Property" for Purposes of Larceny and Theft?

The common law rule was only tangible, personal property could be the subject of larceny: only those items that could literally be touched, taken, and carried away[8] were capable of being "stolen." However, being tangible was not enough to satisfy the "property element;" not everything which could be touched and carried away was property for purposes of larceny. Such things as fixtures to realty,[9] growing trees,[10] and grave markers[11]—or any other items which "savor of the realty" were not "property" within the meaning of the law of larceny, unless there was an interval between the time they were severed from the realty and the time they were taken and carried away.

(i) Animals

Animals were a special case in common law larceny. The common law held that animals of a "base nature" were not considered personalty, so the theft of a cat, for example, was not deemed a larceny. However, domestic animals that were useful for the sustenance of life, including cows, horses, hogs, and chickens, were classified as personalty, capable of being stolen. Wild animals became property only after they were reduced to possession. Thus, the taking of an animal might be a felony, punishable by death, or might be no offense at all, depending on how the animal was classified. In *The Case of the Peacocks*, Y.B. 18 Hen. 8, f. 9, p. 11 (K.B.1526), the chancellor asked the justices of the Court of the King's Bench the question if it was a felony for a man to steal peacocks which are tame and domestic. The opinion states that two justices declared,

> [I]t is not felony, for they are *ferae naturae*. . . . And the law is the same as to a mastiff, a hound, or a spaniel, or a goshawk which is tamed, for they are more properly things for pleasure

---

[8] Criminal liability for theft of, interference with, or unauthorized use of, computer programs, files, or systems, 51 ALR 4th 971.

[9] *See, e.g., Stephens v. Commonwealth*, 304 Ky. 38, 199 S.W.2d 719 (1947). For a current statute incorporating this concept in somewhat archaic terminology, *see* Code of Virginia, § 18.2–99.

[10] *See, e.g., Stansbury v. Luttrell*, 152 Md. 553, 137 A. 339 (1927) (larceny of fallen trees is possible when there was an interval of time between their severance and taking).

[11] *See, e.g., State v. Jackson*, 218 N.C. 373, 11 S.E.2d 149 (1940) (overturning a conviction of larceny for the theft of a gravestone from a cemetery). The North Carolina Supreme Court held that "it was not larceny, at common law, to steal anything adhering to the soil."

than for profit. And similarly the peacock is a bird more for pleasure than for profit. . . .

FitzJames and the other justices disagreed, and said that peacocks are commonly of the same nature of hens or capons, geese or ducks, and that the owner has property in them. They have *animus revertendi* and they are not fowls of warren, like pheasant or partridge . . . as to which taking, even with felonious intent, is not felony. And finally all the justices agreed that the taking of peacocks was felony . . . With respect to "Man's best friend", the Supreme Court of the United States was prompted to say, in *Sentell v. New Orleans & C. Ry. Co.*, 166 U.S. 698, 701 (1897):

While the higher breeds rank among the noblest representatives of the animal kingdom, and are justly esteemed for their intelligence, sagacity, fidelity, watchfulness, affection, and, above all, for their natural companionship with man, others are afflicted with such serious infirmities of temper as to be little better than a public nuisance.[12]

Early decisions in the United States tended to follow the common law rule, distinguishing domestic from wild animals as "property" capable of being stolen. Eventually all animals reduced to possession came to be looked upon as personal property. This change came about both by court decision and by statutes. Consider, for example, the Virginia Criminal Code which has a separate statutory provision, § 18.2–97, for "Larceny of certain animals and poultry," which refers to the theft of a dog, horse, pony, mule, cow, steer, bull or calf, as well as poultry, sheep, swine, lamb, or goat.

(ii) Intangibles

When it came to intangibles, the early common law was clear: intangibles could not be the subject of larceny, because they could not, by definition, be touched or "carried away." This rule persisted until very recently. While intangibles are now recognized as property for many purposes, there remain difficult problems in determining how the traditional law of larceny (or theft) as well as modern criminal fraud statutes should apply to such intangibles as proprietary information, computer source codes, and the like.

---

[12] Dogs seem to be a constant—or at least a recurring—theme in the legal canon. As recently as 1980, in *State v. Wallace*, 49 N.C.App. 475, 271 S.E.2d 760 (1980) overturning a conviction for pursuing deer with dogs, Justice Martin was moved to declare, "This is a case about dogs!" before launching into a multipage *paean* to dogs in the law, ranging from prehistoric time to the present, with excursions into Greek and Roman mythology, poetry, and the English Common Law; he then dismissed the charges based on a defective summons. Concurring in the result only, Justice Hedrick wrote: "I concur completely in the decision that the citation in question does not charge an offense. I am compelled to register, however, my opposition to using the North Carolina Court of Appeals Reports to publish my colleague's totally irrelevant, however learned, dissertation on dogs."

Inevitably, as new forms of property are recognized by law, the criminal codes will have to adapt. Nonetheless, the first person to "steal" a new form of property may benefit from the fact that penal laws are strictly construed. *See, e.g., Lund v. Commonwealth,* 217 Va. 688, 232 S.E.2d 745 (1977) (reversing grand larceny conviction of graduate student who used a university computer without proper authorization and "with intent to defraud." Because Virginia had not then modified the term "larceny" to include labor or services, the court found that Lund's conviction could not stand) (since reversed by statute).

NOTES: PROPERTY CAPABLE OF BEING STOLEN

1. In Lund v. Commonwealth, 217 Va. 688, 232 S.E.2d 745 (1977), the defendant, a graduate student at a state university used computer time without first securing permission and without paying for it. He was charged with using "without authority computer operation time and services of Computer Center Personnel . . . with intent to defraud, such property and services having a value of one hundred dollars or more." The court held that labor and services, and the unauthorized use of the university's computer could not be construed to be subjects of the state's larceny and false pretenses provisions.

The difficulty encountered by the Virginia Supreme Court is obviated in states which have statutes broadly defining "property" to be "anything of value." *See generally* Alois Valerian Gross, *Annot. Criminal Liability for Theft Of, Interference With, or Unauthorized Use Of, Computer Programs, Files, or Systems,* 51 ALR 4th 971 (2007 Update); Computer Fraud and Abuse Act, 18 U.S.C. § 1030 (1994) (2007 supplement); Copyright Act, 17 U.S.C. § 506 (1994) (creating felony offense of copyright infringement) and proposed amendments 2007 CONG. U.S. H.R. 4279, 110th CONGRESS (Introduced Dec. 5, 2007); Economic Espionage Act, 18 U.S.C. §§ 1831–1839 (1996).

As a result of *Lund,* the Virginia General Assembly enacted a new provision codified as § 18.2–98.1, making "computer time" or computer services or data processing services "personal property" within the meaning of the larceny, embezzlement, and false pretenses statutes. In 1984, however, the legislature repealed § 18.2–98.1 as it enacted, at the same time, a comprehensive statute called the "Virginia Computer Crimes Act," codified in § 18.2–152.1 *et seq.* The statute's definitions section, § 18.2–152.2, defines as "property" both tangibles and intangibles, as well as computer services in the broadest sense. The comprehensive act creates also a number of new statutory crimes, such as Computer fraud § 18.2–152.3, Computer trespass § 18.2–152.4, Computer invasion of privacy § 18.2–152.5, Theft of computer services § 18.2–152.6; and Personal trespass by computer § 18.2–152.7.

2. Does it make sense to remove intangibles from theft and to craft new statutes to cover interference with such things as computer networks? Consider Arkansas Revised Statutes § 5–41–203 (2006) Unlawful interference with access to computers—Unlawful use or access of computers.

(a)(1)   A person commits unlawful interference with access to computers if the person knowingly and without authorization interferes with, denies, or causes the denial of access to or use of a computer, system, or network to a person who has the duty and right to use [it]. . . .

(b)(1)   A person commits unlawful use or access to computers if the person knowingly and without authorization uses, causes the use of, accesses, attempts to gain access to, or causes access to be gained to a computer, system, network, telecommunications device, telecommunications service, or information service. . . .

(d)(1)   It is an affirmative defense to a charge made pursuant to this section that at the time of the alleged offense the person reasonably believed that:

(A) The person was authorized to use or access the computer, system, network, telecommunications device, telecommunications service, or information service and the use or access by the person was within the scope of that authorization; or

(B) The owner or other person authorized to give consent would authorize the person to use or access the computer, system, network, telecommunications device, telecommunications service, or information service. . . .

3. In 1990 a 24-year-old Cornell University graduate student was accused of planting a computer virus that crippled 6,000 university, corporate and military computers across the nation. Is such conduct a violation of a computer fraud and abuse statute that makes it a felony to intentionally access the computer of another without authorization, even though the accused "hacker" did not take any information out of the computer nor used it for other purposes?

4. For an interesting and thorough analysis of property and theft issues in the context of intangible property, *see* Geraldine Szott Moohr, *Federal Criminal Fraud and the Development of Intangible Property Rights in Information*, 2000 U. Ill. L. Rev. 683 (2000), in which she notes:

How does one take a thing whose value and essence is independent of a physical form? Conversely, how does one maintain ownership of a *res* that can be simultaneously possessed by others? . . .

Indeed, even the term "taking" is something of a misnomer because intangible property cannot be taken in the strict sense; an interference can only violate an abstract right. . . .

Tangible and intangible property also differ as to the relative significance of economic value. Independent economic value is less significant when stolen property is a tangible object, largely because the owner has also lost the rights of possession and use of that object. In contrast, when intangible property is "taken," the owner generally still possesses the property and may continue to use the information or idea. . . . [and] often the victim's only loss is the diminished value of the intangible property. Hence, the weight of economic value increases when intangible interests are taken. . . .

Criminal law is thought to be more effective than civil law in deterring harmful conduct, and it is, therefore, tempting to use criminal law to protect valuable information. Nevertheless, criminal law is not an appropriate context in which to create property rights. First, the blunt criminal verdict may produce the unintended consequence of overdeterrence. Individuals may then be unwilling to embark upon socially beneficial activities, such as engaging in genetic research or exchanging facts from databases, because those activities risk involvement with the criminal justice system. In addition to reducing the public domain, the social costs include diminished competition when firms are afraid to collect data about their competitors or when employees are reluctant to search for optimal employment. . . .

Keeping the focus of a court on the harm element of the statute is consistent with the purpose of the fraud statutes. . . . and, therefore, has the advantage of tempering the judicial practice of defining new types of fraud in terms of the conduct at issue. . . .

Geraldine Szott Moohr, *Federal Criminal Fraud and the Development of Intangible Property Rights in Information*, 2000 U. Ill. L. Rev. 683 (2000).

(2) What Is Property "of Another"?

Assuming that the goods in question qualify as "property," it still must be property "of another" before it can be the subject of larceny or other misappropriation offenses. It may seem simplistic to say that a thief must steal from "another," but there are numerous factual situations in which the accused thief has some claim to the property. Property that is jointly owned, or to which the defendant has a "claim of right" cannot be the subject of larceny. According to the common law, one co-owner cannot be guilty of larceny from another co-owner. However, the "other" whose property is the subject of the larceny need not be the actual owner. Larceny is a crime against possession, not simply ownership. If the person from whom the property is taken has superior property rights to those of the one who takes it, that is sufficient.[13] Thus, a bailee of property has superior rights to a thief, and even a thief in possession of goods has superior rights to those of another thief not in possession. The only requirement is that the possessor's rights in the property be superior to those of the thief.

Applying these principles, which decision on the prehistoric sunken logs in the following case is better reasoned—the majority or the dissent?

---

[13] *See, e.g., McKee v. State*, 200 Ga. 563, 37 S.E.2d 700 (1946) ("ownership" of stolen property may be laid either in the real owner or in the person in whose possession the property was at the time of the theft).

In re the Personal Restraint of John Tortorelli

Supreme Court of Washington, *en banc*, 2003.
149 Wash.2d 82, 66 P.3d 606.

■ CHAMBERS, J.

John Tortorelli was found guilty of theft, trafficking in stolen property, and criminal profiteering, arising from his business of salvaging stray logs and submerged trees from Lake Washington. Tortorelli made several challenges to his convictions in his direct appeal, which were rejected by the Court of Appeals. In this personal restraint petition he raises numerous additional challenges, including insufficiency of the evidence that the logs and trees were "the property of another," as required by the statute under which he was charged, RCW 9A.56.020(1)(a) . . . We conclude as a matter of law that the State owned the salvaged logs and trees, and we reject his other claims.

FACTS

* * *

[Defendant had conducted salvage operations in Lake Washington to recover logs which had rested on the bottom of the lake for centuries, if not thousands of years. He had acquired a license from the state to do so. The license was acquired in the name of the company which held the license before. He did not disclose that when applying for the new license. As a result, he only had to post bond of $500 for a license instead of the $10,000 bond required of new applicants.]

. . . Charts issued by the National Oceanic and Atmospheric Administration indicate that the forest extends to within 30 feet of the surface of the water. Some trees are anchored in the bed of the lake, but others were uprooted in about 1919 when the Corps of Engineers cleared the channel during construction of the Lake Washington ship canal. The timber the crew found at this site consisted of full length fir trees, about a hundred feet tall, with root balls attached. The crew raised the trees, then cut off the root balls and tops and returned them to the water, retaining only the tree trunks.

In August 1991, while Tortorelli was working in the submerged forest area, he began to cooperate with Dr. Gordon Jacoby and Dr. Patrick Williams, scientists doing a tree ring analysis to date the sunken trees. Tortorelli provided slices from 18 different trees, each of which was found to be at least a thousand years old. In return, the scientists helped locate fallen trees by attaching buoys. Dr. Williams testified at trial that Tortorelli's crane would not be strong enough to lift a tree that was still rooted in the bed of the lake. However, the trees raised by Tortorelli, while not rooted, had been partially buried in the mud, as evidenced by preservation of the outer ring. The trees were still encased in mud when raised from the bed of the lake, and had to be dunked back in the water several times to remove mud.

In March 1992, after spending a few months in Everett, Tortorelli returned to Lake Washington, where he went to work in the Gene L. Coulon Memorial Beach Park area. Toward the end of the month, a metro sewer line was ruptured under the channel between Mercer Island and the eastern shore of Lake Washington, triggering extra scrutiny from DNR [Department of Natural Resources]. On becoming aware of Tortorelli's operations in the area, DNR informed him that he needed to obtain a hydraulics project approval. Tortorelli accordingly applied, but carried on his operations without waiting to receive the permit. . . .

In June 1992, Steve Meacham of DNR and Tortorelli had an "extended discussion about where and when it was legal to collect stray logs," during which Meacham read Tortorelli large portions of the log patrol statute. . . . Four months later, the fisheries department executed a search warrant on Tortorelli's home and log patrol area, and seized records. The State determined that he had illegally seized trees worth $165,000. Tortorelli was arrested in August 1994. He was charged with several offenses, which were consolidated into eight counts for trial. . . .

At trial, Tortorelli did not contest nor concede the State's ownership of all the trees. In fact, Tortorelli had conceded the State's ownership of the logs and trees to a log patrol administrator prior to trial. Instead, he claimed a good faith belief that he had permission to salvage logs under Clearwater's license. The State countered, over Tortorelli's objection, with witness testimony that transfers of log patrol licenses are not legally permissible, a topic on which the statute itself is silent. Tortorelli did not take the stand on his own behalf. At the request of the defense, the trial court gave the entire log patrol statute to the jury as an exhibit, rejecting the State's request for a jury instruction on the statute. Tortorelli was convicted of all counts. He was sentenced to 8 concurrent terms ranging from 12 to 43 months and ordered to pay restitution.

ANALYSIS

* * *

Tortorelli was charged under a statute that requires the jury to find he was stealing "the property of another." RCW 9A.56.020(1)(a). He was not charged under subsection (c), which covers misappropriation of lost property. Thus, one of the elements the State must prove is that the logs and trees belonged to someone other than Tortorelli. At trial, Tortorelli did not contest that the State owned the logs and trees. However, in this restraint petition, Tortorelli argues for the first time that the State did not own the logs or, relatedly, that there is insufficient evidence of state ownership of the logs. We find both arguments unavailing.

First, we find as a matter of law, the State of Washington does own both the ancient forest and unbranded stray logs. Our constitution vests ownership of the "beds and shores of all navigable waters in the state" to the State. Const. art. XVII, § 1. While no Washington court has had occasion to rule on the ownership of logs or trees that have been a part of that lake bed for centuries, generally, the State has title to valuable assets within the beds of navigable waters, with exceptions not relevant here.

Further support of State ownership appears in federal law. When the United States was constituted, the Constitution reserved to the original states the shores and beds of navigable waters within their respective boundaries. Under the equal footing doctrine, states subsequently admitted to the Union obtained "the same rights, sovereignty and jurisdiction . . . as the original States possess within their respective borders." More recently, the Submerged Lands Act of 1953 confirmed that the states took title to natural resources found within navigable waters: . . .

Tortorelli disputes whether the trees and logs were natural resources. "Natural resources" is defined in the Submerged Lands Act as "*without limiting the generality thereof*, oil, gas, and all other minerals, and fish, shrimp, oysters, clams, crabs, lobsters, sponges, kelp, and other marine animal and plant life." 43 U.S.C. § 1301(e) (emphasis added). . . . Trees are "supplied by nature." The legislature has recognized that timber is one of the most valuable natural resources in the state. . . . Thus, we have no difficulty in determining as a matter of law that trees are natural resources. The word "marine" is defined as "of or relating to the commerce of the sea." Because the Submerged Lands Act refers to all navigable waters in the United States, "marine" in this context encompasses navigable waters other than seas. We find no legal or logical reason to exclude the submerged trees from the definition of "natural resources" which also includes oil and gas which, like the trees, are resources as a result of ancient natural disasters and other natural occurrences.

The ancient forest trees are located "within" the waters or soil of Lake Washington. Under state and federal statutory and common law, the State owns the submerged trees. It is well established that unambiguous language does not require nor permit judicial construction.

Once the trees have been cut into logs, it is not so clear that they are natural resources as meant by the statute because cut logs are not "supplied by nature." However, there is a separate basis for state ownership of stray logs, the marks and brands statute, which provides: "Unbranded or unmarked stray logs or forest products become the property of the state when recovered." RCW 76.36.020. Therefore, as a matter of law the State also owned the stray logs left by the Corps of Engineers in about 1919.

Tortorelli argues for the first time that under the "law of finds," the State had no title to the logs and trees. The law of finds is a common law principle granting title to the first party to discover and reduce to possession unknown or abandoned artifacts found in the sea. When the ancient trees slid from Mercer Island into Lake Washington 1,100 years ago, the State of Washington did not exist. Native American tribes do not claim ownership over the trees. Thus, Tortorelli argues that the trees are unowned and under the law of finds he is entitled to salvage them. However, we find the law of finds must give way to our state and federal constitutions and laws, and we decline to apply it to these logs.

* * *

In a similar vein, Tortorelli argues that the evidence was insufficient to convict because the State was allegedly relieved of its burden to prove an element of the crime, that the logs were owned by another. . . . Evidence is sufficient to convict when "viewing the evidence in the light most favorable to the prosecution, *any rational trier of fact* could have found the essential elements of the crime *beyond a reasonable doubt.*" . . . We find Tortorelli has not met his burden for collateral relief. First, we note that the jury was instructed to decide whether the prosecution had proved, beyond a reasonable doubt, that Tortorelli had taken the property of another. It did so find. Second, there was a wealth of evidence on the record from which the jury could so find. Tortorelli has shown no prejudice, and accordingly, we reject this claim. . . .

We hold that the State of Washington had title to both the submerged trees and the stray logs. If admission of the log patrol statute was erroneous, the error was invited, and Tortorelli waived his right to object. The failure to object did not constitute ineffective assistance of counsel as it was based on legitimate trial strategy. We therefore affirm the trial court on all counts.

■ SANDERS, J., dissenting.

As the majority notes, [most] counts . . . are all predicated on the State's asserted ownership of the submerged trees and the stray logs. . . . Tortorelli contends the State submitted insufficient evidence to prove it owns the submerged trees Tortorelli allegedly stole from the state.

. . . Tortorelli raises the common law doctrine of finds. Under this doctrine, "the finder of things that have never been appropriated, or that have been abandoned by a former occupant, may take them into his possession as his own property; and the finder of any thing casually lost is its rightful occupant against all but the real owner." . . . Because the ancient submerged trees fell into Lake Washington prior to the existence of the state and federal governments and none of the previous inhabitants lay claim to the trees, Tortorelli asserts ownership of the submerged trees under the law of finds. Without reaching the merits of Tortorelli's common law claim, the majority concludes as a matter of law that the State owns the submerged trees. . . .

The majority reaches this astonishing conclusion by overstating the State's claim to natural resources under the federal Submerged Lands Act of 1953, 43 U.S.C. § 1301. . . . As the majority notes, the act provides a nonexclusive definition of "natural resources." . . . However, its illustrative examples, "oil, gas, and all other minerals, and fish, shrimp, oysters, clams, crabs, lobsters, sponges, kelp, and other marine animal and plant life," 43 U.S.C. § 1301(e), are all resources that grow or evolve naturally below water, rather than resources that once grew on dry land and then happened to end up beneath the surface by accident or natural disaster.

The majority's conclusion is counterintuitive. The Submerged Lands Act speaks of minerals and marine life, not of sunken trees. Moreover, the rule of lenity requires the court to construe an ambiguous statute in a criminal case favorably to the accused. This assures adequate notice, and thus due process, concerning what conduct will be considered illegal. Today's majority gives short shrift to this vital concern.

I therefore respectfully dissent.

■ ALEXANDER, C.J., concurs.

———

(i)   Property of Another: Partners, Spouses and Children

Property that is jointly owned may or may not be "property of another" subject to misappropriation or trespass. In an unincorporated partnership, partner who steals partnership property is not guilty of larceny under common law rules.[14]

In *People v. Zinke*, 76 N.Y.2d 8, 556 N.Y.S.2d 11, 555 N.E.2d 263 (1990), a limited partnership's sole general partner took more than a million dollars by writing checks on the partnership's money-market account and was charged with larceny. The New York Penal Law § 155.05(1) defined "owner" as a person "who has a right to possession [of the property taken] superior to that of the taker, obtainer, or withholder." The New York Court of Appeals held, as a matter of statutory interpretation, that the general partner was a co-owner of the funds and, as at common law, no other partners had superior rights to the funds. Thus, because "a joint or common owner of property shall not be deemed to have a right of possession thereto superior to that of any other joint or common owner thereof," the general partner had not committed larceny.

The New York legislature had rejected Model Penal Code provisions which would have resulted in a different outcome. *See* Model Penal Code Article 223, Theft and Related offenses, § 223.0. Definitions: . . .

> (7) "property of another" includes property in which any person other than the actor has an interest which the actor is not privileged to infringe, regardless of the fact that the actor also has an interest in the property and regardless of the fact that the other person might be precluded from civil recovery because

---

[14] *Dethlefsen v. Stull*, 86 Cal.App.2d 499, 195 P.2d 56 (1948).

the property was used in an unlawful transaction or was subject to forfeiture as contraband. Property in possession of the actor shall not be deemed property of another who has only a security interest therein, even if legal title is in the creditor pursuant to a conditional sales contract or other security agreement.

The *Zinke* court also rejected the State's argument that partners who misappropriate partnership funds should be treated like officers of a corporation who commit larceny if they misappropriate corporate funds finding that officers or agents of a corporation, unlike partners in a partnership, are not co-owners of corporate property.

Similarly, at common law a spouse could not commit larceny by taking property from the other spouse.[15] In the 1859 case of *Regina v. Avery*,[16] the court said:

> A wife cannot be guilty of larceny in simply taking the goods of her husband; and, if a stranger do no more than merely assist her in the taking, inasmuch as the wife, as principal, cannot be guilty of larceny, the stranger, as accessory, cannot be guilty. It has also been held that a stranger who takes goods with the consent of the wife is not guilty of larceny.[17] Where it is clear to the stranger, however, that the husband has not consented to the taking, the rule is different.

The common law rule that a husband could not commit larceny by taking the property of his wife found disfavor with modern courts and resulted in states passing laws such as Michigan's Married Women's Property Acts, M.C.L. 557.21, M.S.A. 26.165. These provisions "gave married women the power to protect, control, and dispose of property in their own name, free from their husbands' interference."[18] Statutes based on the Model Penal Code, typically specify conditions under which spousal property can or cannot be the subject of theft, *e.g.*:

> **§ 223.1(4) Theft from Spouse.** It is no defense that theft was from the actor's spouse, except that misappropriation of household and personal effects, or other property normally accessible to both spouses, is theft only if it occurs after the parties have ceased living together.

A co-owner *may* be guilty of burglary of the premises "of another" if the co-owner has been legally barred from the premises, as with a restraining order. *See, e.g., Turner v. Commonwealth*, 33 Va.App. 88, 531

---

[15] "The wife cannot commit felony of the goods of her husband, for they are one person in law, . . ." 1 HALE, PLEAS OF THE CROWN 513 (1736). Modern statutes normally alter the common law rules concerning larceny of the goods of a partner or spouse.

[16] 8 Cox C.C. 184, 169 Eng. Rep. 1207 (1859).

[17] *Rex v. Harrison*, 168 Eng. Rep. 126 (1756).

[18] *People v. Wallace*, 173 Mich.App. 420, 434 N.W.2d 422, 426 (1988) (upholding Wallace's conviction of the larceny of his wife's bracelet). *But see Calloway v. State*, 176 Ga.App. 674, 337 S.E.2d 397 (1985) (A person cannot commit theft of property of his/her spouse).

S.E.2d 619 (2000), affirming the conviction of Henry Turner was convicted of multiple offenses, including "break[ing] and enter[ing] in the daytime the residence" of his estranged wife "with the intent to commit murder while armed with a deadly weapon." citing *State v. Singletary*, 344 N.C. 95, 472 S.E.2d 895, 899 (1996) (estranged husband has no marital or proprietary right to re-enter former family residence exclusively occupied by wife); *State v. Harold*, 312 N.C. 787, 325 S.E.2d 219, 222 (1985) (prohibition of burglary protects habitation, not ownership); *Calhoun v. State*, 820 P.2d 819, 821–22 (Okla. Crim. App.1991) (lawful possession of property, not ownership, is dispositive issue in burglary prosecution); *Commonwealth v. Majeed*, 548 Pa. 48, 694 A.2d 336 (1997) (after a year of separation, "Mrs. Majeed and her children, alone, occupied the home[;]" "[Majeed's] license or privilege to enter the premises had expired").

The issue of whether property is that "of another" for purposes of burglary charges can also arise in the cases of juveniles accused of burglarizing or stealing from the family home. In *State v. Howe, State v. Jensen, and State v. Walsh*, 116 Wash.2d 466, 805 P.2d 806 (1991) the Supreme Court of Washington consolidated cases of juvenile defendants convicted of burglarizing their parents' homes. Each raised the issue of "unlawful entry:" "whether a parent can revoke a child's privilege to enter the parental home, and under what conditions is that revocation effective?" Because parents are legally required to provide for their children, a child generally has a privilege to enter the family home. Therefore, the State can only prove burglary if the parent (1) expressly and unequivocally ordered the child out of the parental home, and (2) provided some alternative means of assuring that the parents' statutory duty of care is met. In *State v. Howe*, the juvenile, John, had entered his father's home through an unlocked door, taking his father's car, boat, canteen and gas. John was in foster care, living away from the family home, and had been banned from the home until he could exhibit law-abiding behavior. His needs were provided for through foster care, which gave his father the power to revoke his privilege to enter the house, so John's conviction was affirmed. Similarly, in *State v. Jensen*, similarly, the juvenile's parents had placed him in a temporary home through the Department of Social and Health Services because they could not deal with his drug problem, and had clearly told him he could not enter the home unless one of the parents was present. Jensen's burglary of the family silver was also affirmed.

In *State v. Walsh*, however, 16-year-old Michael Walsh's mother simply changed the locks and locked him out of the house after a series of incidents including a keg party for 50–150 people at the family home when his mother was out of town; the police were called, one child was taken away in an ambulance, and some furniture was smashed. Michael's mother made no other living arrangements for him, and at the time he had no other relatives in the area. Police caught Michael and some friends in the house and arrested them for burglary. He had also forged a check to buy pizza. Michael was convicted of burglary, but the conviction was reversed on appeal, finding that "society has a comparable interest in ensuring that children are provided with basic needs, such as food, shelter and clothing." . . . because his mother did not meet her statutory duty to provide for his care, locking him out of the house without arranging for a place for him to stay or giving him money or food, "she could not revoke his privilege to enter the family home. Therefore, his entry was lawful, and his conviction is reversed."

————

(ii)   Property of Another: Lost, Mislaid or Abandoned Property

Appropriation of lost or mislaid property raises interesting questions. Whose property is it? If the finder converts that property to the finder's own use, is that a larceny? Would it be a theft, under modern statutes? Suppose, for example, the recipient buys a piece of furniture on eBay or at auction, only to find that the property they bought (the furniture) contains other property—for instance, jewelry or money?

In *Merry v. Green*, 7 M. & W. 623, 151 Eng. Rep. 916 (1841), Merry purchased a bureau at a public auction. He later discovered a secret drawer in the bureau containing money and other valuables, which he appropriated to his own use. He was prosecuted for felony; after a series of proceedings, the court stated that if Merry had a reasonable ground for believing that he had purchased both the bureau and any contents, he had a colorable right to the property found in the bureau and would not be guilty of larceny. The court added, however:

> If we assume, as the defendant's case was, that the plaintiff had express notice that he was not to have any title to the contents of the secretary if there happened to be anything in it, and indeed without such express notice if he had no ground to believe that he had bought the contents, we are all of opinion that there was evidence to make out a case of larceny. It was contended that there was a delivery of the secretary, and the money in it, to the plaintiff as his own property, which gave him a lawful possession, and that his subsequent misappropriation did not constitute a felony. But it seems to us, that though there was a delivery of the secretary, and a lawful property in it thereby vested in the plaintiff, there was no delivery so as to give a lawful possession of the purse and money. The vendor had no intention to deliver it, nor the vendee to receive it; both were ignorant of its existence; and when the plaintiff discovered that there was a secret drawer containing the purse and money, it was a simple case of finding, and the law applicable to all cases of finding applies to this case.

———

Under the Model Penal Code, § 223.5 a finder of property known to have been lost or mislaid commits theft "if, with purpose to deprive the owner thereof, he fails to take reasonable measures to restore the property to a person entitled to have it." What is a "reasonable measure?" How, too, is it possible to distinguish between property that is lost or mislaid, on the one hand, and property that has been abandoned?

———

NOTE ON TAKING OF ABANDONED, LOST FOUND GOODS

In Brooks v. State, 35 Ohio St. 46 (1878), a street cleaner found a roll of money and picked it up and put it in his pocket without telling his co-workers. He quit his job and began spending the money. The owner, Newton, had advertised his loss in several local newspapers for a month before Brooks found it, though there was no evidence that Brooks had seen any of the notices. Affirming Brooks' larceny conviction, the Supreme Court of Ohio stated:

> Larceny may be committed of property that is casually lost as well as of that which is not. The title to the property, and its constructive possession, still remains in the owner; and the finder if he takes possession of it for his own use, and not for the benefit of the owner, would be guilty of trespass, unless the circumstances were such to show that it had been abandoned by the owner. . . . In Baker v. The State, 29 Ohio St. 184, . . . it was . . . laid down, that "when a person finds goods that have actually been lost, and takes possession with intent to appropriate them to his own use, really believing, at the time, or having good ground to believe, that the owner can be found, it is larceny." . . .

> If the property has not been abandoned by the owner, it is the subject of larceny by the finder, when, at the time he finds it, he had reasonable ground to believe, from the nature of the property or the circumstances under which it is found, that if he does not conceal but deals honestly with it, the owner will appear or be ascertained. But before the finder can be guilty of larceny, the intent to steal the property must have existed at the time he took it into his possession. . . .

The dissent said:

> I do not think the plaintiff was properly convicted. . . . [The money] had lain there several weeks, and the owner had ceased to make search for it. The evidence fails to show that the plaintiff [in error] had any information of a loss previous to the finding, and in his testimony he denied such notice. There was no mark on the money to indicate the owner, nor was there any thing in the attending circumstances pointing to one owner more than another. . . .

_____

(D) GRADES OF LARCENY

Grades of larceny or theft in modern statutes largely depend on the value of the goods in question. Valuation is part of the prosecution's case in a theft or larceny trial. Value is not an element of common-law larceny, so long as the property has at least some value, and this can create issues as to how to determine the value of the goods, and as to when the value of items should be aggregated, and when they should be treated as individual thefts or larcenies. Determining the value of stolen property is usually a function of the jury, and if the prosecution fails to prove the necessary value for a higher grade of theft or larceny, however, a conviction for a lesser-included theft or larceny can still be sustained if there is a showing of some value.[19]

Some items can be more difficult to value than others. Some items for which there is a verifiable market, such as stamps or coins, for example, can be valued more easily than others through testimony by expert appraisers. Items taken from a retail store can normally be valued based on the items' retail price.[20] Valuation of intangibles, especially in computer crimes, can be more difficult than, for example, valuing store merchandise.

DiMaio v. Commonwealth

Supreme Court of Virginia, 2006.
272 Va. 504, 636 S.E.2d 456.

■ Opinion by LEROY R. HASSELL, SR., C.J.

In this appeal, we consider whether the Commonwealth presented sufficient evidence of value to support convictions for computer fraud in violation of Code § 18.2–152.3 and larceny in violation of Code § 18.2–111.

Jeremy Dion DiMaio was convicted in a bench trial of computer fraud in violation of Code § 18.2–152.3; computer trespass in violation of Code § 18.2–152.4(A); embezzlement in violation of Code § 18.2–111; . . . and attempted extortion in violation of Code §§ 18.2–59 and –26. His convictions were affirmed by the Court of Appeals. We awarded DiMaio an appeal limited to the issues whether the Commonwealth established the value necessary for convictions of computer fraud and larceny.

---

[19] _See, e.g., United States v. Bryant_, 454 F.2d 248 (4th Cir. 1972) (proof of value was required when a defendant was charged with grand larceny, but where the evidence failed to establish such value, a new trial was not required since the defendant would stand convicted of the lesser included misdemeanor offense of larceny of property having a value not exceeding $100).

[20] _See, e.g., Brown v. State_, 143 Ga.App. 678, 239 S.E.2d 556 (1977) (in thefts from retail establishments, the retail value or price is the standard of valuation, and that the wholesale price actually paid by the store is not relevant).

Jeremy Dion DiMaio was employed as the director of human resources for S & M Brands, Inc., trading as Bailey's Cigarettes. William W. Snell served as vice-president and chief financial officer of S & M Brands. In July 2003, S & M Brands made a loan of $6,500 to DiMaio, memorialized in a written loan agreement signed by DiMaio and Stephen Bailey, president of S & M Brands. DiMaio agreed that repayment for the loan, both principal and interest, would be by fixed deduction from his payroll checks commencing in January 2004.

DiMaio informed S & M Brands on April 7, 2004, that he planned to resign as director of human resources effective April 23, 2004. After DiMaio had submitted his letter of resignation, Bailey learned that DiMaio had contacted an employee in the company's payroll department and directed her to refrain from deducting loan payments from his payroll checks and that she had complied with his request. DiMaio was required, pursuant to the terms of the loan agreement, to repay the balance due on the loan within five days from the date of resignation or termination of his employment from S & M Brands. Bailey agreed to extend the period of repayment provided DiMaio gave S & M Brands the proceeds from his final payroll check and return a check that had been issued to DiMaio for his unused vacation time. Even though DiMaio had agreed to this arrangement, he refused to comply. When Bailey learned that DiMaio had failed to honor this agreement, he fired DiMaio and asked him to leave the company's premises immediately.

Bailey appointed Snell to serve as the interim human resources director after DiMaio's termination. When Snell assumed the position, he discovered that certain files that had been located on the computer that S & M Brands had issued to DiMaio were missing. S & M Brands' entire human resource directory, including business forms and templates, had been removed from the computer. Approximately 829 personnel files were missing. Additionally, signed covenants not to compete that S & M Brands had executed with its employees had been physically removed from S & M Brands' premises.

Snell contacted DiMaio and inquired about the missing computer data. DiMaio responded that he had transferred the computer documents to an off-site server and that he would be "willing to provide the files to the company under the right circumstances." "[DiMaio] told me that the documents were not on the computer, and they were not on the server, which has designated password protection for confidential documents in the [human resources] area. I asked him where they were, and he told me that they were on a secure third-party server on the Internet. And that he had placed them there. I didn't have to worry because he had them in a secure location. I asked him how I was going to get ahold of them, and he said that he would be willing to provide the files to the company under the right circumstances. And he expressed some interest in establishing an agreement between himself and the company that would return the files in exchange for forgiveness of the debt that he had personally with S & M Brands."

* * *

Snell, who had experience in evaluating companies and properties, qualified as an expert witness, without objection, and was permitted to render opinions regarding the market value of the 829 personnel files that DiMaio had taken. He testified that the fair market value of the files exceeded $10,000. Snell also testified, over DiMaio's objection that is not the basis of an assignment of error in this appeal, that the value of the personnel files that DiMaio took "would be tens of thousands of dollars or worse . . . that the value of the documents of the company could be much greater."

Everett W. Gee, III, "in-house counsel" for S & M Brands, testified, without objection, that the fair market value of just the computer files that DiMaio took "would run you somewhere at $3,790 . . . for a HR software package that would cover a sliver of the forms that we had." Gee also testified, without objection, that the value of the covenants not to compete exceeded $5,000. He explained that he had researched the jurisprudence in ten states where S & M Brands has employees and that the covenants not to compete were created to comply with the employment laws of those states. . . . Gee also stated that he could receive "$5,000 to $6,000 just for the form" if he sold the form to a willing buyer.

DiMaio argues that the Commonwealth failed to establish the value of the computer records and, therefore, as a matter of law, the evidence was insufficient to support a conviction of computer fraud. . . . We disagree.

Proof that property has some value is sufficient to sustain a conviction of petit larceny, but when the value of the items stolen determines the grade of the offense, the value must be alleged, and the Commonwealth must prove, beyond a reasonable doubt, the value satisfies the statutory requirement for felony larceny. . . . We have stated that "[t]he test is market value, and particularly retail value." *Robinson*, 258 Va. 3, at 5, 516 S.E.2d 475, at 476. The Commonwealth presented sufficient evidence to establish that the value of the computer records that DiMaio took exceeded $200.00. For example, Snell testified, without objection, that the fair market value of the 829 personnel files that DiMaio took had a fair market value in excess of $10,000. . . . Gee testified, without objection, that the files had a value far in excess of $3,790.

DiMaio, relying upon a headnote appended to our decision in *Lund v. Commonwealth*, 217 Va. 688, 232 S.E.2d 745 (1977), argues that the Commonwealth failed to establish that the value of the computer files exceeded $200. We disagree. Initially, we note that headnotes are not authoritative statements of the law of this Commonwealth. Headnotes

are the "abstract of the points decided in each case" required by Code
§ 17.1–322. However, the authoritative statements of case law are
contained in the text of opinions issued by this Court. Additionally, our
decision in *Lund v. Commonwealth* is not pertinent to the resolution of
this appeal. The defendant in *Lund* was indicted for violation of statutes
that related to larceny by false pretense. In *Lund*, we emphasized that
the defendant was charged with certain crimes related to the use of a
computer and the unauthorized use of the computer, but at that time,
those acts did not constitute the crime of larceny. Additionally, we held
that the Commonwealth failed to establish the value of the items that
were purportedly taken. In the appeal before this Court, unlike the
situation in *Lund*, the Commonwealth established fair market value of
the items taken through the testimony of Gee and Snell, and the current
penal statutes prohibit the use of a computer in the commission of a
felony.

DiMaio also argues that the Commonwealth failed to establish the
value of the covenants not to compete and, therefore, his conviction for
larceny cannot be sustained. We disagree. As we previously stated, Gee
testified, without objection, that he had created a specialized form that
complied with the laws of ten states when he drafted the covenants not
to compete and that the market value of the form was between $5,000
and $7,000. . . . This evidence of value is sufficient to satisfy the statutory
requirement for the crime of larceny. . . .

For the foregoing reasons, we will affirm the convictions.

Affirmed.

————

NOTES: VALUATION

1. In State v. Jacquith, 272 N.W.2d 90 (S.D.1978) appellant Norman
Jacquith, Jr., was arrested for breaking into a van and stealing a pair of
prescription sunglasses. He appealed the grand larceny conviction,
contending that the prosecution had failed to prove that the value of the
sunglasses was above the $50.00 statutory threshold for grand larceny. The
State had argued that because there was "no market" for second-hand
prescription sunglasses, a fair market value could not be ascertained.
Therefore, it argued, replacement value was the proper standard. The South
Dakota Supreme Court reversed, finding that "fair market value" was the
proper test. The court held that when the prosecution contends that there is
no fair market value for the goods, the prosecution will have the burden of
proving that no market exists and that a different test should be used. If it
is determined that no market exists from which a fair market value could be
ascertained, then the jury may properly use the "replacement value less
depreciation" test.

Sometimes, of course, replacement value will be as difficult to ascertain
as fair market value. In one such case, testimony of the victim of a burglary

and attempted larceny was held valid to establish the value of an antique cherrywood desk, despite her not being an expert in furniture valuation, where the valuation was based on receipts and documentation in the victim's possession or which the victim had used to form her valuation, and where it was only necessary to establish that the item was worth more than $250, and not to establish its precise value. *See* Thompson v. State, 910 So.2d 60 (Miss.App.2005).

2. Aggregation of Multiple Thefts or Larcenies

Generally, separate thefts can only be aggregated if they are shown to be part of a single plan or scheme. For example, in Buckwalter v. State, 23 P.3d 81 (Alaska App. 2001), a jury convicted Daniel Roy and Donna Buckwalter of first-degree theft and scheme to defraud for stealing more than $25,000 in goods from businesses in Anchorage, Eagle River, and Wasilla and pawning the goods for cash. Though no single theft reached the threshold amount, at trial, the State presented evidence that the Buckwalters had pawned items, many of which Buckwalter had admitted were stolen, for a total of between $22,000 and $26,762.54. Rejecting defendants' aggregation argument, the Alaska Supreme Court noted,

> The common law allowed aggregation of misdemeanor thefts to support a felony charge only if the thefts were from the same owner at the same time and place and were motivated by a single criminal intent.[21] Alaska's aggregation statute, AS 11.46.980(c), is adapted from the less rigid Model Penal Code approach. Model Penal Code § 223.1 takes a "middle ground" between the common law requirement of "unity of place, time, and victim" and the unlimited aggregation of thefts permitted by some state criminal codes.[22] . . .

> Virtually all the jurisdictions that have considered this issue (and that generally follow the Model Penal Code approach) have concluded that a jury must decide whether separate thefts are part of one course of conduct for purposes of aggregation.[23] . . .

> We conclude that Alaska's aggregation statute was enacted to require proof of a single course of conduct. The legislative

---

[21] *See generally* Turner v. State, 636 S.W.2d 189, 195 (Tex. Crim. App.1980); State v. Garman, 100 Wash.App. 307, 984 P.2d 453, 456 (1999); Model Penal Code (MPC) § 223.1(2)(c) cmt. 3(b) at 141–42 (1980); *Larceny—Takings as Single or Separate*, 53 A.L.R.3d 398 (1973).

[22] MPC § 223.1(2)(c) cmt. 3(b) at 141–42 & n. 37 (citing La. Rev. Stat. § 14:67, which permits aggregation of takings "by a number of distinct acts of the offender").

[23] *See, e.g.,* State v. Desimone, 241 Conn. 439, 696 A.2d 1235, 1244 (1997) (citing Conn. Gen. Stat. § 53a–121(b)); State v. Barthell, 554 So.2d 17, 18 (Fla.3d DCA 1989) (citing Fla. Stat. § 812.012(9)(c) (*sic.*, actually Fla. Stat. § 812.012(10)(c) (valuation)); State v. Amsden, 300 N.W.2d 882, 886 (Iowa 1981) (citing Iowa Code § 714.3); State v. Sampson, 120 N.H. 251, 413 A.2d 590, 592 (1980) (citing N.H. Rev. Stat. § 637:2 V(a)); State v. Damiano, 322 N.J.Super. 22, 730 A.2d 376, 392–93 (1999) (citing N.J. Stat. 2C:20–2b(4)); State v. Baca, 123 N.M. 124, 934 P.2d 1053, 1056 (1997) (citing MPC § 223.1(2)(c)); State v. Johnston, 478 N.W.2d 281, 283 (S.D.1991); Turner v. State, 636 S.W.2d 189, 196 (1980) (citing Tex. Penal Code § 31.09); State v. Garman, 100 Wash.App. 307, 984 P.2d 453, 457 (1999) (citing former Wash. Rev. Code 9A.56.010(17)(c) (1998)). *But see* State v. Heslop, 842 S.W.2d 72, 75 (Mo.1992) (*en banc*) (holding that aggregation statute serves the limited purpose of permitting the *state* to combine the value of property stolen during a single course of conduct to determine if the defendant should be charged with a class C felony or a lesser offense).

commentary to the aggregation statute states that its purpose was to increase the potential punishment for individuals who had engaged in a "calculated" series of thefts.[24]

Because the Buckwalters had been convicted of "scheme to defraud" in connection with the series of thefts, the court found that the jury had necessarily found a single course of conduct. They therefore found that any error was harmless, and affirmed the conviction.

C. LARCENY BY TRICK

A crucial element of larceny at early common law was the taking of the property by the defendant. What if the owner of the property willingly gave the property to the defendant though, only to later discover that he had parted with the property because of fraud or trickery? In those cases, the perpetrator had not taken or asported the property in the traditional sense. Does this amount to larceny at common law, or must it be some other crime? And how do modern jurisdictions handle this problem?

The King v. Pear

Central Criminal Court, 1779.
1 Leach 212, 168 Eng. Rep. 208.

The prisoner was indicted for stealing a black horse, the property of Samuel Finch. It appeared in evidence that Samuel Finch was a Livery-Stable-keeper in the Borough; and that the prisoner, on the 2d of July 1779, hired the horse of him to go to Sutton, in the county of Surry, and back again, saying on being asked where he lived, that he lodged at No. 25 in King-street, and should return about eight o'clock the same evening. He did not return; and it was proved that he had sold the horse on the very day he had hired it, to one William Hollist, in Smithfield Market; and that he had no lodging at the place to which he had given the prosecutor directions.

The learned Judge said: There had been different opinions on the law of this class of cases; that the general doctrine then was that if a horse be let for a particular portion of time, and after that time is expired, the party hiring, instead of returning the horse to its owner, sell it and convert the money to his own use, it is felony, because there is then no privity of contract subsisting between the parties; that in the present case the horse was hired to take a journey into Surry, and the prisoner sold him the same day, without taking any such journey; that there were also other circumstances which imported that at the time of the hiring the prisoner had it in intention to sell the horse, as his saying that he lodged at a place where in fact be was not known. He therefore left it with the Jury to consider, Whether the prisoner meant at the time of the

---

[24] Commentary on the Alaska Revised Criminal Code, Senate Journal Supp. No. 47 at 34–35, 1978 Senate Journal 1399.

hiring to take such journey, but was afterwards tempted to sell the horse? for if so he must be acquitted; but that if they were of opinion that at the time of the hiring the journey was a mere pretence to get the horse into his possession, and he had no intention to take such journey but intended to sell the horse, they would find that fact specially for the opinion of the Judges.

The Jury found that the facts above stated were true; and also that the prisoner had hired the horse with a fraudulent view and intention of selling it immediately.

The question was referred to the Judges, Whether the delivery of the horse by the prosecutor to the prisoner, had so far changed the possession of the property, as to render the subsequent conversion of it a mere breach of trust, or whether the conversion was felonious?

The Judges differed greatly in opinion on this case; and delivered their opinions *seriatim* upon it at Lord Chief Justice De Gray's house on 4th February 1780 and on the 22nd of the same month Mr. Baron Perryn delivered their opinion on it. The majority of them thought, That the question, as to the original intention of the prisoner in hiring the horse, had been properly left to the jury; and as they had found, that his view in so doing was fraudulent, the parting with the property had not changed the nature of the possession, but that it remained unaltered in the prosecutor at the time of the conversion; and that the prisoner was therefore guilty of felony.

————

NOTES

1. What is the court holding in *Pear*? How can there be larceny if there was no taking?

2. Is the *Pear* court inventing a new crime? If so, when exactly did Pear commit the offense? And if he did not commit the crime of "larceny" how can he be guilty if he was charged with "larceny" and not some other offense?

3. Why wasn't larceny by trick a recognized offense prior to the *Pear* decision? As Professor George Fletcher has explained:

> The traditional approach to larceny was built on . . . structural principles which expressed the distinction between a public sphere of criminal conduct and a private sphere subject at most to regulation by the rules of private law. One of these structural principles, possessorial immunity, was the explicit rule of the courts that transferring possession of an object conferred immunity from the criminal law on the party receiving possession, for subsequent misuse or misappropriation of the entrusted object. This rule was fundamental in defining the contours of larceny as well as the boundary between larceny and the newer offenses that developed in the eighteenth and nineteenth centuries.

George P. Fletcher, *The Metamorphosis of Larceny*, 89 HARV. L. REV. 469, 472 (1976). Professor Wayne LaFave has similarly explained that:

> . . . The judges who determined the scope of larceny (including its limitations) apparently considered larceny to be a crime designed to prevent breaches of the peace rather than aimed at protecting property from wrongful appropriation. The unauthorized taking of property, even by stealth, from the owner's possession is apt to produce an altercation if the owner discovers the property moving out of his possession and into the possession of the thief. But when the wrongdoer already has the owner's property in his possession at the time he misappropriates it . . . or when he obtains the property from the owner by telling him lies . . . there is not the same danger . . .

WAYNE R. LAFAVE, CRIMINAL LAW § 19.1(a) (2010).

4. Although many states no longer use the terminology of "larceny by trick" the basic problem of gaining possession of property by lying or trickery is very common today. How do modern courts handle the problem? Consider the next case.

———

State v. Bugely

Court of Appeals of Iowa, 1987.
408 N.W.2d 394.

■ SACKETT, JUDGE.

Defendant Mark Kane Bugely appeals from his conviction of theft in the first degree in violation of Iowa Code §§ 714.1(2) and 714.2(1) (1985) for misappropriation of a car he rented. Defendant contends there was insufficient evidence in the record to establish that a final return date had been agreed to by the defendant and Ames National Car Rental (National) agency. As such, defendant argues the state failed to prove beyond a reasonable doubt defendant's retention of the car was inconsistent with the owner's rights in the property as required under Iowa Code § 714.1(2) (1985). We affirm.

On September 14, 1985, defendant entered into a rental agreement with National to rent a car until September 16, 1985. Defendant said he needed the car to get to work while his own was being repaired in Nevada, Iowa. Defendant put down a $100 cash deposit for the rental car, which was valued at $6,500. Before the car was rented National verified the information defendant gave with his bank and place of employment. The rental agreement provided if the car was not returned on time the rate charged could be changed by National. Defendant did not return the car on September 16, 1985. He called National twice and the agreement was extended, first until September 20, 1985, and then until September

27, 1985. Defendant did not return the rental car on September 27, 1985, and did not contact National after that date.

National telephoned defendant's mother, the number defendant had given National to reach him. She said defendant was not there and she did not know when he would return. The defendant did not return National's call. National filed a criminal complaint with the Ames police with regard to the missing car. Cedar Rapids police arrested defendant on October 12, 1985, and the rental car was recovered. The total owed under the rental agreement was $1,497.44. Defendant was charged by trial information with theft in the first degree. After a bench trial the trial court entered findings of fact, conclusions of law and a verdict of guilty. This appeal followed. . . .

II.

Iowa Code § 714.1(2) provides a person commits theft when the person:

> Misappropriates property which the person has in trust, or property of another which the person has in his or her possession or control, whether such possession or control is lawful or unlawful, by using or disposing of it in a manner which is inconsistent with or a denial of the trust or of the owner's rights in such property, or conceals found property, or appropriates such property to his or her own use, when the owner of such property is known to him or her. *Failure by a bailee or lessee of personal property to return the property within seventy-two hours after a time specified in a written agreement of lease or bailment shall be evidence of misappropriation . . . .*

Theft by misappropriation is a general intent crime. The state must prove the following essential elements beyond a reasonable doubt:

1. Defendant had possession of the car owned by National, and

2. Defendant misappropriated the car by using it in a manner inconsistent with the owner's rights (*i.e.*, defendant failed to return the car 72 hours after the time specified in the rental agreement).

The fact finder may *infer* misappropriation from failure to return the property within 72 hours of the rental agreement deadline. Such evidence is a permissive presumption of misappropriation and a rational reference "supported by common sense and experience."

Defendant asserts the state failed to establish a "time specified in a written agreement" as required under § 714.1(2), therefore, his failure to return the car did not constitute misappropriation. Defendant argues the original date in the written agreement cannot be the "time specified" because it was modified at least twice. He also argues there is insufficient evidence to support September 27 was the final deadline. Rather, defendant suggests the rental agreement was an open-ended contract which anticipated returns after the expiration of the agreement because the agreement specified the agency could charge a higher rate for cars returned late. As such, defendant asserts his retention of the car was not inconsistent with National's rights to the property.

Defendant is correct that there must be sufficient evidence of a specified deadline for return to support conviction of theft by a bailee of a rental car. In *People v. McKim*, 99 Mich. App. 829, 298 N.W.2d 625, 627 (1980), the court held that the time within which a defendant is required to return a rental car must be definite and clear to sustain a conviction for theft of a rental car. There, the rental agency extended the defendant's rental agreement twice but the defendant did not return the car. The appellate court reversed the defendant's conviction because the letter the agency sent defendant demanding only that the car be returned "as soon as possible."

On the other hand, in *DeMond v. Superior Court of Los Angeles County*, 368 P.2d 865 (Cal.1962), the court found there was sufficient evidence to sustain a finding of misappropriation for failure to return a rental car. The defendant had obtained an extension of the rental agreement and was told to return the car "in two or three days" but was still driving the car two months beyond the expiration of the agreement without authorization to do so.

We find the factual situation in *State v. Heemer*, 489 P.2d 107 (Utah 1971), is analogous to the instant case. In *Heemer*, the defendant rented a car for one week by making a cash down payment. The car was not returned at the end of that time. Without making any further payments on the agreement the defendant managed, through various excuses given by phone, to extend the rental agreement. While the rental agency had given permission for the defendant to continue to use the car on "a somewhat open-ended contract," the agency told defendant that he must surrender the car "the following Monday." The agency filed a criminal complaint when the defendant did not return the car on the final date. Even though the various extensions had been given, the court found there was sufficient evidence to support defendant's conviction for embezzlement of the car because there was no evidence the agency had ever consented to defendant's retention of the car past the Monday deadline.

In the instant case, viewing the evidence in the light most favorable to the state, we find there is sufficient evidence from the facts in the record and surrounding circumstances to support the trial court's finding that September 27 was the deadline for defendant to return the car. The vehicle status sheets showed National extended the return date until September 20 and then until September 27. There was no status sheet showing additional extensions of the return date. In addition, prior to September 27 defendant called twice to extend the rental agreement. He did not call again after September 27, the required return date. Furthermore, there is no evidence National consented either to an open-ended agreement to start September 27 or to extending the return date past September 27. We therefore find defendant's contention there was "no time specified" to return the rental car to be without merit. We also reject defendant's argument the alleged ambiguity of the return date made the rental agreement an open-ended contract prosecutable only under civil remedies.

We hold defendant's conviction for theft of the rental car is supported by substantial evidence and affirm the trial court.

AFFIRMED.

————

NOTES

1. At early common law, misconduct like that in *Bugely* would not be the business of the criminal justice system. Ames National Car Rental would have to seek redress in civil court. Is the current system preferable to the common law approach? How far should the criminal law venture into breaches of commercial obligations? Is the threat of criminal liability necessary to deter misconduct?

2. Many states have statutes that specifically cover the fact pattern in the *Bugely* case. For instance, in Florida,

> Whoever, after hiring or leasing personal property or equipment under an agreement to return the personal property to the person letting the personal property or equipment or his or her agent at the termination of the period for which it was let, shall, without the consent of the person or persons knowingly abandon or refuse to return the personal property or equipment as agreed, commits a misdemeanor of the second degree . . . unless the value of the personal property or equipment is of a value of $300 or more; in that case the person commits a felony of the third degree . . .

Fla. Stat. Ann. § 812.155(3).

3. Delivery by mistake, in which the possessor of property delivers it inadvertently, did not give rise to larceny at common law, if the recipient took and carried the property away while unaware of the mistake, even if the recipient later appropriates the goods. Under traditional analysis, there was no *actus reus* because the goods had been delivered voluntarily, though mistakenly, and therefore had not been "taken." Further, there was no *mens rea* because the intent to steal was not present at the moment the defendant acquired control of the delivered goods. By contrast, the Model Penal Code § 223.5 provides:

> Theft of Property Lost, Mislaid, or Delivered by Mistake:

> A person who comes into control of property of another that he knows to have been lost, mislaid, or delivered under a mistake as

to the nature or amount of the property or the identity of the recipient is guilty of theft if, with purpose to deprive the owner thereof, he fails to take reasonable measures to restore the property to a person entitled to have it.

D. FALSE PRETENSES

In 1757, Parliament created the crime of obtaining property by false pretenses. The statute was necessary to fill a gap in the law of larceny. As we saw in Section C, larceny by trick involves obtaining possession of property by false representations. What then is the crime of false pretenses? Is it the same behavior, just with a different name? Or does the prosecution have to prove something additional?

Baker v. Commonwealth
Supreme Court of Virginia, 1983.
225 Va. 192, 300 S.E.2d 788.

■ STEPHENSON, JUSTICE.

Robert Lee Baker was indicted for and convicted of grand larceny. The only substantive jury instruction offered by the Commonwealth purported to define larceny by false pretenses. Baker contends this instruction did not set forth all the necessary elements of larceny by false pretenses, and, in any case, the evidence is insufficient to support a conviction on this charge.

Baker and Donald Shumaker went to an automobile dealership in Henrico County. They were aware that the dealership required customers to leave a vehicle as security while they test-drove one of the dealer's automobiles. After receiving a signal from Baker, Shumaker asked to test-drive a Jeep. Leaving as security a truck which he had fraudulently obtained elsewhere, Baker drove the Jeep away and failed to return it. Baker paid Shumaker $100 for his part in the crime.

Baker contends that, to be guilty of larceny by false pretenses, one must make a false representation that induces the victim to pass both title to and possession of the property to the defendant. Since the jury instruction at issue did not state that passage of title was an element of the crime, Baker contends his conviction cannot stand. He further argues that, even if the instruction had been proper, no evidence was presented that the dealership passed title to the Jeep to Baker and Shumaker. We agree.

"An essential element of larceny by false pretenses is that both title to and possession of property must pass from the victim to the defendant (or his nominee)." *Cunningham v. Commonwealth,* 219 Va. 399, 402, 247 S.E.2d 683, 685 (1978). "The gravamen of the offense . . . is the obtainment of ownership of property . . ." *Quidley v. Commonwealth,* 221 Va. 963, 966, 275 S.E.2d 622, 624 (1981). The jury instruction offered by the Commonwealth dealt only with possession and not with title to the property. It was therefore erroneous. Further, no evidence was presented that the dealership passed title to the vehicle to Baker or Shumaker.

The Commonwealth argues that, even if it failed to prove larceny by false pretenses, the evidence at trial was sufficient to sustain a conviction of the common law crime of larceny by trick and that the jury instruction set forth all the elements of this crime. While this may be so, we decline to affirm the conviction on this ground. An accused is entitled to be clearly informed of the charge against him. Va. Const. art. I, § 8. Where, as here, the Commonwealth elects to prosecute a defendant for a specific category of larceny, and no other, its case must either prevail or fail upon that election. The Commonwealth cannot retrospectively argue that Baker should be convicted of a crime for which he was not prosecuted, and on which the jury was not instructed.

For the reasons stated, the judgment of the trial court will be reversed and the indictment dismissed.

Reversed and dismissed.

———

NOTE

Notice how Virginia's continued adherence to the distinction between larceny by trick and false pretenses caused major problems for prosecutors in *Baker*. Also notice how the fact pattern in Baker is actually a "relatively easy [case]" because "vehicles come with paper titles issued by the state." John G. Douglass, *Rethinking Theft Crimes in Virginia*, 38 U. RICH. L. REV. 13, 21 (2003). How would prosecutors have fared with a more complicated set of facts in which the holder of title was not specified on a piece of paper? Consider the next case.

Davies v. Commonwealth
Court of Appeals of Virginia, 1999.
15 Va. App. 350, 423 S.E.2d 839.

■ KOONTZ, CHIEF JUDGE.

In a jury trial, Ralph Donald Davies (Davies) was convicted of two counts of grand larceny by false pretenses. On appeal, he contends that (1) the trial court erred in refusing to instruct the jury that it must find that Davies obtained title to the property, and (2) the evidence was insufficient to prove that title to the property passed. For the reasons that follow, we hold that although the trial court erred in instructing the jury regarding the elements of the offense, the error was harmless. We also hold that sufficient evidence supports the convictions.

On August 21, 1990, Davies filed a credit application in the name of Brian Stark at a Circuit City store. He produced an identification card in the name of Brian Stark. Upon approval of his credit application, Davies purchased on credit a camcorder, a tripod and a car stereo. The value of this property totaled $1,306.16. Davies signed the sales slip acknowledging his receipt of the property and took it from the store premises.

On the same day, Davies also filed a credit application in the name of Brian Stark at a Luskins store. He was approved for credit and purchased on credit a camcorder with a selling price of $799.99. He then removed the camcorder from the store.

On both credit applications, Davies claimed to be Brian Stark, an attorney employed by the firm of Tate and Bywater. However, neither "Brian Stark" nor Davies had ever been employed by that firm. On September 5, 1990, Davies admitted that Brian Stark was not his real name. He further admitted that he had obtained the identification bearing that name from the Division of Motor Vehicles by presenting items taken from a wallet he had found. He then consulted a telephone book to locate someone with the same name so that he could provide an address on the applications.

At trial, Davies offered instruction "F," which would have required the jury, in order to find Davies guilty of grand larceny by false pretenses, to find that the owner of the property parted with both "possession of and title to" the property. Over the objection of defense counsel, the trial court deleted the words "and title to" and granted the instruction as amended.[1] Davies assigns error to the trial court's refusal to instruct the jury that the owner must be deprived of both possession of and title to the property. Moreover, he contends that the evidence was insufficient to prove that the stores parted with title to the property.

"It is elementary that a jury must be informed as to the essential elements of the offense; a correct statement of the law is one of the 'essentials of a fair trial.' " *Darnell v. Commonwealth,* 6 Va.App. 485, 488, 370 S.E.2d 717, 719 (1988) (quoting *Dowdy v. Commonwealth,* 220 Va. 114, 116, 255 S.E.2d 506, 508 (1979)). " 'An essential element of larceny by false pretenses is that both title to and possession of property must pass from the victim to the defendant' . . . 'The gravamen of the offense . . . is the obtainment of ownership of property.' " *Bray v. Commonwealth,* 9 Va.App. 417, 424, 388 S.E.2d 837, 840 (1990) (citations omitted). The requirement that the defendant obtain ownership of the property, rather

---

[1] The amended instruction directed the jury that it must find Davies guilty of each of the following elements beyond a reasonable doubt:

    (1) That the defendant made a false representation of a past event or an existing fact; and

    (2) That when the representation was made, the defendant had an intent to defraud the owner by causing it to part with the possession of its property; and

    (3) That because of the false representation, the owner parted with the possession of its property; and

    (4) That the property taken was worth $200.00 or more.

than mere possession, distinguishes the offense of larceny by false pretenses from the offense of larceny. Therefore, the trial court's refusal to instruct the jury regarding the essential elements of the offense was error.

However, we find that the error in failing to instruct the jury regarding the passage of title was harmless.

The crux of the harmless error analysis is whether the defendant received a fair trial on the merits and substantial justice has been achieved. When an error at trial has affected the verdict, the defendant has been deprived of a fair trial on the merits and substantial justice has not been achieved.

Timmons v. Commonwealth, ___ Va.App. ___, ___, 421 S.E.2d 894, 896 (1992) . . . The issue, then, is whether the erroneous jury instruction affected the jury's verdict so as to deprive Davies of a fair trial. We hold that it did not.

In support of his contention that the erroneous instruction constitutes reversible error, Davies cites *Baker v. Commonwealth,* 225 Va. 192, 300 S.E.2d 788 (1983), where the Court reversed a conviction for false pretenses because the jury was not instructed that the passage of title was an element of the crime. However, Davies' reliance on *Baker* is misplaced because that case involved the larceny of an automobile. Generally, title to a motor vehicle passes upon transfer of the certificate of title. By comparison, in a retail sales transaction involving goods of the nature at issue here, title passes upon the seller's delivery of the goods. Code § 8.2–401(2).[2] . . .

At trial, Davies did not dispute that he obtained possession of the electronics equipment from Circuit City and Luskins. The evidence produced at trial showed that on the basis of the fraudulent information provided in the credit applications, Luskins and Circuit City sold Davies this electronics equipment on credit. At both stores, the property was delivered to Davies, who took possession of the property and left the store with the property. Thus, the evidence produced at trial showed that Davies obtained ownership, or "title," of the property by false pretenses upon the sellers' delivery and Davies' simultaneous receipt of the goods. Consequently, because the undisputed evidence established as a matter of law that ownership (albeit voidable because of his fraud) of the goods passed to Davies, the erroneous instruction did not affect the verdict. We hold, therefore, that the trial court's refusal to instruct the jury that "title" to the property must pass was harmless error.

Moreover, we find Davies' contention that the evidence was insufficient to prove that title to the property had passed to be without

---

[2] Code § 8.2–401(2) provides, in pertinent part: "Unless otherwise explicitly agreed title passes to the buyer at the time and place at which the seller completes his performance with reference to the physical delivery of the goods."

merit. As we have already found, ownership, or title, to the equipment that Davies purchased from the two stores passed upon delivery of the goods to him. The evidence is undisputed that Davies left Circuit City and Luskins in possession of two camcorders, a tripod and a car stereo. Because Davies had both possession of and title to the goods when he received them, the evidence clearly supports his convictions.

For these reasons, the convictions for larceny by false pretenses are affirmed.

Affirmed.

———

NOTES

1. If you take an advanced course in criminal procedure, you may focus in more detail on the harmless error doctrine. In the meantime, for an overview of the doctrine, see WAYNE R. LaFAVE ET AL., CRIMINAL PROCEDURE § 27.6 (5th ed. 2009). For current purposes, all you need to recognize is that an appellate court can determine that there was a mistake at trial—either a violation of the constitution, a statute, or a rule of procedure—and nevertheless uphold the defendant's conviction because the error did not affect the outcome. In other words, the appellate court believes that if the error had not occurred, the defendant still would have been convicted. How can the appellate court say that in this case? Do we know that the jury would have concluded that title passed to Davies when he left the stores?

2. Why did prosecutors only bring false pretenses charges against Davies? Isn't he also guilty of identity theft? Under Virginia law,

> A.   It shall be unlawful for any person, without the authorization or permission of the person or persons who are the subjects of the identifying information, with the intent to defraud, for his own use or the use of a third person, to:
>
> > 1.   Obtain, record or access identifying information which is not available to the general public that would assist in accessing financial resources, obtaining identification documents, or obtaining benefits of such other person;
> >
> > 2.   Obtain money, credit, loans, goods or services through the use of identifying information of such other person;
> >
> > 3.   Obtain identification documents in such other person's name; or
> >
> > 4.   Obtain, record or access identifying information while impersonating a law-enforcement officer or an official of the government of the Commonwealth.

* * *

Va. Code Ann. § 18.2–186.3. Beginning in the 1990s, identity theft exploded as a major problem in the United States. *See* Lynn M. LoPucki, *Did Privacy Cause Identity Theft?* 54 HASTINGS L.J. 1277, 1278 (2003). Accordingly, statutes specifically criminalizing identity theft are fairly new, with Arizona introducing the first one in 1996. *See* David Lish, Comment, *Would the Real David Lish Please Stand Up: A Proposed Solution to Identity Theft*, 38 ARIZ. ST. L.J. 319, 325 (2006). The Virginia statute excerpted above was not codified until 2000.

People v. DeWald

Court of Appeals of Michigan, 2005.
267 Mich. App. 365, 705 N.W.2d 167.

■ PER CURIAM.

. . . [Defendant was convicted of false pretenses and other crimes.] We affirm.

Defendant's convictions stem from his operation of two political action committees (PACs) during the 2000 election campaign and recount. Defendant was the chief of staff of both Friends for a Democratic White House (Friends) and Swing States for a GOP White House (Swing States). Defendant also incorporated PAC Services, with the purpose of providing services to the PACs defendant had formed. Defendant solicited contributions through mailings. A contention at trial was that defendant's mailing lists were stolen from the Federal Election Commission (FEC) disclosure statements of the 2000 presidential campaigns of both Al Gore and George W. Bush. These statements list the contributors to each campaign and appear on the FEC website, along with a warning that the lists are for informational purposes only and may not be used for commercial or solicitation purposes.

Defendant's PACs collected about $700,000 in contributions. Three victims of defendant's solicitation letters testified at trial. All testified that the solicitation letters they received implied an affiliation with either the Bush campaign or the Gore campaign. They also testified that they donated to the PAC that solicited them because the letter led them to believe that their contributions would go to either the Bush campaign or the Gore campaign. They also testified that they would not have given money to the PAC if they had known that the money was not going to either the Bush campaign or the Gore campaign. Defendant's PACs did give money to Democratic and Republican causes, but checks they attempted to give to the Republican National Committee and the Gore campaign were returned, *i.e.*, those entities refused to accept the donations.

Defendant first argues that there was insufficient evidence to sustain his convictions. We disagree. The standard of review for sufficiency of the evidence claims in criminal cases is whether the evidence, viewed in a light most favorable to the people, would warrant a reasonable juror in finding that all the elements of the crime were proven beyond a reasonable doubt. . . .

In order to prove false pretenses, the prosecution must show (1) a false representation concerning an existing fact, (2) knowledge by the defendant that the representation is false, (3) use of the representation with an intent to deceive, and (4) detrimental reliance by the victim. We find that the prosecution presented sufficient evidence on each element to sustain defendant's convictions for false pretenses. Defendant, through the solicitation letters, represented that he was affiliated with either the Bush campaign or the Gore campaign and the language in his letters implied that he knew the individuals to be past donors to the campaign.[1] Defendant used the candidates' names in his solicitation letters. Defendant's later letters represented that he was affiliated with the recount effort of each campaign after the election. These representations were not true because defendant's PACs were not affiliated with either party or its recount effort. It was also undisputed that defendant knew that these representations were false, because he knew that he was not affiliated with either political party's candidate for president.

There was also evidence that defendant used the representations with an intent to deceive. A defendant's intent to deceive can be inferred from the evidence, and minimal circumstantial evidence is sufficient to prove a defendant's intent. There was evidence presented at the trial that defendant used the candidates' names in his solicitation letters, knowing that this use was illegal. Defendant informed an investigator that he learned how to operate a PAC by reading the FEC guide. This guide clearly stated that it was not proper for a PAC to use a candidate's name in its solicitations. There was also testimony from the counsel for the Republican National Committee that he sent defendant a cease-and-desist letter, informing him of his illegal and misleading use of Bush's name in his solicitations. Evidence indicated that defendant mailed additional letters using Bush's name after this letter. The circumstantial evidence presented at trial supported the prosecution's theory that defendant used misrepresentations that he was affiliated with each political party with an intent to deceive potential donors into giving money to his PACs.

There was also detrimental reliance by the victims. Each victim testified that he or she donated money to one of defendant's PACs. The victims also testified that they believed that the money was going to either the Bush campaign or the Gore campaign and that they relied on this in sending the donations. The victims also testified that they would not have sent in the donations if they had known that the money was not

---

[1] Defendant is correct in arguing that false pretenses cannot be based on a misrepresentation of a future event. However, defendant made misrepresentation about an existing fact: that he was affiliated with both the Bush and Gore campaigns.

going to the respective campaigns. In addition, a victim testified that she sent a $200 donation to Friends and that her check was cashed. Another victim testified that he sent a check for $1,000 to Friends because he received the letter in the mail that asked him to assist Gore in his election campaign. And another victim testified that he wrote a check for $100 to Swing States and that check was ultimately cashed.

For these reasons, we find that there was sufficient evidence for the jury to find defendant guilty of false pretenses, $1,000 or more but less than $20,000, and false pretenses, less than $200.

* * *

Affirmed.

————

NOTES

1. The court in *DeWald* states that the crime of false pretenses is based on a misrepresentation of existing fact. This is not the universal rule however. At common law, false pretenses could be based on a misstatement of either a present or past fact. And the modern trend is to recognize misrepresentations of future fact to serve as the basis for a false pretenses charge. *See* WAYNE R. LAFAVE, CRIMINAL LAW § 19.7(b)(5) (2010).

2. Misrepresenting one's professional credentials can also constitute fraud or false pretenses. *See, e.g.* People v. Rohrberg, 22 A.D.3d 421, 802 N.Y.S.2d 682, 2005 N.Y. Slip Op. 07993 (2005) in which an attorney who had been disbarred continued to practice, and was convicted not merely of the misdemeanor of unauthorized practice of law, but also of felony grand larceny by false pretenses. The Appellate Division found that he had been properly convicted of larceny by false pretenses, noting that

> Implicitly and through his conduct, defendant, a former attorney, made false statements to his client regarding his license to practice law, thereby obtaining fees to which he was not entitled. After both his suspension and disbarment, defendant continued to refer to himself as "counsel," bill for and provide legal services to the client, and undertake activities requiring a license to practice law. Moreover, under this Court's rules, defendant was obligated to notify his clients of his disbarment. For this reason, defendant's omission to act (i.e., state that he was no longer an attorney) is itself an act (*i.e.*, a statement that he was an attorney) (*see* Penal Law § 15.00[5]) that properly supported his guilt. Furthermore, the element of reliance was established by testimony that the client would not have hired someone who was not a duly licensed attorney, and would not have paid defendant's fees if it had been aware of his suspension and/or disbarment.

3. Misrepresenting your credentials can amount to false pretenses, but what about puffery. What if an attorney tells you he is regarded as "the best criminal defense attorney in the city" when, in fact, other criminal defense attorneys and prosecutors would never agree with such a statement. If the attorney charges a client a large sum of money based on his puffery, does that make him guilty of the crime of false pretenses?

4. Consider the viewpoint expressed in the A.L.I. Model Penal Code, which provides, in its official Commentary (1980) on § 223.3:

> Theft by Deception
>
> * * *
>
> (3) *Puffing Excepted.* Exaggerated commendation of wares in communications addressed to the public or to a class or group shall not be deemed deceptive if:
>
> (a) it would be unlikely to mislead the ordinary person of the class or group addressed; and
>
> (b) there is no deception other than as to the actor's belief in the commendation; and
>
> (c) the actor was not in a position of special trust and confidence in relation to the misled party.
>
> * * *

The Comment at 181–82 (1980) to M.P.C. § 223.3 notes that the actor need not believe that the impression created is false; for purposes of Theft by Deception, the actor has "purposely deceived" another if the actor "creates the impression that he believes something to be true when in fact he has no belief on the subject."

Problem 7–6. A devastating hurricane swept through south Florida, and Chuckie Darwin saw an opportunity to make a fast buck. Many individuals and businesses in the area were without electrical power and water for several days, and officials managing the relief effort made arrangements for bottled water and ice to be shipped from out of state directly to distribution centers, including a fire station near Darwin's convenience store. Persons receiving the water were not required to fill out an application or to identify themselves. Two cases of water was a normal distribution in the first days of the relief effort but the relief workers would give additional cases on request to people who had special needs or who were taking water for distribution to others. In such instances, the relief workers might ask persons requesting additional cases to explain what they were doing with the water. Darwin made repeated trips, taking away vanloads of water. He joked with the firefighter who gave it to him, "hey, it's not like I'm going to go sell it out of my store." Actually, that is exactly what it was like: The whistle was blown when a customer noticed the same distinct brand (not otherwise available in Florida) for sale in Darwin's store and called authorities. Darwin was charged with "cheating by false pretenses," defined as "any gross fraud or cheat at common law." Has he committed a "gross fraud or cheat" by false pretenses?

E. EMBEZZLEMENT

Larceny in the strict sense can only occur if the stolen property was in someone else's possession, either actual or constructive, at the time of the taking.[25] Embezzlement differs from larceny in that an embezzler initially acquires possession lawfully, through some form of entrustment, while in larceny the property comes into the hands of the thief unlawfully, by a trespassory taking.[26] Thus, one can take possession of goods over which he has mere *custody*, and such a taking amounts to larceny if the other requirements are present.[27] However, if the defendant had actual possession of the goods, no "taking" would be possible, and thus no larceny could occur. The following early case illustrates the problem.

The King v. Bazeley

Central Criminal Court, 1779.
2 Leach 835, 168 Eng. Rep. 517.

. . . Joseph Bazeley was tried . . . for feloniously stealing . . . a Bank-note of the value of one hundred pounds . . . .

The following facts appeared in evidence. The prisoner, Joseph Bazeley, was the principal teller at the house of Messrs. Esdaile's and Hammett's, bankers, in Lombard-street, at the salary of £100 a year, and his duty was to receive and pay, money, notes, and bills, at the counter. The manner of conducting the business of this banking-house is as follows: There are four tellers, each of whom has a separate money-book, a separate money-drawer, and a separate bag. The prisoner being the chief teller, the total of the receipts and payments of all the other money-books were every evening copied into his, and the total balance or rest, as it is technically called, struck in his book, and the balances of the other money-books paid, by the other tellers, over to him. When any monies, whether in cash or notes, are brought by customers to the counter to be paid in, the teller who receives it counts it over, then enters the Bank-notes or drafts, and afterwards the cash, under the customer's name, in his book; and then, after casting up the total, it is entered in the customer's book. The money is then put into the teller's bag, and the Bank-notes or other papers, if any, put into a box which stands on a desk behind the counter, directly before another clerk, who is called the cash book-keeper, who makes an entry of it in the received cash-book in the

---

[25] Abandoned property is therefore not the subject of larceny, inasmuch as it is not in anyone's possession, either actual or constructive. Such property is cast aside, the owner intending to have no further interest therein. *See Commonwealth v. Metcalfe*, 184 Ky. 540, 212 S.W. 434, 436 (1919).

[26] *See, e.g., Simmons v. State*, 79 Ga.App. 390, 53 S.E.2d 772 (1949) (decided under former Code 1933, §§ 26–2602, 26–2603).

[27] One's servant, for example, has mere custody of money that his master has given him to mail. If the servant converts the money to his own use, he has committed larceny. *Rex v. Paradice*, 2 East P.C. 565 (1766).

name of the person who has paid it in, and which he finds written by the receiving teller on the back of the bill or note so placed in the drawer. The prisoner was treasurer to an association called "The Ding Dong Mining Company"; and in the course of the year had many bills drawn on him by the Company, and many bills drawn on other persons remitted to him by the Company. In the month of January 1799, the prisoner had accepted bills on account of the Company, to the amount of £112, 4s. 1d. and had in his possession a bill of £166, 7s. 3d. belonging to the Company, but which was not due until the 9th February. One of the bills, amounting to £100, which the prisoner had accepted, became due on 18th January. Mr. William Gilbert, a grocer, in the Surry-road, Black-friars, kept his cash at the banking-house of the prosecutors, and on the 18th January 1799, he sent his servant, George Cock, to pay in £137. This sum consisted of £122 in Bank-notes, and the rest in cash. One of these Bank- notes was the note which the prisoner was indicted for stealing. The prisoner received this money from George Cock, and after entering the £137 in Mr. Gilbert's Bank-book, entered the £15 cash in his own money-book, and put over the *£22* in Bank-notes into the drawer behind him, keeping back the £100 Bank-note, which he put into his pocket, and afterwards paid to a banker's clerk the same day at a clearing-house in Lombard-street, in discharge of the £100 bill which he had accepted on account of the Ding Dong Mining Company. To make the sum in Mr. Gilbert's Bank-book, and the sum in the book of the banking-house agree, it appeared that a unit had been added to the entry of £37 to the credit of Mr. Gilbert, in the book of the banking-house, but it did not appear by any direct proof that this alteration had been made by the prisoner; it appeared however that he had made a confession, but the confession having been obtained under a promise of favour, it was not given in evidence.

Const and Jackson, the prisoner's Counsel, submitted to the Court, that to constitute a larceny, it was necessary in point of law that the property should be taken from the possession of the prosecutor, but that it was clear from the evidence in this case, that the Bank-note charged to have been stolen, never was either in the actual or the constructive possession of Esdaile and Hammett, and that even if it had been in their possession, yet that from the manner in which it had been secreted by the prisoner, it amounted only to a breach of trust.

The Court left the facts of the case to the consideration of the Jury, and on their finding the prisoner Guilty, the case was reserved for the opinion of the Twelve Judges on a question, whether under the circumstances above stated, the taking of the Bank-note was in law a felonious taking, or only a fraudulent breach of trust.

* * *

. . . [Counsel] after remarking that the prosecutor never had actual possession of the Bank-note, and defining the several offences of larceny, fraud, and breach of trust . . . proceeded to argue the case upon the following points.

First, That the prosecutors cannot, in contemplation of law, be said to have had a constructive possession of this Bank-note, at the time the prisoner is charged with having tortiously converted it to his own use.

Secondly, That supposing the prosecutors to have had the possession of this note, the prisoner, under the circumstances of this case, cannot be said to have tortiously taken it from that possession with a felonious intention to steal it.

Thirdly, That the relative situation of the prosecutors and the prisoner makes this transaction merely a breach of trust; and,

Fourthly, That this is not one of those breaches of trust which the Legislature has declared to be felony.

The first point, viz. That the prosecutor cannot, in contemplation of law, be said to have had a constructive possession of this Bank-note at the time the prisoner is charged with having tortiously converted it to his own use. To constitute the crime of larceny, the property must be taken from the possession of the owner; this possession must be either actual or constructive; it is clear that the prosecutors had not, upon the present occasion, the actual possession of the Bank-note, and therefore the inquiry must be, whether they had the constructive possession of it or, in other words, whether the possession of the servant was, under the circumstances of this case, the possession of the master Property in possession is said by Sir William Blackstone to subsist only where a man hath both the right to, and also the occupation of, the property. The prosecutors in the present case had only a right or title to possess the note, and not the absolute or even qualified possession of it. It was never in their custody or under their controul. There is no difference whatever as to the question of possession between real and personal property; and if after the death of an ancestor, and before the entry of his heir upon the descending estate, or if after the death of a particular tenant, and before the entry of the remainder-man, or reversioner, a stranger should take possession of the vacant land, the heir in the one case, and the remainder-man, or reversioner in the other, would be, like the prosecutor in the present case, only entitled to, but not possessed of, the estate; and each of them must recover possession of it by the respective remedies which the law has in such cases made and provided. Suppose the prisoner had not parted with the note, but had merely kept it in his own custody, and refused, on any pretence whatever, to deliver it over to his employers, they could only have recovered it by means of an action of trover or detinue, the first of which presupposes the person against whom it is brought, to have obtained possession of the property by lawful means, as by delivery, or finding; and the second, that the right of property only, and not the possession of it, either really or constructively, is in the person bringing it. The prisoner received this note by the permission and consent of the prosecutors, while it was passing from the possession of Mr. Gilbert to the possession of Messrs. Esdaile's and Hammett's; and not having reached its destined goal, but having been thus intercepted in its transitory state, it is clear that it never came to the possession of the prosecutors. It was delivered into the possession of the prisoner, upon an implied confidence on the part of the prosecutors, that he would deliver it over into their possession, but which, from the pressure of temporary circumstances, he neglected to do: at the time therefore of the supposed conversion of this note, it was in the legal possession of the prisoner. To divest the prisoner of this possession, it certainly was not necessary that he should have delivered this note into the hands of the prosecutors, or of any other of their servants personally; for if he had deposited it in the drawer kept for the reception of this species of property, it would have been a delivery of it into the possession of his masters; but he made no such deposit: and instead of determining in any way his own possession of it, he conveyed it immediately from the hand of Mr. Gilbert's clerk into his own pocket . . . .

* * *

Secondly, Supposing the prosecutor to have had the possession of this note, yet the prisoner, under the circumstances of this case, cannot be said to have tortiously taken it from that possession with a felonious intent to steal it . . . . [T]here was no evidence whatever to shew that any such intention existed in his mind at the time the note came to his hands . . . . [A]ll the writers on Crown Law agree, that the intent to steal must be when the property comes to his hands or possession; and that if he have the possession of it once lawfully, though he hath the *animus furandi* afterwards, when he carrieth it away, it is no larceny.

. . . [T]he situation which the prisoner held, and the capacity in which he acted in the banking-house of the prosecutors, make this transaction only a breach of trust.

. . . But a breach of trust is not, either by the Common Law or by Act of Parliament, in this case, felony. In the case of *Rex v. Meeres* (1 Show. 49), it is laid down, that if there be such a consent of the owner of the property as argues a trust in the prisoner, and gives him a possession against all strangers, then his breaking that trust, or abusing that possession, though to the owner's utter deceit of all his interest in those goods, it will not be felony: and this rule is confirmed by the case of *Rex v. Waite (ante,* p. 28, case 14) . . . Taking it, therefore, as a settled point, that a breach of trust cannot, by the rules of the common law, be converted into a felonious taking, the next and last inquiry will be, in what cases the Legislature has made this particular breach of trust felony? There are only four statutes upon this subject, viz. the 21 Hen. VIII. c. 7; the 15 Geo. II. c. 13, s. 12; the 5 Geo. III. c. 35, s. 17; and 7 Geo. III. c. 50. The two last Acts relate entirely and exclusively to breaches of trust committed by servants employed in the business of the Post-Offices;

and the second to breaches of trust committed by servants employed in the business of the Bank of England, and of course, cannot affect, in any manner whatever, the present case. Nor can the case of the prisoner be construed within the statute 21 Hen. VIII. c. 7, which enacts, "That all and singular servants to whom any caskets, jewels, money, goods, or chattels, by his or their masters or mistresses, shall be delivered to keep, that if any such servant or servants withdraw themselves from their masters or mistresses, and go away with the caskets, &c. or any part thereof, to the intent to steal the same, and defraud his or their masters or mistresses thereof, contrary to the trust and confidence in him or them put by his or their masters or mistresses; or else being in the service of his or their masters or mistresses, without any assent or command of his master or mistress, embezzle the same casket, jewels, money, goods, or chattels, or any part thereof, or otherwise convert the same to his own use, with like purpose to steal it, it shall be adjudged felony": for it has been determined upon this statute, that it is strictly confined to such goods as are delivered by the master to the servant to keep. But this Bank-note, as has been already shewn, was not in the possession of the master, and therefore it cannot have been delivered by him; it being impossible for a man to deliver, either by himself or his agent, a thing of which he is neither actually nor constructively possessed; but, even admitting that it had been in the master's possession, and delivered by him to the prisoner, it would not have been delivered to him to keep, but for the purpose of entering it faithfully in the book, and handing it over to the Bank-note cashier . . .

. . . [The Crown] argued the case entirely on the question, Whether the prosecutors . . . had such a constructive possession of the Bank-note as to render the taking of it by the prisoner felony? He insisted, that in the case of personal chattels, the possession in law follows the right of property; and, that as Gilbert's clerk did not deposit the notes with Bazeley as a matter of trust to him; for they were paid at the counter, and in the banking-house of the prosecutors, of which Bazeley was merely one of the organs; and, therefore, the payment to him was in effect a payment to them, and his receipt of them vested the property *eo instanter* in their hands, and gave them the legal possession of it.

The Judges, it is said, were of opinion . . . that this Bank-note never was in the legal custody or possession of the prosecutors . . . ; but no opinion was ever publicly delivered; and the prisoner was included in the Secretary of State's letter as a proper object for a pardon.

But in consequence of this case the statute 39 Geo. III. c. 85 was passed, entitled, "An Act to protect Masters and others against Embezzlement, by their Clerks or Servants'; and after reciting, that whereas Bankers, Merchants, and others, are, in the course of their dealings and transactions, frequently obliged to entrust their servants, clerks, and persons employed by them in the like capacity, with receiving, paying, negotiating, exchanging, or transferring money, goods, bonds, bills, notes, bankers' drafts, and other valuable effects and securities; that doubts had been entertained, whether the embezzling the same by such servants, clerks, and others, so employed by their masters, amounts to felony by the laws of England; and that it is expedient that such offences should be punished in the same manner in both parts of the United Kingdom"; it enacts and declares, "That if any servant or clerk, or any person employed for the purpose in the capacity of a servant or clerk to any person or persons whomsoever, or to any body corporate or politic, shall, by virtue of such employment, receive or take into his possession any money, goods, bond, bill, note, banker's draft, or other valuable security or effects, for or in the name, or on the account of his master or masters, or employer or employers, and shall fraudulently embezzle, secrete, or make away with the same, or any part thereof; every such offender shall be deemed to have feloniously stolen the same from his master or masters, employer or employers, for whose use, or in whose name or names, or on whose account, the same was or were delivered to, or taken into the possession of, such servant, clerk, or other person so employed, although such money, &c. was or were no otherwise received into the possession of such master or masters, employer or employers, than by the actual possession of his or their servant, clerk, or other person so employed; and every such offender his adviser, procurer, aider or abettor, shall be liable to be transported for any term not exceeding fourteen years, in the discretion of the Court."

————

NOTES

1. As the court notes in the final paragraph, the *Bazeley* case led Parliament to pass an embezzlement statute, the first of its kind. Two hundred years later, such statutes have largely come and gone. Most states now include embezzlement in the general crime of theft. *See* Stuart P. Green, *Theft By Coercion, Extortion, Blackmail, and Hard Bargaining*, 44 WASHBURN L.J. 553, 565 (2005) (explaining that the Model Penal Code has inspired consolidation of embezzlement and other crimes into the single offense of theft by unlawful taking).

2. Under statutes enacted after *Bazeley,* an employee who could escape liability for larceny could still be guilty of embezzlement. But would separate statutes for larceny and embezzlement make it difficult in some cases to know whether we are dealing with a larceny or embezzlement? For instance, in Gwaltney v. Commonwealth, 19 Va. App. 468, 452 S.E.2d 687 (Va. Ct. App. 1995), a bank teller stole from another teller's cash drawer, rather than taking money from her own drawer. Is this conduct larceny (because the defendant is taking money from another person's drawer), or is it embezzlement (because the defendant is taking money she was generally entrusted to handle as a bank employee)? For a discussion, see John Wesley Bartram, Note, *Pleading for Theft Consolidation in Virginia: Larceny,*

Embezzlement, False Pretenses and § 19.2–284, WASH. & LEE L. REV. 249, 275–278 (1999).

3. What should the result be when a local official—the treasurer of a township—removes funds belonging to the township out of a safe that is located in a secretary's office and which the secretary is primarily responsible for? Is the local official in constructive possession of the funds (such that this is embezzlement) or has he taken the property (such that the crime is larceny)? *See* Loker v. State, 245 A.2d 814 (Md. 1968).

————

State v. Lough

Supreme Court of Rhode Island, 2006.
899 A.2d 468.

■ JUSTICE FLAHERTY, for the Court.

* * *

I

Background

After a jury trial in May 2004, John Lough, a patrolman in the Providence Police Department, was convicted of embezzling and fraudulently converting a child's minibike, valued at approximately $350. Sometime around midnight on July 14, 2003, Lough stopped to aid a fellow officer, Thomas Teft. Officer Teft had detained a juvenile, Shane, because he suspected that the young man was operating a stolen minibike. Officer Teft's suspicions were further aroused because Shane was unable to produce proof of ownership and the vehicle identification number had been partially scratched off the surface of the bike. Despite these dubious circumstances, Officer Teft decided to give Shane a break because the youth insisted that he had recently purchased the bike and he claimed that he had to be at his new job early in the morning. So, rather than arresting him, Officer Teft decided to confiscate the bike and hold it at the police station until Shane could produce proof of ownership.

When Lough arrived at the scene, Officer Teft explained to him that he was unsure about the protocol for confiscating the minibike. Officer Teft's anxiety was heightened because, as a new officer, he still was on probationary status with the department. As a result, the more experienced Lough offered his assistance by volunteering to take possession of the bike and complete the necessary paperwork. Officer Teft accepted this offer and he loaded the bike into the back seat of Lough's police cruiser. After he and Officer Teft went their separate ways, Lough removed the bike from the back seat and placed it in the trunk of the vehicle because it smelled of fuel and had fallen forward against his seat.

A short time later, as Lough and several other officers were responding to a report of a stolen vehicle, his cruiser struck the back of another officer's patrol car, apparently because of faulty brakes. Lough's supervisor instructed him and the officer driving the other vehicle to return to the police station to complete paperwork related to the accident. After finishing the paperwork, Lough left the police station intending to bring his damaged cruiser to a repair facility . . . .

Lough said he remembered that Shane's minibike still was in the trunk of his car while he was on his way to the garage. Lough testified at trial that because he was aggravated by the evening's events and anxious to go home, he "made a wrong decision" and decided to rid himself of the bike by leaving it behind a dumpster. He assumed that the young man would never return to claim the bike, but this assumption proved to be wrong and Shane arrived at the police station the next morning with his mother to reclaim the confiscated bike.

During the hours that followed, department personnel searched the police station and some of the cruisers for the minibike, but they were unable to locate it. The investigation quickly led to Officer Teft, who told the Internal Affairs Division that he had turned the bike over to Lough after he confiscated it the previous night. After this conversation, Officer Teft telephoned Lough regarding the whereabouts of the bike. Lough told him, "Don't worry, I'll take care of it."

Now knowing that Shane intended to reclaim the bike, Lough arranged to meet with Officer Steven Petrella, a fellow officer and friend, at a parking lot in Cranston. According to Lough, he then drove to the dumpster where he had discarded the bike, placed it in his personal vehicle, and drove to the parking lot to meet Officer Petrella. The two officers met around 8 p.m., and Lough placed the minibike into the trunk of Officer Petrella's cruiser.

Later that evening, investigators from Internal Affairs questioned Officers Lough and Petrella about the minibike. Neither officer was forthcoming with details concerning the bike, and neither of them mentioned the parking-lot rendezvous that had taken place earlier that night. Lough told one of the inspectors that after he was involved in the car accident with another officer, he transferred the bike to the trunk of Officer Petrella's car. However, he did not disclose that he left the bike at the dumpster site and transferred it to Petrella's car only after the investigation had started. Officer Petrella told another inspector that the bike had been in the trunk of his car at the start of his shift. But the department knew this statement to be false because the car had been searched earlier that day, and the minibike was not in it.

As the case of the missing minibike continued, Lough eventually came forward with his story about the dumpster, asserting that he had discarded the bike because he believed that Shane would never return to claim it. In August 2003, Lough was indicted on one count of embezzlement and fraudulent conversion in violation of § 11–41–3. Following a four-day trial in May 2004, a jury returned a verdict of guilty and Lough was fined $1,000 and received a one-year suspended sentence. The defendant timely appealed.

On appeal, Lough contends that the trial justice misinterpreted § 11–41–3 and incorrectly instructed the jury that a person could violate the statute by disposing of the property of another. . . . Lough's claims of error all hinge on one central issue: whether a person who is lawfully entrusted with property and throws the property away can be convicted of embezzlement and fraudulent conversion pursuant to § 11–41–3 in the absence of proof that he derived a benefit from using the property. . . .

II

* * *

III

Analysis

To determine whether a conviction for embezzlement and fraudulent conversion under § 11–41–3 requires proof that a defendant derived a benefit from his use of the property, we begin our analysis with the language of the statute itself. Section 11–41–3 provides in relevant part as follows:

> Embezzlement and fraudulent conversion.—Every . . . . officer, agent, clerk, servant, or other person to whom any money or other property shall be entrusted for any specific purpose . . . . who shall embezzle or fraudulently convert to his or her own use . . . . any money or other property which shall have come into his or her possession or shall be under his or her care or charge by virtue of his or her employment . . . shall be deemed guilty of larceny. . . .

In *State v. Oliveira*, 432 A.2d 664 (R.I. 1981) this Court outlined the elements of proof required to sustain a conviction under § 11–41–3. We explained that the state must establish the following:

> (1) that defendant was entrusted with the property for a specific use, (2) that he came into possession of the property in a lawful manner, often as a result of his employment, and (3) that defendant intended to appropriate and convert the property to his own use and permanently deprive that person of the use.

Lough concedes that he was lawfully entrusted with the minibike for the specific purpose of delivering it to the police station. Thus, there is no dispute that the state satisfied the first two elements required to sustain a conviction. He also admitted during trial that when he threw the bike away, he intended to permanently deprive the owner of its use. He maintains, however, that this is insufficient to sustain a conviction because the state also must establish that he "convert[ed] the property to his own use." According to him, this third element of proof requires evidence that he derived some personal gain from using the property.

To support this position, Lough contends that our holding in *State v. Powers*, 644 A.2d 828 (R.I. 1994), stands for the proposition that a person cannot be convicted under § 11–41–3 without evidence that he derived a benefit from using the property in question. In that case, the defendant, Robert Powers, was working as the director of maintenance for a school department when, using a school account, he ordered certain material valued at $1,200 and had it delivered to a private company, all in exchange for goods and services to be used by the school. After school officials learned of the transaction, Powers was charged with embezzlement and fraudulent conversion in violation of § 11–41–3. Although the barter agreement was unauthorized, there was no evidence that Powers had personally used the school department's property or derived a benefit from its use. Therefore, the Superior Court granted his motion to dismiss for lack of probable cause. The state appealed, and we affirmed. Relying on our previous holding in *Oliveira* and the plain language of § 11–41–3, we explained that "an element of the crime charged is that defendant put the property to 'his own use' or used the property for his own benefit."

Citing our language in *Powers*, Lough contends that the trial justice's instruction misstated the elements of proof required to sustain a conviction under § 11–41–3. The disputed instruction stated in part as follows:

> The elements that the State must prove beyond a reasonable doubt in order to convict this defendant are as follows: Number one, that the defendant was entrusted with the property for a specific use or purpose; two, that he came into possession of that property in a lawful manner, and, three, that the defendant intended to appropriate and convert the property to his own use and permanently deprive that person of its use.

> A conversion of property requires a serious act of interference with the owner's rights, using up the property, selling it, pledging it, giving it away, delivering it to one not entitled to it and inflicting serious damage to it, claiming it against the lawful owner, unreasonable withholding possession of it from the owner *or, otherwise, disposing of the property*. Each of these acts seriously interferes with the ownership rights and so constitutes a conversion. (Emphasis added.)

When the jury asked for clarification on what constitutes conversion, the justice stated: "When a person having possession of another's property treats the property as his own, whether he sells it, uses, or *disposes of it*, he is using the property for his own purpose." (Emphasis added.)

Lough argues that by instructing the jury that a person converts property to his own use by disposing of it, the trial justice permitted the jury to return a guilty verdict in the absence of evidence that he derived a benefit from his use of the minibike. This distinction is of paramount importance because Lough conceded in his testimony that he threw the minibike away. Thus, if the act of throwing the minibike away constitutes conversion, Lough's testimony was essentially an admission of guilt.

This Court has not squarely addressed what it means to fraudulently convert property to one's "own use" under § 11–41–3. Contrary to Lough's assertion, however, *Powers* does not hold that a person must derive a personal gain from using the property to be convicted under § 11–41–3. Although we noted that the defendant in *Powers* did not derive a benefit from the bartering transaction, this observation simply underscored the fact that he did not convert the property to his own use, as required by the plain language of the statute. In fact, we clearly stated that the trial court's dismissal of the charge against the defendant was warranted because there was no evidence that he had put the property to his own use. Therefore, under our holding in *Powers* and under the language of the statute, the relevant inquiry is not whether Lough derived a benefit from throwing the bike away, but rather, whether he put the property to "his own use."

Although we have not previously considered whether a person puts property to his own use by disposing of it, other jurisdictions have held that a person puts property to his own use when he treats it as if it were his own, even in the absence of a measurable benefit. For example, in *United States v. Santiago*, 528 F.2d 1130, 1135 (2d Cir. 1976), the Second Circuit Court of Appeals explained as follows:

> The phrase "to his own use" is a carry over from the common-law pleading in trover, . . . and does not require a showing that the misappropriation was for the personal advantage of the defendant. . . . *One's disposition of the property of another, without right, as if it were his own, is a conversion to one's own use.*

The Court of Appeals of New Mexico similarly held in *State v. Archie*, 123 N.M. 503, 943 P.2d 537 (Ct.App.1997), that "[w]hen a person having possession of another's property treats the property as his own, whether he uses it, sells it, or discards it, he is using the property for his own purpose." *Id.* at 540.

When the trial justice rejected Lough's objection to the jury instruction and denied his motions for judgment of acquittal and new trial, he cited *Santiago* and *Archie*, as well as legal treatises, to support his conclusion that disposing of property constitutes conversion within the meaning of § 11–41–3. . . . Lough contends that it was improper for the trial justice to rely on these sources because they are contrary to our holding in *Powers*. However, as noted, *Powers* did not define conversion to require proof of personal gain, nor did it foreclose the possibility that a person may convert property by throwing it away.

In our opinion, a person puts property to his own use when he treats it as his own, and when a person discards property, he treats it as his own. This interpretation of the statute is consistent with the plain meaning of the words used by the Legislature. . . . When Lough decided to dispose of the minibike that had been entrusted to him, he made a decision that was properly vested in its lawful owner; in other words, by discarding the property as if it were his own, Lough converted it to "his . . . own use." We therefore hold that the trial justice correctly instructed the jury on the elements of proof necessary to sustain a conviction under § 11–41–3. In light of this holding, we reject Lough's additional claims of error concerning the denial of his motions for judgment of acquittal and motion for new trial. . . . Because the justice correctly interpreted the statute, we hold that these motions were properly denied.

IV

Conclusion

For the reasons stated herein, we affirm the judgment of the Superior Court. The record in this case shall be remanded to the Superior Court.

————

NOTES

1. Do you believe Lough's story that he threw the bike in a dumpster? What else might have happened?

2. Imagine that in his spare time, a police officer worked as a security guard at a bank. One evening, after the bank closed, the officer took some cash from one of the drawers and kept it for himself. Would the police officer be guilty of embezzlement?

3. Now imagine that it is business hours at the bank. A customer walks up to a teller, fills out a deposit slip, and hands the teller $300. The teller does not put the money in the cash drawer however, but instead slips the money in his own pocket. What crime has the teller committed? *See* State v. Ward, 562 A.2d 1040, 1041–42 (Vt. 1989).

4. Finally, imagine that the teller has been working all day at the bank and he has dutifully placed all cash deposits in the bank drawer. At closing time on Friday evening, the bank manager informs the teller that he will not receive his paycheck because there was a glitch in the payroll department. Upset, the teller waits for the manager to turn her back and then takes $500 out of the bank drawer. The teller thinks to himself, "this is a little more than my salary for the week, but that's what the bank gets for trying to short-change me." What crime has the teller committed? *See* State v. Rathburn, 442 A.2d 452 (Vt. 1981).

————

Problem 7–7. Abel was a buyer in the cabinet division of Zulu's Purchasing Department, and was responsible for finding a supplier and negotiating a suitable price and specifications for cabinets for a new Zulu home-entertainment product. Baker, who owned Baker's Box Co., was a long-time friend of Abel's. Abel chose Baker's, the sole bidder, as supplier of these cabinets. At Abel's request, Baker agreed to pay Abel $1 per cabinet in return for the contract to supply the Zulu cabinets. Abel's supervisor at Zulu found Baker's prices to be fair and reasonable, but without other bids he did not know whether they were competitive. The cabinets supplied were of the required quality and complied in every respect with Zulu's specifications. Another friend, Charlie, did business as Charlie's Consulting Co. Charlie submitted fictitious invoices of Charlie's Consulting Co. to Baker's, even though Charlie's Consulting Co. provided no services to Baker's. After these invoices were paid, Charlie paid part of the proceeds to Abel. Zulu normally allowed its suppliers a maximum of 10% profit, and Baker's prices reflected that profit margin. Zulu had a conflict-of-interest policy of which Abel was aware, forbidding its Purchasing Department employees to accept any gratuities of any kind from suppliers. Zulu was not aware of the payments to Abel via Charlie because records reflecting total payments were altered to conceal the discrepancies. Thus, Zulu's records reflected only the price that Zulu expected to pay. Has Abel committed fraud? embezzlement? or just a breach of contract?

F. RECEIVING AND TRANSPORTING STOLEN PROPERTY AND RELATED OFFENSES

The common law offense of receiving stolen property is closely related to, but distinct from, the crime of larceny. The crime of receiving stolen goods requires *scienter*, in that the receiver must know that the goods have been stolen. Given that those who have purchased stolen goods are likely to lie about it, how will prosecutors be able to prove the *mens rea* element? Consider the cases below.

People v. Rife

Supreme Court of Illinois, 1943.
382 Ill. 588, 48 N.E.2d 367.

■ THOMPSON, JUSTICE.

Plaintiff in error Noah D. Rife, and his wife, Mabel, operators of a junk yard in the city of Danville, were jointly indicted at the January term, 1941, of the circuit court of Vermilion county, charged in three counts with receiving, buying and aiding in concealing 132 pounds of engine brass and 167 pounds of Journal brass, and in a fourth count with receiving, buying and aiding in concealing 299 pounds of brass, all of the property of and stolen from Benjamin Wham, trustee of the Chicago and Eastern Illinois Railway Company, a corporation. Each of the counts charged that defendant knew that said brass had been stolen. Defendants pleaded not guilty and were tried by a jury. Plaintiff in error was found guilty and the value of the property received was found to be

$9.35. His wife, the other defendant, was found not guilty. Motion for a new trial was denied and plaintiff in error was sentenced to the Illinois State Penal Farm at Vandalia for one year and fined $1,000 . . . .

The roundhouse foreman in the Chicago and Eastern Illinois railway yards at Chicago, in October, 1940, supervised the replacing of brass on engines 3643 and 1908. The old brass taken off these engines was loaded into two freight cars, sealed and shipped to the railroad shops or roundhouse at Danville. One of these cars arrived on October 22, 1940, and was unloaded and put in the bins at the Danville shops on October 22 and 23. The other car came in November 2, 1940, and from that time until it was unloaded on November 8, stood upon the company's track at the storeroom in the Danville yards of the C. & E. I. On November 5, 1940, plaintiff in error bought 187 pounds of railroad brass from [a boy] named Henry Brandon. On the day previous he had also bought brass from Brandon. On November 5, 1940, W. B. Sloan, the chief of police of the railway company, Theodore Alberts, general foreman of the company, and Robert Meade, a deputy sheriff, went to the junk yard of plaintiff in error, where they recovered 132 pounds of railway-engine brass and 167 pounds of journal brass. This brass was positively identified by Mr. Alberts from the engine numbers, 3643 and 1908, and the patent number A-D 830 stamped on the various pieces.

The contention is made that the evidence is not sufficient to prove beyond a reasonable doubt that the brass described in the indictment was ever stolen, and also that the evidence is not sufficient to prove beyond a reasonable doubt that plaintiff in error knew the brass had been stolen at the time he purchased it from Henry Brandon. Before there can be a conviction for receiving stolen property the evidence must show beyond a reasonable doubt, first, that the property has, in fact, been stolen by a person other than the one charged with receiving the property; second, that the one charged with receiving its has actually received it or aided in concealing it; third, that the person so receiving the stolen property knew that it was stolen at the time of receiving it; and, fourth, that he received the property for his own gain or to prevent the owner from again possessing it. But while it is true that these four propositions must all be proved beyond a reasonable doubt, it is also true that neither is required to be established by direct evidence. Circumstantial evidence may be resorted to for the purpose of proving the corpus delicti as well as for the purpose of connecting the accused with the crime. There is no invariable rule as to the quantum of proof necessary to establish the corpus delicti. Each case must depend, in a measure, upon its own particular circumstances. Circumstantial evidence is legal evidence and there is no legal distinction between direct and circumstantial evidence so far as weight and effect are concerned. It is not necessary that someone testify, in so many words, to the theft of this brass and that plaintiff in error had knowledge of such theft at the time he purchased the brass from Henry Brandon, but such facts may be shown by circumstantial evidence. The brass found in the Rife junk yard was positively identified as brass which had been removed from the Chicago and Eastern Illinois engines in Chicago and shipped to Danville, within twenty days at the most, previous to that time. It was conclusively proved by the evidence that this brass was shipped from Chicago to Danville for use in the railroad shops there, and received at the C. & E. I. shops at Danville, where it was in the exclusive possession of the railway company on its own private premises. It then disappeared. It must have been taken by somebody. The only conclusion that can follow, under all the circumstances, is that a larceny had been committed. There was no contention by the plaintiff in error on the trial that the brass was not stolen. Indeed, his wife testified that he had told her that Henry Brandon had stolen it. In the case of People v. Feeley ... where department-store merchandise, including shirts, ties, socks, and other wearing apparel, was discovered in an automobile, this court held that the fact that none of the articles had been wrapped in packages by the stores, but had been stuffed in large quantities in cardboard boxes, and the finding of the shoplifters' boxes in the automobile, were circumstances sufficiently proving the theft of such merchandise. In the Feeley case, supra, there was no evidence that the merchandise had been missed or was known to be stolen before found in the automobile. It is not necessary in the instant case, to warrant the jury in finding that a larceny of the brass had been committed, for the evidence to show that it had been missed by the employees of the Chicago and Eastern Illinois Railway Company or that they knew that it had been stolen.

* * *

. . . Plaintiff in error testified that when Brandon sold him the brass, he told him that the brass was not stolen, that he had found it, that it was all right for plaintiff in error to buy it, and that if any one inquired he could say that he had bought it from Brandon. He also testified that the possession of a large amount of heavy brass by [a boy] who claimed to have found it did not arouse his suspicions . . . .

There was no direct evidence that plaintiff in error purchased the brass in question knowing it to have been stolen. The People relied upon circumstantial evidence for such proof, but this does not militate against the prosecution. Knowledge that property was stolen is seldom susceptible of direct proof, but may be inferred from all the surrounding facts and circumstances. Circumstances which will induce a belief in the mind of a reasonable person that property has been stolen are sufficient proof of such guilty knowledge. The knowledge need not be that actual or positive knowledge which one acquires from personal observation of the fact, but it is sufficient if the circumstances accompanying the transaction be such as to make the accused believe the goods had been stolen. This knowledge of the accused is an essential element of the offense and must be found by the jury as a fact. In determining whether the fact existed, the jury will be justified in presuming that the accused acted rationally and that whatever would convey knowledge or induce belief in the mind of a reasonable person, would, in the absence of countervailing evidence, be sufficient to apprise him of the like fact, or induce in his mind the like empression and belief.

In the instant case plaintiff in error, after recent and repeated warnings to be on the alert for stolen railroad brass and to notify the sheriff's office of any suspicious circumstances, failed to report the circumstance to the officers when [a boy] offered him a large amount of such brass with no explanation other than that he had found it and had not stolen it. Plaintiff in error made no inquiry into the details of the [boy's] improbable story of his acquisition of such a large amount of brass. The story of plaintiff in error, of his purchase of this brass in good faith and innocence, is not supported either by any direct or circumstantial evidence. On the countrary, all the evidence points conclusively to, and is sufficient to warrant the jury in believing, beyond a reasonable doubt, that plaintiff in error know when he purchased this brass that he was handling stolen property ... All of the evidence, and facts and circumstances in evidence, in the instant case, when considered together, cannot consistently be reconciled with any theory other than that of the guilt of the accused. Upon a review of the record in a criminal case, it is the duty of this court to consider the evidence, and if it does not establish guilt beyond a reasonable doubt, the conviction must be reversed. We have carefully considered all of the evidence, both that of the People and that of plaintiff in error, and we cannot say that it is not amply sufficient to justify the jury in believing beyond a reasonable doubt that the plaintiff in error is guilty of the crime with which he is charged.

* * *

Judgment affirmed.

_____

NOTES

1. The *Rife* decision states the traditional common law rule that a defendant can only be convicted of receiving stolen property if he knew the property was in fact stolen. Does the court reach the correct result as to Rife's *mens rea*? Was there sufficient evidence that Rife knew the property was stolen? Or does the evidence indicate that he should have known it was stolen?

2. Assume that Rife contended he had made a mistake of fact as to the property being stolen. If he honestly believed that the property was not stolen, should his conviction be upheld under Illinois law? What if the governing law made someone liable for receiving stolen property if "a reasonable person would have believed the property to be stolen"? In that jurisdiction, would Rife's honest mistake of fact suffice?

_____

State v. Chester

Supreme Court of Louisiana, 1997.
707 So.2d 973.

■ PER CURIAM.

With the question of defendant's guilt turning at trial on his knowledge that the property in his possession had been the subject of a theft, the court of appeal reversed his conviction and sentence for possession of stolen property, La.R.S. 14:69, on grounds that "without additional circumstantial evidence concerning the defendant's acquisition of the [stolen property] . . . the state's proof of the crime is not constitutionally sufficient in this case." We granted the state's application for review because the court of appeal's decision appears to conflict with the settled principle of appellate review that "[w]hen a case involves circumstantial evidence, and the jury reasonably rejects the hypothesis of innocence presented by the defendant[ ] . . . that hypothesis falls, and the defendant is guilty unless there is another hypothesis which raises a reasonable doubt." *State v. Captville,* 448 So.2d 676, 680 (La.1984). We now reverse.

On the night of February 22, 1994, the truck owned by John Lawrence disappeared from the carport of his home in Hammond, Louisiana. Lawrence lost not only his vehicle but also several thousand dollars worth of tools he used in his construction business. In the early morning hours of February 23, 1994, the defendant then appeared at the home of Charlie Johnson in Ponchatoula, Louisiana. The defendant was accompanied by a second individual who brought to Johnson's porch a toolbox containing over a dozen straight wrenches and four offset wrenches used to change hydraulic lines in heavy construction equipment. Lawrence's initials appeared on some of the wrenches but were not visible to casual inspection when the defendant opened the box and displayed the wrenches to Johnson. The defendant had known Johnson for several years and offered to sell him the toolbox and wrenches for 35 dollars because he "needed gas" for a trip to New Orleans. He settled for 30 dollars, all of the cash Johnson had with him that morning. The defendant left the tools with Johnson, who asked no questions about the property he had just acquired.

Johnson had occasionally worked for Lawrence clearing land at his construction sites, and he subsequently discovered that the tools had been stolen from his former employer, who reported the theft of his truck to the Tangipahoa Parish Sheriff's Office on February 23, 1994. Two days later, Lawrence recovered his property from the shed at the back of Johnson's home. Lawrence testified at trial that the offset wrenches, specialty tools difficult to find, alone cost 100 dollars each. In all, according to the victim's estimates, the defendant had sold approximately 800 dollars worth of equipment to Johnson for 30 dollars.

In Louisiana, the "mere possession of stolen property does not create a presumption that the person in possession of the property received it with knowledge that it was stolen by someone else." *State v. Ennis,* 414 So.2d 661, 662 (La.1982). The state must therefore prove the defendant's guilty knowledge as it must every other essential element of the offense. Nevertheless, jurors may infer the defendant's guilty knowledge from the circumstances of the offense. *See Barnes v. United States,* 412 U.S. 837, 843, 93 S.Ct. 2357, 2362, 37 L.Ed.2d 380 (1973) ("For centuries courts have instructed juries that an inference of guilty knowledge may be drawn from the fact of unexplained possession of stolen goods."). The inference of guilty knowledge arising from the possession of stolen property is generally a much stronger one than the inference the possessor committed the theft, and for the buyer and seller alike, in a transaction involving stolen goods, "one of the most telling indices of guilt is a low price paid by the receiver." *United States v. Werner,* 160 F.2d 438, 443 (2d Cir.1947); *see* 1 Wayne R. LaFave & Austin W. Scott, Jr., *Substantive Criminal Law,* § 8.10, p. 430 (West 1986) ("The circumstance that the buyer paid an inadequate price for the goods, that the seller was irresponsible, that the transaction between them was secret-these factors all point toward . . . guilty knowledge."); *see United States v. Prazak,* 623 F.2d 152, 154–55 (10th Cir.1980) ("Acquisition of recently stolen property at a ridiculously low price from an unknown person is itself sufficient to support an inference that the one acquiring the property knew the property was stolen."); *State v. Butler,* 9 Ariz.App. 162, 450 P.2d 128, 132 (1969) ("When . . . there is other evidence in addition to possession and sale at a disproportionately low price guilty knowledge may be found."); *Russell v. State,* 583 P.2d 690, 699 (1978) (Thieves "must rid themselves of stolen property as quickly as possible, and willingness to sell at a grossly reduced price betrays or should betray such a predicament.").

In this case, the state presented no direct or circumstantial evidence linking the defendant to the theft of Lawrence's truck. The state also presented no evidence of the circumstances under which the defendant came into possession of the stolen tools. Nevertheless, Lawrence's testimony provided jurors with direct evidence regarding the value of the tools, and jurors had more than simply the disproportionately small sale price with which to gauge defendant's subjective knowledge. The defendant appeared at Johnson's home in the dead of night and in close temporal proximity to the theft of Lawrence's vehicle. He then conducted a transaction in which he volunteered no information about his acquisition or ownership of the tools and Johnson never asked. Under all of these circumstances, we cannot say that the jury's rejection of the hypothesis of innocence offered at trial appears unreasonable and that no rational trier of fact could infer that the defendant knew the wrenches were stolen and that he intended to divest himself of the property quickly with the aid of the greatly reduced price.

* * *

CONVICTION AND SENTENCE REINSTATED; CASE REMANDED TO THE COURT OF APPEAL.

―――――

NOTES

1. Although Johnson purchased the tools for $30, the prosecutors do not appear to have charged him with a crime. Rather, prosecutors charged Chester (the person who sold the property to Johnson) with possession of stolen property. The clear implication of the case is that Chester stole the victim's truck and then sold the property at a very low price to the first person he could find. Why then did prosecutors not charge Chester with the more serious crime of larceny? As a purely intellectual matter, does it make sense to say that Chester received stolen property? Should that label and crime be reserved for pawn shops and individuals who actually purchase the property from thieves?

2. In a case like *Chester*, how does the prosecution prove *mens rea* for possession of stolen property? What facts suggest that Chester had a culpable *mens rea*?

3. In a number of jurisdictions, courts have held that the unexplained possession of recently stolen property gives rise to a presumption or an inference that the possessor is either the thief or the receiver of stolen property. Frequently the jury is so instructed. The presumption of guilt that the jury is allowed to draw in many jurisdictions is far reaching. In the majority of jurisdictions, the presumption might be used to infer the possessor was a criminal receiver. In other jurisdictions, however, the presumption permits a finding that the defendant was the thief. In Ferrell v. Commonwealth, 11 Va.App. 380, 399 S.E.2d 614 (1990), the court said that where the evidence shows a breaking and entering followed by the theft of goods, and the evidence warrants the inference that the breaking and entering and the theft were committed at the same time by the same person as part of the same transaction then the conscious assertion of exclusive possession of the stolen goods shortly thereafter gives rise to the inference that the possessor is guilty of breaking and entering. *Cf.* Mills v. Commonwealth, 1994 WL 410864 (Va.App.1994) (distinguishing *Ferrell*).

4. Consider the possession presumption in the light of Sandstrom v. Montana, *supra* in Chapter 2. In Williamson v. State, 248 Ga. 47, 281 S.E.2d 512 (1981), the Georgia Supreme Court held that *Sandstrom* precludes proof of a material element of a crime by way of a mandatory presumption, but does not affect a permissive inference of guilt from the "recent unexplained" possession of stolen goods, which does not relieve the prosecution of its burden of proof nor require the defense to prove the contrary by any quantum of proof.

5. Some states, although not operating under a comprehensive theft statute, treat receiving stolen property as larceny. Gunter v. Peyton, 287 F.Supp. 928

(W.D.Va.1968). In Cabbler v. Commonwealth, 212 Va. 520, 184 S.E.2d 781 (1971), it was stated that larceny by receiving stolen goods is a lesser offense that is included in the major one of larceny. If the prosecution elects to charge the greater offense under the general larceny statutes, the defendant could nevertheless be found guilty of receiving stolen property.

6. The Model Penal Code § 223.6, Receiving Stolen Property reads:

(1) *Receiving.* A person is guilty of theft if he purposely receives, retains, or disposes of moveable property of another knowing that it has been stolen, or believing that it has probably been stolen, unless the property is received, retained, or disposed with purpose to restore it to the owner. "Receiving" means acquiring possession, control or title, or lending on the security of the property.

(2) *Presumption of Knowledge.* The requisite knowledge or belief is presumed in the case of a dealer who:

(a) is found in possession or control of property stolen from two or more persons on separate occasions; or

(b) has received stolen property in another transaction within the year preceding the transaction charged; . . .

Does the Model Penal Code's approach seem fairer to defendants than the presumption described in Note 3? Or does the Model Penal Code unfairly allow convictions based on prior conduct that is not at issue in the present case? Does the Model Penal Code approach make it too easy to convict someone just because they have committed crimes in the past?

G. CONSOLIDATION OF THEFT OFFENSES

As you have surely noticed, the distinctions between larceny, larceny by trick, false pretenses, embezzlement, and receiving stolen property can be quite confusing. Modern legislatures have tried to simplify the common law rules through a process known as consolidation. Consider the following Texas statutes.

Tex. Pen. Code § 31.02, Consolidation of Theft Offenses

Theft as defined in Section 31.03 constitutes a single offense superseding the separate offenses previously known as theft, theft by false pretext, conversion by a bailee, theft from the person, shoplifting, acquisition of property by threat, swindling, swindling by worthless check, embezzlement, extortion, receiving or concealing embezzled property, and receiving or concealing stolen property.

Tex. Pen. Code § 31.03, Theft

(a) A person commits an offense if he unlawfully appropriates property with intent to deprive the owner of property.

(b) Appropriation of property is unlawful if:

(1) it is without the owner's effective consent;

(2) the property is stolen and the actor appropriates the property knowing it was stolen by another; or

(3) property in the custody of any law enforcement agency was explicitly represented by any law enforcement agent to the actor as being stolen and the actor appropriates the property believing it was stolen by another.

(c) For purposes of Subsection (b):

(1) evidence that the actor has previously participated in recent transactions other than, but similar to, that which the prosecution is based is admissible for the purpose of showing knowledge or intent and the issues of knowledge or intent are raised by the actor's plea of not guilty;

(2) the testimony of an accomplice shall be corroborated by proof that tends to connect the actor to the crime, but the actor's knowledge or intent may be established by the uncorroborated testimony of the accomplice;

(3) an actor engaged in the business of buying and selling used or secondhand personal property, or lending money on the security of personal property deposited with the actor, is presumed to know upon receipt by the actor of stolen property (other than a motor vehicle subject to Chapter 501, Transportation Code) that the property has been previously stolen from another if the actor pays for or loans against the property $25 or more (or consideration of equivalent value) and the actor knowingly or recklessly:

(A) fails to record the name, address, and physical description or identification number of the seller or pledgor;

(B) fails to record a complete description of the property, including the serial number, if reasonably available, or other identifying characteristics; or

(C) fails to obtain a signed warranty from the seller or pledgor that the seller or pledgor has the right to possess the property. It is the express intent of this provision that the presumption arises unless the actor complies with each of the numbered requirements;

(4) for the purposes of Subdivision (3)(A), "identification number" means driver's license number, military identification number, identification certificate, or other official number capable of identifying an individual;

(5) stolen property does not lose its character as stolen when recovered by any law enforcement agency;

(6) an actor engaged in the business of obtaining abandoned or wrecked motor vehicles or parts of an abandoned or wrecked motor vehicle for resale, disposal, scrap, repair, rebuilding, demolition, or

other form of salvage is presumed to know on receipt by the actor of stolen property that the property has been previously stolen from another if the actor knowingly or recklessly:

(A) fails to maintain an accurate and legible inventory of each motor vehicle component part purchased by or delivered to the actor, including the date of purchase or delivery, the name, age, address, sex, and driver's license number of the seller or person making the delivery, the license plate number of the motor vehicle in which the part was delivered, a complete description of the part, and the vehicle identification number of the motor vehicle from which the part was removed, or in lieu of maintaining an inventory, fails to record the name and certificate of inventory number of the person who dismantled the motor vehicle from which the part was obtained;

(B) fails on receipt of a motor vehicle to obtain a certificate of authority, sales receipt, or transfer document as required by Chapter 683, Transportation Code, or a certificate of title showing that the motor vehicle is not subject to a lien or that all recorded liens on the motor vehicle have been released; or

(C) fails on receipt of a motor vehicle to immediately remove an unexpired license plate from the motor vehicle, to keep the plate in a secure and locked place, or to maintain an inventory, on forms provided by the Texas Department of Motor Vehicles, of license plates kept under this paragraph, including for each plate or set of plates the license plate number and the make, motor number, and vehicle identification number of the motor vehicle from which the plate was removed;

(7) an actor who purchases or receives a used or secondhand motor vehicle is presumed to know on receipt by the actor of the motor vehicle that the motor vehicle has been previously stolen from another if the actor knowingly or recklessly:

(A) fails to report to the Texas Department of Motor Vehicles the failure of the person who sold or delivered the motor vehicle to the actor to deliver to the actor a properly executed certificate of title to the motor vehicle at the time the motor vehicle was delivered; or

(B) fails to file with the county tax assessor-collector of the county in which the actor received the motor vehicle, not later than the 20th day after the date the actor received the motor vehicle, the registration license receipt and certificate of title or evidence of title delivered to the actor in accordance with Subchapter D, Chapter 520, Transportation Code, at the time the motor vehicle was delivered;

(8) an actor who purchases or receives from any source other than a licensed retailer or distributor of pesticides a restricted-use pesticide or a state-limited-use pesticide or a compound, mixture, or preparation containing a restricted-use or state-limited-use pesticide is presumed to know on receipt by the actor of the pesticide or compound, mixture, or preparation that the pesticide or compound, mixture, or preparation has been previously stolen from another if the actor:

(A) fails to record the name, address, and physical description of the seller or pledgor;

(B) fails to record a complete description of the amount and type of pesticide or compound, mixture, or preparation purchased or received; and

(C) fails to obtain a signed warranty from the seller or pledgor that the seller or pledgor has the right to possess the property; and

(9) an actor who is subject to Section 409, Packers and Stockyards Act (7 U.S.C. Section 228b), that obtains livestock from a commission merchant by representing that the actor will make prompt payment is presumed to have induced the commission merchant's consent by deception if the actor fails to make full payment in accordance with Section 409, Packers and Stockyards Act (7 U.S.C. Section 228b).

(d) It is not a defense to prosecution under this section that:

(1) the offense occurred as a result of a deception or strategy on the part of a law enforcement agency, including the use of an undercover operative or peace officer;

(2) the actor was provided by a law enforcement agency with a facility in which to commit the offense or an opportunity to engage in conduct constituting the offense; or

(3) the actor was solicited to commit the offense by a peace officer, and the solicitation was of a type that would encourage a person predisposed to commit the offense to actually commit the offense, but would not encourage a person not predisposed to commit the offense to actually commit the offense.

(e) Except as provided by Subsection (f), an offense under this section is:

(1) a Class C misdemeanor if the value of the property stolen is less than:

(A) $50; or

(B) $20 and the defendant obtained the property by issuing or passing a check or similar sight order in a manner described by Section 31.06;

(2) a Class B misdemeanor if:

(A) the value of the property stolen is:

(i) $50 or more but less than $500; or

(ii) $20 or more but less than $500 and the defendant obtained the property by issuing or passing a check or similar sight order in a manner described by Section 31.06;

(B) the value of the property stolen is less than:

(i) $50 and the defendant has previously been convicted of any grade of theft; or

(ii) $20, the defendant has previously been convicted of any grade of theft, and the defendant obtained the property by issuing or passing a check or similar sight order in a manner described by Section 31.06; or

(C) the property stolen is a driver's license, commercial driver's license, or personal identification certificate issued by this state or another state;

(3) a Class A misdemeanor if the value of the property stolen is $500 or more but less than $1,500;

(4) a state jail felony if:

(A) the value of the property stolen is $1,500 or more but less than $20,000, or the property is less than 10 head of sheep, swine, or goats or any part thereof under the value of $20,000;

(B) regardless of value, the property is stolen from the person of another or from a human corpse or grave, including property that is a military grave marker;

(C) the property stolen is a firearm, as defined by Section 46.01;

(D) the value of the property stolen is less than $1,500 and the defendant has been previously convicted two or more times of any grade of theft;

(E) the property stolen is an official ballot or official carrier envelope for an election; or

(F) the value of the property stolen is less than $20,000 and the property stolen is:

(i) aluminum;

(ii) bronze;

(iii) copper; or

(iv) brass;

(5) a felony of the third degree if the value of the property stolen is $20,000 or more but less than $100,000, or the property is:

(A) cattle, horses, or exotic livestock or exotic fowl as defined by Section 142.001, Agriculture Code, stolen during a single transaction and having an aggregate value of less than $100,000; or

(B) 10 or more head of sheep, swine, or goats stolen during a single transaction and having an aggregate value of less than $100,000;

(6) a felony of the second degree if:

(A) the value of the property stolen is $100,000 or more but less than $200,000; or

(B) the value of the property stolen is less than $200,000 and the property stolen is an automated teller machine or the contents or components of an automated teller machine; or

(7) a felony of the first degree if the value of the property stolen is $200,000 or more.

(f) An offense described for purposes of punishment by Subsections (e)(1)–(6) is increased to the next higher category of offense if it is shown on the trial of the offense that:

(1) the actor was a public servant at the time of the offense and the property appropriated came into the actor's custody, possession, or control by virtue of his status as a public servant;

(2) the actor was in a contractual relationship with government at the time of the offense and the property appropriated came into the actor's custody, possession, or control by virtue of the contractual relationship;

(3) the owner of the property appropriated was at the time of the offense:

(A) an elderly individual; or

(B) a nonprofit organization;

(4) the actor was a Medicare provider in a contractual relationship with the federal government at the time of the offense and the property appropriated came into the actor's custody, possession, or control by virtue of the contractual relationship; or

(5) during the commission of the offense, the actor intentionally, knowingly, or recklessly:

(A) caused a fire exit alarm to sound or otherwise become activated;

(B) deactivated or otherwise prevented a fire exit alarm or retail theft detector from sounding; or

(C) used a shielding or deactivation instrument to prevent or attempt to prevent detection of the offense by a retail theft detector.

(g) For the purposes of Subsection (a), a person is the owner of exotic livestock or exotic fowl as defined by Section 142.001, Agriculture Code, only if the person qualifies to claim the animal under Section 142.0021, Agriculture Code, if the animal is an estray.

(h) In this section:

(1) "Restricted-use pesticide" means a pesticide classified as a restricted-use pesticide by the administrator of the Environmental Protection Agency under 7 U.S.C. Section 136a, as that law existed on January 1, 1995, and containing an active ingredient listed in the federal regulations adopted under that law (40 C.F.R. Section 152.175) and in effect on that date.

(2) "State-limited-use pesticide" means a pesticide classified as a state-limited-use pesticide by the Department of Agriculture under Section 76.003, Agriculture Code, as that section existed on January 1, 1995, and containing an active ingredient listed in the rules adopted under that section (4 TAC Section 7.24) as that section existed on that date.

(3) "Nonprofit organization" means an organization that is exempt from federal income taxation under Section 501(a), Internal Revenue Code of 1986, by being described as an exempt organization by Section 501(c)(3) of that code.

(4) "Automated teller machine" means an unstaffed electronic information processing device that, at the request of a user, performs a financial transaction through the direct transmission of electronic impulses to a financial institution or through the recording of electronic impulses or other indicia of a transaction for delayed transmission to a financial institution. The term includes an automated banking machine.

(i) For purposes of Subsection (c)(9), "livestock" and "commission merchant" have the meanings assigned by Section 147.001, Agriculture Code.

(j) With the consent of the appropriate local county or district attorney, the attorney general has concurrent jurisdiction with that consenting local prosecutor to prosecute an offense under this section that involves the state Medicaid program.

———

NOTES

1. Is the Texas statute clearer than the common law rules?

2. Even jurisdictions that have consolidated larceny, embezzlement and other crimes under the umbrella of "theft" still continue to have multiple different theft offenses in their criminal code. For instance, in addition to the offense of "Theft" in section 31.01 of the Texas Penal Code, there are more

Mrs. Morin was without funds at the time. A contingent fee agreement was signed by Mrs. Morin and the firm of Harrington and Jackson, by the respondent. The agreement was dated March 5, 1968 and provided that in the event a satisfactory property settlement was obtained, the respondent's firm was to receive twelve and a half percent of the settlement, in addition to reimbursement for expenses advanced by counsel. Electronic listening and recording equipment was ordered and delivered by air.

On the afternoon of March 6 the respondent and two office associates traveled to St. Johnsbury in two vehicles. Mrs. Mazza continued on to Littleton unaccompanied. She registered on arrival at the Continental 93 Motel under the name of Jeanne Raeder. She called the respondent at St. Johnsbury from a public telephone and informed him of her room number and location. Mrs. Mazza later delivered the key to her room to the respondent to enable him to procure a duplicate. The respondent, representing that he was a book salesman, registered at the motel and procured a room directly above that occupied by Mrs. Mazza. He was accompanied by a junior associate and an investigator—both employed by the respondent's law firm.

During the next day Mrs. Mazza attracted Mr. Morin's attention. The sequence of events which followed led to an invitation by Morin for her to join him at his apartment for a cocktail. Mrs. Mazza accepted. Later she suggested that they go to her room because Mr. Morin's young son was asleep in his quarters. Morin went to Mrs. Mazza's room about midnight. Soon after the appointed hour the respondent and his associates entered the room. With one or more cameras, several photographs were taken of Morin and Mrs. Mazza in bed and unclothed. Morin grabbed for one camera and broke it.

During the time of her stay at the motel Mrs. Mazza carried an electronic transmitter in her handbag. By means of this device, her conversations with Morin were monitored by the respondent and his associates.

The respondent and his companions checked out of the motel at about one in the morning. Before doing so, there was a brief confrontation with Morin. According to Morin's testimony, the respondent demanded $125,000. Morin testified—"at that time I made him an offer of $25,000 to return everything he had, and in a second breath I retracted the offer."

The following day the respondent conferred with Mrs. Morin and reported the events of the trip to New Hampshire. He asked Mrs. Morin to consider reconciliation over the weekend. On March 11, 1968, Mrs. Morin informed the respondent she decided it was too late for reconciliation. With this decision, the respondent dictated, in the presence of Mrs. Morin, a letter which was received in evidence as State's Exhibit 1. The letter was addressed to Armand Morin at Littleton, New

Hampshire, and was placed in the United States mail at Burlington the same day.

The communication is designated personal and confidential. The following excerpts are taken from the full text:

Basically, your wife desires a divorce, and if it can be equitably arranged, she would prefer that the divorce be as quiet and as undamaging as possible.

This letter is being written in your wife's presence and has been completely authorized by your wife. The offer of settlement contained herein is made in the process of negotiation and is, of course, made without prejudice to your wife's rights.

It is the writer's thinking that for the children's sake, for your sake, and for Mrs. Morin's sake, that neither the courts in New Hampshire nor in Vermont, should become involved in this potentially explosive divorce. If a suitable "stipulation or separation agreement" can be worked out, the writer would recommend a Mexican, Stipulation-Divorce. This divorce would be based upon the catch-all grounds "Incompatability." . . .

Mrs. Morin is willing to give up the following:

1. All of her marital rights, including her rights to share in your estate.

2. All of her right, title and interest, jointly or by reason of marital status, that she has in and to, any or all property of the marriage, including the Continental 93 Motel, the three (3) farms in Vermont, the capital stock that you own, the house in Lindenville, the joint venture in land in East Burke, all personal property except as is specifically hereinafter mentioned and in short, all rights that she may now have or might acquire in the future, as your wife. Furthermore, any such settlement would include the return to you of all tape recordings, all negatives, all photographs and copies of photographs that might in any way, bring discredit upon yourself. Finally, there would be an absolute undertaking on the part of your wife not to divulge any information of any kind or nature which might be embarrassing to you in your business life, your personal life, your financial life, of your life as it might be affected by the Internal Revenue Service, the United States Customs Service, or any other governmental agency.

The letter goes on to specify the terms of settlement required by Mrs. Morin, concerning custody of the minor child, her retention of an automobile and the disposition of certain designated personal effects. It further provides:

5. Mrs. Morin would waive all alimony upon receipt of One Hundred Seventy Five Thousand Dollars ($175,000)

The sum of $25,000 is specified to be paid at the signing of the separation agreement, with the balance due according to a schedule of payments over the period of eighteen months.

The letter continues:

At the present time Mrs. Morin is almost without funds. . . . Because of her shortage of money, and, because she is badly missing David, and finally, because she cannot continue for any substantial period of time to live in the present vacuum, the writer must require prompt communication from you with respect to the proposed settlement contained herein. . . . Unless the writer has heard from you on or before March 22, we will have no alternative but to withdraw the offer and bring immediate divorce proceedings in Grafton County. This will, of course, require the participation by the writer's correspondent attorneys in New Hampshire. If we were to proceed under New Hampshire laws, without any stipulation, it would be necessary to allege, in detail, all of the grounds that Mrs. Morin has in seeking the divorce. The writer is, at present, undecided as to advising Mrs. Morin whether or not to file for 'informer fees' with respect to the Internal Revenue Service and the United States Customs Service. In any event, we would file, alleging adultery, including affidavits, alleging extreme cruelty and beatings, and asking for a court order enjoining you from disposing of any property, including your stock interests, during the pendency of the proceeding.

The thought has been expressed that you might, under certain circumstances, decide to liquidate what you could and abscond to Canada or elsewhere. The writer would advise you that this would in no way impede Mrs. Morin's action. You would be served by publication and under those circumstances, I am very certain that all property in New Hampshire and in Vermont, would be awarded, beyond any question, to Mrs. Morin.

With absolutely no other purpose than to prove to you that we have all of the proof necessary to prove adultery beyond a reasonable doubt, we are enclosing a photograph taken by one of my investigators on the early morning of March 8. The purpose of enclosing the photograph as previously stated, is simply to show you that cameras and equipment were in full operating order. . . .

It was stipulated that the letter was received by Morin in Littleton, New Hampshire "in the due course of the mail."

Such is the evidence upon which the respondent was found guilty. . . .

Turning to the other grounds advanced in the motion for acquittal, the respondent maintains his letter (State's Exhibit 1) does not constitute a threat to accuse Morin of the crime of adultery. He argues the implicit threats contained in the communication were "not to accuse of the CRIME of adultery but to bring an embarrassing, reputation-ruining divorce proceeding in Mr. Morin's county of residence unless a stipulation could be negotiated." . . .

In dealing with a parallel contention in *State v. Louanis*, 79 Vt. 463, 467, 65 A. 532, 533, the Court answered the argument in an opinion by Chief Judge Rowell.

> The statute is aimed at blackmailing, and a threat of any public accusation is as much within the reason of the statute as a threat of a formal complaint, and is much easier made, and may be quite as likely to accomplish its purpose. There is nothing in the statute that requires such a restricted meaning of the word "accuse"; and to restrict it thus, would well nigh destroy the efficacy of the act.

The letter, marked "personal and confidential," makes a private accusation of adultery in support of a demand for a cash settlement. An incriminating photograph was enclosed for the avowed purpose of demonstrating "we have all of the proof necessary to prove adultery beyond a reasonable doubt." According to the writing itself, cost of refusal will be public exposure of incriminating conduct in the courts of New Hampshire where the event took place.

In further support of motion for acquittal, the respondent urges that the totality of the evidence does not exclude the inference that he acted merely as an attorney, attempting to secure a divorce for his client on the most favorable terms possible. This of course, was the theory of the defense.

The case presented by the State did not require the court to accept the hypothesis of innocence claimed by the respondent. The acts which he performed and the words that he wrote are established by direct and documentary evidence that is not contradicted. The doctrine . . . advanced by the defense to the effect that the evidence must exclude every reasonable hypothesis except that the respondent is guilty, does not avail him. The rule applies only where the evidence is entirely circumstantial.

The law affords him a presumption of innocence which attends him until the jury returns its verdict. As in all criminal causes, consistent with the right to trial by jury, it was within the province of the triers of the fact to accept the defendant's claim of innocence. After weighing all the evidence in the area of reasonable doubt, the jury might have been persuaded to infer that the accused acted without malicious intent. But the evidence contains the requisite proof to convince the jury to a contrary conclusion.

At the time of the writing, the respondent was undecided whether to advise his client to seek "informer fees." One of the advantages tendered to Morin for a "quiet" and "undamaging" divorce is an "absolute undertaking" on the part of the respondent's client not to inform against him in any way. The Internal Revenue Service, the United States Customs Service and other governmental agencies are suggested as being interested in such information. Quite clearly, these veiled threats exceeded the limits of the respondent's representation of his client in the divorce action. Although these matters were not specified in the indictment, they have a competent bearing on the question of intent.

Apart from this, the advancement of his client's claim to the marital property, however well founded, does not afford legal cause for the trial court to direct a verdict of acquittal in the background and context of his letter to Morin. A demand for settlement of a civil action, accompanied by a malicious threat to expose the wrongdoer's criminal conduct, if made with intent to extort payment, against his will, constitutes the crime alleged in the indictment.

The evidence at hand establishes beyond dispute the respondent's participation was done with preconceived design. The incriminating evidence which his letter threatens to expose was wilfully contrived and procured by a temptress hired for that purpose. These factors in the proof are sufficient to sustain a finding that the respondent acted maliciously and without just cause, within the meaning of our criminal statutes. The sum of the evidence supports the further inference that the act was done with intent to extort a substantial contingent fee to the respondent's personal advantage.

The pronouncement of the jury, in resolving guilt against innocence, does not result from pyramiding inference on inference. Whether the letter threatened to accuse Morin of a crime must be determined from its text. The question of malicious intent similarly depends on the language of the letter. It can also be referred to extraneous facts and circumstances which occurred prior to the writing. . . . The record sustains the court's jurisdiction to try the offense. The evidence of guilt is ample to support the verdict and the trial was free from errors in law.

Judgment affirmed.

———

Problem 7–8. Victoria noticed that her cell phone was missing—either stolen or lost. The next day she called the cell phone number and the person who answered told her "If you want your phone back meet me in front of the Apollo at 263 West 125th Street at 3:00 P.M. tomorrow and if you want it back you will have to give me $160 dollars." Victoria went to the specified location where she met defendant Larson, who asked her, "where is the money?" Larson was arrested and the cell phone was found in his pocket. Assuming that he merely found the phone, has Larson committed extortion?

Larceny? Theft? Explain. What if he purchased it from the thief, without knowing it was stolen—would that change your analysis above?

I. ROBBERY

1. ELEMENTS OF ROBBERY

Robbery was defined at common law as the "felonious taking and carrying away of the personal property of another, from his person or in his presence, by violence, or by putting him in fear."[31] In other words, common law robbery is larceny from the person or presence of another accompanied by the use of force, or by threatening the imminent use of force. Robbery is traditionally classified as a crime against the person; but because the ultimate purpose of the crime is the misappropriation of property, it is included in this section. The common law concept of robbery, however, has been extensively modified by both state and federal statutes, and these changes often require courts to consider to what extent the common law interpretation of terms applies in interpreting a statute.

(A) THE *MENS REA* OF ROBBERY

If a defendant uses force to recover what he believes to be his own property, is that robbery? What if the defendant is owed a monetary debt, can he collect the cash by force?

Thomas v. State

District Court of Appeal of Florida, 1991.
584 So.2d 1022.

■ ZEHMER, JUDGE.

Ronald Anthony Thomas appeals his convictions of first degree murder for violating section 782.04(1)(a), Florida Statutes (1989), and armed robbery with a firearm for violating section 812.13. The jury found him guilty as charged of taking money from the deceased victim and killing him. Thomas raises a single point on appeal, urging reversible error in the trial court's failure to instruct the jury that "a well-founded belief by the defendant that he is the rightful owner of the property in dispute is a complete defense to the charge of robbery." In denying the requested instruction, the trial judge stated that such an instruction is appropriate only where the item taken is a specific identifiable object like a car, bicycle, or piece of furniture, rather than a fungible good like money. Agreeing with the trial court's ruling, we affirm.

The evidence established, primarily through the pretrial confession and trial testimony given by Thomas, the following sequence of events

---

[31] Melvin Wingersky, ed., CLARK & MARSHALL, A TREATISE ON THE LAW OF CRIMES, at 781 (6th ed. 1952).

culminating in the charged robbery and murder. About two weeks before the offense took place, the victim and a girl friend each gave Thomas $10 to purchase some crack cocaine for them. Thomas did not find any in the area, so he sent the money back to the victim through another person. Thomas learned that the victim did not give the girl friend her $10, so Thomas also reimbursed her. On the night of the offenses Thomas, seeing the victim, walked up to him with a revolver in his right hand. Thomas demanded the victim give back the $10 Thomas had paid to the girl friend, and the victim kept saying he did not know what Thomas was talking about. Thomas raised the gun back to hit the victim to make the victim understand that he could not get away with taking his (Thomas's) money, and when he swung the gun to hit the victim in the chest, the victim blocked it with his left arm and the gun went off. At that point, the victim handed Thomas the money and said, "You shot me." Thomas disclaimed any intent to shoot the victim. The jury was instructed on both premeditated murder and felony murder under count one, and armed robbery with a firearm under count two, without the so-called "good faith" or "claim of right" instruction requested by Thomas. The jury found Thomas guilty of both offenses as charged.

Both Thomas and the state agree that no Florida appellate decision has decided whether a claim of right defense is available to a defendant who seeks to collect a debt or recover money by use of force or threat, and our research has not shown any Florida case directly on point. In support of the requested instruction, Thomas relies primarily on *Thomas v. State,* 526 So.2d 183 (Fla. 3d DCA 1988), *rev. denied,* 536 So.2d 245 (Fla.1988), and *Rodriguez v. State,* 396 So.2d 798 (Fla. 3d DCA 1981), arguing that both cases have recognized that a defendant's good faith belief that he has the right to the property taken negates the requisite intent to commit robbery and constitutes a lawful defense to the offense charged. The state, on the other hand, distinguishes those cases from the facts of this case and argues that while many other jurisdictions have considered this issue, the majority of such jurisdictions have concluded that public policy reasons militate against the availability of this defense by any defendant charged with robbery, citing the annotation at 88 A.L.R.3d 1309 and the following cases: *State v. Larsen,* 23 Wash.App. 218, 596 P.2d 1089, 1090 (1979); *Rozika v. State,* 520 N.E.2d 1267 (Ind.1988); *Commonwealth v. Sleighter,* 495 Pa. 262, 433 A.2d 469 (1981); *Austin v. State,* 86 Wis.2d 213, 271 N.W.2d 668 (1978); *State v. Self,* 42 Wash.App. 654, 713 P.2d 142 (1986); *State v. Martin,* 15 Or.App. 498, 516 P.2d 753 (1974); and *State v. Schaefer,* 163 Ariz. 626, 790 P.2d 281 (Ct.App.1990) . . . .

* * *

It appears that most jurisdictions recognize the common law rule that a forcible taking of property under a bona fide claim of right is not robbery where the taker has a good faith belief that he is the owner of the property or is entitled to immediate possession, because this belief negates the taker's intent to steal or commit larceny. The courts of many jurisdictions, including Florida courts, have applied this principle to forcible takings under a bona fide claim of right to specific property, property taken as security, and gambling gains or losses. *See generally* 77 C.J.S. *Robbery* § 22(c) (1952); 67 Am.Jur.2d *Robbery* § 19 (1985); Annot., 88 A.L.R.3d 1309 (1978).

Two recent Florida decisions illustrate the application of this rule. In *Rodriguez v. State,* 396 So.2d 798 (Fla. 3d DCA 1981), the defendants were managers of a motel and had retained and failed to submit to the motel owner the proceeds from three room rentals, claiming that they believed the money was theirs under the terms of a compensation agreement. They were prosecuted and convicted of theft of the money. On appeal, the third district reversed the conviction for a new trial, holding that the trial court erred in refusing to give the following requested jury instruction: "Where it clearly appears that the taking of property was consistent with honest conduct, as where the taker honestly believes that he or she has a right to property, the taker cannot be convicted of theft, even though the taker may have been mistaken." *Id.* at 798–99. In *Thomas v. State,* 526 So.2d 183 (Fla. 3d DCA 1988), a prosecution for armed robbery, the court found reversible error in the trial court's failure to instruct the jury that the defendant's good faith belief that the bicycle he forcibly took from the victim belonged to him was a valid defense to the robbery charge. Relying on *Rodriguez* and the line of older appellate decisions cited therein recognizing the common law rule "that a well-founded belief in one's right to the allegedly stolen property constitutes a complete defense to a charge of theft," the court concluded that since a theft is an essential element of robbery, the trial court was obliged to give the instruction. *Id.* at 184.

On the other hand, in many jurisdictions the claim of right defense has been denied in cases involving charges of robbery where the collection of a debt was honestly believed to be due but force or violent intimidation was used to effect the taking. The underlying rationale for this position has most frequently been said to be that the defendant has no ownership or immediate possessory interest in the specific property taken, i.e., money, and under such circumstances the requisite intent to steal is present. For example, affirming a conviction for robbery in *State v. Larsen,* 23 Wash.App. 218, 596 P.2d 1089 (1979), the court approved an instruction, given over the defendant's objections, stating that "a creditor's intent to collect a debt from his debtor by use or threatened use of immediate force, violence or fear of injury is not a defense to a charge of Robbery." The court explained:

Where self-help is used to recover *specific property,* it is a defense to a charge of robbery that a claim of title is made in good faith . . . Under these circumstances, the defense is allowed because it raises the question of whether the actor proceeded with the intent necessary to constitute the crime of robbery. A contrary rule would prevent an owner of property who caught a thief in the act of carrying away that property from retaking it by force . . . Where, as in this case, a person uses force to collect a debt with no claim of ownership in the specific property acquired, the defense is not allowed because the requisite intent necessary to constitute robbery is present . . . .

Moreover, acceptance of Larsen's argument would sanction debt collection by force contrary to one of the purposes of Washington's Criminal Code, which is "[t]o forbid and prevent conduct that inflicts or threatens substantial harm to individual or public interests." RCW 9A.04.020(1)(a). As stated in *State v. Ortiz,* 124 N.J.Super. 189, 192, 305 A.2d 800, 802 (1973):

> In our view, the proposition not only is lacking in sound reason and logic, but it is utterly incompatible with and has no place in an ordered and orderly society such as ours, which eschews self-help through violence. Adoption of the proposition would be but one step short of accepting lawless reprisal as an appropriate means of redressing grievances, real or fancied. We reject it out of hand.

596 P.2d at 1090 (citations omitted). Similarly, in *State v. Martin,* 516 P.2d at 753, the court rejected the application of the claim of right as a defense to robbery in that case, and explained:

> In so doing, it is important to distinguish between, on the one hand, situations where a person simply uses self-help to recover a specific chattel to which he has the right to immediate possession, and, on the other hand, situations where a person attempts to collect a debt out of another's money, with no pretense of ownership rights in the specific coins and bills. As to the former situation, *State v. Luckey,* 150 Or. 566, 46 P.2d 1042 (1935), holds that intent to steal is absent when a person retakes wrongfully held specific personal property to which he has the right to possession . . . .

> But where, as here, the claim is to money owed, and in order to satisfy the claim, the creditor takes money or other fungible property to which he has no title or right of possession, then the intent to steal is present. Only if the defendant herein had ownership rights in specific coins and bills in Barley's possession would the principle of *State v. Luckey, supra,* be applicable. Here, there was no assertion of such an ownership right; the defendant was attempting to satisfy his alleged claim at gunpoint from whatever cash Barley might have had on his person.

* * *

516 P.2d at 755–56 . . . . We agree with the rationale of these cases, and hold that the common law rule set forth in *Thomas v. State,* 526 So.2d 183, is not available to defeat charges of robbery for forcibly taking money to satisfy a debt owed by the victim to the taker.

* * *

Finding no error in the trial court's denial of the requested instruction, the appealed conviction is **AFFIRMED**.

* * *

———

NOTES ON CLAIM OF RIGHT IN ROBBERY CASES

1. The *Thomas* court draws a distinction between reclaiming a bicycle and reclaiming money because the defendant would not have an ownership or possessory interest in the money. Is that right?

2. Some courts accept a claim of right defense in larceny cases, but reject it in robbery cases. *See* State v. Mejia, 662 A.2d 308, 320 (N.J. 1995) ("[The defendant's argument] hinge[s] on the following syllogism. Robbery equals theft plus assault. Claim of right is a defense to theft. Therefore, it is a defense to robbery . . . . Robbery, however, is a more complex crime than theft plus assault . . . Indeed, the Code's structure indicates that the Legislature intended that not all defenses to theft should apply to robbery.").

3. Perhaps the most famous example of a "claim of right" robbery case involved O.J. Simpson. After Simpson was acquitted of murdering his ex-wife and her friend Ronald Goldman, the family of Ronald Goldman sued Simpson for wrongful death and received a multi-million dollar verdict. Although Simpson did not pay the damages award, the judgment made it more difficult for him to earn money. As a result, Simpson sold his sports memorabilia to generate income. In 2007, Simpson and some associates broke into a Las Vegas hotel to recover memorabilia that Simpson claimed had been stolen from him; at least one person brandished a gun during the break in. Simpson was convicted of robbery and sentenced to 33 years in prison, with parole eligibility after 9 years. *See* Steve Friess, *O.J. Simpson Convicted of Robbery and Kidnapping*, N.Y. TIMES, Oct. 4, 2008. On appeal, Simpson contended, among other things, that the trial judge erred by failing to give the following jury instruction: ". . . [I]f you find the Defendant was under the mistaken impression that he was recovering his own property, then you must find that he lacks the General Intent to commit a prohibited act and render a not guilty verdict." The Supreme Court of Nevada rejected this argument in less than four paragraphs, noting that

> The law in Nevada as to robbery is clear: it is the unlawful taking of property from another by force or fear or violence . . . [A] good faith belief that the property at issue is one's own does not nullify the intent to take property from another by force . . . [I]f the jury

believed that Simpson thought he was recovering his own memorabilia, then, under Nevada law, Simpson was still *not* relieved of criminal liability.

Simpson v. State, No. 53080, 2010 WL 4226452, at *6 (Nev. Oct. 22, 2010).

4. Another interesting *mens rea* issue that can arise in robbery cases is whether a defendant who pays for property can nevertheless be convicted of robbery. In Jupiter v. State, 616 A.2d 412 (Md. 1992), the defendant attempted to purchase beer, but the owner refused because Jupiter was too intoxicated. Jupiter then left the bar and returned with a shotgun. Jupiter placed the shotgun on the counter and asked "Are you going to sell it to me now." The owner agreed and Jupiter paid for the beer in cash. The jury convicted Jupiter of robbery. Can a person be convicted of robbery if he paid for the property he is accused of forcibly stealing? On appeal, the Court of Appeals of Maryland said "yes," because "there is no requirement that the defendant deprive the victim of value; the requirement is simply that the defendant deprives the victim of possession of property of value."

(B) FORCE, FEAR AND INTIMIDATION ISSUES

A common issue in robbery cases is how much force must be applied before a larceny from the person will become a robbery. When the alleged robber believes *he* is the one being robbed, the issue of use of force becomes even more difficult.

Commonwealth v. Cruz

Appeals Court of Massachusetts, 2004.
61 Mass.App.Ct. 1110, 809 N.E.2d 1100.

■ MEMORANDUM AND ORDER PURSUANT TO RULE 1:28.

A jury found the defendant guilty of unarmed robbery (as a lesser included offense under an indictment for armed robbery) and two counts of assault by means of a dangerous weapon in an incident in which the defendant was found to have stolen a $68 pair of blue jeans from a Filene's department store, and thereafter to have assaulted Filene's security personnel who pursued him into the South Shore Plaza parking lot and tried forcibly and unsuccessfully to subdue him. On the defendant's postverdict motion pursuant to Mass. R. Crim. P. 25(b)(2), 378 Mass. 896 (1979), the trial judge then entered a finding of not guilty on the robbery indictment because, in her view, there was "nothing about the facts of this case that fit even the generous contours of robbery." The crux of her decision was that there was insufficient evidence that the "item was taken secretly . . . not from any person" and "[n]o violence or threat of violence occurred within the store, or indeed, within the mall itself."

These are cross appeals by the Commonwealth and by the defendant. The Commonwealth appeals from the judge's action on the defendant's postverdict motion regarding the robbery indictment and from the denial of its motion to reconsider that action. The defendant appeals from the two convictions of assault by means of a dangerous weapon. In the peculiar circumstances of this case, we conclude that the judge's failure to give a required, and requested, instruction on the use of nondeadly force in self-defense was error that deprived the defendant not only of the opportunity to establish that "the basis of the alleged assault . . . was a valid exercise of self-defense for which [he] should be acquitted" but also that any force used by him was to protect himself rather than to complete a taking of property. *Commonwealth v. Galvin*, 56 Mass.App.Ct. 698, 700, 779 N.E.2d 998 (2002). . . .

. . . Here, the defendant testified that he had left Filene's and was proceeding through the mall when he was accosted by two men in their twenties, dressed in casual clothing, with no identified or readily identifiable credentials. . . . They grabbed his arms without telling him who they were. He fled, and they pursued him into the parking lot where they used force in a continued attempt to subdue him. To get them to leave him alone, he told them he had a gun, which he did not have. The defendant believed the two young men were trying to rob him. He was frightened and he was just trying to escape from them.

On such evidence, the defendant was entitled to an instruction on the use of nondeadly force in self-defense. . . . *See Commonwealth v. Cataldo*, 423 Mass. 318, 325, 668 N.E.2d 762 (1996); . . . "Where evidence exists, from whatever source, to support a defendant's claim that he used nondeadly force in self-defense (force neither intended nor likely to cause death or great bodily harm), he is entitled to an instruction on the use of nondeadly force in self-defense." . . . The judge's refusal to give such instruction was error, as it relieved the Commonwealth of the burden of proving that the defendant was not exercising a right to self-defense that arises at a lower level of danger, concern for personal safety. . . .

The judge's failure to give a required instruction on the use of nondeadly force in self-defense not only affected the charge of assault by means of a dangerous weapon by relieving the Commonwealth of the burden of proving that the defendant was not in lawful exercise of his right to use nondeadly force to defend himself, it also hindered his defense to the Commonwealth's case for robbery, which rested on the proposition that the force used by the defendant was to complete a robbery rather than to defend himself. *See Commonwealth v. Sim*, 39 Mass. App.Ct. 212, 217, 654 N.E.2d 340 (1995) ("Escape is an element incident to the crime of robbery"). *See also* Model Penal Code § 221.1(1) & comment 2 (Official Draft 1980). We cannot be "sure that the error did not influence the jury, or had but very slight effect." *Commonwealth v. Alphas*, 430 Mass. 8, 13 n. 7, 712 N.E.2d 575 (1999), quoting from

Commonwealth v. Flebotte, 417 Mass. 348, 353, 630 N.E.2d 265 (1994). Compare *Commonwealth v. Cataldo*, 423 Mass. at 325, 668 N.E.2d 762 (lack of instruction on nondeadly force, although not requested, created a substantial risk of a miscarriage of justice). We therefore conclude that the error in the self-defense instructions extends not only to the charge of assault by means of a dangerous weapon, but also to that of robbery, and requires reversal. . . .

We agree with the Commonwealth, however, that the judge erred in entering the finding of not guilty on the robbery indictment because of her view that, even in the light most favorable to the Commonwealth, the force used was sufficiently attenuated from the taking to establish robbery. "[T]he effect of the decided cases is that the nexus between the force or fear and the taking may be relatively loose and yet encompass a robbery." *Commonwealth v. Lashway*, 36 Mass. App.Ct. 677, 680, 634 N.E.2d 930 (1994). . . . Cf. *Commonwealth v. Novicki*, 324 Mass. 461, 465, 87 N.E.2d 1 (1949) (evidence insufficient to support robbery verdict, but during escape no force used against victim named in indictment); *Commonwealth v. Goldstein*, 54 Mass. App. Ct. 863, 868, 768 N.E.2d 595 (2002) ("The problem with the motion judge's analysis [in dismissing an indictment for robbery] is that it depends upon a precise sequencing of events that is best reserved for a petit jury to sort out under proper instructions from the trial judge").

In light of our holding, we need not address the defendant's other arguments . . . .

Regarding the indictment charging armed robbery, the order allowing the postverdict motion for a required finding is vacated, the finding of not guilty is set aside, and the verdict of guilty of the lesser included offense of unarmed robbery is set aside. . . . The matter is remanded for further proceedings consistent with this memorandum.

So ordered.

Problem 7–9. Pearl was talking on the phone at an outdoor wall-mounted pay telephone, and was wearing a medallion with five diamonds attached to a 20-inch gold rope chain. Teddy approached her from across the street, reached out and snatched the necklace from her neck. Teddy then stared at her for about 10 seconds, took six to seven steps back, and then turned and walked slowly away. When Teddy reached the middle of the street, he turned around and stared at Pearl again. Teddy then ran down an alley. Pearl testified she was scared when Teddy took her necklace, and even more scared by the way in which Teddy stared at her afterwards. Has Teddy satisfied the "force" element that would transform the theft to a robbery?

NOTES ON ROBBERY

1. The common law typically required that the taking in a robbery be from the person or a person's presence. Are these requirements met when a bank teller receives a call from the defendant, who threatens to set off a bomb at the teller's home unless a large sum of money is delivered to a hidden location designated by the caller? *Compare* People v. Smith, 78 Ill.2d 298, 35 Ill.Dec. 761, 399 N.E.2d 1289 (1980) and Brinkley v. United States, 560 F.2d 871 (8th Cir. 1977), cert. denied 434 U.S. 941, 98 S.Ct. 435, 54 L.Ed.2d 302 with United States v. Culbert, 548 F.2d 1355 (9th Cir.), rev'd on other grounds 435 U.S. 371, 98 S.Ct. 1112, 55 L.Ed.2d 349 (1978) and People v. Moore, 184 Colo. 110, 518 P.2d 944 (1974).

2. Statutes have changed some of the common law elements of robbery. *See* Carter v. United States, 530 U.S. 255, 120 S.Ct. 2159, 147 L.Ed.2d 203 (2000) which held that the federal bank robbery statute was not limited to common-law robbery, or larceny by force or fear, and did not include a specific intent *mens rea*. The Court said,

> As to "intent to steal or purloin," it will be recalled that the text of subsection (b) requires a specific "intent to steal or purloin," whereas subsection (a) contains no explicit *mens rea* requirement of any kind. Carter nevertheless argues that such a *specific intent* requirement must be deemed implicitly present in § 2113(a) by virtue of "our cases interpreting criminal statutes to include broadly applicable *scienter* requirements, even where the statute by its terms does not contain them." United States v. X-Citement Video, Inc., 513 U.S. 64 (1994). . . . Properly applied to § 2113, however, the presumption in favor of *scienter* demands only that we read subsection (a) as requiring proof of *general intent*—that is, that the defendant possessed knowledge with respect to the *actus reus* of the crime (here, the taking of property of another by force and violence or intimidation).

3. Imagine that Robin Robber wanted to steal money from a bank. She practiced a threatening speech to give to the teller and she planned to raise her shirt to reveal a gun in her waistband. Robin walked into the bank prepared to give the speech and show the gun. The teller, who was a very nervous person, noticed that Robin had a hand in her jacket pocket. Before Robin could do or say anything, the clerk screamed, "I know you have a gun in your pocket. Don't kill me. Take all the money." The teller filled a bag with cash and threw it on the floor. Robin, who had yet to say or do anything, picked up the bag and left the bank. If Robin is charged with robbery, should she be convicted? *See* United States v. Bellew, 369 F.3d 450 (5th Cir. 2004).

4. Now imagine that Robin walked up to the teller and handed him a blank deposit ticket. The teller was confused and said "Excuse me?" Robin responded by saying "How much money do you have in the drawer?" A police officer overheard the conversation and arrested Robin. Can she be convicted of robbery? *See* United States v. Pina, 889 F.2d 1097 (9th Cir. 1989).

5. Finally, imagine that Robin walked into the bank and held up a long-barreled butane lighter—the type of lighter you use to light candles—and yelled "Give me the money or I will shoot." If Robin is charged under 18 U.S.C. § 2113(d) with robbing a federally insured bank with a "dangerous weapon or device" should she be convicted? *See* United States v. Dixon, 790 F.3d 758 (7th Cir. 2015). For a convincing argument that the Seventh Circuit used the wrong analysis and reached the wrong conclusion, see Cory A. Hutchens, *Is That a Kielbasa in Your Pocket? Applying a Hybrid Standard to the Federal Bank Robbery Act When Bank Robbers Wield Objects as Weapons During a Bank Robbery*, 65 Am. U. L. Rev. 1497 (2016).

---

2. ARMED ROBBERY

A sizeable number of jurisdictions provide, by statute, for an aggravated form of robbery, usually called "armed robbery," for which a greater penalty is provided. Such statutes typically provide that an armed robbery requires the commission of a robbery "while armed with a dangerous weapon."[32] The Supreme Judicial Court of Massachusetts has stated that the gist of the offense of armed robbery is the commission of an offense while armed and it is not necessary to show the use of a dangerous weapon in proving the offense.[33] All that need be shown is that the defendant carried a weapon on his person while he committed the robbery.[34]

NOTES ON ARMED ROBBERY

1. Is an unloaded gun a "dangerous weapon"? Most courts seem to hold that any unloaded firearm that can be used as a bludgeon is a dangerous weapon. *See* Jeffrey F. Ghent, *Annot. Fact that Gun Was Unloaded As Affecting Criminal Responsibility*, 68 A.L.R. 4th 507 (1989) (2007 cum. supp.) and *Annot., Robbery By Means of Toy or Simulated Gun or Pistol*, 81 A.L.R.3d 1006 (1977) (2007 cum. supp.) In People v. Roden, 21 N.Y.2d 810, 288 N.Y.S.2d 638, 235 N.E.2d 776 (1968), the Court of Appeals of New York held that an unloaded gun was a dangerous weapon within the meaning of the former Penal Law under which the appellant was charged, even though there was no evidence that the gun had been used as a bludgeon. *But cf.*, People v. Richards, 28 Ill.App.3d 505, 328 N.E.2d 692 (1975), and People v. Santucci, 48 A.D.2d 909, 369 N.Y.S.2d 490 (1975).

2. Can toy guns be dangerous weapons? It was stated in Johnson v. Commonwealth, 209 Va. 291, 163 S.E.2d 570 (1968), that the use of a pistol with a blocked barrel, capable of firing blank cartridges only, would sustain a charge of robbery with firearms. This seems to be in line with the majority view, although there are a number of jurisdictions holding differently. *See* 81

---

[32] For example, Ill. Rev. Stats., Ch. 38, § 18–2.

[33] *Commonwealth v. Blackburn*, 354 Mass. 200, 237 N.E.2d 35 (1968).

[34] *People v. Magby*, 37 Ill.2d 197, 226 N.E.2d 33 (1967).

A.L.R.3d 1006. In State v. Dye, 14 Ohio App.2d 7, 235 N.E.2d 250 (1968), the Court of Appeals of Ohio suggested that the gravamen of the crime was the fear induced in the victim and this jury instruction had been given: "Even though you find that one of the revolvers used was a toy cap pistol it would make no difference. If those who were held up had reasonable cause to believe that it was a loaded revolver and such put him or them in fear, then you will say the cap pistol becomes a dangerous weapon." It must be pointed out, however, that the toy pistol used in the case and admitted in evidence was described as "so natural in appearance as to be accepted as real. It was of such weight and size that it could, if used as a blackjack or bludgeon, cause severe harm to the head or face of a victim."

3. Would the same reasoning support a conviction for armed robbery where the toy gun used was a plastic one which, though appearing real, was very light in weight and therefore useless as a bludgeon? In People v. Skelton, 83 Ill.2d 58, 46 Ill.Dec. 571, 414 N.E.2d 455 (1980), the Illinois Supreme Court adopted a fact-oriented test to determine whether a weapon that had been used in a robbery is a "dangerous weapon" within the meaning of the armed robbery statute:

> [M]any objects, including guns, can be dangerous and cause serious injury, even when used in a fashion for which they were not intended. Most, if not all, unloaded real guns and many toy guns, because of their size and weight, could be used in deadly fashion as bludgeons. Since the robbery victim could be quite badly hurt or even killed by such weapons if used in that fashion, it seems to us they can properly be classified as dangerous weapons although they were not in fact used in that manner during the commission of the particular offense. It suffices that the potential for such use is present; the victim need not provoke its actual use in such manner. . . .

But cf. People v. Bell, 264 Ill.App.3d 753, 201 Ill.Dec. 182, 636 N.E.2d 614 (1993), in which the court held that *Skelton* was only applicable when the toy or replica gun could not be used as a bludgeon, would not fire blank shells, and would not give off a flash. *See also* Sprouse v. Commonwealth, 19 Va.App. 548, 453 S.E.2d 303 (1995).

4. Treating the use of a firearm in the commission of a robbery as a separate crime is the Virginia Code § 18.2–53.1, which provides:

> It shall be unlawful for any person to use or attempt to use any pistol, shotgun, rifle, or other firearm or display such weapon in a threatening manner while committing or attempting to commit murder, rape, forcible sodomy, inanimate or animate object sexual penetration . . . robbery, carjacking, burglary, malicious wounding . . . , or abduction . . . .

(As amended, 2004).

5. Can a dog be a dangerous weapon within the meaning of the armed robbery statutes? *See* Fern L. Kletter, *Annot., Dog as Deadly or Dangerous*

Weapon for Purposes of Statutes Aggravating Offenses Such as Assault and Robbery, 124 A.L.R.5th 657, § 10 (2004) (collecting cases).

J. BURGLARY: COMMON LAW AND MODERN STATUTES[35]

1. THE ELEMENTS OF COMMON LAW BURGLARY

- At common law, burglary consisted of: breaking and entering of the dwelling house of another, in the nighttime, with intent to commit a felony therein.

The problems which have arisen over the years with respect to each of these elements are perhaps as complex as those concerning the elements of larceny. Modern legislation on burglary has made a number of changes in the common law, generally broadening the scope of the offense. While many of the early troublesome issues have been resolved by statute, familiarity with some of the major common law rules is nevertheless helpful to an understanding of the legislation in this area.

2. INTERPRETING THE COMMON LAW AND MODERN STATUTORY ELEMENTS OF BURGLARY

(A) "BREAKING AND ENTERING"

At common law, the requirement of a "breaking" or "breach" meant that the burglar must have made a trespassory entry involving the creation of an opening into the dwelling.[36] Entering a dwelling which one had a right to enter at the time of entry was not a "breaking" because there was no trespass. Thus, using a key to enter a building which one has an unrestricted right to enter was not a breaking.[37] However, if the entry by use of a key is made at an unauthorized time, a trespass exists and a breaking occurs.[38] A few jurisdictions dispense with the requirement of "breaking," but some of these require a trespass instead. Others provide a higher penalty where a "breaking" occurs. Where breaking is retained as a requirement, some jurisdictions provide that

---

[35] The common law crime of burglary which is discussed in this section, is a crime against the habitation; under modern legislation, however, it has, as here, been grouped with the property offenses.

[36] "Every unwarrantable entry on another's soil the law entitles a trespass by breaking his close; the words of the writ of trespass commanding the defendant to show cause *quare clausum querentis fregit*. For every man's land is in the eye of the law inclosed [sic] and set apart from his neighbor's: and that either by a visible and material fence, as one field is divided from another by a hedge, or by an ideal invisible boundary, existing only in the contemplation of law, as when one man's land adjoins to another's in the same field." 3 BLACKSTONE, COMMENTARIES.

[37] *See, e.g., People v. Kelley*, 253 App. Div. 430, 3 N.Y.S.2d 46 (1938); *Davis v. Commonwealth*, 132 Va. 521, 110 S.E. 356 (1922).

[38] *State v. Corcoran*, 82 Wash. 44, 143 P. 453 (1914).

absent a "breaking in," a "breaking out" will suffice.[39] However, at common law, a "breaking out" was not a burglary.[40]

A common law "breaking," had to involve breaking, moving or putting aside "some material thing, part of the dwelling-house, . . . relied on as a security against intrusion."[41] The breaking may be into any part of a building and need not be a breaking in from the outside. Opening the door of an inner room is sufficient.[42] Merely crossing an imaginary line around the property (called "breaking the close"),[43] is a trespass, but it is not a "breaking" for common law burglary. However, a "constructive breaking" can occur without physical force the burglar gains entry through fraud, deception, or threatened violence. A trick or an artifice to gain entry can be as elaborate as a "Trojan horse" trick of being concealed in a box to gain entry,[44] or by tricking someone into opening a door.[45] Another type of constructive breaking occurs when one who has access to the dwelling, such as a servant, conspires to let another into the house.[46]

The common law "entering" element is satisfied if any part of the burglar's body intrudes into the dwelling, even if it is only a hand or finger.[47] It is also an "entry" within the meaning of burglary if the burglar inserts any object into the dwelling, so long as it is done for the purpose of carrying out the felonious design.[48] The entry must be "consequent upon the breaking," so that if one enters a dwelling through an open door and then opens an inner door but does not go through it, the requirement of entry is lacking.[49] Consent to enter by one who has the authority to

---

[39] *Note, A Rationale of the Law of Burglary*, 57 COLUM. L.REV. 1009 (1951).

[40] *See, e.g.*, 13 AM. JUR. 2D BURGLARY § 14, at 329 (1964) (Virginia, like most of our sister states, follows the view that "breaking out of a building after the commission of a crime therein is not burglary in the absence of a statute so declaring.") (footnote omitted).

[41] *Boon*, 35 N.C. at 246. *Bright*, 4 Va.App. at 252, 356 S.E.2d at 444 (quoting Johnson, 221 Va. at 876, 275 S.E.2d at 594) ([a]ctual breaking involves the application of some force, slight though it may be, whereby the entrance is effected.). *See* BLACK'S LAW DICTIONARY 189 (6th ed. 1990) (as to housebreaking and burglary, [breaking] means the tearing away or removal of any part of a house or of the locks, latches, or other fastenings intended to secure it, or otherwise exerting force to gain an entrance, with criminal intent . . .).

[42] *Davidson v. State*, 86 Tex. Crim.R. 243, 216 S.W. 624 (1919). *See Annot.*, 43 A.L.R.3d 1147 and 70 A.L.R.3d 881. For cases considering whether it is a "breaking" to enter through a partly opened door or window, see cases collected at *Annot.*, 70 A.L.R.3d 881.

[43] *State v. Boon*, 35 N.C. 244, 246 (1852) (crossing the line will sustain an action of trespass *quare clausum fregit* but not for burglary).

[44] *See e.g.*, *Nichols v. State*, 68 Wis. 416, 32 N.W. 543 (1887).

[45] *See, e.g.*, *Le Mott's Case*, 84 Eng. Rep. 1073 (1650), in which burglars told a maid that they wanted to speak to the master, and entered and robbed him when the maid opened the door.

[46] *See, e.g.*, *Regina v. Johnson*, Car. & M. 218, 174 Eng. Rep. 479 (1841).

[47] *State v. Whitaker*, 275 S.W.2d 316 (Mo.1955); *Regina v. O'Brien*, 4 Cox C.C. 400 (1850); *Franco v. State*, 42 Tex. 276 (1875).

[48] If the instrument is used only to carry out the "breaking," however, that will not satisfy the "entering" requirement. *Walker v. State*, 63 Ala. 49 (1879); *Rex v. Rust*, 1 Mood.C.C. 183 (1828); *People v. Williams*, 28 Ill.App.3d 402, 328 N.E.2d 682 (1975).

[49] *Regina v. Davis*, 6 Cox C.C. 369 (1854).

consent; however, is an affirmative defense to burglary.[50] Under modern statutes, some jurisdictions dispense with the requirement of "entry,"[51] and others, following the Model Penal Code, expand the element to "enters or remains." For example, Hawaii Revised Statutes §§ 708–810 Burglary in the first degree provides:

> (1) A person commits the offense of burglary in the first degree if he intentionally enters or remains unlawfully in a building, with intent to commit therein a crime against a person or against property rights, and:
>
> > (a) He is armed with a dangerous instrument in the course of committing the offense; or
> >
> > (b) He intentionally, knowingly, or recklessly inflicts or attempts to inflict bodily injury on anyone in the course of committing the offense; or
> >
> > (c) He recklessly disregards a risk that the building is the dwelling of another, and the building is such a dwelling. . . .

(B) THE DWELLING HOUSE OF ANOTHER

Although many modern statutes have extended the laws of burglary to commercial and even uninhabited structures,[52] the common law required that the structure invaded be a "dwelling house,"[53] and that it be the dwelling house "of another." A "dwelling house," for purposes of common law burglary, is a building habitually used as a place to sleep.[54] Stores and other businesses could be the subject of common law burglary only if someone regularly slept there.[55] Modern statutes on "housebreaking," the day-time burglary of a dwelling offense, still require interpretation on what constitutes a dwelling.

Under some modern statutes, a "dwelling" can include a boat, if someone regularly sleeps there.[56] However, just because someone may

---

[50]   *State v. Hicks*, 421 So.2d 510 (Fla.1982) (because consent is an affirmative defense, the absence of consent need not be alleged in a burglary indictment).

[51]   *Note, A Rationale of the Law of Burglary*, 57 COLUM. L.REV. 1009 (1951).

[52]   While all jurisdictions include virtually all buildings in the scope of burglary, most jurisdictions attach a more severe penalty to the offense where a dwelling is involved. *Note, A Rationale of the Law of Burglary*, 57 COLUM. L.REV. 1009 (1951).

[53]   *See, e.g., Holtman v. State*, 12 Md.App. 168, 278 A.2d 82 (1971), in which a conviction for daytime housebreaking was reversed upon a showing that the defendant had broken into a church. Though it may be the "mansion house of God", the court did not consider it a dwelling within the meaning of the burglary law. On the other hand, an Illinois court construed a "car wash" to be a building falling within the modern Illinois burglary statute above. *People v. Blair*, 1 Ill.App.3d 6, 272 N.E.2d 404 (1971).

[54]   *Rex v. Stock*, Russ. & R. 185, 2 Leach C.C. 1015, 7 Taunt. 339 (1810).

[55]   *State v. Outlaw*, 72 N.C. 598 (1875).

[56]   *See, e.g.*, Illinois Criminal Code (S.H.A. ch. 38):

§ 19–1. Burglary

a) A person commits burglary when without authority he knowingly enters or without authority remains within a building, housetrailer, watercraft, aircraft, motor vehicle

occasionally sleep on the premises does not make a building a "dwelling house" for common law burglary.[57] Seasonal dwellings, such as a summer homes will qualify as dwelling houses, however, even during the period when it is not occupied.[58] The test is whether the occupant intends to return.[59] A building that no one has yet moved into is not considered a dwelling house for purposes of burglary.[60] Rooms in an inn, hotel, or apartment building are the dwellings of the occupants, unless the occupants are merely transients.[61] Where the rooms are occupied by transients, however, the rooms are considered the dwelling house of the landlord, whether or not the landlord lives in the building.[62] The dwelling house must be that "of another," in the sense that it must be occupied by another. It need not be owned by victim, inasmuch as burglary at common law is a crime against the habitation and not against property. An owner may therefore burglarize a building leased to, and occupied by, someone else.[63] The dweller, however, cannot burglarize his own dwelling, even though it has other occupants.[64]

The dwelling house is considered to include not only the dwelling itself but also buildings that are "within the curtilage." The purpose of including buildings used in connection with the dwelling is to protect against the dangers resulting from the likelihood that a dweller who hears a prowler in the nighttime will go forth to protect his family and property. Thus a garage is considered part of the dwelling house where it is in reasonable proximity to the house.[65] A cellar is also within the "curtilage" even though it has no entrance from the dwelling itself and must be entered from the outside.[66] Modern statutes generally preserve

---

(as defined in the Illinois Motor Vehicle Law) railroad car, or any part thereof, with intent to commit therein a felony or theft. . . .

The statute also creates a separate crime of "residential burglary" in § 19–3 of the Criminal Code. Holding that the two offenses are mutually exclusive, the Illinois Supreme Court in *People v. Childress*, 158 Ill.2d 275, 198 Ill.Dec. 794, 633 N.E.2d 635 (1994), remarked: "Residential burglary can be committed only in dwelling places, while simple burglary cannot occur in a dwelling place. The victim in the present case was attacked and killed in her own home, and thus the defendant could not have been guilty of burglary."

[57] *State v. Jenkins*, 50 N.C. 430 (1858). In *Quattlebaum*, 91 N.Y.2d at 748–749, 675 N.Y.S.2d 585, 698 N.E.2d 421 the New York Court of Appeals found that a school building could be considered as a dwelling for purposes of convicting the defendant of burglary. The court held that it could not, though there was a bed in a fifth floor office where someone could have stayed overnight. That holding does not impact the present case, where the building was a dwelling and had been occupied until three days before the burglary.

[58] *State v. Bair*, 112 W.Va. 655, 166 S.E. 369 (1932).

[59] *State v. Meerchouse*, 34 Mo. 344 (1864).

[60] *Woods v. State*, 186 Miss. 463, 191 So. 283 (1939); *Jones v. State*, 532 S.W.2d 596 (Tex.Crim.App.1976), overruled on other grounds sub nom *Moss v. State*, 574 S.W.2d 542 (Tex.Crim.App.1978).

[61] *People v. Carr*, 255 Ill. 203, 99 N.E. 357 (1912).

[62] *See Rodgers v. People*, 86 N.Y. 360 (1881).

[63] *Smith v. People*, 115 Ill. 17, 3 N.E. 733 (1885).

[64] *Clarke v. Commonwealth*, 66 Va. (25 Gratt.) 908 (1874).

[65] *Harris v. State*, 41 Okl. Crim. 121, 271 P. 957 (1928).

[66] *Mitchell v. Commonwealth*, 88 Ky. 349, 11 S.W. 209 (1889).

and expand the applicability of burglary statutes to "separately secured areas" within a structure, but there are limits to the areas that will qualify.

Is it burglary to break into a fenced boat enclosure?

State v. Wentz

Supreme Court of Washington, *en banc.*, 2003.
149 Wash.2d 342, 68 P.3d 282.

■ IRELAND, J.

Defendant Gerald Lee Wentz claims the State produced insufficient evidence to support his conviction for first degree burglary. At the close of his bench trial, the judge found that by entering a locked, six-foot high fence, Wentz had entered a building for the purposes of the burglary statute. The Court of Appeals affirmed. A "fenced area" is included in the statutory definition of building, and the statute is unambiguous. Therefore, we affirm.

FACTS

On the evening of May 29, 1999, police responded to a residential alarm at Patrick Wheeler's home in Spokane. One of the responding officers, Deputy James Melton, found Wentz hiding in the backyard. The officer testified that Wentz said he took a pickup truck from his brother's home in The Dalles, Oregon, without permission that morning. He said he drove the truck to a friend's house and broke in, taking a handgun and some ammunition. Thus prepared, he drove to Spokane, where he intended to confront[16] his ex-wife and sometime girl friend, Janet McFadden, and her new boyfriend, Wheeler.

Wentz told police that upon arriving in Spokane, he proceeded to Wheeler's house, noting McFadden's car in the driveway. He also confirmed that she was there by calling and hanging up when she answered. Parking the truck in a lot a few blocks away, he then walked by and around the house several times. He waited for nightfall before trying to enter Wheeler's home.

Meanwhile, unbeknownst to Wentz, his brother telephoned McFadden in Spokane. Thereafter, she immediately fled, driving back to The Dalles. Wheeler was working a 24-hour shift. Consequently, the house was empty when Wentz arrived. Officer Melton testified that Wentz told him he climbed the fence into the backyard and found an unlocked sliding door. When he slid it partway open, an alarm sounded. Instead of going into the house, he hid in the boat that was parked on a trailer in the backyard. He decided to wait under the boat's cover until McFadden and Wheeler returned.

---

[16] By "confront," Wentz told the police he meant to either shoot them and then himself, or shoot himself in front of them.

A six-foot solid wood fence surrounds the backyard. The fence has two gates, both of which were padlocked. Both Wentz and the police officer who apprehended him had to climb the fence to enter the backyard. Wheeler kept his boat inside the fence next to his house.

Wentz was arrested and charged with [*inter alia*] one count of first-degree burglary. At the close of the trial, the judge found Wentz guilty beyond a reasonable doubt on all counts. The Court of Appeals, Division Three, affirmed the convictions. We granted review solely as to the burglary count. . . .

Is the term "fenced area" in the statutory definition of "building" in RCW 9A.04.110(5) subject to the main purpose test announced in *State v. Roadhs*, 71 Wash.2d 705, 707–09, 430 P.2d 586 (1967)?

Do the qualifying words "used for lodging of persons or for carrying on business therein, or for the use, sale or deposit of goods" apply to the term "fenced area" in RCW 9A.04.110(5)? . . .

ANALYSIS

A.   Standard of Review

* * *

B.   Former Statutory Construction

Whether Wentz had entered Wheeler's *home* was a factual dispute at trial, but the trial court made no finding he had. It nonetheless concluded that Wentz was guilty of first degree burglary based, in part, on the following written findings of fact:

> 19. [The backyard] was secured by a six foot solid wood fence with locked gates. . . . Deputies then checked the back yard and discovered the defendant . . . [hiding] in the yard armed with a Colt .357 revolver and 21 rounds of ammunition . . . .
>
> 33. On May 29, 1999 around 9:23 p.m., the defendant, armed with the Colt firearm, jumped over the locked fence into the secured back yard. . . .
>
> 34. The defendant opened the rear, basement sliding glass door of the house . . . which tripped the security system and caused an alarm to sound.
>
> 35. When the security alarm sounded, the defendant hid himself in the boat in the fenced backyard under a tarp to await [their] return. . . .
>
> 68. On May 29, 1999, the defendant had the specific intent required to commit the offense of first degree burglary and did enter and remain unlawfully on the premises or in the building . . . with the intent to commit a crime against a person or property therein, and, in entering and while on or in such

building or premises and in immediate flight therefrom was armed with a deadly weapon. . . .

Wentz challenges the sufficiency of these findings to support his first degree burglary conviction. To determine whether the evidence is sufficient to sustain a conviction, we view the evidence in the light most favorable to the prosecution and ask whether any rational fact finder could have found the essential elements of the crime beyond a reasonable doubt. *State v. Green*, 94 Wash.2d 216, 221, 616 P.2d 628 (1980), quoting *Jackson v. Virginia*, 443 U.S. 307, 319 (1979).

The trial court entered no written findings regarding whether the fence around Wheeler's backyard was erected mainly for the purpose of protecting property therein, the test announced in *State v. Roadhs*. The issue in *Roadhs* was whether a defendant who unlawfully entered a fenced area could be charged under the burglary statute. Defendant and two other men were apprehended within a public utility district warehouse compound. The compound was fully enclosed by building walls and a cyclone fence topped by barbed wire. The men had cut the barbed wire and climbed over the fence. Defendant was convicted of second degree burglary. He appealed, claiming that the enclosure was not a building under the burglary statute. The second degree burglary statute in effect at the time provided:

> Every person who, with intent to commit some crime therein shall, under circumstances not amounting to burglary in the first degree, enter the dwelling house of another or break and enter, or, having committed a crime therein, shall break out of *any building* or part thereof, or a room or *other structure wherein any property is kept for use, sale or deposit,* shall be guilty of burglary in the second degree. . . . (Former RCW 9.19.020 (1909) (emphasis added).)

As the statute addressed unlawful entry into either a building or a structure, the court first analyzed whether a fenced area was a building. The statutory definition of "building" stated:

> The word "building" shall include every house, shed, boat, watercraft, railway car, tent or booth, whether completed or not, suitable for affording shelter for any human being, or as a place where any property is or shall be kept for use, sale or deposit. (Former RCW 9.01.010(18) (1909).)

Because the statute listed specific items, the court reasoned that the omission of "fenced area" from the building definition was intended by the legislature. *Roadhs*, 71 Wash.2d at 707–08, 430 P.2d 586 (citing the statutory construction principle, "*expressio unius est exclusio alterius*").

The court then turned to the issue of whether a fenced area was a structure. "Structure" was not defined by statute. The court reasoned that the ordinary meaning of "structure" was very broad, conceivably applying to anything from "a building" to "an apple box." Therefore, the court interpreted the general term, "structure," in a manner consistent with the specific term, "building." (citing the statutory construction principle "*noscitur a sociis*"). In doing so, it concluded that:

- Were the fence a mere boundary fence or one erected for the *sole* purpose of esthetic beautification, it would not constitute a "structure" as that term was intended to be interpreted by the legislature. However, where the fence is of such a nature that it is erected mainly for the purpose of protecting property within its confines and is, in fact, an integral part of a closed compound, its function becomes analogous to that of a "building" and the fence itself constitutes a "structure" subject to being burglarized.

This became the test to analyze whether a defendant who entered a fenced area had entered a "structure" and could, therefore, be convicted of burglary. *State v. Livengood*, 14 Wash. App. 203, 209, 540 P.2d 480 (1975) (quoting *Roadhs*, 71 ash.2d at 708–09, 430 P.2d 586).

In 1975, the legislature enacted a new criminal code, Title 9A RCW. Laws of 1975, 1st Ex. Sess., ch. 260. This legislation made sweeping changes to the burglary laws. The statutory definition of "building" now reads: "Building, in addition to its ordinary meaning, includes any dwelling, fenced area, vehicle, railway car, cargo container, or any other structure used for lodging of persons or for carrying on business therein, or for the use, sale or deposit of goods . . . ." RCW 9A.04.110(5). Under the current statutory scheme for burglary, the most serious offense is first degree burglary:

A person is guilty of burglary in the first degree if, with intent to commit a crime against a person or property therein, he or she enters or remains unlawfully in a building and if, in entering or while in the building or in immediate flight therefrom, the actor or another participant in the crime (a) is armed with a deadly weapon, or (b) assaults any person. RCW 9A.52.020(1).

The less serious offenses are those in which the person neither has a deadly weapon nor commits assault. In those cases, the person who enters or remains unlawfully in a building and has the intent to commit a crime against a person or property therein is charged according to the building entered. Thus, if the intent element is satisfied, entry into a dwelling is residential burglary under RCW 9A.52.025(1); entry into a vehicle is vehicle prowling under RCW 9A.52.095–.100; and entry into a building other than a dwelling or a vehicle is second degree burglary under RCW 9A.52.030(1).

"Fenced area" is now expressly included in the "building" definition. RCW 9A.04.110(5). Despite the amendment, the Courts of Appeals continued to apply the *Roadhs* main purpose test for determining whether a fence constitutes a "structure" for purposes of the former burglary statute. . . . This approach fails to track the 1975 legislative change, as the current statutory scheme dispenses with that analysis. Therefore, when a person is charged under the current burglary statute for unlawfully entering or remaining in a fenced area, the State need not show that the fence was erected mainly for the purpose of protecting property within its confines.

C.   Current Statutory Language

We reject Wentz's argument that, even under the current statute, the fenced backyard at issue here is not a building. Wentz asserts that the language following the word "structure" in RCW 9A.04.110(5) modifies each of the named examples, including "fenced area." Therefore, according to Wentz, a fenced area must be "used for lodging of persons or for carrying on business therein, or for the use, sale or deposit of goods," or else it is not a building capable of being burglarized. Before this case, the Courts of Appeals had accepted the reading advocated by Wentz as correct: the modifying language following "any other structure" modifies all of the specific examples, not just "structure."

We disagree. Under the last antecedent rule, "unless a contrary intention appears in the statute, qualifying words and phrases refer to the last antecedent." We determine legislative intent by evaluating the statute as a whole. When reading the statute as a whole, it becomes clear that the legislature did not intend for the qualifying language to refer to all of the antecedents. Such a reading would be unnecessarily limiting in the case of a "vehicle" or a "railway car."

For instance, consider the person who, armed with a deadly weapon, unlawfully enters the following hypothetical spaces with intent to commit a crime against a person or property therein. If we read the qualifying language to modify "vehicle," such a person who unlawfully enters a car that is not used for the noted purposes could only be charged with second degree vehicle prowling, a gross misdemeanor under RCW 9A.52.100. If that same person broke into a delivery van, he could be charged with first degree burglary, a class A felony, because the delivery van is used for the deposit of goods. Similarly, if that person broke into a train's engine car, he could not be charged with first degree burglary. However, it would be first degree burglary if he unlawfully entered a cargo car on the same train.

Because the statute evidences no contrary intention, the qualifying language in RCW 9A.04.110(5) modifies "structure" alone, as the last antecedent. Therefore, the State need not show that the fenced area was used for lodging of persons or for carrying on business therein, or for the use, sale or deposit of goods when prosecuting a person for burglarizing a fenced area.

Unlike some of the other terms in RCW 9A.04.110(5), . . . "fenced area" has no statutory definition. Absent a contrary legislative intent, we give a term that is not defined by statute its ordinary meaning. *Cowiche Canyon Conservancy v. Bosley*, 118 Wash.2d 801, 813, 828 P.2d 549 (1992). The ordinary meaning of "fenced area" clearly encompasses the backyard in this case.

The evidence is sufficient to sustain Wentz's conviction. The trial court found that Wheeler's backyard was surrounded by a six-foot, solid wood fence with padlocked gates. It was secured such that both Wentz and the officer who apprehended him had to climb over the fence to enter the backyard and to gain access to the sliding door. Wentz was discovered in the boat stored within the locked fence. Under these facts, a rational fact finder could have found beyond a reasonable doubt that Wentz entered a fenced area, and therefore a "building". Because we affirm the conviction, we need not reach the State's argument that it has sustained its burden on the lesser-included offense of attempted first degree burglary. . . .

We hold that the term "fenced area" in RCW 9A.04.110(5) is not subject to the test announced in *Roadhs* in order to determine whether it is a building subject to being burglarized, as that case analyzed a separate question under the previous burglary statute. In addition, the language following "structure" in RCW 9A.04.110(5) does not modify "fenced area." The cases that hold otherwise are overruled. The decision by the Court of Appeals in this case is affirmed.

* * *

———

NOTES

1. Were you surprised that Wentz slid open a sliding door to the residence but did not enter? Do you believe his story about never setting foot inside the house before closing the sliding glass door? If his foot crossed the threshold of the door would he be guilty of burglary from that action alone?

2. Early on the morning of November 17, 2012, Michael Jacob Watkins hopped over a fence and entered the Boise Zoo in Idaho. According to Watkins, he wanted to free a monkey held in the zoo; according to a friend, Watkins wanted to steal the monkey to keep as a pet. Regardless of his motive, Watkins' effort failed, with the monkey attacking him and Watkins subsequently killing the monkey. Among other things, prosecutors charged Watkins with burglary. *See* Patrick Orr & Meghann M. Cuniff, *Prosecutor: Accused Boise Monkey Killer Says "He Was Trying To Set It Free" But Friend Says He Wanted a Pet*, IDAHO STATESMAN, Nov. 21. 2012. Can a zoo (or a monkey's cage within a zoo) be a dwelling for purposes of burglary? If not, how could Idaho prosecutors charge Watkins with burglary? Like many states, Idaho has broadened its burglary statute to include more than dwellings and traditional structures. Under Idaho law, burglary includes

> Every person who enters any house, room, apartment, tenement, shop, warehouse, store, mill, barn, stable, outhouse, or other

building, tent, vessel, vehicle, trailer, airplane or railroad car, with intent to commit any theft or any felony, is guilty of burglary.

Idaho Rev. Stat. § 18–401.

Problem 7–10. Penny and Kenny went to the sporting goods store in their home town to steal some fishing reels. Kenny planned to do the actual theft, and Penny agreed to be Kenny's lookout. The fishing reels, with a retail price of $144.00 each, were in a locked, freestanding case, about three feet long, which sat on a counter in the fishing section of the store. Kenny went to the hardware area, took a pair of pliers from a package; and then returned to the sporting goods section, where he attempted to "jimmy" the lock the lock on the fishing reel case intermittently for about ten minutes. After Penny told Kenny that he was being observed by store security personnel, he abandoned his attempts to break into the case, left the pliers in another department, and walked toward the front doors of the store. Kenny was detained by store security personnel for stealing the pliers, the plot unraveled, and ultimately Kenny and Penny were charged with burglary, with Penny charged with aiding and abetting. There is no doubt that Penny helped Kenny; the question is, was the crime burglary?

(C) NIGHTTIME

Originally, burglary only occurred when the breaking and entering occurred in the night time. As an element of burglary, nighttime is the period of time between sunset and sunrise, and it is not considered night if there is enough natural daylight so that one can discern the countenance of a human face.[67] Both the breaking and entering had to occur during the nighttime, but they did not have to occur on the same night.[68] Under modern statutes, all jurisdictions recognize daytime burglaries, although some provide a more severe penalty for burglaries committed at night.[69] *See* Model Penal Code § 221.1 (1980):

> . . . (2) Grading. Burglary is a felony of the second degree if it is perpetrated in the dwelling of another at night, or if, in the course of committing the offense, the actor: (a) . . . inflicts or attempts to inflict bodily injury on anyone; or (b) is armed with explosives or a deadly weapon. Otherwise, burglary is a felony

---

[67] *People v. Griffin*, 19 Cal. 578 (1862). *State v. Billings*, 242 N.W.2d 726 (Iowa 1976).

[68] *Rex v. Smith*, Russ. & Ry. 417, 168 Eng. Rep. 874 (1820). *See* TORCIA, WHARTON'S CRIMINAL LAW § 321, at 247 ("The breaking and entering need not occur on the same night; the defendant may break on one night and enter on another night, so long as he enters through the opening made by his prior break.").

[69] *See, e.g.*, Model Penal Code § 221.1 (1980), which provides:

Burglary Defined. A person is guilty of burglary if he enters a building or occupied structure, or separately secured or occupied portion thereof, with purpose to commit a crime therein. . . . (2) Grading. Burglary is a felony of the second degree if it is perpetrated in the dwelling of another at night, . . . Otherwise, burglary is a felony of the third degree. . . .

Model Penal Code § 221.1, Comment 4, at 81.

of the third degree. An act shall be deemed "in the course of committing" an offense if it occurs in an attempt to commit the offense or in flight after the attempt or commission. "In the course of committing the offense" applies to "conduct that occurs between the period beginning with an attempt to commit the offense of burglary and ending with the conclusion of immediate flight after the attempt or commission of the offense." [Model Penal Code § 221.1, Comment 4, at 81.]

———

(D) WITH INTENT TO COMMIT A FELONY

Jurisdictions define burglarious intent in four principal ways: (a) intent to commit a felony; (b) intent to commit a felony or larceny; (c) intent to commit any crime (with respect to one or more degrees or forms of burglary); and (d) intent to commit certain specified crimes. A few jurisdictions dispense entirely with the requirement of an intent to commit another crime for the lowest degree or form of burglary.

Although burglary is commonly thought of as an offense committed with intent to steal, the required intent actually includes the intent to commit any felony. It is not necessary that the felony in fact be committed;[70] however, both the breaking and entering must be made with the necessary intent.[71] As noted in the section on larceny, at common law both grand and petit larceny were felonies. Petit (or "petty") larceny is now frequently made a misdemeanor by statute, but a vestige of the common law remains in statutes that define burglarious intent as an intent to commit a felony "or to steal."

———

Just because a person is found to have broken and entered another's dwelling in the nighttime, it does not necessarily follow that the person's presence there proves intent to commit a crime, but intent can be inferred from the circumstances of the person's presence, and from supplying an explanation for the person's presence which is at odds with the physical evidence.

Massey v. United States

District of Columbia Court of Appeals, 1974.
320 A.2d 296.

■ GALLAGHER, J.

After a trial by jury appellant was found guilty of second-degree burglary and sentenced to a term of one to three years with execution of

———

[70] *Wilson v. State*, 24 Conn. 57 (1855).

[71] *Colbert v. State*, 91 Ga. 705, 17 S.E. 840 (1893).

two and one-half years suspended and probation imposed in lieu thereof. In this appeal it is argued with considerable force that the trial court erred . . . in denying appellant's motion for judgment of acquittal for failure of proof that appellant entered the premises with the intent to steal. . . . We disagree and affirm.

I

Viewing the evidence in the light most favorable to appellee, as we must, the facts are these. At about 3:00 a. m. on November 30, 1972, Mrs. Beatrice Waiters was in her residence when she heard knocking and hammering on a door. She looked out her back window and observed a man kicking and pounding on a door of the nearby New Jersey Bar and Grill. She saw him stop for a while, run across the street, come back again, pound on the door some more and finally enter the building. Mrs. Waiters then called Mr. Joseph M. Miller, the proprietor of the New Jersey Bar and Grill, and informed him that someone was breaking into his establishment. She then called the police.

Officer Kneiser received the radio run of the incident, responded to the scene, and noticed the splintered door. From her window, Mrs. Waiters advised the officer that she had reported the apparent breaking and entry and that the individual was still inside. The officer then entered the storeroom area and saw someone back in that darkened area. He was asked to halt, but instead the figure disappeared into another room and footsteps were heard running up a stairway.

The building was then surrounded by police and Officer Kneiser prepared to enter the building again with the assistance of the canine patrol. Upon entry he called for anyone in the building to come out and at this time appellant came down the stairs. Appellant was clad only in his underwear and was rubbing his eyes. Appellant followed the officers upstairs, telling them that he was staying with a Mr. Matthews, who resided over the bar and grill, and that he had heard nothing unusual. The search of the upstairs area revealed nothing of a suspicious nature and the officers returned to search the storeroom area.

There they noticed several clothes racks and saw that several items of clothing were folded and stacked on the floor. Appellant, then more fully dressed, came back down the stairs and Officer Kneiser called Mrs. Waiters to her window and asked appellant to step outside. As he did so, Mrs. Waiters pointed at him and said, "Yes, that's him." As they were leaving, the officers recovered appellant's coat and shoes near the storeroom door where the clothes racks were located. They showed the coat to Mrs. Waiters who stated that it "looked like the one the man had on when he broke in."

Mr. Miller, the owner of the bar and grill, testified that appellant frequented his establishment and that he had been there on the evening of November 29. He closed the establishment around 2:40 a. m. and offered appellant a ride home. He drove him to a tourist home a few blocks away. After arriving home himself, Mr. Miller received Mrs. Waiters' call that his premises were being broken into and he immediately returned to the bar and grill. Upon arriving, he noticed that the side door that he had earlier locked and bolted had been broken into. He also noticed that clothing he was keeping for a tailor (which had previously been hanging on racks) was then on the floor next to a box which, although empty earlier, now contained some of the clothes. Mr. Miller had not given appellant permission to enter the premises after hours or to take the clothes off the rack.

Mr. Miller also testified that the second floor of the building was occupied by Gertrude Mitchell, an elderly lady, and Frederick Matthews, [a disabled person who was] cared for by Mr. Miller. At the scene, Officer Kneiser had asked Mr. Matthews whether he had given appellant permission to sleep in the room and he had been "very emphatic with his no's." Ms. Mitchell, the other resident of the second floor, testified that she had not let appellant in and that upon hearing the sound of voices downstairs she had seen a stranger in an undershirt getting into Mr. Matthews' bed.

Appellant took the stand in his own defense. He testified basically that Ms. Mitchell had let him into the premises, that he had taken his shoes and coat off, left them downstairs, and then gone upstairs to sleep with Mr. Matthews. He stated that he entered Mr. Matthews' room, woke him up, motioned to him that he wanted to sleep there and then went to sleep. His next recollection was being awakened by police with flashlights asking if he and Mr. Matthews had heard anything.

II

Appellant's primary contention here is that the "contradictory evidence offered by the government to prove intent was . . . insufficient to permit the jury to find beyond a reasonable doubt that (he) entered with the intent to steal." We disagree.

A requisite element of proof in a prosecution under our burglary statute, D.C.Code 1973, §§ 22–1801(a) and (b), and those of most jurisdictions, is that the defendant have an intent to steal or commit a crime at the time of entry. It is not necessary that the intended theft or crime be consummated. The requisite intent, of course, is a state of mind particular to the accused and unless such intent is admitted, it must be shown by circumstantial evidence. Standing alone, unauthorized presence in another's premises hardly supports an inference of entry with a criminal purpose, but when aided by other circumstances it very well might.

These "other circumstances" need not include the actual commission of a crime within the premises. They are such circumstances as might lead reasonable people, based upon common experience, to conclude beyond a reasonable doubt that the accused possessed the requisite intent. These might include "unexplained presence . . . in (a) darkened house near midnight, access having been by force and stealth through a window," *Washington v. United States*, 105 U.S.App. D.C. 58, 61, 263 F.2d 742, 745, cert. denied, 359 U.S. 1002 (1959); arrest in early morning hours while hiding with gloves, screwdriver and flashlight near site of recently reported entry into home, presence in a building through which entry to another building was being attempted by making a hole through a party wall where dust on trousers matched that in area of attempted entry, forced entry and trying of doors inside home after throwing a brick through a window, or presence in a warehouse amongst scattered papers, opened drawers and office equipment which had been moved into a hall.

In this case it is argued that the evidence was insufficient to support a finding of an intent to steal. In this regard inconsistencies in Mr. Miller's pretrial statements and in-court testimony are pointed up as well as "inherent weaknesses" in his testimony concerning the clothes. Any inconsistencies or weaknesses in this testimony were, however, for the trier of fact to resolve.

Here there was evidence that appellant made an early morning forcible entry, prepared to carry away items of value (clothes), and attempted to conceal his actions inside the premises. We think that there was ample evidence to withstand a motion for judgment of acquittal.

In support of his theory appellant relies mainly on the Circuit Court's opinion in *United States v. Melton*, 491 F.2d 45 (D.C. Cir. 1973).[2] There, the court, over a vigorous dissent, reversed a burglary conviction and, upon grant of rehearing, remanded for entry of an unlawful entry conviction or indictment and prosecution for forcible entry, at the option of the government. But that decision, on the actual state of that record, does not commend itself to us. So that even if the facts here were on all fours, . . . we would not adopt *Melton*. . . . Our basic disagreement with *Melton* is that we see no reason to downgrade as a matter of law the act of breaking and entering the home of another in the dark of night as Melton seems to do. As a matter of fact, those elements have been viewed in some jurisdictions over the years as sufficient in themselves to justify an inference that the entry was with the intent to steal. Though we do not view *Melton* as being especially realistic, there were present here, in any event, additional circumstances from which the jury could reasonably infer an intent to steal.

When a nighttime forcible entry into premises is discovered almost at its inception it would be unrealistic to require stark, undeniable proof of an intent to steal in order to sustain a charge under D.C. Code 1973, § 22–1801. In these times of silent burglar alarms, prompt and efficient law enforcement responses and, as here, an alert citizenry, the available proof of an intent to steal is usually circumstantial. There are no hard

---

[2] *Melton* was decided on September 26, 1973. The government petitioned for rehearing and rehearing *en banc* and upon rehearing the panel decisions was modified and *en banc* consideration denied on January 11, 1974.

and fast rules to be laid down on what is required to establish the element of intent necessary to this crime. Each case will have its own special facts and circumstances. Where the evidence is sufficient to justify a reasonable inference that the requisite intent existed, this court will not disturb the verdict if it otherwise meets the required standards to support a guilty verdict. . . .

There appearing no error requiring reversal, the judgment is Affirmed.

Problem 7–11. Around 10 P.M. on a cold winter night, Mooch broke into Vinnie's two-story house by prying open and breaking the lock to the window of the sun room. Mooch had first attempted to gain entrance through the back door where he cut open the screen door, but had failed to penetrate the locked door. The sun room was used as an unheated storage room by Vinnie, and while in this room Mooch next tried to gain further entrance into the interior of the house through some French doors. However, as Mooch opened these French doors, he knocked over "nine pieces of half-inch thick 2 x 4 plywood" which had been "stacked" against the doors. This noise awakened Vinnie, who, after noticing the disturbed plywood, the open window and the screen-cut on the back door, quickly had called the police from her neighbor's house. Two policemen arrived within two to five minutes. They went into the house, and saw Mooch apparently sleeping in the sun room next to the open window, and arrested him. A clock, a lamp, and some framed paintings were disturbed or broken in the sunroom. Is there enough evidence of an "intent to steal" on Mooch's part to support a burglary conviction?

NOTES

1. When does a habitation cease to be a habitation "of another"? In People v. Barney, 294 A.D.2d 811, 742 N.Y.S.2d 451 (N.Y. App.2002) defendant Barney had learned that the sole occupant of a rented single-family house had died in a traffic accident. Upon learning that the decedent had kept marijuana at the house, Barney broke in in the early morning hours, intending to steal the marijuana. A neighbor spotted lights, called police, and Barney was charged with burglary. At the time Barney broke in, the house remained furnished, the utilities were connected, there was food in the refrigerator and decedent's possessions remained in the house. On appeal, Barney challenged his conviction for breaking into a "dwelling," contending that the building at issue lost its character as a dwelling upon the death of the sole occupant. The New York Appellate division disagreed saying

> A dwelling is defined as "a building which is usually occupied by a person lodging therein at night" . . . A dwelling does not lose its character as a dwelling based on the temporary absence of its occupant . . . In cases where an occupant is temporarily absent, a dwelling retains its character as such if the building was adapted for occupancy at the time of the wrongful entry, the occupant

intended to return, and, on the date of the entry, a person could have occupied the building overnight . . .

Notwithstanding the dissent's position that a deceased occupant could no longer harbor an intent to return to the house, the majority found that the house had not lost its character as a dwelling, because it "ha[d] been used as a residence in the 'immediate past' and ha[d] not been abandoned." *Id. Edwards*, 589 N.W.2d 807, 811; *cf.* People v. Ramos, 52 Cal.App.4th 300, 302, 60 Cal.Rptr.2d 523; People v. Hider, 135 Mich.App. 147, 151–153, 351 N.W.2d 905, 907–908.

2. Many jurisdictions have added new elements to the common law crime of burglary. For example, some make special provisions for armed burglary and burglary involving the use of (or attempt or intent to use) explosives and some require for the offense of first-degree burglary that someone be in the building at the time of the offense. If a burglary statute provides for harsher penalties for breaking and entering "a dwelling house in the night time, with intent to commit a felony," . . . "any person being then lawfully therein," has the defendant violated that statute if the victim arrives home while the defendant is present? *See* Commonwealth v. Mitchell, 67 Mass. App. Ct. 556, 855 N.E.2d 406 (2006) (yes; the more logical reference is to the time during which the burglar is present in the dwelling as a result of his felonious breaking and entering.) The *Mitchell* court said:

> A minority of States require the physical presence of a victim in the dwelling at the time of the breaking and entry in order to constitute a higher degree of the crime of burglary. *See Annot., Occupant's Absence from Residential Structure as Affecting Nature of Offense as Burglary or Breaking and Entering*, 20 A.L.R.4th 349, 355–356 (1983). *See, e.g.*, State v. Nelson, 523 N.W.2d 667, 670 (Minn. Ct. App. 1994) (conviction of burglary in the first degree reversed where the victims were not present in their home when the defendant entered). State v. Tippett, 270 N.C. 588, 595, 155 S.E.2d 269 (1967) (statute . . . requires the presence of someone at the time of the breaking and entering).

> Other States considering this situation have reached the opposite conclusion. See United States v. Hill, 863 F.2d at 1582 n. 5. *See also* State v. Reed, 8 Kan.App.2d 615, 616, 663 P.2d 680 (1983) (possible danger to human life during an aggravated burglary is just as great regardless of when during the burglary the victim comes to be in the building) . . .; Johnson v. Commonwealth, 18 Va.App. 441, 446–447, 444 S.E.2d 559 (1994) (rejecting the argument that the phrase "while said dwelling is occupied" in the relevant statute . . . required that at least one occupant must be physically present in the dwelling at the time of the breaking and entering.)

K. ARSON[72]

At common law, arson was the "willful and malicious burning of the dwelling house of another either by night or by day . . . ."[73] There were four essential elements at common law:

1. The building burned must be a dwelling house, as in burglary (including structures within the curtilage or common enclosure);

2. The dwelling house must be "of another," based on occupancy, not ownership;

3. There must be an actual burning or some part of the house, however slight; and

4. The burning must be willful and malicious.[74]

Modern statutes have considerably expanded the scope of arson: It can now be committed against "any structure," The act may be committed by explosives as well as by fire. What constitutes a "structure," however, may be debatable.

State v. Rogers

Court of Criminal Appeals of Tennessee, 2006.
2006 WL 2716870 (unpublished).

■ MCLIN, J.

The defendant, Matthew Lee Rogers, was convicted by jury of aggravated arson. He was later sentenced to twenty years in confinement as a Range I, violent offender. The defendant now appeals, arguing: (1) the evidence is insufficient to convict him of aggravated arson; (2) the trial court erred in instructing the jury on aggravated arson and reckless burning; and (3) the trial court erred by not granting a new trial after one or more of the jurors consulted an electronic dictionary in order to ascertain the meaning of "structure" as it related to the offense of aggravated arson. After thorough consideration of the record and applicable law, we reverse the defendant's conviction and remand for a new trial.

FACTUAL BACKGROUND

The proof at trial established that on April 23, 2004, a fire was started inside the apartment of Dennis Rollins. At trial, Rollins testified that he lived in an apartment in Town View Towers, a four-story

---

[72] Arson, like burglary, is not strictly a misappropriation offense, but it is included in this chapter because it involves the destruction of property. At common law, it focused more on human habitation, but now encompasses many forms of property destruction by fire or explosion.

[73] Melvin Wingersky, ed., CLARK & MARSHALL, A TREATISE ON THE LAW OF CRIMES, at 893 (6th ed. 1952), citing 1 HAWKINS, PLEASE OF THE CROWN, c. 18 § 2.

[74] Melvin Wingersky, ed., CLARK & MARSHALL, at 893.

apartment building which housed approximately 900 tenants. At the time, his girlfriend, Norma Fish, was living with him. However, unbeknownst to Rollins, his girlfriend was also dating the defendant. Approximately two and one-half weeks before the fire, news of this relationship ignited a minor physical confrontation between the defendant and Rollins. With the defendant's passions inflamed, he told Rollins, "I ain't the one to mess with. . . . She's mine. She's mine."

On April 23, 2004, around 8:30 p.m., Rollins was entertaining several friends in his apartment. After running out of drinks, Rollins and his friends left his apartment to go to the store. After heading back toward his apartment, Rollins received a call from his neighbor who told him that a smoke smell was coming from his apartment. Upon returning to his apartment, Rollins opened his door, smelled smoke and saw a big black spot on the floor; whereupon, he doused the spot with water, sprayed the spot with potpourri, and placed a floor mat over the spot. According to Rollins, when he first smelled the smoke and saw the black spot on the floor, he and his friends were afraid and thought the apartment was on fire. The next day, Rollins called the apartment's management and asked them to investigate. Two days later, an arson investigator showed Rollins a videotape. Because of a hearing problem, Rollins had a paper note on his door advising people to knock loudly. The videotape showed the defendant removing the note off Rollins' door, lighting it on fire, and sliding it under the door.

Donald Sands testified that he lived in the Town View Towers and knew both the defendant and Rollins. According to Sands, the defendant was bitter toward Rollins because he was dating Fish. The defendant told him that he was going to beat up and rob Rollins. However, Sands did not believe the defendant was serious about his threats. Two days later Sands heard about the fire in Rollins' apartment.

Charles Kitts, arson investigator with the Knoxville Fire Department, testified that he viewed a videotape in connection with a reported fire at Town View Towers. After viewing the videotape, Kitts conducted an investigation of Rollins' apartment three days after the fire was reported. During his investigation, Kitts observed light smoke damage to the inside of the door and "burn and melt in the carpet." He took pictures as part of his investigation. The pictures depicted charring damage to a patch of the carpet. Upon conducting his investigation, Kitts surmised that a piece of paper was set on fire and slid under the door thereby causing damage to the carpet. Kitts stated that the defendant was identified in the videotape as the individual who started the fire. Kitts acknowledged that he did not know whether tile or concrete underlay the carpet.

Ray Offenbacher testified that he was working as a security officer for the Town View Towers when Rollins approached and asked him to look at his carpet. Upon entering Rollins' apartment, Offenbacher noted a "significant sized burn to the carpet." However, the carpet was not smoldering or posing any threat. Offenbacher also did not observe any wet spots or water on the carpet. Because it was late Friday evening, Offenbacher told Rollins to wait until Monday then go to the management office and look at the security video. Offenbacher stated that he knew Rollins was hard of hearing and kept a sign on his door. Offenbacher noted that the sign was missing from the door when he came to Rollins' apartment. Offenbacher said he was present when Rollins watched the security video and Rollins identified the defendant as the individual who started the fire. Offenbacher stated that he estimated 200 to 300 people could have been present in the apartment building on a Friday night.

Allison Zong testified that she worked for the Town View Towers' management company. She stated that on Monday morning after the fire, she pulled the video from the camera in the hallway outside of Rollins' apartment. She recalled that Rollins identified the defendant in the video as the person who started the fire. Zong said that the defendant started the fire without permission. Zong stated that Town View Towers consisted of two high rise buildings with 304 units. Zong stated that the apartment complex was 95 to 98 percent occupied. Zong testified that the carpet had to be replaced because the fire had burned the carpet down to the tile underneath. Zong acknowledged, however, that the carpet was not replaced until the middle of July because the damage was not severe enough to warrant immediate attention. According to Zong, the management replaced the entire carpet and vinyl wall base rather than replacing the damaged portion of the carpet.

Gary Haun testified that he worked for Broadway Carpet, which replaced the carpet in Town View Towers as necessary. According to Haun, the carpet installed in Rollins' apartment was not treated with fire retardant. Barry Rice, a private investigator, testified that he specialized in arson investigation. Rice stated that he purchased carpet similar to the type of carpet found in Rollins' apartment. Rice stated that he was unable to set the carpet on fire with a piece of paper though he conducted numerous burn tests. Rice elaborated that he attempted to replicate the burn damage on the carpet by sliding a burning piece of paper under a door and by laying the burning paper on the carpet.

The defendant testified that he went to Rollins' apartment to confront Rollins face to face like a "real man." The defendant knocked on the door but nobody answered. Believing Rollins to be inside, the defendant took the paper sign off the door, lit it, and shoved it under the door. The defendant explained that he was trying to get Rollins' attention and draw him outside. The defendant acknowledged that he knew that a lot of people lived in the apartment complex.

After hearing the evidence and arguments, the jury found the defendant guilty of aggravated arson. The defendant was subsequently sentenced to twenty years in confinement as a Range I, violent offender.

ANALYSIS

I.   Sufficiency of Evidence

On appeal, the defendant first claims that the evidence is insufficient to convict him of aggravated arson. Upon review of this issue, we reiterate the well-established rule that once a jury finds a defendant guilty, his or her presumption of innocence is removed and replaced with a presumption of guilt. Therefore, on appeal, the convicted defendant has the burden of demonstrating to this court why the evidence will not support the jury's verdict. To meet this burden, the defendant must establish that no "rational trier of fact" could have found the essential elements of the crime beyond a reasonable doubt. . . . The state is entitled to the strongest legitimate view of the evidence and all reasonable inferences which may be drawn from that evidence. Questions concerning the credibility of the witnesses, conflicts in trial testimony, the weight and value to be given the evidence, and all factual issues raised by the evidence are resolved by the trier of fact and not this court. We do not attempt to re-weigh or re-evaluate the evidence. Likewise, we do not replace the jury's inferences drawn from the circumstantial evidence with our own inferences.

Relevant to this case, a person can be found guilty of aggravated arson when that person knowingly damages any occupied structure by means of a fire or explosion without the consent of persons who have an ownership interest in the structure. *See* Tenn.Code Ann. § 39–14–301, –302.[1] At trial, the state presented evidence that the defendant started a fire on the carpet of Rollins' apartment without permission and that other tenants were present in the apartment building at the time of the fire. In challenging the sufficiency of the evidence, the defendant does not contest the evidence proving he started a fire inside the apartment building. Instead, he submits that the proof at trial showed that he caused damage to some carpet in Rollins' apartment and not the structure of Town View Towers as charged in the indictment. Therefore, he claims that the state failed to prove that he set fire or burned *any structure* pursuant to the arson and aggravated arson statutes.

We begin our review by noting that the term "structure" is not defined by the arson statute. However, the committee comments to the arson statute denote that the current language of "damages any structure" replaced prior language, which covered "any house, or

---

[1]   Arson is committed when one knowingly damages any structure by means of a fire or explosion: (1) Without the consent of all persons who have a possessory, proprietary, or security interest therein. Tenn. Code Ann. § 39–14–301(a)(1). Aggravated arson occurs when a person commits arson when one or more persons are present inside the structure. Tenn.Code Ann. § 39–14–302(a)(1).

outhouse, or any building, or any other structure. . . ." Also useful to our analysis is the dictionary definition of structure. According to BLACK'S LAW DICTIONARY, structure is any "construction, production, or piece of work artificially built up or composed of parts purposefully joined together." *Id.* at 1464 (8th ed. 2004). According to WEBSTER'S II NEW COLLEGE DICTIONARY, structure is "something constructed, such as a building." Notably, our interpretation of the term "structure" is restricted to the natural and ordinary meaning of the language used in the statute. We are also mindful that our criminal code provisions should be construed according to the fair import of their terms, including reference to judicial decisions and common law interpretations, to promote justice, and effect the objectives of the criminal code.

While there are no Tennessee cases on point, certain out-of-state cases are helpful to our review of this issue. In *In re Jesse L.* 221 Cal. App.3d 161 (Cal. Ct. App.1990), the appellate court was asked to determine whether burn damage to the floors, counters, and light fixtures was sufficient evidence of structural fire damage to support a conviction of arson. After analyzing portions of its civil code, the court determined that "a fixture is a thing, originally personal property, but later affixed or annexed to realty so that it is considered real property." *Id.* at 167. The court then held that "a fixture . . . becomes part of the structure to the extent that a burning or charring or destruction by fire is all that is required to constitute a burning sufficient to support a conviction of arson. . . ." *Id.* at 168. In *People v. Lee*, 24 Cal.App. 4th 1773 (Cal. Ct. App.1994), the court was presented with the issue of whether burn damage to wall-to-wall carpeting inside a house was sufficient to convict the defendant of arson. The court noted that personal property or chattel became a fixture when "it would become essential to the ordinary and convenient use of the property to which it was annexed." *Id.* at 1777 (quoting *M.P. Moller, Inc. v. Wilson*, 8 Cal.2d 31, 38 (Cal.1936)). The court further noted whether personal property had lost its character as personalty and had become a permanent and integral part of the structure was a question of fact to be determined by the jury. *Id.* at 1777–78. The court concluded that "the jury could reasonably find the carpet in this case was a fixture, *i.e.*, originally personal property which was affixed to the real property so securely and permanently it became an integral part of the structure." *Id.* at 1778.

We find the analysis and reasoning set forth in the aforementioned cases to be persuasive and applicable to this case.[2] In this case, evidence

---

[2]   Tennessee courts have considered a "fixture" as "[a]n article in the nature of personal property which has been so annexed to the realty that it is regarded as part of the land." *State ex rel. Comm'r v. Teasley*, 913 S.W.2d 175, 177 (Tenn.Ct.App.1995) (citing Black's Law Dictionary). However, only those chattels/personal property are fixtures "which are so attached to the freehold that, from the intention of the parties and the uses to which they are put, they are presumed to be permanently annexed, or a removal thereof would cause serious injury to the freehold." *Memphis Housing Authority v. Memphis Steam Laundry-Cleaner, Inc.*, 463 S.W.2d 677, 679 (Tenn.1971); *see, e.g., Murphy v. State*, 426 S.W.2d 509, 514 (Tenn.1968)

established that the defendant set fire to a piece of paper, slid it under the door, thereby causing some burn damage to the wall-to-wall carpet inside an occupied apartment building. By their verdict, the jury determined that the damage to the carpet was tantamount to damage to the structure of the apartment building. In our view, it is not unreasonable for the jury to find that the carpet in this case was a permanent and integral part of the structure. Therefore, based upon the evidence presented in this case, we conclude that a reasonable jury could find the defendant guilty of aggravated arson.

II.   Jury Instructions

The defendant next contends that the trial court erred in instructing the jury on the elements of aggravated arson and reckless burning. Specifically, the defendant submits that the trial court declined to provide a definition of the term "structure" in the jury charge. The defendant also submits that the jury charge erroneously reflected that the defendant could be found guilty of reckless burning if the defendant recklessly "started a fire to the structure of another," whereas the reckless burning statute reflects that reckless burning is committed when someone recklessly "starts a fire on the land, building, structure or personal property of another." The defendant asserts that these errors confused the jury and resulted in an unfair trial.

In criminal cases, a defendant has a right to a correct and complete charge of the law. Thus, it follows that the trial court has a duty to give a complete charge of the law applicable to the facts of a case. The material elements of each offense should be described and defined in connection with that offense. The failure to do so deprives the defendant of the constitutional right to a jury trial and subjects the erroneous jury instruction to harmless error analysis. However, not all erroneous jury instruction rises to the level of constitutional error. A jury instruction must be reviewed in its entirety and read as a whole rather than in isolation. A jury instruction is considered "prejudicially erroneous if it fails to fairly submit the legal issues or if it misleads the jury as to the applicable law." *State v. Hodges*, 944 S.W.2d 346, 352 (Tenn.1997).

The record reflects that prior to charging the jury, the trial court determined that it would let the jury use its common sense to determine whether the damage to the carpeting was damage to the structure. The trial court subsequently charged the jury. . . .

In the instant case, the record reflects that the jury instructions fully and fairly state all the elements of aggravated arson and reckless burning. With respect to the trial court's refusal to define the term "structure," we note that a trial court is not required to define or explain words or terms in common use which are understood by persons of

---

(determining under the facts of the case, that a mobile home was a structure since it had become a fixture attached to real estate).

ordinary intelligence. *See State v. Summers*, 692 S.W.2d 439, 445 (Tenn.Crim.App.1985). Also, in this case, it appears that the trial court's initial decision to omit a definition of "structure" was consciously made in deference to the jury's role as the "trier of fact." Thus, pursuant to the aforementioned standard of review, we perceive no error in the trial court's charge on aggravated arson. With respect to the trial court's charge on reckless burning, we determine that the charge was in accordance with the reckless burning statute. Pursuant to the statute, an individual can be convicted of reckless burning if he "recklessly starts a fire on the land, building, structure *or* personal property of another." Tenn. Code Ann. § 39–14–304 (emphasis added). As seen, the language of the statute includes the disjunctive conjunction "or." It is well-established that "when the disjunctive conjunction 'or' is used in a statute, the various elements are to be treated separately, with any one element sufficient to meet the objectives outlined in the statute." *State v. Cleveland*, No. W2004–02892–CCA–R3–CD, 2005 WL 1707975, at *3 (Tenn. Crim. App., at Jackson, July 21, 2005). This disjunctive or alternative construction found in the reckless burning statute is reflected and emphasized in the Tennessee Pattern Jury Instruction. Thus, we perceive no error in the trial court's charge on reckless burning. In sum, the jury charge did not serve to mislead the jury as to the applicable law, nor did it fail to fairly submit the legal issues pertinent to the facts of this case. Consequently, the defendant is not entitled to relief on this issue.

III. Extraneous Information

The defendant next complains that he was denied a fair trial by the jury's exposure to an electronic dictionary when it was used to ascertain the definition of "structure" after the trial court declined to provide such a definition. The state responds by arguing that the defendant failed to show he was prejudiced as a result of the exposure. . . . While the court has a duty to give a complete charge of the law, it is the duty of the jury to apply the law, as directed by the court, to the facts in evidence. . . .

* * *

Although not entirely clear, the record reflects the following: The jury, during its deliberation, submitted a request asking the trial court for a definition of the word "structure." The trial judge declined to provide further definition of the word "structure," deciding instead to let the jury use its common sense to determine whether or not damage to carpet included damage to a structure. One of the jurors, without prior court approval, then consulted an electronic dictionary. The jurors could not find a definition that aided them in deliberation. The jury eventually arrived at a unanimous verdict of guilt. . . .

After considering the whole record in this case, we conclude that the defendant's trial was prejudiced by the jury's consultation of an electronic dictionary. In making this determination, we emphasize the unique circumstances of this case. To begin, it is clear from the record that the jury, as trier-of-fact, was presented with the issue of whether damage to some carpet constituted damage to a structure within the framework of the arson and aggravated arson statutes. It is also clear that the jury struggled with this issue when, during its deliberation, it requested further instruction on the definition of a structure. With no supplemental instruction given, the jury engaged in self-help and consulted an electronic dictionary to gain insight into what constituted a structure. These facts, as argued by the defendant, properly establish a presumption of prejudice. In contrast, the state did not present evidence rebutting the presumption of prejudice. Without sufficient evidence demonstrating the harmlessness of the jury's unsanctioned use of the electronic dictionary, we cannot say with certainty that the jury reached an impartial verdict. Accordingly, the conviction must be reversed and this case is remanded for a new trial.

———

CHAPTER 8

DRUG POSSESSION AND DISTRIBUTION

A. OVERVIEW

Drug crimes are an enormous part of the criminal justice system. By some estimates, drug offenders account for more than twenty percent of America's prison population. Incarceration for drug offenses has ballooned over the last few decades. At present, a staggering fifty percent of federal prison inmates are there for drug convictions. At the state level, the number of people in prison for drug offenses is ten times higher than it was in the 1980s. On any given day, hundreds of thousands of federal and state offenders wake up behind bars serving time for drug crimes. *See The Sentencing Project: Trends in U.S. Corrections* (2014).

On the surface, drug prosecutions are quite simple. An officer searches an individual and finds cocaine in his pocket. Cocaine is an unlawful controlled substance in every state and thus the individual is guilty. While matters are often that straightforward, many drug cases raise difficult legal questions. First, a defendant might assert that the officer's search was unlawful and hope to have the evidence suppressed as a violation of the Fourth Amendment. (You will take up that topic in your Criminal Procedure course.) More particular to our Criminal Law course, a defendant might challenge whether he was truly in possession of the drugs—perhaps the stash of drugs was not in his pocket, but instead lying near his feet. Or the defendant might concede that he was in possession of drugs, but challenge the drug quantity he is charged with possessing. And, then there is the question of drawing the sometimes difficult line between who is a drug user who deserves to be convicted of possession of a controlled substance and who is a drug dealer. This chapter helps you to analyze these issues.

B. POSSESSION OF A CONTROLLED SUBSTANCE

1. PROVING CONSTRUCTIVE POSSESSION

All states criminalize the possession of a controlled substance. For instance, in Virginia, the Legislature has made it "unlawful for any person knowingly or intentionally to possess a controlled substance unless the substance was obtained directly from, or pursuant to, a valid prescription or order of a practitioner while acting in the course of his professional practice." Va. Code § 18.2–250. You do not need to go to law school to know that if you have heroin or cocaine in your pocket, you are in possession of a controlled substance. But many drug dealers are smart enough not to hold the drugs in their pockets. Watch a few episodes of the extraordinary television series *The Wire* and you will see open air drug markets in which drug gangs store drugs in stash houses, behind trees, and under cars. The gangs use runners and lookouts who are near the drugs but not actually holding them. All of this raises the question, can you be in possession of drugs if you are not actually physically holding or touching them?

In re K.A.

Ill. App. Ct. 2nd Dist., 1997.
682 N.E.2d 1233.

■ JUSTICE COLWELL delivered the opinion of the court:

The State filed a second supplemental delinquency petition against the respondent, K.A., seeking to have him adjudicated a delinquent minor and made a ward of the court pursuant to the Juvenile Court Act of 1987. The petition alleged that K.A. had committed the following offenses: unlawful possession of a controlled substance for knowingly and unlawfully possessing less than 15 grams of a substance containing cocaine; unlawful delivery of a controlled substance for knowingly and unlawfully possessing with the intent to deliver less than one gram of a substance containing cocaine; unlawful possession of a controlled substance for knowingly and unlawfully possessing more than 15 but less than 100 grams of a substance containing cocaine; and unlawful delivery of a controlled substance for knowingly and unlawfully possessing with the intent to deliver more than 15 but less than 100 grams of a substance containing cocaine. The trial court subsequently issued an order of adjudication finding K.A. to be a delinquent minor for committing the charged offenses . . . K.A. appeals.

* * *

Testimony at the adjudicatory hearing revealed the following facts. Detective Joe Vincere testified that at approximately 12:10 p.m. on November 1, 1994, several members of the Rockford police department metro narcotics unit executed a search warrant at 313 South Fourth Street. The building at that address was a two-story dwelling containing three or four apartments. The search warrant was executed in a lower apartment.

Detective Vincere knocked on the rear door of the apartment and announced his office. He received no verbal response but heard some type of movement within. At that point, an officer used a battering ram to force open the door.

Detective Vincere was the first officer to enter the apartment. Detective Vincere immediately observed K.A. and Myron Taylor running in the living room toward the front door. K.A. exited the apartment behind Myron but stopped on command after about 40 yards. Myron continued running, was caught, and was returned to the apartment.

Detective Vincere estimated that, when he first observed K.A. and Myron, they were between one foot to three feet away from a McDonald's box under which cocaine was later discovered and five to six feet away from a closet in which cocaine was later discovered in a hole in the floor. The closet was located between the kitchen and the living room.

Detective Vincere testified that K.A. and Myron told him at the scene that they were visiting the apartment. Detective Vincere also testified that K.A. later told him that Myron had told him to go to the apartment the evening before the raid and that he had arrived at the apartment at about 11:45 a.m. to smoke a joint and listen to some music. K.A. explained that he ran because he was afraid. K.A. denied any knowledge of narcotics within the apartment.

Detective Vincere also testified that no cannabis was recovered in the apartment or on K.A. In addition, Detective Vincere admitted on cross-examination that no scales or cutting agents were recovered and that K.A. did not have a key to the apartment.

Detective Vincere further testified to the condition of the interior of the apartment. The apartment contained some McDonald's boxes in a garbage bag, an empty refrigerator, no furniture, except for a kitchen chair and some cushions, and no clothing. He did not recall observing any type of device to play music. He did not observe any indications that someone was staying in the apartment on a regular basis and no documents were located regarding the tenancy of the apartment.

Detective Vincere also testified that the apartment had been raided on three previous occasions within the last four months. The apartment was also under surveillance earlier in the morning prior to the November 1, 1994, raid. K.A. was never observed on any of the prior occasions or on the morning of the raid. Different people were present in the apartment on each occasion.

According to Detective Vincere, the rear door of the apartment was in bad condition from the previous raids. Although the door could be shut and locked, it was not very sturdy, meaning that anyone could enter the apartment through that door.

Detective Mark Welsh's testimony corroborated Detective Vincere's testimony regarding the interior of the apartment. According to Detective Welsh, the apartment was basically vacant of any furniture, food, or clothing, and it appeared no one lived there. He did not observe any machine capable of playing music. Detective Welsh did observe garbage, such as McDonald's boxes, around the apartment.

Detective Welsh also testified that he found a McDonald's box opened up and facing down in the living room. Under the box, Detective Welsh found 10 corners of clear plastic bags which contained an off-white, rock-like substance later identified as cocaine. In a hole in the floor of the closet, Detective Welsh also found two bags, each tied in a knot and containing several smaller corners of clear plastic bags with an off-white, rock-like substance later identified as cocaine. The closet was located between the kitchen and the living room about six to eight feet from the McDonald's box. There were a total of 87 smaller corners of plastic bags.

* * *

In the kitchen cupboards, Detective Welsh observed a large quantity of plastic bags with the corners cut off. The narcotics found in the apartment were wrapped in what appeared to be corners cut from plastic bags. Detective Welsh did not observe any drug paraphernalia, nor did he find any cannabis within the apartment or on K.A. or Myron.

Detective Welsh searched K.A. and found $140 in United States currency in his front pant pocket. K.A.'s mother testified that a few days before November 1, 1994, she gave K.A. $140 so he could buy some clothes.

K.A. testified that Myron told him to go to the apartment and that he arrived at about 11:45 a.m. K.A. knocked on the front door and Myron let him in. Myron was already in the apartment when K.A. arrived. K.A. spent most of his time in the living room without looking around the apartment. K.A. observed a television, some cushions, a boom box, some tapes, and some garbage in the apartment.

K.A. testified that he was listening to music for about 15 minutes when he heard an unusual sound coming from the back door. K.A. then observed the back door caving in and when he turned around he saw Myron unlocking and running out the front door. K.A. then followed Myron out the front door but stopped on command of the police.

K.A. did not think that Myron lived at the apartment but thought one of Myron's relatives lived in the apartment. K.A. testified that he had never been to the apartment before.

* * *

To establish the elements of unlawful possession of a controlled substance, the State must prove the defendant's knowledge of the possession of the controlled substance and that the controlled substance was in the defendant's immediate and exclusive control. Possession may be actual or constructive.

In the instant case, K.A. was clearly not in actual possession of a controlled substance, and the State does not make such a claim. Rather, the State contends that K.A. was in constructive possession of a controlled substance. Constructive possession exists without actual personal present dominion over a controlled substance, but with an intent and capability to maintain control and dominion. Constructive possession may be inferred from the defendant's exclusive control of the premises where narcotics were found. Once it is established that narcotics were found on premises under the defendant's control, it may be inferred that the defendant had the requisite knowledge and possession for a conviction of possession of a controlled substance, absent other facts and circumstances that might leave a reasonable doubt as to guilt in the minds of the jury.

Here, the narcotics were found in the apartment occupied by K.A. during the raid. The mere presence in the vicinity of contraband, however, cannot establish constructive possession. Nonetheless, where other circumstantial evidence is sufficiently probative, proof of proximity combined with inferred knowledge of the presence of contraband will support a finding of guilt on charges of possession.

In the instant case, there is a reasonable doubt, in light of the evidence when viewed as a whole, that the apartment where the drugs were found was under K.A.'s exclusive control. As a result, it cannot be inferred that the narcotics were in his constructive possession.

The record contains no evidence to prove that K.A. owned, rented, or resided in the apartment where the narcotics were found. One way to prove the necessary control over the premises is to show that the defendant lived there. The State presented no evidence of rental receipts, utility bills, or clothing to show that K.A. lived in the apartment. Additionally, K.A. denied residing at the apartment, and Detective Vincere admitted the police were unable to find proof of tenancy for the apartment. Proof of residency, however, "has little if any relevance to the issue of control" when the dwelling is a "drug house." *See People v. Lawton,* 625 N.E.2d 348 (Ill. App. 1993).

A drug house is a dwelling not used primarily as a residence but instead as a center for the packaging and distribution of drugs, and typically it contains very little or no furniture, appliances, food, or clothing. Detectives Vincere and Welsh both testified that the apartment contained very little furniture besides a chair and some cushions, no food, and no clothing. Neither observed any type of device to play music despite K.A.'s testimony that the apartment also contained a television and a radio. It appeared to both detectives that no one lived in the apartment. Thus, K.A. was present in a drug house at the time of the raid. As a result, the fact that K.A. did not own, rent, or reside in the apartment is not fatal to a finding that he controlled the apartment and therefore constructively possessed the drugs found therein.

Even though residence is not a major factor in determining control of a drug house, the State must still prove the defendant's control over a drug house to establish constructive possession. . . .

In this case, however, the State did not present any evidence of K.A.'s fingerprints on the narcotics or on any drug paraphernalia in the apartment. There was no evidence of drug paraphernalia, and the State presented no testimony to characterize the cut plastic bags as drug paraphernalia. In addition, there was no evidence of cocaine residue or any other drugs on K.A. Furthermore, the police never found a key to the apartment and there was no evidence that K.A. admitted owning a key to the apartment. In fact, K.A. testified that Myron was already in the apartment and let K.A. into the apartment when he arrived. Finally, the narcotics were not in plain sight; they were concealed. Detective Welsh testified that the narcotics under the McDonald's box and in the hole in the closet could not be seen.

* * *

In addition, the State presented no evidence to prove that K.A. was ever present at the apartment on any other prior occasion or that he frequently visited the apartment. . . .

The State also presented no evidence to establish that K.A. kept any personal belongings in the apartment or that K.A. was attempting to dispose of the narcotics.

K.A. was also not present at the apartment for a significant amount of time prior to the raid. At most, K.A. was present in the apartment for 25 minutes, and he could have been present for as little as 15 minutes.

Moreover, K.A. was not alone when the police executed the search warrant. Myron was also present during this raid. In addition, Detective Vincere testified that the apartment was basically available to anyone since the rear door was so fragile and other people did access the apartment as evidenced by the presence of different people during each of the prior raids.

* * *

Finally, K.A. did not admit that he possessed or controlled the apartment. On the contrary, K.A. specifically told Detective Vincere that he did not reside at the apartment, that Myron told him to go to the apartment, and that he was there to smoke a joint and listen to some music. In addition, K.A. testified that he thought a relative of Myron's lived at the apartment.

The only factors tending to show K.A.'s control of the apartment are too weak when viewed in light of the overall circumstances. For example, even though K.A. was present when the police executed the search warrant, presence alone is insufficient to prove control over premises. In addition, K.A. was in possession of $140, but his mother testified that she gave him the money. Finally, although K.A. fled from the scene, flight may only be considered along with other factors tending to establish guilt; flight by itself is not sufficient to establish guilt.

In sum, the record shows that the State only proved that K.A. was present in a drug house where the police found drugs and that K.A. fled the apartment. In light of the overall circumstances of this case, the State failed to prove beyond a reasonable doubt that K.A. exercised control over the apartment. Therefore, the State failed to prove K.A.'s possession of the narcotics beyond a reasonable doubt.

* * *

         * * *

———

NOTES

1. Do you believe K.A.'s story? Do you think he was involved in the distribution of drugs? What else could he plausibly be doing in the apartment (particularly if there was no device to play music, as he contended he was there for)?

2. Do you believe K.A.'s mother that the $140 in his pocket was to buy clothes? Does she have an incentive to lie?

3. The court states the rule that proximity to drugs, without more, typically is not enough for constructive possession. Is this a good rule? Have you ever been present at a party where drugs were openly being consumed? Should you be guilty of possession if you fail to leave the party promptly? Is there a difference between being at a party where drugs are present and being in a known drug house that is not used by anyone as a residence and has as its primary purpose the distribution of drugs?

4. What if the police had found a very large amount of drugs hidden in the house? Would that change your opinion about whether K.A. was in constructive possession?

Sierra v. State

District Court of Appeal of Florida, Fifth District, 1999.
746 So.2d 1250.

■ PER CURIAM.

     * * *

In the late evening of October 30, 1997, Deputy Cheryl Kish of the Osceola County Sheriff's Department was patrolling on Osceola Parkway when a white Nissan Maxima caught her attention; the businesses in the area were closed at that time of night, yet the Maxima slowed and made a right turn into a business/warehouse complex. There had been some burglaries in that area, and she felt that no one should have been in that business complex at that time of night. Kish made a u-turn and pulled into the complex where the Maxima had gone.

By this time the Maxima had turned behind the first row of buildings, and Kish lost sight of it for about 15 seconds. She then discovered the Maxima parked next to the complex. Kish did not see anyone around the parked Maxima, and she pulled in behind it and got out of her car. No one was in the Maxima, but the driver's side window was down, the keys were in the ignition, the stereo was playing, and the hood was warm. At the same time Kish put her hand on the hood, she saw an orange garage door coming down, concealing a pair of feet entering one of the warehouses.

By then, a backup unit had arrived, and Kish went to see if anyone was coming out of the front of the building. She backed her car out and drove to the front; about 20 seconds had passed to that point. At the front of the building, Kish saw Sierra standing 3–4 feet from the entrance of the L & C Detail Shop. When Kish came around the corner, Sierra started walking away. Kish asked Sierra to approach her, which he did. While Sierra was being detained, another officer, thinking he heard sounds emanating from the building, was able to raise the garage door, and sent a K-9 unit in to investigate. Meanwhile, Kish entered the building from the front door and went to the rear, where she observed a black nylon duffel bag. Sierra was searched, and while he carried $1195 in cash, no drugs were found on his person. No drugs were found in the Maxima, although Sierra's fingerprints were found in the car, along with other prints which were not his.

Kish acknowledged that she did not know how many people were in the Maxima when she first observed it, and she did not see Sierra in the Maxima or in the building. She never saw Sierra any closer to the building than three or four feet. At the time noises were heard inside the building, Sierra was either with the other officers or in the patrol car.

No one was found in the building. The K-9 unit alerted on a refrigerator, and when it was opened, a deputy found a clear plastic bag with a white substance in it, which later tested to be cocaine. After a search warrant had been obtained, another plastic bag containing what later proved to be cocaine was found behind a couch cushion. No fingerprints were detected on the refrigerator, nor were any of Sierra's prints found on the bags which contained the cocaine. His prints were found on a plastic measuring cup and on an empty roll of baggies, both of which were found in the duffel bag. When the state rested, the defense offered no evidence and moved for a judgment of acquittal, which was denied.

In order to prove a defendant guilty of trafficking by possession, it must be established that the defendant was either in actual or constructive possession of the contraband. There is no evidence of actual possession here. In order to prove constructive possession, the state must prove that the accused had dominion and control over the contraband, that he had knowledge that the contraband is in his presence, and that he had knowledge of the illicit nature of the contraband.

The state did not establish that Sierra had exclusive possession of the warehouse where the drugs were found. In fact, there was no evidence that Sierra had *any* possessory interest in either the warehouse or whatever business may have been conducted therein. Where the premises on which the contraband is found is not in the exclusive possession of a defendant, knowledge of the presence of the contraband on the premises and the accused's ability to maintain control over it will not be inferred, but must be established by independent proof. Mere proximity to contraband is not sufficient to establish constructive possession.

Arguably, the evidence may show Sierra's presence in the warehouse at the time in question, although no one saw him enter or leave. However, his mere presence on the premises is not sufficient to prove that he knew the contraband was there, much less that he had constructive possession of it. Neither the measuring cup nor the unused plastic baggies where his fingerprints were found had any traces of cocaine or other illicit substance. Under this scenario, the most that could be said was that he was present on the premises where cocaine was found. That evidence alone will not support a conviction.

The judgment of conviction is reversed . . . .

———

NOTES

1. The court reverses Sierra's conviction because "the most that can be said was that he was present on the premises where cocaine was found." Do you agree? Are there any other facts that suggest Sierra is guilty? Do those facts help to demonstrate constructive possession?

2. While we can argue about whether the court applies the facts correctly, it does state the correct rule. As Professor Alex Kreit has explained, "Though constructive possession cases remain filled with conflicts, most jurisdictions today have coalesced around at least one basic principle: proximity to contraband, by itself, is insufficient to prove possession." ALEX KREIT, CONTROLLED SUBSTANCES: CRIME, REGULATION, AND POLICY 158 (2013).

3. What should courts do when police find drugs in automobiles that have multiple occupants? Should the front-seat passenger be guilty of drug possession if the police find drugs in the center console? In the absence of additional evidence, the answer is typically "no." *See, e.g.,* C.M. v. State, 818 So.2d 554 (Fla. Dist. App. 2nd District 2002).

4. What about the driver? If police find drugs in the car, is the driver in constructive possession because it is her car? Not necessarily. For instance, in one case a police officer searched a car after removing the driver and front-seat passenger from the vehicle. The front-passenger seat was badly damaged and the officer found a bag of cocaine hidden in a hole in the passenger seat cushion. Although the jury convicted the driver of possessing the cocaine, an appellate court threw out the conviction because there was no evidence the driver knew of the cocaine. The court explained that "[o]wnership of a vehicle where drugs are found and mere proximity to the drugs, though factors . . . are insufficient alone to prove possession." Scruggs v. Commonwealth, 448 S.E.2d 663 (Va. Ct. App. 1994).

5. Should courts require more evidence to find a defendant in an apartment or a warehouse to be in constructive possession of drugs than they would for an occupant of an automobile? After all, an apartment or a warehouse is bigger and the contraband may be further away from the suspect, while an occupant of an automobile is typically sitting right next to contraband that is in the center console or under a floor mat. At least one court has refused to draw a categorical distinction between cars and buildings on the theory that a passenger in a car cannot easily distance herself from contraband because "[t]here is simply no place to go." Rivas v. United States, 783 A.2d 125 (D.C. Ct. App. 2001). Do you agree? Should it be easier to convict passengers in a vehicle on a constructive possession theory?

Cottman v. State

Md. Ct. Spec. App., 2005.
886 A.2d 932.

■ KENNEY, J.

Nathaniel Cottman, Jr., appellant, was convicted in the Circuit Court for Baltimore County of [multiple drug offenses, including possession of cocaine].

* * *

For the following reasons, we shall affirm appellant's convictions.

FACTUAL AND PROCEDURAL HISTORY

In the early morning hours of August 14, 2002, appellant and Ms. Benson were arrested following the completion of a drug deal with Earnest Moore, an undercover Baltimore County Police Detective. . . .

Detective Moore, a member of the Essex Community Drug and Violence Interdiction Team, was the State's only witness. At approximately 5:45 on the morning of August 14, 2002, he was wearing "undercover clothes" and driving an unmarked sport utility vehicle on Dartford Road in Essex. He witnessed several individuals leaning against a car parked in front of 1614 Dartford Road. A woman, later identified as "Ms. Benson," shouted: "Hey, come here." Detective Moore pulled his vehicle to the curb and Benson, along with a male Detective Moore identified as appellant, approached.

Benson stood next to the driver's window. Appellant stood at the driver's mirror and leaned toward the driver's window, approximately two to three feet from Detective Moore. Benson asked Detective Moore whether he was a police officer, and he replied that he was not. Appellant then inquired: "Are you sure you're not police?" Detective Moore repeated his denial. Benson asked Detective Moore if he had been drinking, and lying, Detective Moore claimed that he had. Benson smelled his breath, and said, "Yeah, he's all right." Appellant walked to the front of the police vehicle and looked up and down the street. Detective Moore said that "lookouts" "commonly traveled with drug dealers in that area," and during drug transactions, "will keep a lookout to try to identify any police that are in the area." According to Detective Moore, appellant's actions were consistent with a drug dealer's lookout.

While appellant was standing at the front of the vehicle, Benson asked Detective Moore what he wanted. Detective Moore responded that he wanted $20 worth of cocaine, and Benson retrieved a small bag of cocaine from her mouth. She exchanged the bag for a $20 bill Detective Moore presented. During the transaction, Detective Moore saw appellant's face for "20 seconds, maybe at the most."

As he drove away, Detective Moore witnessed Benson and appellant walk together toward the group in front of 1614 Dartford Road. He notified the surveillance units working with him that he had made a drug purchase and described appellant and Benson. Two to three minutes later, he returned to Dartford Road and walked to where appellant and Benson were being detained. Detective Moore identified both as the individuals involved in the earlier transaction. At trial, Detective Moore again identified appellant and testified that he had no doubt regarding his identification.

Incident to his arrest, appellant was searched, but no drugs or money was found. The substance in the bag Benson gave to Detective Moore was later analyzed and found to contain 0.2 grams of cocaine. Appellant stipulated that the substance in the bag was cocaine, and the drugs were admitted into evidence.

* * *

DISCUSSION

* * *

II.

Appellant . . . contends that the evidence was insufficient to sustain his convictions. . . . [He maintains that] the State "failed to prove that the male subject exercised the requisite dominion and control over the cocaine to justify any rational trier of fact in concluding that he 'possessed' the cocaine at issue."

* * *

Appellant claims that, even if Detective Moore's testimony is credited, the evidence, viewed in the light most favorable to the State, merely demonstrated that appellant was present at the scene at the time the sale occurred. Because there was no evidence that he held the cocaine or the money, or otherwise directed Benson, the evidence was insufficient to permit a rational trier of fact to conclude that he exercised dominion or control over the cocaine.

In response, the State asserts that, although the cocaine was produced from Benson's mouth, there was sufficient evidence presented from which "it could be inferred . . . that this was Benson's and [appellant's] method of concealing their cocaine before it was distributed to their buyers." Therefore, the State maintains, there was sufficient evidence for a rational trier of fact to find that appellant was in constructive possession of the cocaine. . . .

* * *

In the instant case . . . there was sufficient evidence to sustain appellant's conviction for possession of cocaine under . . . a constructive possession theory. Maryland Code (2002), § 5–601(a)(1) of the Criminal Law Article ("C.L."), makes it a crime to "possess or administer to another a controlled dangerous substance, unless obtained directly or by prescription or order from an authorized provider acting in the course of professional practice[.]" C.L. § 5–101(u) defines "possess," in relevant part, as "to exercise actual or constructive dominion or control over a thing by one or more persons." The Court of Appeals has explained that "[t]o prove control, the ' "evidence must show directly or support a rational inference that the control over the prohibited . . . drug in the sense contemplated by the statute, *i.e.,* that [the accused] exercised some restraining or direct influence over it." ' " *White v. State,* 767 A.2d 855 (2001). Moreover, " '[k]nowledge of the presence of an object is normally a prerequisite to exercising dominion and control.' " *Id.* . . .

Possession need not be exclusive, but may be joint. It is also not necessary that the drugs be on appellant's person for him to possess them. In cases where two or more people were charged with the possession of contraband in a home or vehicle, we have relied upon the following factors in determining whether there was joint possession:

> (1) the proximity between the defendant and the contraband, (2) the fact that the contraband was within the view or otherwise within the knowledge of the defendant, (3) ownership or some possessory right in the premises or the automobile in which the contraband is found, or (4) the presence or circumstances from which a reasonable inference could be drawn that the defendant was participating with others in the mutual use and enjoyment of the contraband.

Hall [*v. State*], 705 A.2d 50 (1998).

* * *

[A] rational trier of fact could have concluded that appellant, along with Benson, constructively exercised dominion and control over the cocaine. Appellant approached Detective Moore's vehicle with Benson and stood next to her immediately prior to the sale. As discussed above, his knowledge of the presence of the cocaine can be inferred from his question posed to Detective Moore. Although no money or drugs were found on appellant incident to his arrest, it is a rational inference that appellant had "earned" some portion of the proceeds from the sale or other consideration by acting as a lookout and protecting both Benson and the drugs, such that he shared in the mutual use and enjoyment of the cocaine. His concern that Detective Moore might be a police officer and his acting as a lookout during the transaction permits an inference that appellant exercised a restraining influence over the cocaine. In other words, he could halt the sale in the event that he sensed police involvement or intervention. Viewing the evidence, and the inferences derived therefrom, in the light most favorable to the prosecution, we are persuaded that a reasonable fact finder could have found that appellant was in constructive joint possession of the cocaine.

lookout can stop a sale + they get a cut of the money

* * *

The evidence was, therefore, sufficient to sustain each of appellant's convictions.

* * *

———

NOTES

1. Wasn't the cocaine in Benson's mouth the entire time? How could Cottman have exercised any control over cocaine in another person's mouth?

2. Are you able to reconcile *Cottman* with *In re K.A.* and *Sierra*?

3. Does it make sense, as the *Cottman* court explains, that "[p]ossession need not be exclusive, but may be joint?" Imagine that you are driving home from school with three of your classmates this afternoon. You are sitting in the front passenger seat when the vehicle is stopped and searched by police. The officer opens the center console between you and the driver and discovers cocaine. Are you guilty of possession of a controlled substance via a constructive possession theory? Are the passengers in the back seat also guilty? Can all four of you possess the same cocaine? Would your answer change if it were a very small amount of cocaine? What other facts would be relevant to determining whether you are guilty on a theory of constructive possession?

4. According to the court, Cottman was acting as a lookout. When drugs are sold on the street, there are often other participants in the transaction. As one court explained:

> [A] common pattern [is for] one individual, designated a "runner" [who] would solicit potential customers and direct them to the "holder," who supervised the supply of drugs. A holder in an enterprise rarely keeps the drugs on his person for fear of being caught with incriminating evidence. Instead the holder might stash the drugs in a vehicle, near a tree, or in a bag amongst litter. For the same reason, the participants in an open-air drug enterprise might arrange to have incoming cash stashed separately. Finally . . . an executive lieutenant or captain [is in charge of passing out the drugs] to street lieutenants for selling on the street.

Bullock v. United States, 709 A.2d 87 (D.C. 1998) (excerpted in ALEX KREIT, CONTROLLED SUBSTANCES: CRIME, REGULATION, AND POLICY 177 (2013)). In an open-air drug market, it is possible for the lookout, runner, holder, and lieutenant all to be in constructive possession of the same drugs even if none of them is physically holding them. Can you imagine the difficulty a prosecutor will have in proving guilt?

2. *MENS REA* AS TO DRUG TYPES AND QUANTITIES

United States v. De La Torre
United States Court of Appeals for the Tenth Circuit, 2010.
599 F.3d 1198.

■ MURPHY, CIRCUIT JUDGE.

I.   Introduction

Julio De La Torre was charged in a two-count superseding indictment with possessing with the intent to distribute fifty grams or more of methamphetamine and possessing with the intent to distribute less than fifty kilograms of a substance containing a detectable amount of marijuana, both in violation of 21 U.S.C. § 841(a)(1). After a jury trial, at which he testified, De La Torre was convicted of both counts and was sentenced to 121 months' imprisonment.

De La Torre appeals his methamphetamine conviction and sentence. He argues the district court erred by instructing the jury it could find him guilty of possessing methamphetamine, even if it believed he only knew marijuana was in the backpack and was unaware methamphetamine was present. . . .

II.   Background

. . . At trial, De La Torre testified that for several days prior to February 16, 2007, he was partying in Room 150 of the Comfort Inn in Wichita, Kansas. While there, he admits he smoked marijuana, but claims he neither saw nor used methamphetamine.

On the morning of February 16, 2007, the hotel's desk clerk called the Wichita Police Department and reported what she suspected was a false identification used to rent Room 256. When officers arrived, the clerk provided a copy of the identification card and explained that the people staying in Room 150 were in the process of moving to Room 256. Additionally, the clerk stated other guests had reported the smell of marijuana coming from Room 150.

De La Torre testified he awoke that morning when someone in the room started screaming that the police were at the hotel. At that point, De La Torre claimed one of the people in the room handed him a backpack and instructed De La Torre to follow him. They left the hotel, at which point the other person told De La Torre to get rid of the backpack. Officer Rago, who was in the parking lot, testified he saw De La Torre and another individual run from the hotel and hop over a short fence. Officer

Rago testified De La Torre was carrying a backpack, which he threw into a culvert as he ran away.

Officer Rago informed Officer Springob about what he saw. A few minutes later, De La Torre and a companion walked back to the hotel through the parking lot. Officer Rago recognized them and approached to ask them where they came from and where they were going. Each gave a different answer: one claimed they were coming from the store while the other claimed they were returning from a friend's house. Meanwhile, Officer Springob retrieved the backpack from the culvert. Officer Springob testified he could smell marijuana inside the culvert. When he looked inside the backpack, Officer Springob found a shoe box containing multiple bricks of marijuana, a large bag of methamphetamine, rubber bands, Ziploc bags, and digital scales. As a result, Officer Rago took both men into custody.

Officer Springob read De La Torre his Miranda warnings, and De La Torre agreed to speak with him about the incident. According to Officer Springob, De La Torre admitted knowing the backpack contained marijuana, scales, Ziploc bags, rubber bands, digital scales, and "ice," a form of methamphetamine. Officer Springob also testified De La Torre admitted being in Room 150 for about three days, where he hung out with friends and used marijuana and ecstasy. De La Torre told Officer Springob his friends sold narcotics in the room. He also admitted using methamphetamine in the past, but not at the hotel.

De La Torre testified he did not tell the officer he knew there was methamphetamine in the backpack. Instead, he claimed he told Officer Springob he believed it only contained marijuana because he and others in the hotel room had only used marijuana. Nonetheless, De La Torre admitted the quantities of both the methamphetamine and marijuana discovered in the backpack were distribution quantities. De La Torre also admitted he had used methamphetamine in the past, but claimed he had not used any in the year prior to the incident at the hotel.

* * *

The jury ultimately convicted De La Torre of both counts. . . . The district court ultimately sentenced De La Torre to 121 months' imprisonment to be followed by five years' supervised release.

III. Discussion

A. *De La Torre's Knowledge of the Backpack's Contents*

De La Torre first challenges his conviction for possessing methamphetamine with the intent to distribute. He argues the district court erred in instructing the jury that the Government did not have to prove beyond a reasonable doubt that he knew the precise nature of all controlled substances he possessed. . . .

De La Torre's challenge stems from his testimony that while he believed the backpack contained marijuana, he had no idea it also contained methamphetamine. In support of this argument, he points to his testimony that he only smoked marijuana in the hotel room and did not see methamphetamine while he was there. Specifically, De La Torre argues Tenth Circuit case law does not permit the Government to use his admission that he knew he possessed a single controlled substance, marijuana, to establish the *mens rea* for possessing both marijuana and methamphetamine under 21 U.S.C. § 841(a)(1).

Here, the district court instructed the jury:

To find the defendant guilty of this crime you must be convinced that the government has proved each of the following beyond a reasonable doubt:

First: the defendant knowingly or intentionally possessed a controlled substance;

Second: the controlled substance was methamphetamine;

Third: the defendant possessed the methamphetamine with the intent to distribute it; and

Fourth: the weight of the methamphetamine defendant possessed was at least 50 grams.

It also instructed the jury that the Government did not need "to prove beyond a reasonable doubt that the defendant knew the precise nature of the controlled substance or substances."

Contrary to De La Torre's argument, the district court's instructions were consistent with this court's interpretation of § 841(a)(1). The statute does not require the Government to prove a defendant knew the precise nature of the controlled substance he possessed, so long as he knew he did in fact possess a controlled substance. The Government can establish the *mens rea* for the possession element by proving only that the defendant knew he possessed some controlled substance. Once it proves the defendant had the requisite guilty mind to possess some controlled substance within the universe of all controlled substances, it has established the *mens rea* necessary to establish the possession element with respect to any and all drugs the defendant actually possessed. This is so even if the defendant was unaware of the nature or number of controlled substances he actually possessed. The Government must then prove the defendant did possess the particular controlled substance charged in the indictment. The Government is not required, however, to prove that the controlled substance the defendant actually possessed corresponds to the controlled substance the defendant believed he possessed.

In the instant case, De La Torre's admission established he had the necessary *mens rea* to be convicted of possessing methamphetamine with the intent to distribute it. Even if De La Torre was, as he claimed, wholly unaware of the presence of a second controlled substance in the backpack, he admits he knew the backpack contained a controlled substance. This admission was sufficient to establish his guilty mind as to the possession element with respect to both drugs. Thereafter, De La Torre admitted he did in fact possess distribution amounts of both marijuana and methamphetamine. Consequently, De La Torre's statements were sufficient for the jury to convict him of both counts. The district court did not abuse its discretion or misapply the law in giving the relevant instruction.

* * *

Whitaker v. People

Supreme Court of Colorado, 2002.
48 P.3d 555.

■ JUSTICE HOBBS delivered the Opinion of the Court.

A jury convicted the defendant, David Whitaker, of possessing with intent to distribute over 1,000 grams of methamphetamine, a schedule II controlled substance, and importing methamphetamine into Colorado. Whitaker claimed that his conviction should be reversed because the trial judge did not instruct the jury to apply the *mens rea* of "knowingly" to both the quantity and the importation of the drug. The court of appeals upheld Whitaker's conviction. We agree.

We hold that the General Assembly, in section 18–18–405, did not intend to apply a culpable mental state to the quantity of drugs the defendant distributed, manufactured, dispensed, sold, or possessed. . . .

I.

On January 14, 1998, David Whitaker was a passenger on a Greyhound bus en route from Los Angeles, California to Denver, Colorado. The bus stopped in Grand Junction, Colorado for routine service and to change drivers. Passengers were required to leave the bus during this stop. After the passengers had reboarded, three Grand Junction Police Department officers entered the bus, identifying themselves as police officers. Two of the officers began talking to each of the bus passengers, including Whitaker.

The officers testified that Whitaker appeared nervous while talking to them. When asked about his luggage, Whitaker told the police that he had none. The officers pointed to a black bag near Whitaker and asked if it was his. Whitaker responded that it was not his bag, but said he had placed his jacket and a few other items inside it because no one else appeared to be using it. Whitaker then consented to a search of the bag. The officers discovered 8.8 pounds of uncut methamphetamine contained in several duct tape covered packages inside the bag.

The prosecution charged Whitaker with several drug offenses. At trial, Whitaker argued that he did not possess the drugs and did not know that the packages of drugs were in the bag. The defense did not dispute the facts that the bag contained 8.8 pounds of methamphetamine and that the drugs came across Colorado's state lines via the Greyhound bus. The jury convicted Whitaker of possessing 1,000 grams or more of a schedule II controlled substance with intent to distribute and importation of a schedule II controlled substance. The trial court sentenced him to twenty years in state prison.

The court of appeals affirmed Whitaker's conviction and sentence. . . . It held that the prosecution need not prove that Whitaker "knowingly" imported the controlled substance, nor that the defendant "knew" the drugs weighed more than 1,000 grams. . . .

* * *

II.

We hold that the General Assembly, in section 18–18–405, did not intend to apply a culpable mental state to the quantity of drugs the defendant distributed, manufactured, dispensed, sold, or possessed. We also hold that importation under Colorado's special offender statute, section 18–18–407, does not include a *mens rea* requirement. The jury found beyond a reasonable doubt that the defendant possessed the drug quantity specified by section 18–18–405(3)(a)(III), and imported the drugs across state lines as specified by section 18–18–407(1)(d). Accordingly, we uphold Whitaker's conviction and sentence.

A.

Section 18–18–405 and Quantity of Drug

* * *

. . . Section 18–18–405(3)(a)(III) defines the required sentence for a defendant convicted of unlawful distribution, manufacturing, dispensing, sale or possession of 1,000 grams or more of a schedule I or II controlled substance.[3]

Whitaker argues that the quantity of drugs contained in section 18–18–405(3)(a)(III) is an essential element of the crime of possession with intent to distribute, and the *mens rea* contained in section 18–18–405(1)(a), "knowingly," must apply to it. However, whether the quantity

---

[3]   Section 18–18–405(3)(a)(III), 6 C.R.S. (2001), provides:

(3)(a) Except as otherwise provided in section 18–18–407 relating to special offenders, any person convicted pursuant to paragraph (a) of subsection (2) of this section for knowingly manufacturing, dispensing, selling, distributing, possessing, or possessing with intent to manufacture, dispense, sell, or distribute, or inducing, attempting to induce, or conspiring with one or more other persons, to manufacture, dispense, sell, distribute, possess, or possess with intent to manufacture, dispense, sell, or distribute an amount that is or has been represented to be:

. . .

(III) One thousand grams or one kilogram or more of any material, compound, mixture, or preparation that contains a schedule I or schedule II controlled substance as listed in section 18–18–203 or 18–18–204 shall be sentenced to the department of corrections for a term greater than the maximum presumptive range but not more than twice the maximum presumptive range provided for such offense in section 18–1–105(1)(a).

of drugs involved in the offense requires a *mens rea* is a matter of statutory interpretation. "Our fundamental responsibility in interpreting a statute is to give effect to the General Assembly's purpose and intent in enacting the statute." *Empire Lodge Homeowners' Ass'n v. Moyer,* 39 P.3d 1139, 1152 (Colo.2001). "If the plain language of the statute clearly expresses the legislative intent, then the court must give effect to the ordinary meaning of the statutory language. Likewise, the court should avoid interpreting a statute in a way that defeats the obvious intent of the legislature." *Pediatric Neurosurgery, P.C. v. Russell,* 44 P.3d 1063, 1068 (Colo.2002). We must read the statute as a whole, construing each provision consistently and in harmony with the overall statutory design, if possible.

Here, section 18–18–405(1)(a) defines the offense, and the provisions of 18–18–405(2), (3), (5) and (6) set forth the applicable punishment levels.[4] This statutory structure demonstrates the General Assembly's intent to separate sentencing factors, such as drug type and quantity, from the elements of the crime. Section 18–18–405(3)(a) does not prescribe drug quantity as an element of the offense, nor does it require proof of a culpable mental state in regards to it. . . .

Although section 18–18–405(1)(a) requires the prosecution to prove that the defendant "knowingly" distributed, manufactured, dispensed, sold or possessed the controlled substance, nothing in the statute's language suggests that the prosecution must show that the defendant "knew" the actual weight of the drugs under section 18–18–405(3)(a). To the contrary, section 18–18–405(3)(a) triggers the level of punishment upon proof that the drug quantity involved in the offense was "an amount that is or has been represented to be" the amount specified by subsections (I), (II), or (III) thereunder. . . .

The statute thereby sets forth the drug quantity separately from the elements, with no *mens rea* requirement and with the apparent design of separating the applicable punishment from the creation and definition of the offense.

Any amount of drugs, even less than a usable quantity, can support a conviction under 18–18–405(1)(a). The quantity of drugs turns on objective standards and requires no inquiry into the defendant's state of mind.

The underlying purpose of section 18–18–405(3) is to punish more severely those offenders who deal with large quantities of controlled substances. The legislature's choice to do so is within its prerogative.

---

[4]   Subsection (1) defines the elements of the offense covered by this statute. Subsection (2) defines the level of felony to be applied based upon the type of drug involved in the offense. Subsection (3) defines the required sentence for offenses involving various large quantities of drugs. Subsection (5) works to apply subsection (3) to those defendants who commit a section 18–18–405 offense two or more times within six months and the violations involve an aggregate amount of at least 25 grams of a controlled substance. Subsection (6) requires revocation of the offender's driver's license upon conviction.

Section 18–18–405(3)(a) does not create an additional element for the underlying substantive offense; rather, it defines circumstances that, if proven beyond a reasonable doubt, may require a sentence greater than the presumptive minimum contained in section 18–1–105(1)(a), 6 C.R.S. (2001).

* * *

Accordingly, we affirm the judgment of the court of appeals upholding Whitaker's conviction and sentence.

NOTES

1. The *De La Torre* and *Whitaker* decisions state the majority rules across the United States. Prosecutors must prove that the defendant knew he possessed drugs, but they do not need to show *mens rea* for a particular drug or quantity.

2. One notable thing that De La Torre and Whitaker have in common is the implausibility of their stories. Do you think De La Torre did not know there was methamphetamine in his backpack? How about Whitaker's story about not owning the backpack but placing his possessions in it because "no one else appeared to be using it." Do you think these kind of statements make prosecutors jaded and unwilling to believe criminal defendants even when they are telling the truth?

3. Think back to note 4 after the *Cottman* decision. There are often multiple participants in open air drug markets: lookouts, runners, holders, lieutenants, and possibly other players. Do you think all of them have a good idea of the drug quantity? Is it fair to hold runners and lookouts responsible for the full amount of drugs in the package if they had no idea of the quantity?

4. Would your answer to question 3 above change if the defendant were a lookout standing outside of a stash house and the house contained enough drugs to send the defendant to prison for life? In other words, imagine an eighteen-year old boy being paid $5 an hour to watch in front of a house he knew to contain cocaine. Should the rule in *Whitaker* apply in that situation?

3. DETERMINING DRUG QUANTITY

United States v. Villarreal

United States District Court for the Southern District of Texas, 2012.
2012 WL 401051.

■ JOHN D. RAINEY, SENIOR DISTRICT JUDGE.

* * * [The defendant filed a pre-trial motion for a jury instruction about drug quantity.]

On June 25, 2011, Defendant . . . arrived at the Falfurrias, Texas Border Patrol Checkpoint. Before they arrived, Border Patrol officials had received an anonymous tip that they were carrying illegal drugs. Border Patrol officials searched their car and found ten bundles wrapped in brown postal tape in the trunk of the car. The bundles contained a white powdery substance that the agents believed was methamphetamine. . . .

Subsequent laboratory analysis by the Drug Enforcement Administration (DEA) concluded that the packages instead contained cocaine and had a net weight of 8.4 kilograms. The laboratory separated the ten bundles into two groups. The first group, consisting of two bundles containing wet white powder and 1 bundle containing wet pink powder, had a net weight of 2.5 kilograms and a purity of .41%. The second group, consisting of 7 bundles of compressed white powder, had a net weight 5.9 kilograms and a purity of 3.2%. The laboratory analysis confirmed that each individual bundle contained the controlled substance cocaine.

* * *

Title 21, United States Code, Section 841 makes it an offense to knowingly possess with intent to distribute a substance that contains a detectable amount of cocaine. Section 841 further states that the punishment for the offense depends upon the amount of an illegal substance that is possessed. If that amount is "5 kilograms or more of a mixture or substance containing a detectable amount of" cocaine, the defendant is subject to a mandatory minimum sentence of 10 years in prison and a maximum of life for a first offense. 21 U.S.C. § 841(b)(1)(A). If the amount of the mixture or substance containing cocaine is less than 500 grams, then there is no mandatory minimum and the maximum penalty is up to 20 years in prison for a first offense. 21 U.S.C. § 841(b)(1)(C).

Defendant admittedly possessed a substance that he believed to contain cocaine, and the substance did in fact contain a detectable amount of cocaine. However, Defendant claims that he should not be held responsible for 8.4 kilograms of cocaine at sentencing because the substance he possessed was so diluted that it was essentially unmarketable "garbage." According to Defendant, if the Government fails to prove that the full amount of the mixture or substance Defendant possessed was both marketable as found and weighed more than 5 kilograms, then the jury should have the option of convicting him of the offense of possession with intent to distribute cocaine, with no mandatory minimum and a maximum of 20 years. . . .

* * *

The questions raised by Defendant are: (1) what approach the Court should use when determining the amount of controlled substance for sentencing purposes, and (2) what qualifies as a "mixture or substance."

The United States Supreme Court specifically addressed these issues in Chapman v. United States, 500 U.S. 453, 459, 111 S.Ct. 1919, 114 L.Ed.2d 524 (1991). In Chapman, the Court found that

Congress adopted a "market-oriented" approach to punishing drug trafficking, under which the total quantity of what is distributed, rather than the amount of pure drug involved, is used to determine the length of the sentence. To implement that principle, Congress set mandatory minimum sentences corresponding to the weight of a "mixture or substance containing a detectable amount of" the various controlled substances, including LSD. It intended the penalties for drug trafficking to be graduated according to the weight of the drugs in whatever form they were found-cut or uncut, pure or impure, ready for wholesale or ready for distribution at the retail level. Congress did not want to punish retail traffickers less severely, even though they deal in smaller quantities of the pure drug, because such traffickers keep the street markets going.

As such, the Court concluded that sentences should be based exclusively on the weight of the "mixture or substance," and with respect to drugs like heroin and cocaine, the dilutant, cutting agent, or carrier medium should be included in the weight for sentencing purposes. The Court recognized that "[i]n some cases, the concentration of the drug in the mixture is very low . . . , [b]ut, if the carrier is a 'mixture or substance containing a detectable amount of the drug,' then under the language of the statute the weight of the mixture or substance, and not the weight of the pure drug, is controlling." Id. (citing United States v. Buggs, 904 F.2d 1070 (7th Cir.1990) (1.2% heroin); United States v. Dorsey, 591 F.2d 922 (D.C.Cir.1978) (2% heroin); United States v. Smith, 601 F.2d 972 (8th Cir.1979) (2.7% and 8.5% heroin)).

Federal Circuit Courts have since applied a very factually specific analysis under the "market-oriented" approach of Chapman to determine the quantity of a controlled substance in a "mixture."

For example, in United States v. Segura-Baltazar, 448 F.3d 1281 (11th Cir.2006), officers seized from the defendant's home 1.2 kilograms of a substance with a detectable amount of methamphetamine combined with dimethyl sulfone, a common cutting agent for methamphetamine. Although the mixture contained less than 1% methamphetamine, the court held that it satisfied the legal definition of a "mixture" under 21 U.S.C. § 841 and subjected the defendant to the mandatory minimum sentence of 120 months. The defendant did not disagree that the methamphetamine was combined with a common cutting agent, but instead argued that the mixture was so diluted it would not be marketable or usable on the streets. The district judge rejected the defendant's argument both at trial and at sentencing, noting that "I don't necessarily agree with you that nobody on the street would buy it." The Eleventh Circuit affirmed, holding that the district court correctly considered the combined weight of the cutting agent and the methamphetamine.

* * *

In United States v. Palacios-Molina, 7 F.3d 49 (5th Cir.1993), the defendant was arrested for transporting powder cocaine and two bottles containing cocaine distilled in a thick liquid. Id. at 50. The defendant pled guilty but objected to the drug quantity calculation at sentencing, arguing that the "waste liquid" in the bottles should have been excluded. The district court overruled the defendant's objection and sentenced the defendant based on the greater weight. Id. The Fifth Circuit reversed, distinguishing Chapman on the grounds that the liquid was merely for transportation and concealment, was easily distinguishable from and separable from the cocaine, and would be removed before the cocaine was marketed. As such, the court held that weight of the "waste liquid" should not be included in the amount of controlled substance, since the liquid/cocaine was not a usable mixture that would reach the streets, and the cocaine would be marketable only after the liquid was distilled out. The Fifth Circuit's decision is consistent with a subsequent application note to the Federal Sentencing Guidelines, which provides that "[m]ixture or substance does not include material that must be separated from the controlled substance before the controlled substance can be used." USSG § 2D1 .1, Application Note 1.

In determining whether to include the entire weight of each individual bundle seized from Defendant, the Court must consider whether the "mixture or substance" was in a form recognizable and useable to a consumer, or whether the mixture contained additional matter that would have to be removed before the cocaine could be used.

Here, the Government claims, and Defendant does not dispute, that laboratory analysis by DEA forensic chemist Karen Hall ("Hall") revealed that each individual bundle was found to contain a detectable amount of cocaine. Hall was able to further group the bundles into two identifiable groups, one group consisting of wet powder and the other group consisting of compressed white powder. In addition to cocaine, the 5.9 kilograms of compressed white powder also contained phenyltetrahydroimidazothiazole, which Hall would testify is an adulterant that she has frequently detected in samples of cocaine submitted to the DEA Laboratory. Hall would further testify that the 5.9 kilograms of compressed white powder was similar in appearance and texture to other sample of cocaine submitted to the laboratory and appeared to be in a state that could be ingested by a drug consumer. She would also testify that although the 5.9 kilograms of compressed white powder had a "low" purity of 3.2%, she has tested other substances submitted that contained cocaine with a similarly low purity. Regarding the 2.5 kilograms of wet powder having a purity of .41%, Hall would testify that the sample had a paste like consistency and a foul odor. She would also testify that based on the color and texture, the substance was inconsistent with the cocaine she has personally tested in the laboratory.

Based on the representations made by the Government regarding Hall's testimony, it appears that the 2.5 kilograms of wet powder were not in a form recognizable and useable to a consumer. It further appears that the 5.9 kilograms of compressed white powder were in a form recognizable and useable to a consumer, and thus constitute a "mixture or substance" containing a detectable amount of cocaine within the meaning of the law. Because the 5.9 kilograms of compressed white powder appeared to Hall to be cocaine in a state that could be ingested by a drug consumer, here . . . the Court cannot "necessarily agree with [Defendant] that nobody on the street would buy it." See Segura-Baltazar, 448 F.3d at 1293.

* * *

_____

NOTES

1. It should come as no surprise that drug dealers frequently dilute their product so that they can sell more of it. Quite obviously, illegal drugs are not regulated for purity. And drug users who purchase diluted drugs do not protest in the same way that customers do in the legitimate marketplace. To the contrary, when drug users are addicted, a diluted product will only encourage them to return and purchase more in order to get to the high they are seeking. Furthermore, many of the dilutants used by drug dealers are very dangerous. Accordingly, as the court explains, Congress did not want to create an incentive for drug dealers to dilute their drugs.

2. As *Villarreal* explains, defendants will not succeed by arguing that most of the package was a dilutant or cutting agent, rather than the controlled substance itself. Defendants fare better in court when they argue that the package of drugs was a "gag bag," which is "street parlance for a . . . completely fake container of drugs." United States v. Bedroa-Medrano, 303 F.3d 277 (3rd Cir. 2002). If the package is completely fake and contains no discernable amount of a controlled substance, a defendant cannot be guilty of possession. States do make it illegal to sell or attempt to sell a gag bag. *See, e.g.*, Md. Code Art. 27 § 286b, which makes it unlawful to "distribute, attempt to distribute, or possess with intent to distribute a noncontrolled substance that the person represents as a controlled substance." Of course, selling a gag bag carries not just legal risk but also physical risk because purchasers who have paid money for drugs and received only sugar or some other substance may retaliate against the dealer.

C. POSSESSION WITH INTENT TO DISTRIBUTE

Wells v. Commonwealth

Court of Appeals of Virginia, 1986.
347 S.E.2d 139.

■ KOONTZ, CHIEF JUDGE.

Ruth Ellen Wells was tried and convicted by a jury of possession of marijuana with intent to distribute and her punishment was fixed at confinement in jail for five months and a fine of $1,000. In this appeal, the issue is limited to the sufficiency of the evidence to show intent to distribute marijuana.

On November 13, 1984, officers of the Roanoke City Police Department executed a search warrant at the apartment of Nancy Meadows. This apartment was occupied by Meadows and her two small children. Wells, a friend and frequent visitor of Meadows, was present when the officers entered the apartment. While other officers searched the apartment, one stayed in the living room filling out information cards about the two women. During this process and not in response to any question from the officer, Wells stated: "What you find back there is mine."

Subsequently, in what was described as an adult's bedroom, the police found a brown bag in a dresser drawer. This bag contained seven sandwich baggies, each containing ten baggie corners, for a total of seventy plastic corners containing marijuana. The total weight of the marijuana was 4.2 ounces. The evidence established that the total value of the marijuana was $700. No unusual amounts of money or marijuana related paraphernalia were found during the search of the apartment or on the person of Wells upon her arrest.

* * *

Wells concedes that the evidence was sufficient to prove that she possessed the marijuana. This case therefore presents the question whether the facts proven by the Commonwealth establish intent to distribute rather than mere possession for personal use. In Dukes v. Commonwealth, 227 Va. 119, 313 S.E.2d 382 (1984), the Supreme Court dealt with this question and reviewed some of the prior cases establishing guidelines for its determination.

● When the proof of intent to distribute narcotics rests upon circumstantial evidence, the quantity which the defendant possesses is a circumstance to be considered. Indeed, quantity, alone, may be sufficient to establish such intent if it is greater than the supply ordinarily possessed for one's personal use. However, possession of a small quantity creates an inference that the drug was for the personal use of the defendant.

The Supreme Court in *Dukes* also recognized that the absence of paraphernalia, evidence that the defendant used marijuana, evidence of the method of packaging the marijuana and the absence of unusual amounts of money may all be consistent with the hypothesis of possession for personal use under the facts of a particular case.

The Commonwealth relies heavily on Colbert v. Commonwealth, 219 Va. 1, 244 S.E.2d 748 (1978) to support its position that the evidence was sufficient to establish that Wells possessed the marijuana with intent to distribute. In *Colbert,* the evidence showed that a fight had erupted at the rear of a van parked on the grounds of a rock concert. Later that night, this van was observed on the grounds of a nearby elementary school and the police discovered the defendant in possession of five "nickel bags" of marijuana and a large plastic bag containing "some residue". In addition, the defendant had on his person "over $200 in $10's, $20's and $1's and $5's" which "wasn't folded up or anything together, but it was stuffed down in [his pocket]." The Court concluded that the evidence was sufficient to establish possession with intent to distribute and said:

> In the first place, nothing in the record suggests that the defendant personally used marijuana. Second, the quantity involved is not necessarily indicative of a lack of intent to distribute; indeed, the jury might well have inferred that the quantity seized was what remained from a larger supply held for distribution. Third, the method of packaging does indicate an intent to distribute; from the evidence, the jury might reasonably have found that the marijuana in the "nickel bags" had been transferred from the large plastic bag to facilitate distribution. Finally, considering the foregoing matters along with the testimony concerning the money found "stuffed down" in the defendant's pocket, the jury reasonably could have concluded that the defendant had consummated numerous sales of marijuana at the rock concert.

The facts in *Colbert* strongly suggest possession with intent to distribute and are strikingly dissimilar to those in the present case. In this case, the Commonwealth, by offering Meadows as its witness, established a reasonable inference that the marijuana possessed by Wells was for her personal use. No evidence of intent to distribute was produced by this witness based on activities within the apartment. In fact, Meadows testified that she did not know that the marijuana was there. Officer Day testified that the mode of packaging was as consistent with purchase as with distribution. He further testified that while it was unusual to find this quantity for personal use, he did not testify that it was totally inconsistent with personal use over a period of time.

Additionally, no paraphernalia and no significant amounts of money were found relating to Wells in this case. Consequently, all of the circumstances are consistent with the hypothesis that she hid the marijuana in Meadows's apartment in the packages in which she had obtained possession of them for her personal use. Suspicion of guilt is not sufficient for a conviction. The Commonwealth had the burden to prove beyond a reasonable doubt intent to distribute and having failed to do so, Wells's conviction cannot stand.

Accordingly, we reverse the judgment of the trial court and remand the case for a new trial for possession of marijuana ... if the Commonwealth be so advised.

Reversed and remanded.

————

NOTES

1. The *Wells* court states the general rule: Multiple factors—such as the presence of cash, the method of packaging, and the presence of drug paraphernalia—can factor into determining whether a defendant had an intent to distribute. Thus, someone found with a small amount of drugs can still be convicted of intent to distribute if other evidence is present. However, a large quantity of drugs, without anything else, can also be sufficient to demonstrate intent to distribute.

2. In evaluating the decision in *Wells*, a little math is in order. Wells was found with 4.2 ounces of marijuana. One ounce is equal to 28 grams. A marijuana joint is typically about one gram, and sometimes less than a gram. Thus, a conservative estimate would place Wells in possession of a minimum of 118 joints. Is 118 joints for personal recreational use, or is it an amount that a drug dealer would distribute?

3. According to the court, Wells' marijuana had a street value of $700 in 1986. Adjusted for inflation thirty years later, that marijuana would be worth over $1,500. Does this dollar amount influence your opinion about whether the court was correct?

4. Is it incriminating that there were "seven sandwich baggies, each containing ten baggie corners, for a total of seventy plastic containers containing marijuana?" Does this suggest, as the court believes, that these are the packages Wells purchased the marijuana in? In other words, do you believe that Wells went to a drug dealer and asked for seventy bags of marijuana and the dealer sold her bags that he had wrapped for individual single sales? Or does the seventy bags indicate to you that Wells had separated the marijuana into seventy bags so she could sell them?

Cotton v. State

Court of Appeals of Georgia, 2009.
686 S.E.2d 805, 300 Ga. App. 874.

■ SMITH, PRESIDING JUDGE.

Omali Cotton appeals from his convictions for possession of marijuana with the intent to distribute. . . . In his sole enumeration of error, Cotton contends insufficient evidence exists to support his felony conviction for possessing marijuana with the intent to distribute. We disagree and affirm.

Viewed in the light most favorable to the verdict, the record shows that in a search incident to Cotton's arrest for driving without a license, police officers found three identical small plastic "nickel bags" of marijuana and $60 (two $5 bills, one $10 bill, and two $20 bills) in the same pocket, as well as another identical small bag of marijuana on the ground near his feet. All of the marijuana in the four bags combined weighed 2.7 grams.

The officer who arrested Cotton testified that he spent a lot of time helping a canine officer with "drug enforcement." In his duties as a patrol officer, he would come into contact with drugs at least once a week. The officer testified that he suspected that Cotton was distributing marijuana because he was arrested in an area well-known for drug activity (Ridgecrest Apartments), he did not have a smoking device, he was driving a car that did not belong to him in an apartment complex in which he did not live, personal users normally have all of their marijuana in one bag instead of separate baggies, distributors sell marijuana in small bags like the ones found on Cotton for approximately $10–$20, and the denominations of the cash found in his pocket lent themselves to giving change. The combination of all these facts led the officer to believe that Cotton possessed marijuana with the intent to distribute. The officer acknowledged that his testimony was based upon his experience and information he learned from other officers and people he had previously arrested.

Another officer who assisted with the arrest testified that, based upon his experience patrolling apartments known for being a "high-drug area" where a lot of drugs are bought and sold, as well as his experience with street-level dealers, the drugs and money found on Cotton

> were consistent with a-basically a street level dealer. There were four bags of marijuana separately packaged. The money was in the same location that the drugs were found. There was no wallet. It was easy access for somebody to distribute and take money during a transaction. The . . . money was consistent with the amount of drugs that was on his person. . . .

The amount of the bags was consistent with-like basically a dime bag or a $10 bag would be consistent with the amount of money that he had. He had four bags on him, which isn't a lot of bags, but he had the corresponding money with that.

And my prior experience is if somebody's standing outside of an apartment or something along those lines, they're not going to keep, you know . . . they're not going to keep all 20, 30 on them. They're going to stash them either in a bush or inside an apartment or inside a car and keep them-you know, a minimum amount on their person. And then when they get low, they go back and restock, and then they sell what they have and they conduct business that way.

The officer also found it significant that Cotton did not have a pipe, rolling papers or other smoking device with him which "indicates he wasn't a user, that he was more of a distributor."

Cotton's girlfriend, who lived at Ridgecrest Apartments, testified that Cotton was unemployed at the time of his arrest, that he stayed with her the night before his arrest, that she gave him $80 the day before he was arrested, that he smoked marijuana every day in a blunt made from tobacco cigars, that it was not uncommon for Cotton to possess four $5 bags for his personal use, that he would obtain his marijuana somewhere within Ridgecrest Apartments, and that she had never known him to sell marijuana.

Cotton contends the evidence was insufficient to support a finding that he possessed the marijuana with the intent to distribute. While mere possession will not support a conviction for possession with intent to distribute, the evidence submitted by the State in this case adequately supports Cotton's conviction.

"No bright line rule exists regarding the amount or type of evidence sufficient to support a conviction for possession with intent to distribute." Harper v. State, 285 Ga.App. 261, 265(1)(b), 645 S.E.2d 741 (2007). We have previously held that possession of four individual packages of crack cocaine provided sufficient evidence of intent to distribute. Bowers v. State, 195 Ga.App. 522(1), 394 S.E.2d 141 (1990). In this case, the State also submitted unobjected-to opinion testimony by both officers that the packaging of the marijuana in combination with the denominations of cash found together in Cotton's pants pocket, as well as the absence of a smoking device, demonstrated an intent to distribute. We find this evidence sufficient to support Cotton's intent to distribute conviction. See id.; Helton v. State, 271 Ga.App. 272, 275(b), 609 S.E.2d 200 (2005) (possession of four small bags of methamphetamine, large amount of cash, and expert testimony sufficient to support intent to distribute conviction); Maddox v. State, 227 Ga.App. 602, 603(1), 490 S.E.2d 174 (1997) (possession of four small bags and other evidence sufficient to support intent to distribute 877 conviction).

* * *

Judgment affirmed.

———

NOTES

1. Is it possible to reconcile the decision in *Cotton* with the decision in *Wells*? Cotton had a modest quantity of drugs in a handful of bags—2.7 grams in four bags—while Wells had a much large amount—4.2 ounces in seventy bags. Recall that an ounce contains roughly 28 grams. Therefore, Wells had 43 times more marijuana than Cotton. Are you convinced that Cotton intended to distribute and that Wells did not?

2. The court highlighted the officer's testimony that Cotton did not have a pipe, rolling paper, or other smoking device on his person. The absence of paraphernalia to smoke the drugs with is one factor that courts conclude favors finding an intent to distribute. Should it apply in this case though? Police stopped Cotton while he was driving. If Cotton was venturing out of his home to purchase drugs for personal use, would he have brought his pipe or rolling paper with him?

3. The court also focused on the four bags of marijuana found on and near Cotton and noted that "personal users normally have all of their marijuana in one bag instead of separate baggies" while "distributors sell marijuana in small bags like the ones found on Cotton." The number of bags is a factor courts often look to in determining the difference between possession and intent to distribute. But is four bags of marijuana a lot? And didn't Wells have her marijuana separated into *seventy* different bags and still escape conviction for intent to distribute?

4. The court mentions a few times that Cotton was arrested in a "high drug area." Does that factor help to determine whether Cotton was selling drugs or was merely in possession of them? Wouldn't more of the people in a high drug area be buyers—who come there to purchase drugs—than sellers?

5. Is it fair to pick apart the facts of *Cotton* one by one as we have done in the notes above? If courts and juries are asked to piece together intent to distribute through multiple factors under a totality of the circumstances does individual assessment of specific facts paint an incomplete picture?

6. Does the comparison between *Cotton* and *Wells* begin to show you the difficulty of relying on a multi-factor assessment to demonstrate intent to distribute? Would it be preferable for states to simply set numerical benchmarks in which drug quantities below a certain amount to simple possession and drug quantities above a certain amount constitute intent to distribute? A few states have designed such regimes. *See* ALEX KREIT, CONTROLLED SUBSTANCES: CRIME, REGULATION, AND POLICY 199–200 (2013).

State v. Wilkins

Court of Appeals of North Carolina, 2010.
703 S.E.2d 807, 208 N.C. App. 729.

■ HUNTER, ROBERT C., JUDGE.

Kendrick Wilkins ("defendant") appeals from a judgment entered after a jury found him guilty of felonious possession of marijuana with intent to sell or deliver ("PWISD"). Defendant argues that the trial court erred in denying his motion to dismiss the charge. After careful review, we vacate defendant's sentence and remand for resentencing upon a conviction of possession of a controlled substance.

Background

The evidence at trial tended to establish the following facts: On 17 January 2008, defendant was driving a brown Ford Crown Victoria along Raleigh Road in Rocky Mount, North Carolina. Defendant was driving to his mother's house after purchasing cigars at a convenience store. Defendant passed by Rocky Mount Police Officer T.J. Bunt ("Officer Bunt"), who recognized the Crown Victoria as the car typically driven by Rico Battle ("Battle"). Officer Bunt knew that there were several outstanding warrants for Battle so he activated his blue lights and pulled over the Crown Victoria. When Officer Bunt approached the car, he noticed that defendant was the only occupant of the car and that he was wearing a hat and sunglasses. Officer Bunt testified that when he knocked on the driver's side window, defendant "kind of turned . . . away" and "refused to open" the window or the car door. Officer Bunt then opened the driver's side door, and, upon being asked his name, defendant identified himself as Kendrick Wilkins. Officer Bunt knew that there were outstanding warrants for defendant, and after confirming the existence of the warrants, Officer Bunt arrested defendant.

Upon searching defendant subsequent to the arrest, Officer Bunt discovered a small plastic bag inside of defendant's pocket, which contained three smaller bags. Each of the three bags were "tied off" at the top and contained a substance Officer Bunt believed to be marijuana. The substance was later weighed and determined to be 1.89 grams of marijuana. Defendant testified that he purchased the marijuana for personal use and that typically marijuana can be bought in "nickel" or "dime" bags for $5.00 to $10.00 each.

During the pat down, Officer Bunt also found $1,264.00 in cash separated into 60 $20.00 bills, one $10.00 bill, nine $5.00 bills, and nine $1.00 bills. At trial, defendant testified that approximately $1,000.00 of the cash recovered was for a cash bond that his mother gave to him and the remaining $264.00 was from a check he had cashed. Defendant testified that he was carrying cash because he was "on the run" and if he were arrested the bail bondsman would not accept a check. Defendant was charged with PWISD.

At trial, the jury was instructed on PWISD and misdemeanor possession of marijuana. The jury found defendant guilty of PWISD. Defendant was determined to be a record level III for sentencing purposes and the trial court sentenced defendant to a suspended sentence of 6 to 8 months imprisonment. Defendant was placed on 36 months of supervised probation. Defendant timely appealed to this Court.

Discussion

Defendant's sole argument on appeal is that the trial court erred in denying his motion to dismiss the PWISD charge. We agree.

* * *

Defendant was charged with PWISD pursuant to N.C. Gen. Stat. § 90–95(a)(1) (2009). "While intent [to sell or deliver] may be shown by direct evidence, it is often proven by circumstantial evidence from which it may be inferred." *State v. Nettles,* 612 S.E.2d 172 (2005). "[T]he intent to sell or [deliver] may be inferred from (1) the packaging, labeling, and storage of the controlled substance, (2) the defendant's activities, (3) the quantity found, and (4) the presence of cash or drug paraphernalia." *Id.* at 176. "Although 'quantity of the controlled substance alone may suffice to support the inference of an intent to transfer, sell, or deliver,' it must be a substantial amount." *Id.*

In the present case, only 1.89 grams of marijuana was found on defendant's person, which alone is insufficient to prove that defendant had the intent to sell or deliver. Accordingly, we must examine the other evidence presented in the light most favorable to the State.

The State points to the fact that the marijuana seized from defendant was separated into three smaller packages. Officer Bunt testified that marijuana is typically sold "in bags in different sizes." Based on his training and experience, Officer Bunt believed that each bag of marijuana found in defendant's pocket would sell for between $5.00 and $10.00 each. "The method of packaging a controlled substance, as well as the amount of the substance, may constitute evidence from which a jury can infer an intent to distribute." *State v. Williams,* 321 S.E.2d 561, 564 (1984). The State has not pointed to a case, nor have we found one, where the division of such a small amount of a controlled substance constituted sufficient evidence to survive a motion to dismiss. Moreover, the 1.89 grams was divided into only three separate bags. While small bags may typically be used to package marijuana, it is just as likely that defendant was a consumer who purchased the drugs in that particular packaging from a dealer. Consequently, we hold that the separation of 1.89 grams of marijuana into three small packages, worth a total of approximately $30.00, does not raise an inference that defendant intended to sell or deliver the marijuana.

In addition to the packaging, we must also consider the fact that defendant was carrying $1,264.00 in cash . . . . Upon viewing the evidence of the packaging and the cash "cumulatively," we hold that the evidence is insufficient to support the felony charge. Had defendant possessed more than 1.89 grams of marijuana, or had there been additional circumstances to consider, we may have reached a different conclusion; however, given the fact that neither the amount of marijuana nor the packaging raises an inference that defendant intended to sell the drugs, the presence of the cash as the only additional factor is insufficient to raise the inference.

. . . Defendant possessed a very small amount of marijuana that was packaged in three small bags and he had $1,264.00 in cash on his person. The evidence in this case, viewed in the light most favorable to the State, indicates that defendant was a drug user, not a drug seller.

. . . Consequently, we vacate defendant's sentence and remand for entry of a judgment "as upon a verdict of guilty of simple possession of marijuana."

Vacated and Remanded.

––––––––

NOTES

1. Have you ever walked around town for an extended time period with more than $1,000 in cash in your pocket? Does the large amount of cash found on Wilkins (and the small amount of drugs) suggest that he had a large quantity of drugs earlier in the day but had sold it? If that inference is logical, is it sufficient to convict him of intent to distribute? Or is the government out of luck because the evidence necessary to prove that crime is now gone?

2. Wilkins claimed that he had a lot of cash because he might need it to pay a bail bondsman. Is this story credible? If you find it outlandish, does it make you more likely to believe that the money was from selling drugs?

3. Courts regularly consider a large amount of cash to be a factor suggesting intent to distribute. *See, e.g.*, Jones v. State, 695 S.E.2d 665 (Ga. Ct. App. 2010) (calling $393 a "large amount of cash"). Is this a legitimate factor to consider? Many drug users in poorer communities do not have high credit scores and access to credit cards and traditional banking. As such, they pay for basic life necessities such as groceries and rent with cash. If people living in neighborhoods where drugs are sold pay for legal goods and services in cash, is walking around with hundreds of dollars incriminating?

––––––––

CHAPTER 9

DRIVING WHILE INTOXICATED AND TEXTING WHILE DRIVING

A. OVERVIEW

Drunk driving is an enormous problem in the United States. Every year, nearly 10,000 people are killed because of alcohol-impaired driving. And, of course, there need not be a fatality or even an injury for police to arrest someone for drunk driving. Each year more than one million drivers are arrested in the United States for driving while intoxicated. Drunk driving statutes vary from state to state, and states even have different names for the offense with some calling it driving while intoxicated, while others term it driving under the influence or operating while intoxicated. In all states though the core elements of the offense are nearly identical. To be guilty, a person typically must be (1) operating; (2) a motor vehicle; (3) on a public road; (4) while intoxicated. Each of those four elements can raise complicated legal questions that we explore in this chapter.

Relatedly, the United States is dealing with a growing problem of distracted driving, particularly texting while driving. Distracted driving crashes involving a cell phone have increased from 47,000 in 2010 to over 71,000 in 2013 and the number continues to climb. Legislatures have taken notice and criminalized texting while driving. Those statutes are not nearly as uniform as drunk driving statutes however. And, as we shall see in this chapter, they are often badly drafted and ineffectual.

B. DRIVING WHILE INTOXICATED

1. WHAT DOES IT MEAN TO OPERATE OR CONTROL A VEHICLE?

Murray v. State

Texas Court of Criminal Appeals, 2015.
457 S.W.3d 446.

■ HERVEY, J., delivered the opinion of the Court . . . .

Chad William Murray, Appellant, was charged with misdemeanor driving while intoxicated and was convicted by a jury. He was sentenced to one-year confinement in the county jail and ordered to pay a $1,000 fine. His sentence of confinement was suspended, and Appellant was placed on community supervision for two years. On appeal, Appellant argued that there was insufficient evidence adduced at trial to prove beyond a reasonable doubt that, for purposes of the DWI statute, he was operating a vehicle. . . .

On January 16, 2011, between approximately 1:00 a.m. and 2:00 a.m., Deputy James McClanahan of the Hill County Sheriff's Office was driving on Highway 22 when he saw Appellant's black truck parked on the side of the road. The vehicle, with its headlights on, was parked partially on an improved shoulder and partially in a driveway near a fireworks stand. The officer believed that the engine was running because, due to the cold weather, he could see exhaust vapors leaving the tailpipe of the truck, but he could not see anyone in the vehicle as he drove past it. And because the fireworks stand near Appellant's truck had been broken into recently, Deputy McClanahan suspected that Appellant may have been attempting to steal fireworks, so he parked and approached Appellant's truck on foot. As he neared the vehicle, he saw Appellant reclined in the driver's seat asleep. He also confirmed that the engine was running, the truck transmission was in the "park" position, and the radio was on with the volume turned up. Because of the volume of the radio, McClanahan had to "beat" on the driver's side window for a few minutes to rouse Appellant. Once awake, Appellant rolled down the window, and Deputy McClanahan immediately smelled alcohol in the truck. He also noted that Appellant appeared very intoxicated, his movements were sluggish, and his speech was impaired. He asked Appellant whether he had been drinking alcohol, and Appellant responded that "he'd had a little." There was no one else in Appellant's vehicle or anyone near the area, and no alcoholic substances or containers were found in the vicinity.

McClanahan, who was not certified to administer standard field sobriety tests, radioed for an officer certified to perform those tests. Trooper Frederick Hart from the Department of Public Safety was dispatched to the scene. Hart testified that Appellant failed all of the standard field sobriety tests. Consequently, Trooper Hart arrested Appellant for DWI.

* * *

The [lower court] concluded that the record showed that "[A]ppellant was simply found asleep in a running truck while parked off the roadway and mainly in a private driveway. And, while one can infer that someone had to have driven the truck there, we have no evidence as to when or whether the person was inebriated at the time." Murray v. State, 440 S.W.3d 927, 929 (Tex. App.—Amarillo 2014, pet. granted). We disagree.

The record shows that Appellant's vehicle engine was running, that he was in the driver's seat, that he was the only person in the vehicle, and he was the only person in the vicinity. It also shows that there were no alcoholic beverages or containers in the area. McClanahan testified that, as soon as Appellant rolled down the driver side window, he could immediately smell alcohol, and he thought Appellant was "very intoxicated" based on his observations. Those observations included that Appellant's actions were sluggish, his speech was impaired, and he could not remove his driver's license from his wallet, although he tried and failed multiple times. McClanahan testified that, when he asked Appellant for identification, Appellant pulled business cards out of his wallet and tried to hand them to him, and when McClanahan told Appellant that those were business cards, Appellant handed him a folded $100 bill from his wallet. McClanahan told Appellant he did not want his money, and ultimately, he had to remove the driver's license from Appellant's wallet.

Based on Appellant's admission that he had been drinking, McClanahan's observation that Appellant appeared "very intoxicated," and the fact that no alcoholic beverages were found in the vicinity, a factfinder could have reasonably inferred that Appellant consumed alcoholic beverages to the point of intoxication somewhere other than where he was found. Furthermore, because Appellant was the only person found in the area, a factfinder could have also reasonably inferred that Appellant drove his vehicle to the location at which he was found after drinking to intoxication.

When the evidence is viewed in the light most favorable to the State, a rational factfinder could have found that Appellant operated his vehicle while intoxicated. Consequently, we hold that the evidence in this case was legally sufficient to sustain the jury's finding that Appellant operated his vehicle. We reverse the judgment of the court of appeals and remand this case for the court of appeals to address any other properly raised claims necessary to the disposition of Appellant's appeal.

■ MEYERS, J., filed a dissenting opinion.

The court of appeals decided that there was insufficient evidence in this case for a reasonable jury to conclude beyond a reasonable doubt that Appellant had operated a motor vehicle while intoxicated. I agree.

The majority states that the jury is responsible for "drawing reasonable inferences from basic facts to ultimate facts" and holds that, because the jury could have reasonably inferred that Appellant both consumed alcohol other than where he was found and drove to the location after drinking to intoxication, that the evidence was legally sufficient to support Appellant's conviction. However, I am unfamiliar with this inferral relationship. Since when can juries make inferences that are not based on direct or circumstantial evidence?

There is no evidence in this case at all that speaks to when the vehicle was driven to the location where it was found, or when or where Appellant became intoxicated. Finding the evidence sufficient to support Appellant's conviction would be no different than convicting an individual for possession of marijuana based solely on an officer's observation that the individual was high and smelled of marijuana. I am aware of no possession case where we have allowed this type of attenuated inference, and we should not allow it now in this driving while intoxicated case. Just as the evidence of possession of marijuana by that individual would be insufficient, so is the evidence that Appellant ever drove while intoxicated.

There are certain instances in which inferences are allowed to be made. For example, if an electronics store was robbed, and then an individual was found with electronics that contain serial numbers matching the stolen merchandise, it is allowable to infer that the individual committed the robbery even where there is no additional evidence he was the perpetrator. There, the inference is used to identify the individual who committed the crime. In this case, however, the inference is being used to assert that a crime was committed at all. I cannot condone this type of analysis which has no basis in law. I can only presume that this new procedure for both creating and finding a defendant guilty of a crime should open up a whole new avenue for convictions that are based solely upon a simple inference that a crime was committed.

Although the majority does not directly address whether simply being passed out behind the wheel of a running car is, itself, enough to constitute "operating" a vehicle for purposes of DWI, I would also hold that it is not enough. Operating a vehicle requires taking action in a manner that would enable the vehicle's use, and although turning the ignition would likely meet this definition, there needs to exist some evidence to support a finding that it was done while the defendant was intoxicated. Without such evidence, no rational jury could find beyond a reasonable doubt that the defendant operated a motor vehicle while intoxicated.

I believe the evidence in this case is insufficient to support appellant's conviction and I would affirm the judgment of the court of appeals. For the foregoing reasons, I respectfully dissent.

————

NOTES

1. Is the majority taking the position that Murray was operating the vehicle when the officer found him, or that he had previously operated the vehicle to arrive at the place where he was parked? Or both? Is the evidence stronger under one theory or another?

2. The dissent states that turning the ignition would likely constitute sufficient action to operate a vehicle, but says that "there needs to exist some evidence to support a finding that it was done while the defendant was intoxicated." Is that correct? If the defendant turned on the car and then sat there drinking to the point of intoxication with the car running, would he not still be operating the vehicle while he was intoxicated?

3. If the defendant was drunk, and if there was no evidence he consumed the alcohol anywhere near the vehicle, should it be permissible to allow a jury to infer that the defendant drank the alcohol elsewhere and drove himself (while intoxicated) to the place where he was parked? Should the prosecution have to prove that the defendant did not walk to the vehicle after becoming intoxicated? Should we put the burden on the defendant to prove that he in fact arrived at the vehicle, either by walking or being dropped off? Or should the jury be allowed to make its common sense determination in the absence of any specific evidence about how the defendant got to where he was found by the police?

People v. Eyen

Illinois Court of Appeals, 2nd District, 1997.
683 N.E.2d 193, 291 Ill. App. 3d 38.

■ JUSTICE THOMAS delivered the opinion of the court:

Defendant, John Eyen, was charged by complaint with the offense of driving while under the influence of alcohol (625 ILCS 5/11—501 (West 1994)).... On appeal, defendant argues that ... the State failed to establish defendant's guilt beyond a reasonable doubt. We reverse and remand.

* * *

On April 8, 1995, at approximately 1 a.m., Officer Douglas Olsen of the Village of Addison police department noticed defendant pushing his car northbound on Sable near the intersection of Itasca and Sable in Addison, Illinois. Defendant was pushing the car from the driver's side with the driver's door open. No other passengers were in defendant's car, and no other people were in the area. When he approached defendant, Officer Olsen observed that defendant had glassy, watery eyes; had trouble standing; was wobbling and swaying; and projected a strong odor of alcohol. On the basis of defendant's condition, Officer Olsen concluded that defendant was intoxicated.

Officer Olsen also observed that defendant's car was missing its front license plate and that the car's front bumper and hood were damaged. Officer Olsen asked defendant whether defendant had been driving the vehicle, and defendant responded, "No, I don't drive drunk." Defendant added that someone else had been driving the car, but defendant was unable to provide Officer Olsen with this other person's name. After observing a large amount of oil leaking from defendant's car, Officer Olsen looked under the car and found extensive damage to the car's undercarriage. Officer Olsen asked defendant whether defendant's engine had locked up, and defendant responded, "No, I shut it off."

After placing defendant under arrest, Officer Olsen searched defendant and found a set of car keys in the front right pocket of defendant's pants. Officer Olsen testified that the keys fit in the ignition of defendant's car and turned the engine over. In addition, Officer Olsen testified that defendant's car has an automatic transmission and could be pushed only if the gear shift was in neutral. After attempting to operate the gear shift on defendant's car, Officer Olsen determined that defendant's car could not be placed in neutral unless the key was in the ignition and that the key could not be removed from the ignition if the car was still in neutral. On cross-examination, Officer Olsen testified that he never saw defendant actually driving the car.

Officer James Kaplan of the Village of Addison police department responded to the scene shortly after Officer Olsen's arrival. Officer Kaplan testified that defendant was swaying back and forth, had glassy and bloodshot eyes, was slurring his speech, and there was a strong odor of alcohol on his breath. Officer Kaplan spoke briefly with defendant at the scene, and defendant again insisted that someone else had been driving the car. This time, defendant identified this other driver as Steve Smith. Defendant was unable, however, to provide Officer Kaplan with an address or phone number for Mr. Smith. On cross-examination, Officer Kaplan testified that he never saw defendant actually driving the car.

Defendant neither testified at trial nor called any witnesses on his behalf.

Defendant argues that his conviction of driving while under the influence of alcohol is not supported by the evidence. In particular, defendant argues that the State failed to prove beyond a reasonable doubt that defendant was driving his car. Defendant does not challenge the trial court's finding that defendant was intoxicated.

* * *

. . . Section 11—501 of the Illinois Vehicle Code provides in pertinent part that a person shall not drive or be in actual physical control of any vehicle while the alcohol concentration of his or her blood is 0.10 or more or while the person is under the influence of alcohol. Whether the defendant was in actual physical control of the vehicle is a question of fact.

The Illinois Supreme Court has held recently that a person need not drive in order to be in actual physical control of a vehicle. City of Naperville v. Watson, 175 Ill.2d 399, 402, 222 Ill.Dec. 421, 677 N.E.2d 955 (1997). Likewise, the person's intent to put the vehicle in motion is irrelevant to the determination of actual physical control. Instead, actual physical control is to be determined on a case-by-case basis giving consideration to factors such as whether the motorist is positioned in the vehicle's driver's seat, has possession of the ignition key, and has the physical capability of starting the engine and moving the vehicle.

Although it is one factor to be considered, the presence of the motorist in the driver's seat is not an essential ingredient to a finding of actual physical control. People v. Davis, 205 Ill.App.3d 431, 436, 150 Ill.Dec. 349, 562 N.E.2d 1152 (1990). In Davis, the court held that the evidence supported a finding of actual physical control where the police discovered the defendant asleep inside a zipped sleeping bag in the backseat of the car. In reaching that conclusion, the court in Davis explained that the defendant's location in the backseat in no way makes him harmless because he could in an instant get back into the driver's seat.

In the present case, Officer Olsen testified that defendant was pushing his car by hand along the roadway, that defendant could not push the car unless it was in neutral, and that defendant's car could not be in neutral unless the keys were in the ignition. In addition, Officer Olsen testified that he found the ignition key to defendant's car in the front pocket of defendant's pants. Most importantly, defendant admitted that he had shut off the car's engine. The trial court would not be irrational in concluding, based on these premises, that defendant was in possession of the ignition key, that the key was in the ignition when defendant was pushing his car along the road, and that defendant was physically capable of starting the engine and moving the vehicle. Thus, under Watson, the trial court would not be irrational in concluding that defendant was in actual physical control of his vehicle.

The fact that defendant in the present case was not in the driver's seat is of no consequence. The evidence shows that, like the defendant in Davis, defendant in the present case had physical control of the car, had the keys in the ignition when he was pushing the car down the road, and could in an instant move into the driver's seat. Accordingly, like the defendant in Davis, defendant in the present case was not rendered harmless by virtue of his absence from the driver's seat. Indeed, the trip to the front seat in the present case is a much easier trip than in Davis. In Davis, to enter the driver's seat, the defendant was required to (1) wake up, (2) negotiate the zipper from inside a sealed sleeping bag, and (3) move from the backseat to the front seat by straddling the console between the two front bucket seats. Here, defendant need only sit down.

Finally, we must emphasize that actual physical control is a concept distinct from driving. The Appellate Court, First District, has noted that, if a person is shown to be operating a vehicle, that person is also, by virtue of operating the vehicle, exerting actual physical control over the vehicle. People v. Niemiro, 256 Ill.App.3d 904, 909, 194 Ill.Dec. 715, 628 N.E.2d 212 (1993). The opposite, however, is not always true. A person who is shown to be exerting actual physical control over a vehicle need not be shown to have been operating the vehicle, but only that he or she had the capability or potential to do so. Given this dichotomy, it is difficult to imagine a person possessing greater physical control than defendant who moved his vehicle along the road by hand with the driver's door open and the keys in the ignition. Anything more and defendant would have graduated from actual physical control to actual driving.

Based on the foregoing and reviewing the evidence in the light most favorable to the prosecution, we conclude that the evidence supports a finding that defendant was in actual physical control and thus that defendant was driving while under the influence of alcohol . . . .

* * *

Reversed and remanded.

————

NOTES

1. Notice how broad the Illinois statute is. A defendant need not be driving the vehicle to be guilty. She only has to be in "actual physical control" of the vehicle. The Illinois statute is much broader than some other states' drunk driving statutes. Are there good policy reasons for criminalizing "actual physical control" of a vehicle, even if the intoxicated person is not driving?

2. Where is the stopping point for liability under the Illinois statute? Were you shocked that someone asleep in the backseat inside a sleeping bag could be convicted? Would Illinois allow the conviction of a drunk person who is standing within a few feet of her vehicle, but had at no point unlocked the car?

3. While most state statutes do not go nearly as far as Illinois, it turns out that the common term drunk *driving* is a misnomer. Most states criminalize "operating" a vehicle while intoxicated. And "operating" is a broader term than "driving." *See, e.g.*, Hiegel v. State, 538 N.E.2d 265, 267 (Ind. Ct. App. 1989) ("In those jurisdictions where the word 'drive' is used, it has been interpreted as requiring the vehicle to be in motion, not merely standing still with the engine running. 'Operate,' on the other hand, has been defined more broadly to include merely controlling the vehicle.").

4. Courts differ on what constitutes "operating." Some courts have held that starting the engine of a vehicle is not sufficient to establish operation. *See, e.g.*, State v. Rossi, 734 So.2d 102 (La. Ct. App. 1999); Hiegel v. State, 538 N.E.2d 265 (Ind. Ct. App. 1989). In other states, turning on the ignition is sufficient to demonstrate operation. *See, e.g.*, Sarafin v. Commonwealth, 764 S.E.2d 71, 74 (Va. 2014) (finding defendant to be an operator when seated behind the steering wheel with keys in the ignition); Stewart v. State, 373 S.W.3d 387, 391 (Ark. 2010) (same).

2.   WHAT IS A VEHICLE?

Everton v. District of Columbia

District of Columbia Court of Appeals, 2010.
993 A.2d 595.

■ RUIZ, ASSOCIATE JUDGE:

Baker N. Everton appeals his conviction for operating a vehicle under the influence of alcohol (commonly referred to as "DUI"), in violation of D.C.Code § 50–2201.05 (2001), which appellant claims does not apply to his riding a bicycle while concededly intoxicated. Although the applicable provision of the Traffic Act that incorporates the DUI statute has been in place since the 1920s, this appeal presents an issue of first impression. We conclude that the DUI statute applies to bicycles and affirm the trial court's judgment.

I.   Statement of Facts

On January 12, 2007, at approximately 7:45 p.m., appellant Everton was "yelling and screaming" on the sidewalk at the intersection of Georgia Avenue and Otis Place, N.W., in Washington D.C. Officers Matthew Mahl and Brandon Stagon, members of the Metropolitan Police Department, were on patrol in that area when they heard a loud "commotion" and turned to see appellant standing next to his bicycle.

After approaching appellant, Officer Mahl noticed that appellant had a very strong odor of alcohol on his breath, his eyes were bloodshot and watery, and he was unsteady on his feet, as he "wobbled" and "sway[ed]." In short, Mahl believed that appellant was very intoxicated. Similarly, Officer Stagon observed that appellant's speech was slurred and very loud and that appellant could "hardly stand." The officers asked appellant to quiet down and move on, and told him not to ride his bicycle because he was so intoxicated. Appellant, however, proceeded to ride his bicycle. Officer Mahl repeated his warning not to ride the bicycle, but appellant rode away. As he crossed Otis Place, appellant almost hit a small child who was in the crosswalk. Appellant then lost control of the bicycle and fell on the ground. Officers Mahl and Stagon arrested appellant for violating D.C.Code § 50–2201.05.

Officer Mahl did not administer any of the standard field sobriety tests on the scene out of safety concerns given appellant's level of intoxication and the fear that he could harm himself. Once in the police station, however, Mahl performed the horizontal gaze and nystagmus test and found six clues of impairment evidencing a high level of intoxication.

II.   Is a bicycle a "vehicle" under the DUI statute?

On appeal, Everton claims that D.C.Code § 50–2201.05, part of the Traffic Act of 1925, which criminalizes operating a "vehicle" under the influence of alcohol, does not apply to him because although he was concededly intoxicated, the bicycle he was riding was not a "vehicle" as defined by the statute. We conclude otherwise.

Whether a bicycle is considered a "vehicle" under D.C.Code § 50–2201.05 is a question of statutory interpretation, which we review de novo. "[T]he words of a statute should be construed according to their ordinary sense and with the meaning commonly attributed to them." Thompson v. District of Columbia, 863 A.2d 814, 817–18 (D.C.2004) (quoting Peoples Drug Stores, Inc. v. District of Columbia, 470 A.2d 751, 753 (D.C.1983) (en banc)). "Courts must presume that a legislature says in a statute what it means and means in a statute what it says there." Connecticut Nat'l Bank v. Germain, 503 U.S. 249, 253–54, 112 S.Ct. 1146, 117 L.Ed.2d 391 (1992).

Here, the plain meaning of the Traffic Act does not support Everton's contention that a bicycle is not a "vehicle" for purposes of the DUI statute. D.C.Code § 50–2201.05, provides, in relevant part, that "[n]o person shall operate or be in physical control of any vehicle in the District . . . [w]hile under the influence of intoxicating liquor or any drug or any combination thereof." D.C.Code §§ 50–2201.05(b)(1)(A)(i), –2201.05(b)(1)(A)(i)(II). The Traffic Act defines "vehicle" as "any appliance moved over a highway on wheels or traction tread, including street cars, draft animals, and beasts of burden." Id. at § 50–2201.02(9). Under the Act's clear and unambiguous language defining "vehicle," a bicycle is a "vehicle," as it is an "appliance" consisting of a metal frame mounted on two "wheels" that can move over a "highway." An interpretation of the Traffic Act's definition of "vehicle" as including bicycles comports with the ordinary dictionary definition that a bicycle is a vehicle.

The history of the Traffic Act also supports this interpretation. Relying on a 1926 amendment to the Traffic Act of 1925, which adopted the definition of "vehicle" that remains unchanged to this day, this court's predecessor rejected the notion that the Act "related entirely to motor vehicle traffic" and explained that the amendment was "designed to remove any possible doubt as to its all-encompassing character." District of Columbia v. Wheeler, 57 App. D.C. 106, 106, 17 F.2d 953, 953 (1927).

It is also apparent that the legislature distinguished between the definition of "vehicle" and the narrower category of "motor vehicle." Compare D.C.Code § 50–2201.02(9) (defining "vehicle") with D.C.Code § 50–2201.02(1) (2001) (defining "motor vehicle" as "[a]ll vehicles propelled by internal-combustion engines, electricity, or steam. The term 'motor vehicle' shall not include traction engines, road rollers, vehicles propelled only upon rails or tracks, personal mobility devices, . . . or a battery-operated wheelchair when operated by a person with a disability.").

Furthermore, a comprehensive interpretation of the term "vehicle" is consistent with the intent of the Traffic Act to regulate traffic for the protection of public safety. See, e.g., Cass v. District of Columbia, 829 A.2d 480, 485 (D.C.2003) (holding that "the suspension of driving privileges for violations of the [Traffic] Act by underage persons who possess or consume alcohol" has as "its primary objective . . . traffic safety"); Persham v. United States, 70 App. D.C. 116, 117, 104 F.2d 249, 250 (1939) (holding that under the Traffic Act the District had the power to regulate traffic on public thoroughfares and prosecute and punish for violations). Operating a bicycle while intoxicated poses a serious threat to the safety of pedestrians and other vehicles as it increases the risk of vehicular accidents. We must look no further than the facts of this case, where appellant almost ran over a child who was walking over a crosswalk and fell off his bicycle in a heavily transited city street.

Appellant maintains, however, that if the term "vehicle" is interpreted to include bicycles, a literal application of the DUI statute prohibiting an intoxicated person from "operat[ing] or be[ing] in physical control of any vehicle in the District," D.C.Code § 50–2201.05(b)(1)(A)(i), would lead to an absurd result. According to appellant, "if an intoxicated individual walks or is holding onto the bicycle, as a pedestrian, then the intoxicated individual is still violating the statute." We do not need to decide that question in this case. Everton was not a pedestrian as he was neither walking next to his bicycle nor holding onto it. Rather, he was riding the bicycle across a public street and thus undoubtedly was "operat[ing]" the bicycle as a vehicle. . . .

Giving effect to the clear statutory language of the Traffic Act, and consistently with its purpose, we conclude that a bicycle is a "vehicle" for purposes of the DUI statute of the District of Columbia. Therefore, the trial court did not err in finding Everton guilty of operating a vehicle under the influence of alcohol, in violation of D.C.Code § 50–2201.05. . . .

————

NOTES

1. Is the court correct that a bicycle is a vehicle? Do you need to know what an "appliance" is to answer that question? Does the code tell us what an appliance is? Does the court tell us?

2. The Cambridge English dictionary defines "appliance" as "a device, machine, or piece of equipment, especially an electrical one that is used in the home, such as a refrigerator or washing machine." Does this help or hurt the case for a bicycle being a vehicle?

3. Some states have avoided the interpretive problem in Everton by specifically defining the word vehicle to include bicycles. *See, e.g.*, State v. Bordeaux, 710 N.W.2d 169 (S.D. 2006).

State v. Dellinger

North Carolina Court of Appeals, 1985.
327 S.E.2d 609, 73 N.C. App. 685.

■ EAGLES, JUDGE.

This appeal presents an issue of first impression: whether a horse is a vehicle for the purpose of charging a violation of [the driving while impaired statute]? We hold that it is.

G.S. 20–138.1 provides in pertinent part:

A person commits the offense of impaired driving if he drives any vehicle upon any highway, any street, or any public vehicular area within this state . . . [w]hile under the influence of any impairing substance; or . . . [a]fter having consumed sufficient alcohol that he has, at any relevant time after the driving, an alcohol concentration of 0.10 or more.

Defendant argues that a horse cannot be a "vehicle" and that even if it is, defendant was not "driving" it within the meaning of G.S. 20–138.1. We disagree.

"Vehicle" is defined in G.S. 20–4.01(49) as "every device in, upon, or by which any person or property is or may be transported or drawn upon a highway, excepting devices moved by human power." "Driver" is defined in G.S. 20–4.01(7) as the "operator of a vehicle" and "operator" is defined in G.S. 20–4.01(25) as a "person who is in actual control of a vehicle which is in motion or which has the engine running."

We recognize that a distinction may have been made between driving and operating in prior case law and statutes regulating vehicles. However, no such distinction is supportable under G.S. 20–138.1 since a "driver" is defined as an "operator." It is clear that the legislature intended the two words to be synonymous. State v. Coker, 312 N.C. 432, 323 S.E.2d 343 (1984).

Defendant's main argument is that a horse is not a "device" and therefore cannot be a "vehicle." While we have found no North Carolina decisions defining a saddle horse as a vehicle for the purpose of a prosecution under the driving while impaired statute, we find decisions from other jurisdictions persuasive on this point. In Conrad v. Dillinger, 176 Kan. 296, 270 P.2d 216 (1954), the Kansas Supreme Court held that a saddle horse is a "vehicle" within their statutory definition which is identical to G.S. 20–4.01(49). The Kansas court noted that its legislature expressly made the definition of the word "vehicle" so broad that it included not only automobiles and animal-drawn vehicles, but every device upon or by which any person may be transported, and that this definition is sufficiently broad to cover ridden animals. In addition to defining a horse as a vehicle for the purposes of the traffic laws of the State of Kansas, the court noted that by adoption of G.S. 1949, 8–506, the legislature made all the provisions of Kansas traffic laws applicable to persons riding animals upon a roadway irrespective of whether such animals come under the definition of a vehicle.

North Carolina has a similar statute, G.S. 20–171, that states:

> Every person riding an animal or driving any animal drawing a vehicle upon a highway shall be subject to the provisions of this Article applicable to the driver of a vehicle, except those provisions which by their nature can have no application.

We are convinced that the North Carolina legislature intended the provisions of the traffic laws of North Carolina applicable to the drivers of "vehicles" to apply to horseback riders irrespective of whether a horse is a vehicle.

We are further convinced that by our legislature's broad definition of vehicles in G.S. 20–4.01(49), it was intended that horses are vehicles within the meaning of G.S. 20–138.1 when operated upon a street, highway or public vehicular area by one who is impaired.

We further hold that a horseback rider is an "operator" who is in "control of a vehicle which is in motion" where the horse is ridden upon a street, highway or public vehicular area. Accordingly, where the evidence shows that defendant was riding a horse on a street while defendant had an alcohol concentration of 0.18, the evidence is sufficient from which a jury could find that defendant drove a vehicle upon a street while under the influence of an impairing substance. G.S. 20–138.1.

> * * *

For the reasons herein stated, we find no error in the trial of this action. . . .

————

NOTES

1. Does it defy common sense to say that a horse is a "device?" Is common sense relevant, or should we just focus on the plain language of the statutes?

2. The court focuses on G.S. 20–171 which specifies that "[e]very person riding an animal . . . upon a highway shall be subject to the provisions of this Article to the driver of a vehicle . . . ." Does the fact that North Carolina applies its traffic laws to people riding animals have any bearing on whether an animal is a vehicle?

3. Courts have divided on the question of whether a horse is a vehicle for purposes of drunk driving statutes. For instance, Utah defines motor vehicle as "every device in, upon, or by which an person or property is or may be transported or drawn upon a highway . . . ." The Utah Supreme Court reversed a conviction for a man riding a horse while intoxicated because "[n]o dictionary we have examined defines "device" to encompass an animal." State v. Blowers, 717 P.2d 1321 (Utah 1986).

State v. Brown

Minnesota Court of Appeals, 2011.
801 N.W.2d 186.

■ STONEBURNER, JUDGE.

Appellant, a physically disabled individual who uses a motorized device as a substitute for walking, appeals his conviction of third-degree driving while impaired (DWI) under Minn.Stat. §§ 169A.20, subd. 1(5), .26, subd. 1(a) (2008 & Supp.2009), arguing that the motorized device he uses as a means of mobility is not a "motor vehicle" and that while operating the device he is not the driver of a motor vehicle for purposes of Minn.Stat. § 169A.20, subd. 1 .... Because we conclude that appellant's operation of his motorized device does not make him a driver of a motor vehicle under Minn.Stat. § 169A.20, subd. 1, we reverse appellant's conviction without reaching the constitutional issues.

FACTS

Appellant James Anthony Brown, Jr. was charged with DWI for operating his mobility scooter on the sidewalks of Grand Rapids on July 29, 2009 with an alcohol concentration of more than .08. . . .

The case was submitted to the district court for trial . . . on the following stipulated facts: (1) Brown is physically disabled and uses a battery-operated three-wheel Legend Pride Mobility Scooter (scooter) as a means of mobility to "experience life and complete his day to day necessities"; (2) the scooter has a maximum speed of 5.75 miles per hour; (3) Brown drove his scooter on Grand Rapids city sidewalks to a car dealership; (4) the car dealership contacted the city police department regarding a possibly intoxicated individual in their automobile display lot; (5) the city police arrived and arrested Brown for DWI; (6) Brown consented to a breath test and tested .17 for alcohol concentration; (7) Brown has a 2001 DWI conviction; (8) a driver's license is not required to operate the scooter, vehicle insurance is not required for the scooter, and the scooter cannot be registered at the Department of Public Safety in order to obtain vehicle license plates; (9) Minn.Stat. § 169.212, subd. 2(c) provides that

[a]n electric personal assistive mobility device may be operated on a roadway only:

(1) while making a direct crossing of a roadway in a marked or unmarked crosswalk;

(2) where no sidewalk is available;

(3) where a sidewalk is so obstructed as to prevent safe use;

(4) when so directed by a traffic control device or by a peace officer; or

(5) temporarily in order to gain access to a motor vehicle[;]

and (10) Grand Rapids does not have an ordinance prohibiting a person from public intoxicated in public or an ordinance prohibiting a person from consuming an alcoholic beverage in public.

Based on the stipulated facts, the district court concluded that the state proved beyond a reasonable doubt that, on the relevant date, Brown drove a motor vehicle, as defined by Minn.Stat. § 169A.03, subd. 15, with an alcohol concentration of .08 or more and within ten years of a qualified prior impaired-driving incident. The district court found Brown guilty of third-degree DWI, a gross misdemeanor. . . . Brown was sentenced, and this appeal followed.

ISSUE

Did the district court err as a matter of law by concluding that Brown drove a motor vehicle in violation of Minn.Stat. § 169A.20, subd. 1(5)?

ANALYSIS

This court reviews de novo questions of statutory interpretation. Molde v. CitiMortgage, Inc., 781 N.W.2d 36, 39 (Minn.App.2010). Words and phrases in Minnesota's statutes are interpreted according to their common meaning. Minn.Stat. § 645.08(1) (2010). "We are to read and construe a statute as a whole and must interpret each section in light of the surrounding sections to avoid conflicting interpretations." Am. Family Ins. Group v. Schroedl, 616 N.W.2d 273, 277 (Minn.2000).

"Where the legislature's intent is clearly discernible from plain and unambiguous language, statutory construction is neither necessary nor permitted and [Minnesota's appellate courts] apply the statute's plain meaning." Hans Hagen Homes, Inc. v. City of Minnetrista, 728 N.W.2d 536, 539 (Minn.2007); see also Minn.Stat. § 645.16 (2010) (directing that, when the language of a statute is "clear and free from all ambiguity, the letter of the law shall not be disregarded under the pretext of pursuing the spirit"). In ascertaining the intention of the legislature, we presume that the legislature does not intend a result that is absurd, impossible of execution, or unreasonable. Minn.Stat. § 645.17(1) (2010).

Minnesota Statutes Chapter 169 sets out traffic regulations and defines "motor vehicle," in relevant part, as "every vehicle which is self-propelled," excluding "an electric personal assistive mobility device." Minn.Stat. § 169.011, subd. 42 (2008). "Driver" is defined as "every person who drives or is in actual physical control of a vehicle." Minn.Stat. § 169.011, subd. 24 (2008). "Vehicle" is defined, in relevant part, as "every device in, upon, or by which any person or property is or may be transported or drawn upon a highway." Minn.Stat. § 169.011, subd. 92 (2008).

Additionally, Minn.Stat. § 169.011, subd. 53 (2008), defines "pedestrian" as "any person afoot or in a wheelchair." And section 169.011, subd. 93 (2008) defines "wheelchair" as including "any manual or motorized wheelchair, scooter, tricycle, or similar device used by a disabled person as a substitute for walking."

It is plain that for purposes of traffic regulations contained in Chapter 169, Brown's scooter is a wheelchair and is not a motor vehicle, and Brown, who uses the scooter as a substitute for walking, is, while operating his scooter, a pedestrian. See Boschee v. Duevel, 530 N.W.2d 834, 839 (Minn.App.1995) ("[T]he mere circumstance, that [a person] . . . propels himself or herself along by means of a chair, or by some other mechanical device, does not clothe him or her, in a broad and general sense, with any other character than that of a pedestrian."

Minnesota Statutes Chapter 169A, criminalizing DWI, defines "motor vehicle," in relevant part, as "every vehicle that is self-propelled," including motorboats in operation and off-road recreational vehicles, but not a vehicle moved solely by human power. Minn.Stat. § 169A.03, subd. 15 (2008).

It is a crime for any person to drive, operate, or be in physical control of any motor vehicle, as defined in section 169A.03, subdivision 15, except for motorboats in operation and off-road recreational vehicles, within this state or on any boundary water of this state . . . when the person's alcohol concentration . . . is 0.08 or more . . .

Reading the sections together in a manner that avoids conflict and an absurd result, we conclude that Brown's operation of his scooter as a substitute for walking does not make him the driver of a motor vehicle within the meaning of Minn.Stat. § 169A.20, subd. 1, and does not subject him to criminal charges for operating the scooter while impaired.

As the parties stipulated, scooters used as a substitute for walking are prohibited from being used on highways except in limited circumstances. See Minn.Stat. § 169.21, subd. 5 (2008) (providing, in relevant part, that "[w]here sidewalks are provided and are accessible and usable it shall be unlawful for any pedestrian to walk or move in a wheelchair along and upon an adjacent roadway"). As discussed above, Brown's scooter meets the definition of a wheelchair contained in Minn.Stat. § 169.011, subd. 93, and Minn.Stat. § 169A.03, which does not define "wheelchair," provides that a term defined in section 169.011, but not defined in section 169A.03, "has the meaning given in section 169.011, unless the context clearly indicates otherwise." Minn.Stat. § 169A.03, subd. 1(b) (2008). Therefore, Brown's scooter is, for purposes of Chapter 169A, a wheelchair and does not meet the definition of "vehicle," because it is generally not a "device in, upon, or by which any person or property is or may be transported . . . upon a highway." Because Brown's scooter is not a "vehicle" under the relevant statutory definitions, it is not a "motor vehicle."

* * *

The district court erred by concluding that on July 29, 2009, Brown drove a motor vehicle while impaired in violation of Minn.Stat. § 169A.20, subd. 1(5), and was thereby guilty of gross-misdemeanor DWI.

Reversed.

———

NOTES

1. One of the court's reasons for not finding the mobility scooter to be a vehicle is that they are prohibited from being used on highways. But courts have found a variety of modes of transportation to be vehicles even though they are not typically allowed on highways. *See, e.g.*, Simmons v. State, 635 S.E.2d 849 (Ga. Ct. App. 2006) (golf carts fall within driving while intoxicated statute); State v. Richardson, 832 P.2d 801 (N.M. Ct. App. 1992) (farm tractor is a vehicle for purposes of driving while intoxicated statute).

2. The court briefly quotes from Minn.Stat. § 169.011, subd. 42, which provides that "[m]otor vehicle does not include an electric personal assistive mobility device . . ." Why does the court not make more of this language, which seems to firmly support the position that Brown's motorized scooter could not be a vehicle? The reason is that that definition of "motor vehicle" comes from the traffic section of the Minnesota Code. The driving while intoxicated section of the Minnesota Code has its own definition of "motor vehicle." Minnesota Statute section 169A.120 subd. 1, provides that "[i]t is a crime for any person to drive, operate, or be in physical control of any motor vehicle, as defined in section 169A.03, subdivision 15, except for motorboats in operation and off-road recreational vehicles, within this state or on any boundary water of this state when: (1) the person is under the influence of alcohol . . ." In turn, section 169A.03 defines "motor vehicle" as "every vehicle that is self-propelled and every vehicle that is propelled by electric power obtained from overhead trolley wires. The term includes motorboats in operation and off-road recreational vehicles, but does not include a vehicle moved solely by human power." In light of that definition, is the decision in *Brown* right or wrong? Should the court have included any reference to § 169.011, subd. 42's definition of "motor vehicle" in its opinion?

3. The doctrine of *expressio unius est exclusion alterius* provides that the expression of one thing is the exclusion of another. In other words, when a statute specifies one exception to a general rule, other exceptions are excluded. *See* BLACK'S LAW DICTIONARY (10th ed. 2014). Consider again the definition of "motor vehicle" in the driving while intoxicated section of the Minnesota Code: "Motor vehicle" means every vehicle that is self-propelled and every vehicle that is propelled by electric power obtained from overhead trolley wires. The term includes motorboats in operation and off-road recreational vehicles, but does not include a vehicle moved solely by human power." Does the specific exclusion of vehicles moved solely by human power inform our decision on whether a mobility scooter is a motor vehicle?

4. Minnesota is not alone in concluding a person using a motorized scooter cannot be guilty of driving while intoxicated. For another recent decision reaching the same conclusion, see State v. Greene, 283 Ore. App. 120 (2016) (finding a "legislative intention not to subject people in motorized wheelchairs to the [DWI] statutes when they are traveling as pedestrians in crosswalks." Do these decisions make sense? How can a bicycle and a horse be vehicles for purposes of driving while intoxicated statutes, but a *motorized* scooter not be a vehicle?

3. DETERMINING INTOXICATION

As most people are aware, states typically criminalize driving with a blood alcohol level of .08. That is not the only basis for conviction however. The definition of Intoxication in the Texas Penal Code is similar to that in other states:

"Intoxicated" means:

(A) not having the normal use of mental or physical faculties by reason of the introduction of alcohol, a controlled substance, a drug, a dangerous drug, a combination of two or more of those substances, or any other substance into the body; or

(B) having an alcohol concentration of 0.08 or more.

Tex. Pen. Code § 49.01(2). The cases below explore other approaches that prosecutors can take to prove intoxication and the difficulties they involve.

State v. Thurman

Court of Appeals of Kansas, 2006.
138 P.3d 798 (Table), 2006 WL 2129225.

■ PER CURIAM.

Edward O. Thurman appeals his conviction of misdemeanor driving while under the influence of alcohol (DUI). We affirm.

On February 24, 2005, Thurman was issued a citation for DUI in violation of K.S.A. 8–1567. A bench trial was held, and Trooper Gregory Smith of the Kansas Highway Patrol testified that he was on duty on February 24, 2005, at approximately 8:30 p.m. when he was dispatched to the Lawrence service area on the Kansas turnpike. The dispatcher indicated there had been a hit and run accident. When Trooper Smith arrived, Thurman waved him down. When Trooper Smith approached Thurman, he noticed a strong smell of alcohol coming from Thurman's breath and that Thurman's eyes were bloodshot. Trooper Smith asked Thurman for his driver's license and noticed that Thurman had difficulty removing the license from his wallet.

Thurman advised Trooper Smith that while he was at the turnpike service area, a truck struck his vehicle and left. Thurman advised the trooper that after the accident, he drove east on the turnpike to find the truck that had struck his vehicle. After driving a few miles, Thurman was unsuccessful in locating the truck so he made a U-turn through the concrete barrier wall on the turnpike and returned to the service area. All the openings in the concrete barrier wall have "no U-turn" signs.

Trooper Smith asked Thurman to perform field sobriety tests, and Thurman agreed. Thurman attempted the horizontal gaze nystagmus (HGN) test and the walk-and-turn test. During the walk-and-turn test, Thurman lost his balance, stopped during the walking process, failed to touch heel-to-toe, raised his arms, and took the incorrect number of steps. Exhibiting two clues on this test is considered a failure. With respect to the one-leg stand test, Thurman exhibited three of the four indicators of impairment.

Based on the test results, Trooper Smith determined that Thurman was driving under the influence. Consequently, Thurman was arrested and transported to the Leavenworth County jail. Trooper Smith gave Thurman the implied consent advisories, and Thurman agreed to give a breath sample. Thurman stipulated that his blood alcohol tests were 0.078 percent and the sample was taken within 2 hours of driving. Trooper Smith admitted he did not observe Thurman driving.

Thurman testified he had been up since 4 a.m. that day working and had a few beers around 1 p.m. He admitted driving from the service area to find the vehicle that struck his vehicle but never found it; he also admitted making a U-turn on the turnpike. Thurman explained that he had difficulty getting his license out due to the design of his wallet and he has permanent discoloration of his eyes due to a prior chemical burn.

After hearing all the evidence, the trial court acknowledged that no one observed Thurman's driving but found that making a U-turn on the turnpike with the speed of the traffic showed impaired judgment. The trial court further found that Thurman's admission that he was driving, plus the results of the breath and field sobriety tests, were sufficient to establish he was driving under the influence.

Thurman was sentenced to 6 months in jail and assessed a fine of $500. The jail sentence was suspended after serving 48 hours in jail. Thurman timely appeals.

On appeal, Thurman contends there is insufficient evidence to support his conviction for DUI. Thurman relies on State v. Arehart, 19 Kan.App.2d 879, 878 P.2d 227 (1994), to support his argument. In Arehart, police pulled Arehart over after seeing him leave a liquor store parking lot. The officer did not see any traffic violations and only saw Arehart make a wide turn in the parking lot. In talking with Arehart, the officer noticed a smell of alcohol on his breath, and Arehart admitted that he had consumed two beers over a period of 2 hours. Arehart failed the field sobriety tests and a breath test. However, because of errors in the administration of the breath test, it was not admitted at trial. The trial court convicted Arehart of DUI.

On appeal, this court concluded that the trial court misinterpreted K.S.A. 8–1567(a)(3) and imposed a standard different than required by the statute. Based on the trial court's remarks, this court found the trial court had held that driving after consuming one drink was enough to show the driver was impaired and would support a conviction. Because it appeared this improper standard affected the trial court's finding, the conviction was reversed and the case remanded for a new trial. Significantly, however, this court noted:

"At trial, the court referred to the fact that [the officer] smelled alcohol on defendant's breath, that defendant had difficulty walking, and that defendant made a wide turn with his car while exiting the parking lot. If the court had applied the proper standard, this evidence may have been sufficient to convict defendant. However, by implying that consumption of one drink is sufficient to support a conviction, the trial court downplayed the importance of this evidence." 19 Kan.App.2d at 882.

Here, the trial court did not rely solely on Thurman's dangerous actions in making a U-turn on the turnpike; it also relied on the result of the breath test (just below the legal limit), Thurman's admission he had been drinking, and his poor performance on the field sobriety tests.

The Kansas Supreme Court has taken judicial notice of the relevant manuals published by the National Highway Traffic Safety Administration (NHTSA) dealing with the detection of DUI. Likewise, this court has acknowledged in an unpublished opinion that failure to pass field sobriety tests is sufficient to present a strong likelihood of impairment for purposes of establishing probable cause for arrest. See Sprenkel v. Kansas Dept. of Revenue, Case No. 93,722 (2005).

There was sufficient evidence to support the trial court's finding of Thurman's guilt. * * *

Affirmed.

–––––––

NOTES

1. Under Kansas law, a defendant with a blood alcohol level of .08 or greater can be guilty of driving under the influence. Kan. Rev. Stat. 8–1567(a)(2). If Thurman's blood alcohol level was only .078 how can he be guilty? No provision in the statute allows for the test result to be rounded up. Is a breath sample below .08 the functional equivalent of an acquittal?

2. One theory—seemingly not offered by prosecutors in this case—for showing that Thurman's blood alcohol level exceeded .08 would be regression analysis. Police did not administer the breath test immediately after Thurman was driving. Rather, his car was parked and he was waiting for police to arrive on the scene. Police then transported him to the police station and tested him there. The court does not specify exactly how long this series of events took, but it suggests about two hours passed between Thurman driving and the breathalyzer test. Blood alcohol content dissipates in the blood stream over time. So, if Thurman's blood alcohol level was .078 at the police station, it was almost certainly higher an hour or two earlier when Thurman was driving. Expert witnesses can use a defendant's weight and the time lapse to compute what a defendant's blood alcohol content was while he was driving. *See* Wallis v. Carco Carriage Corp., 124 F.3d 218 (10th Cir. 1997) (explaining retrograde extrapolation and its admissibility). If prosecutors had done that here, Thurman's blood alcohol level likely would have exceeded .08.

3. Many people assume that breathalyzer tests are given on the scene of a traffic stop. It is much more common though for the breath test to be administered at the police station, as it was in this case. *See, e.g.*, State v. Shuler, 858 N.E.2d 1254, 1257 (Ohio App. 2006) (explaining that portable breath test results can be unreliable because they "may register an inaccurate percentage of alcohol present in the breath, and may also be inaccurate as to the presence or absence of any alcohol at all").

4. The Kansas statute allows a conviction for driving under the influence when a person is "under the influence of alcohol to a degree that renders the person incapable of safely driving a vehicle." Kan. Rev. Stat. 8–1567(a)(3). In conducting their analysis, the trial and appellate courts "relied on the result of the breath test." Was that proper? Should the court have looked only to behavioral factors in determining whether Thurman was incapable of safely driving a vehicle?

Paradoski v. State

Texas Court of Appeals, 14th District, 2015.
477 S.W.3d 342.

■ KEM THOMPSON FROST, CHIEF JUSTICE.

In this appeal appellant Cathy Paradoski challenges her conviction for driving while intoxicated (DWI). The record contains evidence that appellant ingested two types of prescription medication. Though appellant concedes she was operating a motor vehicle without the normal use of her faculties, she asserts she suffered a transient ischemic attack (TIA) [a stroke], causing her to lose control of her faculties while driving. On appeal, we address the sufficiency of the evidence supporting her conviction as well as claimed errors in the trial court's admission of evidence. We affirm.

I.   Factual and Procedural Background

A witness called 911 after he saw appellant driving erratically. Shortly thereafter, appellant rear-ended another vehicle. Witnesses reported that appellant slurred her speech and was slow to respond to questions. Appellant could not adequately explain where she was or what happened. Appellant concedes that her mental and physical faculties were impaired. Department of Public Safety Corporal Chad Olive took appellant to a hospital. There, appellant consented to a blood draw. An analysis of appellant's blood showed the presence of hydrocodone, carisoprodol, and meprobamate (a metabolite of carisoprodol). Appellant was charged by information with the misdemeanor offense of driving while intoxicated. Appellant pleaded "not guilty." A jury convicted appellant of the offense and the trial court sentenced her to 180 days' confinement and ordered eighteen months of community supervision.

II.   Analysis

* * *

A person commits the offense of driving while intoxicated if a person is intoxicated while operating a motor vehicle in a public place. Tex. Penal Code Ann. 49.04(a) (West, Westlaw through 2013 3d C.S.). As is relevant in this case, a person is "intoxicated" if she does not have the normal use of her mental and physical faculties by reason of the introduction of a controlled substance into the body. Id. at 49.01(2)(A). Penal Code section 49.04, entitled "Driving While Intoxicated," requires the State to prove that a defendant lost her faculties by reason of the introduction of a substance into her body, but it does not require the State to prove what substance caused the loss of the normal use of mental or physical faculties. Gray v. State, 152 S.W.3d 125, 132 (Tex.Crim.App.2004). A conviction for the offense of driving while intoxicated may be supported solely by circumstantial evidence. Kuciemba v. State, 310 S.W.3d 460, 462 (Tex.Crim.App.2010).

The record contains evidence that appellant did not have the normal use of her faculties while operating a motor vehicle in a public place. Appellant asserts that the evidence is insufficient to prove the cause of the loss of faculties was by reason of the introduction of a controlled substance into her body. Appellant asserts there is no evidence she introduced any substance into her body. She claims there is no evidence that any of the prescription drugs found in her blood caused her to lose control of her mental and physical faculties. Appellant presented evidence at trial that her impairment was caused by a transient ischemic attack.

The record contains the following evidence:

- Appellant left her friend's house between 11:30 p.m. and 11:45 p.m. Her friend's husband testified that appellant was "fine" when appellant left. He did not see appellant take any pills.

- Appellant was swerving in and out of lanes, driving her vehicle in an unsafe manner. A witness called 911 to report the erratic driving. Shortly thereafter, appellant crashed into another vehicle.

- Officer Raymond Hastedt responded to the accident and determined appellant was impaired.

- Corporal Olive took over the scene from Officer Hastedt. Corporal Olive determined appellant was intoxicated. He testified to his belief that appellant was intoxicated by a narcotic because he did not see any evidence appellant was intoxicated by alcohol. * * *

- Corporal Olive transported appellant to the hospital. Appellant's medical records contain notations that say "Lortab," and "Multiple pill bottles." Lortab is a generic hydrocodone. The clinical impression in the medical record is "substance abuse."

- Upon appellant's arrival at the hospital, appellant had a shaky gait and was slurring her speech, but she was "alert and oriented."

- The nurse who saw appellant at the hospital testified that she believed appellant was intoxicated by reason of drugs and/or alcohol and that appellant's behavior was consistent with someone taking hydrocodone and carisoprodol. The nurse opined appellant's behavior was particularly consistent with the side-effects of carisoprodol.

- The nurse testified that she did not believe another medical condition was the cause of appellant's intoxication.

- The nurse stated that she had worked with patients who suffered from a stroke and they are not generally alert and oriented.

- The nurse testified that if there is any suspicion of a stroke, an immediate CAT scan is taken. She explained that usually if a patient is suffering from a stroke there is a "neurological deficit." Appellant's behavior was "[n]ot at all" consistent with her having a stroke. No CAT scan was ordered.

- The nurse testified that she comes into contact with patients experiencing TIAs. According to the nurse, while appellant was in the hospital she was oriented and able to answer questions, but still had slurred speech. The nurse opined that an individual suffering from a TIA could not answer "orienting questions." The nurse stated she had never seen a TIA patient with partial symptoms.

- Appellant consented to a blood draw at the hospital. The blood draw showed appellant's blood contained .02 milligrams of hydrocodone per liter of blood, greater than 15 milligrams per liter of blood of carisoprodol, and greater than 40 milligrams per liter of blood of meprobamate, which is a metabolite of carisoprodol.

- Hydrocone is a narcotic painkiller. The side-effects of this drug include slurred speech and slowed motor skills.

- Carisopodol is a muscle relaxant. Carisoprodol's side-effects include slurred speech, drowsiness, dizziness, and depressed motor skills.

- The State's toxicologist testified that an individual with the levels of hydrocodone and carisoprodol present in appellant's system could lose mental and physical faculties. The State's toxicologist could not discern from the lab results alone whether appellant suffered the loss of her mental and physical faculties and therefore the State's toxicologist could not render an opinion on that subject.

- Appellant presented an expert toxicologist who testified that the amount of hydrocodone and carisoprodol in appellant's blood could cause an individual to become impaired. He explained that both of these drugs have "similar side effects," and when the drugs are taken together, those effects "will be additive." According to appellant's expert, when someone starts taking these drugs, "you would expect they would have some significant side-effects that would occur, meaning drowsiness, sleepiness, and perhaps the loss of mental and physical faculties during that time, but as time progresses both of those side effects parallel in their diminishing in the side effects that are producing that effect."

- Appellant's expert toxicologist testified that a person could take both drugs and have the normal use of mental and physical faculties "with chronic therapy."

- Appellant's expert toxicologist characterized the concentrations in appellant's blood as "high therapeutic, consistent with long-term care, but not consistent with an overdose." Appellant's expert testified that although these drugs "were more than the minimum amount to produce an effect, they were not in the toxic range." Appellant's expert toxicologist testified that he assumed the dosage was "okay" because the doctor continued to prescribe the medication and the doctor would not have continued to do so if the medication caused appellant to be impaired.

- Records from a pharmacy showed appellant filled the prescriptions for hydrocodone and carisoprodol inconsistently. The date of the offense was April 10, 2010. The records revealed appellant received thirty 350 mg tablets of carisoprodol on December 23, 2009, thirty 350 mg tablets on December 29, 2009, twelve 350 mg tablets on January 18, 2010, twelve 350 mg tablets on January 22,

2010, twelve 350 mg tablets on March 16, 2010, twelve 350 mg tablets on March 24, 2010, and twelve 350mg tablets on September 15, 2010. With respect to hydrocodone, appellant received fifteen pills on December 23, 2009, five pills on December 28, 2009, and fifteen pills on December 29, 2009. The record reveals that the dosage of hydrocodone increased in January 2010. Appellant received ten pills of the higher dosage January 18, 2010, ten pills of the higher dosage March 16, 2010, five pills of the higher dosage March 23, 2010, and five pills of the higher dosage September 16, 2010.

- After appellant's accident in April 2010, appellant did not fill a prescription for hydrocodone or carisoprodol until September 2010. * * *

- Appellant also presented an expert neurologist who testified that appellant suffered a TIA and the TIA caused her to be impaired.

Appellant argues the evidence is insufficient to prove that she introduced a substance into her body causing her impairment. Appellant notes her friend's husband testified that appellant was fine when she got into her car and he never saw her take any pills. But, the State's toxicologist testified these medications were present in appellant's blood. Appellant also introduced records indicating that she had a prescription for the medications and filled that prescription. Thus, the jury had sufficient evidence to conclude appellant ingested the prescription medications.

Appellant also asserts that there is no evidence proving she lost her faculties by reason of the prescription drugs in her system. The State's toxicologist provided evidence of the levels of prescription medication in appellant's system. The State's toxicologist testified that the amounts of medication in appellant's system could cause one to lose mental and physical faculties. Appellant's expert toxicologist agreed. The record thus contains evidence that appellant had an amount of prescription medications in her blood that could cause one to lose control of her mental and physical faculties.

Though appellant's expert opined that appellant had developed a tolerance to the drugs based on chronic therapy, his conclusion was based on a belief that appellant's doctor would not have continued prescribing the medication if it was causing appellant problems. Appellant's pharmacy records showed that she refilled her prescriptions inconsistently; she did not fill her prescriptions for a number of months after the accident. The jury reasonably could have concluded that appellant's irregularity in filling the prescriptions prevented appellant from developing the tolerance her expert toxicologist discussed.

Regardless of the jury's conclusion regarding appellant's prescription history, the jury had evidence from the State's expert toxicologist and appellant's expert toxicologist that appellant had prescription medication in her system in a quantity that could cause her to lose her mental and physical faculties. The video taken of appellant the night of the incident showed she had lost control of her mental and physical faculties. And, appellant conceded that she had. Additionally, the nurse who evaluated appellant testified that appellant was impaired by reason of drugs and/or alcohol. The record contains sufficient evidence to support the jury's finding that appellant was intoxicated by reason of the prescription medications in her body.

Appellant argues that she suffered from a TIA and that the TIA (not the controlled substances in her system) caused her symptoms. But, the evidence appellant suffered from a TIA does not render the evidence that she was impaired by reason of prescription medications insufficient.

First, the jury was entitled to disbelieve appellant's witnesses and instead to credit the nurse's testimony that appellant was not suffering from a TIA.

* * *

[Additionally], even if the jury believed appellant suffered from a TIA, the jury reasonably could have concluded that appellant was impaired both by a TIA and the levels of prescription medication in her system. Appellant did not present any evidence that the presence of a TIA somehow negated any side-effects from the prescription medications. In fact, appellant's expert neurologist conceded that if one were on the drugs carisoprodol and hydrocone and also had a TIA, the TIA would not eliminate the effect of those drugs. Accordingly, the evidence presented that appellant suffered a TIA did not negate the State's evidence that appellant was impaired by reason of the prescription medications in her system.

The State presented sufficient evidence to prove that appellant was impaired by reason of prescription medications. Thus, the evidence is sufficient to support the jury's verdict.

* * *

The judgment of the trial court is affirmed.

———

NOTES

1. As *Paradoski* demonstrates, it is possible to convict a defendant of driving while intoxicated without any alcohol being involved. Proving intoxication by controlled substances is more complicated however and typically requires expert testimony like that demonstrated in *Paradoski*. In addition to an expert in toxicology, the prosecution relied heavily on the testimony of a nurse. Is a nurse—as opposed to a doctor—qualified to testify whether a person did or did not have a stroke?

2. Unlike many of the criminal offense you have studied this semester, driving while intoxicated is a fairly low-level offense. In Texas, it is a Class B misdemeanor carrying a maximum sentence of six months in jail. *See* Tex. Pen. Code 49.04(b). In most cases a defendant serves little or no actual jail time though. *See* Adam M. Gershowitz, *12 Unnecessary Men: The Case for Eliminating Jury Trials in Drunk Driving Cases*, 2011 U. ILL. L. REV. 961, 968. Yet, defendants often go to great expense to fight the criminal charges. Think what it must have cost the defendant in *Paradoski* to hire an expert witness and pay for the other trial and appellate costs. Does it give you pause that prosecutors and defendants spend such considerable sums of money on low-level crimes when courts are over-crowded and some very serious felonies get little time and attention from the same prosecutors and defense attorneys?

4.   THE PUBLIC ROAD OR ACCESS REQUIREMENT

Commonwealth v. Virgilio
Massachusetts Court of Appeals, 2011.
947 N.E.2d 1112, 79 Mass. App. Ct. 570.

■ FECTEAU, J.

The defendant appeals from her conviction of operating a motor vehicle under the influence of intoxicating liquor. . . . [S]he contends that the judge erroneously denied her motion for a required finding of not guilty on the ground that the place on which she was operating the vehicle was not within the reach of G.L. c. 90, § 24(1)(a)(1), because it is not a way or place to which members of the public have access as invitees or licensees. . . .[W]e reverse her conviction.

The essential facts are not in dispute. The defendant resides in a single-family cottage located on Burden Street in Sutton. Next door to her house is a two-story, two-family dwelling, in which resides the owner of the other car involved in this scenario. Between the two houses is a paved driveway that widens and ends in a parking area. Only the occupants of the two houses park in this area. There are no businesses or public services of any kind located along or around the driveway parking area. The driveway is the width of two cars; the parking area at the end is several times wider.

* * *

Prior to its amendment, G.L. c. 90, § 24(1)(a)(1) applied only to operation of a motor vehicle "upon any way or in any place to which the public has a right of access." Commonwealth v. Smithson, 41 Mass.App.Ct. 545, 552, 672 N.E.2d 16 (1996). "The original version of the statute was 'passed for the protection of travelers upon highways,' and 'was not intended to make criminal the use of a motor vehicle [while intoxicated] in all places within the Commonwealth.'" Ibid. In Commonwealth v. Paccia, 338 Mass. 4, 6, 153 N.E.2d 664 (1958), the Supreme Judicial Court construed that language to encompass only public ways or ways in which the general public held an easement, and not private ways used by the public merely as licensees or business invitees. In so holding the court said that "[i]f the Legislature had wished to include areas like [the road at issue], to which members of the public have access only as business invitees or licensees, within the penal prohibitions of § 24, it would have been appropriate for it to have made a clear and specific provision to this effect." Ibid. In response, the Legislature amended the statute to add: "any place to which members of the public have access as invitees or licensees." See St.1961, c. 347.

In assessing whether a particular private way falls within the statute, "[i]t is the status of the way, not the status of the driver, which the statute defines . . . . i.e., it is sufficient if the physical circumstances of the way are such that members of the public may reasonably conclude that it is open for travel to invitees or licensees." Commonwealth v. Hart, 26 Mass.App.Ct. at 237–238, 525 N.E.2d 1345. Accordingly, an individual may be held in violation of the statute even if his presence on the way is without benefit of a specific license or invitation. . . .

"If the invitation or license is one that extends (or appears, from the character of the way, to extend) to the general public, the way is covered; if instead the license or invitation is privately extended to a limited class, the way is not covered." Stoddard, supra at 182–183, 905 N.E.2d 114. "Moreover, it is the objective appearance of the way that is determinative of its status, rather than the subjective intent of the property owner." Smithson, supra at 549, 672 N.E.2d 16. Some of the typical physical circumstances that may bear on the question whether a way is accessible to the public within the meaning of the statute are the presence of street lights, hydrants, curbing, and paving. We recognize, however, that the absence of these elements is not dispositive, as some public roadways in many rural communities lack lighting, curbing, and hydrants.

Here, the place in question is a private driveway and parking area that only serves two residences, containing three dwelling units in total. It neither contains nor leads to any businesses or public accommodations. There is nothing in the appearance of the driveway or parking area that would give an impression to the general public or members thereof that it is anything other than a private driveway or that public use was invited, notwithstanding that it is neither gated nor posted. In our view, these circumstances foreclose its consideration, as matter of law, as a way or place to which the public has access as invitees or licensees.

Despite the ways and places to which subsequent case law has extended the statute's reach, it has yet to extend it to all places that an operator may have physical access. In no case brought to our attention has mere physical accessibility by one operating a motor vehicle and who is not a trespasser been deemed minimally sufficient, as matter of law, to qualify as a "way or place to which members of the public have access as invitees or licensees." G.L. c. 90, § 24(1)(a)(1). Here, in our view, the facts beyond its physical accessibility by nontrespassers, namely, that the driveway and parking area were shared by and accessible to the occupants and guests of two residential buildings, are not sufficient to bring these places under the statute's reach. To decide otherwise would be to essentially overrule the requirement that, in cases such as this, members of the public must be able to reasonably conclude, from the physical circumstances of the way, that it is open for travel to invitees or licensees. Doing so would read the word "public" out of the statute or treat as superfluous this word of limitation included by the Legislature, or add words to a statute beyond those the Legislature has chosen to include. . . . The defendant's motion for a required finding of not guilty should have been allowed.

For the foregoing reasons, the judgment is reversed, the verdict is set aside, and judgment shall enter for the defendant.

So ordered.

■ SIKORA, J. (dissenting).

. . . In my view, this case harbors a significant issue of first impression: whether the common area entryways and parking zones of multiple-unit residential buildings constitute "any place to which members of the public have access as invitees or licensees" within the meaning of the Commonwealth's primary statute prohibiting driving impaired by alcohol. G.L. c. 90, § 24(1)(a)(1). None of the cited precedents has addressed that categorical question. It lies open for analysis. The language of the statute permits its application to such places; and its public safety purpose powerfully commends the coverage of those places by the act. The contrary interpretation artificially partitions the field of danger created by the impaired driver.

Some elaboration of the facts is useful. In addition to testimony, the undisputed evidence at trial included two photographic exhibits depicting the scene of the collision. They show two residential buildings set back from a main road. The defendant's single-unit cottage is situated to the left; a two-story, two-unit building is located at the right. The two structures face inward toward each other with their sides toward the main road.

The main road has no sidewalks. A paved wide-mouthed entryway (accommodating two to three car widths) leads directly from the main road, expands to form an apron of about six car widths between the structures, and then enlarges further toward the rear and diagonally behind the buildings. The breadth of the rear apron between and behind the dwellings would accommodate six to eight parked vehicles. No barriers or signs appear at the mouth of the entryway or at any point in the apron. No markings designate or separate any portion of the entire paved area. Four mailboxes stand on the main road to the left of the entryway. Practicably, any visitor by motor vehicle to any of the residential units would drive through the entryway and park at the rear of the apron.

At trial it was undisputed that all the tenants within the two buildings had access to the driveway and parking area and that none of them could restrict access to those places. It was undisputed also that the defendant had driven her automobile into the side of the parked car of a resident of the two-unit building. . . .

Our case turns on the meaning of the statutory clause, "Whoever, upon any way or in any place to which the public has a right of access, or upon any way or in any place to which members of the public have access as invitees or licensees, operates a motor vehicle while under the influence of intoxicating liquor . . . shall be punished." G.L. c. 90, § 24(1)(a)(1), as appearing in St.1994, c. 25, § 3. For the following reasons I conclude that the intoxicated defendant collided with her neighbor's car "in [a] place to which members of the public have access as invitees or licensees." Three methods of construction lead me to that conclusion, all of them approved as traditional guidance: the language of the provision; the cause or occasion for its enactment; and the discoverable legislative intent or purpose.

1.   Literal analysis. We are dealing with a "place" and not a "way" because the common area apron does not constitute an artery of traffic. The clause refers to two places: "any place to which the public has a right of access" and "any place to which members of the public have access as invitees or licensees." We give effect to each substantive term and typically treat none as superfluous. Consequently we have two different categories of "place." The word "any" modifies each and indicates comprehensive categories. The first designates broadly locations to which the public at large has a right of access. The second designates more specifically locations to which "members" within the public have access not by right but by invitation or permission. The word "members" denotes a class smaller than the general public. . . .

Upon those terms, an individual member of the public specifically invited or permitted to drive onto the apron by the owner or by a tenant of the residential buildings here falls within the operation of the clause. Nothing in the language of the clause indicates that a specific invitee or licensee, as distinguished from a random invitee or licensee, no longer qualifies as a "member[ ] of the public."

2.   The cause and occasion of enactment. In Commonwealth v. Paccia, 338 Mass. 4, 6, 153 N.E.2d 664 (1958), the court concluded that a privately owned paved area surrounding a restaurant and a market building and connecting two public ways, and admittedly the location of the defendant's impaired driving, did not qualify under the existing

language of the statute as "a place to which the public has a right of access." The reasoning was

> "that the Legislature has not included within the scope of § 24 privately owned places, not shown to be subject to any general public easement of right. Criminal laws are to be strictly construed and are not to be extended merely by implication. . . . If the Legislature had wished to include areas like [the place at issue], to which members of the public have access only as business invitees or licensees, within the penal prohibitions of § 24, it would have been appropriate for it to have made a clear and specific provision to this effect."

Three years later the Legislature answered by addition of the current second phrase, "or upon any way or in any place to which members of the public have access as invitees or licensees." St.1961, c. 347.4 Significantly the Legislature did not use the limiting phrase suggested by the court, "business invitees or licensees" (emphasis supplied). Instead it employed the unmodified phrase, "invitees or licensees." At Massachusetts common law that phrase encompasses both business and social visitors. . . . The amended statute includes places of both commercial and residential character. . . .

3   Legislative purpose.

* * *

a.   Danger or mischief to be remedied. For decades Massachusetts decisions in various settings have emphasized the lethal risk of impaired driving. . . .

Recidivism multiplies the peril of impaired driving. The addictive nature of alcoholism and the habitual character of abusive social drinking have received legislative recognition in a scheme of progressive sanctions. . . .

The legislative response, developed over decades (often after episodic tragedies) and codified in G.L. c. 90, § 24(1) through (4), and adjoining provisions, has accumulated an array of measures aimed at the criminal law's objectives of deterrence, incapacitation, and reformation of the perpetrator.

b.   Deterrence. "The purpose of G.L. c. 90, § 24, is to . . . 'deter individuals who have been drinking intoxicating liquor from getting into their vehicles, except as passengers.'" Commonwealth v. McGillivary, 78 Mass.App.Ct. 644, 647, 940 N.E.2d 506 (2011).

The words of § 24(1)(a)(1) establish three components of the offense of operating under the influence (OUI): operation of a motor vehicle; impairment by intoxicating liquor; and location accessible to members of the public. The case law has defined operation inclusively. . . . Operation can occur even if the vehicle is motionless or the engine turned off. It is enough for the impaired defendant to have inserted the ignition key and turned it to the "on" position even without activation of the engine. Commonwealth v. McGillivary, 78 Mass.App.Ct. at 646, 940 N.E.2d 506.

The expansive meaning given to the concept of operation reflects the legislative purpose. "Given the well-established relationship between intoxicating liquor and motor vehicle injuries and fatalities [citations omitted], it does no violence to G.L. c. 90, § 24, to conclude that the real purpose of such statutes" is deterrence of the very entry onto the driver's seat of the impaired operator.

c. Lenity. While the purpose of deterrence has characterized the interpretation of the element of operation of the vehicle, a rule of lenity has accompanied the interpretation of the location of its operation. The ambivalent development of the case law has resulted in a seemingly incongruous treatment of the act's purpose of public safety: a stringent definition of operation but a lenient definition of the location of the impaired operation. . . .

. . . [A] rule of lenity should have limited application to the definition of a "place" within the meaning of § 24(1)(a)(1) and to similar provisions employing the same words to proscribe operating under the influence. . . . [T]he rule of lenity operates against ambiguous statutory language depriving an accused of fair warning of punishable conduct. A modern automobile driver does not need more specific notice than the words of the current statutes. Getting behind the wheel in a state of impairment has the character of conduct malum in se. Certainly one could not reason that the defendant in this case would have driven more responsibly if only the statute had provided her a more precise definition of a publicly accessible place.

* * *

The rule of lenity "is a guide for resolving ambiguity, rather than a rigid requirement that we interpret each statute in the manner most favorable to defendants." Simon v. Solomon, 385 Mass. 91, 102–103, 431 N.E.2d 556 (1982) (Hennessy, C.J.). . . .

* * *

Conclusion. The accessible common area at issue here falls within the letter and purpose of the law against driving under the influence of intoxicating liquor. . . . I would affirm the judgment of guilt and the resulting sentence.

State v. Schwein

Supreme Court of Montana, 2000.
16 P.3d 373, 303 Mont. 450.

■ JUSTICE W. WILLIAM LEAPHART delivered the Opinion of the Court.

Michael Schwein (Schwein) appeals from a jury verdict in the Thirteenth Judicial District Court, Yellowstone County, finding him guilty of driving under the influence of alcohol. We affirm the judgment of the District Court.

The following issue [is] raised on appeal:

Did the District Court err in denying Schwein's motion to dismiss the DUI charge on the grounds that the State failed to prove that Schwein's vehicle was upon a way open to the public?

* * *

Factual Background

The facts in this case are not subject to dispute. Around 11 p.m. on March 13, 1999, Yellowstone County Deputy Sheriff Troy Kane (Kane) was driving down State Avenue in Billings when he noticed a black 1995 Chevrolet Corvette parked in the parking lot between the Moose Breath Saloon and Magic City Welding. Kane noticed that, although the car appeared to be unoccupied, its headlights were on. Kane stopped to investigate and found Schwein asleep in the driver's seat, sitting upright with his head tilted toward his chest. Although Schwein had given his keys to the bar owner earlier in the evening, he testified at trial that he had retrieved an extra set from the underside of his car. Kane arrived to find the headlights and dashlights on and the keys in the ignition.

Kane knocked on the car window and Schwein woke up, startled, grabbed for the ignition keys and attempted, but was unable, to start the car. Kane told Schwein to take the keys out of the ignition and hand them to him, which Schwein did. Kane asked Schwein for his license and registration and, in doing so Kane detected the odor of alcohol on Schwein's breath. When asked by Kane, Schwein got out of the car. He refused, however, to perform the field sobriety maneuvers requested and refused to take the preliminary breath test. Kane then arrested Schwein for driving under the influence of alcohol. When Schwein agreed to take the breath test at the Yellowstone County Detention Facility it indicated that his blood alcohol concentration was .229.

Discussion

Did the District Court err in denying Schwein's motion to dismiss the DUI charge on the grounds that the State failed to prove that Schwein's vehicle was upon a way open to the public?

* * *

In order to establish the offense of driving under the influence of alcohol, the State must prove that the defendant, while under the influence of alcohol, drove or was in actual physical control of a vehicle "upon the ways of this state open to the public." Section 61–8–401(1)(a), MCA.

In the present case, Schwein moved for a directed verdict of acquittal arguing that there was no evidence that the parking space in question was a "way of the state open to the public."

Schwein contends that he owns Magic City Welding and that he was parked in front of his own business in a parking space which he leases; that he was asleep and had no intention of driving.

The District Court, relying on our decision in State v. Weis (1997), 285 Mont. 41, 945 P.2d 900, concluded that the parking area between the saloon and the welding shop was a way open to the public and denied Schwein's motion for a directed verdict.

Weis, like Schwein, contended that he was not guilty of DUI because he was operating his vehicle, not on a way of the state open to the public but, rather, in Boulder Lane, which is a privately owned and maintained driveway. We rejected Weis' argument holding that our statutes are not so narrow as to include only those ways or places for travel which are legally dedicated to the public use. Weis, 285 Mont. at 43, 945 P.2d at 902. We noted that "ways of the state open to the public" is defined as including "any highway, road, alley, lane, parking area, or other public or private place adapted and fitted for public travel that is in common use by the public." Weis, 285 Mont. at 43, 945 P.2d at 902 (citing § 61–8–101(1), MCA).

Our decision in City of Billings v. Peete (1986), 224 Mont. 158, 729 P.2d 1268, is particularly relevant to the present dispute. In Peete we held that the parking garage of the Northern Hotel in Billings was a way of the state open to the public notwithstanding that access to the garage could only be obtained via one ramp and only upon obtaining a ticket from the attendant and payment of a fee. The hotel parking garage had a history of public use and the public was encouraged to use the facility. Similarly, the parking lot here in question, though it includes privately leased spaces, is adapted and fitted for public travel and is in common use by the public and customers of adjoining businesses.

The District Court correctly concluded that the Weis decision is controlling and that the parking lot in question falls within the statutory definition of a "way of the state open to the public."

* * *

■ JUSTICE TERRY N. TRIEWEILER, dissenting.

I dissent from the majority opinion. I conclude that there was insufficient evidence to prove that the Defendant, Michael Schwein, operated or was in control of his vehicle "upon the ways of this state open to the public."

On the day of his arrest, Schwein had been drinking at a bar across the lot from his place of business. He left the bar on foot with the intention of spending the night at his shop. However, on his way to his shop, he encountered the owner of the bar who requested his car keys. Schwein gave the owner his car keys, but in the process also gave him the key to his shop. Therefore, he returned to his car where he went to sleep. That is where he was found and arrested.

At the time of his arrest, Schwein's vehicle was parked in a space that he personally leased in front of his shop. During business hours, it is open to customers and no one else. After 5:00 p.m., it is not open to the public. In fact, cars have been towed from that location at Schwein's request.

At the time of his arrest the engine to Schwein's motor vehicle was not running. He had not operated the vehicle after drinking at the bar and he had no intention of doing so.

At the time of his arrest, the parking place in which Schwein's car was located was clearly not "open to the public."

* * *

In all of the cases relied on by the majority, the defendant was actually operating his vehicle at the time of his arrest. Furthermore, the defendant in each of the prior three cases was in an area that actually was "open to the public." Finally, in none of the three prior cases was the defendant on his own private property.

The purpose of our laws prohibiting operating a motor vehicle under the influence of alcohol or drugs is to preserve public safety. The result in this case accomplishes just the opposite. Had Schwein gotten into his vehicle and driven home, there is a chance that he would have arrived without detection. However, it would not have been safe for him to do so.

Schwein did the safest thing apparent to him in his intoxicated condition and he was a threat to no one. In spite of that fact, the majority opinion now extends the reach of the law beyond what was ever intended. I hope that our streets and highways are not a little more dangerous as a result.

For these reasons I dissent from the majority opinion. I conclude that there was insufficient evidence to convict Michael Schwein of operating or being in control of his vehicle while on a public way and under the influence of alcohol.

NOTES

1. As you can tell from *Virgilio* and *Schwein*, different states have different requirements for where a person must be located to be convicted of driving while intoxicated. Massachusetts limits liability to places where "members of the public have access as invitees or licensees." Montana specifies that a driver must be "upon the ways of this state open to the public." Accordingly, we cannot simply say that a parking lot counts for DWI statutes, while a semi-private driveway does not. It is essential to parse each state's statute.

2. Some states do not have a public road or access requirement. For instance, in Georgia, it is unlawful for any person to "drive or be in actual physical control of any moving vehicle" with a blood alcohol level of .08 or more. *See*

Ga. Code Ann. 40–6–391(a)(5). The "statute draws no distinction between driving on public roads versus private thoroughfares." Madden v. State, 555 S.E.2d 832, 834 (Ga. Ct. App. 2001).

3. In *Schwein*, wasn't the defendant on private property after the shopping area had closed? Can that land be a way open to the public if the public was not allowed to be there? Should the case turn on whether drivers would be trespassing at that hour of the evening?

4. Assume that Judge Trieweiler is correct in his dissent that it was safer for Schwein to sleep it off in the parking lot than to try to drive home. Also assume, as Judge Trieweiler insinuates in his dissent, that the court's ruling will in fact make Montana's "streets and highways . . . a little more dangerous as a result." Should the majority have factored those realities into its decision? Should public policy or public safety have any impact on the court's decision?

5. Imagine that the President of the United States became intoxicated one evening, got into the presidential limousine in the front driveway of the White House and drove around inside of the White House gates and parking area. Would the President be guilty of driving while intoxicated under the Massachusetts statute (which includes areas where "members of the public have access as invitees or licensees?" How about the Montana statute which focuses on "the ways of this state open to the public?"

C. TEXTING WHILE DRIVING

Over the last decade, most states have criminalized texting while driving and related types of distracted driving. As with drunk driving, states have not adopted a uniform model statute to ban texting. The scope, language, and levels of fines vary widely by state. A large number of states ban texting while driving but allow hands-free cell phone use. For instance, South Dakota enacted a texting while driving statute in 2014 that provides:

> No person may operate a motor vehicle on a highway while using a handheld electronic wireless communication device to write, send, or read a text-based communication. This section does not apply to a person who is using a handheld electronic wireless communication device:
>
> (1) While the vehicle is lawfully parked;
>
> (2) To contact any emergency public safety answering point or dispatch center;
>
> (3) To write, read, select, or enter a telephone number or name in an electronic wireless communications device for the purpose of making or receiving a telephone call; or
>
> (4) When using voice operated or hands free technology.
>
> . . . . A violation of this section is a petty offense with a fine of one hundred dollars.

S.D. Codified Laws 32–26–47.

Other states have not banned hand-held cell phone use, but have tried to forbid certain specific manual uses of the phone. For instance, Nebraska's statute provides that

> [N]o person shall use a handheld wireless communication device to read a written communication, manually type a written communication, or send a written communication while operating a motor vehicle which is in motion.

> Any person who is found guilty of a traffic infraction under this section . . . shall be fined . . . Two hundred dollars for the first offense.

Neb. Rev. St. § 60–6, 179.01.

Your first reaction to the Nebraska and South Dakota statues might be that the punishments—$100 in South Dakota and $200 in Nebraska—are too low to deter people. As the cases below indicate, there are other more significant problems.

1. PROVING THE USE OF A PROHIBITED FUNCTION ON THE PHONE

United States v. Paniagua-Garcia

United States Court of Appeals for the Seventh Circuit, 2016.
813 F.3d 1013.

■ POSNER, CIRCUIT JUDGE.

An Indiana statute forbids drivers to use a telecommunications device (normally a cellphone) to type, transmit, or read a text message or an electronic-mail message, Ind.Code § 9–21–8–59(a)—in short it prohibits "texting" (sending or receiving textual material on a cellphone or other handheld electronic device; also called "text messaging" or "wireless messaging") or emailing while operating a motor vehicle. All other uses of cellphones by drivers are allowed: making and receiving phone calls, inputting addresses, reading driving directions and maps with GPS applications, reading news and weather programs, retrieving and playing music or audio books, surfing the Internet, playing video games—even watching movies or television. Most of these activities seem dangerous—though no more so, and maybe less so, than texting—and because a driver is more likely to engage in one or more of them than in texting, the most plausible inference from seeing a driver fiddling with his cellphone is that he is not texting.

An Indiana police officer, in the course of passing a car driven by Gregorio Paniagua-Garcia (whom for the sake of brevity we'll call just Paniagua) on an interstate highway, saw that the driver was holding a cellphone in his right hand, that his head was bent toward the phone, and that he "appeared to be texting." Paniagua denies that he was texting, the officer has never explained what created the appearance of texting as distinct from any one of the multiple other—lawful—uses of a cellphone by a driver, and the government now concedes that Paniagua was not texting—that as he told the officer he was just searching for music. An examination of his cellphone revealed that it hadn't been used to send a text message at the time the officer saw him fussing with the cellphone.

Almost all the lawful uses we've listed would create the same appearance—cellphone held in hand, head of driver bending toward it because the text on a cellphone's screen is very small and therefore difficult to read from a distance, a finger or fingers touching an app on the cellphone's screen. No fact perceptible to a police officer glancing into a moving car and observing the driver using a cellphone would enable the officer to determine whether it was a permitted or a forbidden use.

The officer pulled over Paniagua, questioned him at length, eventually asked and received Paniagua's permission to search the car, and discovered in the search five pounds of heroin concealed in the spare tire in the car's trunk. Paniagua was prosecuted in federal court for possession of the heroin . . .

* * *

Indiana is right to be worried about the dangers created by persons who fiddle with their cellphones while driving, but probably wrong to outlaw such fiddling only with respect to texting—if only because the effect of slicing up drivers' use of cellphones in this way has been to make the Indiana statute largely inefficacious, such is the difficulty of distinguishing texting from other uses of cellphones by drivers by glancing into the driver's side of a moving automobile. The contrast with Illinois, which has a "hands-free" law, 625 ILCS 5/12–610.2 (a driver is forbidden to use a cellphone with his hands, as distinct from using bluetooth or other technologies that enable the driver to communicate without manipulating his cellphone), is striking. For while in 2013 only 186 citations were issued for violations of the Indiana texting law, more than 6700 citations were issued in Illinois for violations of the Illinois hands-free law. . . .

REVERSED AND REMANDED

———

NOTES

1. Is Judge Posner correct when he suggests that a police officer would not be able to tell whether a driver was texting as opposed to searching for music on his phone: "No fact perceptible to a police officer glancing into a moving car and observing the driver using a cellphone would enable the officer to determine whether it was a permitted or a forbidden use?" As you will see

* * *

Defendant was found guilty of violating section 23123 and ordered to pay a fine and other penalties, totaling $103. . . .

DISCUSSION

Defendant argues in this appeal, as he argued before the traffic commissioner, that section 23123, subdivision (a) does not prohibit hand-held wireless telephone use while a vehicle is stopped on the public roadways, relying on the Mercer court's definition of "driving." The People argue that section 23123 prohibits such use because the statute applies to persons "operating" their vehicles on the public roadways, and that, in the alternative, substantial evidence of such motion was presented at trial in any event. We conclude defendant listened to his hand-held wireless telephone during a fleeting pause at a traffic light "while driving" in Richmond and, therefore, violated section 23123, subdivision (a), as we now explain.

I.   *The Meaning of "Drive" and "While Driving" in Section 23123*

A.   *The Governing Law*

. . . Subdivision (a) of section 23123 states: "A person shall not drive a motor vehicle while using a wireless telephone unless that telephone is specifically designed and configured to allow hands-free listening and talking, and is used in that manner while driving." (§ 23123, subd. (a).)

* * *

The Vehicle Code does not include definitions for the term "drive" or "while driving," nor are we aware of any cases discussing the application of such terms to the present circumstances . . . .

* * *

Defendant's argument that he was not "driving" is based on our Supreme Court's opinion in Mercer, 53 Cal.3d 753, 280 Cal.Rptr. 745, 809 P.2d 404, in which the court determined the meaning of the term "drive" as it is used in section 23152, which prohibits driving under the influence. Section 23152 provides in relevant part, " 'It is unlawful for any person who is under the influence of any alcoholic beverage or drug . . . to drive a vehicle.' " . . . Mercer was found by police asleep and slumped over the wheel of a car legally parked, its engine running. He refused chemical tests after his warrantless arrest for violation of section 23152. The court extensively analyzed the meaning of the term "drive" [and] drew a distinction between "drive" and "operate."

The Mercer court first looked at the language of section 23152. It determined that, "[i]n everyday usage of the phrase, 'to drive a vehicle,' is understood as requiring evidence of volitional movement of a vehicle" based on numerous dictionary definitions for "drive" that required movement.

Second, the Mercer court looked at the use of similar terms in related statutes. It concluded the Legislature intended "drive," as used in section 23152, subdivision (a) to be construed narrowly. . . .

Third, the Mercer court reviewed decades of case law from other states, which held that the word " 'drive,' when used in a drunk driving statute, requires evidence of a defendant's volitional movement of a vehicle." . . . The court found that most states distinguished between "drive" and "operate," and required volitional movement for the former. . . .

* * *

B. *Defendant's Arguments*

Defendant argues the Mercer court's conclusion that the term "drive" requires evidence of volitional movement means the trial court necessarily was in error because defendant was in a vehicle that was stopped at a red traffic light when he used his wireless telephone. He argues further that, if the trial court were correct, section 23123 "would prohibit the use of a cellular telephone to make a call even in situations where the failure to make the call would clearly be contrary to the interests of public safety and defy common sense." It would, he contends, be a violation to use a hand-held wireless telephone "stopped in traffic behind a major accident that was taking hours to clear," to "call to a child requesting him to come through the rain from inside the school to a parent temporarily stopped, with foot on brake, in a passenger loading zone," or while "waiting for a train to pass or delayed for hours due [to] a road spill." Defendant further contends, "[t]here is no conceivable risk of one using the cell phone in the foregoing circumstances while there are sensible reasons for being able to do so consistent with public policy concerns." Defendant argues the trial court's reasoning is particularly "absurd" when a person sitting in the driver's seat at a traffic light "may lawfully put on make-up, eat a messy sandwich, or focus entirely on changing radio stations or music CDs in the car stereo, yet—under the result below—that same person could not lawfully push one pre-programmed speed dial button on a cell phone to check his or her voicemail."

* * *

Finally, defendant argues that, in the event we find section 23123 ambiguous, we must follow the well-settled rule that "where a penal statute is ambiguous and susceptible to two reasonable interpretations, we must adopt the construction that is most favorable to defendant."

C. *The People's Arguments*

The People argue that the repeated use of the term "operate" in the legislative history for section 23123 indicates that the Legislature intended to regulate the "operation" of motor vehicles, not just the "driving" of them. . . . The People conclude, "all sides in the debate understood the focus of the bill to be reducing the public safety threat posed by a driver using a hand-held cell phone while 'operating' a motor vehicle." Furthermore, "the Legislature did not intend, either expressly or impliedly, to require that the vehicle be moving at the time the motorist was using his or her cell phone." The People argue that the circumstances involved in the present case "show that [defendant] posed the type of threat to public safety envisioned by the Legislature in enacting section 23123."

* * *

D.   *Analysis*

* * *

The People properly argue that the use of the term "operating" in section 23123's legislative history is significant; and, in fact, the term is similarly used in section 23123 itself, which is not the case in section 23152. However, the People ask us to disregard altogether the Legislature's use of the terms "drive" and "while driving" in section 23123, subdivision (a), arguing that the Legislature actually intended "operate" and "while operating." We are not persuaded that we should do so. "Identification of the laudable purpose of a statute alone is insufficient to construe the language of the statute. 'To reason from the evils against which the statute is aimed in order to determine the scope of the statute while ignoring the language itself . . . is to elevate substance over necessary form. The language . . . confines and channels its purpose.' " (Cortez v. Purolator Air Filtration Products Co. (2000) 23 Cal.4th 163, 176, fn. 9, 96 Cal.Rptr.2d 518, 999 P.2d 706.)

However, it is unnecessary for us to further address the People's broader argument because it asks us to decide too much. Neither party focuses sufficiently on the precise circumstances before us. We are not reviewing whether all drivers "operating" their motor vehicles on the public roadways are prohibited from using hand-held wireless telephones, nor are we reviewing the various hypothetical circumstances referred to by defendant, such as whether a hand-held wireless phone may be used by a driver stopped behind a major accident that takes hours to clear. We only review the actions of defendant who, according to the traffic court, was cited for a violation of section 23123, subdivision (a) after a police officer observed him in the driver's seat of a car paused briefly at a red traffic light dialing a wireless telephone and placing it to his ear, and then observed him remove the phone from his ear, close it, and drive through the intersection when the traffic light turned green. . . .

* * *

1. *The Words of Section 23123*

* * *

The language of section 23123, subdivision (a) does not answer the question before us either, because of the ambiguity posed by the terms "drive" and "while driving" with regard to a driver's fleeting pauses as he or she drives on public roadways. . . . Our independent research indicates section 23123, subdivision (a) may be understood to include such fleeting stops because it is not uncommon to use terms like "drive" and "while driving" to refer to a person driving a motor vehicle along the public roadways, regardless of whether he or she stops fleetingly for a red traffic light or other impediments to movement that are beyond his or her control.

Such usage can be readily found in our case law, as indicated by our independent research. For example, in discussing the law of unreasonable searches and seizures, our Supreme Court has recognized the legitimacy of traffic stops because, " ' "in light of the pervasive regulation of vehicles capable of traveling on the public highways, individuals generally have a reduced expectation of privacy while driving a vehicle on public thoroughfares." ' " (People v. Letner and Tobin (2010) 50 Cal.4th 99, 146, 112 Cal.Rptr.3d 746, 235 P.3d 62, italics added.) Although the context of these cases is unrelated to the present circumstances, it nonetheless would be absurd to suggest that the court did not intend this principle to apply to vehicles driving on our thoroughfares that are briefly paused for traffic lights. Elsewhere, being "stopped by a traffic signal" has been characterized as "inherent in city driving." (People v. Cowman (1963) 223 Cal.App.2d 109, 116, 35 Cal.Rptr. 528, italics added [conduct of officers in stopping the defendant's vehicle did not violate his right to privacy or constitutional rights].)

* * *

Given section 23123, subdivision (a)'s ambiguity on the issue, we now examine its legislative history as well.

2. *Section 23123 Legislative History*

* * *

Parts of the Senate Bill Analysis . . . suggest the Legislature intended to prohibit hand-held wireless telephone use beyond the narrow parameters argued by defendant. Its introductory digest states: "This bill prohibits, beginning July 1, 2008, a driver from using a wireless phone while operating a vehicle, unless the phone is specifically designed and configured to allow hands-free operation and is used in that manner. . . ."

The Senate Bill Analysis includes other indications that the Legislature was concerned with restricting drivers' use of hand-held wireless telephones on public roadways, and not only for those times when drivers are moving motor vehicles. It summarizes a 2003 California Highway Patrol report required by the Legislature that recommended giving "serious consideration to requiring use of hands-free cell phones in motor vehicles" without limitation. As the People point out, the analysis also summarizes the opposition's argument "that [the law] unfairly penalizes drivers who are using a hand-held cell phone regardless of whether or not those drivers are operating their vehicle in a safe and responsible manner." These arguments do not limit their concerns to the use of a wireless telephone only when a vehicle is in motion.

. . . [T]he interchangeable use of "drive" and "operate" in the legislative history, and other statements in the history indicate the Legislature was generally concerned about the use of hand-held wireless telephones in motor vehicles on our public roadways, and not just about such use when the vehicles are in motion. In short, the legislative history strongly supports the conclusion that the Legislature intended section 23123 to apply to the circumstances before us.

3. *Possible Consequences*

To the extent any ambiguity remains, we "cautiously take the third and final step in the interpretive process. In this phase of the process, we apply 'reason, practicality, and common sense to the language at hand.' Where an uncertainty exists, we must consider the consequences that will flow from a particular interpretation. . . .

Defendant's narrow interpretation of "drive" and "while driving" in section 23123, subdivision (a) would likely result in significant and numerous public safety hazards on public roadways throughout the state. . . . Were we to adopt defendant's interpretation, we would open the door to millions of people across our state repeatedly picking up their phones and devices to place phone calls and check voice mail (or text-based messages) every day while driving whenever they are paused momentarily in traffic, their car in gear and held still only by their foot on the brake, however short the pause in the vehicle's movement. This could include fleeting pauses in stop-and-go traffic, at traffic lights and stop signs, as pedestrians cross, as vehicles ahead navigate around a double-parked vehicle, and many other circumstances.

* * *

Defendant contends it is safe to use a hand-held device in circumstances such as his because the vehicle is stopped. We disagree. Drivers paused in the midst of traffic moving all around them (behind them, in adjacent lanes, in the roadway in front of them) would likely create hazards to themselves and public safety by their distracted use of their hands on their phones and devices, and would likely cause further traffic delays, whether it be because of a poor response to traffic issues that arise (including if they are hit by another vehicle), distracted drivers' feet letting up on brakes, the failure to promptly move as required by the traffic laws, the inability to resist the temptation to continue their fleeting use of their wireless telephone as they begin moving again, or innumerable other reasons. Construing section 23123 as applying to defendant's circumstances is most consistent with the Legislature's concerns about the public safety hazards caused by drivers' hand-held use of wireless telephones while on the public roadways, and with common sense.

* * *

The trial court's judgment is affirmed.

■ Concurring Opinion of RICHMAN, J.

I concur in the court's opinion. I write separately, however, to say that the scholarly analysis of legislative history and the lengthy discussion of cases are, for me, not necessary to resolution of this appeal, which I would decide this way.

* * *

Any mom or dad driving kids to school can expect to stop while parents in cars in front of them are unloading their kids. A shopper driving to a store near Lake Merritt in Oakland may have to stop while a gaggle of geese crosses the street. A couple going for a Sunday drive in west Marin County may have to stop for a cattle crossing. And, of course, all of us are expected to stop for red lights, stop signs, crossing trains, and funeral processions. In short, all drivers may, and sometimes must, stop. But they do so while "driving." Just like defendant.

––––––––

NOTES

1. The full version of the majority opinion is *much* longer than the excerpt presented here. Is the concurring judge correct that this is a simple case that does not need sophisticated legal analysis?

2. Should the court have looked to the legislative history and practical implications in deciding whether Nelson was driving? Was the court correct that the plain text of the statute was ambiguous? Given that courts have drawn a distinction between operating and driving in the DWI context, should "driving" mean a vehicle that is in motion?

3. How could the California legislature not have foreseen the problem presented by *Nelson*? Other states have been clearer than California in enacting texting while driving legislation. For instance, the Nebraska and South Dakota statutes excerpted at the beginning of this section both use the term "operating" rather than driving. *See* Neb. Rev. St. § 60–6, 179.01.; S.D. Codified Laws 32–26–47.

4. At least one court has reached the opposite conclusion as *Nelson*. *See* People v. Goldstein, 957 N.Y.S.2d 265 (Justice Court, Nassau County 2012) (reversing conviction because the defendant was stopped at a traffic light and "was not moving").

––––––––

CHAPTER 10

UNCOMPLETED CRIMINAL CONDUCT AND CRIMINAL COMBINATIONS

INTRODUCTION

Inchoate crimes, also called anticipatory offenses or incomplete criminal conduct, present some unique problems in criminal law analysis. This chapter will consider crimes of attempt, aiding and abetting, accessoryship, solicitation, and conspiracy. Each type of inchoate crime differs from the others in significant ways. We will begin this chapter by considering attempts—that is, unsuccessful efforts to commit crimes.

A. ATTEMPT

An attempt to commit a crime generally requires the specific intent to commit that crime, and a substantial step, beyond mere preparation, toward committing that crime. Before discussing the complicated question of what constitutes an attempt, it is useful to think about how we should punish defendants who have tried, but failed, to commit the target criminal offense.

1. PUNISHING ATTEMPTS

CALIFORNIA PENAL CODE § 664

Every person who attempts to commit any crime, but fails, or is prevented or intercepted in its perpetration, shall be punished where no provision is made by law for the punishment of those attempts, as follows:

(a) If the crime attempted is punishable by imprisonment in the state prison . . . the person guilty of the attempt shall be punished by imprisonment in the state prison or in a county jail, respectively, for one-half the term of imprisonment prescribed upon a conviction of the offense attempted. However, if the crime attempted is willful, deliberate, and premeditated murder . . . the person guilty of that attempt shall be punished by imprisonment in the state prison for life with the possibility of parole. If the crime attempted is any other one in which the maximum sentence is life imprisonment or death, the person guilty of the attempt shall be punished by imprisonment in the state prison for five, seven, or nine years. The additional term provided in this section for attempted willful, deliberate, and premeditated murder shall not be imposed unless the fact that the attempted murder was willful, deliberate, and premeditated is charged in the accusatory pleading and admitted or found to be true by the trier of fact.

(b) If the crime attempted is punishable by imprisonment in a county jail, the person guilty of the attempt shall be punished by imprisonment in a county jail for a term not exceeding one-half the term of imprisonment prescribed upon a conviction of the offense attempted.

(c) If the offense so attempted is punishable by a fine, the offender convicted of that attempt shall be punished by a fine not exceeding one-half the largest fine which may be imposed upon a conviction of the offense attempted.

(d) If a crime is divided into degrees, an attempt to commit the crime may be of any of those degrees, and the punishment for the attempt shall be determined as provided by this section.

(e) Notwithstanding subdivision (a), if attempted murder is committed upon a peace officer or firefighter, . . . a custodial officer, . . . a custody assistant, . . . or a nonsworn uniformed employee of a sheriff's department whose job entails the care or control of inmates in a detention facility . . . and the person who commits the offense knows or reasonably should know that the victim is a peace officer, firefighter, custodial officer, custody assistant, or nonsworn uniformed employee of a sheriff's department engaged in the performance of his or her duties, the person guilty of the attempt shall be punished by imprisonment in the state prison for life with the possibility of parole.

TEXAS PENAL CODE § 15.01

(a) A person commits an offense if, with specific intent to commit an offense, he does an act amounting to more than mere preparation that tends but fails to effect the commission of the offense intended.

(b) If a person attempts an offense that may be aggravated, his conduct constitutes an attempt to commit the aggravated offense if an element that aggravates the offense accompanies the attempt.

(c) It is no defense to prosecution for criminal attempt that the offense attempted was actually committed.

(d) An offense under this section is one category lower than the offense attempted . . .

PENNSYLVANIA STATUTES, CRIMES AND OFFENSES, 18 PA. C.S.A. § 905

(a) Grading.—Except as otherwise provided in this title, attempt, solicitation and conspiracy are crimes of the same grade and degree as the most serious offense which is attempted or solicited or is an object of the conspiracy.

(b) Mitigation.—If the particular conduct charged to constitute a criminal attempt, solicitation or conspiracy is so inherently unlikely to result or culminate in the commission of a crime that neither such conduct nor the actor presents a public danger warranting the grading of such offense under this section, the court may dismiss the prosecution.

————

NOTES: PUNISHING ATTEMPTS

1. Which statutory scheme—California, Texas, or Pennsylvania—do you find most appropriate?

2. Why should we punish attempts? Consider two circumstances:

> A.   When they were in high school, Bob often teased Mary about her red hair. Twenty years have gone by, but Mary is still upset about it and decides to kill Bob. Mary purchases a rifle, drives downtown, and waits outside the office building where Bob works. When Bob leaves his office at 5:00 p.m., Mary opens the window of her car, aims the rifle, pulls the trigger, and the bullet hits Bob in the shoulder. Bob is taken to the nearest hospital where doctors stabilize him and remove the bullet. A week later Bob is released from the hospital and will suffer no long-term effects from the gunshot wound. The police arrest Mary.

> B.   Assume the same facts as in Scenario A, except this time when Mary fires the rifles she misses Bob completely. The bullet lodges in a nearby building that is under construction. In fact, there is so much noise from the construction site that Bob never hears the gunshot. Bob continues walking and actually strolls past Mary's car. The window is open and Bob sees Mary. It has been so long since high school though that he has no recollection of Mary whatsoever. Stunned by the turn of events, Mary comes to her senses and realizes it is a terrible idea to try to kill Bob. She disposes of the gun and decides to abandon her plot. However, when workers at a nearby parking garage were reviewing their surveillance video, they noticed Mary's attempted murder of Bob. The police subsequently arrest Mary.

Does Mary deserve the same punishment in Scenarios A and B? How do you respond to the objection that Mary deserves a lesser punishment (or no punishment) in Scenario B because she has caused no harm?

3. Think about a different, and possibly more realistic, series of hypotheticals. Your criminal law exam is three hours long. At the end of the three hours, the professor calls time. As all of the students are turning in their exams, one of your classmates—Chris—keeps typing for an extra five minutes. As Chris is typing, students are staring incredulously at him, but he appears not to notice or care. When Chris hands in his exam, the professor says: "You have violated the rules of the exam, I will have to penalize you." Consider the following questions:

> A.   If the professor asks your opinion before she grades the exam, what penalty would you recommend imposing on Chris?

B.   If the professor asks your opinion after the grades have been calculated—and if you knew Chris had the highest grade on the exam—what penalty would you impose on him?

C.   If the professor asks your opinion after the grades have been calculated—and if you knew Chris had received a "D" on the exam, the lowest grade in the class—what penalty would you impose?

D.   Does your answer change if Chris tells the professor that he had not heard her call time because of his earplugs and that taking the extra five minutes was completely accidental? Assume you believe him.

E.   What if Chris had told other students that he planned to take an extra five minutes on the exam, but the professor grabbed away Chris's exam three seconds after calling time?

F.   What if, instead of taking extra time, Chris planned to cheat on the closed-book exam by writing key provisions of the Model Penal Code on his left arm? Chris walks into the exam room at 1:50 p.m., ten minutes before the start of the exam, and he has the MPC written all over his arm. At 1:59 p.m., just as the professor is starting to distribute the exam, Chris runs into the bathroom and washes the MPC off his arm. What punishment?

G.   Assume the same facts as Scenario F, except that the professor distributes the exam at 2:00 p.m. Everyone in the class begins reading the questions (which are all about the MPC). At 2:10 p.m., without ever having looked at his arm, Chris goes to the bathroom and washes the MPC off his arm. Do you impose the same punishment as in Scenario F?

4. In some cases, it is debatable whether the defendant completed the target offense or only made it far enough to have attempted it. For instance, did the defendant actually rob the bank, or merely attempt to rob it? In those cases, if the jury convicts the defendant of the completed offense (for instance, robbery) we do not also punish the defendant for attempted robbery. The attempt "merges" into the completed offense so as not to double-punish. *See, e.g.*, N.J.S.A. 2C:1–8. Relatedly, if a defendant is convicted of aggravated assault, courts will generally not also allow conviction (and hence punishment) for attempted robbery. *See, e.g.*, Commonwealth v. Ayala, 424 A.2d 1260 (Pa. 1981) (concluding that even though the defendant plead guilty to aggravated assault and attempted robbery, they "merged for sentencing purposes" and "cannot be multiply punished by separate consecutive sentences."

———

2.   *MENS REA* ISSUES IN ATTEMPT

Attempt crimes have a <u>specific intent *mens rea,*</u> even when the substantive crime, if completed, would require only a general intent *mens rea.* In a "bad aim" case, in which an unintended victim is struck but not killed, is the specific intent to kill the intended victim sufficient to sustain an attempted murder charge for shooting the unintended victim? Is it possible for a defendant to attempt an accidental crime? Consider the following cases.

Harrison v. State

Court of Appeals of Maryland, 2004.
382 Md. 477, 855 A.2d 1220.

■ BATTAGLIA, J.

Gerard Harrison fired his .38 caliber pistol six times at a man known as "Valentine" but struck James Cook instead. We issued a writ of *certiorari* to determine whether the evidence in this case was sufficient to support Harrison's conviction of attempted second-degree murder. Harrison argues that the evidence was not sufficient to prove the intent element of that crime. For the reasons discussed herein, we agree with Harrison and hold that, under the theory of "concurrent intent," the evidence was insufficient to support a finding that Harrison possessed the requisite intent for attempted second-degree murder. We also hold that the doctrine of "transferred intent" does not support the conviction because "transferred intent" may not be applied to prove attempted murder.

I.   Background

Harrison engaged in a shooting in Baltimore City on July 27, 2001. As a result of the incident, . . . [o]n June 12, 2002, in the Circuit Court for Baltimore City, Harrison was convicted of attempted second-degree murder and use of a handgun in the commission of a felony or crime of violence on an agreed statement of facts, which the prosecutor narrated for the record:

> The facts would be that, on July 27, 2001, in the fifteen hundred block of Clifton Avenue, the victim in this matter, Mr. James Cook, was standing and talking with friends when he was struck in the neck with a bullet. Investigation revealed that [Harrison] and another unknown person were shooting at someone known only to them only as Valentine, and in the course of the shooting, accidentally struck the victim, Mr. Cook.
>
> Your Honor, a witness was identified. He was taken down to the station and shown a photo array. He observed the photo array and picked out [Harrison] who would be identified in court here today as Mr. Gerard Harrison to my right, with counsel, as the person he knows as Fats and as one of the shooters. . . .
>
> During the statement, [Harrison] advised that he and a person known to him as Twin Shitty began firing on a person that they knew as Valentine. [Harrison] stated that he had one gun and

the other person had two guns, stating that he had fired six shots and then they both ran. Found out later that somebody other than their intended target was shot.

[I]f called to testify, the ballistics examiner would have stated that the ballistics evidence recovered from the crime scene was consistent with [Harrison's] confession and that the ballistics show that there were three different firearms used and they matched the caliber that [Harrison] described. The victim was taken to Sinai Hospital where he was operated on. All events occurred in Baltimore City, State of Maryland. That would be the statement supporting the guilty plea as a Count Two, attempted murder in the second degree and Count Six, use of a handgun in the commission of a crime of violence.

The statements made by Harrison during a police interrogation on August 22, 2001, which were referred to in the agreed-upon facts, were as follows:

[Officer]: Okay and if you could, in your own words again tell me what you know and what happened as far as what you knew in this case.

Harrison: All I know is that me and another . . . another dude, a friend of mines walking up on the basketball court and he had two guns, I had one. We just started shooting in the direction of Valentine.

[Officer]: Of Valentine, and why were you all shooting at Valentine?

Harrison: Because he around there selling some dope.

[Officer]: Okay, and was he told something in the past?

Harrison: He was told in the past not to hustle around there.

[Officer]: Okay, and when you all were shooting in the direction of Valentine, what type of gun did you have?

Harrison: I had a .38. . . .

[Officer]: Okay. Now when you all were shooting at Valentine, how many shots did you shoot at him?

Harrison: Six.

[Officer]: So did you have any more shots left?

Harrison: No. . . .

Ct. App Affirmed

The Court of Special Appeals affirmed the convictions. In addition to affirming the handgun conviction, the court held that the evidence was sufficient to sustain Harrison's conviction of attempted second-degree murder of Cook. . . . In reaching this conclusion, the court considered the State's arguments that the intent element of the crime could be supported under theories of "transferred intent," "depraved heart" recklessness, and "concurrent intent." The court concluded that the conviction could not rest on theories of "transferred intent" or "depraved heart" recklessness. The theory of "transferred intent" fails because, according to the court, under *Ford v. State*, 330 Md. 682, 625 A.2d 984 (1993), the doctrine only applies when a defendant shoots at his target, misses, and an unintended victim receives a fatal injury. The court held that "depraved heart" recklessness also does (not) apply because Harrison's conviction of attempted second-degree murder requires that he had a specific intent to kill; depraved heart" murder, on the other hand, "only requires wanton disregard for human life, . . . a mental state [that] falls short" of the necessary mental element of attempted second-degree murder. Nevertheless, in the court's view, the evidence did support a finding of the requisite intent, under the theory of "concurrent intent." The court held that the jury could infer that Harrison "intentionally created a 'kill zone' to accomplish the death of Valentine, the primary victim," and, therefore, the jury could also infer that Harrison had a concurrent intent to kill Cook, who was among those "gathered at the scene of the crime."

[handwritten margin note: you need specific intent to kill]

Harrison petitioned this Court for a writ of *certiorari* and raised two questions, which we have rephrased and combined into one: Is the evidence sufficient to support a conviction of attempted second-degree murder, where Harrison fired six shots at one person, missed that person, but hit another person causing injury and not death?[11] We conclude that the evidence fails to support a conviction for attempted second-degree murder based on the theory of "concurrent intent" because the stipulated facts do not prove that Cook inhabited the "kill zone" when Harrison fired the errant shots. Furthermore, the State's reliance on the doctrine of "transferred intent" also fails inasmuch as that doctrine does not apply to a charge of attempted murder. . . .

[handwritten margin note: issue]

II. Standard of Review

* * *

III. Discussion

"Murder is the killing of one human being by another with the requisite malevolent state of mind and without justification, excuse, or mitigation." The malevolent states of mind that qualify are: (1) the intent to kill, (2) the intent to do grievous bodily harm, (3) the intent to do an act under circumstances manifesting extreme indifference to the value of human life (depraved heart), or (4) the intent to commit a dangerous

---

[11] Harrison phrased his two questions as follows:

    1. Is an intent to kill the named victim a factual and legal prerequisite to a conviction of attempted murder even where the theory is one of "concurrent" intent?

    2. May a conviction for attempted second-degree murder of an unintended victim be sustained on the theory that stipulated facts could support a finding of concurrent intent to kill the intended and unintended victims where the Statement of Facts in support of the conviction states that the defendant shot the victim accidentally, while aiming at another?

felony. The General Assembly has determined that certain murders qualify as murder in the first degree, such as murders committed in the perpetration of enumerated felonies or any kind of willful, deliberate and premeditated killing.

To be guilty of the crime of attempt, one must possess "a specific intent to commit a particular offense" and carry out some overt act in furtherance of the intent that goes beyond mere preparation. For attempted second-degree murder, the State has the burden to prove "a specific intent to kill—an intent to commit grievous bodily harm will not suffice." See, LaFave & Scott, CRIMINAL LAW, § 6.2 at 500–01 (2d ed. 1986) ("[O]n a charge of attempted murder it is not sufficient to show that the defendant intended to do serious bodily harm or that he acted in reckless disregard for human life. . . . [A]ttempted murder requires an intent to bring about the result described by the crime of murder (i.e., the death of another)."); . . .

Harrison challenges his conviction for attempted second-degree murder, arguing that he did not possess the requisite intent to murder Cook because his target was Valentine. In support of this argument, Harrison relies on the agreed-upon facts, which state that Harrison "accidentally" struck the victim, Cook. Harrison contends that the term "accidentally" characterizes his state of mind at the time of the shooting, thereby nullifying the specific intent to kill the victim and obviating guilt of attempted second-degree murder.

The State responds that the term "accidentally" does not characterize Harrison's state of mind, but, rather, "accidentally" refers to the fact that the bullets, by accident, hit Cook instead of Valentine, the intended target. The State argues that the facts support the trial court's determination that Harrison had a specific intent to kill Valentine by shooting six bullets at him. This specific intent to kill, according to the State, should be attributed to Harrison for shooting Cook under two theories: "concurrent intent" and "transferred intent." As to the theory of "concurrent intent," the State argues that, by firing six shots to kill Valentine, Harrison intentionally created a "kill zone." Citing to the considered dicta explicated in Judge Chasanow's discussion for the Court majority in *Ford v. State*, 330 Md. 682, 625 A.2d 984 (1993), the State maintains that the theory of "concurrent intent" functions to apply Harrison's specific intent to kill to everyone in that zone, including Cook. Under the theory of "transferred intent," the State argues, Harrison's intent to kill Valentine transferred to Cook, the person who actually sustained injury.[13]

---

[13] Harrison was not charged with the crime of attempted murder against Valentine, Harrison's primary target, and the State has not argued that Harrison's conviction should be sustained on that basis. Accordingly, we need not discuss the efficacy of the evidence in this case with regard to a conviction of attempted second-degree murder against Valentine.

We first dispose of Harrison's argument that the term "accidentally" in the agreed statement of facts defines his *mens rea* at the time of the shooting. Harrison's reliance on that term is not persuasive. The term "accidentally" describes the outcome of Harrison's act, not his state of mind. Furthermore, in Harrison's statement to the police, which is incorporated by reference in the agreed statement of facts, Harrison admits that he intentionally fired his handgun at Valentine. When a police officer asked what happened, Harrison replied that he and a friend walked to the basketball court and "just started shooting in the direction of Valentine." The officer asked why, and Harrison responded, "Because he around there selling some dope. . . . He was told in the past not to hustle around here." From this evidence, as well as the agreed-upon statement that Harrison "fired six shots at a person [he] knew as Valentine," the trial judge reasonably could have inferred that the shooting was no accident. The trial judge's conclusion that Harrison had a specific intent to kill is supported by the evidence.

Harrison argues, nonetheless, that, even if he did maintain a specific intent to kill, it was directed at Valentine and not at Cook, the one who suffered the injury. Consequently, we must determine whether the necessary specific intent as against Cook could derive from Harrison's specific intent to kill Valentine; or in other words, does Harrison's specific intent to kill Valentine satisfy the requisite intent for attempted second-degree murder, when the actual victim (and who alone was named in the indictment) in this case was a bystander? The State contends that the theories of "concurrent intent" and "transferred intent" support its assertion that Harrison's specific intent to kill fulfills the intent element as against Cook.

A.   Concurrent intent

The Court of Special Appeals upheld Harrison's conviction of attempted murder because a specific intent to murder Cook could be inferred under the theory of "concurrent intent." This theory emerged from the discussion in *Ford v. State*, 330 Md. 682, 625 A.2d 984 (1993), in which the Court expressed its disapproval of the use of "transferred intent" in cases where the defendant faced charges of attempted murder of a bystander. *See* LeEllen Coacher & Libby Gallo, *Criminal Liability: Transferred and Concurrent Intent*, 44 A.F.L. REV. 227, 235 (1998). The *Ford* Court discussed the doctrine of "concurrent intent" to "explain [ ] and justif[y]" the result in *State v. Wilson*, 313 Md. 600, 546 A.2d 1041 (1988), the case in which this Court held that "transferred intent" could be used to prove the specific-intent element of attempted murder of a bystander. Explaining the distinction between "transferred intent" and "concurrent intent," Judge Chasanow for the Court stated:

> In transferred intent, the intended harm does not occur to the intended victim, but occurs instead to a second . . . victim. The actual result is an unintended, unanticipated consequence of

intended harm. For example, consider a defendant who shoots a single bullet at the head of A, standing with B and C. If the defendant misses A and instead kills B, the defendant's intent to murder A will be transferred to allow his conviction for B's murder. The intent is concurrent, on the other hand, when the nature and scope of the attack, while directed at a primary victim, are such that we can conclude the perpetrator intended to ensure harm to the primary victim by harming everyone in that victim's vicinity.

concurrent

To further distinguish between the two theories, the Court offered a hypothetical example of the application of "concurrent intent":

> [A]n assailant who places a bomb on a commercial airplane intending to harm a primary target on board ensures by this method of attack that all passengers will be killed. Similarly, consider a defendant who intends to kill A and, in order to ensure A's death, drives by a group consisting of A, B, and C, and attacks the group with automatic weapon fire or an explosive device devastating enough to kill everyone in the group. . . . When the defendant escalated his mode of attack from a single bullet aimed at A's head to a hail of bullets or an explosive device, the factfinder can infer that, whether or not the defendant succeeded in killing A, the defendant concurrently intended to kill everyone in A's immediate vicinity to ensure A's death. The defendant's intent need not be transferred from A to B, because although the defendant's goal was to kill A, his intent to kill B was also direct; it was concurrent with his intent to kill A.

The Court summed up the rule of "concurrent intent" as follows: "Where the means employed to commit the crime against a primary victim create a zone of harm around that victim, the factfinder can reasonably infer that the defendant intended that harm to all who are in the anticipated zone."

* * *

The doctrine of "concurrent intent" also has found favor in several other jurisdictions. For example, using "concurrent intent," the Supreme Court of California, in *People v. Bland*, 28 Cal.4th 313, 121 Cal. Rptr.2d 546, 48 P.3d 1107 (2002), upheld attempted-murder convictions that arose out of a gang-related shooting resulting in the death of the intended victim and injury to two bystanders. Wilson, a member of the Rolling 20's Crips, was driving through a Long Beach neighborhood with two passengers when he encountered Bland and a friend, both members of the Insane Crips. Bland approached Wilson's car, began shooting into the vehicle, and, along with his friend, continued to shoot as the car started to drive away. Wilson died, and both of his passengers received non-fatal gunshot wounds. During Bland's trial, the jury was instructed according to the doctrine of "transferred intent," after which Bland was convicted of first-degree murder of *Wilson* and attempted first-degree murder of the two injured bystanders.

The Supreme Court of California held that Bland's convictions for attempted murder could not be premised upon "transferred intent" because, in California, that theory did not apply to attempted murder. Nevertheless, the Court concluded that the convictions could rest upon the theory of "concurrent intent." After quoting *Ford* at length, the California court stated the facts before it "virtually compelled" an inference that Bland harbored a specific intent to kill all those in harm's way:

> Even if the jury found that [Bland] primarily wanted to kill Wilson rather than Wilson's passengers, it could reasonably also have found a concurrent intent to kill those passengers when [Bland] and his cohort fired a flurry of bullets at the fleeing car and thereby created a kill zone. Such a finding fully supports attempted murder convictions as to the passengers.

* * *

In concurrent-intent analyses, courts focus on the "means employed to commit the crime" and the "zone of harm around [the] victim." The essential questions, therefore, become (1) whether a fact-finder could infer that the defendant intentionally escalated his mode of attack to such an extent that he or she created a "zone of harm," and (2) whether the facts establish that the actual victim resided in that zone when he or she was injured.

As to the first question, courts have permitted an inference that the defendant created a kill zone when a defendant, like Harrison, fired multiple bullets at an intended target. In *Wilson*, the defendant and his brother fired "multiple bullets" from two handguns. The defendant in *Bland* fired a "flurry of bullets," . . . . Just three random shots directed behind a door gave rise to a permissible inference of a "killing zone" in *Willis*, 46 M.J. at 261–62. These methods of attack are similar to Harrison's six shots at Valentine. We conclude, therefore, that the facts support an inference that Harrison created a "kill zone" around Valentine and that Harrison had the specific intent to kill everyone inside of the zone.

The facts in this case, however, do not permit an inference that Cook, the unintended victim, inhabited the "kill zone" when Harrison's bullet hit him. Courts that have considered the issue all have relied on specific facts showing the location of the unintended victim either in relation to the intended victim or in relation to the defendant. In *Bland*, for example, the unintended victims occupied the same car as the intended victim when the defendant fired a hail of bullets at the car. When . . . the defendant fired multiple "quick fire" shots inside the automobile in which the primary victim sat, the murdered bystander was standing right next to the car.

In the present case, however, the State's argument that Cook was in Harrison's "kill zone" at the time of the shooting lacks adequate support from the evidence. According to the agreed statement of facts, "in the fifteen hundred block of Clifton Avenue, [Cook] was standing and talking with friends when he was struck in the neck with a bullet." Although this statement shows generally where Cook was standing when he was shot, it and the remaining evidence provide no indication where Cook was in relation to Valentine or Harrison. A fact finder, let alone an appellate court, has no idea, based on this meager evidence, whether Cook stood in Harrison's direct line of fire, next to the intended victim, or at a distance from Harrison or his target, Valentine. Absent more specific evidence of Cook's location in relation to the shooter and the intended victim, no inference is permissible that Cook occupied the "kill zone" when he was struck by the bullet. Consequently, we disagree with Court of Special Appeals and conclude that the agreed statement of facts does not provide sufficient evidence to support a finding of "concurrent intent" on the part of Harrison.

* * *

A.   Transferred Intent

The State argues that the theory of "transferred intent" also supports the trial judge's conclusion that Harrison possessed the intent required for attempted second-degree murder. The theory of "transferred intent" has received considerable attention over the years in this Court and the Court of Special Appeals. . . . We first recognized the viability of the doctrine in Gladden v. State, 273 Md. 383, 330 A.2d 176 (1974), which involved a classic question of "transferred intent": whether Gladden was guilty of first-degree murder when he shot and killed a twelve-year-old bystander in the course of attempting to kill a man named Seigel. Judge O'Donnell traced the common law origin of "transferred intent" back to 1576, when the court in Reg. v. Saunders, 2 Plowd. 473, 474a, 75 Eng. Rep. 706, 708 (1576) stated:

> And therefore it is every man's business to foresee what wrong or mischief may happen from that which he does with an ill-intention, and it shall be no excuse for him to say that he intended to kill another, and not the person killed. For if a man of malice prepense shoots an arrow at another with an intent to kill him, and a person to whom he bore no malice is killed by it, this shall be murder in him, for when he shot the arrow he intended to kill, and inasmuch as he directed his instrument of death at one, and thereby has killed another, it shall be the same offense in him as if he had killed the person he aimed at, for the end of the act shall be construed by the beginning of it, and the last part shall taste of the first, and as the beginning of

the act had malice prepense in it, and consequently imported murder, so the end of the act, *viz.* the killing of another shall be in the same degree, and therefore it shall be murder, and not homicide only.

Summarizing the court's holding in *Saunders*, Judge O'Donnell quoted the works of Sir Matthew Hale and Sir William Blackstone. Hale stated:

> To these may be added the cases above mentioned, *viz.* if A. by malice forethought strikes at B. and missing him strikes C. whereof he dies, tho he never bore any malice to C. yet it is murder, and the law transfers the malice to the party slain; . . .

Id. at 391, 330 A.2d at 181 (quoting Sir Matthew Hale, 1 History of the Pleas of the Crown at 466). Blackstone described the same rule as follows:

> Thus if one shoots at A and misses him, but kills B, this is murder; because of the previous felonious intent, which the law transfers from one to the other. The same is the case where one lays poison for A; and B, against whom the prisoner had no malicious intent, takes it, and it kills him; this is likewise murder.

Id. at 391–92, 330 A.2d at 181 (quoting Sir William Blackstone, 4 COMMENTARIES ON THE LAWS OF ENGLAND 201 (Cooley, 3d ed., 1884)).

* * *

Attempting to "invalidate a portion of [the] doctrine that [the Court had] recently and specifically approved in [*Wilson*]." *Id.* at 724, 625 A.2d at 1004 (MCAULIFFE, J., concurring). The three judges viewed the majority's limitation on the transferred-intent doctrine as presenting "interesting problems" for future prosecutions:

The Court revisited the [disagreement between courts] in *Poe v. State*, 341 Md. 523, 671 A.2d 501 (1996), in which Judge Chasanow, again writing for the Court, addressed the factual scenario suggested by Judge McAuliffe in his *Ford* concurrence. Poe, in the course of a heated exchange with his estranged wife, retrieved a shotgun from the trunk of his car and, shouting, "Take this, bitch," fired a single .50 caliber slug at her. The bullet passed through the arm of Ms. Poe, his intended target, and struck a six-year-old bystander in the head. *Id.* Ms. Poe suffered a non-fatal injury, but the child died instantly. At *Poe*'s trial, the judge instructed that "if the jury would have convicted Mr. Poe . . . had she died as a result of the shot, they could convict Mr. Poe of first degree murder of [the child], because the intent to kill Ms. Poe transfers to [the child], the unintended victim." The jury found Poe guilty of first-degree murder of the child and attempted first-degree murder of Ms. Poe.

In *Poe*, the primary issue was whether the trial court erred "in ruling that the doctrine of transferred intent applies where a defendant intends to kill A, shoots and wounds A, but kills B, an unintended victim, by that same shot." Relying on *Ford*, *Poe* maintained that, because he had completed the crime of attempted murder of Ms. *Poe*, his specific intent to kill her could not also be transferred to the child. This Court disagreed, explaining that limitations on "transferred intent" apply only when the defendant shoots at an intended victim and, instead, wounds an unintended victim "without killing either." *Ford*, therefore, was inapposite to the facts of *Poe*, because the unintended victim in *Poe* had been killed, not merely injured. The Court held that "transferred intent" applied to the death of the bystander, despite the fact that *Poe* also had wounded his intended victim. The Court narrowed the question of when to apply "transferred intent" to "what could the defendant have been convicted of had he accomplished his intended act?" and spoke of *Ford* only to note why the defendant's reliance on that case was misplaced.

The Court unanimously agreed with the result in *Poe*, but three judges again joined a concurring opinion to voice concerns over the future use of "transferred intent." Judge Raker, the author of the concurring opinion, took issue with the majority's "overly broad" assertion that "the doctrine of transferred intent does not apply to attempted murder when there is no death." (RAKER, J., concurring). The correct statement of the law, in Judge Raker's view, "is that transferred intent should not apply to attempted murder if no one is injured." For support, Judge Raker cited several cases from England and the United States, in which courts have held the doctrine of "transferred intent" does apply when bystanders received non-fatal injuries. Judge Raker also presented various policy considerations for the application of the doctrine without regard to whether the unintended victim was killed or merely injured, to include that extended application of "transferred intent" would "ensure proportionate punishment of criminal offenses" and prevent increased difficulty in prosecuting criminals for the harm inflicted on bystanders. In support, Judge Raker posed the following hypothetical:

> [A] defendant, A, participates in a drive-by shooting on a public street, intending to kill B, but instead non-fatally injuring B, and non-fatally injuring bystander C. Although A may be convicted of attempted murder of B, it will be difficult to convict A of the attempted murder of C, or of assault with intent to kill C. Without transferred intent, the State will be required to offer separate proof of intent for each victim, *e.g.*, by demonstrating "depraved heart." While firing a "hail of bullets" at a person on a busy street may be prima facie evidence of a depraved heart, numerous factual situations may arise where it will be difficult to demonstrate recklessness.

In conclusion, Judge Raker stated her understanding that the majority held simply that transferred intent may be applied to first-degree murder of a bystander, "regardless of whether the defendant also injured his intended victim," and ergo, *Wilson* remains viable. *Id.* at 540, 671 A.2d at 509.

The question now before us is almost identical to the one debated in *Wilson*, *Ford*, and *Poe*: whether "transferred intent" may apply in an attempted murder case, where a bystander has received a non-fatal injury. Citing *Ford*, the Court of Special Appeals held that the transferred-intent doctrine "[could] not be used to sustain [Harrison's] conviction" because it did not apply in cases charging attempted murder of an unintended victim. We conclude that the Court of Special Appeals was correct in holding that the theory of transferred intent applies only when a bystander has suffered a fatal injury. This holding, as we shall explain, comports with numerous other jurisdictions who have considered the issue and avoids the numerous logical hurdles that arise when "transferred intent" is applied to inchoate offenses.

* * *

The Supreme Court of California extensively discussed the issue of "transferred intent" for attempt crimes in *People v. Bland*, 28 Cal.4th 313, 121 Cal. Rptr.2d 546, 48 P.3d 1107 (2002). That case involved a multiple shooting in which the intended victim was killed and two bystanders received non-fatal injuries. The Supreme Court of California declined to apply the theory of "transferred intent" in considering whether the evidence was sufficient to support the defendant's convictions of attempted first-degree murder of the bystanders. The California court held that "to be guilty of attempted murder, the defendant must intend to kill the alleged victim, not someone else." In other words, "[s]omeone who intends to kill only one person and attempts unsuccessfully to do so, is guilty of attempted murder of the intended victim, but not the others."

Drawing from this Court's discussion in *Ford*, the California court examined the potential pitfalls of applying the doctrine to "inchoate crimes," including the fact that attempted murder does not require a physical injury to the victim. The court wondered, therefore, how a court or prosecuting authority might determine "to whom the defendant's intent should be transferred" when a bystander suffers no physical injury. The court stated that "[t]his concern is real":

> The world contains many people a murderous assailant does not intend to kill. Obviously, intent to kill one person cannot transfer to the entire world. But how can a jury rationally decide which of many persons the defendant did not intend to kill were attempted murder victims on a transferred intent theory? To how many unintended persons can an intent to kill be transferred? Just as acts with implied malice constitute murder of anyone actually killed, but not attempted murder of others, so, too, acts with the intent to kill one person constitute murder of anyone actually killed, but not attempted murder of others.

The *Bland* court also recognized that its limit on "transferred intent" did not preclude the prosecution of the defendant for the injury caused to the unintended victim. For example, in California, the defendant "might be guilty of crimes such as assault with a deadly weapon or firing at an occupied vehicle," and the prosecution can use the theory of "concurrent intent" to establish a specific intent with respect to a bystander.

The most compelling reason why we reject the doctrine of transferred intent as applied to crimes of attempt is that it is not necessary to make "a whole crime out of two halves by joining the intent as to one victim with the harm caused to another victim," the purpose for which it was conceived. *Ford*, 330 Md. at 712, 625 A.2d at 998. When the unintended victim has not suffered a fatal injury, the defendant already has committed a completed crime against the intended victim, and the seriousness of that crime is as great as if the intent were transferred to the unintended victim.

Further, although not in this case, a defendant may be convicted of a crime against an unintended victim with the use of "concurrent intent" and without the use of "transferred intent." Such a defendant also may be convicted of criminal battery, and as Judge Moylan suggested in *Harvey v. State*, 111 Md. App. 401, 430, 681 A.2d 628, 643 (1996), "the crime of reckless endangerment is also available to pick up much of the slack and to make resort to the transferred intent doctrine less compelling." There is little, if any, utility in extending the doctrine of "transferred intent" to inchoate crimes such as attempted murder.

JUDGMENT OF THE COURT OF SPECIAL APPEALS REVERSED; COSTS IN THIS COURT AND IN THE COURT OF SPECIAL APPEALS TO BE PAID BY RESPONDENT.

■ RAKER, J., dissenting.

I would affirm the judgment of conviction based on the doctrine of transferred intent.[1] The majority, in my view, is misguided in its approach in embracing the legal fiction of "concurrent intent" but in rejecting the common law doctrine of "transferred intent" to the circumstances of this case.

---

[1]   The theory underlying the doctrine of transferred intent was well stated in the case of *People v. Scott*, 14 Cal.4th 544, 59 Cal. Rptr.2d 178, 927 P.2d 288 (1996), explaining that intent is not actually transferred. The California Supreme Court explained as follows:

> The legal fiction of transferring a defendant's intent helps illustrate why, as a theoretical matter, a defendant can be convicted of murder when she did not intend to kill the person actually killed. The transferred intent doctrine does not, however, denote an actual "transfer" of "intent" from the intended victim to the unintended victim. Rather, as applied here, it connotes a policy—that a defendant who shoots at an intended victim with intent to kill but misses and hits a bystander instead should be subject to the same criminal liability that would have been imposed had he hit his intended mark. It is the policy underlying the doctrine, rather than its literal meaning, that compels the conclusion that a transferred intent instruction was properly given in this case. *Id.* at 292 (citations omitted).

I.

This is a "bad aim" case, where the intended victim was not harmed, and the unintended victim was injured, but did not die. Petitioner's intent to kill the intended victim should be "transferred" to the unintended victim, thereby holding petitioner accountable for the crime he committed against Mr. Cook, the unintended victim.

Petitioner was convicted of attempted second degree murder of James Cook, and a handgun violation. It is not disputed that petitioner fired six shots from his .38 caliber handgun at a person known as Valentine, missed him and instead struck a bystander, James Cook. Attempted second degree murder requires that petitioner had a specific intent to kill. Although petitioner did not in fact have a specific intent to kill Cook, the State did prove beyond a reasonable doubt that he had a specific intent to kill Valentine. I believe that intent is "transferred" to Cook, and the evidence was sufficient to support the verdict under the doctrine of transferred intent.

* * *

The majority employs the lack of necessity argument in rejecting the doctrine of transferred intent in the context of an attempt, stating that "[t]he most compelling reason why we reject the doctrine of transferred intent as applied to crimes of attempt is that it is not necessary to make 'a whole crime out of two halves by joining the intent as to one victim with the harm caused to another victim.' . . ." (citations omitted). The majority reasons that "[w]hen the unintended victim has not suffered a fatal injury, the defendant already has committed a completed crime against the intended victim, and the seriousness of that crime is as great as if the intent were transferred to the unintended victim." . . . In addition, rationalizing that there is little utility in "extending" the doctrine of transferred intent, the majority concludes that although not in this case, "concurrent intent" rather than transferred intent will apply to defendants who commit crimes against unintended victims.

The majority's reasoning is incomplete and flawed. First, the majority adds an artificial requirement of death of the unintended victim to the transferred intent doctrine.[3] Second, Maryland has repudiated the reasoning that simply because the defendant has committed a completed

---

[3]   The doctrine of transferred intent is not limited to killings. *See* e.g., *State v. Thomas*, 127 La. 576, 53 So. 868, 871 (1910) (citing *The Queen v. Latimer*, 17 Q.B.D. 359 (1886)); Anthony M. Dillof, *Transferred Intent: An Inquiry into the Nature of Criminal Culpability*, 1 BUFF. CRIM. L. REV. 501, 504 (1998). It is instead "a general principle which permits liability for any crime involving a *mens rea* of intent—be it arson, assault, theft or trespass—where the actual object of the crime is not the intended object." *Id.* Neither history nor policy supports a limitation of the transferred intent doctrine to cases resulting in death. *See Poe*, 341 Md. at 537–39, 671 A.2d at 508 (RAKER, J., concurring, noting that American courts, following the English precedents, have applied transferred intent to cases where the unintended victim was injured but not killed).

crime against the intended victim the doctrine does not apply.[4] Finally, the notion that the doctrine is unnecessary because concurrent intent or other crimes are available to the State is wrong, particularly in this case. Most likely, because concurrent intent was not applicable, and transferred intent does not apply, petitioner will escape punishment for the harm he inflicted upon Mr. Cook. This is evident in the mandate, as the current case was not remanded for a new trial.

II.

Transferred intent is a common law doctrine which has long been a part of the law in Maryland. *See State v. Wilson*, 313 Md. 600, 546 A.2d 1041 (1988); Gladden v. *State*, 273 Md. 383, 330 A.2d 176 (1974). . . .

After today's decision, the doctrine of transferred intent will still be a part of Maryland law, albeit more limited in its application. The question arises in this case as to whether transferred intent is applicable when C does not die but is injured. There is an ongoing debate around the country, within the courts and commentators, as to the applicability of the doctrine of transferred intent. Commentators and courts have described the doctrine as "defective," a "curious survival of the antique law," and one having no proper place in the criminal law. Despite the views of detractors, a "roughly equal number of commentators . . . have approved of the doctrine and its result." *Id.* In my view, the doctrine of transferred intent should apply to the crime of attempted murder, for example, when a person, A, intentionally shoots a gun at B, intending to kill B, and because of bad aim or luck, hits but does not kill, or even misses, B, and strikes and injures C. *See Poe*, 341 Md. at 539, 671 A.2d at 509 (RAKER J., concurring, joined by Rodowsky and Karwacki, J.J.). A should not escape punishment for the act committed against C simply because that person had bad aim or good luck.

This Court addressed the question of whether transferred intent applies to attempted murder in *State v. Wilson*, and, noting specifically the split in jurisdictions around the country as to the applicability of transferred intent, we "align[ed] ourselves with the numerous jurisdictions which have applied the transferred intent doctrine to specific intent crimes including attempted murder." In *Wilson*, the intended target, Brown, was not harmed physically, and the unintended victim, Kent, was struck with the bullets but did not die. The defendant was charged with attempted murder of both the intended target and the unintended target. We made clear that the doctrine of "transferred intent" was not limited to homicide cases but extends to all situations where a defendant's intended act " 'affects' or 'inflicts harm upon' an

---

[4] Almost every jurisdiction has rejected the *Ford v. State*, 330 Md. 682, 625 A.2d 984 (1993) opinion reasoning that transferred intent is not applicable where the crime has been "completed" with the death of the intended victim but an unintended victim also dies. *See* e.g., *State v.* Hinton, 227 Conn. 301, 630 A.2d 593, 599 (1993) (noting that "we reject defendant's argument that the successful killing of the intended victim prevents the transfer of that intent to an unintended victim" (citations and internal quotations omitted)).

unintended victim.". . . The Court reasoned that a necessary element of murder is malice and that inasmuch as the State proved the malice element by establishing *Wilson*'s specific intent to kill Brown, *Wilson* would have been guilty of premeditated murder had the unintended victim Kent died. *See id.* Accordingly, the elements of attempted murder were satisfied when Kent survived. *Wilson*, in my view, was decided and reasoned correctly.

* * *

The doctrine of transferred intent in Maryland was set out, and judicially embraced, in *Gladden*. The Court looked at the "classic" doctrine of transferred intent, and held that when an individual kills one person but actually intended to kill another, transferred intent applies. The *Gladden* Court pointed out that under the common law, the doctrine was as follows:

In a student note, *Poe v. State*: *The Court of Appeals of Maryland Limits the Applicability of the Doctrine of Transferred Intent*, 27 U. BALT. L.REV. 167 (1997), the author, Daniel J. Curry, traces the doctrine of transferred intent in Maryland. He concludes that "a defendant who attempts to kill their intended victim but instead injures an unintended victim should be held liable under transferred intent for attempted murder of the unintended, injured victim." Discussing the majority and concurring opinions in *Poe*, the perceptive author concluded that "Judge Raker's reasoning is more sound than the majority's because it does not preclude the use of the doctrine in attempted murder prosecutions. Judge Raker's clarification was in tune with the elements of the doctrine as it is commonly applied." I reiterate my predication in *Poe*:

> If the majority's opinion is interpreted to preclude any use of the doctrine of transferred intent in attempted murder prosecutions, the effect of the decision will be to substantially increase the difficulty of prosecuting criminals for the harm inflicted on innocent bystanders. . . . Without transferred intent, the State will be required to offer separate proof of intent for each victim, *e.g.*, by demonstrating "depraved heart [or concurrent intent]." While firing a "hail of bullets" at a person on a busy street may be *prima facie* evidence of a depraved heart, numerous factual situations may arise where it will be difficult to demonstrate recklessness.

The instant case demonstrates just such a situation. Today's ruling has rewarded petitioner for his bad aim, and will likely result in similar rewards for others in the future.

———

NOTES: *MENS REA* IN CRIMINAL ATTEMPTS

1. The American Law Institute's Model Penal Code § 5.01 retains the basic common law view of attempt, but spells out the requirements as follows:

(1) Definition of Attempt. A person is guilty of an attempt to commit a crime if, acting with the kind of culpability otherwise required for commission of the crime, he:

(a) purposely engages in conduct that would constitute the crime if the attendant circumstances were as he believes them to be; or

(b) when causing a particular result is an element of the crime, does or omits to do anything with the purpose of causing or with the belief that it will cause such result without further conduct on his part; or

(c) purposely does or omits to do anything that, under the circumstances as he believes them to be, is an act or omission constituting a substantial step in a course of conduct planned to culminate in his commission of the crime.

(2) Conduct That May Be Held Substantial Step Under Subsection (1)(c). Conduct shall not be held to constitute a substantial step under Subsection (1)(c) of this Section unless it is strongly corroborative of the actor's criminal purpose. Without negativing the sufficiency of other conduct, the following, if strongly corroborative of the actor's criminal purpose, shall not be held insufficient as a matter of law:

(a) lying in wait, searching for or following the contemplated victim of the

(b) enticing or seeking to entice the contemplated victim of the crime to go to the place contemplated for its commission;

(c) reconnoitering the place contemplated for the commission of the crime;

(d) unlawful entry of a structure, vehicle or enclosure in which it is contemplated that the crime will be committed;

(e) possession of materials to be employed in the commission of the crime, that are specially designed for such unlawful use or that can serve no lawful purpose of the actor under the circumstances;

(f) possession, collection or fabrication of materials to be employed in the commission of the crime, at or near the place contemplated for its commission, if such possession, collection or fabrication serves no lawful purpose of the actor under the circumstances;

(g) soliciting an innocent agent to engage in conduct constituting an element of the crime.

2. For attempts to commit certain offenses, the specific intent requirement may go beyond the specific intent to do the prohibited act. To convict of attempt to commit the federal crime of entering the United States after having been deported and without permission of the Attorney General, the government was required to show that not only did defendant Gracidas intend his attempted re-entry into the United States, it had to show that he also intended not to obtain permission of the Attorney General. United States v. Gracidas-Ulibarry, 231 F.3d 1188. (9th Cir. 2000) (en banc). "There is no general Federal statute proscribing . . . attempt." United States v. Rovetuso, 768 F.2d 809, 821 (7th Cir. 1985), *cert. denied*, 474 U.S. 1076, 106 S.Ct. 838, 88 L.Ed.2d 809 (1986). Thus, under federal law, one is liable for criminal attempt "only where . . . a specific criminal statute makes it impermissible to attempt to commit the crime." *Rovetuso*, 768 F.2d at 821. Federal statutes that specifically prohibit criminal attempt include: 18 U.S.C. § 115(b)(2)–(b)(3) (Influencing, Impeding or Retaliating Against a Federal Official); 18 U.S.C. § 246 (Deprivation of Relief Benefits); 18 U.S.C. § 472 (Uttering Counterfeit Obligations); 18 U.S.C. § 751 (Escape); 18 U.S.C. §§ 793–794 (Espionage); 18 U.S.C. § 844 (Explosives); 18 U.S.C. § 1113 (Murder or Manslaughter); 18 U.S.C. § 1341 (Mail Fraud); 18 U.S.C. § 1344 (Bank Fraud); 18 U.S.C. § 1512 (Tampering with a Witness); 18 U.S.C. § 1708 (Theft or Receipt of Stolen Mail Matter); 18 U.S.C. § 1951 (Interference with Commerce by Threats or Violence); 18 U.S.C. § 2113 (Bank Robbery and Incidental Crimes); and 21 U.S.C. § 846 (Controlled Substances).

3. In People v. Migliore, 170 Ill.App.3d 581, 121 Ill.Dec. 376, 525 N.E.2d 182 (1988) the defendant was convicted of attempted murder on a transferred intent theory, as a result of a drive-by shooting of what turned out not to be the intended victim's house. Migliore had intended to shoot at the home of Bill Knight, against whom he had a grudge, but had mistakenly shot at the home of Dominic Iasparro, against whom Migliore had no grudge. The pattern of the shots indicated to the satisfaction of the jury that Migliore had intended to shoot the person in the house, who he had thought was Knight. Affirming the conviction, the appellate court emphasized that mistaken identity or bad aim could not negate a conviction for attempted murder where the evidence clearly demonstrated both an intent to kill a human being and a substantial, though ineffectual, step toward the killing. Animus against a particular victim is not an element of attempt.

4. In People v. Frysig, 628 P.2d 1004 (Colo. 1981), the court had to interpret the effect upon the elements of the crime of attempt of the legislative change of 1977, which deleted "intentionally" from the criminal attempt statute. Did this mean that the legislature wished to eliminate the requirement that any type of intent accompany the substantial step? The court did not think so:

> One purpose of the general revision was to change certain crimes from specific intent crimes to general intent crimes so that intoxication could not be used to negate the existence of the intent which is an element of the crime charged. . . . We are persuaded that the legislature amended the criminal attempt statute for such

a purpose but did not intend thereby to depart from the tradition of the criminal law in Colorado and elsewhere that an essential element of criminal attempt is the intent "to do an act or to bring about certain consequences which would in law amount to a crime."

However, in 1985, the court rejected a reading of *Frysig* that would require proof of specific intent in a prosecution for attempted aggravated robbery. "[C]ulpability for criminal attempt rests primarily upon the actor's purpose to cause harmful consequences." People v. Krovarz, 697 P.2d 378 (Colo. 1985) (holding that proof of the culpable mental state of "knowledge" was sufficient for an attempt conviction).

State v. Hemmer

Court of Appeals of Nebraska, 1995.
3 Neb. App. 769, 531 N.W.2d 559.

■ IRWIN, JUDGE.

In this case we determine whether the crime of attempted reckless assault on an officer in the second degree exists under the laws of this state. Defendant, Terry L. Hemmer, was charged with such crime in the district court for Pierce County and pled no contest to the charge . . . . We find that the crime of attempted reckless assault on an officer in the second degree does not exist in this state, and we, therefore, reverse Hemmer's conviction.

FACTUAL BACKGROUND

The factual background for this case is taken from the factual basis for Hemmer's plea, which was supplied by the Deputy Pierce County Attorney during the district court proceedings. According to the factual basis, on January 15, 1994, a Platte County sheriff's deputy attempted to stop Hemmer for a speeding violation. When Hemmer would not stop, a high-speed chase ensued. The chase continued from Platte County through Madison County and into Pierce County, at which time there were 8 to 10 law enforcement officers from four different law enforcement agencies involved in the chase.

During the chase, Hemmer ran two roadblocks set up by police. One roadblock had been set up by the Pierce County sheriff in the town of Osmond. As Hemmer's vehicle was being chased through Osmond by a State Patrol trooper, the sheriff parked his vehicle in the middle of a street in the path of the pursuit and exited the vehicle. The sheriff then attempted to "flag the Hemmer vehicle down" as it approached, but when Hemmer's vehicle did not stop, the sheriff was forced to "dive into a snowbank" to avoid being struck. Hemmer was later apprehended in a rural area after his vehicle ran out of gas.

On March 2, 1994, Hemmer was charged with several crimes relating to the incident, including attempted assault on an officer in the second degree. With regard to this charge, the information alleged that

Hemmer attempted to " *intentionally or recklessly* cause bodily injury with a dangerous instrument to a peace officer." (Emphasis supplied.) On March 22, Hemmer filed a motion to quash the attempted assault charge, alleging that it is "legally impossible to commit the crime of attempting to recklessly cause bodily injury with a dangerous instrument to a peace officer."

Subsequently, a plea agreement was reached under which the information was amended to charge only one crime, attempt to "*recklessly* cause bodily injury . . . to a peace officer." (Emphasis supplied.) The plea agreement called for Hemmer to plead guilty to this charge. The court accepted Hemmer's plea and found him guilty as charged in the amended information. The court subsequently sentenced Hemmer to 9 months' imprisonment and ordered him to pay court costs. Hemmer thereafter timely appealed to this court.

* * *

DISCUSSION

* * *

Criminal attempt is defined by § 28–201 as follows:

(1) A person shall be guilty of an attempt to commit a crime if he:

(a) Intentionally engages in conduct which would constitute the crime if the attendant circumstances were as he believes them to be; or

(b) Intentionally engages in conduct which, under the circumstances as he believes them to be, constitutes a substantial step in a course of conduct intended to culminate in his commission of the crime.

(2) When causing a particular result is an element of the crime, a person shall be guilty of an attempt to commit the crime if, acting with the state of mind required to establish liability with respect to the attendant circumstances specified in the definition of the crime, he intentionally engages in conduct which is a substantial step in a course of conduct intended or known to cause such a result.

Assault on an officer in the second degree is defined in § 28–930 as follows:

(1) A person commits the offense of assault on an officer in the second degree if he or she:

(a) Intentionally or knowingly causes bodily injury with a dangerous instrument to a peace officer or employee of the Department of Correctional Services while such officer or employee is engaged in the performance of his or her official duties; or

(b) Recklessly causes bodily injury with a dangerous instrument to a peace officer or employee of the Department of Correctional Services while such officer or employee is engaged in the performance of his or her official duties.

(2) Assault on an officer in the second degree shall be a Class III felony.

Under the amended information, Hemmer was charged only with attempt to "recklessly cause bodily injury with a dangerous instrument to a peace officer." See § 28–930(1)(b).

Hemmer claims that it is legally impossible to commit a crime of attempt to recklessly cause bodily injury because the attempt statute requires that the actor intentionally attempt to commit the underlying crime. Before addressing this argument, we find it necessary to clarify the levels of culpability that are involved in the two statutes at issue in this case.

The attempt statute mentions two levels of culpability, "intentional" and "knowing." See § 28–201(1) and (2). The crime of assault on a peace officer in the second degree has three potential levels of culpability: intentional, § 28–930(1)(a); knowing, § 28–930(1)(a); and reckless, § 28–930(1)(b). However, the information only charged Hemmer with attempted "reckless" assault on an officer in the second degree.

* * *

. . . The criminal code defines "recklessly" nearly the same as it is defined by the Model Penal Code:

Recklessly shall mean acting with respect to a material element of an offense when any person disregards a substantial and unjustifiable risk that the material element exists or will result from his or her conduct. The risk must be of such a nature and degree that, considering the nature and purpose of the actor's conduct and the circumstances known to the actor, its disregard involves a gross deviation from the standard of conduct that a law-abiding person would observe in the actor's situation.

Neb.Rev.Stat. § 28–109(19) (Cum.Supp.1994). *See* Model Penal Code § 2.02(2)(c) (1985).

In *State v. Sodders,* 208 Neb. 504, 304 N.W.2d 62 (1981), the Nebraska Supreme Court discussed the attempt statute and the requisite mental states that accompany § 28–201(1)(a), (1)(b), and (2). In its discussion, the court indicated that where a particular result is an element of the underlying crime, subsections (1)(a) and (b) of the attempt statute require that the actor intended the result, i.e., an intentional *mens rea.* The court then stated:

Subsection (2) of § 28–201 . . . as applied to the defendant in this case, . . . adds nothing to subsections (1)(a) and (b). It simply restates that if one purposefully and with ... premeditated malice intends to kill another and engages in conduct which constitutes a substantial step in a course of conduct *intending to cause such death,* the actor is guilty of attempted murder in the first degree. It does appear to cover an additional situation not applicable here: where the actor *does not intend to cause the specific result* but engages in conduct which is *known* by him in the natural progression of events to cause such result . . . .

Sodders, 208 Neb. at 507–08, 304 N.W.2d at 65.

The above discussion indicates that where a particular result is an element of the underlying crime, § 28–201(1)(a) and b) requires that the actor intend such result for a conviction of criminal attempt. In other words, it must be the actor's conscious object to cause such result. Under § 28–201(2), however, the actor can be convicted of criminal attempt if he *knows* that his conduct will produce the result. In other words, the actor can be convicted of attempt if he is aware of the high probability that such result will occur, even if he does not intend such result.

The underlying crime, as charged in this case, does not contain an intentional or a knowing state of mind as an element, as is required by § 28–201. As charged in the amended information, the crime is not an intentional or knowing one, but, rather, a reckless one. As the Supreme Court stated in *Sodders,* the attempt statute only applies to crimes committed knowingly or intentionally. The attempt statute thus does not apply to a crime such as an attempt to *recklessly* cause bodily injury to a peace officer because the *mens rea* of "reckless" does not rise to the level of "knowing" or "intentional" as required by the attempt statute. This result reflects the position taken by the Model Penal Code.

The comment to § 5.01 of the Model Penal Code discusses the issue of whether the law of attempt should be applied to cases where the underlying crime contains a reckless *mens rea* and has a result as an element:

> Cases will arise where the defendant engaged in conduct that recklessly or negligently created a risk of death, but where the death did not result. Should the law of attempts encompass such cases?

The approach of the Model Code is not to treat such behavior as an attempt . . . The [American Law] Institute's judgment was that the scope of the criminal law would be unduly extended if one could be liable for an attempt whenever he recklessly or negligently created a risk of any result whose actual occurrence would lead to criminal responsibility . . . .

A majority of other jurisdictions addressing this issue has also held that one cannot commit the crime of attempt where the underlying crime contains only a reckless *mens rea.* See, e.g., *People v. Foy,* 155 Misc.2d

81, 587 N.Y.S.2d 111 (1992); *Minshew v. State,* 594 So.2d 703 (Ala.Crim.App.1991); *State v. Dunbar,* 117 Wash.2d 587, 817 P.2d 1360 (1991) (en banc); *Wells v. State,* 555 N.E.2d 1366 (Ind.App.1990); *People v. Coleman,* 131 Ill.App.3d 76, 86 Ill.Dec. 351, 475 N.E.2d 565 (1985); *State v. Zupetz,* 322 N.W.2d 730 (Minn.1982); *State v. Smith,* 21 Or.App. 270, 534 P.2d 1180 (1975); *State v. Melvin,* 49 Wis.2d 246, 181 N.W.2d 490 (1970). Cf. *State v. Tagaro,* 7 Haw.App. 291, 757 P.2d 1175 (1987). But, see, *People v. Thomas,* 729 P.2d 972 (Colo.1986) (en banc); *Gentry v. State,* 437 So.2d 1097 (Fla.1983).

After reviewing the above authority, we conclude that there is no crime in the State of Nebraska for attempted *reckless* assault on a peace officer in the second degree. We note, however, that our decision in no way affects the validity of the crimes of attempted *intentional* or *knowing* assault on a peace officer in the second degree. See § 28–930(1)(a).

CONCLUSION

The crime of attempted reckless assault on a peace officer in the second degree is not a crime under the statutes and case law of Nebraska. Hemmer, therefore, correctly asserts that the amended information was insufficient to charge a crime, and accordingly, we reverse his conviction.

REVERSED.

NOTES: WHAT MAY BE ATTEMPTED?

1. In Charlton v. Wainwright, 588 F.2d 162 (5th Cir. 1979) Karle Charlton, the bouncer at Big Daddy's Lounge in Naples, Florida, tried to eject an intoxicated patron from the bar. In the struggle, the patron fell down a flight of stairs and suffered head injuries, dying several days later. At trial the judge instructed on murder, manslaughter and attempt, and Charlton was found guilty of attempted (negligent) manslaughter. Charlton challenged his conviction in post-conviction proceedings, arguing that "attempted manslaughter by culpable negligence" is a logical absurdity, requiring the specific intent to commit a negligent (involuntary) act. The Fifth Circuit upheld his conviction, but the Florida courts later repudiated the existence of the crime of "attempted manslaughter by culpable negligence." Reid v. State, 656 So.2d 191 (Fla.App. 1995), *review denied,* 663 So.2d 632 (Fla. 1995) (unpublished table decision).

2. In State v. Holbron, 904 P.2d 912, 921 (1995), the Supreme Court of Hawai'i explained that "[o]ur research efforts have failed to discover a single jurisdiction that has recognized the possibility of attempted involuntary manslaughter. On the other hand, the cases holding that attempted involuntary manslaughter is a statutory impossibility are legion." The second part of the court's statement is correct, although the first part is not. The State of Colorado has recognized the crime of attempted reckless manslaughter for decades. For an analysis of the Colorado law and the bigger picture, see Michael T. Cahill, *Attempt, Reckless Homicide, and the Design of Criminal Law*, 78 U. COLO. L. REV. 879 (2007).

3. As Notes 1 and 2 indicate, many courts have held that there cannot be a crime of attempted involuntary manslaughter. Does that rule apply to other homicide crimes? Is it possible to commit the following crimes?

  a. Attempted Depraved Heart Murder?

  b. Attempted Felony Murder?

  c. Attempted Voluntary Manslaughter?

4. The nonexistence of attempt for crimes with a negligence *mens rea* can create certain anomalies, as described in Timothy P. O'Neill, *"With Malice Toward None: A Solution to an Illinois Homicide Quandary,"* 32 DEPAUL L. REV. 107, 107–08 (1982):

> The scene is a tavern in Chicago on a sultry evening in June, 1981. Two friends, Kane and Abel, begin to argue. Suddenly, the argument erupts into a physical altercation. After ten minutes of intense fighting, Kane strangles Abel, breaking the latter's neck. Soon thereafter, the police arrive and arrest Kane. Abel is rushed to the hospital and placed in intensive care. After he is booked, Kane calls his lawyer. Kane voices his concern about the possibility of being charged with murder since he definitely intended to kill Abel. His lawyer responds: Don't worry about murder. There is no question that your actions were performed under a sudden and intense passion resulting from serious provocation. Such an action constitutes [second degree murder], which is a Class [1] felony in Illinois. If you are convicted, the worst you can get is [15] years. . . . Moreover, because you have no prior criminal record, there is a possibility you could even be given probation.' An hour later, Kane's lawyer comes to visit him.
>
> "I'm afraid I have some bad news."
>
> "You mean Abel died?"
>
> "No, the bad news is that Abel did not die."
>
> "I don't understand."
>
> "If he had died, there is no question that you would have been charged with [second degree murder]. He's alive, however and there is no such crime as attempt [second degree (negligent) murder] You admitted you tried to kill Abel and that is attempt [first degree] murder, a Class X felony punishable by up to thirty years in the penitentiary. Moreover, because it is a Class X crime, there is no possibility of probation. Frankly, you made a terrible mistake by not making sure that you actually killed Abel."

Should there be such an offense as attempted reckless or negligent homicide? Is there any other way to resolve the "Kane vs. Abel" anomaly?

———

3.   THE *ACTUS REUS* OF ATTEMPT

Mere intent to commit a particular crime does not constitute an indictable offense. In addition to *mens rea*, all states require some act in furtherance of the intended crime—an *actus reus*—before a defendant can be convicted of attempting a crime. The general rule is that the actor has to go beyond "mere preparation" or, in other words, that the action taken must constitute a "substantial step" toward the commission of the offense. Proximity to the completed crime is not necessarily dispositive in determining whether an attempt has occurred; it is sufficient that the actor has taken any act which "shows the firmness of the accused's criminal intent,"[1] or which is strongly corroborative of his or her criminal purpose.[2] This was not always the general rule. For decades, courts struggled with the proper test to determine whether the *actus reus* of attempt had been satisfied.

People v. Rizzo

Court of Appeals of New York, 1927.
246 N.Y. 334, 158 N.E. 888.

■ CRANE, J.

The police of the city of New York did excellent work in this case by preventing the commission of a serious crime. It is a great satisfaction to realize that we have such wide-awake guardians of our peace. Whether or not the steps which the defendant had taken up to the time of his arrest amounted to the commission of a crime, as defined by our law, is, however, another matter. He has been convicted of an attempt to commit the crime of robbery in the first degree, and sentenced to state's prison. There is no doubt that he had the intention to commit robbery, if he got the chance. An examination, however, of the facts is necessary to determine whether his acts were in preparation to commit the crime if the opportunity offered, or constituted a crime in itself, known to our law as an attempt to commit robbery in the first degree. Charles Rizzo, the defendant, appellant, with three others, Anthony J. Dorio, Thomas Milo, and John Thomasello, on January 14th planned to rob one Charles Rao of a pay roll valued at about $1,200 which he was to carry from the bank for the United Lathing Company. These defendants, two of whom had firearms, started out in an automobile, looking for Rao or the man who had the pay roll on that day. Rizzo claimed to be able to identify the man, and was to point him out to the others, who were to do the actual holding up. The four rode about in their car looking for Rao. They went to the bank from which he was supposed to get the money and to various buildings being constructed by the United Lathing Company. At last they

---

[1]   Commonwealth v. Burton, 16 Pa. D. & C.3d 90, 1980 WL 575 (1980).

[2]   American Law Institute, Model Penal Code § 5.01(2). What conduct amounts to an overt act or acts done toward commission of larceny so as to sustain charge of attempt to commit larceny? *See* 76 A.L.R. 3d 842. What constitutes attempted murder. *See* 54 A.L.R. 3d 612.

came to One Hundred and Eightieth street and Morris Park avenue. By this time they were watched and followed by two police officers. As Rizzo jumped out of the car and ran into the building, all four were arrested. The defendant was taken out from the building in which he was hiding. Neither Rao nor a man named Previti, who was also supposed to carry a pay roll, were at the place at the time of the arrest. The defendants had not found or seen the man they intended to rob. No person with a pay roll was at any of the places where they had stopped, and no one had been pointed out or identified by Rizzo. The four men intended to rob the pay roll man, whoever he was. They were looking for him, but they had not seen or discovered him up to the time they were arrested.

Does this constitute the crime of an attempt to commit robbery in the first degree? The Penal Law, § 2, prescribes:

> "An act, done with intent to commit a crime, and tending but failing to effect its commission, is 'an attempt to commit that crime.'"

The word 'tending' is very indefinite. It is perfectly evident that there will arise differences of opinion as to whether an act in a given case is one *tending* to commit a crime. 'Tending' means to exert activity in a particular direction. Any act in preparation to commit a crime may be said to have a tendency towards its accomplishment. The procuring of the automobile, searching the streets looking for the desired victim, were in reality acts tending toward the commission of the proposed crime. The law, however, had recognized that many acts in the way of preparation are too remote to constitute the crime of attempt. The line has been drawn between those acts which are remote and those which are proximate and near to the consummation. The law must be practical, and therefore considers those acts only as tending to the commission of the crime which are so near to its accomplishment that in all reasonable probability the crime itself would have been committed, but for timely interference. The cases which have been before the courts express this idea in different language, but the idea remains the same. The act or acts must come or advance very near to the accomplishment of the intended crime. In People v. Mills, 178 N. Y. 274, 284, 70 N. E. 786, 789 (67 L. R. A. 131), it was said:

> Felonious intent alone is not enough, but there must be an overt act shown in order to establish even an attempt. An overt act is one done to carry out the intention, and it must be such as would naturally effect that result, unless prevented by some extraneous cause.'

In Hyde v. U. S., 225 U. S. 347, 32 S. Ct. 793, 56 L. Ed. 1114, it was stated that the act amounts to an attempt when it is so near to the result that the danger of success is very great. 'There must be dangerous proximity to success.' . . .

Commonwealth v. Peaslee, 177 Mass. 267, 59 N. E. 55, refers to the acts constituting an attempt as coming *very near* to the accomplishment of the crime.

* * *

How shall we apply this rule of immediate nearness to this case? The defendants were looking for the pay roll man to rob him of his money . . . To constitute the crime of robbery, the money must have been taken from Rao by means of force or violence, or through fear. The crime of attempt to commit robbery was committed, if these defendants did an act tending to the commission of this robbery. Did the acts above described come dangerously near to the taking of Rao's property? Did the acts come so near the commission of robbery that there was reasonable likelihood of its accomplishment but for the interference? Rao was not found; the defendants were still looking for him; no attempt to rob him could be made, at least until he came in sight; he was not in the building at One Hundred and Eightieth street and Morris Park avenue. There was no man there with the pay roll for the United Lathing Company whom these defendants could rob. Apparently no money had been drawn from the bank for the pay roll by anybody at the time of the arrest. In a word, these defendants had planned to commit a crime, and were looking around the city for an opportunity to commit it, but the opportunity fortunately never came. Men would not be guilty of an attempt at burglary if they had planned to break into a building and were arrested while they were hunting about the streets for the building not knowing where it was. Neither would a man be guilty of an attempt to commit murder if he armed himself and started out to find the person whom he had planned to kill but could not find him. So here these defendants were not guilty of an attempt to commit robbery in the first degree when they had not found or reached the presence of the person they intended to rob.

For these reasons, the judgment of conviction of this defendant appellant must be reversed and a new trial granted.

* * *

———

NOTES: THE DIFFICULTY OF DEFINING ATTEMPT

1. Should an attempt conviction turn on whether the defendant is in "dangerous proximity" to completing the crime? What are the benefits and detriments of such a rule?

2. Do you think Rizzo would have gone forward with the robbery if he had encountered Rao or Previti? Is it possible that Rizzo would have backed down from his plan? Does the *Rizzo* decision establish a "chickening out zone" that prevents us from wrongfully convicting defendants who would not have gone through with the crime? *See* Robert Batey, *Minority Report and the Law of Criminal Attempt*, 1 OHIO ST. J. CRIM. L. 689, 695 (2004).

3. In October 2012, police officers arrested one of their colleagues—Officer Gilberto Valle—after they "uncovered several plots to kidnap, rape, cook and eat women." The evidence against Officer Valle consisted of emails and instant messages to other individuals in which he discussed "plans to kidnap, rape, torture, kill, cook and eat body parts of a number of women." A search of Officer Valle's computer found "files pertaining to at least 100 women" including some of his high school classmates. Prosecutors charged Officer Valle with conspiracy, but not attempted murder, kidnapping, or rape. *See* Joseph Goldstein, *Officer Held in Plot to Cook Women and Eat Them*, N.Y. TIMES, Oct. 25, 2012, A26. Would it be possible to charge Officer Valle under the dangerous proximity test?

4. If you do not like the dangerous proximity test that the court formulated in *Rizzo*, can you draft a clearer test? Some state legislatures have either been unable to do so or unwilling to try. For instance, as of the turn of the century, the criminal codes in West Virginia, North Carolina, Rhode Island, Maryland, and New Mexico either did not define attempt or provided "that any act toward the commission of a crime constitutes an attempt." Paul H. Robinson et al., *The Five Worst (and Five Best) American Criminal Codes*, 95 NW. U. L. REV. 1, 47–48 (2000) (internal quotation marks omitted). If you were a legislator, how would you define the difference between the crime of attempt and mere preparation that is not criminal?

United States v. Joyce

United States Court of Appeals for the Eighth Circuit, 1982.
693 F.2d 838.

■ FLOYD R. GIBSON, SENIOR CIRCUIT JUDGE.

Michael Dennis Joyce was convicted after a jury trial on one count of attempting to possess cocaine with the intent to distribute in violation of 21 U.S.C. §§ 841(a)(1) and 846 (1976) (Count I), and one count of traveling in interstate commerce to facilitate an unlawful activity in violation of 18 U.S.C. § 1952 (1976) (Count II). The trial court sentenced Joyce to a term of ten years imprisonment on Count I and a term of five years probation on Count II, to be served consecutively. A timely appeal was filed. Though Joyce raises several issues on appeal, we are primarily concerned here with his claim that the evidence presented at trial was insufficient to sustain his conviction. For the reasons set forth herein, we reverse Joyce's conviction on each count.

I.

The facts as presented to the jury in this case are undisputed and based entirely upon the uncontradicted testimony of the government's only two witnesses: Robert Jones, a St. Louis police officer assigned to the Drug Enforcement Administration Task Force, and James Gebbie, a government informant.

During 1980, the St. Louis Metropolitan Police Department conducted what has been termed a "reverse sting operation," in which undercover police officers posed as drug sellers actively soliciting major drug transactions with reputed drug dealers. As part of that operation, government informant James Gebbie, who testified to having prior drug dealings with Joyce, contacted Joyce by telephone in September and early October, 1980, to inform Joyce about the prospective availability of drugs for purchase in St. Louis. Joyce told Gebbie to call back when Gebbie found out more definite information.

On October 20, 1980 Gebbie again called Joyce, this time informing Joyce that cocaine was available for purchase in St. Louis. Joyce indicated that he had twenty-two thousand dollars and would be in St. Louis the following day, October 21, 1980. Gebbie and Joyce agreed that twenty-two thousand dollars would be more than sufficient to purchase a pound of cocaine.

On October 21, 1980, Joyce flew from Oklahoma City, Oklahoma to St. Louis, Missouri, where he met Gebbie and undercover officer Robert Jones, who was posing as a cocaine seller. Jones and Gebbie took Joyce to a room in a local St. Louis hotel, where Joyce immediately asked to see the cocaine. Jones told Joyce that the cocaine was not in the hotel room, but could be easily obtained by Jones if Joyce was interested in dealing rather than merely talking. After Joyce professed his interest in dealing, Jones recited prices for various quantities of cocaine and Joyce said that he could "handle" a pound of cocaine for twenty thousand dollars. Officer Jones then went to his office and obtained the cocaine.

When Officer Jones returned to the hotel room, he handed Joyce a duct-tape wrapped plastic package said to contain a kilogram of cocaine. Without unwrapping the tape, Joyce immediately returned the package, stating that he could not see the cocaine. Jones then unwrapped about half of the tape covering the plastic package and handed the package back to Joyce. Joyce again returned the package to Jones and asked Jones to open up the package so that Joyce could examine the cocaine more closely. Jones answered that he would only open the plastic package if and when Joyce showed the money that he intended to use to purchase the cocaine. Joyce then replied that he would not produce his money until Jones first opened up the plastic package. After Jones persisted in asking Joyce to produce his money, Joyce again refused, stating that he would not deal with officer Jones no matter how good the cocaine was. Realizing that Joyce was not going to show his money or purchase the cocaine, Jones told Joyce to leave and Joyce left, with no apparent intention of returning at a later time to purchase any cocaine.

As Joyce left the hotel, he was arrested by DEA agents. A search warrant was thereafter obtained and used to search Joyce's luggage revealing twenty-two thousand dollars in cash.

II.

The issue before us is whether the evidence, taken in its entirety and viewed most favorably to the government, is sufficient to prove beyond a reasonable doubt that Joyce attempted to purchase cocaine with the intent to distribute. To resolve this issue we must determine whether Joyce's conduct crossed that shadowy line dividing acts of "mere preparation" to commit a crime and acts constituting an "attempt."

The government argues that Joyce's attempt to possess cocaine was established by evidence that he traveled from Oklahoma City to St. Louis with twenty-two thousand dollars pursuant to a previously discussed drug purchase arrangement, that he expressed an initial willingness to deal with Jones, and that he agreed with Jones on the price for a pound of cocaine. Furthermore, the government adds, Joyce would have purchased the cocaine had it not been for the disagreement between Joyce and Jones resulting from Jones' refusal to open the plastic bag containing the purported cocaine until Joyce first showed his money. The government points out that Jones was acting in compliance with DEA guidelines which prohibit illegal drugs from going into the physical possession of persons under investigation.

Joyce, on the other hand, contends that his conduct did not rise to the level of an attempt to possess cocaine because while he admittedly possessed sufficient money to purchase the cocaine at the agreed upon price, he ultimately refused either to purchase the cocaine or to produce his money. He thus had abandoned any designs he might have had of obtaining cocaine and distributing it before taking the necessary and overt steps of producing the money and obtaining the cocaine.

Although there is no comprehensive statutory definition of attempt in federal law, federal courts have rather uniformly adopted the standard set forth in Section 5.01 of the American Law Institute's Model Penal Code (Proposed Official Draft 1962)[2] that the requisite elements of attempt are (1) an intent to engage in criminal conduct, and (2) conduct constituting a "substantial step" towards the commission of the substantive offense which strongly corroborates the actor's criminal intent. While we adopt this standard here, we are also mindful of Judge Learned Hand's candid, yet poignant, observation that a verbal formulation aimed at dividing mere preparation from attempt is, in itself, not particularly useful. *United States v. Coplon,* 185 F.2d 629, 633 (2nd

---

[2]   The relevant portion of the Model Penal Code provides: Section 5.01. Criminal Attempt. *[handwritten: Model Penal Code]*

(1) Definition of Attempt. A person is guilty of an attempt to commit a crime if, acting with the kind of culpability otherwise required for commission of the crime, he: (a) purposely engages in conduct which would constitute the crime if the attendant circumstances were as he believes them to be; or (b) when causing a particular result is an element of the crime, does or omits to do anything with the purpose of causing or with the belief that it will cause such result without further conduct on his part; or (c) purposely does or omits to do anything which, under the circumstances as he believes them to be, is an act or omission constituting a substantial step in a course of conduct planned to culminate in his commission of the crime. (2) Conduct Which May Be Held Substantial Step Under Subsection (1)(c). Conduct shall not be held to constitute a substantial step under Subsection (1)(c) of this Section unless it is strongly corroborative of the actor's criminal purpose. . . . Model Penal Code (Proposed Official Draft 1962).

Cir.1950), *cert. denied,* 342 U.S. 920, 72 S.Ct. 362, 96 L.Ed. 688 (1952). Indeed, whether conduct represents a "substantial step" toward the commission of the criminal design is, in Justice Holmes' words, "a question of degree," necessarily depending on the factual circumstances peculiar to each case. *Commonwealth v. Peaslee,* 177 Mass. 267, 272, 59 N.E. 55, 56 (1901). However, as the Tenth Circuit analyzed in *United States v. Monholland,* 607 F.2d 1311, 1318 (10th Cir.1979):

> The cases universally hold that mere intention to commit a specified crime does not amount to an attempt. It is essential that the defendant, with the intent of committing the particular crime, do some overt act adapted to, approximating, and which in the ordinary and likely course of things will result in the commission of the particular crime.

With this in mind, we conclude that even assuming Joyce went to St. Louis intending to purchase cocaine, there was clearly insufficient evidence to establish that he engaged in conduct constituting a "substantial step" toward the commission of the crime of possession of cocaine with the intent to distribute. Whatever intention Joyce had to procure cocaine was abandoned prior to the commission of a necessary and substantial step to effectuate the purchase of cocaine. The attempt, of course, need not be successful, but generally the abortion of the attempt occurs because of events beyond the control of the attemptor . . . Here it is undisputed that Joyce, despite having both the opportunity and ability to purchase the cocaine at the agreed upon price, unambiguously refused either to produce his money or to purchase the cocaine. This effectively negated the government's effort to consummate the sale.

This case is comparable to the case of *People v. Miller,* 2 Cal.2d 527, 42 P.2d 308 (1935) where the defendant announced his intention to kill another, obtained a .22 caliber rifle, pursued his intended victim into an open field carrying the .22 caliber rifle, and after loading the rifle apparently changed his mind and voluntarily surrendered the rifle to a third person standing nearby. The Supreme Court of California concluded that the defendant's conduct did not rise to the level of an attempted murder. Similarly in *Wooldridge v. United States,* 237 F. 775 (9th Cir.1916), the defendant, pursuant to a previous arrangement, met a sixteen-year-old girl in a closed store, presumably intending to have intercourse with her. However, after receiving some advice from a friend who was at the store, the defendant decided not to carry through with his criminal intent and left the store without ever approaching the girl. The Ninth Circuit reversed the defendant's conviction for attempted rape, holding that while the defendant may have gone to the store with the intent of having intercourse with the girl, he never committed an overt act toward the commission of the intended crime. *Id.* at 779. Thus, in these two cases and in the instant case, the defendant had the opportunity and ability to commit the completed offense, yet refused to engage in conduct constituting a "substantial step" toward commission of the completed offense.

The government, however, urges that Joyce's initially expressed interest in purchasing a pound of cocaine from Jones at the stated price and his momentary possession of the wrapped package said to contain a kilogram of cocaine constituted a substantial step toward possession of cocaine with the intent to distribute. We disagree. While Joyce professed a desire to purchase cocaine during his preliminary discussions with Jones, Joyce never attempted to carry through with that desire by producing the money necessary to purchase and hence ultimately possess the cocaine. And, although Jones gave Joyce the sealed and wrapped package said to contain a kilogram of cocaine, Joyce did not open the package but immediately returned the package to Jones who in turn refused to open the package because Joyce refused to produce the money necessary to effectuate the purchase of a pound of cocaine. Thus, all we have here is a preliminary discussion regarding the purchase of cocaine which broke down before Joyce had committed any "overt act adapted to, approximating, and which in the ordinary and likely course of things [would] result in the commission of the [crime of possessing cocaine with the intent to distribute]" *Monholland,* 607 F.2d 1311, 1318 (10th Cir. 1979).[4]

We also find unpersuasive the government's claim that Joyce would have purchased the cocaine had it not been for Jones' refusal to open the package of cocaine. We simply fail to see why Joyce's motive for refusing to commit a "substantial step" toward possession of the cocaine is particularly relevant. Joyce's motive for refusing to purchase the cocaine here is no different than had he refused to purchase because he disagreed with Jones as to the price for which the cocaine was offered. And, while we may agree with the government's suggestion that Joyce, who was presumably "street-wise," may have been tipped off that Jones was a DEA undercover agent when Jones refused to open the package, we fail to see how an increased awareness of the risk of apprehension converts what would otherwise be "mere preparation" into an attempt.

Finally, the government makes the rather novel suggestion that because Joyce was only one act away from the completed offense of possession of cocaine with the intent to distribute, he must, therefore, be guilty of attempting to commit the completed offense. First, Joyce was two acts, not one act, away from the completed offense. Before Joyce could have committed the offense of possessing cocaine with the intent to distribute he had to first produce the money necessary to effect the

---

4   In *Monholland,* the Tenth Circuit considered whether a defendant's preliminary discussion with an undercover officer regarding the price at which the defendant could purchase dynamite similar to the sample held by the undercover officer constituted an attempt to receive in interstate commerce an explosive. The court concluded that defendant's preliminary discussion did not constitute an overt act aimed toward commission of the crime defendant was charged with attempting.

purchase of the cocaine and second take actual physical possession of, or exercise dominion and control over, the cocaine. He obviously could not distribute the cocaine before obtaining either actual or constructive possession of it. Nevertheless, whether conduct may be characterized as being one act or two acts away from the completed offense is not particularly helpful in determining if an attempt has been committed. For example, the defendant in *Miller* who while carrying a rifle pursued his intended victim into the open field was only one overt act away from committing the completed offense of murder; all he had left to do was shoot the intended victim. However, the defendant in *Miller,* as Joyce here, had not yet committed an overt act strongly corroborative of the firmness of his criminal purpose. Thus, in *Miller* and in this case the conduct which remained to be done, whether characterized as one act or two acts, was the very conduct which separated mere preparation from a substantial step toward commission of the completed offense.

* * *

Judgment reversed.

———

United States v. Yossunthorn

United States Court of Appeals for the Ninth Circuit, 1999.
167 F.3d 1267.

■ SCHWARZER, SENIOR CIRCUIT JUDGE:

Defendant Paiboon Mekvichitsang appeals his conviction for conspiracy and attempted possession with intent to distribute heroin. Defendant Sunthorn Yossunthorn appeals his conviction for attempted possession with intent to distribute drugs. In this opinion, we decide that the evidence was insufficient to support the convictions for attempted possession with intent to distribute heroin, and reverse these convictions . . . .

FACTS AND PROCEDURAL HISTORY

The essential facts are not in dispute. In 1992, 1993, and 1995, Zagar Kovittamakron and Throngboon Kulkovit made heroin deliveries both directly to Mekvichitsang and, at Mekvichitsang's direction, to Yossunthorn, whom Mekvichitsang described as "one of his workers." The heroin was sometimes fronted to Mekvichitsang and Yossunthorn, i.e., sold to them on credit. From 1992 to 1995, Mekvichitsang and Yossunthorn purchased quantities of heroin from Kovittamakron and Kulkovit ranging from four ounces to one pound. The price also varied: It was $2,700 per ounce in 1992, and $2,600 per ounce during most of 1995. Once during 1995, Mekvichitsang made only partial payment. On at least one occasion, Mekvichitsang returned heroin to Kulkovit, complaining about its poor quality.

On December 4, 1995, Kovittamakron told Mekvichitsang that he expected another heroin shipment. Mekvichitsang expressed interest in purchasing some of it. Later that day, Kovittamakron was arrested and he began cooperating with the government. Kovittamakron recorded a series of phone conversations with Mekvichitsang between December 5 and 7, 1995. On December 6, 1995, Kovittamakron called Mekvichitsang and told him that the heroin had arrived. Mekvichitsang suggested they meet at a McDonald's restaurant near his home at noon the following day to make arrangements for the heroin transaction.

Kovittamakron refused to meet with Mekvichitsang on December 7 as planned. Nevertheless, government agents conducted surveillance and saw Yossunthorn and Mekvichitsang act in ways consistent with conducting countersurveillance. Specifically, at approximately 11:45 a.m., government agents saw Yossunthorn standing in the McDonald's parking lot by his parked car, walking through the parking lot, and looking at cars and people that entered the lot. At about 12:15 p.m., government agents watched as Mekvichitsang drove slowly past the McDonald's, through an adjoining parking lot, and around the block, while looking at the McDonald's parking lot. Mekvichitsang left the area without ever entering the McDonald's lot. Mekvichitsang and Yossunthorn were arrested shortly thereafter.

Both Mekvichitsang and Yossunthorn were convicted of (1) conspiring to distribute and possess with intent to distribute heroin, in violation of 21 U.S.C. §§ 846 and 841(a)(1), during 1992–1995, and (2) attempting to possess with intent to distribute heroin, in violation of 21 U.S.C. § 841(a)(1), during December 5–7, 1995. Kovittamakron and Kulkovit testified for the government . . . .

* * *

DISCUSSION

* * *

III. DEFENDANTS' ATTEMPT CONVICTIONS

Both Mekvichitsang and Yossunthorn challenge the sufficiency of the evidence for their convictions of attempted possession with intent to distribute heroin . . . .

There is no question that there was sufficient evidence that Mekvichitsang intended to possess heroin with intent to distribute. Kovittamakron testified that on December 4–7, he and Mekvichitsang discussed Mekvichitsang's interest in purchasing heroin from Kovittamakron's latest shipment. This testimony was corroborated by recorded phone conversations and by Mekvichitsang's conduct driving around the McDonald's restaurant where Mekvichitsang and Kovittamakron had agreed to meet to discuss arrangements to complete the transaction.

The more critical issue is whether Mekvichitsang's conduct during the period of December 5–7 constituted a substantial step toward acquiring the heroin . . .

The government offers two theories to prove that Mekvichitsang's conduct constituted a substantial step. Neither suffices to uphold Mekvichitsang's attempt conviction.

A. *Countersurveillance*

The government initially argued that by sending Yossunthorn to the McDonald's parking lot and by driving by the McDonald's at the time he had prearranged with a heroin supplier, Mekvichitsang conducted countersurveillance designed to detect law enforcement activity. The government contended that such countersurveillance constituted a substantial step toward possession of heroin with intent to distribute. The government argued that Mekvichitsang drove away from the McDonald's without entering the parking lot because he detected the government agents and/or because he discovered that Kovittamakron had not shown up for the meeting.

Mekvichitsang's countersurveillance activity is similar to the reconnoitering by the defendants in *United States v. Buffington,* 815 F.2d 1292, 1295 (9th Cir.1987), where we found insufficient evidence of a substantial step toward bank robbery. In *Buffington,* the police observed the defendant twice drive slowly by a bank while staring into it, drive to the rear of the bank, enter a nearby store and walk to a window overlooking the bank, leave the store and join his two codefendants as they stood facing the bank. We held that the evidence of reconnoitering was insufficient to uphold the attempt convictions: "Not only did appellants not take a single step toward the bank, they displayed no weapons and no indication that they were about to make an entry. Standing alone, their conduct did not constitute that requisite 'appreciable fragment' of a bank robbery . . ." *Id.* at 1303. The *Buffington* court distinguished *United States v. Stallworth,* 543 F.2d 1038 (2d Cir.1976), where the defendant not only reconnoitered the bank he intended to rob but was armed, had stolen materials for disguises and had moved toward the bank.

* * *

Had Mekvichitsang intended to rob the McDonald's, under these authorities his countersurveillance activities, without more, would clearly be insufficient evidence of an attempt. A fortiori, Mekvichitsang's act of surveying the McDonald's not to rob it or even to take possession of drugs, but merely to ensure the security of an alleged meeting to make arrangements for some future drug purchase, did not constitute an "appreciable fragment" of the crime of drug possession with intent to distribute and, thus, is insufficient evidence of an attempt.

B. *Ordering Drugs from an Established Supplier*

At oral argument, the government argued that Mekvichitsang's substantial step took place before he went to the McDonald's. The government contended that because Mekvichitsang and Kovittamakron had an established relationship in which Kovittamakron fronted heroin to Mekvichitsang at a fixed price, Mekvichitsang's phone call to Kovittamakron ordering heroin constituted a substantial step. As a factual matter, the record does not reflect that Mekvichitsang and his suppliers had agreed on a price for the heroin. Even assuming an agreed price, however, we hold that Mekvichitsang's conduct was not a substantial step toward heroin possession when he ordered drugs from Kovittamakron.

The government's theory rests on the premise that all major elements of the drug transaction were accomplished and that Mekvichitsang's and Kovittamakron's scheduled McDonald's meeting was merely to arrange ministerial details. Yet the government concedes that Mekvichitsang and Kovittamakron had agreed neither on the quantity of heroin that Mekvichitsang would purchase nor on the delivery time and method.[5] Therefore, even assuming that Mekvichitsang and Kovittamakron had a prior agreement to a fixed price, and that the heroin would be fronted to Mekvichitsang by Kovittamakron, there were essential elements of the transaction yet to be arranged.

United States v. Smith, 962 F.2d 923 (9th Cir.1992), is instructive. In *Smith,* we found a substantial step toward possession with intent to distribute cocaine where the defendant arrived at a house where cocaine was picked up by the codefendants, drove off later in another car, and circled the parking lot of the restaurant where the cocaine deal was scheduled to take place before parking there with a shotgun in his lap to fill the role of " 'the heavy in the background.' " *Id.* at 926. In upholding the conviction, we stated that

> [Smith] did all that he could do to ensure the deal's completion. If the deal had been completed as planned, without any interference, Smith would not have been required to engage in any further acts. In fact, he committed all the steps necessary on his part to the completion of the substantive offense. Under those circumstances, a jury could certainly conclude that Smith's conduct went beyond mere preparation.

Id. at 930–31.

---

[5]   The government argues that because it need not prove any particular quantity of heroin for the substantive crime of possession with intent to distribute heroin, it need not show that quantity was established to prove attempt. This argument misses the point. The fewer elements of a drug transaction are agreed upon, the more remains to be done for the possession to be realized. Thus, the fact that the quantity has not been set between drug supplier and purchaser is relevant to ascertaining whether a substantial step (and thus attempted possession) occurred.

Similarly, the defendant cocaine purchaser in *United States v. Davis,* 960 F.2d 820 (9th Cir.1992), had gone beyond mere preparation. Davis entered into negotiations with an undercover DEA agent to purchase cocaine after price and quantity had been negotiated by a middleman, continued the negotiations, arranged for "his people" to deliver the money, and was on his way to pick up the cocaine when he was arrested. *See id.* at 823–24, 826.

In contrast to *Smith* and *Davis,* Mekvichitsang had not "committed all the steps necessary on his part to the completion of the substantive offense." *Smith,* 962 F.2d at 930–31. He merely initiated the transaction by indicating his desire to purchase heroin and scheduling a meeting with Kovittamakron to negotiate a deal. When key elements of the drug deal are incomplete, making an appointment with a known drug supplier, even one who has previously fronted drugs to the defendant at a fixed price, is analogous to the situation in *Harper:* "Making an appointment . . . is not of itself such a commitment to an intended crime as to constitute an attempt, even though it may make a later attempt possible." United v. Harper, 33 F.3d 1143, 1148 (9th Cir. 1994).

* * *

CONCLUSION

The convictions and sentences for attempt are REVERSED . . . .

———

NOTES

1. The courts' decisions in *Joyce* and *Yossunthorn* do an effective job stating the Model Penal Code's substantial step test for attempt. Many states have adopted the substantial step test as their test for attempt; however, courts often look to other tests in an effort to determine if an attempt occurred. *See* Ira P. Robbins, *Double Inchoate Crimes,* 26 HARV. J. ON LEGIS. 1, 107–08 (1989) ("The term 'substantial step' alone adds little precision to an attempt definition. Courts in states that have adopted the substantial-step language often continue to rely on pre-existing common-law formulations of proximity."). Is it possible to formulate a coherent test that differentiates preparation from perpetration?

2. Do *Joyce* and *Yossunthorn* apply the substantial step test correctly to the facts of those cases? In other words, do the courts reach the correct outcome in either or both decisions?

3. In United States v. Harper, 33 F.3d 1143 (9th Cir. 1994), Trina Devay Harper, Aziz Sharrieff, and Carlos Muñoz were arrested in the parking lot of the Home Savings Bank shortly after 10:00 p.m. on the evening of September 21, 1992, while sitting in a rented car. Police seized two loaded handguns, a roll of duct tape, a stun gun, two pairs of latex surgical gloves, six rounds of .357 magnum ammunition and an automated teller machine ("ATM") card, which bore the name of Kimberly Ellis. Harper had used the

Ellis card about an hour earlier in an ATM at a bank next door to the Home Savings parking lot. Harper had requested a twenty dollar withdrawal from the ATM, but had not removed the cash from the cash drawer, creating a "bill trap." The bill trap caused the ATM to shut down and prompted the service technicians to come and repair the ATM. Harper knew about the "bill trap" trick because she had previously worked for both Bank of America and one of its ATM service companies. Harper, Sharrieff, and Muñoz were convicted of conspiracy to rob a federally insured bank, attempted bank robbery, and carrying a firearm during and in relation to a crime of violence, based on the apparent plan to take the ATM money by force when the technician showed up. On appeal, the Ninth Circuit affirmed the firearms and conspiracy charges, but reversed the attempt conviction, saying,

> To obtain a conviction for attempted bank robbery the prosecution must prove (1) culpable intent and (2) conduct constituting a substantial step toward the commission of the crime. . . . ; United States v. Buffington, 815 F.2d 1292, 1301 (9th Cir.1987). Here, there was sufficient evidence to permit a jury to find that the defendants intended to rob the Bank of America. We conclude, however, that under the law of this circuit there was insufficient evidence that the defendants took a substantial step toward commission of the robbery.

4. Under other statutes, the acts of the *Harper* and *Rizzo* defendants would have been more than sufficient to sustain an attempt conviction. *See, e.g.,* Fla. St. Ann. § 777.04. Attempts, solicitation, and conspiracy:

> (1) A person who attempts to commit an offense prohibited by law and in such attempt does any act toward the commission of such offense, but fails in the perpetration or is intercepted or prevented in the execution thereof, commits the offense of criminal attempt. . . .

Kolmeier v. State

Court of Appeals of Georgia, 2008.
289 Ga. App. 709, 658 S.E.2d 261.

■ PHIPPS, JUDGE.

After a traffic stop, Nicholas A. Kohlmeier and his two passengers were arrested; the vehicle was searched; and the three were charged with drug crimes. Kohlmeier appeals his conviction for criminal attempt to manufacture methamphetamine . . . We discern no error and affirm.

Kohlmeier contends that the evidence did not authorize the guilty verdict on the count of criminal attempt to manufacture methamphetamine. "A person commits the offense of criminal attempt when, with intent to commit a specific crime, he performs any act which constitutes a substantial step toward the commission of that crime." An act constituting a "substantial step" is one

[handwritten margin note: Affirmed conviction]

done in pursuance of the intent, and more or less directly tending to the commission of the crime. In general, the act must be inexplicable as a lawful act, and must be more than mere preparation. Yet it can not accurately be said that no preparations can amount to an attempt. It is a question of degree, and depends upon the circumstances of each case. The phrase "inexplicable as a lawful act" does not mean that the act itself must be unlawful. Rather, it means that the act, in light of previous acts, constitutes a substantial step toward the commission of a crime . . . [T]he "substantial step" requirement is intended to (1) ensure firmness of the defendant's criminal intent, (2) insulate from liability "very remote preparatory acts," and (3) allow for apprehension of offenders at an early stage without providing immunity for their actions.[3]

The indictment alleged that Kohlmeier committed criminal attempt to manufacture methamphetamine by performing "an act constituting a substantial step toward the commission of said offense in that [he] did possess methanol, pseudoephedrine, a cookstove and approximately 1000 books of matches containing red phosphorus, essential elements in the manufacture of methamphetamine."

* * *

. . . [T]he evidence showed that on the night of January 31, 2006, a county sheriff's department issued to its officers a BOLO ("be on the lookout") for a certain truck based upon a report from a local merchant, the Food Lion, that two of its customers had left in that truck after purchasing a large quantity of matches. The sheriff's department had requested area merchants to alert it of such a purchase, which the department considered an indication of possible impending methamphetamine manufacturing.

A patrol officer spotted at a Citgo gas station a truck that matched the description in the BOLO. The officer testified that, after the truck passed his patrol car as it left the Citgo parking lot, he "saw that the vehicle . . . didn't have a working tag light on the vehicle and it was dark, which is a violation of Georgia law," and he therefore "turned around and stopped the vehicle." Kohlmeier was the driver, and the male and female passengers matched the descriptions in the BOLO of the two recent purchasers of matches.

A K-9 unit arrived to assist in the traffic stop. As the patrol officer was checking Kohlmeier's driving license, the drug dog alerted at the driver's door seam. Kohlmeier and the passengers stepped out of the truck at the officers' request. The search of the truck yielded a box of cold medicine containing pseudoephedrine, two full bottles of HEET brand

---

[3]   *Dennard v. State,* 243 Ga.App. 868, 871–872, 534 S.E.2d 182 (2000).

fuel treatment, a Coleman camping stove, and a can of kerosene. According to the patrol officer, the type of stove found could be used to make methamphetamine and kerosene could be used to fuel that type of stove. No matches were found at the scene, however.

Another officer, a former narcotics agent with special training regarding the clandestine manufacturing of methamphetamine, was summoned to the scene for his opinion of whether Food Lion's report, coupled with what had been discovered at the traffic stop scene, showed involvement in the manufacture of methamphetamine. He testified that two of the three main ingredients required for manufacturing the drug had been recovered: pseudoephedrine and red phosphorus, the latter being contained in the striker plates of the matchbooks. The officer further testified that HEET was essentially methanol and often used in making the drug to extract the red phosphorus from the striker plates and also to separate the pseudoephedrine out of certain types of cold medicines, including the type found in the truck. Noting the stove, the officer explained that a heat source was required to make methamphetamine. The former narcotics agent suspected impending manufacturing of methamphetamine.

Kohlmeier was handcuffed, placed in the back of a patrol car with his male passenger, and read his *Miranda* rights. Meanwhile, one of the officers returned to the scene with a shopping bag of boxes containing about 5,000 matchbooks, which he had found on the road leading back to the Citgo, the route Kohlmeier had just traveled. A device in the patrol car with Kohlmeier recorded Kohlmeier stating to his male passenger that a store likely had "ratted" about the matchbook purchases. Kohlmeier's female passenger was also arrested and then placed in a separate patrol car. Receipts found in her possession showed recent purchases at Food Lion and a CVS store.

At trial, the former narcotics agent further explained that those involved in the clandestine manufacture of methamphetamine commonly gather the required ingredients and materials surreptitiously to avoid arousing suspicion. To that end, the necessary items generally are not obtained within a single purchase; rather, they are accumulated piecemeal.

In connection with the underlying incident, Kohlmeier's female passenger entered a negotiated guilty plea and then testified as a state witness as follows. She, Kohlmeier, and the male passenger had been friends for years. On several occasions before, the three of them had made and used methamphetamine. On the day in question, Kohlmeier and the male passenger had plans to make a small amount of the drug in a certain wooded area, where they previously had done so using the stove found on Kohlmeier's truck. When stopped by the patrol officer, the three of them were accumulating various items they needed to manufacture methamphetamine. She had purchased the cold medicine from CVS, two boxes of matches from Food Lion, and kerosene from Citgo. The male passenger had purchased three additional boxes of matches from Food Lion. And Kohlmeier had gone into a Fred's store and walked out, pulling from underneath his jacket two bottles of HEET. Somewhere "down the road," however, the male passenger had tossed the matches out the truck window.

* * *

Kohlmeier's challenge to the sufficiency of the evidence on the ground that his conviction rests upon the "mere possession of a Coleman cooking stove and two (2) bottles of HEET" is without merit. The whole of the evidence, construed to uphold the verdict, authorized a finding that Kohlmeier was guilty beyond a reasonable doubt of criminal attempt to manufacture methamphetamine.

* * *

Judgment affirmed.

————

NOTES: EQUIPMENT AND CRIMINAL ATTEMPTS

1. Does the court reach the correct result? If you have seen the popular television series *Breaking Bad*, you know that manufacturing methamphetamine is no easy task. Would Kohlmeier have been able to manufacture the methamphetamine without glass pyrex cookware or chemistry beakers? Wouldn't he have also needed gloves? Can Kohlmeier have been sufficiently close to completing the offense without this additional equipment? Or does having 5,000 matchbooks compensate for the other missing equipment?

2. What if Kohlmeier had 5,000 cold medicine pills (from which he could extract pseudoephedrine) but no other equipment? Does that constitute a substantial step?

3. Consider *State v. O'Brien*, 5 S.W.3d 532 (Mo.App. 1999), in which the court explained:

> The state's evidence against O'Brien consisted only of his possession of ephedrine and pseudoephedrine, toluene, Liquid Fire, and an air tank. While the items found in O'Brien's possession can be used to manufacture methamphetamine, they also have valid uses and are legal to possess. The jury may have been entitled to be suspicious of O'Brien's possession of such chemicals and the air tank, but it did not have a sufficient basis for concluding, without speculation, that O'Brien intended to manufacture methamphetamine or that O'Brien took a substantial step toward the manufacture of methamphetamine. The evidence, therefore, was insufficient to support convictions for possession of ephedrine with the intent to manufacture and attempt to manufacture methamphetamine.

Are you more persuaded by this reasoning than the court's rationale in *Kohlmeier*? What possible legitimate reason would O'Brien have for possessing ephedrine and pseudoephedrine, toluene, Liquid Fire, and an air tank in his car?

4. Some states have attempted to eliminate the attempt problem in methamphetamine cases by instead classifying the offense as "unlawful possession of a methamphetamine-manufacturing chemical with intent to manufacture methamphetamine." People v. Dorsey, 839 N.E.2d 1104, 1108 (Ill.App. 2005). Nevertheless, courts still reference the law of attempt to "provide[ ] some guidance."

5. Consider another situation in which the defendants had the instrumentalities necessary to commit the crime:

> On the evening of January 5, 1993, Tracie Reeves and Molly Coffman, both twelve years of age and students at West Carroll Middle School, spoke on the telephone and decided to kill their homeroom teacher, Janice Geiger. The girls agreed that Coffman would bring rat poison to school the following day so that it could be placed in Geiger's drink. The girls also agreed that they would thereafter steal Geiger's car and drive to the Smoky Mountains. Reeves then contacted Dean Foutch, a local high school student, informed him of the plan, and asked him to drive Geiger's car. Foutch refused this request.
>
> On the morning of January 6, Coffman placed a packet of rat poison in her purse and boarded the school bus. During the bus ride Coffman told another student, Christy Hernandez, of the plan; Coffman also showed Hernandez the packet of rat poison. Upon their arrival at school Hernandez informed her homeroom teacher, Sherry Cockrill, of the plan. Cockrill then relayed this information to the principal of the school, Claudia Argo.
>
> When Geiger entered her classroom that morning she observed Reeves and Coffman leaning over her desk; and when the girls noticed her, they giggled and ran back to their seats. At that time Geiger saw a purse lying next to her coffee cup on top of the desk. Shortly thereafter Argo called Coffman to the principal's office. Rat poison was found in Coffman's purse and it was turned over to a Sheriff's Department investigator. Both Reeves and Coffman gave written statements to the investigator concerning their plan to poison Geiger and steal her car.

The court upheld the girls' convictions. Referencing (but not relying on) the Model Penal Code, the court explained that the MPC:

> contains examples of conduct which, if proven, would entitle, but not require, the jury to find that the defendant had taken a "substantial step;" and that two of these examples are applicable to this case. The section of the model code relied upon by the State, § 5.01(2), provides, in pertinent part, as follows:

(2) Conduct which may be held substantial step under paragraph (1)(c). Conduct shall not be held to constitute a substantial step under paragraph (1)(c) of this Section unless it is strongly corroborative of the actor's criminal purpose. Without negativing the sufficiency of other conduct, the following, if strongly corroborative of the actor's criminal purpose, shall not be held insufficient as a matter of law: . . .

(e) *possession of materials to be employed in the commission of the crime, which are specially designed for such unlawful use or which can serve no lawful purpose of the actor under the circumstances;*

(f) *possession, collection or fabrication of materials to be employed in the commission of the crime, at or near the place contemplated for its commission, where such possession, collection or fabrication serves no lawful purpose of the actor under the circumstances;*

State v. Reeves, 916 S.W.2d 909, 909–12 (Tenn. 1996). Do you think the twelve-year-old girls really would have gone through with killing their homeroom teacher?

6. Does the Model Penal Code language quoted in *Reeves* make you re-think whether the court was correct in *Kohlmeier*?

7. The *Reeves* decision discussed two situations in which the Model Penal Code believes an attempt could have occurred. Section 5.01(2) of the Code provides additional examples:

(2) Conduct That May Be Held Substantial Step Under Subsection (1)(c). Conduct shall not be held to constitute a substantial step under Subsection (1)(c) of this Section unless it is strongly corroborative of the actor's criminal purpose. Without negativing the sufficiency of other conduct, the following, if strongly corroborative of the actor's criminal purpose, shall not be held insufficient as a matter of law:

(a) lying in wait, searching for or following the contemplated victim of the crime;

(b) enticing or seeking to entice the contemplated victim of the crime to go to the place contemplated for its commission;

(c) reconnoitering the place contemplated for the commission of the crime;

(d) unlawful entry of a structure, vehicle or enclosure in which it is contemplated that the crime will be committed;

(e) possession of materials to be employed in the commission of the crime, that are specially designed for such unlawful use or that can serve no lawful purpose of the actor under the circumstances;

(f) possession, collection or fabrication of materials to be employed in the commission of the crime, at or near the place contemplated for its commission, if such possession, collection or fabrication serves no lawful purpose of the actor under the circumstances;

(g) soliciting an innocent agent to engage in conduct constituting an element of the crime.

Problem 10–1. Dillon met Wally at Wally's gun store and said he was looking for a "contractor" because "he wanted someone taken care of." Wally indicated that he knew someone (John) in Detroit who might do the job. Dillon was to call Wally in about a week to find out if Wally was able to locate John in Detroit. Wally was to receive a $3,000 finder's fee for setting it up. Wally called the police and spoke to Detective Johnson, who asked Wally to set up a meeting with Dillon. Wally introduced Dillon to Johnson, whom he referred to as John, and then left them to talk alone. Dillon told Johnson that "he had a job for me, saying that he had a female, his sister, that he wanted taken out" because she owed him a lot of money. Dillon paid $5,000 as a down payment, and said he would need thirty to thirty-two days to get the rest. Dillon provided substantial information about his sister: her name, a physical description, her residence, her vehicle, her place of employment, and other details. Johnson said he could do the job within a week. Johnson asked Dillon if he was sure he wanted his sister killed, "because once I received the money and I left, that I was going to go into action and that the job would be completed, and that his sister would be killed and there is no way to stop me from going forward with this." Dillon responded that he was "100 percent absolutely positive that he wanted the job done. He said that he had never been surer of anything in his life." Dillon has clearly solicited murder, and clearly intends that a murder be committed, but has he committed attempted murder?

Problem 10–2. Bobo had a collection of Persian antiquities that he been unable to sell, so he decided to stage a theft in order to recover an insurance payout. He insured it with Lloyd's of London for $18.5 million, allegedly to protect it while he shipped it from his warehouse in Switzerland to the United States to be offered for sale. He rented a long term storage vault and then contacted one Goren, who arranged with several accomplices to stage an "insurance job." Bobo then arranged for the collection to be handled by a customs brokerage firm and stored at an art packing and customs warehouse. Before the collection was shipped, Bobo took the unusual step of marking his initials in red on each crate, as he had told his accomplices he would do. The goods arrived in New York, and the staged burglary took place, but the thieves were arrested by police who had been tipped off by an informant. Bobo was not present. Has he committed attempted grand larceny?

———

4. IMPOSSIBILITY OF COMPLETION

An intriguing legal issue arises when a would-be felon attempts to commit a crime under circumstances that make it impossible for the crime to be committed. Should a person be punished under the criminal law for attempting to do the impossible? If a would-be pedophile contacts a non-existent child on the Internet, is it legally or factually impossible for him to commit a criminal attempt *vis-à-vis* that fictitious child?

Hix v. Commonwealth
Supreme Court of Virginia, 2005.
270 Va. 335, 619 S.E.2d 80.

■ AGEE, JUSTICE.

Thomas Edward Hix was convicted by a jury in the Circuit Court of Stafford County of attempted indecent liberties with a minor, Code § 18.2–370 (the "attempted indecent liberties statute"), and the use of a computer to solicit a minor, Code § 18.2–374.3 (the "communications statute"). The Court of Appeals denied Hix' petition for appeal, and he timely appealed to this Court. For the reasons set forth, we will affirm the judgment of the Court of Appeals.

I. BACKGROUND AND MATERIAL PROCEEDINGS BELOW

Hix, using the screen name "happyone345," engaged in several electronic communications in an Internet "chat room" with a person using the screen name "heather_boon" ("Heather"). Heather claimed to be a 13-year-old girl[2] but was, in fact, State Police Special Agent C.D. Wells.

On November 14, 2001, Hix contacted Heather, but when Hix learned Heather's age, he terminated the internet conversation saying that she was too young. Five minutes later, Hix contacted Heather again and wrote that he worked in Fredericksburg, lived in Manassas, and worked for the government. The conversation ended with Hix saying again that Heather was too young.

Just minutes later, Hix contacted Heather for a third time. Agent Wells "captured"[3] this third conversation, in which Hix asked Heather

---

[2] Excerpts from the chatroom transcript read as follows:

happyone345: your not a bad girl are you . . . sex and messin around
heather_boon: some times i guess but it is hard at 13

. . .

happyone345: how old are you
heather_boon: 13 u don't remember me do ya
happyone 345: yes you are the girl that said you where a bad girl

. . .

heather_boon: I am 13
happyone345: oh yea

[3] When a chat room conversation is "captured," it is saved verbatim as a text file.

about her prior sexual experiences and asked her to describe her body, with particular reference to her sexual characteristics. Hix also described particular sexual acts that he wanted to engage in with her, invited her to "hook up," and admitted that he "[could] get 30 years in prison." Hix ended the conversation by instructing Heather to add his contact information to her computer "friends" list, and asked her to contact him again later.

On November 27, 2001, Heather observed that Hix was online and contacted him. Hix suggested that he and Heather meet at a local McDonald's restaurant, but Heather replied, "today is not good I don't want 2 give u the flu [sic]." Agent Wells testified that he did not have enough information on Hix' location to arrange a meeting at that time. Hix asked Heather's age and she again told him she was 13. He repeated his desire to engage in certain sexual acts with her. Heather ended the conversation when Hix was no longer responding.

By March 28, 2002, Agent Wells had determined that Hix was using a computer located at the National Guard Armory in Fredericksburg, and Heather initiated a third contact with Hix. Heather reminded Hix that he had previously "wanted 2 [sic] go to lunch." Hix responded that they could "just ride and mess around." Heather reminded Hix that she was 13 years old, and Hix replied, "[S]ee, I'm messed up . . . [T]hey would put me under the jail for messen [sic] with you[,] girl." Nevertheless, Hix told Heather he would be at the McDonald's restaurant near the intersection of Routes 3 and 1, driving a red Ford Thunderbird coupe.

The police observed a vehicle matching the description Hix gave to Heather arrive at the McDonald's restaurant about 20 minutes later. Hix was driving and parked the car near the back of the restaurant. Hix told Lieutenant Bowler, the first law enforcement officer to approach him that he was there to meet a 13 year old girl that he had met on the Internet, that the girl's name was Heather Boone and that she was having problems and he was there to see if he could help her. Wells then approached Hix and introduced himself as "Special Agent Wells with the Virginia State Police . . . also known as Heather Boone." Hix admitted to the police officers that he had participated in the conversations with heather_boon/Agent Wells, and further admitted that he believed that the girl he was going to meet at the McDonald's was, in fact, 13 years old. Hix identified the computer located in the Bravo Company orderly room at the Fredericksburg National Guard Armory as the one he used to communicate with Heather.

At trial, however, Hix testified that Agent Wells' recollection of their conversation at the McDonald's was incorrect and that he, in fact, informed Wells and the other officers that he "was there to meet somebody who said that they were a thirteen year old that [he] didn't believe." Hix' own signed statement affirmed that he agreed to lunch with Heather at her invitation, that he "felt uncomfortable" but "thought that she may be in some kinda [sic] trouble as she [said] she was skipping school."

In his own case-in-chief, Hix testified variously that he was just curious, that he thought that Heather was not really 13 years old, but was an adult "role-playing" and alternately that he was afraid she was in some kind of trouble and needed his help.

At the conclusion of the Commonwealth's evidence, Hix moved to strike the attempted indecent liberties charge on grounds the crime was a "legal impossibility" as there was no actual 13-year-old girl with whom the taking of indecent liberties could have been accomplished . . . . The Court denied the motion to strike at that time and when later renewed. The jury found Hix guilty of attempted indecent liberties with a child and use of a communication system for soliciting sex with children for his conduct on November 14, 2001. The jury fixed Hix' punishment at two and one-half years imprisonment for each offense, and the trial court set the sentences to run concurrently.

On appeal to the Court of Appeals, Hix argued that the evidence was insufficient to support a conviction . . . [H]e contended it was legally impossible under these circumstances to commit the crime of attempted indecent liberties with a child under Code § 18.2–370 because Heather was not a real child . . . .

The Court of Appeals denied Hix' petition for appeal . . . .

* * *

II. ANALYSIS

* * *

A. Code § 18.2–370: Attempted Indecent Liberties with a Child

Hix argues that the crimes described by Code § 18.2–370,[4] whether the completed crime or an attempt, require acts directed toward an actual child. Because the evidence showed that Heather was not an actual child, but an adult law enforcement officer posing as a child, Hix contends the evidence cannot support his conviction for the attempted crime as a matter of law.

---

[4] Code § 18.2–370 provides in pertinent part as follows:

A. Any person eighteen years of age or over, who, with lascivious intent, shall knowingly and intentionally commit any of the following acts with any child under the age of fourteen years shall be guilty of a Class 5 felony:

(1) Expose his or her sexual or genital parts to any child . . . or propose that any such child expose his or her sexual or genital parts to such person; or

. . . .

(3) Propose that any such child feel or fondle the sexual or genital parts of such person or propose that such person feel or fondle the sexual or genital parts of any such child; or

(4) Propose to such child the performance of an act of sexual intercourse or any act constituting an offense under § 18.2–361; or

(5) Entice . . . or invite any such child to enter any vehicle . . . or other place, for any of the purposes set forth in the preceding subdivisions of this section.

Although the issue is framed as one of sufficiency of the evidence, Hix' arguments center on the applicability of the defense of impossibility. In considering such a defense, a distinction must be made between legal impossibility and factual impossibility.[5]

> Legal impossibility occurs when a defendant's actions, even if fully carried out exactly as he intends, would not constitute a crime. Factual impossibility occurs when the actions intended by a defendant are proscribed by the criminal law, but a circumstance or fact unknown to the defendant prevents him from bringing about the intended result.

Parham v. Commonwealth, 2 Va.App. 633, 636, 347 S.E.2d 172, 173–74 (1986) (citing *United States v. Oviedo,* 525 F.2d 881, 883 (5th Cir.1976)).

Hix' explicit communications with Heather and his proposal that they "hook up," if fully carried out exactly as he intended, would constitute a crime under the indecent liberties statute. Only the fact that Agent Wells impersonated a 13-year-old girl "prevent[ed] [Hix] from bringing about his intended result." Thus, we find that Hix' defense is one of factual, not legal impossibility. As Professor LaFave points out, this is an important distinction because

> what is usually referred to as "factual impossibility" is no defense to a charge of attempt. That is, if what the defendant intends to accomplish is proscribed by the criminal law, but he is unable to bring about that result because of some circumstances unknown to him when he engaged in the attempt, then he may be convicted.

2 Wayne R. LaFave & Austin W. Scott, Jr., Substantive Criminal Law, § 11.5(a)(2), at 233 (2d ed.2003). While the distinction between factual and legal impossibility is not always susceptible to a bright line of demarcation, our precedent provides guidance.

Hix argues that the Court of Appeals incorrectly characterized his defense as one of factual impossibility and contends it is one of legal impossibility. He cites *Collins v. Radford,* 134 Va. 518, 536, 113 S.E. 735, 741 (1922), and *Trent v. Commonwealth,* 155 Va. 1128, 1136, 156 S.E. 567 (1931), for the proposition that "[i]f there is some factual condition necessary to the completion of the crime, then the non-existence of that factual condition makes the crime impossible." Hix misreads our decisions.

---

[5] Hix urges this Court to adopt a third kind of impossibility defense: "hybrid legal impossibility." Under this theory, a mistake of fact about the legal status of some necessary element of the crime nullifies a crime of attempt. In accordance with the large majority of jurisdictions, we decline to adopt this position. *See, e.g., United States v. Farner,* 251 F.3d 510, 513 (5th Cir.2001); *United States v. Darnell,* 545 F.2d 595, 598 (8th Cir.1976); *People v. Rojas,* 55 Cal.2d 252, 10 Cal.Rptr. 465, 358 P.2d 921, 923–24 (1961); *State v. Moretti,* 52 N.J. 182, 244 A.2d 499, 503 (1968).

In *Collins,* the defendant was charged with attempting to transfer "ardent spirits." He made arrangements with another to hide a gallon of whiskey in a haystack for him, but before the defendant could retrieve it, a farmer found the whiskey and turned it over to the police. When the defendant returned to retrieve the whiskey, he was arrested.

We rejected the defendant's defense of impossibility because "the impossibility of performance was not of a kind to rob his act of its criminal character." We held that a defense of impossibility is applicable only in those situations where the impossibility is "inherent . . . and not to cases where the impossibility has been brought about by outside interference, or grows out of extraneous facts not within the knowledge and control of the accused." In the defendant's case, he did not know that the farmer had removed the whiskey from the haystack. It was only this extraneous event not within the defendant's knowledge and control, that prevented him from completing the illegal transaction. As such, the transaction was not inherently or legally impossible, but only factually impossible. Had the facts been as the defendant intended them to be, he would have completed the criminal act of transporting ardent spirits. Thus, he was guilty of the attempted act.

In *Trent,* the police discovered an illegal still where the defendant and others were preparing to manufacture illegal spirits. Before the men could complete the process, the police raided the still and apprehended the defendant. He argued that because a "worm" was never found, "it [was] impossible to carry out the processes of distillation" and that this impossibility was a defense. We agreed that if the "worm" were proven not to exist, the defendant's defense could stand, because consummation of the crime would be "inherently impossible." While we found that "the conclusion is inevitable that [the] 'worm' was . . . immediately available" and thus, not proven absent, we rejected the reasoning that the absence of the "worm" would justify an impossibility defense as an "extraneous fact not within the knowledge or control of [the defendant]." Read in context, a defense of impossibility could only be viable for the defendant had he specifically intended to go through the motions of working the still without the "worm." However, if his plans to manufacture the spirits were carried out exactly as he intended, with the "worm" in place, the defendant could be charged with attempting to manufacture illegal spirits, even if the "worm" was not currently present. The fact that his plan was interrupted by law enforcement officers could therefore not bolster the defendant's effort to assert an impossibility defense.

Our decisions in *Collins* and *Trent* differentiate between legal and factual impossibility to the effect that while legal or "inherent impossibility" may be a defense, factual impossibility based upon "some extraneous fact not within the knowledge or control of the accused" is not. The defendant in *Collins* had no knowledge of or control over the farmer's retrieval of the whiskey, and the defendant in *Trent* did not know that the police raid would interrupt the manufacturing process at the still. These cases undergird later decisions of the Court of Appeals which plainly state, "[L]egal impossibility is a defense; factual impossibility is not." *See, e.g., Bloom v. Commonwealth,* 34 Va.App. 364, 372, 542 S.E.2d 18, 21, *aff'd,* 262 Va. 814, 554 S.E.2d 84 (2001).

* * *

In *Bloom,* the Court of Appeals decided a case nearly identical to the case at bar. The defendant was communicating over the internet with an undercover police officer posing as a 13-year-old girl, and "proposed that [he and the girl] meet and have sexual relations." The defendant was apprehended by police when he went to the designated meeting place, but contended at trial that he could not "be convicted because it was impossible to entice a child to engage in sexual acts when he communicated with [a police officer]." The Court of Appeals rejected this argument, stating that

> [t]he defendant thought he was communicating with a young girl with whom he intended to have sexual relations . . . If the defendant intends to violate the law and, but for some impediment, would complete the unlawful act, then he is guilty of the attempted crime.

Id. at 372, 542 S.E.2d at 22.

The Court of Appeals correctly determined that a police officer posing as a child in an internet chat room is only an impediment to the commission of the crime, an extraneous fact outside of the knowledge and control of the defendant. The non-existence of a "real child" does not make the crime of attempted indecent liberties inherently or legally impossible, but only factually impossible. Thus, the fact that Hix and the defendant in *Bloom* were communicating with adult law enforcement officers is not a defense to the attempted crime.

* * *

Hix solicited and intended to have sex with a 13-year-old girl and went to meet her but "was fooled because his target was in reality an undercover law enforcement officer," an extraneous circumstance unknown to him and beyond his control. In such a case, the defense of impossibility is not available for a charge of criminal attempt. As Professor LaFave notes:

> [I]t is clear as a matter of policy that no reason exists for exonerating the defendant because of facts unknown to him which made it impossible for him to succeed . . . [T]he defendant's mental state was the same as that of a person guilty of the completed crime, and by committing the acts in question he has demonstrated his readiness to carry out his illegal venture.

2 LaFave, Substantive Criminal Law § 11.5(a)(2), at 234. The Court of Appeals did not err in its judgment that Hix' claim of impossibility was not a defense to the crime of attempted indecent liberties.

* * *

III. CONCLUSION

For the reasons stated above, we will affirm the judgment of the Court of Appeals.

Affirmed.

———

NOTES: IMPOSSIBLE ATTEMPTS

1. Do you understand the distinction between legal impossibility and factual impossibility? Look again at footnote 5 of the *Hix* opinion. What is hybrid impossibility? Consider the following explanation:

> *Hybrid legal impossibility* exists if D's goal was illegal, but commission of the offense was impossible due to a factual mistake by her regarding the legal status of some factor relevant to her conduct. This version of impossibility is a "hybrid" because, as the definition implies and as is clarified immediately below, D's impossibility claim includes both a legal and a factual aspect to it.
>
> Courts have recognized a defense of legal impossibility or have stated that it would exist if D receives unstolen property believing it was stolen; tries to pick the pocket of a stone image of a human; offers a bribe to a "juror" who is not a juror; tries to hunt deer out of season by shooting a stuffed animal; shoots a corpse believing that it is alive; or shoots at a tree stump believing that it is a human.
>
> Notice that each of the mistakes in these cases affected the legal status of some aspect of the defendant's conduct. The status of property as "stolen" is necessary to commit the crime of "receiving stolen property with knowledge it is stolen"—i.e., a person legally is incapable of committing this offense if the property is not stolen. The status of a person as a "juror" is legally necessary to commit the offense of bribing a juror. The status of a victim as a "human being" (rather than as a corpse, tree stump, or statue) legally is necessary to commit the crime of murder or to "take and carry away the personal property *of another.*" Finally, putting a bullet into a stuffed deer can never constitute the crime of hunting out of season.
>
> On the other hand, in each example of hybrid legal impossibility D was mistaken about a fact: whether property was stolen, whether a person was a juror, whether the victims were human or whether the victim was an animal subject to being hunted out of season.

People v. Thousand, 631 N.W.2d 694, 699 (Mich. 2001). Is it possible to take any claim of legal impossibility or factual impossibility and re-characterize it as hybrid impossibility? As explained in footnote 5 of the *Hix* decision, most courts reject hybrid impossibility. Many commentators agree. *See, e.g.*, Ken Levy, *It's Not Too Difficult: A Plea To Resurrect the Impossibility Defense*, 45 N.M. L. REV. 225, 258 (2014) ("[T]here is no such thing as hybrid impossibility.").

2. Imagine that we live in a jurisdiction in which deer hunting is legal in October, but not in any other month. Martin is hunting on October 5th. Martin is not good at using a calendar however and he believes it is November 5th. What, if anything, can Martin be convicted of?

3. Now imagine that deer hunting is legal in October, but not in any other month. Martin is hunting on November 5th, although he believes that the date is October 5th. What, if anything, can Martin be convicted of? What concepts control the outcome of Martin's case?

4. With the explosion of Internet communication over the last few decades, courts have been called upon to decide more impossibility cases involving older men who incorrectly believe they are communicating with underage children. There are other types of impossibility situations though. For instance, consider a case where a defendant purchases what he believes to be heroin from a drug dealer. In actuality, the dealer is an undercover FBI agent and the defendant has purchased white powder that is not heroin. The defendant cannot be guilty of possession of a controlled substance (because he is not in possession of heroin). But can the defendant be charged with attempted possession of a controlled substance, or is that crime legally impossible? *See* Grill v. State, 651 A.2d 856 (Md. 1995).

5. Congress eliminated the problem raised by Note 2 for federal narcotics cases when it enacted 21 U.S.C. § 841(a)(1) and 21 U.S.C. § 846. These statutes expressly make an "attempt" to possess a controlled substance a crime. As a result, federal courts have consistently ruled that legal impossibility is not a defense in "reverse sting" operations where police substitute a bogus substance for narcotics, sell the substance to an unwary buyer as a narcotic substance, and then effectuate an arrest. *See, e.g.*, United States v. Pennell, 737 F.2d 521 (6th Cir. 1984); United States v. Everett, 700 F.2d 900, 903–08 (3d Cir. 1983).

6. Under federal law, it is a felony to attempt to assassinate the president of the United States. *See* 18 U.S.C. § 1751(c). On October 29, 1994, while Bill Clinton was president of the United States, a man named Dennis Basso visited the White House. Basso looked very much like President Clinton. Another man, Francisco Martin Duran began shooting. "[T]he bullets struck trees and the building in the area where Mr. Basso was standing, and . . . the shooting occurred immediately after two school children mistook a man standing in that location for Bill Clinton." Duran was arrested and at trial the prosecution presented evidence that

> the Defendant had told other people of his desire to kill the President; that he wrote materials that threatened the life of the President and other government officials; that he bought a firearm; that he bought multiple round clips and multiple rounds of

ammunition for that firearm; that he bought a trench coat to conceal the firearm; that he bought a folding stock and pistol grip for the firearm so that it could be folded up and concealed under the trench coat; and that he traveled to Washington, D.C., and waited outside the White House for the opportunity to make an attempt on the life of the President of the United States.

United States v. Duran, 884 F.Supp. 577 (D.D.C. 1995). Is Duran guilty of violating 18 U.S.C. § 1751(c)? Would it affect your answer if President Clinton was not in the White House that day and if he had been thousands of miles away on a foreign trip?

7. At common law an accused under the age of fourteen was conclusively presumed to be incapable of committing the crime of rape and "it logically follows, as a plain legal deduction, that he was also incapable in law of an attempt to commit it." Foster v. Commonwealth, 96 Va. 306, 31 S.E. 503 (1898).

———

5. RENUNCIATION OR ABANDONMENT OF ATTEMPTS

Gravens v. State

Court of Appeals of Indiana, 2005.
836 N.E.2d 490.

■ VAIDIK, JUDGE.

David Gravens appeals his conviction for Attempted Robbery. Specifically, Gravens argues that the trial court's jury instruction on the defense of abandonment is erroneous and that the evidence is not sufficient to support the jury's finding that Gravens did not voluntarily abandon the attempted robbery. Because the case law language added to the pattern jury instruction is necessary to fully inform the jury of the law applicable to the facts and it neither emphasizes a particular evidentiary fact nor states an appellate standard of review, and because there is evidence that Gravens abandoned the attempted robbery as the result of extrinsic circumstances, we affirm.

Facts and Procedural History

Gravens entered the Fifth Third Banking Center in Decatur, Indiana, and walked up to teller Amber Whitman's window. Whitman asked Gravens how she could help him, and Gravens pulled a piece of paper out of his pocket and slid it across the top of the counter. On the top of the piece of paper was printed the following demand: "Give me money from 2 TELLERS." Whitman immediately began to feel nervous and "started getting butterflies in [her] stomach." There was also writing on the bottom of the piece of paper that Whitman was unable to read. As such, Whitman turned the piece of paper around and said to Gravens, in a voice "a little louder" than what she would normally use with a customer, "I can't read this. Can you tell me what you want?" When Whitman questioned him, Gravens became "fluster[ed]" and held up two fingers. Gravens then picked up the note, looked at it, mumbled some words, and finally walked out of the bank.

The State charged Gravens with Attempted Robbery . . . and filed its Notice of Intent to Seek Habitual Offender Status. Gravens then filed his Notice of Affirmative Defense, stating that one of his defenses at trial would be Abandonment.[1] At trial, Gravens tendered Instruction No. 10.17 of the Indiana Pattern Jury Instructions—Criminal ("Pattern Instruction 10.17"), on abandonment. The State objected to instructing the jury on the defense of abandonment. In the alternative, the State tendered its own proposed instruction on abandonment. Gravens objected to the State's proposed instruction, and the trial court overruled the objection. The court gave the jury the State's proposed instruction on abandonment as Preliminary Instruction No. 9 and Final Instruction No. 8 ("the instruction").

The jury found Gravens guilty as charged, and Gravens pled guilty to being a habitual offender. The trial court sentenced Gravens to a term of four years in prison on the attempted robbery conviction and enhanced the sentence by eight years based on the habitual offender finding, for a total executed sentence of twelve years. Gravens now appeals.

Discussion and Decision

* * *

I.   Jury Instruction on Abandonment

Gravens first contends that the trial court abused its discretion by adopting the abandonment instruction proposed by the State rather than instructing the jury in accordance with the pattern instruction that he proposed. . . .

Gravens submitted the following proposed instruction on the issue of abandonment:

> It is an issue whether the Defendant abandoned his effort to commit the crime charged.
>
> It is a defense to a charge of attempted Robbery that the Defendant voluntarily abandoned his effort to commit the Robbery and voluntarily prevented its commission.
>
> The State has the burden of disproving this defense beyond a reasonable doubt.

This proposed instruction tracks the language of Pattern Instruction 10.17.

The State also tendered its own proposed instruction on the issue of abandonment. The State's tendered instruction was identical to

---

[1]   Ind. Code § 35–41–3–10.

Gravens', with the following additional clause ("¶ 3") inserted between the second and third sentences of Pattern Instruction 10.17:

> To be considered voluntary, the Defendant's decision to abandon must originate with the Defendant and must in no way be attributable to the influence of extrinsic circumstances. To be considered voluntary, the Defendant's decision to abandon can not be the product of extrinsic factors that increase the probability of detection or make more difficult the accomplishment of the criminal purpose or because of unanticipated difficulties in carrying out the criminal plan at the precise time and place intended.

This additional language is based largely on decisions of the Indiana Supreme Court. *See Smith v. State*, 636 N.E.2d 124, 127 (Ind.1994); *Barnes v. State*, 269 Ind. 76, 378 N.E.2d 839, 843 (1978). The trial court gave the instruction proposed by the State, and the jury rejected Gravens' abandonment defense when it found him guilty of attempted robbery.

* * *

Gravens makes two arguments as to why it was improper for ¶ 3 to be included in the instruction. First, Gravens contends that ¶ 3 is an "impermissible judicial comment" on particular evidence or types of evidence that intimates the weight the jury must give to that evidence. Second, Gravens argues that ¶ 3 expresses an appellate standard of review that is irrelevant to the jury's role as finder of fact under Article I, § 19 of the Indiana Constitution. The State responds that ¶ 3 was necessary to the abandonment instruction because without it, the jury would have been left with the mistaken impression that abandonment caused by extrinsic factors is sufficient to establish the defense of voluntary abandonment. We agree with the State.

We first address Gravens' argument that ¶ 3 is an "impermissible judicial comment" that "unnecessarily emphasiz[es] certain evidentiary facts and instruct[s] the jury what inference it was required to draw from those facts." Oddly, Gravens does not say which evidentiary fact or facts he believes the instruction as given "unnecessarily emphasized,". . . .

As in *Ham*, Indiana courts have struck down other instructions that improperly emphasize one evidentiary fact. . . . The instruction in this case, on the other hand, does not emphasize any particular piece of evidence. Rather, ¶ 3 informs the jury of what it means for abandonment to be "voluntary," as interpreted by the Indiana appellate courts.

In a variation on the same argument, Gravens, borrowing from *Ham*, contends that "whether certain facts demonstrate that a defendant's decision to abandon an attempt to commit a crime is or isn't voluntary is for the lawyers to argue and the jury to decide,' but not for a court to so instruct." We agree that whether a defendant's abandonment of a criminal effort is voluntary is a question of fact for the jury to decide.

However, whether abandonment caused by extrinsic factors is voluntary for purposes of the abandonment statute is a question of law that has been answered by the Indiana appellate courts. It is well-established that while the jury is to determine both the law and the facts in criminal cases, the trial court's instructions are the best source of the law, and in determining the law, jurors are required to stay within the law as it exists . . . The trial court did not improperly emphasize any particular evidentiary fact or facts when it instructed the jury on the meaning of "voluntary."

* * *

Finally, we apply the three-part test used in reviewing a trial court's decision to give a tendered instruction. *Guyton*, 771 N.E.2d at 1144. First, the instruction correctly states the law. Gravens concedes, "There is no doubt or question that the language which Gravens objected to . . . is a generally correct statement of the law in Indiana." Second, there is evidence in the record to support the giving of the instruction. The fact that Gravens left the bank before getting any money is undisputed, and there was testimony to suggest that Gravens' abandonment may have been the product of extrinsic factors, *e.g.*, Whitman's question. Third and finally, the substance of the instruction is not covered by other instructions that were given. The trial court did not abuse its discretion in giving the instruction.

II. Sufficiency of the Evidence

Next, Gravens argues that the State failed to prove beyond a reasonable doubt that he did not voluntarily abandon his attempt to rob the bank. If there is support in the evidence for the defense of abandonment, the burden is on the State to disprove the defense beyond a reasonable doubt. The State does not dispute that there is support in the evidence for the defense of abandonment, but it argues that it carried its burden of *disproving* the defense by *proving* that Gravens' abandonment was not voluntary, as required by statute. Ind. Code § 35–41–3–10. This is basically a question of the sufficiency of the evidence. When reviewing a challenge to the sufficiency of evidence, we do not reweigh the evidence or judge the credibility of witnesses. We look only to the probative evidence supporting the judgment and the reasonable inferences from that evidence to determine whether a reasonable trier of fact could conclude the defendant was guilty beyond a reasonable doubt. We will uphold the conviction if there is substantial evidence of probative value to support it.

* * *

Here, the State proved that Gravens' abandonment was not voluntary. First, there is no evidence that Gravens had any intention of leaving the bank before Whitman questioned him about his note. Second, Whitman testified that when she spoke to Gravens, she "tried to talk a little louder" than she usually does with customers "so that [the other teller] might take notice." It was reasonable for the jury to infer that Whitman's conduct increased the probability of detection or made more difficult the accomplishment of Gravens' criminal purpose. Third, Whitman testified at Gravens became "fluster[ed]" and left the bank right after she asked him about the note. This testimony supports the inference that Gravens abandoned his criminal plan as a result of the "unanticipated difficulty" of Whitman's questioning. In a related argument, Gravens contends that to the extent that Whitman's question is an "extrinsic factor," "the probability of detection or difficulty in accomplishing the robbery, under this set of circumstances, was increased so infinitesimally by it as to be inconsequential to the question of whether Gravens' decision to abandon his robbery attempt was voluntary." Gravens' argument is an invitation for us to reweigh the evidence, which we may not do. Because there is sufficient evidence in this case to support the jury's finding that Gravens' decision to abandon the attempted robbery did not originate with him but instead was the product of extrinsic factors, we affirm his conviction.

Judgment affirmed. . . .

———

NOTES

1. Model Penal Code § 5.01 provides for a defense of renunciation:

> (4) Renunciation of Criminal Purpose. When the actor's conduct would otherwise constitute an attempt under Subsection (1)(b) or (1)(c) of this Section, it is an affirmative defense that he abandoned his effort to commit the crime or otherwise prevented its commission, under circumstances manifesting a complete and voluntary renunciation of his criminal purpose. The establishment of such defense does not, however, affect the liability of an accomplice who did not join in such abandonment or prevention.
>
> Within the meaning of this Article, renunciation of criminal purpose is not voluntary if it is motivated, in whole or in part, by circumstances, not present or apparent at the inception of the actor's course of conduct, that increase the probability of detection or apprehension or that make more difficult the accomplishment of the criminal purpose. Renunciation is not complete if it is motivated by a decision to postpone the criminal conduct until a more advantageous time or to transfer the criminal effort to another but similar objective or victim.

2. For an interesting assessment of the abandonment issue, see Robert Batey, *Minority Report and the Law of Attempt*, 1 OHIO ST. J. CRIM. L. 689 (2004):

> Whatever test is used or implied, the common-law approach aims to give the defendant a rather large *"locus poenitentiae,"* which

Herbert Packer defines as "a point of no return beyond which external constraints may be imposed but before which the individual is free-not free of whatever compulsions determinists tell us he labors under but free of the very specific social compulsions of the law." . . . The existence of such a "chickening out zone" (how a former student once translated "locus poenitentiae") appears in famous cases like People v. Rizzo and Campbell v. Ward. . . . In *Rizzo*, the defendants drove around New York City looking for a payroll clerk to rob, but attracted the attention of the police before they found the clerk; in *Campbell* one of the defendants entered a parked car, but exited when the owner approached. Despite the fact that all the defendants confessed that they intended to commit robbery and theft, respectively, the courts in both cases found their acts insufficient to render them guilty of an attempt.

The notion behind the granting of a large *locus poenitentiae* seems to be, as one court phrased it, that "the devil may lose the contest, albeit late in the hour." This is certainly the case with Anderton in Minority Report: He has declared his intention to kill Crow and is pointing a loaded weapon at his victim, when he changes his mind and begins invoking Miranda. The fact that he could have a change of heart, even in the moment before firing his gun, means that he is still at that moment in the *locus poenitentiae* and so should arguably be free of criminal liability for attempted murder.

3. In United States v. Stallworth, 543 F.2d 1038 (2d Cir. 1976), involving a foiled bank robbery, the court said:

It seems clear that if the requisite elements of an attempt are present, abandonment due to some extrinsic cause, such as the unexpected arrival of police officers or the intended victim, will be of no effect, but in some cases voluntary abandonment or renunciation can be accepted as a defense even when the elements of attempt are technically complete. . . .

We are persuaded by the trend of modern authority and hold that voluntary abandonment is an affirmative defense to a prosecution for criminal attempt. The burden is on the defendant to establish by a preponderance of the evidence that he or she has voluntarily and completely abandoned his or her criminal purpose. Abandonment is not "voluntary" when the defendant fails to complete the attempted crime because of unanticipated difficulties, unexpected resistance, or circumstances which increase the probability of detention or apprehension. Nor is the abandonment "voluntary" when the defendant fails to consummate the attempted offense after deciding to postpone the criminal conduct until another time or to substitute another victim or another but similar objective. (citations omitted).

4. Professor Murat Mungan has stated that "most jurisdictions either fully excuse an abandoned attempt or do not provide a defense at all. Perhaps due to these features of the law, decision-makers occasionally bend or creatively interpret the law to produce outcomes that comport more with what are presumably their intuitive notions of justice." Murat C. Mungan, *Abandoned Criminal Attempts: An Economic Analysis*, 67 ALA. L. REV. 1, 5 (2015). Can you think of any cases from this chapter that seem to support this argument?

PROBLEM: RENUNCIATION OR ABANDONMENT OF CRIMINAL ATTEMPTS

Problem 10–3. Donald Chump, on a mad impulse, drove his truck to his ex-wife's house and poured the contents of a gasoline can around the house, including the foyer and stairs. A neighbor saw him doing this and asked him what he was doing. Chump replied that the neighbor had better leave because he was going to set the place on fire. The neighbor slapped Chump's lighter out of his hand. Chump left the lighter on the ground and departed. He was arrested shortly thereafter for attempted arson. Did Chump renounce his attempt when he left without picking up the lighter?

B. ACCESSORYSHIP: AIDING AND ABETTING

1. EVOLUTION OF ACCESSORYSHIP

The notion that a criminal defendant can be held responsible for acts done by another is an old one in the common law. By the early fifteenth century, the law divided the parties to crime into principals and accessories of various kinds. A principal was one who committed the *actus reus* of the crime; accessories "at the fact," were present at the crime, "aiding and abetting" the principal. An accessory "before the fact" was not present during the commission of the crime but had advised or encouraged the perpetration of the crime. By the mid-fifteenth century, during the reign of Henry IV, accessories "at the fact" became principals: they were principals in the first degree if they actively participated, and principals in the second degree if they did not actively participate, as long as they were actually or constructively present, aiding and abetting.[3]

While the distinction between principals and accessories persisted in the common law[4] as adopted into the United States, the distinctions became less and less significant. Principals and accessories before the fact received the same punishment,[5] though accessories had some

---

[3]   *See generally* 1 J.W. CECIL TURNER, RUSSELL ON CRIMES 134–81 (11th ed. 1958); 1 JOEL PRENTISS BISHOP, BISHOP ON CRIMINAL LAW § 648 (9th ed. 1923).

[4]   *See, e.g.,* 1 SIR MATTHEW HALE, THE HISTORY OF THE PLEAS OF THE CROWN 615 (1st Am. ed. 1847) (defining an accessory before the fact as, "he, that being absent at the time of the felony commited, doth yet procure, counsel, command, or abet another to commit a felony"); *accord* 4 BLACKSTONE'S COMMENTARIES 36, 37.

[5]   "No distinction was made in the punishment of a principal and of an accessory before the fact by the common law, the principle that what one does by the agency of another he does

advantages in terms of procedure.[6] Even the procedural distinctions eroded somewhat over time.[7] Modern statutes defining the relationships and responsibilities of the parties to criminal offenses have largely eliminated common law distinctions between "principals" and "accessories before the fact."

Accessoryship liability has limits. While it is not necessary for an accessory to know of or endorse every act of the principal felon to be liable, by the same token, one whose innocent acts aid one who commits a crime is not thereby made an accessory to that crime.[8] An accomplice is one who unites with another person or persons in the commission of a crime, voluntarily and with common intent. Mere knowledge that crime is going to be committed is not sufficient to establish liability as accessory if defendant does not encourage or intentionally aid in commission of crime.[9] In any jurisdiction, however, mere presence, without more, is not enough to make one an aider and abettor.[10]

2. WHAT *MENS REA* IS REQUIRED OF AN ACCESSORY?

It is not necessary to prove that each defendant committed all the acts of the crime; each person who does one act that is an ingredient of the crime or immediately connected with it is as guilty as if he committed the whole crime with his own hands.[11] To be guilty as an accessory, one

---

by himself applying equally in criminal and civil cases." Usselton v. People, 149 Ill. 612, 616, 36 N.E. 952, 953 (1894) (citing HUBERT BROOM, A SELECTION OF LEGAL MIXIMS 643 (2d ed. 1848).

[6] At common law, an accessory before the fact had the right to insist upon the conviction of the principal offender before he was put upon trial, on the principle that until the principal felon was convicted, there was no proof that a felony had been convicted, and it would be absurd to convict the accessory one day, and to acquit the principal the next day. *See, e.g.,* 4 BLACKSTONE'S COMMENTARIES 323 (*non constitit* whether any felony was committed or no, till the principal was attainted). Accessories could, of course, waive this privilege if they wished.

[7] It seems that the distinction between accessories before the fact and principals, up to a late date, at least, has been retained in England. By Statute 7. Geo. IV, chap. 64. § 9, it is provided that persons who shall counsel, procure or command any other person to commit a felony shall be deemed guilty of a felony—and may be indicted and convicted—either as accessory before the fact to the principal felony, together with the principal felon, or after his conviction, or may be indicted and convicted of a substantive felony, whether the principal felon shall have been convicted or not, etc. See 11 and 12 Vic. 46, § 1). Usselton v. People, 149 Ill. 612, 616, 36 N.E. 952, 953 (1894).

[8] *See e.g.,* State v. McCalpine, 190 Conn. 822, 463 A.2d 545 (1983). For a complete historical survey of the common law of accountability, see 1 RONALD ABERDEEN ANDERSON, WHARTON'S CRIMINAL LAW AND PROCEDURE §§ 102–116 (1957); WILLIAM LAWRENCE CLARK & WILLIAM LAWRENCE MARSHALL, A TREATISE ON THE LAW OF CRIMES, ch. 8 (6th ed. 1958); Rollin M. Perkins, *Parties To Crime,* 89 U. PA. L. REV. 581 (1941).

[9] State v. Aparo, 223 Conn. 384, 614 A.2d 401 (1992), *cert. denied,* 507 U.S. 972, 113 S.Ct. 1414, 122 L.Ed.2d 785 (1993), *habeas corpus granted by* 956 F.Supp. 118 (1993), *aff'd,* 129 F.3d 113 (1997) (unpublished table decision), *cert. denied,* 522 U.S. 967, 118 S.Ct. 414, 139 L.Ed.2d 317 (1997).

[10] *See, e.g.,* G.C. v. State, 407 So.2d 639 (Fla.App. 1981) (evidence that the defendant knew that another person was going to burglarize apartment, and followed that person to the scene of the crime and watched as other person removed windows from apartment was insufficient to prove that juvenile aided and abetted in attempted burglary).

[11] State v. Churchill, 4 Haw.App. 276, 664 P.2d 757 (1983); State v. Apao, 59 Haw. 625, 586 P.2d 250 (1978).

- must share the criminal intent and community of unlawful purpose with perpetrator of crime and one must knowingly and wilfully assist the perpetrator in the acts which prepare for, facilitate, or consummate it.[12]
- In order for one to be an "accomplice" there must be mutuality of intent and community of unlawful purpose.[13] Accessorial liability does not require that defendant act with conscious objective to cause the result described by statute, and thus, accessory may be liable in aiding another
- if he acts intentionally, knowingly, recklessly or with criminal negligence toward that result, depending on mental state required by substantive crime.[14] Difficult issues arise when an accessory to a crime has a different *mens rea* than the principal. Separate problems occur when the principal commits additional and foreseeable crimes that nevertheless go beyond the particular crime the accessory assisted in. Consider the following cases.

Oates v. State

Court of Special Appeals of Maryland, 1993.
97 Md.App. 180, 627 A.2d 555.

■ MOYLAN, JUDGE.

The single question raised by this appeal is simple: When two defendants are jointly convicted of perpetrating a criminal homicide, must their levels of guilt (blameworthiness) be the same? The answer is equally simple: No.

* * *

The trial lasted seven days, in the course of which twenty-five witnesses testified. Through that testimonial kaleidoscope, a general pattern emerged with modest clarity. On April 14, 1990, a birthday celebration was held at the Classics III Restaurant on Allentown Road in Prince George's County. Neither the appellant nor the codefendant were participants in that celebration but they were present at the restaurant. In the course of the evening, a fight broke out between the appellant and the codefendant, on the one hand, and various party guests, on the other hand. Although a precise chronology is difficult to establish, the level of turbulence was clear. As one party guest testified, a fight started and "people started screaming. Furniture flying in the air. It was very loud. Smashing glass."

During the first phase of hostilities, still within the restaurant, one of the party guests and the ultimate homicide victim, Patrick Stanford,

---

[12] State v. Robertson, 254 Conn. 739, 760 A.2d 82 (2000). Whether the accessorial liability statute allows an accused accomplice to have a different level of intent than the principal, so as to allow the accomplice to be convicted of a lesser-included offense, is undecided in Connecticut. State v. Floyd, 253 Conn. 700, 756 A.2d 799 (2000).

[13] State v. Boles, 223 Conn. 535, 613 A.2d 770 (1992).

[14] State v. Gamble, 27 Conn.App. 1, 604 A.2d 366 (1992), *certification denied*, 222 Conn. 901, 606 A.2d 1329 (1992).

was involved in a fight with both the appellant and the codefendant, Giles. One of the latter two punched Stanford in the mouth, knocking out four teeth. The appellant and Giles then moved on to other fights with other party guests. At some time between 1:30 and 2 A.M., the appellant and Giles left the restaurant and were on the parking lot at the same time that various party guests, including the ultimate homicide victim, Patrick Stanford, were leaving. Threats were hurled between the two opposing camps. One of the departing party guests described how Giles grabbed from his car and then waved menacingly at that witness an object resembling a "butterfly knife."

Patrick Stanford drove away from the scene in a station wagon with two female companions. The appellant and Giles left the scene in Giles's white Jetta. Shortly thereafter, at the intersection of Allentown Road and Branch Avenue, the station wagon was stopped for a traffic light when the Jetta pulled up behind it. The appellant and Giles got out of the Jetta and, with a crowbar, smashed the windows of the station wagon. Stanford was pulled out of the wagon and both assailants proceeded to punch and kick him.

In terms of the final lethal attack on Stanford, Pattina Avery, in whose honor, incidentally, the birthday party had been held, testified that both assailants were "punching and stabbing" Stanford at the same time. An uninvolved witness, a University of Maryland student who was simply driving in the area, testified that one of the assailants was holding the victim while the other was hitting him. After the victim fell to the ground, the two attackers proceeded to kick him. The medical examiner testified that Stanford's body revealed facial injuries, broken teeth, and twelve stab wounds. The cause of death was the multiple stab wounds.

Both Giles and the appellant elected to testify and admitted their participation in the final altercation with Patrick Stanford at the traffic light. After giving his version of the earlier brawl at the Classics III Restaurant, Giles testified that as he and the appellant were driving from the scene, they spotted the car in which Stanford was riding. Giles handed the appellant a crowbar and the appellant jumped out and "began busting out the windows of the car." As the two female passengers ran screaming from the scene, Stanford got out of the car and allegedly attacked Giles with a knife. According to Giles, he and the appellant overpowered Stanford and took the knife away. Giles then described how he began "throwing punches" at Stanford with the knife in his hand but denied any actual stabbing. He testified that the appellant was also punching Stanford, although without a knife. Giles was later shocked to learn that the victim had been stabbed.

In his testimony, the appellant also described the fight at the Classics III Restaurant which, he stated, resulted in a "stampede." The appellant acknowledged getting out of the car at the traffic light and smashing out the back window of the car in which Stanford was riding.

The appellant further testified that it was his intention only to break the window and then leave. He was surprised when Giles began fighting with the victim and he, the appellant, tried to pull Giles off the victim. He disclaimed any intention of hurting anyone that evening.

What the jury concluded and the evidence supported was clear. The death of Patrick Stanford was a criminal homicide. Both the appellant and Giles jointly participated in that criminal homicide. On the basis of the "butterfly knife" earlier observed in Giles's possession and on the basis of Giles's acknowledgement that a knife was in his hand as he repeatedly threw punches at Stanford, the jury obviously concluded that Giles was a principal in the first degree, the wielder of the weapon that struck the fatal blows. From the multiplicity of potentially fatal blows, moreover, the jury concluded that Giles attacked Stanford with a specific intent to kill. The jury gave Giles the benefit of the doubt, however, when it concluded that that specific intent to kill was not premeditated. The obvious verdict under the circumstances was that Giles was guilty of murder in the second degree.

It is equally clear that the jury concluded, with abundant support in the evidence, that the appellant jointly participated with Giles in the criminal homicide. The jury obviously concluded that the appellant was a principal in the second degree, not wielding the lethal weapon but actively aiding and abetting the man who did. Perhaps crediting the exculpatory testimony of the appellant or at least entertaining some doubt thereby, the jury did not conclude that the appellant attacked Stanford with a specific intent to kill or even a specific intent to do grievous bodily harm. Giving the appellant a significant benefit of the doubt, it concluded simply that the appellant was guilty of either 1) grossly negligent, life-endangering conduct toward Stanford or 2) the perpetration of an unlawful act (assault and battery) upon Stanford that resulted in Stanford's death. Either of those closely related states of mind would render the appellant guilty of involuntary manslaughter. That was the verdict the jury returned as to the appellant.

* * *

The appellant now claims that his verdict and Giles's verdict were "legally inconsistent" . . . . How, he asks, can he have aided and abetted in a manslaughter when the person so aided and abetted was found guilty not of manslaughter but of second-degree murder?

The appellant betrays a lack of appreciation of the complex matrix of blameworthiness arising out of a single criminal homicide. The appellant was not in this case an aider and abettor to involuntary manslaughter any more than he was an aider and abettor to second-degree murder or an aider and abettor to first-degree murder. He was, purely and simply, an aider and abettor to criminal homicide, that and nothing more. When two or more persons are joint participants in a crime, they are joint participants only with respect to a single and common *actus reus*. Where, however, a single criminal act has different levels of blameworthiness contingent upon the particular *mens rea* with which it is perpetrated, multiple participants in that crime do not necessarily share the same *mens rea*. Although joint participation ultimately depends upon a mutual tie to the same criminal act, the individual *mentes reae* or levels of guilt of the joint participants are permitted to float free and are not tied to each other in any way. If their *mentes reae* are different, their independent levels of guilt, reflected by nondependent verdicts, will necessarily be different as well.

The classic definition of a crime is the coming together of a guilty act and a guilty mind, an *actus reus* and a *mens rea*. With the vast majority of crimes, there is a single guilty act and a single guilty mind. With criminal homicide as it has evolved over the centuries, however, there is a single guilty act but a rich smorgasbord of guilty minds from which to choose. Picture, for a moment, a body on the floor with a bullet hole between its eyes. Picture the homicidal agent standing over it with smoking gun in hand. We have a homicide (the killing of one human being by another) and we have a homicidal agent, but do we have a crime? We do not know, of course. The act of pulling the trigger could range from the most praiseworthy of acts (resulting in a commendation for valor) to the most blameworthy of acts (resulting in the gas chamber).

Even assuming we have criminal homicide rather than justifiable homicide or excusable homicide, we still have no idea whether it is a garden variety criminal homicide (second-degree murder) in any of its four manifestations, aggravated criminal homicide (first-degree murder) in any of its two clear manifestations, or mitigated criminal homicide (manslaughter) in any of its four manifestations. It all depends upon the state of mind of the homicidal agent (at any level of physical participation). With, as in the case of criminal homicide, finely calibrated levels of venality, the bullet is nothing; the spirit that propels the bullet is everything. . . .

* * *

Two criminals might jointly participate in a murder, one possessing a premeditated intent to kill and the other a mere specific intent to do grievous bodily harm. One would be guilty of murder in the first degree and the other, guilty of murder in the second degree regardless of which was the triggerman and which was the aider and abettor. Each joint participant in a crime enjoys a unique level of blameworthiness that neither controls nor is controlled by the level of blameworthiness of any other joint participant. An aider and abettor of a manslayer may be guilty of murder and an aider and abettor of a murderer may be guilty of manslaughter. The only necessary common denominator is participation in the *actus reus* of the homicide.

Two culprits might jointly perpetrate a killing, one of them cold sober as he acted and the other too drunk to be capable of any specific intent.

If the intoxicated participant were the aider and abettor, he, incapable of any specific intent of his own, would not be charged with the specific intent of his principal. Conversely, if the intoxicated participant were the triggerman, the cold-blooded aider and abettor could not escape responsibility by piggy-backing on the lesser guilt of his principal. According to the appellant's theory, if the triggerman were found to be too mentally incompetent to be criminally responsible, his fully competent aider and abettor might walk from the courtroom. That is not the law.

* * *

The distinguished English scholar Glanville Williams has discussed this same independence of *mentes reae* among joint participants in the same criminal act, tracing the principle as far back as Sir Matthew Hale's HISTORY OF THE PLEAS OF THE CROWN in 1736 and Edward Hyde East's PLEAS OF THE CROWN in 1803. In G. Williams, CRIMINAL LAW 390–391 (1961), Ch. 9, "Principals and Accessories," it is stated: "In one type of case the courts have gone quite far in dissolving the conceptual tie between the responsibility of the principal and that of the accomplice. It is possible for a principal in the first degree to be convicted of murder and a principal in the second degree of manslaughter. Thus if D attacks P intending to murder him, and E enters into the affray thinking that only an assault is intended, and D kills P, this is murder in D and manslaughter in E. There is no reason why a similar result should not be reached for accessories before. P commits a battery upon D; D, in the heat of passion aroused by this, procures E to kill P, which E forthwith does. E (if not affected by the provocation received by D) is guilty of murder; but D is accessory before the fact only to manslaughter. The more interesting situation is the converse, where the guilt of the secondary party is the greater. One who kills without malice aforethought (*e.g.*, as the unintended result of a common assault) may be guilty of manslaughter, while an abettor or instigator, having malice aforethought, may be guilty of murder. . . ."

* * *

JUDGMENT AFFIRMED; COSTS TO BE PAID BY APPELLANT.

———————

NOTES

1. The Model Penal Code has resolved some of the complexities of the common law when it comes to criminal complicity.[15] Consider how the previous case would have been analyzed in a Model Penal Code jurisdiction. Model Penal Code § 2.06. Liability for Conduct of Another, Complicity, provides:

———————

[15] The draft is derived from Model Penal Code cmt. at 19–21 (Tent. Draft No. 4, 1955.)

(1) A person is guilty of an offense if it is committed by his own conduct or by the conduct of another for which he is legally accountable, or both.

(2) A person is legally accountable for the conduct of another person when:

>> (a) acting with the kind of culpability that is sufficient for the commission of an offense, he causes and innocent or irresponsible person to engage in such conduct; or

>> (b) he is made accountable for the conduct of such other person by the Code or by the law defining the offense; or

>> (c) he is an accomplice of such other person in the commission of the offense.

(3) A person is an accomplice of another person in the commission of an offense if:

>> (a) with the purpose of promoting or facilitation the commission of the offense, he

>>> (i) solicits such other person to commit it; or

>>> (ii) aids or agrees or attempts to aid such other person in planning or committing it; or

>>> (iii) having a legal duty to prevent the commission of the offense, fails to make proper effort to do so; or

>> (b) his conduct is expressly declared by law to establish his complicity.

(4) When causing a particular result is an element of an offense, an accomplice in the conduct causing such result is an accomplice in the commission of that offense, if he acts with the kind of culpability, if any, with respect to that result that is sufficient for the commission of the offense.

(5) A person who is legally incapable of committing a particular offense himself may be guilty thereof if it is committed by the conduct of another person for which he is legally accountable, unless such liability is inconsistent with the purpose of the provision establishing his incapacity.

(6) Unless otherwise provided by the Code or by the law defining the offense, a person is not an accomplice in an offense committed by another person if:

>> (a) he is a victim of that offense; or

>> (b) the offense is so defined that his conduct is inevitably incident to its commission; or

>> (c) he terminates his complicity prior to the commission of the offense and

>>> (i) wholly deprives it of effectiveness in the commission of the offense, or

> (ii) gives timely warning to the law enforcement authorities or otherwise makes proper effort to prevent the commission of the offense.

(7) An accomplice may be convicted on proof of the commission of the offense and of his complicity therein, though the person claimed to have committed the offense has not been prosecuted or convicted or has been convicted of a different offense or degree of offense or has an immunity to prosecution or conviction or has been acquitted.

2. Simply being present when a crime is committed, even with knowledge of the crime, is not enough, standing alone, to make one an accomplice. *See* United States v. Garguilo, 310 F.2d 249 (2d Cir. 1962). The Second Circuit noted that

> There may even be instances where the mere presence of a defendant at the scene of a crime he knows is being committed will permit a jury to be convinced beyond a reasonable doubt that the defendant sought "by his action to make it succeed"—for example, the attendance of a 250 pound bruiser at a shake-down as a companion to the extortionist, or the maintenance at the scene of crime of someone useful as a lookout. . . . Yet even in an age when solitude is so detested and "togetherness" so valued, a jury could hardly be permitted to find that the mere furnishing of company to a person engaged in crime renders the companion an aider or abettor. . . .

See also State v. Scott, 289 N.C. 712, 224 S.E.2d 185 (1976) ("The case against Scott then comes to this: he was a friend of the actual perpetrator and was present at the time and place the crime was committed.").

3. In the often-cited Standefer v. United States, 447 U.S. 10, 100 S.Ct. 1999, 64 L.Ed.2d 689 (1980), the issue before the Court was whether a defendant accused of aiding and abetting in the commission of a federal offense may be convicted after the named principal has been acquitted of that offense. The Court first reviewed the history of common law, noting that

> At common law, the subject of principals and accessories was riddled with "intricate" distinctions. 2 J. STEPHEN, HISTORY OF THE CRIMINAL LAW OF ENGLAND 231 (1883). In felony cases, parties to a crime were divided into four distinct categories: (1) principals in the first degree who actually perpetrated the offense; (2) principals in the second degree who were actually or constructively present at the scene of the crime and aided or abetted its commission; (3) accessories before the fact who aided or abetted the crime, but were not present at its commission; and (4) accessories after the fact who rendered assistance after the crime was complete. By contrast, misdemeanor cases "d[id] not admit of accessaries [*sic*] either before or after the fact," . . . .
>
> Because at early common law all parties to a felony received the death penalty, certain procedural rules developed tending to shield accessories from punishment. Among them was one of special

relevance to this case: the rule that an accessory could not be convicted without the prior conviction of the principal offender. Under this rule, the principal's flight, death, or acquittal barred prosecution of the accessory. And if the principal were pardoned or his conviction reversed on appeal, the accessory's conviction could not stand. In every way "an accessory follow[ed], like a shadow, his principal." I. J. BISHOP, CRIMINAL LAW 666 (8th ed. 1892) . . . .

Nonetheless, because a 1909 federal statute had abolished the distinction between principals and accessories the Court affirmed Standefer's conviction.

4. A defendant may be held accountable as an accomplice for crimes he or she could not commit as principals. *See*, *e.g.*, People v. Trumbley, 252 Ill. 29, 96 N.E. 573 (1911). The *Trumbley* Court held that while a woman could not commit the crime of rape as a principal actor, she could nevertheless be punished as an accessory before the fact for aiding and abetting in the commission of the crime of rape. The court said, "Undoubtedly, a woman may be punished for aiding and abetting in the commission of the crime and rape, and as our statute has abolished all distinction between the principal actor and one who is an accessory before or at the fact, the accessory is to be considered as a principal and indicted accordingly." *Accord* People v. Evans, 58 A.D.2d 919, 396 N.Y.S.2d 727 (1977) (holding that a female can be found guilty of rape in aiding and abetting her male codefendant to have sexual intercourse with the female victim, or by beating and holding the victim during the act).

5. Imagine that Bob and Mary are married but don't have a very good relationship. Mary goes out for drinks with her friend Sally. Hours later Mary and Sally come back to Mary's house and find Bob having sex with another woman. Sally takes a deep breath and says to Mary "that good-for-nothing husband of yours should die for this." Mary grabs a kitchen knife and stabs Bob. Sally helps to hold Bob down and Mary stabs Bob a second time. If Bob dies, what should Mary and Sally be charged with? Can they be convicted of different crimes? *See* Parker v. Commonwealth, 201 S.W. 475 (Ky. Ct. App. 1918); Paul H. Robinson, *Criminal Law Defenses: A Systematic Analysis*, 82 COLUM. L. REV. 199, 278 n.307 (1982).

People v. Medina

Supreme Court of California, 2009.
46 Cal.4th 913, 209 P.3d 105.

■ CHIN, J.

In this case, a verbal challenge by defendants (members of a street gang) resulted in a fistfight between defendants and the victim (a member of another street gang). After the fistfight ended, one of the defendants shot and killed the victim as he was driving away from the scene of the fight with his friend. The jury found the gunman guilty of murder and attempted murder of the friend, as the actual perpetrator, and two other participants in the fistfight guilty of those offenses as aiders and abettors. The Court of Appeal affirmed the gunman's convictions, but reversed the participants' convictions. It held there was insufficient evidence that the nontarget offenses of murder and attempted murder were a natural and probable consequence of the target offense of simple assault which they had aided and abetted.

Because a rational trier of fact could have concluded that the shooting death of the victim was a reasonably foreseeable consequence of the assault, on the facts of this case, we reverse the judgment of the Court of Appeal relating to the nonshooting defendants.

I. FACTS AND PROCEDURAL HISTORY

On the evening of January 2, 2004, Manuel Ordenes and his wife Amelia Rodriguez continued their New Year's celebration with a party at their home in Lake Los Angeles, California. Their neighbors Kirk and Abraham, a friend, Lisa, and Jason Falcon were present at their house. Jose Medina ("Tiny"), George Marron, and Raymond Vallejo, self-described members of the Lil Watts gang, were also present. Although Falcon was not identified as a gang member, he was always with Medina, Marron, and Vallejo. Ordenes had formerly been a member of the Lennox gang, a Lil Watts rival, although the two gangs were not rivals in the Lake Los Angeles area. Everyone was drinking alcohol and using methamphetamine.

Around 11:00 p.m., Ernie Barba drove to Ordenes's house with his friend, Krystal Varela, to pick up a CD. Barba went to the house, while Varela stayed at the car. When Ordenes or Rodriguez answered the door, Barba asked, "What's up?" On direct examination, Ordenes stated he heard aggressive voices inside the house saying, "Where are you from?" Later on cross-examination, he clarified that he heard Vallejo say, "Who is that?" and then ask Barba, "Where are you from?" From his experience as a former gang member, Ordenes knew that when a gang member asks another gang member "where are you from?" he means "what gang are you from?" a question which constitutes an "aggression step." He also knew that, if the inquiring gang member was an enemy, the question could lead to a fight or even death. If that gang member had a weapon, he would use it. Wanting to avoid problems in his house, and concerned that somebody was going to get killed, Ordenes ordered, "Take that into the streets, go outside, don't disrespect the house."

Medina, Marron, Vallejo, and Falcon left the house and joined Barba on the front porch. Once outside, Medina, Marron, and Vallejo approached Barba and continued to ask, "Where are you from?" Barba replied, "Sanfer," signifying a San Fernando Valley gang. Vallejo responded, "Lil Watts." Medina remarked, "What fool, you think you crazy?" Vallejo then punched Barba. Medina and Marron joined in the fight. According to Ordenes, Barba, even though outnumbered, defended himself well and held his own against the three attackers. All three "couldn't get [Barba] down." Krystal Varela confirmed that Barba was defending himself well.

Ordenes attempted to break up the fight and pull the attackers off Barba, but Falcon held him back. Eventually, Ordenes was able to pull Barba away and escort him to his car which was parked in front of the house. Barba got into the driver's seat, while Krystal Varela got into the passenger seat. At the car, Ordenes advised Barba to leave.

Varela heard someone in the yard say, "get the heat," which she understood to mean a "gun." Barba closed the driver's side door and drove off. As Ordenes was walking back to his house, he heard Lisa yell from the doorway, "Stop, Tiny. No, stop." Amelia Rodriguez then saw Medina walk into the middle of the street and shoot repeatedly at Barba's car as it drove away. Lisa, who was standing next to Rodriguez, yelled, "Tiny, you know you're stupid. Why you doing that? There's kids here. You f'd up." Barba died of a gunshot wound to the head.

The prosecution charged Medina, Marron, Vallejo, and Falcon with first degree murder (Pen.Code, § 187, subd. (a) and with attempted willful, deliberate, premeditated murder (§§ 664, 187, subd. (a)). Under the prosecution's theory at trial, Medina was guilty as the actual perpetrator, while Marron, Vallejo, and Falcon were guilty as aiders and abettors.

At trial, Hawthorne Police Officer Christopher Port testified as the prosecution's gang expert. Officer Port was assigned to the gang intelligence unit and was familiar with the Lil Watts gang, a violent street gang from Hawthorne. He testified that Lil Watts gang members primarily committed narcotics offenses involving possession and sales, vandalism, and gun-related crimes, including assaults with firearms and semiautomatic firearms, drive-by shootings, and homicides. The police had identified defendants Medina and Vallejo as members of the Lil Watts gang, based on field contacts and their gang tattoos. The police considered Marron to be "affiliated" with the Lil Watts gang, having seen him with Lil Watts gang members, including Medina and Vallejo.

Officer Port testified that the Lake Los Angeles area where Ordenes lived is considered a "transient area for gangs." When a new gang member arrives there, he feels a need to establish himself by demanding respect, which is "the main pride" of a gang member. Officer Port testified that gang members view behavior that disrespects their gang as a challenge and a "slap in the face" which must be avenged. Gang members perceive that, if no retaliatory action is taken in the face of disrespectful behavior, the challenger and others will view the gang member and the gang itself as weak. According to Officer Port, violence is used as a response to disrespectful behavior and disagreements and as a means to gain respect.

Officer Port stated that, when a gang member asks another person, "where are you from?" he suspects that person is in a gang and wants to know what gang he claims as his. In response to hypothetical questions, Officer Port opined that when Barba responded "Sanfer," he was claiming membership in that gang, and that the Lil Watts gang members had viewed Barba's response as disrespectful and had started a fight to avenge themselves. Officer Port stated that a gang member who asks that question could be armed and probably would be prepared to use violence, ranging from a fistfight to homicide. He explained, "In the gang world problems or disagreements aren't handled like you and I would handle a disagreement . . . When gangs have a disagreement, you can almost guarantee it's going to result in some form of violence, whether that be punching and kicking or ultimately having somebody shot and killed."

Ordenes testified that it is important for a gang to be respected and, above all, feared by other gangs. Once a gang is no longer feared, its members lose respect, are ridiculed, and become vulnerable and subject to attack by other gangs. He stated that death is sometimes an option exercised by gang members as a way to maintain respect. Ordenes further stated there are a lot of gang members occupying their "turfs" with guns.

The jury acquitted codefendant Falcon, but found defendants Medina, Marron, and Vallejo guilty as charged . . .

The Court of Appeal affirmed Medina's conviction, but reversed the convictions of Marron and Vallejo on the ground there was insufficient evidence that the nontarget crimes of murder and attempted murder were a reasonably foreseeable consequence of simple assault, the target offense they had aided and abetted.

We granted the Attorney General's petition for review regarding the reversals of Marron's and Vallejo's judgments.

II. DISCUSSION

* * *

It is undisputed that Marron and Vallejo knowingly and intentionally participated in the fistfight that preceded the shooting, that Medina alone shot the victim, and that the jury convicted Marron and Vallejo of murder and attempted murder as aiders and abettors under the natural and probable consequences doctrine.

"A person who knowingly aids and abets criminal conduct is guilty of not only the intended crime [target offense] but also of any other crime the perpetrator actually commits [nontarget offense] that is a natural and probable consequence of the intended crime. The latter question is not whether the aider and abettor *actually* foresaw the additional crime, but whether, judged objectively, it was *reasonably* foreseeable." (*People v. Mendoza* (1998) 18 Cal.4th 1114, 1133, 77 Cal.Rptr.2d 428, 959 P.2d 735.) Liability under the natural and probable consequences doctrine "is measured by whether a reasonable person in the defendant's position would have or should have known that the charged offense was a reasonably foreseeable consequence of the act aided and abetted." (*People v. Nguyen* (1993) 21 Cal.App.4th 518, 535, 26 Cal.Rptr.2d 323.)

. . . "[T]o be reasonably foreseeable '[t]he consequence need not have been a strong probability; a possible consequence which might reasonably have been contemplated is enough . . .' (1 Witkin & Epstein, Cal.Criminal Law (2d ed.1988) § 132, p. 150.)" (*People v. Nguyen, supra,* 21 Cal.App.4th at p. 535, 26 Cal.Rptr.2d 323.) A reasonably foreseeable consequence is to be evaluated under all the factual circumstances of the individual case and is a factual issue to be resolved by the jury.

Here, the Court of Appeal held there was insufficient evidence to support a finding that Medina's act of firing a gun was a reasonably foreseeable consequence of the gang attack in which defendants Marron and Vallejo participated. In so holding, the Court of Appeal reviewed gang violence cases affirming the defendants' liability as aiders and abettors.

In evaluating those cases, the Court of Appeal distilled six factors it considered material to their holdings: "(1) the defendant had knowledge of the weapon that was used before or during his involvement in the target crime; (2) the committed crime took place while the target crime was being perpetrated; (3) weapons were introduced to the target crime shortly after it ensued; (4) the fight which led to the committed crime was planned; (5) the gangs were engaged in an ongoing rivalry involving past acts of violence; or (6) the defendant agreed to or aided the commission of the committed crime." . . .

In evaluating this case, the Court of Appeal found it significant that none of the above factors were present, focusing on facts that were *missing,* rather than on the actual evidence presented. However, as the Attorney General points out, prior knowledge that a fellow gang member is armed is not necessary to support a defendant's murder conviction as an aider and abettor. Likewise, prior gang rivalry, while reflecting motive, is not necessary for a court to uphold a gang member's murder conviction under an aiding and abetting theory. Thus, although evidence of the existence of the above listed factors may constitute sufficient evidence to support an aider and abettor's murder conviction under the natural and probable consequence theory, these factors are not necessary to support such a conviction. We do not view the existence of those factors as an exhaustive list that would exclude all other types and combinations of evidence that could support a jury's finding of a foreseeable consequence. In other words, the absence of these factors alone is not dispositive.

In examining the whole record in the light most favorable to the prosecution, we conclude that a rational trier of fact could have found that the shooting of the victim was a reasonably foreseeable consequence of the gang assault in this case. Medina, Marron, and Vallejo, members of the Lil Watts gang, repeatedly challenged Barba by asking, "Where are you from?" When Barba responded, "Sanfer," Vallejo declared he was a member of another gang, "Lil Watts." Medina remarked, "What fool, you think you crazy?" Apparently viewing Barba's response as disrespectful behavior, Medina, Marron, and Vallejo then attacked Barba.

The Court of Appeal emphasized there was no evidence that the assailants used weapons or were armed during the fistfight, or that the two gangs involved were in the midst of a "war" or had been involved in prior altercations. It further stressed that the shooting occurred after the fistfight had ended. However, the Court of Appeal's analysis ignores the testimony of the gang expert, Officer Port, and of Ordenes, and other evidence.

According to Ordenes, a gang member's query "where are you from?" means "what gang are you from?" and is a verbal challenge, which (depending on the response) could lead to a physical altercation and even death. Officer Port affirmed that a gang member who asks, "where are you from?" could be armed and probably would be prepared to respond with violence, ranging from a fistfight to homicide. As a former gang member, Ordenes foresaw precisely that result. He feared that somebody might get killed after Vallejo verbally challenged Barba, and, because of that fear, ordered defendants to "take that into the streets."

Once the fight ensued, the three men could not get Barba down. Despite being attacked and outnumbered by three aggressors, Barba defended himself well and held his own. Ordenes interrupted the fistfight while Barba was performing well and before the three attackers could vindicate themselves. Given the gang-related purpose of the initial assault and the fact that, despite being outnumbered, Barba exhibited strength against three aggressors who could not avenge themselves in response to what they considered disrespectful behavior by Barba, the jury could reasonably have found that a person in defendants' position (i.e., a gang member) would have or should have known that retaliation was likely to occur and that escalation of the confrontation to a deadly level was reasonably foreseeable as Barba was retreating from the scene.

The record supports that implicit finding by the jury. First, according to the testimony, gang members emphasize the need for respect, primarily in the form of fear. Officer Port testified that gang members view behavior that disrespects their gang as a challenge and "slap in the face" which must be avenged. Gang members perceive that, if no retaliatory action is taken in the face of disrespectful behavior, the challenger and other people will view the gang member and the gang itself as weak. Ordenes, a former gang member, confirmed that once a gang is no longer feared, its members lose respect, are ridiculed, and become vulnerable and subject to attack by other gangs. According to Officer Port, violence is used as a response to disrespectful behavior and disagreements, and as a means to gain respect. Ordenes confirmed that gang members consider death as a means to maintain respect in some circumstances.

Second, the record reveals that Lil Watts was a violent street gang that regularly committed gun offenses. Officer Port testified that Lil Watts members were involved "in all sorts of gun charges," including assaults with firearms, semiautomatic firearms, drive-by shootings, and homicides. Ordenes affirmed that many gang members occupied their turfs with guns. Regarding this specific incident, Ordenes ordered the Lil Watts gang members outside because he was concerned that somebody would be killed. Thus, because Lil Watts members had challenged a rival gang member, the jury could reasonably have inferred that, in backing up that challenge, a Lil Watts member either would have been armed or would have or should have known a fellow gang member was or might be armed.

Third, although there was no evidence the two gangs involved had an ongoing rivalry, Officer Port stated that the Lake Los Angeles area is considered a "transient area for gangs" where newly arrived gang members demand respect to establish themselves in that territory. Ordenes testified that members of Lil Watts, Sanfer, and Pacoima (another gang) live in the Lake Los Angeles area. Thus, escalating the violence with a gun was a foreseeable way for a Lil Watts gang member to exact revenge for Barba's initial disrespect and his later show of strength against the three aggressors, thereby establishing Lil Watts's turf domination in the neighborhood.

Fourth, although Vallejo argues that the fistfight and shooting were not one uninterrupted event, but rather two separate incidents, the evidence showed that Medina, Marron, and Vallejo did not consider the fight to be over and that the shooting resulted directly from that fight. Eyewitnesses testified that the events happened very quickly, in a matter of seconds, not minutes. After Ordenes had broken up the fight, someone yelled, "get the heat," just before the shooting . . . .

* * *

Thus, the evidence shows there was a close connection between the failed assault against Barba (in which Marron, Vallejo, and Medina directly participated) and the murder of Barba; Medina shot Barba because he disrespected Lil Watts; and the shooting and death were " 'not an unreasonable result to be expected from the [assault].' " (*People v. Martinez* (1966) 239 Cal.App.2d 161, 178–179, 48 Cal.Rptr. 521.

* * *

Accordingly, viewing the whole record in the light most favorable to the prosecution, we find there was sufficient evidence to support the murder and attempted murder convictions of defendants Marron and Vallejo.

* * *

■ Dissenting Opinion by MORENO, J.

I dissent. In my view, the Court of Appeal reached the correct conclusion when it reversed the convictions of defendants Marron and Vallejo. I agree with the Court of Appeal that insufficient evidence supported those convictions based on the theory that the shooting of Barba by defendant Medina was a natural and probable consequence of the assault on Barba in which Marron and Vallejo participated. The Court of Appeal did not reach this conclusion lightly. The court applied the deferential substantial evidence standard of review to its inquiry. It also recognized the grim reality that disputes between gang members are in a different category from disputes between civilians. "As gang violence has become more prevalent and innocent bystanders have become victims of the violence in ever increasing numbers, our courts have recognized that a dispute between two neighbors and one between two gang members can lead to different consequences." Nonetheless, the Court of Appeal determined that even in the context of gang violence there was insufficient evidence to support the jury's verdict as to Vallejo and Marron.

* * *

. . . [The Court of Appeal] noted that there was no evidence that either Vallejo or Marron had knowledge that Medina was in possession of a gun before or during the fistfight with Barba. "Indeed," the court observed, "there was no evidence that anyone had a weapon of any kind prior to the shooting." The shooting of Barba did not occur during the assault on him by Medina, Vallejo and Marron. Rather, the testimony of the three percipient witnesses—Ordenes, Rodriguez, and Varela—was that the fight had broken up, Ordenes had walked Barba to his car and put him inside of it, and Barba had begun to drive away when Medina alone walked into the middle of the street and started firing. There was no evidence that the assault on Barba was planned by the defendants, much less that it was a retaliatory act in the course of ongoing gang warfare between the "Lil Watts" and "Sanfer" gangs. In fact, the gang expert, Officer Port, testified that these gangs were not even rivals. Finally, there was no evidence that there was any prior agreement between the defendants to go out looking for a "Sanfer" gang member to assault.

* * *

I must agree with the Court of Appeal: "Notwithstanding the violence which most gang confrontations spawn, on our facts, viewed objectively, we cannot conclude that an unplanned fight between unarmed combatants in front of a residence was reasonably likely to lead to a shooting resulting in death. In essence, the Attorney General is asking us to create a new theory of liability. An aider and abettor would be responsible for any crime that was a natural and *possible* consequence of the target crime. That, we cannot do."

* * *

NOTES

1. Is the dissent correct that Marron and Vallejo are being held responsible for a crime that was only a possible, as opposed to probable, consequence of the target offense?

2. Does the court ever make clear what constitutes "probable"? In the criminal procedure area, probable cause is considered to be a relatively low standard. *See* Bennett L. Gershman, *A Discourse on the ABA's Criminal Justice Standards: Prosecution and Defense Functions*, 62 HASTINGS L.J. 1259, 1267 (2011). Should courts look to criminal procedure decisions on searches, arrests, and charging when ascertaining the scope of substantive criminal law?

————

3. THE *ACTUS REUS* OF ACCESSORYSHIP

As in most other areas of criminal law, prosecutors must demonstrate more than *mens rea* to convict defendants under an accomplice liability theory. Prosecutors must also establish that the defendant committed the *actus reus* of accessoryship by providing actual assistance to the principal. In most instances, proving assistance is not difficult. But for the close cases, how much assistance is required to satisfy the *actus reus* element?

United States v. Ortiz

United States Court of Appeals for the First Circuit, 1992.
966 F.2d 707.

■ SELYA, CIRCUIT JUDGE.

Defendants Felix Nunez Molina (Nunez) and Ruben Ortiz De Jesus (Ortiz) were convicted of aiding and abetting a drug-trafficking operation. Both men appeal. We affirm their convictions . . .

I. BACKGROUND

* * *

On February 19, 1991, a federal Drug Enforcement Administration (DEA) agent, Roberto Izquierdo, using a confidential informant (CI) as a conduit, arranged to buy a half kilo of cocaine from Ernesto Llanos Domenech (Llanos). The men were to meet in front of a local bank. When Llanos arrived, he asked Izquierdo and the CI to come to his house. They refused. Llanos then left to retrieve the cocaine, promising to meet his prospective customer later that evening in a parking area adjacent to a fast-food restaurant.

Unbeknownst to Llanos, he was placed under surveillance at that time. On the way home, Llanos flagged down a passing car operated by Nunez. The two men spoke. They then proceeded to Llanos' house, each driving his own automobile.

After a brief respite, the pair drove to the restaurant in Llanos' car. Llanos was behind the wheel; Nunez was ensconced in the right front seat. When Llanos' car stopped, Izquierdo and the CI (who was wearing a body wire) approached the open window on the passenger's side. They began to rehash the terms of the deal with Llanos, speaking across Nunez. Llanos said that he had brought a package containing a kilogram of cocaine. Izquierdo protested that this was double the amount he had agreed to purchase. Llanos then told the agent that he and Nunez would repair to his house, cut the drug, reweigh it, and return with a half kilogram. During this conversation, Nunez confirmed that he and Llanos would have to reduce, recalibrate, and repackage the contraband. The sellers drove away.

Llanos returned to the restaurant's parking area later that evening, accompanied by Nunez's brother-in-law, defendant Ortiz. An opaque plastic sack lay in the front seat between the two men. Izquierdo approached the vehicle on the driver's side and began discussing the purchase with Llanos. Llanos grabbed the sack, removed a transparent bag of cocaine, and displayed it. After inspecting the bag's contents and engaging in a brief conversation about the previously negotiated sale, Izquierdo left to get the money. At this juncture, the trap snapped shut. DEA agents arrested Llanos and Ortiz. A pat-down search revealed that Ortiz was carrying a beeper.

Nunez and Ortiz were charged with aiding and abetting Llanos' intended cocaine distribution. Llanos was charged as a principal and pled guilty. His alleged myrmidons were tried together and convicted.

II. SUFFICIENCY OF THE EVIDENCE

First and foremost, the appellants strive to convince us that the evidence was insufficient to sustain the jury verdict. We are not persuaded.

* * *

B. *Mere Presence: "Point of Sale" Cases.*

. . . This case, in which Ortiz and Nunez both claim they were merely present at the scene of Llanos' crime and, therefore, the evidence against them was inadequate, presents a paradigmatic example of the sort of problems that can surface. On the one hand, "[m]ere association between the principal and those accused of aiding and abetting is not sufficient to establish guilt; nor is mere presence at the scene and knowledge that a crime was to be committed sufficient to establish aiding and abetting." *United States v. Francomano,* 554 F.2d 483, 486 (1st Cir.1977). On the other hand, "there are circumstances where presence itself implies participation-as where a 250-pound bruiser stands silently by during an extortion attempt, or a companion stands by during a robbery, ready to sound a warning or give other aid if required." *United States v. Martinez,* 479 F.2d 824, 829 (1st Cir.1973). In sum, the line that separates mere presence from culpable presence is a thin one, often difficult to plot.

We think it is important that this case does not involve a claim of mere presence in regard to, say, a seaman aboard a large vessel transporting drugs, *cf. United States v. Mehtala,* 578 F.2d 6 (1st Cir.1978), or an occupier of a multi-occupant dwelling where drugs are stored, *cf. United States v. Ocampo,* 964 F.2d 80 (1st Cir.1992). In situations involving primarily transport or storage, the possibility that an innocent bystander can be on the scene is significantly greater than in a situation where a person is brought to a neutral site by a drug trafficker preliminary to the actual consummation of a narcotics transaction.

Some general principles help us to establish this distinction. When assessing sufficiency challenges in criminal cases, we have remarked, time and again, that factfinders may draw reasonable inferences from the evidence based on shared perceptions and understandings of the habits, practices, and inclinations of human beings. Thus, jurors are neither required to divorce themselves from their common sense nor to abandon the dictates of mature experience. Jurors can be assumed to know that criminals rarely welcome innocent persons as witnesses to serious crimes and rarely seek to perpetrate felonies before larger-than-necessary audiences. Indeed, we held some years ago, on facts highly analogous to those in the instant record, that the "jury could have inferred that, had Appellant been a mere bystander, he would not have joined the two agents and [the principal] in the privacy of the car while the terms of the sale were further discussed." *United States v. Martinez,* 479 F.2d 824 829 (1st Cir. 1973).

In short, when the evidence shows a defendant arriving at the scene of a prearranged drug deal accompanied by, and with the contrivance of, a principal, the most closely applicable precedents are not the cases involving presence during the transport or storage of drugs, but those involving presence at the point of sale. The cases before us fall into the point-of-sale category.[2]

C. *The Evidence Against Nunez.*

In our estimation, the government's case against Nunez passes muster. Before Llanos appeared in the parking lot with Nunez in tow, he spoke with Izquierdo and established a time and place for drugs to be dealt. He mentioned that he had to find his "buddy." From the evidence

---

[2] Of course, the planned sale was temporarily sidetracked after Nunez accompanied Llanos to the restaurant. Yet, the evidence is undisputed that Llanos' intention was to sell cocaine at that meeting. We think it is appropriate, therefore, to treat Nunez's case as a point-of-sale situation.

of subsequent events, the jury could have believed Llanos thereafter cruised the streets until he found Nunez and waved him down. Nunez followed Llanos home, conversed with him, and accompanied him to the parking lot. Once there, Nunez not only listened to the dialogue between buyer and seller but also participated in it, reiterating what Llanos had said earlier: that the drug had to be reworked to effectuate the sale. Although this factual mosaic does not compel a conviction, it adequately supports one.

To be sure, Nunez denies that he remarked the need to cut and reweigh the cocaine. He asserts that since the comment does not appear on the tape recording of the conversation and the trial judge, in denying Nunez's motion for acquittal, acknowledged that Nunez arguably remained silent during the meeting, it was impermissible for the jury to give credence to Izquierdo's testimony about the statement.[3] But, the cases are legion to the effect that, when a jury is presented with conflicting factual statements, the resolution of the conflict, and any concomitant credibility calls, are uniquely within the jury's province . . . In a nutshell, the fact that Nunez's statement was not captured on tape was grist for the jury's mill-but it did not foreclose either the admissibility of the evidence or the jury's right to rely on it.

By the same token, the jury's factfinding mission is not aborted simply because the judge, had he been presiding at a bench trial, might have found the facts differently. The key is whether the jury's decipherment of the record represented a plausible choice among reasonable alternatives, all things considered. In this instance, the judge, despite his articulated doubt about what Nunez said, saw no reason to set aside the verdict. Nor do we.

D. *The Evidence Against Ortiz.*

The case against Ortiz is, admittedly, a bit thinner. Unlike Nunez, Ortiz remained silent during the transaction. Nonetheless, silence does not establish innocence, and the proof as a whole strikes us as sufficient to support Ortiz's conviction.

For one thing, the evidence established that Ortiz and Nunez were brothers-in-law. While innocent association with those involved in illegal activities can never form the sole basis for a conviction, the existence of a close relationship between a defendant and others involved in criminal activity can, as a part of a larger package of proof, assist in supporting an inference of involvement in illicit activity.

For another thing, the government presented evidence that Ortiz was carrying a telephone beeper at the time of his arrest. Although

---

[3] The testimony was blunt and unambiguous. Izquierdo, a percipient witness, testified specifically that Nunez "told me that they have to go and weigh the package so I have my complete half of the cocaine and pack the-in a plastic bag, wrap it around in a plastic bag or whatever the wrapping will be and to weigh it and pack the cocaine and deliver my half kilo of cocaine."

possession of a beeper is not *ipso facto* proof of complicity in the drug trade, *United States v. Duarte,* 950 F.2d 1255, 1260 n. 4 (7th Cir.1991), possession of such an item-on a defendant's person at the scene of an ongoing drug deal—"could justifiably raise the eyebrows of a reasonable jury" when viewed in light of the totality of the evidence. *Id.* at 1260 & n. 4. This sort of inference takes on added cogency in the context of a challenge to evidentiary sufficiency, where a court must construe the evidence and all reasonable inferences therefrom in favor of the government.

Last but not least, Llanos, anticipating that a prearranged drug deal would be consummated, appears purposefully to have brought Ortiz with him to the point of sale. Ortiz, for his part, appears to have come willingly. The bag containing the contraband was in plain view between the two men. Seen in that perspective, the claim of mere presence has the hollow ring of sloganeering. Here, Ortiz's presence patently implied participation.

Ortiz argues vociferously that all the evidence can be explained in a manner perfectly consistent with innocent activity. That argument misses the point. "The fact that [a defendant's] acts appeared not to be illegal when viewed in isolation does not bar his conviction." *United States v. LaChance,* 817 F.2d 1491, 1494 (11th Cir. 1987). In the final analysis, the government's proof at trial "need not exclude every reasonable hypothesis of innocence, provided the record as a whole supports a conclusion of guilt beyond a reasonable doubt." *United States v. Victoria-Peguero,* 920 F.2d 77, 86–87 (1st Cir. 1990). We conclude that the evidence adduced against Ortiz, although perhaps verging toward the margin, was adequate to satisfy this benchmark.

* * *

[Affirmed.]

State ex rel. M.B.

Court of Appeals of Utah, 2008.
198 P.3d 1007.

■ ORME, JUDGE:

The main issue in this appeal is whether a minor can be an accomplice to vehicular burglary and theft when he or she just sits in the front passenger seat of a parked vehicle, without any overt or affirmative action taken to aid in the crime, while two adult companions burglarize a vehicle. We conclude that no definitive inferences regarding such a passenger's involvement in the crime can be drawn without resort to impermissible conjecture or speculation and that a fact-finder could therefore not conclude, beyond a reasonable doubt, that such a person was an accomplice. We accordingly reverse M.B.'s convictions.

BACKGROUND

At around 2:00 a.m. on the morning of April 13, 2007, two men broke into a truck owned by a Salt Lake City couple, damaging the truck and taking its stereo and some CDs. At about the same time, the wife awoke to the sound of a dog barking and a car door shutting. She looked out her window and first observed an unfamiliar car parked on the street across from her driveway. She then saw one man crawling out the back of her truck's camper shell and a second man exiting the driver's side door carrying the stereo and CDs. When the two men returned to the unfamiliar car and opened a door, the dome light came on and she observed the silhouette of M.B. "[j]ust sitting" in the passenger seat. Her husband, who had called the police shortly after she saw the first man exit the camper shell, gave the police information about the vehicle and the direction it was headed. A short time later, police stopped the vehicle and arrested its occupants.

The responding officer stated that M.B. and the two men were wearing dark clothing. Upon investigation of the vehicle, the officer found a screwdriver between the console and the front passenger seat, and some gloves in the console. In the trunk, he found two additional screwdrivers and three more pairs of gloves, along with a car stereo that still had some of the couple's truck's dashboard connected to it.

The State brought the following delinquency allegations against M.B. in juvenile court: (1) vehicular burglary; (2) theft; (3) unlawful possession of burglary tools; and (4) theft by receiving stolen property. After trial, the juvenile court determined that M.B. was guilty of vehicular burglary, theft, and unlawful possession of burglary tools. This appeal followed.

* * *

ANALYSIS

I. Vehicular Burglary and Theft

M.B. claims that his mere passive presence in the front passenger seat of the parked vehicle did not provide enough evidence to support a conclusion that he was an accomplice to vehicular burglary or theft. Specifically, he argues that no evidence admitted in this case could be construed as proving, beyond a reasonable doubt, that "[he] engaged in some active behavior, or at least speech or expression, that served to assist or encourage another to unlawfully enter the vehicle" and take the items in question. We agree.

"Any person who unlawfully enters any vehicle with intent to commit a felony or theft is guilty of a burglary of a vehicle." Utah Code Ann. § 76–6–204 (2003). "A person commits theft if he obtains or exercises unauthorized control over the property of another with a purpose to deprive him thereof." *Id.* § 76–6–404. "Every person, acting with the mental state required for the commission of an offense who directly commits the offense, who solicits, requests, commands, encourages, or intentionally aids another person to engage in conduct which constitutes an offense shall be criminally liable as a party for such conduct." *Id.* § 76–2–202. We only address whether M.B. "encourage[d]" or "intentionally aid[ed]" his two adult companions, as the facts clearly do not support a conclusion that M.B. "directly commit[ted] the offense, . . . [or] solicit[ed], request[ed], [or] command[ed]" that the others commit vehicular burglary or theft.

Our precedents clearly show that "[m]ere presence, or even prior knowledge, does not make one an accomplice to a crime absent evidence showing—beyond a reasonable doubt—that [a] defendant advised, instigated, encouraged, or assisted in perpet[r]ation of the crime." *In re V.T.,* 2000 UT App 189, 5 P.3d 1234. However, "[w]hile mere presence at the scene of a crime affords no basis for a conviction, presence, companionship, and conduct before and after the offense are circumstances from which one's participation in the criminal intent may be inferred." *American Fork City v. Rothe,* 2000 UT App 277, 12 P.3d 108.

In re V.T., 2000 UT App 189, 5 P.3d 1234, is the Utah case most directly on point. There, this court concluded that a juvenile defendant's presence during and after a theft did not support a conclusion that he was an accomplice because no evidence suggested his active involvement. The evidence showed that the defendant had been with friends when they stole a camcorder and that he remained in their presence following the theft while his friends discussed the crime. The State argued that this evidence, coupled with the defendant's friendship with the thieves, supported an inference that the defendant encouraged the theft and was, therefore, guilty of the crime as an accomplice. The juvenile court agreed. We overturned the juvenile court's ruling, concluding that "[t]he facts . . . prove[d] only that [the defendant] was present before, during, and after the theft of the camcorder" and that "[t]he lack of any evidence showing that he at least encouraged the other defendants in stealing the camcorder preclude[d]" a determination that he was culpable as an accomplice. *Id.* ¶ 20.

Other Utah cases show that a defendant's conviction based on accomplice liability will be upheld when the evidence and circumstances show some active participation or involvement in the underlying crime. In *State v. Johnson,* 6 Utah 2d 29, 305 P.2d 488 (1956), for example, the evidence showed that the defendant was spotted "walking rapidly away from the" scene of the burglary, and that another man involved could only have gained access to the burglarized building via a ladder, which the police soon discovered, hidden by cardboard. The Utah Supreme Court observed that the totality of the evidence supported an inference that the defendant had aided the burglary because the other man, who was apprehended inside the building, could not have hidden the ladder after he climbed it and entered the building. Accordingly, the totality of the circumstances allowed an inference beyond a reasonable doubt that the defendant had actively aided the other man and was therefore an accomplice. *See id.* Also, in *American Fork City v. Rothe,* 2000 UT App 277, 12 P.3d 108, this court upheld the conviction of the defendant based on accomplice liability when there was evidence that, beyond his being present during the commission of the crime, the defendant actively looked up and down two separate store aisles, apparently acting as a lookout, while a companion stole items off the shelves of a grocery store.

The State presented no evidence in the instant case suggesting M.B. actually behaved as a lookout or otherwise aided or encouraged the crimes of vehicular burglary and theft. For example, no evidence showed that M.B. looked up and down the street, was in the driver's seat poised to whisk his companions away, handled any of the stolen property, or otherwise acted to ensure that his companions were not discovered or apprehended while they committed vehicular burglary and theft. The only evidence pertaining to M.B. was that he was wearing dark clothes and sat in the passenger seat of the vehicle while his two adult companions broke into the couple's truck, removed CDs and a stereo, and returned to the getaway car, placing the stolen items in the trunk. Without any evidence showing more than just a passive presence, we conclude that the juvenile court's determination that M.B. was guilty of vehicular burglary and theft was erroneous as a matter of law.

The State, relying heavily on federal case law, urges that M.B.'s dark clothing and presence in the idling getaway car allows a fact-finder to draw an inference that he was a lookout ready to give a warning if needed or to otherwise aid the men in their efforts to commit the crimes without being apprehended. The juvenile court also seems to have found that M.B.'s dark clothing, along with his presence in the getaway car, allowed an inference, beyond a reasonable doubt, that M.B. was involved in the crime. We disagree that M.B.'s dark attire solidifies any inference that could be drawn regarding his passive presence in the vehicle at the scene of the crime. We emphasize that there are both innocent and incriminating reasons to explain M.B.'s attire. Considered in a light most favorable to the juvenile court's conclusion, any inferences that may be drawn from M.B.'s dark clothing, along with his passive presence in the passenger seat, are still too weak and speculative to support a conclusion beyond a reasonable doubt that M.B. was an accomplice to vehicular burglary or theft. We also disagree that an idling getaway car, when coupled with the other factors, supports an inference beyond a reasonable doubt that M.B. was an accomplice, given that he was not in the driver's seat.

* * *

The State additionally argues that, as in *United States v. Ortiz,* 966 F.2d 707 (1st Cir. 1992), M.B.'s presence suggests involvement because M.B. was related to the owner and driver of the getaway car. However,

Ortiz is distinguishable because this case involves an adult and a minor. Under the circumstances we do not think the familial relationship, coupled with the difference in age, necessarily supports involvement by M.B., who might have tagged along not knowing criminal activity was afoot or, even knowing it was, planned (or was directed) not to participate. We further note that in this case, the stolen property was placed in the trunk of the vehicle, and any gloves or tools were not in open and plain view of M.B. but in the trunk, console, or between the console and seat. In contrast, we think Ortiz's purposeful presence at the final sale during the drug transaction, with the drugs in plain view on the seat next to him, were the crucial facts supporting an inference of involvement and that the fact regarding Ortiz's relationship with another man who was involved—recited in the *Ortiz* opinion and relied on by the State in the instant case—merely provided further support under the circumstances.

The State further urges that the nature of the crime, i.e., a felony, supports a conclusion that M.B.'s presence was culpable rather than innocent because felons do not want innocent bystanders present while they commit a felony given that such persons might later present incriminating evidence against them. We conclude, however, as previously discussed, that the familial relationship in this case between a minor and an adult creates other explanations for M.B.'s presence besides that of complicit involvement in the criminal activity, e.g., M.B. may have been left with no choice but to accompany his adult relative to the scene of the crime. Moreover, because M.B. was family, his adult relative likely was less concerned that M.B. would "rat him out" given the realities of family loyalty.

We additionally acknowledge that *drivers* of getaway cars are typically found guilty under accomplice liability theories because, as a driver, they inherently show active involvement in the crime. No cases, however, have been called to our attention where a person just sitting as a passenger in a getaway car was found guilty as an accomplice. Accordingly, and for all the reasons discussed, we reverse M.B.'s vehicular burglary and theft convictions.

* * *

Reversed.

———

NOTES

1. The prosecutors in *M.B.* relied heavily on the First Circuit's decision in *Ortiz*, but the Utah appellate court rejected that comparison. Was the court correct? Can you reconcile the appellate decisions in *M.B.* and *Ortiz*?

2. In *Ortiz*, the court focused on the fact that the accomplice had a beeper. If someone other than a doctor is found with a beeper, is that incriminating?

Would it have been incriminating in 1992? In *M.B.*, the prosecution contended that the defendant's dark clothing contributed to the likelihood that he was an accomplice. Is dark clothing incriminating if it is worn at a crime scene?

3. The *Ortiz* and *M.B.* decisions both correctly state the rule that "mere presence" is not sufficient to satisfy the *actus reus* element of accomplice liability. Yet, in both cases it seems as though the prosecutors and the juries were convinced of the defendants' guilt because of their presence at the crime scenes. Do you think most people—particularly prosecutors, defense lawyers, and judges—really believe that mere presence should be insufficient to establish liability?

4. Under the common law, a defendant can only be an accomplice if he actually provides assistance. Thus, if a defendant sought to assist in a burglary and left the front door unlocked, he would not be an accomplice if the principal climbed in the window of the house. *See* JOSHUA DRESSLER, UNDERSTANDING CRIMINAL LAW § 30.04(B)(1) (6th ed. 2012). The Model Penal Code is broader however and provides liability for a defendant who "attempts to aid." *See* Model Penal Code § 2.06(3)(a)(ii).

5. While the common law requires that a defendant provide actual assistance, the prosecution need not prove causation. An accomplice is liable even if the principal did not actually need help to accomplish the offense. Put differently, if the accomplice had the necessary *mens rea* and provided at least some assistance, it does not matter that the principal easily could have completed the crime without the help of the accomplice. For instance, in State v. Tally, 15 So. 722 (Ala. 1894), Judge John Tally knew that four of his relatives planned to murder R.C. Ross because Ross had engaged in sex with their sister. After the four men set out to find and kill Ross, one of Ross's relatives tried to send a telegram warning Ross. Judge Talley learned of the effort to warn Ross, and he instructed the telegram operator not to deliver the warning. The four men killed Ross without ever learning of Judge Talley's efforts to help them. The court concluded that Judge Tally had been an accomplice, even if the result would have been exactly the same without his assistance:

> The assistance given, however, need not contribute to the criminal result in the sense that but for it the result would not have ensued. It is quite sufficient if it facilitated a result that would have transpired without it. It is quite enough if the aid merely rendered it easier for the principal actor to accomplish the end intended by him and the aider and abettor, though in all human probability the end would have been attained without it. If the aid in homicide can be shown to have put the deceased at a disadvantage, to have deprived him of a single chance of life which but for it he would have had, he who furnishes such aid is guilty, though it cannot be known or shown that the dead man, in the absence thereof, would have availed himself of that chance; as, where one counsels murder, he is guilty as an accessory before the fact, though it appears to be probable that murder would have been done without his counsel[.]

Id. at 738–39. For a further analysis of this issue, see Sanford H. Kadish, *Complicity, Cause and Blame: A Study in the Interpretation of Doctrine*, 73 CAL. L. REV. 323 (1985).

4. LIMITATIONS ON ACCESSORYSHIP

Is it possible for anyone to be an accomplice to criminal activity? Are certain categories of people off limits? Consider the materials below.

Miller v. Skumanick

United States District Court for the Middle District of Pennsylvania, 2009.
605 F.Supp.2d 634.

■ JAMES M. MUNLEY, DISTRICT JUDGE.

* * *

Background

At issue in this case is the practice of "sexting," which has become popular among teenagers in recent years. According to the plaintiffs, this is "the practice of sending or posting sexually suggestive text messages and images, including nude or semi-nude photographs, via cellular telephones or over the Internet." Typically, the subject takes a picture of him- or herself with a digital camera or cell phone camera, or asks someone else to take that picture. That picture is stored as a digitized image and then sent via the text-message or photo-send function on a cell phone, transmitted by computer through electronic mail, or posted to an internet website like Facebook or MySpace. This practice is widespread among American teenagers; studies show approximately 20% of Americans age 13–19 have done it.

Images and Threatened Prosecutions

In October 2008, Tunkhannock, Pennsylvania School District officials confiscated several students' cell phones, examined them and discovered photographs of "scantily clad, semi-nude and nude teenage girls." Many of these girls were enrolled in the district. The School District reported that male students had been trading these images over their cell phones.

The School District turned the phones over to Defendant Skumanick, the District Attorney of Wyoming County, Pennsylvania. Skumanick began a criminal investigation. In November 2008, Skumanick stated publically to local newspaper reporters and a district assembly at Tunkhannock High School that students who possess inappropriate images of minors could be prosecuted under Pennsylvania law for possessing or distributing child pornography . . . Skumanick pointed out that these charges were felonies that could result in long prison terms and would give even juveniles a permanent record. Defendant contends that if found guilty of these crimes, the three minor plaintiffs would probably be subject to registration as sex offenders under Pennsylvania's Registration of Sexual Offenders Act ("Meghan's Law") for at least ten years and have their names and pictures displayed on the state's sex-offender website.

On February 5, 2009, Skumanick sent letters to the parents of approximately twenty Tunkhannock students, including the adult plaintiffs in this case. Skumanick sent this letter to the students on whose cell phones the pictures were stored and to the girls shown in the photos. According to the plaintiffs, he did not send the letter to those who had disseminated the images.

The letter informed the parents that their child had been "identified in a police investigation involving the possession and/or dissemination of child pornography." The letter also promised that the charges would be dropped if the child successfully completed a six- to nine-month program focused on education and counseling. The children and parents were invited to a meeting on February 12, 2009 to discuss the issue. The letter warned that "charges will be filed against those that do not participate or those that do not successfully complete the program."

Skumanick held the meeting on February 12, 2009 at the Wyoming County Courthouse. At that meeting, Skumanick reiterated his threat to prosecute unless the children submitted to probation, paid a $100 program fee and completed the program successfully. When asked by a parent at the meeting why his daughter—who had been depicted in a photograph wearing a bathing suit—could be charged with child pornography, Skumanick replied that the girl was posed "provocatively," which made her subject to the child pornography charge. When the father of Marissa Miller asked Skumanick who got to decide what "provocative" meant, the District Attorney replied that he refused to argue the question and reminded the crowd that he could charge all the minors that night. Instead, Skumanick asserted, he had offered them a plea deal. He told Mr. Miller that "these are the rules. If you don't like them, too bad."

The proposed program—which the plaintiffs call a "re-education program"—is divided between girls' and boys' programs. The program is designed to teach the girls to "gain an understanding of how their actions were wrong," "gain an understanding of what it means to be a girl in today's society, both advantages and disadvantages," and "identify nontraditional societal and job roles." Included in the "homework" for the program is an assignment including "[w]hat you did" and "[w]hy it was wrong." The program was initially purported to last six to nine months, but was eventually reduced to two hours per week over five weeks.

At the February 12 meeting, Skumanick asked all those present to sign an agreement assigning the minors to probation and to participation in the program. Only one parent agreed to sign the form for her child. Skumanick gave the parents forty-eight hours to agree to the offer or the minors would be charged. After parents objected, Skumanick extended the time frame for agreeing to his program to a week. Skumanick told parents he would show them the photographs in question at the end of the meeting.

The Photographs Involved

All of the adult plaintiffs here are parents of daughters whose photographs appeared on the confiscated cell phones. They all reside in the Tunkhannock School District, and their children attend the Tunkhannock Schools.

Plaintiff MaryJo Miller and her ex-husband met with Skumanick at his invitation on February 10, 2009. Skumanick showed them the photograph that involved their daughter Marissa. The photograph in question was approximately two years old, and showed Plaintiffs Marissa Miller and Grace Kelly from the waist up, each wearing a white, opaque bra. Marissa was speaking on the phone and Grace using her hand to make the peace sign. The girls were thirteen years old at the time the picture was taken. Despite Ms. Miller's protests to the contrary, Skumanick claimed that this image met the definition of child pornography because the girls were posed "provocatively." The Millers objected to Skumanick's legal claims, insisting that their daughter had a right to a jury trial if charged. Skumanick informed them that no jury trials exists in Juvenile Court. He also promised to prosecute both girls on felony child-pornography charges if they did not agree to his conditions. After the February 12 meeting, Skumanick showed Jane Doe the photograph of her daughter Nancy. The photograph, more than a year old, showed Nancy Doe wrapped in a white, opaque towel. The towel was wrapped around her body, just below her breasts. It looked as if she had just emerged from the shower.

The plaintiffs emphasize that neither of these two photographs depicted any sexual activity . . . At the time that plaintiffs filed their complaint, Skumanick had refused repeated requests to provide plaintiffs' counsel with copies of the pictures. He asserted that he could be charged with a child pornography crime for sharing a copy. The minors insist that they did not disseminate the photographs to anyone else, but that another person sent those pictures "to a large group of people" without their permission.

Potential Charges Against the Plaintiffs

According to the complaint, Skumanick's only basis for the threatened prosecution of the three girls is that they allowed themselves to be photographed. In early March, he asserted to plaintiffs' counsel that the three were accomplices in the production of child pornography. During the hearing on the [temporary restraining order] conducted by this court . . . the defendant reiterated that he intends to charge the girls if they refuse to participate in the education program.

On February 25, 2009, plaintiffs received a letter dated February 23, 2009. This letter advised parents that they were scheduled for a February 28, 2009 appointment at the Wyoming County Courthouse to "finalize the paperwork for the informal adjustment." Plaintiffs contend that an "informal adjustment" amounts to a guilty plea in the juvenile context, since it allows for probation before judgment. Parents who attended the February 28, 2009 meeting informed plaintiffs that agreeing to the informal adjustment would subject plaintiffs to the "re-education" course, six months of probation and drug testing during those six months. All of the parents and minors except the three here involved agreed to the conditions. Defendant has temporarily deferred prosecution to the three minors here to allow plaintiffs' counsel to research the issues in this case. During the hearing on the [temporary restraining order], defendant gave his word as an officer of the court that he would not bring charges against the minor plaintiffs before this court renders a decision.

* * *

. . . While the court emphasizes that its view is preliminary and not intended to absolve the plaintiffs of any potential criminal liability, plaintiffs make a reasonable argument that the images presented to the court do not appear to qualify in any way as depictions of prohibited sexual acts. Even if they were such depictions, the plaintiffs argument that the evidence to this point indicates that the minor plaintiffs were not involved in disseminating the images is also a reasonable one. Thus, a reasonable likelihood exists that plaintiffs will succeed on the merits, and this factor weighs in favor of granting a [temporary restraining order against prosecution].

* * *

———

NOTES

1. On appeal, the Third Circuit upheld the temporary restraining order enjoining prosecution of the girls who had been photographed. *See* Miller v. Mitchell, 598 F.3d 139 (3d Cir. 2010). Shortly thereafter, the district court transformed its temporary restraining order into a permanent injunction and the threatened prosecution of the minors ended. *See* Miller v. Mitchell, No. 3:09cv540, 2010 WL 1779925 (M.D.Pa. Apr. 30, 2010).

2. The *Miller* decision arose in an unusual procedural posture in which individuals went to federal court to civilly enjoin a state prosecutor from filing criminal charges at some point in the future. Because of this procedural posture, the court did not address the viability of the underlying criminal charges. Nevertheless, we know that the prosecutor contended that the three minors were "accomplices in the production of child pornography." Assuming that the prosecutor was correct that the pictures constituted child pornography (a very dubious assumption), would it make sense from a legal perspective to say that the girls assisted in creating child pornography that depicted themselves? Consider the case of In re Meagan R, 49 Cal.Rptr.3d 325 (Cal.App. 1996) in which Oscar Rodriguez broke into the apartment of his ex-girlfriend in order to have sex with his new girlfriend, fourteen-year-old Meagan R. Prosecutors charged Meagan with burglary on a theory of accomplice liability. Burglary was defined as breaking and entering the dwelling house of another with the intent to commit a felony inside, and prosecutors asserted that the felony was statutory rape. In other words, Oscar committed burglary by breaking into his ex-girlfriend's home with the intention to commit statutory rape while inside. Meagan was an accomplice to that crime. A juvenile court agreed and found the charges to be true. On appeal, a California appellate court overturned Meagan's conviction on the ground that the statutory rape law was designed to protect, not punish, the minors who were subjected to statutory rape. The court explained:

> Accordingly, given that Meagan under the circumstances of this case was the victim of statutory rape . . . the juvenile court cannot rely on that crime to serve as the predicate felony in a true finding she committed burglary. When she entered Joani's residence, she had no punishable intent, for she did not have the culpable state of mind required for burglary. Because she could not intend to aid and abet her own statutory rape, she did not enter the residence with the intent to commit that felony therein. While Meagan may have entered the residence with the intent to have sex, she could not commit a felony if she completed that act.

Id. at 330. If Meagan could not have been an accomplice to her own statutory rape because she was a member of the class the statute was designed to protect, can the young girls in *Miller* be accomplices to the production of child pornography that depicts them?

3. Without all the facts, it is difficult to assess the prosecutor's factual claim that the three girls were "accomplices in the production of child pornography." But is there a plausible argument that the prosecutor was incorrect to contend that the three girls were actually accomplices? What other theory of the case could the prosecutor have set forth that might have made more sense?

4. According to the parents who brought the civil suit, the prosecutor "refused repeated requests to provide plaintiffs' counsel with copies of the pictures [because] [h]e asserted that he could be charged with a child pornography crime for sharing a copy." Is that correct? If so, why wasn't it also illegal to show the photographs to the children's parents on February 9th and 12th?

5. Are you surprised the prosecutor wanted to bring criminal charges against the girls whose pictures were disseminated through school? If the district court is correct that twenty percent of teenagers have engaged in "sexting" then school officials have a big problem on their hands. Is this an area where law enforcement should be involved? If so, how could legislatures draft a criminal statute that would seem more reasonable than the actions taken by the prosecutor here?

6. Are there reasons to treat boys and girls differently in sexting cases? If a boyfriend and girlfriend exchange sexually explicit photographs, is it possible that the boyfriend, but not girlfriend, should be charged because of power imbalances in the traditional high-school environment. *See, e.g.*, People v. Interest of T.B., 2016 WL 6123557 (Col. App. Oct. 20, 2016), at *12 (Fox, J., dissenting) ("Here a seventeen-year old and a fifteen-year old each voluntarily sent texts containing partially nude photographs (or sexts) to their then boyfriend, T.B., who was then sixteen-years old . . . . [A]lthough both teen girls also received sexts from T.B., they were not prosecuted.").

7. For additional cases discussing the difficulties facing prosecutors in their charging decisions, see Erik Eckholm, *Proseutors Weigh Teenage Sexting: Folly or Felony?*, N.Y. TIMES, Nov. 13, 2015.

5.   HINDERING PROSECUTION: ACCESSORIES AFTER THE FACT AND RELATED OFFENSES

Those who aid a felon after the crime is completed fall into a different category from those who aid before or during the crime. The common law term for this person is an accessory after the fact, and unlike the accessory before the fact, the accessory *after* the fact does not share in the substantive culpability of the principal felon. Post crime assistance is a separate and distinct offense against public authority.

(A) ACCESSORY AFTER THE FACT

An accessory after the fact, as the name implies, is one who is not one of the principals who committed the crime, but who, "knowing of the commission of the felony by another, gave aid to the felon personally for purpose of hindering the felon's apprehension, conviction, or punishment."[16] Because the accessory after the fact is not a co-participant in the principal felony, it can be important in some cases to determine whether a crime was still in progress when the accused rendered aid. If the crime were still in progress, the defendant rendering aid becomes a co-principal. If, on the other hand, the crime is complete, the defendant is an accessory after the fact, which is a separate, less serious offense. At first glance, it might seem an easy matter to determine whether a defendant helped to commit the crime, or merely assisted "after the fact." However, in the case of continuing offenses, such as many of the misappropriation crimes, it can be more difficult to determine whether the crime is completed, or still in progress. In People v. Zierlion, below, even the justices could not agree.

---

[16]   WAYNE R. LaFAVE, CRIMINAL LAW § 6.9 (3d ed. 2000).

People v. Zierlion

Supreme Court of Illinois, 1959.
16 Ill.2d 217, 157 N.E.2d 72.

■ KLINGBIEL, JUSTICE. After a trial in the criminal court of Cook County before the judge sitting without a jury, Richard Zierlion was convicted of the crime of burglary. He was sentenced to imprisonment in the penitentiary for a term of not less than one nor more than four years. He brings the case to this court for review by writ of error, contending that the evidence is insufficient to prove him guilty of the crime charged.

The evidence shows that on the night of February 4, 1958, four men, namely Tony Gallas, Tom Hills, Paul Petropulos and Ronald Utterbach, entered the office-warehouse of Martin Oil Service, Inc., in Chicago. They pushed a safe belonging to the company out of a second floor window into the yard of the premises. It proved to be too heavy to move. So the four men left for help. In the meantime they had been observed by an employee of the company who came to work at about 11:45 P.M. The police were notified, arrived at the scene, and waited there until about 2:15 A.M. At that time two automobiles appeared, a Cadillac and a Ford, each containing three men. The Cadillac backed up to the safe with the trunk open whereupon the police called to the men. The men fled and the police fired shots killing one and wounding the defendant Zierlion. It further appears that after the original four men left to get assistance they met defendant and one Mike Rudis, the deceased, in a tavern; and that the six of them thereafter went to the yard of the Martin Oil Service to get the safe. There is no evidence that the defendant participated in the affair prior to being called upon to aid in moving the safe.

Defendant argues that to warrant a conviction for burglary it must be shown that the accused entered a building with intent to commit a felony, and that since the evidence fails to show such conduct on the part of defendant the present conviction cannot stand. The contention has merit. Evidence that he was guilty of assisting the burglars after the safe had been removed from the building cannot make him a principal in the crime charged. Proof that a person is an accessory after the fact is proof of an independent offense.

The evidence is insufficient to sustain the judgment, which is accordingly hereby reversed. . . .

■ DAVIS, JUSTICE. I dissent from the conclusions of the court that to warrant a conviction for burglary it must be shown that the accused entered a building with intent to commit a felony, and that evidence that he was assisting the burglars, after the safe had been removed from the building, cannot make him a principal in the crime charged.

Burglary consists of willfully and maliciously entering any dwelling or other building, with or without force, with intent to commit murder, robbery, rape, mayhem, or other felony or larceny. An accessory is defined as "he who stands by, and aids, abets or assists, or who not being present, aiding, abetting, or assisting, hath advised, encouraged, aided or abetted the perpetration of the crime." One who thus "aids, abets, assists, advises or encourages shall be considered as principal, and punished accordingly." Ill.Rev.Stat. 1957, chap. 38, par. 582. While the gist of the offense of burglary is the entering with felonious intent . . ., it does not follow that only those who actually enter the building may be convicted and punished as principals. Thus, one who in furtherance of a common design, stands outside as lookout or waits outside in an automobile, while his confederates enter, is equally guilty with them of the crime of burglary. . . .

The opinion erroneously assumes that the burglary had been completed prior to defendant's participation in efforts to remove the safe from the company premises. While we have held that a burglary is complete upon the breaking and entering with intent to steal . . . , this does not preclude the crime from being a continuing one as long as the participants are still in the process of committing larceny of the property. . . .

It is a general rule of law that "one who withdraws from a criminal enterprise is not responsible for the act of another subsequently committed in furtherance of the enterprise, provided the fact of withdrawal is communicated to the other conspirators." Conversely, one who joins and participates in completing a criminal enterprise should be responsible for both the prior and subsequent acts committed in furtherance of such venture. The evidence establishes that the entry of the building had been accomplished, but the intent to steal the safe had been thwarted at the time the defendant joined the burglars and aided, abetted and participated in furtherance of the original intent to commit larceny of the safe, the purpose of the burglary. Consequently, he is liable as principal even though he did not enter the building. I would affirm the criminal court of Cook County.

––––––––

(B) MISPRISION OF FELONY

Misprision of Felony has been abolished in many jurisdictions, but it still exists as an offense distinct from accessoryship or conspiracy in some jurisdictions in the United States, including the federal courts. United States Code 18 U.S.C. § 4 (2007), provides:

§ 4. Misprision of felony

Whoever, having knowledge of the actual commission of a felony cognizable by a court of the United States, conceals and does not as soon as possible make known the same to some judge or other person in civil or military authority under the United

States, shall be fined under this title or imprisoned not more than three years, or both.

No violation of the statute occurs merely because of the possession of information that another person has committed a federal felony; there must be an affirmative act of concealment. . . .

Nonetheless, the trend in the states is away from recognizing misprision as a crime. In Pope v. State, 38 Md.App. 520, 382 A.2d 880 (1978), the Maryland Supreme Court of Appeals said that because the crime had not been included in the state criminal code, it could not exist except as a common law crime. Commenting on the infrequency with which such a charge has been made, the court concluded as follows:

> If the legislature finds it advisable that the people be obligated under peril of criminal penalty to disclose knowledge of criminal acts, it is, of course, free to create an offense to that end, within constitutional limits, and, hopefully, with adequate safeguards. We believe that the common law offense is not acceptable by today's standards, and we are not free to usurp the power of the General Assembly by attempting to fashion one that would be. We hold that misprision of felony is not a chargeable offense in Maryland.

Pope v. State, 284 Md. 309, 396 A.2d 1054 (1979); *accord* Holland v. State, 302 So.2d 806 (Fla.App. 1974) (reviewing the history of misprision, and concluding, "We agree with Chief Justice Marshall . . . that the crime of misprision of felony is wholly unsuited to American criminal law").

(C) COMPOUNDING A CRIME

One common substitute for misprision is "Compounding a Crime." *See, e.g.*, 720 Ill. Comp. Stat. 5/32–1, which provides:

> Compounding a Crime. (a) A person compounds a crime when he receives or offers to another any consideration for a promise not to prosecute or aid in the prosecution of an offender. (b) Compounding a crime is a petty offense . . .

This offense is most likely to occur in embezzlement case situations where the employer (or his insurer) may seek to recoup a loss, or part of it, in return for withholding a criminal charge.

(D) HINDERING PROSECUTION

Provisions relating to this matter are included in Model Penal Code § 31–5. "Hindering Prosecution" replaces "Accessory After the Fact," "Compounding a Crime," and similar offenses and differs from them in several ways. In State v. Anderson, 10 Neb.App. 163, 626 N.W.2d 627 (2001), the court distinguished these offenses, saying,

While some states, such as Oregon, have replaced the common-law offense of accessory after the fact with the Model Penal Code's "hindering prosecution" approach, which does not require proof that the accused was aware that the principal offender actually committed a crime, Nebraska "adhere[s] to the common law approach by requiring that the defendant have known of the guilt of the person aided."

The *Anderson* court cited State v. Allred, 165 Or.App. 226, 995 P.2d 1210, 1213 (2000), adding,

A prosecution for "hindering prosecution," a crime different from common-law accessory after the fact, is intended to prevent the obstruction of justice and thus does not require that the offender know that he or she is aiding someone who in fact committed a crime.

NOTES: POST-CRIME ASSISTANCE

1. The Supreme Court of Illinois decided People v. Zierlion, 16 Ill.2d 217, 157 N.E.2d 72 (1959), shortly before the enactment of the 1961 Illinois Criminal Code. The drafters' commentary on Section 5, "Accountability for the Conduct of Another", notes that "the crime of accessory after the fact . . . is basically a distinct offense against public authority." 720 Ill. Comp. Stat. 5/31–5 reads:

Concealing or Aiding a Fugitive. Every person not standing in the relation of husband, wife, parent, child, brother or sister to the offender, who, with intent to prevent the apprehension of the offender, conceals his knowledge that an offense has been committed or harbors, aids or conceals the offender, commits a Class 4 felony. This section of the Illinois Criminal Code has been interpreted so that "concealing" means more than a mere failure to come forward with information; there must be an affirmative act toward concealment.

See People v. Donelson, 45 Ill.App.3d 609, 4 Ill.Dec. 273, 359 N.E.2d 1225 (1977) (concealing means more than a mere failure to come forward with information; there must be an affirmative act toward concealment).

2. In State v. Anderson, 10 Neb.App. 163, 626 N.W.2d 627 (2001), defendant Anderson told police that he had been riding around with Randell Fields and "Pookie," aka Shannon Smith, and that Fields and Smith had robbed and shot a man, Carr Hume, in South Omaha. Fields and Smith were charged, but later released when police learned that Hume had actually been killed by one Arlyn Ildefonso, who had no connection either to Anderson or to Fields or Smith. Anderson admitted that he had lied about Fields and Smith because he was scared of them and wanted to pay them back. Everything he had told police he had learned from the television news. Ildefonso was convicted of the Hume murder. Anderson was convicted of being an accessory to first degree murder and appealed, arguing that because he did not know the identity of Hume's murderer he could not, as a matter of law, be an accessory to first degree murder. At most, he argued, his conduct was "false reporting," a misdemeanor. The Nebraska Court of Appeals, in a case of first impression, said.

> At common law, participants in a homicide who lend aid and encouragement while another, the principal, does the killing are classified as accessories. . . . This category includes accessories after the fact, meaning those persons who in some manner are connected with a crime after its perpetration. . . . An accessory after the fact is a person who, knowing that a felony had been committed, intentionally receives, relieves, comforts, or assists the felon, or in any manner aids the felon to escape arrest or punishment. . . .

> At common law, accessory liability requires the accessory to know that "a completed felony was committed, and that the person aided was the guilty party. . . ." The common law emphasized, as a basis for liability, the personal relationship between principal and accessory. . . . Consistent with the notion of derivative liability, the accessory had to have knowledge that the principal committed the crime, . . . and the principal had to be tried and convicted first. . . . [citations omitted]

Thus, the court reasoned, to satisfy the indictment, Anderson must have (1) volunteered false information to the police or obstructed police investigation by deception; (2) had the intent to interfere with, hinder, delay, or prevent the discovery, apprehension, prosecution, conviction, or punishment "of another;" and (3) had knowledge "of the conduct of the other." Distinguishing the Model Penal Code's offense of "Hindering Prosecution," the *Anderson* court found that Anderson could not be Ildefonso's accessory after the fact because he had no knowledge of Ildefonso, "the other" who would be aided by Anderson's false story. The court noted that false reporting was not a lesser-included offense, though the conduct proscribed was similar, and said,

> requiring reliable knowledge of the felon's identity under the requirement that an accessory have general knowledge "of the conduct of the other" serves the purpose of the statute by penalizing those who intentionally "combine" with one they know to help them avoid prosecution, while at the same time preserving the less serious offense of false reporting, even though one's false information leads police astray, but not to the potential benefit of a particular person. . . .

Finding insufficient evidence of such knowledge on Anderson's part, the court reversed his conviction.

C. SOLICITATION

We examine solicitation to commit a crime separately, even though in certain circumstances conduct that would constitute solicitation could also be a form of accessoryship, or even an attempt to commit a crime. The *actus reus* of criminal solicitation is the commanding, hiring, requesting, or encouraging another person to commit a crime, and the *mens rea* is the specific intent that the other person commit the crime. No agreement is needed for criminal solicitation, and it is irrelevant to the guilt of the one soliciting the crime that the person solicited has no intention of committing crime. As long as the defendant made the command, request, or encouragement with the requisite *mens rea* (s)he is guilty.[17] All elements of the crime of solicitation are present when defendant entices or encourages another party to commit the crime, regardless of whether events reached the level of an attempt.[18] If the solicited crime *is* committed, however, the one who successfully solicited another to commit it is guilty of the offense committed.[19] Sometimes, however, it can be difficult to distinguish between a solicitation and an attempt.

State v. Disanto

Supreme Court of South Dakota, 2004.
2004 SD 112, 688 N.W.2d 201.

■ KONENKAMP, J.

Defendant told several people of his intent to murder his former girlfriend and her new boyfriend. Unknown to defendant, his design was revealed to the authorities and they had a police officer pose as a contract killer to interject himself in the plan. Defendant and the "hit man" discussed the murders, wherein defendant wanted each victim shot twice in the head. He directed the feigned killer to the former girlfriend's address, gave him a picture of her, provided details on what valuables could be obtained during the killings, instructed him to kill a child witness if necessary, and issued a final command to proceed with the murders. Shortly afterwards, however, defendant communicated with an intermediary that he wanted to "halt" the murders, saying "I'm not backing out of it, I just want to put it on hold." In his trial for three counts of attempted first-degree murder, defendant unsuccessfully sought a judgment of acquittal claiming that the evidence was insufficient to establish that he went further than mere preparation for the offenses. The jury convicted him on all three charges. We reverse the convictions because defendant's actions amounted to no more than mere preparation: neither he nor the feigned killer committed an act toward the commission of the offenses.

Background

Defendant, Rocco William "Billy" Disanto, and Linda Olson lived together for two years and were engaged for a short time. But their

---

[17]   *See, e.g.*, The Florida Bar v. Marable, 645 So.2d 438 (Fla.1994).

[18]   Metcalf v. State, 614 So.2d 548 (Fla.App.1993), *review granted by* 624 So.2d 267 (Fla.App. 1993) (unpublished table decision), *quashed on other grounds by* 635 So.2d 11 (Fla. 1994).

[19]   Coxwell v. State, 397 So.2d 335 (Fla.App.1981).

turbulent relationship ended in January 2002. Olson soon began a new friendship with Denny Egemo, and in the next month, they moved in together. Obsessed with his loss, defendant began making threatening telephone calls to Olson and Egemo. He told them and others that he was going to kill them. He also sued Olson claiming that she was responsible for the disappearance of over $15,000 in a joint restaurant venture.

On February 17, 2002, while gambling and drinking at the First Gold Hotel in Deadwood, defendant told a woman that he intended "to shoot his ex-girlfriend, to kill her, to shoot her new lover in the balls so that he would have to live with the guilt, and then he was going to kill himself." As if to confirm his intention, defendant grabbed the woman's hand and placed it on a pistol in his jacket. The woman contacted a hotel security officer who in turn called the police. Defendant was arrested and a loaded .25 caliber pistol was taken from him. In a plea bargain, defendant pleaded guilty to possession of a concealed pistol without a permit and admitted to a probation violation. For his probation violation, he was sentenced to two years in the South Dakota State Penitentiary with nine months suspended. . . .

While in the penitentiary, defendant met Stephen Rynders. He told Rynders of his intention to murder Olson and her boyfriend. Rynders gave this information to law enforcement and an investigation began. In June 2002, defendant was released from prison. Upon defendant's release, Rynders, acting under law enforcement direction, picked defendant up and offered him a ride to Lead. Inevitably, the conversation turned to defendant's murder plans. At the suggestion of the investigators, Rynders told defendant that he should hire a contract killer who Rynders knew in Denver.

On the afternoon of June 11, 2002, Rynders and Dale McCabe, a law enforcement officer posing as a killer for hire from Denver, met twice with defendant. Much of their conversation was secretly recorded. Defendant showed McCabe several photos of Olson and gave him one, pointed out her vehicle, led him to the location of her home, and even pointed Olson out to him as she was leaving her home. In between his meetings with McCabe that afternoon, by chance, defendant ran into Olson on the street. Olson exclaimed, "I suppose you're going to kill me." "Like a dog," defendant replied.

Shortly afterwards in their second meeting, defendant told McCabe, "I want her and him dead." "Two shots in the head." With only one shot, he said, "something can go wrong." If Olson's teenage daughter happened to be present, then defendant wanted her killed too: "If you gotta, you gotta, you know what I mean." He wanted no witnesses. He suggested that the murders should appear to have happened during a robbery. Because defendant had no money to pay for the murders, he suggested that jewelry and other valuables in the home might be used as partial compensation. He told McCabe that the boyfriend, Egemo, was known to have a lot of cash. Defendant also agreed to pay for the killings with some methamphetamine he would later obtain. At 3:00 p.m., defendant and McCabe appeared to close their agreement with the following exchange:

McCabe: So hey, just to make sure, no second thoughts or. . . .

Defendant: No, none.

McCabe: You sure, man?

Defendant: None.

McCabe: Okay.

Defendant: None.

McCabe: The deal's done, man.

Defendant: It's a go.

McCabe: OK. Later. I'll call you tonight.

Defendant: Huh?

McCabe: I'll call you tonight.

Defendant: Thank you.

McCabe would later testify that as he understood their transaction, "the deal was sealed at that point" and the killings could be accomplished "from that time on until whenever I decided to complete the task." Less than three hours later, however, defendant, seeking to have a message given to McCabe, called Rynders telling him falsely that a "cop stopped by here" and that Olson had spotted McCabe's car with its Colorado plates, that Olson had "called the cops," that defendant was under intense supervision, and that now the police were alerted because of defendant's threat against Olson on the street. All of this was untrue. Defendant's alarm about police involvement was an apparent ruse to explain why he did not want to go through with the killings.

Defendant: So, I suggest we halt this. Let it cool down a little bit. . . .

Rynders: Okay. . . .

Defendant: So I don't know if that house (Olson's) is being watched, do you know what I'm saying?

Rynders: Okay. . . .

Defendant: And, ah, the time is not right now. I'm just telling you, I, I don't feel it. I feel, you know what I mean. I'm not backing out of it, you know what I'm saying.

Rynders: Um hm.

Defendant: But, ah, the timing. You know what I mean. I just got out of prison, right? . . .

Defendant: So, ah, I'm just telling you right now, put it on hold.

Rynders: Okay.

Defendant: And that's the final word for the simple reason, ah, I don't want nothing to happen to [McCabe], you know what I mean? . . .

Defendant: Let it cool down. Plus let's let 'em make an offer. . . . [referring to defendant's lawsuit against Olson]

Rynders: Well, I have no clue where [McCabe is] at right now.

Defendant: Oh, God. You got a cell number? . . .

Defendant: Get it. . . .

Defendant: I just don't feel good about it to be honest and I'll tell ya, I've got great intuition.

Rynders: Okay. . . .

Defendant: So, I mean, just let him [McCabe] know. Alright buddy?

Rynders: Okay.

Defendant: Get to him. He's gonna call me at 11 tonight.

Despite this telephone call, the next day, McCabe, still posing as a contract killer, came to defendant at his place of employment with Olson's diamond ring to verify that the murders had been accomplished. McCabe drove up to defendant and beckoned him to his car.

McCabe: Hey, man. Come here. Come here. Come here. Jump in, man. Jump in, dude.

Defendant: You sure?

McCabe: Jump in.

Defendant: I can't, I can't leave the bakery. I ain't got the key.

McCabe: . . . It's done, man. . . .

Defendant: Okay. I don't wanna know nothin' about it.

McCabe: All right. Check this out, man. [Showing him Olson's diamond ring.]

Defendant: No.

McCabe: Here.

Defendant: I don't wanna see nothin'. . . .

Defendant was arrested and charged with three counts of attempted murder. He was also charged with one count of simple assault for the threat he made against Olson on the street. The State provided notice that it intended to introduce all the evidence pertaining to defendant's prior arrest and subsequent plea agreement concerning the incident at the First Gold Hotel. Over defendant's objection, the trial court admitted this evidence. A jury convicted defendant of all charges. . . . On appeal, defendant raises the following issues: (1) Whether the trial court erred in denying his motion for judgment of acquittal and motion for judgment notwithstanding the verdict. . . .

Attempted Murder by Hiring Contract Killer

* * *

In defining the crime of attempt, we begin with our statute. SDCL 22–4–1 states that "Any person who attempts to commit a crime and in the attempt does any act toward the commission of the crime, but fails or is prevented or intercepted in the perpetration thereof, is punishable" as therein provided. To prove an attempt, therefore, the prosecution must show that defendant (1) had the specific intent to commit the crime, (2) committed a direct act toward the commission of the intended crime, and (3) failed or was prevented or intercepted in the perpetration of the crime. . . . We need not linger on the question of intent. Plainly, the evidence established that defendant repeatedly expressed an intention to kill Olson and Egemo, as well as Olson's daughter, if necessary. As McCabe told the jury, defendant "was a man on a mission to have three individuals murdered."

Defendant does not claim error in any of the court's instructions to the jury. The jury was instructed in part that

Mere preparation, which may consist of planning the offense or of devising, obtaining or arranging the means for its commission, is not sufficient to constitute an attempt; but acts of a person who intends to commit a crime will constitute an attempt when they themselves clearly indicate a certain, unambiguous intent to commit that specific crime, and in themselves are an immediate step in the present commission of the criminal design, the progress of which would be completed unless interrupted by some circumstances not intended in the original design. The attempt is the direct movement toward commission of the crime after the preparations are made.

Once a person has committed acts which constitute an attempt to commit a crime, that person cannot avoid responsibility by not proceeding further with the intent to commit the crime, either by reason of voluntarily abandoning the purpose or because of a fact which prevented or interfered with completing the crime.

However, if a person intends to commit a crime but before the commission [of] any act toward the ultimate commission of the crime, that person freely and voluntarily abandons the original intent and makes no effort to accomplish it, the crime of attempt has not been committed.

Defendant contends that he abandoned any attempt to murder when he telephoned Rynders to "halt" the killings. The State argued to the jury that defendant committed an act toward the commission of first degree murder by giving the "hit-man" a final order to kill, thus making the crime of attempt complete. If he went beyond planning to the actual commission of an act, the State asserted, then a later abandonment would not extricate him from responsibility for the crime of attempted murder. On the other hand, if he only wanted to postpone the crime, then, the State contended, his attempt was merely delayed, not abandoned. On the question of abandonment, it is usually for the jury to decide whether an accused has already committed an act toward the commission of the murders. Once the requisite act has been committed, whether a defendant later wanted to abandon or delay the plan is irrelevant. . . .

The more perplexing question here is whether there was evidence that, in fulfilling his murderous intent, defendant committed an "act" toward the commission of first degree murder. SDCL 22–4–1. Defendant contends that he never went beyond mere preparation. In *State v. Martinez*, this Court declared that the boundary between preparation and attempt lies at the point where an act "unequivocally demonstrate[s] that a crime is about to be committed." 88 S.D. at 372, 220 N.W.2d at 531 (citing *People v. Miller*, 2 Cal.2d 527, 42 P.2d 308, 310 (1935)). Thus, the term "act" "presupposes some direct act or movement in execution of the design, as distinguished from mere preparation, which leaves the intended assailant only in the condition to commence the first direct act toward consummation of his design." The unequivocal act toward the commission of the offense must demonstrate that a crime is about to be committed unless frustrated by intervening circumstances. However, this act need not be the last possible act before actual accomplishment of the crime to constitute an attempt.

We have no decisions on point in South Dakota; therefore, we will examine similar cases in other jurisdictions. In murder for hire cases, the courts are divided on how to characterize the offense: is it a solicitation to murder or an act toward the commission of murder? Most courts take the view that the mere act of solicitation does not constitute an attempt to commit the crime solicited. This issue is particularly significant in a jurisdiction where any crime can be the subject of attempt but only certain crimes can be the subject of solicitation. As one commentator explained, "[a]lthough in some jurisdictions solicitations are treated as indictable attempts, either by virtue of judicial decisions failing to distinguish them, or by statutory provisions, the great weight of authority is otherwise. Analytically the two crimes are distinct." Francis Bowes Sayre, *Criminal Attempts*, 41 Harv. L. Rev. 821, 857–58 (1928). A majority of courts reason that a solicitation to murder is not attempted murder because the completion of the crime requires an act by the one solicited. We will examine cases espousing both the majority and minority view to discern which ones are consistent with South Dakota law and precedent. However, it is important in examining out-of-state authority to confine our review to decisions using definitions of criminal attempt similar to our own.

Typical of the cases following the majority rule is *State v. Davis*, 319 Mo. 1222, 6 S.W. 2d 609 (Mo.1928) (superceded by statute). There, the defendant and the wife of the intended victim plotted to kill her husband to collect the life insurance proceeds and then to live together. A police officer, posing as an ex-convict, met with the defendant several times. The defendant gave the undercover officer a map showing where the husband could be found and two photographs of him. He promised to pay the agent $600, and later paid that sum. He wanted the matter handled so that the murder would appear to have been committed in the course of a robbery. Because the agent employed to commit the murder did not act toward the consummation of the intended crime, the court held that the defendant's acts amounted to no more than solicitation or preparation. . . .

* * *

[The] cases [cited] are helpful to our analysis because, at the time they were decided, the statutes or case law in those jurisdictions defined attempt in a way identical to our attempt statute. Under this formulation, there must be specific intent to commit the crime and also a direct act done towards its commission, which failed or was intercepted in its perpetration. As the Missouri Supreme Court noted, "[t]his tougher language was couched in terms of preparation and perpetration, and required that '. . . the defendant must have taken steps going beyond mere preparation, by doing something bringing him nearer the crime he intends to commit.'" *State v. Molasky*, 765 S.W.2d 597, 600 (Mo. 1989).

To understand the opposite point of view, we will examine cases following the minority rule. But before we begin, we must first consider the definition of attempt under the Model Penal Code, and distinguish cases decided under its formula. In response to court decisions that hiring another to commit murder did not constitute attempted murder, many jurisdictions created, sometimes at the urging of the courts, the offense of solicitation of murder. As an alternative, another widespread response was to adopt the definition of attempt under the Model Penal Code. This is because the Model Penal Code includes in criminal attempt much that was held to be preparation under former decisions. This is clear from the comments accompanying the definition of criminal attempt in Tentative Draft No. 10 (1960) of the American Law Institute's Model Penal Code, Article 5 § 5.01. The intent was to extend the criminality of attempts by drawing the line further away from the final act, so as to make the crime essentially one of criminal purpose implemented by a substantial step highly corroborative of such purpose. Model Penal Code § 5.01(1) (Proposed Official Draft (1962)).

The Model Penal Code provides in part that "A person is guilty of an attempt to commit a crime if, acting with the kind of culpability otherwise required for commission of the crime, he . . . purposely does or omits to do anything that, under the circumstances as he believes them to be, is

CHAPTER 10   UNCOMPLETED CRIMINAL CONDUCT   1057

an act or omission constituting a *substantial step* in a course of conduct planned to culminate in his commission of the crime." Model Penal Code § 5.01(1)(c) (1985) (emphasis added).[4] The Code then lists in § 5.01(2) several species of conduct that may constitute a "substantial step." The Model Penal Code treats the solicitation of "an innocent agent to engage in conduct constituting an element of the crime," if strongly corroborative of the actor's criminal purpose, as sufficient satisfaction of the substantial step requirement to support a conviction for criminal attempt. Model Penal Code § 5.01(2)(g).

Representative of decisions under the Model Penal Code is *State v. Kilgus*, 128 N.H. 577, 519 A.2d 231 (N.H.1986).[5] There, it was held that the defendant's solicitation of a third party to kill the victim constituted attempted murder, where the defendant had completed all the preliminary steps, including setting and paying the contracted for sum, identifying the victim, and instructing the "killer" that the corpse must be found outside the state. The New Hampshire Supreme Court concluded, "[t]his was more than . . . 'mere' or 'naked' solicitation. It was a 'substantial step' toward the commission of capital murder."

Another decision using the Model Penal Code framework in analyzing the offense of attempt is *State v. Burd*, 187 W.Va. 415, 419 S.E.2d 676 (W.Va.1991). In that case, the court ruled that evidence that the defendant solicited the murder of her boyfriend's wife and child, hired the killer, gave him money for a weapon and an advance on the murder contract, drew a map of the residence of the planned victims, and instructed the killer on how to shoot the victims, supported her conviction for attempted murder. What is curious about *Burd* is that at the time of that decision the State of West Virginia had a definition of attempt similar to our own. Nonetheless, the Court seems to have adopted the Model Penal Code "substantial step" analysis from *Kilgus* to conclude that hiring the feigned assassin was a "substantial act" toward commission of the crime of attempted murder. In support of its position, the Court cited several other murder for hire cases decided under the Model Penal Code definition of attempt.

* * *

In *Braham v. State*, 571 P.2d 631 (Alaska 1977), *cert. denied*, 436 U.S. 910 (1978), evidence that the defendant instructed the hired gunman to visit the intended victim in the hospital for purpose of fostering a relationship of trust and confidence was sufficient to establish the required overt act necessary to prove attempted murder requiring an

---

[4] Many jurisdictions have adopted the "substantial step" framework from the Model Penal Code [Citations omitted.]

[5] Another decision fitting this category is *State v. Sunzar*, 331 N.J.Super. 248, 751 A.2d 627, 632 (1999). By adopting a Model Penal Code type attempt statute the court concluded that "[b]ased on the history outlined above, it appears that our legislature has opted for an expansive version of the attempt law, notwithstanding the 'majority' view, which governs elsewhere." *See also State v. Manchester*, 213 Neb. 670, 331 N.W.2d 776 (1983).

act toward the commission of murder. Alaska's attempt statute at the time is almost identical to ours. The Alaska Supreme Court held that whether an act is merely preparatory or "sufficiently close to the consummation of the crime to amount to attempt, is a question of degree and depends upon the facts and circumstances of a particular case."

In *Duke v. State*, 340 So.2d 727 (Miss.1976), the defendant solicited an employee to kill his business partner. The murder was to take place on a hunting trip. That plan failed and the defendant sought to hire another killer. An FBI agent posed as the killer and collected $11,500 from the defendant after representing to the defendant that the partner was dead. This evidence was held sufficient to sustain the conviction because the court concluded that the defendant's acts went beyond mere preparation.

In *State v. Mandel*, 78 Ariz. 226, 278 P.2d 413 (1954), a woman who made a contract with two pretended accomplices to have her husband murdered, partly executed that contract by paying a portion of the consideration in advance, identified for the intended assassins the home and the car of the intended victim, pointed out a possible site for disposing of the body, and advised them on the time and place where contact could be made for the execution of the murder. The court held that she was properly convicted of attempted murder, stating, "She did everything she was supposed to do to accomplish the purpose. Had it not been for the subterfuge, the intended victim would have been murdered. Under such circumstances she cannot escape by reason of clever, elusive distinctions between preparation, solicitation and acts committed in furtherance of the design." *Id.* at 416.

In *State v. Gay*, 4 Wash.App. 834, 486 P.2d 341 (1971), a wife paid a $1,000 retainer to a feigned killer to assassinate her husband and agreed to pay the killer an additional $9,000 when her husband was dead. She furnished the killer with pictures of her husband so that he would kill the right man and told him about her husband's habits and where he could be found. In upholding her conviction for attempted murder, the court acknowledged that mere solicitation, which involves no more than asking or enticing someone to commit a crime, would not constitute the crime of attempt. However, the court declared that the very act of hiring a contract killer is an overt act directed toward the commission of the target crime. The court ruled that the defendant had done everything that was to be done by her to accomplish the murder of her husband. Since the feigned assassin had made all the contacts and she had no way to contact him, she could not have stopped him after the final planning. The court concluded that the defendant's attempt to murder her husband was clearly established by the following undisputed evidence: (1) the forged assignment of the insurance policy six months before she hired a man to kill her husband, (2) the payment of premiums on her husband's

$50,000 life insurance policy after the divorce had commenced, without the knowledge of her husband, and (3) the hiring of the feigned assassin.

The minority view expressed in *Braham, Duke, Gay*, and *Mandel* is epitomized in the dissenting opinion in *Otto*, where it was noted that efforts to distinguish between "acts of preparation and acts of perpetration" are "highly artificial, since all acts leading up to the ultimate consummation of a crime are by their very nature preparatory." *Otto*, 629 P.2d at 653. For these courts, preparation and perpetration are seen merely as degrees on a continuum, and thus the distinction between preparation and perpetration becomes blurred. In interpreting our law, all "criminal and penal provisions and all penal statutes are to be construed according to the fair import of their terms, with a view to effect their objects and promote justice." Under our longstanding jurisprudence, preparation and perpetration are distinct concepts. Neither defendant nor the feigned "hit man" committed an act "which would end in accomplishment, but for . . . circumstances occurring . . . independent of the will of the defendant."

We cannot convert solicitation into attempt because to do so is obviously contrary to what the Legislature had in mind when it set up the distinct categories of solicitation and attempt. Indeed, the Legislature has criminalized other types of solicitations. *See* SDCL 22–43–2 (soliciting commercial bribe); SDCL 22–23–8 (pimping as felony); SDCL 22–11–20 (solicitation by witnesses); SDCL 22–22–24.5 (solicitation of minor for sex); SDCL 16–18–7 (solicitation by disbarred or suspended attorney). Beyond any doubt, defendant's behavior here was immoral and malevolent. But the question is whether his evil intent went beyond preparation into acts of perpetration. Acts of mere preparation in setting the groundwork for a crime do not amount to an attempt. Under South Dakota's definition of attempt, solicitation alone cannot constitute an attempt to commit a crime. Attempt and solicitation are distinct offenses. To call solicitation an attempt is to do away with the necessary element of an overt act. Worse, to succumb to the understandable but misguided temptation to merge solicitation and attempt only muddles the two concepts and perverts the normal and beneficial development of the criminal law through incremental legislative corrections and improvements. It is for the Legislature to remedy this problem, and not for us through judicial expansion to uphold a conviction where no crime under South Dakota law was committed.

Reversed.

■ SABERS and MEIERHENRY, JJ. (concurring).

I agree because the evidence indicates that this blundering, broke, inept 59-year-old felon, just out of prison, was inadequate to pursue or execute this crime without the motivating encouragement of his "friend from prison" and law enforcement officers. On his own, it would have been no more than a thought.

■ GILBERTSON, C.J. (dissenting).

I respectfully dissent. I would affirm the circuit court. SDCL 22–4–1 defines what constitutes an attempt:

> Any person who attempts to commit a crime and in the attempt does any act toward the commission of the crime, but fails or is prevented or intercepted in the perpetration thereof. . . .

Herein the Defendant was convicted of three counts of attempted murder. The issue before us is whether he committed a direct act toward the commission of the intended crime. . . . In *State v. Miskimins*, 435 N.W.2d 217, 222–23 (S.D.1989) we analyzed the nature of the requirement that a direct act be committed:

> In drawing a distinction between preparation and attempt, this court has held that it is not necessary that the last further act necessary to the actual accomplishment of the crime be taken to be a requisite to make an attempt. The statutes clearly require only that "any" act towards the commission of the crime be done. Any unequivocal act by defendant to insure that the intended result was a crime and not another innocent act constitutes an attempt. "The line between preparation and attempt is drawn at that point where the accused's acts no longer strike the jury as being equivocal but unequivocally demonstrate that a crime is about to be committed."

We also have previously defined preparation as "devising or arranging the means or measures necessary for the commission of the offense" and attempt as "the direct movement toward the commission after the preparations are made." . . . Thus, we must examine the evidence to see whether there was evidence which would allow a jury to find such an act did occur.

* * *

Herein the Defendant hired McCabe, a hit man, gave him instructions on how to kill the intended victims, provided the hit man with a photo of Olson, showed him the location of Olson's home and personally pointed Olson out to the "hit man." All these acts constitute devising or arranging the murder for hire scheme. The Defendant's acts of arriving at a concrete payment arrangement for the "hit man's" services and issuing the final kill order "[i]t's a go," were direct movements that served to actually put Defendant's plan into action. The consummation of the contract and final kill order were "immediate step[s] in the present commission of the criminal design" as required by the jury instructions used in Defendant's trial. This is far more than mere verbal solicitation of a hit man to accomplish the murders. . . .

This evidence, if believed by the jury, was well in excess of the "any act" requirement. It showed Defendant had done everything he could do to carry out his intent to have the killings occur. Defendant had set in motion a course of action that would have resulted in the deaths of two or three individuals "but for" the fact the hit man was in reality an undercover police officer. It appears the only act left was the actual killings themselves. . . . Defendant argues that the evidence clearly demonstrates that Defendant's actions in June 2002 did not go beyond mere preparation. Defendant cites the police's failure to arrest Defendant after the June 11, 2002 meeting as proof of this proposition. Defendant also notes that his phone call to Rynders "clearly shows the Defendant put a halt to the attempted commission of the crime . . . but chose to do so by remaining friendly and cooperative with the hitman."

Two distinct theories can be drawn from Defendant's telephone conversation. The first, posited by Defendant, is that Defendant wished to extricate himself from an agreed upon murder, but leave the "hit man" with the *perception* that the deal remained in place. However, there is a second equally plausible theory which was presented by the State. That is, Defendant merely wanted to delay the previously planned murder, but leave the "hit man" with the *knowledge* that the deal remained in place. Both theories were thoroughly argued to the jury. However, the jury chose to believe the State's theory. Therefore, the jury could have properly concluded Defendant's actions were "done toward the commission of the crime . . . the progress of which would be completed unless interrupted by some circumstances not intended in the original design" and not simply mere preparation.

* * *

Here there was evidence that all that was left was to pull the trigger. As the Court acknowledges "the law of attempts would be largely without function if it could not be invoked until the trigger was pulled." Citing *Dillon*, 194 Cal.Rptr. 390, 668 P.2d at 703.

I also conclude that the two remaining issues raised by the Defendant are without merit and thus would affirm the trial court. Thus, I respectfully dissent.

■ ZINTER, JUSTICE (dissenting).

I join the Court's legal analysis concerning the distinction between solicitations and attempts to commit murder.[6] Therefore, I agree that Disanto's solicitation of McCabe, in and of itself, was legally insufficient . . . to constitute an attempt to commit murder under SDCL 22–4–1. However, I respectfully disagree with the Court's analysis of the facts, which leads it to find as a matter of law that Disanto "committed [no] act toward the commission of the offense." In my judgment, the Court's view of the facts is not supported by the record. On the contrary, even setting aside Disanto's solicitation, he still engaged in sufficient other "acts" toward the commission of the murder such that reasonable jurors could have found that he proceeded "so far that they would result in the

---

[6]   I also join the Court's analysis of Disanto's defense of abandonment.

accomplishment of the crime unless frustrated by extraneous circumstances." The intended victims were clearly in more danger then than they were when Disanto first expressed his desire to kill them.

Specifically, Disanto physically provided McCabe with a photograph of the victim, he pointed out her vehicle, and he took McCabe to the victim's home and pointed her out as she was leaving. None of these acts were acts of solicitation. Rather, they were physical "act[s going] toward the commission" of the murder.

Although it is acknowledged that the cases discussed by the Court have found that one or more of the foregoing acts can be part of a solicitation, Disanto's case has one significant distinguishing feature. After his solicitation was completed, after the details were arranged, and after Disanto completed the physical acts described above, he then went even further and executed a command to implement the killing. In fact, this Court itself describes this act as the "final command" to execute the murder. Disanto issued the order: "It's a go." This act is not present in the solicitation cases that invalidate attempted murder convictions because they proceeded no further than preparation.

Therefore, when Disanto's final command to execute the plan is combined with his history and other acts, this is the type of case that proceeded further than the mere solicitations and plans found insufficient in the case law. This combination of physical acts would have resulted in accomplishment of the crime absent the intervention of the law enforcement officer. Clearly, the victim was in substantially greater danger after the final command than when Disanto first expressed his desire to kill her. Consequently, there was sufficient evidence to support an attempt conviction.

It bears repeating that none of the various "tests" used by courts in this area of the law can possibly distinguish all preparations from attempts. Therefore, a defendant's entire course of conduct should be evaluated in light of his intent and his prior history in order to determine whether there was substantial evidence from which a reasonable trier of fact could have sustained a finding of an attempt. In making that determination, it is universally recognized that the acts of solicitation and attempt are a continuum between planning and perpetration of the offense. Whether acts are so preparatory as to not constitute an attempt or are sufficiently close to consummation of the crime as to constitute an attempt, "is a question of degree and depends upon the facts and circumstances of a particular case." *Braham v. State*, 571 P.2d 631, 637 (Alaska 1977).

However, it is generally the jury's function to determine whether those acts have proceeded beyond mere planning. As this Court itself has noted, where design is shown, "courts should not destroy the practical and common sense administration of the law with subtleties as to what constitutes [the] preparation" to commit a crime as distinguished from acts done towards the commission of a crime. Therefore, it should be a rare case to be decided as a matter of law. . . . We leave this question to the jury because "[t]he line between preparation and attempt is drawn at that point where the accused's acts *no longer strike the jury* as being equivocal but unequivocally demonstrate that a crime is about to be committed."

I would follow that admonition and affirm the judgment of this jury. Disanto's design, solicitation, physical acts toward commission of the crime and his final command to execute the murder, when considered together, unequivocally demonstrated that a crime was about to be committed. This was sufficient evidence from which the jury could have reasonably found that an attempt had been committed. . . .

————

NOTE

1. The *Disanto* Court is not the only one that is divided on the question of how to separate an attempt from a solicitation:

> Pay someone to kill in Idaho, Nevada, or South Dakota, for instance, and you've committed only the lesser crime of solicitation; pay someone to kill in Georgia, Iowa, New York, or Ohio, and you've attempted the murder. We find even greater variation when we consider crimes other than murder. If you ask a child for oral sex, have you attempted sexual battery? If you ask a minister to marry you to your niece, have you tried to marry someone incestuously? If you ask someone to bribe a witness, have you attempted to bribe a witness? If you ask someone to burn down a barn, have you attempted arson? Courts regularly have to answer questions like this. They answer them differently in different places and in different times, and they give different answers when different crimes are involved.

Gideon Yaffe, *Criminal Attempts*, 124 YALE L.J. 92, 121 (2014). Professor Yaffe suggests the following approach:

> [I]f the defendant has asked another person to bring about an event that is a result element of the completed crime, then the defendant may have thereby attempted the crime; if, however, the event that the defendant has asked another person to bring about figures into the definition of an act element of the completed crime, then the defendant has not attempted through his solicitation.

Id. at 122.

D. CONSPIRACY

INTRODUCTION

The elements of common law conspiracy are:

(a)   a combination (agreement) of

(b)   two or more persons

(c)   to accomplish by some concerted action some criminal or unlawful purpose, or some purpose not in itself criminal or unlawful by criminal or unlawful means and

(d)   an overt act by one or more co-conspirators in furtherance of the conspiracy.

While at early common law, the agreement (combination) was enough, the modern rule in most United States jurisdictions is that there must be an "overt act" by at least one co-conspirator before the conspiracy is established.[20] The overt act need not be illegal in itself, and it may be done by any co-conspirator, but in most jurisdictions, the agreement alone is not sufficient without it.[21] Each of these elements can create problems of interpretation and application. In most jurisdictions, the "overt act" can be any act in furtherance of the conspiracy, and need not amount to a "substantial step" which would satisfy the requirements for an attempt.

The Model Penal Code retains the crime of conspiracy, and devotes several sections of code to its various permutations. As Professor Markus D. Dubber has noted,

> American courts have long marveled, in horror, at the unique danger inherent in the very idea of conspiracy. . . . It's no surprise, then, that the treatmentist Model Code would find a prominent place for this traditional crime of exceptional human dangerousness. . . .
>
> As in the common law, the core of conspiracy under the Code is an agreement. . . . It's this agreement that gives rise to criminal liability, by transforming a lonely criminal thought hatched in the mind of a single, powerless, individual into a criminal plan. By entering into an agreement with another person, I reveal myself as one of those persons who suffer from an abnormal disposition to engage in criminal conduct, by distinguishing myself from those untold millions who harbor criminal thoughts, but never share them with others, never mind act on

---

[20]   *But see* State v. LaPlume, 118 R.I. 670, 375 A.2d 938 (1977) ("The common law crime of conspiracy involves a combination of two or more persons to commit some unlawful act or to do some lawful act for an unlawful purpose. . . . The gravamen of the crime is entry into an unlawful agreement and once that occurs the offense is complete. Rhode Island continues to adhere to the common law definition of this crime and, unlike other jurisdictions, it does not require that any overt acts have been committed in execution of the unlawful agreement . . .").

[21]   *See, e.g.*, Mo. Rev. Stat. § 564.016(4).

them in any way. But my decision to seek out like-minded protocriminals, and to join hands with them in the pursuit of a common criminal goal is not only symptomatic of my extraordinary dangerousness. By combining forces with another similarly dangerous person, I multiply my already considerable dangerousness through the magic of cooperation. . . .[22]

Krulewitch v. United States

United States Supreme Court, 1949.
336 U.S. 440, 445, 69 S.Ct. 716, 93 L.Ed. 790.

■ JACKSON, J., concurring.

This case illustrates a present drift in the federal law of conspiracy which warrants some further comment because it is characteristic of the long evolution of that elastic, sprawling and pervasive offense. Its history exemplifies the "tendency of a principle to expand itself to the limit of its logic." The unavailing protest of courts against the growing habit to indict for conspiracy in lieu of prosecuting for the substantive offense itself, or in addition thereto, suggests that loose practice as to this offense constitutes a serious threat to fairness in our administration of justice.

The modern crime of conspiracy is so vague that it almost defies definition. Despite certain elementary and essential elements, it also, chameleon-like, takes on a special coloration from each of the many independent offenses on which it may be overlaid. It is always "predominantly mental in composition" because it consists primarily of a meeting of minds and an intent.

The crime comes down to us wrapped in vague but unpleasant connotations. It sounds historical undertones of treachery, secret plotting and violence on a scale that menaces social stability and the security of the state itself. "Privy conspiracy" ranks with sedition and rebellion in the Litany's prayer for deliverance. Conspirational movements do indeed lie back of the political assassination, the *coup d'état*, the *putsch*, the revolution and seizures of power in modern times, as they have in all history.

But the conspiracy concept also is superimposed upon many concerted crimes having no political motivation. It is not intended to question that the basic conspiracy principle has some place in modern criminal law, because to unite, back of a criminal purpose, the strength, opportunities and resources of many is obviously more dangerous and more difficult to police than the efforts of a lone wrongdoer. . . .

But the conspiracy concept also is superimposed upon many concerted crimes having no political motivation. It is not intended to

---

[22] MARKUS D. DUBBER, CRIMINAL LAW: MODEL PENAL CODE 162–63 (2002).

question that the basic conspiracy principle has some place in modern criminal law, because to unite, back of a criminal purpose, the strength, opportunities and resources of many is obviously more dangerous and more difficult to police than the efforts of a lone wrongdoer. . . .

Conspiracy in federal law aggravates the degree of crime over that of unconcerted offending. The act of confederating to commit a misdemeanor, followed by even an innocent overt act in its execution is a felony and is such even if the misdemeanor is never consummated. The more radical proposition also is well-established that at common law and under some statutes a combination may be a criminal conspiracy even if it contemplates only acts which are not crimes at all when perpetrated by an individual or by many acting severally.

Thus the conspiracy doctrine will incriminate persons on the fringe of offending who would not be guilty of aiding and abetting or of becoming an accessory, for those charges only lie when an act which is a crime has actually been committed.

Attribution of criminality to a confederation which contemplates no act that would be criminal if carried out by any one of the conspirators is a practice peculiar to Anglo-American law. "There can be little doubt that this wide definition of the crime of conspiracy originates in the criminal equity administered in the Star Chamber." In fact, we are advised that "The modern law of conspiracy is almost entirely the result of the manner in which conspiracy was treated by the Court of the Star Chamber." The doctrine does not commend itself to jurists of civil-law countries, despite universal recognition that an organized society must have legal weapons for combatting organized criminality. Most other countries have devised what they consider more discriminating principles upon which to prosecute criminal gangs, secret associations and subversive syndicates. . . .

Of course, it is for prosecutors rather than courts to determine when to use a scatter gun to bring down the defendant, but there are procedural advantages from using it which add to the danger of unguarded extension of the concept.

An accused, under the Sixth Amendment, has the right to trial "by an impartial jury of the State and district wherein the crime shall have been committed." The leverage of a conspiracy charge lifts this limitation from the prosecution and reduces its protection to a phantom, for the crime is considered so vagrant as to have been committed in any district where any one of the conspirators did any one of the acts, however innocent, intended to accomplish its object. The Government may, and often does, compel one to defend at a great distance from any place he ever did any act because some accused confederate did some trivial and by itself innocent act in the chosen district. Circumstances may even enable the prosecution to fix the place of trial in Washington, D.C., where a defendant may lawfully be put to trial before a jury partly or even wholly made up of employees of the Government that accuses him.

When the trial starts, the accused feels the full impact of the conspiracy strategy. Strictly, the prosecution should first establish prima facie the conspiracy and identify the conspirators, after which evidence of acts and declarations of each in the course of its execution are admissible against all. But the order of proof of so sprawling a charge is difficult for a judge to control. As a practical matter, the accused often is confronted with a hodgepodge of acts and statements by others which he may never have authorized or intended or even known about, but which help to persuade the jury of existence of the conspiracy itself. In other words, a conspiracy often is proved by evidence that is admissible only upon assumption that conspiracy existed. The naive assumption that prejudicial effects can be overcome by instructions to the jury . . . all practicing lawyers know to be unmitigated fiction. . . .

The trial of a conspiracy charge doubtless imposes a heavy burden on the prosecution, but it is an especially difficult situation for the defendant. The hazard from loose application of rules of evidence is aggravated where the Government institutes mass trials. Moreover, in federal practice there is no rule preventing conviction on uncorroborated testimony of accomplices, as there are in many jurisdictions, and the most comfort a defendant can expect is that the court can be induced to follow the "better practice" and caution the jury against "too much reliance upon the testimony of accomplices."

A co-defendant in a conspiracy trial occupies an uneasy seat. There generally will be evidence of wrongdoing by somebody. It is difficult for the individual to make his own case stand on its own merits in the minds of jurors who are ready to believe that birds of a feather are flocked together.

———

1. THE AGREEMENT

The *actus reus* for conspiracy has two parts: the agreement, and the overt act. The agreement need not be explicit, so long as it can be proven to exist.[23]

(A) MULTIPLE AGREEMENTS

The agreement may not be a simple agreement to do a single act. When multiple crimes are contemplated, there is often an issue of whether they are within the scope of the same agreement, or of different agreements.

---

[23] Baxter v. State, 586 So.2d 1196 (Fla.App. 1991) (an implied, two-party agreement to commit an inchoate crime and intent of parties to commit that crime may exist with little or no physical evidence to establish them).

Braverman v. United States

Supreme Court of the United States, 1942.
317 U.S. 49, 63 S.Ct. 99, 87 L.Ed. 23.

■ MR. CHIEF JUSTICE STONE delivered the opinion of the Court.

The questions for decision are: (1) Whether a conviction upon the several counts of an indictment, each charging conspiracy to violate a different provision of the Internal Revenue laws, where the jury's verdict is supported by evidence of but a single conspiracy, will sustain a sentence of more than two years' imprisonment, the maximum penalty for a single violation of the conspiracy statute, and (2) whether the six-year period of limitation prescribed by § 3748(a) of the Internal Revenue Code, 26 U.S.C. Int. Rev. Code § 3748(a), is applicable to offenses arising under § 37 of the Criminal Code, 18 U.S.C. 88, 18 U.S.C. § 88 (the conspiracy statute), where the object of the conspiracy is to evade or defeat the payment of a federal tax.

Petitioners were indicted, with others, on seven counts, each charging a conspiracy to violate a separate and distinct internal revenue law of the United States. On the trial there was evidence from which the jury could have found that for a considerable period of time petitioners, with others, collaborated in the illicit manufacture, transportation, and distribution of distilled spirits involving the violations of statute mentioned in the several counts of the indictment. At the close of the trial petitioners renewed a motion which they had made at its beginning to require the Government to elect one of the seven counts of the indictment upon which to proceed, contending that the proof could not and did not establish more than one agreement. In response the Government's attorney took the position that the seven counts of the indictment charged as distinct offenses the several illegal objects of one continuing conspiracy, that if the jury found such a conspiracy it might find the defendants guilty of as many offenses as it had illegal objects, and that for each such offense the two-year statutory penalty could be imposed.

The trial judge submitted the case to the jury on that theory. The jury returned a general verdict finding petitioners "guilty as charged", and the court sentenced each to eight years' imprisonment. On appeal the Court of Appeals for the Sixth Circuit affirmed. . . . It found that "From the evidence may be readily deduced a common design of appellants and others, followed by concerted action" to commit the several unlawful acts specified in the several counts of the indictment. It concluded that the fact that the conspiracy was "a general one to violate all laws repressive of its consummation does not gainsay the separate identity of each of the seven conspiracies." We granted *certiorari* . . . .

Both courts below recognized that a single agreement to commit an offense does not become several conspiracies because it continues over a period of time, and that there may be such a single continuing agreement to commit several offenses. But they thought that in the latter case each contemplated offense renders the agreement punishable as a separate conspiracy.

The question whether a single agreement to commit acts in violation of several penal statutes is to be punished as one or several conspiracies is raised on the present record, not by the construction of the indictment, but by the Government's concession at the trial and here, reflected in the charge to the jury, that only a single agreement to commit the offenses alleged was proven. Where each of the counts of an indictment alleges a conspiracy to violate a different penal statute it may be proper to conclude, in the absence of a bill of exceptions bringing up the evidence, that several conspiracies are charged rather than one, and that the conviction is for each. But it is a different matter to hold, as the court below appears to have done in this case . . . that even though a single agreement is entered into, the conspirators are guilty of as many offenses as the agreement has criminal objects.

The gist of the crime of conspiracy as defined by the statute is the agreement or confederation of the conspirators to commit one or more unlawful acts where "one or more of such parties do any act to effect the object of the conspiracy." The overt act, without proof of which a charge of conspiracy cannot be submitted to the jury, may be that of only a single one of the conspirators and need not be itself a crime. But it is unimportant, for present purposes, whether we regard the overt act as a part of the crime which the statute defines and makes punishable, or as something apart from it, either an indispensable mode of corroborating the existence of the conspiracy or a device for affording a *locus poenitentiae*.

For when a single agreement to commit one or more substantive crimes is evidenced by an overt act, as the statute requires, the precise nature and extent of the conspiracy must be determined by reference to the agreement which embraces and defines its objects. Whether the object of a single agreement is to commit one or many crimes, it is in either case that agreement which constitutes the conspiracy which the statute punishes. The one agreement cannot be taken to be several agreements and hence several conspiracies because it envisages the violation of several statutes rather than one.

The allegation in a single count of a conspiracy to commit several crimes is not duplicitous, for "The conspiracy is the crime, and that is one, however diverse its objects." A conspiracy is not the commission of the crime which it contemplates, and neither violates nor "arises under" the statute whose violation is its object. Since the single continuing agreement, which is the conspiracy here, thus embraces its criminal objects, it differs from successive acts which violate a single penal statute and from a single act which violates two statutes. The single agreement is the prohibited conspiracy, and however diverse its objects it violates but a single statute . . . For such a violation only the single penalty prescribed by the statute can be imposed.

Petitioner Wainer contends that his prosecution was barred by the three-year statute of limitations, since he withdrew from the conspiracy more than three although not more than six years before his indictment. This Court, in *United States v. McElvain*, 272 U.S. 633, 638, and *United States v. Scharlon*, 285 U.S. 518, held that the three-year statute of limitations applicable generally to criminal offenses barred prosecution for a conspiracy to violate the Revenue Acts, since it was not within the exception created by the Act of November 17, 1921, 42 Stat. 220, now § 3748(a)(1) of the Internal Revenue Code, 26 U.S.C. § 3748(a)(1), which provided a six-year statute of limitations "for offenses involving the defrauding or attempting to defraud the United States or any agency thereof, whether by conspiracy or not." To overcome the effect of these decisions, that Act was amended, Revenue Act of 1932, 47 Stat.169, 288, 26 U.S.C. § 3748(a) by the addition of a second exception, which provided a six-year statute of limitations "for the offense of willfully attempting in any manner to evade or defeat any tax or the payment thereof", and by the addition of a new paragraph, reading as follows:

> For offenses arising under § 37 of the Criminal Code . . . where the object of the conspiracy is to attempt in any manner to evade or defeat any tax or the payment thereof, the period of limitation shall also be six years.

To be within this last paragraph it is not necessary that the conspiracy have as its object the commission of an offense in which defrauding or attempting to defraud the United States is an element. It is enough that the conspiracy involves an attempt to evade or defeat the payment of federal taxes, which was among the objects of the conspiracy of which petitioner was convicted. Enlargement, to six years, of the time for prosecution of such conspiracies was the expressed purpose of the amendment.

* * *

The judgment of conviction will be reversed and the cause remanded to the district court where the petitioners will be resentenced in conformity to this opinion.

Reversed.

———

NOTES

1. In U.S. v. Schultz, 333 F.3d 393 (2d Cir. 2003), a wide-ranging conspiracy to smuggle Egyptian antiquities, the Second Circuit found sufficient evidence that the defendant had agreed to the criminal objectives. Evidence including coded communications between conspirators including discussions of possible prison sentences if they were caught was more than enough to establish the defendant's agreement. In U.S. v. Aleskerova, 300 F.3d 286 (2d Cir. 2002), a conspiracy to import artworks stolen from an Azerbaijani museum in violation of National Stolen Property Act, the Second Circuit likewise found that defendant's last-minute trip from Azerbaijan to New York to a meet with co-conspirators, multiple encounters between defendant and co-conspirators with no purpose apart from the conspiracy, defendant's possession of some of the art and evidence that the defendant anticipated profiting from the sale of the stolen art, and false statements when questioned about her activities was enough to establish her agreement with co-conspirators; her later failure to cooperate with her co-conspirators was not sufficient to show abandonment of the conspiracy.

2. In Cartwright v. Commonwealth, 223 Va. 368, 288 S.E.2d 491 (1982), the Supreme Court of Virginia found that the Virginia General Assembly had intended to punish conspiracies to commit more serious crimes more severely; the court held that a single agreement can form the basis for multiple violations of the conspiracy statute. *But see* Mo. Rev. Stat. § 564.016(3) ("If a person conspires to commit a number of offenses, he is guilty of only one conspiracy as long as such multiple offenses are the object of the same agreement.").

3. Chief Justice Shaw of the Massachusetts Supreme Judicial Court described the crime of common law conspiracy in Commonwealth v. Hunt, 45 Mass. (4 Met.) 111, 123 (1842) (citations omitted), saying,

> A conspiracy must be a combination of two or more persons by some concerted action to accomplish some criminal or unlawful purpose, or to accomplish some purpose not in itself criminal or unlawful by criminal or unlawful means. We use the terms criminal or unlawful, because it is manifest that many acts are unlawful, which are not punishable by indictment or other public prosecution; and yet there is no doubt, we think, that a combination by numbers to do them would be an unlawful conspiracy, and punishable by indictment. Of this character was a conspiracy to cheat by false pretences, without false tokens, when a cheat by false pretences only, by a single person, was not a punishable offense. . . . But yet it is clear, that it is not every combination to do unlawful acts, to the prejudice of another by a concerted action, which is punishable as conspiracy.

4. To prove a conspiracy, a few states require prosecutors to demonstrate an action that amounts to a "substantial step." *See, e.g.*, Me. Rev. Stat. tit. 17–A, § 151; Ohio Rev. Code Ann. § 2923.01; Vt. Stat. Ann. tit. 13 § 1404; Wash. Rev. Code § 9A.28.040. Most conspiracy statutes, however, are satisfied if there is "any" overt act done in furtherance of the common undertaking, no matter how remote from the planned execution of the crime.

(B) UNILATERAL AND BILATERAL CONSPIRACIES

The requirement of "two or more" conspirators can cause problems when the defendant "conspires" with another who, unbeknownst to the defendant, is not actually in agreement. Under some modern conspiracy statutes, a conspiracy can be "unilateral" as long as the defendant believes that the other person is actually agreeing to the conspiratorial objectives. At common law, and in many modern jurisdictions, actual agreement by at least two people is required.

State of Connecticut v. Jose Colón

Supreme Court of Connecticut, 2001.
257 Conn. 587, 778 A.2d 875.

■ SULLIVAN, C.J.

A jury found the defendant, Jose Colón, guilty of one count of murder in violation of General Statutes § 53a–54a (a) 2 and one count of conspiracy to commit murder in violation of General Statutes §§ 53a–48 and 53a–54a (a). . . . The defendant appealed from that judgment to the Appellate Court, claiming that the trial court improperly denied his motion for judgment of acquittal on the conspiracy conviction after his sole alleged coconspirator was acquitted of conspiracy in a separate, subsequent trial. The defendant argued that this outcome was in direct conflict with *State v. Grullon*, 212 Conn. 195, 562 A.2d 481 (1989), and *State v. Robinson*, 213 Conn. 243, 567 A.2d 1173 (1989), both of which held that § 53a–48 is strictly a bilateral conspiracy statute. We transferred the appeal to this court. . . . We now conclude that § 53a–48 (a) can be interpreted unilaterally in those cases in which alleged coconspirators are tried separately based on independent evidence of the crime of conspiracy.[5] Accordingly, the defendant's conviction is affirmed.

The jury reasonably could have found the following facts. Sergeant Michael Fischer of the Waterbury police department testified that on April 22, 1996, the Waterbury police received an anonymous telephone call alerting them to a possible homicide at an abandoned building on Ridged Street in Waterbury. When the police arrived, they discovered the bloody body of the victim. The victim had been stabbed several times in the head, neck, arms and torso, and also appeared to have been beaten about the head. A metal pipe and a small buck knife covered in blood and hair were discovered at the crime scene. An autopsy conducted by Edward T. McDonough, the deputy chief medical examiner, revealed that the victim had approximately "125 . . . sharp force injuries . . . he had cuts and stabs over the head, the face, the front of the trunk, the back, and the arms and both legs." The victim also had on his arms, hands and wrists several cuts that were consistent with defensive injuries, as though he had been attempting to protect himself from the blows. The autopsy revealed that the wounds had been inflicted by the buck knife and the metal pipe discovered at the scene, and that another, much

---

[5] We do not, however, overrule *State v. Grullon*, 562 A.2d 481 (Conn.1989), in which we held that a defendant cannot be guilty of conspiracy when the only other co-conspirator is a police officer or agent who never actually intended that the illegally "agreed upon" activity occur.

larger, weapon also had been used in the attack. Michael Silva, a forensic crime scene technician, described the victim's wounds as appearing to have been inflicted by a knife that was "large . . . approximately eight inches long with a fat blade with a brass type of guard to it."[6] Silva also testified that the "cast off" patterns of blood at the crime scene illustrated that the victim had suffered a "severe attack," that the "assailant was swinging very, very violently at the victim," and that the wall behind the victim showed signs of "actual misses . . . [that occurred when] the assailant swung the weapon . . . against the wall. . . ." . . . It was the opinion of McDonough and Silva that, as a result of the combined sharp force injuries, the victim bled to death over a period of time.

Lieutenant Michael Ricci of the Waterbury police department testified that on April 23, 1996, the day after the body was discovered, police officers began questioning local residents about the homicide. After being shown a police photograph, the victim's father identified the victim as his son, Hector Nieves. Once the victim was identified, Ricci and several other officers interviewed area residents in an effort to identify the individual who had made the anonymous call to the Waterbury police. Ricci interviewed Kevin Soto and his girlfriend, Edith Santos, who appeared to have been acquainted with the victim. Ricci requested that the couple come down to the police station the next day to listen to a recording of the unidentified 911 caller. While Soto was at the station, Ricci realized that it was his voice on the 911 tape. Soto then admitted making the call and, after being issued a *Miranda* warning, disclosed his role in the crime and implicated the defendant as the principal actor. . . . Ricci testified that, after Soto's disclosure, several officers were dispatched to Kennedy high school in Waterbury to bring the defendant in for questioning. Shortly after his arrival, and after being issued a *Miranda* warning, the defendant admitted to the officers his participation in the murder.

Ricci testified that, after taking a written statement from the defendant, police officers spoke to Soto a second time about the homicide and also interviewed Santos. Santos gave the police two different statements regarding the events of that day, one before and one after the defendant was placed under arrest. Initially, Santos did not implicate the defendant in the murder. She testified at trial that, when she gave her first statement to the police, she had been afraid that the defendant was still out on the street. Once she knew the defendant was in custody, however, she disclosed to police everything she knew about the murder. Thus, during her second interview with the police, Santos disclosed that she was with Soto at his mother's residence on the day of the murder. She observed Soto leave the residence with the victim and then return about one half hour later. Santos told the police that, when Soto returned

---

[6] Additional witness interviews revealed that a large sword like a machete also had been used in the attack.

to his mother's home after spending time with the defendant, he was acting strangely. When she asked what was wrong, Soto revealed to her that he and the defendant had stabbed the victim. Soto then told Santos that they had to go to her apartment because the defendant was there. When Santos arrived at her apartment and saw the defendant, she could see that he was "full of blood from head to toe." The defendant took a large "sword" out of his sleeve and showed it to her. It also was covered in blood. Santos got the defendant a garbage bag for his bloody clothes, while he showered and changed into clean clothes. Santos testified that, after speaking with Soto, she asked the defendant if the victim was dead and he responded affirmatively. Santos then testified that she, Soto and the defendant left her apartment, and the defendant deposited the bag of bloody clothes behind an abandoned building. When Soto and Santos parted ways with the defendant, they decided to call 911.

Two additional witnesses provided information on the "large sword" Santos described in her statement to the police. Ivan Pagan testified that, on the day of the murder, the defendant came to his house and took a "Pakistani sword" that he was holding for a relative. Ivan Pagan testified that the defendant returned approximately one hour later, in different clothes. and gave the sword back to him with a dent in the tip, covered in fresh blood and hair. The defendant told Ivan Pagan that "he [had] killed [Hector from] up the street." Ivan Pagan took the sword, cleaned it with alcohol and a rag, wrapped it in tape and placed it in his closet. Later that evening, he hid the sword "on the roof by the side of [his] house" covered in branches. Ivan Pagan testified that his fear of the defendant prompted him to take the sword and hide it for him as instructed. Danny Pagan. Ivan Pagan's brother, testified that he saw the defendant speak to Ivan Pagan on April 22, 1996. He testified that he observed the defendant meet Soto up the street, and then place the "Pakistani knife" in his pants.[9] When Danny Pagan asked the defendant where he was going, the defendant answered that he was going up the block "on a mission" with Soto. . . . Later that day, Danny Pagan saw the defendant return to their neighborhood and speak to his brother. Ivan Pagan later told Danny Pagan that the defendant revealed to him that he had killed the victim. The next day, Danny Pagan saw the defendant speak to the police and deny that he was "Cujo," a name the police had learned the defendant was called on the street. After speaking with the police, the defendant approached Danny Pagan and told him that he and Soto had killed somebody with the sword, and he instructed Danny Pagan to move it from its initial hiding place. Danny Pagan testified that after his conversation with the defendant, he moved the sword from the roof where his brother had hidden it, wrapped it in a black plastic bag and placed it in a nearby abandoned garage.

---

[9]   Danny Pagan also described the knife as long, with teeth on one side and a sharp blade on the other.

Mark Deal, a Waterbury police officer, took a statement from the defendant that was read into the record at trial. In his statement, the defendant stated that he met Soto on Hillside Avenue in Waterbury on April 22, 1996. Soto, a member of the Latin Kings gang, told the defendant that the victim had "disrespected the [Latin Kings] nation" and that they had to "work him over." The defendant stated that he and Soto approached the victim and asked him if he wanted to smoke a "blunt," or a marijuana cigarette, in an abandoned building on Ridgewood Street. The defendant walked into the building before Soto and the victim, but turned around when he heard the victim say, "Oh Kevin, why did you do that?" The defendant stated that when he turned around, the victim was holding his throat. When the victim took his hand away, the defendant stated that he saw a lot of blood coming from the victim's throat. Soto had pushed the victim to the floor and shut the door. The defendant then stated that Soto passed him the knife and he stabbed the victim in the chest. When the victim resisted the attack, the defendant punched him and swung at him with the knife, while Soto beat him with a long metal bar. The defendant stated that he remembered stabbing the victim approximately five times before Soto said "let's get out of here." The defendant stated that the victim was still moving when they left him. After the defendant and Soto left the scene, they went to the home of Santos where they cleaned the victim's blood off themselves and changed their clothes. In his statement, the defendant identified Soto as the other participant in the killing and described the murder weapon and the clothing he wore the night of the murder.

The jury began deliberations on October 26, 1998. On October 27, 1998, the jury returned a verdict of guilty on all charges. At the sentencing phase of the trial, the defendant filed a postverdict motion for judgment of acquittal on the conspiracy charges[11] because his sole alleged coconspirator had been acquitted of conspiracy in a separate trial after the defendant's conviction but prior to his sentencing. *See State v. Soto*, 757 A.2d 1156. The defendant relied upon *State v. Grullon*, 562 A.2d 481, and *State v. Robinson*, 567 A.2d 1173, for his argument that, as a matter of law, a defendant cannot be guilty of conspiracy to commit a crime when his sole alleged coconspirator has been acquitted of conspiracy charges stemming from the same crime. The defendant argued that, because his sole alleged coconspirator, Soto, was tried on the same charges, based on identical underlying facts, and acquitted by a jury of the charge of conspiracy to commit murder prior to the defendant's sentencing, he also

---

[11] Defense counsel argued that

[t]he . . . philosophy . . . behind the Robinson decision is that . . . our conspiracy statute is bilateral as was held in Grullon. . . . [I]f there [are] only two coconspirators . . . as there [were] in this case, which I think the evidence is clear that it was [the defendant] and Mr. Soto . . . if one or the other is acquitted after trial, it's a finding on [the] merits; and as a matter of law, then there is no conspiracy because as the case law indicated, you can't have one hand clapping. It's not a unilateral situation, it's a bilateral situation. . . .

must be acquitted of the conspiracy charges. The defendant asserted that, because Connecticut's conspiracy statute requires bilateral agreement, the acquittal of one conspirator necessarily precludes the conviction of the sole alleged coconspirator.[12] The trial court disagreed. Finding *Robinson* to be factually distinguishable from the present case, the trial court made the following finding:

> "[T]he . . . philosophy . . . behind the Robinson decision is that . . . our conspiracy statute is bilateral as was held in Grullon. . . . [I]f there [are] only two coconspirators . . . as there [were] in this case, which I think the evidence is clear that it was [the defendant] and Mr. Soto . . . if one or the other is acquitted after trial, it's a finding on [the] merits; and as a matter of law, then there is no conspiracy because as the case law indicated, you can't have one hand clapping. It's not a unilateral situation, it's a bilateral situation. . . ."

> The court feels the factual pattern here is unlike . . . *Robinson*. I think that the fact pattern here triggers the case law that allow[s] inconsistent verdicts at separate trials. I don't believe it is the policy of the state or the law of the state to undo serious convictions based upon what another jury does in subsequent cases on somewhat different evidence that was presented to that jury.

The trial court went on to state:

> In fact, the Court's recollection . . . [is] that when the two met to gather the sword to move on . . . the evidence against [the defendant] said that they were "going on a mission," which the jury in [this] case could have interpreted to be a conspiracy. That evidence, my recollection [is], was absent in the case of Mr. Soto, so that two juries, one subsequent to the other, [heard] different evidence, allow[ing] inconsistent verdicts.

Accordingly, the trial court denied the defendant's motion for judgment of acquittal. We agree with the trial court's reasoning. General Statutes § 53a–48(a) provides that "[a] person is guilty of conspiracy when, with intent that conduct constituting a crime be performed, he agrees with one or more persons to engage in or cause the performance of such conduct, and any one of them commits an overt act in pursuance of such conspiracy. . . ."[13] Generally, "[i]n construing a statute, [o]ur

---

[12] The defendant recognized that the timing in Robinson was different in that there was an acquittal of the first alleged coconspirator, and therefore the prosecution of the second individual was barred. *State v. Robinson, supra,* 213 Conn. at 253, 567 A.2d 1173. He went on to argue, however, that "[i]t doesn't matter who's convicted first," relying on *Evans v. Commissioner of Correction,* 709 A.2d 1136, cent. denied 714 A.2d 5 (Conn.1998).

[13] The judge instructed the jury on the conspiracy charge as follows:

A person is guilty of conspiracy when with the intent that conduct constituting a crime be performed . . . here murder, he agrees with one or more persons to engage in or cause the performance of such conduct and any one of them commits an overt act in the pursuance of the conspiracy. To constitute the crime of conspiracy, the state must prove

fundamental objective is to ascertain and give effect to the apparent intent of the legislature. . . . In seeking to discern that intent, we look to the words of the statute itself, to the legislative history and circumstances surrounding its enactment, to the legislative policy it was designed to implement, and to its relationship to existing legislation and common law principles governing the same general subject matter." . . . In *Grullon* and *Robinson*, we determined that the language of § 53a–48(a) supported a bilateral interpretation of our conspiracy laws. *State v. Grullon*, 562 A.2d 481; *State v. Robinson*, 567 A.2d 1173. "Our examination of the definition of the crime of conspiracy in § 53a–48 convince[d] us that the legislature [had] determined that conspiracy require[d] a showing that two or more coconspirators intended to engage in or cause conduct that constitute[d] a crime." . . . *State v. Robinson*, 567 A.2d 1173.

In arguing that he could not be convicted of conspiracy once Soto, his sole alleged coconspirator, was acquitted, the defendant relied upon *State v. Grullon*, 562 A.2d 481, and *State v. Robinson*, 567 A. 2d 1173. We now conclude, however, that *Grullon* and *Robinson* are factually distinguishable from one another and, therefore, that the rule in *Grullon* should not have governed our decision in *Robinson*.[14] In *Grullon*, we concluded that a defendant could not be guilty of conspiracy pursuant to § 53a–48 without proof beyond a reasonable doubt that he conspired with another individual who was not a police informant or agent because the statute requires that there be an agreement between coconspirators. *State v. Grullon*, 562 A.2d 481. In *Grullon*, the defendant had conspired with a police agent to deliver a shipment of narcotics. The agent did not have the actual intent to commit the crime. 562 A.2d 481. In *Robinson*, however, the defendant and his coconspirator both were charged with conspiracy to commit murder and both went to trial in different proceedings. *State v. Robinson*, 567 A.2d 1173. The defendant was convicted on the conspiracy charge, but his coconspirator was acquitted. *Id.* Relying on the *Grullon* requirement for bilateral conspiracy, we concluded that the acquittal, at a separate trial, of the defendant's alleged coconspirator foreclosed prosecution of the defendant for

---

the following elements beyond a reasonable doubt: (1) There was an agreement between the defendant and one or more persons to engage in conduct constituting a crime; (2) there was an overt act in furtherance of the subject of the agreement by one of the persons; (3) there was the intent on the part of the defendant that conduct constituting a crime be performed. . . . [W]hat is important is whether the defendant willfully participated in the activities of the conspiracy with knowledge of its illegal ends.

[14] Indeed, the legislature has taken no action since the publication of our decisions in *Grullon* and *Robinson*, both of which interpreted § 53a–48 as a bilateral conspiracy statute. However, "legislative inaction is not necessarily legislative affirmation. . . ." *State v. Hodge*, 726 A.2d 531, cert. denied, 528 U.S. 969 (1999). The legislature's failure to challenge either decision is not dispositive of the issue, however, because "even legislative inaction is not the best of guides to legislative intent." (Internal quotation marks omitted.) *Streitweiser v. Middlesex Mutual Assurance Co.*, 593 A.2d 498 (Conn.1991)

conspiracy because the culpability of the coconspirator was "an essential element of the defendant's offense." 562 A.2d 481.

On the basis of their significant factual differences, however, we now conclude that our reliance on *Grullon* in deciding *Robinson* was improper. "The earlier determination in . . . *Grullon* that General Statutes § 53a–48 is a 'bilateral' conspiracy statute does not offer any real insight in addressing the present issue. Nor does the line of cases holding that the acquittal of one conspirator forecloses the conviction of other conspirators found guilty in the same trial. This rule, while making obvious sense in the context of a single trial for all of the reasons stated in the majority opinion, has been rejected by a number of jurisdictions where, as here, the acquittal occurs in a separate trial." *See United States v. Irvin*, 787 F.2d 1506, 1512–14 (11th Cir.1986), *United States v. Roark*, 753 F.2d 991, 995–96 (11th Cir.), reh. denied, 761 F.2d 698 (11th Cir. 1985); *United States v. Espinosa-Cerpa*, 630 F.2d 328, 330–32 (5th Cir.1980); *Gardner v. State*, 408 A.2d 1317 (Md.1979); *Commonwealth v. Brown*, 375 A.2d 331 (Pa.1977). *State v. Robinson*, 567 A.2d 1173 (COVELLO, J., dissenting).

In *Grullon*, the police agent never intended to commit the underlying crime and, therefore, there was no agreement as required by the statute. *State v. Grullon*, 562 A.2d 481. In *Robinson*, however, the coconspirators were both charged with the underlying, substantive crime of conspiracy, and both coconspirators were charged with having the underlying necessary intent to enter into the conspiracy. *State v. Robinson*, 567 A.2d 1173. Thus, although we recognize that "[t]he doctrine of *stare decisis* counsels that a court should not overrule its earlier decisions unless the most cogent reasons and inescapable logic require it"; . . . *State v. Murray*, 757 A.2d 578 (2000) (McDONALD, C.J., dissenting); it is evident that the facts of these two cases warrant different results and *Robinson* should be overruled. We noted in *Grullon* that "[a]llowing a government agent to form a conspiracy with only one other party would create the potential for law enforcement officers to manufacture conspiracies when none would exist absent the government's presence." . . . *State v. Grullon*, 562 A.2d 481. We reaffirm that principle and decline to overrule *Grullon*.[15] For the following reasons, however, we conclude that the rule

---

[15] Several jurisdictions disagree with our holding in *Grullon*. In *People v. Schwimmer*, 66 A.D.2d 91, 92, 411 N.Y.S.2d 922 (1978), cert. denied, 394 N.E.2d 288 (1979), the New York Appellate Division decided that a defendant could be convicted of conspiracy when all the other members of the alleged conspiracy feigned agreement and never intended to perform the object crime. In *Schwimmer*, the defendant conspired with an undercover New York City police officer and a confidential police informant to illegally sell diamonds owned by the city of New York. The defendant argued that he could not be guilty of conspiracy because his two coconspirators never intended to commit the underlying substantive crimes. *Id*. 411 N.Y.S.2d 922. He argued that his coconspirators' lack of intent rendered a finding of "conspiratorial agreement" impossible and, therefore, that he must be acquitted of the conspiracy charges. *Id*. The New York Appellate Division disagreed and adopted the " 'unilateral approach' exemplified by the [revised] Model Penal Code (10 Uniform Laws Ann., §§ 5.03, 5.04)." *Id*.; *see also People v. Villetto*, 394 N.E.2d 288 (N.Y.1979); *People v. Teeter*, 394 N.E.2d 286 (1979). Other states have followed suit. See *State v. Chan*, 935 P.2d 850 (Ariz. 1997) ("person may be guilty of conspiracy even if

in *Robinson*, although "once believed sound, needs modification to serve justice better. . . ." We now conclude, therefore, that the conviction of a conspirator may be upheld despite the acquittal of his sole alleged coconspirator in a separate trial where there is sufficient evidence to prove, beyond a reasonable doubt, that the defendant was guilty of conspiracy.[16]

In *Robinson*, we held that, "as a matter of law, the conspiracy charge against the defendant was barred after the acquittal of the sole alleged coconspirator." *State v. Robinson*, 567 A.2d 1173. We enumerated therein those jurisdictions that had taken a similar position. 567 A.2d 1173 at n. 8. We also recognized, however, that authorities are split over whether criminal liability under conspiracy laws should be extended to situations where a defendant's coconspirator has been acquitted in a prior trial before a different jury. 567 A.2d 1173 citing 19 A.L.R.4th 192 and cases cited therein. The courts that find liability in such cases have reasoned that "an acquittal is not tantamount to a determination of innocence and that the proof may differ from one trial to another. Central to that reasoning of these courts is their contention that consistent verdicts, even as to conspiracy convictions, are not required at separate trials." 567 A.2d 1173. We now consider the rationale of those jurisdictions persuasive.[17]

When coconspirators are tried separately, the acquittal of one on charges of conspiracy should not dictate the acquittal of the other simply because the state in one case has failed to prove an element necessary to

---

other person in plot is police agent who has no real intention of committing criminal act"); *State v. Null*, 526 N.W.2d 220 (Neb.1995) ("consequence of the unilateral approach to make it immaterial to the guilt of a conspirator whose culpability has been established that the other person . . . with whom he conspired [has] not been or cannot be convicted"); *State v. Sample*, 573 N.W.2d 187 (Wis.1998) (coconspirator's feigned agreement with defendant sufficient to support charge for "inchoate crime of conspiracy"). "Other states have justified the unilateral theory of conspiracy as sound public policy [based on reasoning similar to that of *Schwimmer*]. A person who believes he is conspiring with another to commit a crime is a danger to the public regardless of whether the other person in fact has agreed to commit the crime." *Miller v. State*, 955 P.2d 892, 897 (Wyo.1998).

We note, however, as we did in *Grullon*, that "[a]lthough much of the language of the New York and Connecticut statutes is virtually identical, the New York statute contains a section, not contained in the Connecticut statute, that specifically states that it is not a defense to a conspiracy charge that the defendant's coconspirator lacked the mental state necessary to himself be guilty of conspiracy." *State v. Grullon*, supra, 212 Conn. at 201, 562 A.2d 481. Because the holding in Schwimmer hinges on that section, we are not persuaded by the decision in Schwimmer as it pertains to cases in which the underlying conspiracy charge arose out of a police officer or agent's feigned agreement to commit a crime.

[16] As previously noted, this conclusion does not alter our analysis in *Grullon*, in which we held that there must be "'at least one bona fide co-conspirator'" in order for there to be an underlying substantive charge of conspiracy. *State v. Grullon*, supra, 212 Conn. at 203, 562 A.2d 481. Thus, a defendant's agreement with a police officer or police agent to commit a crime does not satisfy the requirement in § 53a–48 that there be some other person, with culpable intent, who agrees with the defendant to violate the law. Id.

[17] Our analysis of § 53a–48(b) indicates that even when a conspirator successfully thwarts a conspiracy and has a defense to the charge, it does not negate the intent and the guilt of the alleged coconspirator. It is evident, therefore, that it was not the intention of the legislature universally to discharge the guilt of a sole conspirator when, for some evidentiary or procedural reason, his coconspirator is acquitted.

a conspiracy charge. *See United States v. Espinosa-Cerpa*, 630 F.2d at 332 (jury's acquittal of some coconspirators should not be taken to negate fact of possible criminal complicity with any remaining alleged coconspirators); *People v. Berkowitz*, 406 N.E.2d 783 (N.Y.1980) (principles of collateral estoppel do not bar prosecution of one conspirator after acquittal of sole coconspirator in criminal trial). The acquittal of a codefendant in a separate trial "could . . . [result] from a multiplicity of factors completely unrelated to the actual existence of a conspiracy;" *United States v. Strother*, 458 F.2d 424, 426 (5th Cir.), cert. denied, 409 U.S. 1011 (1972); for example, certain evidentiary issues that might render evidence inadmissible in one trial but not in another. *See Rosecrans v. United States*, 378 F.2d 561, 567 (5th Cir.1967); *Marquiz v. People*, 726 P.2d 1105, 1107 (Colo.1986). In separate trials, "[t]he evidence presented to the juries and the manner in which that evidence is presented may be significantly different and certainly will never be identical." *Marquiz v. People*, *supra*, at 1107. As a result, "[d]ifferent juries may rationally come to different conclusions, especially when differing evidence is presented." *United States v. Roark*, 753 F.2d at 995.

An . . . unsuccessful prosecution of an alleged coconspirator in a separate trial means nothing more than that on a given date the prosecution failed to meet its burden of proving the defendant guilty beyond a reasonable doubt of all of the elements constituting conspiracy. It certainly does not mean . . . that a conspiracy did not occur. It has long been recognized that criminal juries in the United States are free to render not guilty verdicts resulting from compromise, confusion, mistake, leniency or other legally and logically irrelevant factors.

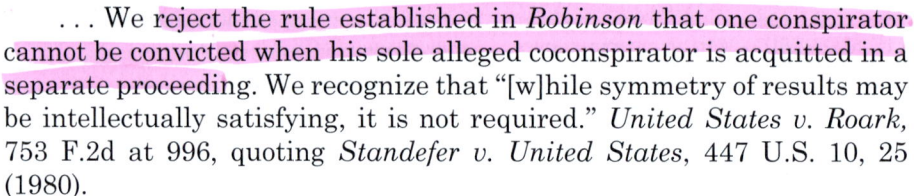

. . . We reject the rule established in *Robinson* that one conspirator cannot be convicted when his sole alleged coconspirator is acquitted in a separate proceeding. We recognize that "[w]hile symmetry of results may be intellectually satisfying, it is not required." *United States v. Roark*, 753 F.2d at 996, quoting *Standefer v. United States*, 447 U.S. 10, 25 (1980).

The defendant in this case was tried and convicted by a jury that was presented with a specific body of facts, some of which were not presented in Soto's trial. For example, the jury in this case heard testimony of the "mission" upon which the defendant and his coconspirator embarked when they conspired to murder the victim. That evidence was inadmissible at the trial of the defendant's coconspirator, which may have been a factor in his acquittal on the conspiracy charge. The acquittal of the defendant's coconspirator did not nullify the defendant's conviction of the same charge, where the two defendants were tried separately, and their respective juries were presented with separate, independent evidence of their agreement to commit the crime in question. Accordingly, we conclude that the trial court properly concluded that the defendant's conviction should stand despite Soto's acquittal and, therefore, that it properly denied the defendant's motion for judgment of acquittal.

The judgment is affirmed.

■ In this opinion the other JUSTICES concurred.

———

NOTES

1. Even in a state requiring proof of bilateral conspiracy, it is possible to charge and convict a defendant of conspiring with persons whose names are unknown; all that is required is that the evidence produced at trial show that unnamed co-conspirator did exist and that defendant conspired with him. State v. Rodriguez-Jimenez, 439 So.2d 919 (Fla.App. 1983).

2. Should the rule of consistency for joint conspirators be retained? Courts in different states do not agree. *See, e.g.*, Smith v. State, 250 Ga. 264, 297 S.E.2d 273 (1982), which held:

> In a joint trial of co-conspirators. a failure of proof as to one co-conspirator would amount to a failure of proof as to both, the evidence presented being identical. Co-conspirators, alleged to be the only two parties to the conspiracy, may not receive different verdicts when they are tried together. With two trials, the issue before the court in each case is the guilt or innocence of that particular defendant, which must be proved beyond a reasonable doubt. When the jury returns a verdict of guilty, it indicates that as to this defendant the burden of proving the conspiracy and the defendant's participation has been met. Where the trials are severed, it is highly possible that co-conspirators could receive different verdicts without those verdicts being fatally inconsistent. In the first trial the evidence may be properly presented. the burden of proving X guilty of conspiracy may be met, and the jury can properly return a verdict of guilty. In the subsequent trial of conspirator Y. However, the death or unavailability of certain witnesses, the failure of the prosecution to present all available evidence. the ineffectiveness of the prosecution in presenting its case, or the difference in jury composition could all affect the verdict. The failure of the prosecution to prove all elements of the conspiracy in the subsequent case would justify a directed verdict of acquittal, as happened in this case, without being inconsistent with the earlier conviction.

Florida law provides that it is not necessary, to sustain a conviction for conspiracy, that coconspirators be charged. Filer v. State, 285 So.2d 669 (Fla.App. 1973). However, a conspiracy conviction for one defendant cannot be sustained where all other co-defendant charged with conspiracy have been acquitted. State v. Russell, 611 So.2d 1265 (Fla.App.1992).

3. At common law, a husband and wife were legally one person, and therefore could not conspire with each other. That rule has long since been abrogated.

See United States v. Dege, 364 U.S. 51, 80 S.Ct. 1589, 4 L.Ed.2d 1563 (1960) (" '[W]e free our minds from the notion that criminal statutes must be construed by some artificial and conventional rule,' . . . and therefore do not allow ourselves to be obfuscated by medieval views regarding the legal status of woman and the common law's reflection of them." (citations omitted)).

———

(C) WHARTON'S RULE AND NECESSARY PARTIES

Regardless of whether a jurisdiction follows a bilateral or unilateral theory of conspiracy, the question of "necessary parties," or "Wharton's Rule" still has to be addressed. The two rules, while not identical, have the same practical effect: that in conspiracies to commit certain crimes, a combination of more than two people will be required.

People v. Lee

Court of Appeal, Fifth District, California, 2006.
136 Cal.App.4th 522, 38 Cal.Rptr.3d 927.

■ ARDAIZ, P.J.

* * *

FACTS

As a result of monitored telephone conversations between Lee, an inmate in the Substance Abuse Treatment Facility (SATF) at Corcoran State Prison, and his wife, Felicia Rush, correctional officers suspected Rush would be smuggling drugs into the prison at Lee's behest on July 12, 2003.[2] A search warrant was obtained for Rush, who was intercepted upon her arrival for visitation that day. During the search, she relinquished a green condom containing three bindles of marijuana and loose tobacco; and a clear condom containing three small bindles of marijuana, two separately-packaged rocks of cocaine base, and loose tobacco. The items had been secreted in her bra.

In her initial statements to investigators, Rush maintained that, although she had had a conversation with Lee confirming the items she was to bring in, she had been told to bring in the drugs by a noninmate she knew only as Stephon. This person was subsequently identified as Stephon Devine, an employee of the counseling program provider at SATF. By the time he was identified, he was no longer employed at the institution. Rush agreed to help the district attorney's office in its investigation of him, then informed the investigator that she had lied

———

[2] Drugs can be passed from visitor to inmate during contact visits, or, in the case of noncontact visits, with the assistance of inmate porters who work in the visiting room.

about Lee's lack of involvement. Further investigation revealed that Devine, Lee, and Rush were working together.[3]

Rush testified at trial while facing a felony charge of bringing drugs into a state prison. She admitted that, prior to July 12, she had brought in tobacco and marijuana quite a few times. If she and Lee had noncontact visits, he would signal her when she was supposed to give the contraband to one of the inmate workers in the visiting room. If they had contact visits, she usually would give the drugs directly to Lee. According to Rush, she started bringing drugs into the prison because she was afraid of Lee. She initially received a telephone call at her office in Santa Monica. The caller told her to buy drugs and bring them to the prison. She thought it was a joke, but, a few hours later, two individuals came to her office and threatened her. She also received a telephone call from Lee's aunt, telling her that she had to give him money and cooperate with him because she was always putting him in a bind. Lee subsequently telephoned her and told her to cooperate in bringing the items into the prison. He confirmed that he knew about the people who came to her office. In addition to the items she brought to Lee, he and Devine, who were working together, had her bring tobacco and money to the prison and leave it for Devine at prearranged locations. She sent money to Devine, as well.

The drugs Rush brought into the prison on July 12 were intended for Lee, who was the one who told her to bring them in. In an earlier visit, Lee had told her what she was supposed to do, because she would "cost him, put him in a bind and all his people." He told her how to package the items, as well as the number of items to bring.

DISCUSSION

I

AN INMATE CAN BE CONVICTED OF CONSPIRACY TO VIOLATE § 4573.9

Section 4573.9 provides, in pertinent part: "Notwithstanding any other provision of law, any person, *other than a person held in custody*, who sells, furnishes, administers, or gives away, or offers to sell, furnish, administer, or give away to any person held in custody in any state prison . . . any controlled substance, the possession of which is prohibited by Division 10 (commencing with § 11000) of the Health and Safety Code, if the recipient is not authorized to possess the same . . . is guilty of a felony punishable by imprisonment in the state prison for two, four, or six years." (Italics added.)[4]

---

[3]   Following his September 25 arrest for conspiracy to introduce narcotics into a state prison, Devine told investigators that, while employed as a counselor in Lee's facility, he brought tobacco to Lee, and Rush paid him for doing so. He adamantly denied being involved in any drug transactions.

[4]   Marijuana, cocaine, and cocaine base are among the prohibited controlled substances. (Health & Saf.Code, §§ 11054, subds. (d)(13), (f)(1), 11055, subd. (b)(6), 11350, 11357.)

The parties agree that Lee could not commit the substantive offense because, as an inmate, he was not a person "other than a person held in custody." Lee was not convicted of violating § 4573.9, however, but of *conspiracy* to violate that statute. Lee says he could not properly be charged with, or convicted of, conspiracy because the language of § 4573.9 specifically precludes him from punishment and, inasmuch as other statutes provide for lesser punishment for inmates, to apply the law of conspiracy under the circumstances present here would run contrary to the expressed legislative intent. Respondent counters that conspiracy is a separate and distinct offense from the substantive crime committed, and Lee has not shown the existence of an affirmative legislative intent that he go unpunished for his role in the charged criminal conduct.

Pursuant to § 182, subdivision (a)(1), a conspiracy consists of two or more persons conspiring to commit any crime. A conviction of conspiracy requires proof that the defendant and another person had the specific intent to agree to conspire to commit an offense, as well as the specific intent to commit the elements of that offense, together with proof of the commission of an overt act "by one or more of the parties to such agreement" in furtherance of the conspiracy. . . . Criminal conspiracy is an offense distinct from the actual commission of a criminal offense that is the object of the conspiracy. . . . "In contemplation of law the act of one [conspirator] is the act of all. Each is responsible for everything done by his confederates, which follows incidentally in the execution of the common design as one of its probable and natural consequences. . . ." *People v. Morante*, 20 Cal.4th 403, 416–417, 84 Cal.Rptr.2d 665, 975 P.2d 1071 (1999) (fns. omitted.)

"[T]he basic conspiracy principle has some place in modern criminal law, because to unite, back of a criminal purpose, the strength, opportunities and resources of many is obviously more dangerous and more difficult to police than the efforts of a lone wrongdoer." . . . Collaboration magnifies the risk to society both by increasing the likelihood that a given quantum of harm will be successfully produced and by increasing the amount of harm that can be inflicted. As the United States Supreme Court wrote in *Callanan v. United States* (1961) 364 U.S. 587, 593–594 [81 S.Ct. 321, 5 L.Ed.2d 312]: "Concerted action both increases the likelihood that the criminal object will be successfully attained and decreases the probability that the individuals involved will depart from their path of criminality. Group association for criminal purposes often, if not normally, makes possible the attainment of ends more complex than those which one criminal could accomplish. Nor is the danger of a conspiratorial group limited to the particular end toward which it has embarked. Combination in crime makes more likely the commission of crimes unrelated to the original purpose for which the group was formed. In sum, the danger which a conspiracy generates is not confined to the substantive offense which is the immediate aim of the enterprise." . . . "Thus wrongful conduct by such combination should be criminally punished even when the same acts would be excused or receive a lesser punishment when performed by an individual; group criminal conduct calls for enhanced punishment, and society has a justifiable right and obligation to intervene at an earlier stage." *People v. Williams* 101 Cal.App.3d 711, 721, 161 Cal.Rptr. 830 (1980).

In light of the foregoing, "[t]here are many cases . . . in which it has been recognized that a defendant may be liable to prosecution for conspiracy to commit a given crime even though he is incapable of committing the crime itself. . . ." Lee now relies on narrowly-drawn, interconnected exceptions to this general rule, all of which are founded, however implicitly, on the notion that legislative intent is paramount in determining whether a party can be prosecuted for conspiracy in a given situation.

The first such exception is Wharton's Rule (1 ANDERSON, WHARTON'S CRIMINAL LAW AND PROCEDURE (1957) p. 191), which provides that where "the cooperation of two or more persons is necessary to the commission of the substantive crime, and there is no ingredient of an alleged conspiracy that is not present in the substantive crime, then the persons necessarily involved cannot be charged with conspiracy to commit the substantive offense and also with the substantive crime itself. . . . The rule is considered in modern legal thinking as an aid in construction of statutes, a presumption that the Legislature intended the general conspiracy section be merged with the more specific substantive offense. . . ." (. . . *see, e.g., Pinkerton v. United States* (1946) 328 U.S. 640, 643); . . . It applies only where it is impossible to have the substantive offense "*without concerted effort amounting to conspiracy.* . . ."

As the United States Supreme Court explained in *Iannelli v. United States* (1975) 420 U.S. 770, 783–784 Wharton's Rule "has current vitality only as a judicial presumption, to be applied in the absence of legislative intent to the contrary. The classic Wharton's Rule offenses—adultery, incest, bigamy, duelling—are crimes that are characterized by the general congruence of the agreement and the completed substantive offense. The parties to the agreement are the only persons who participate in commission of the substantive offense, and the immediate consequences of the crime rest on the parties themselves rather than on society at large. . . . Finally, the agreement that attends the substantive offense does not appear likely to pose the distinct kinds of threats to society that the law of conspiracy seeks to avert. It cannot, for example, readily be assumed that an agreement to commit an offense of this nature will produce agreements to engage in a more general pattern of criminal conduct. . . ."

Section 4573.9 is not the type of crime usually seen as a classic Wharton's Rule offense. *See Iannelli v. United States, supra,* 420 U.S. at pp. 782–785. More importantly, it is possible to have the substantive offense without concerted effort amounting to conspiracy. For instance, one may administer a controlled substance without the consent, or against the will, of the person to whom it is administered, and one may offer to sell or give away a controlled substance to one who does not accept the offer. Thus, while two people may act in concert to violate the statute, such cooperation is not necessary. *See, e.g., Gebardi v. United States* (1932) 287 U.S. 112, 121–122 [where woman consents to own transportation, Mann Act violation not prosecutable as conspiracy because it is impossible to commit substantive offense without cooperative action]; . . . Moreover, while the person who buys or obtains a drug is not generally an accomplice of the person who sells or furnishes it (*People v. Label* (1974) 43 Cal.App.3d 766, 770–771, 119 Cal.Rptr. 522), an exception exists where, as here, the participants "conspire together in a prearranged plan. . . ." (*People v. Lima* (1944) 25 Cal.2d 573, 577, 154 P.2d 698) [although thief and receiver of stolen goods generally are not accomplices, exception exists where they conspire together in prearranged plan for one to steal and deliver property to other, and, pursuant to such plan, one does steal and deliver to other].[7] In light of the foregoing, Wharton's Rule does not prevent Lee from being charged with, and convicted of, conspiring to violate § 4573.9.

The second exception is found in cases holding that, where the Legislature has dealt with crimes which necessarily involve the joint action of two or more persons and where no punishment is provided for the conduct of one of the parties, that person cannot be charged as a principal, coconspirator, or aider and abettor if (1) a different and more lenient criminal statute is found to be controlling as to such person, or (2) there is an affirmative legislative intent that such participant go unpunished. As Lee primarily relies on this exception, we examine the various cases.

In *Gebardi v. United States, supra*, 287 U.S. 112, 53 S.Ct. 35, the United States Supreme Court, noting that criminal transportation under the Mann Act could be effected without the woman's consent, "perceive[d] in the failure of the Mann Act to condemn the woman's participation in those transportations which are effected with her mere consent, evidence of an affirmative legislative policy to leave her acquiescence unpunished." Accordingly, it held, the woman could neither violate the Mann Act nor be convicted of conspiracy to do so.

---

[7] Respondent points to the fact that Devine and perhaps others were also involved in the conspiracy. An exception to Wharton's Rule exists "where one of the actors joins with third persons on his side of the transaction. . . ." *People v. Lewis* (1963) 214 Cal.App.2d 799, 800, 29 Cal.Rptr. 825; *Iannelli v. United States, supra*, 420 U.S. at p. 782, fn. 15, 95 S.Ct. 1284. "The rationale supporting this exception appears to be that the addition of a third party enhances the dangers presented by the crime." (*Iannelli*, at p. 782, fn. 15, 95 S.Ct. 1284.) We do not rely on this exception because, given the evidence adduced at trial, it is impossible to determine whether Devine was involved in a conspiracy to smuggle anything other than tobacco, a substance which does not fall within the provisions of § 4573.9, or whether anyone else was involved in the conspiracy between Lee and Rush.

In *Ex parte Cooper* (1912) 162 Cal. 81, 121 P. 318, the California Supreme Court determined that only a married person could commit the then-existing crime of adultery. As a result, the statute which made "only the person 'who lives in a state of . . . adultery' guilty of the public offense therein defined, thus impliedly exclud[ed] the idea of any guilt of such offense on the part of the unmarried participant whose only part in the affair has been to live with the married party in the state forbidden to him by the law." Where the idea of guilt of one participant "is thus excluded by the terms of the statute defining the offense," that person cannot be punished as an aider and abettor in the offense, even though he or she may be considered an accomplice under § 31.[8]

In *People v. Clapp* (1944) 24 Cal.2d 835, 151 P.2d 237, the defendants were convicted of performing an abortion in violation of former § 274. The convictions were based on the testimony of the woman who underwent the operation, and of her mother-in-law and sister-in-law, who were present. On appeal, the defendants claimed that, since all three witnesses were accomplices, their testimony required corroboration under § 1111. The California Supreme Court found it necessary to determine whether the witnesses were subject to prosecution under the provisions the defendants were accused of violating, or whether the acts of the witness participating in the transaction constituted a separate and distinct offense. The court stated:

> If a statutory provision so defines a crime that the participation of two or more persons is necessary for its commission, but prescribes punishment for the acts of certain participants only, and another statutory provision prescribes punishment for the acts of participants not subject to the first provision, it is clear that the latter are criminally liable only under the specific provision relating to their participation in the criminal transaction. The specific provision making the acts of participation in the transaction a separate offense supersedes the general provision in § 31 . . . that such acts subject the participant in the crime of the accused to prosecution for its commission. . . .

Accordingly, because a separate provision of the Penal Code (former § 275) prescribed punishment for a woman who submits to an illegal abortion, the witness who underwent the abortion could not be punishable as a principal for the crime of abortion, the distinct offense for which the defendants were on trial, and so was not an accomplice for purposes of the corroboration requirement. In *People v. Buffum, supra*, 40 Cal.2d 709, 256 P.2d 317, the defendants were convicted of conspiring to induce miscarriages under former § 274. The trial court refused to

---

[8] Section 31 provides, in part: "All persons concerned in the commission of a crime, whether it be felony or misdemeanor, and whether they directly commit the act constituting the offense, or aid and abet in its commission, or, not being present, have advised and encouraged its commission, . . . are principals in any crime so committed."

instruct that the women involved were accomplices for purposes of § 1111. The defendants argued that while, under *Clapp*, the women were not accomplices with respect to an actual violation of the statute, they were coconspirators of the person who performed the abortion and, accordingly, subject to prosecution for the identical offense of conspiracy to violate the anti-abortion statute. The court found § 182 to be closely analogous to § 31, which the *Clapp* court had construed, and held:

> [T]he same reasoning which precludes the application of § 31 for the purpose of prosecuting a woman as a principal under § 274 likewise precludes the use of § 182 in prosecuting her for conspiracy to violate § 274. Since ... the Legislature has expressed an intent that a woman who consents and voluntarily submits to an abortion is not punishable under § 274, it clearly did not intend that she should be punished for conspiracy to violate that statute. Although the language of § 182, standing alone, is sufficiently broad to include any agreement to procure an abortion, the provision, like that in § 31, is general and must yield to the specific provision in § 275. Any other construction would mean that the conspiracy law could be used as a device for defeating the legislative intention of imposing a lesser penalty on a woman who violates § 275 than is prescribed for a person convicted under § 274.

The court acknowledged the line of cases recognizing that a defendant may be prosecuted for conspiracy to commit a certain crime even though he or she is incapable of committing the crime itself, but reasoned: "This rule ... does not apply where the statutes defining the substantive offense disclose an affirmative legislative policy that the conduct of one of the parties involved shall be unpunished. ... Similarly, the rule should not be applied where, as here, the Legislature singles out one of the parties for special treatment by enacting a statute which deals only with the conduct of that person and provides for a lesser punishment than is given to the other party." Accordingly, the court concluded that the women in question were not subject to prosecution for conspiracy to violate § 274; hence, none was an accomplice.

In *Williams v. Superior Court* (1973) 30 Cal.App.3d 8, 106 Cal.Rptr. 89 (*Williams*), the issue before the court was whether a prostitute could be charged with both prostitution and with conspiring with her pimp to commit prostitution. (*Id.* at p. 10, 106 Cal. Rptr. 89.) After examining many of the foregoing opinions, as well as *People v. Berger* (1960) 185 Cal.App.2d 16, 19–20, 7 Cal.Rptr. 827 (which held that the woman who is exploited by a male in violation of § 266h is not an accomplice of the man who exploits her), the appellate court concluded:

> Since the Legislature provided for a lesser penalty for prostitution (a misdemeanor) than for pimping (266h) and pandering (266i), which are both felonies, it would defeat the

legislative classification to permit a prostitute to be charged with conspiracy in a case in which the alleged co-conspirator is either a pimp or panderer. . . . From these cases a rule emerges, applicable to the limited area in which Congress or the Legislature has dealt with crimes which necessarily involve the joint action of two or more persons, and where no punishment at all, or a lesser penalty, is provided for the conduct, or misconduct, of one of the participants. Thus, the female 'transportee' in a Mann Act situation and the unmarried participant in adulterous intercourse, whose participation is not denounced by the statute, cannot be charged with criminal conduct by the improper use of the conspiracy statute. By the same token, abortees and prostitutes for whose criminal participation with aborters or with pimps and panderers the Legislature has prescribed a lesser punishment, may not be subjected to greater punishment by the misuse of the conspiracy statute. (*Williams*, at pp. 14–15, 106 Cal.Rptr. 89.)

In *People v. Mayers, supra*, 110 Cal.App.3d 809, 168 Cal.Rptr. 252, the three-card monte case, the defendant argued that the specific provision of § 332, proscribing three-card monte, prevailed over the general sanction against conspiracy to defraud contained in subdivision 4 of § 182. The appellate court agreed, stating: "It is a firmly established principle where specific conduct is prohibited by a special statute, a defendant cannot be prosecuted under a general statute. . . . The foregoing rule is necessary to prevent a general statute from swallowing up the exceptions contained in specific enactments." The court observed that § 332 made the defendant's offense a misdemeanor, whereas, if § 182 applied, "any § 332 misdemeanor violation would be automatically elevated to a felony. . . ." The court found it "[n]oteworthy" that the Legislature had revised § 332 from a pure felony statute to one in which felony or misdemeanor status depended upon the value of the money or property fraudulently obtained, and concluded that "[p]unishment as a conspiracy would void § 332's specifically sanctioned misdemeanor punishment of three-card monte where the value of defrauded property did not exceed" a specified amount.

In *People v. Pangelina* (1981) 117 Cal.App.3d 414, 172 Cal.Rptr. 661, two prostitutes residing in a house of prostitution were charge with conspiracy to keep a house of prostitution, a felony, although the underlying substantive offense (§ 315) was a misdemeanor. The court noted prior appellate decisions that recognized an affirmative legislative intent to punish prostitutes less severely than pimps or panderers, because, "rather than being accomplices or coconspirators of those charged with felony pimping or pandering, prostitutes are criminally exploited by such persons. . . ." *Pangelina*, at p. 422, 172 Cal. Rptr. 661. The court concluded that, in light of the legislative intent behind the statutory scheme, "the use of the conspiracy law to impose felony punishment upon persons merely residing in a house of prostitution . . . directly violates an affirmative legislative intent to punish those parties as misdemeanants. Such a conclusion is strengthened by a consideration of the policy behind the prohibition of criminal conspiracies [citation], which is not served where, as here, the presence of more than one prostitute in a house of prostitution does nothing to further the criminal objective of the prostitute, or make more likely the commission of other crimes. . . . Permitting appellants to be convicted and punished as felons pursuant to § 182 would effectively elevate any misdemeanor violation of § 315 to a felony whenever more than one prostitute was found to 'willfully reside' in a house of prostitution—an increased punishment clearly repugnant to legislative intent. . . ."

* * *

None of the foregoing authorities persuade us that Lee cannot be liable for conspiring to violate § 4573.9. In each, the overriding consideration is the Legislature's intent—whether divined from statutory language or from application of principles, such as Wharton's Rule or the rule that a specific statute controls over a general one, which are, fundamentally, aids to discerning legislative intent (see *In re Williamson* (1954) 43 Cal.2d 651, 654, 276 P.2d 593; *People v. Mayers, supra*, 110 Cal.App.3d at pp. 813, 815, 168 Cal.Rptr. 252)—that one party escape punishment, or be punished less severely, for participation in the conduct at issue. We discern no such intent here. Section 4573.9 is one of a series of statutes, which are to be construed together and which demonstrate that the Legislature "chose to take a prophylactic approach to" "the ultimate evil [of] drug use by prisoners" "by attacking the very presence of drugs and drug paraphernalia in prisons and jails. . . ." (*People v. Gutierrez* (1997) 52 Cal.App.4th 380, 386, 60 Cal.Rptr.2d 561; cf. *People v. Buese* (1963) 220 Cal.App.2d 802, 807, 34 Cal.Rptr. 102.) The obvious purpose of these statutes is "to deter the presence of illicit drugs in custodial institutions"; the statutes are "deemed necessary to ensure orderly administration and security within such institutions. . . ." *People v. Superior Court (Ortiz)* (2004) 115 Cal. App.4th 995, 1002, 9 Cal.Rptr.3d 745.

In pertinent part, § 4573 makes it a felony, punishable by imprisonment for two, three, or four years, for "any person" to "knowingly bring[ ] or send [ ] into, or knowingly assist[ ] in bringing into, or sending into, any state prison," any controlled substance or related paraphernalia. Section 4573.5 makes it a felony, punishable by imprisonment for sixteen months, or two or three years (see § 18), for "[a]ny person" to "knowingly bring[ ] into any state prison" drugs other than controlled substances or related paraphernalia. Section 4573.6 makes it a felony, punishable by imprisonment for two, three, or four years, for "[a]ny person" to "knowingly [have] in his or her possession in any state prison, . . . , any controlled substances" or related paraphernalia. Section 4573.8 makes it a felony, punishable by imprisonment for sixteen months, or two or three years (see § 18), for "[a]ny person" to "knowingly [have] in his or her possession in any state prison, . . . , drugs in any manner, shape, form, dispenser, or container," or any paraphernalia for consuming drugs. "Notwithstanding any other provision of law," § 4573.9 makes it a felony, punishable by imprisonment for two, four, or six years, for "any person, other than a person held in custody," to furnish, etc., or offer to furnish, etc., any controlled substance to a prison inmate.

Section 4573.9 is the only one of the statutes that specifically attacks the deliberate use of a noninmate to smuggle drugs to an inmate. That the potential harm addressed by this statute reaches well beyond that of the other statutes, cannot be gainsaid. Although the drugs might be intended merely for the recipient inmate's personal use, the existence of what amounts to a smuggling operation makes it much more likely there will be further distribution within the prison. Moreover, according to information before the Legislature in support of the enactment of § 4573.9, the actions of noninmates (such as visitors, teachers, maintenance workers, and correctional officers) in bringing drugs into prisons "are violative of the public trust, and exacerbate problems in internal control." Sen. Rules Com., Off. of Sen. Floor Analyses, Analysis of Sen. Bill No. 2863 (1989–1990 Reg. Sess.) as amended Aug. 28, 1990, p. 2. The same bill also increased penalties under the other related statutes, thus clearly indicating how serious a problem the Legislature considered the presence of controlled substances in prisons, and especially the sale or furnishing of those substances to inmates.

It is apparent that, by seeking to deter illicit activities on the part of visitors and correctional personnel . . . the Legislature sought to reduce the flow of drugs into the prison system. Although the increased penalty for the substantive offense of in-prison sale, etc., of controlled substances is restricted to noninmates, nothing in the legislative history of § 4573.9 or in the overall statutory scheme suggests the Legislature intended to exempt from this increased penalty those inmates who actively join with noninmates in a criminal conspiracy to introduce controlled substances into prison. To hold otherwise would lead to the absurd result of an incarcerated drug kingpin, using noninmate "mules" to smuggle into prison contraband that is then sold to other inmates in a profit-making business enterprise, and yet escaping the increased penalties to which the "mules," who operate at his or her direction, are subject.

In sum, we conclude that, while the Legislature reasonably could (and did) determine that, in order to deter the introduction of controlled substances into prisons, only noninmates should be subject to increased penalties for commission of the substantive offense proscribed by § 4573.9, the more lenient related statutes are not controlling with respect to a person in Lee's situation, and there is no affirmative legislative intent that such a participant go unpunished or be punished less severely. The situation shown by the evidence in the present case is precisely the type in which collaborative criminal activities pose a greater potential threat than the individual substantive offense; hence, there is no logical reason why the Legislature would want conspiracy to violate § 4573.9 and a violation of the statute itself to be merged for prosecution and punishment. *See Iannelli v. United States, supra*, 420 U.S. at pp. 778–779;. . . . Since we do not find, "from all of the circumstances that there was an *affirmative* legislative intent to create an exception to the general rule of liability of . . . conspirators" . . . it follows that Lee was properly charged with, and convicted of, conspiracy to violate § 4573.9.[10] . . . The judgment is affirmed.

NOTES

1. Wharton's Rule owes its name to Francis Wharton, whose treatise on criminal law identified the doctrine and its fundamental rationale:

> When to the idea of an offense plurality of agents is logically necessary, conspiracy, which assumes the voluntary accession of a person to a crime of such a character that it is aggravated by a plurality of agents, cannot be maintained. . . . In other words, when the law says, "a combination between two persons to effect a particular end shall be called, if the end be effected, by a certain name," it is not lawful for the prosecution to call it by some other name; and when the law says, such an offense—*e.g.*, adultery— shall have a certain punishment, it is not lawful for the prosecution to evade this limitation by indicting the offense as conspiracy.

2 FRANCIS WHARTON, WHARTON'S CRIMINAL LAW § 1604 (12th ed. 1932).

2. In Iannelli v. United States, 420 U.S. 770, 95 S.Ct. 1284, 43 L.Ed.2d 616 (1975), Iannelli, along with seven unindicted coconspirators and six co-defendants, was charged with conspiring to violate and with violating 18 U.S.C. § 1955, a federal gambling statute making it a crime for five or more persons to conduct, finance, manage, supervise, direct, or own a gambling business prohibited by state law. Each petitioner was convicted and sentenced under both counts. The Court of Appeals for the Third Circuit affirmed, finding that a recognized exception to Wharton's Rule permitted prosecution and punishment for both offenses. The United States Supreme Court, per Justice Powell, affirmed, after considering at length the application of Wharton's Rule to such a statute. The Court noted that

---

[10] Lee says the impropriety of his prosecution and conviction are further demonstrated by the trial court's purportedly erroneous failure to instruct, as an element of the offense, that the person charged must be "any person, other than a person held in custody." We do not view this as a claim of instructional error, but simply a contention made for illustrative purposes. Were we to find the instruction somehow incomplete, we would conclude that any error was harmless beyond a reasonable doubt. (*People v. Hughes* (2002) 27 Cal.4th 287, 353, 116 Cal.Rptr.2d 401, 39 P.3d 432; *see Neder v. United States* (1999) 527 U.S. 1, 7–20, 119 S.Ct. 1827, 144 L.Ed.2d 35.)

Wharton's Rule had originated in Shannon v. Commonwealth, 14 Pa. 226 (1850), in which the Pennsylvania Supreme Court ordered dismissal of an indictment for conspiracy to commit adultery (filed after the government had failed to obtain conviction for the substantive offense). The *Shannon* Court held that "where concert is a constituent part of the act to be done, as it is in fornication and adultery, *a party acquitted of the major cannot be indicted of the minor.*" Francis Wharton later articulated the Rule in its present form. The *Iannelli* Court said,

> This Court's prior decisions indicate that the broadly formulated Wharton's Rule ... has current vitality only as a judicial presumption, to be applied in the absence of legislative intent to the contrary. The classic Wharton's Rule offenses—adultery, incest, bigamy, duelling—*are crimes that are characterized by the general congruence of the agreement and the completed substantive offense.* . . .

> Wharton's Rule applies only to offenses that *require* concerted criminal activity, a plurality of criminal agents. In such cases, a closer relationship exists between the conspiracy and the substantive offense because *both* require collective criminal activity. The substantive offense therefore presents some of the same threats that the law of conspiracy normally is thought to guard against, and it cannot automatically be assumed that the Legislature intended the conspiracy and the substantive offense to remain as discrete crimes upon consummation of the latter. Thus, absent legislative intent to the contrary, the Rule supports a presumption that the two merge when the substantive offense is proved.

Even though the gambling statute required that five or more persons and a certain volume of cash be involved, the Court noted that the persons gambling and the persons conspiring need not necessarily be the same persons, unlike the classic Wharton's Rule crimes in which the persons conspiring to commit adultery were the adulterers themselves. After a lengthy examination of the legislative history and statutory language, the Court found no such congruence of agreement between the violation of § 1955 and the conspiracy to violate it. Finding a clear Congressional intent to impose punishment for both, the Court rejected petitioner's argument and affirmed all of the co-conspirators' convictions.

———

(D) "WHEEL AND SPOKE" AND "CHAIN" CONSPIRACIES

Conspiracies may have many members, and difficult issues arise in determining whether the relationships that exist between the various individuals involve all of them in one single conspiracy, or whether several distinct conspiracies exist involving a smaller number of individuals—different ones for each offense charged. New parties may join a conspiracy at any time, while others may terminate their relationship without terminating the original conspiracy.[24] In solving the problems thus encountered, courts and legal commentators have referred to the "rimless wheel" and the "chain" relationships.

State v. Samuel Maduro

Supreme Court of Vermont, 2002.
174 Vt. 302, 816 A.2d 432.

■ MORSE, J.

Defendant Samuel Maduro, also known as Samuel Penney, appeals from the district court's judgment of conviction following a jury trial on charges of delivery of cocaine in violation of 18 V.S.A. § 4231(b)(3) and conspiracy to sell cocaine in violation of 13 V.S.A. § 1404(a). He argues on appeal that the trial court improperly admitted evidence of prior uncharged bad acts as direct evidence of the conspiracy, as well as evidence of intent on the delivery charge, and that the court erroneously denied his motion for judgment of acquittal on the charge of delivery. Because we agree that the evidence was erroneously admitted, we reverse and remand for a new trial.

The charges at issue stem from events occurring in the spring of 1999. The affidavit submitted in support of the charges alleged that, between February 1999 and May 1999, defendant engaged in a conspiracy to sell cocaine. As laid out in the affidavit, the conspiracy consisted of the defendant providing materials such as crack cocaine, cash and scales to a juvenile, K.M., to hold for him when police searched his apartment pursuant to conditions of his furlough status, and included, on one occasion, asking K.M. to give crack cocaine to an individual in exchange for cash at defendant's apartment while he was not there. The affidavit also alleged that on May 1, 1999, defendant delivered to K.M. roughly seventy-seven grams of crack cocaine to hold for him, which K.M. provided to the police when they contacted her in the course of investigating defendant's activities. Defendant was charged with the above crimes in June 1999. A little less than a month before the case was set to go to trial in September 2000, the State disclosed an additional witness it intended to call who would provide "prior bad act" evidence. Specifically, the State intended to call Keith Merrow to testify that defendant provided him with powder and crack cocaine at their common workplace to sell between January and May 1999. Defendant moved in limine to exclude the evidence. In response, the State argued that the evidence was not only admissible to show intent with regard to the conspiracy charge, but was also direct evidence of the conspiracy itself because Merrow also formed part of that conspiracy. The court heard argument on the motion the first day of trial and denied defendant's motion. The court decided to let the evidence in, both as

---

[24] Cam v. State, 433 So.2d 38 (Fla.App. 1983).

direct evidence of the conspiracy itself and for the purpose of showing plan and intent on the conspiracy offense.

The trial resulted in a hung jury on both charges. Prior to defendant's new trial, he again moved to exclude Merrow's testimony. In response, the State simply renewed its previous arguments in opposition to defendant's motion. . . . Following a short discussion revisiting its original ruling, the court indicated that it would not change the ruling and thus would make the same ruling on defendant's new motion.

Accordingly, Merrow testified at trial that he had met defendant in jail and then later worked with him for the same employer. He stated that defendant approached him at work and asked if he would sell cocaine for him. Merrow agreed to do so and worked out an arrangement in which he found customers, found out how much of the drug they wanted, and then procured it from defendant. He would then receive a percentage of the sale. Merrow stated that defendant did not know who his customers were and that he never brought the customers to defendant's apartment. He then testified that he remembered seeing a young girl at defendant's apartment on some of the occasions when he would visit to pick up drugs. He also testified, however, that K.M.— presumably the young girl, although never directly identified by Merrow—did not participate in any of his transactions, did not provide him with drugs or money, and was never a witness to the transfers from defendant.

Following Merrow's testimony, the trial court determined that the whole of his testimony went to the charged conspiracy and thus there was no need for any limiting instructions to the jury at that point in the trial. Defendant objected, and the court overruled his objection. At the close of trial, during the jury charge, the court affirmatively instructed the jury that it could consider Merrow's testimony as direct evidence of the conspiracy charge involving K.M. It also added, however, that, if the jury determined that Merrow's testimony was related to a separate uncharged conspiracy, it could still consider the evidence as proof of the opportunity to commit the crimes of which the defendant is charged; the defendant's intent to commit the crimes of which he is charged; the defendant's preparation for and plan to commit the crimes of which he is charged; the defendant's knowledge and absence of mistake in committing the crimes he is accused of.

After the charge to the jury, defendant objected to the above-quoted portion, requesting that the court limit the instruction to the conspiracy charge and direct the jury not to consider it as evidence of opportunity, etc., with regard to the delivery charge. Defendant argued that the testimony did not demonstrate those things with respect to the charged delivery, and that it also was unfairly prejudicial with respect to the delivery charge. The court declined to do so. Defendant now appeals to this Court. Defendant argues that the trial court's decision that the evidence was admissible as direct evidence of the charged conspiracy, as well as its ultimate admission of the evidence for somewhat more limited purposes under V.R.E. 404(b) on the delivery charge, was reversible error. More specifically, defendant first argues that the trial court erroneously determined that V.R.E. 404(b) did not apply to the evidence with regard to the conspiracy charge. He contends that the testimony was *not* direct evidence of the charged conspiracy, but was instead evidence of a separate uncharged conspiracy. In other words, defendant argues that the trial court erroneously determined that the Merrow testimony was directly relevant as res gestae evidence with respect to the charged conspiracy.

We have previously noted that crimes which form a body of evidence relating to the events surrounding the crime of which a defendant is charged are part of the *res gestae.* As such, they do not require a limiting instruction that would otherwise accompany evidence of uncharged bad acts. As another court has noted, res gestae evidence "is generally linked in time and circumstances with the charged crime, or forms an integral and natural part of an account of the crime," and "is not subject to the general rule that excludes evidence of prior criminality." *People v. Quintana*, 882 P.2d 1366, 1373 (Colo.1994) (internal quotation marks and citations omitted) (holding three separate statements threatening to kill other people, made in the course of killing another individual, each constituted part of res gestae of a single incident of murder, as opposed to separate uncharged bad acts). In fact, the trial court explicitly relied on *Quintana* when it concluded that Merrow's testimony described acts that formed part of the charged conspiracy.

The determination of what acts constitute the *res gestae* of a single conspiracy, as opposed to multiple separate conspiracies, presents special challenges for a court, however. *Cf.* 2 W. LaFave & A. Scott, SUBSTANTIVE CRIMINAL LAW § 6.5(a), at 89 (1986) ("The breadth of the law of conspiracy makes it subject to prosecutorial and judicial abuse.") (footnotes omitted); . . . The United States Supreme Court addressed the problem and the ensuing consequences of conflating multiple conspiracies with a single conspiracy in *Kotteakos v. United States*, 328 U.S. 750, 769–77 (1946), a case in which the government charged a single conspiracy involving thirty-two defendants. It noted the confusion of "the common purpose of a single enterprise with the several, though similar, purposes of numerous separate adventures of like character," in a scenario involving "separate spokes meeting in a common center, though . . . without the rim of the wheel to enclose the spokes."

Notably in this case, the charge involves only defendant, and the affidavit in support of the charge names only K.M. as a coconspirator. No mention is made of defendant's activities with Merrow in the charging documents. Nevertheless, the court determined that the activities formed part of the conspiracy and thus allowed the evidence in directly. We cannot agree. When determining whether one or multiple conspiracies exist, courts have looked for the existence of "(1) a common goal, (2) interdependence among the participants,' and (3) overlap among the participants." In a "wheel" conspiracy such as one at issue here, where the State argues defendant formed the hub, and K.M. and Merrow formed the spokes, there must be a "rim" for there to be one conspiracy. *See United States v. Rosnow*, 977 F.2d 399, 405 (8th Cir.1992) (". . . [T]hose people who form the wheel's spokes must have been aware of each other and must do something in furtherance of some single, illegal enterprise.") . . .

An agreement among co-conspirators need not be explicit, however, and may be inferred from the participants' acts or other circumstantial evidence. Nowhere in its proffer of Merrow's testimony did the State point to evidence of such factors as listed above.

Furthermore, Merrow's and K.M.'s testimony at trial at best established that they simply recognized one another from defendant's apartment. It did not establish an awareness of each other's participation in any way, general or otherwise, in the charged conspiracy. And the State did not offer to prove, nor did the testimony demonstrate, that Merrow and K.M. were interdependent in any way, or shared a community of interest. Thus, the wheel in this case lacks a rim to connect the two spokes to support one conspiracy instead of two. *Cf. Rosnow*, 977 F.2d at 406 (evidence insufficient to show single conspiracy instead of several). Defendant's activities with Merrow were not part and parcel of the charged conspiracy involving K.M. as determined by the trial court. Therefore, Merrow's testimony was not relevant as direct evidence of defendant's conspiracy with K.M. Because the trial court improperly admitted the Merrow testimony as direct evidence of the charged conspiracy, and specifically instructed the jury that they could use it for that purpose, we must reverse defendant's conviction on that charge and remand for a new trial. In essence, the admission, in combination with the court's instruction, allowed the jury to convict defendant on the conspiracy charge based on his activities with Merrow—a separate and *uncharged* conspiracy—as opposed to his activities with K.M. . . .

This resolution does not dispose of the delivery charge, however. The question remains whether the trial court also improperly admitted the evidence under V.R.E. 404(b) with respect to the charge of delivering crack cocaine to K.M. We briefly address defendant's challenge to the sufficiency of the evidence supporting the charge, however, as resolution in defendant's favor would obviate the potential for remand on the evidentiary issue. Defendant contends that the State has failed to prove that he had possession of the cocaine originally, prior to delivering it to K.M. K.M. testified, however, that defendant physically gave it to her to hold for him while she was visiting him in his apartment in early May. This sufficiently establishes that it was in defendant's possession before he transferred it to K.M. To the degree that defendant challenges K.M.'s reliability as a witness, such determinations are matters for the fact finder.

We now turn to defendant's V.R.E. 404(b) argument. As described above, the State originally offered the Merrow testimony under V.R.E. 404(b) only to show intent on the conspiracy charge. In response to defendant's motion in limine to exclude the evidence, the trial court determined that, in addition to coming in as direct evidence, it could alternately be admitted to show both plan and intent on the conspiracy charge. At defendant's retrial, it renewed its ruling. Although the Merrow testimony went only to the conspiracy charge and not to the delivery charge, the court issued no limiting instruction whatsoever at the time Merrow testified. Furthermore, when it came time to charge the jury, the court instructed that the Merrow testimony could not only be used with respect to the delivery charge—going beyond its original ruling in that respect—but that is could be used to show opportunity, preparation, knowledge and lack of mistake, in addition to just plan and intent. Defendant objected.

As we have emphasized, when uncharged bad acts are at issue:

> The State has the burden to show precisely how the proffered evidence is relevant to the theory advanced, how the issue to which it is addressed is related to the disputed elements in the case, and how the probative value of the evidence is not substantially outweighed by its prejudicial effect. The evidence must relate to an element of the offense or the defense *that is genuinely in issue.*

State v. Winter, 162 Vt. 388, 393, 648 A.2d 624, 627 (1994) (citations omitted; emphasis added).

Arguably defendant placed his opportunity to possess the seventy-seven grams of crack—a substantial amount—in issue by advancing the theory that the possibility of frequent, random searches of his apartment resulting from his furlough status would preclude him from having drugs on the premises. Additionally, defendant advanced the theory that the crack belonged to the boyfriend of K.M.'s mother and not him. Nevertheless, the State never linked the Merrow testimony to dispelling either of these theories of defense to the delivery charge. . . .

Because of the open-ended instruction, which was varied from its original ruling that the evidence would be admitted only to show intent and plan to commit the offense of conspiracy, we cannot affirm. The court's admission cannot be said to be harmless with respect to the delivery charge given that the only evidence in support of that charge is K.M.'s testimony that the crack she gave to the police was provided to her by defendant. Thus, we cannot say beyond a reasonable doubt that Merrow's testimony to repeated drug deals with defendant involving crack and powder cocaine did not contribute to the verdict. . . .

Reversed and remanded for proceedings consistent with this opinion.

————

NOTES

1. In a "wheel" relationship, a central individual, who is at the "hub" of the wheel, has criminal dealings with different individuals, each one of whom might be symbolized by a spoke of the wheel. There is a different conspiracy in existence between the hub and each spoke of the wheel, but there is no conspiracy between the spokes themselves, unless there were a rim on the wheel that, independently, would connect all of the spokes. *See, e.g.,* Kotteakos v. United States, 328 U.S. 750, 66 S.Ct. 1239, 90 L.Ed. 1557 (1946). In *Kotteakos,* the "hub" was a broker who procured loans for thirty-two different individuals (the spokes) by false and fraudulent applications to the Federal Housing Administration. The government charged all individuals as members of a single conspiracy to obtain fraudulent loans. The Supreme Court reversed the conspiracy conviction based on failure to prove a "rim"—i.e., a connection between the various spokes.

2. In a "chain" relationship, a single conspiracy exists that links a number of individuals together. *See, e.g.,* Blumenthal v. United States, 332 U.S. 539, 68 S.Ct. 248, 92 L.Ed. 154 (1947). In *Blumenthal,* A and B agreed to sell C's product and A knew that C existed but was unaware of who he was. The Court said that A, B and C were "links" in a criminal chain, rather than "spokes" in a wheel. Some courts have abandoned the wheel, spoke, rim, and chain metaphor, finding that they can interfere with understanding given conspiracies. *See, e.g.,* State v. Desantos, 233 Wis.2d 274, 610 N.W.2d 230 (App.2000) (unpublished table decision) (finding that the artificial construction of wheel and spoke interfered with analysis of many real-life conspiracies).

3. In State v. Jackson, 276 Wis.2d 697, 688 N.W.2d 688 (2004), Jackson and two other men conspired to fire bomb a police officer's house, enabling two others to shoot people fleeing from the building. Jackson was convicted of one count of possession of a firebomb, and two counts of conspiracy: conspiracy to commit arson, and conspiracy to commit intentional homicide. In Braverman v. United States, 317 U.S. 49, 63 S.Ct. 99, 87 L.Ed. 23 (1942), the Court interpreted 18 U.S.C. § 371[25] and found that an agreement to commit several crimes was one conspiracy if there was one agreement, Jackson challenged the dual convictions, arguing that there was only one conspiracy to do multiple crimes. Affirming his conviction, the Wisconsin Court of Appeals distinguished *Braverman* on the grounds that the Wisconsin

————

[25] 18 U.S.C. § 371 reads:

> If two or more persons conspire either to commit any offense against the United States, or to defraud the United States, or any agency thereof in any manner or for any purpose, and one or more of such persons do any act to effect the object of the conspiracy, each shall be fined under this title or imprisoned not more than five years, or both.

The pertinent language of § 371 has remained unchanged since the statute was interpreted in Braverman v. United States, 317 U.S. 49, 63 S.Ct. 99, 87 L.Ed. 23 (1942).

statute, unlike the federal statute interpreted in *Braverman*, broke down conspiracy charges based on the name of the target crime(s)—in this case, arson and murder. After ruling out a double jeopardy challenge, it affirmed the dual convictions, saying. "Jackson conspired to commit two crimes, arson and murder. Accordingly, under Wis. Stat. § 939.31, he may be charged with two counts of conspiracy, one incorporating the crime of arson, another incorporating murder. Each charge requires proof of facts that the other does not; they are different in fact and in law. . . . *Braverman* does not help Jackson."

———

2. SCOPE OF CO-CONSPIRATOR LIABILITY

Co-conspirator liability can be exceptionally broad. Once a person is shown to be part of a conspiracy, he is potentially responsible for a host of additional crimes. However, there are limits on establishing co-conspirator liability in the first place. Are you guilty of conspiracy simply because you sell your product to a person who you believe will use it for a criminal offense? In the first case below, we examine who can be characterized as a co-conspirator. In the following case we address what offenses a co-conspirator can be held responsible for.

United States v. Falcone
Supreme Court of the United States, 1940.
311 U.S. 205, 61 S.Ct. 204, 85 L.Ed. 128.

■ MR. JUSTICE STONE delivered the opinion of the Court.

The question presented by this record is whether one who sells materials with knowledge that they are intended for use or will be used in the production of illicit distilled spirits may be convicted as a coconspirator with a distiller who conspired with others to distill the spirits in violation of the revenue laws.

Respondents were indicted with sixty-three others in the Northern District of New York for conspiring to violate the revenue laws by the operation of twenty-two illicit stills in the vicinity of Utica, New York. The case was submitted to the jury as to twenty-four defendants, of whom the five respondents and sixteen operators of stills were convicted. The Court of Appeals for the Second Circuit reversed the conviction of the five respondents on the ground that as there was no evidence that respondents were themselves conspirators, the sale by them of materials, knowing that they would be used by others in illicit distilling, was not sufficient to establish that respondents were guilty of the conspiracy charged. . . .

All of the respondents were jobbers or distributors who, during the period in question, sold sugar, yeast or cans, some of which found their way into the possession and use of some of the distiller defendants. The indictment while charging generally that all the defendants were parties to the conspiracy did not allege specifically that any of respondents had knowledge of the conspiracy, but it did allege that respondents Alberico and Nole brothers sold the materials mentioned knowing that they were to be used in illicit distilling. The Court of Appeals reviewing the evidence thought, in the case of some of the respondents, that the jury might take it that they were knowingly supplying the distillers. As to Nicholas Nole, whose case it considered most doubtful, it thought that his equivocal conduct "was as likely to have come from a belief that it was a crime to sell the yeast and the cans to distillers as from being in fact any further involved in their business". But it assumed for purposes of decision that all furnished supplies which they knew ultimately reached and were used by some of the distillers. Upon this assumption it said, "In the light of all this, it is apparent that the first question is whether the seller of goods, in themselves innocent, becomes a conspirator with—or, what is in substance the same thing, an abettor of—the buyer because he knows that the buyer means to use the goods to commit a crime." And it concluded that merely because respondent did not forego a "normally lawful activity, of the fruits of which he [knew] that others [were making] an unlawful use" he is not guilty of a conspiracy.

The Government does not argue here the point which seems to be implicit in the question raised by its petition for certiorari, that conviction of conspiracy can rest on proof alone of knowingly supplying an illicit distiller, who is not conspiring with others. In such a case, as the Government concedes, the act of supplying or some other proof must import an agreement or concert of action between buyer and seller, which admittedly is not present here. But the Government does contend that one who with knowledge of a conspiracy to distill illicit spirits sells materials to a conspirator knowing that they will be used in the distilling, is himself guilty of the conspiracy. It is said that he is, either because his knowledge combined with his action makes him a participant in the agreement which is the conspiracy, or what is the same thing he is a principal in the conspiracy as an aider or abettor by virtue of § 332 of the Criminal Code, 18 U.S.C. § 550, 18 U.S.C. § 550, which provides: "Whoever directly commits any act constituting an offense defined in any law of the United States, or aids, abets, counsels, commands, induces, or procures its commission, is a principal."

The argument, the merits of which we do not consider, overlooks the fact that the opinion below proceeded on the assumption that the evidence showed only that respondents or some of them knew that the materials sold would be used in the distillation of illicit spirits, and fell short of showing respondents' participation in the conspiracy or that they knew of it. We did not bring the case here to review the evidence, but we are satisfied that the evidence on which the Government relies does not do more than show knowledge by respondents that the materials would be used for illicit distilling if it does as much in the case of some.[1] In the case of Alberico. as in the case of Nicholas Nole, the jury could have found that he knew that one of their customers who is an unconvicted defendant was using the purchased material in illicit distilling. But it could not be inferred from that or from the casual and unexplained meetings of some of respondents with others who were convicted as conspirators that respondents knew of the conspiracy. The evidence respecting the volume of sales to any known to be distillers is too vague and inconclusive to support a jury finding that respondents knew of a conspiracy from the size of the purchases even though we were to assume what we do not decide that the knowledge would make them conspirators or raiders or abettors of the conspiracy. Respondents are not charged with aiding and abetting illicit distilling, and they cannot be brought within the sweep of the Government's conspiracy dragnet if they had no knowledge that there was a conspiracy.

---

[1]   The two Falcones, who were in business as sugar jobbers, were shown to have sold sugar to three wholesale grocers who in turn were shown to have sold some of the sugar to distillers. To establish guilty knowledge the Government relies upon evidence showing that the volume of their sales was materially larger during the periods of activity of the illicit stills; that Joseph Falcone was shown on two occasions, at one of which Salvatore Falcone was present, to have been in conversation with one of the conspirators who was a distiller, and on one occasion with another distiller conspirator who was his brother-in-law; that Joseph Falcone had been seen at the Venezia Restaurant which was patronized by some of the conspirators and knew its proprietor, and on two occasions Salvatore Falcone had visited the restaurant, on one to collect funds for the Red Cross and on another for a monument to Marconi.

Respondent Alberico was a member of a firm of wholesale grocers who dealt in sugar and five-gallon tin cans among other things. They sold sugar to wholesale grocers and jobbers. To establish Alberico's guilty knowledge the Government relies on evidence that his total purchases of sugar materially increased during the period when the illicit stills were shown to be in operation; that some of his sugar purchases from a local wholesaler were at higher prices than he was then paying others; that on the premises of one of the distillers there were found fifty-five cardboard cartons, each suitable for containing one dozen five-gallon cans, on one of which was stenciled the name of Alberico's firm; that on eight to ten occasions Alberico sold sugar and cans in unnamed amounts to Morreale, one of the defendant distillers who was not convicted, and on one occasion was overheard to say, in refusing credit to Morreale, "I could not trust you because your business is too risky."

Respondent Nicholas Nole was shown to be proprietor of Acme Yeast Company and also the Utica Freight Forwarding Company, to which one and one-half tons of K & M yeast was consigned by the seller. Wrappers bearing the distinctive marks of the Acme Yeast Company and K & M yeast, quantity not stated, were found at one of the stills; and a K & M yeast container was found at another. To show guilty knowledge of Nicholas Nole the Government relies on the circumstance that he registered the Acme Yeast Company in the county clerk's office in the name of a cousin; that the order for the consignment of K & M yeast was placed in the name of an unidentified person; that Nole had been seen in conversation with some of the convicted distillers at a time when some of the illicit stills were in operation, and that on one occasion during that period he sold and delivered fifteen five-gallon cans of illicit alcohol from a source not stated. Respondent John Nole was shown to be a distributor for the National Grain Yeast Company in Utica during the period in question. Yeast wrappers bearing the National labels were found at three of the stills. To show guilty knowledge of John Nole the Government relies on evidence that he had assisted his brother Nicholas in unloading yeast at the Utica Freight Forwarding Co.; that he was a patron of the Venezia Restaurant; that on one occasion he was seen talking with Morreale, the unconvicted distiller. in the vicinity of a store in Utica, whose store it does not appear. On three occasions Morreale and another convicted defendant procured yeast in cartons and some in kegs at the store and on one occasion John Nole told the person in charge of the store to let them have the yeast; that John Nole's information return required by the Government of all sales of yeast in excess of five pounds to one person did not show in February or March, 1938, any sale of yeast to Morreale or any sale of keg yeast.

The gist of the offense of conspiracy as defined by § 37 of the Criminal Code, 18 U.S.C. § 88, 18 U.S.C. § 88, is agreement among the conspirators to commit an offense attended by an act of one or more of the conspirators to effect the object of the conspiracy. Those having no knowledge of the conspiracy are not conspirators; and one who without more furnishes supplies to an illicit distiller is not guilty of conspiracy even though his sale may have furthered the object of a conspiracy to which the distiller was a party but of which the supplier had no knowledge. On this record we have no occasion to decide any other question.

Affirmed.

———

NOTES

1. In footnote 1, the Court noted that to "establish Alberico's guilty knowledge the Government relies on evidence that his total purchases of sugar materially increased during the period when the illicit stills were shown to be in operation." The Court also explained that "some of his sugar purchases from a local wholesaler were at higher prices than he was then paying others." Should these factors make the Court more willing to uphold Alberico's guilt as a party to the conspiracy? Put differently, do increased sales or charging a higher price suggest that Alberico has a stake in the conspiratorial venture? Consider People v. Lauria, 59 Cal. Rptr. 628, 632–634 (Cal. App. 1967), in which (prior to the advent of answering machines and voicemail) the defendant ran a message answering service. Lauria was aware that some of the clients using his answering service were prostitutes. Lauria even acknowledged that he "had personally used [the] services" of at least one prostitute who paid for his answering service. Some of the prostitutes paid Lauria to take as many as 500 messages per month. Prosecutors charged Lauria and three prostitutes with conspiracy to commit prostitution. Relying in part on the *Falcone* decision, the court concluded that while Lauria knew about the prostitution he lacked the intent to become a part of the conspiracy itself. Although the court rejected the contention that Lauria was a conspirator, it noted instances in which providing goods or services would permit a jury to infer a conspiracy:

> Intent may be inferred from knowledge, when the purveyor of legal goods for illegal use has acquired a stake in the venture. For example, in Regina v. Thomas (1957), 2 All.E.R. 181, 342, a prosecution for living off the earnings of prostitution, the evidence showed that the accused, knowing the woman to be a convicted prostitute, agreed to let her have the use of his room between the hours of 9 p.m. and 2 a.m. for a charge of 3 a night. The Court of Criminal Appeal refused an appeal from the conviction, holding that when the accused rented a room at a grossly inflated rent to a prostitute for the purpose of carrying on her trade, a jury could find he was living on the earnings of prostitution.

In the present case, no proof was offered of inflated charges for the telephone answering services furnished the codefendants.

Intent may be inferred from knowledge, when no legitimate use for the goods or services exists. The leading California case is People v. McLaughlin, 111 Cal.App.2d 781, 245 P.2d 1076, in which the court upheld a conviction of the suppliers of horse-racing information by wire for conspiracy to promote bookmaking, when it had been established that wireservice information had no other use than to supply information needed by bookmakers to conduct illegal gambling operations.

* * *

Intent may be inferred from knowledge, when the volume of business with the buyer is grossly disproportionate to any legitimate demand, or when sales for illegal use amount to a high proportion of the seller's total business. In such cases an intent to participate in the illegal enterprise may be inferred from the quantity of the business done. For example, . . . the sale of narcotics to a rural physician in quantities 300 times greater than he would have normal use for provided potent evidence of an intent to further the illegal activity . . .

No evidence of any unusual volume of business with prostitutes was presented by the prosecution against Lauria.

Inflated charges, the sale of goods with no legitimate use, sales in inflated amounts, each may provide a fact of sufficient moment from which the intent of the seller to participate in the criminal enterprise may be inferred. In such instances participation by the supplier of legal goods to the illegal enterprise may be inferred because in one way or another the supplier has acquired a special interest in the operation of the illegal enterprise. His intent to participate in the crime of which he has knowledge may be inferred from the existence of his special interest.

Do the three factors enunciated in *Lauria* make you re-think whether the Supreme Court could have upheld the convictions of some of the defendants in *Falcone*?

2. If Lauria did have a stake in the venture, would that make him a conspirator or an accessory? Courts have recognized that a defendant can simultaneously be both an accessory *and* a co-conspirator. *See* Commonwealth v. Schoff, 2006 Pa.Super. 307, 911 A.2d 147 (2006) (affirming wife's conviction of first-degree murder for hire (as an accessory) *and* criminal conspiracy to commit first-degree murder of her ex-husband where wife and her mother solicited four different people before finding one who was willing to kill the husband). Was Lauria both an accessory and a conspirator?

3. The common law rule is that the goal of the conspiratorial agreement need not be a crime, as long as either the means to achieve the goal or the goal itself is illegal.[26] The Model Penal Code and many state statutes now require that the conspiratorial objective be a crime, but issues still arise as to the requirement of *scienter* as to the goals of the conspiracy. Each coconspirator must have the requisite intent. In Commonwealth v. Benesch, 290 Mass. 125, 194 N.E. 905 (1935), defendants, Benesch, Davison, and Tibbetts were convicted of conspiring to have registered brokers or salesmen sell securities in violation of the applicable laws and regulations. Because the conspiracy involved the specific intent to violate the applicable securities laws, the Massachusetts Supreme Judicial Court reversed, saying,

> While no decision in this commonwealth directly in point has been called to our attention, it has been held by excellent authority in other jurisdictions that in order to sustain an indictment for conspiracy to commit an offence which, like that here involved, is *malum prohibitum* only, belonging to a general type of offences which has been greatly extended by modern legislation in many fields, it must appear that the defendant knew of the illegal element involved in that which the combination was intended to accomplish. . . .

> Perhaps as to Benesch alone there was evidence of the necessary intent. . . . But one cannot be a conspirator alone. We are of opinion that the evidence is insufficient to support a verdict that any of the other alleged conspirators had the knowledge both of the existence of the prohibition and of its violation which is necessary to prove affirmatively a criminal intent. . . . [to violate the securities laws].

4. *Scienter* is also required as to the illegality in the conspiracy. In Davidson v. United States, 61 F.2d 250 (8th Cir. 1932), defendants were convicted of conspiracy to violate the National Motor Vehicle Theft Act. In reversing their conviction, the court said:

> If this verdict on the first count charging conspiracy is to be sustained, it must not only appear that the car in question constituted interstate commerce, but also that these defendants. when they received the car, had knowledge of the interstate character of the transaction. In other words, it must appear that they knew where this car came from, in order to warrant a conclusion that by receiving and selling the car, they participated in the furtherance of a conspiracy as alleged in count 1 of this indictment.

However, in *United States v. Feola*, 420 U.S. 671, 95 S.Ct. 1255, 43 L.Ed.2d 541 (1975), the United States Supreme Court held that knowledge that the intended victim is a federal officer is not an element of a 18 U.S.C. § 371 conspiracy to assault a federal officer while engaged in the performance of his official duties, under 18 U.S.C. § 111. The Court held that § 111 requires only "an intent to assault, not an intent to assault a federal

---

[26] *See, e.g.*, Commonwealth v. Dyer, 243 Mass. 472, 138 N.E. 296 (1923) (affirming convictions for common-law conspiracy to create a monopoly in fresh fish, so as to "fix, regulate, control, and to enhance exorbitantly and unreasonably the price of fresh fish, and thus to cheat and defraud the public").

officer." Dissenting, Justices Stuart and Douglas argued that of § 111 is an aggravated assault statute, requiring proof of *scienter*.

The *Feola* Court distinguished United States v. Crimmins, 123 F.2d 271 (2d Cir.1941), in which the defendant had been found guilty of conspiring to receive stolen bonds that had been transported in interstate commerce, though there was no evidence to prove that Crimmins actually knew the stolen bonds had moved into the State. Accepting for the sake of argument the assumption that such knowledge was not necessary to sustain a conviction on the substantive offense, Judge Learned Hand nevertheless concluded that to permit conspiratorial liability where the conspirators were ignorant of the federal implications of their acts would be to enlarge their agreement beyond its terms as they understood them. He capsulized the distinction in what has become well known as his "traffic light" analogy: "While one may, for instance, be guilty of running past a traffic light of whose existence one is ignorant, one cannot be guilty of conspiring to run past such a light, for one cannot agree to run past a light unless one supposes that there is a light to run past."

The *Feola* Court said,

> One may run a traffic light "of whose existence one is ignorant," but assaulting another "of whose existence one is ignorant," probably would require unearthly intervention. Thus, the traffic light analogy, even if it were a correct statement of the law, is inapt. . . . We hold here only that where a substantive offense embodies only a requirement of *mens rea* as to each of its elements, the general federal conspiracy statute requires no more.

5. In State v. Shriver, 741 S.W.2d 836 (Mo.App. 1987), the Missouri Court of Appeals declined to find that the three-year statute of limitations had run on a conspiracy, even though the objective of the conspiracy had not been achieved and more than three years had passed since the last overt act. The court said,

> conspiracy is a continuing offense, chargeable by an agreement and an overt act. It continues until termination by its successful completion, abandonment of the agreement by the conspirators, or withdrawal by the defendant; from the point of termination the statute of limitations begins to run. If the conspiracy has not terminated in one of these three manners, it continues until the filing of the information. Abandonment is not necessarily presumed to occur upon the commission of the last overt act in furtherance of the conspiracy; rather, it remains a matter to be determined from the evidence. Here, the information indicates the conspiracy had not terminated, and, therefore, it continued until the filing of the information.

Pinkerton v. United States

Supreme Court of the United States, 1946.
328 U.S. 640, 66 S.Ct. 1180, 90 L.Ed. 1489.

■ Mr. JUSTICE DOUGLAS delivered the opinion of the Court.

Walter and Daniel Pinkerton are brothers who live a short distance from each other on Daniel's farm. They were indicted for violations of the Internal Revenue Code. The indictment contained ten substantive counts and one conspiracy count. The jury found Walter guilty on nine of the substantive counts and on the conspiracy count. It found Daniel guilty on six of the substantive counts and on the conspiracy count . . .

A single conspiracy was charged and proved. Some of the overt acts charged in the conspiracy count were the same acts charged in the substantive counts. Each of the substantive offenses found was committed pursuant to the conspiracy . . . .

* * *

It is contended that there was insufficient evidence to implicate Daniel in the conspiracy. But we think there was enough evidence for submission of the issue to the jury.

There is, however, no evidence to show that Daniel participated directly in the commission of the substantive offenses on which his conviction has been sustained, although there was evidence to show that these substantive offenses were in fact committed by Walter in furtherance of the unlawful agreement or conspiracy existing between the brothers. The question was submitted to the jury on the theory that each petitioner could be found guilty of the substantive offenses, if it was found at the time those offenses were committed petitioners were parties to an unlawful conspiracy and the substantive offenses charged were in fact committed in furtherance of it.

Daniel relies on United States v. Sall, 116 F.3d 745 (3rd Cir. 1940). That case held that participation in the conspiracy was not itself enough to sustain a conviction for the substantive offense even though it was committed in furtherance of the conspiracy. The court held that, in addition to evidence that the offense was in fact committed in furtherance of the conspiracy, evidence of direct participation in the commission of the substantive offense or other evidence from which participation might fairly be inferred was necessary.

We take a different view. We have here a continuous conspiracy. There is here no evidence of the affirmative action on the part of Daniel which is necessary to establish his withdrawal from it . . . . And so long as the partnership in crime continues, the partners act for each other in carrying it forward. It is settled that 'an overt act of one partner may be the act of all without any new agreement specifically directed to that act.' Motive or intent may be proved by the acts or declarations of some of the conspirators in furtherance of the common objective. A scheme to use the mails to defraud, which is joined in by more than one person, is a conspiracy. Yet all members are responsible, though only one did the mailing. The governing principle is the same when the substantive offense is committed by one of the conspirators in furtherance of the unlawful project. The criminal intent to do the act is established by the formation of the conspiracy. Each conspirator instigated the commission of the crime. The unlawful agreement contemplated precisely what was done. It was formed for the purpose. The act done was in execution of the enterprise. The rule which holds responsible one who counsels, procures, or commands another to commit a crime is founded on the same principle. That principle is recognized in the law of conspiracy when the overt act of one partner in crime is attributable to all . . .

A different case would arise if the substantive offense committed by one of the conspirators was not in fact done in furtherance of the conspiracy, did not fall within the scope of the unlawful project, or was merely a part of the ramifications of the plan which could not be reasonably foreseen as a necessary or natural consequence of the unlawful agreement. But as we read this record, that is not this case.

Affirmed.

■ Mr. JUSTICE RUTLEDGE, dissenting in part.

The judgment concerning Daniel Pinkerton should be reversed. In my opinion it is without precedent here and is a dangerous precedent to establish.

Daniel and Walter, who were brothers living near each other, were charged in several counts with substantive offenses, and then a conspiracy count was added naming those offenses as overt acts. The proof showed that Walter alone committed the substantive crimes. There was none to establish that Daniel participated in them, aided and abetted Walter in committing them, or knew that he had done so. Daniel in fact was in the penitentiary, under sentence for other crimes, when some of Walter's crimes were done.

* * *

The court's theory seems to be that Daniel and Walter became general partners in crime by virtue of their agreement and because of that agreement without more on his part Daniel became criminally responsible as a principal for everything Walter did thereafter in the nature of a criminal offense of the general sort the agreement contemplated, so long as there was not clear evidence that Daniel had withdrawn from or revoked the agreement. Whether or not his commitment to the penitentiary had that effect, the result is a vicarious criminal responsibility as broad as, or broader than, the vicarious civil liability of a partner for acts done by a co-partner in the course of the firm's business.

Such analogies from private commercial law and the law of torts are dangerous, in my judgment, for transfer to the criminal field . . . .

* * *

———

NOTES: CONSPIRATOR LIABILITY

1. The *Pinkerton* rule provides that a conspirator may be held liable for a crime to which the conspirator never agreed and which is committed by a co-conspirator with whom the conspirator never personally dealt, as long as the crime is reasonably foreseeable and is committed in furtherance of the conspiracy. Does the *Pinkerton* doctrine provide for liability that is too far ranging? Aren't conspirators being held liable for the actions of others under a simple negligence theory? Shouldn't courts disfavor liability when an individual is not personally aware (i.e., at least reckless, as opposed to negligent) that a crime is occurring?

2. Some states, as well as the Model Penal Code, have rejected the *Pinkerton* doctrine because it provides too broad of liability. *See* Neal Katyal, *Conspiracy Theory*, 112 YALE L.J. 1307 (2003). Consider State ex rel. Woods v. Cohen, 173 Ariz. 497, 844 P.2d 1147 (1992), in which Cohen was indicted for conspiracy to defraud the Arizona Health Care Cost Containment System and for various offenses committed by his co-conspirators in carrying out that conspiracy. The state had argued that under the *Pinkerton* rule, Cohen was liable for twelve counts in the indictment that were committed solely by his co-conspirators, without his participation. The Arizona Supreme Court declined to follow *Pinkerton*, finding the Arizona conspiracy statute to be substantially distinguishable from the one at issue in *Pinkerton*, commenting,

> This scheme, in contrast to the provisions of the prior code and its federal analogue, exclusively defines when one may be held liable for acts committed by others and makes judicial adoption of the *Pinkerton* theory inappropriate unless it is otherwise within the statutory list. . . . Clearly, one who has not agreed to the commission of a crime and has not aided in its planning or commission could not be convicted of the crime as an accomplice. *Pinkerton* liability is not, therefore, the equivalent of accomplice liability. A conspirator to a completed offense is not always an accomplice to that offense.

> To sum up in a syllogism, the statute defines the universe of vicarious liability. *Pinkerton* liability is not within the statutory universe. Therefore, *Pinkerton* liability is not the law of Arizona.

3. Given the broad scope of *Pinkerton* liability, defendants in gangs are potentially responsible for a wide array of crimes. Thus, the ability to withdraw from a gang conspiracy is quite important. Yet, as one prominent judge has noted "[g]etting involved in a conspiracy, particularly a gang, is a risky endeavor because of the difficulty to get out." United States v. Randall,

661 F.3d 1291, 1294 (10th Cir. 2011). In *Randall,* the court concluded that a former gang member did not withdraw from the conspiracy even though he claimed to have left the gang, found legitimate employment as a mechanic, and started attending church. In another case, a court rejected a withdrawal claim by a former motorcycle gang member who had added "out of date" to his gang tattoo, sold his bike, joined a church, and cut off "virtually all" contact with other gang members. *See* United States v. Starrett, 55 F.3d 1525, 1550 (11th Cir. 1995). In these cases, and others, the courts concluded that successful withdrawal required the gang member to inform law enforcement of the scheme or communicate his withdrawal to his co-conspirators. "Simply not spending time with coconspirators is not enough." *Randall,* 661 F.3d at 1295. Expert testimony from a gang expert that members "mature out of" a gang through disassociation is insufficient to support a withdrawal claim. *Id.* For an argument that the withdrawal doctrine is unusable to gang members in its current form see Cecelia M. Harper, *How Do I Divorce My Gang? Modifying the Defense of Withdrawal for a Gang-Related Conspiracy,* 50 VAL. U. L. REV. 765 (2016).

4. The *Pinkerton* doctrine is not the only area of conspiracy law that critics target. The sweeping nature of conspiracy prosecutions has raised concerns about possible abuse and unfairness. As Professor Paul Marcus has explained:

> The other matter particularly linked to conspiracy relates to guilt by association. Here, too, complaints have been asserted for decades. Defense counsel would state the matter in this way:
> - "Juries do not differentiate between individual defendants in large conspiracy cases."

Paul Marcus, *Criminal Conspiracy Law: Time to Turn Back From an Ever Expanding, Ever More Troubling Area,* 1 WM. & MARY BILL RTS. J. 1, 7–8 (1992). Are critics correct to attack conspiracy doctrine? Does the law of conspiracy make it too easy for prosecutors to convict defendants who may be less culpable and to use guilt-by-association to influence the jury?

5. There is more than one way for prosecutors to charge defendants who combine together in illegal activity. In the federal system, prosecutors often utilize the federal conspiracy statute. *See* 18 U.S.C. § 371. But sometimes they have another prominent option. In 1970, Congress enacted the Racketeer Influenced and Corrupt Organizations Act 18 U.S.C. § 1961 *et seq.,* or RICO, which provides that

> - It shall be unlawful for any person employed by or associated with any enterprise engaged in, or the activities of which affect, interstate or foreign commerce, to conduct or participate, directly or indirectly, in the conduct of such enterprise's affairs through a pattern of racketeering activity or collection of unlawful debt."

18 U.S.C. § 1962(c). The statute defines "pattern of racketeering activity" to include "at least two acts of racketeering activity." 18 U.S.C. § 1961(5). "Racketeering activity," in turn, is defined to include dozens of crimes, including:

(A) any act or threat involving murder, kidnapping, gambling, arson, robbery, bribery, extortion, dealing in obscene matter, or dealing in a controlled substance or listed chemical (as defined in section 102 of the Controlled Substances Act), which is chargeable under State law and punishable by imprisonment for more than one year; (B) any act which is indictable under any of the following provisions of title 18, United States Code: Section 201 (relating to bribery), section 224 (relating to sports bribery), sections 471, 472, and 473 (relating to counterfeiting), section 659 (relating to theft from interstate shipment) if the act indictable under section 659 is felonious, section 664 (relating to embezzlement from pension and welfare funds), sections 891–894 (relating to extortionate credit transactions), section 1028 (relating to fraud and related activity in connection with identification documents), section 1029 (relating to fraud and related activity in connection with access devices), section 1084 (relating to the transmission of gambling information), section 1341 (relating to mail fraud), section 1343 (relating to wire fraud), section 1344 (relating to financial institution fraud), section 1425 (relating to the procurement of citizenship or nationalization unlawfully), section 1426 (relating to the reproduction of naturalization or citizenship papers), section 1427 (relating to the sale of naturalization or citizenship papers), sections 1461–1465 (relating to obscene matter), section 1503 (relating to obstruction of justice), section 1510 (relating to obstruction of criminal investigations), section 1511 (relating to the obstruction of State or local law enforcement), section 1512 (relating to tampering with a witness, victim, or an informant), section 1513 (relating to retaliating against a witness, victim, or an informant), section 1542 (relating to false statement in application and use of passport), section 1543 (relating to forgery or false use of passport), section 1544 (relating to misuse of passport), section 1546 (relating to fraud and misuse of visas, permits, and other documents), sections 1581–1592 (relating to peonage, slavery, and trafficking in persons)., section 1951 (relating to interference with commerce, robbery, or extortion), section 1952 (relating to racketeering), section 1953 (relating to interstate transportation of wagering paraphernalia), section 1954 (relating to unlawful welfare fund payments), section 1955 (relating to the prohibition of illegal gambling businesses), section 1956 (relating to the laundering of monetary instruments), section 1957 (relating to engaging in monetary transactions in property derived from specified unlawful activity), section 1958 (relating to use of interstate commerce facilities in the commission of murder-for-hire), section 1960 (relating to illegal money transmitters), sections 2251, 2251A, 2252, and 2260 (relating to sexual exploitation of children), sections 2312 and 2313 (relating to interstate transportation of stolen motor vehicles), sections 2314 and 2315 (relating to interstate transportation of stolen property), section 2318 (relating to trafficking in counterfeit labels for phonorecords, computer programs or computer program documentation or packaging and copies of motion pictures or other audiovisual works), section 2319 (relating to criminal infringement of a copyright), section 2319A (relating to unauthorized fixation of and trafficking in sound recordings and music videos of live musical performances), section 2320 (relating to trafficking in goods or services bearing counterfeit marks), section 2321 (relating to trafficking in certain motor vehicles or motor vehicle parts), sections 2341–2346 (relating to trafficking in contraband cigarettes), sections 2421–24 (relating to white slave traffic), sections 175–178 (relating to biological weapons), sections 229–229F (relating to chemical weapons), section 831 (relating to nuclear materials), (C) any act which is indictable under title 29, United States Code, section 186 (dealing with restrictions on payments and loans to labor organizations) or section 501(c) (relating to embezzlement from union funds) . . .

18 U.S.C. § 1961(1). Significantly for purposes of this chapter, the RICO statute contains a conspiracy provision that simply says: "It shall be unlawful for any person to conspire to violate any of the provisions of subsection (a), (b), or (c) of this section." 18 U.S.C. § 1962(d). While the RICO conspiracy provision in many ways overlaps the general conspiracy statute, it actually permits prosecutors to push the envelope of group liability even further. *See* Gerald E. Lynch, *RICO: The Crime of Being a Criminal, Parts III & IV*, 87 COLUM. L. REV. 920, 945–55 (1987).

The RICO statute was originally designed to target mafia activity. *See* Michael Vitiello, *More Noise From the Tower of Babel: Making "Sense" Out of* Reves v. Ernst & Young, 56 OHIO ST. L.J. 1363, 1371–72. (1995). Nevertheless, prosecutors have used the RICO statute to prosecute "corrupt government agencies, health care fraud, securities fraud, and drug trafficking by police." Matthew C. Heger, Note, *Bringing RICO to the Ring: Can the Anti-Mafia Weapon Target Dogfighters?*, 89 WASH. U. L. REV. 241, 243–44 (2011).

The RICO statute raises many complicated issues, including what constitutes a criminal enterprise, what conduct affects interstate commerce, what must motivate the criminal purpose, how to compute the statute of limitations, and what it means to "participate" in a criminal enterprise. The issues are of considerable importance because RICO violations carry up to twenty years in prison, hefty fines, and forfeiture of assets. *See* 18 U.S.C. § 1963. For an early assessment of the importance of RICO to prosecutors, see Gerald E. Lynch, *RICO: The Crime of Being a Criminal, Parts I & II*, 87 COLUM. L. REV. 661 (1987). For a recent overview of RICO, see Sean M. Douglass & Tyler Layne, *Racketeer Influenced and Corrupt Organizations*, 48 AM. CRIM. L. REV. 1075 (2011).

———

SPECIAL DEFENSES TO CRIMINAL PROSECUTIONS

CHAPTER 11

ENTRAPMENT

A. THE DEVELOPMENT OF AN AMERICAN LEGAL DEFENSE TO CRIME

INTRODUCTION

Entrapment is a particularly American legal product. No mention of it can be found in the early English criminal law writings of luminaries like Hale, Hawkins, and Stephen. An in-depth look at how the doctrine of entrapment developed can be found at Mikell, *The Doctrine of Entrapment in the Federal Courts*, 90 PA. L.REV. 245 (1942). See also, Dean Marcus, *The Development of Entrapment Law*, 33 WAYNE L.REV. 5 (1986). The earliest reference to entrapment as a defense to crime in an American case may be found in United States v. Whittier, 28 F.Cas. 591 (C.C.E.D.Mo.1878)—concurring opinion, where the idea was rejected. While some other cases made mention of it subsequently, probably the first court decision wherein the defendant was acquitted on the ground of entrapment was Woo Wai v. United States, 223 F. 412 (9th Cir.1915), but the theoretical basis for it was not laid, nor were the procedural details worked out. See also, James F. Pensoldt & Stephen Marsh, *Entrapment When the Spoken Word Is the Crime*, 65 FORDHAM L.REV. 1199 (2000).

It was not until the 1932 decision by the United States Supreme Court in Sorrells v. United States, 287 U.S. 435, 53 S.Ct. 210, 77 L.Ed. 413 (1932)—mentioned in the first leading case in this Chapter—that the contours of the defense began to take shape. The *Sorrels* case was remarkable for the Court's opinion, which focused on the lack of predisposition of the defendant, and its concurring opinion of Justice Roberts, which went much farther and saw the defense of entrapment not as a protection for innocent individuals who were entrapped by the police, but rather as a protection of the government from itself for its unfair and overbearing governmental acts. A seminal work by Professor Groot describes the difference between the Court's opinion and the concurrence in this manner:

> The majority implements the entrapment defense through statutory construction. The act done by the accused is not condemned by the statute if he was entrapped into doing it. The defense is a negation of the existence of the crime. Justice Roberts would deny the use of a forum to convict an accused who has been entrapped. In his opinion the entrapment defense does not negate crime, for the existence of crime is a necessary precondition to the application of the defense as either a plea in bar or an excuse.

Roger Douglas Groot, The Serpent Beguiled Me and I (Without Scienter) Did Eat—Denial of Crime and the Entrapment Defense, 1973 ILL. L.FORUM 254, 257. See also, Brian Thomas Feeney, Scrutiny for the Serpent: The Court Refines Entrapment Law in Jacobson v. United States (Note), 42 CATH. U. L.REV. 1027 (1993); John Cirace, An Interesting Balancing Test for Entrapment, 18 PACE L.REV. 51 (1997). In Sherman v. United States, also mentioned in the lead case, the Supreme Court essentially reaffirmed Sorrells.

United States v. Russell

Supreme Court of the United States, 1973.
411 U.S. 423, 93 S.Ct. 1637, 36 L.Ed.2d 366.

■ MR. JUSTICE REHNQUIST delivered the opinion of the Court.

There is little dispute concerning the essential facts in this case. On December 7, 1969, Joe Shapiro, an undercover agent for the Federal Bureau of Narcotics and Dangerous Drugs, went to respondent's home on Whidbey Island in the State of Washington where he met with respondent and his two codefendants, John and Patrick Connolly. Shapiro's assignment was to locate a laboratory where it was believed that methamphetamine was being manufactured illicitly. He told the respondent and the Connollys that he represented an organization in the Pacific Northwest that was interested in controlling the manufacture and distribution of methamphetamine. He then made an offer to supply the defendants with the chemical phenyl-2-propanone, an essential ingredient in the manufacture of methamphetamine, in return for one-half of the drug produced. This offer was made on the condition that Agent Shapiro be shown a sample of the drug which they were making and the laboratory where it was being produced.

During the conversation, Patrick Connolly revealed that he had been making the drug since May 1969 and since then had produced three pounds of it. John Connolly gave the agent a bag containing a quantity of methamphetamine that he represented as being from "the last batch that we made." Shortly thereafter, Shapiro and Patrick Connolly left respondent's house to view the laboratory which was located in the Connolly house on Whidbey Island. At the house, Shapiro observed an empty bottle bearing the chemical label phenyl-2-propanone.

By prearrangement, Shapiro returned to the Connolly house on December 9, 1969, to supply 100 grams of propanone and observe the manufacturing process. When he arrived he observed Patrick Connolly and the respondent cutting up pieces of aluminum foil and placing them in a large flask. There was testimony that some of the foil pieces accidentally fell on the floor and were picked up by the respondent and Shapiro and put into the flask. Thereafter, Patrick Connolly added all of the necessary chemicals, including the propanone brought by Shapiro, to make two batches of methamphetamine. The manufacturing process having been completed the following morning, Shapiro was given one-half of the drug and respondent kept the remainder. Shapiro offered to buy, and the respondent agreed to sell, part of the remainder for $60.

About a month later, Shapiro returned to the Connolly house and met with Patrick Connolly to ask if he was still interested in their "business arrangement." Connolly replied that he was interested but that he had recently obtained two additional bottles of phenyl-2-propanone and would not be finished with them for a couple of days. He provided some additional methamphetamine to Shapiro at that time. Three days later Shapiro returned to the Connolly house with a search warrant and, among other items, seized an empty 500-gram bottle of propanone and a 100-gram bottle, not the one he had provided, that was partially filled with the chemical.

There was testimony at the trial of respondent and Patrick Connolly that phenyl-2-propanone was generally difficult to obtain. At the request of the Bureau of Narcotics and Dangerous Drugs, some chemical supply firms had voluntarily ceased selling the chemical.

At the close of the evidence, and after receiving the District Judge's standard entrapment instruction,[4] the jury found the respondent guilty on all counts charged. On appeal, the respondent conceded that the jury could have found him predisposed to commit the offenses, . . . but argued that on the facts presented there was entrapment as a matter of law. The Court of Appeals agreed, although it did not find the District Court had misconstrued or misapplied the traditional standards governing the entrapment defense. Rather, the court in effect expanded the traditional notion of entrapment, which focuses on the predisposition of the defendant, to mandate dismissal of a criminal prosecution whenever the court determines that there has been "an intolerable degree of governmental participation in the criminal enterprise." In this case the court decided that the conduct of the agent in supplying a scarce ingredient essential for the manufacture of a controlled substance established that defense.

This new defense was held to rest on either of two alternative theories. One theory is based on two lower court decisions which have found entrapment, regardless of predisposition, whenever the government supplies contraband to the defendants. United States v. Bueno, 447 F.2d 903 (C.A.5 1971); *United States v. Chisum*, 312 F.Supp. 1307 (C.D.Cal.1970). The second theory, a nonentrapment rationale, is based on a recent Ninth Circuit decision that reversed a conviction because a government investigator was so enmeshed in the criminal

---

[4]   The District Judge stated the governing law on entrapment as follows: "Where a person already has the willingness and the readiness to break the law, the mere fact that the government agent provides what appears to be a favorable opportunity is not entrapment." He then instructed the jury to acquit respondent if it had a "reasonable doubt whether the defendant had the previous intent or purpose to commit the offense . . . and did so only because he was induced or persuaded by some officer or agent of the government." No exception was taken by respondent to this instruction.

activity that the prosecution of the defendants was held to be repugnant to the American criminal justice system, *Greene v. United States*, 454 F.2d 783 (C.A.9 1971). The court below held that these two rationales constitute the same defense, and that only the label distinguishes them. In any event, it held that "[b]oth theories are premised on fundamental concepts of due process and evince the reluctance of the judiciary to countenance 'overzealous law enforcement.'" . . .

This Court first recognized and applied the entrapment defense in *Sorrells v. United States*, 287 U.S. 435 (1932). In *Sorrells*, a federal prohibition agent visited the defendant while posing as a tourist and engaged him in conversation about their common war experiences. After gaining the defendant's confidence, the agent asked for some liquor, was twice refused, but upon asking a third time the defendant finally capitulated, and was subsequently prosecuted for violating the National Prohibition Act.

Mr. Chief Justice Hughes, speaking for the Court, held that as a matter of statutory construction the defense of entrapment should have been available to the defendant. Under the theory propounded by the Chief Justice, the entrapment defense prohibits law enforcement officers from instigating a criminal act by persons "otherwise innocent in order to lure them to its commission and to punish them." . . . Thus, the thrust of the entrapment defense was held to focus on the intent or predisposition of the defendant to commit the crime. "[I]f the defendant seeks acquittal by reason of entrapment he cannot complain of an appropriate and searching inquiry into his own conduct and predisposition as bearing upon that issue.". . .

Mr. Justice Roberts concurred but was of the view "that courts must be closed to the trial of a crime instigated by the government's own agents.". . . The difference in the view of the majority and the concurring opinions is that in the former the inquiry focuses on the predisposition of the defendant, whereas in the latter the inquiry focuses on whether the government "instigated the crime."

In 1958 the Court again considered the theory underlying the entrapment defense and expressly reaffirmed the view expressed by the *Sorrells* majority. *Sherman v. United States* [356 U.S. 369]. In *Sherman* the defendant was convicted of selling narcotics to a Government informer. As in *Sorrells*, it appears that the Government agent gained the confidence of the defendant and, despite initial reluctance, the defendant finally acceded to the repeated importunings of the agent to commit the criminal act. On the basis of *Sorrells*, this Court reversed the affirmance of the defendant's conviction.

In affirming the theory underlying *Sorrells*, Mr. Chief Justice Warren for the Court, held that "[t]o determine whether entrapment has been established, a line must be drawn between the trap for the unwary innocent and the trap for the unwary criminal." . . .

In the instant case, respondent asks us to reconsider the theory of the entrapment defense as it is set forth in the majority opinions in *Sorrells* and *Sherman*. His principal contention is that the defense should rest on constitutional grounds. He argues that the level of Shapiro's involvement in the manufacture of the methamphetamine was so high that a criminal prosecution for the drug's manufacture violates the fundamental principles of due process. The respondent contends that the same factors that led this Court to apply the exclusionary rule to illegal searches and seizures, . . . and confessions, . . . should be considered here. But he would have the Court go further in deterring undesirable official conduct by requiring that any prosecution be barred absolutely because of the police involvement in criminal activity. The analogy is imperfect in any event, for the principal reason behind the adoption of the exclusionary rule was the Government's "failure to observe its own laws." . . . Unlike the situations giving rise to the holdings in *Mapp* and *Miranda*, the Government's conduct here violated no independent constitutional right of the respondent. Nor did Shapiro violate any federal statute or rule or commit any crime in infiltrating the respondent's drug enterprise.

Respondent would overcome this basic weakness in his analogy to the exclusionary rule cases by having the Court adopt a rigid constitutional rule that would preclude any prosecution when it is shown that the criminal conduct would not have been possible had not an undercover agent "supplied an indispensable means to the commission of the crime that could not have been obtained otherwise, through legal or illegal channels." Even if we were to surmount the difficulties attending the notion that due process of law can be embodied in fixed rules, and those attending respondent's particular formulation, the rule he proposes would not appear to be of significant benefit to him. For, on the record presented, it appears that he cannot fit within the terms of the very rule he proposes.

The record discloses that although the propanone was difficult to obtain, it was by no means impossible. The defendants admitted making the drug both before and after those batches made with the propanone supplied by Shapiro. Shapiro testified that he saw an empty bottle labeled phenyl-2-propanone on his first visit to the laboratory on December 7, 1969. And when the laboratory was searched pursuant to a search warrant on January 10, 1970, two additional bottles labeled phenyl-2-propanone were seized. Thus, the facts in the record amply demonstrate that the propanone used in the illicit manufacture of methamphetamine not only *could* have been obtained without the intervention of Shapiro but was in fact obtained by these defendants.

While we may some day be presented with a situation in which the conduct of law enforcement agents is so outrageous that due process principles would absolutely bar the government from invoking judicial processes to obtain a conviction, *cf. Rochin v. California*, 342 U.S. 165

(1952), the instant case is distinctly not of that breed. Shapiro's contribution of propanone to the criminal enterprise already in process was scarcely objectionable. The chemical is by itself a harmless substance and its possession is legal. While the Government may have been seeking to make it more difficult for drug rings, such as that of which respondent was a member, to obtain the chemical, the evidence described above shows that it nonetheless was obtainable. The law enforcement conduct here stops far short of violating that "fundamental fairness, shocking to the universal sense of justice," mandated by the Due Process Clause of the Fifth Amendment. *Kinsella v. United States ex rel. Singleton*, 361 U.S. 234, 246 (1960).

The illicit manufacture of drugs is not a sporadic, isolated criminal incident, but a continuing, though illegal, business enterprise. In order to obtain convictions for illegally manufacturing drugs, the gathering of evidence of past unlawful conduct frequently proves to be an all but impossible task. Thus in drug-related offenses law enforcement personnel have turned to one of the only practicable means of detection; the infiltration of drug rings and a limited participation in their unlawful present practices. Such infiltration is a recognized and permissible means of investigation; if that be so, then the supply of some item of value that the drug ring requires must, as a general rule, also be permissible. For an agent will not be taken into the confidence of the illegal entrepreneurs unless he has something of value to offer them. Law enforcement tactics such as this can hardly be said to violate "fundamental fairness" or "shocking to the universal sense of justice," *Kinsella*, supra.

Respondent also urges, as an alternative to his constitutional argument, that we broaden the nonconstitutional defense of entrapment in order to sustain the judgment of the Court of Appeals. This Court's opinions in *Sorrells v. United States*, supra, and *Sherman v. United States*, supra, held that the principal element in the defense of entrapment was the defendant's predisposition to commit the crime. Respondent conceded in the Court of Appeals, as well he might, "that he may have harbored a predisposition to commit the charged offenses." . . . Yet he argues that the jury's refusal to find entrapment under the charge submitted to it by the trial court should be overturned and the views of Justices Roberts and Frankfurter, in *Sorrells* and *Sherman*, respectively, which made the essential element of the defense turn on the type and degree of governmental conduct, be adopted as the law.

We decline to overrule these cases. *Sorrells* is a precedent of long standing that has already been once re-examined in *Sherman* and implicitly there reaffirmed. Since the defense is not of a constitutional dimension, Congress may address itself to the question and adopt any substantive definition of the defense that it may find desirable.

Critics of the rule laid down in *Sorrells* and *Sherman* have suggested that its basis in the implied intent of Congress is largely fictitious, and have pointed to what they conceive to be the anomalous difference between the treatment of a defendant who is solicited by a private individual and one who is entrapped by a government agent. Questions have been likewise raised as to whether "predisposition" can be factually established with the requisite degree of certainty. Arguments such as these, while not devoid of appeal, have been twice previously made to this Court, and twice rejected by it, first in *Sorrells* and then in *Sherman*.

We believe that at least equally cogent criticism has been made of the concurring views in these cases. Commenting in *Sherman* on Mr. Justice Roberts' position in *Sorrells* that "although the defendant could claim that the Government had induced him to commit the crime, the Government could not reply by showing that the defendant's criminal conduct was due to his own readiness and not to the persuasion of government agents," *Sherman v. United States*, 356 U.S., at 376–377, Mr. Chief Justice Warren quoted the observation of Judge Learned Hand in an earlier stage of that proceeding:

> "Indeed, it would seem probable that, if there were no reply [to the claim of inducement], it would be impossible ever to secure convictions of any offences which consist of transactions that are carried on in secret." United States v. Sherman, 200 F.2d 880, 882. *Sherman v. United States*, 356 U.S., at 377 n. 7.

Nor does it seem particularly desirable for the law to grant complete immunity from prosecution to one who himself planned to commit a crime, and then committed it, simply because government undercover agents subjected him to inducements which might have seduced a hypothetical individual who was not so predisposed. We are content to leave the matter where it was left by the Court in *Sherman*:. . . .

Several decisions of the United States district courts and courts of appeals have undoubtedly gone beyond this Court's opinions in *Sorrells* and *Sherman* in order to bar prosecutions because of what they thought to be, for want of a better term, "overzealous law enforcement." But the defense of entrapment enunciated in those opinions was not intended to give the federal judiciary a "chancellor's foot" veto over law enforcement practices of which it did not approve. The execution of the federal laws under our Constitution is confined primarily to the Executive Branch of the Government, subject to applicable constitutional and statutory limitations and to judicially fashioned rules to enforce those limitations. We think that the decision of the Court of Appeals in this case quite unnecessarily introduces an unmanageably subjective standard which is contrary to the holdings of this Court in *Sorrells* and *Sherman*.

Those cases establish that entrapment is a relatively limited defense. It is rooted, not in any authority of the Judicial Branch to dismiss prosecutions for what it feels to have been "overzealous law enforcement," but instead in the notion that Congress could not have intended criminal punishment for a defendant who has committed all the elements of a proscribed offense, but was induced to commit them by the Government.

Sorrells and *Sherman* both recognize "that the fact that officers or employees of the Government merely afford opportunities or facilities for the commission of the offense does not defeat the prosecution," 287 U.S., at 441; 356 U.S., at 372. Nor will the mere fact of deceit defeat a prosecution, . . . for there are circumstances when the use of deceit is the only practicable law enforcement technique available. It is only when the Government's deception actually implants the criminal design in the mind of the defendant that the defense of entrapment comes into play.

Respondent's concession in the Court of Appeals that the jury finding as to predisposition was supported by the evidence is, therefore, fatal to his claim of entrapment. He was an active participant in an illegal drug manufacturing enterprise which began before the Government agent appeared on the scene, and continued after the Government agent had left the scene. He was, in the words of *Sherman*, supra, not an "unwary innocent" but an "unwary criminal." The Court of Appeals was wrong, we believe, when it sought to broaden the principle laid down in *Sorrells* and *Sherman*. Its judgment is therefore

Reversed.

■ MR. JUSTICE DOUGLAS, with whom MR. JUSTICE BRENNAN concurs, dissenting.

A federal agent supplied the accused with one chemical ingredient of the drug known as methamphetamine ("speed") which the accused manufactured and for which act he was sentenced to prison. His defense was entrapment, which the Court of Appeals sustained and which the Court today disallows. Since I have an opposed view of entrapment, I dissent.

. . . .

In my view, the fact that the chemical ingredient supplied by the federal agent might have been obtained from other sources is quite irrelevant. Supplying the chemical ingredient used in the manufacture of this batch of "speed" made the United States an active participant in the unlawful activity. . . .

Mr. Justice Roberts in *Sorrells* put the idea in the following words:

The applicable principle is that courts must be closed to the trial of a crime instigated by the government's own agents. No other issue, no comparison of equities as between the guilty official and the guilty defendant, has any place in the enforcement of this overruling principle of public policy.

May the federal agent supply the counterfeiter with the kind of paper or ink that he needs in order to get a quick and easy arrest? The Court of Appeals in Greene v. United States, 454 F.2d 783, speaking through Judges Hamley and Hufstedler, said "no" in a case where the federal agent treated the suspects "as partners" with him, offered to supply them with a still, a still site, still equipment, and an operator and supplied them with sugar. . . .

The Court of Appeals in the instant case relied upon this line of decisions in sustaining the defense of entrapment, 459 F.2d 671. In doing so it took the view that the "prostitution of the criminal law," as Mr. Justice Roberts described it in *Sorrells*, 287 U.S., at 457, was the evil at which the defense of entrapment is aimed.

Federal agents play a debased role when they become the instigators of the crime, or partners in its commission, or the creative brain behind the illegal scheme. That is what the federal agent did here when he furnished the accused with one of the chemical ingredients needed to manufacture the unlawful drug.

■ MR. JUSTICE STEWART, with whom MR. JUSTICE BRENNAN and MR. JUSTICE MARSHALL join, dissenting.

It is common ground that "[t]he conduct with which the defense of entrapment is concerned is the *manufacturing* of crime by law enforcement officials and their agents." *Lopez v. United States*, 373 U.S. 427, 434 (1963). For the Government cannot be permitted to instigate the commission of a criminal offense in order to prosecute someone for committing it. *Sherman v. United States*, 356 U.S. 369, 372 (1958). As Mr. Justice Brandeis put it, the Government "may not provoke or create a crime and then punish the criminal, its creature." *Casey v. United States*, 276 U.S. 413, 423 (1928) (dissenting opinion). It is to prevent this situation from occurring in the administration of federal criminal justice that the defense of entrapment exists. *Sorrells v. United States*, 287 U.S. 435 (1932); *Sherman v. United States*, supra. Cf. *Masciale v. United States*, 356 U.S. 386 (1958); *Lopez v. United States*, supra. But the Court has been sharply divided as to the proper basis, scope, and focus of the entrapment defense, and as to whether, in the absence of a conclusive showing, the issue of entrapment is for the judge or the jury to determine.

I

In *Sorrells v. United States*, supra, and *Sherman v. United States*, supra, the Court took what might be called a "subjective" approach to the defense of entrapment. In that view, the defense is predicated on an unexpressed intent of Congress to exclude from its criminal statutes the prosecution and conviction of persons, "otherwise innocent," who have been lured to the commission of the prohibited act through the Government's instigation. . . . [ ] The key phrase in this formulation is "otherwise innocent," for the entrapment defense is available under this approach only to those who would not have committed the crime but for the Government's inducements. Thus, the subjective approach focuses on the conduct and propensities of the particular defendant in each individual case: if he is "otherwise innocent," he may avail himself of the defense; but if he had the "predisposition" to commit the crime, or if the "criminal design" originated with him, then—regardless of the nature and extent of the Government's participation—there has been no entrapment. . . .

The concurring opinion of Mr. Justice Roberts, joined by Justices Brandeis and Stone, in the *Sorrells* case, and that of Mr. Justice Frankfurter, joined by Justices Douglas, Harlan, and Brennan, in the *Sherman* case, took a different view of the entrapment defense. In their concept, the defense is not grounded on some unexpressed intent of Congress to exclude from punishment under its statutes those otherwise innocent persons tempted into crime by the Government, but rather on the belief that "the methods employed on behalf of the Government to bring about conviction cannot be countenanced." . . . Thus, the focus of this approach is not on the propensities and predisposition of a specific defendant, but on "whether the police conduct revealed in the particular case falls below standards, to which common feelings respond, for the proper use of governmental power." Id., at 382. Phrased another way, the question is whether—regardless of the predisposition to crime of the particular defendant involved—the governmental agents have acted in such a way as is likely to instigate or create a criminal offense. Under this approach, the determination of the lawfulness of the Government's conduct must be made—as it is on all questions involving the legality of law enforcement methods—by the trial judge, not the jury.

In my view, this objective approach to entrapment advanced by the Roberts opinion in *Sorrells* and the Frankfurter opinion in *Sherman* is the only one truly consistent with the underlying rationale of the defense. Indeed, the very basis of the entrapment defense itself demands adherence to an approach that focuses on the conduct of the governmental agents, rather than on whether the defendant was "predisposed" or "otherwise innocent." I find it impossible to believe that the purpose of the defense is to effectuate some unexpressed congressional intent to exclude from its criminal statutes persons who committed a prohibited act, but would not have done so except for the Government's inducements. For, as Mr. Justice Frankfurter put it, "the only legislative intention that can with any show of reason be extracted from the statute is the intention to make criminal precisely the conduct in which the defendant has engaged." *Sherman v. United States*, supra, at 379. See also *Sorrells v. United States*, supra, at 456 (ROBERTS, J., concurring). Since, by definition, the entrapment defense cannot arise unless the defendant actually committed the proscribed act, that defendant is manifestly covered by the terms of the criminal statute involved.

Furthermore, to say that such a defendant is "otherwise innocent" or not "predisposed" to commit the crime is misleading, at best. The very fact that he has committed an act that Congress has determined to be illegal demonstrates conclusively that he is not innocent of the offense.

He may not have originated the precise plan or the precise details, but he was "predisposed" in the sense that he has proved to be quite capable of committing the crime. That he was induced, provoked, or tempted to do so by government agents does not make him any more innocent or any less predisposed than he would be if he had been induced, provoked, or tempted by a private person—which, of course, would not entitle him to cry "entrapment." Since the only difference between these situations is the identity of the tempter, it follows that the significant focus must be on the conduct of the government agents, and not on the predisposition of the defendant.

The purpose of the entrapment defense, then, cannot be to protect persons who are "otherwise innocent." Rather, it must be to prohibit unlawful governmental activity in instigating crime. As Mr. Justice Brandeis stated in *Casey v. United States*, supra, at 425: "This prosecution should be stopped, not because some right of Casey's has been denied, but in order to protect the Government. To protect it from illegal conduct of its officers. To preserve the purity of its courts." . . . If that is so, then whether the particular defendant was "predisposed" or "otherwise innocent" is irrelevant; and the important question becomes whether the Government's conduct in inducing the crime was beyond judicial toleration.

Moreover, a test that makes the entrapment defense depend on whether the defendant had the requisite predisposition permits the introduction into evidence of all kinds of hearsay, suspicion, and rumor—all of which would be inadmissible in any other context—in order to prove the defendant's predisposition. It allows the prosecution, in offering such proof, to rely on the defendant's bad reputation or past criminal activities, including even rumored activities of which the prosecution may have insufficient evidence to obtain an indictment, and to present the agent's suspicions as to why they chose to tempt this defendant. This sort of evidence is not only unreliable, as the hearsay rule recognizes; but it is also highly prejudicial, especially if the matter is submitted to the jury, for, despite instructions to the contrary, the jury may well consider such evidence as probative not simply of the defendant's predisposition, but of his guilt of the offense with which he stands charged.

More fundamentally, focusing on the defendant's innocence or predisposition has the direct effect of making what is permissible or impermissible police conduct depend upon the past record and propensities of the particular defendant involved. Stated another way, this subjective test means that the Government is permitted to entrap a person with a criminal record or bad reputation, and then to prosecute him for the manufactured crime, confident that his record or reputation itself will be enough to show that he was predisposed to commit the offense anyway. . . .

This does not mean, of course, that the Government's use of undercover activity, strategy, or deception is necessarily unlawful. . . .

Indeed, many crimes, especially so-called victimless crimes, could not otherwise be detected. Thus, government agents may engage in conduct that is likely, when objectively considered, to afford a person ready and willing to commit the crime an opportunity to do so. *Osborn v. United States*, 385 U.S. 323, 331–332 (1966). . . .

But when the agents' involvement in criminal activities goes beyond the mere offering of such an opportunity, and when their conduct is of a kind that could induce or instigate the commission of a crime by one not ready and willing to commit it, then—regardless of the character or propensities of the particular person induced—I think entrapment has occurred. For in that situation, the Government has engaged in the impermissible manufacturing of crime, and the federal courts should bar the prosecution in order to preserve the institutional integrity of the system of federal criminal justice.

II

In the case before us, I think that the District Court erred in submitting the issue of entrapment to the jury, with instructions to acquit only if it had a reasonable doubt as to the respondent's predisposition to committing the crime. Since, under the objective test of entrapment, predisposition is irrelevant and the issue is to be decided by the trial judge, the Court of Appeals, I believe, would have been justified in reversing the conviction on this basis alone. But since the appellate court did not remand for consideration of the issue by the District Judge under an objective standard, but rather found entrapment as a matter of law and directed that the indictment be dismissed, we must reach the merits of the respondent's entrapment defense. . . .

It is undisputed that phenyl-2-propanone is an essential ingredient in the manufacture of methamphetamine; that it is not used for any other purpose; and that, while its sale is not illegal, it is difficult to obtain, because a manufacturer's license is needed to purchase it, and because many suppliers, at the request of the Federal Bureau of Narcotics and Dangerous Drugs, do not sell it at all. It is also undisputed that the methamphetamine which the respondent was prosecuted for manufacturing and selling was all produced on December 10, 1969, and that all the phenyl-2-propanone used in the manufacture of that batch of the drug was provided by the government agent. In these circumstances, the agent's undertaking to supply this ingredient to the respondent, thus making it possible for the Government to prosecute him for manufacturing an illicit drug with it, was, I think, precisely the type of governmental conduct that the entrapment defense is meant to prevent.

Although the Court of Appeals found that the phenyl-2-propanone could not have been obtained without the agent's intervention—that "there could not have been the manufacture, delivery, or sale of the illicit drug had it not been for the Government's supply of one of the essential ingredients," . . . the Court today rejects this finding as contradicted by the facts revealed at trial. The record, as the Court states, discloses that one of the respondent's accomplices, though not the respondent himself, had obtained phenyl-2-propanone from independent sources both before and after receiving the agent's supply, and had used it in the production of methamphetamine. This demonstrates, it is said, that the chemical was obtainable other than through the government agent; and hence the agent's furnishing it for the production of the methamphetamine involved in this prosecution did no more than afford an opportunity for its production to one ready and willing to produce it. . . . Thus, the argument seems to be, there was no entrapment here, any more than there would have been if the agent had furnished common table salt, had that been necessary to the drug's production.

It cannot be doubted that if phenyl-2-propanone had been wholly unobtainable from other sources, the agent's undercover offer to supply it to the respondent in return for part of the illicit methamphetamine produced therewith—an offer initiated and carried out by the agent for the purpose of prosecuting the respondent for producing methamphetamine—would be precisely the type of governmental conduct that constitutes entrapment under any definition. For the agent's conduct in that situation would make possible the commission of an otherwise totally impossible crime, and, I should suppose, would thus be a textbook example of instigating the commission of a criminal offense in order to prosecute someone for committing it.

But assuming in this case that the phenyl-2-propanone was obtainable through independent sources, the fact remains that that used for the particular batch of methamphetamine involved in all three counts of the indictment with which the respondent was charged—*i.e.*, that produced on December 10, 1969—was supplied by the Government. This essential ingredient was indisputably difficult to obtain, and yet what was used in committing the offenses of which the respondent was convicted was offered to the respondent by the Government agent, on the agent's own initiative, and was readily supplied to the respondent in needed amounts. If the chemical was so easily available elsewhere, then why did not the agent simply wait until the respondent had himself obtained the ingredients and produced the drug, and then buy it from him? The very fact that the agent felt it incumbent upon him to offer to supply phenyl-2-propanone in return for the drug casts considerable doubt on the theory that the chemical could easily have been procured without the agent's intervention, and that therefore the agent merely afforded an opportunity for the commission of a criminal offense.

. . . .

It is the Government's duty to prevent crime, not to promote it. Here, the Government's agent asked that the illegal drug be produced for him, solved his quarry's practical problems with the assurance that he could provide the one essential ingredient that was difficult to obtain, furnished that element as he had promised, and bought the finished product from the respondent—all so that the respondent could be prosecuted for producing and selling the very drug for which the agent had asked and for which he had provided the necessary component. . . .

I would affirm the judgment of the Court of Appeals.

Hampton v. United States

Supreme Court of the United States, 1976.
425 U.S. 484, 96 S.Ct. 1646, 48 L.Ed.2d 113.

■ MR. JUSTICE REHNQUIST announced the judgment of the Court in an opinion in which THE CHIEF JUSTICE and MR. JUSTICE WHITE join.

This case presents the question of whether a defendant may be convicted for the sale of contraband which he procured from a government informer or agent. The Court of Appeals for the Eighth Circuit held he could be, and we agree.

I

Petitioner was convicted of two counts of distributing heroin in violation of 21 U.S.C. § 841(a)(1) in the United States District Court for the Eastern District of Missouri and sentenced to concurrent terms of five years' imprisonment (suspended). The case arose from two sales of heroin by petitioner to agents of the Federal Drug Enforcement Administration (DEA) in St. Louis on February 25 and 26, 1974. The sales were arranged by one Hutton, who was a pool-playing acquaintance of petitioner at the Pud bar in St. Louis and also a DEA informant.

According to the Government's witnesses, in late February 1974, Hutton and petitioner were shooting pool at the Pud when petitioner, after observing "track" (needle) marks on Hutton's arms told Hutton that he needed money and knew where he could get some heroin. Hutton responded that he could find a buyer and petitioner suggested that he "get in touch with those people." Hutton then called DEA agent Terry Sawyer and arranged a sale for 10 p.m. on February 25.

At the appointed time, Hutton and petitioner went to a pre-arranged meeting place and were met by Agent Sawyer and DEA Agent McDowell, posing as narcotics dealers. Petitioner produced a tinfoil packet from his cap and turned it over to the agents who tested it, pronounced it "okay," and negotiated a price of $145 which was paid to petitioner. Before they parted, petitioner told Sawyer that he could obtain larger quantities of heroin and gave Sawyer a phone number where he could be reached.

The next day Sawyer called petitioner and arranged for another "buy" that afternoon. Petitioner got Hutton to go along and they met the agents again near where they had been the previous night.

They all entered the agents' car, and petitioner again produced a tinfoil packet from his cap. The agents again field-tested it and pronounced it satisfactory. Petitioner then asked for $500 which Agent

Sawyer said he would get from the trunk. Sawyer got out and opened the trunk which was a signal to other agents to move in and arrest petitioner, which they did.

Petitioner's version of events was quite different. According to him, in response to petitioner's statement that he was short of cash, Hutton said that he had a friend who was a pharmacist who could produce a non-narcotic counterfeit drug which would give the same reaction as heroin. Hutton proposed selling this drug to gullible acquaintances who would be led to believe they were buying heroin. Petitioner testified that they successfully duped one buyer with this fake drug and that the sales which led to the arrest was solicited by petitioner in an effort to profit further from this ploy.

Petitioner contended that he neither intended to sell, nor knew that he was dealing in heroin and that all of the drugs he sold were supplied by Hutton. His account was at least partially disbelieved by the jury which was instructed that in order to convict petitioner they had to find that the Government proved "that the defendant knowingly did an act which the law forbids, purposely intending to violate the law." Thus the guilty verdict necessarily implies that the jury rejected petitioner's claim that he did not know the substance was heroin, and petitioner himself admitted both soliciting and carrying out sales. The only relevance of his version of the facts, then, lies in his having requested an instruction embodying that version. He did not request a standard entrapment instruction but he did request the following:

> The defendant asserts that he was the victim of entrapment as to the crimes charged in the indictment.
>
> If you find that the defendant's sales of narcotics were sales of narcotics supplied to him by an informer in the employ of or acting on behalf of the government, then you must acquit the defendant because the law as a matter of policy forbids his conviction in such a case.
>
> Furthermore, under this particular defense, you need not consider the predisposition of the defendant to commit the offense charged, because if the governmental involvement through its informer reached the point that I have just defined in your own minds, then the predisposition of the defendant would not matter.

The trial court refused the instruction and petitioner was found guilty. He appealed to the United States Court of Appeals for the Eighth Circuit, claiming that if the jury had believed that the drug was supplied by Hutton he should have been acquitted. The Court of Appeals rejected this argument and affirmed the conviction. . . .

II

In *Russell* we held that the statutory defense of entrapment was not available where it was conceded that a government agent supplied a necessary ingredient in the manufacture of an illicit drug. We reaffirmed the principle of Sorrells v. United States, . . . and Sherman v. United States . . . , that the entrapment defense "focus[es] on the intent or predisposition of the defendant to commit the crime," . . . rather than upon the conduct of the Government's agents. We ruled out the possibility that the defense of entrapment could ever be based upon governmental misconduct in a case, such as this one, where the predisposition of the defendant to commit the crime was established.

. . . In view of these holdings, petitioner correctly recognizes that his case does not qualify as one involving "entrapment" at all. He instead relies on the language in *Russell* that "we may some day be presented with a situation in which the conduct of law enforcement agents is so outrageous that due process principles would absolutely bar the government from invoking judicial processes to obtain a conviction. . . .["]

In urging that this case involves a violation of his due process rights, petitioner misapprehends the meaning of the quoted language in *Russell*, supra. Admittedly petitioner's case is different from Russell's but the difference is one of degree, not of kind. In *Russell* the ingredient supplied by the Government agent was a legal drug which the defendants demonstrably could have obtained from other sources besides the Government. Here the drug which the government informant allegedly supplied to petitioner was both illegal and constituted the *corpus delicti* for the sale of which the petitioner was convicted. The Government obviously played a more significant role in enabling petitioner to sell contraband in this case than it did in *Russell*.

But in each case the Government agents were acting in concert with the defendant, and in each case either the jury found or the defendant conceded that he was predisposed to commit the crime for which he was convicted. The remedy of the criminal defendant with respect to the acts of Government agents, which, far from being resisted, are encouraged by him, lies solely in the defense of entrapment. But, as noted, petitioner's conceded predisposition rendered this defense unavailable to him.

. . . .

The limitations of the Due Process Clause of the Fifth Amendment come into play only when the Government activity in question violates some protected right of the *defendant*. Here, as we have noted, the police, the Government informant, and the defendant acted in concert with one another. If the result of the governmental activity is to "implant in the mind of an innocent person the disposition to commit the alleged offense and induce its commission . . . ," . . . the defendant is protected by the defense of entrapment. If the police engage in illegal activity in concert with a defendant beyond the scope of their duties the remedy lies, not in freeing the equally culpable defendant, but in prosecuting the police under the applicable provisions of state or federal law. . . . But the police conduct here no more deprived defendant of any right secured to him by the United States Constitution than did the police conduct in *Russell* deprive Russell of any rights.

Affirmed.

■ [The concurring opinion of MR. JUSTICE POWELL, with whom MR. JUSTICE BLACKMUN joined, is omitted].

■ MR. JUSTICE BRENNAN, with whom MR. JUSTICE STEWART and MR. JUSTICE MARSHALL concur, dissenting.

I joined my Brother Stewart's dissent in United States v. Russell, . . . and Mr. Justice Frankfurter's opinion concurring in the result in Sherman v. United States. . . . Those opinions and the separate opinion of Mr. Justice Roberts in *Sorrells* . . . express the view, with which I fully agree, that "courts refuse to convict an entrapped defendant, not because his conduct falls outside the proscription of the statute, but because, even if his guilt be admitted, the methods employed on behalf of the Government to bring about conviction cannot be countenanced." . . .

In any event, I think that reversal of petitioner's conviction is also compelled for those who follow the "subjective" approach to the defense of entrapment. As Mr. Justice Rehnquist notes, the Government's role in the criminal activity involved in this case was more pervasive than the Government involvement in *Russell*. Ante, at 489. In addition, I agree with Mr. Justice Powell that *Russell* does not foreclose imposition of a bar to conviction—based upon our supervisory power or due process principles—where the conduct of law enforcement authorities is sufficiently offensive, even though the individuals entitled to invoke such a defense might be "predisposed." . . . In my view, the police activity in this case was beyond permissible limits.

Two facts significantly distinguish this case from Russell. First, the chemical supplied in that case was not contraband. It is legal to possess and sell phenyl-2-propanone and, although the Government there supplied an ingredient that was essential to the manufacture of methamphetamine, it did not supply the contraband itself. In contrast, petitioner claims that the very narcotic he is accused of selling was supplied by an agent of the Government. . . .

Second, the defendant in Russell "was an active participant in an illegal drug manufacturing enterprise which began before the Government agent appeared on the scene, and continued after the Government agent had left the scene." . . . Russell was charged with unlawfully manufacturing and processing methamphetamine, . . . and his crime was participation in an ongoing operation. In contrast, the two sales for which petitioner was convicted were allegedly instigated by Government agents and completed by the Government's purchase. The beginning and end of this crime thus coincided exactly with the Government's entry into and withdrawal from the criminal activity involved in this case, while the Government was not similarly involved in Russell's crime. . . .

. . . Where the Government's agent deliberately sets up the accused by supplying him with contraband and then bringing him to another agent as a potential purchaser, the Government's role has passed the point of toleration. . . . The Government is doing nothing less than buying contraband from itself through an intermediary and jailing the intermediary. . . . There is little, if any, law enforcement interest promoted by such conduct; plainly it is not designed to discover ongoing drug traffic. Rather, such conduct deliberately entices an individual to commit a crime. That the accused is "predisposed" cannot possibly justify the action of government officials in purposefully creating the crime. No one would suggest that the police could round up and jail all "predisposed" individuals, yet that is precisely what set-ups like the instant one are intended to accomplish. . . . Thus, this case is nothing less than an instance of "the Government . . . seeking to punish for an alleged offense which is the product of the creative activity of its own officials."
. . .

. . . For the reasons stated I would at a minimum engraft the Bueno principle upon that defense and hold that conviction is barred as a matter of law where the subject of the criminal charge is the sale of contraband provided to the defendant by a Government agent. . . .

Jacobson v. United States

Supreme Court of the United States, 1992.
503 U.S. 540, 112 S.Ct. 1535, 118 L.Ed.2d 174.

■ JUSTICE WHITE delivered the opinion of the Court.

I

In February 1984, petitioner, a 56-year-old veteran-turned-farmer who supported his elderly father in Nebraska, ordered two magazines and a brochure from a California adult bookstore. The magazines, entitled Bare Boys I and Bare Boys II, contained photographs of nude preteen and teenage boys. The contents of the magazines startled petitioner, who testified that he had expected to receive photographs of young men 18 years or older. On cross-examination, he explained his response to the magazines:

> [PROSECUTOR]: [Y]ou were shocked and surprised that there were pictures of very young boys without clothes on, is that correct?
>
> [JACOBSON]: Yes, I was.
>
> [PROSECUTOR]: Were you offended?
>
> . . .
>
> [JACOBSON]: I was not offended because I thought these were a nudist type publication. Many of the pictures were out in

a rural or outdoor setting. There was—I didn't draw any sexual connotation or connection with that.

The young men depicted in the magazines were not engaged in sexual activity, and petitioner's receipt of the magazines was legal under both federal and Nebraska law. Within three months, the law with respect to child pornography changed; Congress passed the Act illegalizing the receipt through the mails of sexually explicit depictions of children. In the very month that the new provision became law, postal inspectors found petitioner's name on the mailing list of the California bookstore that had mailed him Bare Boys I and II. There followed over the next 2 1/2 years repeated efforts by two Government agencies, through five fictitious organizations and a bogus pen pal, to explore petitioner's willingness to break the new law by ordering sexually explicit photographs of children through the mail.

The Government began its efforts in January 1985 when a postal inspector sent petitioner a letter supposedly from the American Hedonist Society, which in fact was a fictitious organization. The letter included a membership application and stated the Society's doctrine: that members had the "right to read what we desire, the right to discuss similar interests with those who share our philosophy, and finally that we have the right to seek pleasure without restrictions being placed on us by outdated puritan morality." Petitioner enrolled in the organization and returned a sexual attitude questionnaire that asked him to rank on a scale of one to four his enjoyment of various sexual materials, with one being "really enjoy," two being "enjoy," three being "somewhat enjoy," and four being "do not enjoy." Petitioner ranked the entry "[p]re-teen sex" as a two, but indicated that he was opposed to pedophilia.

For a time, the Government left petitioner alone. But then a new "prohibited mailing specialist" in the Postal Service found petitioner's name in a file, and in May 1986, petitioner received a solicitation from a second fictitious consumer research company, "Midlands Data Research," seeking a response from those who "believe in the joys of sex and the complete awareness of those lusty and youthful lads and lasses of the neophite [sic] age." The letter never explained whether "neophite" referred to minors or young adults. Petitioner responded: "Please feel free to send me more information, I am interested in teenage sexuality. Please keep my name confidential."

Petitioner then heard from yet another Government creation, "Heartland Institute for a New Tomorrow" (HINT), which proclaimed that it was "an organization founded to protect and promote sexual freedom and freedom of choice. We believe that arbitrarily imposed legislative sanctions restricting your sexual freedom should be rescinded through the legislative process." The letter also enclosed a second survey. Petitioner indicated that his interest in "[p]reteen sex-homosexual" material was above average, but not high. In response to another question, petitioner wrote: "Not only sexual expression but freedom of the press is under attack. We must be ever vigilant to counter attack right wing fundamentalists who are determined to curtail our freedoms."

HINT replied, portraying itself as a lobbying organization seeking to repeal "all statutes which regulate sexual activities, except those laws which deal with violent behavior, such as rape. HINT is also lobbying to eliminate any legal definition of 'the age of consent.'" These lobbying efforts were to be funded by sales from a catalog to be published in the future "offering the sale of various items which we believe you will find to be both interesting and stimulating." HINT also provided computer matching of group members with similar survey responses; and, although petitioner was supplied with a list of potential "pen pals," he did not initiate any correspondence.

Nevertheless, the Government's "prohibited mailing specialist" began writing to petitioner, using the pseudonym "Carl Long." The letters employed a tactic known as "mirroring," which the inspector described as "reflect[ing] whatever the interests are of the person we are writing to." Petitioner responded at first, indicating that his interest was primarily in "male-male items." Inspector "Long" wrote back:

> My interests too are primarily male-male items. Are you satisfied with the type of VCR tapes available? Personally, I like the amateur stuff better if its [sic] well produced as it can get more kinky and also seems more real. I think the actors enjoy it more.

Petitioner responded:

> As far as my likes are concerned, I like good looking young guys (in their late teens and early 20's) doing their thing together.

Petitioner's letters to "Long" made no reference to child pornography. After writing two letters, petitioner discontinued the correspondence.

By March 1987, 34 months had passed since the Government obtained petitioner's name from the mailing list of the California bookstore, and 26 months had passed since the Postal Service had commenced its mailings to petitioner. Although petitioner had responded to surveys and letters, the Government had no evidence that petitioner had ever intentionally possessed or been exposed to child pornography. The Postal Service had not checked petitioner's mail to determine whether he was receiving questionable mailings from persons—other than the Government—involved in the child pornography industry.

At this point, a second Government agency, the Customs Service, included petitioner in its own child pornography sting, "Operation Borderline," after receiving his name on lists submitted by the Postal Service. Using the name of a fictitious Canadian company called "Produit Outaouais," the Customs Service mailed petitioner a brochure advertising photographs of young boys engaging in sex. Petitioner placed an order that was never filled.

The Postal Service also continued its efforts in the Jacobson case, writing to petitioner as the "Far Eastern Trading Company Ltd." The letter began:

> As many of you know, much hysterical nonsense has appeared in the American media concerning "pornography" and what must be done to stop it from coming across your borders. This brief letter does not allow us to give much comments; however, why is your government spending millions of dollars to exercise international censorship while tons of drugs, which makes yours the world's most crime ridden country are passed through easily.

The letter went on to say:

> [W]e have devised a method of getting these to you without prying eyes of U.S. Customs seizing your mail.... After consultations with American solicitors, we have been advised that once we have posted our material through your system, it cannot be opened for any inspection without authorization of a judge.

The letter invited petitioner to send for more information. It also asked petitioner to sign an affirmation that he was "not a law enforcement officer or agent of the U.S. Government acting in an undercover capacity for the purpose of entrapping Far Eastern Trading Company, its agents or customers." Petitioner responded. A catalog was sent, and petitioner ordered Boys Who Love Boys, a pornographic magazine depicting young boys engaged in various sexual activities. Petitioner was arrested after a controlled delivery of a photocopy of the magazine.

When petitioner was asked at trial why he placed such an order, he explained that the Government had succeeded in piquing his curiosity:

> Well, the statement was made of all the trouble and the hysteria over pornography and I wanted to see what the material was. It didn't describe the—I didn't know for sure what kind of sexual action they were referring to in the Canadian letter.

In petitioner's home, the Government found the Bare Boys magazines and materials that the Government had sent to him in the course of its protracted investigation, but no other materials that would indicate that petitioner collected, or was actively interested in, child pornography.

Petitioner was indicted for violating 18 U.S.C. § 2252(a)(2)(A). The trial court instructed the jury on the petitioner's entrapment defense,[1]

---

[1]   The jury was instructed:

As mentioned, one of the issues in this case is whether the defendant was entrapped. If the defendant was entrapped he must be found not guilty. The government has the burden of proving beyond a reasonable doubt that the defendant was not entrapped.

petitioner was convicted, and a divided Court of Appeals for the Eighth Circuit, sitting en banc, affirmed, concluding that "Jacobson was not entrapped as a matter of law." . . .

II

There can be no dispute about the evils of child pornography or the difficulties that laws and law enforcement have encountered in eliminating it. Likewise, there can be no dispute that the Government may use undercover agents to enforce the law. "It is well settled that the fact that officers or employees of the Government merely afford opportunities or facilities for the commission of the offense does not defeat the prosecution. Artifice and stratagem may be employed to catch those engaged in criminal enterprises." Sorrells v. United States (1932); Sherman v. United States (1958); United States v. Russell (1973).

In their zeal to enforce the law, however, Government agents may not originate a criminal design, implant in an innocent person's mind the disposition to commit a criminal act, and then induce commission of the crime so that the Government may prosecute. Where the Government has induced an individual to break the law and the defense of entrapment is at issue, as it was in this case, the prosecution must prove beyond reasonable doubt that the defendant was disposed to commit the criminal act prior to first being approached by Government agents.[2]

Thus, an agent deployed to stop the traffic in illegal drugs may offer the opportunity to buy or sell drugs and, if the offer is accepted, make an arrest on the spot or later. In such a typical case, or in a more elaborate "sting" operation involving government-sponsored fencing where the defendant is simply provided with the opportunity to commit a crime, the entrapment defense is of little use because the ready commission of the criminal act amply demonstrates the defendant's predisposition. Had the agents in this case simply offered petitioner the opportunity to order child pornography through the mails, and petitioner—who must be presumed to know the law—had promptly availed himself of this criminal

---

If the defendant before contact with law-enforcement officers or their agents did not have any intent or disposition to commit the crime charged and was induced or persuaded by law-enforcement officers o[r] their agents to commit that crime, then he was entrapped. On the other hand, if the defendant before contact with law-enforcement officers or their agents did have an intent or disposition to commit the crime charged, then he was not entrapped even though law-enforcement officers or their agents provided a favorable opportunity to commit the crime or made committing the crime easier or even participated in acts essential to the crime.

[2] Inducement is not at issue in this case. The Government does not dispute that it induced petitioner to commit the crime. The sole issue is whether the Government carried its burden of proving that petitioner was predisposed to violate the law before the Government intervened. The dissent is mistaken in claiming that this is an innovation in entrapment law and in suggesting that the Government's conduct prior to the moment of solicitation is irrelevant. The Court rejected these arguments six decades ago in Sorrells v. United States when the Court wrote that the Government may not punish an individual "for an alleged offense which is the product of the creative activity of its own officials" and that in such a case the Government "is in no position to object to evidence of the activities of its representatives in relation to the accused" . . .

opportunity, it is unlikely that his entrapment defense would have warranted a jury instruction.

But that is not what happened here. By the time petitioner finally placed his order, he had already been the target of 26 months of repeated mailings and communications from Government agents and fictitious organizations. Therefore, although he had become predisposed to break the law by May 1987, it is our view that the Government did not prove that this predisposition was independent and not the product of the attention that the Government had directed at petitioner since January 1985.

The prosecution's evidence of predisposition falls into two categories: evidence developed prior to the Postal Service's mail campaign, and that developed during the course of the investigation. The sole piece of preinvestigation evidence is petitioner's 1984 order and receipt of the Bare Boys magazines. But this is scant if any proof of petitioner's predisposition to commit an illegal act, the criminal character of which a defendant is presumed to know. It may indicate a predisposition to view sexually oriented photographs that are responsive to his sexual tastes; but evidence that merely indicates a generic inclination to act within a broad range, not all of which is criminal, is of little probative value in establishing predisposition.

Furthermore, petitioner was acting within the law at the time he received these magazines. Receipt through the mails of sexually explicit depictions of children for noncommercial use did not become illegal under federal law until May 1984, and Nebraska had no law that forbade petitioner's possession of such material until 1988. Evidence of predisposition to do what once was lawful is not, by itself, sufficient to show predisposition to do what is now illegal, for there is a common understanding that most people obey the law even when they disapprove of it. This obedience may reflect a generalized respect for legality or the fear of prosecution, but for whatever reason, the law's prohibitions are matters of consequence. Hence, the fact that petitioner legally ordered and received the Bare Boys magazines does little to further the Government's burden of proving that petitioner was predisposed to commit a criminal act. This is particularly true given petitioner's unchallenged testimony that he did not know until they arrived that the magazines would depict minors.

The prosecution's evidence gathered during the investigation also fails to carry the Government's burden. Petitioner's responses to the many communications prior to the ultimate criminal act were at most indicative of certain personal inclinations, including a predisposition to view photographs of preteen sex and a willingness to promote a given agenda by supporting lobbying organizations. Even so, petitioner's responses hardly support an inference that he would commit the crime of receiving child pornography through the mails. Furthermore, a person's inclinations and fantasies are his own and beyond the reach of government.

On the other hand, the strong arguable inference is that, by waving the banner of individual rights and disparaging the legitimacy and constitutionality of efforts to restrict the availability of sexually explicit materials, the Government not only excited petitioner's interest in sexually explicit materials banned by law but also exerted substantial pressure on petitioner to obtain and read such material as part of a fight against censorship and the infringement of individual rights. For instance, HINT described itself as "an organization founded to protect and promote sexual freedom and freedom of choice" and stated that "the most appropriate means to accomplish [its] objectives is to promote honest dialogue among concerned individuals and to continue its lobbying efforts with State Legislators." These lobbying efforts were to be financed through catalog sales. Mailings from the equally fictitious American Hedonist Society, and the correspondence from the nonexistent Carl Long, endorsed these themes.

Similarly, the two solicitations in the spring of 1987 raised the spectre of censorship while suggesting that petitioner ought to be allowed to do what he had been solicited to do. The mailing from the Customs Service referred to "the worldwide ban and intense enforcement on this type of material," observed that "what was legal and commonplace is now an 'underground' and secretive service," and emphasized that "[t]his environment forces us to take extreme measures" to ensure delivery. The Postal Service solicitation described the concern about child pornography as "hysterical nonsense," decried "international censorship," and assured petitioner, based on consultation with "American solicitors," that an order that had been posted could not be opened for inspection without authorization of a judge. It further asked petitioner to affirm that he was not a Government agent attempting to entrap the mail order company or its customers. In these particulars, both Government solicitations suggested that receiving this material was something that petitioner ought to be allowed to do.

Petitioner's ready response to these solicitations cannot be enough to establish beyond reasonable doubt that he was predisposed, prior to the Government acts intended to create predisposition, to commit the crime of receiving child pornography through the mails. The evidence that petitioner was ready and willing to commit the offense came only after the Government had devoted 2 1/2 years to convincing him that he had or should have the right to engage in the very behavior proscribed by law. Rational jurors could not say beyond a reasonable doubt that petitioner possessed the requisite predisposition prior to the Government's investigation and that it existed independent of the Government's many and varied approaches to petitioner. As was explained in Sherman, where entrapment was found as a matter of law, "the Government [may not] pla[y] on the weaknesses of an innocent party and beguil[e] him into committing crimes which he otherwise would not have attempted."

Law enforcement officials go too far when they implant in the mind of an innocent person the disposition to commit the alleged offense and induce its commission in order that they may prosecute. Like the *Sorrells* Court, we are unable to conclude that it was the intention of the Congress in enacting this statute that its processes of detection and enforcement should be abused by the instigation by government officials of an act on the part of persons otherwise innocent in order to lure them to its commission and to punish them. When the Government's quest for convictions leads to the apprehension of an otherwise law-abiding citizen who, if left to his own devices, likely would have never run afoul of the law, the courts should intervene.

Because we conclude that this is such a case and that the prosecution failed, as a matter of law, to adduce evidence to support the jury verdict that petitioner was predisposed, independent of the Government's acts and beyond a reasonable doubt, to violate the law by receiving child pornography through the mails, we reverse the Court of Appeals' judgment affirming the conviction of Keith Jacobson.

It is so ordered.

■ JUSTICE O'CONNOR, with whom THE CHIEF JUSTICE and JUSTICE KENNEDY join, and with whom JUSTICE SCALIA joins except as to Part II, dissenting.

Keith Jacobson was offered only two opportunities to buy child pornography through the mail. Both times, he ordered. Both times, he asked for opportunities to buy more. He needed no Government agent to coax, threaten, or persuade him; no one played on his sympathies, friendship, or suggested that his committing the crime would further a greater good. In fact, no Government agent even contacted him face to face. The Government contends that from the enthusiasm with which Mr. Jacobson responded to the chance to commit a crime, a reasonable jury could permissibly infer beyond a reasonable doubt that he was predisposed to commit the crime. I agree. . . .

The first time the Government sent Mr. Jacobson a catalog of illegal materials, he ordered a set of photographs advertised as picturing "young boys in sex action fun." He enclosed the following note with his order: "I received your brochure and decided to place an order. If I like your product, I will order more later." For reasons undisclosed in the record, Mr. Jacobson's order was never delivered.

The second time the Government sent a catalog of illegal materials, Mr. Jacobson ordered a magazine called "Boys Who Love Boys," described as: "11 year old and 14 year old boys get it on in every way possible. Oral, anal sex and heavy masturbation. If you love boys, you will be delighted with this." Along with his order, Mr. Jacobson sent the following note:

"Will order other items later. I want to be discreet in order to protect you and me."

Government agents admittedly did not offer Mr. Jacobson the chance to buy child pornography right away. Instead, they first sent questionnaires in order to make sure that he was generally interested in the subject matter. Indeed, a "cold call" in such a business would not only risk rebuff and suspicion, but might also shock and offend the uninitiated, or expose minors to suggestive materials. . . . Mr. Jacobson's responses to the questionnaires gave the investigators reason to think he would be interested in photographs depicting preteen sex.

The Court, however, concludes that a reasonable jury could not have found Mr. Jacobson to be predisposed beyond a reasonable doubt on the basis of his responses to the Government's catalogs, even though it admits that, by that time, he was predisposed to commit the crime. The Government, the Court holds, failed to provide evidence that Mr. Jacobson's obvious predisposition at the time of the crime "was independent and not the product of the attention that the Government had directed at petitioner." In so holding, I believe the Court fails to acknowledge the reasonableness of the jury's inference from the evidence, redefines "predisposition," and introduces a new requirement that Government sting operations have a reasonable suspicion of illegal activity before contacting a suspect.

I

This Court has held previously that a defendant's predisposition is to be assessed as of the time the Government agent first suggested the crime, not when the Government agent first became involved. Until the Government actually makes a suggestion of criminal conduct, it could not be said to have implanted in the mind of an innocent person the disposition to commit the alleged offense and induce its commission. Even in Sherman v. United States, in which the Court held that the defendant had been entrapped as a matter of law, the Government agent had repeatedly and unsuccessfully coaxed the defendant to buy drugs, ultimately succeeding only by playing on the defendant's sympathy. The Court found lack of predisposition based on the Government's numerous unsuccessful attempts to induce the crime, not on the basis of preliminary contacts with the defendant.

. . .

The rule that preliminary Government contact can create a predisposition has the potential to be misread by lower courts as well as criminal investigators as requiring that the Government must have sufficient evidence of a defendant's predisposition before it ever seeks to contact him. Surely the Court cannot intend to impose such a requirement, for it would mean that the Government must have a reasonable suspicion of criminal activity before it begins an investigation, a condition that we have never before imposed. The Court denies that its new rule will affect run-of-the-mill sting operations, and one hopes that it means what it says. Nonetheless, after this case, every defendant will claim that something the Government agent did before soliciting the crime "created" a predisposition that was not there before. For example, a bribetaker will claim that the description of the amount of money available was so enticing that it implanted a disposition to accept the bribe later offered. A drug buyer will claim that the description of the drug's purity and effects was so tempting that it created the urge to try it for the first time. In short, the Court's opinion could be read to prohibit the Government from advertising the seductions of criminal activity as part of its sting operation, for fear of creating a predisposition in its suspects. That limitation would be especially likely to hamper sting operations such as this one, which mimic the advertising done by genuine purveyors of pornography. No doubt the Court would protest that its opinion does not stand for so broad a proposition, but the apparent lack of a principled basis for distinguishing these scenarios exposes a flaw in the more limited rule the Court today adopts.

II

The second puzzling thing about the Court's opinion is its redefinition of predisposition. The Court acknowledges that petitioner's responses to the many communications prior to the ultimate criminal act were indicative of certain personal inclinations, including a predisposition to view photographs of preteen sex. If true, this should have settled the matter; Mr. Jacobson was predisposed to engage in the illegal conduct. Yet, the Court concludes, "petitioner's responses hardly support an inference that he would commit the crime of receiving child pornography through the mails."

The Court seems to add something new to the burden of proving predisposition. Not only must the Government show that a defendant was predisposed to engage in the illegal conduct, here, receiving photographs of minors engaged in sex, but also that the defendant was predisposed to break the law knowingly in order to do so. The statute violated here, however, does not require proof of specific intent to break the law; it requires only knowing receipt of visual depictions produced by using minors engaged in sexually explicit conduct. Under the Court's analysis, however, the Government must prove more to show predisposition than it need prove in order to convict.

The Court ignores the judgment of Congress that specific intent is not an element of the crime of receiving sexually explicit photographs of minors. The elements of predisposition should track the elements of the crime. The predisposition requirement is meant to eliminate the entrapment defense for those defendants who would have committed the crime anyway, even absent Government inducement. . . .

The crux of the Court's concern in this case is that the Government went too far and "abused" the " 'processes of detection and enforcement' " by luring an innocent person to violate the law. Consequently, the Court holds that the Government failed to prove beyond a reasonable doubt that Mr. Jacobson was predisposed to commit the crime. It was, however, the jury's task, as the conscience of the community, to decide whether Mr. Jacobson was a willing participant in the criminal activity here or an innocent dupe. The jury is the traditional defense against arbitrary law enforcement. Indeed, in *Sorrells*, in which the Court was also concerned about overzealous law enforcement, the Court did not decide itself that the Government conduct constituted entrapment, but left the issue to the jury. There is no dispute that the jury in this case was fully and accurately instructed on the law of entrapment, and nonetheless found Mr. Jacobson guilty. Because I believe there was sufficient evidence to uphold the jury's verdict, I respectfully dissent.

NOTES AND QUESTIONS

1. In the states, the defense of entrapment developed by court decision—as in the federal courts—and also by statutory recognition. The California Supreme Court adopted an unusual approach to entrapment defenses in People v. Barraza, 23 Cal.3d 675, 153 Cal.Rptr. 459, 591 P.2d 947 (1979):

MOSK, J.

* * *

The principle currently applied in California represents a hybrid position, fusing elements of both the subjective and objective theories of entrapment. In People v. Benford (1959) 53 Cal.2d 1, 9, 345 P.2d 928, this court unanimously embraced the public policy/deterrence rationale that Justices Roberts and Frankfurter had so persuasively urged. In doing so, we ruled inadmissible on the issue of entrapment the most prejudicial inquiries that are allowed under the subjective theory, i.e., evidence that the defendant "had previously committed similar crimes or had the reputation of being engaged in the commission of such crimes or was suspected by the police of criminal activities. . . ." Despite the lessons of *Benford*, however, this court has continued to maintain that entrapment depends upon where the intent to commit the crime originated. People v. Moran (1970) 1 Cal.3d 755, 760, 83 Cal.Rptr. 411, 463 P.2d 763.

Chief Justice Traynor, dissenting in *Moran*, in an opinion joined by two other justices of this court, recognized that in thus departing from the rationale adopted in *Benford*, we have seriously undermined the deterrent effect of the entrapment defense on impermissible police conduct. He reasoned that attempts to fix the origin of intent or determine the defendant's criminal predisposition divert the court's attention from the only proper subject of focus in the entrapment defense: the dubious police conduct which the court must deter. The success of an entrapment defense should not turn on differences among defendants; we are not concerned with who first conceived or who willingly, or reluctantly, acquiesced in a criminal project. What we do care about is how much and what manner of persuasion, pressure, and cajoling are brought to bear by law enforcement officials to induce persons to commit crimes. Even though California courts do not permit introduction of the highly prejudicial evidence of subjective predisposition allowed in jurisdictions following the federal rule, our more limited focus on the character and intent of the accused is still misplaced and impairs our courts in their task of assuring the lawfulness of law enforcement activity.

Commentators on the subject have overwhelmingly favored judicial decision of the issue by application of a test which looks only to the nature and extent of police activity in the criminal enterprise. . . . In recent years several state courts (see Grossman v. State (Alaska 1969) 457 P.2d 226; People v. Turner (1973) 390 Mich. 7, 210 N.W.2d 336; State v. Mullen (Iowa 1974) supra, 216 N.W.2d 375) and legislatures (see N.D.Cent.Code, § 12.1–05–11 (1976); N.H.Rev.Stat.Ann., § 626:5 (1974); Pa.Const.Stat.Ann., tit. 18, § 313 (Purdon 1973); Haw.Rev.Stat., § 702–237) have recognized that such a test is more consistent with and better promotes the underlying purpose of the entrapment defense. Such support for the position no doubt derives from a developing awareness that "entrapment is a facet of a broader problem. Along with illegal search and seizures, wiretapping, false arrest, illegal detention and the third degree, it is a type of lawless law enforcement. They all spring from common motivations. Each is a substitute for skillful and scientific investigation. Each is condoned by the sinister sophism that the end, when dealing with known criminals or the 'criminal classes,' justifies the employment of illegal means." (Donnelly, *Judicial Control of Informants, Spies, Stool Pigeons, and Agent Provocateurs* (1951) 60 YALE L.J. 1091, 1111.)

For all the foregoing reasons we hold that the proper test of entrapment in California is the following: was the conduct of the law enforcement agent likely to induce a normally law-abiding person to commit the offense? For the purposes of this test, we presume that such a person would normally resist the temptation to commit a crime presented by the simple opportunity to act unlawfully. Official conduct that does no more than offer that opportunity to the suspect—for example, a decoy program—is therefore permissible; but it is impermissible for the police or their agents to pressure the suspect by overbearing conduct such as badgering, cajoling, importuning, or other affirmative acts likely to induce a normally law-abiding person to commit the crime.

Although the determination of what police conduct is impermissible must to some extent proceed on an ad hoc basis, guidance will generally be found in the application of one or both of two principles. First, if the actions of the law enforcement agent would generate in a normally law-abiding person a motive for the crime other than ordinary criminal intent, entrapment will be established. An example of such conduct would be an appeal by the police that would induce such a person to commit the act because of friendship or sympathy, instead of a desire for personal gain or other typical criminal purpose. Second, affirmative police conduct that would make commission of the crime unusually attractive to a normally law-abiding person will likewise constitute entrapment. Such conduct would include, for example, a guarantee that the act is not illegal or the offense will go undetected, an offer of exorbitant consideration or any similar enticement.

Finally, while the inquiry must focus primarily on the conduct of the law enforcement agent, that conduct is not to be viewed in a vacuum; it should also be judged by the effect it would have on a normally law-abiding person situated in the circumstances of the case at hand. Among the circumstances that may be relevant for this purpose, for example, are the transactions preceding the offense, the suspect's response to the inducements of the officer, the gravity of the crime, and the difficulty of detecting instances of its commission. We reiterate, however, that under this test such matters as the character of the suspect, his predisposition to commit the offense, and his subjective intent are irrelevant.

RICHARDSON, J.

I respectfully dissent, . . . from that portion of the majority's opinion which establishes a new test for the defense of entrapment.

As the majority concedes, in determining the existence of an entrapment, the United States Supreme Court has consistently rejected the "objective" ("hypothetical person") test which the majority adopts in favor of the "subjective" ("origin of intent") test.

In Sorrells v. United States (1932) 287 U.S. 435, 53 S.Ct. 210, Sherman v. United States (1958) 356 U.S. 369, 78 S.Ct. 819, and recently in United States v. Russell (1973) 411 U.S. 423, 93 S.Ct. 1637, the high court has approved and reapproved the "subjective" test. Following this lead, the federal courts and the courts of the overwhelming majority of states, including California, apply the "subjective" test, thereby keeping attention properly focused on the unique interrelationship of the police and the particular defendant who is asserting the defense of entrapment.

The majority now proposes to ban consideration of the particular defendant and replace him with a hypothetical "normally law-abiding person" who is described as "a person [who] would normally resist the temptation to commit a crime presented by the simple opportunity to act unlawfully." The briefest reflection reveals the difficulties inherent in this definition. The individual who has *never* committed a criminal act can safely be categorized as a "normally law-abiding person" since presumably his unblemished record is proof of his ability to resist temptation. However, what of the individual who has transgressed in the past either once or several times? Is he no longer "*normally* law-abiding"? Is "normally" synonymous with "generally"? If it may be drawn at all, the line between "normally law-abiding" individuals and "others" is not so easily fixed as the majority suggests.

The fallacy underlying the majority's thesis, of course, is that in the very real world of criminal conduct there are no hypothetical people. To attempt to judge police conduct in a vacuum is to engage in a futile and meaningless exercise in semantics. It is the recognition of this precise fact that has restrained the United States Supreme Court from discarding the subjective test whereby attention is pointed at the particular defendant rather than on some imaginary or fictitious person. The majority abandons the actual for the hypothetical. It thereby substitutes the unreal for the real, with unnecessary complications that inevitably result therefrom.

Further, by adopting an "objective" test, the majority does not really eliminate the "subjective" test. Even if the jury makes a finding adverse to the defendant pursuant to the "objective" test, the defendant may still presumably argue entrapment to the jury using the "subjective" standard to negate intent. The question of what the defendant intended is always relevant. Indeed, in the present case defendant admitted commission of the act. He denied only the requisite intent. The majority ignores entirely this problem of the double assertion of the entrapment defense.

The issue of entrapment is a factual matter, the determination of which is of critical importance to both parties. Regardless of any salutary effect which a trial court opinion might have on police administration, the matter is properly entrusted to the jury and should remain within its province.

2. Some crimes do not involve a victim in the traditional sense because all are actually participants and no one sees himself as victimized. Hence, no one files a complaint with the police following the criminal offense. Examples of so-called victimless crimes include illicit narcotics transactions and dealing in non-taxed alcoholic beverages. In these kinds of cases, entrapment frequently becomes an issue. While use of full-time government undercover agents, as in *Russell, Hampton,* and *Jacobson* is one answer to the difficult enforcement problem, often agents need a long time to infiltrate the "criminal" world to such a degree that they are trusted. Witness the delay between the first contact of the target and prosecution in *Jacobson*. Further, the procedure is often dangerous. To save time, reduce the danger to government employees, and assist undercover agents, a law enforcement agency will sometimes use an underworld person to bait the trap, thereby stimulating the unlawful conduct by the defendant. Thus, in Williamson v. United States, 311 F.2d 441 (5th Cir. 1962), the Court reversed Williamson's conviction for possession of untaxed whiskey because the government's informer was to be paid a $200 fee contingent upon his securing evidence against Williamson. In United States v. Curry, 284 F. Supp. 458 (N.D.Ill.1968), the Court granted Curry's post-trial motion for acquittal largely because the unlawful narcotic sale had been arranged by an informer who himself was a defendant in a federal narcotics complaint and had been offered a dismissal of the charge by government agents if he would develop other narcotic cases for the government.

However, not all contingent arrangements are condemned to the extent of reversing convictions. In United States v. Costner, 359 F.2d 969 (6th Cir. 1966), the Court affirmed a conviction, distinguishing the contingent fee arrangement from that in *Williamson* because although Williamson was named as the object of the investigation, no one in particular was singled out in *Costner*.

In accord with *Costner*, see People v. Mills, 40 Ill.2d 4, 237 N.E.2d 697 (1968). *See also* United States v. Baxter, 342 F.2d 773 (6th Cir. 1965), cert. denied 381 U.S. 934, 85 S.Ct. 1766, 14 L.Ed.2d 699.

Heard v. United States, 414 F.2d 884 (5th Cir. 1969), distinguished *Williamson* because in *Heard* the contingent fee informer was instructed to develop an unlawful narcotics sale against a person named Walker. Heard was an unexpected participant with Walker. Hence, while the contingent arrangement might have tainted a prosecution against Walker, the contingent arrangement played no part in Heard's prosecution.

In Hill v. United States, 328 F.2d 988 (5th Cir. 1964), another case dealing with possession of untaxed whiskey, the informer who induced the sale of untaxed whiskey was offered a $300 reward if Hill were caught. However, the Court refused to reverse the conviction distinguishing its own Fifth Circuit Williamson case from *Hill* on the basis that Hill had a past record of convictions for the same offense and the complaint of Hill's neighbors about Hill's illegal activities initiated the investigation.

The outstanding article by Dean Marcus, *The Development of Entrapment Law*, 33 WAYNE L. REV. 5 (1986) mentioned in the Introduction was adopted from the book by Marcus, THE ENTRAPMENT DEFENSE, 1986.

3. For another excellent overview of entrapment issues, see Park, *The Entrapment Controversy*, 60 MINN. L. REV. 163 (1976). Professor Park has thought through the implications of alternative approaches to entrapment in various factual situations and has offered some original insights.

B. LIMITATIONS ON USE OF THE DEFENSE

Mathews v. United States

Supreme Court of the United States, 1988.
485 U.S. 58, 108 S.Ct. 883, 99 L.Ed.2d 54.

■ CHIEF JUSTICE REHNQUIST delivered the opinion of the Court.

This case requires the Court to decide whether a defendant in a federal criminal prosecution who denies commission of the crime may nonetheless have the jury instructed, where the evidence warrants, on the affirmative defense of entrapment. The United States Court of

Appeals for the Seventh Circuit upheld the ruling of the District Court, which had refused to instruct the jury as to entrapment because petitioner would not admit committing all of the elements of the crime of accepting a bribe. This holding conflicts with decisions of other Courts of Appeals, which have taken a variety of approaches to the question. We granted certiorari to resolve this conflict, and we now reverse.

Petitioner was employed by the Small Business Administration (SBA) in Milwaukee, Wisconsin, and was responsible for the SBA's "8A Program," which provided aid to certain small businesses. Under the program, the SBA obtained government contracts and subcontracted them to program participants. The SBA would then assist the participants in performing the contracts. Midwest Knitting Mills, whose president was James DeShazer, was one of the participants in the 8A Program. DeShazer's principal contact at the SBA was petitioner.

In October 1984, DeShazer complained to a government customer that petitioner had repeatedly asked for loans. DeShazer believed that petitioner was not providing Midwest with certain 8A Program benefits because DeShazer had not made the requested loans. In early 1985, the FBI arranged for DeShazer to assist in the investigation resulting from his complaint. Under FBI surveillance, DeShazer offered petitioner a loan that, according to DeShazer, petitioner had previously requested. Petitioner agreed to accept the loan, and two months later, DeShazer met petitioner at a restaurant and gave him the money. Petitioner was immediately arrested and charged with accepting a gratuity in exchange for an official act. 18 U.S.C. § 201(g).

Before trial petitioner filed a motion *in limine* seeking to raise an entrapment defense. The District Court denied the motion, ruling that entrapment was not available to petitioner because he would not admit all of the elements (including the requisite mental state) of the offense charged. The District Court did, however, allow petitioner to argue as his first line of defense that his acts "were procurred [sic] by the overt acts of the principle [sic] witness of the Government, Mr. DeShazer."

At trial, the Government argued that petitioner had accepted the loan in return for cooperation in SBA matters. The Government called DeShazer, who testified both that petitioner had repeatedly asked for loans and that he and petitioner had agreed that the loan at issue would result in SBA-provided benefits for Midwest. The Government also played tape recordings of conversations between DeShazer and petitioner in which they discussed the loan. Petitioner testified in his own defense that although he had accepted the loan, he believed it was a personal loan unrelated to his duties at the SBA. Petitioner stated that he and DeShazer were friends and that he had accepted a personal loan from DeShazer previously. According to petitioner, he was in dire financial straits when DeShazer broached the possibility of providing a loan. Petitioner also testified that DeShazer had stated that he needed quickly to get rid of the money that he was offering to petitioner because he had been hiding the money from his wife and was concerned that she would be upset if she discovered this secret; DeShazer had also stated at one point that if petitioner did not take the money soon, DeShazer would be tempted to spend it.

At the close of the trial, petitioner moved for a "mistrial" because of the District Court's refusal to instruct the jury as to entrapment. The District Court noted that the evidence of entrapment was "shaky at best," but rather than premise its denial of petitioner's motion on that ground, the court reaffirmed its earlier ruling that as a matter of law, petitioner was not entitled to an entrapment instruction because he would not admit committing all elements of the crime charged. The jury subsequently found petitioner guilty.

The United States Court of Appeals for the Seventh Circuit affirmed the District Court's refusal to allow petitioner to argue entrapment . . .

We granted certiorari, to consider under what circumstances a defendant is entitled to an entrapment instruction. We hold that even if the defendant denies one or more elements of the crime, he is entitled to an entrapment instruction whenever there is sufficient evidence from which a reasonable jury could find entrapment.

Because the parties agree as to the basics of the affirmative defense of entrapment as developed by this Court, there is little reason to chronicle its history in detail. Suffice it to say that the Court has consistently adhered to the view, first enunciated in *Sorrells v. United States* (1932), that a valid entrapment defense has two related elements: government inducement of the crime, and a lack of predisposition on the part of the defendant to engage in the criminal conduct. Predisposition, "the principal element in the defense of entrapment," focuses upon whether the defendant was an "unwary innocent" or instead, an "unwary criminal" who readily availed himself of the opportunity to perpetrate the crime. The question of entrapment is generally one for the jury, rather than for the court.

The Government insists that a defendant should not be allowed both to deny the offense and to rely on the affirmative defense of entrapment. Because entrapment presupposes the commission of a crime, a jury could not logically conclude that the defendant had both failed to commit the elements of the offense *and* been entrapped. According to the Government, petitioner is asking to "clai[m] the right to swear that he had no criminal intent and in the same breath to argue that he had one that did not originate with him."

As a general proposition a defendant is entitled to an instruction as to any recognized defense for which there exists evidence sufficient for a reasonable jury to find in his favor. Stevenson v. United States, 162 U.S. 313, 16 S.Ct. 839, 40 L.Ed. 980 (1896); 4 C. Torcia, WHARTON'S CRIMINAL PROCEDURE § 538, p. 11 (12th ed. 1976) (hereinafter Wharton). . . . In *Stevenson*, this Court reversed a murder conviction arising out of a gunfight in the Indian Territory. The principal holding of the Court was that the evidence was sufficient to entitle the defendant to a manslaughter instruction, but the Court also decided that the defendant was entitled as well to have the jury instructed on self-defense. The affirmative defense of self-defense is, of course, inconsistent with the claim that the defendant killed in the heat of passion.

* * *

The Government argues that allowing a defendant to rely on inconsistent defenses will encourage perjury, lead to jury confusion, and subvert the truthfinding function of the trial. These same concerns are, however, present in the civil context, yet inconsistency is expressly allowed under the Federal Rules of Civil Procedure. We do not think that allowing inconsistency necessarily sanctions perjury. Here petitioner wished to testify that he had no intent to commit the crime, and have his attorney argue to the jury that if it concluded otherwise, then it should consider whether that intent was the result of government inducement. The jury would have considered inconsistent defenses, but the petitioner would not have necessarily testified untruthfully.

We would not go so far as to say that charges on inconsistent defenses may not on occasion increase the risk of perjury, but particularly in the case of entrapment we think the practical consequences will be less burdensome than the Government fears. The Court of Appeals in United States v. Demma, 523 F.2d 981, 985 (C.A.9 1975) (en banc), observed:

> Of course, it is very unlikely that the defendant will be able to prove entrapment without testifying and, in the course of testifying, without admitting that he did the acts charged. . . . When he takes the stand, the defendant forfeits his right to remain silent, subjects himself to all the rigors of cross-examination, including impeachment, and exposes himself to prosecution for perjury. Inconsistent testimony by the defendant seriously impairs and potentially destroys his credibility. While we hold that a defendant may both deny the acts and other elements necessary to constitute the crime charged and at the same time claim entrapment, the high risks to him make it unlikely as a strategic matter that he will choose to do so.

The Government finally contends that since the entrapment defense is not of "constitutional dimension," and that since it is "relatively limited," Congress would be free to make the entrapment defense available on whatever conditions and to whatever category of defendants it believed appropriate. Congress, of course, has never spoken on the subject, and so the decision is left to the courts. We are simply not persuaded by the Government's arguments that we should make the availability of an instruction on entrapment where the evidence justifies it subject to a requirement of consistency to which no other such defense is subject.

The Government contends as an alternative basis for affirming the judgment below that the evidence at trial was insufficient to support an instruction on the defense of entrapment. Of course evidence that government agents merely afforded an opportunity or facilities for the commission of the crime would be insufficient to warrant such an instruction. But this question was pretermitted by the Court of Appeals, and it will be open for consideration by that court on remand.

Reversed.

■ JUSTICE KENNEDY took no part in the consideration or decision of this case.

■ JUSTICE BRENNAN, concurring.

I join the Court's opinion. I write separately only because I have previously joined or written four opinions dissenting from this Court's holdings that the defendant's predisposition is relevant to the entrapment defense. Although some governmental misconduct might be sufficiently egregious to violate due process, my differences with the Court have been based on statutory interpretation and federal common law, not on the constitution. Were I judging on a clean slate, I would still be inclined to adopt the view that the entrapment defense should focus exclusively on the government's conduct. But I am not writing on a clean slate; the Court has spoken definitively on this point. Therefore I bow to *stare decisis*, and today join the judgment and reasoning of the Court.

■ JUSTICE SCALIA, concurring.

I concur in the judgment of the Court because in my view the defense of entrapment will rarely be genuinely inconsistent with the defense on the merits, and when genuine inconsistency exists its effect in destroying the defendant's credibility will suffice to protect the interests of justice.

The typical case presenting the issue before us here is one in which the defendant introduces evidence to the effect that he did not commit the unlawful acts, or did not commit them with the requisite unlawful intent, and also introduces evidence to show his lack of predisposition and inordinate government inducement. There is nothing inconsistent in these showings. The inconsistency alleged by the Government is a purely formal one, which arises only if entrapment is defined to require not only (1) inordinate government inducement to commit a crime, (2) directed at a person not predisposed to commit the crime, but also (3) causing that person to commit the crime. If the third element is added to the definition, counsel's argument to the jury cannot claim entrapment without admitting the crime. But I see no reason why the third element is essential, unless it is for the very purpose of rendering the defense unavailable without admission of the crime. Surely it does not add anything of substance to the findings the jury must make, since findings of (1) inordinate inducement plus (2) lack of predisposition will almost inevitably produce a conclusion of (3) causality. To be sure, entrapment cannot be available as a defense unless a crime by the object of the entrapment is established, since if there is no crime there is nothing to defend against; but in that sense all affirmative defenses assume commission of the crime.

My point is not that entrapment must be defined to exclude element (3). Whether it is or not, since that element seems to me unnecessary to achieve the social policy fostered by the defense I am not willing to declare the defense unavailable when it produces the formal inconsistency of the defendant's simultaneously denying the crime and asserting entrapment which assumes commission of the crime. I would not necessarily accept such formal inconsistency for other defenses, where the element contradicted is a functionally essential element of the defense.

Of course in the entrapment context, as elsewhere, the defendant's case may involve genuine, *non* formal inconsistency. The defendant might testify, for example, that he was not in the motel room where the illegal drugs changed hands, and that the drugs were pressed upon him in the motel room by agents of the Government. But that kind of genuine inconsistency here, as elsewhere, is self-penalizing. There is nothing distinctive about entrapment that justifies a special prophylactic rule.

■ JUSTICE WHITE, with whom JUSTICE BLACKMUN joins, dissenting.

At his criminal trial, petitioner took the stand and flatly denied accepting a loan "for or because of any official act." Petitioner later moved for a mistrial because the District Court would not permit him to rely on that testimony while he simultaneously argued that, in fact, he *had* accepted a loan for an official act, but only at the Government's instigation. Today, the Court holds that this rather sensible ruling on the part of the District Court constitutes reversible error. The reasons the Court offers for reaching this conclusion are not at all persuasive, and I respectfully dissent.

I

The Court properly recognizes that its result is not compelled by the Constitution. As the Court acknowledges, petitioner has no Fifth or Sixth Amendment right to conduct the inconsistent entrapment defense that he wished to mount at trial. And yet, if the Constitution does not compel reversal of the decision below, then what does?

Certainly not any Act of Congress, or the Federal Rules of Criminal Procedure. As the majority candidly admits, "Congress . . . has never spoken on the subject [at issue here], and so the decision is left to the courts." Moreover, the Court also frankly notes that while the Federal Rules of Civil Procedure contain a provision expressly authorizing inconsistent defenses, Federal Rule Civil Procedure 8(e)(2), the Federal Criminal Rules are without any such authorization. Indeed, the rather scant authority the majority cites in support of its view that inconsistent defenses are generally permitted in criminal trials is strongly suggestive of just how extraordinary such pleadings are in the criminal context.

Nor is the result the Court reaches urged by a predominance of authority in the lower courts. As the Court recognizes, only two Circuits have held, as the Court does today, that a criminal defendant may deny committing the elements of a crime, and then contend that the Government entrapped him into the offense. The remaining Circuits are far more restrained in their allowance of such inconsistent defenses, divided along the lines the majority discusses in its opinion.

Thus, neither the Constitution, nor a statute, nor the Criminal Rules, nor the bulk of authority compels us to reverse petitioner's conviction. Nor does the Court claim support from any of these sources for its decision. Instead, the majority rests almost exclusively on an application of the "general proposition [that] a defendant is entitled to an instruction as to any legally sufficient defense for which there exists evidence sufficient for a reasonable jury to find in his favor." There are several reasons, however, why this "general proposition" is inapposite here.

II

First, there is the unique nature of the entrapment defense. There is a valuable purpose served by having civil litigants plead alternative defenses which may be legally inconsistent. Allowing a tort defendant to claim both that he owed no duty-of-care to the plaintiff, but that if he did, he met that duty, preserves possible alternative defenses under which the defendant is entitled to relief. It prevents formalities of pleadings, or rigid application of legal doctrines, from standing in the way of the equitable resolution of a civil dispute. The same may be true for *some* criminal defenses (such as "self-defense" or "provocation") where a defendant may truthfully testify as to the facts of the crime, leaving it to his counsel to argue that these facts make out, as a matter of law, several possible defenses.

But the entrapment defense, by contrast, "is a relatively limited defense;" it is only available to "a defendant who has committed all the elements of a proscribed offense." Thus, when a defendant (as petitioner did here) testifies that he did not commit the elements of the offense he is charged with, the defense of entrapment is *not* a plausible alternate legal theory of the case; rather, it is a proper defense *only* if the accused is lying. We have rejected before the notion that a defendant has a right to lie at trial, or a right to solicit his attorney's aid in executing such a defense strategy. And there is respectable authority for concluding that no legitimate end of the criminal justice system is served by requiring a trial court to entertain such tactics, in the form of an entrapment defense which is at odds with the defendant's own testimony.

Allowing such inconsistency in defense tactics invites the scourge of an effective criminal justice system: perjury. In the past, we have taken extraordinary steps to combat perjury in criminal trials; these steps have even included permitting the admission of otherwise inadmissible evidence to prevent a defendant from procuring an acquittal via false testimony. Yet today, the Court reaches a result which it concedes "may . . . on occasion" increase the risk of perjury. This is reason enough to reject the Court's result. Worse still, the majority's prognostication may well be an understatement. Even if—as the Court suggests,— inconsistent defenses do not measurably increase the frequency of perjury in civil trials, the risk of perjury in a criminal trial is always greater than in a civil setting because the stakes are so much higher. Absent some constitutional or statutory mandate to conduct criminal trials in a particular way, we should be taking steps to minimize, not increase, the danger of perjured testimony.

* * *

Finally, even if the Court's decision does not result in increased perjury at criminal trials, it will—at the very least—result in increased confusion among criminal juries. The lower courts have rightly warned that jury confusion is likely to result from allowing a defendant to say "I did not do it" while his lawyer argues "He did it, but the government tricked him into it." Creating such confusion may enable some defendants to win acquittal on the entrapment defense, but only under the peculiar circumstances where a jury rejects the defendant's own stated view of the facts. We have not previously endorsed defense efforts to prevail at trial by playing such "shell games" with the jury; rather, we have written that "[a] defendant has no entitlement to the luck of a lawless decisionmaker." Nor, it should be added, is there any entitlement to a baffled decisionmaker.

III

Ultimately, only the petitioner knows whether he accepted a loan in exchange for an official act, or whether he obtained it as a personal favor. Today, the Court holds that petitioner has a right to take the stand and claim the latter, while having his attorney argue that he was entrapped into doing the former. Nothing counsels such a result—let alone compels it. Hence this dissent.

NOTES

1. State courts have not been kind to the *Mathews* approach. The majority of state courts that have considered the issue continue to hold that the entrapment defense "is one in which the defendant admits doing the act but seeks to justify, excuse, or mitigate it." People v. Hendrickson, 45 P.3d 786 (Colo. App. 2001). See, for instance, the Supreme Courts of Florida and Arizona, which have also rejected the *Mathews* rule and decided to continue to follow earlier precedents prohibiting a defendant from interposing an entrapment defense unless she first admits commission of the crime charged. Since *Mathews* involved a non-constitutional interpretation of federal rules of criminal procedure, the state courts were not required to follow it, and both courts declined the opportunity to do so voluntarily.

In *Wilson v. State*, 577 So.2d 1300 (Fla. 1991), the defendant was charged with the sale of cocaine and possession with intent to distribute. Because he denied committing the offenses, the trial judge refused to give an entrapment instruction based on evidence that a police officer gave him $20 with which to buy, and give to her, a small piece of crack cocaine. The Supreme Court was persuaded by Justice White's dissent in *Mathews* that permitting inconsistent defenses fosters perjury, and therefore adhered to its earlier decisions refusing to allow a defendant to argue entrapment unless she admits commission of the charged offense. However, the court would permit a defendant to plead both entrapment and innocence if the two positions are not inconsistent.

In *State v. Soule*, 168 Ariz. 134, 811 P.2d 1071 (1991), the court's majority was satisfied to adhere to existing state precedent, which follows the traditional and prevailing view, requiring a defendant to admit all elements of an offense before he can avail himself of the defense of entrapment. The court said, "To allow a defendant to testify as to two defenses that cannot *both* be true is equivalent to sanctioning a defendant's perjury." Furthermore, said the court, the jury is likely to be confused by allowing inconsistent defenses: "What must the jury think when the defendant testifies that he had nothing to do with the sale of narcotics and then the defendant's attorney tells the jury that, yes, the defendant did commit the crime but was entrapped?"

The dissenting justices would have followed the *Mathews* rule, maintaining that the defense will not truly be inconsistent in many cases, and that where it is, the jurors will be able to handle it.

2. For some other writings on the issues covered in these cases, see, Jacqueline E. Ross, *Tradeoffs in Undercover Investigations: A Comparative Perspective*, 69 U.CHICAGO L. REV. 1501 (2002); Fred Warren Bennett, *From Sorrells to Jacobson: Reflections on Six Decades of Entrapment Law, and Related Defenses, in Federal Court*, 27 WAKE FOREST L. REV. 829 (1992); Christopher D. Moore, *The Elusive Foundation of the Entrapment Defense*, NW. U. L. REV. 1151 (1995); Laura Gardner Webster, *Building a Better Mousetrap: Reconstructing Federal Entrapment Theory From Sorrells to Matthews*, 32 ARIZ. L. REV. 605 (1990); Bennett L. Gershman, *Abscam, The Judiciary, and the Ethics of Entrapment (Comment)*, 91 YALE L.J. 1565 (1982); Elliott Rothstein, *United States v. Hollingsworth: The Entrapment Defense and the Neophyte Criminal—When the Commission of a Criminal Act Does Not Constitute A Crime*, 17 W.NEW ENG. L. REV. 3–3 (1995).

C. DUE PROCESS VIOLATIONS *OR* ENTRAPMENT AS A MATTER OF LAW

The objective approach urged upon the Court by the *Sorrells* concurring opinion of Justice Roberts, supra, has been seen as a rule wherein entrapment was established as a matter of law if the governmental conduct was deemed to be so outrageous that a prosecution ought not to be permitted, even if the putative defendant was predisposed toward committing the offense. While the *Russell* Supreme Court had never encountered such outrageous conduct, it left the door open for that eventuality. The Court's opinion stated:

> While we may some day be presented with a situation in which the conduct of law enforcement agents is so outrageous that due process principles would absolutely bar the government from invoking judicial processes to obtain a conviction, . . . the instant case is distinctly not of that breed. *Russell, supra* at p. 1097.

The language of the Court seems to couch "entrapment as a matter of law" in constitutional due process terms. The eventuality of encountering such "outrageous" police conduct is one that many lower courts seem to believe is not nearly as remote as the *Russell* court intimates.

1. ENTRAPMENT AS A MATTER OF LAW

United States v. Knox

United States Court of Appeals, Fifth Circuit, 1997.
112 F.3d 802.

■ DeMoss, Circuit Judge:

Defendant/Appellant Reverend David Brace was pastor of the Faith Metro Church in Wichita, Kansas. Faith Metro had financial difficulties and, by late 1993, was heavily in debt. The church had to pay over $60,000 per month in debt service and needed to raise $10 million to pay its bondholders and other creditors. In an effort to raise the money, Brace hired a Houston financial consulting firm, First Diversified Financial Services, in early 1994. Brace met with Mike Clark, the president of First Diversified, and Clark's assistant, 24-year-old Defendant/Appellant Shannon Knox. Brace paid First Diversified $75,000 to prepare a prospectus for a $10.8 million limited private offering by Faith Metro.

Under the terms of the prospectus, Faith Metro offered 432 units of senior secured notes bearing 12.5% interest. The units were $25,000 each, with a minimum subscription of two units ($50,000). If all units were sold, $10.8 million would be raised, of which $9.375 million went to the church. Payment on the notes would begin in September 1995 with quarterly payments of $337,500. Thus, interest of $112,500 accrued monthly on the notes. The church could begin repaying the principal any time after December 31, 1996, and the notes matured on December 31, 1999. Thus, under the terms of the prospectus, Faith Metro would have use of $9.375 million for up to five years, accruing $112,500 per month in interest (paid quarterly), with the principal of $10.8 million due for repayment on December 31, 1999.

The first printing of the prospectus was on September 1, 1994. Knox sent the prospectus to approximately 40 broker dealers, and received responses from two. The second printing of the prospectus was on December 1, 1994. Copies were sent to 32 or 33 broker dealers, and Knox received responses from three. None of these responses proved fruitful and, ultimately, no money was raised through the private offering.

In October or November 1994, Knox met Roy Clarkston, who worked for the Brazos Valley Small Business Development Center. Clarkston had several clients in the Bryan-College Station area interested in private placements, so Clark, who was also at the meeting, gave Clarkston a copy of the Faith Metro prospectus. In mid to late February 1995, Clarkston told Knox that he had several potential investors in San Antonio. Clarkston told Knox that he knew them through his business dealings in South and Central America. Brace was not present at any of these meetings and did not meet Clarkston until March 24, 1995.

At the same time Clark and Knox were seeking financing for Faith Metro, undercover federal agents were running an elaborate sting operation in San Antonio designed to catch money launderers. Beginning in October 1994, undercover agents from the United States Drug Enforcement Agency, the Internal Revenue Service, and United States Customs were involved in the operation. As part of the sting operation, undercover agents investigated Clarkston, who they suspected was a money launderer. The undercover agents told Clarkston that they were seeking to launder cocaine proceeds and requested his assistance. Clarkston suggested several long-term laundering schemes, including investing in a cattle business and a sports bar, but the undercover agents rejected the ideas, saying they were interested in short-term investments.

In early March 1995, Clarkston told the undercover agents that he had a "major big time guy," a church group, anxious to do business. At this time the undercover agents had no knowledge of Brace or Knox. On March 17, 1995, Clarkston met with the undercover agents in San Antonio and explained that he knew a minister who was interested in laundering cocaine funds, and that the preacher's representative, his financial advisor, was in town and anxious to meet with them. The undercover agents explained to Clarkston that they did not want innocent people involved in the business, and asked him if the minister knew they were cocaine traffickers and that the money would be cocaine proceeds. Clarkston replied that the preacher and the other person knew and did not care.

Later that day, Knox met with Clarkston and the undercover agents. Knox said that he was representing Brace and that he was there to negotiate a deal. Early in the conversation, the undercover agents told Knox that the money was from drug proceeds; Knox said that this was not a problem.[4] Knox showed the prospectus to the undercover agents, who indicated that they might be able to lend Brace $3 million.

On March 24, the undercover agents met Brace for the first time at a meeting also attended by Knox and Clarkston. The undercover agents told Brace that they would be able to loan him the entire $10 million, not just the $3 million previously discussed. To make sure that Brace and Knox could handle such a large sum, the undercover agents told them that they would have a practice transfer of $100,000, a condition to which Brace readily agreed. The undercover agents then informed Brace that the money came from the sale of cocaine, and that he was being asked to launder it. Brace stated that he was not troubled by the money's source.[5] At the end of the meeting, Brace said he was ready to start the test money, but the undercover agents told him to have patience.

Brace and Clarkston met with the undercover agents on April 26. Before the meeting, Knox told the undercover agents that he and Brace had already "contrived a system" to quickly deposit and transfer the first $100,000. At the meeting, the undercover agents gave Brace an account number for an undercover account in a London bank where Brace was to wire the $100,000 in the first test. Brace was given $100,000 in cash, which he wired to the English bank the next week.

On May 5, the undercover agents again met with Brace in San Antonio. The undercover agents suggested another $100,000 test, this time to a domestic account controlled by the undercover agents. Brace agreed to this, stating that to conceal the source of the money, he would carry it on his books as a loan. The undercover agents again gave Brace $100,000 in cash. As he counted it, he commented, "I have a feeling that neither one of you, have ever come across a pastor like me." Brace took the money and wired it to the account.

Knox called one of the undercover agents on May 10. During the conversation, Knox mentioned that he "kn[e]w a couple of people that deserve a bullet," and inquired, "can we work on that." Knox then stated that "I got a couple of problems, that I'm trying to alleviate but if, uh they don't alleviate I, uh I might need some services of some kind," referring to having someone killed.[7]

On May 12, the undercover agents met with Brace, Clarkston and Knox, and delivered the cash for another test, this time $150,000. Four

---

[4]   This conversation, unlike later ones, was not taped. Knox testified that the undercover agents did not tell him they were drug dealers. The veracity of this testimony, however, was a credibility issue for the jury.

[5]   One of the undercover agents actually said, "he is asking you to launder money." The government informed Brace that the money was from drugs only six pages into the transcript of the meeting.

[7]   Knox never brought up the subject again, but the undercover agent questioned him about it often. Knox argues that it was plain error for the district court to admit the extrinsic evidence of Knox's solicitation of murder. We address this issue below. [The court determined that the admission of evidence of solicitation of murder against Knox was admissible to show his predisposition to launder money. Editor.]

days later Brace and Knox wired the money to the English bank. The undercover agents told Brace and Knox that they would soon be ready to transfer the entire $10 million.

On June 21, the final meeting took place. The undercover agents met Brace and Knox in a San Antonio parking lot and gave them three canvas bags purportedly containing $10 million. The bags actually contained an amount of newspaper clippings approximating the weight of $10 million in cash. Brace and Knox were arrested as they left the parking lot.

Brace and Knox were charged with money laundering in a four count indictment. In Count One, Brace and Knox were charged with conspiring to launder money in violation of 18 U.S.C. § 1956(h). In Count Two, Brace was charged with laundering $100,000, and aiding and abetting Clarkston, in violation of 18 U.S.C. §§ 2 and 1956(a)(2)(B)(I). In Count Three, Brace was charged with laundering $100,000 in violation of 18 U.S.C. § 1956(a)(3)(B). In Count Four, Brace and Knox were charged with laundering $150,000, and aiding and abetting each other, in violation of 18 U.S.C. §§ 2 and 1956(a)(2)(B)(I). After a jury trial, Brace and Knox were convicted on all counts . . .

DISCUSSION

Entrapment as a Matter of Law

Brace argues that, as a matter of law, he was entrapped.[9] . . . The government concedes that Brace was induced; therefore, the evidence must prove beyond reasonable doubt that Brace was predisposed to launder money. Because this is a sufficiency review, we will reverse only if no rational juror could have found predisposition beyond a reasonable doubt.

The Supreme Court most recently addressed entrapment and predisposition in Jacobson v. United States (1992).

The *en banc* Seventh Circuit recently wrestled with the meaning of Jacobson in United States v. Hollingsworth, 27 F.3d 1196 (7th Cir.1994) (en banc). Writing for the majority, Chief Judge Posner stated that in examining predisposition, we must ask ourselves what the defendant would have done, had the government not been involved. To properly answer that question, we must look to more than the defendant's mental state; we must also consider the defendant's skills, background and contacts. As Chief Judge Posner explained, predisposition "has positional as well as dispositional force. The defendant must be so situated by reason of previous training or experience or occupation or acquaintances that it is likely that if the government had not induced him to commit the crime some criminal would have done so. . . ." A defendant may have the desire to commit the crime, but may be without any ability to do so. The defendant is able to commit the crime only when the government steps in and provides the means to do so. In those cases, we cannot say that,

---

[9]   In his brief, Knox does not argue that he was entrapped as a matter of law. Accordingly he waived the issue and we do not address it.

absent government involvement, the defendant would likely have committed the crime.

The facts of Hollingsworth illustrate the Seventh Circuit's point. The Hollingsworth defendants were an orthodontist and a farmer, both from Arkansas. The pair, who had attempted and failed at many business ventures, decided to become international financiers, a vocation for which neither had any training, contacts, aptitude, or experience. They secured two foreign banking licenses, one from Grenada, and attempted to make money. Unfortunately, they had no customers and were rapidly going broke. The orthodontist, deciding to raise capital by selling the Grenadan banking license, placed an ad in USA Today offering the license for $29,950.

A Customs agent saw the ad and, knowing that foreign banks are sometimes used for money laundering, assumed that someone who wanted to sell one would possibly be interested in money laundering. The agent, acting undercover, contacted the orthodontist and, ultimately, persuaded him to launder money. The orthodontist and farmer were convicted of money laundering.

The en banc Seventh Circuit reversed, stating that, "[h]ad the government left [him] 'to his own devices' . . . in all likelihood [the orthodontist], a middle-aged man who so far as anyone knows had never before committed any crime, would never have committed a money-laundering or related offense." The government "turned two harmless, though weak, foolish, . . . and greedy, men into felons." Chief Judge Posner made clear that "[w]hatever it takes to become an international money launderer, they did not have it." "Even if they had wanted to go into money laundering before they met [the agent,] . . . the likelihood that they could have done so was remote. They were objectively harmless." It was "highly unlikely that if [the agent] had not providentially appeared someone else would have guided them into money laundering. No real criminal would do business with such [novices]."

We recognize that the Seventh Circuit's reading of Jacobson has not been universally embraced. The Ninth Circuit has rejected the Seventh Circuit's positional predisposition requirement and the First Circuit has adopted a different test. See United States v. Thickstun, 110 F.3d 1394, 1398 (9th Cir.1997); United States v. Gendron, 18 F.3d 955, 962–63 (1st Cir.1994); see also *Hollingsworth*, 27 F.3d at 1211 (EASTERBROOK, J., dissenting) (criticizing positional predisposition requirement). In *Gendron*, then Chief Judge (now Justice) Breyer held that Jacobson stands for the proposition that in trying to induce the target of a sting to commit a crime, the government may not confront him with circumstances that are different from the ordinary circumstances a real criminal would use in inducing one to engage in wrongdoing. Thus, the government must show that a defendant would have committed the crime when "faced with an ordinary 'opportunity' to commit the crime rather than a special 'inducement.' "

Nonetheless, we are persuaded that the Seventh Circuit's *Hollingsworth* decision is correct. The Supreme Court instructs that in determining predisposition we are to ask what the defendant would have done absent government involvement. To give effect to that command, we must look not only to the defendant's mental state (his "disposition"), but also to whether the defendant was able and likely, based on experience, training, and contacts, to actually commit the crime (his "position").

We are called upon to determine whether the government proved beyond a reasonable doubt that Brace was predisposed to launder money. Following *Hollingsworth*, we look to Brace's position, as well as his mental disposition. The evidence of Brace's mental disposition to launder money is close. Nonetheless, we must reverse because the government failed to prove that Brace, absent government involvement, was in a position to launder money. Therefore, the evidence is insufficient to prove that Brace was predisposed to launder money.

The government argues that the evidence shows that Brace was predisposed to launder money. The government, however, fails to address the positional and dispositional aspects of pre-disposition. All of the evidence the government adduced at trial went solely to Brace's mental disposition. The government offered no evidence that Brace was in a position to launder money. The government offered no evidence that real drug dealers would use a novice such as Brace to launder money. Brace had never been convicted of a crime, and, as far as the record shows, had never committed a crime worse than speeding before he met the undercover agents. The evidence shows that Brace certainly had never laundered money before, and knew little, if anything, about the subject. In fact, he had to send an associate to the library to figure out the mechanics of laundering money. It is possible that real drug dealers often use such ignorant and naive individuals to launder millions of dollars. If that is the case, the government offered no proof of it.

The government failed to prove that real drug dealers would use a church to launder money. The only evidence that a church might be useful in money laundering came when Brace's counsel was cross-examining one of the undercover agents. When asked whether a real drug dealer would use someone who "didn't know what the hell he was doing," and "was totally inefficient," the undercover agent responded that: "Perhaps, perhaps not, depending on what he—in the whole gist of the thing, the fact that he had a church, that was golden to me. That would have been golden because nobody looks at a church." This statement is too vague and non-committal to be evidence of anything. The undercover agent says "perhaps, perhaps not," and then says that a church would be "golden" to him, not whether a real drug dealer would find it so.

The government never adduced evidence that a church would be valuable in money laundering, or that a church has ever been used in money laundering. The only evidence the government offered on the subject established that no church has ever knowingly been used to launder drug money. On cross-examination of Knox, the Assistant United States Attorney ("AUSA") asked whether Knox could "identify even a single church company in the United States that's ever knowingly taken purported drug proceeds." Knox responded that he had no information regarding that, and the AUSA asked, "Never heard of that before?" To which Knox responded, "No, sir. Not thus far." It is possible that drug dealers regularly use churches to launder money, and that a willing, though inexperienced, pastor would be an invaluable asset. That, however, is not in the record, and this is an issue upon which the government bore the burden of proof. On the record before us, the government failed to prove that any church has ever been used to launder money, or that a church would even be useful in laundering money.

After examining the record, we must conclude that the government failed to prove that Brace was in a position to launder money. When we ask the question of what Brace would have done if he had never met the undercover agents, we cannot answer "launder money for real drug dealers." In all likelihood, Brace never would have laundered money, but instead would have missed his bond payments and been forced into bankruptcy, as ultimately happened. Because the government failed to establish that Brace would have laundered money absent government involvement, the evidence is insufficient to prove predisposition. Accordingly, we hold that Brace was entrapped as a matter of law, and his convictions must be reversed.

[The discussion on evidentiary and sentencing issues is omitted.]

CONCLUSION

The government failed to prove beyond a reasonable doubt that Brace would likely have laundered money absent the government's involvement. Accordingly, we hold that Brace was entrapped as matter of law, and his convictions and sentence on all counts are REVERSED. . . . Knox's convictions and sentences are, in all respects, AFFIRMED.

State v. Blanco

District Court of Appeal of Florida, Fourth District., 2005.
896 So.2d 900.

ON MOTION FOR REHEARING EN BANC

■ MAY, J.

We grant the State's motion for rehearing en banc, withdraw our previous opinion, and substitute the following opinion in its place.

The State appeals an order dismissing charges against the defendant based upon entrapment. . . .

Law enforcement received information that drugs were being sold at a bar without any detailed information. Undercover officers went to the bar to attempt to find the dealers. Upon arrival, one of the officers approached the bar and sat next to the defendant. A conversation ensued. The officer indicated that he liked to "party", and explained to the defendant that he meant the use of cocaine.

The defendant left the bar at some point and went to the restroom. Upon his return, he told the officer no one was selling cocaine, but he found someone selling "Tina" or crystal meth for $60. The officer gave money to the defendant, who returned with the drugs. The officer bought the defendant a beer and talked for awhile. The officer exchanged numbers with the defendant and called him during the following days. The defendant was arrested two weeks later.

The defendant moved to dismiss the case on the grounds of entrapment. The court heard testimony from the defendant and the officer. They both testified to a conversation taking place and the use of the term "party". However, the defendant's interpretation of the word, and who said what, differed from that of the officer.

The trial court granted the defendant's motion to dismiss. The court explained:

> I have to kind of disagree with [the State]. . . . [T]his particular defendant was not a target of an investigation. He had not been previously noted as someone who dealt in drugs and that they were targeting him. This officer walks into knowingly—knowing it's a gay bar—and, as he testified, he approached this man who was sitting alone. He was the one that began the conversation. If it had been a woman sitting there I think she would have felt the same way. This was a man who was interested in her or him. The manner of procedure here and the talk that resulted would certainly seem to me objectionable, denied this man of his due process rights. And I am going to grant the motion to dismiss.

It is from this ruling that the State appeals.

Unlike subjective entrapment, which focuses on the issues of inducement and the defendant's predisposition, an objective analysis of entrapment on due process grounds focuses on the conduct of law enforcement. Munoz v. State, 629 So.2d 90 (Fla.1993).[1] The type of conduct held to violate due process is that which so offends decency or a sense of justice that judicial power may not be exercised to obtain a conviction.

In this case, the defendant's version of the facts differed from that of the officer. But, even assuming the facts in the light most favorable to

---

[1]   As Justice Kogan noted in his concurrence in *Munoz*, "[t]he due-process entrapment defense recognized in *Cruz, Glosson*, and [State v. Hunter, 586 So.2d 319 (Fla.1999)] essentially is the same as 'objective entrapment.' Thus, the majority appears to toss objective entrapment out the front door but then readmits essentially the same concept into Florida law via the rear entrance, with some minor tinkering as to analysis."

the defendant, law enforcement's conduct was not so outrageous that dismissal was warranted.

The trial court failed to limit its consideration to the conduct of law enforcement. Rather, it focused its attention on the effect of the officer's conduct on the defendant, the defendant's subjective perception of the situation, and his apparent lack of predisposition to commit the offense. Respectfully, those factors are irrelevant to a ruling when it is objectively analyzed on due process grounds.

Law enforcement was alerted that drugs were being sold at this bar. As it does on a daily basis, it engaged undercover officers to find the dealers at the suspected location. We conclude the officer's conduct did not rise to that level of "outrageous" as required under the case law to support a finding of entrapment on due process grounds.

Accordingly, we reverse the trial court's order of dismissal and remand the case for reinstatement of the charges. The factual dispute between the State and the defendant prevents the resolution of subjective entrapment on a motion to dismiss. A jury may very well find the defendant not guilty on the basis of subjective entrapment. That, however, is a decision for another day.

REVERSED AND REMANDED.

■ STONE, WARNER, KLEIN, STEVENSON, SHAHOOD, GROSS, TAYLOR, JJ., concur.

■ FARMER, C.J., dissents with opinion, in which Gunther and Polen, JJ., concur.

■ HAZOURI, J., Recused.

■ FARMER, C.J., dissenting.

I see no need to repeat what we said in the panel opinion affirming the decision of the trial judge dismissing this case. I write instead to make the following points.

The rationale of the en banc majority's position is this. In considering dismissal under the objective test for entrapment a trial Judge may not engage in any fact-finding, that the statute requires the jury to resolve the facts underlying an entrapment defense. *See* § 777.201(2), Fla. Stat. (2004) ("The issue of entrapment shall be tried by the trier of fact."). And so, in the majority's view, a *pretrial* motion to dismiss on the grounds of entrapment must be decided solely on undisputed facts—i.e., only on those facts which the State will concede—because otherwise the court would be invading the function the statute gave to the jury. The majority reasons that when the underlying facts for entrapment are disputed "law enforcement's conduct was not so outrageous that dismissal was warranted . . ." One should carefully note that this reasoning is *not* followed by any citation of authority. Nor does the majority advance any explanation why its proposition might be sustainable.

Judge Lebow did not specify which test for entrapment she relied on in dismissing this case. This is significant because entrapment takes two forms in Florida. The first form is essentially an affirmative defense centered around the accused's alleged lack of any predisposition to commit the crime. The second form is not an affirmative defense. In this second form of entrapment, the conduct of the government operates as a legal bar to the entire prosecution. In this second form, predisposition is not a material consideration. The first form is called the *subjective* test; the second form is the *objective* test. *Munoz v. State*, 629 So.2d 90, 98–99 (Fla.1993); *Cruz v. State*, 465 So.2d 516, 520 (Fla.1985) ("The subjective view recognizes that innocent, unpredisposed, persons will sometimes be ensnared by otherwise permissible police behavior. However, there are times when police resort to impermissible techniques. In those cases, the subjective view allows conviction of predisposed defendants. The objective view requires that all persons so ensnared be released."); *Soohoo v. State*, 737 So.2d 1108, 1109 (Fla. 4th DCA 1999) ("Thus, as it stands today, Florida courts embrace both the subjective and objective standards of entrapment."). Under the objective test, the contention is that as a matter of due process courts should not tolerate the conduct of the government regardless of the predisposition of the accused.

I do not think the majority's proposition banning all judicial fact-finding in objective entrapment cases is a correct statement of Florida law. Although the Legislature has reshaped the *subjective* test on entrapment into a specific statute under which the jury has a leading role, the supreme court made clear in *Munoz* that the entrapment statute does not bar the trial Judge from evaluating police conduct under the Due Process Clause:

Because the legislature cannot abrogate an accused's due process rights, section 777.201 is inapplicable whenever a judge determines as a matter of law that law enforcement personnel have violated an accused's due process rights.

Accordingly, it is now established law in this state that the trial judge *is* authorized to dismiss a criminal case when the conduct of the government should not be tolerated. The majority's view thus raises the question just how the trial judge is to carry out judicial authority to assess police conduct under constitutional law without engaging in some fact finding to determine precisely what that conduct is.

Before *Munoz*, the supreme court had already made clear that while the subjective test is *ordinarily* (but not exclusively, as I shall presently show) for the jury, the objective test is for the court alone:

"The due process defense based upon governmental misconduct is an objective question of law *for the trial court*, as opposed to the subjective predisposition question submitted to the jury in the usual entrapment defense." [e.s.] *State v. Glosson*, 462 So.2d 1082, 1084 (Fla.1985). *Munoz* explained later that: "section 777.201 neither prohibits the judiciary from objectively reviewing the issue of entrapment to the extent such a review involves the due process clause . . . of the Florida Constitution, nor prohibits the judiciary from determining under the subjective test that, in certain circumstances, entrapment has been established as a matter of law." *Munoz*, 629 So.2d at 101. In other words, even though the entrapment statute seems to require that all entrapment cases be submitted to a jury, actually the trial judge may take the issue from the jury when the evidence does not legally involve a true conflict. As for objective entrapment, *Munoz* held: "the legislature cannot enact a statute that overrules a judicially established legal principle enforcing or protecting a . . . constitutional right. Accordingly, section 777.201 cannot overrule a decision of this Court regarding entrapment in any case decided under the due process provision of . . . the Florida Constitution."

There is not so much as a word here suggesting that under the *objective* test the judicial assessment of the police conduct may be made only when the state stipulates to defendant's pretrial testimony.

It is inconceivable that any rule of law or principle would operate in a factual void. All legal rules and principles are drawn upon a background of pertinent facts. If some government conduct passes muster under the Due Process Clause, but some does not, the only basis to differentiate the good from the bad is on the facts involved. Someone has to decide what those facts are. If the objective test is solely for the judge and not the jury (as *Glosson* and *Munoz* hold), then the only person who is qualified to ascertain what the facts are raising a Due Process question must be the Judge. And to do that, it may be necessary to ascertain or resolve some of those facts.

Indeed the essence of the objective test on entrapment is that the very prosecution of the crime itself must be stopped because it was begotten by police conduct that our society does not want to tolerate under its organic law. It takes but a moment's reflection to understand that the evidence admitted during the criminal trial is unlikely to include all the facts relevant to an objective entrapment issue. This is so because the guilt of the accused in objective entrapment is largely irrelevant. Some of the police conduct may be outside the corpus of the alleged crime. Therefore a holding that all objective entrapment cases must turn on undisputed facts would mean that only when the government has admitted the facts implicating a due process issue can the law enforcement officials be found to have acted outside the constitutional norm.

Depending on officials to admit that they have engaged in acts raising a due process bar to prosecution, in order to evaluate the propriety of such conduct, is logically indistinguishable from asking the actor to decide whether the acts should be tolerated. Human beings have a bent of failing to recognize the invidious nature of their own conduct, especially when they are imbued with a sense of "mission" in a cause they conceive to be noble—like punishing persons believed to be involved in the drug trade. A holding that government conduct deemed intolerable under the Due Process Clause may be condemned by the court only when those engaged in such conduct trouble themselves to admit it would truly be against reason and experience. And because objective entrapment is meant to be preemptive and not an affirmative defense, it should ordinarily be determined before an accused is put to the burden of the trial. If the claim of objective entrapment is valid, any outcome of the trial in favor of the government will be nugatory anyway.

* * *

And even if the state had not waived the jury determination, when the testimony at the hearing is properly analyzed it is apparent that there is no real conflict in the testimony for purposes of objective entrapment. The majority's argument of factual conflict hinges entirely on whether Mike or defendant introduced the subject of drugs through the use of the word *party*. In other words, the only material thing truly disputed by Mike's testimony at that hearing is whether it was Mike who introduced the subject of drugs during the encounter between the two men at the bar. But Mike's testimony is legally ineffective to create a real conflict in the evidence for due process purposes.

According to Mike, the term *party* referred to illegal drugs. To recap the pertinent testimony, defendant had initially testified that it was Mike who first used the word *party* and that he thought Mike was referring to sex. In rebuttal, Mike testified that it was defendant who first used the word *party* and that *Mike* (but not necessarily the whole world) understood it to refer to drugs. Yet, in fact, Mike admitted to having to clarify to defendant that he was referring to drugs rather than sex in using the word *party*. Mike's testimony thus does not refute defendant's testimony that Mike was using both sex and drugs to induce a crime.

* * *

Giving the evidence its proper legal import, the testimony from both participants in the encounter establishes inducement by the police as a matter of law. Nothing in Mike's testimony challenges the assertion that he was using implied sex to induce a drug transaction. That means that government promoted the crime—instead of detecting a crime already in the planning or operational stages. From this testimony the trial court found that Mike, the government agent, used sex to entice defendant into a drug transaction.

In addition to improperly understanding the testimony and its absence of real conflict, the majority's holding as to the jury requirement in objective entrapment cases is mistaken for another reason. Any rule that all objective entrapment cases must be submitted to the jury unless the prosecution effectually admits its own misconduct would be in striking contrast with *subjective* entrapment cases where *Munoz* holds that the law allows some subjective entrapment cases to be decided before trial by the judge—even though the defendant has the burden of proving lack of predispositon. The majority advance no reason why the standard for removing an objective entrapment case from a jury should be any more difficult than it now is for subjective entrapment.

The *Munoz* court explained that a trial Judge may take a subjective entrapment case from the jury and decide it as a matter of law:

> "Section 777.201 directs that the issue of entrapment be submitted to the trier of fact. Such direction is consistent with the subjective evaluation of entrapment because the two factual issues above ordinarily present questions of disputed facts to be submitted to the jury as the trier of fact. However, *if the factual circumstances of a case are not in dispute, if the accused establishes that the government induced the accused to commit the offense charged, and if the State is unable to demonstrate sufficient evidence of predisposition prior to and independent of the government conduct at issue, then the trial judge has the authority to rule on the issue of predisposition as a matter of law.*" [e.s.]

It is apparent from this statement that only three things are necessary for a judicial determination of entrapment: (1) the critical circumstances are not in dispute; (2) the accused establishes government inducement; and (3) the police are unable to present legally sufficient evidence of predisposition before, and unconnected with, the government conduct. All three things are made here.

The critical circumstances are not in dispute. Defendant was unknown to the police before Mike sat next to him at the bar. Defendant had no arrests or any record for criminal activities. Although police had received information that illegal drugs were being sold at the bar, no one mentioned or referred to defendant as being involved in any such activity. He was not a target of any police investigation. When Mike sat next to him he was but a face in the crowd.

* * *

The accused has established government inducement. As I have just shown, properly understood, the testimony is clear that it was Mike who introduced the subject of drugs, not defendant. Thus the record is uncontradicted that the conduct of the officer did in fact promote defendant into committing the crime. The unrebutted testimony of defendant was found by the trial judge to involve using sex as a lure to induce an unsuspecting man into a drug transaction promoted by the police. The dismissal on the basis of objective entrapment is therefore based on legally proper procedures and represented a decision founded on a matter of law.

* * *

Plainly all of the State's evidence on predisposition deals with events arising during the encounter between defendant and Mike. The State did not suggest the existence of any evidence of any predisposition on defendant's part *before the encounter*. As the trial judge noted, defendant was not a target of any investigation. The police had no previous basis to believe that he had been identified or named as someone dealing in drugs. The state did not even know of his existence until Mike sat down next to him in the bar. The State had no information about him, by tip or otherwise. When Mike began making advances to defendant at the bar, it was with absolutely no reason to suspect him of anything.

In short, the state's entire evidence on predisposition relates to events involving Mike's encounter with defendant and ensuing events. This is plainly insufficient. *Munoz* requires a defendant initially to offer evidence that, if believed, would constitute inducement by the police and that he was not predisposed to commit the crime.

Defendant's pretrial testimony was sufficient to make out a prima facie case of inducement by the officer. There is no evidence that defendant was predisposed to commit the crime until his encounter with Mike had begun. A number of cases after *Munoz* have held that the trial court was authorized to dismiss the entire case then and there, without awaiting a jury determination . . . Therefore, entrapment rather than crime was at hand, and as a matter of law, the trial court should have granted Farley's motion to dismiss.

* * *

Upon consideration of either test, there is no legal basis to reverse the trial judge. Nor is there any reason to take up this case en banc to reverse the trial judge without running into conflict with the supreme court, with our own decision in *Farley*, and with the other district courts in *Robichaud* and *Ramos* and *Beattie*.

I therefore dissent.

2. SENTENCING ENTRAPMENT, SENTENCING MANIPULATION, AND THE DUE PROCESS DEFENSE

People v. Smith et al.

Supreme Court of California, 2003.
31 Cal.4th 1207, 80 P.3d 662, 7 Cal.Rptr.3d 559.

■ BROWN, J.

In our order granting the petitions for review in this case, we limited the issues to be briefed and argued to: (1) Whether the doctrine of "sentencing entrapment" recognized in some federal cases affords a defense to charged drug offenses or enhancements in state court; and (2) whether the federal defense of outrageous governmental conduct (see, e.g., *United States v. Bogart* (9th Cir.1986) 783 F.2d 1428 (*Bogart*)) applies in state courts in addition to the entrapment defense under state law, which itself looks to the allegedly entrapping government conduct.

A jury convicted defendants of, among other crimes, attempting to transport a controlled substance—cocaine. The jury also found true an allegation that the quantity of cocaine involved exceeded 80 kilograms. Accordingly, defendants were each sentenced to an additional term of 25 years.

Defendants contend their sentences on the transportation counts should be modified by reducing the additional terms from 25 years to 15 years, the enhancement terms provided for transportation of quantities of controlled substances in excess of 20, but less than 40, kilograms. In arguing for the modification, defendants rely, first, on the related doctrines of "sentencing entrapment" and "sentencing manipulation."

While sentencing entrapment and sentencing manipulation are terms that some courts have used interchangeably, as we shall use them, *sentencing entrapment focuses primarily on the subjective intent of the defendant*, while *sentencing manipulation focuses primarily on the objective conduct of the police*.

Under the theory of sentencing entrapment, a defendant's sentence should be reduced if he was *predisposed* to commit a lesser offense, but was entrapped by the police into committing an offense subject to greater punishment.

Under the theory of sentencing manipulation, a sentence should be reduced if law enforcement officials, for the purpose of increasing a defendant's sentence, engaged in conduct so *outrageous* as to violate the defendant's right to *due process*.

While the Court of Appeal rejected the doctrine of sentencing entrapment, it not only accepted the doctrine of sentencing manipulation, it significantly lowered the bar for finding a violation. "We do not believe a showing of 'outrageous' conduct is required in order to establish sentence manipulation. . . . Rather, we believe defendants establish sentence manipulation for purposes of the quantity enhancement when they show the police selected the amount of drugs for *no legitimate law enforcement purpose* but solely to maximize the defendants' sentence."

We reject the doctrine of sentencing entrapment as inconsistent with California entrapment doctrine, under which "the character of the suspect, his predisposition to commit the crime, and his subjective intent are irrelevant."

In this case, the conduct of the undercover officer was far from outrageous; indeed, it was quite unexceptionable. Therefore, we need not decide here whether the doctrine of sentencing manipulation should be adopted in California. However, we do take this occasion to express our disapproval of the less rigorous test of sentencing manipulation adopted by the Court of Appeal—that the allegedly manipulative conduct has "no legitimate law enforcement purpose but [was undertaken] solely to maximize the defendants' sentence." Were the doctrine of sentencing manipulation to be adopted in California, the predicate conduct should be truly *outrageous*. By contrast, garden variety manipulation claims are largely a waste of time.

In arguing for modification of their sentences, defendants also invoke a due process defense based on outrageous government conduct (outrageous conduct defense).

The federal test of entrapment, unlike the California test, is subjective and focuses on "the intent or predisposition of the defendant to commit the crime." . . . In *Russell*, the Supreme Court, while reaffirming the federal subjective test for entrapment, left open the possibility of an objective constitutional defense based on due process: "While we may some day be presented with a situation in which the conduct of law enforcement agents is so outrageous that due process principles would absolutely bar the government from invoking judicial processes to obtain a conviction [citation], the instant case is distinctly not of that breed." (Russell v. United States, 411 U.S. at pp. 431–432, 93 S.Ct. 1637.)

In California, unlike in federal courts, the test for entrapment focuses on the police conduct and is objective. Entrapment is established if the law enforcement conduct is likely to induce a *normally law-abiding person* to commit the offense.

We are, therefore, presented with this question: In California, in the context of an entrapment claim, is the outrageous conduct defense *superfluous* because our entrapment defense itself focuses on the conduct of law enforcement? Just as this case is the wrong case in which to address the viability in California of the doctrine of sentencing manipulation because the conduct of law enforcement here was quite unexceptionable, so, too, is it the wrong case in which to address the viability in this state of the outrageous conduct defense.

The facts bearing on the limited issues before us may be briefly stated. Juan Martinez was an undercover narcotics officer. An informant of demonstrated reliability told Officer Martinez that defendant Edaleene Sherrie Smith was involved in drug trafficking and "ripping off" other drug dealers, and that Smith was very excited about the prospect of robbing a home where, on the instructions given him by another officer, the informant had told Smith that 200 kilograms of cocaine would be found.

In furtherance of the sting, Officer Martinez then met with Smith. Officer Martinez told Smith that he wanted to "rip off" a major drug dealer he worked for, and that the amount of cocaine involved would be between 30 and 100 kilograms. Smith assured Officer Martinez that she made her living that way, that she knew exactly what she was doing, and that she always used the same experienced three-person crew. Smith then informed Officer Martinez of her fee schedule: If the robbery yielded

30 kilograms of cocaine, she was to receive five kilograms for herself and nine more to divide among her crew, with the remainder going to the officer. If more than 50 kilograms were involved, the officer's share, Smith said, would be 60 percent.

In subsequent conversations, Officer Martinez gave Smith the address of a house and informed her that 85 kilograms of cocaine would be located in a van parked in an adjoining garage. Prior to the arrival of defendants, the officers had withdrawn, pursuant to a court order, 85 kilograms of cocaine from the property division of the police department and placed it in the van parked in the garage. The key was left in the ignition of the van. When defendants arrived, Smith remained in the car, while codefendants Waymond Thomas and Obed Gonzalez entered the house and then the garage. As Thomas and Gonzalez began backing the van out of the garage, the police activated a remote-controlled switch that shut off the engine. Thomas and Gonzalez, as well as Smith, were then arrested.

[A] jury convicted defendants of attempting to transport cocaine, and the jury found true an allegation that the quantity of cocaine involved exceeded 80 kilograms. Smith and Thomas were also convicted of conspiracy to commit robbery, attempted robbery, grand theft of an automobile, and grand theft of personal property. Smith received a sentence of 36 years in prison including the 25-year quantity enhancement for attempting to transport more than 80 kilograms of cocaine. Thomas was given a prison sentence of 47 years eight months, including the 25-year enhancement. Gonzalez, who was convicted of the same charges, except for conspiracy to commit robbery, received a sentence of 33 years, including the 25-year enhancement.

The Court of Appeal affirmed defendants' judgments of conviction, but modified each defendant's sentence by reducing the sentence enhancement from 25 years to 15 years.

We reverse the judgment of the Court of Appeal insofar as it reduces defendants' 25-year sentence enhancement for attempting to transport more than 80 kilograms of cocaine. In all other respects, the Court of Appeal's judgment is affirmed.

I.   SENTENCING ENTRAPMENT

Four federal circuit courts of appeals—the First, Seventh, Eighth, and Ninth—appear to accept the doctrine of sentencing entrapment. The United States Courts of Appeals of the District of Columbia and the Eleventh Circuit, and possibly also the Tenth Circuit, reject it. In the remaining federal circuits, the status of the doctrine is unclear. [Cite discussions omitted.]

We reject the doctrine of sentencing entrapment because, as the Court of Appeal below observed, the concept simply "does not fit with California's criminal law." The federal doctrine of sentencing entrapment, like the federal doctrine of entrapment generally, focuses on the intent of the defendant and is subjective. The California test of entrapment, by contrast, "focuses on the police conduct and is objective." Under the California test, "such matters as the character of the suspect, his predisposition to commit the offense, and his subjective intent are irrelevant."

Another reason for rejecting the doctrine of sentencing entrapment, relied upon by the Court of Appeal in this case, is that "California courts do not follow the same rigid sentencing guidelines as federal courts, so the need for a specific basis for departure from a guideline is not present Defendants here received 25-year quantity enhancements ..." Subdivision (e) of Health and Safety Code section 11370.4 provides: "Notwithstanding any other provision of law, the court may strike the additional punishment for the enhancements provided in this section if it determines there are circumstances in mitigation of the additional punishment and states on the record its reasons for striking the additional punishment." Rule 4.428(a) of the California Rules of Court provides in pertinent part: "If the judge has statutory discretion to strike the additional term for an enhancement, the court may consider and apply any of the circumstances in mitigation enumerated in these rules. . . ." The circumstances in mitigation enumerated in the rules include the fact that the defendant, "with no apparent predisposition to do so, was induced by others to participate in the crime."

II.   SENTENCING MANIPULATION

Again, under the theory of sentencing manipulation, as it is usually defined by the federal courts discussing the concept, a defendant's sentence should be reduced if law enforcement officials, for the purpose of increasing the defendant's sentence, engaged in conduct that was so outrageous or extraordinary as to violate the defendant's right to due process of law.

While several federal circuit courts have discussed sentencing manipulation in dicta, not a single case has been brought to our attention where a federal circuit court approved a downward departure from the federal sentencing guidelines on this basis.

At least four states have addressed the doctrine of sentencing manipulation. The Court of Appeals of New Mexico has apparently left the question open. (*State v. Rael* (Ct.App.1999) 127 N.M. 347, 981 P.2d 280, 287 [under some circumstances continuing transactions may constitute unfair manipulation of a defendant's sentence, but no sentencing manipulation found in case at bar].) The Superior Court of Pennsylvania has adopted the doctrine of sentencing manipulation as defined by the outrageous conduct standard. (*Commonwealth v. Petzold* (Pa.Super.Ct.1997) 701 A.2d 1363, 1366–1367 [sentence reduction an appropriate and just response to outrageous government conduct designed solely to increase a defendant's term of incarceration].) The District Court of Appeal of Florida has adopted the lesser standard of sentencing manipulation embraced by the Court of Appeal here. (*State v.*

Steadman (Fla.Dist.Ct.App.2002) 827 So.2d 1022, 1024–1025 [no legitimate law enforcement purpose given for undisputed sentencing manipulation].) The Court of Criminal Appeals of Tennessee apparently accepts the doctrine of sentencing manipulation under the rubric of sentencing entrapment, but has not spelled out whether it adopts the outrageous conduct standard or some lesser standard. (*State v. Thornton* (Tenn.Crim.App.1999) 10 S.W.3d 229, 244 [imposition of consecutive sentences for sale of narcotics may be inappropriate, " 'depending upon the number of specific buys the officers [choose] to conduct and the amounts purchased in each buy' "].)

A. The Conduct of the Undercover Officer Here Was Unexceptionable, Hence We Need Not Decide Whether We Accept the Doctrine of Sentencing Manipulation.

To reiterate, defendants were each sentenced to an additional term of 25 years for having attempted to transport more than 80 kilograms of cocaine, and they contend they should instead have received the 15-year additional terms applicable to more than 20 but less than 40 kilograms, because the undercover officer manipulated them into agreeing to steal more than 80 kilograms.

Even assuming arguendo that we accepted the doctrine of sentencing manipulation, defendants' contention would fail for the simple reason that it lacks any factual basis.

Sentencing manipulation, as we have said, focuses primarily on the objective conduct of the police. However, the conduct of the police does not occur in a vacuum, especially in a sting operation. The court's assessment of an officer's objective conduct will inevitably be colored by, for example, whether the defendant was from the start an enthusiastic proponent of the proposed crime or initially declined and was only gradually worn down.

When initially approached by the informant, defendant Smith expressed nothing but enthusiasm at the prospect of robbing a home where she was told 200 kilograms of cocaine would be found. When the undercover officer himself first met with Smith, he told her the amount of cocaine involved would be 30 to 100 kilograms. Smith did not express any preference for a transaction at the lower end of that range. To the contrary, Smith sought to reassure the officer that she was up to the job as described, telling him she made her living that way, that she knew exactly what she was doing, and that she always used the same experienced three-person crew. Indeed, rather than expressing a concern about the large amount of cocaine potentially involved, Smith set out a fee schedule that actually gave the officer a discount for quantity: If the robbery yielded 30 kilograms of cocaine, Smith was to receive five kilograms for herself and nine more to divide among her crew, with the remainder of the cocaine, which would work out to 54 percent of it, for the officer. If more than 50 kilograms were involved, the officer's share, Smith said, would be 60 percent. In a subsequent conversation, the officer told Smith 85 kilograms of cocaine would be found at the designated location, and that was the sum actually found there. Again, there is no indication whatsoever that Smith expressed any qualms about the prospect of stealing 85 kilograms of cocaine, an amount that was well within the range that had been discussed from the outset. To borrow a phrase from the Third Circuit Court of Appeals, Smith "was an experienced drug courier who demonstrated what can only be characterized as a yeoman's attitude towards this venture."

It is quite clear that none of the federal circuit courts that accept the doctrine would find sentencing manipulation on these facts.

* * *

The defendants here were merely given an apparent opportunity to do what Smith so proudly proclaimed they did for a living. Nevertheless, the Court of Appeal concluded that defendants were victims of sentencing manipulation because Smith had indicated that they "would do the theft for 30 kilos." However, stings are permissible stratagems in the enforcement of criminal law, and the purpose of a sting is to catch criminals at work, not to find out how cheaply they will work. . . .

B.   The Standard for Sentencing Manipulation Proposed by the Court of Appeal is Rejected.

It is unnecessary for us to decide in this case whether we accept the doctrine of sentencing manipulation because the conduct of the police here was not overreaching by any reasonable standard.

III. THE OUTRAGEOUS CONDUCT DEFENSE

We now come to the question embedded in the outrageous conduct defense asserted by defendants: In California, in the context of an entrapment claim, is the defense of outrageous law enforcement conduct superfluous because our entrapment defense itself focuses on the conduct law enforcement?

The outrageous conduct defense has been called the "deathbed child of objective entrapment." (*United States v. Santana* (1st Cir.1993) 6 F.3d 1, 3.) In *Russell, supra*, 411 U.S. 423, 93 S.Ct. 1637, 36 L.Ed.2d 366, the Supreme Court reaffirmed the subjective test for entrapment focusing on the intent or predisposition of the defendant to commit the crime. However, the high court left open the possibility of an objective constitutional defense based on due process: While we may some day be presented with a situation in which the conduct of law enforcement agents is so outrageous that due process principles would absolutely bar the government from invoking judicial processes to obtain a conviction [citation], the instant case is distinctly not of that breed. . . . The law enforcement conduct here stops far short of violating that fundamental fairness, shocking to the universal sense of justice mandated by the Due Process Clause of the Fifth Amendment.

The vast majority of the federal circuit courts of appeals allow the outrageous conduct defense ... While the test for entrapment in California is objective and focuses on the conduct of law enforcement this court, like the United States Supreme Court, has left open the possibility that we might accept the outrageous conduct defense.

The Court of Appeal here treated outrageous conduct as a viable defense, but found "nothing shocking about the police conduct." In *People v. Wesley* (1990) 224 Cal.App.3d 1130, 274 Cal.Rptr. 326, one of its own earlier decisions, this Court of Appeal identified four factors a court should consider in determining whether due process principles had been violated by outrageous police conduct: (1) whether the police manufactured a crime that otherwise would not likely have occurred, or merely involved themselves in an ongoing criminal activity; (2) whether the police themselves engaged in criminal or improper conduct repugnant to a sense of justice; (3) whether the defendant's reluctance to commit the crime is overcome by appeals to humanitarian instincts such as sympathy or past friendship, by temptation of exorbitant gain, or by persistent solicitation in the face of unwillingness; and (4) whether the record reveals simply a desire to obtain a conviction with no reading that the police motive is to prevent further crime or protect the populace. These factors, the *Wesley* court said, are only illustrative and no one is, in itself, determinative. Each factor should be viewed in context with all pertinent aspects of the case and proper law enforcement objectives.

None of he factors it had identified in *Wesley*, the Court of Appeal found, are present in this case. . . .

The record does not show the police in this case were motivated simply by a desire to obtain a conviction but rather demonstrates they were motivated by a desire to stop a robbery ring that had operated undetected for the past decade and to protect the public from the violence which could easily result when a gang of thieves attempts to steal pure cocaine from a drug lord.

We are left with the question we started with: In California, in the context of an entrapment claim, is the defense of outrageous law enforcement conduct superfluous because our entrapment defense itself focuses on the conduct of law enforcement? This case, in which the conduct of law enforcement was entirely unexceptionable, is the wrong case in which to resolve this question.

DISPOSITION

The judgment of the Court of Appeal is reversed insofar as it reduces defendants' 25-year sentence enhancement for attempting to transport more than 80 kilograms of cocaine. In all other respects, the Court of Appeal's judgment is affirmed.

■ WE CONCUR: BAXTER, CHIN, and MORENO, JJ. Concurring Opinion by WERDEGAR, J.

I concur in the result, but decline to join the majority in its unnecessary, potentially confusing, and questionable discussion of certain issues.

* * *

The due process "defense" of outrageous law enforcement conduct is actually a *bar to prosecution* rather than a defense to the charge; as such, it is properly raised by motion and decided by the court. *People v. Wesley* (1990) 224 Cal.App.3d 1130, 1138, 274 Cal.Rptr. 326 In contrast, entrapment is a *defense to the charge* and is decided by jury trial. The constitutional bar of outrageous law enforcement conduct, moreover, may be invoked against police or prosecutorial conduct that does not involve inducement to crime and therefore cannot serve as the basis for an entrapment defense. The two doctrines are therefore distinct both substantively and procedurally. They do overlap substantively in a particular factual context, i.e., in cases where the thrust of the defense is that the government improperly instigated the crime. But that an area of overlap exists does not make either doctrine redundant and provides no reason to doubt that in a proper case of outrageous conduct, whether or not including government inducement to crime, the defendant may be able to obtain dismissal of the action on due process grounds.

■ WE CONCUR: GEORGE, C.J., and KENNARD, J.

NOTES AND QUESTIONS

Problem 11-1. Police enlist the aid of a confidential informant (CI), a person with an impressive prior record of narcotic offenses and currently awaiting trial on theft and burglary charges, to make drug purchases in exchange for which the CI's pending charges will be "forgotten." The CI furnishes police with the names of five to six persons from whom he thinks he can buy drugs. The defendant is one of these persons and furnishes drugs in several "small-time" marijuana transactions. In raising the defense of outrageous government conduct, is defendant permitted to show that the police conduct constitutes a due process violation because the police used the services of a serious offender whose crimes were forgiven to catch a "small-time" drug dealer? Also, is the claim of outrageous government conduct one that should be decided by the court, or submitted to the jury? *Cf.* State v. Plough, 2001 WL 637813 (Ohio Court of Appeals, 11th Dist., 2001).

Problem 11-2. A female police officer encourages defendant, a male known to have a drug habit, to have an intimate sexual relationship with her, and tells him that he can use drugs in her presence and that she would not arrest him. In stating this, she knows, however, that other police officers are observing their exchanges and plan to arrest defendant as soon as any crime is spotted. Is defendant entitled to an entrapment defense? Is this entrapment as a matter of law in a jurisdiction that follows the "objective" test for entrapment of the *Russell* concurrence? Does it constitute a due process violation? *See, e.g.*, State v. Eichel, 495 So.2d 787 (Fla. App. 1986); United States v. Gamache, 156 F.3d 1 (1st Cir. 1998); State v. Tookes, 67

Haw. 608, 699 P.2d 983 (1985); Municipality of Anchorage v. Flanagan, 649 P.2d 957 (Alaska App. 1982); State v. Putnam, 31 Wash. App. 156, 639 P.2d 858 (1982).

Question 11-3. A divorced, lonely, middle-aged man forced into early retirement by the Air Force, begins to trawl the Internet and visits "alternate lifestyle" discussion groups. After contacting Sharon, whose ad had indicated she was looking for someone who understood her family's "unique needs" and that she preferred servicemen, defendant responded that he was looking for a "long-term relationship leading to marriage." Sharon responds favorably, says she is divorced and has three daughters, and many email exchanges occur thereafter. While the tenor of the exchanges is "normal" at first, with defendant indicating repeatedly he is not aware of what the "special needs" she refers to entails, Sharon gradually indicates she is looking for a man who will be a sexual mentor for her daughters. After some period of time, defendant finally gets the hint and expresses his willingness to play sex instructor to Sharon's children. They eventually make plans for defendant to travel to California from his Florida home, where he meets Sharon in a hotel room. She offers him some pornographic magazines featuring children, and shows pictures of her three daughters, ages 7, 10, and 12. She then directs him to an adjoining room to meet her children, "presumably to give them their first lesson under their mother's protective supervision." Upon entering the room, defendant is met by FBI, military personnel, and sheriff's department officers. Defendant is charged with attempted lewd acts with a minor in violation of law. Does he have an entrapment defense? Is the government's conduct "outrageous" enough to raise a due process defense? See Judge Kozinski's opinion in United States v. Poehlman, 217 F.3d 692 (9th Cir. 2000).

Problem 11-4. A male IRS undercover agent pretending to be a big-time financier who is seeking "safe and discrete placements" for large amounts of money induces a woman lawyer to have sexual intercourse with him after a relationship is established. In the course of the relationship, the agent wines and dines the lawyer in plush hotels, gives her gifts, and then induces her to participate in a money laundering scheme for which she is arrested. Entrapment as a matter of law? *Cf.*, United States v. Nolan-Cooper, 155 F.3d 221 (3d Cir. 1998).

Problem 11-5. An undercover police agent develops a close relationship with the defendant. The agent takes the defendant to one of his "friends"—a person who is drug addicted though he is trying to "kick" his habit. The "friend" is going through withdrawals, looking "pinkish, yellowish, sick," shaking and "tweaking and twitching." When the "friend" approaches defendant, the "friend" asks if defendant could please "get him something." Begging for help and repeatedly and stating "I am hurting, I need a fix" for some twenty minutes, defendant and the "friend" go to a place where defendant uses a twenty-dollar bill to exchange it for cocaine. Defendant is arrested when he gives the cocaine to the "friend" and charged with trafficking. Does he have a defense of outrageous government conduct? *See* Bradley v. W.A. Duncan, 315 F.3d 1091 (9th Cir. 2002).

1. In United States v. Thickstun, 110 F.3d 1394 (9th Cir.1997), defendant urged the court to follow the Hollingsworth case cited in the Knox opinion in holding that a defendant is predisposed only "if she is actually in a position to commit the crime without government assistance." The court declined the follow Hollingsworth:

> We read Jacobson as not creating a requirement of positional readiness but as applying settled entrapment law. The inference that the government's methods had persuaded an otherwise law-abiding citizen to break the law, coupled with the absence of evidence of predisposition, established entrapment as a matter of law under the existing two-part test. It was not necessary for the court to expand the entrapment defense, nor is there language in the opinion that it did so. While our reading conflicts with that of the Seventh Circuit in *Hollingsworth*, it accords with then-Judge Breyer's opinion in United States v. Gendron, 18 F.3d 955 (1st Cir.1994).

2. In People v. Auld, 815 P.2d 956 (Colo. App. 1991), the court rejected an appeal by the state, which sought to reverse the trial court's dismissal of charges of receiving and possession of a dangerous weapon in a sting operation directed against an attorney-defendant, in the exercise of its "supervisory power in protecting judicial integrity in the face of governmental misconduct."

A drug enforcement police task force, operating on a tip that Auld might accept drugs as payment for services, induced the prosecutor to draft a false drugs and weapons complaint against an undercover agent. The prosecutor's wife notarized the complaint. When the undercover agent was first brought to court for a bond hearing, he was questioned by the judge and made false statements to the judge, who was unaware of the sting operation. The agent then sought to retain Auld as his attorney, making an initial cash payment for legal fees and offering to pay the balance by giving the lawyer drugs. Auld refused the drugs but said he might take a gun at a "black market price." The agent then gave the defendant an Uzi semi-automatic rifle. Auld's acceptance of the weapon lead to the charge of receiving stolen property and possession of a dangerous weapon. The trial court rejected Auld's motions based on alleged due process violations in targeting defendant without probable cause or reasonable suspicion, on failure to cease the sting operation when he first refused drugs, and on invasion of the attorney-client relationship. The judge granted the motion to dismiss, however, on alleged outrageous governmental conduct that had enmeshed the judiciary in law enforcement activities without its knowledge. In upholding the trial court's dismissal of the charges, the appeals court said:

> The People in effect admit that the district attorney here has perpetrated a fraud upon the court of this state by filing false documents, making false statements to a judge, and creating a counterfeit prosecution. They further concede that as a result of the district attorney's activities, the county court was duped into playing an active part in the prosecutorial function of the executive branch. . . .

* * *

. . . [T]he trial court [properly] exercised its supervisory power in protecting judicial integrity in the face of governmental misconduct. The trial court found, with evidentiary support, that the conduct of the district attorney, an officer of the court, and the law enforcement agencies may have violated the Colorado Criminal Code relating to perjury and false swearing.

> In addition, the district attorney may very well have violated the Code of Professional Responsibility by using perjured testimony, making false statements to the court, and by the manner in which he performed his duties as a public prosecutor. Also to be considered is ABA, Standards for Criminal Justice, Standard 3–2.8(a) (1980) which denotes as unprofessional conduct the intentional misrepresentation by a prosecutor of matters of fact or law to the court.

---

3. PERJURY ENTRAPMENT

U.S. v. Sarihifard

United States Court of Appeals, Fourth Circuit, 1998.
155 F.3d 301.

■ CHAMBERS, DISTRICT JUDGE:

Mohammad Sarihifard ("Petitioner") was convicted after a jury trial in the Eastern District of Virginia of perjury before a grand jury. The trial judge sentenced Petitioner to twenty-one months in prison pursuant to the federal sentencing guidelines.

The charges against Petitioner initially stem from a conversation with federal agents where Petitioner provided the agents with inaccurate information. The federal agents were conducting an investigation into alleged money laundering and drug trafficking at Eagle Motors. Eagle Motors was a small used car dealership in Arlington, Virginia, owned by Ali Galadari ("Galadari"). Galadari was a target of the government's investigation. From 1994 to 1995, Petitioner, a close friend of Galadari, worked as a used car salesman for Eagle Motors. Petitioner apparently was not the primary target of the government's investigation. However, the agents were seeking information concerning Petitioner's purchase and resale of a new 1995 Nissan Pathfinder. According to the government, the 1995 Pathfinder was purchased in Petitioner's name and sold two weeks later. The government agents theorized that the Pathfinder represented the profits of a drug transaction and that Petitioner was simply a "straw" owner of the vehicle. In January 1996, Petitioner told the government agents that he purchased the Pathfinder for his own use and that he sold it to another buyer named Deborah Mills two weeks later for a profit of $1000.00. After Petitioner relayed his version of events, the agents called Petitioner a "liar." However, Petitioner adhered to his story. Petitioner told the same story to a grand jury later that month. Prior to his testimony before the grand jury, the United States Attorney apprized Petitioner of his rights under the Fifth Amendment to the United States Constitution. After Petitioner testified before the grand jury, the United States Attorney informed the grand jury that Petitioner had not provided truthful testimony. The United States Attorney instructed the grand jury to disregard Petitioner's testimony for the purposes of examining the possible illegal activity at Eagle Motors.

During the following months, the government intensified its investigation of Eagle Motors. In February 1996, Jockery Jones ("Jones"), a suspect in the money laundering scheme, testified under a grant of immunity that he was the actual purchaser of the Nissan Pathfinder. Later that month, Galadari entered into a plea agreement with the government where he agreed to cooperate with government agents. In July 1996, Galadari testified before the grand jury. Galadari told the grand jury that Petitioner was merely a straw owner of the vehicle. On July 17, 1996, Mahmoud Moshrefi ("Moshrefi"), Petitioner's roommate and a salesperson at Eagle Motors, also entered into a plea agreement with the government. Moshrefi testified before the grand jury that the sale of the Pathfinder was consummated in furtherance of a money laundering scheme and that Petitioner fulfilled a pivotal role in the scheme by acting as the straw owner of the vehicle. After Jones and the Eagle Motors' employees testified, the grand jury indicted Petitioner. He was charged with perjury before a grand jury and making false statements to government agents.

Petitioner's trial on the grand jury perjury and false statements charges commenced in October 1996. At trial, Moshrefi and Jones testified for the United States ("Respondent"). The two witnesses told the jury that Jones was the actual purchaser of the Nissan Pathfinder. They described a scheme where Eagle Motors' employees needed to account for $31,500 in cash so they asked Petitioner if he would agree to have his name listed as the purchaser of the Nissan. Petitioner agreed and received $1000.00 in cash as payment for his minor role in the scheme. In addition, Deborah Mills testified that Petitioner never sold her a Nissan Pathfinder, that she never purchased a Nissan Pathfinder and that she never even visited Eagle Motors. Moshrefi and Galadari also testified that Petitioner never purchased, borrowed, possessed or drove the Pathfinder that was actually sold to Jones. The transcript of Petitioner's January 1996 testimony before the grand jury was introduced into evidence. On October 29, 1996, Petitioner was convicted of the charges as contained in the indictment.

PERJURY ENTRAPMENT

Perjury entrapment occurs when a government agent coaxes a defendant to testify under oath for the sole purpose of eliciting perjury.

See United States v. Shuck, 895 F.2d 962, 966 (4th Cir.1990); *Brown*, 245 F.2d at 555. In the instant case, Petitioner argues that he is a victim of perjury entrapment because the government was aware of his prior false statements to the agents. Petitioner asserts that the government coaxed him into testifying before the grand jury for the sole purpose of eliciting perjury. This argument is unpersuasive.

Entrapment is an affirmative defense. Hence, the Petitioner must demonstrate that the government induced him to commit a crime. Based upon the information presented by the Petitioner, the Court concludes that there is no evidence suggesting that the government's purpose in questioning the defendant was the solicitation of perjured testimony. At the time that Petitioner testified before the grand jury, the government was conducting an investigation into possible money laundering at Eagle Motors. Petitioner's testimony was a source of possible evidence into several individuals' involvement in criminal activity. The government did suspect that Petitioner provided false statements to the government agents in a prior interview. However, this does not mean that the government did not have a valid purpose in eliciting Petitioner's testimony before the grand jury. It also does not show that the government knew Petitioner would testify falsely before the grand jury. Prior to his grand jury testimony, Petitioner knew that the government agents did not believe his statements. Moreover, Petitioner was provided with Fifth Amendment warnings before he testified. He was explicitly told that he could refuse to answer any question on the ground that it might incriminate him. Arguably, Petitioner's prior false statements provided the government with notice that he might testify falsely before the grand jury. However, this falls far short of proving that the government asked him to testify for the purpose of eliciting perjury. When the government has a legitimate reason for asking a witness to testify before the grand jury and the witness is provided with adequate warnings, the mere fact that the government knows that the witness possibly may provide false testimony does not establish the requisite showing of inducement. *See United States v. Vesich,* 724 F.2d 451, 460–61 (5th Cir.1984). Absent sufficient evidence that the government asked defendant to testify for the purpose of eliciting perjury, the defense of perjury entrapment must fail.

NOTE

See United States v. Rodriguez-Rodriguez, 453 F.3d 458, 462 (7th Cir. 2006) (holding that the entrapment doctrine does not apply to venue "manufactured" by the conduct of government agents).

———

CHAPTER 12

COMPULSION, INTOXICATION, AUTOMATISM AND OTHER NON-CONTROLLABLE FACTORS

A. COMPULSION

1. DURESS

State v. St. Clair
Supreme Court of Missouri, 1953.
262 S.W.2d 25.

■ HOLLINGSWORTH, JUDGE. Convicted in the Circuit Court of Jackson County of robbery in the first degree, defendant has appealed from a sentence of imprisonment in the State Penitentiary for a term of five years imposed upon him in conformity with the verdict returned by the jury. At the trial he admitted physical perpetration of the act of robbery as charged in the information but pleaded not guilty by reason of insanity and duress. The trial court submitted and instructed the jury on the issue of insanity but refused his request for an instruction submitting the issue of duress. He assigns error in the refusal of the court to so instruct. . . .

The victim of the robbery was William Rieken, who lived and operated a truck garden in or near Kansas City in Jackson County and sold the produce thereof from a roadside stand in front of his home. On the night of August 19, 1950, at about 11 o'clock and after he had retired, someone knocked at his rear bedroom door. He did not answer. The door was pushed open, a man entered and stated, "We want your money." The man held a pistol in one hand and a flashlight in the other. The flashlight enabled Rieken to see the intruder. Rieken went into another room, took $325 from his overalls and brought it to the intruder who took it and said to him, "Now you stay in there. We are going to be around here awhile, if you come out we will shoot you." When the intruder left the house, Rieken looked through a window, and saw a truck driven away with men in it. He promptly reported the matter to the police and, at the trial, identified defendant as the man who entered his home and robbed him.

On August 26, 1950, defendant and Loren Young and Calvin McNeal were arrested at defendant's home near Blue Springs in Jackson County, where were found a stolen automobile, several flashlights, numerous firearms and a large quantity of ammunition. Defendant, upon being questioned by the officers, readily admitted participation in the robbery as above detailed by Rieken, but also asserted that Young and McNeal had forced him to do so. Young and McNeal are now serving terms of imprisonment in the penitentiary. . . .

Defendant lived with his wife and son and collected and sold used automobile parts. He testified that in July, before the robbery in August, Young and McNeal first came to his home to buy an automobile part; that thereafter they made frequent visits to his home and soon began to stay there practically all of the time, in the house and yard, slept on his premises in their automobile and had his wife cook for them; that Young and McNeal there engaged in extensive target practice with firearms; that he tried to stop them but they wouldn't stop; that they shot at him and threatened him, and that he came to fear them greatly and was afraid to report them to the sheriff's office; they told him that if he did report them, they would kill both him and his wife before the officers could get them.

Defendant further testified that on the night of the robbery Young and McNeal asked him to drive his truck to Kansas City to "haul some stuff" for them; that he did not want to go, but they threatened to "punch" him; that at their direction he drove his truck with them accompanying him, to some place in Kansas City; that he did not know where they were, but one finally said, "Here is where the job is going to be", and he started to stop, but Young told him to drive on; that they went to a little town somewhere, where Young told him it was going to be a holdup of old man Rieken; that he started to argue, but they said that if he didn't do what they said to do, they were going to "blow my head out"; that they said to him, "If you get out [of Rieken's house] and run away, we are going back out and shoot your wife and boy", and he was afraid he would be shot if he did not go through with the holdup; that McNeal gave him a pistol and McNeal displayed a sawed-off shotgun. Young stayed in the truck. McNeal went with defendant to the door of Rieken's home, hammered on the door with the end of the sawed-off shotgun, and told defendant to go in and ask for the money; that he went in and held up Rieken in the manner testified by Rieken; that he then ran back to the truck preceded by McNeal, and all sped away; that McNeal took the money and the pistol from him; that Young then laughed, saying, "You robbed a man with a gun that wasn't even loaded", and showed him that the pistol which he had used in holding up Rieken had no ammunition in it.

The appellate courts of this State seem not to have dealt with duress or coercion as a defense to an otherwise criminal act. At least, we have not been cited nor have we found any such case. However, the question has been considered with some frequency in other jurisdictions. Numerous cases are cited in WHARTON'S CRIMINAL LAW, Vol. 1 § 384, p. 514. From these cases and others cited below it is established by the great weight of authority that although coercion does not excuse taking the life of an innocent person, yet it does excuse in all lesser crimes. But, to constitute a defense to a criminal charge, the coercion must be present, imminent, and impending and of such a nature as to induce a well grounded apprehension of death or serious bodily injury if the act is not done. Threat of future injury is not enough. Nor can one who has a reasonable opportunity to avoid doing the act without undue exposure to death or serious bodily injury invoke the doctrine as an excuse. . . .

We are convinced that the evidence in this case made a submissible issue under defendant's plea of duress. If the evidence above set forth was believed by the jury, it would have justified a finding that defendant committed the robbery not of his volition, but because of a well grounded fear of present, imminent and impending death or serious bodily injury at the hands of Young and McNeal. Furthermore, if believed by the jury, his testimony that he was under the immediate surveillance of McNeal who stood at the door with a drawn shotgun at the time he was in the Rieken home would warrant a finding that he had no reasonable opportunity to avoid committing the robbery without immediate exposure to death or great bodily injury. Under these circumstances, the court erred in refusing to instruct the jury on the issue of duress. . . .

The judgment is reversed and the cause remanded.

NOTES AND QUESTIONS

1. Is the defense of duress a defense of justification, or a defense of excuse? Why should it matter?

A considerable amount of thought has been given to that issue. In his seminal article on the topic, Professor Joshua Dressler states that though at first glance the common law defense of duress looks like a justification defense, he suggests that duress excuses, rather than justifies, wrongdoing. *See* Dressler, *Exegesis of the Law of Duress: Justifying the Excuse and Searching for its Proper Limits*, 62 SO. CA. L. REV. 1331, 1385 (1989). He concludes his study by observing:

> . . . [D]uress is at once a fascinating and very troubling excuse, for it requires us to ask ourselves what level of moral courage we have a right to demand of others through the criminal justice system. In seeking to draw the proper outer limits of the defense, we must avoid acting hypocritically or overzealously, yet we should be prepared to make moral judgments about those who were unluckily confronted with dilemmatic choices we have only faced on our nightmares. . . .

See also Bayles, *Reconceptualizing Necessity and Duress*, 33 WAYNE L. REV. 1191 (1987).

2. At common law the defense of duress was not available in a murder prosecution; this view is based on the statement expressed by Blackstone, that "he ought rather to die himself than escape by the murder of an innocent." (4 Blackstone Comm. [7th ed.] 30.) This view is followed in most American jurisdictions. Why not make the defense available to murder?

Recent commentators, such as Prof. Dressler (supra) would "allow juries to excuse persons who kill under duress." Professor Yale Kamisar, in commenting on Prof. Dressler's article, stated:

> . . . I think the reason the common law doesn't recognize it, is because it never had an honest-to-God duress case. It is very easy to dismiss the defense of duress when you're convinced the guy is lying and the whole thing is a fantasy.
>
> But take the case where the coercer says: "I have your wife and three kids captive and unless you agree to lure Mr. So and So to a place where my associates and I can kill him, I'm going to kill one of your kids every twenty-four hours." The defendant does nothing. At the end of the first day the body of his oldest son is sent to him. The defendant then decides to do whatever the person holding his wife and kids wants him to do.
>
> I don't see why there should be any question about duress being an excuse in such a case. . . . [Criminal law conference discussions reported at 19 RUTGERS L.J. at 722–723 (1988).]

Do you agree with Prof. Kamisar?

In Director of Public Prosecutions v. Lynch, [1975] A.C. 653, [1975] 2 W.L.R. 641, [1975] 1 All E.R. 913, the English House of Lords debated the applicability of the duress defense to murder cases. Lynch alleged that he had been forced by members of the Irish Republican Army to drive them to the home of a constable who was then killed by the IRA. If duress is held not to be a defense to murder, should it nevertheless be a defense to complicity to murder?

3. Assume that St. Clair had been forced by Young and McNeal to help them rob "old man Rieken," and that during the robbery Rieken had been accidentally shot and killed by McNeal. If in the jurisdiction duress is not available as a defense to murder, should it nevertheless be considered as a defense to felony-murder? See, People v. Serrano, 286 Ill.App.3d 485, 222 Ill.Dec. 47, 676 N.E.2d 1011 (1st Dist. 1997); State v. Hunter, 241 Kan. 629, 740 P.2d 559 (1987); Tully v. State, 730 P.2d 1206 (Okla.Crim.App.1986); People v. Petro, 13 Cal.App.2d 245, 56 P.2d 984 (1936). Compare, People v. Roper, 259 N.Y. 170, 181 N.E. 88 (1932).

4. Patty Hearst, kidnapped and held confined by members of the Symbionese Liberation Army for months, participated during her "captivity" in a bank robbery. She appeared to be involved rather willingly when one viewed the bank's film tape that had been made during the commission of the crime. At her trial, the ordinary duress question was presented (threats of death), but, in addition, could not her participation in the crime be excused as coerced because of the pressures of psychological indoctrination or "brainwashing?"

See, in this regard, Delgado, *Ascription of Criminal States of Mind: Toward a Defense Theory for the Coercively Persuaded ("Brainwashed") Defendant*, 63 MINN. L. REV. 1 (1978), and a further exchange of views on the article in 63 MINN. L. REV. 335 and 361 (1979).

In Lunde & Wilson, *Brainwashing as a Defense to Criminal Liability: Patty Hearst Revisited,* 13 CRIM. L. BULL. 341, 358 (1977), the authors state: "a true case of coercive persuasion ['brainwashing'] cannot fit under the duress rubric. The coercive aspects of the indoctrination process may occur long before the commission of the crime for which the accused stands charged. At the time of the commission of the offense . . . the defendant may be under no immediate duress." *See also* Alldridge, *Brainwashing as a Criminal Defense,* 1984 CRIM. L. REV. 726.

5. Consider the following excerpt from LaFave & Scott, CRIMINAL LAW, 2d ed., 1986, at 440:

> The common law rule was that, except for murder and treason, a married woman was not punishable for crime if she acted under the coercion of her husband; and, if she committed the criminal act in her husband's presence, there was a rebuttable presumption that he had coerced her. Something less in the way of pressure was required for a wife to be coerced than for an ordinary person to meet the requirements of the defense of duress; one early English case held that the husband's mere command would do.

> The modern trend, however, is to do away with the presumption. In a North Carolina case its appellate court held that the "long recognized and applied" presumption had outlived its necessity and usefulness. State v. Smith, 33 N.C.App. 511, 235 S.E.2d 860 (1977). *See also* Conyer v. United States, 80 F.2d 292 (6th Cir.1935); State v. Renslow, 211 Iowa 642, 230 N.W. 316 (1930); Morton v. State, 141 Tenn. 357, 209 S.W. 644 (1919).

6. With reference to the above, see the Model Penal Code, § 2.09(1) which provides:

> It is an affirmative defense that the actor engaged in the conduct charged to constitute an offense because he was coerced to do so by the use of, or threat to use, unlawful force against the person, or the person of another, which a person of reasonable firmness in his situation would have been unable to resist.

7. In Williams v. State, 101 Md. App. 408, 646 A.2d 1101 (1994), the defendant claimed that he was forced to participate in a break-in by a drug gang, of which he was a member. Consider, in this regard, Model Penal Code § 2.09(2), which provides:

> The defense provided by this section is unavailable if the actor recklessly placed himself in a situation in which it was probable that he would be subjected to duress. The defense is also unavailable if he was negligent in placing himself in such a situation, whenever negligence suffices to establish culpability for the offense charged.

8. On whom rest the burdens of proof and persuasion when a defendant claims to be acting under duress? See, in this regard, the case of Dixon v. United States, 548 U.S. 1, 126 S.Ct. 2437, 165 L.Ed.2d 299 (2006), discussed supra in Chapter 2, Section D.

2. NECESSITY

In the year 1884, a yacht was caught in a storm 1600 miles from the nearest land. Its crew of four had to abandon the vessel and put to sea in an open lifeboat which contained no water and no food except two small cans of vegetables. For three days there was no other food. On the fourth day they caught a small turtle which was their only food for the next eight days. From then on, until their twentieth day at sea, they had nothing to eat, and only a very small amount of rain water to drink. On the eighteenth day, as their boat was still drifting at sea and was still more than a thousand miles from land, one of the seamen proposed to two of the others that they kill and eat the fourth member, a boy about seventeen years of age who was then in an extremely weakened condition. Although one seaman dissented from this proposal, two days later the boy was killed. The survivors, including the one who had refused to participate in the killing, fed upon the boy's body. On the fourth day after the killing, they were rescued by a passing vessel.

Were the two seamen who killed the boy guilty of a criminal homicide? What of the third seaman? Would your answer be any different if all four members, including the boy, had drawn lots, with the boy as the loser?

Or, suppose the men in the lifeboat were in the Navy and the Captain of their vessel ordered that the youngest and weakest person in the boat be killed for this purpose. Would such a command be a defense to the men who carried out the Captain's orders?

Or, suppose the lifeboat contained both passengers and crew and that, rather than the lack of food, the difficulty had been occasioned by the unseaworthiness of the lifeboat, a condition which had been compounded by a torrential downpour. To keep the boat from sinking, the members of the crew cast fourteen male passengers overboard. Two women—sisters of one of the male victims—jumped out of the boat to join their brother in death. As a result of this human jettisoning, the boat remained afloat and the survivors were rescued a short time later. Were the members of the crew guilty of criminal homicide with respect to the male passengers who were cast overboard? With respect to the two women who jumped overboard? Would your answer be different if the crewmen, in an attempt to lighten the boat, had not thrown passengers overboard but rather had thrown overboard other members of the crew who were unnecessary to the operation of the lifeboat?

NOTES

1. Consider, Fuller, *The Case of the Speluncean Explorers*, 62 HARV. L. REV. 616 (1949) in which Professor Lon Fuller poses a hypothetical case in which some trapped cave explorers kill and eat one of their number in order to survive until rescue. Among the views advanced for disposing of the criminality issue in the case presented, consider the following:

"... [P]ositive law is predicated on the possibility of men's coexistence in society. When a situation arises in which the coexistence of men becomes impossible, then the condition that underlies all of our precedents and statutes ceases to exist. When that condition disappears ... the force of positive law disappears with it." Under such circumstances, therefore, endangered persons are not in a "state of civil society" but in a "state of nature." Id. at 620, 621.

Compare Cardozo, Law and Literature, 113 (1931): "There is no rule of human jettison.... Who shall choose in such an hour between the victims and the saved? Who shall know when masts and sails of rescue may emerge out of the fog?"

See also Hall, GENERAL PRINCIPLES OF CRIMINAL LAW 425–36 (2d ed. 1960).

2. Consider the possible disposition of the case situations presented under the Model Penal Code provision, § 3.02:

(1) Conduct which the actor believes to be necessary to avoid harm or evil to himself or to another is justifiable, provided that:

(a) the harm or evil sought to be avoided by such conduct is greater than that sought to be prevented by the law defining the offense charged; and

(b) neither the Code nor other law defining the offense provides exceptions or defenses dealing with the specific situation involved; and

(c) a legislative purpose to exclude the justification claimed does not otherwise plainly appear.

United States v. Bailey

Supreme Court of the United States, 1980.
444 U.S. 394, 100 S.Ct. 624, 62 L.Ed.2d 575.

■ MR. JUSTICE REHNQUIST delivered the opinion of the Court.

In the early morning hours of August 26, 1976, respondents Clifford Bailey, James T. Cogdell, Ronald C. Cooley, and Ralph Walker, federal prisoners at the District of Columbia jail, crawled through a window from which a bar had been removed, slid down a knotted bedsheet, and escaped from custody. Federal authorities recaptured them after they had remained at large for a period of time ranging from one month to three and one-half months. Upon their apprehension, they were charged with violating 18 U.S.C. § 751 (a), which governs escape from federal custody. At their trials, each of the respondents adduced or offered to adduce evidence as to various conditions and events at the District of Columbia jail, but each was convicted by the jury. The Court of Appeals for the District of Columbia Circuit reversed the convictions by a divided vote, holding that the District Court had improperly precluded consideration by the respective juries of respondents' tendered evidence. We granted certiorari, and now reverse the judgments of the Court of Appeals.

Reversed

In reaching our conclusion, we must decide the state of mind necessary for violation of § 751(a) and the elements that comprise defenses such as duress and necessity. . . .

I

* * *

The prosecution's case in chief against Bailey, Cooley, and Walker was brief. The Government introduced evidence that each of the respondents was in federal custody on August 26, 1976, that they had disappeared, apparently through a cell window, at approximately 5:35 a.m. on that date, and that they had been apprehended individually between September 27 and December 13, 1976.

Respondents' defense of duress or necessity centered on the conditions in the jail during the months of June, July, and August 1976, and on various threats and beatings directed at them during that period. In describing the conditions at the jail, they introduced evidence of frequent fires in "Northeast One," the maximum-security cellblock occupied by respondents prior to their escape. Construed in the light most favorable to them, this evidence demonstrated that the inmates of Northeast One, and on occasion the guards in that unit, set fire to trash, bedding, and other objects thrown from the cells. According to the inmates, the guards simply allowed the fires to burn until they went out. Although the fires apparently were confined to small areas and posed no substantial threat of spreading through the complex, poor ventilation caused smoke to collect and linger in the cellblock.

Respondents Cooley and Bailey also introduced testimony that the guards at the jail had subjected them to beatings and to threats of death. Walker attempted to prove that he was an epileptic and had received inadequate medical attention for his seizures.

Consistently during the trial, the District Court stressed that, to sustain their defenses, respondents would have to introduce some evidence that they attempted to surrender or engaged in equivalent conduct once they had freed themselves from the conditions they described. But the court waited for such evidence in vain. Respondent Cooley, who had eluded the authorities for one month, testified that his "people" had tried to contact the authorities, but "never got in touch with anybody." He also suggested that someone had told his sister that the FBI would kill him when he was apprehended.

Respondent Bailey, who was apprehended on November 19, 1976, told a similar story. He stated that he "had the jail officials called several times," but did not turn himself in because "I would still be under the threats of death." Like Cooley, Bailey testified that "the FBI was telling my people that they was going to shoot me."

Only respondent Walker suggested that he had attempted to negotiate a surrender. Like Cooley and Bailey, Walker testified that the FBI had told his "people" that they would kill him when they recaptured him. Nevertheless, according to Walker, he called the FBI three times and spoke with an agent whose name he could not remember. That agent allegedly assured him that the FBI would not harm him, but was unable to promise that Walker would not be returned to the D.C. jail. Walker testified that he last called the FBI in mid-October. He was finally apprehended on December 13, 1976.

At the close of all the evidence, the District Court rejected respondents' proffered instruction on duress as a defense to prison escape.[3] The court ruled that respondents had failed as a matter of law to present evidence sufficient to support such a defense because they had not turned themselves in after they had escaped the allegedly coercive conditions. After receiving instructions to disregard the evidence of the conditions in the jail, the jury convicted Bailey, Cooley, and Walker of violating § 751(a).

Two months later, respondent Cogdell came to trial before the same District Judge who had presided over the trial of his co-respondents. When Cogdell attempted to offer testimony concerning the allegedly inhumane conditions at the D.C. jail, the District Judge inquired into Cogdell's conduct between his escape on August 26 and his apprehension on September 28. In response to Cogdell's assertion that he "may have written letters," the District Court specified that Cogdell could testify only as to "what he did . . . [n]ot what he may have done." Absent such testimony, however, the District Court ruled that Cogdell could not present evidence of conditions at the jail. Cogdell subsequently chose not to testify on his own behalf, and was convicted by the jury of violating § 751(a).

By a divided vote, the Court of Appeals reversed each respondent's conviction and remanded for new trials. The majority concluded that the District Court should have allowed the jury to consider the evidence of coercive conditions in determining whether the respondents had formulated the requisite intent to sustain a conviction under § 751(a). According to the majority, § 751(a) required the prosecution to prove that

---

[3] Respondents asked the District Court to give the following instruction:

"Coercion which would excuse the commission of a criminal act must result from:

"1) Threathening [sic] conduct sufficient to create in the mind of a reasonable person the fear of death or serious bodily harm;

"2) The conduct in fact caused such fear of death or serious bodily harm in the mind of the defendant;

"3) The fear or duress was operating upon the mind of the defendant at the time of the alleged act; and

"4) The defendant committed the act to avoid the threatened [sic] harm."

a particular defendant left federal custody voluntarily, without permission, and "with an intent to avoid confinement." 190 U.S.App.D.C., at 148, 585 F.2d, at 1093. The majority then defined the word "confinement" as encompassing only the "normal aspects" of punishment prescribed by our legal system. Thus, where a prisoner escapes in order to avoid "non-confinement" conditions such as beatings or homosexual attacks, he would not necessarily have the requisite intent to sustain a conviction under § 751(a). According to the majority:

> When a defendant introduces evidence that he was subject to such "non-confinement" conditions, the crucial factual determination on the intent issue is . . . whether the defendant left custody only to avoid these conditions or whether, in addition the defendant *also* intended to avoid confinement. In making this determination the jury is to be guided by the trial court's instructions pointing out those factors that are most indicative of the presence or absence of an intent to avoid confinement. (emphasis in original).

Turning to the applicability of the defense of duress or necessity, the majority assumed that escape as defined by § 751(a) was a "continuing offense" as long as the escapee was at large. Given this assumption, the majority agreed with the District Court that, under normal circumstances, an escapee must present evidence of coercion to justify his continued absence from custody as well as his initial departure. Here, however, respondents had been indicted for "flee[ing] and escap[ing]" "[o]n or about August 26, 1976," and not for "leaving *and staying away from* custody." (emphasis in original). Similarly, "[t]he trial court's instructions when read as a whole clearly give the impression that [respondents] were being tried only for leaving the jail on August 26, and not for failing to return at some later date." Under these circumstances, the majority believed that neither respondents nor the juries were acquainted with the proposition that the escapes in question were continuing offenses. This failure, according to the majority, constituted "an obvious violation of [respondents'] constitutional right to jury trial."

The dissenting judge objected to what he characterized as a revolutionary reinterpretation of criminal law by the majority. He argued that the common-law crime of escape had traditionally required only "general intent," a mental state no more sophisticated than an "intent to go beyond permitted limits." (emphasis deleted) . . .

II

Criminal liability is normally based upon the concurrence of two factors, "an evil-meaning mind [and] an evil-doing hand. . . ." Morissette v. United States. In the present case, we must examine both the mental element, or *mens rea*, required for conviction under § 751(a) and the circumstances under which the "evil-doing hand" can avoid liability under that section because coercive conditions or necessity negate a conclusion of guilt even though the necessary *mens rea* was present.

A

Few areas of criminal law pose more difficulty than the proper definition of the *mens rea* required for any particular crime. In 1970, the National Commission on Reform of Federal Criminal Laws decried the "confused and inconsistent ad hoc approach" of the federal courts to this issue and called for "a new departure." . . . Although the central focus of this and other reform movements has been the codification of workable principles for determining criminal culpability, see e.g., American Law Institute, Model Penal Code §§ 2.01–2.13 (Prop. Off. Draft 1962) (hereinafter Model Penal Code); S. 1, 94th Cong., 2d Sess. §§ 301–303 (1976), a byproduct has been a general rethinking of traditional *mens rea* analysis.

At common law, crimes generally were classified as requiring either "general intent" or "specific intent." This venerable distinction, however, has been the source of a good deal of confusion. As one treatise explained:

> Sometimes "general intent" is used in the same way as "criminal intent" to mean the general notion of *mens rea*, while "specific intent" is taken to mean the mental state required for a particular crime. Or, "general intent" may be used to encompass all forms of the mental state requirement, while "specific intent" is limited to the one mental state of intent. Another possibility is that "general intent" will be used to characterize an intent to do something on an undetermined occasion, and "specific intent" to denote an intent to do that thing at a particular time and place. W. LaFave & A. Scott, HANDBOOK ON CRIMINAL LAW § 28, pp. 201–202 (1972) (footnotes omitted) (hereinafter LAFAVE & SCOTT).

This ambiguity has led to a movement away from the traditional dichotomy of intent and toward an alternative analysis of *mens rea*. See id., at 202. This new approach, exemplified in the American Law Institute's Model Penal Code, is based on two principles. First, the ambiguous and elastic term "intent" is replaced with a hierarchy of culpable states of mind. The different levels in this hierarchy are commonly identified, in descending order of culpability, as purpose, knowledge, recklessness, and negligence. Model Penal Code § 2.02. Perhaps the most significant, and most esoteric, distinction drawn by this analysis is that between the mental states of "purpose" and "knowledge." As we pointed out in United States v. United States Gypsum Co., 438 U.S. 422, 445 (1978), a person who causes a particular result is said to act purposefully if " 'he consciously desires that result, whatever the likelihood of that result happening from his conduct,' " while he is said to act knowingly if he is aware " 'that that result is practically certain to follow from his conduct, whatever his desire may be as to that result.' "

* * *

In certain narrow classes of crimes, however, heightened culpability has been thought to merit special attention. Thus, the statutory and common law of homicide often distinguishes, either in setting the "degree" of the crime or in imposing punishment, between a person who knows that another person will be killed as the result of his conduct and a person who acts with the specific purpose of taking another's life. . . . Similarly, where a defendant is charged with treason, this Court has stated that the Government must demonstrate that the defendant acted with a purpose to aid the enemy. See Haupt v. United States, 330 U.S. 631, 641 (1947). Another such example is the law of inchoate offenses such as attempt and conspiracy, where a heightened mental state separates criminality itself from otherwise innocuous behavior. . . .

In a general sense, "purpose" corresponds loosely with the common-law concept of specific intent, while "knowledge" corresponds loosely with the concept of general intent. . . . Were this substitution of terms the only innovation offered by the reformers, it would hardly be dramatic. But there is another ambiguity inherent in the traditional distinction between specific intent and general intent. Generally, even time-honored common-law crimes consist of several elements, and complex statutorily defined crimes exhibit this characteristic to an even greater degree. Is the same state of mind required of the actor for each element of the crime, or may some elements require one state of mind and some another? In United States v. Feola, 420 U.S. 671 (1975), for example, . . . we concluded that Congress intended to require only "an intent to assault, not an intent to assault a federal officer." What *Feola* implied, the American Law Institute stated: "[C]lear analysis requires that the question of the kind of culpability required to establish the commission of an offense be faced separately with respect to each material element of the crime." MPC Comments 123. See also Working Papers 131; LAFAVE & SCOTT 194.

Before dissecting § 751(a) and assigning a level of culpability to each element, we believe that two observations are in order. First, in performing such analysis courts obviously must follow Congress' intent as to the required level of mental culpability for any particular offense. . . . In the case of § 751(a), however, neither the language of the statute nor the legislative history mentions the *mens rea* required for conviction.[6]

Second, while the suggested element-by-element analysis is a useful tool for making sense of an otherwise opaque concept, it is not the only principle to be considered. The administration of the federal system of

---

[6]   This omission does not mean, of course, that § 751(a) defines a "strict liability" crime for which punishment can be imposed without proof of any *mens rea* at all. As we held in Morissette v. United States, supra, at 263, "mere omission [from the statute] of any mention of intent will not be construed as eliminating that element from the crimes denounced." . . .

criminal justice is confided to ordinary mortals, whether they be lawyers, judges, or jurors. This system could easily fall of its own weight if courts or scholars become obsessed with hair-splitting distinctions, either traditional or novel, that Congress neither stated nor implied when it made the conduct criminal.

As relevant to the charges against Bailey, Cooley, and Walker, § 751(a) required the prosecution to prove (1) that they had been in the custody of the Attorney General, (2) as the result of a conviction, and (3) that they had escaped from that custody. As for the charges against respondent Cogdell, § 751(a) required the same proof, with the exception that his confinement was based upon an arrest for a felony rather than a prior conviction. Although § 751(a) does not define the term "escape," courts and commentators are in general agreement that it means absenting oneself from custody without permission. . . .

Respondents have not challenged the District Court's instructions on the first two elements of the crime defined by § 751(a). It is undisputed that, on August 26, 1976, respondents were in the custody of the Attorney General as the result of either arrest on charges of felony or conviction. As for the element of "escape," we need not decide whether a person could be convicted on evidence of recklessness or negligence with respect to the limits on his freedom. A court may someday confront a case where an escapee did not know, but should have known, that he was exceeding the bounds of his confinement or that he was leaving without permission. Here, the District Court clearly instructed the juries that the prosecution bore the burden of proving that respondents "knowingly committed an act which the law makes a crime" and that they acted "knowingly, intentionally, and deliberately. . . ." . . . The sufficiency of the evidence to support the juries' verdicts under this charge has never seriously been questioned, nor could it be.

The majority of the Court of Appeals, however, imposed the added burden on the prosecution to prove as a part of its case in chief that respondents acted "with an intent to avoid confinement." While . . . the word "intent" is quite ambiguous, the majority left little doubt that it was requiring the Government to prove that the respondents acted with the purpose—that is, the conscious objective—of leaving the jail without authorization. . . .

We find the majority's position quite unsupportable. Nothing in the language or legislative history of § 751(a) indicates that Congress intended to require either such a heightened standard of culpability or such a narrow definition of confinement. . . . Accordingly, we hold that the prosecution fulfills its burden under § 751(a) if it demonstrates that an escapee knew his actions would result in his leaving physical confinement without permission. . . .

B

Respondents also contend that they are entitled to a new trial because they presented (or, in Cogdell's case, could have presented) sufficient evidence of duress or necessity to submit such a defense to the jury. . . .

Common law historically distinguished between the defenses of duress and necessity. Duress was said to excuse criminal conduct where the actor was under an unlawful threat of imminent death or serious bodily injury, which threat caused the actor to engage in conduct violating the literal terms of the criminal law. While the defense of duress covered the situation where the coercion had it source in the actions of other human beings, the defense of necessity, or choice of evils, traditionally covered the situation where physical forces beyond the actor's control rendered illegal conduct the lesser of two evils. Thus, where A destroyed a dike because B threatened to kill him if he did not, A would argue that he acted under duress, whereas if A destroyed the dike in order to protect more valuable property from flooding, A could claim a defense of necessity. . . .

Modern cases have tended to blur the distinction between duress and necessity. In the court below, the majority discarded the labels "duress" and "necessity," choosing instead to examine the policies underlying the traditional defenses. In particular, the majority felt that the defenses were designed to spare a person from punishment if he acted "under threats or conditions that a person of ordinary firmness would have been unable to resist," or if he reasonably believed that criminal action "was necessary to avoid a harm more serious than that sought to be prevented by the statute defining the offense." The Model Penal Code redefines the defenses along similar lines. See Model Penal Code § 2.09 (duress) and § 3.02 (choice of evils).

We need not speculate now, however, on the precise contours of whatever defenses of duress or necessity are available against charges brought under § 751(a). Under any definition of these defenses one principle remains constant: if there was a reasonable, legal alternative to violating the law, "a chance both to refuse to do the criminal act and also to avoid the threatened harm," the defenses will fail. . . . Clearly, in the context of prison escape, the escapee is not entitled to claim a defense of duress or necessity unless and until he demonstrates that, given the imminence of the threat, violation of § 751(a) was his only reasonable alternative. . . .

* * *

We need not decide whether such evidence as that submitted by respondents was sufficient to raise a jury question as to their initial departures. This is because we decline to hold that respondents' failure to return is "just one factor" for the jury to weigh in deciding whether the initial escape could be affirmatively justified. On the contrary, several considerations lead us to conclude that, in order to be entitled to an instruction on duress or necessity as a defense to the crime charged, an escapee must first offer evidence justifying his continued absence from custody as well as his initial departure and that an indispensable element of such an offer is testimony of a bona fide effort to surrender or return to custody as soon as the claimed duress or necessity had lost its coercive force.

First, we think it clear beyond peradventure that escape from federal custody as defined in § 751(a) is a continuing offense and that an escapee can be held liable for failure to return to custody as well as for his initial departure. Given the continuing threat to society posed by an escaped prisoner, "the nature of the crime involved is such that Congress must assuredly have intended that it be treated as a continuing one." Moreover, every federal court that has considered this issue has held, either explicitly or implicitly, that § 751(a) defines a continuing offense. . . .

* * *

We therefore hold that, where a criminal defendant is charged with escape and claims that he is entitled to an instruction on the theory of duress or necessity, he must proffer evidence of a bona fide effort to surrender or return to custody as soon as the claimed duress or necessity had lost its coercive force. We have reviewed the evidence examined elaborately in the majority and dissenting opinions below, and find the case not even close, even under respondents' versions of the facts, as to whether they either surrendered or offered to surrender at their earliest possible opportunity. Since we have determined that this is an indispensable element of the defense of duress or necessity, respondents were not entitled to any instruction on such a theory. Vague and necessarily self-serving statements of defendants or witnesses as to future good intentions or ambiguous conduct simply do not support a finding of this element of the defense.

* * *

This case presents a good example of the potential for wasting valuable trial resources. In general, trials for violations of § 751(a) should be simple affairs. The key elements are capable of objective demonstration; the *mens rea*, as discussed above, will usually depend upon reasonable inferences from those objective facts. Here, however, the jury in the trial of Bailey, Cooley, and Walker heard five days of testimony. It was presented with evidence of every unpleasant aspect of prison life from the amount of garbage on the cellblock floor, to the meal schedule, to the number of times the inmates were allowed to shower. Unfortunately, all this evidence was presented in a case where the defense's reach hopelessly exceeded its grasp. Were we to hold, as respondents suggest, that the jury should be subjected to this potpourri even though a critical element of the proffered defenses was concededly absent, we undoubtedly would convert every trial under § 751(a) into a hearing on the current state of the federal penal system. . . .

Because the juries below were properly instructed on the *mens rea* required by § 751(a), and because the respondents failed to introduce evidence sufficient to submit their defenses of duress and necessity to the juries, we reverse the judgments of the Court of Appeals.

Reversed.

■ MR. JUSTICE MARSHALL took no part in the consideration or decision of this case.

■ [MR. JUSTICE STEVENS' concurring opinion is omitted.]

■ MR. JUSTICE BLACKMUN, with whom MR. JUSTICE BRENNAN joins, dissenting.

The Court's opinion, it seems to me, is an impeccable exercise in undisputed general principles and technical legalism: The respondents were properly confined in the District of Columbia jail. They departed from that jail without authority or consent. They failed promptly to turn themselves in when, as the Court would assert by way of justification, the claimed duress or necessity "had lost its coercive force." Therefore, the Court concludes, there is no defense for a jury to weigh and consider against the respondents' prosecution for escape violative of 18 U.S.C. § 751(a).

It is with the Court's assertion that the claimed duress or necessity had lost its coercive force that I particularly disagree. The conditions that led to respondents' initial departure from the D.C. jail continue unabated. If departure was justified—and on the record before us that issue, I feel, is for the jury to resolve as a matter of fact in the light of the evidence, and not for this Court to determine as a matter of law—it seems too much to demand that respondents, in order to preserve their legal defenses, return forthwith to the hell that obviously exceeds the normal deprivations of prison life and that compelled their leaving in the first instance. The Court, however, requires that an escapee's action must amount to nothing more than a mere and temporary gesture that, it is to be hoped, just might attract attention in responsive circles. But life and health, even if convicts and accuseds, deserve better than that and are entitled to more than pious pronouncements fit for an ideal world.

The Court, in its carefully structured opinion, does reach a result that might be a proper one were we living in that ideal world, and were our American jails and penitentiaries truly places for humane and rehabilitative treatment of their inmates. Then the statutory crime of escape could not be excused by duress or necessity, by beatings, and by guard-set fires in the jails, for these would not take place, and escapees would be appropriately prosecuted and punished.

But we do not live in an ideal world "even" (to use a self-centered phrase) in America, so far as jail and prison conditions are concerned. The complaints that this Court, and every other American appellate court, receives almost daily from prisoners about conditions of incarceration, about filth, about homosexual rape, and about brutality are not always the mouthings of the purely malcontent. . . . I therefore dissent.

I

The atrocities and inhuman conditions of prison life in America are almost unbelievable; surely they are nothing less than shocking. The dissent in the *Bailey* case in the Court of Appeals acknowledged that "the circumstances of prison life are such that at least a colorable, if not credible, claim of duress or necessity can be raised with respect to virtually every escape." And the Government concedes: "In light of prison conditions that even now prevail in the United States, it would be the rare inmate who could not convince himself that continued incarceration would be harmful to his health or safety."

A youthful inmate can expect to be subjected to homosexual gang rape his first night in jail, or, it has been said, even in the van on the way to jail. Weaker inmates become the property of stronger prisoners or gangs, who sell the sexual services of the victim. Prison officials either are disinterested in stopping abuse of prisoners by other prisoners or are incapable of doing so, given the limited resources society allocates to the prison system. Prison officials often are merely indifferent to serious health and safety needs of prisoners as well.

Even more appalling is the fact that guards frequently participate in the brutalization of inmates. The classic example is the beating or other punishment in retaliation for prisoner complaints or court actions.

The evidence submitted by respondents in these cases fits that pattern exactly. Respondent Bailey presented evidence that he was continually mistreated by correctional officers during his stay at the D.C. jail. He was threatened that his testimony in the Brad King case would bring on severe retribution. Other inmates were beaten by guards as a message to Bailey. An inmate testified that on one occasion, three guards displaying a small knife told him that they were going "to get your buddy, that nigger Bailey. We're going to kill him." The threats culminated in a series of violent attacks on Bailey. Blackjacks, mace, and slapjacks (leather with a steel insert) were used in beating Bailey.

Respondent Cooley also elicited testimony from other inmates concerning beatings of Cooley by guards with slapjacks, blackjacks, and flashlights. There was evidence that guards threatened to kill Cooley.

It is society's responsibility to protect the life and health of its prisoners. "[W]hen a sheriff or a marshal [*sic*] takes a man from the courthouse in a prison van and transports him to confinement for two or three or ten years, *this is our act. We* have tolled the bell for him. And whether we like it or not, we have made him our collective responsibility. We are free to do something about him; he is not" (emphasis in original). Address by The Chief Justice, 25 Record of the Assn. of the Bar of the City of New York 14, 17 (Mar. 1970 Supp.). Deliberate indifference to serious and essential medical needs of prisoners constitutes "cruel and unusual" punishment violative of the Eighth Amendment. Estelle v. Gamble, 429 U.S. 97, 104 (1976). . . .

. . . The reasons that support the Court's holding in Estelle v. Gamble lead me to conclude that failure to use reasonable measures to protect an inmate from violence inflicted by other inmates also constitutes cruel and unusual punishment. Homosexual rape or other violence serves no penological purpose. Such brutality is the equivalent of torture, and is offensive to any modern standard of human dignity. Prisoners must depend, and rightly so, upon the prison administrators for protection from abuse of this kind.

There can be little question that our prisons are badly overcrowded and understaffed and that this in large part is the cause of many of the shortcomings of our penal systems. This, however, does not excuse the failure to provide a place of confinement that meets minimal standards of safety and decency.

Penal systems in other parts of the world demonstrate that vast improvement surely is not beyond our reach. "The contrast between our indifference and the programs in some countries of Europe—Holland and the Scandinavian countries in particular—is not a happy one for us." Address by The Chief Justice, supra, at 20. . . . Sweden's prisons are not overcrowded, and most inmates have a private cell. Salomon, *Lessons from the Swedish Criminal Justice System: A Reappraisal*, 40 FED. PROBATION 40, 43 (Sept. 1976). The prisons are small. The largest accommodate 300–500 inmates; most house 50–150. . . .

II

The real question presented in this case is whether the prisoner should be punished for helping to extricate himself from a situation where society has abdicated completely its basic responsibility for providing an environment free of life-threatening conditions such as beatings, fires, lack of essential medical care, and sexual attacks. To be sure, Congress in so many words has not enacted specific statutory duress or necessity defenses that would excuse or justify commission of an otherwise unlawful act. The concept of such a defense, however, is "anciently woven into the fabric of our culture." J. Hall, GENERAL PRINCIPLES OF CRIMINAL LAW 416 (2d ed. 1960), quoted in Brief for United States 21. And the Government concedes that "it has always been an accepted part of our criminal justice system that punishment is inappropriate for crimes committed under duress because the defendant in such circumstances cannot fairly be blamed for his wrongful act."

Although the Court declines to address the issue, it at least implies that it would recognize the common-law defenses of duress and necessity to the federal crime of prison escape, if the appropriate prerequisites for assertion of either defense were met. Given the universal acceptance of these defenses in the common law, I have no difficulty in concluding that Congress intended the defenses of duress and necessity to be available to persons accused of committing the federal crime of escape.

I agree with most of the Court's comments about the essential elements of the defenses. . . . I therefore agree that it is appropriate to treat unduly harsh prison conditions as an affirmative defense.

I also agree with the Court that the absence of reasonable less drastic alternatives is a prerequisite to successful assertion of a defense of necessity or duress to a charge of prison escape. One must appreciate, however, that other realistic avenues of redress seldom are open to the prisoner. Where prison officials participate in the maltreatment of an inmate, or purposefully ignore dangerous conditions or brutalities inflicted by other prisoners or guards, the inmate can do little to protect himself. Filing a complaint may well result in retribution, and appealing to the guards is a capital offense under the prisoners' code of behavior. In most instances, the question whether alternative remedies were thoroughly "exhausted" should be a matter for the jury to decide.

I, too, conclude that the jury generally should be instructed that, in order to prevail on a necessity or duress defense, the defendant must justify his continued absence from custody, as well as his initial departure. I agree with the Court that the very nature of escape makes it a continuing crime. But I cannot agree that the only way continued absence can be justified is evidence "of a bona fide effort to surrender or return to custody." The Court apparently entertains the view, naive in my estimation, that once the prisoner has escaped from a life- or health-threatening situation, he can turn himself in, secure in the faith that his escape somehow will result in improvement in those intolerable prison conditions. While it may be true in some rare circumstance that an escapee will obtain the aid of a court or of the prison administration once the escape is accomplished, the escapee, realistically, faces a high probability of being returned to the same prison and to exactly the same, or even greater, threats to life and safety.

The rationale of the necessity defense is a balancing of harms. If the harm caused by an escape is less than the harm caused by remaining in a threatening situation, the prisoner's initial departure is justified. The same rationale should apply to hesitancy and failure to return. A situation may well arise where the social balance weighs in favor of the prisoner even though he fails to return to custody. The escapee at least should be permitted to present to the jury the possibility that the harm that would result from a return to custody outweighs the harm to society from continued absence.

Even under the Court's own standard, the defendant in an escape prosecution should be permitted to submit evidence to the jury to demonstrate that surrender would result in his being placed again in a life- or health-threatening situation. The Court requires return to custody once the "claimed duress or necessity had lost its coercive force." Realistically, however, the escapee who reasonably believes that surrender will result in return to what concededly is an intolerable prison situation remains subject to the same "coercive force" that prompted his escape in the first instance. It is ironic to say that that force is automatically "lost" once the prison wall is passed.

The Court's own phrasing of its test demonstrates that it is deciding factual questions that should be presented to the jury. It states that a "bona fide" effort to surrender must be proved. Whether an effort is "bona fide" is a jury question. The Court also states that "[v]ague and necessarily self-serving statements of defendants or witnesses as to future good intentions or ambiguous conduct simply do not support a finding of this element of the defense." Traditionally, it is the function of the jury to evaluate the credibility and meaning of "necessarily self-serving statements" and "ambiguous conduct."

Finally, I of course must agree with the Court that use of the jury is to be reserved for the case in which there is sufficient evidence to support a verdict. I have no difficulty, however, in concluding that respondents here did indeed submit sufficient evidence to support a verdict of not guilty, if the jury were so inclined, based on the necessity defense. . . .

In conclusion, my major point of disagreement with the Court is whether a defendant may get his duress or necessity defense to the jury when it is supported only by "self-serving" testimony and "ambiguous conduct." It is difficult, to imagine any case, criminal or civil, in which the jury is asked to decide a factual question based on completely disinterested testimony and unambiguous actions. The very essence of a jury issue is a dispute over the credibility of testimony by interested witnesses and the meaning of ambiguous actions.

Ruling on a defense as a matter of law and preventing the jury from considering it should be a rare occurrence in criminal cases. "[I]n a criminal case the law assigns [the factfinding function] solely to the jury." . . . The jury is the conscience of society and its role in a criminal prosecution is particularly important. . . . Yet the Court here appears to place an especially strict burden of proof on defendants attempting to establish an affirmative defense to the charged crime of escape. That action is unwarranted. If respondents' allegations are true, society is grossly at fault for permitting these conditions to persist at the D.C. jail. The findings of researchers and government agencies, as well as the litigated cases, indicate that in a general sense these allegations are credible. . . . In an attempt to conserve the jury for cases it considers truly worthy of that body, the Court has ousted the jury from a role it is particularly well-suited to serve.

NOTES

1. Some other courts have taken cognizance of the fact that brutality and homosexual attacks are commonplace within some prisons and penitentiaries. In Esquibel v. State, 91 N.M. 498, 576 P.2d 1129 (1978), the court said it was not error to instruct on the defense of duress to a charge of escape when there was substantial evidence of a prolonged history of beatings and serious threats toward the defendant by certain guards and prison personnel. In People v. Harmon, 53 Mich.App. 482, 220 N.W.2d 212 (1974), affirmed 394 Mich. 625, 232 N.W.2d 187 (1975), the defendant's conviction for prison escape was reversed, holding that the evidence justified submission to the jury of the defense of duress by reason of fear of corroborated threatened homosexual attacks by other inmates. In People v. Lovercamp, 43 Cal.App.3d 823, 118 Cal.Rptr. 110 (1974), the court held that a prison escape by women prisoners induced by a threatened lesbian homosexual assault by other female inmates could be justified as a matter of necessity as long as the inmate does not resort to violence in the escape and reports to the proper authorities when he or she has reached a position of safety from the immediate threat. See, in this connection, Gardner, *The Defense of Necessity and the Right to Escape from Prison—A Step Toward Incarceration Free from Sexual Assault*, 49 SO.CAL. L. REV. 110 (1975). *See also* State v. Reese, 272 N.W.2d 863 (Iowa 1978); Jorgensen v. State, 100 Nev. 541, 688 P.2d 308 (1984).

South Dakota's statute on the defense of "justification" requires a broader scope for the defense in escape cases than was approved in the foregoing Bailey Case. A majority of the South Dakota Supreme Court, in State v. Miller, 313 N.W.2d 460 (S.D.1981), said that the defense of necessity was properly raised "when the offered evidence, if believed by the jury, would support a finding by them that the offense of escape was justified by a reasonable fear of death or great bodily harm so imminent or emergent that, according to ordinary standards of intelligence and morality, the desirability of avoiding the injury outweighs the desirability of avoiding the public injury arising from the offense committed. . . ." *See also* State v. Baker, 598 S.W.2d 540 (Mo.App.1980), holding that a post-escape effort to surrender is not an essential element for the invocation of the necessity defense; and People v. Unger, 66 Ill.2d 333, 5 Ill.Dec. 848, 362 N.E.2d 319 (1977).

2. A person may, at times, be forced to do an act other than prison escape that he knows is against the criminal laws, but which he feels compelled to do under the duress of special circumstances to prevent a greater harm from occurring. The traditional example of the intentional destruction of property in order to save lives may be found in the Bible: "Then the mariners were afraid, and cried every man unto his god, and cast forth the wares that were in the ship into the sea, to lighten it of them." (Jonah, c. 1, v. 5.) With such an ancient origin, the defense of necessity has long been recognized as a justification for some crimes, although its precise limits have never been clearly defined. It is generally stated that the special circumstances which create a dangerous condition must have been occasioned by natural forces rather than by human agency. Thus, the Model Penal Code suggests these examples of the proper application of the defense of necessity: destruction of property to prevent the spread of fire; mountain climbers breaking into a house, and stealing provisions, when caught in a storm; jettisoning of cargo at sea to save the vessel; or a druggist dispensing a drug without the prescription to alleviate distress in an emergency. There are decided cases, however, where the circumstances that forced a defendant to choose the lesser of two evils were created, at least in part, by human agency. Thus, the defense of necessity was held available to drunk driving to get medical aid for another person unconscious in the vehicle in State v. Noyes, 149 Wis.2d 401, 439 N.W.2d 646 (1989); again to driving under the influence to avoid abusive husband and seek medical attention in State v. Shotton, 142 Vt. 558, 458 A.2d 1105 (1983); to a violation of speeding laws in an attempt to apprehend a felon in State v. Gorham, 110 Wash. 330, 188 P. 457 (1920); and to a doctor performing an abortion to save the life of the mother in Rex v. Bourne, 3 All E.R. 615 (1938).

3. Consider again, in this regard, the text that was presented prior to the *Bailey* case. The first paragraph of the hypothetical presents, in essence, the facts in the case of The Queen v. Dudley & Stephens, 14 Q.B.D. 273, 15 Cox C.C. 624 (1884), in which it was held that there was no justification for the killing and that the surviving crewmen were therefore guilty of murder. Accordingly, they were sentenced to death; however, their sentences were commuted to six months' imprisonment.

The fourth paragraph of the text presents, in essence, the facts of United States v. Holmes, 26 Fed.Cas. 360, No. 15383 (C.C.Pa.1842). Although most of the crew disappeared following the rescue, one of their number, Holmes, stood trial and was convicted of manslaughter. He was sentenced to six months' imprisonment.

United States v. Oakland Cannabis Buyers' Cooperative and Jeffrey Jones

Supreme Court of the United States, 2001.
532 U.S. 483, 121 S.Ct. 1711, 149 L.Ed.2d 722.

■ Justice Thomas delivered the opinion of the Court.

The Controlled Substances Act, 84 Stat. 1242, 21 U.S.C. § 801 *et seq.*, prohibits the manufacture and distribution of various drugs, including marijuana. In this case, we must decide whether there is a medical necessity exception to these prohibitions. We hold that there is not.

I

In November 1996, California voters enacted an initiative measure entitled the Compassionate Use Act of 1996. Attempting "to ensure that seriously ill Californians have the right to obtain and use marijuana for medical purposes," Cal. Health & Safety Code Ann. § 11362.5 (West

Supp. 2001), the statute creates an exception to California laws prohibiting the possession and cultivation of marijuana. These prohibitions no longer apply to a patient or his primary caregiver who possesses or cultivates marijuana for the patient's medical purposes upon the recommendation or approval of a physician. In the wake of this voter initiative, several groups organized "medical cannabis dispensaries" to meet the needs of qualified patients. Respondent Oakland Cannabis Buyers' Cooperative is one of these groups.

The Cooperative is a not-for-profit organization that operates in downtown Oakland. A physician serves as medical director, and registered nurses staff the Cooperative during business hours. To become a member, a patient must provide a written statement from a treating physician assenting to marijuana therapy and must submit to a screening interview. If accepted as a member, the patient receives an identification card entitling him to obtain marijuana from the Cooperative.

In January 1998, the United States sued the Cooperative and its executive director, respondent Jeffrey Jones (together, the Cooperative), in the United States District Court for the Northern District of California. Seeking to enjoin the Cooperative from distributing and manufacturing marijuana, the United States argued that, whether or not the Cooperative's activities are legal under California law, they violate federal law. Specifically, the Government argued that the Cooperative violated the Controlled Substances Act's prohibitions on distributing, manufacturing, and possessing with the intent to distribute or manufacture a controlled substance. 21 U.S.C. § 841(a). Concluding that the Government had established a probability of success on the merits, the District Court granted a preliminary injunction.

The Cooperative did not appeal the injunction but instead openly violated it by distributing marijuana to numerous persons. To terminate these violations, the Government initiated contempt proceedings. In defense, the Cooperative contended that any distributions were medically necessary. Marijuana is the only drug, according to the Cooperative, that can alleviate the severe pain and other debilitating symptoms of the Cooperative's patients. The District Court rejected this defense, however, after determining there was insufficient evidence that each recipient of marijuana was in actual danger of imminent harm without the drug. The District Court found the Cooperative in contempt and, at the Government's request, modified the preliminary injunction to empower the United States Marshal to seize the Cooperative's premises. Although recognizing that "human suffering" could result, the District Court reasoned that a court's "equitable powers [do] not permit it to ignore federal law." Three days later, the District Court summarily rejected a motion by the Cooperative to modify the injunction to permit distributions that are medically necessary.

* * *

The Cooperative appealed both the contempt order and the denial of the Cooperative's motion to modify. Before the Court of Appeals for the Ninth Circuit decided the case, however, the Cooperative voluntarily purged its contempt by promising the District Court that it would comply with the initial preliminary injunction. Consequently, the Court of Appeals determined that the appeal of the contempt order was moot. 190 F.3d 1109, 1112–1113 (1999).

. . . [T]he Court of Appeals reversed and remanded. According to the Court of Appeals, the medical necessity defense was a "legally cognizable defense" that likely would apply in the circumstances. . . . Remanding the case, the Court of Appeals instructed the District Court to consider "the criteria for a medical necessity exemption, and, should it modify the injunction, to set forth those criteria in the modification order." Following these instructions, the District Court granted the Cooperative's motion to modify the injunction to incorporate a medical necessity defense.

The United States petitioned for certiorari to review the Court of Appeals' decision that medical necessity is a legally cognizable defense to violations of the Controlled Substances Act. Because the decision raises significant questions as to the ability of the United States to enforce the Nation's drug laws, we granted certiorari.

II

The Controlled Substances Act provides that, "except as authorized by this subchapter, it shall be unlawful for any person knowingly or intentionally . . . to manufacture, distribute, or dispense, or possess with intent to manufacture, distribute, or dispense, a controlled substance." 21 U.S.C. § 841(a)(1). The subchapter, in turn, establishes exceptions. For marijuana (and other drugs that have been classified as "schedule I" controlled substances), there is but one express exception, and it is available only for Government-approved research projects, § 823(f). Not conducting such a project, the Cooperative cannot, and indeed does not, claim this statutory exemption.

The Cooperative contends, however, that notwithstanding the apparently absolute language of § 841(a), the statute is subject to additional, implied exceptions, one of which is medical necessity. According to the Cooperative, because necessity was a defense at common law, medical necessity should be read into the Controlled Substances Act. We disagree.

As an initial matter, we note that it is an open question whether federal courts ever have authority to recognize a necessity defense not provided by statute. A necessity defense "traditionally covered the situation where physical forces beyond the actor's control rendered illegal conduct the lesser of two evils." *United States* v. *Bailey*, 444 U.S. 394, 410, 62 L.Ed.2d 575, 100 S.Ct. 624 (1980). Even at common law, the defense of necessity was somewhat controversial. See, *e.g.*, *Queen* v. *Dudley & Stephens*, 14 QB 273 (1884). And under our constitutional system, in which federal crimes are defined by statute rather than by common law, it is especially so. As we have stated: "Whether, as a policy matter, an exemption should be created is a question for legislative judgment, not judicial inference." *United States* v. *Rutherford*, 442 U.S. 544, 559, 61 L.Ed.2d 68, 99 S.Ct. 2470 (1979). Nonetheless, we recognize that this Court has discussed the possibility of a necessity defense without altogether rejecting it. See *e.g.*, *Bailey*, *supra*, at 415.

We need not decide, however, whether necessity can ever be a defense when the federal statute does not expressly provide for it. In this case, to resolve the question presented, we need only recognize that a medical necessity exception for marijuana is at odds with the terms of the Controlled Substances Act. The statute, to be sure, does not explicitly abrogate the defense. But its provisions leave no doubt that the defense is unavailable.

Under any conception of legal necessity, one principle is clear: The defense cannot succeed when the legislature itself has made a "determination of values." 1 W. LaFave & A. Scott, SUBSTANTIVE CRIMINAL LAW § 5.4, p. 629 (1986). In the case of the Controlled Substances Act, the statute reflects a determination that marijuana has no medical benefits worthy of an exception (outside the confines of a Government-approved research project). Whereas some other drugs can be dispensed and prescribed for medical use, see 21 U.S.C. § 829, the same is not true for marijuana. Indeed, for purposes of the Controlled Substances Act, marijuana has "no currently accepted medical use" at all. § 811.

The structure of the Act supports this conclusion. The statute divides drugs into five schedules, depending in part on whether the particular drug has a currently accepted medical use. The Act then imposes restrictions on the manufacture and distribution of the substance according to the schedule in which it has been placed. Schedule I is the most restrictive schedule. The Attorney General can include a drug in schedule I only if the drug "has no currently accepted medical use in treatment in the United States," "has a high potential for abuse," and has "a lack of accepted safety for use . . . under medical supervision." §§ 812(b)(1)(A)–(C). Under the statute, the Attorney General could not put marijuana into schedule I if marijuana had any accepted medical use.

* * *

The Cooperative further argues that use of schedule I drugs generally . . . can be medically necessary, notwithstanding that they have "no currently accepted medical use." According to the Cooperative, a drug may not yet have achieved general acceptance as a medical treatment but may nonetheless have medical benefits to a particular patient or class of patients. We decline to parse the statute in this manner. It is clear from the text of the Act that Congress has made a determination that marijuana has no medical benefits worthy of an exception. The statute expressly contemplates that many drugs "have a useful and legitimate medical purpose and are necessary to maintain the health and general welfare of the American people," § 801(1), but it includes no exception at all for any medical use of marijuana. Unwilling to view this omission as an accident, and unable in any event to override a legislative determination manifest in a statute, we reject the Cooperative's argument.

* * *

For these reasons, we hold that medical necessity is not a defense to manufacturing and distributing marijuana.[7] The Court of Appeals erred when it held that medical necessity is a "legally cognizable defense." . . .

III

The Cooperative contends that, even if the Controlled Substances Act forecloses the medical necessity defense, there is an alternative ground for affirming the Court of Appeals. This case, the Cooperative reminds us, arises from a motion to modify an injunction to permit distributions that are medically necessary. According to the Cooperative, the Court of Appeals was correct that the District Court had "broad equitable discretion" to tailor the injunctive relief to account for medical necessity, irrespective of whether there is a legal defense of necessity in the statute. To sustain the judgment below, the argument goes, we need only reaffirm that federal courts, in the exercise of their equity jurisdiction, have discretion to modify an injunction based upon a weighing of the public interest.

* * *

. . . [T]he mere fact that the District Court had discretion does not suggest that the District Court, when evaluating the motion to modify the injunction, could consider any and all factors that might relate to the public interest or the conveniences of the parties, including the medical needs of the Cooperative's patients. On the contrary, a court sitting in equity cannot "ignore the judgment of Congress, deliberately expressed in legislation." A district court cannot, for example, override Congress'

---

[7] Lest there be any confusion, we clarify that nothing in our analysis, or the statute, suggests that a distinction should be drawn between the prohibitions on manufacturing and distributing and the other prohibitions in the Controlled Substances Act. Furthermore, the very point of our holding is that there is no medical necessity exception to the prohibitions at issue, even when the patient is "seriously ill" and lacks alternative avenues for relief. Indeed, it is the Cooperative's argument that its patients are "seriously ill," and lacking "alternatives." We reject the argument that these factors warrant a medical necessity exception. If we did not, we would be affirming instead of reversing the Court of Appeals.

Finally, we share JUSTICE STEVENS' concern for "showing respect for the sovereign States that comprise our Federal Union." However, we are "construing an Act of Congress, not drafting it." Because federal courts interpret, rather than author, the federal criminal code, we are not at liberty to rewrite it. Nor are we passing today on a constitutional question, such as whether the Controlled Substances Act exceeds Congress' power under the Commerce Clause.

policy choice, articulated in a statute, as to what behavior should be prohibited. "Once Congress, exercising its delegated powers, has decided the order of priorities in a given area, it is . . . for the courts to enforce them when enforcement is sought." Courts of equity cannot, in their discretion, reject the balance that Congress has struck in a statute. . . .

In this case, the Court of Appeals erred by considering relevant the evidence that some people have "serious medical conditions for whom the use of cannabis is necessary in order to treat or alleviate those conditions or their symptoms," that these people "will suffer serious harm if they are denied cannabis," and that "there is no legal alternative to cannabis for the effective treatment of their medical conditions." As explained above, in the Controlled Substances Act, the balance already has been struck against a medical necessity exception. Because the statutory prohibitions cover even those who have what could be termed a medical necessity, the Act precludes consideration of this evidence. It was thus error for the Court of Appeals to instruct the District Court on remand to consider "the criteria for a medical necessity exemption, and, should it modify the injunction, to set forth those criteria in the modification order."

The judgment of the Court of Appeals is reversed, and the case is remanded for further proceedings consistent with this opinion.

It is so ordered.

■ JUSTICE BREYER took no part in the consideration or decision of this case.

■ JUSTICE STEVENS, with whom JUSTICE SOUTER and JUSTICE GINSBURG join, concurring in the judgment.

Lest the Court's narrow holding be lost in its broad dicta, let me restate it here: "We hold that medical necessity is not a defense to *manufacturing* and *distributing* marijuana." This confined holding is consistent with our grant of certiorari, which was limited to the question "whether the Controlled Substances Act, 21 U.S.C. 801 *et seq.*, forecloses a medical necessity defense to the Act's prohibition against *manufacturing* and *distributing* marijuana, a Schedule I controlled substance." And, at least with respect to distribution, this holding is consistent with how the issue was raised and litigated below. As stated by the District Court, the question before it was "whether [respondents'] admitted *distribution* of marijuana for use by seriously ill persons upon a physician's recommendation violates federal law," and if so, whether such distribution "should be enjoined pursuant to the injunctive relief provisions of the federal Controlled Substances Act."

Accordingly, in the lower courts as well as here, respondents have raised the medical necessity defense as a justification for distributing marijuana to cooperative members, and it was in that context that the Ninth Circuit determined that respondents had "a legally cognizable defense." The Court is surely correct to reverse that determination. Congress' classification of marijuana as a schedule I controlled substance—that is, one that cannot be distributed outside of approved research projects, see 21 U.S.C. §§ 812, 823(f), 829—makes it clear that "the Controlled Substances Act cannot bear a medical necessity defense to *distributions* of marijuana."[1]

Apart from its limited holding, the Court takes two unwarranted and unfortunate excursions that prevent me from joining its opinion. First, the Court reaches beyond its holding, and beyond the facts of the case, by suggesting that the defense of necessity is unavailable for anyone under the Controlled Substances Act. Because necessity was raised in this case as a defense to distribution, the Court need not venture an opinion on whether the defense is available to anyone other than distributors. Most notably, whether the defense might be available to a seriously ill patient for whom there is no alternative means of avoiding starvation or extraordinary suffering is a difficult issue that is not presented here.[2]

Second, the Court gratuitously casts doubt on "whether necessity can ever be a defense" to *any* federal statute that does not explicitly provide for it, calling such a defense into question by a misleading reference to its existence as an "open question." By contrast, our precedent has expressed no doubt about the viability of the common-law defense, even in the context of federal criminal statutes that do not provide for it in so many words. *See e.g.*, *United States* v. *Bailey*, 444 U.S. 394, 415, 62 L.Ed.2d 575, 100 S.Ct. 624 (1980). . . . The Court's opinion on this point is pure dictum.

The overbroad language of the Court's opinion is especially unfortunate given the importance of showing respect for the sovereign States that comprise our Federal Union. That respect imposes a duty on federal courts, whenever possible, to avoid or minimize conflict between federal and state law, particularly in situations in which the citizens of a State have chosen to "serve as a laboratory" in the trial of "novel social and economic experiments without risk to the rest of the country." In my view, this is such a case. By passing Proposition 215, California voters have decided that seriously ill patients and their primary caregivers

---

[1] In any event, respondents do not fit the paradigm of a defendant who may assert necessity. The defense "traditionally covered the situation where physical forces beyond the actor's control rendered illegal conduct the lesser of two evils." *United States* v. *Bailey*, 444 U.S. 394, 410, 62 L.Ed.2d 575, 100 S.Ct. 624 (1980); see generally 1 W. LaFave & A. Scott, SUBSTANTIVE CRIMINAL LAW § 5.4, pp. 627–640 (1986). Respondents, on the other hand, have not been forced to confront a choice of evils—violating federal law by distributing marijuana to seriously ill patients or letting those individuals suffer—but have thrust that choice upon themselves by electing to become distributors for such patients. Of course, respondents also cannot claim necessity based upon the choice of evils facing seriously ill patients, as that is not the same choice respondents face.

[2] As a result, perhaps the most glaring example of the Court's dicta is its footnote 7, where it opines that "nothing in our analysis, or the statute, suggests that a distinction should be drawn between the prohibitions on manufacturing and distributing and the other prohibitions in the Controlled Substances Act."

should be exempt from prosecution under state laws for cultivating and possessing marijuana if the patient's physician recommends using the drug for treatment.[4] This case does not call upon the Court to deprive *all* such patients of the benefit of the necessity defense to federal prosecution, when the case itself does not involve *any* such patients.

* * *

I join the Court's judgment of reversal because I agree that a distributor of marijuana does not have a medical necessity defense under the Controlled Substances Act. I do not, however, join the dicta in the Court's opinion.

NOTES AND QUESTIONS

1. Some state courts have agreed with the United States Supreme Court that the medical necessity defense is not available as a matter of state law to the use of marijuana. *See* State v. Poling, 207 W.Va. 299, 531 S.E.2d 678 (2000) (medical necessity defense not available as treatment for multiple sclerosis); Commonwealth v. Hutchins, 410 Mass. 726, 575 N.E.2d 741 (1991) (denying medical necessity defense for use of marijuana to treat scleroderma, a chronic debilitating disease that results in the buildup of scar tissue throughout the body); State v. Tate, 102 N.J. 64, 505 A.2d 941 (1986) (defense not available to relieve spasticity caused by quadriplegia). However, as Justice Stevens opinion concurring in the judgment in *Oakland Cannabis Buyers'* notes, a number of other states have adopted marijuana medical necessity by voter initiative or statute and at least one state has recognized the defense by judicial decision. *See* Jenks v. State, 582 So.2d 676 (Fla. App. 1991).

Problem 12–1. Since the United States Supreme Court held in *Oakland Cannabis Buyers' Cooperative* that there is no medical necessity defense available for marijuana offenses (or did it), how is it possible for the states mentioned above to recognize such a defense? Is the U.S. Supreme Court not the highest court in the Country?

2. *The "Home Alone" Syndrome.* Consider the availability of a necessity defense to a couple, charged with cruelty to children, who left their two children in an automobile for three hours at night in freezing conditions while they worked. They testified that they were unable to locate a babysitter, feared losing their jobs and becoming homeless again, and had "received mixed signals from [their] . . . supervisors concerning whether the children could stay inside the building." *See* People v. Turner, 249 Ill.App.3d 474, 189 Ill.Dec. 80, 619 N.E.2d 781 (1993).

---

[4] Since 1996, six other States—Alaska, Colorado, Maine, Nevada, Oregon, and Washington—have passed medical marijuana initiatives, and Hawaii has enacted a similar measure through its legislature. See Alaska Stat. Ann. §§ 11.71.090, 17.37.010 to 17.37.080 (2000); Colo. Const., Art. XVIII, § 14; Haw. Rev. Stat. §§ 329–121 to 329–128 (Supp. 2000); Me. Rev. Stat. Ann., Tit. 22, § 2383–B(5) (2000); Nev. Const., Art. 4, § 38; Ore. Rev. Stat. §§ 475.300 to 475.346 (1999); Wash. Rev. Code §§ 69.51A.005 to 69.51A.902 (1997 and Supp. 2000–2001).

3. The statutory defense of "competing harms" (N.H. Rev. Stat. Ann. § 627.3) is not available in a charge of criminal trespass based on an incident where the defendant occupied the construction site of a nuclear power plant. In State v. Dorsey, 118 N.H. 844, 395 A.2d 855 (1978), the defendant argued that he believed his conduct was necessary to avoid greater harm to himself and others, which is akin to the common law defense of necessity, but the court, in rejecting the defense, stated:

> Defendant and others who oppose nuclear power have other lawful means of protesting nuclear power; therefore, they are not justified in breaking the law. . . . The act of criminal trespass was a deliberate and calculated choice and not an act that was urgently necessary to avoid a clear and imminent danger. . . . Nothing in this opinion should be construed as favoring or not favoring nuclear power. We deal only with the law as it relates to the defense relied upon. Nor do we pass upon the motives of the defendant. Good motives are not a defense to the commission of crime, except in a case of emergency not present here.

Similarly, in State v. Warshow, 138 Vt. 22, 410 A.2d 1000 (1979), the defendants were convicted of unlawful trespass when they joined a rally at a nuclear power plant known as Vermont Yankee for the purpose of preventing workers from gaining access to the plant and placing it on-line. In affirming the conviction, the majority of the court said: "There is no doubt that the defendants wished to call attention to the dangers of low-level radiation and nuclear waste, and nuclear accident. But low-level radiation and nuclear waste are not the types of imminent danger classified as an emergency sufficient to justify criminal activity. . . . Where the hazards are long term, the danger is not imminent, because the defendants have time to exercise options other than breaking the law."

Problem 12–2. Defendants entered a clinic and tried to bar access to rooms where first trimester abortions were being performed. In their prosecution for disorderly conduct, they contended that they were entitled to rely on the defense of necessity because they were acting to prevent the death of fetuses whose deaths were imminent. The situation was therefore unlike *Dorsey* and *Warshow, supra*. What result? *See* People v. Stiso, 93 Ill.App.3d 101, 48 Ill.Dec. 687, 416 N.E.2d 1209 (1981); Cleveland v. Municipality of Anchorage, 631 P.2d 1073 (Alaska 1981); State v. O'Brien, 784 S.W.2d 187 (Mo.App.1989); Hill v. State, 688 So.2d 901 (Fla.1996). *See also*, the federal Freedom of Access to Clinic Entrances Act of 1994, 18 U.S.C. § 248.

B. INTOXICATION

1. VOLUNTARY INTOXICATION

People v. Langworthy

Supreme Court of Michigan, 1982.
416 Mich. 630, 331 N.W.2d 171.

■ FITZGERALD, CHIEF JUSTICE.

The common ground of these cases is that, at their trials, both defendants attempted to utilize voluntary intoxication as a defense to charges of crimes which Michigan appellate courts previously have held to be general-intent crimes. Both defendants request this Court to expand the category of specific-intent crimes to include the offenses they were convicted of, *i.e.*, first-degree criminal sexual conduct and second-degree murder, in order to make available to them the defense of voluntary intoxication.

FACTS

Defendant Lundy was found guilty but mentally ill of three counts of first-degree criminal sexual conduct ... and sentenced to three concurrent life terms. The convictions arose from the October 30, 1978, rape of his adult sister. The crime, carried out with the use of a knife as a threatening weapon, involved three penetrations.

At Lundy's bench trial, the major issue centered on defendant's mental state at the time of the commission of the crime. His defense was predicated upon expert testimony regarding his mental state as well as evidence that he had been sniffing glue and drinking alcohol immediately prior to the crime. The trial court rejected Lundy's insanity defense as well as his intoxication defense, ruling as to the latter that first-degree criminal sexual conduct is a general-intent crime.

The Court of Appeals affirmed in a memorandum opinion.

Defendant Langworthy was convicted of second-degree murder ... and was sentenced to 60 to 90 years in prison.

After a bench trial, the trial judge found that on the night of November 5, 1976, defendant, Roy Schipani, and Alan Parker were together indulging in alcohol and drugs in a house in Ypsilanti. Parker left sometime during the early morning hours to purchase cigarettes at a gas station. There he met the decedent, William Wedge, who returned to the house with Parker.

The trial judge further found that Wedge was intoxicated and offensive and that Wedge made certain comments which irritated defendant. Wedge then passed out and the three others discussed robbing Wedge. Defendant suggested that they "blow him away" and then he turned up the stereo, went to a closet where he got a rifle and shot Wedge in the mouth and in the chest.

The trial judge determined that the defendant was not mentally ill or legally insane at the time of the commission of the crime. He found that defendant had taken at least 400 milligrams of Valium and some codeine and Nembutal and had been drinking Southern Comfort and Coke at the time of the crime. The trial judge concluded:

> However, the Court finds that as a result of the drugs and alcohol his judgment and his appreciation of the consequence of his actions was grossly impaired.

That he committed the act knowingly with malice but "without a real concept of the consequence of the act." That he had a conscious intent to commit the crime but that his judgment and appreciation of the consequence of his act was grossly impaired as the result of the drugs and alcohol.

The Court of Appeals affirmed in an unpublished opinion per curiam, ruling, *inter alia*, that second-degree murder is not a specific-intent crime and that, therefore, voluntary intoxication was not a defense.

A.   THE VOLUNTARY INTOXICATION DEFENSE

Every jurisdiction in this country recognizes the general principle that voluntary intoxication is not any excuse for crime. This is in accord with the common-law rule dating back to the sixteenth century which allowed no concession to a defendant because of his intoxication. However, by the early nineteenth century, the English courts began to fashion a doctrine to mitigate the harshness and rigidity of the traditional rule. The doctrine, which has come to be known as the exculpatory rule, was stated by Judge Stephen as follows:

> "[A]lthough you cannot take drunkenness as any excuse for crime, yet when the crime is such that the intention of the party committing it is one of its constituent elements, you may look at the fact that a man was in drink in considering whether he formed the intention necessary to constitute the crime."

It is said that the theory behind this exculpatory doctrine is that it does not hold that drunkenness will excuse crime; rather, it inquires whether the very crime which the law defines has in fact been committed. Almost every state, by statute or by common law, has adopted the exculpatory rule, and Michigan is no exception.

"While it is true that drunkenness cannot excuse crime, it is equally true that when a certain intent is a necessary element in a crime, the crime cannot have been committed when the intent did not exist." *People v. Walker*, 38 Mich. 156, 158 (1878). See, also, *People v. Crittle*, 390 Mich. 367, 212 N.W.2d 196 (1973).

The applicability of the exculpatory rule rests entirely on the determination whether the offense involved is categorized as a general- or specific-intent crime.

> It is important in this decision to emphasize that intoxication may only negative the existence of *specific intent*. Examination of the cases reveals that where the rule was applied, it was done so in cases where the crime charged also involved a specific intent. *People v. Guillett*, 342 Mich. 1, 6, 69 N.W.2d 140 (1955). See also *Roberts v. People*, 19 Mich. 401 (1870).

Thus, if a crime is determined to require only a general intent, the defendant's voluntary intoxication during the commission of an offense may not be asserted as a defense to the existence of the mental element of that crime.

The general intent-specific intent dichotomy arose as a compromise between the perceived need to afford some relief to the intoxicated offender whose moral culpability was considered less than that of a sober person who committed the same offense and the view that a person who voluntarily becomes drunk and commits a crime should not escape the consequences. Although the rule seems logical on the surface, it has proven to be far from logical in application. While specific intent can easily be defined as "a particular criminal intent beyond the act done"[9] (whereas general intent is the intent simply to do the physical act), the ease of stating the definition belies the difficulty of applying it in practice. In order to appreciate the problem, one need only note the divergence of opinion among the jurisdictions as to which crimes require a specific intent and, therefore, to which crimes the exculpatory rule applies.

It has been noted that the law with respect to voluntary intoxication and criminal responsibility has shown little tendency to change or develop despite advances socially and medically in this area; and, we might add, despite strong criticism from treatise writers, law review commentators, case law, and the drafters of the Model Penal Code. My Brother Levin summarized the major criticisms of the exculpatory rule while on the Court of Appeals:

> It has also been maintained that the availability of the intoxication defense should not depend on whether a court chooses to characterize an element of the crime charged as separate from the element of general intent. It has been observed that neither common experience nor psychology knows of any such phenomenon as "general intent" distinguishable from "specific intent." It does seem incongruous to make the

---

[9]   *People v. Depew*, 215 Mich. 317, 320, 183 N.W. 750 (1921). See, also, *Roberts v. People*, 19 Mich. 401, 414 (1870); LaFave & Scott, CRIMINAL LAW, § 28, p. 202:

"[T]he most common usage of 'specific intent' is to designate a special mental element which is required above and beyond any mental state required with respect to the *actus reus* of the crime."

admissibility of mitigating evidence depend on whether the statutory definition of a crime includes a separately stated intent, and other methods of defining specific intent are highly manipulable.

The clumsiness of the exculpatory device has been criticized. A defendant who is charged with a specific intent crime may go free if he can prove he was intoxicated; this result contrasts sharply with the absolute denial of relief to the intoxicated offender charged with a crime of general intent.

If the function of the general/specific intent distinction is to eliminate the defense as to lesser included offenses, *e.g.*, assault and battery, but to retain it for the more serious offenses, *e.g.*, armed robbery, and in that manner mitigate the general rule that intoxication is not a defense, then manifestly this should be done on a consistent basis. The right to interpose this defense should depend on something more substantial than a technical distinction that was seized upon by a judge 130 years ago and adopted by other judges to reach results thought sound in the cases then before them.

While we recognize the illogic and incongruity of the general intent-specific intent dichotomy, the remedy is not clear-cut. One solution, of course, would be to join the ranks of those few states which do not allow the voluntary intoxication defense even where a specific intent is required. We agree, however, with Professors LaFave and Scott that this view is clearly wrong. It would require us to ignore basic concepts of criminal culpability as well as modern scientific views on alcoholism.

The alternative would be to allow the intoxication defense to be asserted against any charge of crime which traditionally has required general or specific intent. Although this Court has the power to so modify the common-law rule, we believe that it would be imprudent to take that step at this time. While abolishing the general intent-specific intent distinction may rid the courts of an illogical rule, it would do nothing to help solve the problem of the intoxicated offender, both from the standpoint of the offender and from the standpoint of society which suffers from the acts of the intoxicated offender. . . .

The problem of alcoholism and crime is complex, requiring studies and policy considerations beyond the ability of any judicial body. Various solutions which have been proposed would require legislative action. We urge the Legislature to consider the intoxicated-offender problem and to modernize Michigan law on this subject. Until the Legislature takes action or until we are persuaded to modify the common-law rule in an appropriate case in the future, we shall continue to struggle with applying the rule case by case.

B.   IS FIRST-DEGREE CRIMINAL SEXUAL
CONDUCT A SPECIFIC INTENT CRIME?

* * *

This case requires us to decide whether first-degree criminal sexual conduct is a general- or specific-intent crime. We have previously held, under the predecessor to the criminal sexual conduct statute, that rape is not a specific-intent crime. *People v. Phillips*, 385 Mich. 30, 187 N.W.2d 211 (1971). This comports with the overwhelming weight of authority which holds that rape is a general-intent crime.

An examination of the statute convinces us that the Legislature did not intend to include specific intent as an element of first-degree criminal sexual conduct. Neither the first-degree criminal sexual conduct statute nor the corresponding statutory definition of "sexual penetration" contains any language whatsoever regarding intent. The fact that the Legislature must have been cognizant, in enacting the first-degree criminal sexual conduct provision, of the established rule that rape does not require specific intent, combined with the absence of any provision regarding intent, considerably weakens defendant's argument that his crime is a specific-intent offense. If the Legislature wanted to add specific intent as an element, knowing that the predecessor statute had been consistently construed as a general-intent crime, it would have specifically done so. The fact that it did not leads us to conclude that the Legislature intended to maintain the general rule that "no intent is requisite other than that evidenced by the doing of the acts constituting the offense", *i.e.*, general intent.

Moreover, one of the purposes of the new act was to strengthen the laws against sexual violence by removing certain evidentiary obstacles to the prosecution of sexual assault. This further strengthens our conclusion that it is unlikely that a new element of proof would be added without specific mention.

* * *

Accordingly, we conclude that first-degree criminal sexual conduct is a general-intent crime for which the defense of voluntary intoxication is not available.

C.   IS SECOND-DEGREE MURDER A GENERAL
OR SPECIFIC INTENT CRIME?

Defendant Langworthy petitions this Court to extend to second-degree murder cases the rule in *People v. Garcia*, 398 Mich. 250, 247 N.W.2d 547 (1976), that non-felony first-degree murder is a specific-intent crime. . . .

In support of his position, defendant has cited for our consideration cases from other jurisdictions which allow murder to be reduced to manslaughter through the successful assertion of the voluntary intoxication defense. We have reviewed these cases and others, and we have concluded that they are not applicable to the situation existing in Michigan.[27] An examination of the jurisdictions which defendant relies upon demonstrates why the cases are clearly distinguishable.

Unlike that of Michigan, the statutory schemes of some states do not divide murder into degrees. To further complicate comparison, these states may require, as an element of their single crime of murder, premeditation or some other specific mental element (such as intent to kill) not required for second-degree murder in Michigan. These states do no more than Michigan already does with respect to first-degree murder, *i.e.*, allow intoxication to negate the element of premeditation (or intent to kill) and reduce the degree of the offense. The difference is that in these states negation of premeditation, for example, means that murder has not been proven at all, whereas in Michigan it only means that first-degree murder has not been proven. This difference is due to the legislative classification of homicide, which we have no control over and, consequently, which makes these cases distinguishable.

* * *

Thus, we find that all of the jurisdictions which defendant relies upon as persuasive authority for his position are not applicable to our circumstances in Michigan. In any event, despite the existence of cases which allow a proper voluntary intoxication defense to reduce murder or second-degree murder to manslaughter, the majority rule remains as follows:

> It is now generally held that intoxication may be considered where murder is divided into degrees, and in many states, may have the effect of reducing homicide from murder in the first degree to murder in the second degree. In fact, in most states the only consideration given to the fact of drunkenness or intoxication at the time of the commission of the homicide is to enable the court and jury to determine whether the prisoner may be guilty of murder in the second degree, rather than of murder in the first degree. The rule followed by most courts is that intoxication will not reduce a homicide from murder to manslaughter. 40 Am Jur 2d, Homicide, § 129 at 420–421. See also 40 CJS, Homicide, § 5 at 831. ("Voluntary intoxication does not of itself negative the malice required to constitute murder in the second degree and thereby reduce murder in the second degree to voluntary manslaughter."); Annot. 12 ALR 861, 888

---

[27] The difficulty with reliance on case law from other jurisdictions in this area of law is that we are dealing with three concepts, each of which is necessary to the decision of the question involved here, and each of which is unique to the jurisdiction under consideration. Those three concepts are the definition of second-degree murder, the definition of malice, and the particular voluntary intoxication rule involved, whether statutory or common-law. The lack of identity of the three concepts makes comparison difficult. The divergence of result depending on the rule followed by a particular jurisdiction is noted in 40 Am.Jur.2d, Homicide, § 129, p. 421.

("the great weight of authority is that intoxication will not reduce a homicide from murder to manslaughter"), 79 ALR 897, 904.[33]

* * *

We find that there is more than a sufficient basis to distinguish between the degrees of murder to require that specific intent be demonstrated for first-degree murder only. In *People v. Garcia, supra*, we held that "wilful" killing means the "intent to accomplish the result of death". Moreover, specific intent to kill is a necessary constituent of the elements of premeditation and deliberation. It would be difficult, if not impossible, to premeditate and deliberate a killing without at the same time possessing the specific intent to kill. This logic, however, does not apply to second-degree murder.

The *mens rea* requirement for second-degree murder is supplied by the element of malice. While the intent to kill satisfies the malice requirement, it is not a necessary element of second-degree murder. An intent to inflict great bodily harm or a wanton and willful disregard of the likelihood that the natural tendency of a person's behavior is to cause death or great bodily harm may also satisfy the malice requirement. *People v. Aaron*, 409 Mich. 672, 299 N.W.2d 304 (1980).

With respect to the element of malice encompassing wanton and willful disregard, we concur with the majority rule that voluntary intoxication is not a defense. We agree with the analysis of Professors LaFave and Scott:

> The person who unconsciously creates risk because he is voluntarily drunk is perhaps morally worse than one who does so because he is sober but mentally deficient. At all events, the cases generally hold that drunkenness does not negative a depraved heart by blotting out consciousness of risk, and the Model Penal Code, which generally requires awareness of the risk for depraved-heart murder (and for recklessness manslaughter), so provides.[35]

Because second-degree murder does not require intent to kill, but rather, only wanton and willful disregard malice need be shown; and, because we have concluded that voluntary intoxication may not negate this latter category of malice, we believe that voluntary intoxication should not be a defense to a charge of second-degree murder. We are aware that there may be second-degree murder cases which involve only

---

[33] *State v. Hall*, 214 N.W.2d 205, 208–209 (Iowa, 1974). See, also, LaFave & Scott, fn. 9 *supra*, pp. 345, 586; Model Penal Code (Tentative Draft No. 9, 1958), § 2.08, p. 5, Comment 2; . . . p. 534; State v. Bunn, 283 N.C. 444, 196 S.E.2d 777 (1973).

[35] LaFave & Scott, fn. 9 *supra*, p. 545. See, also, . . . *Rogers v. State*, 196 Tenn. 263, 265 S.W.2d 559 (1954); *Jones v. State*, 70 Wis.2d 41, 233 N.W.2d 430 (1975); *Commonwealth v. Cambric*, 475 Pa. 454, 380 A.2d 1224 (1977); *People v. LeGrand*, 61 A.D.2d 815, 402 N.Y.S.2d 209 (1978); N.Y.Penal Law, § 15.05, N.D.Cent.Code, § 12.1–04–02.

the intent to kill or the intent to do great bodily harm types of malice. We are further aware that these two categories of malice sound suspiciously akin to the traditional language of specific intent. However, we decline to extend the defense of voluntary intoxication to these cases on the grounds of public policy.

* * *

We hold that second-degree murder is not a specific-intent crime for which the defense of voluntary intoxication may be asserted.

* * *

■ Levin, Justice (*dissenting*).

* * *

I

The critical element of second-degree (common-law) murder is malice aforethought. Malice aforethought, for purposes of second-degree murder, is established by evidence tending to show that the defendant acted with either "the intention to kill, the intention to do great bodily harm, or the wanton and willful disregard of the likelihood that the natural tendency of [his] behavior is to cause death or great bodily harm".

In *People v. Garcia*, 398 Mich. 250, 259, 247 N.W.2d 547 (1976), this Court recognized, in the context of first-degree murder, that intent to kill is a specific intent which voluntary intoxication can negate. Similarly, malice aforethought based upon intent to inflict great bodily harm is, by definition, a specific intent although there has not been any need to rule thereon until now. The opinion of the Court seems to agree.

The reason the Court gives for its conclusion that second-degree murder is not a specific-intent offense is that the malice requirement may be satisfied by showing "willful and wanton disregard". This ignores that it is rare for a person to be charged with second-degree murder on the theory that he acted with willful and wanton disregard. Where the evidence does not support a finding of intent to kill or to inflict great bodily harm, the charge is usually . . . manslaughter and not second-degree murder. It is letting the tail wag the dog to classify second-degree murder as a general-intent crime because willful and wanton disregard may in a few isolated cases be the prosecution's theory.

* * *

There are indeed some offenses (*e.g.*, common-law rape, see part II *infra*) which have not been deemed to include an element of specific intent. It is *not* asserted that second-degree murder is such an offense. The intents to kill or to inflict great bodily harm are specific intents. It cannot thus properly be said that second-degree murder does not include a specific intent. It can only be said that a person may—in some other case—be convicted of second-degree murder without a finding of specific intent upon a finding of wanton and willful disregard.

To be sure, the intoxication defense deserves legislative consideration. Until the Legislature acts, we should apply the judicially crafted specific-general-intent distinction on a reasoned basis. We should not ignore that where second-degree murder is charged, the people's theory is almost universally intent to kill or to inflict great bodily harm and only rarely if ever willful and wanton disregard. It is hypertechnical to classify second-degree murder, which has "intent to" elements, as a general-intent crime because in a rare case a person might be convicted on a theory of willful and wanton disregard.

In the instant case, the prosecution did not claim willful and wanton disregard. The people rather introduced evidence tending to show that Langworthy killed with premeditation, deliberation and malice. The judge found "that the defendant consciously and knowingly shot the deceased intending to kill him". Langworthy was thus convicted on the basis of specific intent to kill, and voluntary intoxication should be a defense.

———

■ [In Part II of his dissenting opinion, JUDGE LEVIN concludes, based on a careful statutory analysis, that Michigan's first-degree sexual conduct statute also requires specific intent.]

NOTES AND QUESTIONS

Problem 12–3. Both in the reduction of murder to voluntary manslaughter and the claim of self defense, is an intoxicated defendant entitled to rely on the fact of voluntary intoxication to explain either provocation or a belief in the need to use force? You may recall that the doctrines surrounding voluntary manslaughter and self defense rely upon reasonableness. Does this eliminate voluntary intoxication from the defense? *See* Bishop v. United States, 107 F.2d 297 (D.C.Cir.1939); United States v. Weise, 89 F.3d 502 (8th Cir.1996); LaFave, CRIMINAL LAW 3d ed., §§ 4.10(d)–(e), pp. 417–18.

1. Is the general/specific intent dichotomy an adequate way to handle the issue of voluntary intoxication? Neither the majority nor dissenting Justice Levin in *Langworthy* seemed particularly enamored with this approach, both suggesting that the Michigan Legislature visit the issue. How should the Michigan Legislature have responded? On this question, consider Model Penal Code §§ 2.08(1) and (2), which provide:

> (1) . . . [I]ntoxication of the actor is not a defense unless it negatives an element of the offense.

> (2) When recklessness establishes an element of the offense, if the actor, due to self-induced intoxication, is unaware of a risk of which he would have been aware had he been sober, such unawareness is immaterial.

2. Referring back to Chapter 2, Section D., where should the burden of proof with respect to the issue of voluntary intoxication properly be placed? Does your conclusion make sense as a policy matter?

3. Can voluntary intoxication ever operate as a defense to driving under the influence of alcohol or drugs? *See* Menard v. State, 16 Ark.App. 219, 699 S.W.2d 412 (1985).

4. Could a jurisdiction eliminate the availability of voluntary intoxication as a defense to any crime, including those requiring specific intent?

See Montana v. Egelhoff, 518 U.S. 37, 116 S.Ct. 2013, 135 L.Ed.2d 361 (1996). The Montana Supreme Court ruled that MONT. CODE ANN. § 45–2–203, which provided that an "intoxicated condition" could not be considered "in determining the existence of a mental state which is an element of the offense," violated the Due Process Clause because it prevented the defendant from introducing "clearly relevant" evidence on an element of the crime, and therefore relieved the state of part of its burden of proof.

The United States Supreme Court, in a plurality opinion by Justice Scalia, reversed. Justice Scalia concluded that the Due Process Clause does not guarantee the right to introduce all relevant evidence, but limits the restriction on the right to introduce evidence only when the restriction "offends some principle of justice so rooted in the traditions and conscience of our people as to be ranked as fundamental." The plurality concluded the respondent had failed to establish that the right to have a jury consider evidence of voluntary intoxication in determining the presence of the requisite mental state was a "fundamental principle of justice."

Justice Ginsburg concurred on the ground that the Montana Code provision was not simply a rule of evidence, but a substantive judgment by the Montana legislature redefining *mens rea* to hold equally culpable an actor whose voluntary intoxication has reduced his capacity for self control. Four Justices dissented in three separate dissenting opinions, essentially agreeing with the Montana Supreme Court's conclusion that the Montana law violated Due Process.

2.   INVOLUNTARY INTOXICATION

State v. Hall

Supreme Court of Iowa, 1974.
214 N.W.2d 205.

■ UHLENHOPP, JUSTICE.

The principal legal question in this appeal from a conviction of first-degree murder relates to the effect upon criminal responsibility of a mental condition resulting from voluntary ingestion of a drug. The principal factual dispute is whether defendant Allen Lee Hall did ingest a drug and if so, its effect upon him.

The fact is not disputed that defendant slew Gilford Eugene Meacham in a car at the time and place charged. Defendant left a fingerprint in the car and also an overnight bag containing his social security card. A few days later he turned himself in and voluntarily disclosed that he shot Meacham. At trial, defendant testified about his version of what happened. Much of the testimony was by defendant himself, as only he and Meacham were present at the occurrence.

The State's version is that the homicide was a cold-blooded murder by defendant in the course of robbing Meacham. Defendant was hitchhiking in the West, and Meacham offered him a ride from Oregon to Chicago, with defendant to drive. Defendant was then to split off and hitchhike to his home in North Carolina, while Meacham was to drive on to Connecticut to get married. According to the State, after defendant had passed Des Moines, Iowa, he shot Meacham in the head, robbed him of $208, dumped his body on a side road, drove on to Davenport, Iowa, took a bus from there to Chicago, Illinois, and then hitchhiked to the Southwest. . . .

state's version

Defendant's version is more extensive. According to him, he grew up in North Carolina, his father abandoned the family penniless when defendant was small, defendant's stepfather later shot defendant's dog when it was frothing at the mouth with rabies, leaving an indelible impression on defendant, defendant subsequently dropped out of school but eventually obtained a high school equivalency certificate, he served in the army but was discharged as undesirable, at one time he drove a car in Utah without the owner's consent and was convicted and sentenced to ten years, and at another time he was convicted of a federal offense for which he received five years probation that he violated by leaving North Carolina on the present occasion. He testified that he was married but had no children, worked in a factory in North Carolina, lived with his wife in that State, and on this occasion had left to hitchhike through the West.

Regarding the incident involved here, defendant testified that casual acquaintances in California gave him a pill and told him it was a "little sunshine" and would make him feel "groovy." He met Meacham in Oregon and they made the arrangement for the trip east. Meacham had a pistol. Defendant drove all the way to Iowa without rest and was exhausted. He testified he took the pill at Des Moines, it made him feel funny, and the road turned different colors and pulsated. Meacham was sleeping on the passenger side. Defendant testified he heard strange noises from Meacham's throat, like growling. Meacham's face grew and his nose got long, and his head turned into a dog like the one defendant's stepfather had shot. Defendant testified he got scared, picked up Meacham's gun, and shot him three times.

took drugs + had hallucinations

Defendant stated he did not remember much that happened for awhile. The next he clearly remembered anything he was in a cemetery at What Cheer, Iowa. He testified he had periods thinking Meacham was human and periods thinking Meacham was a dog. He drove back to the highway and traveled awhile, then turned off on a side road and removed Meacham's body from the car.

Defendant testified further he drove to What Cheer and tried there to wipe the blood from his hands. He then returned to see if Meacham was alive, kicked something in the road, saw it was Meacham's billfold, and took it. He removed the money from the billfold, discarded the billfold itself, and later used some of the money and threw away some of it. He also threw away the gun.

Defendant testified he drove to Davenport, abandoned the car, took a bus to Chicago, hitchhiked through the Southwest, and turned himself in to officials in the State of Nevada. He voluntarily told officers about the incident, although in his original version he did not say anything about the claimed pill or its aftermath.

The County Attorney of Jasper County, Iowa, charged defendant with murder. A separate trial was held on the question of defendant's sanity to stand trial. A jury found him sane. Defendant pleaded insanity at the time of the act and stood trial on the murder charge; a jury found him guilty of first-degree murder. After the trial court overruled defendant's motion for new trial and sentenced him, he appealed.

* * *

I. *Drug Intoxication as Complete Defense.* The case is different from the usual one in which the accused contends only that use of alcohol or other drugs prevented him from forming specific intent. Here defendant first contends the drug caused temporary insanity, which constitutes a complete defense. Defendant is right that insanity, if established, is a complete defense. Under our law the test of insanity is "whether defendant had capacity to know the nature and quality of his acts and [the] distinction between right and wrong." *State v. Harkness*, 160 N.W.2d 324, 334 (Iowa). In addition to himself as a witness, defendant introduced testimony by two physicians who opined the drug was LSD and answered hypothetical questions about defendant's mental condition. By himself and those witnesses, defendant adduced substantial evidence which would meet the Harkness test in an ordinary case of an insanity defense. This evidence assumed the truth of defendant's testimony that he ingested the drug and sustained hallucinations as a result.

Defendant requested an instruction on insanity as a complete defense, tailored to include temporary insanity induced by drugs. The trial court refused it, and instructed that the jury should consider the claimed mental condition in connection with intent, as reducing the offense but not as exonerating it.

This court has held that a temporary mental condition caused by voluntary intoxication from alcohol does not constitute a complete defense. Is the rule the same when the mental condition results from voluntary ingestion of other drugs? We think so, and the cases so hold. *Commonwealth v. Campbell*, 445 Pa. 488, 495, 284 A.2d 798, 801 ("there should be no legal distinction between the voluntary use of drugs and the voluntary use of alcohol in determining criminal responsibility"); *People v. Corson*, 221 Cal.App.2d 579, 34 Cal.Rptr. 584; *DeBerry v. Commonwealth*, 289 S.W.2d 495 (Ky.); *State v. Bellue*, 194 S.E.2d 193 (S.C.). See *State v. Christie*, 243 Iowa 1199, 53 N.W.2d 887, on reh. 54 N.W.2d 927 (alcohol and phenobarbital); *State v. Church*, 169 N.W.2d 889 (Iowa) (glue sniffing); *State v. Clark*, 187 N.W.2d 717 (Iowa) (tranquilizer).

Holding

Defendant does not contend that extended use of drugs caused him "settled or established" insanity. He does argue that he did not take the pill voluntarily. But assuming he did take a drug, according to his own testimony no one tricked him into taking it or forced him to do so. Such is the language of defendant's own citations involving involuntary intoxication. *People v. Nichol*, 34 Cal. 211, 215 ("fraud, contrivance, or force of some other person"); *McCook v. State*, 91 Ga. 740, 17 S.E. 1019 (same); *Bartholomew v. People*, 104 Ill. 601, 606 (same); *Choate v. State*, 19 Okl.Cr. 169, 177, 197 P. 1060, 1063 ("fraud or artifice"); 22 C.J.S. Criminal Law § 69 at 220–221 ("being compelled to drink against his will, or through another's fraud or strategem"—"fraud or duress"); Annot. 30 A.L.R. 761, 764 ("by strategem, or the fraud of another"). Defendant did not take the pill by mistake—thinking, for example, it was candy. If his own testimony is believed, he knew it was a mind-affecting drug. See *Bennett v. State*, 161 Ark. 496, 257 S.W. 372 (no excuse that whisky had different effect than accused anticipated, if he knew it was whisky); *Commonwealth v. Campbell, supra*, 445 Pa. at 495, 284 A.2d at 801 (LSD—"nonpredictability of effect on the human body is devoid of any adequate legal justification based upon legal precedent, or reason, or policy considerations for a radical change and departure from our law of criminal responsibility").

We hold that the trial court properly refused the requested instruction.

* * *

■ LeGrand, Judge (dissenting).

Dissent

I dissent from . . . the majority opinion because of its erroneous treatment of defendant's claimed defense of insanity. Consequently, I dissent, too, from the result.

The insanity issue arose at trial because plaintiff testified he had ingested a quantity of LSD shortly before the events in question without knowing what it was and without realizing its possible harmful effects. The majority concedes there was ample medical testimony produced by defendant as to the properties of this hallucinogenic drug to support a finding defendant was suffering from a mental illness or temporary insanity and to require its submission to the jury. However, the majority then deprives defendant of this defense by holding his condition resulted from the voluntary ingestion of drugs, which it equates with voluntary alcoholic intoxication.

Arguments

I find this portion of the majority opinion unacceptable on two grounds. First, I cannot agree that drug intoxication should be treated the same as that resulting from the use of alcohol. Second, even assuming the two are legally indistinguishable, the evidence here presents a fact question on the voluntariness of defendant's conduct, which should have taken the issue to the jury.

* * *

Drug v. Alcohol intoxication

I.   My first disagreement with the majority opinion deals with its premise that drug intoxication and alcohol intoxication are legally the same when considering them as a possible defense to the commission of a crime. There is authority to support that view, although not as much as the majority says there is. . . .

* * *

[The] ... authorities relied on are unimpressive ... except *Commonwealth v. Campbell* (1971), 445 Pa. 488, 284 A.2d 798, 801. Even that case drew a hesitant special concurrence from one member of the court, who went along with the result only because he felt the "present state of our scientific knowledge" did not permit a distinction between the use of alcohol and the use of drugs to be made. South Carolina apparently adopts that same view. See *State v. Bellue* (S.C.1973), 194 S.E.2d 193, 195.

* * *

On the other side of the coin are cases like *State v. Flores*, 82 N.M. 480, 483 P.2d 1320 (1971) where, under circumstances quite like those here, failure to instruct on the issue of insanity was held to be reversible error.

And in *State v. Trantino*, 44 N.J. 358, 209 A.2d 117, 123 (1965), the New Jersey Supreme Court held the question of temporary insanity allegedly resulting from the use of liquor and dexedrine had been properly submitted for jury determination.

* * *

I point out, too, that the problem presented here was recognized (but not decided) in *Pierce v. Turner* (10th Cir.1968), 402 F.2d 109, 113, cert. denied 394 U.S. 950, 89 S.Ct. 1290, 22 L.Ed.2d 485 where the court said:

> We anticipate, of course, that the demands of due process may require adjustments and refinement in traditional and "stock" instructions on the subject of criminal responsibility in view of the frightening effects of the hallucinatory drugs.

I believe the time has come for this "adjustment and refinement" in our instructions dealing with this subject. The fallacy in the majority's position is that it puts the issue on a *time* basis rather than an *effect* basis. It says the use of drugs is no defense unless mental illness resulting from long established use is shown because that's what we have said of alcoholic intoxication. See *State v. Booth*, 169 N.W.2d 869, 873 (Iowa 1969). But we have said that about alcohol because ordinarily the use of alcohol produces no mental illness except by long continued excessive use. On the other hand that same result can be obtained overnight by the use of modern hallucinatory drugs like LSD.

The reason for our alcohol-intoxication rule disappears when we discuss the use of these drugs. See G. Lunter, "The Effect of Drug-Induced Intoxication on the Issue of Criminal Responsibility," 8 Cr. Law Bulletin, page 731 (1972) and Comment in 17 DePaul Law Rev., page 365 (1968), "LSD—Its Effect on Criminal Responsibility."

Several quotations from the latter are significant. At page 370 the author says:

LSD can cause a breakdown in the normal functioning of the mind because hallucinations and a complete break with reality is one result of the use of the drug.

At page 371 this appears:

The LSD reaction may be equated, for legal purposes, with delirium tremens. In many ways they have the same effect on the human mind, and it would appear that both should render the subject legally insane.

Our intoxication rationale as applied to alcohol simply does not fit the use of modern hallucinatory drugs; and it was never meant to. It was adopted before such drugs, as we now know them, were in common use. That is why I would say they *are* dissimilar and should be so regarded. There is no justifiable reason for equating the effects of so-called "hard" drugs, particularly those classified as hallucinatory, with the use of alcohol.

In the present case there is testimony of some 90 drug categories. Each has its own properties and each has its own effects. To treat all alike simply because each is classified generally as a drug strikes me as a judicial cop-out which completely disregards the realities of the situation.

In the case of alcohol, we have long experience which teaches us the usual and ordinary effects of alcohol upon the human mind and body. We are therefore justified in formulating general rules as to alcoholic intoxication, even though they may not operate with precise fairness in every case. We do not yet have the same scientific reliability on the effect of the use of drugs as far as criminal responsibility is concerned. But this should not tempt us to slough the matter off by lumping *all* drugs together with alcohol, where obviously many of them do not belong.

* * *

II. Assuming, however, there is no merit to what I have said in Division I, there is still another reason why I cannot agree with the majority opinion. Even under that view, it is only *voluntary* intoxication which may not be relied upon as a defense to the commission of a criminal act. The majority finds that the use of drugs here was voluntary. I believe that finding entirely overlooks the real import of the evidence.

The testimony shows defendant took a pill which he knew to be a drug but which he did not know to be LSD and which he testified he thought to be harmless, although he had been told it would make him feel groovy. There is nothing to indicate he knew it could induce hallucinations or lead to the frightening debilitating effects of mind and body to which the doctors testified. The majority nevertheless holds the defendant's resulting drug intoxication was voluntary. I disagree.

* * *

In other words, does voluntary in this context refer to the *mechanical act of ingesting the pill* or does it refer to a *willing and intelligent assumption of the possible harmful consequences of that act?*

I am convinced voluntary as here used should relate to a knowledgeable acceptance of the danger and risk involved. Applied to the instant case, that rule would demand submission of the issue to a jury. See *De Berry v. Commonwealth* (Ky.1956), 289 S.W.2d 495, 497, where the court held one who commits a crime under the influence of drugs should be held guilty if he takes the drug *knowing the effect it is likely to have.* See also *Saldiveri v. State* (Md.App.1958), 217 Md. 412, 143 A.2d 70, 77, where it was held administration of an excess dosage of drug by mistake could not result in voluntary drug intoxication.

In my opinion the trial court erred in holding defendant was not entitled to have the issue of temporary insanity submitted to the jury under proper instruction. I would reverse and remand for a new trial, because of the court's failure to give such an instruction.

■ MASON and RAWLINGS, JJ., join in this dissent.

NOTES AND QUESTIONS

1. Why should *involuntary* intoxication be treated differently than *voluntary* intoxication? Why do you suppose the former is assimilated to insanity, which can be a complete defense to crime, whereas the latter cannot be a complete defense, only reducing the degree of the offense where it is such as to eliminate a particular mental component? See, for example, the Model Penal Code, § 2.08(4), which provides:

Intoxication which (a) is not self-induced or (b) is pathological is an affirmative defense if by reason of such intoxication the actor at the time of his conduct lacks substantial capacity either to appreciate its criminality [wrongfulness] or to conform his conduct to the requirements of the law.

See, e.g., Brancaccio v. State, 698 So.2d 597 (Fla. App. 1997) (defendant who was taking prescribed Zoloft, an antidepressant, entitled to instruction on involuntary intoxication); City of Minneapolis v. Altimus, 306 Minn. 462, 238 N.W.2d 851 (1976) (defendant claiming unusual reaction from Valium—confusion and hyperexcitability—entitled to involuntary intoxication instruction).

2. Who has the better of the argument in *State v. Hall*, Justice Uhlenhopp for the majority or Judge LeGrand for the dissent? Can you articulate the difference between the voluntary drinking of alcohol and the voluntary taking of a hallucinatory drug like LSD? Should whatever differences that might occur in either anticipated results or risk assessment make a legal difference? Should it make a difference whether it is 1974 (as in *Hall*) or the 21st Century?

3. Can voluntary drug usage (or for that matter voluntary alcohol consumption) ever amount to a complete defense to crime? Is an affirmative answer suggested by the opinions in *Hall*? *See* Porreca v. Maryland, 49 Md.App. 522, 433 A.2d 1204 (1981); Barrett v. United States, 377 A.2d 62 (D.C.App.1977); People v. Kelly, 10 Cal.3d 565, 111 Cal.Rptr. 171, 516 P.2d 875 (1973).

3.   ADDICTION

At this point, you should read or reread *Robinson v. California* in Chapter 4, p. 349, *supra*.

Powell v. Texas

Supreme Court of the United States, 1968.
392 U.S. 514, 88 S.Ct. 2145, 20 L.Ed.2d 1254.

■ MR. JUSTICE MARSHALL announced the judgment of the Court and delivered an opinion in which THE CHIEF JUSTICE, MR. JUSTICE BLACK, and MR. JUSTICE HARLAN join.

In late December 1966, appellant was arrested and charged with being found in a state of intoxication in a public place, in violation of Vernon's Ann.Texas Penal Code, Art. 477 (1952), which reads as follows:

Whoever shall get drunk or be found in a state of intoxication in any public place, or at any private house except his own, shall be fined not exceeding one hundred dollars.

. . . His counsel urged that appellant was "afflicted with the disease of chronic alcoholism," that "his appearance in public (while drunk was) . . . not of his own volition," and therefore that to punish him criminally for that conduct would be cruel and unusual, in violation of the Eighth and Fourteenth Amendments to the United States Constitution.

The trial judge in the county court, sitting without a jury, . . . ruled as a matter of law that chronic alcoholism was not a defense to the charge. He found appellant guilty, and fined him $50. . . .

I.

The principal testimony was that of Dr. David Wade, a Fellow of the American Medical Association, duly certificated in psychiatry. . . . Dr. Wade sketched the outlines of the "disease" concept of alcoholism; noted that there is no generally accepted definition of "alcoholism"; alluded to the ongoing debate within the medical profession over whether alcohol is actually physically "addicting" or merely psychologically "habituating"; and concluded that in either case a "chronic alcoholic" is an "involuntary drinker," who is "powerless not to drink," and who "loses his self-control over his drinking." He testified that he had examined appellant, and that appellant is a "chronic alcoholic," who "by the time he has reached (the state of intoxication) . . . is not able to control his behavior, and (who) . . . has reached this point because he has an uncontrollable compulsion to drink." Dr. Wade also responded in the negative to the question whether appellant has "the willpower to resist the constant excessive consumption of alcohol." He added that in his opinion jailing appellant without medical attention would operate neither to rehabilitate him nor to lessen his desire for alcohol.

On cross-examination, Dr. Wade admitted that when appellant was sober he knew the difference between right and wrong, and he responded affirmatively to the question whether appellant's act in taking the first drink in any given instance when he was sober was a "voluntary exercise of his will." Qualifying his answer, Dr. Wade stated that "these individuals have a compulsion, and this compulsion, while not completely overpowering, is a very strong influence, an exceedingly strong influence, and this compulsion coupled with the firm belief in their mind that they are going to be able to handle it from now on causes their judgment to be somewhat clouded."

Appellant testified concerning the history of his drinking problem. He reviewed his many arrests for drunkenness; testified that he was unable to stop drinking; stated that when he was intoxicated he had no control over his actions and could not remember them later, but that he did not become violent; and admitted that he did not remember his arrest on the occasion for which he was being tried. On cross-examination, appellant admitted that he had had one drink on the morning of the trial and had been able to discontinue drinking. . . .

Evidence in the case then closed. . . . [T]he State contented itself with a brief argument that appellant had no defense to the charge because he "is legally sane and knows the difference between right and wrong."

Following this abbreviated exposition of the problem before it, the trial court indicated its intention to disallow appellant's claimed defense of "chronic alcoholism." Thereupon defense counsel submitted, and the trial court entered, the following "findings of fact":

(1) That chronic alcoholism is a disease which destroys the afflicted person's will power to resist the constant, excessive consumption of alcohol.

(2) That a chronic alcoholic does not appear in public by his own volition but under a compulsion symptomatic of the disease of chronic alcoholism.

(3) That Leroy Powell, defendant herein, is a chronic alcoholic who is afflicted with the disease of chronic alcoholism.

Whatever else may be said of them, those are not "findings of fact" in any recognizable, traditional sense in which that term has been used in a court of law; they are the premises of a syllogism transparently designed to bring this case within the scope of this Court's opinion in Robinson v. State of California, 370 U.S. 660, 82 S.Ct. 1417, 8 L.Ed.2d 758 (1962). Nonetheless, the dissent would have us adopt these "findings" without critical examination; it would use them as the basis for a constitutional holding that "a person may not be punished if the condition essential to constitute the defined crime is part of the pattern of his disease and is occasioned by a compulsion symptomatic of the disease."

. . .

The difficulty with that position, as we shall show, is that it goes much too far on the basis of too little knowledge. In the first place, the record in this case is utterly inadequate to permit the sort of informed and responsible adjudication which alone can support the announcement of an important and wide-ranging new constitutional principle. We know very little about the circumstances surrounding the drinking bout which resulted in this conviction, or about Leroy Powell's drinking problem, or indeed about alcoholism itself. . . .

Furthermore, the inescapable fact is that there is no agreement among members of the medical profession about what it means to say that "alcoholism" is a "disease." One of the principal works in this field states that the major difficulty in articulating a "disease concept of alcoholism" is that "alcoholism has too many definitions and disease has practically none." This same author concludes that "a disease is what the medical profession recognizes as such." In other words, there is widespread agreement today that "alcoholism" is a "disease," for the simple reason that the medical profession has concluded that it should attempt to treat those who have drinking problems. There the agreement stops. Debate rages within the medical profession as to whether "alcoholism" is a separate "disease" in any meaningful biochemical, physiological or psychological sense, or whether it represents one peculiar manifestation in some individuals of underlying psychiatric disorders.

* * *

The trial court's "finding" that Powell "is afflicted with the disease of chronic alcoholism," which "destroys the afflicted person's will power to resist the constant, excessive consumption of alcohol" covers a multitude of sins. Dr. Wade's testimony that appellant suffered from a compulsion which was an "exceedingly strong influence," but which was "not completely overpowering" is at least more carefully stated, if no less mystifying. . . . [C]onceptual clarity can only be achieved by distinguishing carefully between "loss of control" once an individual has commenced to drink and "inability to abstain" from drinking in the first place. Presumably a person would have to display both characteristics in order to make out a constitutional defense, should one be recognized. Yet the "findings" of the trial court utterly fail to make this crucial distinction, and there is serious question whether the record can be read to support a finding of either loss of control or inability to abstain.

Dr. Wade did testify that once appellant began drinking he appeared to have no control over the amount of alcohol he finally ingested. Appellant's own testimony concerning his drinking on the day of the trial would certainly appear, however, to cast doubt upon the conclusion that he was without control over his consumption of alcohol when he had sufficiently important reasons to exercise such control. However that may be, there are more serious factual and conceptual difficulties with reading this record to show that appellant was unable to abstain from drinking. Dr. Wade testified that when appellant was sober, the act of taking the first drink was a "voluntary exercise of his will," but that this exercise of will was undertaken under the "exceedingly strong influence" of a "compulsion" which was "not completely overpowering." Such concepts, when juxtaposed in this fashion, have little meaning.

* * *

It is one thing to say that if a man is deprived of alcohol his hands will begin to shake, he will suffer agonizing pains and ultimately he will have hallucinations; it is quite another to say that a man has a "compulsion" to take a drink, but that he also retains a certain amount of "free will" with which to resist. It is simply impossible, in the present state of our knowledge, to ascribe a useful meaning to the latter statement. This definitional confusion reflects, of course, not merely the undeveloped state of the psychiatric art but also the conceptual difficulties inevitably attendant upon the importation of scientific and medical models into a legal system generally predicated upon a different set of assumptions.

II.

* * *

There is as yet no known generally effective method for treating the vast number of alcoholics in our society. . . . Thus it is entirely possible that, even were the manpower and facilities available for a full-scale attack upon chronic alcoholism, we would find ourselves unable to help the vast bulk of our "visible"—let alone our "invisible"—alcoholic population.

However, facilities for the attempted treatment of indigent alcoholics are woefully lacking throughout the country. It would be tragic to return large numbers of helpless, sometimes dangerous and frequently unsanitary inebriates to the streets of our cities without even the opportunity to sober up adequately which a brief jail term provides. . . .

One virtue of the criminal process is, at least, that the duration of penal incarceration typically has some outside statutory limit; this is universally true in the case of petty offenses, such as public drunkenness, where jail terms are quite short on the whole. "Therapeutic civil commitment" lacks this feature; one is typically committed until one is "cured." Thus, to do otherwise than affirm might subject indigent alcoholics to the risk that they may be locked up for an indefinite period of time under the same conditions as before, with no more hope than before of receiving effective treatment and no prospect of periodic "freedom."

Faced with this unpleasant reality, we are unable to assert that the use of the criminal process as a means of dealing with the public aspects of problem drinking can never be defended as rational. The picture of the penniless drunk propelled aimlessly and endlessly through the law's "revolving door" of arrest, incarceration, release and re-arrest is not a pretty one. But before we condemn the present practice across-the-board, perhaps we ought to be able to point to some clear promise of a better world for these unfortunate people. Unfortunately, no such promise has yet been forthcoming. If, in addition to the absence of a coherent approach to the problem of treatment, we consider the almost complete absence of facilities and manpower for the implementation of a rehabilitation program, it is difficult to say in the present context that the criminal process is utterly lacking in social value. . . .

* * *

III.

* * *

Appellant, however, seeks to come within the application of the Cruel and Unusual Punishment Clause announced in Robinson v. State of California, 370 U.S. 660, 82 S.Ct. 1417, 8 L.Ed.2d 758 (1962), which involved a state statute making it a crime to "be addicted to the use of narcotics." This Court held there that "a state law which imprisons a person thus afflicted (with narcotic addiction) as a criminal, even though he has never touched any narcotic drug within the State or been guilty of any irregular behavior there, inflicts a cruel and unusual punishment. . . ."

On its face the present case does not fall within that holding, since appellant was convicted, not for being a chronic alcoholic, but for being in public while drunk on a particular occasion. The State of Texas thus has not sought to punish a mere status, as California did in Robinson; nor has it attempted to regulate appellant's behavior in the privacy of his own home. Rather, it has imposed upon appellant a criminal sanction for public behavior which may create substantial health and safety hazards, both for appellant and for members of the general public, and which offends the moral and esthetic sensibilities of a large segment of the community. This seems a far cry from convicting one for being an addict, being a chronic alcoholic, being "mentally ill, or a leper. . . ."

Robinson so viewed brings this Court but a very small way into the substantive criminal law. And unless Robinson is so viewed it is difficult to see any limiting principle that would serve to prevent this Court from becoming, under the aegis of the Cruel and Unusual Punishment Clause, the ultimate arbiter of the standards of criminal responsibility, in diverse areas of the criminal law, throughout the country.

It is suggested in dissent that Robinson stands for the "simple" but "subtle" principle that "(c)riminal penalties may not be inflicted upon a person for being in a condition he is powerless to change." In that view, appellant's "condition" of public intoxication was "occasioned by a compulsion symptomatic of the disease" of chronic alcoholism, and thus, apparently, his behavior lacked the critical element of *mens rea*. Whatever may be the merits of such a doctrine of criminal responsibility, it surely cannot be said to follow from Robinson. The entire thrust of Robinson's interpretation of the Cruel and Unusual Punishment Clause is that criminal penalties may be inflicted only if the accused has committed some act, has engaged in some behavior, which society has an interest in preventing, or perhaps in historical common law terms, has committed some *actus reus*. It thus does not deal with the question of whether certain conduct cannot constitutionally be punished because it is, in some sense, "involuntary" or "occasioned by a compulsion."

Likewise, as the dissent acknowledges, there is a substantial definitional distinction between a "status," as in Robinson, and a "condition," which is said to be involved in this case. . . .

Ultimately, then, the most troubling aspects of this case, were Robinson to be extended to meet it, would be the scope and content of what could only be a constitutional doctrine of criminal responsibility. In dissent it is urged that the decision could be limited to conduct which is "a characteristic and involuntary part of the pattern of the disease as it

afflicts" the particular individual, and that "(i)t is not foreseeable" that it
would be applied "in the case of offenses such as driving a car while
intoxicated, assault, theft, or robbery." That is limitation by fiat. In the
first place, nothing in the logic of the dissent would limit its application
to chronic alcoholics. If Leroy Powell cannot be convicted of public
intoxication, it is difficult to see how a State can convict an individual for
murder, if that individual, while exhibiting normal behavior in all other
respects, suffers from a "compulsion" to kill, which is an "exceedingly
strong influence," but "not completely overpowering." Even if we limit our
consideration to chronic alcoholics, it would seem impossible to confine
the principle within the arbitrary bounds which the dissent seems to
envision.

* * *

Traditional common-law concepts of personal accountability and
essential considerations of federalism lead us to disagree with appellant.
We are unable to conclude, on the state of this record or on the current
state of medical knowledge, that chronic alcoholics in general, and Leroy
Powell in particular, suffer from such an irresistible compulsion to drink
and to get drunk in public that they are utterly unable to control their
performance of either or both of these acts and thus cannot be deterred
at all from public intoxication. And in any event this Court has never
articulated a general constitutional doctrine of *mens rea*.

* * *

Affirmed.

■ MR. JUSTICE BLACK, whom MR. JUSTICE HARLAN joins, concurring.

While I agree that the grounds set forth in Mr. Justice MARSHALL's
opinion are sufficient to require affirmance of the judgment here, I wish
to amplify my reasons for concurring.

Those who favor the change now urged upon us rely on their own
notions of the wisdom of this Texas law to erect a constitutional barrier,
the desirability of which is far from clear. To adopt this position would
significantly limit the States in their efforts to deal with a widespread
and important social problem and would do so by announcing a
revolutionary doctrine of constitutional law that would also tightly
restrict state power to deal with a wide variety of other harmful conduct.

I.

* * *

Apart from the value of jail as a form of treatment, jail serves other
traditional functions of the criminal law. For one thing, it gets the
alcoholics off the street, where they may cause harm in a number of ways
to a number of people, and isolation of the dangerous has always been
considered an important function of the criminal law. In addition,
punishment of chronic alcoholics can serve several deterrent functions—

it can give potential alcoholics an additional incentive to control their drinking, and it may, even in the case of the chronic alcoholic, strengthen his incentive to control the frequency and location of his drinking experiences.

These values served by criminal punishment assume even greater significance in light of the available alternatives for dealing with the problem of alcoholism. Civil commitment facilities may not be any better than the jails they would replace. . . .

* * *

II.

I agree with MR. JUSTICE MARSHALL that the findings of fact in this case are inadequate to justify the sweeping constitutional rule urged upon us. I could not, however, consider any findings that could be made with respect to "voluntariness" or "compulsion" controlling on the question whether a specific instance of human behavior should be immune from punishment as a constitutional matter. When we say that appellant's appearance in public is caused not by "his own" volition but rather by some other force, we are clearly thinking of a force that is nevertheless "his" except in some special sense. The accused undoubtedly commits the proscribed act and the only question is whether the act can be attributed to a part of "his" personality that should not be regarded as criminally responsible. Almost all of the traditional purposes of the criminal law can be significantly served by punishing the person who in fact committed the proscribed act, without regard to whether his action was "compelled" by some elusive "irresponsible" aspect of his personality. As I have already indicated, punishment of such a defendant can clearly be justified in terms of deterrence, isolation, and treatment. On the other hand, medical decisions concerning the use of a term such as "disease" or "volition," based as they are on the clinical problems of diagnosis and treatment, bear no necessary correspondence to the legal decision whether the overall objectives of the criminal law can be furthered by imposing punishment. For these reasons, much as I think that criminal sanctions should in many situations be applied only to those whose conduct is morally blameworthy . . . I cannot think the States should be held constitutionally required to make the inquiry as to what part of a defendant's personality is responsible for his actions and to excuse anyone whose action was, in some complex, psychological sense, the result of a "compulsion."

III.

The rule of constitutional law urged by appellant is not required by Robinson v. State of California . . . In that case we held that a person could not be punished for the mere status of being a narcotics addict. We explicitly limited our holding to the situation where no conduct of any kind is involved, . . .

The argument is made that appellant comes within the terms of our holding in Robinson because being drunk in public is a mere status or "condition." Despite this many-faceted use of the concept of "condition," this argument would require converting Robinson into a case protecting actual behavior, a step we explicitly refused to take in that decision.

Punishment for a status is particularly obnoxious, and in many instances can reasonably be called cruel and unusual, because it involves punishment for a mere propensity, a desire to commit an offense; the mental element is not simply one part of the crime but may constitute all of it. This is a situation universally sought to be avoided in our criminal law; the fundamental requirement that some action be proved is solidly established even for offenses most heavily based on propensity, such as attempt, conspiracy, and recidivist crimes. . . .

The reasons for this refusal to permit conviction without proof of an act are difficult to spell out, but they are nonetheless perceived and universally expressed in our criminal law. Evidence of propensity can be considered relatively unreliable and more difficult for a defendant to rebut; the requirement of a specific act thus provides some protection against false charges. Perhaps more fundamental is the difficulty of distinguishing, in the absence of any conduct, between desires of the day-dream variety and fixed intentions that may pose a real threat to society; extending the criminal law to cover both types of desire would be unthinkable, since "(t)here can hardly be anyone who has never thought evil. When a desire is inhibited it may find expression in fantasy; but it would be absurd to condemn this natural psychological mechanism as illegal."

In contrast, crimes that require the State to prove that the defendant actually committed some proscribed act involve none of these special problems. In addition, the question whether an act is "involuntary" is, as I have already indicated, an inherently elusive question, and one which the State may, for good reasons, wish to regard as irrelevant. In light of all these considerations, our limitation of our Robinson holding to pure status crimes seems to me entirely proper.

IV.

The rule of constitutional law urged upon us by appellant would have a revolutionary impact on the criminal law, and any possible limits proposed for the rule would be wholly illusory. If the original boundaries of Robinson are to be discarded, any new limits too would soon fall by the wayside and the Court would be forced to hold the States powerless to punish any conduct that could be shown to result from a "compulsion," in the complex, psychological meaning of that term. . . .

The real reach of any such decision, however, would be broader still, for the basic premise underlying the argument is that it is cruel and unusual to punish a person who is not morally blameworthy. I state the proposition in this sympathetic way because I feel there is much to be said for avoiding the use of criminal sanctions in many such situations. But the question here is one of constitutional law. The legislatures have always been allowed wide freedom to determine the extent to which moral culpability should be a prerequisite to conviction of a crime. The criminal law is a social tool that is employed in seeking a wide variety of goals, and I cannot say the Eighth Amendment's limits on the use of criminal sanctions extend as far as this viewpoint would inevitably carry them.

But even if we were to limit any holding in this field to "compulsions" that are "symptomatic" of a "disease," in the words of the findings of the trial court, the sweep of that holding would still be startling. Such a ruling would make it clear beyond any doubt that a narcotics addict could not be punished for "being" in possession of drugs or, for that matter, for "being" guilty of using them. A wide variety of sex offenders would be immune from punishment if they could show that their conduct was not voluntary but part of the pattern of a disease. More generally speaking, a form of the insanity defense would be made a constitutional requirement throughout the Nation, should the Court now hold it cruel and unusual to punish a person afflicted with any mental disease whenever his conduct was part of the pattern of his disease and occasioned by a compulsion symptomatic of the disease. . . .

* * *

■ MR. JUSTICE WHITE, concurring in the result.

If it cannot be a crime to have an irresistible compulsion to use narcotics, Robinson v. California, I do not see how it can constitutionally be a crime to yield to such a compulsion. Punishing an addict for using drugs convicts for addiction under a different name. Distinguishing between the two crimes is like forbidding criminal conviction for being sick with flu or epilepsy but permitting punishment for running a fever or having a convulsion. Unless Robinson is to be abandoned, the use of narcotics by an addict must be beyond the reach of the criminal law. Similarly, the chronic alcoholic with an irresistible urge to consume alcohol should not be punishable for drinking or for being drunk.

Powell's conviction was for the different crime of being drunk in a public place. Thus even if Powell was compelled to drink, and so could not constitutionally be convicted for drinking, his conviction in this case can be invalidated only if there is a constitutional basis for saying that he may not be punished for being in public while drunk. . . .

The trial court said that Powell was a chronic alcoholic with a compulsion not only to drink to excess but also to frequent public places when intoxicated. Nothing in the record before the trial court supports the latter conclusion, which is contrary to common sense and to common knowledge. The sober chronic alcoholic has no compulsion to be on the public streets; many chronic alcoholics drink at home and are never seen drunk in public. Before and after taking the first drink, and until he becomes so drunk that he loses the power to know where he is or to direct his movements, the chronic alcoholic with a home or financial resources is as capable as the nonchronic drinker of doing his drinking in private, of removing himself from public places and, since he knows or ought to know that he will become intoxicated, of making plans to avoid his being found drunk in public. For these reasons, I cannot say that the chronic alcoholic who proves his disease and a compulsion to drink is shielded from conviction when he has knowingly failed to take feasible precautions against committing a criminal act, here the act of going to or remaining in a public place. On such facts the alcoholic is like a person with smallpox, who could be convicted for being on the street but not for being ill, or, like the epileptic, who would be punished for driving a car but not for his disease.

* * *

. . . For the purposes of this case, it is necessary to say only that Powell showed nothing more than that he was to some degree compelled to drink and that he was drunk at the time of his arrest. He made no showing that he was unable to stay off the streets on the night in question.[5]

Because Powell did not show that his conviction offended the Constitution, I concur in the judgment affirming the [lower] court.

■ MR. JUSTICE FORTAS, with whom MR. JUSTICE DOUGLAS, MR. JUSTICE BRENNAN, and MR. JUSTICE STEWART join, dissenting.

* * *

I.

* * *

The sole question presented is whether a criminal penalty may be imposed upon a person suffering the disease of "chronic alcoholism" for a condition—being "in a state of intoxication" in public—which is a characteristic part of the pattern of his disease and which, the trial court found, was not the consequence of appellant's volition but of "a compulsion symptomatic of the disease of chronic alcoholism." . . . We deal here with the mere condition of being intoxicated in public.[2]

---

[5] I do not question the power of the State to remove a helplessly intoxicated person from a public street, although against his will, and to hold him until he has regained his powers. The person's own safety and the public interest require this much. A statute such as the one challenged in this case is constitutional insofar as it authorizes a police officer to arrest any seriously intoxicated person when he is encountered in a public place. Whether such a person may be charged and convicted for violating the statute will depend upon whether he is entitled to the protection of the Eighth Amendment.

[2] It is not foreseeable that findings such as those which are decisive here—namely that the appellant's being intoxicated in public was a part of the pattern of his disease and due to a compulsion symptomatic of that disease—could or would be made in the case of offenses such as driving a car while intoxicated, assault, theft, or robbery. Such offenses require independent acts or conduct and do not typically flow from and are not part of the syndrome of the disease of

II.

As I shall discuss, consideration of the Eighth Amendment issue in this case requires an understanding of "the disease of chronic alcoholism" with which, as the trial court found, appellant is afflicted, which has destroyed his "will power to resist the constant, excessive consumption of alcohol," and which leads him to "appear in public (not) by his own volition but under a compulsion symptomatic of the disease of chronic alcoholism." . . .

. . . Although there is some problem in defining the concept, its core meaning, as agreed by authorities, is that alcoholism is caused and maintained by something other than the moral fault of the alcoholic, something that, to a greater or lesser extent depending upon the physiological or psychological makeup and history of the individual, cannot be controlled by him. . . .

* * *

III

* * *

Robinson stands upon a principle which, despite its sublety, must be simply stated and respectfully applied because it is the foundation of individual liberty and the cornerstone of the relations between a civilized state and its citizens: Criminal penalties may not be inflicted upon a person for being in a condition he is powerless to change. In all probability, Robinson at some time before his conviction elected to take narcotics. But the crime as defined did not punish this conduct.[29] The statute imposed a penalty for the offense of "addiction"—a condition which Robinson could not control. Once Robinson had become an addict, he was utterly powerless to avoid criminal guilt. He was powerless to choose not to violate the law.

In the present case, appellant is charged with a crime composed of two elements—being intoxicated and being found in a public place while in that condition. The crime, so defined, differs from that in Robinson. The statute covers more than a mere status. But the essential constitutional defect here is the same as in Robinson, for in both cases the particular defendant was accused of being in a condition which he had no capacity to change or avoid. . . .

* * *

---

chronic alcoholism. If an alcoholic should be convicted for criminal conduct which is not a characteristic and involuntary part of the pattern of the disease as it afflicts him, nothing herein would prevent his punishment.

[29]   The Court noted in Robinson that narcotic addiction "is apparently an illness which may be contracted innocently or involuntarily." In the case of alcoholism it is even more likely that the disease may be innocently contracted, since the drinking of alcoholic beverages is a common activity, generally accepted in our society, while the purchasing and taking of drugs are crimes. As in Robinson, the State has not argued here that Powell's conviction may be supported by his "voluntary" action in becoming afflicted.

The findings in this case, read against the background of the medical and sociological data to which I have referred, compel the conclusion that the infliction upon appellant of a criminal penalty for being intoxicated in a public place would be "cruel and inhuman punishment" within the prohibition of the Eighth Amendment. This conclusion follows because appellant is a "chronic alcoholic" who, according to the trier of fact, cannot resist the "constant excessive consumption of alcohol" and does not appear in public by his own volition but under a "compulsion" which is part of his condition.

I would reverse the judgment below.

NOTES AND QUESTIONS

1. A number of the Justices in the various opinions in *Powell* address how the purposes of imposing criminal sanctions relate to the prosecution of chronic alcoholics for public drunkenness. Does the use of the criminal law in this fashion serve the goals of criminal punishment? Can you articulate why or why not? If the goals are not well served, why do you think the Court decided *Powell* the way it did? Is the holding consistent with *Robinson v. California*? On these issues, see Sanford H. Kadish, *Fifty Years of Criminal Law; An Opinionated Review*, 87 CALI. L. REV. 943, 962–66 (1999).

2. Not all states, as a matter of state law, have agreed with the conclusion reached by the U.S. Supreme Court in *Powell*. At least two state courts have concluded that, as a matter of statutory construction or state constitutional law, an alcoholic cannot be prosecuted for public intoxication. *See* State v. Fearon, 283 Minn. 90, 166 N.W.2d 720 (1969) (chronic alcoholics not "voluntarily drinking" within meaning of statute); State *ex. rel.* Harper v. Zegeer, 170 W.Va. 743, 296 S.E.2d 873 (1982) (rejecting justifications for incarcerating chronic alcoholics). A number of states have also decriminalized public intoxication by statute. *See* David Robinson, Jr., *Powell v. Texas: The Case of the Intoxicated Shoeshine Man—Some Reflections a Generation Later by a Participant*, 26 AM. J. CRIM. L. 401 (1999).

Problem 12–4. Justice Marshall's opinion for himself and three other Justices, Justice White's concurring opinion, and Justice Fortas' dissenting opinion for four members of the Court all to some extent frame the issue in terms of whether "a person [may be] punished if the condition essential to constitute the defined crime is part of the pattern of his disease and is occasioned by a compulsion symptomatic of the disease." *Robinson v. California* held that it was cruel and unusual punishment in violation of the Eighth Amendment to prosecute a person for the status or condition of being a narcotics addict. Does this mean that the Eighth Amendment would also be violated when an addict is charged with possession of drugs, say heroin? *See* United States v. Moore, 486 F.2d 1139 (D.C.Cir.1973); People v. Davis, 33 N.Y.2d 221, 351 N.Y.S.2d 663, 306 N.E.2d 787 (1973).

3. Is there an alternative solution to the problem of addiction and the use of intoxicants other than criminal prosecution versus non-prosecution? Would diversion of these offenders through drug courts or other treatment programs be preferable? If so, why is this alternative not more often utilized? *See* Steven Belenko, *The Challenges of Integrating Drug Treatment Into the Criminal Justice Process*, 63 Alb. L. Rev. 833 (2000).

C. Automatism

Fulcher v. State

Supreme Court of Wyoming, 1981.
633 P.2d 142.

■ Brown, Justice.

On November 17, 1979, the appellant consumed seven or eight shots of whiskey over a period of four hours in a Torrington bar, and had previously had a drink at home.

Appellant claims he got in a fight in the bar restroom, then left the bar to find a friend. According to his testimony, the last thing he remembers until awakening in jail, is going out of the door at the bar.

Appellant and his friend were found lying in the alley behind the bar by a police office who noted abrasions on their fists and faces. Appellant and his friend swore, were uncooperative, and combative. They were subsequently booked for public intoxication and disturbing the peace. During booking appellant continued to swear, and said he and his friend were jumped by a "bunch of Mexicans." Although his speech was slurred, he was able to verbally count his money, roughly $500 to $600 in increments of $20, and was able to walk to his cell without assistance.

Appellant was placed in a cell with one Martin Hernandez who was lying unconscious on the floor of the cell. After the jailer left the cell, he heard something that sounded like someone being kicked. He ran back to the cell and saw appellant standing by Hernandez. When the jailer started to leave again, the kicking sound resumed, and he observed appellant kicking and stomping on Hernandez's head. Appellant told the officer Hernandez had fallen out of bed. Hernandez was bleeding profusely and was taken to the hospital for some 52 stitches in his head and mouth. He had lost two or three teeth as a result of the kicking.

Appellant was released later in the day, November 18, 1979, and went home. He went back to Torrington on November 22, 1979, to see a doctor. Appellant testified that the doctor diagnosed he had a concussion, although there is no evidence in the record of medical treatment.

At his arraignment in district court, appellant first entered a plea of "not guilty by reason of temporary mental illness." Upon being advised by the trial judge that he would have to be committed for examination pursuant to § 7–11–304, W.S.1977, he withdrew that plea and entered a plea of not guilty.

In preparation for trial, appellant was examined by Dr. Breck LeBegue a forensic psychiatrist. The doctor reviewed the police report and conducted a number of tests.

At the trial Dr. LeBegue testified that in his expert medical opinion appellant suffered brain injury and was in a state of traumatic automatism at the time of his attack on Hernandez. Dr. LeBegue defined traumatic automatism as the state of mind in which a person does not have conscious and willful control over his actions, and lacks the ability to be aware of and to perceive his external environment. Dr. LeBegue further testified that another possible symptom is an inability to remember what occurred while in a state of traumatic automatism.

Dr. LeBegue was unable to state positively whether or not appellant had the requisite mental state for aggravated assault and battery, but thought appellant did not because of his altered state of mind. He could not state, however, that the character of an act is devoid of criminal intent because of mind alteration.

* * *

I

We hold that the trial court properly received and considered evidence of unconsciousness absent a plea of "not guilty by reason of mental illness or deficiency."

The defense of unconsciousness perhaps should be more precisely denominated as the defense of automatism. Automatism is the state of a person who, though capable of action, is not conscious of what he is doing. While in an automatistic state, an individual performs complex actions without an exercise of will. Because these actions are performed in a state of unconsciousness, they are involuntary. Automatistic behavior may be followed by complete or partial inability to recall the actions performed while unconscious. Thus, a person who acts automatically does so without intent, exercise of free will, or knowledge of the act.

Automatism may be caused by an abnormal condition of the mind capable of being designated a mental illness or deficiency. Automatism may also be manifest in a person with a perfectly healthy mind. In this opinion we are only concerned with the defense of automatism occurring in a person with a healthy mind. To further narrow the issue to be decided in this case, we are concerned with alleged automatism caused by concussion.

The defense of automatism, while not an entirely new development in the criminal law, has been discussed in relatively few decisions by American appellate courts, most of these being in California where the defense is statutory. Some courts have held that insanity and automatism are separate and distinct defenses, and that evidence of automatism may be presented under a plea of not guilty. Some states have made this distinction by statute. In other states the distinction is made by case law.

> A defense related to but different from the defense of insanity is that of unconsciousness, often referred to as automatism: one who engages in what would otherwise be criminal conduct is not guilty of a crime if he does so in a state of unconsciousness or semi-consciousness. * * * LaFave & Scott, Criminal Law, § 44, p. 337 (1972).

> The defenses of insanity and unconsciousness are not the same in nature, for unconsciousness at the time of the alleged criminal act need not be the result of a disease or defect of the mind. As a consequence, the two defenses are not the same in effect, for a defendant found not guilty by reason of unconsciousness, as distinct from insanity, is not subject to commitment to a hospital for the mentally ill.

The principal reason for making a distinction between the defense of unconsciousness and insanity is that the consequences which follow an acquittal will differ. The defense of unconsciousness is usually a complete defense. That is, there are no follow-up consequences after an acquittal; all action against a defendant is concluded.

However, in the case of a finding of not guilty by reason of insanity, the defendant is ordinarily committed to a mental institution.

* * *

The mental illness or deficiency plea does not adequately cover automatic behavior. Unless the plea of automatism, separate and apart from the plea of mental illness or deficiency is allowed, certain anomalies will result. For example, if the court determines that the automatistic defendant is sane, but refuses to recognize automatism, the defendant has no defense to the crime with which he is charged. If found guilty, he faces a prison term. The rehabilitative value of imprisonment for the automatistic offender who has committed the offense unconsciously is nonexistent. The cause of the act was an uncontrollable physical disorder that may never recur and is not a moral deficiency.

If, however, the court treats automatism as insanity and then determines that the defendant is insane, he will be found not guilty. He then will be committed to a mental institution for an indefinite period. The commitment of an automatistic individual to a mental institution for rehabilitation has absolutely no value. Mental hospitals generally treat people with psychiatric or psychological problems. This form of treatment is not suited to unconscious behavior resulting from a bump on the head.

It may be argued that evidence of unconsciousness cannot be received unless a plea of not guilty by reason of mental illness or deficiency is made pursuant to Rule 15, W.R.Cr.P. We believe this approach to be illogical.

* * * Insanity is incapacity from disease of the mind, to know the nature and quality of one's act or to distinguish between right and wrong in relation thereto. In contrast, a person who is completely unconscious when he commits an act otherwise punishable as a crime cannot know the nature and quality thereof or whether it is right or wrong. * * *

It does not seem that the definition of "mental deficiency" in § 7–11–301(a)(iii), W.S.1977, which includes "brain damage," encompasses simple brain trauma with no permanent aftereffects. It is our view that the "brain damage" contemplated in the statute is some serious and irreversible condition having an impact upon the ability of the person to function. It is undoubtedly something far more significant than a temporary and transitory condition. The two defenses are merged, in effect, if a plea of "not guilty by reason of mental illness or deficiency" is a prerequisite for using the defense of unconsciousness.

The committee that drafted Wyoming Pattern Jury Instructions Criminal, apparently recognized mental illness or deficiency and unconsciousness as separate and distinct defenses. See § 4.301, Wyo. P.J.I.Cr. A copy is attached hereto as Appendix A. Admittedly the instructions in Wyo.P.J.I.Cr. are not authoritative, because they were not approved by the Wyoming Supreme Court, and this was a matter of design. Still they are the product of a distinguished group of legal scholars, including judges, attorneys and teachers of the law. The comment to this pattern jury instruction notes that it is limited to persons of sound mind, and the comment distinguishes persons suffering from "mental deficiency or illness." In this respect, it tracks the case law from other jurisdictions, which authorities hold that unconsciousness and insanity are completely separate grounds of exemption from criminal responsibility.

Although courts hold that unconsciousness and insanity are separate and distinct defenses, there has been some uncertainty concerning the burden of proof. We believe the better rule to be that stated in State v. Caddell, supra, 215 S.E.2d at 363:

> We now hold that, under the law of this state, unconsciousness, or automatism, is a complete defense to the criminal charge, separate and apart from the defense of insanity; that *it is an affirmative defense; and that the burden rests upon the defendant to establish this defense, unless it arises out of the State's own evidence*, to the satisfaction of the jury. (Emphasis added.)

The rationale for this rule is that the defendant is the only person who knows his actual state of consciousness. Hill v. Baxter, 1 All E.R. 193 (1958), 1 Q.B. 277.

Our ruling on the facts of this case is that the defense of unconsciousness resulting from a concussion with no permanent brain damage is an affirmative defense and is a defense separate from the defense of not guilty by reason of mental illness or deficiency.

II

The appellant's conviction must, nevertheless, be affirmed. Dr. LeBegue was unable to state positively whether or not appellant had the requisite mental state for aggravated assault. He could not state that the character of the act was devoid of criminal intent because of the mind alteration. The presumption of mental competency was never overcome by appellant and the evidence presented formed a reasonable basis on which the trial judge could find and did find that the State had met the required burden of proof.

Further, the trial judge was not bound to follow Dr. LeBegue's opinion. The trier of the facts is not bound to accept expert opinion evidence in the face of other substantial and credible evidence to the contrary. State v. Peterson, 24 N.C.App. 404, 210 S.E.2d 883 (1975). Cf., Reilly v. State, Wyo., 496 P.2d 899 (1972), reh. denied, 498 P.2d 1236 (1972). There was an abundance of other credible evidence that appellant was not unconscious at the time of the assault and battery for which he was convicted.

Affirmed.

■ RAPER, JUSTICE, specially concurring, with whom ROONEY, JUSTICE, joins.

I concur only in the result reached by the majority, except to the extent I otherwise herein indicate.

The reasoning of the majority with respect to the defense of unconsciousness in this case is contrary to clear legislative will and has judicially amended the statutes of this state pertaining to mental illness or deficiency excluding criminal responsibility.

I

Dr. LeBegue's testimony was inadmissible in its entirety. " 'Mental deficiency' means a defect attributable to mental retardation, *brain damage* and learning disabilities." Section 7–11–301, W.S.1977. "A person is not responsible for criminal conduct if at the time of the criminal conduct, as a result of mental illness or deficiency, he lacked substantial capacity either to appreciate the wrongfulness of his conduct or to conform his conduct to the requirements of law." Section 7–11–304(a), W.S.1977. This was appellant's defense.

Section 7–11–304(c), W.S.1977 provides that, "[e]vidence that a person is not responsible for criminal conduct by reason of mental illness or deficiency is not admissible at the trial of the defendant unless a plea of 'not guilty by reason of mental illness or deficiency' is made. * * * "No such plea was entered.

The appellant apparently does not dispute the fact that he did in fact commit the assault on his victim as charged. While the appellant argued to the trial judge by way of a written brief that the plea of unconsciousness was not mental deficiency as contemplated by § 7–11–301 et seq., W.S.1977, the testimony of Dr. LeBegue makes it clear that appellant's condition, which he opines to have existed at the time of the crime, involved a head injury. He testified specifically:

> "In my opinion he did suffer a brain injury, in my opinion did suffer *brain damage*. He suffered a concussion which is essentially a brain bruise." (Emphasis added.)

This, according to the doctor's testimony, translated into "traumatic automatism" as well as explained the appellant's amnesia, his inability to remember kicking and stomping the victim, Hernandez. Appellant cannot avoid the effects of the statute by use of the clinical language of traumatic automatism.

* * *

I am not concerned with the fact that unconsciousness may be a defense in this case but am distressed that the procedure for taking advantage of it has been cast aside. In order to reach the conclusion of the majority that it is not necessary to plead mental deficiency as a defense in the case of unconsciousness, it is indispensable that it be pretended that § 7–11–301, supra, does not exist. The appellant's disorder, if it existed, was caused by "brain damage" according to the appellant's own testimony. That is "mental deficiency" by statutory definition. The majority has feebly attempted to jump the hurdle of a statutory definition by saying "unconsciousness" is not "insanity," but we no longer use that term. It must be pointed out that under the old statutes and before adoption of the current law pertaining to mental deficiency, "insanity" was not legislatively defined. The majority is attempting to adopt the law of an era gone by-by, rather than what the authors of the new legislation considered a more informed and modern concept.

When the legislature amends a statute, it must be presumed that some change in existing law was intended and courts should endeavor to make such amendment effective. It is not reasonable that the legislature would enact a law to declare what is already the law. The legislature will not be presumed to intend futile things. When the legislature declared that mental deficiency was a defect attributable to brain damage (§ 7–11–301), that was a definition it had never before undertaken. That was then collated by the legislature with a declaration that a person is not responsible for his criminal conduct when, because of mental deficiency (which includes brain damage), he lacked the capacity to conform his conduct to the requirements of the law (§ 7–11–304(a)). Appellant's position is that being unconscious because of a blow on the head causing brain damage rendered him not responsible for kicking his victim around. We, then, now have before us a defense of mental deficiency defined by the legislature as including brain damage, not insanity which was never defined by the legislature nor this court to either include or exclude brain damage.

* * *

It follows that damage to the brain causing a defect in its function would bring the appellant within the statute requiring conformity with all its provisions, i.e., commitment for examination and necessity of plea of "not guilty by reason of mental illness or deficiency."

* * *

I conclude that the majority opinion has no authoritative basis whatsoever; not a single case or reference cited supports their position. I would have affirmed the district court, but would not have created the new defense of unconsciousness, at least as to traumatic automatism (brain damage) clearly included as a mental deficiency by § 7–11–301(a)(iii), supra. There is no need for the court to go beyond the point. I can safely predict that defendants will disregard the plea of "not guilty by reason of mental illness or deficiency" and claim unconsciousness for many mental diseases and deficiencies which include that symptom.

■ [The opinion of ROONEY, JUSTICE, specially concurring, is omitted.]

NOTES

1. Recall that the first case in Chapter 2, State v. Hinkle, dealt with a similar claim that the court referred to as unconsciousness. Do the two courts treat the claims in the same fashion? What are the similarities and differences? The West Virginia Court in *Hinkle* seemed to use automatism and unconsciousness interchangeably. Automatism manifests itself in a wide range of disorders recognized by courts including organic brain disorders (*Hinkle*), concussional states following head injuries (*Fulcher*), epilepsy, somnambulism (sleepwalking), hypnotic states, metabolic disorders, acute emotional trauma, and more recently, sleep deprivation (McClain v. State, 678 N.E.2d 104 (Ind.1997)). *See generally*, 27 A.L.R. 4th 1067 (1984); LaFave, CRIMINAL LAW 3d Ed., § 4.9, pp. 405–11.

2. Prof. Michael Corrado rejects the view that automatism is properly equated with an "unconsciousness" defense. In his article, *Automatism and the Theory of Action*, 39 EMORY L.J. 1191 (1990), he states:

> If automatism is a defense, it is not because of unconsciousness; the actors in these cases are not unconscious in any ordinary sense. It is also not because intent is lacking, or because the behavior does not amount to action . . . because the behavior in these cases is not random or accidental but purposive. * * *

> If automatism is a defense, it is because the action involved, while conscious and purposive, is not voluntary. The action is not voluntary because, although it involves what used to be called an

act of will (being purposive), the act of will is itself caused by
something beyond the actor's control—a blow on the head, a sleep
disorder, epilepsy, hypnotic suggestion. . . .

Problem 12–5. Assume that a group of terrorists kidnap an airline pilot and
hold him captive for ten weeks during which time he is subjected to both
torture and extensive propaganda about the evil ways of the United States
government. The intensity of this experience eventually leads the pilot to
acquiesce in the views of his captors and his willingness to join them in a
suicide mission to hijack and fly a jetliner into a government building in
Washington, D.C. The group is captured, however, during the attempted
hijacking and the pilot is charged with various acts of terrorism. This sounds
remarkably similar to the case of the heiress Patty Hearst who was
kidnapped by the Symbionese Liberation Army on February 4, 1974, and
participated in a bank robbery with them on April 15, 1974. Can the airline
pilot, like Patty Hearst attempted to do with respect to the bank robbery
charges lodged against her, claim a defense of "brainwashing" to the
terrorism charges? *See* Donald T. Lunde & Thomas E. Wilson, *Brainwashing
as a Defense to Criminal Liability: Patty Hearst Revisited*, 13 CRIM. L. BULL.
341 (1977); Richard Delgado, *Ascription of Criminal States of Mind: Toward
a Defense Theory for the Coercively Persuaded ("Brainwashed") Defendant*,
63 MINN. L. REV. 1 (1978); Joshua Dressler, *Professor Delgado's
"Brainwashing" Defense: Courting A Deterministic Legal System*, 63 MINN.
L. REV. 335 (1979).

3. Should a person suffering from a multiple personality disorder be
permitted to rely on some form of an unconsciousness claim when she
performs a criminal act while disassociated from her primary personality
and in the state of consciousness of her secondary personality? *See* State v.
Grimsley, 3 Ohio App.3d 265, 444 N.E.2d 1071 (1982).

D. SYNDROME DEFENSES

Consider again, at this point, the "battered spouse" defense
discussed as a part of self-defense in Chapter 5, in the case of
Commonwealth v. Cary, 211 Va. 87 (2006) and Notes (in the Self Defense
section, on pp. 570–574).

State v. Stewart

Supreme Court of Kansas, 1988.
243 Kan. 639, 763 P.2d 572.

■ LOCKETT, JUSTICE.

A direct appeal by the prosecution upon a question reserved
(K.S.A.1987 Supp. 22–3602[b][3]) asks whether the statutory
justification for the use of deadly force in self-defense provided by K.S.A.
21–3211 excuses a homicide committed by a battered wife where there is
no evidence of a deadly threat or imminent danger contemporaneous with

the killing. An *amicus curiae* brief has been filed by the Kansas County and District Attorney Association.

Peggy Stewart fatally shot her husband, Mike Stewart, while he was sleeping. She was charged with murder in the first degree. Defendant pled not guilty, contending that she shot her husband in self-defense. Expert evidence showed that Peggy Stewart suffered from the battered woman syndrome. Based upon the battered woman syndrome, the trial judge instructed the jury on self-defense. The jury found Peggy Stewart not guilty.

The State stipulates that Stewart "suffered considerable abuse at the hands of her husband," but contends that the trial court erred in giving a self-defense instruction since Peggy Stewart was in no imminent danger when she shot her sleeping husband. We agree that under the facts of this case the giving of the self-defense instruction was erroneous. We further hold that the trial judge's self-defense instruction improperly allowed the jury to determine the reasonableness of defendant's belief that she was in imminent danger from her individual subjective viewpoint rather than the viewpoint of a reasonable person in her circumstances.

Following an annulment from her first husband and two subsequent divorces in which she was the petitioner, Peggy Stewart married Mike Stewart in 1974. Evidence at trial disclosed a long history of abuse by Mike against Peggy and her two daughters from one of her prior marriages. Laura, one of Peggy's daughters, testified that early in the marriage Mike hit and kicked Peggy, and that after the first year of the marriage Peggy exhibited signs of severe psychological problems. Subsequently, Peggy was hospitalized and diagnosed as having symptoms of paranoid schizophrenia; she responded to treatment and was soon released. It appeared to Laura, however, that Mike was encouraging Peggy to take more than her prescribed dosage of medication.

In 1977, two social workers informed Peggy that they had received reports that Mike was taking indecent liberties with her daughters. Because the social workers did not want Mike to be left alone with the girls, Peggy quit her job. In 1978, Mike began to taunt Peggy by stating that Carla, her 12-year-old daughter, was "more of a wife" to him than Peggy.

Later, Carla was placed in a detention center, and Mike forbade Peggy and Laura to visit her. When Mike finally allowed Carla to return home in the middle of summer, he forced her to sleep in an un-air conditioned room with the windows nailed shut, to wear a heavy flannel nightgown, and to cover herself with heavy blankets. Mike would then wake Carla at 5:30 a.m. and force her to do all the housework. Peggy and Laura were not allowed to help Carla or speak to her.

When Peggy confronted Mike and demanded that the situation cease, Mike responded by holding a shotgun to Peggy's head and threatening to kill her. Mike once kicked Peggy so violently in the chest and ribs that she required hospitalization. Finally, when Mike ordered Peggy to kill and bury Carla, she filed for divorce. Peggy's attorney in the divorce action testified in the murder trial that Peggy was afraid for both her and her children's lives.

One night, in a fit of anger, Mike threw Carla out of the house. Carla, who was not yet in her teens, was forced out of the home with no money, no coat, and no place to go. When the family heard that Carla was in Colorado, Mike refused to allow Peggy to contact or even talk about Carla.

Mike's intimidation of Peggy continued to escalate. One morning, Laura found her mother hiding on the school bus, terrified and begging the driver to take her to a neighbor's home. That Christmas, Mike threw the turkey dinner to the floor, chased Peggy outside, grabbed her by the hair, rubbed her face in the dirt, and then kicked and beat her.

After Laura moved away, Peggy's life became even more isolated. Once, when Peggy was working at a cafe, Mike came in and ran all the customers off with a gun because he wanted Peggy to go home and have sex with him right that minute. He abused both drugs and alcohol, and amused himself by terrifying Peggy, once waking her from a sound sleep by beating her with a baseball bat. He shot one of Peggy's pet cats, and then held the gun against her head and threatened to pull the trigger. Peggy told friends that Mike would hold a shotgun to her head and threaten to blow it off, and indicated that one day he would probably do it.

In May 1986, Peggy left Mike and ran away to Laura's home in Oklahoma. It was the first time Peggy had left Mike without telling him. Because Peggy was suicidal, Laura had her admitted to a hospital. There, she was diagnosed as having toxic psychosis as a result of an overdose of her medication. On May 30, 1986, Mike called to say he was coming to get her. Peggy agreed to return to Kansas. Peggy told a nurse she felt like she wanted to shoot her husband. At trial, she testified that she decided to return with Mike because she was not able to get the medical help she needed in Oklahoma.

When Mike arrived at the hospital, he told the staff that he "needed his housekeeper." The hospital released Peggy to Mike's care, and he immediately drove her back to Kansas. Mike told Peggy that all her problems were in her head and he would be the one to tell her what was good for her, not the doctors. Peggy testified that Mike threatened to kill her if she ever ran away again. As soon as they arrived at the house, Mike forced Peggy into the house and forced her to have oral sex several times.

The next morning, Peggy discovered a loaded .357 magnum. She testified she was afraid of the gun. She hid the gun under the mattress of the bed in a spare room. Later that morning, as she cleaned house, Mike kept making remarks that she should not bother because she would not be there long, or that she should not bother with her things because she could not take them with her. She testified she was afraid Mike was going to kill her.

Mike's parents visited Mike and Peggy that afternoon. Mike's father testified that Peggy and Mike were affectionate with each other during the visit. Later, after Mike's parents had left, Mike forced Peggy to perform oral sex. After watching television, Mike and Peggy went to bed at 8:00 p.m. As Mike slept, Peggy thought about suicide and heard voices in her head repeating over and over, "kill or be killed." At this time, there were two vehicles in the driveway and Peggy had access to the car keys. About 10:00 p.m., Peggy went to the spare bedroom and removed the gun from under the mattress, walked back to the bedroom, and killed her husband while he slept. She then ran to the home of a neighbor, who called the police.

When the police questioned Peggy regarding the events leading up to the shooting, Peggy stated that things had not gone quite right that day, and that when she got the chance she hid the gun under the mattress. She stated that she shot Mike to "get this over with, this misery and this torment." When asked why she got the gun out, Peggy stated to the police:

> I'm not sure exactly what . . . led up to it . . . and my head started playing games with me and I got to thinking about things and I said I didn't want to be by myself again. . . . I got the gun out because there had been remarks made about me being out there alone. It was as if Mike was going to do something again like had been done before. He had gotten me down here from McPherson one time and he went and told them that I had done something and he had me put out of the house and was taking everything I had. And it was like he was going to pull the same thing over again.

Two expert witnesses testified during the trial. The expert for the defense, psychologist Marilyn Hutchinson, diagnosed Peggy as suffering from "battered woman syndrome," or post-traumatic stress syndrome. . . .

The State's expert, psychiatrist Herbert Modlin, neither subscribed to a belief in the battered woman syndrome nor to a theory of learned helplessness as an explanation for why women do not leave an abusive relationship. . . . He stated that Peggy was unable to escape the abuse because she suffered from schizophrenia, rather than the battered woman syndrome.

At defense counsel's request, the trial judge gave an instruction on self-defense to the jury. The jury found Peggy not guilty.

* * *

The traditional concept of self-defense has posited one-time conflicts between persons of somewhat equal size and strength. When the defendant claiming self-defense is a victim of long-term domestic violence, such as a battered spouse, such traditional concepts may not apply. Because of the prior history of abuse, and the difference in strength and size between the abused and the abuser, the accused in such cases may choose to defend during a momentary lull in the abuse, rather than during a conflict. However, in order to warrant the giving of a self-defense instruction, the facts of the case must still show that the spouse was in imminent danger close to the time of the killing.

* * *

Where self-defense is asserted, evidence of the deceased's long-term cruelty and violence towards the defendant is admissible. *State v. Hundley*, 236 Kan. 461, 464, 693 P.2d 475 (1985); *State v. Gray*, 179 Kan. 133, 292 P.2d 698 (1956). In cases involving battered spouses, expert evidence of the battered woman syndrome is relevant to a determination of the reasonableness of the defendant's perception of danger. *State v. Hodges*, 239 Kan. 63, 716 P.2d 563 (1986). Other courts which have allowed such evidence to be introduced include those in Florida, Georgia, Illinois, Maine, New Jersey, New York, Pennsylvania, Washington, and Wisconsin. However, no jurisdictions have held that the existence of the battered woman syndrome in and of itself operates as a defense to murder.

In order to instruct a jury on self-defense, there must be some showing of an imminent threat or a confrontational circumstance involving an overt act by an aggressor. There is no exception to this requirement where the defendant has suffered long-term domestic abuse and the victim is the abuser. In such cases, the issue is not whether the defendant believes homicide is the solution to past or future problems with the batterer, but rather whether circumstances surrounding the killing were sufficient to create a reasonable belief in the defendant that the use of deadly force was necessary.

In three recent Kansas cases where battered women shot their husbands, the women were clearly threatened in the moments prior to the shootings. . . .

* * *

On appeal, none of these cases raised the issue of the propriety of the self-defense instruction. Each case involved a threat of death to the wife and a violent confrontation between husband and wife, contemporaneous with the shooting. Here, however, there is an absence of imminent danger to defendant: Peggy told a nurse at the Oklahoma hospital of her desire to kill Mike. She later voluntarily agreed to return home with Mike when he telephoned her. She stated that after leaving the hospital Mike

Reasoning

threatened to kill her if she left him again. Peggy showed no inclination to leave. In fact, immediately after the shooting, Peggy told the police that she was upset because she thought Mike would leave her. Prior to the shooting, Peggy hid the loaded gun. The cars were in the driveway and Peggy had access to the car keys. After being abused, Peggy went to bed with Mike at 8 p.m. Peggy lay there for two hours, then retrieved the gun from where she had hidden it and shot Mike while he slept.

Under these facts, the giving of the self-defense instruction was erroneous. Under such circumstances, a battered woman cannot reasonably fear imminent life-threatening danger from her sleeping spouse . . .

Holding

. . . We . . . hold that when a battered woman kills her sleeping spouse when there is no imminent danger, the killing is not reasonably necessary and a self-defense instruction may not be given. To hold otherwise in this case would in effect allow the execution of the abuser for past or future acts and conduct.

One additional issue must be addressed. In its *amicus curiae* brief, the Kansas County and District Attorney Association contends the instruction given by the trial court improperly modified the law of self-defense to be more generous to one suffering from the battered woman syndrome than to any other defendant relying on self-defense. We agree and believe it is necessary to clarify certain portions of our opinion in *State v. Hodges*, 239 Kan. 63, 716 P.2d 563.

Here, the trial judge gave the instruction approved in *State v. Simon*, 231 Kan. 572, 575, 646 P.2d 1119 (1982), stating:

> The defendant has claimed her conduct was justified as self-defense.
>
> A person is justified in the use of force against an aggressor when and to the extent it appears to him and he reasonably believes that such conduct is necessary to defend himself or another against such aggressor's imminent use of unlawful force. Such justification requires both a belief on the part of the defendant and the existence of facts that would persuade a reasonable person to that belief.

The trial judge then added the following:

> You must determine, from the viewpoint of the defendant's mental state, whether the defendant's belief in the need to defend herself was reasonable in light of her subjective impressions and the facts and circumstances known to her.

This addition was apparently encouraged by the following language in *State v. Hodges*, 239 Kan. 63, Syl. & 4, 716 P.2d 563:

> Where the battered woman syndrome is an issue in the case, the standard for reasonableness concerning an accused's

belief in asserting self-defense is not an objective, but a subjective standard. The jury must determine, from the viewpoint of defendant's mental state, whether defendant's belief in the need to defend herself was reasonable.

The statement that the reasonableness of defendant's belief in asserting self-defense should be measured from the defendant's own individual subjective viewpoint conflicts with prior law. Our test for self-defense is a two-pronged one. We f irst use a subjective standard to determine whether the defendant sincerely and honestly believed it necessary to kill in order to defend. We then use an objective standard to determine whether defendant's belief was reasonable—specifically, whether a reasonable person in defendant's circumstances would have perceived self-defense as necessary. See *State v. Simon*, 231 Kan. at 573–74, 646 P.2d 1119. In *State v. Hundley*, 236 Kan. at 467, 693 P.2d 475, we stated that, in cases involving battered spouses, "[t]he objective test is how a reasonably prudent battered wife would perceive [the aggressor's] demeanor."

Hundley makes clear that it was error for the trial court to instruct the jury to employ solely a subjective test in determining the reasonableness of defendant's actions. Insofar as the above-quoted language in *State v. Hodges* can be read to sanction a subjective test, this language is disapproved.

The appeal is sustained.

■ PRAGER, C.J., dissents.

■ HERD, JUSTICE, dissenting:

The sole issue before us on the question reserved is whether the trial court erred in giving a jury instruction on self-defense. We have a well-established rule that a defendant is entitled to a self-defense instruction if there is any evidence to support it, even though the evidence consists solely of the defendant's testimony. *State v. Hill*, 242 Kan. 68, 78, 744 P.2d 1228 (1987). It is for the jury to determine the sincerity of the defendant's belief she needed to act in self-defense, and the reasonableness of that belief in light of all the circumstances.

It is not within the scope of appellate review to weigh the evidence. An appellate court's function is to merely examine the record and determine if there is any evidence to support the theory of self-defense. If the record discloses any competent evidence upon which self-defense could be based, then the instruction must be given. In judging the evidence for this purpose, all inferences should be resolved in favor of the defendant. *State v. Hill*, 242 Kan. at 79, 744 P.2d 1228.

* * *

It is evident . . . appellee met her burden of showing some competent evidence that she acted in self-defense, thus making her defense a jury question. She testified she acted in fear for her life, and Dr. Hutchinson corroborated this testimony. The evidence of Mike's past abuse, the escalation of violence, his threat of killing her should she attempt to leave him, and Dr. Hutchinson's testimony that appellee was indeed in a "lethal situation" more than met the minimal standard of "any evidence" to allow an instruction to be given to the jury.

* * *

The majority implies its decision is necessary to keep the battered woman syndrome from operating as a defense in and of itself. It has always been clear the syndrome is not a defense itself. Evidence of the syndrome is admissible only because of its relevance to the issue of self-defense. The majority of jurisdictions have held it beyond the ordinary jury's understanding why a battered woman may feel she cannot escape, and have held evidence of the battered woman syndrome proper to explain it. The expert testimony explains how people react to circumstances in which the average juror has not been involved. It assists the jury in evaluating the sincerity of the defendant's belief she was in imminent danger requiring self-defense and whether she was in fact in imminent danger.

* * *

It is a jury question to determine if the battered woman who kills her husband as he sleeps fears he will find and kill her if she leaves, as is usually claimed. Under such circumstances the battered woman is not under actual physical attack when she kills but such attack is imminent, and as a result she believes her life is in imminent danger. She may kill during the tension-building stage when the abuse is apparently not as severe as it sometimes has been, but nevertheless has escalated so that she is afraid the acute stage to come will be fatal to her. She only acts on such fear if she has some survival instinct remaining after the husband-induced "learned helplessness."

* * *

The majority claims permitting a jury to consider self-defense under these facts would permit anarchy. This underestimates the jury's ability to recognize an invalid claim of self-defense. Although this is a case of first impression where an appeal by the State has been allowed, there have been several similar cases in which the defendant appealed on other grounds. In each of these cases where a battered woman killed the sleeping batterer, a self-defense instruction has been given when requested by the defendant. See *e.g., People v. Emick*, 103 App.Div.2d 643, 481 N.Y.S.2d 552 (1984); *People v. Powell*, 102 Misc.2d 775, 424 N.Y.S.2d 626, *aff'd* 83 App.Div.2d 719, 442 N.Y.S.2d 645 (1981); *State v. Leidholm*, 334 N.W.2d 811.

The most recent case on this issue is *State v. Norman*, 89 N.C.App. 384, 393, 366 S.E.2d 586 (1988), which held the trial court erred in refusing to instruct on self-defense where a battered wife shot her husband as he slept. The court stated:

> [W]ith the battered spouse there can be, under certain circumstances, an unlawful killing of a passive victim that does not preclude the defense of perfect self-defense. Given the characteristics of battered spouse syndrome, we do not believe that a battered person must wait until a deadly attack occurs or that the victim must in all cases be actually attacking or threatening to attack at the very moment defendant commits the unlawful act for the battered person to act in self-defense. Such a standard, in our view, would ignore the realities of the condition. This position is in accord with other jurisdictions that have addressed the issue.

* * *

The majority bases its opinion on its conclusion appellee was not in imminent danger, usurping the right of the jury to make that determination of fact. The majority believes a person could not be in imminent danger from an aggressor merely because the aggressor dropped off to sleep. This is a fallacious conclusion. For instance, picture a hostage situation where the armed guard inadvertently drops off to sleep and the hostage grabs his gun and shoots him. The majority opinion would preclude the use of self-defense in such a case.

* * *

The majority disapproves *State v. Hodges*, 239 Kan. 63, 716 P.2d 563, where we adopted the subjective test for self-defense in battered wife cases. We adopted the subjective test because there is a contradiction in the terms "reasonably prudent battered wife." One battered into "learned helplessness" cannot be characterized as reasonably prudent. Hence, the *Hodges* modification of *State v. Hundley*, 236 Kan. 461, 693 P.2d 475, was necessary and properly states the law.

In *State v. Hundley*, we joined other enlightened jurisdictions in recognizing that the jury in homicide cases where a battered woman ultimately kills her batterer is entitled to all the facts about the battering relationship in rendering its verdict. The jury also needs to know about the nature of the cumulative terror under which a battered woman exists and that a batterer's threats and brutality can make life-threatening danger imminent to the victim of that brutality even though, at the moment, the batterer is passive. Where a person believes she must kill or be killed, and there is the slightest basis in fact for this belief, it is a question for the jury as to whether the danger was imminent. I confess I am an advocate for the constitutional principle that in a criminal prosecution determination of the facts is a function of the jury, not the appellate court.

I would deny this appeal.

NOTES AND QUESTIONS

1. Exactly how does syndrome evidence fit with other defensive claims? Is it a separate defense? Is such evidence and testimony relevant only to self defense or can it be utilized in other ways?

2. With respect to the second question (the breadth of expert testimony regarding the relevant syndrome), see United States v. Azure, 801 F.2d 336 (8th Cir. 1986), in which the court reversed a conviction where a prosecution expert was permitted to say he could see no reason why the alleged victim of child sex abuse was not telling the truth. The court said the expert "might have aided the jurors without usurping their exclusive function [of determining the facts] by generally testifying about a child's ability to separate truth from fantasy . . . and expressing his opinion as to whether it was consistent with [the victim's] story that she was sexually abused." But to put the expert's stamp of approval on the victim's believability went "too far." Accord: State v. Heath, 316 N.C. 337, 341 S.E.2d 565 (1986).

3. Among the veritable catalogue of "syndrome" evidence that behavioral experts attempt to offer to the courts, we note, *e.g.*:

Postpartum Psychosis. Post Partum Psychosis is a psycho-medical disorder peculiar to women, asserted as a defense to infanticide. See, generally, *Postpartum Psychosis as a Defense to Infant Murder*, 5 TOURO L. REV. 287 (1989); *Postpartum Psychosis: A Way Out For Murderous Moms?*, 18 HOFSTRA L. REV. 1133 (1990); *Postpartum Psychosis As an Insanity Defense: Underneath a Controversial Defense Lies a Garden Variety Insanity Defense Complicated by Unique Circumstances for Recognizing Culpability in Causing*, 21 RUTGERS L. REV. 669 (1990); *Postpartum Depression Defense: Are Mothers Getting Away with Murder?*, 24 NEW. ENG. L. REV. 953 (1990); Reece, *Mothers Who Kill: Postpartum Disorders and Criminal Infanticide*, 38 U.C.L.A. L. REV. 699 (1991).

Premenstrual Syndrome. Among the extensive recent literature on the subject, see, e.g.: Dalton, PREMENSTRUAL SYNDROME AND PROGESTERONE THERAPY (2d ed.), 1984; Norris, PMS: PREMENSTRUAL SYNDROME, 1983; Dalton, *Premenstrual Syndrome*, 9 Hamline L. Rev. 143 (1986); Keye & Trunnell, *Premenstrual Syndrome: A Medical Perspective*, 9 Hamline L. Rev. 165 (1986); *Riley, Premenstrual Syndrome As A Legal Defense*, 9 Hamline L. Rev. 193 (1986); Heggestad, *The Devil Made Me Do It: The Case Against Using Premenstrual Syndrome As A Defense In a Court of Law*, 9 Hamline L. Rev. 155 (1986); Holtzman, *Premenstrual Symptoms: No Legal Defense*, 60 St. John's L. Rev. 712 (1986); Oakes, *PMS: A Plea Bargain in Brooklyn Does Not A Rule of Law Make*, 9 Hamline L. Rev. 203 (1986); Chait, *Premenstrual Syndrome and Our Sisters in Crime: A Feminist Dilemma*, 9 Women's Rts. L. Rep. 267 (1986); Pahl-Smith, *Premenstrual Syndrome As A Criminal Defense: The Need For a Medico-Legal Understanding*, 15 N.C. Cent. L.J. 246 (1985); Press, *Premenstrual Stress Syndrome As a Defense in Criminal Cases*, 1983 Duke L.J. 176 (1983).

State v. Grecinger

Supreme Court of Minnesota, 1997.
569 N.W.2d 189.

Defendant Leonard Allen Grecinger, Sr., was convicted of attempted murder in the second degree and assault in the third degree and was sentenced to 153 months in prison. The court of appeals affirmed this conviction. We must determine whether expert testimony on battered woman syndrome is admissible in the prosecution's case-in-chief against an alleged batterer.

Grecinger had been in an on-and-off relationship with the victim, Barbara Skoglund, for about three years, during which they lived together at various times. On September 28, 1991, Grecinger and Skoglund attended a memorial run for the BPM motorcycle club and a party that took place afterward. The events that took place on that day and the day before are in drastic dispute. At trial, Skoglund testified that on the night before the party, Grecinger grabbed her by her hair, slapped her, threw her to the floor, and choked her until she lost consciousness. The next day, Skoglund said that she did not want to attend the party but, according to her testimony, Grecinger insisted that she go. Once at the party, Skoglund found Grecinger kissing a woman who was sitting on his lap. She testified that she threw the woman off his lap but did not get into a fight with the woman. Skoglund then told Grecinger that their relationship was over and went into the bathroom.

Skoglund further testified that Grecinger followed her into the bathroom, closed the door, and beat her. Grecinger grabbed her by the hair, threw her to the floor, kicked her, and choked her until she lost consciousness. During this time, Grecinger allegedly told her, "[I]f you leave me, I'm gonna kill you; if I can't have you, * * * no one's gonna." When Skoglund regained consciousness, she started screaming for help, and Grecinger choked her again until she lost consciousness. When she regained consciousness a second time, Grecinger demanded that she get on her knees, hug him, and apologize for making him angry. Grecinger then told her to walk out of the bathroom with her head up high without crying or looking at anyone. Grecinger followed Skoglund outside and told her to get on his motorcycle. Skoglund started to run away from Grecinger, but he caught her and dragged her back over the dirt road to his motorcycle. Again, he told her to get on the motorcycle. She complied, and they drove off.

Skoglund testified that during the motorcycle ride, Grecinger slapped her in the face. Upon arriving at Grecinger's house, Skoglund broke away and ran down the street, screaming for help. Two women stopped and let her into their car. Skoglund asked them to take her to the home of her friend, Char Copiskey, where she spent the night. The next morning, Copiskey suggested that they go to the Battered Women's Coalition ("Coalition"). At the Coalition, pictures were taken of Skoglund.

Skoglund was then taken to the emergency room because she was fading in and out of consciousness.

Skoglund was admitted to the hospital under an assumed name out of concern for her safety, and she remained there for five days. She suffered from numerous injuries, including swelling and bruising around both eyes; a fracture in her left orbital bone; bleeding in her right eye; bruising and abrasions on her face, ear, and neck; a swollen lip; swelling around her vocal cords consistent with choking; bruising and swelling on her shoulders, chest, arms, and legs; an abrasion on her abdomen; and a tender scalp.

Two law enforcement officers visited Skoglund in the hospital and tried to get a statement from her. Initially, Skoglund refused to talk to them because she did not want to involve the police; however, after being assured that Grecinger would not be arrested except upon her request, she agreed to give a statement. She told one of the officers that the night before the party, Grecinger had choked her until she passed out, and that at the party, he followed her into the bathroom, where he threw her to the floor, slapped her, and again choked her into unconsciousness. When she gave the statement to police, Skoglund asked them not to press charges against Grecinger at that time.

Skoglund also testified that while she was in the hospital, Copiskey brought her a letter from Grecinger in which he apologized for what he did and asked that she speak with him. When Skoglund called Grecinger, he promised he would leave her alone if she did not press charges against him. He also promised her he would seek treatment for his anger.

Skoglund testified that she went back to the Coalition after leaving the hospital to retrieve the pictures that were taken of her. She then gave the pictures to one of her sisters for safekeeping. A few weeks later, Skoglund resumed her relationship with Grecinger, after he told her that he had stomach cancer and would not live much longer. At Grecinger's insistence, Skoglund called the sheriff's department and recanted, claiming that her injuries actually had been inflicted by two unknown men who assaulted her when she left the party.

In her testimony, Skoglund admitted that she lied to some people about the cause of her injuries because she was afraid of Grecinger. However, Skoglund also testified that she had previously identified Grecinger as her assailant to others, including Copiskey, a police investigator, a worker from the Coalition, and two of her sisters. On several occasions in 1992 and 1993, Skoglund petitioned for orders for protection against Grecinger; however, she either sought to have the petitions dismissed or failed to follow through on them, because she feared that Grecinger would harm her. Finally, in June 1994, Skoglund sought to reopen the investigation against Grecinger for the alleged September 1991 assault, because she was afraid he was going to kill her.

When Grecinger took the stand, his version of events drastically differed from Skoglund's. Grecinger testified that the day before the memorial run, he told Skoglund he did not want her to accompany him to the run because she often embarrassed him in public. Grecinger denied that he was physically violent toward Skoglund that day.

Grecinger testified that at the party following the memorial run, a woman was sitting on his lap when Skoglund walked into the kitchen, grabbed the woman by her hair, and pulled her off of him. Although Grecinger tried to break up the fight, Skoglund wound up with her shirt torn, hair pulled out, scratches on her face, and a bloody lip. After fighting with the woman, Skoglund grabbed Grecinger by his hair and dragged him to the bathroom. According to Grecinger, Skoglund "went completely bananas" in the bathroom and kicked the toilet seat off the toilet, hit him with the toilet tank cover, and ripped the medicine cabinet off the wall. Skoglund then asked him to hug her and tell her he loved her. Grecinger denied hitting or choking Skoglund in the bathroom and maintained that he only tried to prevent her from hurting him and herself.

Grecinger testified that they then left the party to go home. As they neared his house, Skoglund jumped off the motorcycle and started running. Grecinger ran after her out of concern for her, but gave up after she jumped into a car with two men whom he believed she knew.

To support this testimony, numerous friends of Grecinger's testified that they did not witness any violence between Grecinger and Skoglund at the party. Several defense witnesses also corroborated Grecinger's testimony that Skoglund got into a fight with another woman at that party. The defense also attacked Skoglund's credibility, suggesting that the three-year gap between the time the incident occurred and the time Skoglund pursued prosecution demonstrated that she was not credible. For instance, during opening statements, Grecinger's attorney stated that for nearly three years, Skoglund had used the alleged incident to control Grecinger. Furthermore, Grecinger's attorney cross-examined Skoglund regarding her delay in seeking prosecution.

In response to the defense's attack on Skoglund's credibility, the prosecution sought to introduce expert testimony on battered woman syndrome. The court admitted the expert testimony over Grecinger's objection. As foundation for the expert testimony, a psychologist testified that she first treated Skoglund in October 1992. The psychologist testified that Skoglund reported symptoms of anxiety stemming from a physically abusive episode with her boyfriend one year earlier. The psychologist subsequently diagnosed Skoglund as suffering from posttraumatic stress disorder.

After Skoglund and the psychologist who treated her had testified, an expert witness testified regarding battered woman syndrome, which she described as a subset of posttraumatic stress disorder. The expert further testified that the symptoms of a woman suffering from battered woman syndrome can include feelings of terror, acceptance of blame for the battering, a negative self-image, isolation, denial or minimization of the abuse, and depression. She explained that many battered women do not report the abuse out of fear for their safety, denial of the abuse, fear that no one will listen, or hope that the batterer will change.

The jury convicted Grecinger of attempted murder in the second degree and assault in the third degree, and he was sentenced to 153 months in prison. On appeal to this court, Grecinger argues that the expert testimony was improperly admitted, because it was not helpful to the jury and because it was merely duplicative of other witnesses' testimony about the reasons for the delayed prosecution.

We note at the outset that traditionally we have proceeded with great caution when admitting testimony of expert witnesses, especially in criminal cases. An expert with special knowledge has the potential to influence a jury unduly. Special care must be taken by the trial judge to ensure that the defendant's presumption of innocence does not get lost in the flurry of expert testimony and, more importantly, that the responsibility for judging credibility and the facts remains with the jury. Thus, the court must ascertain whether such testimony is relevant, whether it is helpful to the trier of fact, and whether its prejudicial effect substantially outweighs its probative value.

Under Minn. R. Evid. 608(a), the credibility of a witness can be supported by evidence in the form of an opinion only when the character of that witness has been attacked in that respect. Because the victim's credibility can be attacked during cross-examination of the victim or even during opening statements, the prosecution need not wait until rebuttal to present expert testimony on battered woman syndrome. Rather, such testimony may be presented as rehabilitative evidence during the state's case-in-chief.

Consequently, the admission of battered woman syndrome testimony during the state's case-in-chief in this case was proper under Minn. R. Evid. 608(a). By the time the expert testimony on battered woman syndrome was presented, Skoglund's credibility regarding her delay in seeking prosecution of Grecinger was already at issue. During opening statements, Grecinger's attorney suggested that during the gap in time, Skoglund used the alleged incident to control Grecinger. Furthermore, when cross-examining Skoglund, Grecinger's attorney briefly questioned Skoglund regarding her delay in seeking prosecution.

Although the prosecutor asserted only that battered woman syndrome testimony was being offered to explain the delay in prosecution, such testimony arguably was responsive to other attacks against Skoglund's credibility. For instance, Grecinger's attorney stated that Skoglund was a liar because of the various stories she had told to explain her injuries. Furthermore, Grecinger's attorney questioned

Skoglund about why she returned to her relationship with Grecinger after the alleged assault, and why she recanted statements she had made when seeking an order for protection against Grecinger. Having concluded that expert testimony about battered women syndrome could properly be admitted to rehabilitate Skoglund's credibility under Rule 608(a), we must ascertain whether it is admissible under Minn. R. Evid. 702 when introduced as part of the prosecution's case-in-chief. In State v. Hennum, 441 N.W.2d 793 (1989), this court considered the admissibility of expert testimony on battered woman syndrome to support a defendant's self-defense claim for the shooting death of her husband. We decided two important issues in Hennum. First, we held that battered woman syndrome has gained sufficient scientific acceptance to warrant admissibility as expert testimony. We held that such testimony satisfied the helpfulness test of Minn. R. Evid. 702, because it helped to explain a phenomenon that was not understood by the average person. Second, this court held that expert testimony on battered woman syndrome should be limited to a description of the syndrome and its characteristics. We held that the expert should not be permitted to testify on the ultimate fact of whether the particular defendant actually suffers from battered woman syndrome.

The question raised by this case is under what circumstances our holding in Hennum should be extended to allow for prosecutorial use of expert testimony on battered woman syndrome. Grecinger does not argue that expert testimony on battered woman syndrome should be categorically excluded from the prosecution's case-in-chief against an alleged batterer. Rather, he argues that under Minn. R. Evid. 702, expert testimony on battered woman syndrome should be admissible only to address an issue that is inherently confusing to the jury and only when there is no other evidence to address it.

The basic consideration in admitting expert testimony under Rule 702 is the helpfulness test—that is, whether the testimony will assist the jury in resolving factual questions presented. Thus, "[i]f the subject of the testimony is within the knowledge and experience of a lay jury and the testimony of the expert will not add precision or depth to the jury's ability to reach conclusions about that subject which is within their experience, then the testimony does not meet the helpfulness test."

In this case, Grecinger contends that the expert testimony did not meet the helpfulness test because it was cumulative of other evidence in the case. He observes that prior to the expert witness' testimony, several other witnesses had testified as to why the prosecution was delayed. For example, Skoglund testified that she did not immediately pursue prosecution because Grecinger forced her to recant her statement to the sheriff's department. Furthermore, a deputy sheriff testified that he did not pursue prosecution at the time of the alleged incident because he had promised Skoglund he would not arrest Grecinger unless she requested that he do so.

However, such testimony does not explain why Skoglund did not seek prosecution at the time of the assault. Instead, the jury might believe that a woman who is beaten by her mate would immediately seek to have him arrested and that such a woman would not recant such a statement despite threats made by the batterer. Consequently, the expert testimony on battered woman syndrome was not duplicative of prior testimony; rather, it was necessary to explain the complexity of Skoglund's behavior and the reasons for her behavior.

The helpfulness of expert testimony on battered woman syndrome was decided by this court in Hennum, where we held that expert testimony on battered woman syndrome would help to explain a phenomenon not within the understanding of an ordinary lay person. Thus, it seems clear that the expert's testimony on battered woman syndrome could help the jury understand why Skoglund returned to the relationship with Grecinger after the incident, told contradictory stories about how her injuries were inflicted, waited almost three years to pursue prosecution of Grecinger, and recanted statements she made to the police and the district court regarding Grecinger's abuse. As this court recognized in Hennum, the expert testimony on battered woman syndrome would help the jury to understand the behavior of a woman suffering from the syndrome, which might otherwise be interpreted as a lack of credibility.

Grecinger also argues that the admission of expert testimony on battered woman syndrome was unfairly prejudicial because such testimony shifted attention away from the case and focused on the problem of domestic violence. Unlike circumstances in which expert testimony on battered woman syndrome is presented to support a defendant's claim of self-defense, prosecutorial use of such testimony raises the added concern for the rights of the alleged batterer in such a proceeding. Because of the special knowledge that expert witnesses possess, we are concerned about the potential for expert testimony on battered woman syndrome to influence a jury unduly, particularly in cases such as this where there are two entirely different accounts of the events in controversy. Thus, to minimize the potential for unfair prejudice to the defendant, we caution trial judges that careful inquiry and balancing must be made under Minn. R. Evid. 403.

Under Rule 403, relevant and even helpful expert testimony may be excluded if the probative value of such testimony is substantially outweighed by the danger of unfair prejudice or of misleading the jury. Although this court has not previously considered the admissibility of expert testimony on battered woman syndrome under Rule 403, other state courts have addressed this precise issue. Compare State v. Battista, 31 Conn.App. 497, 626 A.2d 769, 779–80 (prosecutorial use of testimony on battered woman syndrome was not prejudicial, particularly because of the court's limiting instruction), cert. denied, 227 Conn. 907, 632 A.2d 696 (1993), and State v. Ciskie, 110 Wash.2d 263, 751 P.2d 1165, 1173–74 (1988) (prosecutorial use of battered woman syndrome testimony was not unfairly prejudicial to defendant, particularly because expert was not permitted to assess the victim's credibility), with State v. Pargeon, 64 Ohio App.3d 679, 582 N.E.2d 665, 666–67 (1991) (trial court erred by permitting state to present testimony during its case-in-chief in which expert opined that victim suffered from battered woman syndrome; such testimony created unfairly prejudicial inference of defendant's propensity to batter victim).

We decided in Hennum that the theory underlying battered woman syndrome is beyond the experimental stage and has gained substantial acceptance in the scientific community. When the scientific reliability of expert testimony is not at issue, this court has upheld the presentation of expert testimony by the prosecution to explain complainant's behavior under Rule 403. For instance, this court has held that the prosecution's presentation of expert testimony on the typical reporting practices of adolescent victims of sexual assault was not unfairly prejudicial to a defendant charged with criminal sexual conduct.

Thus, a defendant need not be unfairly prejudiced by the prosecution's use of expert testimony on battered woman syndrome, if adequate limitations are placed on the presentation thereof. In Hennum, this court held that an expert testifying on battered woman syndrome may not testify as to whether the defendant actually suffers from the syndrome. This holding similarly applies to expert testimony on battered woman syndrome presented by the prosecution. Such a limitation provides one means of ensuring that such testimony will not unfairly prejudice the alleged batterer.

In addition, because of our concern about the impact expert testimony on battered woman syndrome may have on the jury, we emphasize that the expert may not suggest that the complainant was battered, was truthful, or fit the battered woman syndrome. Likewise, the expert may not express an opinion as to whether the defendant was in fact a batterer.

In the case at hand, the expert testimony was adequately limited and was not unfairly prejudicial to Grecinger. Earlier in the trial, the testimony of a psychologist who had treated Skoglund laid the foundation for the expert testimony on battered woman syndrome. The psychologist merely testified to characteristics possessed by Skoglund which were consistent with those found in someone suffering from battered woman syndrome. Although the psychologist testified that she diagnosed Skoglund with posttraumatic stress disorder, she did not give testimony on the ultimate fact of whether Skoglund suffered from battered woman syndrome. Similarly, when the expert witness took the stand, her testimony was limited to a definition of battered woman syndrome, an explanation of the general symptoms of posttraumatic stress disorder as exhibited by battered women, and a description of common characteristics shared by battered women. The expert did not testify as to whether Skoglund suffered from battered woman syndrome, whether or when Skoglund had told the truth, or whether Grecinger was a batterer. Consequently, the issue of Skoglund's credibility remained in the hands of the jury, and Grecinger was not unfairly prejudiced.

In summary, we hold that expert testimony on battered woman syndrome presented during the prosecution's case-in-chief is admissible if it is introduced after the victim's credibility has been attacked by the defense, see Minn. R. Evid. 608(a), if it helps the jury understand the victim's inconsistent statements or delay in seeking prosecution of the batterer, see Minn. R. Evid. 702, and if the expert merely describes the syndrome and its characteristics and does not offer an opinion as to whether the victim suffers from it, thereby reducing the risk of unfair prejudice to the defendant.

Affirmed.

———

CHAPTER 13

Insanity at Time of the Prohibited Act and Competency to Stand Trial

Insanity is not a medical condition. Rather, it is a legal term of art for the legal effects, if any, of a person's mental condition. Whether a mental disease or defect will be a defense to conduct that would otherwise be criminal depends in large part on what legal test the jurisdiction has adopted to determine sanity. The insanity defense in United States jurisdictions reflects, to a large degree, two principal tests: the *M'Naghten* test, and the American Law Institute's Model Penal Code test. There are multiple permutations of these tests, however, as well as several additional insanity tests. As you read the materials below, consider whether you find one approach to defining insanity to be more persuasive or whether defining insanity is simply impossible.

A. Distinguishing Competency from Insanity

Before defining insanity, it is important to distinguish the separate concept of competency. When courts assess a defendant's competency they are inquiring whether (s)he is able to stand trial, not whether (s)he was insane at the time of the crime. The test of competency is succinctly stated in one state statute in the following terms: ". . . a defendant is unfit to stand trial or be sentenced if, because of a mental or physical condition, he is unable: (1) to understand the nature and purpose of the proceedings against him; or (2) to assist in his defense."

Consider the case of R. Allen Stanford, a billionaire financier who was convicted of fraud in 2012 for running a $7 billion ponzi scheme. Stanford was a savvy businessman who managed a complicated investment portfolio and frequently appeared on television to promote his financial products. Following his arrest, Stanford did not claim to be insane; he claimed instead that prosecutors misunderstood his financial empire and that all of his businesses were perfectly legitimate. Because of his wealth and his duel citizenship in Antigua, Stanford was denied bail following his arrest. While incarcerated pending trial, Stanford was savagely beaten by another prisoner. Stanford's lawyers subsequently contended that the beating led to medical problems including depression, amnesia, and post-traumatic stress disorder. Stanford's lawyers argued that the prison assault and medical problems rendered him incapable of consulting with his attorneys and assisting in his own defense. Put simply, Stanford argued that he had become incompetent to stand trial while being detained, not that he was insane at the time of the alleged crime. Although the trial was temporarily delayed because of Stanford's mental health issues, the judge eventually found Stanford competent to stand trial, and he was later convicted and sentenced to 110 years in prison. *See* Clifford Krauss, *Stanford Sentenced to 110-Year Term in $7 Billion Ponzi Case*, N.Y. TIMES, June 14, 2012.

Burden usually on D

Most courts place the burden on the defendant to demonstrate incompetency, although some courts allocate the burden to the government. *See Competency to Stand Trial*, 45 GEO. L.J. ANNUAL REVIEW OF CRIMINAL PROCEDURE, 512, 517 (2016).

Although competency is an important legal question, it is primarily a question of criminal procedure, rather than the substantive criminal law covered in this course. For purposes of deciding whether a defendant's mental health problems excuses him from criminal liability, the key question is not his present mental condition, but whether he was sane at the time of the crime. The materials below analyze that question.

B. THE *M'NAGHTEN* (RIGHT/WRONG) TEST

Daniel M'Naghten's Case
House of Lords, 1843.
0 Cl. & F. 200, 8 Eng. Reprint 718.

The prisoner had been indicted for [the murder of Edward Drummond, private secretary to Sir Robert Peel.] . . . The prisoner pleaded Not guilty.

Evidence having been given of the fact of the shooting of Mr. Drummond, and of his death in consequence thereof, witnesses were called on the part of the prisoner, to prove that he was not, at the time of committing the act, in a sound state of mind . . .

■ LORD CHIEF JUSTICE TINDAL (in his charge): "The question to be determined is, whether at the time the act in question was committed, the prisoner had or had not the use of his understanding, so as to know that he was doing a wrong or wicked act." If the jurors should be of opinion that the prisoner was not sensible, at the time he committed it, that he was violating the laws both of God and man, then he would be entitled to a verdict in his favour: but if, on the contrary they were of opinion that when he committed the act he was in a sound state of mind, then their verdict must be against him.

Found not guilty

Verdict, Not guilty, on the ground of insanity.

This verdict, and the question of the nature and extent of the unsoundness of mind which would excuse the commission of a felony of this sort, having been made the subject of debate in the House of Lords, it was determined to take the opinion of the Judges on the law governing such cases . . .

■ LORD CHIEF JUSTICE TINDAL . . . The first question proposed by your Lordships is this: "What is the law respecting alleged crimes committed by persons afflicted with insane delusion in respect of one or more particular subjects or persons: as, for instance, where at the time of the commission of the alleged crime the accused knew he was acting contrary to law, but did the act complained of with a view, under the influence of insane delusion, of redressing or revenging some supposed grievance or injury, or of producing some supposed public benefit?"

In answer to which question, assuming that your Lordships inquiries are confined to those persons who labour under such partial delusions only, and are not in other respects insane, we are of opinion that, notwithstanding the party accused did the act complained of with a view, under the influence of insane delusion, of redressing or revenging some supposed grievance or injury, or of producing some public benefit he is nevertheless punishable according to the nature of the crime committed, if he knew at the time of committing such crime that he was acting contrary to law; by which expression we understand your Lordships to mean the law of the land.

Your Lordships are pleased to inquire of us, secondly, "What are the proper questions to be submitted to the jury, where a person alleged to be afflicted with insane delusion respecting one or more particular subjects or persons, is charged with the commission of a crime (murder, for example), and insanity is set up as a defence?" And, thirdly, "In what terms ought the question to be left to the jury as to the prisoner's state of mind at the time when the act was committed?" And as these two questions appear to us to be more conveniently answered together, we have to submit our opinion to be, that the jurors ought to be told in all cases that every man is to be presumed to be sane, and to possess a sufficient degree of reason to be responsible for his crimes, until the contrary be proved to their satisfaction; and that to establish a defence on the ground of insanity, it must be clearly proved that, at the time of the committing of the act, the party accused was labouring under such a defect of reason, from disease of the mind, as not to know the nature and quality of the act he was doing; or, if he did know it, that he did not know he was doing what was wrong. The mode of putting the latter part of the question to the jury on these occasions has generally been, whether the accused at the time of doing the act knew the difference between right and wrong: which mode, though rarely, if ever, leading to any mistake with the jury, is not, as we conceive, so accurate when put generally and in the abstract, as when put with reference to the party's knowledge of right and wrong in respect to the very act with which he is charged. If the question were to be put as to the knowledge of the accused solely and exclusively with reference to the law of the land, it might tend to confound the jury, by inducing them to believe that an actual knowledge of the law of the land was essential in order to lead to a conviction; whereas the law is administered upon the principle that every one must be taken conclusively to know it, without proof that he does know it. If the accused was conscious that the act was one which he ought not to do, and if that act was at the same time contrary to the law of the land, he is punishable; and the usual course therefore has been to leave the question to the jury, whether the party accused had a sufficient degree of reason to know that he was doing an act that was wrong; and this course we think is correct, accompanied with such observations and explanations as the circumstances of each particular case may require.

The fourth question which your Lordships have proposed to us is this: "If a person under an insane delusion as to existing facts, commits an offence in consequence thereof, is he thereby excused?" To which question the answer must of course depend on the nature of the delusion: but, making the same assumption as we did before, namely, that he labours under such partial delusion only and is not in other respects insane, we think he must be considered in the same situation as to responsibility as if the facts with respect to which the delusion exists were real. For example, if under the influence of his delusion he supposes another man to be in the act of attempting to take away his life, and he kills that man, as he supposes, in self-defence, he would be exempt from punishment. If his delusion was that the deceased had inflicted a serious injury to his character and fortune, and he killed him in revenge for such supposed injury, he would be liable to punishment . . .

NOTES

1. On the history behind the *M'Naghten* Rules, consider the following from the opinion of Chief Judge Biggs of the Third Circuit Court of Appeals in United States v. Currens, 290 F.2d 751 (3d Cir.1961), at pp. 448–449:

> The *M'Naghten* Rules . . . were engendered by the excitement and fear which grew out of the acquittal of Daniel M'Naghten who had attempted to assassinate Sir Robert Peel, Prime Minister of England, but who instead shot Peel's private secretary, Drummond, because M'Naghten had mistaken Drummond for Peel. The offense against Drummond followed a series of attempted assassinations of members of the English Royal House, including Queen Victoria herself, and attacks on the Queen's ministers. Some of these were considered to have grown out of Anti-Corn-Law League plots. When M'Naghten was acquitted at his trial . . . public indignation, led by the Queen, ran so high that the Judges of England were called before the House of Lords to explain their conduct. A series of questions were propounded to them. Their answers, really an advisory opinion which were delivered by Lord Chief Justice Tindal for all fifteen Judges, save Mr. Justice Maule, constitute what are now known as the M'Naghten Rules . . . The *M'Naghten* Rules, which applied primarily the test of knowing the difference between right and wrong, are set out in the ancient book, written by William Lambard of Lincolns Inn, Eirenarcha or of the

Office of the Justices of Peace, reprinted at least seven times between 1582 and 1610. At 'Cap. 21.218' of this work Lambard stated: 'If a mad man or a natural foole, or a lunatike in the time of his lunacie, or a childe y apparently hath no knowledge of good nor euil do kill a man, this is no felonious acte, nor any thing forfeited by it . . . for they cannot be said to haue any understanding wil. But if upon examination it fal out, y they knew what they did, & y it was ill, the seemth it to be otherwise.' It will be observed that Lambard laid down as his test of criminal responsibility 'knowledge of good or evil.' The phraseology quoted is as antique and creaking as the doctrine of criminal responsibility it announces. For the words 'knowledge of good or evil,' the phrase 'knowledge of right and wrong' was substituted. This essential principle, embodied in the M'Naghten Rules, is not 118 years old. The substance of the M'Naghten Rules was set out in the Eirenarcha over 375 years ago, published in a year in which belief in witchcraft and demonology, even among well educated men, was widespread. The Eirenarcha itself contains a statute imposing severe penalties for injuries or death caused by witchcraft. The principles of law embodied in the volume were, of course, typical of the thinking of the times . . .

2. The name of the defendant in the principal case has been spelled several different ways. In an article in the LONDON TIMES it was spelled "M'Naughten." The late Justice Frankfurter wrote to the TIMES and chided it for the error, whereupon the TIMES replied that the spelling it used was based upon a letter signed by the man himself. Justice Frankfurter, displaying (as Judge Irving R. Kaufman phrased it) "that pixy humor which delighted so many of his intimates," wrote to the editor of the TIMES as follows: "To what extent is a lunatic's spelling even of his own name to be deemed an authority?" (See fn. 2 of Judge Kaufman's opinion in United States v. Freeman, 357 F.2d 606, 608 (2d Cir.1966).)

3. The *M'Naghten* test is the most common insanity test in the United States. Twenty-one jurisdictions utilize the *M'Naghten* test. Another eight states use a broader version of the *M'Naghten* test that still focuses on cognition but asks whether defendants can "appreciate" the criminality of their conduct. *See* Paul H. Robinson, *Murder Mitigation in the Fifty-Two American Jurisdictions: A Case Study in Doctrinal Interrelational Analysis*, 47 TEX. TECH. L. REV. 19, 21 (2014).

4. Does the *M'Naghten* rule seem like an appropriate test, or is it too simplistic? Are juries, which lack any psychological training, in a position to determine if the defendant knew the difference between right and wrong? Would a psychiatrist diagnose a patient using that terminology?

5. In 2001, Andrea Yates—a former nurse who was married to a NASA engineer—killed her five children in a suburb outside Houston, Texas. Yates had a history of severe depression and was being treated by a psychiatrist who instructed her husband not to leave her alone with the children. On the morning of June 20th, Yates's husband left for work an hour before Yates's mother was to come to the house to supervise her. During the hour she was unattended, Yates drowned her children one at a time in the bathtub. The eldest child tried to run from her, but Yates caught him and drowned him as well. Prosecutors charged Yates with capital murder and sought the death penalty. Yates claimed insanity. Texas utilizes a variation of the *M'Naghten* rule. What result would you expect at trial? How could a mother who drowns her five young children be anything but insane? Or does the fact that she waited for her husband to leave for work show that she knew right from wrong? For an overview of the Yates case and the applicable law, see Christopher Slobogin, *The Integrationist Alternative to the Insanity Defense: Reflections on the Exculpatory Scope of Mental Illness in the Wake of the Andrea Yates Case*, 30 AM. J. CRIM. L. 315 (2003).

6. Consider the case of William White, a hitchhiker who stopped at a motel and killed a man by stabbing him to death 27 times. White contended that he had been commanded by God to stop at the motel and kill the victim. White's medical expert was prepared to testify that this psychotic episode was caused by the use of illegal drugs. Specifically, the medical expert explained that White:

> [H]as a history of one prior psychiatric hospitalization while in Louisiana. This occurred about three months ago. The records for this hospitalization were not available at the time of this evaluation. Mr. White reports that he was treated through use of Haldol, an antipsychotic medication, which would suggest that he was being treated for psychotic symptoms at that time. The lack of psychiatric symptoms prior to age 27 or 28 and Mr. White's description of rather heavy cocaine abuse at that time would suggest that he likely was experiencing a drug-induced psychosis at the time of that hospitalization. Mr. White discontinued his Haldol once he got out of the hospital and, by his report, almost immediately began abusing cocaine, marijuana, and alcohol (as well as ecstasy) again.

White v. Commonwealth, 636 S.E.2d 353, 358 (Va. 2006). The medical expert concluded that "Mr. White was suffering from a drug-induced psychosis. This condition resulted from his abuse of cocaine, antihistamines and marijuana." He further explained that "Mr. White's psychosis was almost surely the result of his substance abuse and not some other mental condition." *Id.* The trial court refused to allow White to present this evidence of so-called "settled insanity." The Virginia Supreme Court affirmed White's conviction, explaining that "[i]n order to establish the existence of a mental disease or defect caused by alcohol or drug abuse, i.e., settled insanity, White's evidence would have to demonstrate long-term, chronic, and habitual abuse. White's proffered evidence on this question was insufficient to establish a prima facie defense of insanity." Does this decision seem correct to you? Should it matter how long White suffered from substance abuse to determine whether he fell under the *M'Naghten* test? Should this have been a question for the jury?

7. If it is legitimate for courts to exclude the insanity defense for persons who have caused their own "settled insanity" through abuse of alcohol and other substances, should it be possible to claim insanity based on psychosis-causing brain damage sustained as a result of other anti-social or illegal conduct, such as brawling or reckless driving? Many legislatures have not carefully thought through this question in drafting insanity and other excuse defenses. *See* Paul H. Robinson, *Causing the Conditions of One's Own Defense: A Study of the Limits of Theory in Criminal Law Doctrine*, 71 VA. L. REV. 1 (1985).

8. Closely related to the *M'Naghten* test is the "Bonnie" standard, proposed by Professor Richard J. Bonnie and endorsed by the American Psychiatric Association. Under this test, a defendant would not be criminally responsible if he proved, by the greater weight of the evidence, that, as a result of mental disease or mental retardation, he was unable to appreciate the wrongfulness of his conduct at the time of the offense. The phrase "mental disease or mental retardation" is defined as "only those severely abnormal mental conditions that grossly and demonstrably impair a person's perception or understanding of reality, and that are not attributable primarily to the voluntary ingestion of alcohol or other psychoactive substances." The Bonnie test is similar to *M'Naghten* but it drops the term "defect," and defines insanity in terms of the defendant's ability to distinguish reality from fantasy as well as to "appreciate the wrongfulness of his conduct." *See, e.g.*, Richard J. Bonnie & Christopher Slobogin, *The Role of Mental Health Professionals in the Criminal Process: The Case for Informed Speculation*, 66 VA. L. REV. 427 (1980) (advocating changes in standards for medical testimony in insanity cases); Am. Psychiatric Ass'n, THE INSANITY DEFENSE POSITION STATEMENT 5 (1982), available at http://www.psych.org/edu/other_res/lib_archives/archives/198503.pdf.

9. The Bonnie standard would presumably cover certain conditions excluded by *M'Naghten* including brain tumors which can at times cause psychotic-seeming behavior. Is the exclusion of "settled insanity"—*i.e.*, organic damage resulting from substance abuse—a legitimate exclusion if the actual result is the person's inability to control his or her behavior? *See* Greider v. Duckworth, 701 F.2d 1228, 12 Fed. Rules Evid. Serv 1338 (7th Cir.1983) (while temporary mental incapacity induced by voluntary intoxication is generally not a defense, the law will not hold an accused responsible for his acts where ingestion of intoxicants has been abused to the point that it has produced mental disease such that the accused is unable to appreciate wrongfulness of his conduct or is unable to conform his conduct to requirements of the law). *See also* People v. McCarthy, 110 Cal.App.3d 296, 167 Cal.Rptr. 772 (1980) ("[W]hen an effort is made to establish insanity due to alcohol, it must be shown that there exists a 'settled insanity' and not the type of a temporary mental condition produced by current use of alcohol. In other words, your friendly local lush cannot get sloshed, commit a horrendous crime and slip into a state hospital free from criminal sanctions. If an alcoholic wants to use his problem as an escape hatch, he must drink enough to develop a mental disorder that continues when he is stone sober even though the damage is not permanent in the sense it is beyond repair.").

———

People v. Serravo

Supreme Court of Colorado, 1992.
823 P.2d 128.

■ JUSTICE QUINN delivered the Opinion of the Court.

We granted certiorari to review the decision of the court of appeals in People v. Serravo, 797 P.2d 782 (Colo.App.1990), in order to determine the meaning of the phrase "incapable of distinguishing right from wrong" in Colorado's statutory definition of insanity codified at section 16–8–101(1), 8A C.R.S. (1986). The trial court, in the insanity phase of a criminal prosecution, instructed the jury that the phrase "incapable of distinguishing right from wrong" refers to a person who appreciates that his conduct is criminal but, due to a mental disease or defect, believes that the conduct is morally right. The prosecution, pursuant to section 16–12–102(1), 8A C.R.S. (1986), appealed the trial court's ruling on the question of law, and the court of appeals approved the ruling. The court of appeals held that the meaning of "incapable of distinguishing right from wrong" is not confined to a defendant's knowledge of legal right or legal wrong but rather refers to a defendant's cognitive inability to distinguish right from wrong under societal standards of morality, and that the trial court's instruction did not inject a subjective standard of morality into the test of legal insanity. The court of appeals also held that a deific-decree delusion is an exception to the societal standard of moral wrong and that, under such an exception, a defendant may be adjudicated insane if the defendant knew that the act was illegal and morally wrong under societal standards of morality but, due to a mental disease or defect, believed that God had ordained the act.

Although we disagree with the court of appeals' conclusion that the trial court's instruction did not incorporate a subjective standard of morality into the right-wrong test for legal insanity, we affirm that part of the court of appeals' decision which holds that the phrase "incapable of distinguishing right from wrong" refers to a cognitive inability to distinguish right from wrong under existing societal standards of morality rather than, as implied by the trial court's instruction, under a purely subjective and personal standard of morality. In addition, rather than characterizing the deific-decree delusion as an exception to the right-wrong test for legal insanity, we hold that a defendant may be judged legally insane where, as here, the defendant's cognitive ability to distinguish right from wrong with respect to an act charged as a crime has been destroyed as a result of a psychotic delusion that God has ordered him to commit the act. Finally, we hold that federal and state principles of double jeopardy prohibit the retrial of the defendant on the issue of his sanity or insanity at the time of the commission of the acts charged against him.

I.

Serravo was charged in a multi-count information with crimes of attempt to commit first degree murder after deliberation, assault in the first degree, and the commission of crimes of violence. The charges arose out of the stabbing of his wife, Joyce Serravo, on May 10, 1987. After the charges were filed, Serravo entered a plea of not guilty by reason of insanity and was thereafter examined by several psychiatrists. The issue of legal insanity was tried to a jury, which returned a verdict of not guilty by reason of insanity.

The evidence at the insanity trial established that the stabbing occurred under the following circumstances. On the evening of May 9, 1987, Serravo, who was a King Soopers union employee, visited striking employees at the King Soopers store near his home. Serravo returned home at approximately 12:30 a.m. on May 10. After sitting in the kitchen and reading the Bible, he went upstairs to the bedroom where his wife was sleeping, stood over her for a few minutes, and then stabbed her in the back just below the shoulder blade. When his wife awoke, Serravo told her that she had been stabbed by an intruder and that she should stay in bed while he went downstairs to call for medical help.

Police officers were later dispatched to the home. Serravo told the officers that he had gone to the King Soopers store and had left the garage door open, that the door leading to the house from the garage was unlocked, that when he returned from King Soopers and was reading the Bible he heard his front door slam, and that he went upstairs to check on his wife and children and saw that his wife was bleeding from a wound in her back. Serravo signed a consent to search his home and gave the police clothes that he was wearing at the time of his discovery of his wife's injury.

Several weeks after the stabbing Serravo's wife found letters written by Serravo. In these letters Serravo admitted the stabbing, stating that "[o]ur marriage was severed on Mother's Day when I put the knife in your back," that "I have gone to be with Jehovah in heaven for three and one-half days," and that "I must return for there is still a great deal of work to be done." After reading the letters, Serravo's wife telephoned him in order to confront him about the letters. Serravo told his wife that God had told him to stab her in order to sever the marriage bond. Mrs. Serravo informed the police of these facts and Serravo was thereafter arrested and charged.

The prosecution presented expert psychiatric testimony on Serravo's sanity at the time of the stabbing. Doctor Ann Seig, a resident psychiatrist in training at the University of Colorado Health Sciences Center, examined Serravo pursuant to a court ordered evaluation of his mental state. Serravo gave the doctor a history of having worked on a plan, inspired by his relationship to God, to establish a multi-million dollar sports complex called Purely Professionals. This facility, according to Serravo, would enable him to achieve his goal of teaching people the path to perfection. On the night of the stabbing, Serravo, according to the history given to Doctor Seig, was excited because he finally believed that he had received some positive encouragement in his endeavor from some King Soopers union members, but he was discouraged by some inner "evil spirits" who kept raising troublesome questions about how he would deal with his wife's lack of encouragement and support. Doctor Seig diagnosed Serravo as suffering either from an organic delusional disorder related to left temporal lobe damage as a result of an automobile accident some years ago or paranoid schizophrenia. Either diagnosis, in Doctor Seig's opinion, would adequately account for Serravo's delusional belief that he had a privileged relationship with God as the result of which he was in direct communication with God. Doctor Seig testified that Serravo was operating under this delusional system when he stabbed his wife and these delusions caused him to believe that his act was morally justified. Doctor Seig, however, was of the view that Serravo, because he was aware that the act of stabbing was contrary to law, was sane at the time of the stabbing.

Serravo presented four psychiatrists and a clinical psychologist on the issue of his legal insanity. The first psychiatrist, Doctor Frederick Miller, was of the opinion that on the night of the stabbing Serravo was under the psychotic delusion that it was his divine mission to kill his wife and that he was morally justified in stabbing her because God had told him to do so. Doctor Miller was not quite certain whether Serravo's psychotic disorder was paranoid schizophrenia, a paranoid delusional disorder, or an organic delusional disorder. Although uncertain of the exact diagnostic label applicable to Serravo, Doctor Miller was of the opinion that Serravo's mental illness made it impossible for him to distinguish right from wrong even though Serravo was probably aware that such conduct was legally wrong.

Another psychiatrist, Doctor Eric Kaplan, was the attending psychiatrist at the University of Colorado Health Services and a member of the faculty of the medical school. Doctor Kaplan supervised Doctor Ann Seig during her examination of Serravo and also made an independent evaluation of Serravo's mental condition. It was Doctor Kaplan's opinion that Serravo was suffering from paranoid schizophrenia at the time of the stabbing and was laboring under the paranoid delusion that his wife stood in the way of his divine mission of completing the large sports complex, that Serravo believed that the stabbing was the right thing to do, and that Serravo, as a result of his mental illness, was unable to distinguish right from wrong with respect to the stabbing. Two other psychiatrists, Doctor Geoffrey Heron and Doctor Seymour Sundell, offered the opinion that Serravo, at the time of the stabbing, was suffering from paranoid schizophrenia and a paranoid delusion about God which so affected his cognitive ability as to render him incapable of distinguishing right from wrong as normal people would be able to do in accordance with societal standards of morality.

Doctor Leslie Cohen, a clinical psychologist, also testified about Serravo's mental condition at the time of the stabbing. Having conducted extensive psychological testing of Serravo, Doctor Cohen was able to offer an opinion on Serravo's reality testing, his emotional reactivity, and his volition, all of which were relevant to the functioning of his conscience. The doctor was of the opinion that Serravo's conscience was based on a false belief or delusion about his magical powers as a result of his direct communication with God. Serravo, in the doctor's view, was suffering from a psychotic disorder that rendered him incapable of distinguishing right from wrong at the time of the stabbing. Although Doctor Cohen acknowledged that Serravo appeared to cover up his conduct when the police arrived at his home, the doctor explained that conduct as the product of a small part of his still intact reality testing. According to Doctor Cohen, Serravo is "not an incoherent man who can't figure out what's going on," but rather "senses that people don't understand his reasoning very well" and thus apparently believed that the police "wouldn't understand the complex reasoning that went behind the stabbing and that it would be better if he kept it to himself."

At the conclusion of the evidence, the trial court instructed the jury, in accordance with the statutory definition of insanity, that a person "is not accountable who is so diseased or defective in mind at the time of the commission of the act as to be incapable of distinguishing right from wrong, with respect to the act." The court also gave the following jury instruction, to which the prosecution objected, on the meaning of the phrase "incapable of distinguishing right from wrong":

Instruction No. 5

As used in the context of the statutory definition of insanity as a criminal defense, the phrase "incapable of distinguishing right from wrong" includes within its meaning the case where a person appreciates that his conduct is criminal, but, because of a mental disease or defect, believes it to be morally right.

In objecting to the jury instruction, the prosecution stated that it would permit the jury to return an insanity verdict based solely on a purely subjective moral standard rather than a legal standard of right and wrong. The trial court, however, was of the view that, because the statutory definition of insanity was not cast in terms of either legal or moral wrong, it was appropriate to instruct the jury that legal insanity included an incapacity, due to a mental disease or defect, to distinguish right from wrong in a moral sense.

The jury returned a verdict of not guilty by reason of insanity at the time of the commission of the alleged crimes, and the court committed Serravo to the custody of the Department of Institutions until such time as he is found to be eligible for release. The prosecution appealed the district court's ruling on the challenged jury instruction to the court of appeals, which approved the ruling. The court of appeals concluded that the statutory definition of insanity "reflects the General Assembly's intent to define wrong under a societal standard of moral wrong" and that, "as society's moral judgment is usually identical to the legal standard, the test is not broadened much if 'wrong' is determined by a societal moral standard." The court of appeals also concluded that the jury instruction did not apply a subjective moral standard to the defendant's capacity to distinguish right from wrong. Finally, the court adopted the so-called "deific-decree" exception to the societal standard of moral wrong. Based on that exception, the court of appeals determined that, although there was some evidence indicating that Serravo knew the stabbing of his wife was illegal and contrary to societal standards of morality, there was evidentiary support for the insanity verdict because there was expert testimony that Serravo was inspired by an insane delusion that God had decreed the act. We thereafter granted the People's petition to consider whether the court of appeals correctly interpreted the meaning of the phrase "incapable of distinguishing right from wrong" in the statutory definition of insanity.

II.

We initially consider whether the phrase "incapable of distinguishing right from wrong" should be measured by legal right and wrong, as argued by the People, or instead, should be measured by a societal standard of morality, as determined by the court of appeals. The phrase in question appears in section 16–8–101, 8A C.R.S. (1986), which defines legal insanity as follows:

The applicable test of insanity shall be, and the jury shall be so instructed: "A person who is so diseased or defective in mind at the time of the commission of the act as to be incapable of distinguishing right from wrong with respect to that act is not accountable. But care should be taken not to confuse such mental disease or defect with moral obliquity, mental depravity, or passion growing out of anger, revenge, hatred, or other motives, and kindred evil conditions, for when the act is induced by any of these causes the person is accountable to the law."

Because Colorado's statutory definition of insanity is based on the right-wrong test of legal insanity articulated in M'Naghten's Case, our resolution of the issue before us must begin with a review of that case.

A.

* * *

B.

* * *

We acknowledge that some cases subsequent to M'Naghten have interpreted the right-wrong test as limiting the insanity defense to a cognitive inability to distinguish legal right from legal wrong, with the result that a person's simple awareness that an act is illegal is a sufficient basis for finding criminal responsibility. We believe, however, that such an analysis injects a formalistic legalism into the insanity equation to the disregard of the psychological underpinnings of legal insanity. A person in an extremely psychotic state, for example, might be aware that an act is prohibited by law, but due to the overbearing effect of the psychosis may be utterly without the capacity to comprehend that the act is inherently immoral. A standard of legal wrong would render such a person legally responsible and subject to imprisonment for the conduct in question notwithstanding the patent injustice of such a disposition. Conversely, a person who, although mentally ill, has the cognitive capacity to distinguish right from wrong and is aware that an act is morally wrong, but does not realize that it is illegal, should nonetheless be held responsible for the act, as ignorance of the law is no excuse.

Construing the term "wrong" as moral wrong finds support in several cases which have basically followed the well-reasoned opinion of the New York Court of Appeals in People v. Schmidt, 216 N.Y. 324, 110 N.E. 945 (1915). The Schmidt opinion, written by then Judge Benjamin Cardozo, rejected the view that the term "wrong" means "contrary to the law of the state." After a careful analysis of M'Naghten and the history of the insanity defense, Judge Cardozo remarked:

The [M'Naghten] judges expressly held that a defendant who knew nothing of the law would none the less be responsible if he knew that the act was wrong, by which, therefore, they must have meant, if he knew that it was morally wrong. Whether he would also be responsible if he knew that it was against the law, but did not know it to be morally wrong, is a question that was not considered. In most cases, of course, knowledge that an act is illegal will justify the inference of knowledge that it is wrong. But none the less it is the knowledge of wrong, conceived of as moral wrong, that seems to have been established by that decision as the controlling test. That must certainly have been the test under the older law when the capacity to distinguish between right and wrong imported a capacity to distinguish between good and evil as abstract qualities.[10] There is nothing to justify the belief that the words right and wrong,

---

[10] In the early nineteenth century, prior to M'Naghten, English law treated the phrase "good and evil," which connotes the moral quality of an act, as synonymous and interchangeable with the phrase "right and wrong."

The first known substitution of "right and wrong" for "good and evil" was in Parker's Case (1812), in which the Attorney-General argued that "before it could have any weight in rebutting a charge [treason] so clearly made out, the jury must be perfectly satisfied, that at the time when the crime was committed, the person did not really know right from wrong." In Bellingham's Case (1812), both phrases were used, and Lord Chief Justice Mansfield instructed the jury that "the single question was, whether, at the time this fact [murder] was committed, [the defendant] . . . possessed a sufficient degree of understanding to distinguish good from evil, right from wrong." In the United States, these two phrases were also used synonymously in both infancy and insanity cases.

when they became limited by [M']Naughten's Case to the right and wrong of the particular act, cast off their meaning as terms of morals, and became terms of pure legality.

In resolving the ostensible tension between the legal standard of wrong in the answer to the first *M'Naghten* question (i.e., a person is legally responsible if the person acted with knowledge that an act is contrary to the "law of the land") and the moral standard suggested in the answer to the second and third *M'Naghten* questions (i.e., actual knowledge of codified law is not required for a conviction, but rather a person may be punished for conduct if the person knows that the act is one that "he ought not do"), the *Schmidt* opinion stated that the first answer "presupposes the offender's capacity to understand that violation of the law is wrong" and that the offender is sane except for a delusion that his act will redress a supposed grievance or attain some public benefit. The first *M'Naghten* answer, in other words, "applies only to persons who 'are not in other respects insane'" The delusion that an act will redress a supposed grievance or result in a public benefit, in Cardozo's words, "has no such effect in obscuring moral distinctions as a delusion that God himself has issued a command," inasmuch as "[t]he one delusion is consistent with knowledge that the act is a moral wrong, [but] the other is not."

Because the delusion emanating from an imagined grievance or public benefit does not obscure moral distinctions—as would an insane belief that God has issued a command—there is really no conflict between "the commands of law and morals" in a case where a defendant knows that the act is morally wrong but commits the act because he believes that either personal or public good will result. There is an obvious difference in kind, however, between that case and the person who suffers from an insane delusion that virtually destroys the cognitive ability to distinguish the morality or immorality of an act, even though the person may be aware the act is contrary to law. Although in most instances the very same forms of criminal conduct classified as felonies would also be considered violative of basic ethical norms, we are of the view that limiting the definition of "wrong" to "legal wrong" results in stripping legal insanity of a significant part of its psychological components. Various forms of mental diseases or defects can impair a person's cognitive ability to distinguish moral right from moral wrong and yet have no effect whatever on the person's rather sterile awareness that a certain act is contrary to law. To be sure, a person should not be judged legally insane merely because that person has personal views of right or wrong at variance with those which find expression in the law. It is quite another matter, however, to say that a mentally ill person suffering from an insane delusion that overbears the mental capacity to distinguish right from wrong should nonetheless be held criminally responsible for conduct solely because the person was aware that the act charged in the criminal prosecution was contrary to law. Such a result, in our view, proceeds from a narrowly legalistic interpretation that accords little weight to the baneful effects of various forms of mental illness on the cognitive capacity of the human mind.

In urging that the phrase "incapable of distinguishing right from wrong" in section 16–8–101, 8A C.R.S. (1986), should be limited to legal right and wrong, the People focus on that part of the insanity definition which states that "care should be taken not to confuse such mental disease or defect with moral obliquity" and argue that this statutory language manifests a legislative intent to define legal insanity in terms of an incapacity to distinguish legal right from legal wrong. We acknowledge, as asserted by the People, that the term "moral obliquity" refers to a deviation from moral rectitude. Webster's Third New International Dictionary 1557 (1986). Accepting that definition, however, does not lead us to the construction urged by the People.

The purpose served by the statutory reference to "moral obliquity" is not to provide a definitional component for legal insanity, which has been defined in the preceding sentence of section 16–8–101 as an incapacity to distinguish right from wrong with respect to the act due to a mental disease or defect existing at the time of the commission of the act. Rather, the purpose served by the reference to "moral obliquity" is to distinguish, on the one hand, an act committed by a person capable of distinguishing right from wrong but nonetheless acting out of a perverse and culpable rejection of prevailing moral standards and, on the other hand, an act committed by a person in a state of mental illness that renders the person incapable of distinguishing right from wrong with respect to the act. In the case of a person acting out of moral obliquity, rather than a mental disease or defect rendering the actor incapable of distinguishing right from wrong, the person is accountable to the law. In our view, therefore, the statutory definition of legal insanity in terms of an incapacity to distinguish right from wrong due to a mental disease or defect, along with the statutory distinction between an act resulting from legal insanity and an act resulting from moral obliquity, serves to confirm the fact that the General Assembly intended the concepts of right and wrong to be measured by a moral rather than a legal standard. If the General Assembly intended otherwise, we reasonably may assume that it would have cast the statutory definition of insanity in terms of an incapacity to distinguish "legality from illegality" or "lawfulness from unlawfulness" rather than in terms of an incapacity to distinguish "right from wrong" with respect to the act charged as a crime. We thus conclude that the term "wrong" in the statutory definition of insanity refers to moral wrong.

C.

Moral wrong can be measured either by a purely personal and subjective standard of morality or by a societal and presumably more objective standard. We believe that the better reasoned interpretation of "wrong" in the term "incapable of distinguishing right from wrong" refers to a wrongful act measured by societal standards of morality.

The concepts of "right" and "wrong" are essentially ethical in character and have their primary source in the existing societal standards of morality, as distinguished from the written law. A person's awareness and appreciation of right and wrong derive primarily from a variety of experiences and relationships including, but not necessarily limited to, behavioral rules endorsed by the social culture as well as ethical principles transmitted through the family, the community, the formal educational process, and religious associations. Simply put, legal insanity combines concepts of law, morality and medicine with the moral concepts derived primarily from the total underlying conceptions of ethics shared by the community at large. Defining "wrong" in terms of a purely personal and subjective standard of morality ignores a substantial part of the moral culture on which our societal norms of behavior are based.[11]

Construing the term "wrong" in accordance with societal standards of morality results in a substantially more objective standard of moral wrong than the purely personal and subjective moral standard, under which an accused could be adjudicated insane even if he knew that the act in question was both forbidden by law and condemned by society, but nonetheless harbored a personal belief that the act was right. A personal and subjective standard of morality should not be permitted to exonerate a defendant any more than an ignorance of the law, engendered by a mental illness, should be equated with legal insanity. In sum, the appropriate construction of the term "incapable of distinguishing right from wrong with respect to [the] act" in section 16–8–101 should be measured by existing societal standards of morality rather than by a defendant's personal and subjective understanding of the legality or illegality of the act in question.

D.

We turn then to Jury Instruction No. 5, which stated that the phrase "incapable of distinguishing right from wrong" includes the case of a person who "appreciates that his conduct is criminal but, because of a mental disease or defect, believes it to be morally right." Although the court of appeals concluded that this instruction did not incorporate a

---

[11] The traditional reluctance to hold children under a certain age responsible for criminal acts is a good illustration of the fact that moral standards are learned through a dynamic societal process. Society has determined that both insane persons and children under a certain age are not responsible moral agents, in the former case because a mental disease or defect has prevented an adequate assimilation of societal moral standards, and in the latter case because immaturity has prevented an adequate opportunity for acquiring a moral sense of right and wrong. Like the *M'Naghten* test, the test for measuring infant incapacity has generally involved the inquiry of whether the child could distinguish between right and wrong. See generally, Platt & Diamond, *The Origins of the "Right and Wrong" Test of Criminal Responsibility and Its Subsequent Development in the United States: An Historical Survey*, 54 Calif.L.Rev. 1227, 1237–47 (1966).

subjective moral standard to the determination of whether defendant understood right from wrong, we are of a contrary view. Jury Instruction No. 5 was cast in terms so general that it well could have been interpreted by the jury to incorporate a personal and subjective standard of moral wrong rather than a societal standard of right and wrong. The court of appeals' approval of the instruction, in our view, is inconsistent with its adoption of a societal standard of moral wrong for purposes of legal insanity.

We emphasize here that in most cases involving the defense of legal insanity there will be no practical difference between a definition of "wrong" in terms of legal wrong and a definition of "wrong" in terms of societal standards of morality. This is so because, for the most part, the proscriptions of the criminal law generally reflect the moral prohibitions of the social order. As previously discussed, however, the concept of legal insanity, while part of our positive law, incorporates psychological and moral components that are not necessarily limited by the confines of positive law. A clarifying instruction on the definition of legal insanity, therefore, should clearly state that, as related to the conduct charged as a crime, the phrase "incapable of distinguishing right from wrong" refers to a person's cognitive inability, due to a mental disease or defect, to distinguish right from wrong as measured by a societal standard of morality, even though the person may be aware that the conduct in question is criminal. Any such instruction should also expressly inform the jury that the phrase "incapable of distinguishing right from wrong" does not refer to a purely personal and subjective standard of morality.

III.

We next consider the relationship between the so-called "deific-decree" delusion and Colorado's test of legal insanity. The court of appeals, after holding that the term "wrong" in the statutory definition of insanity refers not to legal wrong but moral wrong under societal standards of morality, held that the "deific-decree" delusion was an exception to the societal standards of moral wrong. Drawing on the opinion of the Washington Supreme Court in State v. Crenshaw, 98 Wash.2d 789, 659 P.2d 488 (1983), the court of appeals limited the so-called deific-decree exception to those situations in which a person commits a criminal act, knowing it is illegal and morally wrong according to society's standards but, because of a mental defect, believes that God has decreed the act. This exception, the court of appeals went on to conclude, must be distinguished from the case in which a person acts in accordance with a duty imposed by a particular faith. In our view, the "deific-decree" delusion is not so much an exception to the right-wrong test measured by the existing societal standards of morality as it is an integral factor in assessing a person's cognitive ability to distinguish right from wrong with respect to the act charged as a crime.

In discussing the deific-decree delusion in *Schmidt*, the court stated:

We must not . . . exaggerate the rigor of the rule by giving the word "wrong" a strained interpretation, at war with its broad and primary meaning, and least of all, if in so doing, we rob the rule of all relation to the mental health and true capacity of the criminal. The interpretation placed upon the statute by the trial judge may be tested by its consequences. A mother kills her infant child to whom she has been devotedly attached. She knows the nature and quality of the act; she knows that the law condemns it; but she is inspired by an insane delusion that God has appeared to her and ordained the sacrifice. It seems a mockery to say that, within the meaning of the statute, she knows that the act is wrong. If the definition propounded by the trial judge is right, it would be the duty of a jury to hold her responsible for the crime. We find nothing either in the history of the rule, or in its reason and purpose, or in judicial exposition of its meaning, to justify a conclusion so abhorrent . . .

. . .

. . . Knowledge that an act is forbidden by law will in most cases permit the inference of knowledge that, according to the accepted standards of mankind, it is also condemned as an offense against good morals. Obedience to the law is itself a moral duty. If, however, there is an insane delusion that God has appeared to the defendant and ordained the commission of a crime, we think it cannot be said of the offender that he knows the act to be wrong.

If a person insanely believes that "he has a command from the Almighty to kill, it is difficult to understand how such a man can know that it is wrong for him to do it." *Schmidt*, 110 N.E. at 948 (quoting Guiteau's Case, 10 Fed. 161, 182 (1882)). A person acting under such a delusion is no less insane even though the person might know that murder is prohibited by positive law. It thus seems clear to us that a person is legally insane if that person's cognitive ability to distinguish right from wrong with respect to the act has been destroyed as a result of a psychotic delusion that God has commanded the act. We thus conclude that, although the court of appeals mischaracterized the deific-decree delusion as an exception to the right-wrong test for legal insanity, a defendant nonetheless may be judged legally insane where, as here, the defendant's cognitive ability to distinguish right from wrong with respect to the act has been destroyed as a result of a psychotic delusion that God has decreed the act.

IV.

The question remains whether, in light of our disapproval of the trial court's jury instruction on the meaning of "wrong" in Colorado's test of legal insanity, we should remand the case for a new trial on the issue of insanity. This case was filed in the court of appeals as a prosecutorial appeal pursuant to section 16–12–102(1), 8A C.R.S. (1986), on a question of law—namely, the correctness of the jury instruction on the meaning of the term "wrong" in the statutory definition of insanity. Although we disagree with the court of appeals' conclusion that the challenged jury instruction did not apply a subjective standard of morality to the right-wrong test for legal insanity, we conclude that a retrial of the defendant would violate the federal and state constitutional prohibitions against placing an accused twice in jeopardy for the same offense.

In Colorado, while the issue of an accused's sanity must be tried separately from the issue of guilt, insanity remains an affirmative defense to a crime. Once any credible evidence of this affirmative defense is introduced into evidence, the prosecution bears the burden of proving the defendant's sanity beyond a reasonable doubt. In People ex rel. Juhan v. District Court, 165 Colo. 253, 265, 439 P.2d 741, 747 (1968), this court held that "[m]ental capacity to commit a crime is a material part of total guilt for there can be no crime without the *mens rea*." A jury verdict of not guilty by reason of insanity, therefore, is an adjudication on the merits which absolves the defendant of criminal responsibility, and results in a commitment of the defendant to the custody of the Department of Institutions until such time as the defendant is eligible for release.

* * *

Because [earlier precedent] holds that an appellate determination of evidentiary insufficiency to sustain a verdict is an adjudication on the merits that bars retrial, it necessarily follows that the Double Jeopardy Clause of the United States Constitution prohibits retrial after a jury verdict of not guilty by reason of insanity. Such a verdict represents a judicial determination that, irrespective of any error in a trial court's instructional rulings, the prosecution has failed to prove the defendant's sanity beyond a reasonable doubt and that, consequently, the defendant lacked the mental capacity to commit the crime charged against him. Allowing a retrial on the issue of a defendant's sanity after the jury has returned a verdict of not guilty by reason of insanity is nothing less than giving the state the impermissible "second bite at the apple." * * *

The judgment of the court of appeals is accordingly approved in part and disapproved in part.

■ VOLLACK, J., dissents.

■ JUSTICE VOLLACK dissenting:

The majority holds that the phrase, "incapable of distinguishing right from wrong," means a mental incapacity to know that an act is wrong under existing societal standards of morality. In addition, the majority rejects the characterization of the deific decree as an exception to the right-from-wrong test and holds that a defendant may be judged legally insane when the defendant's cognitive ability to distinguish right from wrong with respect to an act has been destroyed as a result of a psychotic delusion that God has ordered the act. Finally, the majority holds that federal and state principles of double jeopardy prohibit the retrial of the defendant on the issue of his sanity at the time of the commission of the act charged against him. I disagree with the majority's holdings in this case.

I.

The issue raised in this case is the meaning of the phrase, "incapable of distinguishing right from wrong," in section 16–8–101(1), 8A C.R.S. (1986). In determining the meaning of "incapable of distinguishing right from wrong," this court must look first and foremost to the language of the statute to determine whether the General Assembly adopted a legal or moral standard for determining criminal insanity when they enacted section 16–8–101(1).

A.

The origin of criminal insanity tests is M'Naghten's Case. In M'Naghten, the judges determined that a defendant is not criminally responsible (1) where the defendant does not know the nature and quality of his act, or (2) where he does not know right from wrong with respect to that act. Since the M'Naghten decision in 1843, American courts and legislatures have adopted various tests to determine criminal responsibility. Some courts have adopted the M'Naghten test, other courts have adopted the American Law Institute Model Penal Code (Official Draft and Revised Comments 1985) [hereinafter cited as "Model Penal Code"] test (the ALI-MPC test), while still other courts have adopted modifications of these two tests or completely different tests.

In Colorado, the test of criminal responsibility, which has been codified in section 16–8–101(1), is the "right from wrong" prong of the test announced in M'Naghten. Section 16–8–101(1) states:

> (1) The applicable test of insanity shall be, and the jury shall be so instructed: "A person who is so diseased or defective in mind at the time of the commission of the act as to be incapable of distinguishing right from wrong with respect to that act is not accountable. But care should be taken not to confuse such mental disease or defect with moral obliquity, mental depravity, or passion growing out of anger, revenge, hatred, or other motives, and kindred evil conditions, for when the act is induced by any of these causes the person is accountable to the law."

(Emphasis added.)

B.

Next, the language in section 16–8–101(1) must be placed in context with the language from other tests for insanity. Section 16–8–101(1) does not follow the language from the American Law Institute Model Penal Code (ALI-MPC) test . . . Under this test, jurisdictions have the option to adopt either the "wrongfulness" or "criminality" standard. The "wrongfulness" standard was intended by the drafters of the ALI-MPC test to establish a broader, moral criterion for determining criminal responsibility. Courts that have adopted the ALI-MPC "wrongfulness" language have followed the intent of the ALI-MPC drafters and defined "wrongfulness" as morally wrong.

Colorado has not adopted the ALI-MPC "wrongfulness" language. On the contrary, section 16–8–101(1) adopted the "right from wrong" language enumerated in *M'Naghten*. Accordingly, case law defining criminal responsibility based on the "wrongfulness" language is not persuasive, or even applicable, to our determination of the meaning of "incapable of distinguishing right from wrong" in section 16–8–101(1).

C.

The majority fails to define the phrase, "incapable of distinguishing." However, the General Assembly's adoption of this language is important for two reasons. First, because *M'Naghten* focuses on the cognitive capacity of the person, this phrase indicates the level of cognition that is necessary for a person to be determined insane. Second, the General Assembly's use of this phrase indicates the legislature's intent to adopt a rigid test of insanity similar to the original *M'Naghten* test.

The original *M'Naghten* formulation was a rigid standard and required that a person be totally devoid of cognitive ability before they could be found insane. Accordingly, modern tests, such as the ALI-MPC test, the ABA standard, and the federal standard, adopted language such as "unable to appreciate the wrongfulness" or "lacks substantial capacity to appreciate the wrongfulness." These tests discarded the term "know," which was used in *M'Naghten*, in favor of language that provided more flexibility and indicated that the defendant was not required to be totally incapacitated in order to be found criminally insane.

The General Assembly did not adopt the "unable to appreciate" language. In fact, use of the phrase, "incapable of distinguishing," indicates an intent to adopt a restrictive standard similar to the original interpretation of *M'Naghten* that a defendant must be totally devoid of cognitive capacity to satisfy the test of insanity in section 16–8–101(1). The majority, by not defining the phrase, "incapable of distinguishing," disregards the language in the statute and the intent of the General Assembly.

The phrase, "incapable of distinguishing right from wrong," incorporates the same limited meaning of criminal insanity that the *M'Naghten* judges enumerated . . . Thus, the focus under *M'Naghten*, and section 16–8–101(1), is whether the defendant is so devoid of cognitive capacity that the defendant's mental status prevented the defendant from being "conscious" that his or her conduct was forbidden by the law.

D.

The majority concludes, relying on what is essentially dicta from a 1915 New York case, People v. Schmidt, 216 N.Y. 324, 110 N.E. 945

(1915), that "wrong" means whether the defendant knows that an act is wrong by society's morals. The express language of the *M'Naghten* decision, however, supports neither the majority's nor the *Schmidt* opinion, but instead indicates that "right from wrong" was meant to be legal right from wrong.

First, nowhere in any of the *M'Naghten* judges' answers does the word "moral" appear. Secondly, the *M'Naghten* judges' answer to the first question clearly expresses the view that a person is punishable if that person "knew at the time of committing their crime that he was acting contrary to law." Both the *Schmidt* court and the majority, however, relied on the answer to the second and third questions in *M'Naghten* to support their conclusion.

In *Schmidt*, the court stated that the "judges [in *M'Naghten*] expressly held that a defendant who knew nothing of the law would nonetheless be responsible if he knew that the act was wrong." From this premise, the *Schmidt* court concluded "by which, therefore, [the *M'Naghten* judges] must have meant, if you knew that it was morally wrong." This conclusion is unsupported, however, because nowhere in the answer to the second and third questions do the *M'Naghten* judges "expressly" or impliedly hold what the *Schmidt* court states they hold.

Relying on the tenuous reasoning in *Schmidt*, the majority states that the *M'Naghten* judges' answer to the second and third questions "qualifies the reference to 'law of the land' in the first answer" and "suggests that a person may be considered legally sane as long as the person commits an act contrary to law and knows that the act was morally wrong without regard to the person's actual knowledge of its illegality under positive law." The majority, and *Schmidt*, opinions' interpretation of the answer to the second and third questions, in my view, disregards the plain meaning of the *M'Naghten* answers.

The answer to the second and third questions does not "qualify" the first answer, as the majority states, but instead explains the first answer by stating how the jury should be instructed. The best way to demonstrate this is with the aid of a hypothetical. A defendant is charged with murder and pleads insanity. In such a case, the *M'Naghten* judges state that the question of the defendant's sanity should not be put to the jury "generally and in the abstract." By this they meant that the jury should not be asked whether the defendant knew that murder was against the law. If the court submits the instruction "generally and in the abstract," the court would be asking the jury, on the one hand, whether the defendant actually knew murder was against the law, while on the other hand, the defendant is presumed to know the law. Such a request would confuse the jury.

To avoid such confusion, the judges stated that the question should be put to the jury "with reference to the party's knowledge of right and wrong, in respect to the very act with which he is charged." By this they meant whether the defendant was "conscious" that the particular act he or she committed (whatever it is labeled by the state) was against the law. Such an interpretation flows logically from a reading of the answer to the second and third questions and complements, instead of conflicts with, the answer to the first question.

Section 16–8–101(1) is a codification of the *M'Naghten* right from wrong test. The *M'Naghten* rule looks exclusively to the cognitive capacity of the accused, and contemplates as insane a person who is totally devoid of cognitive capacity. Under *M'Naghten*, even though the defendant committed the act under a delusion, "he is nevertheless punishable . . . if he knew at the time of committing such crime that he was acting contrary to . . . the law of the land."

We should not leave to the jury the question of whether some particular act is morally right or wrong . . . This court should follow the intent of the General Assembly, and the plain meaning of *M'Naghten*, and conclude that the General Assembly adopted a legal standard for determining criminal insanity in section 16–8–101(1).

II.

I also disagree with the majority's decision concerning the deific decree exception recognized by the court of appeals. The deific decree exception is a narrow exception recognized by a small minority of those states which define wrong by society's moral standards. State v. Crenshaw, 659 P.2d 488, 494 (Wash.1983). This exception has been applied in cases where a defendant knew an act was legally wrong but believed, because of a mental defect, that God decreed the act. A person qualifies as insane under this exception only if their free will has been overcome by their belief in the deific decree . . .

In Colorado, neither the General Assembly nor this court has accepted subjective tests to determine criminal responsibility. In the 1983 revision of section 16–8–101, the legislature deleted the volitional prong of the insanity definition. By deleting the volitional prong, the legislature eliminated any focus on an individual's subjective behavior and restricted the insanity defense only to those cases where the defendant was incapable of distinguishing right from wrong.

. . . Accordingly, under the current statute, I would reject the subjective deific decree exception, either in the form adopted by the court of appeals or in the form adopted by the majority.

III.

I also disagree with the majority's conclusion "that a retrial of the defendant would violate the federal and state constitutional prohibitions against placing an accused twice in jeopardy for the same offense." I disagree because, under the bifurcated trial system, a defendant is not placed in jeopardy during the sanity phase of the trial.

* * *

The jury in a sanity trial is only asked to determine whether the defendant is sane or insane, and not whether the defendant lacked the requisite culpable mental state to commit the crime. Thus, under our statute and procedures, a not-guilty-by-reason-of-insanity verdict is not an adjudication on the merits, as the majority contends.

In this case, the sanity trial was not aimed at reaching a final determination of the defendant's guilt or innocence, and was not the equivalent of an adjudication on the merits. Accordingly, the sanity trial does not preclude the retrial of the defendant.

I would reverse the court of appeals and district court, and remand the case for a new sanity trial.

NOTES

1. For a discussion of the so-called "deific decree" doctrine, in which defendants are excused from crimes because God told them to do it, see Rabia Belt, *When God Demands Blood: Unusual Minds and the Troubled Juridical Ties of Religion, Madness, and Culpability*, 69 U. MIAMI L. REV. 755 (2015).

2. Should defendants be excused if God told them to commit a crime, but not if Satan did? Does your answer depend on whether the defendant belonged to a Satanic *religion*? If the defendant were "merely" delusional in following Satan, rather than following an instruction from a deity, should he not be excused from criminal liability?

3. Should a defendant be able to invoke the insanity defense if he realizes his conduct is illegal? Colorado and roughly twenty other states allow a defendant to be found insane if he believes his conduct is morally rightful, even while recognizing it violates the jurisdiction's criminal code. *See* Ken Levy, *Dangerous Psychopaths: Criminally Responsible But Not Morally Responsible, Subject to Criminal Punishment and Preventive Detention*, 48 SAN DIEGO L. REV. 1299, 1351 (2011). How do juries in these jurisdictions know that the defendant truly believed his illegal conduct was morally rightful?

4. Why is there such variation among the experts in *Serravo*? Two scholars suggest that the experts might not have been given the same legal standard to work with prior to giving their opinions. *See* Kate E. Bloch & Jeffrey Gould, *Legal Indeterminacy in Insanity Cases: Clarifying Wrongfulness and Applying a Triadic Approach to Forensic Evaluations*, 67 HASTINGS L.J. 913, 941–42 (2016).

C. THE IRRESISTIBLE IMPULSE TEST

As a supplement to the *M'Naghten* test, a number of jurisdictions have adopted the so-called "irresistible impulse" test. The test originated as early as 1844 in a Massachusetts case, Commonwealth v. Rogers, 48

Mass. (7 Metc.) 500, 502 (1844), and it was developed in greater detail nearly a half-century later in the Alabama decision below.

Parsons v. State

Supreme Court of Alabama, 1887.
81 Ala. 577, 2 So. 854.

■ SOMERVILLE, J.

In this case the defendants have been convicted of the murder of Bennett Parsons, by shooting him with a gun; one of the defendants being the wife and the other the daughter of the deceased. The defense set up in the trial was the plea of insanity, the evidence tending to show that the daughter was an idiot, and the mother and wife a lunatic, subject to insane delusions, and that the killing on her part was the offspring and product of those delusions.

. . . The earliest English decisions, striving to establish rules and tests on the subject [of insanity], including alike the legal rules of criminal and civil responsibility, and the supposed tests of the existence of the disease of insanity itself, are now admitted to have been deplorably erroneous, and, to say nothing of their vacillating character, have long since been abandoned. The views of the ablest of the old text writers and sages of the law were equally confused and uncertain in the treatment of these subjects, and they are now entirely exploded. Time was in the history of our laws that the veriest lunatic was debarred from pleading his providential affliction as a defense to his contracts. It was said, in justification of so absurd a rule, that no one could be permitted to stultify himself by pleading his own disability. So great a jurist as Lord COKE, in his attempted classification of madmen, laid down the legal rule of criminal responsibility to be that one should " *wholly* have lost his memory and understanding;" as to which Mr. Erskine, when defending Hadfield for shooting the king, in the year 1800, justly observed: "No such madman ever existed in the world." . . . [O]ther judges had ventured to decide that, to be non-punishable for alleged acts of crime, "a man must be totally deprived of his understanding and memory, so as not to know what he was doing, no more than an infant, a brute, or *a wild beast.*" *Arnold's Case*, 16 How. State Tr. 764. All these rules have necessarily been discarded in modern times in the light of the new scientific knowledge acquired by a more thorough study of the disease of insanity . . .

In view of . . . the new light thrown on the disease of insanity by the discoveries of modern psychological medicine, the courts of the country may well hesitate before blindly following in the unsteady footsteps found upon the old sandstones of our common-law jurisprudence a century ago . . .

[Margin note: Old view of insanity]

* * *

In ancient times, lunatics were not regarded as "unfortunate sufferers from disease, but rather as subjects of demoniacal possession, or as self-made victims of evil passions." They were not cared for humanely in asylums and hospitals, but were incarcerated in jails, punished with chains and stripes, and often sentenced to death by burning or the gibbet . . . The exposure of these evils not only led to the establishment of that most beneficent of modern civilized charities,-the hospital and asylum for the insane,-but also furnished hitherto unequaled opportunities to the medical profession of investigating and treating insanity on the pathological basis of its being a disease of the mind. Under these new and more favorable conditions, the medical jurisprudence of insanity has assumed an entirely new phase. The nature and exciting causes of the disease have been thoroughly studied and more fully comprehended. The result is that the "right and wrong test," [as] it is sometimes called, which, it must be remembered, itself originated with the medical profession, in the mere dawn of the scientific knowledge of insanity, has been condemned by the great current of modern medical authorities, who believe it to be "founded on an ignorant and imperfect view of the disease." 15 Encyclop. Brit. (9th Ed.) tit. "Insanity."

The question, then, presented seems to be whether an old rule of legal responsibility shall be adhered to, based on theories of physicians promulgated a hundred years ago, which refuse to recognize any evidence of insanity, except the single test of mental capacity to distinguish right and wrong, or whether the courts will recognize as a possible fact, if capable of proof by clear and satisfactory testimony, the doctrine, now alleged by those of the medical profession who have made insanity a special subject of investigation, that the old test is wrong, and that there is no single test by which the existence of the disease, to that degree which exempts from punishment, can in every case be infallibly detected . . .

It is everywhere admitted, and as to this there can be no doubt, that an idiot, lunatic, or other person of diseased mind, who is afflicted to such extent as not to know whether he is doing right or wrong, is not punishable for any act which he may do while in that state. Can the courts justly say, however, that the only test or rule of responsibility in criminal cases is the power to distinguish right from wrong, whether in the abstract, or as applied to the particular case? Or may there not be insane persons, of a diseased brain, who, while capable of perceiving the difference between right and wrong, are, as matter of fact, so far under *the duress of such disease* as to destroy *the power to choose* between right and wrong? Will the courts assume as a fact, not to be rebutted by any amount of evidence, or any new discoveries of medical science, that there is and can be no such state of mind as that described by a writer on psychological medicine as one "in which the reason has lost its empire over the passions, and the actions by which they are manifested, to such a degree that the individual can neither repress the former, nor abstain from the latter?" Dean, Med. Jur. 497.

. . . The rule in *McNaghten's Case* arrogates to the court, in legal effect, the right to assert, as matter of law, the following propositions: (1) That there is but a single test of the existence of that degree of insanity such as confers irresponsibility for crime; (2) that there does not exist any case of such insanity in which that single test-the capacity to distinguish right from wrong-does not appear; (3) that all other evidences of alleged insanity, supposed by physicians and experts to indicate a destruction of the freedom of the human will, and the irresistible duress of one's actions, do not destroy his mental capacity to entertain a criminal intent.

* * *

In the present state of our law, under the rule in *McNaghten's Case,* we are confronted with this practical difficulty, which itself demonstrates the defects of the rule. The courts, in effect, charge the juries, as matter of law, that no such mental disease exists as that often testified to by medical writers, superintendents of insane hospitals, and other experts; that there can be, as matter of scientific fact, no cerebral defect, congenital or acquired, which destroys the patient's power of self control,- his liberty of will and action . . .

* * *

In the learned treatise of Drs. Bucknill and Tuke on Psychological Medicine, 269, (4th Ed., London, 1879,) the legal tests of responsibility are discussed, and the adherence of the courts to the right and wrong test is deplored as unfortunate; the true principle being stated to be "whether, in consequence of congenital defect or acquired disease, *the power of self-control* is absent altogether, or is so far wanting as to render the individual irresponsible." It is observed by the authors: "As has again and again been shown, the unconsciousness of right and wrong is one thing, and the powerlessness, through cerebral defect or disease, to do right, is another . . ."

* * *

Other distinguished writers on the medical jurisprudence of insanity have expressed like views, with comparative unanimity. And nowhere do we find the rule more emphatically condemned than by those who have the practical care and treatment of the insane in the various lunatic asylums of every civilized country. A notable instance is found in the following resolution, unanimously passed at the annual meeting of the British Association of Medical Officers of Asylums and Hospitals for the Insane, held in London, July 14, 1864, where there were present fifty-four medical officers: "Resolved, that so much of the legal test of the mental condition of an alleged criminal lunatic as renders him a responsible agent, because he knows the difference between right and wrong, is inconsistent with the fact, well known to every member of this meeting, that the power of distinguishing between right and wrong exists very frequently in those who are undoubtedly insane, and is often associated with dangerous and uncontrollable delusions." Judicial Aspects Insan. (Ordronaux, 1877,) 423, 424.

* * *

It is no satisfactory objection to say that the rule above announced by us is of difficult application. The rule in *McNaghten's Case, supra,* is equally obnoxious to a like criticism. The difficulty does not lie in the rule, but is inherent in the subject of insanity itself. The practical trouble is for the courts to determine in what particular cases the party on trial is to be transferred from the category of sane to that of insane criminals; where, in other words, the border line of punishability is adjudged to be passed. But, as has been said in reference to an every-day fact of nature, no one can say where twilight ends or begins, but there is ample distinction nevertheless between *day* and *night.* We think we can safely rely in this matter upon the intelligence of our juries, guided by the testimony of men who have practically made a study of the disease of insanity; and enlightened by a conscientious desire, on the one hand, to enforce the criminal laws of the land, and, on the other, not to deal harshly with any unfortunate victim of a diseased mind, acting without the light of reason or the power of volition.

* * *

. . . We think it sufficient if the insane delusion—by which we mean the delusion proceeding from a *diseased mind*—sincerely exists at the time of committing the alleged crime, and the defendant, believing it to be real, is so influenced by it as either to render him incapable of perceiving the true nature and quality of the act done, by reason of the depravation of the reasoning faculty, or so subverts his will as to destroy his free agency by rendering him powerless to resist by reason of *the duress of the disease.* In such a case, in other words, there must exist either one of two conditions: (1) Such mental defect as to render the defendant unable to distinguish between right and wrong in relation to the particular act; or (2) the overmastering of defendant's will in consequence of the insane delusion under the influence of which he acts, produced by disease of the mind or brain.

In conclusion of this branch of the subject, that we may not be misunderstood, we think it follows very clearly from what we have said that the inquiries to be submitted to the jury, then, in every criminal trial where the defense of insanity is interposed, are these: *First.* Was the defendant at the time of the commission of the alleged crime, as matter of fact, afflicted with a *disease of the mind,* so as to be either idiotic, or otherwise insane? *Second.* If such be the case, did he know right from wrong, as applied to the particular act in question? If he did not have such knowledge, he is not legally responsible. *Third.* If he did have such knowledge, he may nevertheless not be legally responsible if the two following conditions concur: (1) If, by reason of the duress of such mental disease, he had so far lost the *power to choose* between the right and wrong, and to avoid doing the act in question, as that his free agency was at the time destroyed; (2) and if, at the same time, the alleged crime was so connected with such mental disease, in the relation of cause and effect, as to have been the product of it *solely*.

2 other conditions to avoid legal responsibility

* * *

———

NOTES

1. Can a person have a true "irresistible impulse" without being, at the same time, deficient or defective with respect to the nature and quality of the act or the defendant's ability to distinguish between right and wrong?

2. Although the test in *Parsons* is usually described as the "irresistible impulse" test, most jurisdictions that have adopted the test do not actually use that terminology. Rather, the test is typically referred to as a "volitional" or "control" test. Juries are usually asked to assess a defendant's capacity for self-control, not whether he suffered an irresistible impulse. *See* Richard E. Redding, *The Brain Disorder Defendant: Neuroscience and Legal Sanity in the Twenty-First Century*, 56 AM. U. L. REV. 51, 81–82 (2006).

3. In the years following *Parsons*, the irresistible impulse test was adopted by more than a dozen states. *See* ABRAHAM S. GOLDSTEIN, THE INSANITY DEFENSE 67–70, 241–42 n.1 (1967). Although the test gained favor, no state has ever adopted the irresistible impulse test as the sole test for determining insanity. *See* Stephen J. Morse, *Protecting Liberty and Autonomy: Desert/Disease Jurisprudence*, 48 SAN DIEGO L. REV. 1077, 1113–1114 (2011). Rather, as in *Parsons*, it has been used in conjunction with a cognitive test for insanity.

4. A central premise of the *Parsons* decision was that science had advanced to the point of recognizing that some defendants would know right from wrong but be unable to control themselves. One hundred years later, some very prominent experts disagree with that premise. According to Professor Stephen Morse, there are no irresistible impulses because every action carries a degree of voluntariness with it. *See* Stephen J. Morse, *Culpability and Control*, 142 U. PA. L. REV. 1587, 1600–1601 (1994).

5. Not all experts (not to mention lay people) agree with Professor Morse that irresistible impulses are a fiction. Assuming you disagree with Professor Morse, how would you determine what is an irresistible impulse as opposed to an impulse that a person chose not to resist? Consider the following remark from Professor Christopher Slobogin who, after looking at social science research, concluded that "when we discuss 'impulsivity,' we literally do not know what we are talking about." Christopher Slobogin, *The Integrationist Alternative to the Insanity Defense: Reflections on the Exculpatory Scope of Mental Illness in the Wake of the Andrea Yates Trial*,

30 AM. J. CRIM. L. 315, 323 (2003). If we cannot set criteria for impulsivity, how can it be a test for insanity?

6. Irresistible impulse is not the same as "temporary insanity." In State v. Kolisnitschenko, 84 Wis.2d 492, 267 N.W.2d 321 (1978), the Court said, "[W]e are not willing to hold . . . that a temporary psychotic state which lasts only for the period of intoxication and which is brought into existence by the interaction of a stormy personality and voluntary intoxication constitutes a mental disease which is a defense to the crime charged [murder]."

Commonwealth v. Shin

Appeals Court of Massachusetts, 2014.
16 N.E.3d 1122.

■ HANLON, J.

* * *

At approximately five o'clock in the evening on January 20, 2011, the victim boarded a Massachusetts Bay Transportation Authority (MBTA) Green Line subway train at Park Street station, heading for Cleveland Circle. It was rush hour and the train was crowded; she stood with her back against the wall by the "accordion bend" in the middle of the train in an attempt to allow space for other passengers.

At the Copley stop, many people entered the train and it became very crowded; the defendant boarded with the other passengers and he went to stand "very close" to the victim, so close that he made her uncomfortable, "and he was touching [her] arm on [her] left side." After the train left Copley and before the next stop (Hynes Convention Center), the defendant lifted his hand and touched the victim between her legs on her upper thigh, within "two inches" of her genital area. She testified that "[i]t was very high on [her] leg." As soon as the defendant put his hand on the victim's leg, she lifted up her left arm and, pushing him in the center of his chest, "said watch your hands. [She] pushed him as far as [she] could push him away from [her]."

The victim got off the train at the Hynes Convention Center stop because she "wanted to get out of the enclosed train car"; the defendant also got off the train at that stop, and the victim watched from the platform as he passed through the fare gate and climbed the stairs toward the station exit. She then felt safe enough to get back on the next train and continue to her intended stop.

MBTA transit officers obtained videotape footage from the Hynes Convention Center station; the victim identified the defendant on the tape and the officers then obtained "fare gate information" for the time shown on the videotape. They determined the defendant's name and home address from his "transportation access pass" or "Charlie" card.

The following day, three transit officers went to the defendant's home and spoke with him. At their request, he provided his Charlie card and, "immediately" after checking the numbers on the card, the officers gave the defendant a Miranda warning. The defendant then asked for privacy because "[h]e did not want the other people in the home to know what [they] were talking about"; as a result, the defendant and all three officers moved into a room adjacent to the entrance door to continue their conversation. The defendant later agreed to accompany the officers back to the MBTA transit police headquarters; while traveling in the officers' unmarked car, the defendant stated that "he did have a problem" relating to the incident that they were investigating, and that he had medication but was not presently taking it.

* * *

At the jury-waived trial, the defendant's primary defense was lack of criminal responsibility, specifically that he was unable to "conform [his] conduct to the requirements of the law." *Commonwealth v. Berry*, 457 Mass. 602, 612, 931 N.E.2d 972 (2010). His sole witness was Dr. Susan Lewis, a forensic psychologist at the Worcester Division of the District Court Department. Dr. Lewis had seen the defendant first in 2005 for an "aid in sentencing examination" at the Erich Lindemann Mental Health Center (Lindemann Center). At that time, the defendant had been charged with indecent assault and battery on a person fourteen years old or older; "he was experiencing auditory hallucinations," along with "grandiosity in terms of the stories he was telling at that time." Dr. Lewis diagnosed him in 2005 with schizophrenia. In connection with the proceedings in this case, she also reviewed diagnoses from other doctors who had seen the defendant between 2005 and her evaluation in 2011, and testified that "there's no dispute that he's been suffering from schizophrenia."

The defendant has a significant history of hospitalization for mental illness. Specifically, between 2005 and 2009, he was hospitalized by court order on six different occasions. In May, 2007, a guardian was appointed for the defendant with . . . [authority] to consent to medication.

Apparently, there are no records available for the time period between November, 2009, when the defendant was released from the Lindemann Center—with an ankle bracelet that he immediately removed—and December, 2010, when the defendant met with a psychiatrist, presenting "with hypomanic symptoms." At that time, the defendant made it clear that "he was not going to take his medication." "He had refused it. He was experiencing manic symptoms, very agitated, irritable." In addition, apparently, the defendant was experiencing some difficulty obtaining the medication. Dr. Lewis's report states that the defendant was "insisting his Mass Health card was being declined. *Problems with his card were remedied* and the pharmacy was notified" (emphasis supplied).

In summary, Dr. Lewis opined that the defendant "has a confirmed severe and persistent mental illness that has been ongoing for the previous [seven] years. . . . [O]ne consistent finding is that his ability to perceive reality is significantly impaired. When he willingly takes his medication his symptoms are muted although never in complete remission." In addition, the defendant

> "suffers from the paraphilia called Frotteurism. Frotteurism refers to the paraphilic interest in rubbing against a non-consenting person for sexual gratification. It may involve touching any part of the body including the genital area. . . . With the overlay of non-compliance with taking his medication and the subsequent resulting psychotic symptoms it is difficult to clearly discern the relative weight of each state. By [the defendant's] present report and previous findings of psychosis from earlier evaluations, it seems likely that [the defendant] was experiencing active symptoms of mental illness at the time of the alleged events. As previously noted, at these times, [the defendant] misreads social cues and misinterprets the cues of his victims as beckoning and provocative and that she may welcome his advances. . . . It is more likely than not that during the index event [the defendant's] ability to conform his behaviors to the requirements of the law was significantly impaired by this mental state. In addition, when [the defendant] refuses to take his medication his psychotic symptoms become exacerbated and prominent affecting his impulse control. . . . His mental stability at this time is distorted by psychosis and his sexualized state, compromising his ability to appreciate the wrongfulness of his conduct."

At trial, Dr. Lewis testified that, at the time at issue, "[the defendant] was not taking his medication . . . was experiencing an increase in some of the symptoms that he's experienced over the seven years, that he misinterprets his social cues in the environment thinking an individual is communicating something to him when in actuality they are not, he is agitated, he's irritable, he is likely experiencing ideas of reference which is that an individual engages in a particular act that has nothing whatsoever to do with him and he interprets it as a message to him in some way, that given those circumstances, that he's unable to appreciate the wrongfulness of his conduct or conform his behaviors to the requirements of the law."

After hearing all the evidence, the judge requested further arguments and briefing from both counsel on the issue whether the defendant knew that his failure to take his medication would cause him to act in a manner that was against the law and, if so, whether that would permit a finding that he was criminally responsible. After reviewing those arguments, the judge found that the defendant was criminally responsible, stating that the defendant "was aware that if he failed to take his medication, it would result in this kind of behavior once again. . . . He has had enough contact with the court system and enough treatment by this doctor who testified and other doctors that make it very clear to him that he needs to take his medication or he would be right back where he started." . . . Specifically, the judge found that the defendant "knew that if he didn't take his medication" he was likely to commit further crimes "and he went ahead anyway and stopped taking his medication." On that basis, the judge found the defendant criminally responsible.

Discussion . . . .

Some things are not in dispute. The defendant is mentally ill, suffering from a major mental illness as well as a separate personality disorder. As noted, despite some history of exaggeration of symptoms when it served his purposes, he also has a long history of treatment and hospitalization for mental illness. In addition, the defendant has a significant history of noncompliance with his prescribed medication and the evidence indicates that the symptoms of his mental illness never disappear completely.

In *Commonwealth v. Berry,* 457 Mass. at 617 n. 9, 931 N.E.2d 972, the court set out a jury instruction for cases "[w]here the Commonwealth offers evidence that the defendant knew or had reason to know of the effects of drugs or alcohol on [his] . . . mental disease." The instruction explained that, "if the Commonwealth has proved beyond a reasonable doubt that the defendant consumed drugs or alcohol knowing or having reason to know that the drugs or alcohol would activate a latent mental disease or intensify an active mental disease, causing [him] to lose the substantial capacity to appreciate the wrongfulness of [his] conduct or the substantial capacity to conform [his] conduct to the requirements of the law, then you would be warranted in finding the defendant criminally responsible."

The court refined that holding the next year in *Commonwealth v. DiPadova,* 460 Mass. 424, 436–437, 951 N.E.2d 891 (2011), saying, "there was evidence . . . indicating that [the defendant] knew at the time of the murder that drugs intensified the symptoms of his mental illness. In light of that evidence, it was critical that the instructions given to the jury clarify how the defendant's knowledge was to be considered. Specifically, the jury should have been instructed that (1) if the defendant's mental illness did not reach the level of a lack of criminal responsibility until he consumed drugs, he was criminally responsible if he knew (or should have known) that the consumption would have the effect of intensifying or exacerbating his mental condition; and, in contrast, (2) if the defendant's mental illness *did* reach the level of lack of criminal responsibility even in the absence of his consumption of drugs, it was irrelevant whether he took drugs knowing that they would exacerbate that condition."

The issue in this case is arguably similar, but distinguishable in a number of ways. Obviously, here, the question is not whether the defendant knowingly and voluntarily consumed alcohol or drugs that exacerbated his inability to understand the wrongfulness of his behavior or undermined his capacity to conform his behavior to the requirements of the law, but whether his *failure* to take prescribed medication had those effects. It is not at all clear that the situations are analogous; mentally ill people fail to take prescribed medication for a myriad of reasons, including, for example, side effects that may be otherwise dangerous to their health.[12] In addition, some people are unable to obtain the appropriate medication because of lack of money or access to medical care, or problems with necessary paperwork such as may have occurred in this case. A decision not to take a prescribed medicine, though it may be ill-advised, is different in kind from a decision to ingest alcohol or drugs that are not prescribed. In addition, some medications work better than others, or take time to become effective, and the difficulty of discerning when, exactly, someone stopped taking medication and what his mental state was at that time would be challenging at best. Finally, as noted, a guardian had been appointed for this defendant in [a] 2007 [proceeding]. . . . Such a proceeding necessarily would have involved a decision that the defendant was not competent to make medical decisions at least at that time.

Ordinarily, a determination that a defendant lacks criminal responsibility by reason of mental disease or defect ends the inquiry and requires an acquittal. *Berry* and *DiPadova* represent an exception to that general rule. Those decisions each start with the proposition that the defendant in that case was not criminally responsible at the time of the crime; the question was whether the lack of responsibility was produced by the voluntary consumption of drugs or alcohol with the knowledge that it would render that defendant not criminally responsible. "The *source* of the lack of substantial capacity [was] the critical factor in determining whether the defendant [was] criminally responsible" in those cases. *DiPadova,* 460 Mass. at 431, 951 N.E.2d 891. It strains that analysis considerably to apply it to a defendant such as this, because his mental illness is not *caused* by his failure to take medication, even though the medication might alleviate it somewhat or even entirely. Whether the *Berry-DiPadova* analysis is proper in a case such as this is a difficult question and one for which our cases—and those of other jurisdictions— provide little guidance. On balance, we are persuaded that it does not apply on the facts of this case. That is, *Berry* and *DiPadova* have no applicability in a circumstance where the allegation is that the

---

[12] "Apart from side effects and illness insight, main reasons for non-compliance . . . were forgetfulness, distrust in therapist, and no subjective need for treatment. Other notable reasons were stigma and advice of relatives/acquaintances against neuroleptic medication. Gain from illness was a reason for non-compliance in 11–18% of the psychosis patients." Moritz, Peters, Karow, Deljkovic, Tonn, & Naber, Cure or Curse? Ambivalent Attitudes Towards Neuroleptic Medication in Schizophrenia and Non-Schizophrenia Patients, 1 Mental Illness 4, 4 (2009).

defendant's lack of criminal responsibility arises only from a failure to take prescribed medication. The appropriate analysis was simply whether, at the time of the incident, the defendant was criminally responsible.

Here, in seeking to resolve the question of the defendant's criminal responsibility, the judge erroneously took an additional step of inquiring whether the defendant's lack of criminal responsibility was caused by his failure to take prescribed medications. As a result, we cannot discern whether she actually made a determination that this defendant in fact lacked the requisite capacity at the time of the crime and, if so, whether that lack of capacity was due to a mental disease or defect.

In addition, even if the *Berry-DiPadova* analysis were appropriately applied to this case, the important question would be whether, at the time that the defendant refused his medication, he was criminally responsible. The evidence suggests the answer may very well be no. The Commonwealth argues that the judge addressed this issue when she said "it has also been established that whenever [the defendant] is compliant with his medication he's fine. Every single time he has had an issue, and he's a very intelligent young man from all accounts, every time he has had a problem with the court system, it has been because he is non-compliant with the medications prescribed for him." In fact, the evidence may not have been so clear cut; Dr. Lewis's testimony was only that "if he's compliant with taking his medication, the symptoms of his mental illness diminish substantially."

Second, even if the evidence established that the defendant was criminally responsible when he was compliant with his medication, there is no evidence that this defendant ever was compliant with his medication between the time that he was released from the Lindemann Center in November, 2009, and the date of this crime on January 20, 2011. There is a gap in the record of the defendant's mental health history from November, 2009, until December, 2010, when he was back in contact with his doctors. During the time between December, 2010, and January, 2011, when this offense occurred, the medical records show that the defendant appeared with "manic symptoms," was "irritable" and "agitated," and refused medication. There is also some evidence indicating that the defendant had had difficulty obtaining his medication because of insurance problems. Finally, we note that the Commonwealth's argument, taken to its logical extreme, could be used to argue that every mentally ill defendant who had ever taken helpful medication in the past, but discontinued it, was criminally responsible.

. . . [T]he question of the appropriate analysis for a situation in which a mentally ill defendant stops taking prescribed medication and the effect of that action on his criminal responsibility is a matter for which there is no guiding case law. After careful review, we are persuaded that it was prejudicial error to apply the *Berry-DiPadova* analysis here. The defendant, therefore, is entitled to a new trial. The judgment is reversed and the finding set aside.

So ordered.

———

NOTES

1. Does the *Shin* court reach the correct result? If insanity is an excuse defense used to protect those who are not morally blameworthy for their conduct, should it apply to a defendant who knows he suffers from mental illness and does not take his medication? For an argument to that effect, see Michael D. Slodov, *Criminal Responsibility and the Noncompliant Psychiatric Offender: Risking Madness*, 40 CASE. W. RES. L. REV. 271 (1989).

2. As you know from the discussion of actions and omissions, the criminal law generally punishes actions, but not omissions. In *Shin*, the court follows a similar logic by drawing a distinction between taking drugs and alcohol on the one hand, and refusing medication on the other hand. Is the court on firm ground in drawing the action/omission distinction? Isn't the discontinuation of taking medicine a type of act?

3. In *Shin*, the court focused on the unaffordability of prescriptions and side effects of medication. Should the defendant have to demonstrate financial hardship and/or side effects in his or her *own* particular case in order to invoke the insanity defense? How severe should the hardship and side effects have to be? Does the *Shin* court require inquiry into these types of questions? *See* Michael Pierce, *Commonwealth v. Shin*, 97 MASS. L. REV. 15, 16 (2015).

D. THE "PRODUCT" TEST

Durham v. United States

United States Court of Appeals, District of Columbia Circuit, 1954.
94 U.S. App. D.C. 228, 214 F.2d 862.

■ BAZELON, CIRCUIT JUDGE.

Monte Durham was convicted of housebreaking, by the District Court sitting without a jury. The only defense asserted at the trial was that Durham was of unsound mind at the time of the offense . . .

I.

Durham has a long history of imprisonment and hospitalization. In 1945, at the age of 17, he was discharged from the Navy after a psychiatric examination had shown that he suffered 'from a profound personality disorder which renders him unfit for Naval service.' In 1947 he pleaded guilty to violating the National Motor Theft Act and was placed on probation for one to three years. He attempted suicide, was taken to Gallinger Hospital for observation, and was transferred to St. Elizabeth's Hospital, from which he was discharged after two months. In

January of 1948, as a result of a conviction in the District of Columbia Municipal Court for passing bad checks, the District Court revoked his probation and he commenced service of his Motor Theft sentence. His conduct within the first few days in jail led to a lunacy inquiry in the Municipal Court where a jury found him to be of unsound mind. Upon commitment to St. Elizabeths, he was diagnosed as suffering from 'psychosis with psychopathic personality.' After 15 months of treatment, he was discharged in July 1949 as 'recovered' and was returned to jail to serve the balance of his sentence. In June 1950 he was conditionally released. He violated the conditions by leaving the District. When he learned of a warrant for his arrest as a parole violator, he fled to the 'South and Midwest obtaining money by passing a number of bad checks.' After he was found and returned to the District, the Parole Board referred him to the District Court for a lunacy inquisition, wherein a jury again found him to be of unsound mind. He was readmitted to St. Elizabeths in February 1951. This time the diagnosis was 'without mental disorder, psychopathic personality.' He was discharged for the third time in May 1951. The housebreaking which is the subject of the present appeal took place two months later, on July 13, 1951.

* * *

. . . [T]he psychiatric testimony was unequivocal that Durham was of unsound mind at the time of the crime. Dr. Gilbert, the only expert witness heard, so stated at least four times . . . And though the prosecution sought unsuccessfully in its cross- and recross-examination of Dr. Gilbert to establish that Durham was a malingerer who feigned insanity whenever he was trapped for his misdeeds, it failed to present any expert testimony to support this theory. In addition to Dr. Gilbert's testimony, there was testimony by Durham's mother to the effect that in the interval between his discharge from St. Eliabeths in May 1951, and the crime 'he seemed afraid of people' and had urged her to put steel bars on his bedroom windows.

Apparently the trial judge regarded this psychiatric testimony as 'no testimony' on two grounds: (1) it did not adequately cover Durham's condition on July 13, 1951, the date of the offense; and (2) it was not directed to Durham's capacity to distinguish between right and wrong. We are unable to agree . . .

* * *

On re-direct examination, Dr. Gilbert was asked whether he would say that Durham 'knew the difference between right and wrong on July 13, 1951; that is, his ability to distinguish between what was right and what was wrong.' He replied: 'As I have stated before, if the question of the right and wrong were propounded to him he could give you the right answer.' Then the court interrupted to ask:

'The Court. No, I don't think that is the question, Doctor- not whether he could give a right answer to a question, but whether he, himself, knew the difference between right and wrong in connection with governing his own actions. * * * If you are unable to answer, why, you can say so; I mean, if you are unable to form an opinion.

'The Witness. I can only answer this way: That I can't tell how much the abnormal thinking and the abnormal experiences in the form of hallucinations and delusions- delusions of persecution- had to do with his anti-social behavior.

'I don't know how anyone can answer that question categorically, except as one's experience leads him to know that most mental cases can give you a categorical answer of right and wrong, but what influence these symptoms have on abnormal behavior or anti-social behavior-

The Court. Well, your answer is that you are unable to form an opinion, is that it?

'The Witness. I would say that that is essentially true, for the reasons that I have given.'

* * *

II.

It has been ably argued by counsel for Durham that the existing tests in the District of Columbia for determining criminal responsibility, i.e., the so-called right-wrong test supplemented by the irresistible impulse test, are not satisfactory criteria for determining criminal responsibility. We are argued to adopt a different test to be applied on the retrial of this case. This contention has behind it nearly a century of agitation for reform.

A. The right-wrong test, approved in this jurisdiction in 1882, was the exclusive test of criminal responsibility in the District of Columbia until 1929 when we approved the irresistible impulse test as a supplementary test . . . The right-wrong test has its roots in England . . . [T]oward the middle of the nineteenth century, the House of Lords in the famous M'Naghten case restated what had become the accepted 'right-wrong' test . . . which has since been followed, not only in England but in most American jurisdictions as an exclusive test of criminal responsibility . . .

* * *

As early as 1838, Isaac Ray, one of the founders of the American Psychiatric Association, in his now classic Medical Jurisprudence of Insanity, called knowledge of right and wrong a 'fallacious' test of criminal responsibility. This view has long since been substantiated by enormous developments in knowledge of mental life. In 1928 Mr. Justice Cardozo said to the New York Academy of Medicine: 'Everyone concedes that the present (legal) definition of insanity has little relation to the truths of mental life.'

... The science of psychiatry now recognizes that a man is an integrated personality and that reason, which is only one element in that personality, is not the sole determinant of his conduct. The right-wrong test, which considers knowledge or reason alone, is therefore an inadequate guide to mental responsibility for criminal behavior ...

* * *

The fundamental objection to the right-wrong test, however, is not that criminal irresponsibility is made to rest upon an inadequate, invalid or indeterminable symptom or manifestation, but that it is made to rest upon any particular symptom. In attempting to define insanity in terms of a symptom, the courts have assumed an impossible role, not merely one for which they have no special competence ... In this field of law as in others, the fact finder should be free to consider all information advanced by relevant scientific disciplines.

... [I]n 1929, we ... added the irresistible impulse test as a supplementary test for mining criminal responsibility ...

... The term 'irresistible impulse,' however, carries the misleading implication that 'diseased mental condition(s)' produce only sudden, momentary or spontaneous inclinations to commit unlawful acts.

* * *

We find that as an exclusive criterion the right-wrong test is inadequate in that (a) it does not take sufficient amount of physic realities and scientific knowledge, and (b) it is based upon one symptom and so cannot validly be applied in all circumstances. We find that the 'irresistible impulse' test is also inadequate in that it gives no recognition to mental illness characterized by brooding and reflection and so relegates acts caused by such illness to the application of the inadequate right-wrong test. We conclude that a broader test should be adopted.

* * *

The rule we now hold must be applied ... is simply that an accused is not criminally responsible if his unlawful act was the product of mental disease or mental defect.

We use 'disease' in the sense of a condition which is considered capable of either improving or deteriorating. We use 'defect' in the sense of a condition which is not considered capable of either improving or deteriorating and which may be either congenital, or the result of injury, or the residual effect of a physical or mental disease.

Whenever there is 'some evidence' that the accused suffered from a diseased or defective mental condition at the time the unlawful act was committed, the trial court must provide the jury with guides for determining whether the accused can be held criminally responsible. We do not, and indeed could not, formulate an instruction which would be either appropriate or binding in all cases. But under the rule now announced, any instruction should in some way convey to the jury the sense and substance of the following: If you the jury believe beyond a reasonable doubt that the accused was not suffering from a diseased or defective mental condition at the time he committed the criminal act charged, you may find him guilty. If you believe he was suffering from a diseased or defective mental condition when he committed the act, but believe beyond a reasonable doubt that the act was not the product of such mental abnormality, you may find him guilty. Unless you believe beyond a reasonable doubt either that he was not suffering from a diseased or defective mental condition, or that the act was not the product of such abnormality, you must find the accused not guilty by reason of insanity. Thus your task would not be completed upon finding, if you did find, that the accused suffered from a mental disease or defect. He would still be responsible for his unlawful act if there was no causal connection between such mental abnormality and the act. These questions must be determined by you from the facts which you find to be fairly deducible from the testimony and the evidence in this case.

The questions of fact under the test we now lay down are as capable of determination by the jury as, for example, the questions juries must determine upon a claim of total disability under a policy of insurance where the state of medical knowledge concerning the disease involved, and its effects, is obscure or in conflict. In such cases, the jury is not required to depend on arbitrarily selected 'symptoms, phases or manifestations' of the disease as criteria for determining the ultimate questions of fact upon which the claim depends. Similarly, upon a claim of criminal irresponsibility, the jury will not be required to rely on such symptoms as criteria for determining the ultimate question of fact upon which such claim depends. Testimony as to such 'symptoms, phases or manifestations,' along with other relevant evidence, will go to the jury upon the ultimate questions of fact which it alone can finally determine. Whatever the state of psychiatry, the psychiatrist will be permitted to carry out his principal court function which, as we noted in Holloway v. U.S. [148 F.2d 665, 667 (D.C. Cir. 1945)], 'is to inform the jury of the character of (the accused's) mental disease (or defect). The jury's range of inquiry will not be limited to, but may include, for example, whether an accused, who suffered from a mental disease or defect did not know the difference between right and wrong, acted under the compulsion of an irresistible impulse, or had 'been deprived of or lost the power of his will * * * .' [State v. White, 270 P.2d 727, 730 (N.M. 1954).]

Finally, in leaving the determination of the ultimate question of fact to the jury, we permit it to perform its traditional function which, as we said in Holloway, is to apply 'our inherited ideas of moral responsibility to individuals prosecuted for crime * * * .' [Holloway, 148 F.2d at 667.] Juries will continue to make moral judgments, still operating under the fundamental precept that 'Our collective conscience does not allow punishment where it cannot impose blame.' [Id. at 666–667.] But in making such judgments, they will be guided by wider horizons of knowledge concerning mental life. The question will be simply whether the accused acted because of a mental disorder, and not whether he displayed particular symptoms which medical science has long recognized do not necessarily, or even typically, accompany even the most serious mental disorder.

The legal and moral traditions of the western world require that those who, of their own free will and with evil intent (sometimes called *mens rea*), commit acts which violate the law, shall be criminally responsible for those acts. Our traditions also require that where such acts stem from and are the product of a mental disease or defect as those terms are used herein, moral blame shall not attach, and hence there will not be criminal responsibility. The rule we state in this opinion is designed to meet these requirements.

Reversed and remanded for a new trial.

————

NOTES

1. The product test was actually first adopted in New Hampshire, more than eighty years before *Durham*. *See* State v. Pike, 49 N.H. 399 (1870). The decision in *Durham*—authored by nationally recognized Judge David Bazelon—gave the test far more prominence though.

2. The *Durham* decision tells us that a defendant is insane if his conduct is "the product" of a mental disease or defect. What does "product" mean though?

3. The product test announced in *Durham* initially received some favorable commentary. For example, in Sauer v. United States, 241 F.2d 640 (9th Cir. 1957) the court explained that the advantage of the *Durham* test was that "the jury is no longer required to rely on specific and particular mental symptoms in determining criminal responsibility, [and] that all relevant evidence as to mental condition goes to the jury on the ultimate question of fact." The court further noted that the "*Durham* opinion has generally been regarded as a response by the law to progress achieved in the field of psychiatry." As the *Sauer* court noted, one of the key premises of the *Durham* decision was to return power to the jury. Is that effectively what happens under a test that asks whether behavior was the product of mental illness? Doesn't the *Durham* test actually do the opposite of its intended goal by leaving it to expert witnesses to tell the jury what behavior was the product of mental illness and what behavior wasn't? Imagine that a student—Dana Defendant—in your criminal law class kills the instructor. At trial, Defendant asserts an insanity defense. An expert witness testifies that Defendant suffered from "Criminal Law Anxiety Syndrome" and that her actions were a product of that mental disease or defect. How is a jury to evaluate that testimony?

4. The product test was short lived. Less than twenty years after adopting the test, the Court of Appeals for the District of Columbia abandoned it. *See* United States v. Brawner, 471 F.2d 969 (D.C. Cir.1972). The court's principal reason for rejecting the product test was the undue dominance gained by experts giving testimony on insanity. Even Judge Bazelon, who authored the *Durham* opinion, concurred in part in *Brawner* and acknowledged flaws in the product test. *See id.* at 1010 (Bazelon, C.J. concurring in part and dissenting in part).

E. THE AMERICAN LAW INSTITUTE (A.L.I.) MODEL PENAL CODE TEST, AND ITS RECENT MODIFICATIONS

The American Law Institute, in Section 4.01 of the Model Penal Code, proposed the following insanity test:

> (1) A person is not responsible for criminal conduct if at the time of such conduct as a result of mental disease or defect he lacks substantial capacity either to appreciate the criminality [wrongfulness] of his conduct or to conform his conduct to the requirements of law.

> (2) As used in this Article, the terms "mental disease or defect" do not include an abnormality manifested only by repeated criminal or otherwise anti-social conduct.

At the outset, you should notice that while the Model Penal Code test resembles the *M'Naghten* test, it contains several important differences. First, the Model Penal Code standard modifies the *M'Naghten* standard by substituting "appreciate" for "know," and providing that a person is not guilty because of mental disease or defect who "lacks substantial capacity" to "appreciate" the "wrongfulness (or criminality)," of the conduct in question. The Model Penal Code standard is therefore less absolute than *M'Naghten*'s cognitive "right-wrong" test. Second, the Model Penal Code standard includes a volitional prong, relating to the person's capacity to conform his or her conduct to the requirements of the law. Yet, the test is careful not to use the word "impulse" and instead asks whether the defendant can "conform" his conduct. Third, the Model Penal Code test explicitly excludes mental diseases or defects whose sole manifestation is repeated criminal or other antisocial conduct (although some jurisdictions which follow the MPC have not enacted this proviso).

In adopting the Model Penal Code test (and abandoning the product test), the Court of Appeals for the District of Columbia explained that the Model Penal Code

> formulation retains the core requirement of a meaningful relationship between the mental illness and the incident charged. The language in the ALI rule is sufficiently in the common ken that its use in the courtroom, or in preparation for trial, permits a reasonable three-way communication—between

(a) the law-trained, judges and lawyers; (b) the experts and the jurymen—without insisting on a vocabulary that is either stilted or stultified, or conducive to a testimonial mystique permitting expert dominance and encroachment on the jury's function. There is no indication in the available literature that any such untoward development has attended the reasonably widespread adoption of the [Model Penal Code] rule in the Federal courts and a substantial number of state courts.

United States v. Brawner, 471 F.2d 969 (D.C. Cir. 1972).

In an appendix to its opinion the Court of Appeals for the District of Columbia in *Brawner* suggested the following instruction on insanity to be given at trial:

> The defendant in this case asserts the defense of insanity.

> You are not to consider this defense unless you have first found that the Government has proved beyond a reasonable doubt each essential element of the offense. One of these elements is the requirement [of premeditation and deliberation for first degree murder] [or of specific intent for _____], on which you have already been instructed. In determining whether that requirement has been proved beyond a reasonable doubt you may consider the testimony as to the defendant's abnormal mental condition.

> If you find that the Government has failed to prove beyond a reasonable doubt any one or more of the essential elements of the offense, you must find the defendant not guilty, and you should not consider any possible verdict relating to insanity.

> If you find that the Government has proved each essential element of the offense beyond a reasonable doubt, then you must consider whether to bring in a verdict of not guilty by reason of insanity.

> The law provides that a jury shall bring in a verdict of not guilty by reason of insanity if, at the time of the criminal conduct, the defendant, as a result of mental disease or defect, either lacked substantial capacity to conform his conduct to the requirements of the law, or lacked substantial capacity to appreciate the wrongfulness of his conduct.

> Every man is presumed to be sane, that is, to be without mental disease or defect, and to be responsible for his acts. But that presumption no longer controls when evidence is introduced that he may have a mental disease or defect.

> The term insanity does not require a showing that the defendant was disoriented as to time or place.

Mental disease [or defect] includes any abnormal condition of the mind, regardless of its medical label, which substantially affects mental or emotional processes and substantially impairs behavior controls. The term "behavior controls" refers to the processes and capacity of a person to regulate and control his conduct and his actions.

In considering whether the defendant had a mental disease [or defect] at the time of the unlawful act with which he is charged, you may consider testimony in this case concerning the development, adaptation and functioning of these mental and emotional processes and behavior controls.

mental disease v. defect

The term "mental disease" differs from "mental defect" in that the former is a condition which is either capable of improving or deteriorating and the latter is a condition not capable of improving or deteriorating.

* * *

NOTES: A.L.I.-MPC DEFINITION OF INSANITY

1. Is the Model Penal Code's more nuanced terminology—using the word "appreciate" rather than "know" and asking whether a defendant "lacks substantial capacity"—more effective than the *M'Naghten* test? Or is the more nuanced language simply semantics?

2. Following its introduction, the Model Penal Code test was widely adopted and quickly became the majority test in the United States. However, in 1981, John Hinckley attempted to assassinate President Reagan. Hinckley was subsequently found not guilty by reason of insanity under the Model Penal Code test. Public outrage then led to the Model Penal Code test falling out of favor and a national move back towards the *M'Naghten* test. *See* Paul H. Robinson & Markus D. Dubber, *The American Model Penal Code: A Brief Overview*, 10 NEW CRIM. L. REV. 319, 339–340 (2007).

3. In September, 1978, the Supreme Court of California in People v. Drew, 22 Cal.3d 333, 149 Cal.Rptr. 275, 583 P.2d 1318 (1978), discarded the *M'Naghten* rule it had followed for over a century and, instead, adopted the Model Penal Code test. The dissenting opinion of Justice Richardson felt that "a major change of the type contemplated by the majority should be made by the Legislature." How valid is that argument? Should it be the legislature or the courts that determines the language and scope of the insanity test?

4. Switching insanity tests is not as simple as it might seem. The Model Penal Code test embraced in *People v. Drew* was effectively nullified when California voters, in 1982, passed Proposition 8. Subsequently the legislature enacted California Penal Code § 25(b), which provided:

In any criminal proceeding, including any juvenile court proceeding, in which a plea of not guilty by reason of insanity is entered, this defense shall be found by the trier of fact only when the accused person proved by a preponderance of the evidence that he or she was incapable of knowing or understanding the nature and quality of his or her act *and* of distinguishing right from wrong at the time of the commission of the offense.

In People v. Horn, 158 Cal.App.3d 1014, 205 Cal.Rptr. 119 (1984), the defendant would have been insane under both the A.L.I. and the *Durham* tests; but the trial court found him legally sane on the ground that the new statute was stricter than *M'Naghten*, in that it required both prongs to be met. The appeals court reversed, and after a series of cases addressing the issue, held, in People v. Skinner, 39 Cal.3d 765, 217 Cal.Rptr. 685, 704 P.2d 752 (1985), that as a matter of judicial construction, § 25(b) was intended to restore the law to "the pre-*Drew* California version of the *M'Naghten* test."

5. The Model Penal Code test provides two possible formulations of insanity: (1) when the defendant cannot appreciate the "criminality" of his conduct; or (2) when the defendant cannot appreciate the "wrongfulness" of his conduct. What is the difference, and which one is preferable? Professor Henry Weihofen advocated for the latter approach:

> If we are to hold a person mentally responsible for his criminal act unless he is so disordered as to be unable to appreciate its criminality, we shall have to condemn as responsible and fit for punishment some of the most wildly disordered persons ever seen— for example, persons with elaborately developed delusions who hear "voices" and who kill while believing that the deed was commanded by God. Such a person may know full well that the act was a violation of the temporal law. He may even commit it precisely because he knows it is criminal: believing that he is the reincarnation of Jesus Christ, ordained again to suffer execution, he commits an act that will bring about that result. As long ago as 1800, just such a case was tried in England. That was the famous case of Hadfield, a war veteran who had been discharged from the British army on the ground of insanity. He was suffering from systematized delusions that, like Christ, he was called upon to sacrifice himself for the world's salvation. He therefore shot at King George III, so that by the appearance of crime he might be condemned, and thereby lay down his life as he felt divinely called upon to do. Hadfield was acquitted on the ground of insanity, largely because of the brilliant handling of the case by his counsel, Lord Erskine. Under the "criminality" wording of the Model Code formula, it would seem that latter-day Hadfields would have to be condemned.

Henry Weihofen, *Capacity to Appreciate "Wrongfulness" or "Criminality" Under the A.L.I.-Model Penal Code Test of Mental Responsibility*, 58 J.C.L., C. & P.S. 27, 27–28 (1967). Do you agree?

F. THE FEDERAL TEST

In 1984, Congress, for the first time, passed a statute to formulate a uniform test for insanity for use in federal criminal trials. The Insanity Defense Reform Act of 1984, 18 U.S.C. § 17 (1984) provides:

§ 17. Insanity Defense

(a) Affirmative Defense. It is an affirmative defense to a prosecution under any Federal statute that, at the time of the commission of the acts constituting the offense, the defendant, as a result of severe mental disease or defect, was unable to appreciate the nature and quality or the wrongfulness of his acts. Mental disease or defect does not otherwise constitute a defense.

(b) Burden of Proof. The defendant has the burden of proving the defense of insanity by clear and convincing evidence.

Under previous federal practice, once the presumption of sanity had been overcome by evidence of insanity produced by the defendant, the burden of proving sanity beyond a reasonable doubt then shifted to the government. The Insanity Defense Reform Act shifted the burden of proving insanity to the defendant by clear and convincing evidence, and further requires that proof of the underlying disabling illness show "severe" mental disease or defect. Does such a shifting of the burden of proof run afoul of the cases discussed in Chapter 2D on constitutional requirements related to the presumption of innocence?

PROBLEMS

Problem 13–1. Bridget took an infant from the hospital where she worked with the intent to keep it as her own. She is charged with violating the federal kidnaping statute. Prior to trial, a psychiatric report was prepared for the court and a panel of three psychiatrists agreed that Bridget was suffering from a multiple personality disorder (MPD) and that one of Bridget's alter personalities, "Rina," was controlling Bridget's conduct at the time of the kidnaping, and that the defendant's dominant or host personality, "Bridget," did not consciously participate in the abduction. At the trial, the defense plead insanity under the Federal Statute and put on the experts who testified to the above. Neither of the three examining experts could establish positively that the *alter* personality in control of Bridget at the time of the offense was legally insane, *i.e.*, "unable to appreciate the nature and quality or the wrongfulness" of her acts. Was Bridget legally insane?

Problem 13–2. Dora was a 19-year-old college student who was seeing a college counselor for some as yet undetermined psychological problems, when she became pregnant. She did not want to admit the pregnancy to herself, however, and continued with her life just as if she weren't, claiming she was eating too much and gaining weight. At nine months pregnant, the baby was born while she was alone in her college dorm room. She called 9-1-1 and when rescue and police arrived, they found the infant on the floor of the room, dead from head wounds. Dora told police she felt stomach cramps as she was doing aerobic exercises, and "then the baby dropped and the baby's head hit the floor." Dora is charged with murder. The defense wants to present expert testimony that Dora suffered from hysterical denial pregnancy syndrome. Is such testimony relevant under the federal statute on insanity?

G. DIMINISHED RESPONSIBILITY

Fisher v. United States

Supreme Court of the United States, 1946.
328 U.S. 463, 66 S.Ct. 1318, 90 L.Ed. 1382.

■ MR. JUSTICE REED delivered the opinion of the Court.

This writ of *certiorari* brings here for review the sentence of death imposed upon petitioner by the District Court of the United States for the District of Columbia after a verdict of guilty on the first count of an indictment which charged petitioner with killing by choking and strangling Catherine Cooper Reardon, with deliberate and premeditated malice. The United States Court of Appeals for the District of Columbia affirmed the judgment and sentence of the District Court.

The errors presented by the petition for certiorari and urged at our bar were, in substance, that the trial court refused to instruct the jurors that they should consider the evidence of the accused's psychopathic aggressive tendencies, low emotional response and borderline mental deficiency to determine whether he was guilty of murder in the first or in the second degree. The aggregate of these factors admittedly was not enough to support a finding of not guilty by reason of insanity. Deliberation and premeditation are necessary elements of first degree murder. . . .

The homicide took place in the library building on the grounds of the Cathedral of Saint Peter and Saint Paul, Washington, D.C., between eight and nine o'clock, a.m., on March 1, 1944. The victim was the librarian. She had complained to the verger a few days before about petitioner's care of the premises. The petitioner was the janitor. The verger had told him of the complaint. Miss Reardon and Fisher were alone in the library at the time of the homicide. The petitioner testified that Miss Reardon was killed by him immediately following insulting words from her over his care of the premises. After slapping her impulsively, petitioner ran up a flight of steps to reach an exit on a higher level but turned back down, after seizing a convenient stick of firewood, to stop her screaming. He struck her with the stick and when it broke choked her to silence. He then dragged her to a lavatory and left the body to clean up some spots of blood on the floor outside. While Fisher was doing this cleaning up, the victim "started hollering again." Fisher then took out his knife and stuck her in the throat. She was silent. After that he dragged her body down into an adjoining pump pit, where it was found the next morning. The above facts made up petitioner's story to the jury of the killing . . .

The effort of the defense is to show that the murder was not deliberate and premeditated; that it was not first but second degree murder. A reading of petitioner's own testimony, summarized above, shows clearly to us that there was sufficient evidence to support a verdict of murder in the first degree, if petitioner was a normal man in his mental and emotional characteristics . . . But the defense takes the position that the petitioner is fairly entitled to be judged as to deliberation and premeditation, not by a theoretical normality but by his own personal traits. In view of the status of the defense of partial responsibility in the District and the nation no contention is or could be made of the denial of due process. It is the contention of the defense that the mental and emotional qualities of petitioner were of such a level at the time of the crime that he was incapable of deliberation and premeditation although he was then sane in the usual legal sense. He knew right from wrong . . . His will was capable of controlling his impulses . . . Testimony of psychiatrists to support petitioner's contention was introduced. An instruction charging the jury to consider the personality of the petitioner in determining intent, premeditation and deliberation was sought and refused.

From the evidence of the psychiatrists for the defense, the jury might have concluded the petitioner was mentally somewhat below the average with minor stigma of mental subnormalcy. An expert testified that he was a psychopathic personality of a predominantly aggressive type. There was evidence that petitioner was unable by reason of a deranged mental condition to resist the impulse to kill Miss Reardon. All evidence offered by the defense was accepted by the trial court. The prosecution had competent evidence that petitioner was capable of understanding the nature and quality of his acts. Instructions in the usual form were given by the court submitting to the jury the issues of insanity, irresistible impulse, malice, deliberation and premeditation. Under these instructions . . . the jury could have determined from the evidence that the homicide was not the result of premeditation and deliberation . . .

The error claimed by the petitioner is limited to the refusal of one instruction. The jury might not have reached the result it did if the theory of partial responsibility for his acts which the petitioner urges had been submitted. Petitioner sought an instruction from the trial court which would permit the jury to weigh the evidence of his mental deficiencies, which were short of insanity in the legal sense, in determining the fact of and the accused's capacity for premeditation and deliberation . . .

Petitioner urges forcefully that mental deficiency which does not show legal irresponsibility should be declared by this Court to be a relevant factor in determining whether an accused is guilty of murder in the first or second degree, upon which an instruction should be given, as requested. It is pointed out that the courts of certain states have adopted this theory. Others have rejected it. It is urged, also, that since evidence of intoxication to a state where one guilty of the crime of murder may not be capable of deliberate premeditation requires in the District of Columbia an instruction to that effect . . . courts from this must deduce that disease and congenital defects, for which the accused may not be responsible, may also reduce the crime of murder from first to second degree. This Court reversed the Supreme Court of the Territory of Utah for failure to give a partial responsibility charge upon evidence of drunkenness in language which has been said to be broad enough to cover mental deficiency . . . It should be noted, however, that the Territory of Utah had a statute specifically establishing such a rule.

No one doubts that there are more possible classifications of mentality than the sane and the insane . . . Criminologists and psychologists have weighed the advantages and disadvantages of the adoption of the theory of partial responsibility as a basis of the jury's determination of the degree of crime of which a mentally deficient defendant may be guilty. Congress took a forward step in defining the degrees of murder so that only those guilty of deliberate and premeditated malice could be convicted of the first degree. It may be that psychiatry has now reached a position of certainty in its diagnosis and prognosis which will induce Congress to enact the rule of responsibility for crime for which petitioner contends. For this Court to force the District of Columbia to adopt such a requirement for criminal trials would involve a fundamental change in the common law theory of responsibility.

We express no opinion upon whether the theory for which petitioner contends should or should not be made the law of the District of Columbia. Such a radical departure from common law concepts is more properly a subject for the exercise of legislative power or at least for the discretion of the courts of the District . . .

Affirmed.

■ MR. JUSTICE FRANKFURTER, dissenting.

. . . According to the more enlightened rule appellate courts may review the facts in a capital case . . . Were such the scope of our review of death sentences, I should think it would be hard to escape what follows as the most persuasive reading of the record . . .

The evidence in its entirety hardly provides a basis for a finding of premeditation. He struck Miss Reardon when she called him "black n*****." He kept on when her screaming frightened him. He did not know he had killed her. There is not the slightest basis for finding a motive for the killing prior to her use of the offensive phrase. Fisher, to be sure, had Miss Reardon's ring in his possession. But it came off in his hand while he was dragging her, and he put it away when he reached home to conceal its possession from his wife. He did not run away and he cleaned up the blood "because [he] did not want to leave the library dirty, leave awful spots on the floor, [he] wanted to clean them up." He treated the spots on the floor not as evidence of crime but as part of his job to keep the library clean. Fisher was curiously unconnected with the deed, unaware of what he had done. His was a very low grade mentality, unable to realize the direction of his action and its meaning. His whole behavior seems that of a man of primitive emotions reacting to the sudden stimulus of insult and proceeding from that point without purpose or design. Premeditation implies purpose and purpose is excluded by instantaneous action. Fisher's response was an instinctive response to provocation, and premeditation means nothing unless it precludes the notion of an instinctive and uncalculated reaction to stimulus. Accordingly, if existing practice authorized us to review the facts in a capital case I should be compelled to find that the ingredients of murder in the first degree were here lacking. I would have to find that the necessary premeditation and deliberation for the infliction of a death sentence were wanting, as did the New York Court of Appeals in a case of singularly striking similarity . . .

As I have already indicated, I do not believe that the facts warrant a finding of premeditation. But, in any event, the justification for finding first-degree murder premeditation was so tenuous that the jury ought not to have been left to founder and flounder within the dark emptiness of legal jargon. The instructions to the jury on the vital issue of premeditation consisted of threadbare generalities, a jumble of empty abstractions equally suitable for any other charge of murder with none of the elements that are distinctive about this case, mingled with talk about mental disease. What the jury got was devoid of clear guidance and illumination. Inadequate direction to a jury may be as fatal as misdirection . . .

The judgment should be reversed and a new trial granted.

■ MR. JUSTICE MURPHY, dissenting.

. . . The existence of general mental impairment, or partial insanity, is a scientifically established fact. There is no absolute or clear-cut dichotomous division of the inhabitants of this world into the sane and the insane. "Between the two extremes of 'sanity' and 'insanity' lies every shade of disordered or deficient mental condition, grading imperceptibly one into another." . . .

More precisely, there are persons who, while not totally insane, possess such low mental powers as to be incapable of the deliberation and premeditation requisite to statutory first degree murder. Yet under the rule adopted by the court below, the jury must either condemn such persons to death on the false premise that they possess the mental requirements of a first degree murderer or free them completely from criminal responsibility and turn them loose among society. The jury is forbidden to find them guilty of a lesser degree of murder by reason of their generally weakened or disordered intellect.

Common sense and logic recoil at such a rule. And it is difficult to marshal support for it from civilized concepts of justice or from the necessity of protecting society. When a man's life or liberty is at stake he should be adjudged according to his personal culpability as well as by the objective seriousness of his crime. That elementary principle of justice is applied to those who kill while intoxicated or in the heat of passion; if such a condition destroys their deliberation and premeditation the jury may properly consider that fact and convict them of a lesser degree of murder. No different principle should be utilized in the case of those whose mental deficiency is of a more permanent character. Society, moreover, is ill-protected by a rule which encourages a jury to acquit a partially insane person with an appealing case simply because his mental defects cannot be considered in reducing the degree of guilt.

It is undeniably difficult, as the Government points out, to determine with any high degree of certainty whether a defendant has a general mental impairment and whether such a disorder renders him incapable of the requisite deliberation and premeditation. The difficulty springs primarily from the present limited scope of medical and psychiatric knowledge of mental disease. But this knowledge is ever increasing. And juries constantly must judge the baffling psychological factors of deliberation and premeditation, Congress having entrusted the ascertainment of those factors to the good sense of juries. It seems senseless to shut the door on the assistance which medicine and psychiatry can give in regard to these matters, however inexact and incomplete that assistance may presently be. Precluding the consideration of mental deficiency only makes the jury's decision on deliberation and premeditation less intelligent and trustworthy.

It is also said that the proposed rule would require a revolutionary change in criminal procedure in the District of Columbia and that this Court should therefore leave the matter to local courts or to Congress. I cannot agree. Congress has already spoken by making the distinction between first and second degree murder turn upon the existence of deliberation and premeditation. It is the duty of the courts below to fashion rules to permit the jury to utilize all relevant evidence directed toward those factors. But when the courts below adopt rules which substantially impair the jury's function in this respect, this Court should exercise its recognized prerogative.

If, as a result, new rules of evidence or new modes of treatment for the partly defective must be devised, our system of criminal jurisprudence will be that much further enlightened. Such progress clearly outweighs any temporary dislocation of settled modes of procedure.

Only by integrating scientific advancements with our ideals of justice can law remain a part of the living fiber of our civilization.

■ MR. JUSTICE FRANKFURTER and MR. JUSTICE RUTLEDGE join in this dissent.

■ MR. JUSTICE RUTLEDGE, dissenting.

. . . Congress introduced the requirements of premeditation and deliberation into the District of Columbia Code . . . I do not think it intended by doing so to change the preexisting law only in cases of intoxication. Hence, I cannot assent to the view that the instructions given to the jury were adequate on this phase of the case. I think the defendant was entitled to the requested instruction which was refused or one of similar import . . .

NOTES ON DIMINISHED RESPONSIBILITY

1. In 1984, Professor Stephen Morse identified two variants of so-called diminished capacity: (1) the "*mens rea* variant" which is not really a defense at all but one which, through the use of evidence of a defendant's mental condition, seeks to create a reasonable doubt in the minds of the jurors as to whether the statutorily required *mens rea* element of the crime is present; and (2), the "true" diminished capacity, which he called the defense of "partial responsibility," where the actor commits the prohibited act with the required mental state but is adjudged guilty of a lesser crime because of mental or emotional impairment short of insanity, that quantitatively reduces his moral responsibility. Professor Morse advocates abolishing the second branch of the diminished capacity concept. *See* Stephen J. Morse, *Undiminished Confusion in Diminished Capacity*, 75 J. CRIM. L. & CRIMINOLOGY 1 (1984). Which category does *Fisher* fall into?

2. The diminished responsibility (or what Professor Morse calls "partial responsibility") doctrine has not been widely adopted. The influential California Supreme Court adopted the doctrine in People v. Wolff, 61 Cal.2d 795, 40 Cal. Rptr. 271, 394 P.2d 959 (1964). Following the infamous Dan White murder trial which became known for the so-called "Twinkie" defense—the argument that junk food exacerbated his mental problems— the defense of diminished capacity was abolished in California by ballot initiative in 1982. The California Penal Code, provides: "*The defense of diminished capacity is hereby abolished . . . there shall be no defense of diminished capacity, diminished responsibility, or irresistible impulse . . .*" Cal. Pen. Code § 25 also now places the burden of proof of insanity on the defendant by a preponderance of the evidence. Under the new provision, evidence of diminished capacity may still be considered as part of the sentencing determination however.

3. Most other states have likewise rejected the idea of partial responsibility. *See Mental or Emotional Condition as Diminishing Responsibility for Crime*, 22 A.L.R.3d 1228 (cataloging cases from across the country). Why might courts decline to follow the lead of the California Supreme Court and judicially adopt the doctrine of diminished responsibility? Consider the explanation offered by the Court of Appeals of Maryland:

> We here affirm our position that the concepts of both diminished capacity and insanity involve a moral choice by the community to withhold a finding of responsibility and its consequence of punishment, and on this basis are indistinguishable. Accordingly, because the legislature, reflecting community morals has, by its definition of criminal insanity already determined which states of mental disorder ought to relieve one from criminal responsibility, this court is without authority to impose our views in this regard even if they differed.

Johnson v. State, 292 Md. 405, 439 A.2d 542 (1982). Is the court correct that insanity is the only available option because the legislature has declined to adopt any other formulation for reducing responsibility? Put differently, is insanity all or nothing?

4. Do you have a firm opinion on whether states should adopt a diminished responsibility doctrine that allows for conviction on a lower offense? The leading authority on diminished responsibility—Professor Morse—has wavered. After decades of criticizing it, Professor Morse advocated a doctrine of "guilty but partially responsible." In a 1998 article, he noted that "I should confess at the outset that in previous writing I have rejected the adoption of a generic partial responsibility defense on the grounds that morality did not require it and that the practical costs of adopting it would be unacceptably large. I now believe, on further reflection, that the moral claim is sufficiently weighty to justify bearing the potential practical costs." Stephen J. Morse, *Excusing and the New Excuse Defenses: A Legal and Conceptual Review*, 23 CRIME & JUST. 329, 373 (1998).

5. As noted above, even though California now rejects diminished responsibility at the guilt stage of trials, it is relevant at sentencing. This is not an unusual approach. The Federal Sentencing Guidelines provide for downward departures from the guideline sentence for nonviolent offenders in cases where a "significantly reduced mental capacity . . . contributed to the commission of the offense." UNITED STATES SENTENCING GUIDELINES MANUAL § 5K2.13 (2011); *See, e.g.*, United States v. Checoura, 176 F. Supp. 2d 310 (D.N.J. 2001) (compulsive gambling disorder). A United States District Court in the prosecution of a Chicago lawyer, who had defrauded her law firm of more than $900,000, used the defendant's "diminished mental capacity" resulting from the taking of asthma medication and other prescription as a justification for a departure from federal sentencing guidelines. *See* Laura Gatland, *Lawyer Sentenced*, ABA J. Oct. 1997, at 24. In another infamous case, a defendant embezzled more than $240,000 from her employer to fuel her compulsive shopping addiction. Rather than sentence her to a prison term under the Federal Sentencing Guidelines, the trial judge found diminished responsibility from the compulsive shopping and sentenced the defendant to probation. The Court of Appeals reversed on the grounds that there was a lack of evidence of impaired capacity. *See* United States v. Roach, 296 F.3d 565 (7th Cir. 2002). Assuming there was sufficient evidence of mental impairment, should compulsive shopping be a valid reason for a sentencing reduction?

H. ABOLISHING OR LIMITING THE INSANITY DEFENSE

In the wake of the successful insanity defense (under the *Durham* standard) on behalf of John W. Hinckley, Jr. at his 1982 federal trial for the attempted assassination of President Ronald Reagan in 1981, Congress and a number of state legislatures focused attention on the perceived need for abolition or modification of the insanity defense. Over thirty separate bills were introduced in Congress proposing to abolish or modify the insanity defense. Ironically, in the Hinckley case, had he been prosecuted for violation of a law of the District of Columbia (attempted murder, for example) the burden would have been upon him to prove insanity by a preponderance of the evidence; however, because he was tried for violating the Presidential Assassination Statute, a Congressional nationwide offense, the general federal law then existing imposed upon the prosecution the burden of proving sanity beyond a reasonable doubt.

Efforts in the states toward abolition of the insanity defense date back almost to *M'Naghten* itself and have continued to recur in the intervening decades.[1] Montana, for example, passed a statute providing that evidence of "insanity" would be excluded unless relevant to the mental state requirement for the offense charged. Is that approach constitutional? Is it sound public policy? Consider the next case.

State v. Korell

Supreme Court of Montana, 1984.
213 Mont. 316, 690 P.2d 992.

■ HASWELL, CHIEF JUSTICE.

Jerry Korell appeals the judgment of the Ravalli County District Court finding him guilty of attempted deliberate homicide and aggravated assault. Korell was sentenced to concurrent sentences of thirty-five and fifteen years at the Montana State Prison. Korell's defense

---

[1]   See, e.g., Rood, Abolition of the Defense of Insanity in Criminal Cases, 9 MICH. L.REV. 126 (1910); Keedy, Insanity and Criminal Responsibility, 30 HARV. L. REV. 535 (1917); Wilbur, Should the Insanity Defense to a Criminal Charge be Abolished?, 8 A.B.A.J. 631 (1922); e.g., Goldstein & Katz, Abolish the "Insanity Defense"—Why Not?, 72 YALE L.J. 853 (1963); Morris, Madness and the Criminal Law, 1982; Dershowitz, Abolishing the Insanity Defense; The Most Significant Feature of the Administration's Criminal Code—An Essay, 9 CRIM. L. BULL. 434 (1973); Morris, Psychiatry and the Dangerous Criminal, 41 SO. CAL. L. REV. 514 (1968); Thomas, Breaking of the Stone Tablet: Criminal Law Without the Insanity Defense, 19 IDAHO L. REV. 239 (1983); Morris, The Criminal Responsibility of the Mentally Ill, 33 SYRAC. L. REV. 477 (1982). Taking a different position, see e.g., Wexler, An Offense-Victim Approach to Insanity Defense Reform, 26 ARIZ. L. REV. 17 (1984); Arenella, Reflections on Current Proposals to Abolish or Reform the Insanity Defense, 8 AM.J.L. & MED. 271 (1982); Morse, Excusing the Crazy: The Insanity Defense Reconsidered, 58 SO.CAL.L.REV. 777 (1985).

at trial was that he lacked the requisite criminal mental state by reason of his insanity. On appeal his primary contention is that the Montana statutory scheme deprived him of a constitutional right to raise insanity as an independent defense.

Jerry Korell is a Viet Nam veteran who had several disturbing experiences during his tour of duty. The exact nature of the trauma was never fully documented. Friends and family agree that he was a different person when he returned from the service. Between Korell's honorable discharge in 1970 and the present events, he was twice admitted to VA hospitals for psychological problems and treated with anti-psychotic drugs. In 1976 he was jailed briefly in Boise, Idaho, for harassing and threatening the late Senator Frank Church.

The basic nature of Korell's problems was that he would periodically slip into paranoid phases during which he had trouble relating to male authority figures. His mental health varied dramatically. In the poorer times his family entertained thoughts about having him civilly committed. His VA hospitalizations were voluntary and neither of the stays were of such length that he was fully evaluated or treated.

In 1980 Korell entered a community college program for echocardiology in Spokane, Washington. Echocardiology is the skill associated with recording and interpreting sonograms of the heart for diagnostic purposes. In March 1982 he was sent to Missoula to serve a clinical externship at St. Patrick's Hospital. Korell's supervisor at the hospital was Greg Lockwood, the eventual victim of this crime.

Korell's relationship with Lockwood deteriorated for a variety of work-related reasons. Foremost was Korell's belief that he was worked excessively by Lockwood. At this time Korell was subjected to what expert testimony labeled psychological stressors: a divorce by his wife, financial problems and the pressures of graduation requirements.

In April 1982 Korell wrote a letter to the hospital administrator complaining about his supervisor, Lockwood. Korell was transferred to an externship in Spokane, and Lockwood was placed on probation. Both men retained very bitter feelings about the incident. Lockwood stated to friends he would see to it that Korell was never hired anywhere in echocardiology. Korell may have learned of Lockwood's statements.

Korell's actions in the next two months indicate a great deal of confusion. He set fire to a laundromat because he lost nine quarters in a machine and was tired of being ripped off. He set fire to a former home of his wife because she had bad feelings about it.

Released on bail from these incidents, he returned to Missoula in June 1982. Psychiatric testimony introduced at trial indicates that Korell felt he had to kill Lockwood before Lockwood killed him. He removed a handgun from a friend's home, had another acquaintance purchase ammunition, and on the evening of June 25, 1982, drove to the Lockwood home in the Eagle Watch area of the Bitterroot Valley. Shirley Lockwood, Greg's wife, saw the unfamiliar vehicle approach the house. Greg Lockwood was lying on the living room floor at the time watching television. Korell entered the house through a side door and began firing. Although wounded, Greg Lockwood managed to engage the defendant in a struggle. A shot was fired in the direction of Lockwood's wife. Korell grabbed a kitchen knife and both men were further injured before Lockwood was able to subdue Korell.

Korell was charged with attempted deliberate homicide and aggravated assault. The defendant gave notice of his intent to rely on a mental disease or defect to prove that he did not have the particular state of mind which is an essential element of the offense charged. Prior to trial he sought a writ of supervisory control declaring that he had a right to rely on the defense that he was suffering from a mental disease or defect at the time he committed the acts charged. The writ was denied by this Court on December 20, 1982, and the case proceeded to trial.

Several psychologists and psychiatrists testified on Korell's mental condition. The defense sought to establish by its expert witnesses and numerous character witnesses that Korell was a disturbed man who was psychotic at the time the crimes were committed. It was argued that his actions when he entered the Lockwood home were not voluntary acts. The State produced its own expert witnesses who testified on Korell's mental condition. Four doctors testified in all, two for the prosecution and two for the defense. Three of the four stated Korell had the capacity to act knowingly or purposely, the requisite mental state for the offenses, when he entered the Lockwood home.

* * *

In keeping with Montana's current law on mental disease or defect, the jury was instructed that they could consider mental disease or defect only insofar as it negated the defendant's requisite state of mind. The jury returned guilty verdicts for the attempted deliberate homicide and aggravated assault.

[This case raises the question of whether there is a constitutional right to raise insanity as an independent defense to criminal charges.]

* * *

I. CONSTITUTIONAL CHALLENGE

A. *Background*

In 1979 the Forty-Sixth Session of the Montana Legislature enacted House Bill 877. This Bill abolished use of the traditional insanity defense in Montana and substituted alternative procedures for considering a criminal defendant's mental condition. Evidence of mental disease or defect is now considered at three phases of a criminal proceeding.

Before trial, evidence may be presented to show that the defendant is not fit to proceed to trial. Section 46–14–221, MCA. Anyone who is unable to understand the proceedings against him or assist in his defense may not be prosecuted. Section 46–14–103, MCA.

During trial, evidence of mental disease or defect is admissible when relevant to prove that, at the time of the offense charged, the defendant did not have the state of mind that is an element of the crime charged, e.g., that the defendant did not act purposely or knowingly. Section 46–14–102, MCA. The State retains the burden of proving each element of the offense beyond a reasonable doubt. Defendant may, of course, present evidence to contradict the State's proof that he committed the offense and that he had the requisite state of mind at that time.

Whenever the jury finds that the State has failed to prove beyond a reasonable doubt that the defendant had the requisite state of mind at the time he committed the offense, it is instructed to return a special verdict of not guilty "for the reason that due to a mental disease or defect he could not have a particular state of mind that is an essential element of the offense charged . . ."

Finally at the dispositional stage following the trial and conviction, the sentencing judge must consider any relevant evidence presented at the trial, plus any additional evidence presented at the sentencing hearing, to determine whether the defendant was able to appreciate the criminality of his acts or to conform his conduct to the law at the time he committed the offense for which he was convicted.

The sentencing judge's consideration of the evidence is not the same as that of the jury. The jury determines whether the defendant committed the offense with the requisite state of mind, e.g., whether he acted purposely or knowingly. The sentencing judge determines whether, at the time the defendant committed the offense, he was able to appreciate its criminality or conform his conduct to the law.

If the court concludes the defendant was not suffering from a mental disease or defect that rendered him unable to appreciate the criminality of his conduct or to conform his conduct to the requirements of law, normal criminal sentencing procedures are invoked.

Whenever the sentencing court finds the defendant was suffering from mental disease or defect which rendered him unable to appreciate the criminality of his conduct or to conform his conduct to the requirements of law, mandatory minimum sentences are waived. The defendant is committed to the custody of the director of institutions and placed in an appropriate institution for custody, care and treatment not to exceed the maximum possible sentence. As a practical matter, this means the defendant may be placed in the Warm Springs State Hospital under the alternative sentencing procedures. The institutionalized defendant may later petition the District Court for release from the hospital upon a showing that the individual has been cured of the mental disease or defect. If the petition is granted, the court must transfer the defendant to the state prison or place the defendant under alternative confinement or supervision. The length of this confinement or supervision must equal the original sentence.

In summary, while Montana has abolished the traditional use of insanity as a defense, alternative procedures have been enacted to deal with insane individuals who commit criminal acts.

Much has been written concerning criminal responsibility and insanity. Professor Norval Morris commented that "[r]ivers of ink, mountains of printer's lead, forests of paper have been expended on this issue . . ." Morris, *Psychiatry and the Dangerous Criminal,* 41 S.Cal.L.R. 514, 516 (1968). Yet there is a paucity of judicial opinions construing the constitutional parameters of the traditional insanity defense or the various reform proposals. This case is the first direct constitutional challenge to Montana's abolition of the affirmative insanity defense and adoption of alternative procedures in its place.

* * *

While some jurisdictions, most notably the federal courts, have given the prosecution the burden of proving the defendant's sanity beyond a reasonable doubt, such practice is not the rule in Montana. Prior to 1979, insanity was treated as an affirmative defense that had to be established by the accused by a preponderance of the evidence . . . [I]t is sufficient that the State prove beyond a reasonable doubt the requisite mental state, e.g., purposely or knowingly, that is an element of the offense charged.

* * *

Review of our case law reveals that the constitutionality of the legislature's abolition of the affirmative defense of insanity has not previously been decided. Korell's present challenge is based on the Fourteenth Amendment guarantee of due process of law and the Eighth Amendment prohibition against cruel and unusual punishment.

B. *Due Process Considerations*

1. Fundamental Rights

The due process clause of the Fourteenth Amendment was intended in part to protect certain fundamental rights long recognized under the common law. Appellant contends that the insanity defense is so embedded in our legal history that it should be afforded status as a fundamental right. He argues that the defense was firmly established as a part of the common law long before our federal constitution was adopted and is essential to our present system of ordered liberty.

The United States Supreme Court has never held that there is a constitutional right to plead an insanity defense. Moreover, the Court has noted that the significance of the defense is properly left to the states:

"We cannot cast aside the centuries-long evolution of the collection of interlocking and overlapping concepts which the common law has utilized to assess the moral accountability of an individual for his antisocial deeds. The doctrines of *actus reus, mens rea,* insanity, mistake, justification, and duress have historically provided the tools for a constantly shifting adjustment of the tension between the evolving aims of the criminal law and changing religious, moral, philosophical, and medical views of the nature of man. This process of adjustment has always been thought to be the province of the States."

Powell v. Texas (1968), 392 U.S. 514, 535–536, 88 S.Ct. 2145, 2156, 20 L.Ed.2d 1254, 1269.

* * *

For centuries evidence of mental illness was admitted to show the accused was incapable of forming criminal intent. Insanity did not come to be generally recognized as an affirmative defense and an independent ground for acquittal until the nineteenth century. Morris, *The Criminal Responsibility of the Mentally Ill,* 33 Syracuse L.R. 477, 500 (1982); American Medical Association, *The Insanity Defense in Criminal Trials and Limitations of Psychiatric Testimony,* Report of the Board of Trustees, at 27 (1983). The defense grew out of the earlier notions of *mens rea.*

We reject appellant's contention that from the earliest period of the common law, insanity has been recognized as a defense. What we recognize is that one who lacks the requisite criminal state of mind may not be convicted or punished.

Three older state court decisions have found state statutes abolishing the insanity defense to be unconstitutional. *State v. Lange* (1929), 168 La. 958, 123 So. 639; *Sinclair v. State* (1931), 161 Miss. 142, 132 So. 581; *State v. Strasburg* (1910), 60 Wash. 106, 110 P. 1020. These decisions are distinguishable in that they interpret statutes that precluded *any* trial testimony of mental condition, including that which would cast doubt on the defendant's state of mind at the time he committed the charged offense. The Montana statutes in question expressly allow evidence of mental disease or defect to be introduced to rebut proof of defendant's state of mind.

The United States Supreme Court refused in 1952 to accept the argument that the Due Process Clause required the use of a particular insanity test or allocation of burden of proof. *Leland v. Oregon* (1952), 343 U.S. 790, 72 S.Ct. 1002, 96 L.Ed. 1302. The Oregon statute upheld in *Leland* required the defendant to prove insanity beyond a reasonable doubt. This allocation of proof was found constitutionally sound because the State retained the burden to prove the requisite state of mind and other essential criminal elements. The State's due process burden of proof was further emphasized in *In Re Winship* (1970). *Winship* established that the prosecution must prove beyond a reasonable doubt every element constituting the crime charged.

The Montana statutory scheme is consistent with the dictates of *Leland* and *Winship*. The 1979 amendments to the criminal code do not unconstitutionally shift the State's burden of proof of the necessary elements of the offense. The State retains its traditional burden of proving all elements beyond a reasonable doubt.

2. The Delusional Defendant

In addition to asserting that the insanity defense is a fundamental constitutional right, the appellant contends that insanity is a broader concept than *mens rea*. Korell argues that individuals may be clearly insane yet also be capable of forming the requisite intent to commit a crime. For example, an accused may form intent to harm under a completely delusional perception of reality or act without volitional control. It is defendant's position that the due process of these defendants is compromised by state law which permits conviction of delusional defendants and those who act without volitional control.

Addressing the delusional defendant first, we note that planning, deliberation and a studied intent are often found in cases where the defendant lacks the capacity to understand the wrongfulness of his acts. Fink & Larene, *In Defense of the Insanity Defense,* 62 Mich.B.J. 199 (1983). Illustrations include the assassin acting under instructions of God, the mother drowning her demonically-possessed child, and the man charging up Montana Avenue on a shooting spree believing he is Teddy Roosevelt on San Juan Hill. Defendant contends that these people could properly be found guilty by a jury under current Montana law.

As some commentators have noted, the 1979 amendments to the law on mental disease or defect may actually have lowered the hurdle mentally disturbed defendants must clear to be exculpated. In order to be acquitted, the defendant need only cast a reasonable doubt in the minds of the jurors that he had the requisite mental state. See, Bender, *After Abolition: The Present State of the Insanity Defense in Montana,* 45 Mont.L.R. 133, 141 (1984). As a practical matter, the prosecutor who seeks a conviction of a delusional and psychotic defendant will be faced with a heavy burden of proof.

Assuming the delusional defendant is found guilty by a jury, factors of mitigation must be considered by the sentencing judge in accordance with section 46–14–311, MCA. The fact that the proven criminal state of mind was formed by a deranged mind would certainly be considered. In addition, a defendant can be sentenced to imprisonment only after the sentencing judge specifically finds that the defendant was *not* suffering, at the time he committed the offense, from a mental disease that rendered him unable to appreciate the criminality of his conduct or to conform his conduct to the requirements of law.

3. The Volitionally-Impaired Defendant

The test of mental disease or defect that was afforded defendants prior to 1979 read as follows:

> "A person is not responsible for criminal conduct if at the time of such conduct as a result of mental disease or defect he is unable either to appreciate the criminality of his conduct or to conform his conduct to the requirements of the law."

Section 46–14–101, MCA (1978).

It is the second prong of this standard, the volitional aspect of mental disease or defect, that appellant claims has been eliminated. He argues that there are those who lack the ability to conform their conduct to the law and that elimination of the involuntariness defense is unconstitutional.

The volitional aspect of mental disease or defect has not been eliminated from our criminal law. Consideration of a defendant's ability to conform his conduct to the law has been moved from the jury to the sentencing judge. The United States Supreme Court found in *Leland,* that the "irresistible impulse" test of insanity was not implicit in the concept of ordered liberty. Additionally, the minimum requirements of any criminal offense are still a voluntary act and companion mental state. Section 45–2–202, MCA, provides that "[a] material element of every offense is a voluntary act . . . ."

This Court has not judicially recognized the automatism defense. Applications of the defense may exist where a defendant acts during convulsions, sleep, unconsciousness, hypnosis or seizures. Our criminal code's provisions requiring a voluntary act and defining involuntary conduct adequately provide for such defenses. See sections 45–2–202 and 45–2–101(31), MCA.

To the extent that the 1979 criminal code revisions allegedly eliminated the defense of insanity-induced volitional impairment, we find no abrogation of a constitutional right.

C. *Eighth Amendment Considerations*

Appellant next contends that abolition of the affirmative defense of insanity violates the Eighth Amendment's prohibition of cruel and unusual punishment . . .

* * *

Prior to sentencing, the court is required to consider the convicted defendant's mental condition at the time the offense was committed. This review is mandatory whenever a claim of mental disease or defect is raised. The plain language of the statute reads: ". . . the sentencing court *shall* consider any relevant evidence . . ." Section 46–14–311, MCA (emphasis added). Whenever the sentencing court finds the defendant suffered from a mental disease or defect, as described in section 46–14–

311, MCA, the defendant must be placed in an "... appropriate institution for custody, care and treatment ..." Section 46–14–312(2), MCA.

These requirements place a heavy burden on the courts and the department of institutions. They serve to prevent imposition of cruel and unusual punishment upon the insane. Since the jury is properly preoccupied with proof of state of mind, it is imperative that the sentencing court discharge its responsibility to independently review the defendant's mental condition.

It is further argued that subjecting the insane to the stigma of a criminal conviction violates fundamental principles of justice. We cannot agree. The legislature has made a conscious decision to hold individuals who act with a proven criminal state of mind accountable for their acts, regardless of motivation or mental condition. Arguably, this policy does not further criminal justice goals of deterrence and prevention in cases where an accused suffers from a mental disease that renders him incapable of appreciating the criminality of his conduct. However, the policy does further goals of protection of society and education. One State Supreme Court Justice who wrestled with this dilemma observed: "In a very real sense, the confinement of the insane is the punishment of the innocent; the release of the insane is the punishment of society." *State v. Stacy* (Tenn.1980), 601 S.W.2d 696, 704 (Henry, J., dissenting).

Our legislature has acted to assure that the attendant stigma of a criminal conviction is mitigated by the sentencing judge's personal consideration of the defendant's mental condition and provision for commitment to an appropriate institution for treatment, as an alternative to a sentence of imprisonment.

For the foregoing reasons we hold that Montana's abolition of the insanity defense neither deprives a defendant of his Fourteenth Amendment right to due process nor violates the Eighth Amendment proscription against cruel and unusual punishment. There is no independent constitutional right to plead insanity.

* * *

■ SHEEHY, JUSTICE, dissenting:

It is a matter of coincidence that I dictate this dissent on Sunday, November 11, 1984. This used to be called Armistice Day, and the television news is full of reports of a reunion of Viet Nam war veterans in Washington, D.C. Coincident with their reunion is the dedication of a memorial statuary to Viet Nam war veterans, the seven-foot tall representation of three Viet Nam war servicemen who seem to be peering intently at an earlier Viet Nam war memorial on which is inscribed the names of more than 58,000 servicemen who lost their lives in that war.

It was a war in which nothing was won and much was lost. A part of that loss, not recognized or admitted by the authorities at first, was the damaging effect to the cognitive abilities of some that served in the war. Only recently has there been positive acceptance that there does exist in some ex-servicemen a post-Viet Nam war traumatic syndrome.

Jerry Korell, the evidence is clear, is a victim of that syndrome. Before his term of service, he was a mentally functional citizen. After his return from service, he is mentally dysfunctional. We can measure our maturity about how we meet such problems by the fact that Jerry Korell now will inevitably spend a great part of his life in jail for his actions arising out of that dysfunction.

Jerry Korell's dysfunction can be traced almost directly to the Viet Nam war. There are thousands of others whose mental aberrations have no such distinct origins. From genes, from force of environment, from physical trauma, or from countless other causes, their actions do not meet the norm. You know them well—the strange, the different, the weird ones.

Sometimes (not really often it should be said) these mentally aberrant persons commit a criminal act. If the criminal act is the product of mental aberration, and not of a straight-thinking cognitive direction, it would seem plausible that society should offer treatment, but if not treatment, at least not punishment. The State of Montana is not such a society.

I would hold that Montana's treatment of the insanity defense is unconstitutional . . .

* * *

Before 1979, it was clear in Montana that persons suffering from a mental disease or defect were not responsible for their criminal conduct. Former section 95–501, R.C.M. 1947, provided:

> "(1) A person is not responsible for criminal conduct if at the time of such conduct as a result of mental disease or defect he is unable either to appreciate the criminality of his conduct or to conform his conduct with the requirements of law."

> "(2) As used in this chapter, the term 'mental disease or defect' does not include an abnormality manifested only by repeated criminal or other antisocial conduct."

The provisions of former section 95–501, R.C.M. 1947, reflected the American Law Institute position with respect to the insanity defense. The language found in subsection (2) of section 95–501, R.C.M. 1947, was a caveat formed by the ALI to restrict the definition of mental disease or defect.

In 1979, the legislature acted to repeal and eliminate what was subdivision (1) of section 95–501, R.C.M. 1947. What remains are only the provisions of present section 46–14–101, MCA, which defines mental disease or defect in the same manner as subdivision (2) of former section 95–501, supra.

Thus, the 1979 legislature removed any statutory direction that a person is not responsible for criminal conduct if at the time of the conduct, as a result of mental disease or defect, he was unable to appreciate the criminality of his conduct or to conform his conduct to the requirements of law.

The 1979 legislature went further. While one may not use the defense of mental disease or defect unless within ten days of entering plea one files a written notice of a purpose to rely on such mental disease or defect to prove that one did not have a particular state of mind which is the essential element of the offense charged (section 46–14–201, MCA), once one has filed such a notice, the court thereupon appoints a psychiatrist or requests the superintendent of the Montana State Hospital to designate a qualified psychiatrist to examine and report upon the mental condition of the defendant. Section 46–14–202, MCA.

* * *

Section 46–14–213, MCA, provides that when the psychiatrist who has examined the defendant testifies, his testimony may include his *opinion* "as to the ability of the defendant *to have a particular state of mind* which is an element of the offense charged." The statute takes away from the psychiatrist, and from the jury, the previous test of whether the defendant lacked the capacity to appreciate the criminality of his conduct or his ability to conform his conduct to the requirements of the law. The statute instead places in the power of the psychiatrist, and takes from the jury, the determination of *whether the defendant had the particular state of mind* which is an element of the offense charged. Thus is the defendant deprived of his right of trial by jury as to every element of the crime charged against him. See, *In Re Winship* (1970), 397 U.S. 358, 90 S.Ct. 1068, 25 L.Ed.2d 368.

The elements of the crime of deliberate homicide in Montana are a voluntary act (section 45–2–202, MCA), coupled with either purpose or knowledge (section 45–5–102, MCA). Thus the jury must be instructed, even where the insanity is an issue, that if the defendant acted purposely, or with knowledge, he is guilty of the offense. The jury is then instructed that a person acts knowingly if, with respect to the conduct, he is aware of his conduct. Section 45–2–101(33), MCA.

The jury is also instructed that the defendant acts purposely if it is his conscious object to engage in that conduct or to cause that result. Section 45–2–101(58), MCA. No consideration is given by the jury as to whether the defendant lacks substantial capacity to appreciate the criminality of his conduct, or whether he is unable to conform his conduct to the requirements of the law. If the psychiatrist has testified that the defendant had the state of mind required as an element of the crime, that is, in the case of deliberate homicide, purpose or knowledge, the defendant is criminally guilty. The jury never gets to determine if the defendant acted by force of mental aberration.

In a case under present Montana law, therefore, when the defendant relies on insanity to explain the crime of deliberate homicide, the jury is led to the inevitable conclusion by *managed testimony* that he is indeed guilty of the crime.

Montana's statutory scheme seeks to ameliorate the managed conviction of the insane defendant by providing that at his *sentencing,* he having been convicted of a criminal act, the sentencing judge may take into consideration his insanity! At the sentencing, the judge, and not the jury, shall for the first time consider whether the defendant was suffering from a mental disease or defect which rendered him unable to appreciate the criminality of his conduct or to conform his conduct to the requirements of law.

For the reasons foregoing, I would hold the statutory scheme pertaining to insane defendants in Montana unconstitutional. I do not hold with the majority that there is no independent constitutional right to plead insanity. I consider that position the ultimate insanity. I would hold that he has an independent constitutional right to trial by jury of the fact of his ability to commit a crime by mental aberration.

* * *

I would reverse and remand for a new trial, and direct the District Court to instruct the jury on the ALI formulations respecting insanity as applied to criminal acts.

I suggest a retrial on the basis of the ALI formulations not because I consider those formulations the last word on the subject, but because we do have remaining in our statutes some recognition of the ALI formulations with respect to the insanity defense. Under present law the District Court must look to the ALI formulations to determine the extent of the sentence to be imposed, section 46–14–311, MCA. The real problem facing this Court is that the abolition by the legislature in 1979 of mental disease or defect as an exculpatory defense leaves a cavity in our criminal law that is the obligation of the legislature to fill. Unless we now recognize the ALI formulations on the basis that there is legislative recognition of their validity in the sentencing process, we have no legislative direction in the statutes for the insanity defense.

It is curious that Montana abolished the insanity defense in 1979, before the onset of the Hinckley trial. Hinckley's attack on President Reagan, and the subsequent acquittal of Hinckley in June 1982, prompted a rash of enactments and proposals for enactments with respect to the insanity defense. The Standing Committee on Association Standards for Criminal Justice of the American Bar Association at the time of the Hinckley verdict had been considering mental health law and criminal justice issues for close to a year and a half. The Hinckley verdict triggered the Committee's consideration of key issues in order to advise Congress, state legislatures and the public in the aftermath of the concern arising from the Hinckley verdict. At least part of the credit must be given to that Standing Committee for the fact that Congress has refused so far to abolish the insanity defense.

* * *

. . . Montana's abolition of the insanity defense in 1979 been held up for criticism and disrespect by national authorities and scholars. It behooves our legislature, which will be meeting in a few months, to reexamine its mental health laws as they pertain to criminal justice and to revamp the same . . .

* * *

In the meantime, I would reverse the conviction of Jerry Korell, and return this cause for a trial on his insanity defense.

NOTES ON ABOLISHING OR LIMITING THE INSANITY DEFENSE

1. Which opinion, the majority or the dissent, do you find more persuasive? As a matter of fairness, particularly when dealing with a war veteran, is it proper to primarily leave mental illness questions to sentencing? Even if a judge imposes a lighter sentence because of mental illness, isn't there something stigmatizing about being a convicted felon? On the other hand, people who commit crimes with the requisite *mens rea* are dangerous, aren't they? Is the majority correct to say that "the release of the insane is the punishment of society"?

2. A handful of other states have adopted the same approach as Montana. *See, e.g.*, Kan. Stat. Ann. Sec. 22–3220 (providing that it is a defense to prosecution of any criminal offense that "the defendant, as a result of mental disease or defect, lacked the mental state required as an element of the offense charged. Mental disease of defect is not otherwise a defense."); Idaho Code § 18–207 ("Mental condition shall not be a defense to any charge of criminal conduct."). The Idaho Supreme Court reaffirmed the constitutionality of abolishing the insanity defense. *See* State v. Delling, 152 Idaho 122, 267 P.3d 709 (Idaho 2011). In response, a group of prominent law professors filed an amicus curiae brief urging the Supreme Court of the United States to grant certiorari in *Delling* and find the insanity defense is constitutionally required. *See* Brief of Amici Curiae 52 Criminal Law and Mental Health Professors in Support of Petitioner, Delling v. Idaho, No. 11–1515 (June 2012). Over the dissent of three justices, the Supreme Court declined to hear the case however. *See* Delling v. Idaho, 133 S. Ct. 504 (2012).

3. Not all courts are willing to defer to legislative decisions to abolish the insanity defense. In 1995, the Nevada Legislature abolished the insanity defense. In Finger v. State, 117 Nev. 548, 27 P.3d 66 (2001), the *en banc* Supreme Court decided that Nevada's statutory scheme "would permit an individual to be convicted of a criminal offense under circumstances where the individual lacked the mental capacity to form the applicable intent to commit the crime, a necessary element of the offense." The court stated that "legal insanity is a well-established and fundamental principle of the law of the Unites States" and concluded that "[s]uch a statutory scheme violates the due process clauses of the United States and Nevada Constitutions." Is the insanity defense so engrained in our history, principles, and values that states must continue to provide for it?

4. Arizona has taken a different approach in limiting claims of mental illness. Unlike Montana, Arizona recognizes an affirmative defense of insanity. *See* Ariz. Rev. Stat. Sec. 13–502. A defendant in Arizona cannot be found insane unless he demonstrates that "at the time of the commission of the criminal act [he] was afflicted with a mental disease or defect of such severity that [he] did not know the criminal act was wrong." However, a defendant cannot point to mental illness to rebut the prosecution's claim that he had the requisite *mens rea*. Put differently, Arizona does not allow evidence of a mental disorder other than insanity, thus eliminating claims of lack of *mens rea* and diminished capacity. It is nearly the opposite of the approach taken by Montana. In Clark v. Arizona, 548 U.S. 735, 776 (2006), the Supreme Court upheld the Arizona framework, explaining that "[b]ecause allowing mental-disease evidence on *mens rea* can ... easily mislead, it is not unreasonable to address that tendency by confining consideration of this kind of evidence to insanity, on which a defendant may be assigned the burden of persuasion." Unfortunately, the *Clark* decision was not a model of clarity and legal scholars disagree about the Court's actual holding. *See* Peter Westen, *The Supreme Court's Bout with Insanity: Clark v. Arizona*, 4 OHIO ST. J. CRIM. L. 143 (2006) (arguing that the Court did not actually answer the questions it posed); Ronald J. Allen, *Clark v. Arizona: Much (Confused) Ado About Nothing*, 4 OHIO ST. J. CRIM. L. 135 (2006) ("Unlike Professor Westen, . . . I think the Court actually did what it purported to do, which is to hold that the exclusion of evidence in this case on certain issues was not sufficiently unreasonable or ill justified to amount to a due process violation. . .").

5. Should defendants effectively get two bites at the apple: first to argue that mental illness precluded them from forming the *mens rea* required for the crime, and second to argue that even if they had the *mens rea* that they did not understand their conduct was wrongful? Or is it legitimate for states to eliminate one of those avenues? Put differently, do we really need a stand-alone insanity defense? If we punish people based on retribution and what they deserve, should mental illness simply factor into questions of whether a person acted with the required *mens rea*, in self defense, or under duress? For a compelling argument in this regard, see Christopher Slobogin, *An End to Insanity: Recasting the Role of Mental Disability in Criminal Cases*, 86 VA. L. REV. 1199 (2000).

6. As a matter of policy, does it make sense to excuse people from criminal liability because of their mental health problems? Many people in society have lots of different types of problems. Some defendants grew up in abusive families; others received inadequate education from failing public schools; still others live in impoverished neighborhoods where it is practically impossible to find legitimate employment and selling illegal drugs is the only viable option for earning a living. Why do we excuse the insane, but not others who have faced major life obstacles? Is it because the insane had no choice in their actions, while the poor, uneducated, and abused had an (albeit difficult) choice not to commit crime?

7. Although only a few states sought to abolish the insanity defense altogether in the aftermath of the Hinckley verdict, a large number of states adopted a less dramatic, but nevertheless important, change. In addition to the traditional verdicts of guilty, not guilty, or not guilty by reason of insanity, states provided the jury with the option to find defendants "guilty but mentally ill." Although the formulations vary by state, the general idea was that a guilty but mentally ill defendant would be sentenced to prison but would have the opportunity to receive treatment in prison or a mental hospital. Critics were quick to pounce, contending that the new verdict did not increase the number of prisoners receiving mental health treatment and that it therefore was really no difference than a guilty verdict. *See* Christopher Slobogin, *Guilty But Mentally Ill: An Idea Whose Time Should Not Have Come*, 53 GEO. WASH. L. REV. 494 (1985). More colorfully, consider the description of a leading mental health expert and a prominent judge:

> GBMI is a politically expedient "third-way" fraud. It has nothing to do with responsibility and nothing to do with treatment. It is the equivalent of a verdict of "guilty but herpes," with no guarantee that the herpes will be treated or even noticed once the defendant leaves the courtroom. Its only purpose is to give legislatures political cover and to lull jurors into mistakenly believing their GBMI verdicts might mean that defendants with mental disorder who receive this verdict will be given special treatment and attention, or otherwise dealt with more mercifully at sentencing or in prison.

Stephen J. Morse & Morris B. Hoffman, *The Uneasy Entente Between Legal Insanity and Mens Rea: Beyond Clark v. Arizona*, 97 J. CRIM. L. & CRIMINOLOGY 1071, 1122–1123 (2007). Inevitably, defendants raised unsuccessful constitutional challenges to the guilty but mentally ill verdict. *See, e.g.*, State v. Hornsby, 326 S.C. 121, 484 S.E.2d 869, 872–873 (1997); Taylor v. State, 440 N.E.2d 1109 (Ind.1982). Today, approximately a dozen states provide the jury with the option to find the defendant guilty but mentally ill. *See* Clark v. Arizona, 548 U.S. 735, 752 n.19 (2006) (collecting statutes).

8. Does the public focus on the wrong topics when thinking about the criminal justice system? For instance, everyone from average citizens to legislators, to judges pay a tremendous amount of attention to capital punishment. Yet, for all of the media, legislative, and judicial attention it receives, death sentences are rarely handed down and even more rarely carried out. *See* Douglas A. Berman, *A Capital Waste of Time: Examining the Supreme Court's "Culture of Death,"* 34 Ohio N.U. L. Rev. 861 (2008). Is the focus on the insanity defense—and the efforts to limit or abolish it—similarly out of proportion with its impact in the real world? One study found that not guilty by reason of insanity verdicts occurred in only ½ of 1 percent of all cases handled by public defenders in New Jersey. *See* NATIONAL MENTAL HEALTH ASSOCIATION, MYTHS & REALITIES: A REPORT OF THE NATIONAL COMMISSION ON THE INSANITY DEFENSE (1983). In light of how rarely the insanity defense is successfully invoked, should legislators, courts, and academics be spending time focusing on other more common criminal justice problems?

I. THE WEIGHT OF PSYCHIATRIC TESTIMONY

People v. Wolff

Supreme Court of Califoria, 1964.
61 Cal.2d 795, 40 Cal.Rptr. 271, 394 P.2d 959.

■ SCHAUER, JUSTICE . . .

Defendant, a fifteen year old boy at the time of the crime, was charged with the murder of his mother. The juvenile court found him to be "not a fit subject for consideration" under the Juvenile Court Law, and remanded him to the superior court for further proceedings in the criminal action. To the information accusing him of murder defendant entered the single plea of "not guilty by reason of insanity," thereby admitting commission of the basic act which, if not qualified under the special plea, constitutes the offense charged . . . After considering reports of three alienists appointed to examine defendant . . . the court declared a doubt as to his mental capacity to stand trial . . . At a hearing on that issue, however, the court found defendant to be "mentally ill but not to the degree that would preclude him from cooperating with his counsel in the preparation and presentation of his defense." The plea of not guilty by reason of insanity was then tried to a jury and resulted in a verdict that defendant was legally sane at the time of the commission of the jurisdictional act of killing . . . The court determined the crime to be murder in the first degree; . . .

* * *

The Sufficiency of the Evidence of Sanity

Turning now to defendant's more specific contentions, it is first urged that "As a matter of law, [defendant] was legally insane at the time of the commission of the offense." In support of this proposition defendant stresses the fact that each of the four psychiatrists who testified at the trial stated (1) that in his *medical* opinion defendant suffers from a permanent form of one of the group of mental disorders generically known as "schizophrenia" and (2) that defendant was also *legally* insane at the time he murdered his mother. Much confusion has been engendered in this and similar cases by failure to distinguish between these two branches of the testimony and by uncritical acceptance of both as equally "expert." The bases of the psychiatrists' "legal" opinion will be explored hereinafter; on the purely medical question these witnesses agreed (and in this litigation no one disputes their findings) that defendant's illness is characterized by a "disintegration of the personality" and a "complete disassociation between intellect and emotion," that defendant "is not capable of conceptual thinking" but only of "concrete" thinking, and that although his memory is not impaired his judgment is affected "to a considerable degree."

However impressive this seeming unanimity of expert opinion may at first appear (and we give it due consideration not only on the issue of sanity, but also in a subsequent portion of this opinion wherein we discuss the degree of the crime), our inquiry on this just as on other factual issues is necessarily limited at the appellate level to a determination whether there is substantial evidence in the record to support the jury's verdict of sanity (and the trial court's finding as to the degree of the murder) under the law of this state . . . It is only in the rare case when "the evidence is uncontradicted and entirely to the effect that the accused is insane" . . . that a unanimity of expert testimony could authorize upsetting a jury finding to the contrary. While the jury may not draw inferences inconsistent with incontestably established facts . . . nevertheless if there is substantial evidence from which the jury could infer that the defendant was legally sane at the time of the offense such a finding must be sustained in the face of any conflicting evidence, expert or otherwise, for the question of weighing that evidence and resolving that conflict "is a question of fact for the jury's determination" . . . Indeed, *the code specifically requires that the jury be instructed* (and they were so instructed in the case at bench) that "The jury is not bound to accept the opinion of any expert as conclusive, but should give to it the weight to which they shall find it to be entitled. The jury, may, however, disregard any such opinion if it shall be found by them to be unreasonable." (Pen. Code, § 1127b.)

The question of what may constitute substantial evidence of legal sanity cannot be answered by a simple formula applicable to all situations . . .

[I]t is settled that "the conduct and declarations of the defendant occurring within a reasonable time before or after the commission of the alleged act are admissible in proof of his mental condition at the time of the offense." . . . In the present case such evidence was introduced, both of defendant's conduct and of his declarations.

Conduct of Defendant as Evidence of Legal Sanity. Among the kinds of conduct of a defendant which our courts have held to constitute evidence of legal sanity are the following: "an ability on the part of the accused to devise and execute a deliberate plan" . . . ; "the manner in which the crime was conceived, planned and executed" . . . ; the fact that witnesses "observed no change in his manner and that he appeared to be normal" . . . ; the fact that "the defendant walked steadily and calmly, spoke clearly and coherently and appeared to be fully conscious of what he was doing" . . . ; and the fact that shortly after committing the crime the defendant "was cooperative and not abusive or combative" . . . , that "questions put to him . . . were answered by him quickly and promptly" . . . , and that "he appeared rational, spoke coherently, was oriented as to time, place and those persons who were present" . . .

In the case at bench there was evidence that in the year preceding the commission of the crime defendant "spent a lot of time thinking about sex." He made a list of the names and addresses of seven girls in his community whom he did not know personally but whom he planned to anesthetize by ether and then either rape or photograph nude. One night about three weeks before the murder he took a container of ether and attempted to enter the home of one of these girls through the chimney, but he became wedged in and had to be rescued. In the ensuing weeks defendant apparently deliberated on ways and means of accomplishing his objective and decided that he would have to bring the girls to his house to achieve his sexual purposes, and that it would therefore be necessary to get his mother (and possibly his brother) out of the way first.

The attack on defendant's mother took place on Monday, May 15, 1961. On the preceding Friday or Saturday defendant obtained an axe handle from the family garage and hid it under the mattress of his bed. At about 10 p.m. on Sunday he took the axe handle from its hiding place and approached his mother from behind, raising the weapon to strike her. She sensed his presence and asked him what he was doing; he answered that it was "nothing," and returned to his room and hid the handle under his mattress again. The following morning . . . He returned to the kitchen, approached his mother from behind and struck her on the back of the head. She turned around screaming and he struck her several more blows. They fell to the floor, fighting. She called out her neighbor's name and defendant began choking her. She bit him on the hand and crawled away. He got up to turn off the water running in the sink, and she fled through the dining room. He gave chase, caught her in the front room, and choked her to death with his hands. Defendant then took off his shirt and hung it by the fire, washed the blood off his face and hands, read a few lines from a Bible or prayer book lying upon the dining room table, and walked down to the police station to turn himself in. Defendant told the desk officer, "I have something I wish to report . . . I just killed my mother with an axe handle." The officer testified that defendant spoke in a quiet voice and that "His conversation was quite coherent in what he was saying and he answered everything I asked him right to a T."

Defendant's counsel repeatedly characterizes as "bizarre" defendant's plan to rape or photograph nude the seven girls on his list. Certainly in common parlance it may be termed "bizarre;" likewise to a mature person of good morals, it would appear highly unreasonable. But many a youth has committed—or planned—acts which were bizarre and unreasonable. This defendant was immature and lacked experience and judgment in sexual matters. But it does not follow therefrom that the jury were precluded as a matter of law from finding defendant *legally* sane at the time of the murder. From the evidence set forth hereinabove the jury could infer that defendant had a motive for his actions (gratification of his sexual desires), that he planned the attack on his mother for some time (obtaining of the axe handle from the garage several days in advance; abortive attempt to strike his mother with it on the evening before the crime), that he knew that what he was doing was wrong (initial concealment of the handle underneath his mattress; excuse offered when his mother saw him with the weapon on the evening before the crime; renewed concealment of the handle under the mattress), that he persisted in the fatal attack (pursuit of his fleeing mother into the front room; actual infliction of death by strangling rather than bludgeoning), that he was conscious of having committed a crime (prompt surrender to the police), and that he was calm and coherent (testimony of desk officer and others). We need not determine whether such conduct would alone constitute substantial evidence from which the jury could find defendant legally sane at the time of the murder, for as will next be shown the record contains further evidence on this issue.

Declarations of Defendant as Evidence of Legal Sanity. Oral declarations made by a defendant during the period of time material to his offense may constitute evidence of legal sanity . . . In *People v. Darling* (1962) . . . we referred *inter alia* to statements made by a defendant relating to his "reason for first committing the homicide and later surrendering himself," and held that "such evidence firmly establishes that defendant was aware at all times that his actions were wrong and improper." . . .

In the case at bench defendant was questioned by Officers Stenberg and Hamilton shortly after he came to the police station and voluntarily announced that he had just killed his mother. The interrogation was transcribed and shown to defendant; he changed the wording of a few of his answers, then affixed his signature and the date on each page. When asked by Officer Hamilton why he had turned himself in, defendant replied, "Well, for the act I had just committed." Defendant then related the events leading up to and culminating in the murder, describing his conduct in the detail set forth hereinabove. With respect to the issue of his state of mind at the time of the crime, the following language is both relevant and material: When asked how long he had thought of killing his mother, defendant replied, "I can't be clear on that. About a week ago, I would suppose, the very beginning of the thoughts. First I thought of giving her the ether . . . Then Thursday and Friday I thought of it again. Q. Of killing your mother? A. Not of killing. Well, yes I think so. Then Saturday and Sunday the same." After stating that he struck her the first blow on the back of the head, defendant was asked: "Q. Did you consider at the time that this one blow would render her unconscious, or kill her?

A. I wasn't sure. I was hoping it would render her unconscious. Q. Was it your thought at this time to kill her? A. I am not sure of that. Probably kill her, I think." Defendant described the struggle in which he and his mother fell to the floor, and was asked: "Q. Then what happened . . . A. She moved over by the stove, and she just laid still. She was breathing, breathing heavily. I said "I shouldn't be doing this'—not those exact words, but something to that effect, and laid down beside her, because we were on the floor. Q. Were you tired? A. Yes." After defendant had choked her to death he said, "God loves you, He loves me, He loves my dad, and I love you and my dad. It is a circle, sort of, and it is horrible you have done all that good and then I come along and destroy it."

Detective Stenberg thereafter interrupted Officer Hamilton's interrogation, and asked the following questions: "Q. (Det. W.R. Stenberg) You knew the wrongfulness of killing your mother? A. I did. I was thinking of it. I was aware of it. Q. You were aware of the wrongfulness. Also had you thought what might happen to you? A. That is a question. No. Q. Your thought has been in your mind for three weeks of killing her? A. Yes, or of just knocking her out. Q. Well, didn't you feel you would be prosecuted for the wrongfulness of this act? A. I was aware of it, but not thinking of it." . . . Officer Hamilton asked: "Q. Can you give a reason or purpose for this act of killing your mother? Have you thought out why you wanted to hurt her? A. There is a reason why we didn't get along. There is also the reason of sexual intercourse with one of these other girls, and I had to get her out of the way. Q. Did you think you had to get her out of the way permanently? A. I sort of figured it would have to be that way, but I am not quite sure."

Thus, contrary to the misunderstanding of counsel and amicus curiae, Officer Stenberg's question ("You knew the wrongfulness of killing your mother?") related unequivocally to defendant's knowledge *at the time of the commission of the murder*; and defendant's equally unequivocal answer ("I did. I was thinking of it. I was aware of it.") related to the same period of time. This admission, coupled with defendant's uncontradicted course of conduct and other statements set forth hereinabove, constitutes substantial evidence from which the jury could find defendant legally sane at the time of the matricide.

It is contended that the foregoing evidence of defendant's conduct and declarations is equally consistent with the type of mental illness (*i.e.*, a form of "schizophrenia") from which according to the psychiatric witnesses, defendant is said to be suffering. But this consistency establishes only that defendant is suffering from the diagnosed mental illness—a point that the prosecution readily concedes; it does not compel the conclusion that on the very different issue of legal sanity the evidence is insufficient as a matter of law to support the verdict. To hold otherwise would be in effect to substitute a trial by "experts" for a trial by jury, for it would require that the jurors accept the psychiatric testimony as conclusive on an issue—the legal sanity of the defendant—which under our present law is exclusively within the province of the trier of fact to determine.

To guard against misunderstanding of our rules it is pertinent to observe that we do not reject expert testimony simply or solely because it may *also* answer the ultimate question the jury is called upon to decide . . .; but strictly speaking, a psychiatrist is not an "expert" at all when it comes to determining whether the defendant is *legally* responsible under the terms of the California rule. Thus Dr. Alfred K. Baur, psychiatrist and Chief of Staff of the Veteran's Administration Hospital at Salem, Virginia, has recently warned that the question of a defendant's "insanity" (which he defines as *legal* irresponsibility) should not even be asked of members of his profession: "As psychiatrists, we can testify as to our findings regarding the 'mental condition' of the person in question . . .; but, to ask the psychiatric witness, 'Doctor, in your opinion is this person insane (or sane)?' is the same as asking an expert witness in a criminal trial, 'In your opinion, is the accused guilty or not guilty?' Yet, many lawyers ask psychiatrists to state opinions on the sanity of the accused and, unfortunately, many psychiatrists perpetuate the problem by accepting the role of oracle and answering the question, even thinking it properly within their functions." (Baur, *Legal Responsibility and Mental Illness* (1962) 57 N.W.U.L. REV. 12, 13; for similar views, *see* Address of Dr. Karl Menninger to the Judicial Conference of the 10th Circuit (1962) 32 F.R.D. 566, 571; Glueck, LAW AND PSYCHIATRY (1962) pp. 65–67; *cf. People v. O'Brien* (1932) 122 Cal. App. 147, 150154[2], 9 P.2d 902.)

In the light of the authorities which have been brought to our attention it thus appears that a psychiatrist's conclusion as to the *legal* insanity of a schizophrenic is inherently no more than tentative. As Dr. Manfred S. Guttmacher observes, "in the most malignant type of psychosis schizophrenia, the decision is often extremely difficult and the psychiatrist, conscientiously attempting to assay the individual's capacity to distinguish right and wrong will be able to do little more than conjecture. Much, indeed is known about the schizophrenic disorders at a descriptive level and valid generalizations about the symptomatology can be made. But our methods of examination do not permit us to particularize convincingly in regard to the individual patient." (Guttmacher, *Principal Difficulties with the Present Criteria of Responsibility and Possible Alternatives*, in Model Pen. Code, Tent. Draft No. 4 (1955), p. 171.) In this uncertain state of knowledge, the fact that the four psychiatrists in the case at bench happened each to diagnose defendant's *medical* condition as "schizophrenia" did not preclude the jury from weighing, as they were required to do, these witnesses' further opinions that defendant was *legally* insane at the time of the murder. Nor is this case unusual in this respect: in accordance with the just mentioned principle, jury verdicts of legal sanity have been upheld in a long line of cases in which the expert medical testimony was unanimous that the defendant was suffering from schizophrenia [Citations omitted] . . .

To the extent, moreover, that the psychiatric witnesses in the case at bench were asked their opinion as to defendant's legal sanity, a close examination of their responses discloses still further grounds in support of the verdict . . . Dr. Nielsen testified on direct examination that at the time of the murder defendant "knew right from wrong" but was "acting impulsively" and "didn't think it through"; that during the period of the final outburst, "He knew what he was doing after all. He studied his mother to see whether she was dead and when she wasn't, he went ahead and finished it." On cross-examination Dr. Nielsen was asked whether defendant's compulsion to kill his mother resembled an "irresistible impulse;" he replied, "It was not resisted and it was an impulse." The doctor further agreed that defendant "was capable at the time of knowing the difference between right and wrong, but that he didn't bother to think about it"; . . .

The next psychiatric witness, Dr. Smith, testified that when defendant killed his mother "He was acting on an impulse"; that "his expressions of intention to go out and have intercourse and his intention to knock out his mother and the aunt, if she came, are evidence of his ability to think because of his ability to plan. Now beyond that point of having struck his mother, this is an impulsive schizophrenic piece of behavior which is entirely separated in my opinion from some planned piece of activity."

The final psychiatric witness, Dr. Skrdla, testified on direct examination that at the time of the killing defendant "knew that he had committed a wrong act, at least morally wrong, and possibly legally wrong, because, according to the story he gave me, he washed the blood from himself and changed his clothes, and, a few minutes after the murder, went to the police station to report it. This would indicate that he recognized that his act was wrong." On cross-examination Dr. Skrdla testified that when defendant killed his mother "he probably did know the difference between right and wrong" but that he was one of those schizophrenics who "because of their emotional problems, their own conflicts, . . . are not able to prevent themselves from going ahead and acting on whatever ideas or compulsions they may have." . . .

The doctrine of "irresistible impulse" as a defense to crime is, of course not the law of California; to the contrary, the basic behavioral concept of our social order is free will . . .

It is true that certain other psychiatric testimony was to the effect that at the time of the murder defendant did not know the nature and quality of his acts and that what he was doing was wrong. But this created only a conflict in the evidence, which was for the jury to resolve. From the testimony quoted above the jury could infer that even though some or all of the psychiatric witnesses concluded that defendant was "legally insane," there was no basis for that conclusion under the California *M'Naghten* rule.

Finally, to accept defendant's thesis would be tantamount to creating by judicial fiat a new defense plea of "not guilty by reason of schizophrenia." To do so (assuming *arguendo* that it were within our power) would be bad law and apparently still worse medicine. It would require the jurors to accept as beyond dispute or question the opinions of the psychiatric witnesses as to the defendant's *legal* sanity. But it is doubtful that any reputable psychiatrist today would claim such infallibility; clearly the four who testified in the case at bench did not do so. Thus, Dr. Daryl D. Smith agreed with counsel's assertion with respect to schizophrenia that "there is quite a bit of divergence of [psychiatric] opinion relative to this disease." Indeed, it is often acknowledged that the causes and cure of schizophrenia are unknown (*e.g.*, Diamond, *From M'Naghten to Currens, and Beyond* (1962) 50 CAL. L. REV. 189, 195; Weihofen, MENTAL DISORDER AS A CRIMINAL DEFENSE (1954) p. 16), and that "schizophrenia" is not even a single disease as such but merely a label or term of convenience encompassing a variety of more or less related symptoms or conditions of mental disorder; thus in the case at bench Dr. J.M. Nielsen agreed that "schizophrenia" is "just a psychiatric classification, . . . simply an abstract definition as applied to the behavior pattern."

Such a classification covers a broad spectrum of mental conditions. As Dr. Alfred K. Baur emphasizes, "Some people are sophisticated enough to know that schizophrenia is one of the 'major psychoses' and contributes to many in the 'insane' category. But it is very difficult to get across to lay people the idea that a person diagnosed schizophrenic may be quite competent, responsible, and not dangerous, and, in fact, a valuable member of society, albeit at times a personally unhappy one. The same can be said of every psychiatric diagnosis or so-called mental illness." (Baur, *Legal Responsibility and Mental Illness* (1962) 57 N.W.U.L. REV. 12, 16–17.) The argument for defendant, in short, ignores our often-repeated admonition that " 'sound mind' and 'legal sanity' are not synonymous." . . .

———

NOTES

1. As the *Wolff* court notes (and as we noted at the outset of this chapter) insanity is a legal construct, not a medical condition. As Professor Morse has explained:

> When the legal system must decide if a person is crazy enough to warrant special legal treatment, it should recognize the social and moral nature and significance of the decision. Consequently, the question of who is crazy should be decided by society's representatives—judges and juries of laypersons.

Stephen J. Morse, *Crazy Behavior, Morals, and Science: An Analysis of Mental Health Law*, 51 SO. CAL. L. REV. 527, 560 (1978). Does this make sense to you? If four expert witnesses testify that a defendant was suffering from a mental disease or defect when he committed the crime, why shouldn't we trust their expert opinions instead of those of non-expert jurors?

2. Are experts practically a necessity in insanity cases? Consider Oliver v. State, 850 S.W.2d 742 (Tex. App.—Hous. 1993) in which a defendant with a long history of mental illness was charged with killing her infant child. Oliver's evidence of insanity included her own testimony about her psychiatric problems and three clinical psychologists who believed Oliver was insane. The prosecution did not present a medical expert and instead sought to rebut the insanity claim through cross-examination of Oliver's experts. In particular, prosecutors focused on Oliver's background as a nurse and that she suffered from Munchausen's Syndrome, a condition where people fabricate non-existent symptoms in order to be admitted to the hospital. The jury convicted Oliver, but the court of appeals reversed the conviction for insufficient evidence. The court explained that "[t]he State did not present any expert testimony to contradict the expert testimony of the three doctors. After reviewing all the evidence in the record relevant to the issue of appellant's sanity, we must conclude that the verdict of the jury, which implicitly rejected the affirmative defense of insanity, is so against the great weight and preponderance of the evidence as to be manifestly unjust." Do cases like *Oliver* signal to prosecutors that it is too big of a risk to go without an expert in an insanity case even if, as the *Wolff* case demonstrates, an expert is not absolutely required?

McCulloch v. Commonwealth

Court of Appeals of Virginia, 1999.
29 Va. App. 769, 514 S.E.2d 797.

■ BUMGARDNER, JUDGE.

James C. McCulloch appeals his conviction of first degree murder of his wife. He argues that the trial court erred (1) in denying his request for a second expert to evaluate his sanity at the time of the offense, and (2) in not permitting lay witness testimony about his sanity at the time of the offense. Concluding that the trial court did not err, we affirm.

The defendant's wife entered a grocery store bleeding from a stab wound. Just as she entered, two customers saw a man run past the front of the store. They chased him and saw him holding a knife. The two followed the man, who turned out to be the defendant, to his home. When the police arrived, they found a bloodstained knife in the kitchen sink, and the defendant admitted to them that he stabbed his wife.

Pursuant to the defendant's motion, the trial court appointed Dr. Jerome S. Nichols, a licensed clinical psychologist, to evaluate defendant's competency to stand trial and mental state at the time of the offense. Dr. Nichols reported that the defendant was competent to stand trial. Only the defendant's attorney was given the evaluation on sanity at the time of the offense. It would show that the defendant was sane.

The defendant attempted suicide while in jail. Following further evaluation, Dr. Nichols found the defendant no longer competent to stand trial. The trial court continued the trial and committed him to Central State Hospital. After treatment, the hospital found the defendant competent and returned him for trial. The trial court again continued the trial when Dr. Nichols indicated the defendant needed additional treatment. Though the doctor changed that opinion, the trial court still continued the case to allow additional medical treatment.

The defendant filed an insanity defense notice on June 25 pursuant to Code § 19.2–168. The Commonwealth then moved for an examination of the defendant by a qualified mental health expert pursuant to Code § 19.2–168.1. The trial court granted the motion and returned the defendant to Central State Hospital for the evaluation. That evaluation found him sane at the time of the offense.

On the day before the trial, the defendant moved for appointment of a psychiatrist to determine sanity at the time of the offense. The trial court ruled that the initial appointment of Dr. Nichols, a psychologist, had satisfied all legal requirements and that the defendant was not entitled to another court-appointed expert. The trial court found that the defendant offered no more than a possibility that a second opinion would reveal anything different. The trial court denied the motion but emphasized that it would reconsider its ruling at any time the defendant presented a factual basis indicating by more than a mere possibility that a second opinion would assist the defense.

At the pretrial hearing the day before trial, the trial court ruled that unless the defendant presented expert testimony that he suffered from a disease of the mind, he could not present evidence that he was insane at the time of the offense. Until the defendant proffered expert testimony that he was insane under the law of Virginia, he could not offer during the guilt phase testimony about his mental state at the time of the offense.

The defendant also sought to prove insanity through the testimony of lay witnesses who observed his behavior, demeanor, and actions. The defendant proffered the testimony of several witnesses. The court ruled that the affirmative defense of insanity required the defendant to introduce "into evidence [ ] someone's opinion that the defendant is 'insane' . . . , [and] all that a lay witness can do is to give observations about facts." Having no expert opinion that the defendant was insane, the trial court precluded the defendant from introducing other testimony about his mental condition at the time of the offense.

During the trial, the defendant proffered that one witness would testify that after his arrest the defendant spoke to her as if she were his wife. Another would testify that before the murder he "didn't seem right." Still another would testify that a month before the murder the defendant "was not acting like himself." The testimony of seven jail inmates would indicate variously that the defendant "was crazy"; "acted very nervous all the time like he didn't have it all together"; "cried a lot"; "would sit in his cell and bark like a dog"; "acts like he is in another world and just kind of hangs to himself"; "acted very depressed"; and "acted like he had a split personality." Two additional witnesses would testify that the defendant lost forty pounds, thought his wife was alive, had blackouts and was not sleeping and that the defendant lost sixty pounds and "hears and sees things."

The trial court excluded some lay testimony because it concerned the defendant's conduct and demeanor after the offense was committed. It excluded other testimony because it was impermissible lay opinion. The trial court permitted one lay witness to testify about the defendant's habits before the murder because it corroborated the defendant's testimony. It also permitted the defendant to testify about his state of mind at the time of the offense.

Indigent defendants are entitled to the appointment of a psychiatrist to assist in their defense, but this right is not absolute. *See Ake v. Oklahoma,* 470 U.S. 68, 77, 105 S.Ct. 1087, 84 L.Ed.2d 53 (1985). The defendant must demonstrate "that his sanity at the time of the offense is to be a significant factor at trial . . ." *Id.* at 83, 105 S.Ct. 1087. A request unaccompanied by a showing of reasonableness is properly denied. *See Caldwell v. Mississippi,* 472 U.S. 320, 323 n. 1, 105 S.Ct. 2633, 86 L.Ed.2d 231 (1985). The trial court did appoint an expert, Dr. Nichols, who determined that, in his opinion, the defendant was sane at the time of the offense.

The defendant argues that his case required the appointment of an additional expert because Dr. Nichols is not a psychiatrist. The Supreme Court in *Ake* recognized the obligation of the trial court to provide a defendant with "one competent psychiatrist." *Ake,* 470 U.S. at 79, 105 S.Ct. 1087. However, that Court "did not intend to restrict to psychiatrists those mental health professionals who could perform evaluations of insanity at the time of the offense." *Funk v. Commonwealth,* 8 Va.App. 91, 96, 379 S.E.2d 371, 373 (1989).

The only reason given to support the request for appointment of a psychiatric expert was the suggestion that a psychologist was not competent to evaluate any relevant effect upon defendant resulting from a previous bullet wound to his head. Dr. David Hartman, the psychiatrist who treated the defendant for ten years after that shooting, stated that the gunshot wound had not entered the brain and had caused no organic brain damage. When Dr. Hartman was unable to offer an opinion about the defendant's mental state at the time of the offense, the trial court excluded his testimony.

The trial court did not err in refusing to appoint a psychiatrist as a second expert. The court found that the defendant had not established a factual basis to support his request. Determining whether the defendant has made an adequate showing is a decision that lies within the trial court's discretion.

The trial court did not abuse its discretion. There was no indication that a further evaluation would turn out differently. The basis for the request was supposition that was not supported by the defendant's own doctor. When denying the motion, the trial court emphasized that it would reconsider the ruling if the defendant presented anything to indicate there was more than the mere possibility that a second expert would conclude differently. The defendant presented nothing to suggest more than a mere possibility. All medical evaluations concluded that the defendant was sane at the time of the offense. The first appointment met the obligation to provide a mental health expert, and the defendant never showed a particularized need for an additional evaluation.

Next, the defendant argues that the trial court erred in ruling that expert testimony was a necessary predicate to his asserting an insanity defense and erred in excluding the proffered lay witness testimony. The trial court held the defendant had to present expert testimony before he could introduce lay evidence to support his insanity defense. We conclude that the holding was correct in this case. The evidence did not support the defendant's insanity defense, though in an appropriate case factual testimony alone may be sufficient to establish the defense.

The defendant must prove to the satisfaction of the jury that he was insane at the time of the offense. He has the burden of affirmatively raising the issue of insanity and proving his mental disease or defect by a preponderance of the evidence . . . Although lay testimony may support a plea of insanity, 'it is generally recognized that it is advisable to adduce expert testimony to better resolve such a complex problem.'" *Herbin v. Commonwealth,* 28 Va.App. 173, 183, 503 S.E.2d 226, 231 (1998) (quoting *Shifflett v. Commonwealth,* 221 Va. 760, 769, 274 S.E.2d 305, 311 (1981)).

"While lay witnesses may testify to the attitude and demeanor of the defendant, '[l]ay witnesses cannot express an opinion as to the existence of a particular mental disease or condition.'" *Id.* (quoting *Mullis v. Commonwealth,* 3 Va.App. 564, 573, 351 S.E.2d 919, 925 (1987)). In *Mullis,* a lay witness was not permitted to explain the defendant's actions by testifying that he was "paranoid" because this might suggest to the jury that the defendant had been diagnosed "paranoid." Here, no medical evidence supporting an insanity defense was introduced, and the lay testimony defendant proffered was insufficient to establish a *prima facie* case for an insanity defense.

The trial court excluded lay witness testimony that addressed the defendant's state of mind when offered for the purpose of establishing his sanity at the time of the offense . . . We hold that the trial court did not err in excluding testimony for the purpose for which it was offered, and we will not consider an argument presented by a party for the first time on appeal.

Concluding that the trial court did not err, we affirm the conviction.

Affirmed.

NOTES

1. There is a general perception that you can find an expert witness to testify to anything. *See* Samuel Gross, *Expert Evidence*, 1991 WIS. L. REV. 1113, 1114–1115. Does the *McCulloch* case make you rethink that assessment?

2. Experts often disagree in their assessment of the defendant's sanity. For instance, in a study of 165 Hawaii cases, scholars reviewed 483 experts' decisions about whether a defendant was sane. (In 153 cases, three experts assessed the defendants' sanity. In 12 cases, two experts assessed sanity.) The study found that in only 55.1% of cases did all of the evaluators agree upon the defendant's mental state at the time of the crime. *See* W. Neil Gowensmith et al., *How Reliable are Forensic Evaluations of Legal Sanity?* 37 L. & HUM. BEHAV. 98 (2013). If experts agree in only about half of Hawaii insanity cases, does that suggest the importance of having at least two or three expert assessments in each case?

3. Like McCulloch, the vast majority of criminal defendants—upwards of 80%—are indigent and cannot afford to pay for their own lawyers or experts. *See* Adam M. Gershowitz, *The Invisible Pillar of Gideon*, 80 IND. L.J. 571, 585 (2005). While these defendants are entitled to free appointed counsel (*see* Gideon v. Wainwright, 372 U.S. 335 (1963)) and free expert witnesses (*see* Ake v. Oklahoma, 470 U.S. 68 (1985)), they are not entitled to the counsel of their choice or to unlimited experts. The story is different for affluent defendants however. Richer defendants can hire as many experts as they like and (consistent with the general perception) may be able to find an expert witness to say anything. Does this type of criminal justice system make sense? Should all expert witnesses—for defendants and prosecutors—simply be chosen off a pre-determined list as was apparently done in *McCulloch*? Professor Robertson has proposed a similar framework in the civil context. *See* Christopher Tarver Robertson, *Blind Expertise*, 85 N.Y.U. L. REV. 174 (2010). If all experts were chosen off a single list, would perceptions of the criminal justice system and the appropriateness of the insanity defense improve?

4. As noted in the opinion, McCulloch's trial was delayed after he attempted suicide and the court found him incompetent to stand trial. However, "after treatment" the court moved forward with the trial. Could McCulloch have refused the treatment and thereby prevented his trial from occurring? The answer is generally no. The Supreme Court of the United States has upheld the forcible medication and treatment of defendants in order to make them competent for trial. Forcible medication is constitutionally permissible so long as the treatment is medically appropriate, it is unlikely that the side effects would undermine the fairness of the trial, and the forced medication would further important government interests by bringing a defendant charged with a serious offense to trial. *See* Sell v. United States, 539 U.S. 166 (2003).

5. Does a defendant absolutely need expert testimony to present a successful insanity defense? The court in *McCulloch* says expert testimony is advisable but that it is not required. The court correctly states the rule. *See* WAYNE R. LAFAVE, CRIMINAL LAW 453 (5th ed. 2010) ("Although a persuasive case is unlikely to be made on lay testimony alone, courts have not infrequently upheld verdicts based upon a jury's acceptance of lay testimony of sanity over expert testimony of insanity, and have likewise indicated that an insanity defense may be supported by lay witnesses alone."). Yet, while the *McCulloch* court accurately states the rule, does it properly apply the rule to the facts? If expert testimony is not necessary, why does the court not reject the trial court's evidentiary decision and reverse McCulloch's conviction? Didn't McCulloch proffer enough lay testimony to demonstrate that he was insane? The court explains that lay witnesses cannot testify to the existence of a mental disease. But if insanity is a legal construct and jurors serve to provide the moral conscience of the community, shouldn't jurors be permitted to infer the existence of a mental disease based on lay testimony about McCulloch's behavior? Has the court over-privileged the importance of expert testimony?

J. SPECIAL PROBLEMS WITH DETENTION OF INSANITY ACQUITTEES

In *Jones v. United States* 463 U.S. 354, 103 S.Ct. 3043, 77 L.Ed.2d 694 (1983), the United States Supreme Court held that insanity acquittees belong to a special class of persons whose dangerousness has already been demonstrated by the criminal acts they have committed. The Court thus ruled that a finding of insanity at a criminal trial by a preponderance of the evidence is sufficiently probative of mental illness to justify commitment to a mental institution for an indefinite period of time until an acquittee regains his sanity or is no longer dangerous, without regard to the length of an acquittee's hypothetical criminal sentence. The Supreme Court further held that this procedure does not violate due process of law. The Court ruled that it was reasonable for Congress to determine that a finding of mental illness at a criminal trial constitutes an adequate basis for hospitalization and continued confinement of a defendant acquitted by reason of insanity.

To what extent does the issue of insanity acquittees overlap with the detention of "sexually dangerous persons?" In this regard, *see* the discussion *supra* Chapter 6.

K. SPECIAL ISSUES OF PROOF IN INSANITY DEFENSE CASES

Legal insanity is most often regarded as an affirmative defense in which the burden of proof may constitutionally be placed on the defendant, who is generally required to give notice of his or her intent to raise the defense. Use of the insanity defense does not, however, relieve the prosecution of proving *mens rea* as well as every other element of the charged crime beyond a reasonable doubt. This creates a certain tension between what the defendant must prove to establish the defense once the prosecution has established the elements of the offense.

NOTES: ISSUES OF PROOF IN INSANITY DEFENSE CASES

1. *See* 18 U.S.C. § 17(b), placing the burden of proving the defense of insanity on the defendant, and specifying that the quantum of proof required to satisfy this burden is "clear and convincing evidence." Statutes have been held constitutional which require that the defense of insanity be pleaded specially, and that there shall be separate trials—one as to guilt and the other to determine insanity. This represents the so-called bifurcated trial concept, adopted by statute in California and Colorado. In practice, the procedure is not much used and frequently defendants raise the defense of partial insanity in the guilt phase of the trial in an attempt to reduce a murder from first to second degree. In Wisconsin, where the bifurcated trial was judicially adopted in State ex rel. La Follette v. Raskin, 34 Wis.2d 607, 150 N.W.2d 318 (1967), it was held that evidence concerning mental condition is not admissible during the guilt phase of the trial. *See* Curl v. State, 40 Wis.2d 474, 162 N.W.2d 77 (1968). In Commonwealth v. McCusker, 448 Pa. 382, 292 A.2d 286, 293 (1972), the court suggested that holding that "psychiatric evidence is admissible as an aid in determining whether an accused acted in the heat of passion at the time of his offense is only a natural and logical application of the orderly and authoritative development of the law of evidence in such cases."

2. May the defense attorney assert an insanity defense on behalf of a defendant, over her client's objection, if the lawyer believes that a serious question exists as to the client's sanity? In State v. Bean, 171 Vt. 290, 762 A.2d 1259 (2000), the Vermont Supreme Court's majority held that the decision to pursue an insanity defense ultimately rests with the defendant, and not with his or her counsel. The Court said that if an acquittal on the grounds of insanity were to be obtained, the finding would often result in involuntary institutionalization as well as stigmatization. The defendant ought to be permitted to decide whether such consequences are preferable to the stigma resulting from a criminal conviction.

3. While a defendant ultimately has the choice whether to plead insanity, a lawyer's failure to secure a mental-health evaluation can constitute ineffective assistance of counsel. *See, e.g.* Antwine v. Delo, 54 F.3d 1357 (8th Cir. 1995). In that case, defense counsel's failure to procure second mental evaluation of defendant, which would have discovered defendant's bipolar disorder, constituted ineffective assistance of counsel, as counsel could have presented evidence of disorder at penalty phase, and, since there were only two aggravating factors, evidence might have altered sentencing outcome.

4. Prosecutors often counter insanity defense arguments by showing that the defendant engaged in some form of planning before carrying out the crime charged. Consider the following statement of the Supreme Court of North Carolina in State v. Cooper, 286 N.C. 549, 213 S.E.2d 305, 321 (1975):

> We may take judicial notice of the well known fact that a dog, a wild animal or a completely savage, uncivilized man may have the mental capacity to intend to kill and patiently to stalk his prey for that purpose. The law, however, does not impose criminal responsibility upon one who has this level of mental capacity only. For criminal responsibility it requires that the accused have, at the time of the act, the higher mental ability to distinguish between right and wrong with reference to that act. It requires less mental ability to form a purpose to do an act than to determine its moral quality . . .

APPENDIX

RELEVANT PROVISIONS OF THE UNITED STATES CONSTITUTION AND ITS AMENDMENTS

Provisions of the Constitution of the United States, and certain Amendments thereto, of particular significance in the administration of criminal justice:

Preamble

We the People of the United States, in Order to form a more perfect Union, establish Justice, insure domestic Tranquility, provide for the common defense, promote the general Welfare, and secure the Blessings of Liberty to ourselves and our Posterity, do ordain and establish this Constitution for the United States of America.

Article I.

SECTION 8. The Congress shall have Power To lay and collect Taxes, Duties, Imposts and Excises, to pay the Debts and provide for the common Defence and general Welfare of the United States; but all Duties, Imposts and Excises shall be uniform throughout the United States; . . .

To regulate Commerce with foreign Nations, and among the several States and with the Indian Tribes; . . .

To provide for the Punishment of counterfeiting the Securities and current Coin of the United States; . . .

To constitute Tribunals inferior to the supreme Court;

To define and punish Piracies and Felonies committed on the high Seas, and Offences against the Law of Nations;

To declare War, grant Letters of Marque and Reprisal, and make Rules concerning Captures on Land and Water; . . .

To make Rules for the Government and Regulation of the land and naval Forces;

To provide for calling forth the Militia to execute the Laws of the Union, suppress Insurrections and repel Invasions;

To provide for organizing, arming, and disciplining, the Militia, and for governing such Part of them as may be employed in the Service of the United States, reserving to the States respectively, the Appointment of the Officers, and the Authority of training the Militia according to the discipline prescribed by Congress;

To exercise exclusive Legislation in all Cases whatsoever, over such District (not exceeding ten Miles square) as may, by Cession of particular States, and the Acceptance of Congress, become the Seat of the Government of the United States, and to exercise like Authority over all Places purchased by the Consent of the Legislature of the State in which the Same shall be, for the Erection of Forts, Magazines, Arsenals, Dock-Yards, and other needful Buildings;—And

To make all Laws which shall be necessary and proper for carrying into Execution the foregoing Powers, and all other Powers vested by this Constitution in the Government of the United States, or in any Department or Officer thereof.

SECTION 9.

No Bill of Attainder or *ex post facto* Law shall be passed.

Article III.

SECTION 1. The judicial Power of the United States, shall be vested in one supreme Court, and in such inferior Courts as the Congress may from time to time ordain and establish. The Judges, both of the supreme and inferior Courts, shall hold their Offices during good Behaviour, and shall, at stated Times, receive for their Services, a Compensation, which shall not be diminished during their Continuance in Office.

SECTION 2.

. . . the supreme Court shall have appellate Jurisdiction, both as to Law and Fact, with such Exceptions, and under such Regulations as the Congress shall make.

The Trial of all Crimes, except in Cases of Impeachment, shall be by Jury; and such Trial shall be held in the State where the said Crimes shall have been committed; but when not committed within any State, the Trial shall be at such Place or Places as the Congress may by Law have directed.

SECTION 3. Treason against the United States, shall consist only in levying War against them, or in adhering to their Enemies, giving them Aid and Comfort. No Person shall be convicted of Treason unless on the Testimony of two Witnesses to the same overt Act, or on Confession in open Court.

The Congress shall have Power to declare the Punishment of Treason, but no Attainder of Treason shall work Corruption of Blood, or Forfeiture except during the Life of the Person attainted.

Article VI.

This Constitution, and the Laws of the United States which shall be made in Pursuance thereof; and all Treaties made, or which shall be made, under the Authority of the United States, shall be the supreme Law of the Land; and the Judges in every State shall be bound thereby, any Thing in the Constitution or Laws of any State to the Contrary notwithstanding.

AMENDMENTS

Amendment I.

Congress shall make no law respecting an establishment of religion, or prohibiting the free exercise thereof; or abridging the freedom of speech, or of the press; or the right of the people peaceably to assemble, and to petition the Government for a redress of grievances.

Amendment II.

A well regulated militia, being necessary to the security of a free State, the right of the people to keep and bear arms, shall not be infringed.

Amendment III.

No Soldier shall, in time of peace be quartered in any house, without the consent of the owner, nor in time of war, but in a manner to be prescribed by law.

Amendment IV.

The right of the people to be secure in their persons, houses, papers, and effects, against unreasonable searches and seizures, shall not be violated, and no warrants shall issue, but upon probable cause, supported by oath or affirmation, and particularly describing the place to be searched, and the persons or things to be seized.

Amendment V.

No person shall be held to answer for a capital, or otherwise infamous crime, unless on a presentment or indictment of a Grand Jury, except in cases arising in the land or naval forces, or in the militia, when in actual service in time of war or public danger; nor shall any person be subject for the same offence to be twice put in jeopardy of life or limb; nor shall be compelled in any criminal case to be a witness against himself, nor be deprived of life, liberty, or property, without due process of law; nor shall private property be taken for public use, without just compensation.

Amendment VI.

In all criminal prosecutions, the accused shall enjoy the right to a speedy and public trial, by an impartial jury of the State and district wherein the crime shall have been committed, which district shall have been previously ascertained by law, and to be informed of the nature and cause of the accusation; to be confronted with the witnesses against him; to have compulsory process for obtaining witnesses in his favor, and to have the assistance of Counsel for his defence.

Amendment VII.

In Suits at common law, where the value in controversy shall exceed twenty dollars, the right of trial by jury shall be preserved, and no fact tried by a jury, shall be otherwise re-examined in any Court of the United States, than according to the rules of the common law.

Amendment VIII.

Excessive bail shall not be required, nor excessive fines imposed, nor cruel and unusual punishments inflicted.

Amendment IX.

The enumeration in the Constitution, of certain rights, shall not be construed to deny or disparage others retained by the people.

Amendment X.

The powers not delegated to the United States by the Constitution, nor prohibited by it to the States, are reserved to the States respectively, or to the people.

Amendment XIII.

SECTION 1. Neither slavery nor involuntary servitude, except as a punishment for crime whereof the party shall have been duly convicted, shall exist within the United States, or any place subject to their jurisdiction.

SECTION 2. Congress shall have power to enforce this article by appropriate legislation.

Amendment XIV.

SECTION 1. All persons born or naturalized in the United States, and subject to the jurisdiction thereof, are citizens of the United States and of the State wherein they reside. No State shall make or enforce any law which shall abridge the privileges or immunities of citizens of the United States; nor shall any State deprive any person of life, liberty, or property, without due process of law; nor deny to any person within its jurisdiction the equal protection of laws. . . .

SECTION 5. The Congress shall have power to enforce, by appropriate legislation, the provisions of this article.

Amendment XV.

SECTION 1. The right of citizens of the United States to vote shall not be denied or abridged by the United States or by any State on account of race, color, or previous condition of servitude.

SECTION 2. The Congress shall have power to enforce this article by appropriate legislation.

Amendment XVI.

The Congress shall have power to lay and collect taxes on incomes, from whatever source derived, without apportionment among the several States, and without regard to any census or enumeration. . . .

INDEX

References are to Pages